18/5

99p

GOOD BEER GUIDE 1994

EDITED BY JEFF EVANS

D1328810

CAMRA BOOKS

Campaign for Real Ale Ltd.
34 Alma Road, St Albans,
Herts. AL1 3BW

CONTENTS

Editor: Jeff Evans. **Deputy Editor:** Jill Adam. **Behind the Scenes:** Iain Dobson MBE, Iain Loe, Steve Cox, Malcolm Harding, Roger Protz, Andrew Sangster, Jo Bates, Catherine Dale, Su Tilley, Jean Jones, Clare Stevens, Cressida Feiler. **Design:** Rob Howells. **Cover Photograph:** Tom Dobbie. **Pump Clip:** Porter Lancastrian, Blackburn. **Maps:** David Perrott. **Illustrations:** Stephen Holmes *(pages 10-17)*. **Cartoons:** Larry.

Published by: Campaign for Real Ale Ltd., 34 Alma Road, St Albans, Herts. AL1 3BW. Tel. (0727) 867201. **Typeset by** Create Publishing Services, Bath. **Printed by** Bath Press, Bath.

ISBN 1 85249 006 3

Nearly 40,000 CAMRA members make this guide possible. Special thanks to CAMRA Regional Directors, to those members who helped with pub surveys and those who provided information on beers and breweries.

INTRODUCTION

IT'S OFFICIAL. Real ale is the drink of the nineties, even the big brewers say so. Keg beer is fading fast and lager is past its peak. But this is not news to those of us who keep a keen eye on the brewing world. A mere glance at the breweries section of the *Good Beer Guide* has shown a remarkable increase in the number of real ale breweries in recent years, culminating this year with nearly thirty new producers entering the Independents section.

Sadly, prices continue to rise well ahead of inflation and the threat of take-overs remains in the air, with Greenalls already swooping upon its fellow pub operator Devenish. Such a take-over clearly has implications for choice and competition in the trade, and it comes on top of one of the most disgraceful acts by any brewer or pub company for many a year. In February 1993, Greenalls demolished the famous Tommy Ducks pub in Manchester, ignoring local planning legislation and not even telling the bar staff of its intentions. It was bulldozed during the night.

Undoubtedly the most pressing problem for the British brewing industry in the nineties is the question of beer duty. The Single Market, Maastricht and all that are now behind us, with the legacy an open-door trading arrangement across Europe and few restrictions on the import and export of beer between European countries. Cross-Channel trade in bottled and canned French, Belgian, Dutch and German beer has been heavy, as drinkers and those making a fast buck have taken advantage of lower beer prices on the Continent. The prices are lower simply because governments in Europe do not tax their brewers as heavily as we do. Only the Irish in the EC pay more duty on beer than British producers. The French pay eight times less. It is clearly time for the Government to take another look at beer duty. All British brewers, big and small, would benefit from a reduction in beer tax, as, of course, would drinkers. It would help stem the flow of poor quality imports and keep alive our pub industry.

The Government has already reneged on a review of the brewing industry, a review which had been promised ever since the Beer Orders introduced such radical changes in 1989. There are signs that it may go back on a second assurance: that it would implement Section 43 of the Weights and Measures Act. This clause sounds technical but, in simple terms, means that a publican would be obliged to give you a full pint for your money, with any froth or foam not counted as part of the measure. It would counteract the current trend of encouraging thick, creamy heads on pints, which are fine for certain northern beers but quite inappropriate for many others, damaging their flavour and consistency. With less beer and more air in a deep head, the brewers are gaining financially from this method of service and we, the drinkers, are losing out.

CAMRA AND REAL ALE

THE CAMPAIGN FOR REAL ALE (CAMRA) was founded in 1971 as a consumer movement to protect Britain's brewing heritage. At the time, brewery take-overs and closures were commonplace, and traditional British beer was on its deathbed. As the giant breweries were closing down small producers all across the country, choice was diminishing and, in place of beers brewed for local palates, nationally advertised keg beers were finding their way onto the bar.

Unlike traditional ale (or real ale, as CAMRA christened it), keg beer is a dead product. It does not continue to mature in the keg because it has been filtered and pasteurised to remove all life-giving yeast. It even needs to be pumped full of gas to send it to the bar and to give it some fizz. Real ale is drawn into the glass by simple methods, without the use of extra gas. The handpump is the most common means of dispense, but electronic pumps are also used, or the beer can simply be tapped from the cask itself. In Scotland, air pressure is still used in some parts. Nor does real ale need added gas to give it life. The continuous fermentation creates its own effervescence, as well as a good, fresh taste. Producing real ale takes skill and craftsmanship, as Roger Protz describes on page 10: keg beer is a factory product, designed more for profit and ease of use than customer satisfaction. Thankfully, CAMRA has been hugely successful in its fight against keg and has also campaigned against lager — not the classic beer style perfected by some of our European neighbours, but the pale imitation of it touted by British brewers. Whereas genuine lagers can be wonderfully flavoursome and fresh-tasting, the weaker British lagers, being pasteurised and over-gassed, are as dispiriting as keg beer.

ABOUT THE GOOD BEER GUIDE

THE GOOD BEER GUIDE is a celebration of real ale. It is CAMRA's flagship publication, first published in 1974, with the purpose of guiding drinkers to those pubs which served top quality traditional ale. The principle is still the same today. In the *Guide*, you will find around 5,000 pubs serving the best real ale in Britain, as well as full details of all breweries currently in operation, with information on the beers they brew. The *Good Beer Guide* is unique amongst national pub guides in that the criterion for entry is the quality of a pub's beer. All kinds of pub are featured, from quiet village locals to bustling town boozers and they are selected annually for the *Guide* by CAMRA members. We do not employ inspectors to visit pubs once or twice before making up their minds, nor do we rely simply on reader recommendations. Our surveyors are real enthusiasts who use the pubs all year-round and know just how consistently good or bad the pubs in their area are. The final list of entries for each area is drawn up at a selection meeting of the local CAMRA branch. No payment is ever taken for entry to the *Guide*.

Readers' views are, of course, always taken into account. Any recommendations or criticisms are forwarded to the local CAMRA branch and are carefully considered when choosing pubs. Correspondence is very much appreciated, so please continue to write. A recommendation form is provided on page 509.

All pubs are formally surveyed each year and all the information is checked and updated, right up to the very last minute. As with all guide books, changes are likely during the currency of the *Good Beer Guide* and some beers or facilities may be different on your visit. However, major amendments to pub entries are published throughout the year in *What's Brewing*, the monthly CAMRA newspaper, delivered free to all members (see page 512).

How the Entries are Arranged

PUBS ARE ARRANGED ALPHABETICALLY in counties, with English counties first, then Welsh, followed by Scottish regions, Northern Ireland and the offshore islands. An at-a-glance guide to reading the pub entries is provided on the inside front cover, with all the symbols for pub facilities explained. Where meals and accommodation are indicated, no assessment of quality is made, except where mentioned in the pub description. Only the pub's real ales are included, with beers listed by brewery, in alphabetical order. Where more than one beer is available from the same brewery, they are listed in increasing order of original gravity (approximate strength). Seasonal beers, like winter ales, are included but are clearly not available all year-round. Full details of all beers mentioned can be found in the breweries section. Pubs in England and Wales can open from 11am to 11pm, though not all choose to do so. Some areas have special licensing arrangements for opening earlier or closing later (on market days, for example). Full opening hours are given for each pub, including any variations to the statutory Sunday hours, which are 12-3, 7-10.30. In Scotland, later closing is commonplace and many pubs now stay open all day Sunday, though standard Sunday hours are 12.30-2.30, 6.30-11.

Licensing Reform

Stephen Cox looks at the Government's proposals and calls for sanity in pub opening laws

WE'D LOST OUR WAY TRYING TO FIND THE PUB, tucked away in the woods. It was crowded, and half past ten on Friday night. As I struggled to the bar, I made some comment to my Dutch friends along the lines of "Only another half an hour before closing time."

Their reaction was distinctly sour. Their normal good humour was tempered by thirst and inconvenience. "Why do you English put up with these stupid laws?", they asked. It was a good question. Here was an excellent pub, where people were happily drinking and chatting. The staff were

pouring beer as fast as they could and, shortly, t
would have to begin the unpleasant business of thr
his customers out into the cold. Quite frank,
shouldn't that pub have stayed open as long as the li
wanted?

SUNDAY WORST

I WAS SHOWING AN AMERICAN FRIEND around St Albans on a hot Sunday afternoon. He'd been looking forward to visiting some of our famous pubs — but, of course, none of them was open. Thirsty tourists were lining up for ice-creams, and outside the tea-shops, but there was no chance of a cool pint and it was two hours until the pubs opened. We debated going into a pizza parlour, and ordering two lagers and a round of garlic bread. "Why do you English put up with this?", he asked. "You let your pubs open some of the time on Sundays. Why not Sunday afternoons, too?"

The sun beat down, the tourists thought of cool pubs and cooler beer, and I didn't have much to say. Except to point out that, apparently, Parliament trusts the Scots to drink on Sunday afternoons, and people who use clubs, and people going to restaurants... but not English and Welsh pub-goers.

NO KID-IN

WE WERE DISCUSSING where to take the kids for a pub lunch. There were pubs with beer gardens, but what if it rained? And there were pubs with tiny cramped family rooms, which didn't much appeal to the adults. There were only big chain restaurant pubs that would take kids, plastic soulless places that they are, a sort of burger bar with handpumps. So, in the end, we broke the law.

We went to a great country pub, which does real ale, real cider, excellent food, and has a splendid pub cat. I won't name it for fear of reprisals. The governor simply ignores the law, and lets children into the bar. He's not the only one.

Watching the youngest tucking away into his chips, I wondered what evil influence the law was trying to hide from him. He's seen both his parents drinking, in beer gardens, in family rooms, at home, at beer festivals, in restaurants... As my boss once explained to his kid: "Son, you're allowed to watch me drink, you're just not allowed to watch me pay for it. "

Children are allowed into pubs at the licensee's discretion in Ireland, France, Spain, Belgium and the Netherlands, just for starters. Why do the English and Welsh put up with these stupid laws?

The Proposals

AT LEAST THE CHILDREN issue may be resolved. In March 1993, the Government launched a consultative paper on the licensing system in England and Wales. There were four main proposals: to introduce a children's certificate system like Scotland, to define the powers of licensing magistrates to refuse new licences, to abolish the Welsh local polls on Sunday opening, and to introduce a new 'continental café-style premises' licence.

The children's certificate is straightforward enough, though still a very timid reform by continental standards. The licensee applies for the certificate — so pubs that don't want to admit kids don't have to. The local justices decide whether the pub is suitable — so kids aren't admitted to the local licensed knocking shop. Accompanied children are then permitted in pubs with certificates. CAMRA warmly supports this proposal. Our main concern is that it should not be too hedged around with restrictions, unless these genuinely protect the interests of children.

At present, licensing justices have complete discretion in considering licence applications, and they don't even have to reveal their reasons for refusing a licence. Clearly this is unfair and absurd. The Government, and CAMRA, wants to move to specific statutory reasons for refusal, with reasons for refusal given in writing. Sensible enough.

Currently, every seven years, a referendum may be called in a Welsh district to see if pubs there may open on Sunday. To describe this as unfair and anachronistic is an understatement. The last polls cost taxpayers £400,000, saw

an average turnout of only 9 per cent of registe
and saw only one district, Dwyfor, remain dry o.
CAMRA wants this law scrapped and the 1996 po.
doned.

Where we get into Cloud Cuckoo Land is the new
licence. The problem is not whether cafés should be licen
to sell alcohol — there are clearly times and places whe
this is perfectly sensible. Indeed, café-style premises can be
licensed under the existing law.

What the Government wants to do, it seems, is rig the licensing system, so that thousands of cafés open, at the expense of traditional pubs. They want to tie justices' hands, so that it is 'Oui' to the café, but a possible 'Non' to any new pub.

The logic behind this seems infused with a *Toujours Provence* sentimentalism. The Consultative Paper explains that pubs are full of heavy drinking young men, who create public disorder. What we need, they say, is nice, clean continental-style cafés, where this won't happen. What has not occurred to the Government is that any sandwich bar owner with an eye to the main chance will buy in a few crates of Heineken, and install a jukebox. You may get exactly that sort of problem drinker flocking to cafés, where, to be blunt, the owner may not know what's hit him. How will the mere absence of a bar stop punch-ups?

If we do need a new type of licence — and I'm not persuaded — then we need some common sense here. The local justices must have powers to look at cafés and pubs on similar grounds.

The Home Office even suggests that foreign tourists want to come to Britain to drink in a British person's half-baked idea of what a continental-style café might look like. Why not promote the great British pub instead? Foreign visitors love it. Increasingly, pubs do food and coffee as well as booze, and better than most continental cafés. Just let the pubs open sensible grown-up hours, and let children into suitable pubs. And that's where I started.

Stephen Cox is CAMRA's Campaigns Manager.

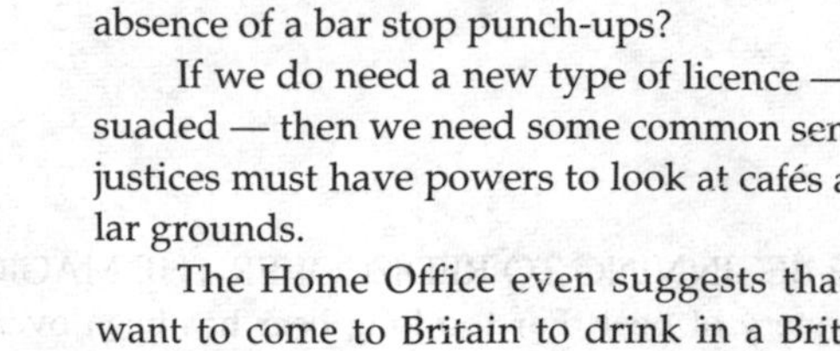

…UGHT ON THE HOP

…er Protz visits Elgood's and rediscovers …e art of the brewer

"Those who look upon beer as something coarse, common and low; who regard it as something to be drunk in secret but not in public, as something not quite 'nice', should cast away all associations and come to beer afresh and taste it afresh...I do not ask them to go through any of the ritual of the connoisseur or to titlillate their palates. I ask them merely to drink with an open gullet and an open mind."

ANONYMOUS BRITISH WRITER, 1934.

WE ARE BEGINNING TO REDISCOVER THE MAGIC and the mystery of beer. For too long beer has been overshadowed not so much by wine itself but by a wine snobbery that suggests, often stridently, that the product of the grape is infinitely superior to that of barley.

It is not the case in countries where beer is placed on its rightful pedestal and where brewers are honoured with the title of 'brewmaster'. But the British have a great capacity for understating their own achievements and so we have tended to dismiss our own great beer culture and wax lyrical instead about the undoubted merits of imported wine.

The aim of this article is not to downgrade wine, but to attempt to sketch the enormous skills that go into brewing and the fascinating chain of bio-chemical reactions that make beer possible.

I followed the brewing process in Elgood's splendid Georgian brewery in Wisbech, Cambridgeshire. No two breweries are identical. The beauty of a traditional plant such as Elgood's is that the process flows logically from floor to floor and room to room in artisanal vessels. It is far removed from the functional but soulless, high-tech modern plants where brewing takes place behind tiled walls and inside enclosed conical fermenters.

THE MALT

THE MAKING OF BEER BEGINS IN A MALTIN some distance from the brewery. It is the transform barley into malt that begins to release the sugars that can feed on.

British beer is brewed from two-row maritime barley is called two-row because of the number of rows of grain i each ear, and it is maritime as a result of its proximity to the sea, which means the finest malting barley in Britain comes from East Anglia and the Scottish Lowlands.

There are two basic varieties of barley suitable for brewing: winter varieties such as Maris Otter and its offshoots Halcyon and Pipkin, sewn in the autumn and harvested the following summer, and spring barleys such as Triumph, sewn when the worst of the winter is over.

Each grain of barley consists of an inner cell called the endosperm, composed mainly of starch, and an outer wall which not only protects the endosperm but also contains vital proteins that release enzymes during the mashing process in the brewery. One common misconception of the malting process is that it turns the starch in the endosperm into sugar. In fact, malting renders the starch soluble but it becomes sugar only in the brewery mash tun.

Why barley? The world is rich in other cereals, and many of them are used to a greater or lesser extent in brewing. But, as the father of the American micro-brewing revo-

lution, Fritz Maytag of the Anchor Brewery, puts it: "Barley is the finest grain, the sweetest grain". Natural selection over centuries has led to barley becoming the preferred cereal of brewers, not only because of its quality and rich flavours but also because it has a husk that acts as a natural filter during the mashing process.

The art of the maltster is to take the raw grain, allow it to partially germinate then gently roast it to produce malt. Malt looks little different to barley grains, but malting crucially changes its character. When the barley reaches the maltings it is steeped in tanks of water to encourage germination. The grains are then spread on floors where the temperature is kept at 15 degrees C and constantly turned and raked to ensure the heat reaches every layer of grain.

Only partial germination, with rootlets breaking through, takes place. The grain is then moved to a kiln room where searing heat toasts it. The heat depends on the type of malt required by the brewer: pale malt makes up the bulk of all brewing malt. A higher temperature produces crystal or amber malts, which add colour and a delicious cob nuts character to beer. Chocolate black and roasted malt have little fermentable material in them because of the savage roasting they receive and they are used for colour and flavour .

And now, and only now, the essential and vital ingredient in brewing is ready for the trip to the brewery. At Elgood's, the malt is first cleaned to remove any unwanted material, such as small stones from the barley field. It is then ground or cracked in a mill to make a coarse powder called grist. The cracked malt is held in a large box, the grist case, and mixed with other malts according to recipe.

At Wisbech, the two bitters, Cambridge and Greyhound, are made up of pale malt, roast barley and small amounts of maize and wheat. Roast barley, which has not been malted, is widely used in Scotland, and in dark beers in England and Wales, but is rare in English bitters. It is used by Elgood's in place of crystal malt and gives colour to the beer and a slightly vinous fruitiness to the palate. Flaked maize is used to control the proteins in the mash while torrefied wheat, a posh name for popcorn, gives a good head on the finished beer.

The Mash

WHEN THE MASH STARTS EARLY IN THE MORNING, the grist pours from the case into the mash tun, a vessel dating back to the turn of the century and made from copper. A thousand kilos of malt are used for every brew, mixed with water in the ratio of one kilo of malt to two barrels of 'liquor', as brewing water is known. Elgood's liquor comes from the public supply, though many breweries use their own natural springs. At Wisbech, the water is treated to remove hardness but a measured amount of calcium sulphate is put in to 'Burtonise' the liquor and to replicate the gypsum-rich waters of Burton upon Trent, where pale ales were first developed.

During the mashing process, enzymes in the malt convert the starches into sugar, a process known as saccharification. The sugars produced are maltose and dextrin. Maltose is highly fermentable while dextrins are not, but are important to give a good 'malty body' to beer. If all sugars turned to alcohol, the finished beer would be strong, but too dry and thin for comfort.

The temperature of the mash must be maintained at 66 degrees C as enzymes are extremely sensitive to heat: too high and they are destroyed, too slow and they will work only sluggishly, refusing to convert sufficient sugar. The temperature of the mash must start higher than 66 degrees, as the liquor will cool when it first mixes with the grist. So the mash starts at a 'strike heat' of about 75 degrees. This can be achieved in the mash tun but Elgood's uses a Steele's Masher, placed above the mash tun, a large tube with an

ELGOOD'S MASH TUN, WITH THE STEELE'S MASHER ABOVE ENSURING A PERFECT STRIKE HEAT FOR THE MALT GRIST AND LIQUOR AT THE START OF THE MASH

Archimedes screw which precisely mixes grist and liquor at strike heat temperature before the mix goes into the tun.

The thick, porridge-like mash is repeatedly stirred and stands for between 1½ and two hours. At the end of mashing, the sweet liquid, called wort, is run off through the slotted base of the tun into an underback where it is held while the spent grains are sprayed, or sparged, with more hot liquor by revolving perforated tubes in the roof of the mash tun. This washes out any remaining sugars.

No wort leaves the tun until it is running clear. The brewer checks the wort by running some off through side taps. The first runnings are usually thick and are returned to the tun until satisfactory clarity is achieved. The wort has to be pumped to the copper quickly to avoid its losing heat and becoming hazy and tainted. Elgood's copper is a splendid vessel built in 1950. It is a pressurised boiler with a central device known as a calandria that acts in just the same way as a coffee percolator to keep the boiling wort circulating.

THE HOPS

IT IS IN THE COPPER that beer-in-the-making meets its next vital ingredient. Is there a more fascinating plant than the hop, humulus lupulus? The Latin name means the wolf plant, for it runs riot across the ground or in hedges, unless trained and controlled to climb up string and wire frames. The Romans ate it as a delicacy like asparagus and its use in brewing has been recorded since the tenth century.

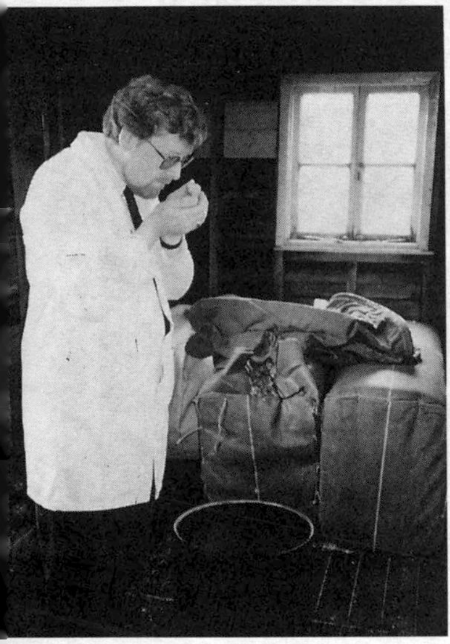

SAVOURING THE AROMA OF THE HOP FLOWERS IN THE HOP STORE. AT ELGOOD'S, ONLY THE DEEPLY BITTER FUGGLES HOPS ARE USED

The hop adds more to beer than aroma and bitterness. The tannins and acids contained in the cone of the plant play an important part in warding off infections in the wort. While the hop has no 'fermentable material' — starch — it does contribute to the aroma and palate of the finished beer. The tart, citric and perfumy aroma of low gravity beers comes from the hop, not from the malt.

Hops are grown primarily in Kent and Worcestershire. When they are picked in early autumn they are dried in warm oast houses, crammed into large sacks called pockets and sold to breweries. Hops, like grapes, come in a multitude of varieties. The favoured varieties in British ale brewing are the Fuggle and the Golding, the first giving a deep and pungent bitterness to beer, the second a resiny, peppery aroma. Wye College in Kent has developed several new hop varieties that are less prone to attack by aphids and wilt than Fuggles and Goldings and many brewers are also using the likes of Challenger, Northdown and Target.

Hop balance is essential in beer. At Elgood's, only Fuggles are used, which gives the beers a marvellous deep bitterness but little aroma, but a new head brewer is considering introducing an aroma hop as well.

During the 1½-hour copper boil, essential alpha acids, beta acids and oils are extracted from the hops and absorbed into the wort. The hops are not all added at the start of the boil, as some of the aroma and bittering qualities are distilled off. Hops are added at stages during the boil, often as late as fifteen minutes from the end.

The system of 'dry hopping', that is adding a of hops to each cask of beer as it leaves the brewery, ing favour. Elgood's head brewer speaks for many wh says dry hopping can lead to inconsistency of flavour. T is now a trend towards either late copper hopping or add hops in the hop back, the vessel that holds the hopped wo after it has been strained through the base of the copper.

At Elgood's, the whole flower of the hop is used. Others prefer compressed pellet hops, though they require a centrifuge to separate liquid and spent hops. Most brewers frown on the use of hop oils and extract which tend to leave an unpleasant bite at the back of the drinker's throat.

In the Copper

AT ELGOOD'S, INVERT SUGAR — sugar inverted into its component parts of glucose and fructose — is added during the boil, though glucose, brown sugar and other types can be used. Sugar is a controversial addition to beer. It was a useful tool when breweries were working flat out, for it meant that more wort could be pushed through the mash tuns as another fermentable material was added in the copper. It is less necessary today and too heavy a hand on the sugar bag can lead to a thin and dry beer, for glucose is highly fermentable and the yeast will attack it first before moving on to the maltose.

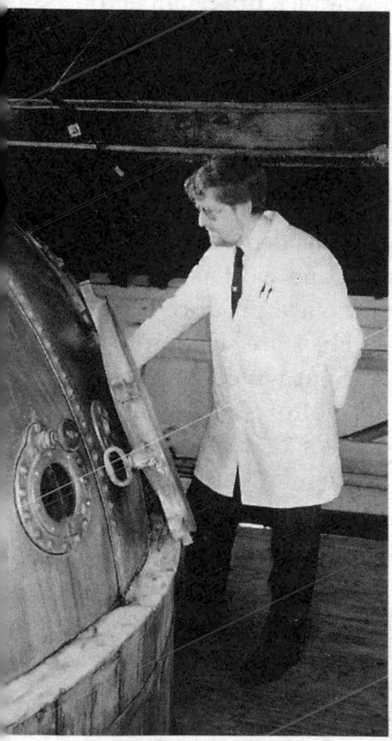

ELGOOD'S SPLENDID 1950S COPPER, WHERE THE MASH IS BOILED WITH THE HOPS

During the copper boil, the proteins come out of solution and coagulate into a sticky substance. This moment is known as the Hot Break. Copper finings, made from Irish moss, a type of seaweed, are used to clarify the hopped wort and the mess of protein, called trub, settles to the base of the copper along with the spent hops.

The hopped wort is held in the hop back and then cooled rapidly in preparation for the titanic battle to come in the fermenters. Most brewers cool the wort in heat exchangers but Elgood's has a beguiling system of open copper cooling trays where the prevailing air temperature cools the wort. As the liquid is open to the atmosphere, wild yeasts could begin to attack the wort in the trays but Elgood's says it never suffers such problems.

ENTATION

THE WORT IS COOLED TO 20 DEGREES C, run into the fermenting vessels and then mixed — or pitched — with yeast. The brewer will check his starting, or original, gravity carefully. If he wants a beer with a gravity of 1036 degrees — which means 36 parts of malt sugars and other sugars have been added to water, which has a gravity of 1000 degrees — he may have to add liquor to bring the wort down to that level.

At Elgood's, Cambridge Bitter and Greyhound Bitter come from the same wort. They are separated in the fermenters, with extra liquor added to reduce the gravity of Cambridge. This is known as parti-gyling: each new brew is called a 'gyle'.

Yeast is often thought of as a neutral substance that turns sweet liquids into alcohol. This single-celled fungus is far more complex than that. Used from brew to brew, often for decades and even centuries, a particular yeast strain will pick up, retain and pass on the flavours of beer from one batch to another. Take a yeast strain out of one brewery and transfer it to another and both the yeast and the beer will rapidly change flavour characteristics.

HIGH-SIDED SLATS ON THE WOODEN FERMENTING VESSELS KEEP IN THE EXPANDING YEAST AND WORT

At Elgood's, the wooden and lined fermenters have high-sided slats added to contain the yeast and wort as alcohol and carbon dioxide are produced. At first just a few bubbles are seen on the surface of the wort but within 24 hours a thick, heaving, yellow-white head with darker streaks of protein has formed, rising to regular cauliflower-like peaks. Elgood's yeast, in common with all ale yeasts, is a top-fermenting strain that works best at a warm temperature. A lager yeast works at a cooler one. Splendid aromas, known as esters, are produced and, according to the volume and mix of malt, such tantalising smells as apples, oranges, blackcurrants, pear drops and liquorice can be detected.

Fermentation lasts for four to five days. The great head of yeast is skimmed and kept for future use while the remaining yeast slowly sinks to the base of the vessel. The brewer will not let all the sugars turn to alcohol, for the finished beer would be too attenuated, or brewed out, and would lack body. The 'green beer' is run into conditioning tanks where it rests for a few days, purging itself of rougher esters and higher alcohols. But the brewer will want to retain many of the delectable fruity notes that mark ale out from the world's other great beer style, lager. Finings, a glutinous substance made from the bladder of the sturgeon fish, is added to begin the lengthy process of clearing the beer that will continue in the cask in the pub cellar. When the brewer is satisfied that the first stage of conditioning is complete, he will run — or rack — the beer into casks, adding priming sugar to encourage a powerful second fermentation and, in some cases, additional hops for aroma. The care that goes into each final stage of cask beer production is in sharp contradiction to keg brewing where, after primary fermentation, the beer is chilled, filtered to remove yeast, pasteurised to ensure total death and racked into sealed and pressurised kegs.

THE BREWERY CAT, GUARDING THE ELGOOD'S GRAIN STORE

Cask-conditioned beer is not yet ready to drink. It will continue to ferment and condition in the pub cellar for a few days more before it can delight and refresh the drinker. The publican or his cellarman will have to use skill and experience to know when best to tap and vent each cask as the beer ferments and breathes.

Venting — knocking a porous peg of wood into a small shive hole on top of the cask — allows excess gas to escape but it is vital to retain some gas to give the beer sparkle and a good head. At the right moment, the cellarman will replace the soft peg with a hard one to keep in sufficient gas. As the second fermentation dies down, the finings will drag the yeast and proteins to the belly of the cask. The cellarman will draw off small amounts of beer and when he is satisfied it has 'dropped bright' and has a good aroma, free from yeasty off-flavours, he will connect the tap to the beer lines and the fresh ale is ready to serve.

The brewer's work is done. He has taken the raw ingredients, the skills of maltster and hop grower, added his own craftsmanship and produced a beer unique to Britain and, increasingly, the envy of the rest of the beer-drinking world.

■ Thanks to Alan Pateman, head brewer at Elgood's, for his help, patience and assistance.

Roger Protz edits CAMRA's newspaper, What's Brewing, and writes for the Morning Advertiser and The Guardian. His books include The Village Pub, The Real Ale Drinker's Almanac and Brew Your Own Real Ale at Home. (with Graham Wheeler)

THE NAME GAME

Editor Jeff Evans contemplates the logic behind strange names

A PINT OF PIGSWILL", I ordered somewhat gingerly. I'm pleased to say my adventure was well rewarded when the landlord returned with an excellent brew, full of malt and hop flavour. There were no hints of potato peel, no bouquet of rancid apple, not even a lingering cabbage and turnip finish. A more pedantic drinker might have returned it for a refund or complained to Trading Standards. I simply wondered why a good beer a like this should be saddled with such an ugly name.

There turned out to be some logic to the madness: the beer was originally brewed by Bunces as a house beer for a pub called The Two Pigs in Corsham, but the episode left me considering just how many other fine brews had struggled to gain respect, held back by a ridiculous and unjust title.

I was not the first to address the issue. In the 1980s, the Paul Daniels quiz show *Every Second Counts* demanded that contestants picked out the real ales from a list of bizarre names. Presumably Old Wiggy Wizard was not amongst the proffered titles. But matters really came to a head a year ago, with Whitbread's infamous beer bore advert, in which three ale aficionados held pints of Old Grumblebelly up to the light and launched into a stream of adjectives in an attempt to describe their pints. Meanwhile, across the bar, three discerning Flowers Original drinkers merely sat and supped, in awe of the ale-tasters' creative wordpower. It was a fine, amusing advert, but lessons in outrageous beer descriptions are difficult to take from Whitbread. To close breweries, feebly copy the beers elsewhere and still call them Higsons, Wethered's, Fremlins and Strong's, now that's what I call imagination.

Whitbread, it has to be said, is not prone to the fits of name madness which occasionally overcome brewers. It is a disease which needs urgent treatment, akin to the ailment which encourages sad parents to name their offspring after the entire Chelsea football team. You only have to explore the Beers Index to discover such graphic offerings as Headcracker, Skullsplitter, Hammerhead and Dragonslayer. Well, you can't say you weren't warned. Presumably, St

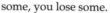

Austell's occasional brew, Crippledick, is sponsored by Cornish Family Planning Association, though I must qu ly state that Brown Willy, from the Min Pin Inn, innocent derives its name from Cornwall's highest hill. But if fu marks in this section go to Barry Parish of Parish Brewery for his enigmatic Baz's Bonce Blower, spare a thought for Archers of Swindon. At last realising that Headbanger was a less than suitable name for their excellent strong brew, they changed it to Old Cobleigh's. Sadly, it hasn't taken long for the new nickname of Old Cobblers to take hold. You win some, you lose some.

Of course, the strangest of beer names can have an appropriate and fitting origin and some breweries like to develop their beer range along a theme. The Hampshire Brewery has launched a series of mystic titles broadly based around King Alfred, whose parliament was based in Andover, the brewery's home town. The Titanic brewery recalls the great ship and its skipper, Captain Smith, who hailed from Stoke-on-Trent, where the brewery is based, and the Lakeland Brewery at The Masons Arms in Cumbria celebrates the works of local *Swallows and Amazons* writer Arthur Ransome.

Other breweries also allude to their geographical, historical and cultural associations. The Pendle Witches of the 17th century are remembered by Moorhouse's, and Hesket Newmarket's ales are named after Lake District fells. University connections are well to the fore amongst Morrells Oxford brews, with names like Varsity, College and Graduate established well before Inspector Morse began to link ale and academia, and neighbour Morland's Old Speckled Hen is not named after a chicken, but after the MG motor car built on the Oxfordshire assembly lines. Theakston's Old Peculier takes its name from the Peculier, or ecclesiastical court, of Masham in medieval times and, like Hanby's Drawwell and Whitby's Woblle, is one of those beer names everyone thinks you have spelled incorrectly.

Some beer titles reflect modern influences, such as television. We've seen Black Adder and Baldric, and now Bushy's have introduced Lovely Jubbely Christmas Ale to the Isle of Man. Not only is Douglas a long way from

Peckham, but I could have sworn Del Boy's favourite tipple was Drambuie and Lucozade.

Of course, the pump clip has long been used as an arena for word games, for clever and not-so-clever plays on words, intended to give the beer a gimmicky introduction. David Bruce has been master of the art, teasing the drinking public with near the knuckle puns on words like 'firkin', 'fox' and 'phoenix'.

The Jolly Roger brewery has been more subtle, with its delicately-titled Goodness stout, much in the same vein as West Coast's Guiltless stout. I grew up in the South Wales valleys and was assailed by a keg beer from the Crown brewery appallingly labelled Same Again, which I remembered with a shudder on seeing the beer Banks & Taylor decided to call 2XS. And surely there's some confusion in Cropton pubs when you order one pint of Two Pints. My spirits were lifted, however, on hearing that Reindeer Brewery had decided against calling its stout Janet Street Porter. At least that gives libel lawyers less to get their teeth into.

One of the more appealing uses of the pump clip is to pay someone a tribute. Brewery forefathers have long been remembered in this way but more recent achievers are now beginning to feature, too. The fighter aces of World War II have been honoured in Shepherd Neame's Spitfire Ale, originally brewed to commemorate the Battle of Britain. More parochially, Elgood's has named a porter after its recently retired head brewer, Sir Henry Holder, and Charles Wells Bombardier takes its name from Bombardier Billy Wells, the man who beat the gong at the start of Rank films. In 1993, Tolly Cobbold created Tollyshooter to thank Sir John Harvey-Jones for his advice in the *Troubleshooter* TV series. But to many CAMRA members, Maclay's kind gesture in naming Kane's Amber Ale after the late Dan Kane, a popular Scottish real ale campaigner, is the most appreciated.

Sadly, though, it looks like we shall still be plagued by names which do the beers no justice and the real ale cause little good. I've always time for dreamy rustic titles like Farmer's Glory or Tally Ho, the historically reflective Cromwell Bitter or the literally inspired Tom Brown's Best Bitter, but do we really need Dr Thirsty's Draught, Son of a Bitch or Old Fart?

How about a pint of Auld Soxx, Dogbolter or Dizzy Dick? Give me Pigswill any day.

BEER AROUND BRITAIN

Iain Loe, CAMRA's Research Manager, offers a traveller's guide to the local flavour of British beer

WITH BREWERS SPENDING massive sums promoting their national ales — Draught Bass, Tetley Bitter, John Smith's Bitter and so on — you could be forgiven for thinking that wherever you go in Britain you will end up drinking the same brands of beer.

However, different regions of the country do have their own identities. Local breweries, offering variations in style and taste, differentiate the regions. The British drinking scene might be dominated by the national brewers but there are still plenty of smaller producers around to make a drinking visit to Burton, Bradford or Barnstable worthwhile. Here are a few clues to help you track down the flavour of each region of the country.

SOUTH-WEST

Avon, Cornwall, Devon, Gloucestershire

We start our journey in the South-West, where the region's two largest (and national) breweries, Courage and Whitbread, dominate. However, the region is regarded by many as the heartland of the microbrewery revolution. Successful established micros include Butcombe, Exmoor, Exe Valley, Smiles, Otter, Uley and Blackawton, and newcomers Freeminer and Bridgwater have started since the publication of the last *Good Beer Guide*. The region is also home to one of the prettiest breweries, Donnington, whose pubs still grace the Cotswold countryside.

Cornwall may be regarded by some as showing less variety, but even here new breweries are in the planning stage and the well-established St Austell offers local colour to the visitor, as does the famous home-brew pub, the Blue Anchor in Helston. Whitbread, through its supply agreement with the Devenish pub company (now acquired by Greenalls), has most influence, with the Redruth brewery centrating on canned beers and only producing one real ale — Cornish Original, for Whitbread to supply to Devenish pubs! The take-over by Greenalls may change the face of Devenish pubs, particularly in Devon and Cornwall, with some houses earmarked for disposal. Whilst in the West Country, look out for so-called 'Boy's Bitters', such as Courage Bitter Ale and Whitbread West Country Pale Ale. They can be found in quite a few outlets but there is little promotion for these low-gravity bitters.

Central-South

Berkshire, Buckinghamshire, Dorset, Hampshire, Isle of Wight, Oxfordshire, Wiltshire

Part of this region was once known to travellers on the Waterloo to Bournemouth line as 'Strong Country', courtesy of the signs that welcomed them at the trackside. The Strong Brewery in Romsey was taken over by Whitbread in 1968 and closed in 1981, but even today large sections of the region are dominated by Whitbread, most notably the coastal strip from Portsmouth to Bournemouth.

However, there are some oases for the beer drinker. Wiltshire, following the management buy-out at Ushers, has no less than nine independent breweries, and offers the best choice of real ale. In Dorset, the Heart of Wessex, independents Hall & Woodhouse, Eldridge Pope and Palmers are joined by minnow Poole brewery, though Mild is conspicuous by its absence from this county. In Hampshire, Ringwood, a pioneer in the small brewery revolution, is well represented in the free trade and the Gale's tied estate extends over much of the county. What might surprise the visitor is the sizeable presence of Marston's, who acquired the Winchester Brewery in 1923. Across the Solent, the name of Burts will soon live again, following its purchase by Isle of Wight neighbour Island Brewery.

Berkshire, bereft of breweries, apart from Courage's mega-keggery by the side of the M4, is well supplied by independents such as Brakspear, Fuller's and Morland. And Oxfordshire, as well as five independent breweries of its own, has Fuller's, Young's and Ushers tied houses. But don't ignore Morrells pubs in Oxford city, or Brakspear's excellent country houses around Henley-on-Thames.

The Wethered name, now fading from pubs in the Bucks and Berks area, is a sad reminder of the fine Marlow brewery closed by Whitbread in 1988. Wethered Bitter is now brewed by McMullen in Hertford, but the new Rebellion Beer Company, Old Luxters and Chiltern keep Bucks brewing traditions alive in the free trade.

South-East

Kent, Surrey, Sussex

Real ale will greet the visitor in over 90 per cent o region's pubs, though most of it will come from the natic brewers, despite the fact that the last national brewer Fremlins of Faversham, was closed by Whitbread in 1990 The liveries of other former local producers, such as Friary Meux, bought and closed by Allied, can still be seen around the region.

The largest independent is Shepherd Neame, whose pub estate has almost doubled since the pub sell-offs by the national brewers, and the region has also acquired a number of Morland pubs, picked up by the Oxfordshire brewery in a deal with Courage. Sussex is home for two stalwart family brewers, King & Barnes of Horsham and Harveys of Lewes. Harveys beers are also available through Beards pubs, though Beards itself gave up brewing in the 1950s.

Prices vary but, apart from the odd bargain, are not cheap. In coastal resorts, prices are comparable with Central London.

Greater London

The capital now has only four breweries of any size: independents Fuller's and Young's, and the Courage and Guinness keg plants at Mortlake and Park Royal. However, independents such as Sam Smith, Shepherd Neame and Greene King have a presence and new pub chains like Wetherspoon and Regent Inns have provided a refreshing change from the otherwise drab uniformity of the national brewers' pubs. The Nicholson's pub chain is a notable exception, having pubs of high quality and often historic value, albeit coupled with expensive pints of beer.

London is also home to the Firkin chain of brew pubs, established by David Bruce, but now owned by Taylor Walker. Several other brew pubs may also be discovered.

East Anglia

Bedfordshire, Cambridgeshire, Essex, Hertfordshire, Norfolk, Suffolk

Another national brewery-free zone, following the closure of Ind Coope's Romford brewery in 1993. However, there are seven long-established 'family' breweries, eleven small independents set up in recent years and three home-brew pubs. Two of the independents, Mauldons, with its Black Adder, and Woodforde's, with Norfolk Nog, are recent winners of CAMRA's *Champion Beer of Britain* award.

The largest pub owner in the region is Greene King, with over 800 pubs, but the nationals still have a strong esence through Grand Metropolitan (a.k.a. Watney) in orfolk, Ind Coope in Essex, Whitbread in the western parts of the region and Benskins in Hertfordshire. Pubmaster, the Brent Walker pub chain, operates the former Tolly Cobbold estate, as well as a number of former Grand Met houses, whilst the Tolly Cobbold brewery is itself operating again after a management buy-out and the beers are becoming increasingly available.

East Anglia is awash with real ale, but for sheer diversity head for Norwich or Cambridge. Visit Southwold in Suffolk for Adnams, Wisbech for Elgood's, Hertford for McMullen and Bedford for Charles Wells, although all these beers are fairly widely available.

East Midlands

Leicestershire, Lincolnshire, Northamptonshire, Nottinghamshire, South Humberside

This is another region where national brewers tend to dominate, Tetley, Bass, Boddingtons and Ind Coope Burton Ale being the most common beers, alongside Marston's Pedigree. Scottish & Newcastle's Home Brewery Mild is now being brewed by Mansfield and a fight has begun to ward off the threat to the entire Home Brewery. Mansfield now offers a good supply of its own cask brands, resuming real ale production in 1982, after a decade of keg-only brewing. In Nottingham, look out for Hardys & Hansons, and, in Leicester, Everards and the tiny Hoskins & Oldfield. The original Hoskins brewery, however, has experienced some boardroom turmoil and a question mark remains over its future.

Derby and Lincoln offer the best opportunities for discovering interesting beers, and don't miss a diversion to Wainfleet and Bateman's brewery. Pub chains such as Greenalls (with former Shipstone's pubs supplied from Tetley Walker in Warrington), and Inntrepreneur are well represented, but smaller companies such as Tynemill offer a more positive input to the beer scene.

West Midlands

Birmingham, Hereford and Worcester, Shropshire Staffordshire, Warwickshire

Ansells (Carlsberg-Tetley) and M&B (Bass) dominate this region but Batham, Sarah Hughes, Holden's and other smaller breweries add extra choice and value for money. Banks's beer offers good value, too, and although its sister brewery, Hanson's, has been closed, many of the pubs still bear the Hanson's name. They serve Banks's beers and possibly beers from Camerons, also now owned by Wolverhampton & Dudley.

Burton-upon-Trent is the birthplace of pale ale and still has six working breweries of various sizes. Guest beers are increasingly available in the West Midlands and, if you are looking for mild, this is where to come. The very pale and sweetish beers of the Black Country, such as Batham's, are also well-known, though, sadly, Simpkiss is no more, thanks to Greenalls, which has destroyed much of the brewing heritage of the Midlands. All the same, the area is becoming popular with tourists taking 'beer weekends'.

An important note: electric dispense from plastic bar founts is very common in the West Midlands, so don't be confused and think nearly all the beer is keg!

South and Mid Wales

Dyfed, Mid, South and West Glamorgan, Gwent, Powys

Welsh Brewers (Bass's Welsh trading division), Whitbread (in South-East Wales) and Tetley (in Gwent) dominate here, but Brains (strong in Cardiff), Felinfoel and Crown Buckley (following its management buy-out from Guinness) add extra variety.

Beer choice is generally poorer than in England, but has increased in the last ten years. The industrial valleys north of Pontypridd, Rhymney Valley north of Caerphilly and Gwent's western valleys are still pretty poor bets for real ale, but the situation is improving, although guest beers, where sold, are largely confined to Brains and Crown Buckley. Look in rural South-East Wales for the best choice, even though here the guest beer availability has been diminished with the sale of Courage pubs to the newly independent Ushers brewery.

The area, unfortunately, has not been a fruitful base for microbreweries. Several have opened, but all have closed in the last decade, the most recent being Sam Powell of Newtown, whose beers are now brewed by Wood. Greenalls has also destroyed choice in northern Powys, by closing Shropshire's Wem brewery and filling its pubs with Tetley Walker brews.

Prices tend to be on a par with the Midlands and there are two plus points: a lot of pubs seem to have adopted afternoon opening, and no area in the region is dry on Sunday!

MERSEYSIDE AND NORTH WALES

Cheshire, Clwyd, Gwynedd, Merseyside

Tetley (with Peter Walker in Liverpool) and Greenalls are the major players in this region, with the best areas for interesting beers Liverpool, Warrington and Chester, and the worst, Deeside, Wrexham and Ellesmere Port. The high spots of recent years have been the opening of the Cains brewery, in the old Higsons site, and the Coach House brewery, in Warrington, and the low spots, the closure of both Higsons and Greenalls. New small breweries are opening in North Wales and, with Vaux moving in to join Lees of Manchester in this patch, the real ale scene is improving all the time. However, Marston's seems intent on ruining the pub estate of the former Border brewery, which it closed in the mid-80s.

A word of warning: Dwyfor in the Anglesey area of North Wales is still dry on Sundays and all day opening is still very patchy in this region.

NORTH-WEST

Lancashire, Greater Manchester, Cumbria

Independent breweries Hydes', Holt, Robinson's and Lees continue to offer choice and competition which helps keeps Manchester the best value for money city in the country, with pints a fraction of their cost in southern England. The area is rich in milds, including two produced by its best-known brewery, Boddingtons, now owned by Whitbread. The Strangeways site has increased production by over 100 per cent in recent years, whilst the separate Boddington Pub Company remains a big player in the local pub scene. Greenalls, also now just a pub group, has achieved infamy for its sly demolition of the Manchester city-centre outlet Tommy Ducks, and several other inner-City houses are threatened by redevelopment plans. Local CAMRA branches are working with planners to ensure that as many as possible are saved.

Independents such as Jennings, Thwaites, Moorhouse's and Mitchell's successfully vie with the nationals in Lancashire and Cumbria, and new breweries such as Preston (now being rechristened the Atlas Brewery) have introduced yet more variety. Sadly, Matthew Brown in Blackburn was closed by S&N, despite assurances to the contrary, and Hartleys of Ulverston's brewing days have been brought to an end by Robinson's. Production of the one remaining Hartleys beer has been transferred to Stockport.

YORKSHIRE

West, South and North Yorkshire, Cleveland, North Humberside

Nationals are well to the fore in Yorkshire, with Carlsberg-Tetley, Bass, Courage and Scottish & Newcastle all having breweries in the region, but this has not prevented an explosion of small breweries offering more choice. The marketing term 'Yorkshire Bitter' has become rather clichéd of late, over-used for promoting beers nationwide. Thank goodness the talking horses have now been pensioned off. Genuine quality does exist, though, amongst Yorkshire brews and Tadcaster has long been known as the Burton of the North. It still boasts three breweries: Sam and John Smith's, and the Bass brewery, now, unfortunately, keg only. And with Timothy Taylor in Keighley, Wards of Sheffield and a host of new micros, there is a generous variety of proper Yorkshire ale to be supped. Masham is home to the famous Theakston brewery, though only about ten per cent of Theakston beers originate there, the rest coming from S&N's factory in Newcastle.

Choose York for pubs historic, Bradford for beer variety, Leeds if you like Tetley, and the Moors and Dales for fabulous scenery and country pubs.

NORTH-EAST

Durham, Northumberland, Tyne and Wear

This region is dominated by Scottish & Newcastle but the other Nationals, as well as Vaux and Camerons (now owned by Wolverhampton & Dudley), have a presence.

Best bets for beer choice are the centres of Newcastle, Darlington, Durham and Sunderland, and beer black spots include eastern Durham and the non-tourist parts of Northumberland. Pub groups such as Legendary Yorkshire Heroes, Sir John Fitzgerald, Northumbria Inns, Tap & Spile (Pubmaster) and T&J Bernards (S&N) offer some variety, but S&N beers are usually sold in these houses, too. Micros such as Hadrian, Big Lamp, Border, Hexhamshire, Butterknowle and Longstone increase choice, though Federation, the common drink in clubs, is keg more often than not.

SCOTLAND

There are still vast areas, notably in the Highlands, where real ale is the exception rather than the rule. The cities of Edinburgh, Glasgow and Aberdeen offer a good choice of beers, many from South of the Border, but at a price. Scotland has not been a happy hunting ground for micro-breweries, though established firms, such as Maclay and

Belhaven, with a few newcomers like Broughton, Harviestoun and Orkney do sterling (excuse the pun) work to refresh the tastebuds. Several new breweries are in the planning stages and these will be welcomed by Scottish beer hunters. S&N's T&J Bernards pub chain is expanding, and Pubmaster's Tap & Spile now has outlets at both Glasgow and Aberdeen airports.

Scotland, a big barley growing country, but not known for its hops, has a tradition of darker, sweeter, maltier beers than the rest of Britain and air pressure is the distinctive form of dispense, using air (not carbon dioxide) to force the beer to the bar. But be warned: keg dispense does now masquerade in the guise of the tall air fount. Opening hours are the big plus, being far more generous than elsewhere in the UK, with midnight closing and Sunday afternoon opening commonplace in towns and cities.

NORTHERN IRELAND, ISLE OF MAN AND THE CHANNEL ISLANDS

Real ale in Northern Ireland meant, until recently, only Hilden Ale or bottled Worthington White Shield. However, thanks to the campaigning efforts of the local CAMRA branch, mainland brewers such as Scottish & Newcastle are now actively looking to export their cask-conditioned ales to the province.

On the Isle of Man, too, beer choice has increased, largely thanks to the work of Bushy's Brewery, which has offered Isle of Man Breweries some much needed competition. Active CAMRA work has also brought cask ales, including Bass, Cains, Marston's and Tetley, from the mainland.

In the Channel Islands, though Randalls of Jersey has stopped brewing, Ann Street now once again produces cask beer, the Tipsy Toad pub brewery has opened and Guernsey still has two independents. The local CAMRA branches on the islands also run beer festivals and several mainland brews, such as Fuller's, Ringwood, Bass and Boddingtons, are now regularly available. Visitors should be careful to specify 'real ale' when ordering, as many pubs stock both cask and keg.

This 'region' exemplifies what good campaigning by CAMRA members can do to persuade brewers and pub owners to offer cask ales to their customers. Next time you're there, raise a glass of real ale to their efforts.

■ One more tip: keep your *Good Beer Guide* handy when travelling. Even in areas of poor choice, it'll help you find a pint worth drinking.

Avon

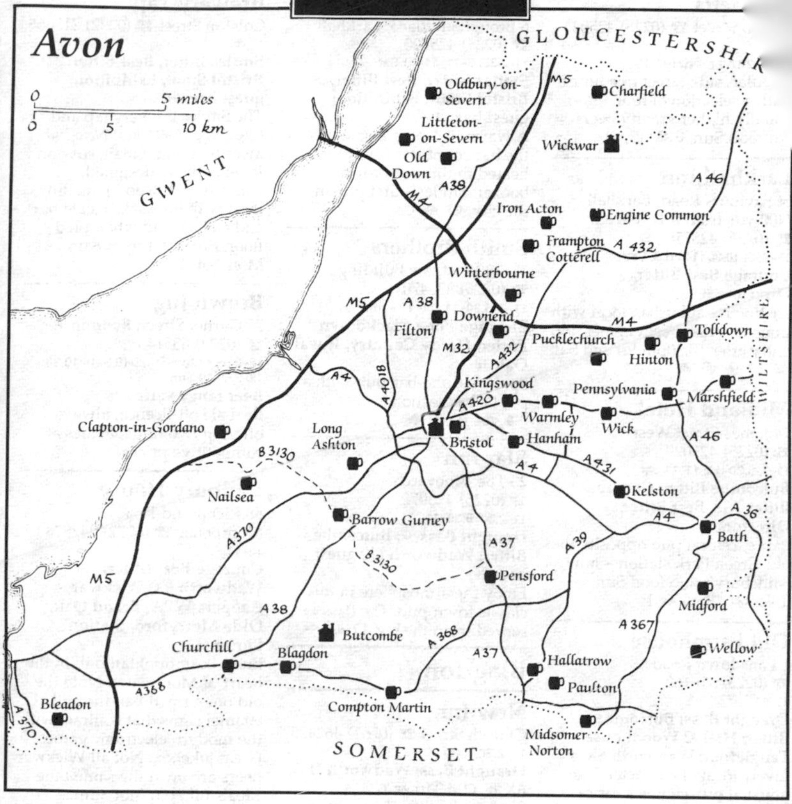

***Butcombe,** Butcombe; **Hardington, Ross, Smiles,** Bristol; **Wickwar,** Wickwar*

Barrow Gurney

Princes Motto
Barrow Street ☎ (0275) 472282
11–2.30, 6–11
Draught Bass Ⓖ; Butcombe Bitter; Marston's Pedigree; Smiles Best Bitter Ⓗ; Wadworth 6X Ⓖ; Whitbread Boddingtons Bitter Ⓗ
Friendly, unspoilt local, adorned with old sketches and maps. The bar, divided in two, can get busy. ⛫ ❀ ♣ P

Bath

Bell Inn
103 Walcot Street
☎ (0225) 460426
11.30–11
Adnams Bitter; Courage Best Bitter, Directors; Fuller's ESB; Smiles Best Bitter, Exhibition; guest beers Ⓗ
Open-plan bar renowned for its jazz and soul music. Games include chess and backgammon. ❀ ♣

Belvedere Wine Vaults
25 Belvedere, Lansdown Road
☎ (0225) 330264
12–3, 5.30–11
Bass Worthington BB, Draught Bass Ⓗ
Welcoming, unpretentious local with a quiet lounge.
Q ⊞ ♣

Bladud Arms
Gloucester Road, Lower Swainswick (A46)
☎ (0225) 420152
11–3, 7–11
Draught Bass; Butcombe Bitter; Marston's Pedigree; Wadworth IPA, 6X; guest beer Ⓗ
A long lounge bar with a public bar section. Skittle alley.
❀ ◐ ♣ P

Cross Keys
Midford Road, Combe Down (B3110) ☎ (0225) 832002
11–2.30 (3 Sat), 6–11
Courage Best Bitter; John Smith's Bitter; Ushers Best Bitter, Founders Ⓗ
Attractive Bath stone building with two traditional bars. Large aviary in the beer garden. Interesting food; good regular trade. ⛫ Q ❀ ◐ ◑ P

Fairfield Arms
1 Fairfield Park Road, Fairfield
☎ (0225) 310594
11–2.30 (3 Sat), 6–11
Courage Best Bitter; Ushers Best Bitter Ⓗ
Welcoming local, with an award-winning garden, on the north-eastern outskirts.
❀ ⊞ ♣

Golden Fleece
1–3 Avon Buildings, Lower Bristol Road ☎ (0225) 429572
11–2.30 (3 Sat), 5.30 (4.30 Fri)–11
Courage Best Bitter; John Smith's Bitter; guest beers Ⓗ
Very popular, street-corner local. The landlord changes his guest beers on a daily basis; the range includes Eldridge Pope Hardy Country alternating with Wadworth 6X and Marston's Pedigree. Weekday lunches. ◐ ⊞ ♣ P

...etts
... Street ☎ (0225) 425045
...
...range varies [H]
...ular, side-street free house ...h a selection of four, ...ually higher gravity beers. ...o food Sun. ◖ ⇌ (Spa)

Larkhall Inn
St Saviours Road, Larkhall (400 yds from A4/A46 jct)
☎ (0225) 425710
11–2, 6–10.30 (11 Fri & Sat)
Courage Best Bitter, Directors [H]
Distinctive suburban local with unusual brass beer engines. No entry after 10.30pm Fri and Sat.
♛ Q ❀ ⊞ ♣

Midland Hotel
14 James Street West
☎ (0225) 425029
11–3, 5.30–11; 11–11 Sat
Butcombe Bitter; Courage Bitter Ale, Best Bitter, Directors [H]
Large, central pub opposite the old Green Park station – now Sainsbury's. No food Sun.
◖ ⊞ ⇌ (Spa) ♣ P

Old Farmhouse
1 Lansdown Road
☎ (0225) 316162
12–11
Draught Bass; Butcombe Bitter; Hall & Woodhouse Tanglefoot; Wadworth 6X [H]
Lively local of character. The unusual pub sign is a caricature of its landlord. Meals Wed–Sat. ♛ ❀ ◖◗ ⊞ ♣

Old Green Tree
12 Green Street
☎ (0225) 462357
11–11; closed Sun lunch
Beer range varies [H]
Small, popular and traditional city-centre pub: three panelled rooms with parquet floors and no gimmicks. Five local beers. Dress restrictions.Q ◖ ⚟

Pig & Fiddle
2 Saracen Street
☎ (0225) 460868
11–3, 5–11 (11–11 summer)
Ash Vine Bitter, Challenger, Tanker, Hop & Glory, Black Bess Porter; guest beer [H]
A former fish restaurant, and Ash Vine's first pub in the county. No food Sun. ❀ ◖ ⇌ (Spa) ♣ ⊖

Porter Butt
York Place, London Road
☎ (0225) 425084
12–3, 5.30–11; 12–11 Sat
Courage Bitter Ale, Best Bitter, Directors; Fuller's London Pride; Marston's Pedigree [H]
Two-bar local by the bus depot. No food Sun. ❀ ◖ ⊞ ♣ P

Rose & Crown
6 Brougham Place, Larkhall
☎ (0225) 425700
11–2.30, 5–11; 11–11 Sat
Smiles Bitter, Best Bitter, Bristol Stout, Exhibition; guest beer [H]
A warm welcome awaits you – the bar counter is centrally heated in this out-of-town boozer. Smiles's first pub in the city. ⊞ ♣ ⊖

Smith Brothers
11–12 Westgate Buildings
☎ (0225) 330470
11–3, 5.30–11 (11–11 summer)
Eldridge Pope Blackdown Porter, Hardy Country, Royal Oak [H]
Spacious, one-bar pub with a public bar section.
◖◗ ⇌ (Spa) ♣

Star Inn
23 The Vineyards
☎ (0225) 425072
11–2.30, 5.30–11
Draught Bass [G]**; Butcombe Bitter; Wadworth 6X; guest beer** [H]
Enjoy the atmosphere in this classic town pub. The Bass is served from the jug. Q ⊞ ♣

Blagdon

New Inn
Church Street ☎ (0761) 462475
11–2.30, 7–11
Draught Bass; Wadworth IPA, 6X [H]**, Old Timer** [G]
Stone pub with a horse-brass decor. The garden offers beautiful views over Blagdon Lake and outboard motors can be hired. Good value food.
♛ Q ❀ ◖◗ ♣ P

Bleadon

Queens Arms
Celtic Way ☎ (0934) 812080
11–2.30, 7–11; 11–11 Sat
Ringwood Best Bitter, Fortyniner, Old Thumper [G]**; Whitbread Flowers IPA** [H]**; guest beers**
Two-bar, cottage-style pub with three separate drinking areas. The beers are served from a central stillage. Skittles and darts are popular. Overall, a gem. No food Sun.
Q ♘ ❀ ◖ ▲ ♣ P

Bristol

Albert
1 West Street, Bedminster
☎ (0272) 661968
11.30–2.30, 7.30–11
Courage Best Bitter; Smiles Best Bitter; Wadworth 6X [H]
Popular two-bar pub. The main bar is papered with record sleeves and photographs. Live jazz and folk. ◖

Brewery Tap
Colston Street ☎ (0272) 213668
11–11
Smiles Bitter, Best Bitter, Bristol Stout, Exhibition; guest beer [H]
The Smiles brewery tap and CAMRA's 1991 *Best New Pub* award-winner. Small, cosy and imaginatively designed, featuring ash wood panelling, inset with hopsack, a slate bar and a black and white tiled floor. Breakfast from 8am Mon–Sat. Q ◖

Brown Jug
77 Garnet Street, Bedminster
☎ (0272) 635145
12–2 (not Mon–Fri), 5 (6 Sat)–10.30; 12–2, 7–10 Sun
Beer range varies [H]
Real ale off-licence, always offering two unusual ales at competitive prices.

Cadbury House
68 Richmond Road, Montpelier ☎ (0272) 247874
12–11
Courage Best Bitter; Wadworth 6X; Wickwar Coopers WPA, Brand Oak, Olde Merryford, Station Porter [H]
Busy, cosmopolitan pub in the heart of Montpelier. Note the old one-armed bandits and enamel signs that contrast with the modern electronic games. Great jukebox. Not all Wickwar beers are on at the same time. Meals till 7pm (not Sun).
♛ ❀ ◖ ⇌ (Montpelier) ♣

Cambridge Arms
Coldharbour Road, Westbury Park ☎ (0272) 735584
11–11
Draught Bass; Courage Bitter Ale, Best Bitter [H]
Busy pub, comfortable and warm, attracting a wide age range. Occasional live music. Barbecues in summer in a good garden. ❀ ◖ P

Highbury Vaults
164 St Michael's Hill, Kingsdown ☎ (0272) 733203
12–11
Brains SA; Smiles Bitter, Best Bitter, Bristol Stout, Exhibition; guest beers [H]
Highly original and popular with all, a pub with Victorian/Edwardian fittings and a tiny snug. Eve meals Mon–Fri (till 8.30) Q ❀ ◖◗

Humpers Off-Licence
26 Soundwell Road, Staple Hill
☎ (0272) 565525
12–2, 4.30–10.30; 12–2, 7–10.30 Sun
Draught Bass; Smiles Best Bitter, Exhibition; Wickwar Brand Oak; guest beers [E]
Friendly, well-run off-licence, an oasis for guest beers (three

from far and wide. Low prices, and discounts for quantity. Strong ale in winter. ⌓

Kellaway Arms
Kellaway Avenue, Horfield
☎ (0272) 246694
11–2.30 (3 Fri & Sat), 6–11
Courage Best Bitter; Marston's Pedigree; Smiles Best Bitter Ⓗ
Comfortable, two-bar suburban local close to Horfield Common: a large public bar and a smaller lounge. Slides in the garden. No food Sun. Q ❀ ◐ ♣

King Charles
11 Kings Square Avenue (off Stokes Croft) ☎ (0272) 424451
11.30–11
Hardington Traditional; Ushers Best Bitter Ⓗ**; guest beer**
Small, friendly, cosmopolitan city-centre pub. Backgammon Tue. No food Sun. ◐ ♣

Kings Head
60 Victoria Street
☎ (0272) 277860
11–3 (not Sat), 5.30 (7.30 Sat)–11; 12–3, 7.45–10.30 Sun
Courage Bitter Ale, Best Bitter; Smiles Best Bitter Ⓗ
Small Victorian gem, restored but unspoilt: boasts a superb barback and a tramcar bar, full of character. Four-pint beer jug discount. Highly praised lunchtime snacks.
Q ⇌ (T Meads)

Knowle Hotel
Leighton Road, Knowle
☎ (0272) 777019
11.30–2.30, 5.30–11; 11–3, 6–11 Sat
Ind Coope Burton Ale; Smiles Best Bitter; Tetley Bitter Ⓗ
Large, friendly, two-bar pub with a good view over Bristol. Good value food. Several sports teams. Q ❀ ◐ ♿ ♣

Lion
19 Church Lane, Cliftonwood
☎ (0272) 268492
11–2.30 (4 Sat), 6–11
Butcombe Bitter; Courage Best Bitter, Directors; Ruddles Best Bitter Ⓗ
Small, two-bar pub, a bit out of the way, but popular with locals. Jazz-oriented jukebox; pinball machines in the back bar. Excellent Sun lunches, but no food Sun eve. ◐ ◑

Phoenix
15 Wellington Road, Broadweir ☎ (0272) 558327
11.30–11
Draught Bass; Oakhill Bitter, Black Magic Ⓗ**, Yeoman** Ⓖ**; Smiles Best Bitter** Ⓗ**; Wadworth 6X** Ⓖ**; guest beers**
Basic, no-frills oasis for real ales; up to ten normally on sale, with an emphasis on local independents' brews. Given a *Special Merit* award by Avon CAMRA in 1992 to mark many years of excellence. Warm and friendly – a must for visitors to Bristol. Wheelchair access to ladies' WC only. Q ❀ ♿

Prince of Wales
5 Gloucester Road, Bishopston
☎ (0272) 245552
11–2.30, 5.30–11; 11–11 Sat
Courage Directors; Hardington Best Bitter; John Smith's Bitter Ⓗ
Popular, Victorian two-bar pub with a courtyard. Always busy eves. Q ❀ ◐ ♣

Prince of Wales
84 Stoke Lane, Westbury on Trym ☎ (0272) 623715
11–3, 5.30–11; 11–11 Sat
Courage Bitter Ale, Best Bitter; Hardington Best Bitter; Ushers Best Bitter Ⓗ
Friendly, well-run, comfortable pub in a residential area. Probably the biggest seller of Bitter Ale, which is sold as Boys' Bitter. No food Sun. ❀ ◐

Printers Devil
10 Broad Plain, St Philips (back of Evening Post building) ☎ (0272) 264290
11.30–3 (not Sat), 5–9 (8–11 Sat); closed Sun
Courage Best Bitter; John Smith's Bitter; Ushers Best Bitter, Founders Ⓗ
One-bar city pub, HQ for the Cartoonists' Club of GB; the walls are adorned with cartoons. A centre for the business community at lunchtimes – dress appropriately. Mixed clientele in the eve. No food weekends.
◐ ◑ ⇌ (T Meads)

Rose of Denmark
6 Dowry Place, Hotwells (near flyover) ☎ (0272) 290472
11–11
Ind Coope Burton Ale; Smiles Bitter; Tetley Bitter Ⓗ
Pub with a classic, listed Georgian exterior and a friendly atmosphere. Good value beer and food.
🛏 ◐ ◑ ♣

Royal Oak
The Mall, Clifton
☎ (0272) 738846
11–3, 5.30–11
Courage Best Bitter, Directors; John Smith's Bitter; Wadworth 6X Ⓗ
Welcoming, split-level pub with a slightly old-fashioned, timbered decor. ◐

Ship Inn
8 Lower Park Row
☎ (0272) 265022
12–11
Beer range varies Ⓗ
Popular split-level pub with a nautical theme, close to Bristol Royal Infirmary. Can get busy on Fri and Sat nights. ❀ ◐

Star Inn
4–6 North Street, Bedminster
☎ (0272) 663588
11–2.30, 5.30–11
Ind Coope Burton Ale; Smiles Best Bitter; Tetley Bitter Ⓗ
Large, popular pub with a central hexagonal bar. Good darts facilities. ❀ ◐ ♿ ♣

Swan with Two Necks
12 Little Ann Street, St Judes (near end of M32)
☎ (0272) 551893
11–3 (may extend in summer), 5–11; 11–11 Fri; 12–11 Sat
Hardington Traditional, Best Bitter, Moonshine, Jubilee, Old Lucifer Ⓗ**, Old Ale** Ⓖ**; guest beer** Ⓗ
Hardington's first pub: a real one-bar boozer in simple style with a varied clientele. Unusual guest beers from far afield. Q ◐

White Lion
Quay Head, Colston Avenue (opp. Cenotaph)
☎ (0272) 254819
11–11
Draught Bass; Smiles Best Bitter; Wickwar Brand Oak; guest beer Ⓗ
Small city-centre bar, popular lunchtime and early eve. The Victorian spiral staircase to the gents' is reputedly from Bristol's old gaol. Local independent guest beers. ❀ ◐

Charfield

Pear Tree
Wotton Road ☎ (0454) 260663
11.30–2.30, 7–11
Whitbread WCPA Ⓗ**; guest beers**
Small, two-bar, village local on the main road, with a good range of pub games. Friendly local clientele. The three constantly-changing guest beers are the main attraction.
🔥 Q ❀ ◐ ♣ P

Churchill

Crown Inn
Skinners Lane (off A368, W of A38 jct) OS446596
☎ (0934) 852995
11.30–3, 5.30–11
Draught Bass; Butcombe Bitter; Cotleigh Old Buzzard; Eldridge Pope Dorchester, Hardy Country; Palmers IPA Ⓖ**; guest beers**
Multi-roomed, unspoilt pub with real fires. Always a good range of beers, usually from the South-West; Batch Bitter (the house beer) is brewed by Cotleigh. Beware keg cider on handpump. Dress restrictions.
🔥 Q 🐴 ❀ ◐ ⛺ ♣ P

Clapton-in-Gordano

Black Horse
Clevedon Lane OS472739
☎ (0275) 842105
11–2.30 (3 Sat), 6–11
Courage Bitter Ale, Best Bitter; Smiles Best Bitter [G]
14th-century stone pub with a flagstone floor, inglenook and high-back settles. Formerly the village lock-up and now the centre of village life.
♛ Q ☋ ❀ ◐ ♣ ⌂ P

Compton Martin

Ring O' Bells
Bath Road ☎ (0761) 221284
11.30–2.30, 6.30–11
Draught Bass; Butcombe Bitter; Wadworth 6X [H]**; guest beer** (occasionally)
Very pleasant, two-bar roadside pub, offering wonderful food, a well-equipped family room, and a safe garden.
♛ Q ☋ ❀ ◐ ◑ ♣ ⌂ P

Downend

Beaufort Hunt
64 Downend Road
☎ (0272) 570688
11–11
Courage Best Bitter; Marston's Pedigree; guest beer [H]
Two-bar local with a friendly atmosphere, weekly-changing guest beer and a wide range of good food. Q ❀ ◐ ♿ ♣ P

Engine Common

Cross Keys
North Road, Yate (300 yds off A482) ☎ (0454) 228314
11.45–2.30, 5.45–11
Courage Best Bitter; Wadworth 6X; Wickwar Brand Oak [H]
Very pleasant, two-bar, 17th-century village local. The public bar has a flagstone floor. Lively clientele; wide range of pub games. No lunches Sun.
♛ Q ◐ ⊟ ⇌ (Yate) ♣ P

Filton

Filton Recreation Centre
Elm Park ☎ (0272) 791988
12–2 (11.30–2.30 Thu & Fri; 11.30–2 Sat), 6.30 (4 Wed, 6 Sat)–11
Butcombe Bitter; Furgusons Dartmoor Best Bitter; Ind Coope Burton Ale; Tetley Bitter [H]
Part of Filton Recreation Centre but open to the public. Key ring collection in the bar. The landlord is a Burton *Master Cellarman*. Q ♿ P

Frampton Cotterell

Rising Sun
Ryecroft Road ☎ (0454) 772330
11.30–3, 7–11
Draught Bass; Smiles Best Bitter; Wadworth 6X; Wickwar Olde Merryford [H]
At least six ales are always available and meals are freshly cooked (eves Fri and Sat only) in this genuine free house with a single bar and a skittle alley. Cider in summer.
Q ❀ ◐ ◑ ⌂ P

Hallatrow

Old Station Inn
Wells Road (A39, 400 yds from A37) ☎ (0761) 452228
11–3, 5 (6 Sat)–11
Ash Vine Challenger; Draught Bass; Eldridge Pope Dorchester, Hardy Country [H]
Old railway hotel on the disused GWR North Somerset line. A busy, main-road free house with a friendly atmosphere. ♛ Q ❀ 🛏 ◐ ◑ ♣ P

Hanham

Swan Inn
Conham Hill ☎ (0272) 673947
12–3, 7–11
Draught Bass; Courage Bitter Ale, Best Bitter [H]
Deservedly popular, unspoilt, old-fashioned, three-bar pub, with pictures of bygone Hanham.
Q ☋ ❀ ◐ ⊟ ♿ ♣ P

Hinton

Bull
1 mile SW of M4 jct 18
OS735768 ☎ (0272) 372332
11.30–2.30, 6 (7 winter)–11
Draught Bass; Wadworth IPA, 6X [H]**, Old Timer** [G]
Mature, country local with a children's garden, an attractive bar, a lounge and a restaurant.
♛ ❀ ◐ ◑ ⊟ ▲ ♣ P

Iron Acton

Rose & Crown
High Street ☎ (0454) 228423
5–11; 12–2.30, 6–11 Sat; closed Mon–Fri lunch
Draught Bass; Hook Norton Old Hooky; Marston's Pedigree; Smiles Exhibition; Whitbread WCPA [H]
Very attractive, old, two-bar pub. Warm welcome.
♛ Q ❀ 🛏 ♣

Kelston

Old Crown
Bath Road ☎ (0225) 423032
11.30–3, 5–11
Draught Bass; Butcombe Bitter; Smiles Best Bitter, Exhibition (summer)**; Wadworth 6X, Old Timer** [H]
Wonderful 18th-century coaching inn with a large garden. Note the original beer engines and flagstone floor. No food Sun; eve meals Thu–Sat in the restaurant.
♛ Q ❀ ◐ ♣ P

Kingswood

Highwayman
Hill Street ☎ (0272) 671613
12–2.30 (11.30–3 Fri; 11–3 Sat), 7.30–11
Ind Coope Burton Ale; Tetley Bitter; Wadworth 6X [H]
Pre-war traditional building with a modern interior and a single central bar. Extensive, good value menu (English and foreign). No-smoking area Mon–Fri lunchtimes. Large family area and a safe garden play area. ☋ ❀ ◐ ◑ ♿ ♣ P ⊬

Littleton-on-Severn

White Hart
1½ miles off B4461 at Elberton
OS596900 ☎ (0454) 412275
11.30–2.30, 6–11; 11.30–11 Sat
Smiles Bitter, Best Bitter, Exhibition; Wadworth 6X; guest beer [H]
Popular 17th-century farmhouse, tastefully enlarged into a two-bar, multi-roomed pub. Avon CAMRA *Pub of Year* 1990 and 1991, and winner of national CAMRA *Pub Refurbishment Award* 1990. Not to be missed.
♛ Q ☋ ❀ 🛏 ◐ ◑ ♣ P

Long Ashton

Angel Inn
172 Long Ashton Road (near B3128 jct) ☎ (0275) 392244
11–2.30 (3 Sat), 5.30 (6 Sat)–11
Draught Bass; Courage Best Bitter; Eldridge Pope Hardy Country; Oakhill Bitter; Wadworth 6X [H]
Lovely old, unspoilt village pub with a courtyard seating area. Priest hole in a corner of the fireplace. ♛ ❀ ◐ ◑

Miners Rest
42 Providence Lane
☎ (0275) 393449
11–2.30, 6.30–11
Draught Bass; Courage Best Bitter; guest beers [G]
Pleasant, friendly, old cottage-style pub near the top of a steep lane, with extensive views over the valley. Eve meals and Sun lunch by arrangement. Up to six guest beers and Taunton cider.
♛ ☋ ❀ ◐ ♣ ⌂ P

Marshfield

Catherine Wheel
High Street ☎ (0225) 892220
11–2.30 (not Mon), 6–11

Courage Bitter Ale [H], **Best Bitter** [G]; **Wadworth 6X** [H]
Thriving 17th-century local with a warm welcome. The rear lounge area was formerly a coal cellar. No food Mon.
♨ Q ⛟ ◐ ♣ P

Midford

Hope & Anchor
On B3110 ☎ (0225) 832296
11–3, 6.30–11
Butcombe Bitter; Marston's Pedigree; Smiles Best Bitter; Wadworth 6X [H]
Nestling beneath a disused but impressive Somerset and Dorset Railway viaduct, this 300-year-old country pub has a large bar, half split into a restaurant area, but excellent food (some Spanish) is available throughout. ♨ ❀ ◐ P

Midsomer Norton

White Hart
The Island ☎ (0761) 418270
11–3, 5.30–11
Draught Bass [G]
Victorian establishment with many rooms. A minor classic. No food Sun.
♨ ☗ ◐ ⊞ ♣ ⛢

Nailsea

Blue Flame
West End OS449690
☎ (0275) 856910
12–3, 6–11 (may vary summer)
Draught Bass; Smiles Best Bitter, Exhibition; guest beer (occasionally) [G]
The pub on the moor: a popular, unspoilt local, often busy in summer.
♨ Q ☗ ❀ ♿ ♣ ⛢ P

Sawyers Arms
High Street ☎ (0275) 853798
11–3, 5.30–11
Courage Best Bitter, Directors; Eldridge Pope Hardy Country, Royal Oak; Marston's Pedigree; Webster's Yorkshire Bitter [H]
Popular and friendly, two-bar local; often busy. Good value food. ❀ ◐ ♿ ♣ ⛢ P

Oldbury-on-Severn

Anchor Inn
Church Road ☎ (0454) 413331
11.30–2.30 (3 Sat), 6.30 (6 Sat)–11
Draught Bass [G]; **Butcombe Bitter; Marston's Pedigree; S&N Theakston Best Bitter** [H], **Old Peculier** [G]
Converted 16th-century mill near the River Severn. Excellent food with a daily-changing menu in the bar and restaurant. Deservedly popular, with a friendly atmosphere. A quality pub.
♨ Q ❀ ◐ ⊞ ♣ P

Old Down

Fox
Inner Down OS617873
☎ (0454) 412507
11.30–3, 6 (5.30 Fri & Sat)–11
Draught Bass; Hook Norton Best Bitter; Whitbread Flowers IPA; guest beer [H]
150-year-old, picturesque village pub, built from local stone. Beamed ceilings give a cosy yet spacious atmosphere. Attractive flowers and hanging baskets, plus a children's play area in the garden. ♨ Q ❀ ♣ ⛢ P

Paulton

Somerset Inn
Bath Road (off B3355) OS660572 ☎ (0761) 412828
12–2.30, 7–11
Courage Bitter Ale, Best Bitter; Ushers Founders [H]
One-bar local, outside the village, with fine views over the Cam valley. Renowned for its food. ♨ Q ❀ ◐ ⛢ P

Pennsylvania

Swan Inn
On A46, ¼ mile N of A420
☎ (0225) 891022
11–3, 5–11 (11–11 Easter–Mid-Sept)
Archers Village; Draught Bass; Marston's Pedigree; Smiles Bitter; guest beer [H]
Excellent free house in a rural setting: a comfortable, split-level building with a busy, but not too crowded bar, and a quieter lounge/eating area. Avon CAMRA *Pub of the Year* 1992. ♨ ◐ ♣ P

Pensford

Rising Sun
Church Street ☎ (0761) 490402
11.30–2.30, 7–11
Ind Coope Burton Ale; Tetley Bitter; Wadworth 6X [H]
15th-century stone pub with a garden leading down to the River Chew (unfenced). Cosy, comfortable and friendly. No eve meals Sun or Mon (book Sun lunch). ♨ ❀ ◐ ♣ ⛢ P

Pucklechurch

Rose & Crown
Parkfield Road
☎ (0272) 372351
11–2.30, 6.30–11
Draught Bass [H]; **Hall & Woodhouse Tanglefoot** [G]; **Wadworth IPA, 6X, Farmer's Glory** (summer) [H], **Old Timer** [G]
Large village pub and restaurant. The building dates back to the 1700s, with low beams and open fireplaces. Comfortably furnished, offering a friendly atmosphere in several quiet drinking areas.

No bar food Sun, no food a[…] Sun and Mon eves.
♨ Q ❀ ◐ ♣ P

Tolldown

Crown
On A46, ½ mile S of M4 jct 18
☎ (0225) 891231
11–2.30, 6–11
Hall & Woodhouse Tanglefoot; Wadworth IPA, 6X, Old Timer [H]
16th-century, Cotswold stone roadside inn, near Dyrham House. ♨ ❀ ⛟ ◐ ♣ P

Warmley

Midland Spinner
London Road ☎ (0272) 674204
11–11
Courage Best Bitter; John Smith's Bitter; guest beers [H]
Very popular pub with a railway theme, near the old Midland line, used by walkers and cyclists. Pleasant atmosphere. ♨ ❀ ◐ ♣ P

Wellow

Fox & Badger
Railway Lane (2 miles W of B3110 at Hinton Charterhouse) OS741583 ☎ (0225) 832293
11–3, 6–11
Butcombe Bitter; Courage Bitter Ale; Morland Old Speckled Hen; Wadworth 6X; guest beer [G]
Pretty Wellow's only pub, a two-bar local where, unusually, the public bar is carpeted and the lounge flagstoned. ♨ ◐ ⊞ ♣ ⛢

Wick

Rose & Crown
High Street ☎ (0272) 372198
11.30–2.30, 5.30 (6 Sat)–11
Courage Best Bitter, Directors; John Smith's Bitter; Wadworth 6X [H]
Comfortable, spacious inn dating from 1640. Old photographs and bric-a-brac depict a bygone era. The restaurant has a varied, sensibly priced menu (book Sun lunch; no meals Sun eve).
♨ Q ❀ ◐ ♣ P ⚟

Winterbourne

Mason's Arms
41 North Road, Watleys End
☎ (0454) 772065
11–3, 5.30–11; 11–11 Sat
Courage Best Bitter; Marston's Pedigree; Wadworth 6X [H]
Welcoming village pub with strong sporting connections. Bar meals are very reasonably priced and excellent quality.
❀ ◐ ♿ ♣ ⛢ P

Bedfordshire

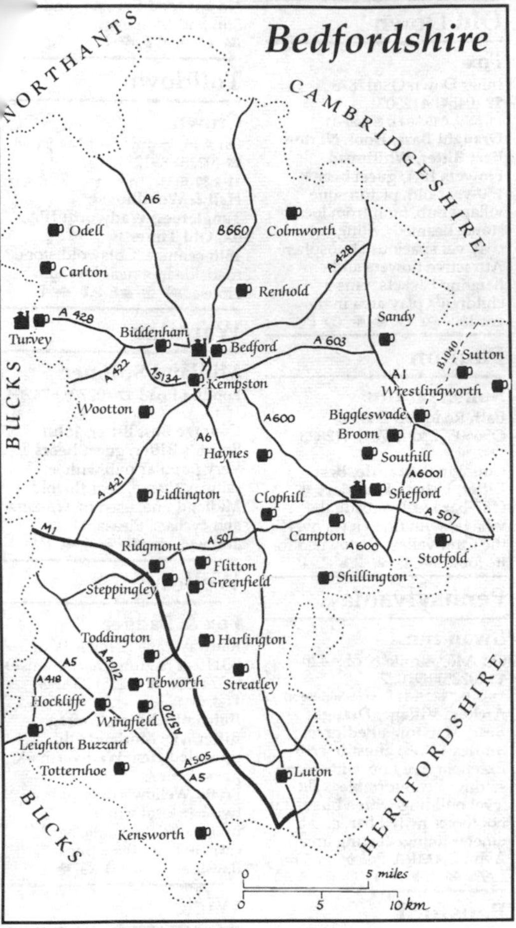

Banks & Taylor, *Shefford*; **Nix Wincott**, *Turvey*; **Wells**, *Bedford*

Bedford

Castle

17 Newnham Street (E off High St, A6) ☎ (0234) 353295
11–3, 5.30 (7 Sat)–11; 11–11 Fri
Adnams Broadside; Wells Eagle, Bombardier; Mansfield Riding Bitter Ⓗ
Country pub within the town, with a walled garden. Busy at weekends. Excellent meals are served Mon–Sat lunchtime and Mon–Thu eve.
❀ 🛏 ◑ ◐ ⊟ ♿ P

Fleur de Lis

12 Mill Street (off High St, A6)
☎ (0234) 211004
10.30–2.30 (4 Sat), 5.30 (7 Sat)–11; 10.30–11 Thu & Fri; 12–2, 7–10.30 Sun
Adnams Broadside; Wells Eagle Ⓗ
Very well run, one-bar town-centre pub with a mixed clientele and an upstairs meeting room. Parking is difficult lunchtimes. No lunches weekends. Twenty-first year in this guide. ◑

Three Cups

Newnham Street (E off High St, A6) ☎ (0234) 352153
11–11; 10.30–4, 7–11 Sat
Greene King IPA, Rayments Special, Abbot Ⓗ
Warm and welcoming, wood-panelled, two-bar pub opposite a large auction house which is well worth a visit. No lunches Sun. ❀ ◑ ⊟ ♣ P

Biddenham

Three Tuns

Main Road (S of A428, village loop) OS022499
☎ (0234) 354847
11.30–2.30, 6–11
Greene King IPA, Rayments Special, Abbot Ⓗ
Delightful village inn with an excellent range of home-cooked food. Children are permitted in the dining area; no food Sun eve. Skittles played. ❀ ◑ ◐ ⊟ ♣ P

Biggleswade

Rising Sun

38 Sun Street ☎ (0767) 313737
12–2.30 (11.30–3 Sat), 6–11
Adnams Broadside; Hall & Woodhouse Tanglefoot; Mansfield Riding Mild, Riding Bitter; Morland Old Speckled Hen; Wells Eagle Ⓗ; **guest beers**
Popular, welcoming pub on the northern edge of town, offering a good range of guest ales. Superb tandoori opposite.
❀ ◑ ◐ ⊟ ≋ ♣ P

Try also: Crown Hotel, High St (Greene King)

Broom

Cock

High Street (100 yds N of B658) ☎ (0767) 314411
12–3, 6–11
Greene King IPA, Abbot Ⓖ
Multi-roomed village local where the beer is served direct from the cellar. A skittles room, two cosy snugs and a carefully added restaurant complete the picture in this 21-year *Guide* entry. No food Sun and Mon eves.
🜲 ❀ ◑ ◐ ♣ P

Campton

White Hart

Mill Lane (off A507)
☎ (0462) 812657
12–3, 7–11; 11–11 Sat
S&N Theakston Best Bitter; Wadworth 6X Ⓗ
Popular, three-bar, open-plan village free house with a comfortable lounge and dining area. Games dominate the public bar, which has a flagstone floor and an inglenook. Petanque is played all year. No lunches Sun.
🜲 ❀ ◑ ◐ ♿ ♣ P

Carlton

Fox

35 High Street (3 miles N of A428 at Turvey) OS953553
☎ (0234) 720235
12–3, 6–11
Wells Eagle; guest beers Ⓗ

18th-century, friendly, thatched village inn serving excellent restaurant and bar food (not Sun eve or Mon). Children are welcome in the restaurant. Near the Odell and Harrold country park.
Q ❀ ◖◗ P

Clophill

Stone Jug
Back Street ☎ (0525) 60526
11–3, 6–11
Courage Directors; S&N Theakston Best Bitter; John Smith's Bitter Ⓗ; guest beers
Deservedly popular free house where guest beers complement the regular range. Check before arriving with children. No food Sun. ⛴ ❀ ◖ P

Colmworth

Wheatsheaf
Wilden Road ½ mile E of B660) OS101574 ☎ (0234) 376370
12–2.30, 6.30–11
Adnams Bitter; Draught Bass; Marston's Pedigree; guest beers Ⓗ
17th-century country pub, south of Colmworth village. Low oak beams are a regular headbanger. Wide variety of bar meals. Children's play area in the garden.
⛫ Q ❀ ◖◗ ⊟ ♣ P

Flitton

White Hart
Brook Lane ☎ (0525) 861486
12–3, 7–11
Adnams Broadside; Hall & Woodhouse Tanglefoot *or* **Morland Old Speckled Hen; Wells Eagle Ⓗ**
Attractive village pub: the public bar has games and the lounge has a dining area, offering a very good range of meals at reasonable prices. (No eve meals Sun.) Barbecues in the summer. Camping/caravanning must be booked in advance. ❀ ◖◗ ⊟ ⛺ ♣ P

Greenfield

Compasses
44 High Street ☎ (0525) 71344
11–11
Morland Old Speckled Hen; Wells Eagle Ⓗ
A T-shaped, split-level bar, a former butcher's shop. The building and implements used for curing and smoking remain at the rear of the main building. Live music most weekends. Eve meals Mon–Fri only. ⛫ ❀ ◖◗ ♣ P

Harlington

Carpenters Arms
Sundon Road
☎ (0525) 872384
12–2.30, 5.30–11; 11–11 Sat
Banks's Bitter; Wadworth 6X; Webster's Yorkshire Bitter Ⓗ
17th-century village pub featuring a low-ceilinged lounge with copper-topped tables, and a small snug. The public bar has pool, darts, etc. Lounge bar users can watch the dumb waiter being used to supply the (highly recommended) upstairs restaurant. No food Sun eve.
⛫ ❀ ◖◗ ⇌ ♣ P

Haynes

Greyhound
68 Northwood End Road (W off A600) ☎ (023 066) 239
11–3, 5.30–11
Greene King IPA, Rayments Special, Abbot Ⓗ
Large, friendly pub with a quiet lounge, plus a conservatory and a garden. Home-cooked food is served at all sessions.
⛴ ❀ ◖◗ ⊟ ♣ P

Hockliffe

Red Lion
Watling Street
☎ (0525) 210240
12–2.30 (3 Sat), 5.30 (6 Sat)–11
Marston's Pedigree; Tetley Bitter Ⓗ
Friendly roadside pub with one long bar, where one end is oriented towards games, and the other towards food. The sizeable garden is used for barbecues and petanque in summer.
⛫ ❀ 🛏 ◖◗ ♣ P

Kempston

Griffin
174 Bedford Road (opp. police station) ☎ (0234) 854775
11–3, 6–11
Greene King XX Mild, IPA, Abbot Ⓗ
Refurbished pub with three bars catering for a mixed clientele. Excellent food is served at all times at good prices. The lounges and the restaurant area feature landscape paintings.
❀ ◖◗ ♣ P

King William IV
56 High Street
☎ (0234) 854533
11.30–3, 5.30–11
Wells Eagle, Bombardier Ⓗ; guest beers
Attractive, genuine oak-beamed building which caters for a mixed clientele, with one bar and a games room. Always one or two guest beers available. The garden has swings. ❀ ◖◗ ♣ P

Kensworth

Farmers Boy
216 Common Road
☎ (0582) 872207
11–11
Fuller's London Pride, ESB Ⓗ
Comfortable and well-kept, friendly village pub. The small public bar is dominated by a pool table; locals tend to frequent the lounge bar which can be boisterous! Note the original Mann, Crossman & Paulin leaded windows. Excellent home-cooked food. Occasional dwile flonking!
⛫ ❀ ◖◗ ⊟ ♣ P

Leighton Buzzard

Black Lion
20 High Street
☎ (0525) 382510
11–2.30, 5.30–11
Ansells Mild; Ind Coope Burton Ale; Tetley Bitter Ⓗ; guest beers
Smart town-centre pub with a central bar and a video jukebox. Lively Fri and Sat eve but quiet during the week.
❀ ◖ ♣

Stag
Heath Road ☎ (0525) 372710
12–2.30 (3 Sat), 6–11
Fuller's Hock, Chiswick, London Pride, ESB Ⓗ
Pub re-opened in March 1993 after an extensive and expensive refit, which shows in the quality of the fittings. Now has a separate food bar, but retains a street-corner, local atmosphere, due to its popularity with all ages.
Q ◖◗ ♣ P

Star
230 Heath Road (A418)
☎ (0525) 377294
11–2.30, 5.30 (6 Sat)–11
Adnams Bitter; Draught Bass; Ind Coope ABC Best Bitter; Wadworth 6X Ⓗ
Pub where the interior is crammed with interesting articles, including sewing machines, cricket bats, cameras and pictures of aeroplanes. Situated in a smart area and accented toward food (recommended). Smoking restrictions apply only at lunchtime.
Q ❀ ◖◗ ♿ ♣ P ⍻

Try also: Ship, Wing Rd (Grand Met)

Lidlington

Green Man

High Street ☎ (0525) 402869
12–2.30 (3 Sat), 6–11
Greene King IPA, Abbot [H]
17th-century thatched pub and restaurant in a quiet village. Traditional games, a varying menu and a cosy lounge ensure a popular local following. Handy for ramblers on the Greensand Ridge path. Food not available Sun and Mon eve.
⚲ ❀ ◖◗ ♿ ▲ ⇌ ♣ P

Luton

Bird & Bush

Hancock Drive, Bushmead (off A6, behind Barnfield College)
☎ (0582) 480723
12–2.30, 6–11; 12–11 Sat
Adnams Bitter; Draught Bass; Charrington IPA; guest beer [H]
Opened in May 1991, a 'community tavern' with attractive Yorkshire flagstone and quarry-tiled floors. Up-to-date facilities include a no-smoking area, wheelchair WC and a children's play area in the garden. The good bar food includes vegetarian options; no food Sun.
❀ ◖ ♿ ♣ P ⚟

Mother Redcap

80 Latimer Road
☎ (0582) 30913
11–3, 5–11; 11–11 Fri & Sat
Greene King IPA, Abbot [H]
Large pub where a chimney breast separates the lounge from the games area. Originally a row of houses which were converted in the 1920s. Watercolour sketches and old photos of Luton decorate the walls. No food Sun. ❀ ◖ ♣

Two Brewers

43 Dumfries Street
☎ (0582) 23777
11–11
Banks & Taylor Shefford Bitter, SOD, SOS; guest beers [H]
Friendly back-street local, popular with bricklayers, bankers and bikers. Offers an ever-changing range of guest beers, plus regular beer festivals and Weston's cider and perry. The home-cooked food is recommended.
⚲ ❀ ◖ ♣ ⌽

Wheelwrights Arms

34 Guildford Street
☎ (0582) 20023
10.30–11
Fuller's Chiswick, London Pride, ESB; guest beers [H]
Lively, one-bar, town-centre free house, handy for the bus and railway stations, and Arndale shoppers. Six beers are normally available. No food Sun. ◖ ⇌ ♣

Try also: Bricklayers Arms, Hightown Rd (Banks & Taylor)

Odell

Mad Dog

Little Odell (W end of village)
☎ (0234) 720221
11–2.30, 6–11
Greene King IPA, Rayments Special, Abbot [H]
Thatched pub near the Odell and Harrold Country Park. A ghost occasionally appears near the inglenook. The generous home-cooked food includes vegetarian dishes, and the pub can be busy at mealtimes. Children's roundabout in the garden.
Q ❀ ◖◗ P

Try also: Bell (Greene King)

Renhold

Three Horseshoes

42 Top End (1 mile N of A428)
☎ (0234) 870218
11–2.30, 6–11; 11–11 Sat
Greene King XX Mild, IPA, Rayments Special *or* Abbot [H]
Friendly village pub with a children's play area in the garden. Good value, home-cooked food includes fresh steaks and soup. No food Tue eve or Sun.
⚲ Q ❀ ◖◗ ⊟ ♣ P

Try also: Polhill Arms (Greene King)

Ridgmont

Rose & Crown

89 High Street (A507, near M1 jct 13) ☎ (0525) 280245
10.30–2.30, 6–11
Adnams Broadside; Mansfield Riding Bitter; Wells Eagle, Bombardier [H]
Popular, welcoming pub and restaurant (booking advised). The public bar has a games area, whilst the large grounds offer facilities for camping/caravanning and barbecues in summer. In every edition of this guide.
⚲ ❀ ◖◗ ⊟ ▲ ♣ P

Sandy

Bell

Station Road (50 yds S of B1042) ☎ (0767) 680267
12–2.30, 5–11; 12–11 Sat
Greene King IPA, Rayments Special [H]
Friendly one-bar local opposite the station and handy for the RSPB HQ. An extensive range of free bar-top food is available Sun lunchtimes, but otherwise no meals Sun.
⚲ ❀ ◖◗ ⇌ ♣ P

Shefford

White Hart

2 North Bride Street
☎ (0462) 811144
11–3, 6.30 (7 Sat)–11
Banks & Taylor Shefford Mild, Shefford Bitter [H]**, SPA, SOD** [G]**, SOS** [H]**, 2XS** [G]
Public bar with an open fire, a cosy lounge and a dining room (no food Sun eve). The full range of Banks & Taylor beers is served.
⚲ ❀ ⛟ ◖◗ ♣ P

Shillington

Noah's Ark

Hillfoot Road ☎ (0462) 711611
11.30–11; 11.30–3, 7–11 Tue
Greene King IPA, Abbot [H]
Welcoming, two-bar country pub. Good value, home-cooked food is served lunchtime and early eve (not Tue or Sun eves). Petanque is played, and there is a children's play area in the garden. ❀ ◖◗ ♣ P

Southill

White Horse

High Road (1 mile E of B658)
☎ (0462) 813364
11–3, 6–11; 11–11 summer Sat (one hour supper licence extension weekday eves)
Whitbread Boddingtons Bitter, Flowers IPA [H]
Large country pub and restaurant featuring a miniature diesel railway in the garden. A brief walk from Southill Park cricket ground. Children are welcome in the restaurant. ⚲ ❀ ◖◗ ⊟ ♣ P

Steppingley

Drovers Arms

Flitwick Road ☎ (0525) 712196
11.30–3, 6 (7 winter)–11
Wells Eagle, Bombardier [H]
Solid, red-brick building housing an angular bar and lounge areas. The friendly atmosphere is evident on both sides of the bar. Games include darts, cribbage and dominoes. No meals Sun.
⚲ Q ❀ ◖◗ ♣ P

Stotfold

Stag

35 Brook Street
☎ (0462) 730261
12 (5 Mon–Wed)–11

Hop Back Summer Lightning; Mitchell's Fortress; Samuel Smith OBB; Summerskills Whistle Belly Vengeance; Tetley Bitter; Wadworth 6X Ⓗ; guest beers
Ex-Whitbread pub, completely transformed by its new owners who offer 10–12 real ales per week (over 250 different ales last year). Also stocks a large range of foreign bottled beers. Very friendly atmosphere. Beware the Saracen armoured car guarding the car park. Lunches served Thu–Sat only.
♛ ❀ ◑ ◗ ▲ ♣ ⌓ P

Streatley

Chequers
Sharpenhoe Road (off A6)
☎ (0582) 882072
11–3 (4 winter Sat), 5 (4.30 summer, 6 winter Sat)–11; 11–11 summer Sat
Greene King XX Mild, IPA, Abbot Ⓗ
Friendly village pub next to the church: one large bar which houses a collection of old games and sports equipment, with framed pictures depicting their use. Floodlit boules pitch. No meals Sun eve.
♛ ❀ ◑ ◗ ♣ P

Sutton

John O' Gaunt
High Street ☎ (0767) 260377
12–3, 7–11
Greene King IPA, Abbot Ⓗ
Attractive pub in a picturesque village, near the golf course and the ford crossing the High Street. Good range of bar food (not served Sun). Skittles played; boules court in the garden. ♛ Q ❀ ◑ ◗ ⊟ ♣ P

Tebworth

Queens Head
The Lane ☎ (0525) 874101
11–3 (3.30 Sat), 6 (7 Sat)–11
Adnams Broadside Ⓖ; Wells Eagle Ⓗ
Very welcoming, good-humoured pub with two small, popular bars. Limited menu, but well prepared and good value (not served Sun).
♛ ❀ ◑ ◗ ♣ P

Toddington

Angel
1 Luton Road ☎ (0525) 872380
11–3, 6–11
Banks & Taylor Shefford Bitter; Courage Best Bitter; Fuller's London Pride; John Smith's Bitter; Wadworth 6X; Whitbread Boddingtons Bitter Ⓗ; guest beer
Lively and enterprising pub, dating in part from the 16th century. The lounge is decorated with musical instruments and the lower bar is now a thriving jazz venue with live music nightly and Sun lunchtime. The café offers cream teas, while the restaurant is open Wed–Sun eve. Ring before taking children. ♛ ♘ ❀ ◑ ◗ P

Sow & Pigs
19 Church Square
☎ (0525) 873089
11–11
Greene King IPA, Rayments Special, Abbot Ⓗ
Unpretentious and unpredictable. Apart from a piano, an harmonium and stuffed fish, the bar area features a number of pigs (even flying!). The pool room to the rear has Breughel prints and stuffed birds. A sense of humour can be an asset for visitors! ♛ Q ❀ ◑ ♣ P

Totternhoe

Old Bell
Church Road ☎ (0582) 662633
12–3, 6–11
Adnams Bitter; Bateman XXXB; Exmoor Gold; Greene King IPA; Hook Norton Old Hooky; Palmers IPA Ⓗ; guest beers
Comfortable, friendly village free house offering a wide choice of real ales, many of which are rare in the area. The good range of bar food features an extensive sausage menu. No meals Sun.
♛ ❀ ◑ ◗ ♣ P

Old Farm Inn
Church Road ☎ (0582) 661294
11–3, 6–11
Fuller's Chiswick, London Pride Ⓗ
Popular, friendly, old village pub: a traditional public bar and a cosy, quiet lounge with a large fireplace. No meals Sun. ♛ Q ❀ ◑ ⊟ ♣ P

Turvey

Three Cranes
High Street (off A428)
☎ (0234) 881305
11–3, 6–11
Adnams Bitter; Draught Bass; Fuller's London Pride, ESB; Hook Norton Best Bitter; guest beer Ⓗ
17th-century coaching inn with an excellent range of food, including vegetarian dishes, in all bars and a restaurant area. Holds Sun eve quizzes. ♛ Q ❀ ⛟ ◑ ◗ P

Wingfield

Plough
Tebworth Road
☎ (0525) 873077
12–3, 6–11
Banks & Taylor Shefford Bitter; Fuller's London Pride Ⓗ; guest beers
Attractive, thatched one-bar pub with a children's/pool room to the rear. Two or three guest beers also normally on offer. Eve meals served Fri–Sun only.
♛ ♘ ❀ ◑ ◗ ♣ P

Wootton

Chequers
Hall End Road, Hall End
☎ (0234) 768394
11–3, 5.30–11
Hall & Woodhouse Tanglefoot; Wells Eagle, Bombardier; guest beers Ⓗ
16th-century coaching inn boasting three real fires, oak beams and brasses. Large garden. No eve meals Sun in winter. ♛ ❀ ◑ ◗ ⊟ P

Wrestlingworth

Chequers
43 High Street ☎ (0767) 23256
12–2.30, 6 (7 winter)–11
Greene King XX Mild, IPA, Abbot Ⓗ
Brass-bedecked old village pub with a large open fire. The dining area offers imaginative, home-cooked food. Boules played in the large garden.
♛ Q ❀ ◑ ◗ ♣ P

Opening Hours

Permitted opening hours in England and Wales are 11–11, though not all pubs choose to take advantage of the full session and many close in the afternoons. Some pubs have special licences and there are sometimes special local arrangements for market days and other events. Standard Sunday hours are 12–3, 7–10.30. Scottish licensing laws are more generous and pubs may stay open longer.

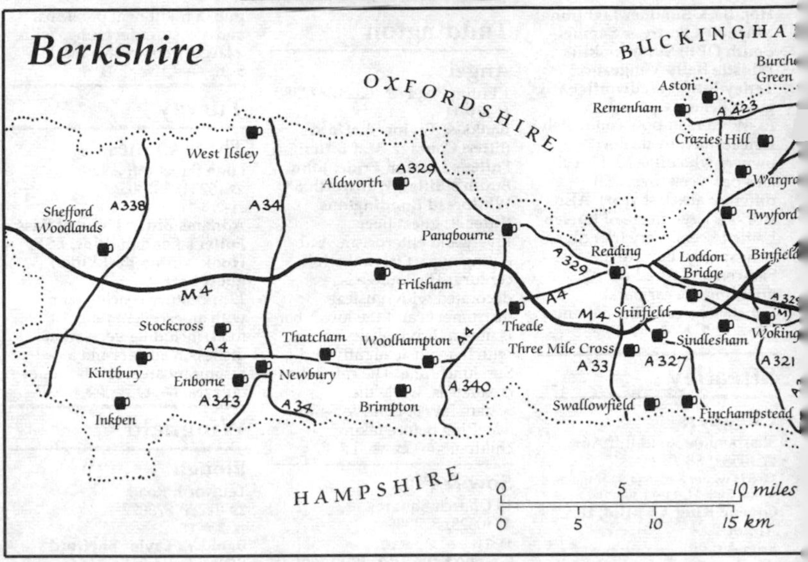

Aldworth

Bell
Off B4009 ☎ (0635) 578272
11–3, 6–11; closed Mon except bank hols
Arkell's 3B, Kingsdown; Hall & Woodhouse Badger Best Bitter; Hook Norton Best Bitter; Morrells Mild Ⓗ
Excellent atmosphere in a haven for traditionalists: a pub in the same family for over 250 years and little changed during this time. A splendid, one-handed clock monitors the passage of time in the tranquil tap room. Hot rolls and soup served. National CAMRA *Pub of the Year* 1990.
⛫ Q ♞ ❀ ♣ P

Ascot

At The Station
Station Hill ☎ (0344) 22361
10.30–3, 5–11; 10.30–11 Sat
Courage Best Bitter, Directors Ⓗ
Traditional pub built in the 1850s. Piano player Sat eves. The garden bar is open all day but does not serve real ale.
Q ❀ ◐ ⊟ ⇌ ♣ P

Aston

Flower Pot
Ferry Lane (off A423) OS784842 ☎ (0491) 574721
11–3, 6–11
Brakspear Mild, Bitter, Old (winter), **Special** Ⓗ
Wonderful old inn, a short walk from its own landing on the River Thames. Traditional wood floor in the public bar, and a lounge with armchairs. Breakfasts served from 8am. A refurbishment may remove the family area. ⛫ Q ♞ ❀ 🛏 ◐ ◗ ▲ ♣ P

Binfield

Jack O'Newbury
Terrace Road North (B3018)
☎ (0344) 483856
11–3, 6–11
Hogs Back TEA; Old Luxters Barn Ale; Wychwood Best, Dr Thirsty's Draught, Hobgoblin Ⓗ
Plush, comfortable pub with 15th-century stables converted into a skittle alley alongside. Interesting collection of bric-a-brac, including bells.
⛫ Q ❀ ◐ ♣ P

Jolly Farmer
Howe Lane (Maidenhead road, near B3018) OS852741
☎ (0734) 343343
11–3, 5.30–11
Morland Bitter Ⓖ
Real, unspoilt, two-bar, stone-floor country pub.
⛫ Q ❀ ⊟ P

Stag & Hounds
Forest Road (B3018/B3034 jct)
☎ (0344) 483553
11–3, 5.30–11
Courage Best Bitter, Directors; Ruddles County; John Smith's Bitter Ⓗ
Charming, historic, 14th-century coaching inn with a bar full of oak beams and curios. Lots of separate drinking areas add character. Warm and cosy on winter nights. No bar meals weekends; eve meals in the bistro (not Sun).
⛫ Q ❀ ◐ ◗ P

Try also: Victoria Arms, Terrace Rd North (Fuller's)

Bracknell

Blue Lion
Broad Lane (near Horse & Groom roundabout, A322)
☎ (0344) 425875
11–3, 5–11; 11–11 Sat
Draught Bass; Charrington IPA; Wadworth 6X Ⓗ
Comfortable, open-plan, modern pub catering for all tastes. Eve meals in summer only. ❀ ◐ ◗ ♿ ⇌ ♣ P

Brimpton

Three Horseshoes
School Road ☎ (0734) 712183
11–3, 6–11
Fuller's London Pride, ESB; Wadworth IPA Ⓗ
Delightful early Victorian, two-bar village pub, built by Mays of Basingstoke. The landlord used to be a champion cyclist. Interesting old photographs of the pub and village. ❀ 🛏 ◐ ♣ P

Burchett's Green

Crown
Burchett's Green Road
☎ (0628) 822844
11–11
Morland Bitter, Old Masters, Old Speckled Hen Ⓗ
Small, interesting village local where aircraft prints decorate the walls. The landlord cooks

the food with outstanding results. ⛫ Q ❀ ◑◗ ♣ P

Crazies Hill

Horns

Between A4 and A423, towards Warren Row/Wargrave OS799809
☎ (0734) 401416
11–2.30, 5.30–11
Brakspear Mild, Bitter, Old, Special Ⓗ
Wonderful country pub, recently refurbished and now run as a pub not as a restaurant. Well worth finding for all Brakspear's beers. No food Sun/Mon.
⛫ Q ♉ ❀ ◑ ♿ ▲ ♣ P

Enborne

Craven Arms

Enborne Road OS427647
☎ (0635) 253336
11–3, 6–11
Wadworth IPA, 6X, Farmer's Glory (summer), **Old Timer** Ⓗ**; guest beer**
Pleasant, ancient, rural pub with a warm welcome for families. Local newspaper *Pub of the Year* for two out of the last three years. Excellent garden for children.
♉ ❀ ◑◗ ♣ P

Eton Wick

Pickwick

32 Eton Wick Road
☎ (0753) 861713
11.30 (12 Sat)–2.30, 5.30 (6 Sat)–11
Young's Bitter, Porter (summer), **Special, Winter Warmer** Ⓗ
The only Young's pub in Berkshire, well known for its Malaysian food (eve meals Wed and Sat only). Live music every other Fri. Quiz night Sun. The landlord likes a philosophical debate. Awards for floral displays.
❀ ◑◗ ♣ P

Try also: Greyhound, Common Rd (Morland)

Finchampstead

Queens Oak

Church Lane ☎ (0734) 734855
11.30–2.30 (3 Sat, may extend), 6–11
Brakspear Bitter, Old, Special Ⓗ
Pleasant country pub on a walkers' route, right opposite the church. Interesting key fob collection in the right-hand bar; the left-hand bar is no-smoking. Great garden for kids. Pizzas recommended.
Q ❀ ◑◗ ▲ ♣ P ⍻

Frilsham

Pot Kiln

On Yattendon to Bucklebury road; not in Frilsham village OS552731 ☎ (0635) 201366
12–2.30, 6.30–11; 12–2.30, 7–10.30 Sun
Arkell's 3B; Morland Bitter, Old Speckled Hen; guest beer (summer) Ⓗ
Earth has nothing to show more fair than the rustic idyll unfolding before this pub, which was built in front of former kilns, with superb Flemish bond brickwork. Intimate bar; comfortable lounge – both free of distractions. The clientele reflects its rural nature. No food Sun or Tue. ⛫ Q ❀ ◑◗ ♣ P ⍻

Holyport

Belgian Arms

Holyport Street
☎ (0628) 34468
11–2.30, 5.30 (7.30 winter)–11
Brakspear Bitter, Old, Special Ⓗ
Old, wisteria-clad local just off the green. Renamed during WWI, after German prisoners held locally saluted the pub sign (it was the Eagle at the time). An upper room was used as a Wesleyan chapel until 1835; a Brakspear pub for 97 years. No meals Sun eve.
⛫ Q ❀ ◑◗ P

George

The Green ☎ (0628) 28317
11–3, 5.30–11; 11–11 Sat
Courage Best Bitter, Directors; John Smith's Bitter Ⓗ
Low-beamed, large single bar, incorporating a restaurant area, in a 600-year-old building which was once the village butcher's and barber's. No eve meals Sun/Mon.
⛫ Q ❀ ◑◗ ♣ P

Inkpen

Swan

Craven Road, Lower Green (Hungerford to Combe and Inkpen road) OS359643
☎ (0488) 668326
12–2.30, 6.30–11
Brakspear Bitter; Ringwood Best Bitter; guest beer Ⓗ
Large, 16th-century inn near famous Combe Gibbet. The menu features excellent Singaporean and English dishes. A comfortable and popular pub with very reasonably priced beer and three open fires. Children welcome. ⛫ ❀ ◑◗ ⌓ P

Kintbury

Blue Ball

High Street ☎ (0488) 58515
11–2.30, 6–11; 11–11 Sat
Courage Best Bitter; Smiles Best Bitter; guest beer Ⓗ
Beams, brick and wood panels, a warm welcome and a fire to match in this typical, busy, village pub. Dogs permitted on a lead, but no children inside. Small car park.
⛫ Q ❀ ◑ ⊟ ♿ ⇌ ♣ P

Dundas Arms

Station Road ☎ (0488) 58263
11–2.30, 6–11; 12–2.30, 7–10.30 Sun
Fuller's London Pride; Morland Bitter; Wells Bombardier; guest beer Ⓗ
Attractive, 18th-century inn by the Kennet and Avon Canal (lock 78). Named after Lord Dundas, who opened the canal in 1810. Note the old penny-covered bar. Good food; separate noted restaurant. No bar meals Sun, or Mon eve.
Q ❀ 🛏 ◑◗ ⇌ P

Loddon Bridge

George

479 Wokingham Road (A329)
☎ (0734) 268144
11–2.30 (3 Sat), 5.30 (5 Thu & Fri)–11
Courage Best Bitter, Directors; John Smith's Bitter Ⓗ
Interesting pub overlooking the river, with a large, attractive garden, great for summer drinking. Lively at lunchtimes with office workers; local eve trade. ❀ ◑
⇌ (Winnersh Triangle) P

Maidenhead

Cricketers Arms

16 Park Street (opp. town hall)
☎ (0628) 38332

Berkshire

11–2.30 (3 Fri & Sat), 5.30–11
Morland Bitter, Old Masters H
Two-bar pub with bar billiards in the small public. The saloon is comfortable and open-plan. No food Sun. ◐ ⇌ ♣

Hand & Flowers
15 Queen Street
☎ (0628) 23800
10.30–3, 5.30 (7 Sat)–11; 12–2.30, 7–10.30 Sun
Brakspear Bitter, Old, Special H
Small Victorian pub in the town centre. Popular with office workers at lunchtime; relaxing atmosphere in the eve. Mild is occasionally available. No meals Sun.
♛ Q ◐ ⇌

Vine
20 Market Street (behind Sainsbury's) ☎ (0628) 782112
10.30–11
Brakspear Bitter, Special H
Boisterous locals' pub with a friendly welcome, the home of several sports teams. Almost surrounded by new development but externally unchanged. No food weekends. ❀ ◐ ⇌ ♣

Newbury

Coopers Arms
39 Bartholomew Street (SW of Kennet Centre) ☎ (0635) 47469
11–3, 5–11; 11–11 Fri & Sat
Arkell's 3B, Kingsdown H
Horribly run-down Courage pub rescued by Arkell's and now a pleasant town local. The boisterous public bar remains, but prices are the same throughout. No smoking in the lounge/dining area lunchtimes (no food Sun); children welcome in this room.
◐ ⇌ ♣ P

Try also: Nag's Head, Bartholomew St (Courage)

Oakley Green

Olde Red Lion
Oakley Green Road (B3024, off A308) ☎ (0753) 863892
11–11
Brakspear Bitter; Greene King IPA; Ind Coope Friary Meux Best Bitter H
400-year-old country inn where Aunt Sally can be played in the large rear garden. The separate restaurant boasts an extensive menu of home-cooked food (eve meals Tue–Sat); bar snacks also served. Strictly no electronic entertainment here.
Q ❀ ◐ ◑ ♣ P

Old Windsor

Oxford Blue
Crimp Hill (off A308)
☎ (0753) 861954
11–11
Brakspear Bitter; Ind Coope Burton Ale; Tetley Bitter H
300-year-old verandah-fronted pub with an adventure playground for children. The back bar is full of airline models and memorabilia. Separate, very popular restaurant. Q ❀ 🛏 ◐ ◑ P

Pangbourne

Cross Keys
Church Road ☎ (0734) 843268
11–3, 6–11
Morland Bitter, Old Speckled Hen; guest beer H
Unspoilt, 17th-century pub with a patio garden backing onto the River Pang (small aviary and regular summer barbecues). Traditional meals cooked on the premises with senior citizen discounts. Small snug bar for children.
❀ 🛏 ◐ ◑ ⊟ ⇌

Pinkneys Green

Robin Hood
Marlow Road (A308)
☎ (0628) 26686
11.30–2.30, 5–11; 11–3.30, 6–11 Sat
Morland Bitter, Old Masters H**; guest beers**
Small, busy ex-Courage pub, built as a greengrocer's in the 17th century. Can get very crowded. ❀ ◐ ◑ ♣ P

Stag & Hounds
1 Lee Lane (SW corner of the green) ☎ (0628) 30268
11–2.30, 6–11
S&N Theakston Best Bitter, XB H**; guest beers**
Originally a Nicholson's beer house from the 1820s. The raised open porch leads to the bar, now mainly devoted to food. Off-road parking opposite. Live music Sun eve.
♛ ❀ ◐ ◑

Waggon & Horses
112 Pinkney Road (S of green)
☎ (0628) 24429
11–3, 5–11
Morland Bitter, Old Masters H
Very welcoming and popular locals' pub. The quiet saloon at the rear is accessed via the alley to the right. The public is plain but can get very busy. No meals weekends.
♛ Q ❀ ◐ ♣

Reading

Fisherman's Cottage
Orts Road, Kennetside (on canal tow path)
☎ (0734) 571553
11.30–3, 5–11 (usually 11–11 summer)
Fuller's Chiswick, London Pride, Mr Harry, ESB H
A tastefully extended gazebo area adds to the ambience of this traditional pub on the canalside. Quiz and foodie eves to delight all tastes. Great for a stop on summer walks.
♛ ❀ ◐ ◑ P

Horn
2 Castle Street (corner of St Mary's Butts) ☎ (0734) 574794
11–3, 5.30–11; 11–11 Wed–Sat
Courage Best Bitter, Directors H
Ancient inn in a conservation area, close to shops and the market. ❀ ◐ ♣

Sweeney & Todd
10 Castle Street (off St Mary's Butts) ☎ (0734) 586466
11–11; closed Sun eve
Adnams Bitter; Eldridge Pope Hardy Country, Blackdown Porter, Royal Oak; Wadworth 6X H
Splendid little bar at the rear of a pie shop, with a cellar restaurant and a covered patio. Always a cheery atmosphere, where diners mix easily with drinkers. House wines and port are recommended, as are the home-made pies.
Q ❀ ◐ ◑

Wallingford Arms
2 Caroline Street (off ring road near swimming pool)
☎ (0734) 575272
11 (12 Fri)–11
Morland Bitter, Old Masters, Old Speckled Hen; Wells Bombardier H
Popular back-street local with a pleasant public bar and a cosy lounge. A real gem.
❀ ◐ ♿ ♣ P

Remenham

Two Brewers
Wargrave Road (A321/A423, just before Henley bridge)
☎ (0491) 574375
11–3, 6–11
Brakspear Bitter, Old (winter), **Special** H
Pleasant, near-riverside pub within sight of the brewery, just a short walk to Henley.
♛ Q ☋ ❀ 🛏 ◐ ◑ ⇌ (Henley: not winter Sun)
♣ P

Shefford Woodlands

Pheasant Inn
Baydon Road ☎ (0488) 648284
11–3, 5.30–11
Brakspear Bitter; Hall & Woodhouse Hard Tackle; Wadworth IPA, 6X; guest beer Ⓗ
Excellent, two-bar country pub (once known as the Boarden House). A basic public bar with Ring the Bull, a smart saloon and a small dining room with a wide range of imaginative food. Very popular with itinerant rugby fans. 🔥 Q ❀ ◖ ◗ ⊟ ♣ P

Shinfield

Bell & Bottle
School Green ☎ (0734) 883563
11–11
Courage Best Bitter; Hook Norton Best Bitter; S&N Theakston Best Bitter, XB, Old Peculier; guest beers Ⓗ
Recently refurbished village pub where enthusiastic young owners offer a wide choice of guest beers. Two bars, one with darts. 🔥 ❀ ◖ ◗ ♣ P

Sindlesham

Walter Arms
Bearwood Road (off B3030/A329, near Bearwood College)
☎ (0734) 780260
11–2.30 (3 Sat), 5–11
Courage Best Bitter, Directors Ⓗ
Impressive, refurbished country pub, always busy. Friendly service; good reputation for excellent, home-cooked food.
🔥 Q ❀ 🛏 ◖ ◗ P

Stockcross

Lord Lyon
On B4000 ☎ (048 838) 366
11–3, 5.30–11
Arkell's 2B, 3B, Kingsdown Ⓗ
Large, well-kept pub named after a local racehorse: a single bar split into several areas. Well deserved reputation for its food. Note the unusual carved sign over the front door. 🔥 ❀ ◖ ◗ ♿ ♣ P

Try also: Rising Sun (Free)

Swallowfield

Crown
The Street (off B3349)
☎ (0737) 883260
11–3, 6–11
Morland Bitter, Old Masters Ⓗ
Pub with a basic, friendly, village public bar and a smarter and smaller lounge bar. Eve meals Thu–Sat only.
🔥 ❀ ◖ ◗ ⊟ ♿ ♣ P

Thatcham

Old Chequers
The Broadway
☎ (0635) 863312
11–11
Tetley Bitter; Wadworth 6X; guest beer Ⓗ
17th-century pub with a traditional atmosphere, old wood flooring, a low, beamed ceiling and plenty of photos depicting old Thatcham village scenes. Church pew benches. A lively mix of business types at lunchtime and the younger set at night. No eve meals Fri–Sun. ❀ ◖ ◗ ♿ P

Try also: Spotted Dog, Cold Ash (Free)

Theale

Falcon
31 High Street
☎ (0734) 302523
10.30–11
Archers Best Bitter; Courage Best Bitter, Directors; Wadworth 6X Ⓗ**; guest beers**
Old inn near the site of the former Blatch's brewery. Car park through the classic coaching arch. No food Sun.
❀ ◖ ≢ ♣ P

Three Mile Cross

Swan
Off A33 S of M4 jct 11
☎ (0734) 883674
11–11
Courage Best Bitter, Directors; Marston's Pedigree; Webster's Yorkshire Bitter Ⓗ
Smart roadhouse on the old A33, now bypassed. The landlady is an experienced canine judge which explains the dog pictures around the bars. The lunchtime and early eve emphasis is on freshly cooked food. 🔥 ❀ ◖ ◗ P

Twyford

Duke of Wellington
High Street ☎ (0734) 340456
11–2.30, 6–11
Brakspear Mild, Bitter, Old, Special Ⓗ
Friendly, 16th-century village pub: a popular public bar and a quieter lounge. Large, sheltered garden.
Q ❀ ◖ ⊟ ≢ P

Kings Arms
Wargrave Road (by central traffic lights) ☎ (0734) 340014
11–3, 6–11
Brakspear Mild, Bitter, Old, Special Ⓗ
Busy, modern, two-bar pub with lots of games.
◖ ◗ ⊟ ≢ ♣

Wargrave

Bull
High Street ☎ (0734) 403120
11–2.30, 6–11
Brakspear Bitter, Special Ⓗ
17th-century village pub with beams and a huge log fire. Busy food trade (no meals Sun eve). 🔥 Q ❀ 🛏 ◖ ◗
≢ (not winter Sun)

West Ilsley

Harrow
High Street (off A34)
☎ (0635) 28260
11–3, 6–11
Morland Bitter, Old Masters, Old Speckled Hen Ⓗ
Beautifully refurbished village pub in the Berkshire downs. Cricket can be viewed on the ground opposite without leaving the front garden. Handy for walkers on the nearby Ridgeway. Very good food: home-made rabbit pie is a speciality.
🔥 ❀ ◖ ◗ ♿ ⛺ ♣ P

White Waltham

Beehive
Waltham Road
☎ (0628) 822877
11–3, 5.30–11
Brakspear Bitter; Gale's Best Bitter; Whitbread Flowers IPA, Original; guest beers Ⓗ
Traditional country local opposite the cricket pitch and near the airfield. Popular with all tastes. Regulars make all feel welcome. Trips arranged to breweries and beer festivals. Petanque and mini-zoo in the back garden. The sort of place you want to move next door to. 🔥 Q ❀ ◖ ◗ ⊟ ♣ ⌓ P

Windsor

Prince Albert
2 Clewer Hill Road (B3022 S of centre) ☎ (0753) 864788
11–11
Courage Best Bitter; Marston's Pedigree; Wadworth 6X Ⓗ
Cosy and friendly, two-bar pub, a former 19th-century hunting lodge. No food Sun.
❀ ◖ ♣ P

Prince Christian
11 Kings Road
☎ (0753) 860980
11–3, 5–11; 11–11 Fri
Fuller's London Pride; S&N

Berkshire

Theakston Best Bitter Ⓗ**; guest beer**
Windsor's longest established free house, a short stroll (down Sheet Street) from the town centre and castle. One guest beer always available, reasonably priced for the locality. No food weekends.
◖ ⇌ (Central)

Trooper
97 St Leonards Road (opp. arts centre) ☎ (0753) 861717
11.30–2.30, 5.30–11; 11–11 Fri, 12–11 Sat
Beer range varies Ⓗ
One-bar pub divided into two areas, featuring TV, pinball, fruit machine, jukebox and bar billiards. Popular with the young and can be noisy.
❀ 🛏 ◖◗ P

Vansittart Arms
Vansittart Road
☎ (0753) 865988
11–11
Fuller's Chiswick (summer), **London Pride, ESB** Ⓗ
Warm welcome in a comfortable, open-plan pub which was originally called the World Upside Down but is now named after a local land-owning family. All food is home cooked, with some unusual dishes, including game. Free fresh mussels on the bar Sun lunch. No food Sun eve. ❀ ◖◗ ⇌ ♣

Try also: Court Jester, Church Lane, nr castle (Ind Coope)

Winkfield Row

Old Hatchet
Hatchet Lane OS922713
☎ (0344) 882303
11–11
Draught Bass; Charrington IPA; Fuller's London Pride; Young's Bitter Ⓗ
Attractive pub converted from three woodcutters' cottages. Good food is served in a homely atmosphere; separate restaurant area. 🔥 ❀ ◖◗ P

Wokingham

Crooked Billet
Honey Hill (off B3430, 2 miles SE of town) OS826667
☎ (0734) 780438
11–11
Brakspear Bitter, Old, Special Ⓗ
Excellent, extended country pub; an old building retaining all its character. The bar is split into three areas, with a separate restaurant. Ramp access for wheelchairs to the bar. Interesting collection of chiming clocks. Eve meals Tue–Sat only. Well worth seeking out.
🔥 Q ❀ ◖◗ ♣ P

Dukes Head
56 Denmark Street
☎ (0734) 780316
11.30–3, 5.30 (4.30 Fri, 6 Sat)–11
Brakspear Bitter, Old, Special Ⓗ
Town pub popular with business and passing trades, converted from three cottages in 1795. The skittle alley building is over 200 years old. Separate area with games; comfortable, well-furnished lounge. Unusual bar top. No food Sun. ❀ ◖ ⇌ ♣

Queens Head
23 The Terrace (A329, top of Station Rd) ☎ (0734) 781221
11–3, 5.30–11
Morland Bitter, Old Masters, Old Speckled Hen Ⓗ
Charming single-bar pub retaining much olde-worlde character. Popular with locals and business people. Active darts and quiz teams; Aunt Sally matches in the garden (access through the bar). No food Sun. ❀ ◖ ⇌ ♣

Woolhampton

Rowbarge Inn
Station Road ☎ (0734) 712213
11–2.30, 6–11
Courage Best Bitter; Fuller's London Pride; Ruddles County; Wadworth 6X; guest beer Ⓗ
Old, civilised, canalside pub, displaying a collection of objects way above the average pub tat – is this the national collection of blowlamps? Strong food emphasis.
❀ ◖◗ ⇌ (Midgham) P ⚟

Try also: Rising Sun, on A4 1 mile E (Free)

Buckinghamshire

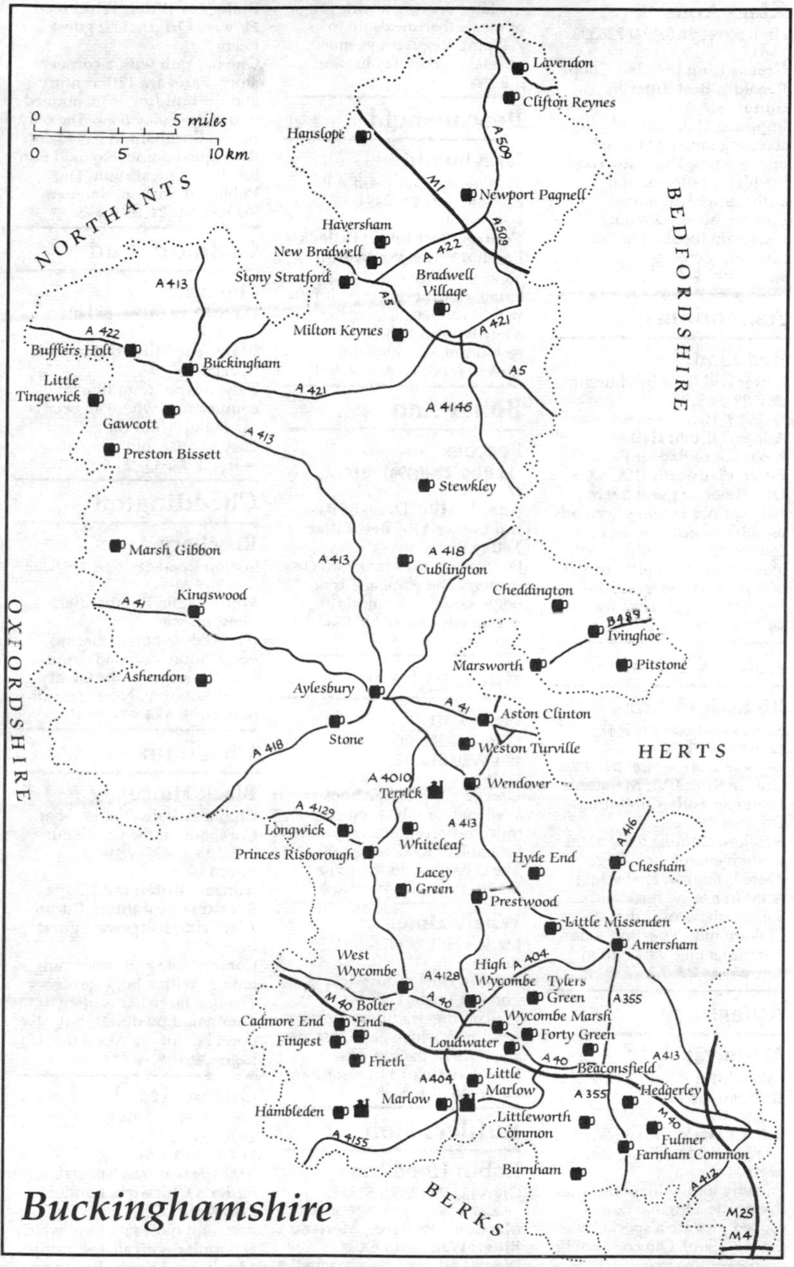

Chiltern, *Terrick;* **Old Luxters,** *Hambleden;*
Rebellion, *Marlow*

Amersham

Eagle

High Street ☎ (0494) 725262
11–3, 6–11

Fuller's London Pride; Greene King IPA; Tetley Bitter Ⓗ
Old-town pub at the western end of the High Street. Comfortable and highly polished, the bar is geared towards diners at lunchtimes (eve meals Sat only). A footbridge allows access to the rear of the pub.
♛ Q ❀ ☾ ♣

Kings Arms
High Street ☎ (0494) 726333
11–11
Greene King IPA; Ind Coope Benskins Best Bitter Ⓗ, **Burton Ale** Ⓖ
Imposing 15th-century coaching inn, now free of brewery ties. The many rooms are highly polished and authentically decorated. Popular, award-winning restaurant (book). The beer range may change.
♔ Q ❀ ◐ ◑ P

Ashendon

Red Lion
Lower End (lane by church)
☎ (0296) 651296
12–2.30, 7–11; closed Mon
Adnams Bitter; Hall & Woodhouse Badger Best Bitter; Wadworth IPA, 6X Ⓗ, **Old Timer** Ⓖ; **guest beers**
400-year-old building formerly used by magistrates as a courtroom, on a hilltop overlooking the northern Vale of Aylesbury. Separate dining area with imaginative food.
♔ Q ❀ ⛟ ◐ ◑ P

Aston Clinton

Rothschild Arms
82 Weston Road (B4544)
☎ (0296) 630320
12–2.30, 5.30 (4 Fri)–11; 11.30–11 Sat
Greene King IPA; Marston's Pedigree; Tolly Cobbold Original Ⓗ
Small, welcoming local at the western end of the village (there is another Rothschild Arms in nearby Buckland). Superb views over distant Chiltern hills. Function room. Eve meals till 8.30; no food Sun. ♔ ❀ ⛟ ◐ ◑ ♿ ♣ P

Aylesbury

Aristocrat
1 Wendover Road (A413)
☎ (0296) 415366
11–3, 5–11
Fuller's Hock, Chiswick, London Pride, ESB; guest beers Ⓗ
Friendly local with occasional live music. Original home-cooked pies are a speciality (no food Sun). Quizzes. Public car park at the rear.
❀ ◐ ◑ ♿ ⇌ ♣

Grapes
Market Square ☎ (0296) 83735
11 (8am Wed, Fri & Sat)–11
Courage Best Bitter, Directors; S&N Theakston XB Ⓗ; **guest beers**
Narrow bar where wooden floorboards and Victorian decor provide a pleasant atmosphere. Restaurant upstairs, serving a wide range of meals (bar meals up to 7.45pm). Regular live music. Special market day licence.
◐ ◑ ⇌

Beaconsfield

Greyhound
33 Windsor End (S off A40 roundabout) ☎ (0494) 673823
11–2.30, 5.30–11
Courage Best Bitter; Fuller's London Pride; Wadworth 6X Ⓗ
Small, charming, unspoilt pub with a very cosy, snug bar and a newly refurbished restaurant, serving home-cooked food. Q ❀ ◐ ◑ ♿ P

Bolter End

Peacock
On B482 ☎ (0494) 881417
11–2.30, 6–11
Ansells Mild; Draught Bass; Ind Coope ABC Best Bitter; Tetley Bitter Ⓗ
Popular country pub with cosy corners. The emphasis is on home-cooked bar meals at reasonable prices. No food Sun eve. ♔ Q ❀ ◐ ◑ ♣ P

Buckingham

New Inn
18 Bridge Street
☎ (0280) 815713
10–11
Greene King IPA, Abbot Ⓗ
Well-run, family-oriented pub, much involved in local affairs. Sri Lankan food a speciality. The cellar bar doubles as a family room. ♔ ♞ ❀ ◐ ◑

Whale Hotel
Market Hill ☎ (0280) 815537
10–11
Fuller's Hock, Chiswick, London Pride, ESB Ⓗ
Welcoming, traditional market town pub where gas lights are a feature of the bar. The lounge doubles as a restaurant.
♔ ❀ ⛟ ◐ ◑ ♿ ♣

Bufflers Holt

Robin Hood Inn
On A422 ☎ (0280) 813387
11–2.30, 6.30–11; 12–2, 7–10.30 Sun
Marston's Pedigree; Morland Bitter; Wadworth 6X Ⓗ
Warm and cosy, two-roomed bar in an old drovers' inn. Interesting selection of English wines. Beware keg cider on a fake handpump.
♔ Q ♞ ❀ ⛟ ◐ ◑ ♿ ♣ P

Burnham

Old Five Bells
14 Church Street (off High St)
☎ (0628) 604276
11–11
Brakspear Bitter; Whitbread Flowers Original Ⓗ; **guest beers**
One-bar pub with a conservatory. Parts are 12th century and the building is mentioned in the *Domesday Book*. The only pub in Burnham to have kept its original name. No food Sun lunch; eve meals Sun–Thu. Public car park in Summers Rd behind. ♞ ❀ ◐ ◑ ♿ ♣

Cadmore End

Old Ship
On B482 ☎ (0494) 881404
11–3, 6–11
Brakspear Mild, Bitter, Old, Special Ⓖ
Tiny, unspoilt, traditional country pub where all beer is carried up from the cellar. Easy to miss, but you will regret it. ♔ Q ❀ ♣

Cheddington

Rosebery Arms
Station Road ☎ (0296) 668222
11–2.30, 5.30–11
Wells Eagle, Bombardier; guest beer Ⓗ
Fine, old ex-hotel, offering good value food and drink, near the scene of the Great Train Robbery. No eve meals Sun. ♔ ❀ ◐ ◑ ⇌ ♣ P

Chesham

Black Horse
Chesham Vale (2 miles N of Chesham on the Cholesbury road) ☎ (0494) 784656
11–2.30, 6–11
Adnams Bitter; Ind Coope Benskins Best Bitter, Burton Ale; Tring Ridgeway; guest beer Ⓗ
Comfortable and welcoming, old inn with a huge garden. The one large bar is often dominated by diners, but don't be put off! Mind the beam. ❀ ◐ ◑ ♿ P

Queens Head
Church Street (B485)
☎ (0494) 783773
11–2.30, 5.30 (6 Sat)–11
Brakspear Bitter, Special; Fuller's Chiswick, London Pride Ⓗ
Excellent old-town local which is popular with all age groups: a traditional public bar and a comfortable and airy lounge, with a small courtyard to the rear. No meals Sun eve.
♔ Q ❀ ◐ ◑ ⊟ ⊖ ♣ P

Clifton Reynes

Robin Hood
☎ (0234) 711574
11.30–2.30, 6.30–11; 12–2.30, 7–10.30 Sun
Greene King IPA, Abbot Ⓗ

Nice country inn, off the beaten track and a haven for ramblers. Warm and cosy, with good food (no meals Mon).
♨ Q 🚼 ❀ ◖ ◗ ♿ ♣ P

Cublington

Unicorn
High Street ☎ (0296) 681261
12–3, 5.30–11
Fuller's London Pride; Hardys & Hansons Best Bitter; Taylor Landlord Ⓗ
Low-beamed village local with open fires at each end of a long bar. Separate dining room (no meals Sun eve). Five ales from a changing range, but beware the keg cider on a fake handpump. Petanque played.
♨ ❀ ◖ ◗ ♣ P

Farnham Common

Yew Tree
Collinswood Road (A355)
☎ (0753) 643223
11–11
Morland Bitter, Old Masters, Old Speckled Hen; guest beer Ⓗ
Very small and simple country pub, named after a yew tree which stood outside. The lounge is given over to food but the lively public is popular. Stone-cooked food is a speciality.
♨ ❀ ◖ ◗ ⊞ ▲ ♣ P

Try also: Foresters, The Broadway (Bass)

Fingest

Chequers
☎ (0491) 638335
11–3, 6–11
Brakspear Bitter, Old, Special Ⓗ
Smart, comfortable pub with distinct areas. The spacious garden is a feature. Outstanding bar food and a restaurant (no meals Sun eve).
♨ Q 🚼 ❀ ◖ ◗ ♣ P ⊘

Forty Green

Royal Standard of England
Forty Green Road, Knotty Green (off B474) OS923919
☎ (0494) 673382
11–3, 5.30–11
Courage Best Bitter; Eldridge Pope Hardy Country, Royal Oak; Marston's Pedigree, Owd Rodger Ⓗ
Ancient, rambling and historic pub, in the same private ownership since 1961. Hard to find, but busy, though seldom crowded. House bitter from Morland. Wide range of meals.
♨ Q 🚼 ❀ ◖ ◗ P

Frieth

Prince Albert
Moor End (100 yds from Lane End to Frieth road)
☎ (0494) 881683
11–3, 5.30–11
Brakspear Mild, Bitter, Old Special Ⓗ
The sort of pub you don't want to tell other people about, enjoying superb atmosphere, location and hospitality. Josie's platefuls are a bonus at lunchtime (Tue–Sat). ♨ Q ❀ ◖ ♣

Fulmer

Black Horse
Windmill Road
☎ (0753) 663183
11–2.30, 5.30–11
Courage Best Bitter, Directors Ⓗ
Three-bar pub dating from the early 17th century. None of the bars is particularly large, and the central bar is the smallest – plain and simple with wood flooring. The public can get crowded on darts nights. Snacks only on Sun.
♨ Q ❀ ◖ ⊞ ♣ P

Gawcott

Cuckoos Nest
New Inn Lane
10.30–3 (not Mon), 6–11
Hook Norton Best Bitter, Old Hooky; Marston's Pedigree Ⓗ**; guest beers** (occasionally)
Popular, welcoming, two-bar, 18th-century village local. Tiny car park. ♨ ❀ ⊞ ♿ ♣ P

Hambleden

Stag & Huntsman
N of A4155 ☎ (0491) 571227
11–2.30, 6–11
Brakspear Bitter, Special; Old Luxters Barn Ale; Wadworth 6X, Farmer's Glory, Old Timer Ⓗ
Unspoilt, three-bar pub in a picturesque, brick and flint NT village. Extensive menu (not served Sun eve), with seafood a speciality; fish and chip specials Tue eve in winter.
♨ Q ❀ 🛏 ◖ ◗ ♣

Hanslope

Globe
50 Hartwell Road, Long Street
☎ (0908) 510336
12–2.30, 6–11
Banks's Mild, Bitter Ⓔ**; Marston's Pedigree** Ⓗ
Very pleasant, roadside pub north of the village. Friendly atmosphere, combined with excellent country fare. Good car park, garden and play area. Booking advised for meals Fri night and weekends.
Q ❀ ◖ ⊞ ♿ ♣ P

Haversham

Greyhound
High Street ☎ (0908) 313487
11.30–2.30, 5.30–11; 12–3, 6.30–11 Sat; 12–2.30, 7–10.30 Sun
Greene King IPA, Rayments Special, Abbot Ⓗ
300-year-old pub with two cosy bars. Warm welcome.
♨ Q 🚼 ❀ ◖ ◗ ♣ P

Hedgerley

One Pin
One Pin Lane ☎ (0753) 643035
11–4, 5.30–11
Courage Best Bitter, Directors Ⓗ
Traditional two-bar pub with an air of class in the saloon. In the public, with its parquet flooring, bar billiards can be played. The landlord has been here 29 years. Part of the film *Genevieve* was filmed here. No food Sun. ◖ ◗ ♣ P

High Wycombe

Bird in Hand
81 West Wycombe Road (A40)
☎ (0494) 523502
11.30–3, 5.30 (6 Sat)–11
Courage Best Bitter, Directors; Marston's Pedigree; Ruddles Best Bitter; Wadworth 6X Ⓗ
Recent refurbishment has not ruined the character of this pub with distinctive wood panelling. No eve meals Sun.
♨ ❀ ◖ ◗ ♣ P

Rose & Crown
Desborough Road
☎ (0494) 527982
11–11
Courage Best Bitter; Gale's HSB; Marston's Pedigree; Morland Old Speckled Hen; Ruddles County; Wadworth 6X Ⓗ**; guest beers**
Wycombe's most interesting selection of beers in an L-shaped, corner pub with busy office lunchtime trade (no meals weekends). ◖ ⇌ ♣

Hyde End

Barley Mow
Chesham Road (B485, between Gt Missenden and Chesham)
☎ (024 06) 5625
11–3, 6–11 (11–11 summer)
Brakspear Special; Courage Best Bitter; Marston's Pedigree; guest beer Ⓗ
Isolated pub on a hill above Gt Missenden. One large, L-shaped bar. Biannual beer festivals. ♨ 🚼 ❀ ◖ ◗ ♣ P

Buckinghamshire

Ivinghoe

Rose & Crown

Vicarage Lane (turn opp. church, then first right)
☎ (0296) 668472
12–2.30 (3 Sat), 6–11
Adnams Bitter; Greene King IPA; Morrells Mild; guest beer Ⓗ
Tucked-away in a back street, a thriving ex-Allied pub. The elevated rear public bar is home to a keen darts team; the lower lounge bar is small, intimate and can get crowded. No food Sun. Parking can be difficult. ♨ Q ◖ ◗ ▲ ♣

Kingswood

Crooked Billet

Ham Green (A41)
☎ (0296) 770239
11–3, 5–11; 11–11 Fri, Sat & summer
Draught Bass; Ind Coope Burton Ale; Tetley Bitter; Wadworth 6X Ⓗ
Rambling 17th-century pub with an historic inn sign, large gardens and a banqueting suite. Breakfast from 9am. ♨ ♞ ❀ ⌸ ◖ ◗ ♣ P

Lacey Green

Pink & Lily

Pink Road, Parslow's Hillock (1 mile from village) OS827019
☎ (0494) 488308
11.45 (11 Sat)–3, 6–11
Brakspear Bitter; Courage Directors; Wadworth 6X; Whitbread Boddingtons Bitter, Flowers Original; Wychwood Hobgoblin Ⓗ
Roomy and popular country pub, with an enclosed patio and an original snug bar. Always eight ales available and good, home-cooked meals – no chips! Splendid log fires. ♨ Q ❀ ◖ ◗ ♣ P

Lavendon

Horseshoe

High Street ☎ (0234) 712641
11–3, 5.30–11; 11–11 Sat
Hall & Woodhouse Tanglefoot; Wells Eagle Ⓗ
Lively village inn, on the main trunk road between Northampton and Bedford. Two low-beamed bars: a fine example of a 16th-century coaching inn. No meals Sun–Tue. ♨ Q ♞ ❀ ◖ ◗ ♣

Little Marlow

King's Head

Church Road ☎ (0628) 484407
11–3, 5–11
Brakspear Bitter; Greene King Abbot; Wadworth 6X; guest beer Ⓗ
Village pub, dating from the 14th century: two bars with much character. Varied, home-cooked meals are always available, along with six ales. Function room. ♨ ❀ ◖ ◗ ♿ P

Little Missenden

Crown

Off A413 ☎ (024 06) 2571
11–2.30, 6–11; 12–2.30, 7–10.30 Sun
Hook Norton Best Bitter; Marston's Pedigree; Morrells Varsity Ⓗ**; guest beer** Ⓖ
Genuine village pub with an equally genuine welcome. Warm and comfortable, the bar is decorated with brass and farm implements. No food Sun. ♨ Q ❀ ◖ ♣ ⌓ P

Little Tingewick

Red Lion

Mere Road ☎ (0280) 847836
12–3.30, 6–11
Fuller's Chiswick, London Pride, ESB Ⓗ
Lively, village local with civil war connections – ask the landlord. Traditional Sun lunch a speciality.
♨ Q ♞ ❀ ◖ ◗ ♣ P ⊬

Littleworth Common

Blackwood Arms

Common Lane (SE of Burnham to Beaconsfield road, near Beech Tree pub) OS937863 ☎ (0753) 642169
11–2.30, 5.30–11; 11–11 Fri & Sat
Beer range varies Ⓗ
Very highly recommended free house in idyllic woodland surroundings; popular with cyclists and ramblers. A beer festival. Good value food.
♨ Q ❀ ◖ ◗ ▲ ♣ ⌓ P

Longwick

Red Lion

Thame Road (A4130)
☎ (084 44) 4980
12–2.30, 6–11
Fuller's London Pride; Hook Norton Best Bitter; Tetley Bitter Ⓗ
Comfortable and friendly, roadside inn with steam rail memorabilia. Substantial meals; separate dining area. No eve meals Sun. En suite bedrooms. Q ⌸ ◖ ◗ ♣ P

Loudwater

Derehams Inn

Derehams Lane (just N of A40) OS903907 ☎ (0494) 530965
11 (12 Sat)–3, 5.30–11
Brakspear Bitter; Fuller's London Pride; Gibbs Mew Salisbury; S&N Theakston Best Bitter; Wadworth 6X; Young's Bitter Ⓗ
Cosy pub, hard to find so mainly catering for local trade. The beer range varies. Lunches weekdays only. Small car park. ♨ ❀ ◖ ♣ P

Marlow

Clayton Arms

Quoiting Square, Oxford Road
☎ (0628) 483037
10.30–2.30 (3 Fri & Sat), 6–11; 12–2.30, 7–10.30 Sun
Brakspear Mild, Bitter, Old Ⓗ
Town-centre gem with two small bars. The landlord has lived here since 1929. The original and genuine local.
♨ Q ♞ ⊞ ⇶ ♣

Prince of Wales

1 Mill Road (off Station Rd)
☎ (0628) 482970
11–11
Brakspear Bitter; Wadworth 6X; guest beers Ⓗ
Friendly back-street local with two connecting bars: a comfortable public and a lounge with a dining area (families welcome). No food Sun eve. ❀ ◖ ◗ ⇶ ♣ P

Marsh Gibbon

Greyhound

West Edge ☎ (0869) 277365
12–4, 6–11
Fuller's London Pride; Greene King Abbot; Hook Norton Best Bitter; S&N Theakston Best Bitter Ⓗ
Listed building, probably of Tudor origin, with 17th-century brickwork. Burned down in 1725 and rebuilt in 1740 for £50. Thai and continental food (no meals Tue eve). ♨ Q ♞ ❀ ◖ ◗ ▲ P

Marsworth

Red Lion

Vicarage Road (off B489 near canal bridge) OS919147
☎ (0296) 668366
11–3, 6–11
Draught Bass; Fuller's London Pride; Hook Norton Best Bitter; Morrells Varsity; Tring Ridgeway Ⓗ
Idyllic, canalside, village pub: a comfortable upper bar, with a food section, and a long, tile-floored public bar with games. A true gem with a mixed clientele. No food Sun.
♨ Q ❀ ◖ ◗ ♣ ⌓ P

Milton Keynes: *Bradwell Village*

Prince Albert

17 Vicarage Road
☎ (0908) 312080
11–2.30 (3 Fri, 5 Sat), 6–11

Wells Eagle, Bombardier Ⓗ**; guest beers**
Victorian building in an older village, now surrounded by modern housing. 🏠 ❀ ◐ ◑ P

New Bradwell

New Inn
Bradwell Road
☎ (0908) 312094
11–11; 11–4, 6.30–11 Sat
Hall & Woodhouse Tanglefoot; Morland Old Speckled Hen; Wells Eagle, Bombardier Ⓗ
Lively, canalside inn with good value bar food and a separate restaurant upstairs. Ideal for narrow boaters.
🏠 Q 🐎 ❀ ◐ ◑ ⊟ ♣ P

Newport Pagnell

Green Man
92 Silver Street
12–3, 5.30–11; 11–11 Sat
Banks's Mild, Bitter; Marston's Pedigree; guest beer Ⓗ
Corner pub re-opened and admirably extended. Well worth finding. 🏠 ❀ ⊟ ♣ P

Pitstone

Duke of Wellington
Cooks Wharf OS927161
☎ (0296) 661402
12–2.30 (3 Sat), 6–11
Fuller's London Pride; Marston's Pedigree Ⓗ**; guest beer** (Easter–Nov)
One-bar country pub. The Grand Union Canal passes immediately behind. Special rates for meals for senior citizens. 🏠 ❀ ◐ ◑ ♣ P

Preston Bissett

Old Hat
Main Street ☎ (028 04) 355
11–2.30, 7 (6 Sat)–11
Hook Norton Best Bitter Ⓗ
Grade II-listed, thatched pub, a step back in time. Classic settle in front of the fire. A must on cold nights, or any time really. 🏠 Q P

Prestwood

King's Head
188 Wycombe Road (A4128)
☎ (024 06) 2392
11–11
Brakspear Mild, Bitter, Old, Special; Fuller's London Pride; Greene King Abbot; guest beers Ⓖ
The ultimate antidote to the modern pub: traditional decor and atmosphere – no machines, no music, no draught lager, no meals (snacks only).
🏠 Q ❀ ⊟ ♣ ⌓

Princes Risborough

Bird in Hand
Station Road ☎ (084 44) 5602
11–3, 6–11
Greene King IPA, Rayments Special, Abbot Ⓗ**, Winter Ale** Ⓖ
Cosy cottage pub – a real local, with the accent on games. Immaculate collection of brass trinkets and darts trophies. No food Sun. ❀ ◐ ⇌ ♣

Stewkley

Swan
High Street North
☎ (0525) 240285
11.30–3, 6–11
Courage Best Bitter, Directors; Marston's Pedigree; John Smith's Bitter Ⓗ
Fine Georgian pub in the village centre. Good atmosphere in an old, beamed interior. Bar billiards; monthly live music Sun eves (no food Sun). ❀ ◐ ◑ ♣ P

Stone

Waggon & Horses
39 Oxford Road (A418)
☎ (0296) 748740
11–2.30 (3 Fri & Sat), 5.30–11
Ind Coope ABC Best Bitter, Burton Ale Ⓗ
Immaculate roadside pub with two bars. The landlord has the Burton Ale cellarmanship award. Good, home-cooked food.
Q ❀ ◐ ◑ ⊟ ♣ P

Stony Stratford

Bull Hotel (Vaults Bar)
High Street ☎ (0908) 567104
12–11
Bass Worthington BB, Draught Bass; Eldridge Pope Royal Oak; Fuller's London Pride; Hook Norton Best Bitter; Wadworth 6X Ⓗ
Small Victorian bar next to an old coaching inn (involved in the original 'Cock & Bull' story). Folk club Sun lunch. Beers change regularly.
🏠 ❀ 🛏 ◐ ◑ P

Tylers Green

Horse & Jockey
Church Road (off B474)
☎ (0494) 815963
11–2.30, 5.30–11
Ansells Mild; Fuller's London Pride; Ind Coope Burton Ale; Tetley Bitter; guest beers Ⓗ
Spacious pub serving food at all hours. Fine collection of horse brasses and livery.
❀ ◐ ◑ ♿ ⌓ P

Wendover

King & Queen
17 South Street (A413 S of High St) ☎ (0296) 623272
12–3, 6–11; 12–11 Sat
Ansells Mild Ⓖ**; Greene King IPA; Tetley Bitter** Ⓗ
Small, 16th-century pub with a mainly local trade. The excellent, stone-flagged public bar has an inglenook. A rare outlet in this area for dark mild (not in hot summer months) and real cider.
🏠 ❀ ◐ ◑ ♿ ⇌ ♣ ⌓ P

Weston Turville

Plough
5 Brook End (B4544, E end of village) ☎ (0296) 612546
11–2.30, 6–11
Fuller's Hock, Chiswick, London Pride Ⓗ**, Mr Harry, ESB** Ⓖ
Well-kept, well-run, one-bar pub with a vintage jukebox and a strong games following. Eve meals end at 8 Thu; no food Sun. 🏠 ❀ ◐ ◑ ♣ P

West Wycombe

George & Dragon Hotel
High Street ☎ (0494) 464414
11–2.30, 5.30–11; 11–11 Sat; 12–2.30, 7–10.30 Sun
Courage Best Bitter, Directors Ⓗ**; guest beer**
18th-century coaching inn in a NT village, with an original timbered bar. Noted for its food. Meals every day. Excellent garden. Function room. 🏠 Q 🐎 ❀ 🛏 ◐ ◑ P

Whiteleaf

Red Lion
Upper Icknield Way (off A4010) ☎ (084 44) 4476
11–3, 5.30–11
Brakspear Bitter; Hook Norton Best Bitter; Morland Bitter; Wadworth 6X Ⓗ
Attractive 17th-century inn in a quiet Chilterns village. Good food and quiet conversation.
🏠 Q ❀ 🛏 ◐ ◑ P

Wycombe Marsh

General Havelock
114 Kingsmead Road (parallel to A40) ☎ (0494) 520391
11–2.30 (3 Fri & Sat), 5.30 (5 Fri & Sat)–11
Fuller's Hock, Chiswick, London Pride, Mr Harry, ESB Ⓗ
Traditional family pub, smart and friendly. Noted for its lunches (eve meals in summer only). 🏠 ❀ ◐ ◑ ♿ ♣ P

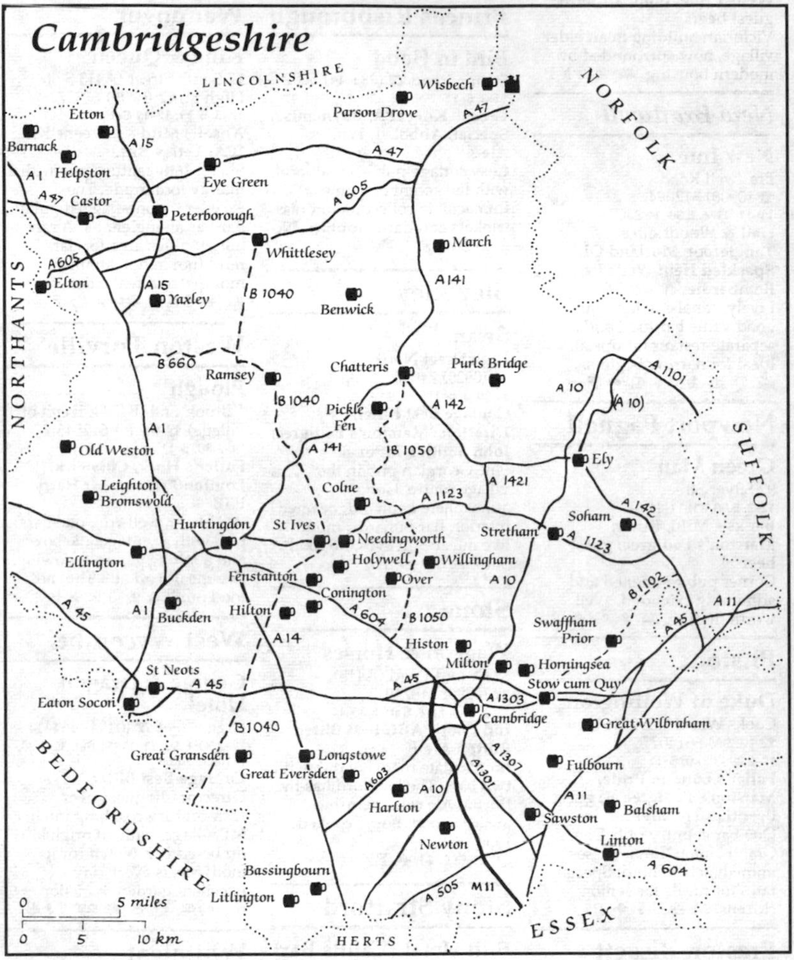

Elgood's, Wisbech

Balsham

Bell

2 West Wickham Road
☎ (0223) 894415
11–2.30, 6–11; 11–11 Sat
Greene King XX Mild, IPA Ⓗ
Two-bar, village local where games and music cater for the younger element in the public, while the saloon lends itself to conversation, being the hub of village life. ♛ ❀ ♣ P

Barnack

Millstone

Millstone Lane
☎ (0780) 740296
11–2.30, 6–11
Everards Tiger, Old Original; Ridleys IPA; guest beer Ⓗ
Stone-built village local close to 'Hills and Holes' – a former stone quarry for churches. The restaurant is open every session. Function suite.
❀ ◐ ◑ ♿ P ⊁

Bassingbourn

Pear Tree

North Road ☎ (0763) 44068
11–2.30, 6–11
Eldridge Pope Hardy Country, Royal Oak; Greene King IPA; Whitbread Boddingtons Bitter Ⓗ
Village-centre pub with a social club discount for pensioners: a lively public bar and a dining area. Noted for the poetry etched on its windows. ♛ ⊨ ◐ ◑ ♣ P

Benwick

Five Alls

High Street ☎ (035 477) 520
11–3, 6–11; 11–11 Fri & Sat
John Smith's Bitter Ⓗ
'I govern all' – a queen; 'I plead for all' – a barrister; 'I pray for all' – a priest; 'I fight for all' – a soldier; 'I pay for all' – a ploughman; a community pub named after the working man's timeless complaint. Fishing parties by prior arrangement. Own bowling green. ♛ ❀ ◐ ♿ ▲ ♣ P

Buckden

Falcon
Mill Road ☎ (0480) 811612
12–4, 7–11; 12–11 Sat
Mansfield Riding Mild; Morland Old Speckled Hen; Wells Eagle Ⓗ
Situated just outside the main village, on the road to Offords: a single lounge bar with a games room at the rear. Traditional games include Northants skittles, now sadly rare this far east. Two gardens; one is enclosed, with a patio. Beware Scrumpy Jack cider on false handpump.
P

Try also: Spread Eagle (Wells)

Cambridge

Ancient Druids
Napier Street ☎ (0223) 324514
11–3, 5.30 (6 Sat)–11
Ancient Druids Mild, Kite Bitter, Druids Special, Merlin; Wells Bombardier; guest beers Ⓗ
The micro brewery attached to this modern, open-plan pub is an obvious attraction, but there's always a good range of other beers, plus good value food (not served Sun/Mon eves). Public car parks nearby.

Cambridge Blue
Gwydir Street ☎ (0223) 61382
12–2.30 (3.30 Sat), 6–11
Nethergate IPA, Bitter, Old Growler; guest beers Ⓗ
Bustling, friendly pub with a no-smoking bar and a snug. Exotic guest beers usually include a mild. The landlord has been a parliamentary candidate for the Monster Raving Loony Party.
Q

Champion of the Thames
King Street ☎ (0223) 352043
11–11
Greene King XX Mild, IPA Ⓗ, **Abbot** Ⓖ
Delightful little pub with a local atmosphere, rare in the city centre. Splendid etched windows show the Champ in action. No food Sun.
Q

Cow & Calf
St Peters Street
☎ (0223) 311919
12–3, 5.30 (7 Sat)–11
Courage Best Bitter, Directors; Nethergate Bitter; S&N Theakston Best Bitter; John Smith's Bitter; guest beers Ⓗ
Superb, street-corner local catering for a wide clientele. Meals served weekdays only. Use Shire Hall car park eves.

Elm Tree
Orchard Street ☎ (0223) 63005
11–11
Mansfield Riding Mild; Wells Eagle, Bombardier Ⓗ
Small, friendly, oddly-shaped, one-bar pub in an area rich in good boozers.

Free Press
Prospect Row ☎ (0223) 68337
12–3, 6–11
Greene King IPA, Abbot Ⓗ
Hearty pub, packed with interesting features. No music and no fruit machines but imaginative, high-quality food and a sun-trap patio garden where furry beasties roam free. Q

Haymakers
High Street, Chesterton
☎ (0223) 67417
11–2.30 (3 Sat), 6–11
Ind Coope Burton Ale; Tetley Bitter; Tolly Cobbold Original; Whitbread Flowers Original Ⓗ
Welcoming, one-bar community pub serving good value food (no meals Sun). Live music Fri and Sat eve.
P

Mitre
Bridge Street ☎ (0223) 358403
11–11
Adnams Bitter; Ind Coope Burton Ale; Tetley Bitter; guest beers Ⓗ
Attractively 'demodernised' pub in a non-clichéd alehouse style. Up to five guest beers, plus regular beer festivals. Eve meals finish at 8.

Portland Arms
129 Chesterton Road
☎ (0223) 357268
11–2.30, 5–11
Greene King XX Mild, IPA, Rayments Special, Abbot Ⓗ
Spacious, comfortable pub which overlooks the peace and tranquillity of the Mitchams Corner gyratory system! Strong nautical flavour in the lounge.

St Radegund
King Street ☎ (0223) 311794
12–11; closed Sun
Fuller's London Pride; Hook Norton Best Bitter; Nethergate Bitter; guest beer Ⓗ
The smallest pub in Cambridge but bursting with atmosphere and character. Starting point for the (in)famous King Street Run. Greek meze and huge crusty sandwiches available.

Tram Depot
Dover Street (off East Rd)
☎ (0223) 324553
11–3, 5–11; 11.30–11 Sat
Adnams Bitter; Everards Tiger, Old Original; Hall & Woodhouse Tanglefoot; guest beers Ⓗ
Characterful, award-winning pub that used to be the stables of a horse tram depot. Now owned by Everards, so the Earl Soham beers have gone. Public car park at the rear.

Wrestlers
337 Newmarket Road
☎ (0223) 358777
11–11
Adnams Broadside; Hall & Woodhouse Tanglefoot; Mansfield Riding Bitter; Morland Old Speckled Hen; Wells Eagle, Bombardier Ⓗ
Boisterous town pub, with live music twice a week. Authentic Thai food, including take-away (no food Sun). Notable collection of bottles.

Zebra
80 Maids Causeway
☎ (0223) 464116
12–3, 6–11
Greene King IPA, Rayments Special, Abbot Ⓗ
Although basically open-plan, this busy, comfy pub has several distinct drinking areas. Food is good, cheap and plentiful (not served Sun eve).

Try also: Empress, Thoday St (Whitbread)

Castor

Royal Oak
24 Peterborough Road
☎ (0773) 380217
11–2.30, 6–11
Ind Coope Burton Ale; Tetley Bitter; guest beer Ⓗ
Listed building with a thatched roof and a low-beamed ceiling. A friendly village pub with a warm welcome. Weekly guest beer; bar snacks Mon–Sat lunchtime.
Q P

Chatteris

Honest John
24–26 South Park Street
☎ (0354) 692698
11–2.30, 5–11
Morland Old Speckled Hen; Whitbread Boddingtons Bitter, Wethered Bitter Ⓗ
Former Labour Exchange, which became a pub in 1973. The landlord is a bit of a poet.
P

Cambridgeshire

Colne

Green Man
East Street ☎ (0487) 840368
12–3, 7–11
Greene King IPA; Ind Coope Burton Ale Ⓗ
Comfortable, friendly two-bar village pub, dating from the 17th century. Take care with the deep step down into the pub and the low, uneven door to the lounge. ❀ ◑ ◗ ⊞ ♣ P

Conington

White Swan
☎ (095 47) 251
11–2.30 (3 Sat), 6–11
Greene King XX Mild Ⓖ, IPA, Rayments Special Ⓗ, Abbot Ⓖ
Victorian pub in a splendid pastoral setting, featuring fine tiled floors and a choice of (free) snuffs. Very busy at weekends. No meals Sun eve.
⛫ ♞ ❀ ◑ ◗ ⊞ ♿ ♣ P

Eaton Socon

Crown
Great North Road (A45, St Neots bypass) ☎ (0480) 212232
11–2.30, 5.30–11
Tetley Bitter; guest beer Ⓗ
Ivy-clad free house, just off the A1, often crowded. At least six real ales on offer. Bookings are advised for the restaurant. Campsite at nearby Wyboston Lakes. ❀ ◑ ◗ ▲ P

Millers Arms
Ackerman Street (off A1)
☎ (0480) 405965
12–2, 6–11; 11–11 Fri, & Sat
Greene King XX Mild, IPA, Abbot Ⓗ
Small village pub on the larger of Eaton Socon's greens. The large garden boasts many children's facilities and a boules pitch; summer barbecues. Popular with boat owners from the nearby river moorings. Children welcome until 8pm. ⛫ ♞ ❀ ◑ ♣

Ellington

Mermaid
Off A14 ☎ (0480) 891450
11.30–2.30, 6–11; 11.30–11 Sat
Draught Bass Ⓗ
One-bar village free house, which has an unusual alcoved wood-burning stove.
⛫ ❀ ♣

Elton

Crown
Duck Street ☎ (0832) 280232
11.30–2.30, 6–11
Greene King IPA, Rayments Special, Abbot; guest beers Ⓗ
Grade II-listed building on the village green, rebuilt in 1985 after a major fire. A large comfortable bar and a restaurant. Boules played.
⛫ ❀ ◑ ♣ P

Ely

Prince Albert
62 Silver Street
☎ (0353) 663494
11.30–2.30 (3 Fri, 3.30 Sat), 6.30–11
Greene King XX Mild, IPA, Abbot Ⓗ
The emphasis is firmly on good ale and good company at Cambridge CAMRA's *Pub of the Year* 1993, which also has a delightful award-winning garden. Public car park across the street (entrance in Barton Road). No food Sun.
⛫ Q ❀ ◑ ♣

West End House
West End ☎ (0353) 662907
11.30–2.30, 6–11
Draught Bass; Courage Directors; Marston's Pedigree; Ruddles Best Bitter; Webster's Yorkshire Bitter Ⓗ
Four drinking areas with a plethora of beams and low ceilings. The cat remains unfriendly, though. ⛫ ❀ ♣

Etton

Golden Pheasant
Main Street (Helpston turn off A15, then 1st right)
☎ (0733) 252387
11–11
Adnams Bitter; Draught Bass; Bateman XXXB; Courage Directors; Greene King IPA; Ruddles County Ⓗ; guest beers
Former 19th-century manor farmhouse: a large, comfortable lounge bar, a family room and a restaurant. Paintings displayed in the lounge are for sale. The large garden gets very busy in summer.
⛫ Q ♞ ❀ ◑ ◗ ♿ ▲ ♣ P

Eye Green

Greyhound
41 Crowland Road
☎ (0733) 222487
11 (12 Sat)–3, 7–11
Wells Eagle, Bombardier Ⓗ
Popular village local; basic but comfortable with a large garden. ❀ ⊞ ♣ P

Fenstanton

King William
High Street (off A604)
☎ (0480) 62467
11–2.30, 6.30–11
Greene King IPA, Abbot, Rayments Special Ⓗ
Village pub opened-up, but separated into eating and drinking areas by original beams and settles. Pleasantly situated on the village green which is complete with a clock tower and a pond. ❀ ◑ ◗

Fulbourn

Bakers Arms
2 Hinton Road
☎ (0223) 880606
11–11
Greene King XX Mild, IPA, Rayments Special, Abbot Ⓗ
Two distinct drinking areas, a lounge and hall-like conservatory, overlook the outstanding garden with its children's attractions. The food is all home cooked; Sun barbecues and afternoon teas. Splendid hanging basket display.
⛫ ♞ ❀ ◑ ◗ ▲ ♣ P

Great Eversden

Hoops
High Street ☎ (0223) 262185
12–2.30 (may vary summer), 7–11
Adnams Broadside; Wells Eagle Ⓗ, Bombardier Ⓖ
17th-century village inn with a heavily-timbered seating area separated from the public bar by a conversational lobby.
⛫ ❀ ⊞ ♣ P

Great Gransden

Crown & Cushion
On B1046 ☎ (076 77) 214
12–11; 12–2.30, 6–11 Mon
Adnams Broadside; Mansfield Riding Mild; Wells Eagle, Bombardier Ⓗ
Traditional, thatched village pub where the split-level interior is divided into areas. Good home-cooked food. Small menagerie in the garden. Live music Tue and Thu eves. Ten years in this guide.
⛫ ❀ ◑ ◗ P

Great Wilbraham

Carpenters Arms
High Street ☎ (0223) 880202
11–2.30, 6.30 (7 winter)–11
Greene King XX Mild, IPA, Rayments Special, Abbot Ⓗ
Two-bar country local. Large fireplaces and an affable landlord create real warmth. Keenly priced, home-cooked, bar meals (not served Sun eve). ⛫ ❀ ◑ ◗ ♣ P

Harlton

Hare & Hounds
High Street ☎ (0223) 262672
11–11
Wells Eagle, Bombardier Ⓗ

Welcoming, single-roomed, country pub. The outstanding garden has an adventure playground, skittle alley, petanque pitch, crazy golf and a children's zoo (see Mildred, the pot-bellied pig). A haunt of traction engines and 2CVs.
❀ ◑ ♣ P

Helpston

Bluebell

Woodgate ☎ (0733) 252394
11–2.30, 7–11; 12–2, 7–10.30 Sun
Draught Bass; Bateman XXXB; John Smith's Bitter; Webster's Yorkshire Bitter H
Pub dating from the 1600s; its wood-panelled lounge features a famed collection of teapots and Toby jugs. Simple public bar. John Clare, the peasant-poet, used to be the pub's pot boy. No keg bitter sold.
Q ❀ ♣ P

Hilton

Prince of Wales

Potton Road (B1040)
☎ (0480) 830257
11–2.30, 6–11; 11–11 Sat
Adnams Bitter; Draught Bass; Banks & Taylor Shefford Bitter; guest beer H
Village free house which retains a public bar, offering a warm welcome and good value food (not served Mon).
◑ ♣ P

Histon

Boot

High Street ☎ (0223) 233745
11–3, 6–11
Greene King IPA; Tetley Bitter; Tolly Cobbold Original; Whitbread Flowers Original H
Very friendly, comfortable pub with a growing reputation for its food (not served Tue eve). Superb fireplace in the public bar. ❀ ◑ ♣ P

Red Lion

High Street ☎ (0223) 232288
11.30–2.30 (4 Sat), 5.30 (6 Sat)–11
Adnams Bitter; Greene King IPA; Samuel Smith OBB; Taylor Landlord; Tetley Bitter; Woodforde's Wherry H
Pub with a relaxing lounge bar and a pine-panelled, games-oriented public. A rare local outlet for Landlord. Good, home-cooked weekday lunches. ❀ ♣ P

Holywell

Ferry Boat Inn

(A1123 to Needingworth, then signed) OS343707
☎ (0480) 63227
11–3, 6–11
Adnams Bitter, Broadside; Fuller's London Pride; Greene King IPA, Abbot H
Partly-thatched, riverside pub, reputedly haunted; now very much a lounge bar pub. Popular with rivergoers in the summer, it features in the *Guinness Book of Records* as one of England's oldest pubs. Much extended.
❀ ◑ P

Horningsea

Plough & Fleece

High Street ☎ (0223) 860795
11.30–2.30, 7–11; 12–2, 7–10.30 Sun
Greene King IPA, Abbot H
A conservatory extension adds interest to the lounge, but the public bar is the real gem here. Superb food is based on old English recipes – try the Northamptonshire chocolate pudding. Eve meals Tue–Sat.
Q ❀ ◑ P

Huntingdon

Old Bridge

High Street (just off ring road)
☎ (0480) 52681
11–11
Adnams Bitter; Banks & Taylor Shefford Bitter; guest beer H
Large, impressive, ivy-clad hotel by the River Ouse. Good quality meals, but expensive. Happy hour 6.30–7.30. Plush lounge bar surroundings.
Q ◑ P

Leighton Bromswold

Green Man

The Avenue (off A14)
☎ (0480) 890238
12 2.30 (not Tue–Thu), 7–11; closed Mon
S&N Theakston Old Peculier; Taylor Landlord; guest beer H
CAMRA East Anglia *Pub of the Year* 1992: a comfortable, rural free house with a collection of brewery memorabilia. Wide and ever-changing range of guest beers, and good value food. Hood skittles played. Always a warm welcome.
❀ ◑ ♣ P

Linton

Crown

High Street ☎ (0223) 891759
12–2.30, 5.30–11
Fuller's Chiswick; Whitbread Boddingtons Bitter, Flowers IPA; guest beer H
Long, narrow, comfy pub and restaurant situated in one of the county's finest streets. No meals Sun eve.
❀ ◑ P

Litlington

Crown

Silver Street ☎ (0763) 852439
11–2.30, 6–11
Greene King IPA, Abbot H
Enlarged village pub retaining two bars; the lounge bar has memorabilia from the nearby WWII American airbase. Don't be confused by the village's one-way system. In 20 editions of this guide. ❀ ◑ ♣

Longstowe

Golden Miller

High Street
11.30–2.30, 7–11
Adnams Bitter; Bateman XXXB; Greene King Abbot H**; guest beers**
One-bar free house and restaurant in rural surroundings with a large garden. Named after the famous racehorse which used to be stabled nearby. ❀ ◑ P

Try also: Queen Adelaide, Croydon (Free)

March

Ship

Nene Parade ☎ (0354) 56999
10.30–11
Greene King XX Mild, IPA, Abbot H
17th-century, thatched, one-bar pub with unusual carved beams. Benches in front overlook the old River Nene, which offers extensive moorings. Pool room.
♣

Milton

Waggon & Horses

High Street ☎ (0223) 860313
12–2.30 (4 Sat), 5 (7 Sat)–11
Bateman XB; Nethergate Bitter; guest beers H
Pub with two guest beer pumps, one for a strong beer, the other alternating mild and bitter. Fri night is curry night (no meals Sat lunch or Sun eve). Cider varies.
❀ ◑ P

Needingworth

Queens Head

High Street (A1128)
☎ (0480) 63946
11–11
Courage Directors; Greene King IPA; Taylor Landlord; Woodforde's Wherry H**; guest beer**
Friendly, two-bar village local with a strong domino following in the public bar.

Two large fish tanks feature in the lounge bar (which has no handpumps). Good range of guest beers. Specialises in curries (take-away available).
❀ ◐ ◑ ⊞ ♣ ⌂ P

Newton

Queens Head
Fowlmere Road
☎ (0223) 870436
11.30 (11 Sat)–2.30, 6–11
Adnams Bitter, Old, Broadside Ⓖ
Idyllic village pub offering simple but delicious food to complement the ale. The goose which used to patrol the car park now resides in the public bar. ⛰ Q ❀ ◐ ◑ ⊞ ♣ ⌂ P

Old Weston

Swan
☎ (083 23) 400
12–3 (not Mon or Tue), 6.30–11
Adnams Bitter; Greene King Abbot; Hook Norton Old Hooky; Webster's Yorkshire Bitter Ⓗ
Olde-worlde free house and restaurant with beams and low ceilings. ⛰ 🛏 ◐ ◑ ♣ P

Over

Exhibition
2 King Street (off Longstanton road) ☎ (0954) 30790
11.30–2.30, 6.30–11
Greene King IPA; Tetley Bitter; Whitbread Flowers Original; guest beer Ⓗ
Former beer house named after the Great Exhibition of 1851; now twice extended. Swimming pool for children in summer. No meals Sun or Mon eves. ❀ ◐ ◑ ♣ P

Parson Drove

Swan
Main Road (B1187/B1166 jct near A47) ☎ (0945) 700291
12–2 (11–3 Sat; not Tue), 7–11
Elgood's Cambridge Bitter; guest beers Ⓗ
Largely unspoilt, Fen village pub built in 1541. The public bar has darts and bar billiards; the lounge is named after Samuel Pepys, who had his horse stolen the night he stayed here. Friendly welcome, and good food in the bar or restaurant. Live music Sat eve.
⛰ Q ❀ 🛏 ◐ ◑ ⊞ ♿ ♣ P

Peterborough

Blue Bell
6 The Green, Werrington
☎ (0733) 571264
11–3, 6.30–11
Elgood's Cambridge Bitter, GSB; guest beer Ⓗ
Friendly, welcoming, large village pub. Excellent food is cooked by the landlord (not served Wed eve). The guest beer changes monthly and includes all Elgood's seasonal special brews; the best Elgood's in the area.
❀ ◐ ◑ ⊞ ♿ ♣ P

Bogarts Bar & Grill
17 North Street
☎ (0733) 349995
11–11
Draught Bass; Bateman XB; Moorhouse's Pendle Witches Brew; Taylor Landlord; Young's Porter Ⓗ**; guest beers**
Once the Ostrich pub, then a home-brew shop; now an oasis in the real ale desert of Peterborough's city centre. Winner of the 1991 Peterborough CAMRA *Pub of the Year* award. Interesting food. ❀ ◐ ⇌

Charter's Café Bar
Town Bridge ☎ (0733) 315700
12–3 (extends summer), 5–11 (check hours when football matches are on)
Adnams Broadside; Bass Worthington BB, Draught Bass; Hook Norton Mild; Maclay Kane's Amber Ale; Pitfield Hoxton Heavy Ⓗ**; guest beers**
Converted Dutch barge built in 1907, moored against the Town Bridge and providing the largest and busiest real ale venue in town. Its extensive range, including milds and porters, changes weekly. Lively, informal atmosphere for all ages. Restaurant and garden. ❀ ◐ ◑ ⇌

Coach & Horses
High Street, Fletton (1½ miles from centre, towards Whittlesey) ☎ (0733) 343400
11.30–2.30, 6–11; 11–11 Sat
Ansells Mild; Ruddles Best Bitter, County; guest beers Ⓗ
Early 19th-century, two-bar pub with a friendly atmosphere. Home-cooked food includes Sun lunch. Large garden. ❀ ◐ ◑ ♣ P

Crown
749 Lincoln Road (old A15, N of centre) ☎ (0733) 341366
11–11
Adnams Bitter; Draught Bass; M&B Highgate Mild; S&N Theakston Old Peculier; Stones Best Bitter Ⓗ**; guest beers**
Street-corner pub where there is always something going on; live music and discos at weekends. Good choice of reasonably-priced food.
⛰ ☕ ❀ ◐ ◑ ⊞ ♿ ♣ P

Hand & Heart
12 Highbury Street (near bus depot at Millfield)
☎ (0733) 69463
10.30–2.30 (3 Sat), 6–11
Courage Directors; John Smith's Bitter, Magnet; Wilson's Mild; guest beer Ⓗ
Gem of a back-street local, with a diverse clientele in the bar and quiet lounge. Also corridor service. Note the original Warwicks' Brewery windows and the whisky collection. The cheapest beer in town. ⛰ Q ⊞ ♣ ⌂

Nags Head
22 Whalley Street (off Eastfield Rd about ½ mile from centre)
☎ (0733) 66788
11–2.30, 7–11
Marston's Pedigree; John Smith's Bitter Ⓗ
Small, back-street pub built in 1862. Strong on pub games with a real community feel and a friendly atmosphere. The Pedigree is sometimes changed for a guest beer.
❀ ◑ ♣

Nolia's
5 Fitzwilliam Street (near central library)
☎ (0733) 343200
12–midnight
Draught Bass; Bateman XB, XXXB; guest beers Ⓗ
Small pub in the town centre, specialising in Malaysian food. Three drinking areas all have bare floorboards. Can be quite crowded, especially at weekends. Sometimes frequented by thespians from the local theatre. Q ◐ ◑ ♣

Ramblewood Inn
The Village, Orton Longueville
☎ (0733) 391111
11–3, 5.30–11
Adnams Bitter, Broadside; Draught Bass; Fuller's London Pride; Greene King IPA; guest beer Ⓗ
Pub in the former stables of Orton Hall, a restored 17th-century country house. Popular with both locals and the business community. Busy at weekends. ❀ ◐ ◑ ♿ ⛺ P

Try also: Royal Arms, Eye Rd (Elgood's)

Pickle Fen

Crafty Fox
London Road (B1050)
☎ (0354) 692266
11–11
Home Bitter; S&N Theakston XB Ⓗ
Small, isolated pub, supposedly haunted. Jazz bands and barbecues in summer; horse-riding

available at weekends. Children are welcome in the conservatory. ❀ ◐◗ P

Purls Bridge

Ship
OS477868 ☎ (035 478) 578
12–3, 7–11; closed Mon
Greene King IPA Ⓗ
Isolated pub, two miles down a country lane from Manea. Boat moorings are available on the Bedford river.
♔ ❀ ◐◗ P

Ramsey

Three Horseshoes
Little Whyte ☎ (0487) 812452
11–2.30, 6–11
S&N Theakston Best Bitter; Younger IPA Ⓗ
Busy, back-street pub with a distinctly northern flavour.
🛏 ◐◗ ⊞ ♣

Try also: George (Free)

St Ives

Oliver Cromwell
Wellington Street
☎ (0480) 65601
10.30–2.30, 6–11
Adnams Broadside; Greene King IPA Ⓗ
Busy one-bar pub largely unchanged in recent years, situated by the riverside quay and the historic bridge. Note the ornate wrought iron on the exterior, once part of a ship. The pub's clock keeps to GMT.
Q

Try also: Aviator, Ramsey Rd (Free)

St Neots

Wheatsheaf
Church Street ☎ (0480) 477435
11–2.30, 7 (6 Fri)–11
Greene King XX Mild, IPA, Abbot Ⓗ**, Winter Ale** Ⓖ
Cheerful local, a rare outlet for the excellent XX Mild. Successful quiz team.
♔ ❀ ♣

Try also: Old Sun, Huntingdon St (Whitbread)

Sawston

Kings Head
High Street ☎ (0223) 833541
11–2.30, 7–11
Greene King XX Mild, IPA, Rayments Special, Abbot Ⓗ
Thriving, low-ceilinged, two-bar local. Its award-winning garden has a petanque pitch, children's play equipment and a garden bar. No food Sun. ❀ ◐ ⊞ ♣ P

Soham

Carpenters Arms
Brook Street (off Staple Lane from Fordham Rd roundabout) ☎ (0353) 720869
11–11
Greene King IPA; guest beers Ⓗ
Edge-of-town free house: an L-shaped bar with a lounge beyond and a pool room at the back. Aircraft interest is reflected in the decor. Three guest beers; beer festivals in June and November. No food Sun. ❀ ◐ ♣ P

Stow cum Quy

Prince Albert
Newmarket Road (A1303, off A45 at Quy roundabout)
☎ (0223) 811294
11.30–3, 5–11
Greene King IPA; guest beers Ⓗ
The 1992 Cambridge CAMRA *Pub of the Year* which has offered over 700 guest beers without recourse to the big brewers. The range always includes a mild and light, medium and strong bitters. Lively, friendly and welcoming. Interesting vegetarian options on the menu (booking advisable for eve meals). ♔ ◐◗ ♣ P

Stretham

Red Lion
High Street ☎ (0353) 648132
11–3, 6.30–11; 11–11 Sat
Fuller's London Pride; Greene King IPA; M&B Highgate Mild; Nethergate Bitter; Webster's Yorkshire Bitter; guest beer Ⓗ
Superbly renovated and extended village inn, run with style and imagination. Good food at all times. The Highgate is sold as Red Lion Dark. Teenager's amusements in the first-floor club room.
♔ ⛵ ❀ 🛏 ◐◗ ⊞ ♿ ♣ P

Swaffham Prior

Red Lion
High Street ☎ (0638) 742303
12–2.30, 7–11
Greene King IPA, Rayments Special; guest beers Ⓗ
Successful combination of a village local and a country restaurant; exposed beams and brickwork lend atmosphere. The large garden is overlooked by two church towers. Meeting place of the Devils Dyke Morris Men. No food Sun eve or Mon. ♔ ❀ ◐◗ P

Whittlesey

Bricklayers Arms
9 Station Road
John Smith's Bitter; Webster's Yorkshire Bitter Ⓗ
Popular town local with a very friendly atmosphere in both the large bar and smaller lounge. Eve meals Sat only, by arrangement.
♔ Q ❀ ⊞ ⇌ ♣ P

Willingham

Three Tuns
Church Street ☎ (0954) 60437
11–2.30, 6–11; 12–2.30, 7–10.30 Sun
Greene King XX Mild, IPA, Abbot Ⓗ
Village local in the classic mould – no frills, no fuss, just good ale and good company. Basic lunchtime snacks.
Q ❀ ⊞ ♣ P

Wisbech

Rose Tavern
53 North Brink
☎ (0945) 588335
12–3, 5.30–11
Butterknowle Bitter, Conciliation Ale; Cains FA; guest beers Ⓗ
Cosy, one-room pub on the riverside; a listed, 200-year-old building. The closest pub to Elgood's brewery. The present landlord reinstated the pub's original name. ❀ 🛏 ◐◗ ♣

Try also: Red Lion, North Brink; **Three Tuns**, Norwich Rd (both Elgood's)

Yaxley

Royal Oak
106 Main Street
☎ (0733) 240464
12–2, 4.30–11; 12–11 Sat
Courage Directors; John Smith's Bitter; guest beer Ⓗ
Thatched village pub in the Grand Met monopoly area.
♔ ❀ ⊞ ♣ P

Neighbours

Remember: roads do not end at county boundaries! Check the pages of neighbouring counties for an even bigger choice of great pubs.

Cheshire

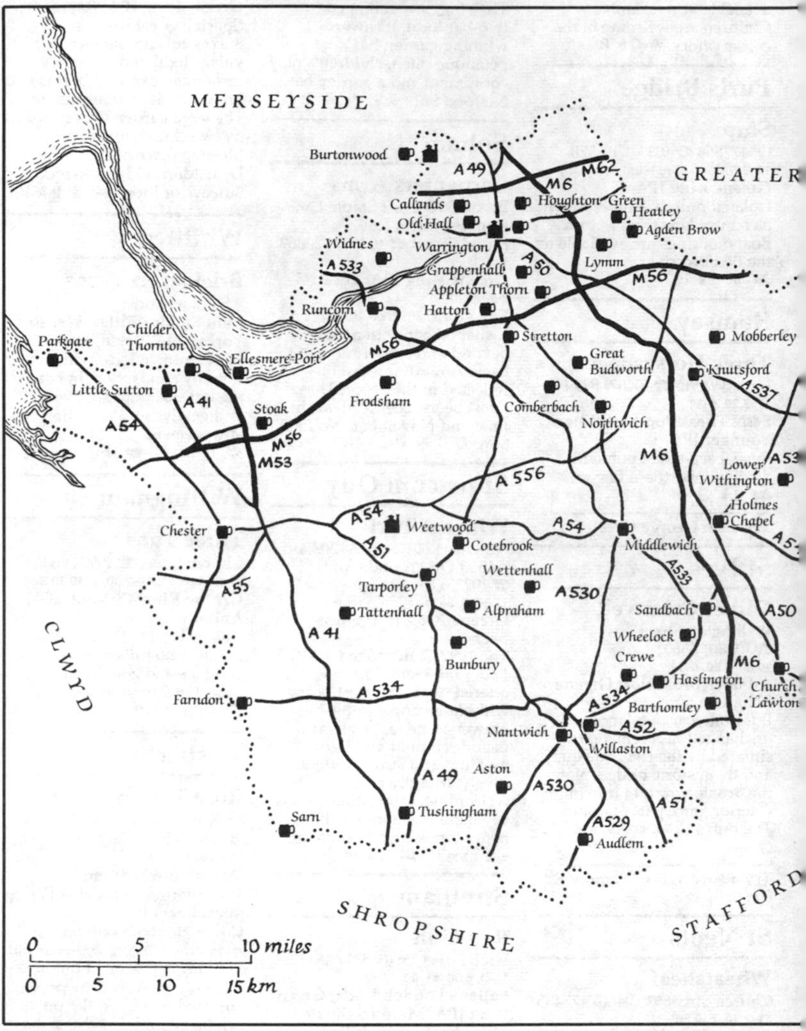

Burtonwood, Burtonwood; **Coach House**, Warrington; **Weetwood**, Weetwood

Agden Brow

Wheatsheaf

Higher Lane, Broomedge (A56) ☎ (092 575) 2567
11.30–3, 5.30–11

Hydes' Anvil Mild, Bitter Ⓔ

Roadside pub, over 200 years old but extended in the late 1980s with an open-plan layout and a central bar, plus a games area. One of three Hydes' pubs in the area.
❀ ◖◗ P

Try also: Jolly Thresher, (Hydes' Anvil)

Alpraham

Travellers Rest

Chester Road (A51, 7 miles from Nantwich towards Chester)
☎ (0829) 260523
12–3 (not Mon–Fri), 6–11

McEwan 70/-; Tetley Walker Mild, Bitter Ⓗ

Quiet village local, unchanged for years, with its own bowling green.
⩕ Q ❀ ♣ P

Appleton Thorn

Appleton Thorn Village Hall

Stretton Road ☎ (0925) 261187
Closed lunchtime; 8.30–11 Thu–Sat only; 8.30–10.30 Sun

Moorhouse's Black Cat Mild; guest beers Ⓗ

Award-winning, cosy lounge attached to a village hall, run by a charitable trust in old school buildings. Hours are restricted, but it may also open first Sun lunch each month. Extra guest beers have now

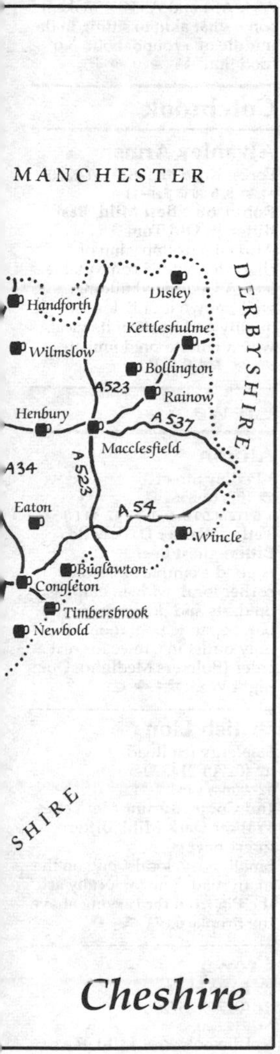

been added. The Old School Bitter is brewed by Coach House. Q ❀ ♿ ♣ P

Aston

Bhurtpore Inn

Wrenbury Road
☎ (0270) 780917
12–2.30, 5.30–11
Whitbread Boddingtons Bitter H; **guest beers**
Former farmhouse with photographs of local interest and also of India, from where the name is derived. Recently returned to the family of a previous owner. Belgian bottled beers also on sale; four guest beers, always including a mild. Restaurant open Fri–Sun. 🔥 Q ❀ ◑◗ ♿ P

Audlem

Bridge

Shropshire Street
☎ (0270) 811267
12 (11 summer)–3, 7 (5.30 summer)–11
Banks's Mild; Marston's Bitter, Merrie Monk, Pedigree H
Mainly a locals' pub but during the summer busy with canal-users tackling the long flight of locks nearby.
🔥 Q ❀ ◑◗ ▲ ♣ P

Try also: Lord Combermere, The Square (Free)

Barthomley

White Lion

Audley Road ☎ (0270) 882242
11.30–3, 6–11; 11.30–11 Sat
Burtonwood Mild, Bitter, Forshaw's, Top Hat H
Black and white, thatched pub at the centre of a small, picturesque village. Dated 1614, but a list of landlords on the wall shows only 18 names. The church opposite was the scene of a massacre in the Civil War. Popular with motorcyclists.
🔥 Q ❀ 🛏 ♣ P

Bollington

Church House

Chapel Street ☎ (0625) 574014
11–3, 5.30–11
Jennings Bitter; Marston's Pedigree; S&N Theakston Best Bitter; Tetley Walker Bitter; Whitbread Boddingtons Bitter H
Popular corner-terrace pub with a reputation for good food at all times. Renovated church pews in the lounge.
🔥 Q ◑◗

Cotton Tree

3–5 Ingersly Road
☎ (0625) 576883
11–11
Vaux Bitter, Samson; Wards Mild H
Stone-built corner local. The Bollington Building Society met here in the 1830s in the days when such societies were simple and friendly. Recently taken over by Vaux and pleasantly decorated throughout. Now a good village pub. 🔥 Q ♣

Queens Arms

High Street ☎ (0625) 573068
2 (12 Fri & Sat)–11
Robinson's Best Mild, Best Bitter H
Solidly-built stone pub, set back slightly from the rest of the terrace. Modernised in Robinson's style. ❀ ◑◗ ♣

Buglawton

Church House

Buxton Road ☎ (0260) 272466
11–3, 5.30–11
Robinson's Best Mild, Best Bitter E
Roomy pub with excellent bar meals and a grill room (closed Sat eve). Its unusual pub sign is combined with a pigeon cote. Very good outside facilities for children. Boules pitch. 🔥 🛝 ❀ ◑◗ ♣ P

Try also: Robin Hood (Marston's)

Bunbury

Dysart Arms

Opp. church OS569581
☎ (0829) 260183
12–3.30, 5.30–11; 12–11 Sat
Tetley Walker Bitter; Thwaites Bitter H
18th-century former farmhouse opposite an historic church. The stone-floored public bar has a pool table; the lounge boasts a large inglenook and an aquarium. Wheelchair access via the back door. 🔥 Q ❀ ◑◗ ♿ ♣ P

Burtonwood

Bridge Inn

Phipps Lane ☎ (0925) 225709
11.30–11
Burtonwood Mild, Bitter, Forshaw's H
Four-roomed pub, games and sports oriented; the licensee's mementoes from his rugby-playing days are displayed. Also has a bowling green and children's play area. No food at weekends. 👶 ❀ ◑ ♣ P

Callands

Hoop & Mallet

Callands Road (off A49, near Ikea) ☎ (0925) 413257
11.30–3, 5.30–11; 11.30–11 Fri & Sat
Hydes' Anvil Mild, Bitter E
Large, alcoved, 1980s new-town pub, wood-panelled with comfortable furnishings. Home-made, reasonably-priced lunches are popular with local business people. The walls are adorned with breweriana, and there is an accent on sport: a golf and two football teams. No food weekends. ◑ ♣ P

Chester

Albion

Park Street (off Newgate St)
11.30–3, 5.30–11
Cains Bitter; Greenalls Mild,

Bitter, Thomas Greenall's Original; Stones Best Bitter [H]
Traditional back-street local, popular with a wide range of drinkers. No admittance after 10.30 Fri and Sat nights (no pub crawlers allowed). No fried food (eve meals Fri and Sat only). Enjoy! ♨ Q ◐ ◑

Boathouse Inn
The Groves (via Dee Lane)
☎ (0244) 328709
11–4, 6–11 (11–11 summer)
Home Mild; Marston's Pedigree; S&N Theakston XB [H]**; guest beers**
Two separate pubs: a riverside lounge with a patio, and an 'ale-taster' bar with a range of seven beers. Plus, the only children's room in Chester.
♨ ♘ ❀ ◐ ◑ ♿ P

Boot
Eastgate Street
11–3.30, 5.30–11; 11–11 Fri & Sat
Samuel Smith OBB, Museum [H]
Old pub still retaining some 17th-century walls, with a glass panel revealing its construction. ◐

Centurion
1 Oldfield Road, Vicars Cross (off A51, 1 mile from centre)
☎ (0244) 347623
11.30–3, 6–11; 11–11 Sat
Cains Bitter; Jennings Bitter; Robinson's Best Bitter; Tetley Walker Mild, Bitter, Winter Warmer [H]**; guest beers** (occasionally)
Energetic modern pub that holds regular beer festivals and charity functions. Roman maps add interest to the comfortable lounge and pool is popular in the bar. The landlord may vary the beer range. Q ❀ ♿ P

Mill Hotel
Milton Street ☎ (0244) 350035
11–11
Beer range varies [H]
Modern hotel alongside the canal, serving at least five guest beers, mostly from independents. Good value bar meals are served daily from 11am to 10pm. ❀ 🛏 ◐ ◑ P

Old Custom House
Watergate Street
☎ (0244) 324335
11.30–3, 5.30–11
Banks's Mild; Marston's Bitter, Pedigree [H]**, Owd Rodger** (winter) [G]
Friendly, never-changing pub, a quarter of a mile from the Cross. The building dates back to 1637 and features ornate bar carvings and splendid fireplaces. Still home to unsuccessful sports teams. No food Sun. ♨ Q ◐ ⊞ ♣

Try also: Cherry Orchard, Boughton (Courage); **Clavertons**, Lower Bridge St (Lees); **Pop In Off-Licence**, Boughton (Free); **Union Vaults**, Egerton St (Boddingtons)

Childer Thornton

White Lion
New Road (200 yds off A41)
☎ (051) 339 3402
11.30–3, 5–11; 11.30–11 Fri & Sat
Thwaites Best Mild, Bitter, Craftsman [H]
Unspoilt, two-roomed country local with a warm reception for all. The snug is used by families at lunchtime but can get busy at weekends. No food Sun. ♨ Q ❀ ◐ P

Church Lawton

Lawton Arms
Liverpool Road West (at A50/B5077 jct)
☎ (0270) 873743
11.30–3.30, 5.30 (4.30 Fri)–11
Robinson's Best Mild, Best Bitter [E]
Georgian locals' pub with a snug and a games room, serving the cheapest Robinson's in the area.
♨ ❀ ♣ P

Comberbach

Drum & Monkey
The Avenue (off A559)
☎ (0606) 891417
11–3, 5.30–11; 11–11 Sat
Tetley Walker Dark Mild, Bitter [H]
Popular, small, one-roomed village local where a brass monkey dominates. Overflow car park opposite.
❀ ◐ ▲ ♣ P

Congleton

Rose & Crown
44 West Road ☎ (0260) 273423
11–2.30, 6–11; 11–11 Fri & Sat
Burtonwood Bitter [H]
Small pub with a large bar. Popular with locals and close to the football ground.
♿ ♣ P

Waggon & Horses
Newcastle Road, West Heath
☎ (0260) 274366
11.30–3, 6–11
Marston's Bitter, Pedigree [H]
Large, well-established inn standing on the western edge of town. The tables outside in summer – with the pub's situation (at the junction of the A34, A54 and A534) – make it somewhat akin to sitting in the middle of a roundabout. No food Sun. ♨ ❀ ◐ ♣ P

Cotebrook

Alvanley Arms
Forest Road ☎ (0829) 760200
11.30–3, 5.30 (6 Sat)–11
Robinson's Best Mild, Best Bitter [H]**, Old Tom** [G]
Attractive country inn of character, with a comfortable feel. A Georgian building, well-known locally for the quality and value of its meals, which tend to predominate.
♨ ❀ 🛏 ◐ ◑ P

Crewe

Albion
1 Pedley Street
☎ (0270) 256234
1–3 (12–4.30 Sat), 7–11; 12–11 Fri
Tetley Walker Dark Mild, Bitter; guest beer [H]
A good example of a street-corner local, with an emphasis on darts and dominoes in the bar. Separate pool room. The only outlet in Crewe for real cider (Bulmers Medium). Quiz night Wed. ⇌ ♣ ⌽

British Lion
58 Nantwich Road
☎ (0270) 214379
12–4 (may vary), 7–11
Ind Coope Burton Ale; Tetley Walker Dark Mild, Bitter; guest beer [H]
Small, busy, locals' pub on the main road. Known locally as the Pig from the carving above the fireplace. ♨ ⇌ ♣

Crown
25 Earle Street
☎ (0270) 257295
11–5 (6 Sat), 7–11
Robinson's Best Mild, Best Bitter [H]
Small, four-roomed town-centre pub full of character. One of a dying breed of town pubs. ⊞ ♣

Horseshoe
26 North Street
☎ (0270) 584265
12–3 (4 Mon & Fri, 5 Sat), 7–11
Robinson's Best Mild, Best Bitter [H]
Old, multi-roomed, high-ceilinged pub. ♨ ⊞ ♣ P

Kings Arms
56 Earle Street
☎ (0270) 584134
11–4 (11.30–3 Tue–Thu), 7–11
Whitbread Chester's Mild, Chester's Best Bitter, Boddingtons Bitter, Trophy [H]
Large pub with rooms for all tastes ⊞ ♿ ♣

Disley

White Horse
Buxton Old Road
11–3, 5.30–11
Robinson's Best Mild, Best Bitter [H]
Imposing building at the village centre. Dates from 1869 although its open-plan interior now conforms to Robinson's format. A pub which suffers few vices and smoke is kept to an acceptable level thanks to good ventilation. Quieter than neighbouring trendy hostelries. Good value food till 8pm. ◐ ◑ ♿ ⇌ P

Try also: Crescent, Buxton Rd (Robinson's)

Eaton

Waggon & Horses
Manchester Road (A34)
☎ (0260) 224229
11–3, 5.30 (6 Sat)–11
Robinson's Best Mild, Best Bitter [H]
Pleasant roadside pub with a vast car park. Meeting place for the S Cheshire and N Staffs MG Owners Club. Dining room. 🔥 Q ❀ ◐ ◑ ♣ P

Try also: Plough, Macclesfield Rd (Banks's)

Ellesmere Port

Straw Hat
Hope Farm Road, Great Sutton
☎ (051) 356 3335
12–11
Courage Directors; John Smith's Bitter [H]
Sports-oriented estate pub with an unusual glass-fronted corridor linking the bar and the lounge. Live music and aerobics alternate in the eve.
🐴 ❀ ⊞ ♿ ♣ P

Sutton Way Hotel
Thelwell Road
☎ (051) 348 0144
11–11
John Smith's Bitter [H]**; guest beers**
Noisy, boisterous ale house where sport and Sky TV are prominent. Frequent live music and a lively social scene. Despite its distance from the coast, sea angling is very popular. ❀ ⊞ ♣ P

Try also: Sir Robert, Overpool Rd (Whitbread)

Farndon

Greyhound Hotel
High Street ☎ (0829) 270244
12–3 (not Mon–Fri), 5.30 (7 Sat)–11
Greenalls Mild, Bitter, Thomas Greenall's Original [H]
Friendly hotel by the River Dee, whose residents include two donkeys and four goats. Handy for a pint before trying your luck fishing for the famous Dee salmon. Beware the keg cider on fake handpump.
🔥 Q ❀ 🛏 ⊞ ♣ P

Frodsham

Rowlands Bar
31 Church Street (50 yds from station) ☎ (0928) 33361
11–11
Whitbread Boddingtons Bitter; guest beers [H]
Pub with three fast-changing guest beers (soon increasing; 200 different beers each year) and a wide variety of good food in the bar and restaurant. Now very busy, with a good atmosphere and clientele. An award-winner with no jukebox or bandit. Q ◐ ◑ ⇌ ⌓

Grappenhall

Parr Arms
Church Lane (off A56/A50)
☎ (0925) 267393
11–3, 5.30–11; 12–2, 7–10.30 Sun
Greenalls Bitter, Thomas Greenall's Original [H]
Quiet, well-ordered pub which attracts a mature local clientele, set in a quaint cobbled village close to the Bridgewater Canal. A central bar services a public bar and two lounges. Q ❀ ◐ ⊞ P

Great Budworth

George & Dragon
High Street ☎ (0606) 891317
12–3, 7–11
Ind Coope Burton Ale; Tetley Walker Bitter [H]**; guest beer**
Pub located opposite the church in a picturesque village. Burton Ale is sometimes replaced by a second guest beer. Beware the exit from the car park – on a sharp, blind bend.
🔥 🐴 ❀ ◐ ◑ ♿ ▲ ♣ P

Handforth

Railway
Station Road ☎ (0625) 523472
11–3, 5.30–11
Robinson's Best Mild, Best Bitter [E]
Large, multi-roomed pub facing the station. Smart, and popular with the locals. No food Sun. ◐ ⇌ P

Haslington

Hawk
137 Crewe Road
☎ (0270) 582181
11–11; 12–2.30, 7–10.30 Sun
Robinson's Best Mild, Best Bitter [E]
15th-century roadside inn and restaurant. An exposed panel inside reveals an original wattle wall. Dick Turpin reputedly once stayed here. Eve meals served Thu–Sat.
🔥 ❀ ◐ ◑ P

Hatton

Hatton Arms
Warrington Road
☎ (0925) 730314
11–11
Greenalls Mild, Bitter, Thomas Greenall's Original [H]
Traditional rural village pub based on old cottages, retaining multiple rooms and real fires, with beams and character. Run by a village-born couple who care.
🔥 Q 🐴 ❀ ◐ ♿ P

Heatley

Railway
Mill Lane (B5159)
☎ (0925) 752742
12–11
S&N Theakston Best Bitter; Whitbread Boddingtons Bitter; guest beer [H]
Large, old-style pub, catering for most needs with a folk club on Thu and a large, open grassed garden. An ideal base for a family stroll along the new Trans-Pennine Trail to enjoy the countryside of the River Bollin plain. No food Sun, but sandwiches always available. 🐴 ❀ ◐ ♣ P

Henbury

Cock Inn
Chelford Road (A537)
☎ (0625) 423186
11–3, 5.30–11
Robinson's Best Mild, Best Bitter [H]
Comfortable main-road pub situated just outside Macclesfield, serving both local and passing trades. Children are welcome in the restaurant. Q ❀ ◐ ◑ ♣ P

Holmes Chapel

Swan
Station Road ☎ (0477) 532259
11–3, 4.30–11; 11–11 Fri & Sat
Samuel Smith OBB, Museum [H]
Former coaching inn with good food. The car park is reached by driving under the pub. Interesting old black stove on display. Very large pizzas are a speciality.
Q ❀ ◐ ◑ ⇌ P

Houghton Green

Millhouse
Ballater Drive, Cinnamon Brow (off A574)
☎ (0925) 811405
12–3.30, 5.30 (7 Sat)–11
Holt Mild, Bitter Ⓗ
Large, spacious 1980s estate pub, serving new town residential areas. The basic bar and the two-roomed lounge are equally popular. Holt's most westerly tied house and the best value pint for miles. Quiz night Tue.
❀ ☾ ⊟ ♣ P

Kettleshulme

Bulls Head
Macclesfield Road
☎ (0663) 733225
12–3 (summer only), 7–11
Whitbread Boddingtons Bitter; guest beer Ⓗ
Friendly, country-stone, terraced pub situated in the centre of a village in the Peak National Park. Time has little changed its traditional character, with its cosy lounge, public bar and darts area.
♛ ❀ ♣ P

Knutsford

Builders Arms
Mobberley Road (off A537)
☎ (0565) 634528
11.30–3, 5.30–11; 12–2, 7–10.30 Sun
Banks's Mild; Marston's Bitter, Pedigree Ⓗ
Delightful pub in an attractive terrace on the outskirts of the town centre. A former Taylor's Eagle brewery pub, busy, with a keen games emphasis. Best approached from the road opposite the Legh Arms.
Q ❀ ⇌ ♣

White Bear
1 Canute Place
☎ (0565) 632120
11–11
Greenalls Mild, Bitter Ⓗ
Old coaching inn, dating from 1634, which has witnessed much of the town's history from its position facing the former cattle market. An excellent community pub with small, low-ceilinged rooms and a thatched roof.
Q ❀ ⇌ ♣

White Lion
94 King Street
☎ (0565) 632018
11.30–11
Cains Bitter; Tetley Walker Bitter Ⓗ**; guest beers**
Tasteful, black and white-timbered, town-centre pub, dating, probably, from the mid 17th-century: certainly in existence long before soldiers were billeted here during the 1745 Jacobite rebellion. No food Sun. ♛ Q ❀ ☾ ⇌ ♣

Little Sutton

Travellers Rest
14 Ledsham Road
☎ (051) 339 2176
11.30–11
Walker Mild, Bitter, Best Bitter, Winter Warmer; guest beers Ⓗ
Large, roadside pub with a split-level lounge and a busy public bar. Emphasis on food lunchtimes. Eve meals end early.
♛ ❀ ☾ ☽ ⊟ ♿ ⇌ ♣ P

Lower Withington

Red Lion
Trap Street, Dicklow Hill (B5392) ☎ (0477) 71248
11.45–2.30 (3 Sat), 5.30–11
Robinson's Dark Best Mild, Best Bitter Ⓗ
Large, rural pub with a restaurant, and a tap room for locals. Close to Jodrell Bank radio telescope. Even though the pump clip says 'Robinson's Best Mild' it is actually a very rare outlet for the Dark Mild.
♛ ❀ ☾ ☽ ♣ P

Lymm

Spread Eagle
Eagle Brow (A6144)
☎ (092 575) 5939
11.30–11
Lees GB Mild, Bitter Ⓗ**, Moonraker** Ⓔ
Ornate, old village pub near Lymm Cross and canal moorings. Three varying rooms: a large, plush split-level lounge, a cosy snug, particularly popular with locals, and a basic bar extension. ♛ ☾ ⊟

Macclesfield

Baths
40 Green Street
11–4 (not Mon–Fri), 6.30–11
Banks's Hanson's Mild, Bitter Ⓗ
Small but thriving local, just off the A537 Buxton road, a few minutes' walk uphill from the station. A local bowling green inspired its original name – Bowling Green Tavern – as did a public bath its current name; the pub has survived both. Note: lunchtime opening only at weekends. ⇌ ♣

Evening Star
87–89 Jame Street (400 yds from A536/A523 jct)
☎ (0625) 424093
11–3, 5.30–11; 12–2, 7–10.30 Sun
Banks's Mild; Marston's Bitter, Pedigree Ⓗ
Friendly little local tucked away in the back streets, made difficult to find by car by a maze of blocked streets. Quiet lunchtimes but busier eves and weekends. Q ⇌ ♣

George & Dragon
23 Sunderland Street
☎ (0625) 421898
11–4 (3 Tue & Wed), 5.30 (7 Sat)–11
Robinson's Best Mild, Best Bitter Ⓔ
Friendly pub with good value food (not served Sun; eve meals finish at 6.45). Pool, darts and skittles played. Close to both bus and rail stations. ❀ ☾ ☽ ⇌ ♣

Navigation
161 Black Road
☎ (0625) 611249
11–3 (not Mon–Fri), 7–11
Tetley Walker Bitter Ⓗ**; guest beer**
One-room, Victorian pub built at the time of the canal construction. Keen sports emphasis, including a Sun football team. Guest beer once a week. Note: lunchtime opening only at weekends. ♣

Prince of Wales
33 Roe Street ☎ (0625) 424796
11.30–11
Greenalls Bitter, Thomas Greenall's Original; Stones Best Bitter Ⓗ
Pleasant pub, handy for shoppers in the town centre and opposite the Silk Heritage Centre. ☾ ☽ ⇌ ♣

Ship
61–63 Beech Lane
☎ (0625) 423279
2 (12 Sat)–11
Coach House Coachman's; Whitbread Boddingtons Bitter Ⓗ**; guest beers**
Formerly two cottages converted 35 years ago and now a single-roomed pub. An old 1940s boiler provides the heat. Guest beers come mainly from Coach House.
♛ ❀ ☾ ⇌ ♣ P

Middlewich

Boar's Head
Kinderton Street
☎ (060 683) 3191
12–3.30, 5.30–11; 11–11 Fri & Sat
Robinson's Best Mild, Best Bitter Ⓔ
Large, multi-roomed pub.
☕ ❀ ⛍ ☾ ☽ ♿ ♣ P

Mobberley

Bird in Hand

☎ (0565) 873149
11.30–3, 5.30 (5 Fri)–11
Samuel Smith OBB, Museum Ⓗ
Popular, 18th-century pub on the eastern outskirts of the village. Modernised, but retaining local charm with a number of wood-panelled alcoves. A wide selection of freshly prepared food is available (not Mon eve or Sun). ⛼ Q ❀ ◑ ◐ ♿ P

Try also: Bulls Head, Town Lane (Tetley Walker)

Nantwich

Rifleman

68 James Hall Street (by playing fields)
☎ (0270) 629977
12–4, 6.30–11; 12–11 Fri; 11–11 Sat
Robinson's Best Mild, Best Bitter Ⓔ
Small, back-street pub which can be difficult to find.
⛼ ❀ ◑ ♿ ♣ P

Newbold

Horseshoe

Fence Lane (left off A34 at Astbury church, right after ½ mile, follow bends for 1½ miles) OS863602
☎ (0260) 272205
11–3, 6–11
Robinson's Best Mild, Best Bitter Ⓔ
Isolated country pub, formerly part of a farmhouse. Difficult to find but worth the effort.
⛼ ☎ ❀ ◑ ◐ ♣ P

Try also: Egerton Arms, Astbury (Robinson's)

Northwich

Beehive

High Street
11–11
Greenalls Mild, Bitter, Thomas Greenall's Original; Stones Best Bitter Ⓗ
Attractive town-centre pub with a red-brick exterior, and an open, split-level interior. Popular throughout the day. The excellent value lunches and congenial atmosphere entice both locals and shoppers alike. ◑

Old Hall

Bewsey Farm

Bewsey Farm Close (off A57 W of Warrington) ☎ (0925) 33705
11.30–3, 5.30–11; 11–11 Fri & Sat
Cains Mild, Bitter; Tetley Walker Bitter; Whitbread Boddingtons Bitter; guest beers Ⓗ
Long, narrow, open-plan pub converted in the 1980s from old farm buildings close to Bewsey Old Hall. The decor is a blend of woodwork and brick, with ornaments reflecting its former use. Quiz night Tue; barbecues in summer. At least two guest beers per week. ❀ ◑ ♣ P

Parkgate

Red Lion

The Parade ☎ (051) 336 1548
12–11
Ind Coope Burton Ale; Tetley Walker Dark Mild, Walker Best Bitter Ⓗ
Pub since at least 1822, offering a traditional lounge and a bar with a pool table and dartboard. Draws mainly local people during the winter, but a good passing trade in summer, due to its location, with excellent views of Wales.
Q ◑ ♣

Rainow

Highwayman

On B5470, N of Rainow
☎ (0625) 573245
11.30–3, 7–11
Thwaites Bitter Ⓗ
Remote and windswept inn, known as the Blacksmiths Arms until 1949 and locally as the Patch. A maze of connecting rooms with a small tap room in the far corner. Three blazing fires during the winter months. Breathtaking views from the front door.
⛼ Q ❀ ◑ ◐ ♣ P

Runcorn

Windmill

Windmill Hill (off A558, 1½ miles from A56 jct)
☎ (0928) 710957
11.30–3, 5–11; 11.30–11 Fri & Sat
Hydes' Anvil Light, Bitter Ⓔ
Large, modern, octagonal pub built in the late 1980s, with a split-level lounge and a public bar. Quiz night Tue.
☎ ❀ ◑ ♿ ♣ P

Sandbach

Lower Chequers

Crown Banks ☎ (0270) 762569
11–3 (2.30 Wed & Fri), 5.30–11; 11.30–11 Sat
Ruddles Best Bitter; guest beers Ⓗ
The oldest pub in town, dating back to 1570; a former money changing house, with a striking frontage and an unusually-shaped interior. Note the historic Saxon cross in the square outside. Seven guest beers a week (up to five at a time). Lunches served Wed–Sun. ⛼ Q ❀ ◑

Sarn

Queens Head

Off B5069, S of Threapwood OS440447 ☎ (094 881) 244
12–3, 5–11
Marston's Bitter Ⓗ
Small pub by a stream which forms the English/Welsh border. Small bistro attached.
⛼ Q ❀ ◑ ◐ ♣ P

Stoak

Bunbury Arms

Little Stanney Lane
☎ (0244) 301665
Cains Bitter; Whitbread Boddingtons Bitter Ⓗ
Excellent traditional pub near Ellesmere Port motorway junctions and the Shropshire Union Canal. Recently refurbished, with an enlarged lounge plus a small, basic bar. Weekday lunches.
⛼ Q ❀ ◑ ⊟ ♿ ♣ P

Stretton

Hollow Tree

Tarporley Road (off A49, at M56 jct 10) ☎ (0925) 730733
11–3, 5.30–11
S&N Theakston Best Bitter, XB, Old Peculier Ⓗ
Renovated Georgian farmhouse; a 1980s conversion featuring a central bar with a roomy, plush, alcoved lounge area, a function room and a restaurant (closed Mon). Large garden. Beware keg Scrumpy Jack cider on handpump.
❀ ◑ ◐ P

Ring O'Bells

Northwich Road, Lower Stretton (300 yds from M56 jct 10) ☎ (0925) 730556
12–3, 5.30 (7 Sat)–11; 12–3, 7.30–10.30 Sun
Greenalls Mild, Bitter, Thomas Greenall's Original Ⓗ
Small, welcoming roadside pub, once a row of cottages and still comprised of small rooms. A charity library, and a horseshoe post make up the entertainment. ⛼ Q ❀ ♣ P

Tarporley

Rising Sun

High Street ☎ (0829) 732423
11.30–3, 5.30–11
Robinson's Best Mild, Best Bitter Ⓗ
15th-century listed building with beamed ceilings: a cosy village pub with a good reputation for food; the lounge is often full of diners. No food Sun eve. In every edition of this guide. ◑ ◐ P

Cheshire

Tattenhall

Letters Inn
High Street ☎ (0829) 70221
11–3 (may extend), 5.15–11; 11–11 Sat
Thwaites Bitter; Whitbread Boddingtons Bitter, Castle Eden Ale Ⓗ**; guest beer**
Rustic village pub with a large, attractive fireplace and a separate eating area. Bar meals always available.

Try also: Sportsmans Arms, High St (Thwaites)

Timbersbrook

Coach & Horses
Dane in Shaw Bank (1 mile N of Congleton, off A527, on Rushton Spencer road) OS890619 ☎ (0260) 273019
11–3, 6–11
Robinson's Best Mild, Best Bitter Ⓔ
Situated high in the hills above Congleton: a small brick-built pub with associated farm buildings, which is half-hidden from the main road as it winds upwards from the A537. A through-lounge with a tap room behind the fireplace, popular with locals.
P

Tushingham

Blue Bell
Off A41, 4 miles N of Whitchurch ☎ (0948) 2172
12–3, 6–11
Hanby Drawwell Ⓗ**; guest beers**
Historic, 17th-century coaching inn, reputedly haunted by a duck! Once on the A41, but now by passed. A truly international pub, with an American landlord and a Russian landlady.
Q P

Try also: Wheatsheaf, Nomansheath (S&N)

Warrington

Causeway
233 Wilderspool Causeway (A49 S of town)
☎ (0925) 31955
11–3, 5.30–11; 12–11 Sat
Coach House Coachman's; Greenalls Mild, Bitter Ⓗ
Large four-roomed pub close to the rugby league ground. A rare outlet for Coach House in its home town – effectively the brewery tap. Q P

Lord Rodney
67 Winwick Road (off A49 opp. Tetley Walker brewery)
☎ (0925) 234296
12–3.30, 5 (7 Sat)–11; 12–11 Wed–Fri
Cains Bitter; Robinson's Best Bitter; Tetley Walker Bitter, Walker Best Bitter, Winter Warmer Ⓗ**; guest beers**
Extremely popular Victorian-style pub. The long bar has a bank of handpumps serving four or five guest beers. Quiz night Tue; live music Fri. Holds a couple of two-three-week beer festivals a year. CAMRA regional *Pub of the Year* 1992. Eve meals Mon–Thu only. (Central)

Lower Angel
27 Buttermarket Street
☎ (0925) 33299
11–4, 7–11
Ind Coope Burton Ale; Tetley Walker Mild, Bitter, Best Bitter, Winter Warmer Ⓗ**; guest beers**
Small, popular town-centre pub offering usually up to ten guest beers a week. Often the first pub to offer new beers from the nearby Coach House brewery. Beware: the Addlestones cider is on blanket pressure.
(Central)

Wettenhall

Boot & Slipper
Long Lane OS625613
☎ (0270) 73238
11.30–3, 5.30–11; 11.30–11 Sat
M&B Highgate Mild; Marston's Pedigree Ⓔ/Ⓗ
16th-century country pub with beams and a friendly atmosphere. A full menu is served in the restaurant, but bar meals are also popular.
P

Wheelock

Cheshire Cheese
466–468 Crewe Road
☎ (0270) 760319
11.30–11
Banks's Mild, Bitter Ⓗ
Split-level canalside pub. Cartoon caricatures of regulars adorn the walls.
P

Commercial
Crewe Road
☎ (0270) 760122
8–11; 12–2, 8–10.30 Sun
Marston's Pedigree; Thwaites Bitter; Whitbread Boddingtons Bitter; guest beers (occasionally) Ⓗ
Exceptional free house with signs of its former Birkenhead brewery ownership. The fine games room has a full-sized snooker table and table skittles. Bulmers traditional cider is also available, often served with a slice of lemon.
Q

Widnes

Eight Towers
Weates Close ☎ (051) 424 8063
11–11
Banks's Mild, Bitter Ⓔ**; Camerons Strongarm** Ⓗ
New pub on the outskirts of town, in the shadow of Fiddler's Ferry power station.
P

Willaston

Horse Shoe
Newcastle Road
☎ (0270) 69404
12–3, 6–11; 12–11 Fri
Robinson's Best Mild, Bitter, Best Bitter, Old Tom (winter) Ⓗ
Small, three-roomed pub with a wood-panelled lounge and a locals' bar. The garden has children's swings. Eve meals Wed–Sun. Q P

Wilmslow

Farmers Arms
71 Chapel Lane (off A34)
☎ (0625) 532443
11–11
Whitbread Boddingtons Mild, Bitter Ⓗ**; guest beers** (occasionally)
Traditional, Victorian town pub: several rooms (including a tap room) with brasses and antiques. Very busy at times due to its friendly atmosphere. Nice garden in summer. Quiz night Tue. No food Sun.
Q P

New Inn
Alderley Road
☎ (0625) 523123
11.30–3 (3.30 Fri & Sat), 5.30–11
Hydes' Anvil Light, Bitter Ⓔ
Large, extensive modernisation of a much smaller pub, designed to cater almost exclusively for the appetites of the shoppers trooping from the Sainsbury's supermarket next door. No eve meals Sun or Mon.
P

Wincle

Wild Boar
On A54 OS960672
☎ (0260) 227219
12–3, 7–11
Robinson's Best Bitter Ⓔ
Traditional, welcoming stone pub, high on the moors, with warming open fires in cold weather. Fortnightly clay pigeon shoots can make Sun lunchtimes very busy. A popular venue for sledging and skiing during snowy weather.
P

Cleveland

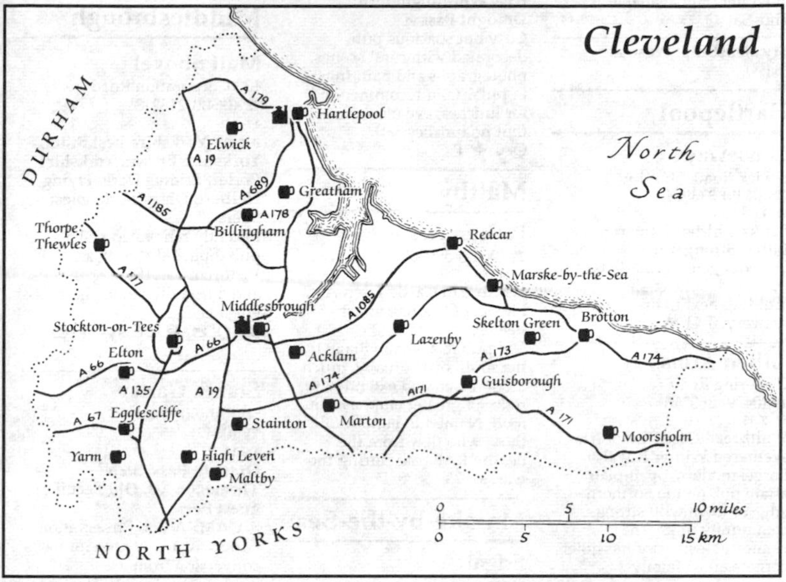

Camerons, *Hartlepool;* **North Yorkshire,** *Middlesbrough*

Acklam

Master Cooper
291 Acklam Road
☎ (0642) 819429
11–11
Samuel Smith OBB Ⓗ
Listed building, a former fish and chip shop and restaurant. A large, L-shaped room with original beams and ceilings.
♛ ❀ ♣ P

Billingham

Smiths Arms
Green ☎ (0642) 554405
11–11
Banks's Bitter; Camerons Strongarm Ⓗ
One of Billingham's original pubs, facing the village green. Recently refurbished function room. ☾ ♣ P

Brotton

Green Tree
90 High Street ☎ (0287) 76377
7–11
Camerons Strongarm Ⓗ
Stone-built former manor house dating from the 14th century. The cosy interior has several small rooms. Caters for a strong local trade.
♛ Q ⛟ ⊞ ♿ ♣

Egglescliffe

Pot & Glass
Church Road (off A135 into Butts Lane, then right)
☎ (0642) 780145
11–3, 5.30–11
Draught Bass Ⓗ
Charming village pub with two bars and a separate children's/function room. The ornate bar fronts were carved by a former licensee. Long and fascinating history, plus a ghost. Eve meals on request.
Q ⛟ ❀ ☾ ⊞ ♣ P

Elton

Sutton Arms
Off A66 ☎ (0642) 582350
12–3, 5.30–11
Camerons Strongarm; Tetley Bitter; Whitbread Castle Eden Ale, Flowers Original Ⓗ
Large, imposing pub at the edge of the village. Food-oriented, but stocks a good range of ales. ❀ ☾ ◗ ⊞ ♣ P

Elwick

McOrville Arms
The Green (400 yds off A19)
11–3, 7–11
Brakspear Bitter; Whitbread Boddingtons Bitter, Flowers IPA, Castle Eden Ale Ⓗ
Modernised local on the village green – scene of great bonfire night celebrations.
♛ ❀ ☾ ♣ P

Greatham

Hope & Anchor
High Street (400 yds off A689)
☎ (0429) 870451
11–4, 6–11
Tetley Bitter Ⓗ
Well modernised pub in a quiet village near Hartlepool.
⛟ ❀ ☾ ◗ ♣ P

Guisborough

Globe Hotel
Northgate ☎ (0287) 632778
2 (11.30 Sat)–3, 6.30–11
Camerons Bitter, Strongarm Ⓗ
Traditional local with regular patronage. Stages a comedy night on the last Thu of each month. ❀ ⊞ ♣ P

Tap & Spile
Westgate ☎ (0287) 632983
11–3, 5.30–11; 11–11 Thu–Sat
Big Lamp Prince Bishop Ale; Camerons Strongarm; Marston's Merrie Monk; guest beers Ⓗ
Old town-centre pub refurbished in traditional style and with a regular patronage. The rooms are set around a central bar. Quiz night Tue. Occasional draught cider. Eve meals until 7pm; lunches

in winter only available Thu–Sat. Q

Try also: Ship, Westgate (Bass)

Hartlepool

Causeway

Elwick Road, Stranton
(0429) 273954
11–11
Banks's Bitter; Camerons Bitter, Strongarm H
Unspoilt gem, formerly part of the Tap & Spile chain, standing next to the Camerons brewery.

Gillen Arms

Clavering Road
(0429) 860218
11–2.30, 5.30–11
Whitbread Castle Eden Ale, Wethered Winter Royal H
Large, modern, open-plan estate pub on the northern edge of town with strong community links. The comfortable interior has quiet corners and a family conservatory. P

Jackson Arms

Tower Street (0429) 862413
11–4, 5.30–11
Draught Bass; S&N Theakston Old Peculier; Taylor Landlord; Whitbread Castle Eden Ale; guest beer H
Two-roomed pub with typical Fitzgerald's pub chain antique touches. No food Tue or Sun.

New Inn

Durham Street (on headland)
(0429) 267797
11–3, 5.30–11
Camerons Strongarm H
Fine street-corner local which has featured in this guide for almost two decades. CAMRA Cleveland branch *Pub of the Year* 1991. Not to be missed.
Q

High Leven

Fox Covert

Low Lane (A1044 Yarm–Thornaby road)
(0642) 760033
11–3, 5–11
Vaux Samson, Double Maxim H
Distinctive cluster of whitewashed brick buildings of obvious farmhouse origin. The comfortable open-plan interior offers a warm welcome for all. Large function room upstairs.
P

Lazenby

Nags Head

High Street (0642) 440149
11.30–3, 7–11; 12–3, 7–10 Sun
Bass Worthington BB, Draught Bass H
Cosy but spacious pub, decorated with rural scenes, photographs and paintings. Popular (and recommended) for lunches; eve meals Sat only (but no lunches Sat).
Q P

Maltby

Pathfinders

(0642) 590300
11–11
Whitbread Castle Eden Ale, Flowers Original; guest beer H
Old pub in a small village to the south of Thornaby, much modernised and extended to reflect a greater emphasis on food. Named in honour of those who flew from the nearby RAF base during the war. P

Marske-by-the-Sea

Frigate

Hummershill Lane
(0642) 484302
12–3, 6.30–11; 12–11 Fri & Sat
John Smith's Bitter, Magnet H
Pleasant estate pub with a large lounge. The bar offers pool and darts but a quiet room is also available. Live entertainment every Tue night, and Fri night once a month.
P

Zetland Hotel (Top House)

9 High Street (0642) 483973
12–4, 7–11
Vaux Samson, Double Maxim, Extra Special; guest beer H
Large, spacious lounge and a separate bar. Quiz nights, folk and domino eves are held in the bar and upstairs room. Barbecues during the summer. Guest beers are from the Vaux list. Tiny car park. Local CAMRA *Pub of the Year* 1992.
Q P

Marton

Apple Tree

38 The Derby (opp. Stewart Park) (0642) 310564
11.30–11
Bass Worthington BB, Draught Bass H
Modern pub in a private housing estate serving a local patronage. The large lounge is divided to create a cosy atmosphere. Children are welcome in the conservatory. Good bar lunches.
P

Try also: Rudds Arms, Stokesley Rd (Whitbread)

Middlesbrough

Malt Shovel

133 Corporation Road
(0642) 213213
11–11
North Yorkshire Best Bitter, Yorkshire Brown, Yorkshire Porter, Erimus Dark, Flying Herbert, Dizzy Dick; guest beers H
Recently renovated real ale pub (built 1886) with a Victorian bar, three open fires and a friendly atmosphere. Six guest beers.
Q

Star & Garter

Southfield Road
(0642) 245307
11–11
Draught Bass; S&N Theakston XB, Old Peculier; guest beer
A CAMRA Pub Preservation Group award-winner for its conversion from a workingmen's club. The fine Victorian-style bar uses features from former pubs. A discrete games area plus a large, L-shaped lounge with a quiet eating area.
P

Tap & Barrel

86 Newport Road (by bus station)
(0642) 219995
11–11
North Yorkshire Best Bitter, IPA, Yorkshire Porter, Erimus Dark, Flying Herbert, Dizzy Dick; guest beers H
Cosy pub near the town centre, converted from a shop. Dining/function room upstairs. (Wheelchair access to ground floor only.) Cider varies.

Try also: Southfield, Southfield Rd (Camerons)

Moorsholm

Toad Hall Arms

High Street (1½ miles off A171)
(0287) 660155
7–11 (may open Sat lunch in summer)
Tetley Bitter H
Family pub on the edge of the North Yorks moors but only 20 mins from industrial Teesside, offering fine views out to sea from the garden. The cosy interior has 'toad' bric-a-brac. Children are welcome in the dining room. Self-contained flat to rent.
Q P

Redcar

Pig & Whistle
43 West Dyke Road
☎ (0642) 482697
11–11
Courage Directors; Marston's Pedigree; Ruddles Best Bitter; John Smith's Magnet; guest beer Ⓗ
Once known as the Alexandra Hotel and still retaining etched-glass windows, a smoke room and a central bar. A friendly, busy local with a collection of 2,000 miniature pigs. The pool room can be used for functions. No food Sun. Children welcome lunchtime only.
Q ☾ ⊞ ⇌ ♣

Yorkshire Coble
West Dyke Road (next to racecourse) ☎ (0642) 482071
11–3, 6–11
Samuel Smith OBB Ⓗ
Large, typical Sam Smith's estate pub with a strong regular clientele. A comfortable lounge, a large functional bar and a games room.
❀ ◐ ⊞ ⇌ (Central) ♣ P

Try also: Hop & Grape, High St (John Smith's)

Skelton Green

Miners Arms
5 Boosbeck Road
☎ (0287) 650372
12–4 (5.30 Sat), 7–11
Vaux Samson Ⓗ
Terraced local with a long, narrow lounge, a separate family room and a central corridor with a serving hatch. Shove-ha'penny played.
Q ♿ ♣ P

Stainton

Stainton Inn
☎ (0642) 599902
11–3, 6–11
Camerons Bitter, Strongarm Ⓗ
Victorian red-brick pub, at the village centre, extended in 1987. Very popular for food. Part of the Banks's chain after the aquisition of Camerons brewery.
Q ❀ ◐ ⊞ ♿ ♣ P

Stockton-on-Tees

Cricketers Arms
2 Portrack Lane
☎ (0642) 675468
11–11
Whitbread Boddingtons Bitter, Trophy, Castle Eden Ale; guest beer Ⓗ
Friendly corner local with a pleasant atmosphere. Eve meals finish at 8.
◐ ♣ P

Fitzgeralds
9–10 High Street
☎ (0642) 678220
11–3 (3.30 Fri), 6.30–11; 11–11 Sat
Draught Bass; McEwan 80/-; S&N Theakston Old Peculier; Taylor Landlord; guest beers Ⓗ
Impressive, stone-built pub with granite pillars. The interior has been restored to its 1903 condition. Draught cider occasionally.
☾ ⇌ ♣ ⌓

Senators
Bishopton Road
☎ (0642) 672060
11–4, 7 (6.30 Fri)–11
Vaux Double Maxim Ⓗ
Modern pub built onto the Whitehouse Farm shopping complex. The plain exterior hides a warm and comfortable interior. ❀ ◐

Sun
Knowles Street
☎ (0642) 615676
11–4, 5.30–11; 11–11 Wed, Fri & Sat
Draught Bass Ⓗ
Excellent, deservedly popular drinkers' pub just off the High Street. Venue of Stockton folk club, and claims Britain's largest sales of Draught Bass.
⇌ ♣

Try also: Clarendon, Dovecot St.; **Wild Ox,** Norton Rd (both Camerons)

Thorpe Thewles

Vane Arms
Durham Road
☎ (0740) 30548
11–3, 6.30–11
Vaux Double Maxim Ⓗ
Typical one-roomed village pub: functional and friendly.
Q ❀ ◐ ▲ ♣ P

Yarm

Ketton Ox
100 High Street
☎ (0642) 788311
11–11
Vaux Samson Ⓗ
One of several fine coaching inns in a marvellous village conservation area. A warm and welcoming pub where blocked-in oval windows on the facade betray the site of old cock-fighting rooms. Children welcome lunch and early eve. Occasional gourmet eves – ring for details. No eve meals at weekends (other eves till 8). ❀ ◐ ♣

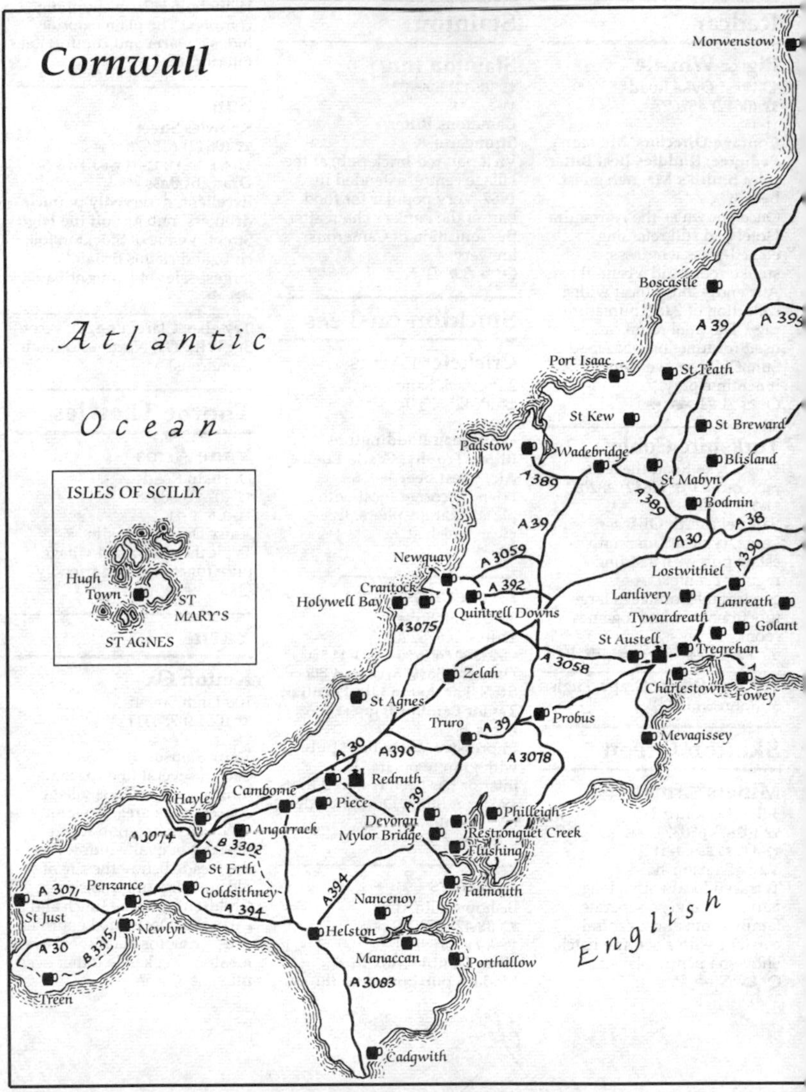

Redruth, Redruth; **St Austell**, St Austell

Altarnun

Rising Sun
Off A30, on Camelford road
OS825215 ☎ (0566) 86636
11–3, 6–11
Cotleigh Old Buzzard; Exmoor Ale; Whitbread Flowers Original Ⓗ; guest beers
Lively, 16th-century country pub on the edge of Bodmin Moor. Ever-changing guest beers and good fare. Popular with both locals and visitors.
P

Angarrack

Angarrack Inn
32 Steamer's Hill (off A30 N of Hayle) ☎ (0736) 752380
11–2.30, 6–11; 12–2, 7–10.30 Sun
St Austell Bosun's, XXXX Mild, HSD Ⓗ
Very welcoming and comfortable village pub offering an extensive and good value menu of home-prepared food (vegetarian option).
P

Blisland

Royal Oak
Village Green ☎ (0208) 850739
12–3, 6–11
Draught Bass Ⓗ; guest beers
Simply furnished country pub overlooking the green in an attractive moorland village; built from granite with stone mullion windows. Large family-cum-games room with a patio. Up to three guest

beers. No eve meals Sun.
P

Bodmin

Hole in the Wall

Crockwell Street (A389)
☎ (0208) 72379
11–2.30, 5–11; 11–11 Sat
Draught Bass; Whitbread Boddingtons Bitter Ⓗ; guest beers
Formerly the town's debtors' prison, containing an unusual collection of antiques and bric-a-brac. Entered through the gardens or via a walkway direct from the main town car park. Eve meals in summer only. Q

Masons Arms

5–9 Higher Bore Street (A389)
☎ (0208) 72607
11–3, 5–11; 11–11 Fri & Sat
Draught Bass; Wadworth 6X Ⓗ
Historic town pub, built before the Napoleonic Wars and reputed to hold the oldest continuous licence in Cornwall. Quiet lounge. Good value food. Friendly.
Q P

Boscastle

Cobweb

On B3263 ☎ (0840) 250278
11–3, 6–11; 11–12 Sat
Draught Bass; St Austell XXXX Mild, Tinners Ⓗ
Very popular pub with a constantly changing range of guest beers. An inn full of character, with slate floors and old artefacts hanging from the beams. Old ship's figurehead behind the bar. Live music Sat night. P

Napoleon

High Street ☎ (0840) 250204
11–3, 6–11
Draught Bass; St Austell Bosun's, Tinners, HSD Ⓖ
16th-century inn, once a recruitment centre for the Napoleonic Wars. A friendly, comfortable pub with several small rooms, granite walls and slate floors. Beers kept behind the bar are plumbed into the cooling system.
Q P

Botus Fleming

Rising Sun

Off A388, 4 miles from Tamar bridge ☎ (0752) 842792
12–3, 6–11 (may vary)
Draught Bass; Morland Old Speckled Hen Ⓗ; guest beers
Unspoilt and unpretentious country pub with 12th-century origins, tucked away in a quiet village on the outskirts of Saltash. A happy, friendly pub now in the third generation of family ownership. Good value cider; raucous euchre sessions. Boules. P

Cadgwith

Cadgwith Cove Inn

☎ (0326) 290513
11–11 (12–2.30, 7–11 winter)
Devenish Cornish Original; Marston's Pedigree; Whitbread Flowers IPA Ⓗ
17th-century, unspoilt smuggling inn in the heart of Cadgwith Cove and the fishing village of Cadgwith.

Callington

Coachmakers Arms

Newport Square
☎ (0579) 82567
11–2.30, 6.30–11
Draught Bass; Fuller's London Pride; Greene King Abbot Ⓗ; guest beers
17th-century coaching inn with a friendly atmosphere. Good food and en suite accommodation; popular public bar area.
Q P

Camborne

Tyacks Hotel

Commercial Street
☎ (0209) 612424
11–11
St Austell Bosun's, XXXX Mild, Tinners, HSD Ⓗ
18th-century, former coaching inn providing a very high standard of comfort, with a good range of ales, wines and excellent cuisine.
Q P

Charlestown

Rashleigh Arms

☎ (0726) 73635
11–11
Draught Bass; Ruddles County; John Smith's Bitter; Wadworth 6X; Whitbread Flowers Original Ⓗ; guest beers
Large, friendly inn overlooking the famous port, comprising two large bars, a restaurant and a family room. At least two guest ales. AA three-star accommodation.
P

Crantock

Old Albion Inn

Langurroc Road
☎ (0637) 830243
11–11
Courage Best Bitter, Directors; John Smith's Bitter; guest beers Ⓗ
A good place for refreshment after a church visit or a walk on the beach, dunes and cliffs: a thatched inn offering good food, including vegetarian.
Q P

Devoran

Old Quay Inn

St Johns Terrace (off A39)
☎ (0872) 863142
11–3, 6–11
Whitbread Boddingtons Bitter, Flowers IPA Ⓗ; guest beers
Friendly, welcoming pub with fine views over Devoran Quay and Creek. Various guest beers. P

Cornwall

Falmouth

Seven Stars
The Moor ☎ (0326) 312111
11–3, 6–11
Draught Bass [G]; Ruddles County [H]; St Austell HSD; guest beers [G]
Unspoilt by 'progress', a pub in the same family for five generations. The present landlord is an ordained priest. A lively tap room with barrels on display, and a quiet snug. Forecourt benches. Q ❀ ⊟

Flushing

Royal Standard
St Peters Hill (off A393 at Penryn) ☎ (0326) 374250
11–2.30 (3 Fri & Sat), 6.30–11; 12–2, 7–10.30 Sun (varies in winter)
Draught Bass; Whitbread Flowers IPA; guest beers (summer) **[H]**
Friendly local near the village entrance. Beware of swans in the road nearby. ♨ ❀ ☾ ☽ ♣

Fowey

Safe Harbour
Lostwithiel Street
☎ (0726) 833379
11–3, 6–11
St Austell Bosun's, Tinners, HSD, Winter Warmer [H]
300-year-old pub at the top end of town, a lounge and public bar on two levels. Friendly atmosphere, with piano music at times. ♨ Q ❀ 🛏 ☾ ☽ ⊟ ♿ ▲ ♣ P

Golant

Fishermans Arms
☎ (0726) 832453
11–3, 6–11
Courage Best Bitter; Ushers Best Bitter, Founders [H]
Charming village pub in a delightful waterside setting, with views across the River Fowey. Home-cooked food. Cider in summer. ♨ Q ♘ ❀ ☾ ☽ ♿ ▲ ♣ ◡ P

Goldsithney

Crown
Fore Street ☎ (0736) 710494
11–3 (extends summer), 6–11
St Austell Bosun's, XXXX Mild, HSD [H]
Attractive, comfortable village pub with a warm atmosphere. Very popular restaurant (bookings advisable) and excellent, home-cooked bar meals. ♨ ❀ 🛏 ☾ ☽ ▲

Gunnislake

Rising Sun
Calstock Road
☎ (0822) 832201
11.30–2.30, 5–11
Draught Bass; Courage Best Bitter; Fuller's London Pride; Hook Norton Old Hooky; St Austell HSD [H]; guest beers
17th-century village inn with spectacular views over the Tamar valley. A friendly pub welcoming to locals and visitors. Fine collection of china, glass and brass. The landlord is an international chef and is building up a good reputation for bar meals.
♨ Q ❀ ☾ ☽ ▲ ⇌ ♣ ◡ P

Hayle

Bird in Hand
Trelissick Road
☎ (0736) 753974
11–11 (11–3, 6.30–11 winter)
Courage Best Bitter, Directors; Paradise Bitter, Miller's Ale, Artists Ale; Wadworth 6X [H]; guest beers
Set in a former coach house with its own brewery, an imposing pub adjacent to Paradise Park bird gardens. Excellent range of own and guest ales. Restaurant upstairs. Bar meals in summer.
❀ ☾ ☽ ♿ ▲ ⇌ ♣ P

Helston

Blue Anchor
Coinagehall Street
☎ (0326) 562821
11–3, 6–11
Blue Anchor Middle, Best, Special [H]
An inn for all reasons: a superb, unspoilt, rambling granite and thatch, 15th-century building. The world-famous 'Spingo' beers come from the old brewhouse (a might strong for some). Two friendly bars offer good chat and no jukebox. Mind the gunnel when leaving.
♨ Q ♘ ▲

Holywell Bay

Treguth Inn
Holywell Road (off A3075)
☎ (0637) 830248
11.30–11 (11.30–2.30, 7–11 winter)
Courage Best Bitter, Directors; Ruddles County; John Smith's Bitter; guest beers [H]
Well situated on the hill down to a sandy beach, this thatched pub has genuine low beams (watch your head in the doorway) and a good mix of locals and holidaymakers. Popular for meals. Choice of camping or self-catering sites, plus a leisure park nearby.
♨ Q ♘ ❀ ☾ ☽ ▲ ♣ P

Isles of Scilly: *St Mary's*

Bishop & Wolf
Main Street, Hugh Town
☎ (0720) 22790
11–3, 5–11
St Austell Tinners, HSD [H]
Lovely pub with marine decor: a large bar, a pool room and an upstairs restaurant. Named after the two famous lighthouses. The beer is fined at the pub after the sometimes arduous crossing from the mainland. ♘ ☾ ☽ ▲ ♣

Kingsand

Rising Sun
Village Green ☎ (0752) 822840
11–3, 7–11
Draught Bass; Courage Best Bitter; Wadworth 6X [H]
Traditional pub in a Cornish fishing village. The cosy bar is well stocked with old local photos. Good value, wholesome, home-cooked food. ♨ Q ❀ ☾ ☽ ♿ ▲ ♣

Lanlivery

Crown Inn
Off A 390, 1½ miles W of Lostwithiel ☎ (0208) 872707
11–3 (may extend), 6–11
Bass Worthington BB, Draught Bass [H]; guest beer (occasionally)
Comfortable and old-fashioned pub in a 12th-century, listed building. The popular restaurant has an inglenook and a low-beamed ceiling. Accommodation in separate buildings. Large car park. ♨ Q ♘ ❀ 🛏 ☾ ☽
⊟ ♿ ▲ ♣ P

Lanreath

Famous Punch Bowl Inn
Off B3359 ☎ (0503) 220218
11–3, 6–11
Draught Bass; S&N Theakston Old Peculier (summer); **Whitbread Boddingtons Bitter [H]**
Velveteen chaises longues in the lounge and an enormous, flagstoned farmer's kitchen as the public bar are amongst the features of this 17th-century coaching house. Excellent food. ♨ Q ♘ ❀ 🛏 ☾ ☽
⊟ ▲ ◡ P

Launceston

Westgate Inn
Westgate Street
☎ (0566) 772493
11–11
Courage Best Bitter [H]
Busy and popular town pub still kept in the traditional style, with two bars. Good value, home-cooked bar meals. Cosmopolitan clientele. Next to a large car park.
☾ ☽ ⊟ ♿ ♣

Liskeard

Albion
Dean Street ☎ (0579) 342643
11–3, 7–11
Marston's Pedigree; John Smith's Bitter; Wadworth 6X; guest beers [H]
Friendly town pub close to the market, popular with farmers at lunchtime, and darts and pool players eves. Happy hour 7–8. Cider in summer; at least one guest beer.
☋ ❀ ◖ ◗ ⇌ ♣ ⍥ P

Lostwithiel

Royal Oak
Duke Street ☎ (0208) 872552
11–11
Draught Bass; Fuller's London Pride; Marston's Pedigree; Whitbread Flowers Original; [H]**; guest beers**
Busy, friendly, 13th-century inn, well-known for good food. A traditional public bar and a comfortable lounge with a restaurant. Specialises in guest beers from small independent breweries.
Q ☋ ❀ 🛏 ◖ ◗ ⊞ ▲ ⇌ ♣ P

Manaccan

New Inn
☎ (0326) 231323
11–3, 6–11
Devenish Cornish Original; Whitbread Boddingtons Bitter [G]
Very traditional, thatched pub in the village centre. Prides itself on good, home-cooked food. No jukebox or fruit-machines. The car park is tiny.
♨ Q ❀ ◖ ◗ ▲ P

Mevagissey

Fountain Inn
☎ (0726) 842320
11–11
St Austell Bosun's, Tinners [H]
Traditional, olde-worlde inn, licensed for 500 years: two bars, a slate floor and wood beams. Collection of historic photos. Home-cooked lunches; separate restaurant open March–Oct. Piano played Fri and Sat. ♨ ☋ 🛏 ◖ ◗ ▲

Morwenstow

Bush Inn
Crosstown OS208151
☎ (0288) 83242
11.30–3, 7–11 (closed winter Mon)
St Austell HSD [H]
Pleasant pub with a long history, simply furnished with wooden benches and tables. Popular in summer; handy for the coastal footpath. Isolated, but worth finding. No food Sun. ♨ Q ❀ ◖ ⊞ ♣ P

Mylor Bridge

Lemon Arms
Off A393 at Penryn
☎ (0326) 373666
11–3, 6–11
St Austell Tinners, HSD [H]
Friendly, one-bar, village-centre pub serving good food.
♨ ❀ ◖ ◗ ▲ ♣ P

Nancenoy

Trengilly Wartha
Off B3291 OS731282
☎ (0326) 40332
11–3, 6–11 (may vary)
Furgusons Dartmoor Best Bitter; St Austell XXXX Mild [G]**; Tetley Bitter** [H]**; guest beers** [G]
Delightful, remote country pub with beer-loving owners who ring the changes with a variety of guest beers. Renowned for its food. Excellent walks nearby.
♨ Q ☋ ❀ 🛏 ◖ ◗ ♿ ♣ ⍥ P

Newlyn

Fishermans Arms
Fore Street ☎ (0736) 63399
10.30–2.30, 5.30–11
St Austell XXXX Mild, Tinners, HSD [H]
Popular old local with superb views over the busy fishing harbour and Mount's Bay. Note the inglenook and memorabilia display. Good value, simple food. Limited parking. ♨ ❀ ◖ ◗ ♣ P

Newquay

Tavern
Mellanvrane Lane, Trenninick (off Treloggan Rd, near boating lake) ☎ (0637) 873564
11–3, 6.30–11
Bass Worthington BB, Draught Bass; guest beer [H]
Once a gentleman's house; the area surrounding has all now been developed for housing, leaving this pub tucked away. Much of the oak panelling and beams survive. Large games room and frequent live entertainment. Steak meals a speciality. ☋ ❀ ◖ ◗ ▲ ♣ P

Padstow

London Inn
6–8 Lanadwell Street
☎ (0841) 532554
11–4, 6–11
St Austell Bosun's, Tinners, HSD [H]
Set in what were fishermen's cottages, a nice old pub just off the harbour and decorated with a strong nautical theme. Large range of malt whiskies.
♨ Q 🛏 ◖ ◗ ♣

Penzance

Fountain Tavern
St Clare Street ☎ (0736) 62673
11–2.30, 5.30–11
St Austell Bosun's, HSD [H]
Unpretentious local with a real community spirit and a warm, family atmosphere. Off the town centre. Limited parking.
♨ ❀ 🛏 ◖ ♣ P

Mount's Bay Inn
The Promenade, Werrytown
☎ (0736) 63027
11–2.30, 5.30–11
Draught Bass [H]**; guest beers**
Small, friendly free house situated towards Newlyn, offering three guest ales changed regularly. An open bar with an eating area to one side. Worth a visit. ♨ Q ◖ ◗

Philleigh

Roseland Inn
2 miles off A3078, on King Harry Ferry road
☎ (0872) 580254
11–3, 6–11
Devenish Cornish Original; Marston's Pedigree; Whitbread Flowers Original [H]
Classic pub at the heart of the Roseland peninsula: an unspoilt, 17th-century inn, with a slate floor, wood beams, and a lot of character. Excellent, home-cooked fare; separate restaurant. No eve bar meals in winter. Worth finding. ♨ Q ❀ ◖ ◗ ▲ P

Piece

Countryman
On the Four Lanes–Pool road
☎ (0209) 215960
11–11
Courage Best Bitter, Directors; Ruddles County; John Smith's Bitter; Wadworth 6X; guest beer [H]
Former count house for the local tin mining community, said to be haunted by three maidens. A warm welcome in a popular country pub with a variety of entertainments.
♨ ☋ ❀ ◖ ◗ ♿ ▲ ♣ P

Polbathic

Half Way House
On A387 ☎ (0503) 30202
11–3, 5.30 (6 Sat)–11
Courage Best Bitter; Ushers Best Bitter, Founders [H]
Large, 16th-century, roadside coaching inn with several bars. Home-cooked bar food is served in addition to the restaurant. Families and pets welcome. ♨ Q ☋ ❀ 🛏
◖ ◗ ⊞ ▲ ⇌ (St Germans) ♣

Cornwall

Polperro

Blue Peter
The Quay ☎ (0503) 72743
11–11
St Austell Tinners, HSD [H]; guest beer
Superb, small pub on the end of the quay, reached via steps cut out of local rock. Atmospheric ambience and admirable fare. Live music regularly. Well worth the walk.
♛ Q ♉ ❀ ◖ ◗ ♿ ♣ ⌓

Porthallow

Five Pilchards
☎ (0326) 280256
11–2.30, 6–11
Draught Bass; Devenish Cornish Original; Greene King Abbot [H]
Attractive, rural pub on the beach, with views over to Falmouth. Boasts a fine collection of brass ships' lamps, model ships and wreck histories. Self-catering accommodation. ♛ Q ❀ ⛟ ◖

Port Isaac

Golden Lion
13 Fore Street ☎ (0208) 880336
11–11 (12–3, 6–11 winter)
St Austell Tinners, HSD [H]
Friendly, 18th-century village pub, a popular watering hole in a busy, picturesque fishing port. The main bar, overlooking the harbour, has a decorative ceiling. Linked to smuggling in olden days.
♛ ♉ ◖ ◗ ⊞ ♣

Probus

Hawkins Arms
Fore Street ☎ (0726) 882208
11–3, 5.30–11; 11–11 Sat
St Austell Bosun's, XXXX Mild, Tinners [H], HSD [G]/[H]
Pub with a landlord who enjoys both his beer and home cooking. Good value meals in generous portions.
♛ ♉ ❀ ⛟ ◖ ◗ ▲ ♣ P

Quintrell Downs

Two Clomes
East Road ☎ (0637) 873485
12–2.30, 7–11
Beer range varies [H]
18th-century free house which takes its name from the old clome ovens either side of the large log fire. Self-catering chalets in the pub grounds are ideal as a holiday base for Newquay and the North Coast. Up to four beers, constantly changed. ♛ Q ♉ ❀ ⛟ ◖ ◗ ♿ ▲ ⇌ ♣ P

Redruth

Tricky Dickies
Tolgus Mount (off the old Redruth bypass)
☎ (0209) 219292
11–3, 6–11 (midnight Tue & Thu)
Greene King Abbot; Wadworth 6X; Whitbread Boddingtons Bitter [H]; guest beer
Tastefully renovated, old tin mine smithy. Squash/exercise facilities available; a meeting point for hash runners. Good food. Children welcome. Jazz on Tue and other entertainment on Thu.
♉ ❀ ◖ ◗ ♿ ▲ ♣ P

Restronguet Creek

Pandora Inn
End of Restronguet Hill, near A39 OS814371
☎ (0326) 372678
11–11 (12–2.30, 6.30–11 winter)
Draught Bass; St Austell Bosun's, Tinners, HSD [H]
13th-century, thatched pub at the waterside, reachable by both road and water. Restaurant upstairs (à la carte).
♛ Q ♉ ❀ ◖ ◗ ▲ P

Rilla Mill

Manor House Inn
Off B3254 at Upton Cross
☎ (0579) 62354
12–2.30 (3 Sat), 7–11
Draught Bass; Greene King Abbot; Hook Norton Old Hooky [H]; guest beers
Comfortable and welcoming, 17th-century country inn and restaurant, in the delightful Lynher valley. Good reputation for excellent, home-cooked food. Six self-catering cottages in the grounds. Heated outdoor swimming pool.
♛ Q ❀ ⛟ ◖ ◗ ▲ ♣ P

St Agnes

Railway Inn
Vicarage Road
☎ (0872) 552310
11–3, 6–11 (maybe 11–11 summer)
Marston's Pedigree; Whitbread Boddingtons Bitter, Flowers IPA [H]
Pub named when the railway arrived. The trains have long gone, but this pleasant village inn remains. Copper and horse brasses, plus much more.
♛ Q ❀ ◖ ◗ ▲ ♣ P

St Austell

Carlyon Arms (Sandy)
Sandy Hill ☎ (0726) 72129
11–2.30, 5–11; 11–11 Sat
St Austell XXXX Mild, Tinners, HSD [H]
Friendly local, a recently refurbished St Austell house. Good, home-cooked food. Lively eve clientele: darts, pool, and live music Wed and Fri. ♛ ❀ ⛟ ◖ ⇌ ♣ P

St Breward

Old Inn
Churchtown ☎ (0208) 850711
12–3, 6–11
Draught Bass; Ruddles County; John Smith's Bitter [H]; guest beers
Set high on Bodmin Moor, next to the church: a solidly-built, granite building with slate floors and beamed ceilings. An old stone cross stands in front. Separate games room and restaurant. Selection of malt whiskies.
♛ ♉ ❀ ◖ ◗ ⊞ ♣ P

St Erth

Star Inn
Near A30, signed from Hayle
☎ (0736) 752068
11–3, 5–11
Marston's Pedigree; Whitbread WCPA, Boddingtons Bitter [H]
Fine village pub with a welcoming atmosphere. Bric-a-brac of all descriptions abounds, including the largest collection of snuff boxes in the country. Excellent food.
♛ ◖ ◗ ▲ ⇌ ♣ P

St Just

Star
Fore Street ☎ (0736) 788767
11–3, 5.30–11
St Austell Tinners, HSD [G]
Proper pub in this once-great tin mining town. Atmospheric bar and friendly staff (and cat). ♛ ♉ ❀ ⛟ ◖ ◗ ▲

St Kew

St Kew Inn
Churchtown ☎ (0208) 84259
11–2.30, 6–11; 12–2.30, 7–10.30 Sun
St Austell Tinners, HSD [G]
Attractive, 15th-century inn: a plain public bar with a slate floor and a large fireplace, and a comfortable lounge where beer used to be brewed. Good food, especially steaks.
♛ Q ❀ ◖ ◗ ⊞ ♣ P

St Mabyn

St Mabyn Inn
Churchtown ☎ (0208) 84266
11.30–3, 6–11
Draught Bass; S&N Theakston Best Bitter, XB [H]

Attractive, 15th-century pub next to the church, popular with locals and offering a warm, friendly welcome. Decorated with some interesting, if not unusual, items. ♨ ♘ ❀ ◖ ◗ ⊟ ♣ P

St Mellion

Coryton Arms
☎ (0579) 50322
11–11
Draught Bass; Cotleigh Tawny; Exmoor Gold; Furgusons Dartmoor Best Bitter; guest beers [H]
12th-century village inn now comfortably refurbished, with flagstoned floors in the bar. The village is about to be bypassed which will improve access. Panoramic views over the Tamar valley and Dartmoor. Close to the golf course. ♨ ❀ ◖ ◗ ♣ ⌓ P

St Teath

White Hart Hotel
☎ (0208) 850281
11–2.30, 6–11
Ruddles County; Ushers Best Bitter [H]
Bustling village pub, dating from the 1700s. Three bars each offer a different ambience, ranging from a noisy public (with satellite TV) to a quiet snug. Popular for food. Garden play area.
♨ Q ♘ ❀ 🛏 ◖ ◗ ⊟ ♣ P

Saltash

Two Bridges
Albert Road ☎ (0752) 848952
12–11
Courage Best Bitter, Directors; Ushers Best Bitter, Founders [H]
Pub with a cosy, country-cottage interior and a large garden with excellent river views. Barbecues Sat in summer; live music Wed and Fri. ♨ Q ❀ ≢ ♣ P

Stratton

Bideford Inn
Maiden Street ☎ (0288) 352033
11–3, 6–11
Draught Bass; Courage Best Bitter [H]
Extensively refurbished, 400-year-old coaching inn, with spacious, wood-panelled bars and beamed ceilings. A friendly pub with a children's play area in the garden.
♨ ♘ ❀ 🛏 ◖ ◗ ♣

Kings Arms Inn
Howells Road (A3092)
☎ (0288) 352396
11–3, 6–11 (may extend summer)
Exmoor Gold; Fuller's London Pride; Hall & Woodhouse Tanglefoot; Hook Norton Best Bitter; Smiles Exhibition; Whitbread Boddingtons Bitter [H]
Delightful, 17th-century village pub on the outskirts of Bude, run by an experienced landlord. Two cosy, inter-connecting bars with slate flags, and a separate dining area. Good value meals. A friendly pub. ♨ Q ❀ 🛏 ◖ ◗ ⊟ ♿ ▲ ♣ ⌓ P

Treburley

Springer Spaniel
On A388 ☎ (0579) 370424
11–3, 5.30–11
Exmoor Ale; Furgusons Dartmoor Best Bitter; Ind Coope Burton Ale [H]
Excellent, roadside country pub with 17th-century origins, now tastefully refurbished in a cosy, comfortable style by a professional landlord with a sense of humour. Renowned for high quality, value bar and dining room food. ♨ Q ♘ ❀ ◖ ◗ ⊟ ♿ ▲ ♣ ⌓ P

Treen

Logan Rock Inn
☎ (0736) 810495
10.30–3, 5.30–11 (10.30–11 summer)
St Austell Tinners, HSD [H]
Good, small pub near Minack Open Air Theatre. The characterful bar offers good food. Try a walk to the cliffs.
♨ ♘ ❀ ◖ ◗ ♿ ▲ P

Tregrehan

Britannia
On A390, 3 miles E of St Austell ☎ (0726) 812889
11–11
Bass Worthington BB, Draught Bass; Courage Directors; St Austell Tinners [H]**; guest beer**
16th-century inn on the main road. Well-known for its good food (all day), it has a separate restaurant and a safe, large garden with a play area. Fruit machines in the entrance.
Q ♘ ❀ ◖ ◗ ⊟ ♿ ▲ ♣ P

Trematon

Crooked Inn
☎ (0752) 848177
11–3, 6–11
Furgusons Dartmoor Best Bitter; St Austell XXXX Mild, HSD; Wadworth 6X [H]
Good selection of traditional ales and homely bar meals in a 17th-century inn. Luxurious accommodation; extensive outdoor children's play area, with wildlife. Enjoy the rustic drive. ♨ ♘ ❀ 🛏 ◖ ◗ ▲ P

Truro

City Inn
Pydar Street (just N of cathedral) ☎ (0872) 72623
11–3, 5–11; 11–11 Fri, Sat & summer
Courage Bitter Ale, Best Bitter, Directors; John Smith's Bitter; Wadworth 6X [H]**; guest beer**
Originally the Railway, renamed after a fire in 1876; a pub with a large collection of jugs in a pleasant bar with a convivial atmosphere. Garden and aviary at the back. Excellent food. Cornwall CAMRA *Pub of the Year* 1992.
🛏 ◖ ◗ ≢ ♣

Old Ale House
Quay Street ☎ (0872) 71122
11–3, 5–11
Draught Bass; Tetley Bitter; Whitbread Boddingtons Bitter [H]**, Flowers Original** [G]**; guest beers** [H]/[G]
Forerunner of the alehouse style of pub: sawdust, peanuts and bric-a-brac abound. A no-nonsense drinking pub with regular live music, including jazz jam sessions. The beer range is constantly varied. ◖ ◗ ≢

Tywardreath

New Inn
Fore Street ☎ (0726) 813901
11–2.30, 6–11
Draught Bass [G]**; St Austell XXXX Mild** [H]**, Tinners** [G]
Popular village pub near the coast. A secluded garden leads off the lounge and there is a separate room for darts and the jukebox. Popular with all age groups. Recently awarded a certificate for 20 years in the *Guide*.
Q ❀ ⊟ ▲ ≢ ♣ ⌓ P

Wadebridge

Ship Inn
Gonvena Hill ☎ (0208) 812839
11–2.30, 5.30–11
Whitbread Boddingtons Bitter [H]
Small, friendly, 16th-century coaching inn with a fine leaded window inset with the pub's name. Three small, comfortable drinking areas. Live folk music first Sat every month. ♨ ♘ ◖ ◗ ♣ P

Zelah

Hawkins Arms
High Road (off A30)
☎ (0872) 540339
11–3, 6–11
Butcombe Bitter; Ind Coope Burton Ale; Tetley Bitter; guest beers [H]
Well worth turning off the bypass for the excellent value meals and the range of beers, which varies almost weekly. Safe garden play area for children; B&B at good rates.
♨ Q ♘ ❀ 🛏 ◖ ◗ ▲ ♣ P

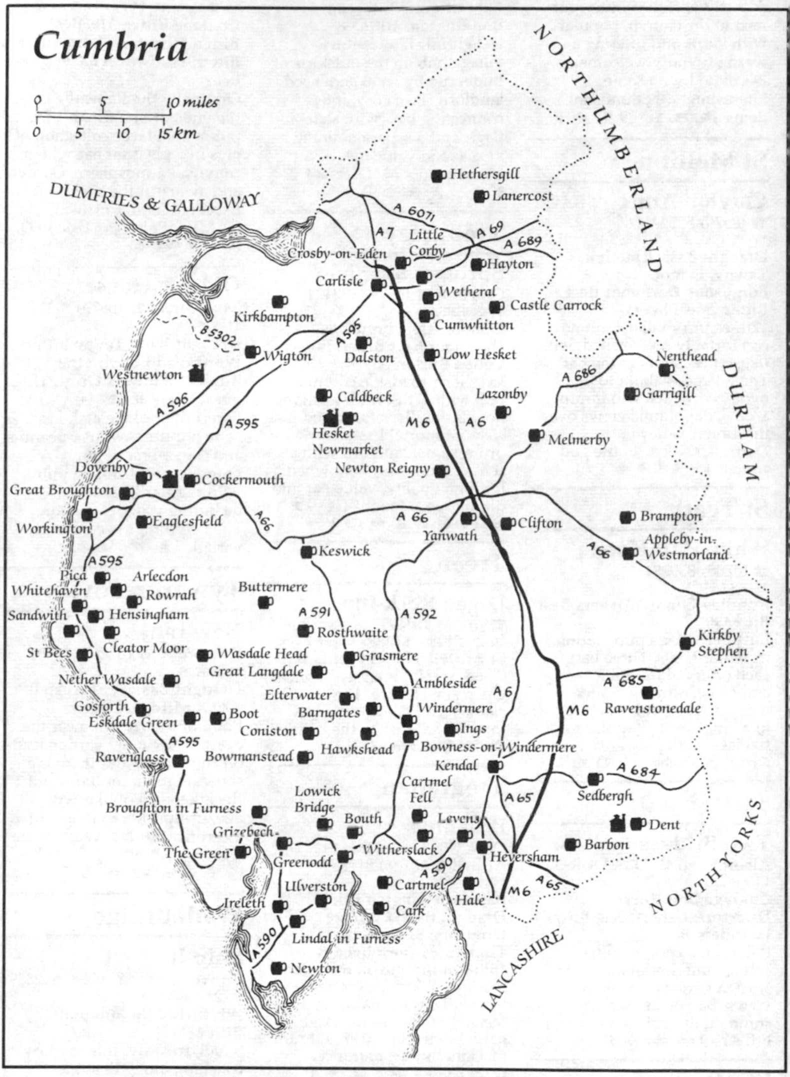

Dent, *Dent*; **Hesket Newmarket**, *Hesket Newmarket*; **Jennings**, *Cockermouth*; **Yates**, *Westnewton*

Ambleside

Golden Rule

Smithy Brow (off A591, towards Kirkstone)
☎ (053 94) 32257
11–11
Robinson's Mild, Bitter, Hartleys XB Ⓗ

Unhesitatingly recommended as an unspoilt, genuine pub with no modern trappings. Much favoured by students, climbers, paragliders, locals and all who appreciate traditional values. Well-filled rolls are made daily. Very limited parking.
⛰ Q ❀ ♣ P

Appleby-in-Westmorland

Golden Ball

High Wiend ☎ (076 83) 51493
11.30–3, 7–11 (11–11 summer)
Jennings Bitter, Cumberland Ale Ⓗ

Friendly, popular, two-roomed pub, formerly owned by Marston's. A fine example of an honest, no-frills, town-centre 'boozer'. Toasties made to order. 🛏 ≠ ♣

Royal Oak Inn
Bongate ☎ (076 83) 51463
11–3, 6–11
Draught Bass; Caledonian Deuchars IPA; Yates Bitter; Younger Scotch [H]; guest beers
Stylish, well-appointed, former coaching inn on the southern edge of town; a wood-panelled tap room, a lounge bar and a dining room. Usually has four guest beers, plus cider in summer. Cumbria CAMRA *Pub of the Year* 1992.
♔ Q ❀ 🛏 ◖ ◗ ♣ ⌓ P

Arlecdon

Sun Inn
☎ (0946) 862011
11.30–2.30, 6–11
Jennings Bitter; Nethergate Old Growler; Tetley Bitter [H]
Friendly, village local serving good food. Children welcome. The beer range may vary.
♔ ◖ ◗ ♣ P

Barbon

Barbon Inn
☎ (052 42) 76233
12–3, 6.30–11
S&N Theakston Best Bitter, Old Peculier [H]
Former coaching inn, circa 17th century. Quiet, cosy front bar; a lounge with deep armchairs and oak settles; separate dining room. Fishing, walking and pony trekking can be arranged for guests. Four-poster beds – Oliver Cromwell may have slept in one of them.
Q ❀ 🛏 ◖ ◗ P

Barngates

Drunken Duck
Off B5286, near Hawkshead OS351012
☎ (053 94) 36347
11.30–3, 6–11
Jennings Bitter; Marston's Pedigree; S&N Theakston XB, Old Peculier; Whitbread Boddingtons Bitter; Yates Bitter [H]
Amongst the best-known and most difficult to find pubs in the Lake District, reputed to be some 400 years old. An amusing legend about the pub's name can be read inside. Nearly always busy, especially in summer. Good food, including vegetarian. Fishing.
♔ Q ⛀ ❀ 🛏 ◖ ◗ ▲ P

Boot

Burnmoor Inn
☎ (094 67) 23224
11–3, 5–11
Jennings Bitter, Cumberland Ale [H]
Traditional Lakeland inn dating from 1578 in parts. Meals include authentic Austrian dishes. Scafell Pike, Laal Ratty (Dalegarth station), waterfalls and superb walks are all nearby.
♔ Q ❀ 🛏 ◖ ◗ P

Bouth

White Hart
Off A590 between Newby Bridge and Ulverston
☎ (0229) 861229
12–3, 6–11 (12–11 Thu–Sat in summer)
Jennings Bitter; Robinson's Hartleys XB, Best Bitter; Tetley Mild, Bitter; Whitbread Boddingtons Bitter [H]
17th-century coaching inn, popular with tourists and locals. Live music and quizzes; games room. Good food.
♔ Q ⛀ ❀ 🛏 ◖ ◗ ▲ ♣ P

Bowmanstead

Ship Inn
On A593, 1 mile S of Coniston
☎ (053 94) 41224
11–3 (summer only), 5–11
Robinson's Hartleys XB [H]
Comfortable old local with a genuine welcome. The snug adjoining the main bar is used as a family/games room.
♔ Q ❀ 🛏 ◖ ◗ ▲ ♣ P

Bowness-on-Windermere

Hole in T'Wall (New Hall Inn)
Lowside ☎ (053 94) 43488
11–11
Robinson's Best Mild, Hartleys XB, Best Bitter [H]
Popular pub near the village centre, with a reputation for good food, in a building of considerable character. Two bars on the split-level ground floor, a family/games room upstairs and a large patio.
♔ Q ⛀ ❀ ◖ ◗ ♣

Brampton

New Inn
Near Appleby
☎ (076 83) 51231
11.30–2.30, 7–11 (11–3, 6–11 summer, may vary)
S&N Theakston Best Bitter; Whitbread Boddingtons Bitter, Castle Eden Ale; Younger Scotch [H]
Formerly a farmhouse, now a comfortable, characterful pub in a pleasant hamlet overlooking the River Eden. Solid fuel range in the dining room.
♔ Q ❀ 🛏 ◖ ◗ ▲ ♣ P

Broughton in Furness

Manor Arms
The Square ☎ (0229) 716286
2 (12 Fri & Sat)–11 (12–11 summer)
S&N Theakston Best Bitter; Taylor Landlord; Yates Bitter [H]; guest beers
Local CAMRA *Pub of the Year* for the last two years. Children are welcome at this popular village local. Constantly changing guest beers. Snacks at all times.
♔ Q ❀ 🛏 ▲ ♣

Buttermere

Bridge Hotel
☎ (076 87) 70252
11–11
Black Sheep Special Strong; S&N Theakston Best Bitter, XB, Old Peculier; Younger No. 3 [H]
Originally a cornmill, first licensed in 1735: a pub which has had various names, including the Victoria, after the queen who stayed here. Note the farm memorabilia. Good choice of traditional Cumbrian and ale dishes. Walkers and families welcome. Local CAMRA *Pub of the Year* 1992. ♔ Q ❀ 🛏 ◖ ◗ ⊟ ▲ ⌓ P

Caldbeck

Oddfellows Arms
☎ (069 74) 78227
12–3, 6.30–11
Jennings Bitter, Cumberland Ale [H]
Pleasant village inn which has undergone sympathetic refurbishment, previously known as the John Peel. Excellent value food is freshly prepared, and served in the new restaurant area.
♔ Q ❀ 🛏 ◖ ◗ ♿ ♣ P

Cark

Engine Inn
Station Road ☎ (053 95) 58341
12–4 (5 summer), 7–11; 11–11 Sat
S&N Matthew Brown Mild, Theakston Best Bitter; Younger Scotch [H]
18th-century alehouse near the old mill house on the village square. ♔ ⛀ ❀ 🛏 ◖ ◗ ♿ ▲ ≠ ♣ P

Cumbria

Carlisle

Caledonian Cask House
Botchergate ☎ (0228) 28468
11–11
Whitbread Boddingtons Bitter, Castle Eden Ale; guest beers Ⓗ
City-centre pub, which has undergone a major transformation. With 12 handpumps, guest beers are featured all the time. Stone-flagged floors and bare wood boards; Carlisle has waited a long time for a pub like this! ◐ ⇌

Carlisle Rugby Club
Warwick Road (just off A69)
☎ (0228) 21300
7 (5.30 Fri, 6 Sat)–11; closed Mon–Sat lunch (12.30–11 Sat during rugby season)
Tetley Bitter; Yates Bitter; guest beer Ⓗ
Friendly club with a cosy lounge and a large bar. Very handy for rugby union and soccer fans. Show this guide or CAMRA membership to be signed in. Guest beers in the rugby season. ♔ ☕ ❀ ♣ P

Chaplins
Crosby Street ☎ (0228) 29055
11–3, 7–11; 7–10.30 Sun, closed Sun lunch
S&N Theakston Best Bitter; Younger No. 3 Ⓗ
Popular and comfortable, city-centre bar and restaurant, serving excellent value bar lunches. The self-serve salad bar is recommended; restaurant meals are served upstairs eves. Rare outlet for No. 3 in this area. ◐ ⇌

Howard Arms
Lowther Street ☎ (0228) 32926
11–11
S&N Theakston Best Bitter, XB Ⓗ
Deservedly regular *Guide* entry, where partitions give a multi-roomed effect. Can be a squeeze most nights. A large number of State Management bottles are in evidence. Impressive tiled frontage.
❀ ◐ ⇌

Turf Tavern
Newmarket Road
☎ (0228) 515367
11–11
Marston's Pedigree; Robinson's Hartleys XB; Whitbread Boddingtons Bitter, Castle Eden Ale Ⓗ
Formerly a racecourse grandstand, which stood derelict for years. Renovated in fine style and now a large, comfortable and popular pub. Interesting fans in the roof. Has its own 'study'.
❀ ◐ ⇌ P

Woolpack Inn
Milbourne Street
☎ (0228) 32459
11–3, 5.30–11; 11–11 Fri & Sat
Jennings Mild, Bitter, Cumberland Ale, Oatmeal Stout, Sneck Lifter Ⓗ
Nineteen consecutive years in the *Guide*: a large local with an extraordinarily warm welcome in a spacious lounge, a snug bar and a games room. A mural depicts Carlisle's past. Large selection of whiskies. Live jazz Thu and Sun night and Sun lunch; other music Fri. ❀ 🛏 ◐ ◑ ♿ ⇌ ♣ P

Cartmel

Cavendish Arms
Cavendish Street
☎ (053 95) 36240
11.30–11
Draught Bass; John Smith's Bitter Ⓗ**; guest beer**
Large, comfortable and friendly pub in the village centre. Well known for the high standard of its meals, it gets packed on bank hols, especially on race days. Regular food theme nights.
♔ Q ❀ 🛏 ◐ ◑ ♿ ♣ P

Cartmel Fell

Masons Arms
Strawberry Bank (between Gummers How and Bowland Bridge) OS413895
☎ (053 95) 68486
11.30–3, 6–11
Lakeland Amazon, Great Northern, Big Six, Damson Ⓗ**; guest beers**
Extremely popular brew pub. Enormous selection of bottled beer from all over the world, and a wide range of food. Busy at all times; large parties are discouraged. Now makes its own cider. Self-catering accommodation available.
♔ Q ☕ ❀ 🛏 ◐ ◑ ⌓ P

Castle Carrock

Duke of Cumberland
☎ (0228) 70341
12–3, 7–11 (may vary summer)
Jennings Cumberland Ale, Oatmeal Stout; S&N Theakston Best Bitter Ⓗ
Comfortable village local, now re-opened after being sold by Marston's. Pool room behind the bar area. ♔ ❀ ◐ ◑ ▲ ♣ P

Cleator Moor

Derby Arms
Ennerdale Road
☎ (0946) 810779
11–4, 5–11
S&N Theakston Best Bitter, XB Ⓗ
Lively and interesting pub for the adventurous drinker. ❀ ♣

Clifton

George & Dragon
On A6 ☎ (0768) 65381
11–3, 6–11 (may vary)
Ind Coope Burton Ale; Tetley Bitter Ⓗ
Traditional local with two bars, a dining room and a games room. A large forecourt, with benches set out in summer, doubles as a car park. Sun lunch is very popular. Wheelchair WC.
♔ ❀ 🛏 ◐ ◑ ♿ ▲ ♣ P

Cockermouth

Bush Hotel
Main Street ☎ (0900) 822064
11–11; 11–3, 6.30–11 Sat
Jennings Mild, Bitter, Cumberland Ale, Oatmeal Stout, Sneck Lifter Ⓗ**; guest beers**
Refurbished town-centre pub; Jennings's very successful first venture into guest beers. Also stocks a wide variety of continental bottled beers. Children welcome when not too busy. Quiz Tue. Eve meals in summer. ♔ Q ◐ ◑ ♣

Swan Inn
Kirkgate ☎ (0900) 822425
11–3, 7–11
Jennings Bitter, Cumberland Ale (summer)**, Oatmeal Stout, Sneck Lifter** Ⓗ
Popular pub on a cobbled Georgian square which stocks a huge selection of whiskies. Parking nearby. Q ▲ ♣

Coniston

Sun Hotel
☎ (053 94) 41428
11–11
Draught Bass (summer)**; Jennings Bitter; Tetley Bitter** Ⓗ
Comfortable, well-appointed hotel with a popular public bar. Convenient for travellers returning from the fells and mountains. Meals weekends only in January.
♔ Q ❀ 🛏 ◐ ◑ ▲ ♣ P

Crosby-on-Eden

Stag Inn
☎ (0228) 573210
11–2.30, 6–11
Jennings Mild, Bitter, Cumberland Ale Ⓗ
Delightful, olde-worlde pub with low-beamed ceilings and stone-flagged floors. Good

home-cooked food available in the bar and upstairs restaurant. ♛ ❀ ◖ ◗ ♣ P

Cumwhitton

Pheasant Inn

A69 from Carlisle, turn right at Warwick Bridge, follow signs
☎ (0228) 560102
12–3, 5.30–11; 11–11 Sat
Jennings Cumberland Ale, Sneck Lifter; Marston's Pedigree; S&N Theakston Best Bitter Ⓗ; guest beers
Pub built in 1690 and retaining a lot of character with its original stone-flagged floor, fireplace, beams, antique furniture and old prints of local interest. Good, home-made fresh food.
♛ Q ❀ 🛏 ◖ ◗ ▲ ♣ P

Dalston

Bridge End Inn

☎ (0228) 710161
11–3.30, 5.30–11; 11–11 Sat & summer
Greenalls Thomas Greenall's Original Ⓗ
Interesting watering hole near the northern end of the Cumbria Way. Good basic food with a take-away menu that serves the village. Good outdoor play area for children.
♛ Q ❀ ◖ ◗ ▲ ⇌ ♣ P

Dent

Sun Inn

Main Street ☎ (053 96) 25208
11–3, 6.30–11 (11–11 summer, may vary)
Dent Bitter, Ramsbottom, T'Owd Tup Ⓗ; Younger Scotch Ⓔ
The original Dent Brewery tied house. A typical Dales village inn with original beams. No-smoking dining area; eve meals till 8.30 (Cumberland sausage is a speciality). The games room has a jukebox. Rare outside gents'.
♛ Q ❀ 🛏 ◖ ◗ ▲ ♣ P

Dovenby

Ship Inn

On A594, Maryport–Cockermouth road ☎ (0900) 828097
11–3, 5.30–11; 11–11 Sat
Jennings Bitter, Cumberland Ale Ⓗ
Friendly village pub with a garden play area for children.
♛ ❀ 🛏 ◖ ◗ ♣ P

Eaglesfield

Black Cock Inn

☎ (0900) 822989
11–3.30, 6–11; 11–11 Sat
Jennings Bitter Ⓗ
Cosy, panelled and brass-hung village local, where a roaring fire and friendly welcome awaits. Birthplace of John Dalton, Fletcher Christian and Robert Eaglesfield. Easy parking outside. ♛ Q ❀ ♣

Elterwater

Britannia

☎ (053 94) 37210
11–11
Jennings Mild, Bitter; Marston's Pedigree; Whitbread Boddingtons Bitter Ⓗ
Popular pub in the centre of a delightfully situated village. The patio is adjacent to the village green which is often required as an overflow area. Dining room and a small back bar. Good value food.
♛ Q ❀ 🛏 ◖ ◗ ▲ ♣ 🍎

Eskdale Green

King George IV Inn

☎ (094 67) 23262
11–3, 6–11
Draught Bass; Jennings Cumberland Ale; Whitbread Boddingtons Bitter Ⓗ
Pleasant, many-roomed pub, on several levels with unusual bar stools and stone-flagged floors. Busy meals trade, with daily specials. Handy for the Ravenglass and Eskdale Railway (Eskdale Green station).
♛ Q 🚼 ❀ 🛏 ◖ ◗ ▲ ♣ P

Garrigill

George & Dragon

Signed off B6277 from Alston (on the Pennine Way)
☎ (0434) 381293
12–3, 7–11 (may be 12–11 summer)
McEwan 70/-; S&N Theakston Best Bitter, XB, Old Peculier Ⓗ; guest beer
Excellent free house and restaurant, popular with fell walkers. The stone-flagged floor has been retained in front of the large open fire.
♛ Q 🚼 🛏 ◖ ◗ ▲ ♣ P

Gosforth

Horse & Groom

Kell Bank (Eskdale road)
☎ (094 67) 25254
11–3.30, 5.30–11; 11–11 Sat
Jennings Bitter; Tetley Bitter; Whitbread Boddingtons Bitter Ⓗ
Lively, popular village local, with a paved area for outdoor drinking. ❀ 🛏 ◖ ◗ ▲ ♣ P

Grasmere

Travellers Rest

On A591 ☎ (053 94) 35378
11–11
Jennings Bitter, Cumberland Ale Ⓗ
Popular, roadside inn on the Coast to Coast walk with a games/family room and a dining room serving good quality meals. Roaring fire in winter; great views all year.
♛ 🚼 ❀ 🛏 ◖ ◗ ▲ ♣ P

Great Broughton

Punchbowl Inn

Main Street ☎ (0900) 824708
11–3 (not Mon, except bank hols), 6.30–11 (may vary)
Jennings Bitter Ⓗ
Small, friendly village pub with a cosy atmosphere. Parking very limited. ♛ ♣ P

Great Langdale

Old Dungeon Ghyll Hotel

☎ (053 94) 37272
11–11
Jennings Cumberland Ale; Marston's Pedigree; S&N Theakston Mild, XB, Old Peculier; Yates Bitter; guest beers Ⓗ
One of the best-known pubs in Lakeland. The Climbers Bar has flagged floors, basic seating, a cast iron range (noted for steaming socks) and an informal atmosphere. A more sedate bar and dining room are available in the hotel. Surrounded by the very best views/fells/walks/climbs.
♛ Q ❀ 🛏 ◖ ◗ ▲ ♣ 🍎 P

The Green

Punchbowl Inn

Off A595, between Broughton and Millom ☎ (0229) 772605
11–3, 6–11 (11–11 summer, may vary)
Whitbread Boddingtons Bitter Ⓗ; guest beers
Friendly pub for diners, locals and drinkers. Varied live music. A traditional meeting place for the cattle round up!
♛ ❀ ◖ ◗ ♿ ▲ ♣ P

Greenodd

Machells Arms

Main Street ☎ (0229) 861246
11–3, 6–11
Greenalls Thomas Greenall's Original; Ind Coope Burton Ale; Tetley Bitter Ⓗ
Small, friendly village local offering good, home-cooked food and reasonably priced B&B. The landlord always finds time for a good crack.
♛ Q 🛏 ◖ ◗ ♣ P

Grizebeck

Greyhound Inn

Off A595 ☎ (0229) 89224

12–3, 6–11
Courage Directors; John Smith's Bitter Ⓗ
Pub with a warm atmosphere and a stone-flagged floor. Beware of the sloping bar!
♔ ❀ ◑ ◗ ♿ ▲ ♣ P

Hale

Kings Arms Hotel

On A6 ☎ (053 95) 63203
11–3, 6–11
Mitchell's Best Bitter, ESB Ⓗ
Unspoilt, roadside pub with an L-shaped bar area. Artefacts and plates adorn the walls. No dogs allowed at mealtimes. A bowling green adjoins. ♔ Q ⚘ ❀ ◑ ◗ ▲ ♣ P

Hawkshead

Kings Arms Hotel

The Square ☎ (053 94) 36372
11–11
S&N Theakston Best Bitter, Old Peculier; Tetley Bitter, Whitbread Boddingtons Bitter, Flowers Original Ⓗ
Cosy, olde-worlde pub and restaurant with oak beams and a log fire. Set in a picturesque village. ♔ ❀ 🛏 ◑ ◗ ▲ ♣

Hayton

Stone Inn

☎ (0228) 70498
11–3, 5.30–11; 11–11 Sat
Federation Buchanan's Original; Jennings Cumberland Ale, Oatmeal Stout; S&N Theakston Best Bitter Ⓗ
Popular, village local with an attractive stone bar and fireplace. ♔ Q ♣ P

Hensingham

Sun Inn

Main Street ☎ (0946) 695149
12–4, 6.30–11
Jennings Bitter Ⓗ
Small, traditional pub with loyal regulars. Q ♣

Hesket Newmarket

Old Crown Inn

☎ (069 74) 78288
12–3 (Sat & school hols), 5.30–11
Hesket Newmarket Great Cockup Porter, Skiddaw Special, Blencathra, Doris's 90th Birthday Ale, Old Carrock Ⓗ
Very friendly, fellside village local with good home-cooking and its own brewery (tours followed by a meal are available if booked). Shelves full of books and an assortment of games. ♔ Q ◗ ▲ ♣

Hethersgill

Black Lion

Off A6071, 2½ miles NE of Smithfield ☎ (0228) 75318
11–3, 7–11; 11–11 Sat
Draught Bass; Maclay 80/- Ⓗ
Welcoming village local, which also serves as the post office. Good value snacks served; self-catering cottage available. ♔ ❀ ♿ ♣ P

Heversham

Blue Bell Hotel

Princes Way ☎ (053 95) 62018
11–3, 6–11
Samuel Smith OBB, Museum Ⓗ
Much enlarged during the heyday of the A6, this 500-year-old former vicarage has a bar/games room, a lounge bar and a dining room. ♔ Q ⚘ ❀ 🛏 ◑ ◗ ♿ ▲ ♣ P

Ings

Watermill Inn

Just off A591 ☎ (0539) 821309
12–3, 6–11
S&N Theakston Best Bitter, XB, Old Peculier Ⓗ**; guest beers**
Family-run oasis, offering a wide range of guest beers, and cider in summer. Good value, home-cooked meals use local produce; the specials often contain beer. Warm welcome. Wheelchair WC. ♔ Q ❀ 🛏 ◑ ◗ ♿ ▲ ⌓ P ⚟

Ireleth

Bay Horse

☎ (0229) 463755
12–2 (summer only), 7–11; 12–2, 7–10.30 Sun
Jennings Mild, Bitter, Cumberland Ale, Sneck Lifter Ⓗ
Friendly, 18th-century country pub, popular with locals and visitors alike. The games room hosts regular darts, pool and quiz nights. ♔ Q ❀ ⇌ (Askam in Furness) ♣ P

Kendal

Burgundy's Wine Bar

Lowther Street
☎ (0539) 733803
11–2.30 (not Mon), 6.30–11; 7–10.30 Sun, closed Sun lunch
Draught Bass; Stones Best Bitter Ⓗ**; guest beers**
Thriving, European-style wine bar in a former Labour Exchange. Guest beers change rapidly. The origin of the house beer is a secret. Eve meals May–Sept, and by arrangement in winter.
Q ◑ ◗ ⇌

Cask House

Allhallows Lane
☎ (0539) 724060
11–11
Whitbread Boddingtons Bitter Ⓗ**; guest beers**
Formerly the Roebuck, a town-centre pub with bare wood floors, next to the old public wash house. Three guest beers plus real cider. Popular with office staff lunchtime and the younger set eves and weekends. Eve meals Easter–Oct. ◑ ◗ ⇌ ⌓

Ring O'Bells

Kirkland ☎ (0539) 720326
11–3, 6–11; 11–11 Sat (may vary summer)
Vaux Lorimers Best Scotch, Samson; Wards Sheffield Best Bitter Ⓗ
Unspoilt pub, reputed to be the only one in England to stand on consecrated ground. The ring of bells from the superb parish church can be heard on Wed eve. Eve meals June–Sept. The snug is a real gem. ♔ Q ❀ 🛏 ◑ ◗ ♣

Sawyers Arms

139 Stricklandgate
☎ (0539) 729737
11.30–4, 6.30–11; 11–11 Fri, Sat & summer
Robinson's Hartleys XB, Best Bitter Ⓗ**, Old Tom** (winter) Ⓖ
Popular local with a warm welcome. Look out for the Hartleys etched window, and the 1936 Gaskell & Chambers Dalex handpumps. 1950s/60s music played. 🛏 ⇌ ♣

Keswick

Bank Tavern

Main Street ☎ (076 87) 72663
11–11
Jennings Mild, Bitter, Cumberland Ale, Sneck Lifter Ⓗ
Popular local in the town centre, with a village atmosphere. Q ⚘ ❀ 🛏 ◑ ◗ ▲ ♣

Packhorse Inn

Packhorse Court
☎ (076 87) 71389
11–11
Jennings Mild, Bitter, Cumberland Ale, Oatmeal Stout, Sneck Lifter Ⓗ
Unusually and attractively refurbished pub, with comfy settees, prints and books. Beers may not all be available in winter, but usually at least four are on. Children welcome for meals. Q ◑ ◗ ♿

Kirkbampton

Rose & Crown

☎ (0228) 576492
7–11

Webster's Yorkshire Bitter; guest beer Ⓗ
Unspoilt, two-roomed local with friendly service. Doubles as the village shop/post office during the day. 🏠 Q ❀ ⊟ ♣

Kirkby Stephen

White Lion
Market Street ☎ (076 83) 71481
10.30–3, 5.30–11 (may vary)
Jennings Bitter, Cumberland Ale Ⓗ
Open-plan, town-centre pub formerly owned by Marston's. Keen interest in darts and dominoes. The Jennings beers may vary. Q ◐ ◗ ▲ ♣

Lanercost

Abbey Bridge Inn (Blacksmiths Bar)
Off A69, 2 miles outside Brampton ☎ (069 77) 2224
12–2.30, 7–11; 12–2.30, 7–10.30 Sun
Yates Bitter Ⓗ**; guest beers**
An absolute gem. A split-level bar area with a stone-flagged floor and a spiral staircase leading up to a restaurant, serving quality food. Always two or three changing guest beers. Not to be missed. 🏠 Q ❀ 🛏 ◐ ◗ ▲ ♣ P

Lazonby

Joiners Arms
☎ (0768) 898728
11–11
Draught Bass; Stones Best Bitter Ⓗ
Warm and friendly village local, recently extended to include a pool room. Owned by a former head brewer of Stones Brewery. Handy for the Settle to Carlisle line. 🏠 ❀ 🛏 ◐ ◗ ⇌ P

Levens

Hare & Hounds
400 yds off A590
☎ (053 95) 60408
11–3, 6–11
Vaux Samson; Wards Thorne Best Bitter, Sheffield Best Bitter Ⓗ
Village pub with a lounge for diners, a snug, and a games room. No eve meals Sun–Tue, Nov–Mar. Q ❀ ◐ ◗ ♣ P

Lindal in Furness

Railway Inn
London Road ☎ (0229) 462889
7.30 (12 Sat)–11
Jennings Bitter Ⓗ**; guest beers**
Very friendly village local, offering regularly changing guest beers. Children's play area. 🏠 Q ❀ ♣

Little Corby

Haywain
☎ (0228) 560598
12–3, 7–11
Robinson's Hartleys XB, Best Bitter Ⓗ
Two-roomed village local; the long lounge bar has a piano. Q ❀ ◐ ◗ ♿ ♣ P

Low Hesket

Rose & Crown
On A6 ☎ (0228) 73346
12–3, 7–11
Jennings Mild, Bitter, Cumberland Ale Ⓗ
Comfortable village pub with a warm, friendly atmosphere, and good value food from a varied menu. No food Mon eve, except bank hols. 🏠 ☕ ❀ ◐ ◗ P

Lowick Bridge

Red Lion
On A5084, 3 miles S of foot of Coniston Lake
☎ (0229) 885366
11–3, 6–11
Robinson's Best Mild, Hartleys XB, Best Bitter Ⓗ
Excellent country pub, a focal point for the community and popular with visitors. Good food; excellent Sun lunches. Families welcome. Fine view. 🏠 Q ❀ ◐ ◗ ▲ ♣ P

Melmerby

Shepherds Inn
Off A686 ☎ (0768) 881217
10.30–3, 6–11
Jennings Cumberland Ale, Sneck Lifter; Marston's Pedigree Ⓗ**; guest beers**
Deservedly popular free house in an attractive location on the edge of the village green by the northern Pennines. Superb food. 🏠 Q ❀ ◐ ◗ ▲ ♣ P ⊁

Nenthead

Miners Arms
A689 from Alston towards Stanhope ☎ (0434) 381427
12–3, 7–11
Beer range varies Ⓗ
At 1,500 ft above sea level, probably the highest village pub in England, offering national prize-winning cuisine and a friendly atmosphere. Three handpumps serve different ales, changed weekly. 🏠 Q ❀ 🛏 ◐ ◗ ♿ ▲ ♣ P

Nether Wasdale

Screes Hotel
☎ (094 67) 26262
12–3 (may vary winter), 6–11
S&N Theakston Best Bitter, Old Peculier; Yates Bitter Ⓗ**; guest beers** (summer)
Homely hotel with public bars on split levels, in a village one mile west of Wastwater. An ideal base for walks around Wasdale. Fifty malt whiskies. 🏠 ☕ ❀ 🛏 ◐ ◗ ▲ ♣ P

Newton

Farmers Arms
☎ (0229) 462607
11–3 (not Mon–Wed), 6.30–11; 11–11 Sat
Thwaites Best Mild, Bitter Ⓗ
Large, welcoming village local with a very attractive interior of beams and stone fireplaces. Lunches Thu–Sun. Bar billiards and bar skittles played. 🏠 Q ❀ ◐ ◗ ♣ P

Newton Reigny

Sun Inn
W of Penrith ☎ (0768) 67055
11–3, 6–11; 11–11 Sat
Beer range varies Ⓗ
Large village pub with a pool room. The jukebox offers a wide range of music. 🏠 ☕ ❀ 🛏 ◐ ◗ ♿ ▲ ♣ P

Pica

Greyhound Inn
1 mile E of Pica
☎ (0946) 830366
12–2.30 (not Mon), 6.30–11; 12–2, 6.30–10.30 Sun
Jennings Mild, Bitter, Cumberland Ale Ⓗ**; guest beer**
Cosy, roadside pub offering a warm welcome, and first-class home cooking and accommodation at reasonable rates. 🏠 ❀ 🛏 ◐ ◗ ♿ ▲ ♣ P

Ravenglass

Ratty Arms
☎ (0229) 717676
11–3, 6–11 (11–11 Easter–Oct)
Jennings Bitter; Ruddles Best Bitter, County Ⓗ**; guest beer**
Cheerful, friendly local, converted from a railway station, with lots of railway memorabilia. Next to the main line and the narrow gauge steam (La'al Ratty) stations. Also handy for the Roman bathhouse, Muncaster Castle and a children's playground. Tasty, wholesome food Easter–Oct. 🏠 Q ☕ ❀ ◐ ◗ ▲ ⇌ P

Ravenstonedale

Black Swan Hotel
☎ (053 96) 23204
12–3, 6–11

Cumbria

Robinson's Hartleys XB, Best Bitter; S&N Theakston Best Bitter; Younger Scotch Ⓗ**; guest beer** (summer)
Hotel in an area of natural beauty: a locals' bar, a lounge and a dining room. Good food. Three bedrooms are adapted for guests with disabilities.
⛰ Q ❀ 🛏 ◐ ◗ ♿ ▲ ♣ P

Rosthwaite

Scafell Hotel (Riverside Bar)

☎ (076 87) 77208
11–11
S&N Theakston Mild (summer), **Best Bitter, XB, Old Peculier** Ⓗ
Refurbished and enlarged bar at the rear of a country hotel, in a beautiful valley. Children, walkers, climbers (boots and all) welcome. Open 8.30am for breakfasts, sandwiches and flask filling. A popular stop on the Coast to Coast walk. Live music (trad. folk).
⛰ Q ♘ 🛏 ◐ ◗ ▲ P

Rowrah

Stork Hotel

☎ (0946) 861213
11–3, 6–11
Jennings Mild, Bitter; Marston's Pedigree Ⓗ
Well-established, family-run local, near a karting track and the Coast to Coast walk. The bar features stuffed animals.
⛰ Q ❀ 🛏 ▲ ♣

St Bees

Queens Hotel

Main Street ☎ (0946) 822287
12–3, 5.30–11
S&N Theakston Best Bitter; Whitbread Boddingtons Bitter; Younger Scotch Ⓗ
Small hotel with two bars and a comfortable, relaxed atmosphere. Limited parking.
⛰ Q ♘ ❀ 🛏 ◐ ◗ ▲ ≹ P

Sandwith

Dog & Partridge

☎ (0946) 692671
12–4, 7–11 (12–11 summer if busy)
Yates Bitter Ⓗ
Cosy, friendly village pub at the St Bees end of the Coast to Coast walk. Occasional guest beers or another from the Yates range. Children welcome. ⛰ Q 🛏 ◐ ◗ ♣ P

Sedbergh

Red Lion

Finkle Street ☎ (053 96) 20433
11–3, 6.30–11
Jennings Mild, Bitter, Cumberland Ale, Oatmeal Stout, Sneck Lifter Ⓗ
Excellent, friendly local with a warm welcome for visitors. No junk food served. Unusual covered outside area at the rear. At the heart of the Howgill Fells, and popular with walkers, riders and cyclists. ❀ ◐ ◗ ▲ ♣

Ulverston

Kings Head

Queen Street ☎ (0229) 582892
11–3 (5.30 Sat), 6 (6.30 Sat)–11
S&N Theakston Best Bitter; Younger No. 3 Ⓗ**; guest beer**
Friendly, market town pub about 300 years old, with its own bowling green. Resident ghost. ⛰ ❀ 🛏 ◐ ≹

Wasdale Head

Wasdale Head Inn

OS187089 ☎ (094 67) 26229
11–11 (winter: open weekends only, phone first)
Jennings Bitter; S&N Theakston Best Bitter, Old Peculier; Yates Bitter Ⓗ**; guest beer** (summer)
In the shadow of England's highest mountain, and at the head of England's deepest lake, set in a hauntingly beautiful landscape. Popular with climbers and walkers. CAMRA West Pennines *Pub of the Year* 1991.
⛰ Q ♘ ❀ 🛏 ◐ ◗ ▲ ♣ P

Wetheral

Wheatsheaf Inn

☎ (0228) 560686
11–3, 6–11
Greenalls Bitter, Thomas Greenall's Original Ⓗ
Cosy, one-roomed village pub with a real fire and a warm welcome. Good, home-cooked food. ⛰ ❀ ◐ ◗ ♿ ≹ ♣ P

Whitehaven

Central

104 Duke Street
☎ (0946) 692796
11–4, 6.30–11; 11–11 Fri & Sat
S&N Theakston Mild, Best Bitter, XB Ⓗ
Pub with a popular and busy front lounge with railway paintings; quieter back bar. Lunches weekends. ◐ ≹ ♣

Golden Fleece

Chapel Street ☎ (0946) 63194
11–11
Jennings Bitter, Cumberland Ale, Sneck Lifter Ⓗ
Popular, back-street pub, worth the trouble of finding. The walls are graced by local characters, captured by a local artist. The Jennings beers may vary. ❀ ≹ ♣

Wigton

Victoria

King Street ☎ (069 73) 42672
11–11
Jennings Mild, Bitter Ⓗ
Comfortable local in the town centre, virtually opposite the bus station. ♿ ≹ ♣

Windermere

Grey Walls Hotel (Greys Inn)

Elleray Road ☎ (053 94) 43741
11–11
S&N Theakston Mild, Best Bitter, XB, Old Peculier; guest beer Ⓗ
Popular pub just off the village-centre, offering games, family and dining areas. The jumbo mixed grill is renowned – available all day Sat. Guest beers are a bonus in this Nationals-dominated area.
⛰ ♘ ❀ 🛏 ◐ ◗ ≹ ♣ P

Witherslack

Derby Arms

Off A590 ☎ (053 95) 52207
12–2.30 (11–3 summer), 6–11
Vaux Samson; Wards Thorne Best Bitter Ⓗ
Former coaching inn: two-rooms on the ground floor, plus a cellar bar. Beers vary within the Vaux range. Home-cooked meals from local produce (not served winter Mon or Tue, or Sun eve). Garden play area.
⛰ Q ♘ ❀ 🛏 ◐ ◗ ▲ ♣ P

Workington

George IV

Stanley Street (near harbour)
☎ (0900) 602266
11–3, 7–11
Jennings Bitter Ⓗ
Cosy end-of-terrace pub, on probably the oldest street in town. Convenient for the rugby league, football and greyhound stadia. ⛰ Q ≹

Yanwath

Gate Inn

☎ (0768) 62386
12–3, 7 (6 summer)–11
S&N Theakston Best Bitter; Yates Bitter Ⓗ**; guest beer** (summer)
Refurbished village pub retaining a cosy feel. It has a games area and a dining room, with an imaginative menu.
⛰ Q ❀ ◐ ◗ ▲ ♣ P

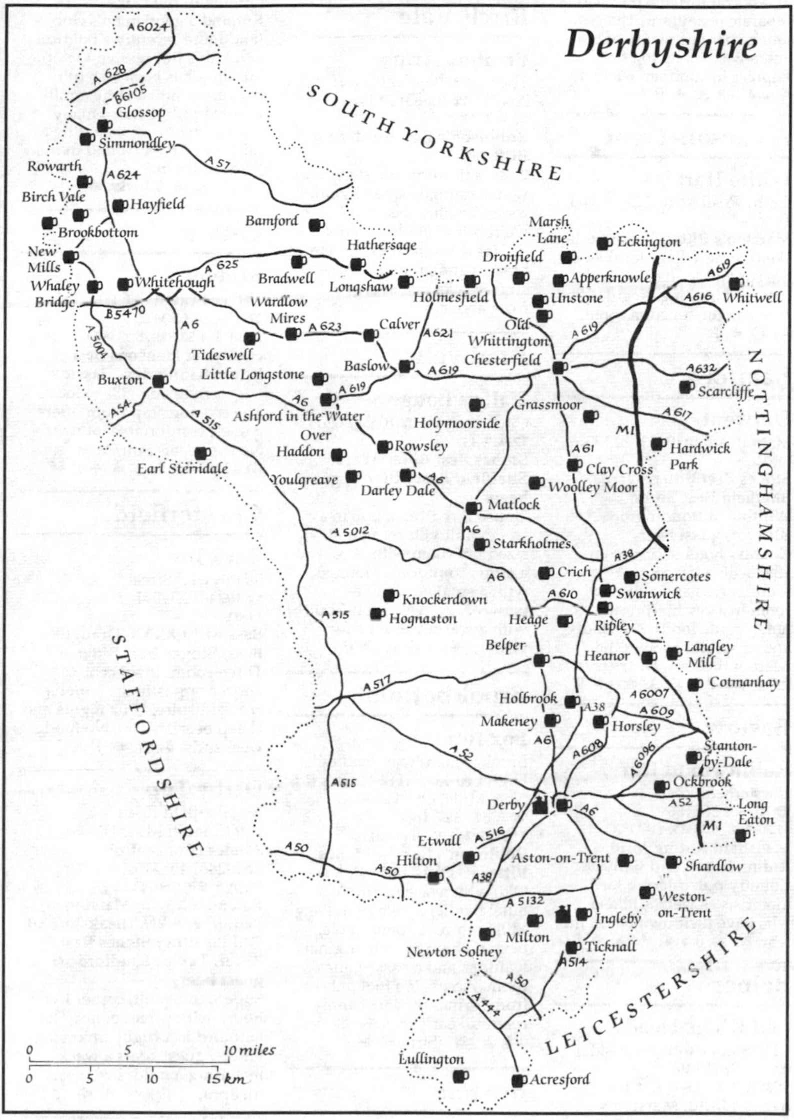

Brunswick, Derby; **Lloyds**, Ingleby

Acresford

Cricketts Inn

On A444 ☎ (0283) 760359
11–3, 6.30–11; 12–2.30, 7–10.30 Sun
Draught Bass; Marston's Pedigree Ⓗ; guest beers
18th-century former coaching inn. Its name means 'wooded copse' and is not derived from an insect or a game. Tidy basic bar; smart lounge; good reputation for food (not served Mon eve). ♔ ❀ ◐ ◑ ⊟ ♣ P

Apperknowle

Yellow Lion

High Street ☎ (0246) 413181
12–2 (3 Sat), 6–11
Bass Worthington BB; Greene King Abbot; Stones Best Bitter; Tetley Bitter Ⓗ; guest beers
Busy, stone-built village free house with a comfortable lounge and a separate, no-smoking restaurant. The extensive menu includes vegetarian dishes. Winner of CAMRA awards. ❀ ◐ ◑ P

Ashford in the Water

Ashford Hotel

1 Church Street
☎ (0629) 812725
11–11
Bass Worthington BB, Draught Bass; Stones Best Bitter Ⓗ; guest beers (summer)

Smart, comfortable pub with a separate restaurant. The cosy lounge bar has plenty of brass and a welcoming log fire. Popular in summer. Q P

Aston-on-Trent

White Hart

Derby Road (0332) 792264
11–11
Marston's Bitter, Pedigree [H]
Welcoming village local where the bar and lounge are both cosy and inviting. Regular live music in the function room. Q P

Bamford

Derwent

Main Road (0433) 51395
11–11
Stones Best Bitter; Wards Sheffield Best Bitter; Whitbread Boddingtons Bitter [H]**; guest beers**
Country hotel dating from 1890 with a tap room, two lounge areas and a dining room (reasonably-priced, home-made food). A friendly and unspoilt haven in the heart of the Peak District. P

Baslow

Robin Hood Inn

Chesterfield Road
(0246) 583186
11.30–3.30, 6.30–11; 11–11 Sat
Mansfield Riding Mild, Riding Bitter, Old Baily [H]
Country pub catering for motorists as well as hikers, who have their own bar at the rear. P

Belper

Old Kings Head

1 Days Lane (off Cheapside)
(0773) 821497
11.30–3, 7–11; 11–11 Fri & Sat
Banks's Mild; Marston's Pedigree [H]
Early 15th-century inn on a quiet lane near the town centre: a multi-roomed centre of local activity. Lunches Thu–Sat. Parking difficult. Q

Queens Head

29 Chesterfield Road
(0773) 825525
12 (4 Mon)–11
Ansells Mild; Ind Coope ABC Best Bitter, Burton Ale; Tetley Bitter [H]**; guest beers**
Large pub with a roomy lounge and a delightful snug with bench seats. Across the corridor is a family room. Q

Birch Vale

Printers Arms

Thornsett, New Mills (off A6015) (0663) 743843
12–2, 7–11
Robinson's Best Mild, Best Bitter [H]
Cosy, mid-terraced, stone pub with a lounge, bar and games room. The low-beamed bar is welcoming and has an open fire (as does the lounge). Horse brasses and antique tack. A stuffed pike oversees events from above the bar. P

Bradwell

Valley Lodge

Church Street (0433) 620427
12–4, 7–11
Stones Best Bitter; Wards Sheffield Best Bitter [H]**; guest beers**
Unusual red-brick pub in a stone-built village: a good-sized tap room with pool, and a large, comfortable lounge, with a smaller room in-between. A lively locals' pub with a warm welcome for visitors. P

Brookbottom

Fox Inn

Brookbottom Road (end of High Lea Rd, off St Mary's Rd, New Mills) OS985864
(061) 427 1634
11.30–3, 7 (5.30 summer)–11
Robinson's Best Mild, Best Bitter [H]**, Old Tom** (winter) [G]
Old, whitewashed pub in a quiet hamlet a mile from New Mills centre: a comfortable, beamed lounge with original features, and a basic games room. Access (on foot only) from Strines Station. Family room till early eve. (Strines) P

Buxton

Bakers Arms

26 West Road (0298) 24404
12–3, 6 (7 Sat)–11
Ind Coope Burton Ale; Tetley Bitter [H]**; guest beers**
Cosy, two-roomed pub close to the market place. Recently introduced guest beers, with regular appearances from Burton Bridge. Also has an excellent range of malts. A welcoming pub. P

Old Clubhouse

3 Water Street (follow signs to Opera House) (0298) 70117
11–11
Ind Coope Burton Ale; Tetley Bitter [H]
Originally the Duke of Rutland's gentleman's club (and more recently a political club), this impressive Victorian building has been tastefully converted into a large, multi-roomed pub. Retains many original features, including a mirrored fire surround in the 'Ladies' Room'. Q

Calver

Bridge

Calver Bridge (A623)
(0433) 630415
11.30–3 (4.30 Sat), 5.30 (6 Sat)–11
Hardys & Hansons Best Bitter, Kimberley Classic [H]
Large, roadside village local. The spacious tap room offers games; comfortable lounge. No eve meals Sun/Mon. Q P

Chesterfield

Buck Inn

5 Holywell Street
(0246) 239091
11–11
Bass Mild XXXX, Draught Bass; Stones Best Bitter [H]
Three-room, town-centre boozer opposite the famous crooked spire. Quiz nights and cheap beer on Thu. No food weekends. P

Derby Tup

387 Sheffield Road, Whittington Moor (B6052, 2 miles N of centre)
(0246) 454316
11.30–3, 5 (6 Sat)–11
Bateman XXXB; Marston's Pedigree; S&N Theakston XB, Old Peculier; Stones Best Bitter; Taylor Landlord [H]**; guest beers**
Superb, unspoilt, corner free house with three rooms. The landlord is a rugby union fan. Fifteen guest beers a week, including a mild. Eve meals till 8pm. Q

Portland Hotel

Market Square, West Bars
(0246) 234502
11–3, 5.30–11
Courage Directors; John Smith's Bitter [H]
Imposing former station hotel. The unspoilt exterior is of significant historical importance; inside, the original wooden fire surround has escaped modernisation. No-smoking pool room. Q P

Royal Oak

43 Chatsworth Road, Brampton (A627)
(0246) 277854

11–3, 6–11; 11–11 Fri & Sat
S&N Theakston Mild, Best Bitter, XB, Old Peculier; Younger IPA, No. 3 [H]; guest beers
Lively pub with a good atmosphere, on the main road from the Peak District. Quiz Sun; live entertainment twice a week. Major stockist of world-wide bottle-conditioned beers (70 varieties). ❀ ⊟ ♣ ⌓ P

Star Inn
422 Chatsworth Road, Brampton (A627)
☎ (0246) 277714
12–4 (5 Sat), 5.30 (6.30 Sat)–11
Ind Coope Burton Ale; Stones Best Bitter; Tetley Bitter [H]
Clean local on the outskirts of Chesterfield. Friendly clientele in a good, long bar. ♣ P

Victoria
21–23 Victoria Street West, Brampton (off A619 near mini-roundabout)
☎ (0246) 273832
12–3.30, 7–11
Wards Thorne Best Bitter, Sheffield Best Bitter [H]; guest beers (occasionally)
Two-roomed, traditional local with a welcome. Guest beers from the Vaux group. Winner of brewery and CAMRA awards. Q ❀ ⊟ ♿ ♣

Clay Cross

Cannon
Thanet Street ☎ (0246) 250078
12–3, 7–11
Courage Directors; Ruddles Best Bitter; Webster's Yorkshire Bitter [H]
Large, well-appointed pub with a mock-Tudor interior. A separate restaurant offers a good value menu. Quiz nights. ♛ ⛑ ❀ ◖ ◗ P ⊬

Prince of Wales
Thanet Street ☎ (0246) 865698
12–4 (4.30 Sat), 7–11
S&N Theakston Best Bitter; Stones Best Bitter [H]
Comfortable, small, traditional village pub with a lounge and a public. No gimmicks, just great atmosphere. ❀ ⊟ ♣

Cotmanhay

Bridge Inn
Bridge Street (off A6007)
☎ (0602) 322589
11–11
Hardys & Hansons Best Mild, Best Bitter [E]
Traditional village local by the Erewash Canal, frequented by a good mix of locals, fishermen and boaters. Frequent visitors include eagles and goats. No swearing in the bar. A rare find. Q ❀ ⊟ ♣ P

Crich

Cliff Inn
Cromford Road
☎ (0773) 852444
11–3, 6–11
Hardys & Hansons Best Mild, Best Bitter, Kimberley Classic [H]
Popular, stone-built local with two small rooms. Near the National Tramway Museum. ❀ ◖ ◗ ⊟ P

Darley Dale

Grouse Inn
Dale Road North (A6)
☎ (0629) 734357
12–3, 7–11
Hardys & Hansons Best Mild, Best Bitter, Kimberley Classic (summer) **[H]**
Roadside local, renovated but keeping a traditional atmosphere. Popular with all ages and handy for tourists. Good children's playground. ♛ ⛑ ❀ ◖ ◗ ♿ Å ♣ P

Derby

Alexandra Hotel
203 Siddals Road
☎ (0332) 293993
11–2.30, 4.30 (6 Sat)–11
Bateman Mild, XB; Courage Bitter Ale; Marston's Pedigree [H]; guest beers
Friendly pub with pleasing, subtle decor and wooden floors. Bottled beer collection and train memorabilia in the bar. At least five guest beers; over 500 different beers last year. Guest ciders. No food Sun. Q ❀ ◖ ♿ ⇌ ⌓ P

Brunswick Inn
1 Railway Terrace
☎ (0332) 290677
11–11
Brunswick Celebration Mild, First Brew, Old Accidental; Marston's Pedigree [H]; S&N Theakston Old Peculier [G]; Taylor Landlord [H]; guest beers
The oldest purpose-built railwayman's pub, where 14 handpumps serve beers from all around the country, as well as the on-site brewery. Annual beer festival first week Oct. Eve meals by arrangement. Q ⛑ ❀ ◖ ♿ ⇌ ♣ ⌓ ⊬

Crompton Tavern
46 Crompton Street
☎ (0332) 292259
11–11
Marston's Pedigree; Taylor Landlord; Wards Mild, Sheffield Best Bitter [H]; guest beers
U-shaped community pub. Friendly and unpretentious. Rotating guest beers. ❀ ◖ ♣

Dolphin Inn
Queen Street ☎ (0332) 49115
10.30–11
Bass Worthington BB, Draught Bass; M&B Highgate Mild, Springfield Bitter; Stones Best Bitter [H]
The oldest and most picturesque pub in the city, built in 1530, the same year as the cathedral tower. One of the four rooms is devoted to memorabilia of Offiler's brewery. Food 9.30am–10.30pm. ♛ Q ❀ ◖ ◗ ♣ P

Drill Hall Vaults
1 Newlands Street
☎ (0332) 298073
12–2.30, 7–11
Marston's Pedigree [H]
One-roomed, friendly, comfortable pub, with brass items on the walls and beams on the ceiling. Pool. ♛ ◖ ♣

Friargate
114 Friargate ☎ (0332) 297065
11.30–3, 6–11
Bateman Mild; Hoskins Beaumanor Bitter, Penn's Ale, Old Nigel [H]; guest beers
One-roomed, out-of-town pub in town, decorated with beer mats and bottles. ◖

Station Inn
Midland Road
☎ (0332) 360114
11–11
Draught Bass [G]
Narrow pub used by postal workers. Pool table off the bar; function room. ⇌ ♣

Victoria Inn
12 Midland Place
☎ (0332) 45156
11–3, 7–11
Bass Worthington BB, Draught Bass; M&B Highgate Mild [H]
Friendly, L-shaped local with live music (most styles) in the function room. ❀ ⇌

Vine Inn
37 Whitaker Street
☎ (0332) 41473
11–3, 7–11
Banks's Hanson's Mild; Draught Bass; M&B Highgate Mild [H]
Long-established, back-street local, popular with all sections of the community. Offiler's brewery started here in 1856. Food on Derby County match days only. ❀ ♣

Woodlark
80 Bridge Street (off Friargate)
☎ (0332) 32910
11.30–2.30, 5 (7.30 Sat)–11
Adnams Bitter; Bass Worthington BB, Draught Bass [H]; guest beers

Derbyshire

Former brew pub, now a free house, built in the early 19th century. A small bar and a larger lounge, with brass-topped tables. Two rotating guest beers. Q ❀

York Tavern
York Street (via Friargate and Vernon St) ☎ (0332) 362849
12–3, 6–11
Marston's Pedigree Ⓗ**; guest beers**
Busy, friendly, back-street local with a U-shaped drinking area, a pool table and a darts area. ❀ ♣

Dronfield

Old Sidings
91 Chesterfield Road
☎ (0246) 410023
12–11
Bass Worthington BB, Draught Bass; Stones Best Bitter Ⓗ**; guest beers**
Lively pub with an L-shaped lounge on two levels. Comfortably furnished with a railway theme. Restaurant in the basement. Eve meals Wed–Sat. Regular entertainment. ❀ ◖◗ ≠ ♣ P

Earl Sterndale

Quiet Woman
☎ (0298) 83211
11–3 (may extend), 6–11
Banks's Mild; Marston's Bitter, Pedigree Ⓗ
Superb example of a village local, overlooking the green; two-roomed with the bar and games room both having real fires. Dominoes tables can be found in the low beamed lounge and free-range eggs can be bought over the bar. A classic. ♨ Q ❀ ▲ ♣ P

Eckington

Prince of Wales
Church Street ☎ (0246) 423966
11.30–3, 7–11
Marston's Bitter, Pedigree, Owd Rodger (winter) Ⓗ
Stone-built, friendly, two-room local with a well-equipped garden. Separate room for Sun lunches and functions. Q ❀ ◖ ♣ P

White Hart
Church Street ☎ (0246) 434855
12–3.30, 7–11
Home Bitter; S&N Theakston XB; Younger Scotch Ⓗ
Historic inn in the old centre of the village, next to the church: a traditional tap room with a pool table, a comfortable lounge and a function room. Occasional live music. Eve meals end at 8.30. ❀ ⛿ ◖◗ ⊞ ♿ ♣ P

Etwall

Hawk & Buckle
Main Street ☎ (0283) 733471
11.30–2.30, 7–11
Marston's Bitter, Pedigree Ⓗ
Smart, modern village local with a comfortable lounge and a smaller bar with a games area. Parking opposite. ♨ ❀ ⊞ ♣ P

Glossop

Crown Inn
142 Victoria Street
☎ (0457) 862824
11.30–11
Samuel Smith OBB, Museum Ⓗ
A regular *Guide* entry for a decade: two small, comfortable snugs, an active games room and an attractive central bar. A true locals' ale house. ♨ ☕ ≠ ♣ ⚡

Friendship Inn
Arundel Street
☎ (0457) 855277
12–3 (4 Sat), 5 (7 Sat)–11
Robinson's Best Mild, Best Bitter Ⓗ
Corner of terrace pub, just off the main shopping street, with always a pleasant atmosphere. Families welcome. Typical Robinson's decor, with wood panelling. ♨ Q ♿ ≠ ♣

Surrey Arms
133 Victoria Street
☎ (0457) 853192
11.30–11
Whitbread Boddingtons Bitter; guest beers Ⓗ
Warm, comfortable pub with a welcoming atmosphere. Two pumps are devoted to guest ales, one usually a premium bitter. ≠ ♣

Whiteley Nab
1 Charlestown (A624, 1 mile from centre) ☎ (0457) 852886
12–11
Vaux Lorimers Best Scotch; Wards Sheffield Best Bitter Ⓗ
Formerly the Commercial, but renamed in 1992 (shortly after Vaux acquired it), after the hill it nestles under. Local reputation for good food at all times (including all day Sun). Occasional jazz. ❀ ◖◗ ♣ P

Grassmoor

Boot & Shoe
302 North Wingfield Road
☎ (0246) 850251
11–4, 7–11
Mansfield Riding Bitter Ⓗ
Friendly, two-roomed village local catering for all age groups. Organist at weekends in the lounge. ❀ ⊞ ♿ ♣ P

Hardwick Park

Hardwick Inn
1 mile S of M1 jct 29
☎ (0246) 850245
11.30–3, 6–11
S&N Theakston XB, Old Peculier; Younger Scotch Ⓗ
17th-century inn owned by the National Trust, at the exit gates of Hardwick Hall. Excellent food (no eve meals Sun). ♨ Q ☕ ❀ ◖◗ P

Hathersage

Plough
Leadmill Bridge (B6001, 1 mile from centre) ☎ (0433) 650319
11.30–3, 6.30–11; 11–11 Sat
Ind Coope Burton Ale; Tetley Bitter Ⓗ
Comfortable pub with a spacious, split-level lounge and a small, intimate tap room. Converted from a farmhouse on the banks of the Derwent, and popular with walkers, campers and locals. ♨ ❀ ⛿ ◖◗ ⊞ ▲ ≠ ♣ P

Scotsman's Pack
School Lane ☎ (0433) 50253
12–3, 7 (6 summer)–11 (12–11 summer Sat)
Burtonwood Mild, Bitter, Forshaw's Ⓗ
Comfortable village pub with three lounge areas served by a central bar. A feature is 'Little John's Chair', made for a giant but perhaps not the one who lies in the churchyard. ❀ ⛿ ◖◗ ♿ ▲ ≠ ♣ P

Hayfield

George Hotel
14 Church Street
☎ (0663) 743691
12–11
Burtonwood Mild, Bitter Ⓗ
Listed building entered below street level. Oak beam ceilings and a kitchen range fireplace feature in the lounge. Separate snug, games and bar areas. ♨ Q ❀ ⛿ ◖◗ ♿ ▲ ♣ P

Sportsman
Kinder Road (½ mile from village) ☎ (0663) 741565
12–3 (usually Fri–Sun only), 7–11
Thwaites Best Mild, Bitter, Craftsman Ⓗ
Smartly presented pub in a stone-built terrace on the north bank of the Kinder. Function room. ♨ Q ⛿ ◖◗ ▲ ♣

Heage

Black Boy
Old Road ☎ (0773) 856799
11.30–3, 6.30–11
Mansfield Riding Bitter, Old Baily Ⓗ

Modernised, large and open-plan: a bright and friendly, lounge-based pub. Restaurant meals eves. ♨ ❀ ◖ ♣ P

White Hart
2 Church Street
☎ (0773) 852302
11.30–3.30, 6–11
Draught Bass [H]
Large, attractive pub of early 17th-century origin, with many rooms. ☋ ◖ ◗ ⊞ ♣ P

Heanor

New Inn
Derby Road ☎ (0773) 719609
11–3.30, 7–11
Home Mild, Bitter; S&N Theakston Best Bitter [H]
Popular, friendly and compact local on Tag Hill.
❀ ◖ ⊞ ♣ P

Hilton

White Swan
Egginton Road
☎ (0283) 732305
11.30–11
Bass Worthington BB, Draught Bass; M&B Highgate Mild; Marston's Pedigree; Stones Best Bitter [H]**; guest beers**
100-year-old country pub with fireplaces featuring ancient beams: one is over 300 years old. Famed for its meals, especially the 'Desperate Dan Pie'. Quiz Mon. Children's garden assault course. No food Sun/Mon eves.
♨ ❀ ◖ ◗ ▲ ♣ P ⊬

Hognaston

Red Lion
Main Street ☎ (0335) 370396
11–3, 6–11
Marston's Pedigree [H]
Typical, upland village pub; a main U-shaped room, warm and friendly, and a small pool room (families welcome). Also sells eggs and cheese.
♨ ❀ ◖ ▲ ♣ P

Holbrook

Wheel Inn
Chapel Street ☎ (0332) 880006
Mansfield Riding Mild, Old Baily; Taylor Landlord; Wards Thorne Best Bitter; Whitbread Boddingtons Bitter, Flowers Original [H]**; guest beers**
Warm, friendly country pub with traditionally-beamed rooms complemented by a large, covered patio and a leisure garden with a rockery and ponds. Informal bistro-style dining, with innovative, sensibly-priced meals. Annual beer festival. ♨ Q ❀ ◖ ◗

Holmesfield

Traveller's Rest
Main Road ☎ (0742) 890446
12–4, 7–11
Home Bitter; Younger No. 3 [H]
Pleasant pub with pool in the tap room and a spacious, comfortable lounge. Live entertainment Thu and occasional Mons. ❀ ⊞ ▲ ♣

Holymoorside

Lamb Inn
Loads Road ☎ (0246) 556167
12–3 (not Mon–Thu), 7–11
Home Bitter; S&N Theakston XB [H]**; guest beers**
Unspoilt village inn offering a variety of guest beers and a warm welcome. Popular with locals. ♨ Q ❀ ♿ ♣ P

Horsley

Coach & Horses
47 Church Street
☎ (0332) 880581
11.30–2.30, 6–11
Banks's Mild; Marston's Bitter, Pedigree [H]
Popular village pub, smart and comfortable, with a conservatory and a children's garden play area. ❀ ◖ P

Ingleby

John Thompson Inn
☎ (0332) 862469
10.30–2.30, 7–11
Draught Bass; JTS XXX [H]
Pub opened in 1969 after conversion from a 15th-century farmhouse. The interior features a wealth of oak and displays a collection of paintings and antiques. Upmarket (motor cyclists not welcome). Brewery in the car park. ♨ ☋ ❀ ◖ ♿ ♣ P ⊬

Knockerdown

Knockerdown
On B5035 ☎ (0629) 85209
11–3, 7–11
Banks's Mild; Marston's Pedigree [H]
Isolated, friendly country pub. China hangs from the beams in both rooms. ♨ ◖ ◗ ♣ P

Langley Mill

Railway Tavern
Station Road ☎ (0773) 764711
11 (12 Mon)–4, 6 (7 Mon, Tue & Sat)–11
Home Mild, Bitter [E]
Busy and popular roadside pub. ❀ ◖ ⊞ ⇌ ♣ P

Little Longstone

Packhorse
Main Street ☎ (0629) 640471
11–3, 5 (6 Sat)–11
Marston's Bitter, Pedigree [H]
Ancient, unspoilt village local, a pub since 1787. The small, comfortable lounge has an adjoining intimate dining room (open Wed–Sat). The separate tap room is well used by ramblers and offers live folk music alternate Weds.
♨ Q ❀ ◖ ◗ ▲ ♣

Long Eaton

Hole in the Wall
Regent Street (off Market Place, near the Green)
☎ (0602) 734920
11–3, 6–11; 11–11 Mon, Fri & Sat
Draught Bass [H]**; guest beers**
Smart, two-roomed town pub with a narrow lounge and an off-sales hatch. The bar has Sky TV and pool. Pleasant garden with an aviary and skittle alley. ❀ ◖ ⊞ ♣ ⌓

Longshaw

Grouse
On B6054 ☎ (0433) 30423
12–3, 6–11
Vaux Double Maxim; Wards Sheffield Best Bitter, Kirby [H]
Originally built as a farmhouse in 1804 and the hayloft, barn doors and stone trough survive. A comfortable lounge at the front leads to a conservatory overhung with vines, and an adjoining tap room. No meals Mon or Tue.
♨ Q ❀ ◖ ◗ ⊞ ♣ P

Lullington

Colvile Arms
Coton Road ☎ (082 786) 212
12–3 (not Mon–Fri), 7–11
Draught Bass; Marston's Pedigree [H]
18th-century village pub: a basic, wood-panelled bar, a smart lounge, plus a function room. Bowling green.
♨ ❀ ♣ P

Makeney

Hollybush
Hollybush Lane OS352447
☎ (0332) 841729
12–3, 6–11; 11–11 Sat
Marston's Pedigree [H]**, Owd Rodger** [G]**; Ruddles County** [H]**; S&N Theakston Old Peculier** [G]**; guest beers**
Old pub with many rooms in a Grade II listed building. Beer is brought from the cellar in jugs. Very popular in summer.
♨ Q ☋ ❀ 🛏 ◖ ◗ ♣ P

Derbyshire

Marsh Lane

Fox & Hounds
Main Road ☎ (0246) 432974
12–3, 7 (6 summer)–11
Burtonwood Bitter, Forshaw's 🄷
Pub with a comfortable lounge and a traditional tap room; also a large beer garden and play area. Extensive menu.
Q ❀ ◗ ⊞ ♿ ♣ P

Matlock

Thorntree
48 Jackson Road (on hillside N of town, behind County Offices) ☎ (0629) 582923
11.30–3 (not Mon & Tue), 7–11
Draught Bass; Mansfield Old Baily 🄷
Small, unspoilt local off the beaten track, with a warm welcome and a fine atmosphere. No food Sun. Q ❀ ◖ ♣

Milton

Swan Inn
Main Street ☎ (0283) 703188
12–2.30, 7–11
Marston's Pedigree 🄷
Popular, friendly village pub with a smart lounge and a locals' bar. No food Sun eve or Mon. ♛ ◖ ◗ ⊞ ♣ P

New Mills

Crescent
Market Street ☎ (0663) 746053
11.30–3, 5.30–11; 11.30–11 Sat
Tetley Mild, Bitter 🄷**; guest beers**
Two-roomed pub with shop-front windows – a clue to its former use. A large lounge and a lively vault. The jukebox in the lounge can be intrusive.
❀ ◖ ◗ ≢ ♣

Newton Solney

Unicorn Inn
Repton Road (B5008)
☎ (0283) 703324
11.30–3, 5–11; 11.30–11 Fri & Sat
Draught Bass 🄷**; guest beers**
Busy village local with a bar created from the original separate rooms, but a small lounge and a meeting room also remain. Cosy. No food Sun. Q ❀ 🛏 ◖ ◗ ♿ ♣ P

Ockbrook

Royal Oak
Green Lane ☎ (0332) 662378
11.30–2.30, 7–11
Draught Bass 🄷
Characterful, village meeting place with four rooms. No food Sun. ♛ Q ❀ ◖ ♣ P

Old Whittington

Cock & Magpie
2 Church Street North
☎ (0246) 454453
11.30–3, 6 (7 Sat)–11
Mansfield Riding Bitter, Old Baily 🄷
Good village local next to the old Cock & Magpie (now a museum), where the plot to bring William of Orange to the throne was hatched. Walled garden. No food Sat or Sun eves, but excellent value other times. ❀ ◖ ◗ ⊞ ♿ ♣ ⌓ P

White Horse
High Street ☎ (0246) 450414
11.45–3, 5–11
Whitbread Boddingtons Mild, Bitter, Trophy, Castle Eden Ale 🄷**; guest beers**
Good village local with a large lounge, where excellent value food is served (no meals Sun eves). ❀ ◖ ◗ ⊞ ♿ ♣ P

Over Haddon

Lathkil Hotel
☎ (0629) 812501
11–2.30 (3 summer), 6–11
Wards Mild, Thorne Best Bitter, Sheffield Best Bitter 🄷
Free house in an idyllic setting: a fine, oak-panelled bar with leather and wood furnishings. Excellent food. Children welcome lunchtime.
♛ Q 🛏 ◖ ◗ ⊞ P

Ripley

Sitwell Arms
Wall Street ☎ (0773) 742747
11–3 (4 Sat), 7–11
Hardys & Hansons Best Mild, Best Bitter 🄷
Basic, friendly, two-roomed local. Pool in the back room, skittles in the yard. ❀ ♣

Rowarth

Little Mill Inn
Off Marple Bridge–Mellor–Hayfield road OS011889
☎ (0663) 743178
11–11
Banks's Bitter; Camerons Strongarm; Marston's Pedigree 🄷**; guest beers**
Busy, convivial pub serving good home-made food. A veritable adventure park for children. Up to three guest beers.
♛ Q ♞ ❀ 🛏 ◖ ◗ ▲ P

Rowsley

Grouse & Claret
Station Yard, Station Road
☎ (0629) 733233
11–11
Mansfield Riding Mild, Riding Bitter, Old Baily 🄷
Large, well-appointed pub. The emphasis is on traditional, home-cooked food. B&B, caravan and camping facilities. Family room only in summer.
♛ ♞ ❀ 🛏 ◖ ◗ ⊞ ♿ ▲ ♣ P ⊬

Scarcliffe

Horse & Groom
Mansfield Road (B6417)
☎ (0246) 823152
12–3, 7–11
Home Bitter; S&N Theakston XB 🄷
Beamed coaching inn with a play area. Good home cooking. ♛ ❀ ◖ ⊞ ♣ P

Shardlow

Canal Tavern
196 Shardlow Road
☎ (0332) 792844
11.30–3, 5–11, (11–11 summer)
Bateman Mild; Hoskins Beaumanor Bitter, Penn's Ale 🄷**; guest beers**
1780 warehouse converted into a busy canalside real ale pub, with an adjoining restaurant. Decorated with breweriana. Beer festivals. ❀ ◖ ◗ ♣ P

Malt Shovel
The Wharf (off A6 at Navigation pub) ☎ (0332) 799763
11–3, 5–11
Banks's Mild; Marston's Pedigree 🄷
Characterful, canalside tavern converted from an old maltings. Popular with the boating fraternity. Recently refurbished. ♛ Q ❀ ◖ ♣ P

Simmondley

Hare & Hounds
Simmondley Road
☎ (0457) 852028
12–3, 5.30–11; 12–11 Sat
Ind Coope Burton Ale; Tetley Walker Dark Mild, Bitter 🄷**; guest beers**
Former 19th-century textile mill with extensive views of Glossopdale. The landlord is a Burton Ale *Master Cellarman*. Beer festival in June.
❀ ◖ ◗ ♣ P ⊬

Somercotes

Horse & Jockey
Leabrooks Road
☎ (0773) 602179
11–3, 7–11
Home Mild, Bitter; S&N Theakston XB 🄷
Popular, multi-roomed, unspoilt local, worth a visit. Parking can be difficult. ❀

Stanton-by-Dale

Chequers
Dale Road
11–2.30 (3 Thu–Sat), 7–11
Draught Bass; M&B Mild [E]
Superb cottage-style pub of exceptional character, with a raised lounge area where an old water pump takes pride of place. Excellent lunches, all home made. No meals Sun.
Q ❀ ◖ ♿ ♣ P

Starkholmes

White Lion
195 Starkholmes Road (between Matlock Green and Cromford) ☎ (0629) 582511
12–2.30, 7–11
Home Bitter; S&N Theakston XB [H]
Olde-worlde pub with a low-beamed interior and views of Matlock Bath. Home-made traditional food (not served Sun–Tue lunch). Boules. ♘ ❀ ◖ ◗ ♿ ♣ P

Swanwick

Gate Inn
The Delves (E of A61, via the Green) ☎ (0773) 602039
11.30–3, 7–11
Courage Directors; Marston's Pedigree; John Smith's Bitter [H]
Smart, open-plan pub with a bar, a lounge and an eating area. Pool in the bar. ◖ ◗ ♣ P

Ticknall

Chequers
High Street ☎ (0332) 864392
12–2.30, 6–11
Marston's Pedigree; Ruddles Best Bitter, County [H]
Small, friendly, two-roomed local offering many games.
♨ Q ❀ ♣ P

Staff of Life
High Street ☎ (0332) 862479
11.30–2.30, 7 (6 Apr–Oct)–11
Marston's Pedigree, Owd Rodger; Moorhouse's Pendle Witches Brew; S&N Theakston XB, Old Peculier; Taylor Landlord [H]**; guest beers**
Food house with a real ale bar offering an excellent choice – at least ten guests. ❀ ◖ ◗ P

Tideswell

Anchor
Four Lane Ends (A623/B6049 jct) ☎ (0298) 871371
11–3 (may extend), 6–11
Robinson's Hartleys XB (summer), **Best Bitter** [H]
500-year-old pub on a crossroads: a traditional tap room with a dartboard, a spacious, oak-panelled lounge and a dining room.
♨ Q ❀ 🛏 ◖ ◗ ⊟ ▲ ♣ P

George
Commercial Road
☎ (0298) 871382
11–3, 7–11
Hardys & Hansons Best Mild, Best Bitter, Kimberley Classic [H]
Substantial, stone-built country hotel in the village centre: a comfortable lounge with a dining room, and a small snug leading to a tap room with pool.
♨ Q ❀ 🛏 ◖ ◗ ⊟ ▲ ♣ P

Unstone

Fleur de Lys Hotel
Main Road ☎ (0246) 412157
12–3 (not Mon–Thu), 5 (7 Sat)–11
S&N Theakston Best Bitter, XB, Old Peculier; Younger Scotch [H]
Conspicuous old coaching inn, standing on a wishing well. Live entertainment Thu and Sun eves. ♨ ❀ ◖ ♿ ♣ P

Wardlow Mires

Three Stags' Heads
At A623/B6465 jct
☎ (0298) 872268
7–11; 11–11 Sat, summer & bank hols
S&N Theakston Old Peculier; Springhead Bitter [H]**; guest beers**
Carefully restored, 17th-century farmhouse pub with two rooms. The bar is heated by an ancient range. Popular with hikers; dogs welcome.
♨ Q ❀ ◖ ◗ ▲ ♣ P

Weston-on-Trent

Coopers Arms
Weston Hall ☎ (0332) 690002
11–3, 6–11
Draught Bass [H]
Built in 1633, Weston Hall, visible for miles, was converted into a pub in 1991. Large fireplace in each room; well in the lounge. Virtually all the beams are original.
♨ Q ♘ ❀ ◖ ◗ P

Whaley Bridge

Shepherd's Arms
7 Old Road ☎ (0663) 732384
11.30–3, 7–11
Banks's Mild; Marston's Bitter, Pedigree [H]
Ageless local above the main street. The lounge is softly lit and quiet, in contrast to the excellent vault with its stone-flagged floor, unvarnished table, settles and stools.
♨ Q ❀ ⊟ ⇌ ♣ P

White Horse
1 Lower Macclesfield Road, Horwich End ☎ (0663) 732617
12–3 (not Wed), 5.30–11; 12–11 Sat
Whitbread Boddingtons Mild, Bitter [H]
Sociable, lounge-style Victorian pub in local stone, offering a relatively rare mild. Prominently placed on the old A6 and handy for the Goyt Valley leisure area. Look for the Timex!
❀ ◖ ◗ ⇌ ♣ P

Whitehough

Oddfellows Arms
Whitehead Lane
☎ (0663) 750306
12–3, 5–11 (12–11 summer)
Banks's Mild; Marston's Bitter, Pedigree [H]
Proper country pub, attracting a large cross-section of the community with its warm atmosphere. A fourth (Marston's) ale is available on rotation.
♨ Q ♘ ❀ ♣

Whitwell

Jug & Glass
Portland Street
☎ (0909) 720289
11–3, 6.30–11
John Smith's Bitter, Magnet [H]
Unspoilt, two-roomed stone local with a timber bar, doors and matching fireplace. A listed building at the centre of the old village, a genuine mining community. All welcome.
♨ ❀ ⊟ ♣ P

Woolley Moor

White Horse Inn
White Horse Lane (400 yds off B6014) ☎ (0246) 590319
11.30–2.30, 6.30–11
Bass Worthington BB, Draught Bass; M&B Highgate Mild [H]**; guest beers**
Pub almost legendary for its fine ale and food. Set in excellent walking country. Children's adventure playground. Inventive menu (no food Sun eve). Don't miss.
Q ❀ ◖ ◗ ⊟ ♣ P

Youlgreave

George Inn
Church Street ☎ (0629) 636292
11–2.30, 6.30–11
Home Mild, Bitter [H]
Large, lively local opposite one of the finest churches in the county. Historic Haddon Hall and Arbor Low are nearby.
♘ ❀ 🛏 ◖ ◗ ⊟ ♿ ▲ ♣

Devon

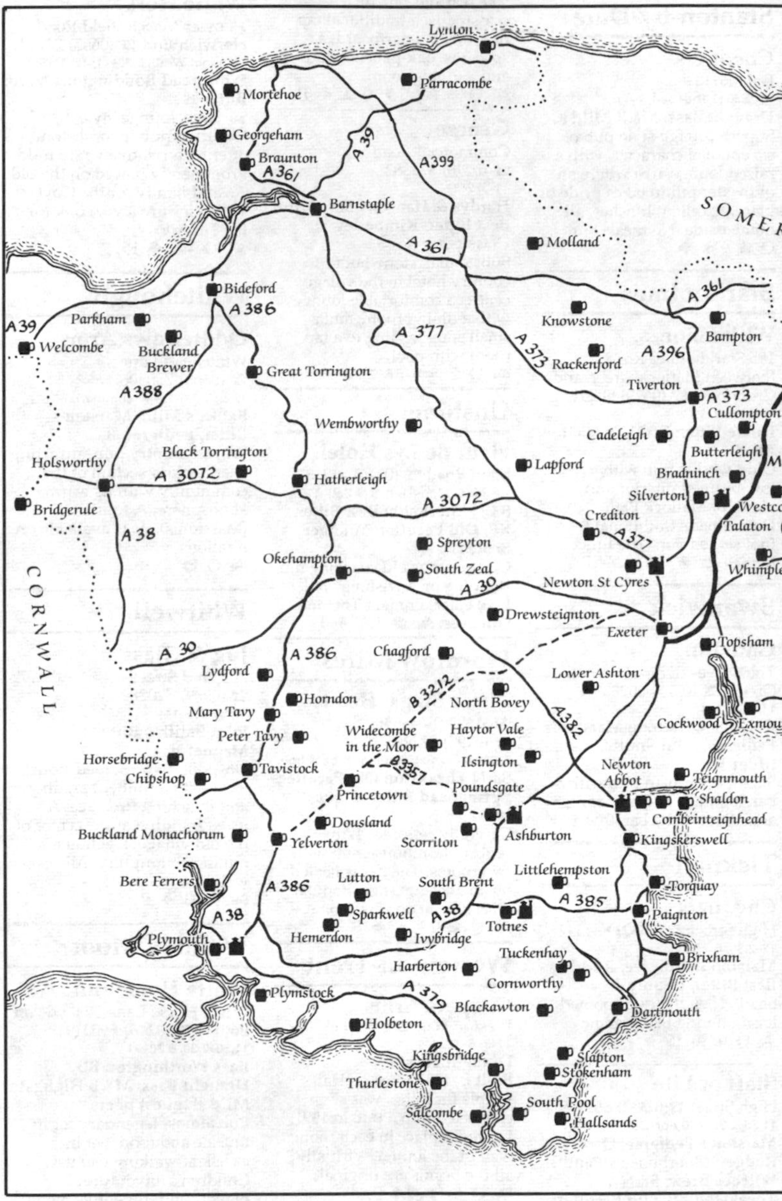

Beer Engine, *Newton St Cyres;* ***Blackawton,*** *Totnes;* ***Branscombe Vale,*** *Branscombe;* ***Exe Valley,*** *Silverton;* ***Mill,*** *Newton Abbot;* ***Otter,*** *Mathayes, Luppitt;* ***Summerskills,*** *Plymouth;* ***Thompson's,*** *Ashburton*

Ashburton

London Hotel

West Street ☎ (0364) 52478

11–2.30, 5.30–11

Thompson's Best Bitter, IPA, Botwrights, Figurehead Ⓗ; **guest beers** (occasionally)

Famous 15th-century inn, recently refurbished throughout, with two bars and a large restaurant. Thompson's brewery is situated to the rear and parties are welcome to tour. ♨ Q ⛟ ◐ ◑ P

Try also: Exeter Inn (Free)

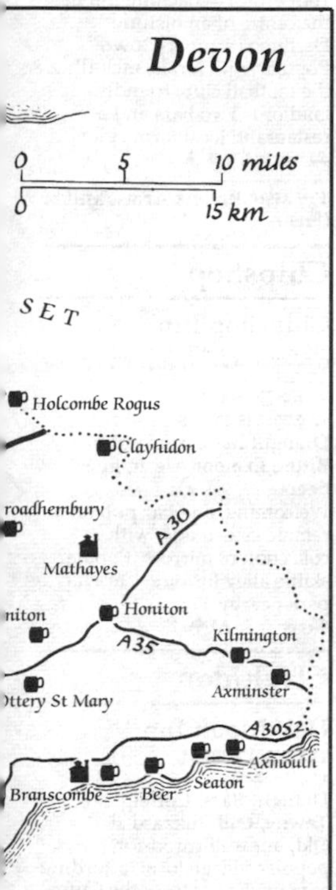

Axminster

Axminster Inn
Silver Street
☎ (0297) 34947
11–11
Palmers BB, IPA, Tally Ho! Ⓗ
Basic, town-centre pub with a wide range of facilities.
♨ ❀ 🛏 ◐ ⊞ ♿ ⇌ ♣ ♁ P

Millwey
Chard Road ☎ (0297) 32774
11–2.30, 7–11
Palmers BB, IPA Ⓗ
Modern pub on the edge of a housing estate, north of the centre. Lunches Tue–Sat.
⚇ ❀ ◐ ⊞ ♿ ♣ P

Axmouth

Ship Inn
☎ (0297) 21838
11.30–2 (11–2.30 summer), 6–11
Devenish Cornish Original; Whitbread Flowers Original Ⓗ
Well-known pub with an excellent menu served in a large dining room. Convalescent owls make unusual drinking companions. One of only two pubs in Devon to appear in every edition of the *Guide*. ♨ Q
⚇ ❀ ◐ ◑ ⊞ ♿ ▲ ♣ ♁ P

Try also: Harbour Inn (Free)

Bampton

Exeter Inn
Tiverton Road
☎ (0398) 331345
11–2.30, 6–11
Exmoor Ale; Freetraders Twelve Bore Bitter Ⓗ
Pub offering excellent value bar snacks. Good atmosphere.
♨ Q ⚇ ❀ 🛏 ◐ ◑ ⊞ ♿ ♣

Barnstaple

Barnstaple Inn
12 Trinity Street
☎ (0271) 43483
11–2.30 (4 Sat), 5 (7 Sat)–11; 11–11 Fri
Courage Best Bitter; John Smith's Bitter Ⓗ
Traditional, friendly town local in the Victorian part of Barnstaple, severed by new road schemes. Currently tenanted but under threat of an Inntrepreneur lease.
Q ⊞ ♣

Corner House
108 Boutport Street
☎ (0271) 43528
11–2.30, 5.30–11
Draught Bass Ⓗ; guest beers
Welcoming town alehouse retaining its 1930s wood-panelled interior and curved bar. An unspoilt pub appealing to discerning drinkers from all walks of life.
⚇ ♣

Rolle Quay
Across Rolle Bridge, N of centre ☎ (0271) 45182
11–11
Ruddles County; Ushers Best Bitter; guest beers Ⓗ
Established town pub next to the still working quay, just off the town centre.
❀ 🛏 ◐ ◑ ⊞ ♣

Beer

Anchor Hotel
Fore Street ☎ (0297) 20386
11–2.30, 5.30–11 (11–11 summer)
Furgusons Dartmoor Best Bitter, Strong (summer); Wadworth 6X Ⓗ
Hotel with three large bars overlooking the sea. ♨ Q
❀ 🛏 ◐ ◑ ⊞ ♿ ▲ ♣ P

Bere Ferrers

Old Plough
Signed from Bere Alston, off A386 ☎ (0822) 840358
12–3 (4 Sat), 7–11 (supper licence)
Draught Bass Ⓖ; Courage Best Bitter Ⓗ; Summerskills Best Bitter Ⓖ; Whitbread Boddingtons Bitter Ⓗ; guest beers
16th-century village inn by the River Tavy in an area of outstanding beauty. 1991 local *Seafood Pub of the Year*. Moorings for visitors; check tides first! Cider in summer.
♨ Q ❀ ◐ ◑ ♿ ⇌ ♣ ♁

Bideford

Joiners Arms
Market Place ☎ (0237) 472675
12–3, 7–11
Draught Bass Ⓖ; Fuller's London Pride; Furgusons Dartmoor Best Bitter Ⓗ
Lively local with a display of joiner's tools. At the bar is pictured the money the pub used to have minted to give in prize money. ♨ 🛏 ◐ ◑ ♣

Blackawton

Normandy Arms
1 mile from A3122
☎ (080 421) 316
12 (11 summer)–2.30, 7 (6 summer)–11
Draught Bass; Blackawton Bitter, Devon Gold, 44 Special; Ruddles Best Bitter Ⓗ
A pub since 1836, renamed in 1952 to commemorate the Normandy landings. Plenty of military memorabilia on the walls. Home of the International Worm Charming Festival (held in early May); Blackawton Wiggly X is specially brewed for the event.
♨ Q ⚇ ❀ 🛏 ◐ ◑ ▲ ♣ P

Black Torrington

Torridge Inn
Broad Street (off A3072)
☎ (0409) 23243
12–3, 6.30–11; 11–11 Sat
Courage Directors; Eldridge Pope Hardy Country, Blackdown Porter; Whitbread Boddingtons Bitter Ⓗ; guest beers

Devon

Large, L-shaped bar, with a small restaurant. Guest ales from independent breweries, plus Inch's cider. ⌂ Q
☺ ❀ ⛟ ◑ ◗ ▲ ♣ ⌓ P

Bradninch

Castle Inn
Fore Street ☎ (0392) 881378
12–3, 6–11
Furgusons Dartmoor Best Bitter; Ind Coope Burton Ale [H]
Old coaching house with a warm, friendly atmosphere and comfortable surroundings. Good value, home-cooked meals. The landlord is a member of the *Guild of Master Cellarmen*. ☺ ❀ ◑ ◗ P

Branscombe

Fountainhead
☎ (029 780) 511
11–2 (2.30 summer), 6.30–10.30 (11 summer)
Branscombe Vale Branoc, Olde Stoker; Hall & Woodhouse Badger Best Bitter [H]
Unpretentious, 14th-century pub, whose lounge bar was formerly the village blacksmith's and the central fireplace, the forge. ⌂ Q
❀ ⛟ ◑ ◗ ⊞ ♿ ▲ ♣ ⌓ P

Braunton

Mariners Arms
South Street ☎ (0271) 813160
11–3, 6–11
Exmoor Ale; Wadworth 6X; guest beer [H]
Busy, open-plan local. The L-shaped bar has a solid oak, rough-cut bar top. ❀ ◑ ◗ ♣

Bridgerule

Bridge Inn
☎ (028 881) 316
12–3, 6–11
Wadworth 6X; Whitbread Flowers IPA; guest beer [H]
Welcoming pub close to the Cornish border, popular throughout the year. Unusual guest beers. ⊞ ♣

Brixham

Blue Anchor
Fore Street ☎ (0803) 859373
11–11
Blackawton Headstrong; Furgusons Dartmoor Strong [H]
Historic, 16th-century, harbourside pub, where the food is very reasonable; look for the 'two for the price of one' offers (no food Sun). The building used to be a sail loft, which is evidenced by its nautical character. Live music twice weekly. Very popular with tourists. ⌂ Q ◑ ◗ ♣

Broadhembury

Drewe Arms
☎ (040 484) 267
11–2.30, 6–11
Draught Bass; Cotleigh Tawny; Otter Bitter; guest beers (occasionally) [G]
Largely unspoilt inn in a village of thatched, white-washed cottages. Well-behaved children admitted. Otter Ale and Head are sometimes among the guest beers. No food Sun eve.
⌂ Q ☺ ❀ ◑ ◗ ⊞ ▲ ♣ ⌓

Buckland Brewer

Coach & Horses
☎ (0237) 451395
11.30–2.30, 6–11
Wadworth 6X; Whitbread Flowers IPA, Original [H]
Old coaching inn at the village centre, with a low-beamed interior and a sloping floor. Friendly atmosphere.
⌂ ☺ ❀ ⛟ ◑ ◗ ⊞ ♣ P

Buckland Monachorum

Drake Manor Inn
The Village ☎ (0822) 853892
11.30–2.30, 6.30–11
Courage Best Bitter; John Smith's Bitter; Ushers Best Bitter, Founders [H]
Lively village pub with two bars and an eating area. Note the collection of tea and coffee cups in the lounge. Real cider in summer. Small car park.
⌂ Q ☺ ❀ ◑ ◗ ⊞ ♣ ⌓ P

Butterleigh

Butterleigh Inn
☎ (0884) 855407
12–2.30, 6 (5 Fri)–11; 12–2.30, 7–10.30 Sun
Cotleigh Harrier, Tawny, Old Buzzard [H]; guest beers (occasionally)
Popular village inn featuring a stained-glass porch. Good food.
⌂ Q ❀ ⛟ ◑ ◗ ⊞ ♿ ♣ P

Cadeleigh

Cadeleigh Arms
2 miles W of Bickleigh
☎ (0884) 855238
11–11
Draught Bass; Butcombe Bitter; Cotleigh Harrier; Tawny, Old Buzzard [H]
Country pub with a warm, friendly atmosphere and wonderful views across the Exe and Dart valleys.
☺ ❀ ◑ ◗ ♿ ▲ ♣ ⌓ P

Chagford

Globe Inn
High Street ☎ (0647) 433485
11–3, 6 (7 winter)–11
Draught Bass [H]**; guest beers**
16th-century coaching inn in the centre of an historic Dartmoor stannery town. Popular with locals, including the football club; friendly landlord. Two bars and a restaurant; local farm cider.
⌂ ❀ ⛟ ◑ ◗ ▲ ⌓

Try also: Bullers Arms, Mill St (Free)

Chipshop

Chipshop Inn
2½ miles off A384, W of Tavistock OS437751
☎ (0822) 832322
12–2.30, 7 (6.30 Fri & Sat)–11
Draught Bass; Butcombe Bitter; Exmoor Ale [H]**; guest beers**
Welcoming, one-bar pub on a remote crossroads, with a collection of mirrors. Popular skittle alley for hire. Caravan park nearby.
⌂ ❀ ◑ ◗ ▲ ♣ P

Clayhidon

Half Moon Inn
☎ (0823) 680291
12–2.30, 7–11
Draught Bass; Cotleigh Tawny, Old Buzzard [H]
Old, but well-cared-for, popular village local, affording superb views across the Culm valley. ⌂ Q ☺ ❀ ◑ ◗ ♿ ▲
♣ ⌓ P

Cockwood

Anchor
Between Dawlish Warren and Starcross ☎ (0626) 890203
11–2.30 (3 Fri, 4 Sat), 6–11
Draught Bass [G]**; Eldridge Pope Hardy Country; Marston's Pedigree; Whitbread Boddingtons Bitter, Porter** [H]
Small, cosy, unspoilt pub by the old harbour. One room is split into three distinct areas by wooden screens. Popular with tourists but a real gem out of season. Famous for its seafood.
⌂ Q ❀ ◑ ◗ ♣ ⌓ P

Combeinteignhead

Wild Goose Inn
On B3195 ☎ (0626) 872241
11.30–2.30, 6.30–11
Exe Valley Dob's Best Bitter; Mill Janner's Ale; Wadworth 6X; guest beers [H]
17th-century inn, set in a picturesque village, with always a good range of West Country ales and malt whiskies. Popular with locals and tourists, providing an extensive menu, including vegetarian dishes. Trad. jazz Mon. ⌂ Q ❀ ◑ ◗ ▲ ♣ P

Cornworthy

Hunters Lodge Inn
☎ (0803) 732204
11.30–3, 6.30–11
Blackawton 44 Special; Ushers Best Bitter [H]
Popular pub with a genial host, German shepherd dog and magnificent food in the bar or restaurant. ❀ ◖ ◗ ♣ P

Crediton

Crediton Inn
Mill Street ☎ (0363) 772882
11–11
Draught Bass [H]**; guest beers**
Lively local, dating from 1852, with a function room-cum-skittle alley. ♉ ◖ ◗ ⇌ ♣

Exchange
High Street ☎ (0363) 775853
11–11
Courage Best Bitter, Directors; Webster's Yorkshire Bitter [H]
Comfortable one-bar pub with a steak and wine bar in the cellar. Function room. ❀ ◖ ◗

Cullompton

Manor House
Fore Street ☎ (0884) 32281
11–11
Draught Bass; Eldridge Pope Hardy Country [H]
16th-century, town-centre hotel serving good food.
⛰ ♉ ❀ 🛏 ◖ ◗ ♿ ♣ P

Dartmouth

Cherub Inn
Higher Street ☎ (0803) 832571
11–3, 5–11
Blackawton Bitter; Wadworth 6X; Whitbread Flowers Original [H]
Dartmouth's oldest building, dating from 1380 and Grade I-listed. Named after a type of boat built locally for carrying wool. Flora dominates the frontage. Q ❀ ◖ ◗ ⌓

Dousland

Burrator Inn
☎ (0822) 853121
11–11
Bass Worthington BB, Draught Bass; St Austell HSD; Wadworth 6X [H]**; guest beers**
Former Victorian hotel in Dartmoor National Park, near the Burrator reservoir. Ideal for walkers. Large garden and play area. Food all day.
⛰ ♉ ❀ 🛏 ◖ ◗ ♿ ▲ ♣ P

Drewsteignton

Drewe Arms
The Square ☎ (0647) 21224
11–2.30, 6–11; 12–2, 7–10.30 Sun
Whitbread Flowers IPA [G]
Thatched pub untouched for 100 years, with the country's oldest and longest serving landlady. Close to Fingle Bridge and Castle Drogo. In every edition of this guide.
⛰ Q ♉ ❀ ⊞ ♣ ⌓ P

Exeter

Double Locks
Canal Banks OS933900
☎ (0392) 56947
11–11
Greene King Abbot [H]**; Eldridge Pope Royal Oak** [G]**; Everards Old Original** [H]**; Exe Valley Dob's Best Bitter; Wadworth 6X** [G]**; guest beers**
Remote but very popular pub on the edge of Exeter, with a large garden on the banks of Exeter Canal. Good value food; large variety of games.
⛰ ♉ ❀ ◖ ◗ ♿ ▲ ♣ ⌓ P

Exeter & Devon Arts Centre
Bradninch Place, Gandy Street
☎ (0392) 219741
12–2.30, 5–11; closed Sun
Branscombe Vale Branoc; Furgusons Dartmoor Best Bitter; Wadworth 6X [H]**; guest beers**
Small bar in an arts/community centre. Excellent lunches (including vegetarian). Frequent live music and other events in the theatre bar.
◖ ♿ ⇌ (Central) ⊬

Great Western Hotel
Station Approach
☎ (0392) 74039
11–3, 5–11; 11–11 Sat
Bass Worthington BB, Draught Bass; Exe Valley Devon Glory [H]
Smart pub/hotel bar outside the station; good food and a pleasant atmosphere.
🛏 ◖ ◗ ⇌ (St Davids)

Hole in the Wall
Little Castle Street
☎ (0392) 73341
11–3, 6–11; closed Sun
Eldridge Pope Hardy Country, Royal Oak [H]
Oak-panelled and beamed bars above a wine library/shop. Boasts a collection of farm implements and pressure gauges. Quiz Mon; pool in the games bar. ◖ ⇌ (Central) ♣

Jolly Porter
St Davids Hill ☎ (0392) 54848
11–11
Courage Best Bitter, Directors; John Smith's Bitter; Wadworth 6X [H]**; guest beers**
Friendly pub with three drinking areas. Popular with students, locals and passing trade. ◖ ◗ ⇌ (St Davids)

North Bridge
St Davids Hill ☎ (0392) 56296
4 (3 Fri, 12 Sat)–11
Draught Bass; Furgusons Dartmoor Best Bitter; Ind Coope Burton Ale [H]
Friendly but basic pub close to the city centre. Possibly the first in Exeter to introduce over-sized glasses. ⇌ (St Davids/Central) ♣

On the Waterfront
6–10 Southern Warehouses, The Quay ☎ (0392) 210590
12–2.30, 5.30–11 (may be 12–11 Mon–Fri in summer)
Courage Best Bitter, Directors; John Smith's Bitter [H]
Excellent pub/restaurant serving superb pizzas (arrive hungry as they are enormous). Very popular, and handy for the Maritime Museum. Gets loud in the eve.
❀ ◖ ◗ ♿ ⇌ (St Thomas)

Royal Oak
Fore Street, Heavitree (B3183, 1 mile from centre)
☎ (0392) 54121
11–3 (extends in summer), 5.30–11
Draught Bass; Marston's Pedigree; Whitbread Flowers IPA [H]**; guest beer** (occasionally)
Thatched pub, formerly a forge, in an Exeter suburb. An abundance of artefacts decorates the walls and ceiling; spot the cell door from Dartmoor Prison. Generous-portioned, hot snacks at lunchtime (not served Sun) as well as meals. ♉ ❀ ◖ ♣ P

Well House
Cathedral Close
☎ (0392) 58464
11–2.30, 5–11 (closed when Exeter City FC are at home)
Beer range varies [H]
Popular bar attached to the Royal Clarence hotel. Good value lunches and a constantly changing range of six beers.
◖ ⇌ (Central)

Try also: Prospect, The Quay (Free); **Vines**, Gandy St (Free)

Exmouth

Country House Inn
176 Withycombe Village Road
☎ (0395) 263444
11–2.30 (3.45 Sat), 5–11
Devenish Royal Wessex [H]**; Marston's Pedigree; Wadworth 6X** [E]
Lively village-type pub, formerly a blacksmith's; now comfortably furnished, with an enormous garden and aviary to the rear. Excellent food (weekday lunchtimes and Sat night); barbecues in summer.
Q ❀ ◖ ♿ ▲ ♣ ⌓ P

Grove
The Esplanade
☎ (0395) 272101
11–3, 5.30–11 (11–11 May–Sept)

Devon

Brakspear Special; Exe Valley Devon Glory; Greene King Abbot; Wadworth 6X; Whitbread Boddingtons Bitter [H]
Spacious, well-appointed seafront pub with a continuously changing beer menu and monthly beer nights (nine beers) in winter. Good food; large garden; live music.
❀ ◖◗ ♿ ⇌ P

Feniton

Nog Inn
Ottery Road ☎ (0404) 850210
11–2.30, 6–11
Cotleigh Tawny; Otter Ale [H]**; guest beers**
Lively village pub with a squash court and a possessive cat. Regular guest ales from a wide range of breweries.
♛ ♉ ❀ 🛏 ⊞ ♿ ⇌ ♣ P

Georgeham

Rock Inn
Rock Hill (just off B3231)
☎ (0271) 890322
11–3, 5–11; 11–11 Fri, Sat & summer
Fuller's ESB; Marston's Pedigree; Ruddles Best Bitter, County; Tetley Bitter; Ushers Best Bitter [H]
Unspoilt village pub offering good food and a range of traditional games. Pleasant rear garden. Believed to be the only pub in North Devon serving six real ales all year round, plus cider in summer.
♛ ❀ 🛏 ◖◗ ♣ ⌓ P

Great Torrington

Black Horse Inn
High Street ☎ (0805) 22121
11–3, 6–11
Courage Directors; John Smith's Bitter; Ushers Best Bitter; Wadworth 6X [H]**; guest beer**
By far the oldest and most attractive inn in town (circa 12th century). The base of General Halifax during the Civil War battle of Torrington.
♛ ♉ 🛏 ◖◗ ▲ ♣

Hallsands

Hallsands Hotel
3 miles S of Stokenham
OS818387 ☎ (054 851) 264
11–11
Draught Bass [H]/[G]**; guest beer** (summer)
Isolated coaching inn of character, on the Devon South Coast path; built in 1906 to replace an inn washed into the sea in 1903. A diving hotel with boat hire, air and a resident auxiliary coastguard/diver. Impressive sea views; the patio is on a low cliff edge. Stancombe cider in summer.
♛ ♉ ❀ 🛏 ◖◗ ♣ ⌓ P

Harberton

Church House Inn
☎ (0803) 863707
12–2.30, 6–11
Draught Bass; Courage Best Bitter; guest beers [H]
13th-century pub with an enormous, heavily-beamed lounge and a listed wooden screen. The family room has a highchair. Good food.
♛ Q ♉ ❀ ◖◗ ⌓

Hatherleigh

Tally Ho Country Inn
Market Street ☎ (0837) 810306
11–3, 6–11
Tally Ho Mild, Potboiler's Brew, Tarka Tipple, Nutters, Janni Jollop [H]
Friendly inn with its own brewery at the rear, two fires and a great atmosphere. The small, intimate restaurant offers a large, mostly Italian, menu; barbecues in summer. Thurgia, a bottle-conditioned beer, is also available occasionally on draught.
♛ ❀ 🛏 ◖◗ ♣ P

Haytor Vale

Rock Inn
Near Haytor Rocks
☎ (0364) 661305
11–2.30, 6.30–11
Draught Bass; Eldridge Pope Dorchester, Hardy Country, Royal Oak [H]
200-year-old coaching inn inside Dartmoor National Park, offering excellent food and accommodation.
♛ Q ❀ 🛏 ◖◗ ▲ ⊬

Hemerdon

Miners Arms
On Plympton–Cornwood road
☎ (0752) 343252
11–2.30 (3 Sat), 5.30–11
Draught Bass [H]/[G]**; Ruddles County** [H]**; Ushers Best Bitter; Whitbread Boddingtons Bitter** [H]
Former tin miners' pub on the edge of Dartmoor, near a derelict mine and workings, on a hill overlooking the outskirts of Plymouth. Children's garden play equipment.
♛ Q ♉ ❀ ♿ ♣ P

Holbeton

Dartmoor Union
Fore Street (2½ miles off A379)
☎ (075 530) 288
11.30–3, 6–11
Draught Bass; Summerskills Best Bitter [H]
Ancient former workhouse which celebrated its 200th year as a pub in 1993. Noted for its food.
♛ Q ♉ ❀ ◖◗ ▲ ⌓ P

Holcombe Rogus

Prince of Wales
☎ (0823) 672070
12–3, 7–11
Draught Bass; Cotleigh Harrier, Tawny, Old Buzzard [H]**; guest beers**
Pleasant country pub with interesting cash register handpumps. Good food.
♛ Q ♉ ❀ ◖◗ ▲ ♣ P

Holsworthy

Golden Fleece
Bodmin Street
☎ (0409) 253263
11–11
St Austell Tinners [H]
Well-renovated pub with a welcoming atmosphere. Its exposed beams, panelling and slate floor offer a relaxing environment. Q ◖◗ ⊞

Kings Arms
The Square ☎ (0409) 253517
11–11
Draught Bass; Furgusons Dartmoor Best Bitter [H]
Popular Victorian hostelry in the centre of this attractive market town; friendly atmosphere. Splendid stained-glass windows; welcoming snug. ♛ Q ◖◗ ⊞ ♣

Honiton

Red Cow
High Street ☎ (0404) 47497
11–3, 6–11
Bass Worthington BB; Otter Ale; Ruddles County; John Smith's Bitter [H]
Cosy town pub with a friendly atmosphere.
♛ ❀ 🛏 ◖ ⇌ ♣

Vine Inn
Vine Passage ☎ (0404) 42889
11–2.30, 6–11
Otter Ale [H]
Town local with keen skittles, darts and crib teams.
♛ Q ❀ ⇌ ♣

Horndon

Elephant's Nest
1¾ miles off A386 at Mary Tavy ☎ (0822) 810273
11.30–2.30, 6.30–11
Palmers IPA; St Austell HSD; Whitbread Boddingtons Bitter [H]**; guest beers**
Popular, 16th-century moorland pub offering an extensive menu. Apparently named after the size of a previous landlord! Cider varies. ♛ Q ♉ ❀ 🛏 ◖◗ ▲ ♣ ⌓ P

Horsebridge

Royal Inn
OS750400 ☎ (0822) 87214
12–2.30, 7–11; 12–2.30, 7–10.30 Sun
Draught Bass; Horsebridge Best, Tamar, Heller; Marston's Pedigree Ⓗ
15th-century brew pub, sympathetically converted from a nunnery into two bars. Very isolated, it stands near an old bridge over the River Tamar. Occasional special brews. 🔥 Q ❀ ◖◗ ♿ ♣ P

Ilsington

Carpenters Arms
☎ (0364) 661215
11–2.30, 6–11
Whitbread Flowers IPA Ⓖ
Timeless, one-bar village local run by a very experienced couple. Popular with darts and card players. 🔥 ❀ ◖◗ ♣ 🍎

Ivybridge

Imperial
Western Road ☎ (0752) 892269
11–3, 5.30–11; 11–11 Fri, Sat & summer
Courage Best Bitter; Ruddles Best Bitter; Wadworth 6X; guest beers Ⓗ
Friendly atmosphere in a pub with a large open fire. High quality food and a wide range of guest beers, including local breweries. Summer barbecues. 🔥 👶 ❀ ◖◗ ♿ ▲ ♣ 🍎 P

Kilmington

New Inn
The Hill (signed off A35)
☎ (0297) 33376
10.30–11 (11–3, 7–11 winter)
Palmers BB, IPA Ⓗ
Superb, quiet village pub with fine views from the garden. Q 👶 ❀ ◖◗ ⊞ ♿ ▲ ♣ P

Kingsbridge

Ship & Plough
The Promenade
☎ (0548) 852485
11–11
Draught Bass; Blewitt's Best Bitter; Whitbread Flowers Original Ⓗ
Oak beams, open fires and stone walls in a pub with its own brewery. Occasional live music. Home-cooked food in the bar and restaurant, which includes a pizza bar. Occasional mini-beer festivals. 🔥 👶 ❀ 🛏 ◖◗ ▲ ♣

Kingskerswell

Bickley Mill Inn
Stoneycombe ☎ (0803) 873201
11–2.30, 6–11
Draught Bass; Greene King IPA; Wadworth 6X Ⓗ
Large free house converted from a 13th-century mill in 1971, enjoying an attractive situation in the Stoneycombe valley. 🔥 👶 ❀ 🛏 ◖◗ P ⊬

Knowstone

Masons Arms
☎ (039 84) 231
11–3, 7–11
Cotleigh Tawny; Hall & Woodhouse Badger Best Bitter Ⓖ
Charming, 16th-century, Grade II-listed building on the edge of Exmoor and the Two Moors Way. Thatched roof, rendered walls and a superb, unspoilt interior with an impressive open fireplace provide a welcoming atmosphere. North Devon CAMRA *Pub of the Year* 1993. Occasional ciders. 🔥 Q 👶 ❀ 🛏 ◖◗ ⊞ ▲ ♣ 🍎 P

Lapford

Old Malt Scoop
☎ (0363) 83330
11.30–2.30, 6–11
Adnams Broadside Ⓖ**; Butcombe Bitter; Hook Norton Best Bitter** Ⓗ**; Wadworth 6X** Ⓖ
Superb, friendly village pub with many rooms, including a 'kitchen bar' with an inglenook. 🔥 Q 👶 ❀ 🛏 ◖◗ ⊞ ♿ ▲ ⇌ ♣ 🍎 P

Littlehempston

Tally Ho!
Off A381 ☎ (0803) 862316
11–2.30 (3 summer), 6–11
Draught Bass; Furgusons Dartmoor Best Bitter Ⓗ
14th-century inn situated in a quiet village, but very close to the main line railway, with an open, low-beamed interior. Popular with locals and tourists, mainly for its good, varied menu.
🔥 Q ❀ ◖◗ ▲ P

Lower Ashton

Manor Inn
Off B3193 ☎ (0647) 52304
12–2.30, 6–11; closed Mon
Draught Bass; Cotleigh Tawny; Wadworth 6X Ⓗ**; guest beers**
Small, friendly local with a reputation for good, home-cooked food. A 19th-century pub with little alteration. Constantly changing guest ales. 🔥 Q ❀ ◖◗ ▲

Try also: **Royal Oak**, Dunsford (Free)

Lutton

Mountain Inn
Off A38 at Plympton
☎ (0752) 537247
11–3, 6 (7 Mon–Wed in winter)–11
Furgusons Dartmoor Best Bitter; Ind Coope Burton Ale; Summerskills Best Bitter; Wadworth 6X Ⓗ**; guest beers**
Exposed cob walls and a large granite fireplace make this pub worth visiting. Families very welcome. Burton Ale is sold as Mountain Ale; 'Mountain' is a corruption of Montain, the local land owners centuries ago. Cider in summer; large hot rolls all year.
🔥 Q 👶 ❀ ◖◗ ▲ ♣ 🍎 P

Lydford

Castle Inn
On B3278 ☎ (082 282) 242
11.30–3, 6–11
Draught Bass; Furgusons Dartmoor Best Bitter; Palmers IPA Ⓗ**; guest beers**
16th-century inn near the castle, with a pleasant, welcoming atmosphere: low-beamed ceilings, slate floors and large stone fireplaces. 🔥 Q 👶 ❀ 🛏 ◖◗ ⊞ ♿ ▲ ♣ P ⊬

Lynton

Royal Castle Hotel
Castle Hill ☎ (0598) 52348
11–3, 6.30 (6 summer)–11
Butcombe Bitter; Exmoor Ale (summer)**; Tetley Bitter** Ⓗ
Elegant clifftop hotel with spectacular views along the coast and across the Bristol Channel. The historic building was badly damaged by fire some years ago, but has been well restored. Q ❀ 🛏 ◖◗ P

Mary Tavy

Mary Tavy Inn
Lane Head (A386)
☎ (0822) 810326
11.30 (11 summer)–3, 6–11
Draught Bass; St Austell Tinners, HSD Ⓗ
Charming, 16th-century inn on the western edge of Dartmoor. Good value, home-cooked food.
🔥 👶 ❀ 🛏 ◖◗ ▲ ♣ P

Molland

Black Cock
Off A361, 2 miles S of Molland
☎ (0769) 550297
11–2.30, 5.30–11
Cotleigh Harrier, Tawny Ⓗ**; guest beer** (summer)
Pub in attractive countryside south of Exmoor, with camping facilities opposite. The interior has been opened up. Well signposted.
🔥 👶 ❀ 🛏 ◖◗ ▲ 🍎 P

Devon

London Inn

☎ (0769) 550269
11–2.30, 7–11
Draught Bass; Whitbread Flowers IPA [G]
Cosy, 18th-century, Grade II-listed building, nestling at the foot of the Exmoor National Park; recently renovated. The adjacent church is worth visiting. Q P

Mortehoe

Ship Aground

The Square ☎ (0271) 870856
11–3, 5.30–11 (may vary in summer)
Butcombe Bitter; Whitbread Boddingtons Bitter; guest beer [H]
Attractive pub converted from old cottages, next to the village church. Handy for coastal walks and golden beaches. The beer range varies; cider in summer. Busy in the season.

Newton Abbot

Dartmouth Inn

East Street (opp. hospital)
☎ (0626) 53451
11–11
Draught Bass [H]; guest beers
Probably the oldest pub in Newton Abbot, retaining its period character. South Devon CAMRA *Pub of the Year* 1992. The wide range of guest beers from all over the country changes daily. No food Sun. Occasional oriental food served.

Newton St Cyres

Beer Engine

By station, off A377
☎ (0392) 851282
11.30–2.30, 6–11 (8–midnight downstairs Fri & Sat); 11–11 Sat & bank hols
Beer Engine Rail Ale, Piston, Sleeper [H]
Comfortable, friendly pub/ brewery with good food. Live music in the Boiler Room bar downstairs Fri and Sat nights. Q P

North Bovey

Ring of Bells

Between Manaton and Moretonhampstead OS741839
☎ (0647) 40375
11–3, 6–11
Furgusons Dartmoor Best Bitter; Ind Coope Burton Ale; Wadworth 6X [H]; guest beer
Rambling, low-beamed pub in an attractive Dartmoor village. May have been built originally to house masons building the nearby church. Good food. Luscombes cider in summer. Q P

Okehampton

Plume of Feathers Hotel

Fore Street ☎ (0837) 52815
10.30–3.30, 6.30–11
Courage Best Bitter, Directors [H]; guest beers
Large town pub with two bars, a former coaching inn displaying archive pictures of old stables. Situated on the edge of Dartmoor and ideal for day trips. Frequent independent south-western guest beers. P

Ottery St Mary

London

Gold Street ☎ (0404) 814763
10.30–2, 5.30–11
Draught Bass [H]; guest beer
18th-century coaching house with oak beams and horse brasses. Olde-worlde restaurant; skittle alley and a pool room. Q P

Paignton

Polsham Arms

35 Lower Polsham Road
☎ (0803) 558360
11–11
Whitbread Boddingtons Bitter; guest beers [H]
Two-bar pub with a friendly atmosphere, near the seafront. Regular mini-beer festivals and live entertainment. Q P

Parkham

Bell Inn

1 mile S of A39
☎ (0237) 451201
11–3, 6–11 (12–2.30, 7–11 winter)
Draught Bass [G]; Whitbread Flowers IPA [H]; guest beers (summer)
Delightful thatched inn at the edge of a thriving village. The low-beamed interior has a grandfather clock set into the wall. Q P

Parracombe

Hunters Inn

Heddons Mouth (signed off A39 and A399, not in Parracombe village) OS655482
☎ (059 83) 230
11–2.30, 7–11 (11–11 summer)
Ind Coope Burton Ale; Wadworth 6X; Whitbread Flowers Original [H]; guest beers (summer)
Edwardian country house hotel, set in a wooded valley on the edge of Exmoor, close to spectacular coastal walks. Peacocks patrol the balconies. Family room and Hancocks cider, both in summer only. P

Peter Tavy

Peter Tavy Inn

Off A386 ☎ (0822) 810348
11.30–2.30 (3 Sat), 6.30–11
Furgusons Dartmoor Strong; Summerskills Whistle Belly Vengeance; Whitbread Fremlins Bitter [H]; guest beers
Ancient moorland pub with low ceilings and flagstoned floors. Access to the garden is via steps from the car park: not suitable for small children. Q P

Plymouth

China House

Sutton Wharf (off Sutton Rd)
☎ (0752) 260930
11.30–3, 5–11
Furgusons Dartmoor Best Bitter, Dartmoor Strong; Wadworth 6X [H]
A gem of a pub, well worth finding, built within the shell of an old china warehouse. Occasional live music. Great view over the Barbican. P

Clifton

35 Clifton Street
☎ (0752) 266563
11.30–3, 7–11
Draught Bass; Furgusons Dartmoor Strong; Summerskills Best Bitter [H], Ninjabeer [G]; Tetley Bitter [H]; guest beers
Warm, friendly atmosphere in a pub fielding numerous teams. Ignore the large wall clock, it's never right. Guest beers unusual to Plymouth.

Dolphin Hotel

The Barbican ☎ (0752) 660876
10–11
Draught Bass [G]; guest beer (very occasionally)
Historic pub on the Barbican, used by local fishermen and serious drinkers. The Tolpuddle Martyrs stayed here on their first night back from Australia. 100 yards from the Mayflower memorial, the Pilgrim Fathers' departure point for North America.

Fishermans Arms

31 Lambhay Street, Barbican
☎ (0752) 661457
11–11
St Austell HSD [H]
200-year-old Barbican local, with a friendly atmosphere; families welcome. Look for the unusual electric weather vane.

Little Mutton Monster
240 James Street, Mutton Cove, Devonport
☎ (0752) 560938
11.30–3, 6–11
Draught Bass; Fuller's London Pride; Marston's Pedigree; Morland Old Speckled Hen [H]; guest beers
Large, 200-year-old, one-bar pub adjoining the dockyard, displaying a large collection of rugby programmes. Good value food. Q ❀ ◐◑ ♣ P

London Inn
8 Church Road, Plympton St Maurice ☎ (0752) 337025
12–2.30 (11–3 May–Dec), 7–11
Courage Best Bitter; Ruddles County; John Smith's Bitter [H]; guest beers
17th-century coaching pub, reputed to be haunted by Roundheads and Cavaliers who died here after a local Civil War battle. The lounge has not been altered since 1945. Large collection of ships' crests. ⛼ ◐ ⊟ ▲ ♣ P

Prince Maurice
3 Church Hill, Eggbuckland (off B3413) ☎ (0752) 771515
11–3, 7–11; 11–11 Sat
Draught Bass; Courage Best Bitter; St Austell XXXX Mild, HSD; S&N Theakston Old Peculier; Wadworth 6X [H]; guest beer
Excellent, friendly pub, named after the nephew of Charles I, who stayed locally whilst commanding the Royalist troops during the Civil War. Parts of the pub date from the 16th century. ⛼ ❀ ♣ P

Pym Arms
16 Pym Street, Devonport
☎ (0752) 561823
11–3, 6–11
Draught Bass; Charrington IPA; St Austell XXXX Mild, HSD; Wadworth 6X; guest beers [H]/[G]
Friendly, side-street pub near the dockyard, frequented by students. ≠ (Devonport) ♣ ⌓

Royal Albert Bridge Inn
930 Wolseley Road, St Budeaux ☎ (0752) 361108
11–11
Draught Bass; Courage Best Bitter [H]
Friendly, riverside local in the shadow of Brunel's bridge, with picturesque views across the River Tamar to Cornwall. Opposite stands a monument to the American troops who left from the slipway for the D-Day landings. ❀ ◐◑ ♣

Shipwrights Arms
13 Sutton Road, Coxside (off A374) ☎ (0752) 665804
11–3, 6–11
Courage Best Bitter, Directors [H]
Convivial, one-bar pub near the city centre, Sutton Harbour and the yacht marina. Piano sing-along Sat eve. No food Sun. ⛼ ❀ ◐ ♿ ♣ P

Stopford Arms
172 Devonport Road, Stoke
☎ (0752) 562195
11–2.30 (3 Sat), 6–11
Courage Best Bitter [H]; guest beers
Clean, smart, traditional, two-bar local. The best Courage outlet in the area. Q ◐ ≠ (Devonport) ♣

Thistle Park Tavern
32 Commercial Road, Coxside
☎ (0752) 667677
11–11
Eldridge Pope Royal Oak; Greene King Abbot; Ruddles County; St Austell HSD; Summerskills Best Bitter [H]; guest beers
Warm, friendly atmosphere in a pub which holds two regular beer festivals – May Day weekend and the last weekend of Oct. Plans to brew its own beer. ⛼ ♿ ♣

Unity
50 Eastlake Street
☎ (0752) 262622
11–11
Furgusons Dartmoor Best Bitter; Ind Coope Burton Ale [H]
Good pub, ideally placed for shoppers. Friendly staff. ◐

Plymstock

Boringdon Arms
Boringdon Terrace, Turnchapel ☎ (0752) 402053
11–3, 5.30–11; 11–11 Fri, Sat & summer
Draught Bass; Butcombe Bitter; Fuller's London Pride; St Austell HSD; Summerskills Whistle Belly Vengeance, Ninjabeer [H]; guest beers
Friendly, two-bar local, an ex-quarrymaster's house with many artefacts on display. Features a conservatory, a beer garden in the old quarry, and accommodation with sea views. Regular beer festivals. ⛼ ♘ ❀ 🛏 ◐◑ ▲ ♣

Poundsgate

Tavistock Inn
On Ashburton–Dartmeet road
☎ (036 43) 251
11.30–2.30, 6–10.30 (11 Fri & Sat) (11–3, 6–11 summer)
Courage Best Bitter; Ushers Best Bitter [H]
700-year-old unspoilt pub in a small Dartmoor village, with a cosy, rugged front bar. ⛼ Q ♘ ❀ ◐◑ ⌓ P

Princetown

Plume of Feathers
☎ (082 289) 240
11–11
Bass Worthington BB, Draught Bass; St Austell HSD [H]
Reputedly Princetown's oldest building: slate floors, exposed beams, granite walls. Has its own camping site and an adventure play area for children. Used by walkers, and near the prison. ⛼ ♘ ❀ 🛏 ◐◑ ♿ ▲ ♣ ⌓ P

Rackenford

Stag Inn
1 mile S of A361(T)
☎ (088 488) 369
12–2.30, 6–11
Cotleigh Tawny [H]; guest beer (summer)
Inn dating back to 1237, with a thatched roof, cob walls and an unusual cobbled tunnel entrance. The low-beamed interior boasts an open fireplace and wood panelling. ⛼ Q ♘ ❀ 🛏 ◐◑ ♣

Salcombe

Ferry Inn
Ferry Steps (off the High St)
☎ (0548) 844000
11–11
Palmers IPA, Tally Ho! [H]
Waterside pub with two bars and a Mediterranean bistro. Ferry Bitter is Palmers Bridport Bitter. Large garden with live music every weekend in summer. One of the best pub sites in the South-West. ⛼ Q ❀ ◐◑ ♣

Scorriton

Tradesmans Arms
☎ (036 43) 206
12–2 (2.30 Sat & summer), 7–11
Furgusons Dartmoor Best Bitter; Wadworth 6X; guest beer [H]
Free house in an unspoilt village on the edge of Dartmoor. Friendly, relaxing atmosphere in the main and snug bars; good family room with splendid views. Live music alternate Fri and Sun. A weekly guest beer replaces one of the regulars. No food Mon eve. ⛼ ♘ ❀ ◐◑ ⌓ P

Seaton

Hook & Parrot
Esplanade ☎ (0297) 20222
11–11
Draught Bass; Devenish Royal Wessex; Whitbread Castle Eden Ale, Flowers Original [H]

Large bar/lounge area with sea vistas. The adjoining coffee bar acts as a restaurant; the downstairs bar caters for the younger generation and has pool. Q 🐎 ❀ 🛏 ◖◗ ⊟ ♣

Sleeper
Marine Place ☎ (0297) 24380
11–2.30 (3 Sat & Mon–Thu in summer), 6.30–11 (midnight Fri & Fri/Sat in summer)
Beer Engine Rail Ale, Piston, Sleeper [H]
Pleasant, two-bar pub near the seafront. Q 🐎 ◖◗ ⊟ ▲ ♣

Shaldon

Clifford Arms
Fore Street ☎ (0626) 872311
11–2.30, 6–11
Draught Bass; Furgusons Dartmoor Best Bitter; Palmers IPA [H]
18th-century pub in the heart of the village, specialising in home-cooked food, especially fresh local fish in summer. Cider in summer.
🐎 ❀ ◖◗ ▲ ♣ ⌓

Silverton

Silverton Inn
Fore Street ☎ (0392) 860196
12–3, 5.30–11; 11–11 Sat
Draught Bass; Exe Valley Dob's Best Bitter [H]; guest beers
Pub with a recently modernised interior and a restaurant upstairs. ♛ ❀ ◖◗

Slapton

Queens Arms
☎ (0548) 580800
11.30–3, 6–11
Furgusons Dartmoor Best Bitter; Palmers IPA; guest beers [H]
14th-century pub with an inglenook; families are welcome. Suntrap garden. Good value food.
♛ ❀ ◖◗ ♣ ⌓ P

South Brent

Royal Oak Hotel
Station Road ☎ (0364) 72133
11–2 (4 Sat), 7 (5 Sat)–11
Furgusons Dartmoor Best Bitter, Strong; Wadworth 6X [H]
Former posting house where the local court was held and the judge's seat can still be seen. The locals' room is now part of the one large bar. Fields 22 skittles teams and has its own Dartmoor letterbox stamp. 🛏 ◖◗ ▲ ♣

South Pool

Millbrook Inn
1½ miles S of Frogmore OS775402 ☎ (0548) 531581
11.30–2.30, 6 (5.30 summer)–11 (times vary depending on tides)
Draught Bass [G]; Ruddles Best Bitter; John Smith's Bitter [H]
Small, popular pub near the head of Southpool Creek; pontoon moorings at high tide only. Special local crab sandwiches. Q ❀ ◖◗ ♣ ⌓

South Zeal

Oxenham Arms
☎ (0837) 840244
11–2.30, 6–11; 12–2.30, 7–10.30 Sun
Draught Bass; St Austell Tinners [G]
Superb hostelry on the edge of Dartmoor, dating back to the 17th century. A flagstone entrance, a granite monolith, stone mullioned windows and open fireplaces betoken its historic character. Excellent food and accommodation.
♛ Q 🛏 ◖◗ ⊟ ▲ P

Sparkwell

Treby Arms
Off A38 at Plympton
☎ (0752) 537363
11–3, 6.30–11
Draught Bass; Webster's Yorkshire Bitter; Whitbread Boddingtons Bitter [H]; guest beers
Pub dating from circa 1750, next to the Dartmoor Wildlife Park. No eve meals winter Mon. ♛ Q ❀ ◖◗ ♿ ▲ ♣ P

Spreyton

Tom Cobley
☎ (064 723) 314
12–2.30 (not Mon), 6 (7 Mon)–11
Cotleigh Tawny; Exe Valley Dob's Best Bitter; guest beers [G]
Quiet village local with a small bar and a function room with an indoor barbecue. All food is home-cooked; no meals Mon.
♛ Q 🐎 ❀ 🛏 ◖◗ ♿ ♣ P

Stokenham

Tradesman's Arms
50 yds N of A379
☎ (0548) 580313
12–2.30 (3 summer), 7–11 (closed Sun–Thu eves in winter)
Draught Bass; Hook Norton Best Bitter [H]; guest beers
Small, 15th-century, thatched cottage inn in an attractive setting. The restaurant offers fish specialities at weekends and is famous for its curry Sun. Over 100 malt whiskies. Luscombe cider in summer.
♛ Q ❀ ◖◗ ⌓ P

Talaton

Talaton Inn
☎ (0404) 822214
12–2.30, 7–11
Wadworth 6X [H]
Friendly village local. Good food in the lounge/restaurant.
Q 🐎 ❀ ◖◗ ⊟ ♣ P

Tavistock

Tavistock Inn
Brook Street ☎ (0822) 612661
11.30–3, 5.30–11; 11.30–11 Fri & Sat; 12.30–3, 7–10.30 Sun
Courage Best Bitter; John Smith's Bitter; Ushers Best Bitter, Founders [H]
Friendly locals' town pub next to the former site of Tavistock Brewery. The ex-chef landlord does the cooking. Q ◖

Teignmouth

Blue Anchor
22 Teign Street (near quay)
☎ (0626) 772741
11–11
Adnams Broadside; Marston's Pedigree; S&N Theakston Old Peculier; Whitbread Boddingtons Bitter [H]; guest beers
Roomy one-bar pub, with a friendly, cosmopolitan atmosphere; lively, with an excellent jukebox. Opens for breakfast at 8am.
♛ ❀ ◖◗ ⇌ ♣ P

Golden Lion
85 Bitton Park Road (A381)
☎ (0626) 776442
12–3, 6–11; 11–11 Sat & summer
Beer range varies [H]
Two, constantly changing guest beers in a two roomed pub, popular with locals and tourists alike. Good sports teams (darts, pool, etc.); occasional live music.
Q ◖◗ ⊟ ⇌ ♣ ⌓ P

Thurlestone

Village Inn
☎ (0548) 560382
11.30–2.30, 6–11
Draught Bass; Courage Directors; Palmers BB [H]; guest beer
Two-bar, beamed pub with a family dining area; owned by the adjacent hotel. Selection of foreign bottled beers. No Sun eve meals in winter.
🐎 ❀ ◖◗ ⌓ P

Tiverton

Racehorse
Wellbrook Street
☎ (0884) 252606
11–11
Ruddles County; Ushers Best Bitter; Webster's Yorkshire Bitter [H]
Popular local with a friendly atmosphere. Food is available all day. Function room at the rear. ♛ 🐎 ❀ ◖◗ ♿ ♣ P

White Horse
Gold Street ☎ (0884) 252022
11–11
Draught Bass; Greene King IPA [H]
Small but friendly, town-centre pub serving good value food. ♞ ❀ ⛟ ◐ ◗ ♿ ♣

Topsham

Bridge Inn
Bridge Hill ☎ (0392) 873862
12–2, 6–10.30 (11 Sat); 12–2, 7–10.30 Sun
Branscombe Vale Branoc; Exe Valley Devon Glory; Exmoor Ale; Fuller's ESB; Marston's Owd Rodger; S&N Theakston Old Peculier [G]
Unspoilt, multi-roomed pub with around 12 ales at any one time (the range may vary). A local institution.
Q ♞ ❀ ⇌ P

Lighter Inn
The Quay ☎ (0392) 875439
11–11
Hall & Woodhouse Badger Best Bitter, Hard Tackle, Tanglefoot [H]
Comfortable, open-plan pub. The most westerly Hall & Woodhouse tied house.
♞ ❀ ⛟ ◐ ◗ ▲ ⇌ P

Try also: Globe Hotel (Free)

Torquay

Crown & Sceptre
2 Petitor Road, St Marychurch
☎ (0803) 328290
11–3, 6–11; 11–11 Sat
Courage Best Bitter, Directors; Marston's Pedigree; Ruddles County; guest beer [H]
Once a village pub, now part of Torquay. Regular live music. Near the model village.
♨ ♞ ❀ ⊞ ♿ ▲ ♣ P

Devon Dumpling
108 Shiphay Lane, Shiphay (behind hospital)
☎ (0803) 613465
11–2.30 (3 Fri), 5.30–11; 11–11 Sat
Courage Best Bitter, Directors; Ruddles County; John Smith's Bitter; Wadworth 6X [H]**; guest beer**
16th-century converted farmhouse, with a warm atmosphere; very popular with locals. Good range of home-cooked food. Rumoured to be haunted by a farmhand who hanged himself in what is now the bar. Family room upstairs.
♨ ♞ ❀ ◐ ◗ ♿ ♣ P

Old Market Inn
9 Torwood Street
☎ (0803) 294334
11–11
Adnams Broadside [G]**; Fuller's London Pride** [H]**; Morland Old Speckled Hen; Palmers Tally Ho!** [G]**; Whitbread Porter** [H]**; guest beers**
Whitbread cask ale pub offering a wide range of guest beers. ◗

Totnes

Kingsbridge Inn
9 Leetchwell Street
☎ (0803) 863324
11–2.30, 5.30–11
Draught Bass; Courage Best Bitter; Furgusons Dartmoor Best Bitter; Thompson's Figurehead [H]**; guest beers**
Comfortable, low-lit bar with an eating area, where Thompson's Figurehead is sold as Bridge Best. Home-made food, made with local produce, is a speciality. Varied guest ales. Live music weekly, but no piped music. Historic leech wells nearby.
Q ♞ ❀ ◐ ◗ ▲ ♣ ⌓ ⚟

Rumours
High Street ☎ (0803) 864682
10–11; 7–10.30 Sun, closed Sun lunch
Draught Bass; Wadworth 6X; guest beers [H]
Dutch 'Brown' café or French brasserie-type pub with murals and exhibitions by local artists. Regular guest beers and plenty of food. Attracts a wide spectrum of Totnes people. Cider in summer. ♞ ◐ ◗ ▲ ⇌ ⌓ ⚟

Tuckenhay

Floyd's Inn
Bow Creek (2 miles E of A381, S of Totnes) OS817602
☎ (0803) 732350
11–3, 5.30–11
Draught Bass; Blackawton Bitter; Exmoor Ale; Furgusons Dartmoor Best Bitter [H]
16th-century creekside pub and restaurant, owned by TV cook Keith Floyd. Interesting food – as is to be expected. Cosy snug. ♨ ♞ ❀ ◐ ◗ P

Try also: Watermans Arms, Bow Bridge (Free)

Welcombe

Old Smithy Inn
2 miles off A39 OS232178
☎ (028 883) 305
12–3, 7–11 (12–11 summer); 12–2.30, 7–10.30 Sun
Butcombe Bitter; Marston's Pedigree (summer) [H]
Popular, 13th-century, thatched inn, set in attractive countryside. Extremely busy during the summer. Take the superb coastal walk to the Bush in Cornwall.
♨ ♞ ❀ ⛟ ◐ ◗ ▲ ⌓ P

Wembworthy

Lymington Arms
Lama Cross (2 miles W of Eggesford station, off A377)
☎ (083 783) 572
11–3, 6–11
Eldridge Pope Dorchester, Hardy Country, Royal Oak; Palmers IPA [H]
Large country inn where the main bar is split in half: on one side is a comfortable lounge area with a woodburning stove, where children are welcome. Large function room at the rear. Close to the Taw and the Tarka Trail, and a great base for walks.
♨ ❀ ⛟ ◐ ◗ ♣ ⌓ P

Westcott

Merry Harriers
On B3181 S of Cullompton
☎ (0392) 881254
12–2.30, 7–11; 12–2, 7–10.30 Sun
Draught Bass [H]
Friendly roadside pub with a restaurant and good food.
♨ Q ❀ ◐ ◗ ♿ ▲ P

Whimple

New Fountain
Church Road ☎ (0404) 822350
11–3, 6–11
Oakhill Bitter; Tetley Bitter [H]**; guest beers** (occasionally)
Family-run local with a warm, friendly atmosphere, serving a varied menu of good value home-cooked food.
♨ ♞ ❀ ◐ ◗ ⊞ ⇌ ♣ P

Widecombe in the Moor

Rugglestone Inn
Just outside village, past the church ☎ (036 42) 327
11.30–2.30, 6 (6.30 spring, 7 winter)–11; 11–3, 6–11 Sat
Draught Bass [G]
Basic, two-room pub, converted from an old cottage. Popular with locals and walkers. ♨ Q ◐ ▲

Yelverton

Rock Inn
Rock Complex (near A386/B3212 jct) ☎ (0822) 852022
11–3, 5.30–11; 11–11 Sat & summer
Draught Bass; Charrington IPA; St Austell HSD; Whitbread Boddingtons Bitter [H]**; guest beers**
Large, popular, well-run pub with three bars and a lively games room. Worthington White Shield available.
♨ Q ♞ ❀ ◐ ◗ ⊞ ♣ P

Dorset

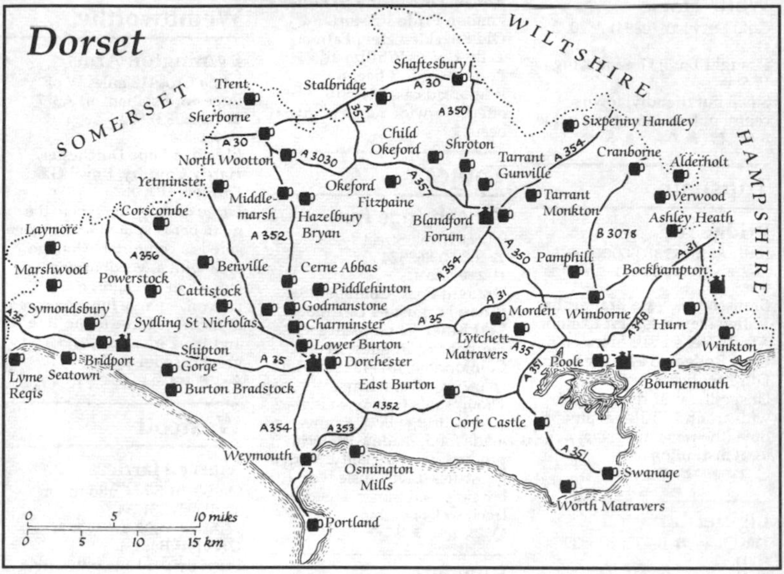

Cook's, *Bockhampton;* **Eldridge Pope, Goldfinch,** *Dorchester;* **Hall & Woodhouse,** *Blandford Forum;* **Palmers,** *Bridport;* **Poole,** *Poole*

Alderholt

Churchill Arms
Daggons Road
☎ (0425) 652147
11–3, 6–11
Hall & Woodhouse Badger Best Bitter H
Home of the local rugby club, alongside a defunct railway. Pleasant decor and wood panelling. ♣ P

Ashley Heath

Struan Hotel
Horton Road (½ mile N of A31/A338 roundabout)
☎ (0425) 473553
11–3, 6–11
Hall & Woodhouse Badger Best Bitter, Tanglefoot; Wells Eagle H
Superb country inn set in natural-wooded surroundings near the New Forest. The atmosphere is warm and friendly, with traditional furnishings, oak beams and panelling. Celebrates Burns Night. P

Benville

Talbot
1½ miles off A356
☎ (0935) 83381
11.30–2.30, 6.30–11
Butcombe Bitter; Greene King Abbot H
Village pub and restaurant, offering a friendly welcome. Butcombe Bitter may be swapped with Young's Special. Q ♣ P

Blandford Forum

Half Moon Inn
Whitecliff Mill Street (Shaftesbury road)
☎ (0258) 452318
10–11
Hall & Woodhouse Badger Best Bitter; Wells Eagle H
Unspoilt, basic town pub with a friendly atmosphere. The licensees are Hall & Woodhouse's longest serving. Holds events in support of the RNLI. Children admitted to the pool room. Q ♣ P

Kings Arms
Whitecliff Mill Street (Shaftesbury road)
☎ (0258) 452163
11–2.30, 6–11; 11–11 Fri & Sat
Draught Bass; Ringwood Best Bitter; guest beer H
Historic Georgian hotel with a comfortable interior; the former JL Marsh's brewery tap, built where the 1731 great fire of Blandford started. Games and electronic music room, popular with the younger set; multi-beamed main room. P

Bournemouth

Grove Tavern
Poole Hill (½ mile from square) ☎ (0202) 290016
11–3, 5–11
Marston's Bitter, Pedigree H**; guest beer**
Typical locals' town pub; its attractive frontage has stained-glass windows. Quiet TV. Home-made food.

Porterhouse
113 Poole Road
☎ (0202) 768586
11–3, 5–11; 11–11 Sat
Ringwood Best Bitter, XXXX Porter, Fortyniner, Old Thumper H**; guest beers**
Lively town pub for all, with friendly staff. Recently refurbished but keeping its old atmosphere, if not quieter. ⇌ (Branksome)

Bridport

Ropemakers
West Street ☎ (0308) 421255
11–3, 7–11; 11–11 Fri & Sat
Palmers BB, IPA, Tally Ho! (summer) H

Lively town pub near the market square, popular with young people and very busy at times. ❀ ◖ ♿ ▲ ♣ ⌓ P

Burton Bradstock

Three Horseshoes

Mill Street ☎ (0308) 897259
11–2.30, 6–11
Palmers BB, IPA, Tally Ho! [H]
Superb, friendly, thatched inn in a picturesque coastal village. Food has a deservedly high reputation. ⛫ Q ♘ ❀ 🛏 ◖ ◗ ♿ ▲ ♣ P

Cattistock

Fox & Hounds

Duck Street ☎ (0300) 20444
12–3 (not Mon), 7–11
Beer range varies [H]
Former medieval longhouse with original fireplaces and oak panelling. Always two ales from a selection of a dozen breweries; cider in summer. ⛫ Q ♘ ❀ 🛏 ◖ ◗ ⊟ ▲ ♣ P

Cerne Abbas

Red Lion

Long Street ☎ (0300) 341441
11.30–2.30, 6.30–11
Wadworth IPA, 6X [H]; guest beers
Large local with a striking Victorian frontage, near the hillside giant. Good food, including vegetarian.
⛫ Q ❀ ◖ ◗ ♿ ♣

Charminster

New Inn

North Street ☎ (0305) 264694
12–2.30 (3 Sat), 7–11 (11–3, 6–11 summer)
Draught Bass; Wadworth 6X [H]
Comfortable local with a large conservatory and streamside garden. Jazz Thu.
⛫ ♘ ❀ ◖ ◗ ▲ ♣ ⌓ P

Child Okeford

Saxon Inn

Gold Hill (narrow lane at N end of village)
☎ (0258) 860310
11.30–2.30, 7–11
Draught Bass; Whitbread Boddingtons Bitter; guest beer [H]
Pub taking its name from the Saxons who lived in the hill fort above the village. Plenty of wildlife in the garden.
⛫ ♘ ❀ ◖ ◗ ▲ ♣ P

Corfe Castle

Fox Inn

West Street ☎ (0929) 480449
11–2.30, 6–11 (may vary summer)
Gibbs Mew Bishop's Tipple; Greene King Abbot; Ind Coope Burton Ale [G]; guest beers
Historic 16th-century building with garden views of the castle and a recently found well in the food bar. Home of the Ancient Order of the Purbeck Marblers. ⛫ Q ❀ ◖ ▲

Corscombe

Fox Inn

Off A356 ☎ (0935) 891330
12–2.30, 7–11
Exmoor Ale, Beast; Greene King Abbot [G]
Superb country inn attracting a mixed clientele. Unspoilt both inside and out, featuring a slate floor and bar top. ⛫ Q
❀ ◖ ◗ ⊟ ♿ ▲ ♣ ⌓ P

Cranborne

Sheaf of Arrows

4 The Square ☎ (0725) 517456
12 (11 summer)–4, 6–11
Draught Bass; Ringwood Best Bitter [G]; guest beer
Traditional local. The lively public bar has a wood floor and oak beams. Comfortable lounge and a skittle alley.
Q ❀ 🛏 ◖ ◗ ⊟ ▲ ♣ ⌓ P

Dorchester

Tom Brown's

47 High East Street
☎ (0305) 264020
11–3, 6–11
Goldfinch Tom Brown's, Flashman's Clout, Midnight Blinder [H]
Wood-floored home of the Goldfinch Brewery. New management has increased the pub's popularity, but it has retained its atmosphere. Two crib teams; good jukebox.
⛫ 🛏 ◖ ◗ ♿ ⇌ (South) ♣

White Hart

53 High East Street
☎ (0305) 263545
11–3, 6–11
Hall & Woodhouse Badger Best Bitter, Tanglefoot [H]
Popular riverside pub used by cricketers in summer and skittlers in winter. Also has crib and pool teams. Good value ales for the area. Commended in a Hall & Woodhouse cellar competition. Eve meals finish at 8.30.
⛫ Q ❀ 🛏 ◖ ◗ ♿
⇌ (South) ♣ P

East Burton

Seven Stars

East Burton Road
☎ (0929) 462292
11–3, 6.30 (6 summer)–11
Ind Coope Burton Ale; Tetley Bitter; Whitbread Castle Eden Ale [H]; guest beer
Large free house with a friendly country atmosphere. The landlord has won a national award for his Tetley Bitter. Good value food.
⛫ ❀ ◖ ◗ ♿ ▲ ♣ ⌓ P

Godmanstone

Smiths Arms

Main Road ☎ (0300) 341236
11–3, 6–11
Ringwood Best Bitter [G]
England's smallest inn, as stated in the *Guinness Book of Records*. Granted a licence by Charles II when he stopped here to have his horse shod. Riverside garden. Summer cider. ⛫ Q ❀ ◖ ◗ ♿ ♣ ⌓ P

Hazelbury Bryan

Antelope

Pidney (1 mile E of B3143)
OS745091 ☎ (0258) 817295
11–3, 6–11
Hall & Woodhouse Badger Best Bitter [G]
Step back in time to this remote village local where the handpumps are just for show. Probably the cheapest beer in E Dorset.
⛫ Q ❀ 🛏 ◖ ◗ ♣ ⌓

Hurn

Avon Causeway Hotel

Off B3073 ☎ (0202) 482714
11–11
Everards Beacon [G]; Ringwood Best Bitter, Old Thumper [H]; Wadworth IPA [G], 6X, Old Timer [H]
Converted from the old Hurn railway station (closed 1935), an ideal pub for families. Large bar area with old railway memorabilia. Two full-sized railway carriages are parked by the platform.
♘ ❀ 🛏 ◖ ◗ ♿ P

Laymore

Squirrel

Off B3165 ☎ (0460) 30298
11–2.30, 6–11
Cotleigh Harrier; Oakhill Yeoman [H]; guest beers
Unspoilt village local. Two or three guest beers change each week, at very low prices.
⛫ Q ❀ 🛏 ◖ ◗ ♿ ▲ ♣ ⌓ P

Lower Burton

Sun Inn

½ mile N of Dorchester
☎ (0305) 250445
11–2.30, 6.30–11
Fuller's London Pride; Smiles Bitter [H]; guest beers

Dorset

Former Devenish house, reopened as a free house in 1992. A superb range of good value food complements the four ales, two of which change regularly. Very busy at weekends. P

Lyme Regis

Angel Inn

Mill Green (down Monmouth St, off High St)
(0297) 443267
11–2.30, 7–11
Palmers BB, IPA [G]
Northern, 1950s-type local giving good value, run by an ex-GWR steam railwayman. Ever expanding collection of bottled beers (now over 800).
P

Royal Standard

Marine Parade
(0297) 442637
11–3, 7–11 (11–11 summer)
Palmers BB, IPA, Tally Ho! [H]
Historic, 400-year-old pub on the beach, popular with young people and tourists. Extended, but its character remains unchanged. Eve meals in summer.

Volunteer

Broad Street (0297) 442214
11–3, 7–11
Draught Bass; Wadworth 6X [H]**; guest beer**
Town pub near the cinema. Two guest beers, but prices on the expensive side.

Lytchett Matravers

Chequers

High Street (0202) 622215
11–2.30, 6–11
Draught Bass; Ringwood Fortyniner; guest beer [H]
Large, one-bar pub and restaurant in a setting on the edge of a conurbation. The garden has children's play equipment and farm animals.
Q P

Marshwood

Bottle Inn

On B3165 (0297) 678254
11–2 (3 summer), 6–11
Hook Norton Best Bitter; Ruddles Best Bitter; Wadworth 6X [H]
Attractive roadside local in a beautiful wooded location. Home-cooked food.
Q

Middlemarsh

White Horse

(0963) 210219
11.30–2.30, 7–11
Draught Bass; Pitfield ESB; Wiltshire Old Grumble [H]
One-bar pub on the Dorchester to Sherborne road; welcoming, with a large log fire. Note the collection of old cameras.
P

Morden

Cock & Bottle

On B3075 (092 945) 238
11–2.30, 6 (6.30 winter)–11
Hall & Woodhouse Badger Best Bitter, Tanglefoot; Wells Eagle [H]
Unspoilt, friendly, village pub in a rural setting. Two contrasting but linked bar areas. Home-cooked food.
P

North Wootton

Three Elms

(0935) 812881
11–2.30, 6.30 (6 Fri & Sat)–11
Fuller's London Pride; Greene King Abbot; Hook Norton Mild; Smiles Best Bitter; Wadworth 6X [H]**; guest beers**
Large, popular rural free house offering a wide range of ales and foreign beers, with a house beer and two guests on tap. P

Okeford Fitzpaine

Royal Oak

Lower Street (0258) 860308
11–2.30, 6.30–11
Fuller's London Pride; Ringwood Best Bitter [H]
Homely pub in a picture-postcard village; the nearby telephone box really is painted green! CAMRA E Dorset *Pub of the Year* 1992. No food Wed.
P

Osmington Mills

Smugglers Inn

Off A353 (0305) 833125
11–3, 6–11
Courage Best Bitter, Directors; Ruddles County [H]
A spacious pub situated in a valley close to the cliff top, with a family area and restaurant. The garden has a stream running through it. Popular, and crowded in summer. The beer range may vary.
P

Pamphill

Vine Inn

Vine Hill (off B3082) OS995004
(0202) 882259
11–2.30, 7–11
Whitbread Strong Country [H]**; guest beer** [G]
Split-level country pub built into the hillside: two very small bars, with a stairway leading to an alternative drinking area with darts. The garden is well equipped for children. Q

Piddlehinton

Thimble Inn

(030 04) 270
12–2.30, 7–11.30
Eldridge Pope Hardy Country; Hall & Woodhouse Badger Best Bitter, Hard Tackle; Ringwood Old Thumper [H]
Enlarged, pretty country inn astride the River Piddle. A well and an island fireplace are features. Good value food.
Q P

Poole

Antelope Hotel

High Street (0202) 672029
12–3, 5.30–11
Whitbread Boddingtons Bitter; guest beers [H]
A 15th-century coaching inn, now a plush hotel. The large bar has bar billiards, a food bar (not Sun), and regular live music. Prices on the high side but offset by regular happy hours.

Beehive

234 Sandbanks Road, Lilliput
(0202) 708641
10.30–2.30, 6–11
Eldridge Pope Dorchester, Hardy Country, Royal Oak [H]
Large family pub (adventure garden for children), on the way to the beach and ferry. Comfortable and cosy with a youngish clientele.
P

Bricklayers Arms

41 Parr Street, Lower Parkstone (0202) 740304
11–2.30, 7–11
Eldridge Pope Dorchester, Hardy Country, Blackdown Porter, Royal Oak [H]
Friendly, fairly small, one-bar local which gets crowded most eves. The bar features cigarette card collections. Regular live rock/blues bands in the music-cum-function room.
(Parkstone)

Conjurors Half Crown

Commercial Road, Parkstone
(0202) 740302
11–3, 5 (6 Sat)–11
Hall & Woodhouse Badger Best Bitter, Hard Tackle, Tanglefoot [H]
Large Dickensian-style pub with many alcoves and different levels. The wooden floorboards, old beams and wall panelling give a relaxing atmosphere. Good range of food. (Parkstone) P

Darby's Corner

2 Waterloo Road (A349)
(0202) 693780
12–11; 11–2.30, 6–11 Sat

Gribble Ale, Reg's Tipple; Hall & Woodhouse Badger Best Bitter, Hard Tackle, Tanglefoot [H]
Strange-looking, flat-roofed pub of Mediterranean appearance. Popular with business people and locals alike. Good food trade; breakfast is served daily 8.30–10. Wheelchair WC.
❀ ◑ ◗ ♿ P

Foundry Arms
Lagland Street
☎ (0202) 672769
11–2.30, 6–11 (may vary in summer)
Eldridge Pope Hardy Country, Royal Oak [H]
Comfortable, town-centre pub: an L-shaped, single bar with two dartboards and photos of old Poole. Good home-cooked food (not served Sun or Mon eves). Beers may vary.
❀ ◑ ◗ ⇌ ♣ P ⚡

Inn in the Park
Pinewood Road, Branksome Park ☎ (0202) 761318
11–2.30 (3 Sat), 5.30 (6 Sat)–11
Draught Bass; Wadworth IPA, 6X [H]
Plush inn near the sea, featuring a cigarette card collection. Meals served in the dining area (not Sun).
♨ Q 🛏 ◑ ◗ P

Lord Nelson
The Quay ☎ (0202) 673774
11–11
Hall & Woodhouse Badger Best Bitter, Hard Tackle, Tanglefoot; Wells Eagle [H]
Busy pub with nautical artefacts and flagstoned floors. Regular live bands and loud blues/rock music. A well-furnished, no-smoking children's room provides a quiet alternative. No food Sun.
♘ ❀ ◑ ♿ ⚡

Portsmouth Hoy
The Quay ☎ (0202) 673517
11–2.30, 6–11; 11–11 Fri & Sat (10–11 summer)
Eldridge Pope Dorchester, Hardy Country, Blackdown Porter, Royal Oak [H]
Pub with a nautical flavour and a cross-section of clientele. Warm atmosphere; family games. Q ❀ ◑ ◗ ♿ ♣ ⚡

Portland

Corner House
49 Straits, Easton
☎ (0305) 822526
11–3, 6–11
Eldridge Pope Dorchester, Hardy Country, Blackdown Porter, Royal Oak [H]**; guest beer**
Unchanged, 19th-century corner alehouse with a small, cosy bar and a games room. Winner of Eldridge Pope's *Cellar Supremo*. ❀ 🛏 ♣

Cove House
Chesil Beach, Chiswell
☎ (0305) 820895
11.30–2.30, 6.30–11 (varies in summer)
Marston's Pedigree; Whitbread Flowers Original [H]**; guest beers**
Old inn at the end of Chesil beach, hidden away from the road. Virtually rebuilt after the storms of 1990 when struck by a 60-ft wave. Two guest beers from Whitbread's list.
❀ ◑ ◗ P

Powerstock

Three Horseshoes
OS961516
☎ (030 885) 328
11–3, 6–11
Palmers BB, IPA [H]
Pub at the foot of Eggardon Hill, affording lovely views. The menu offers many fish dishes, also vegetarian options. Prices on the high side. No eve meals winter Sun.
♨ Q ❀ 🛏 ◑ ◗ ♿ ▲ ♣ ⌓ P

Seatown

Anchor Inn
☎ (0297) 89215
11–2.30, 7–11 (11–11 summer)
Palmers IPA, Tally Ho! [E]
Small, cosy pub next to a stony beach, within walking distance of Golden Cap, the highest point on the south coast. Busy in summer. No eve meals winter Sun. Beers are pricey.
♨ ♘ ❀ ◑ ◗ ▲ ♣ P

Shaftesbury

Fountain Inn
Breach Lane, Enmore Green
☎ (0747) 52062
11–3, 6.30–11; 11–11 Sat
Brains SA; Wadworth 6X [H]**; guest beers**
Comfortable, well-used, split-level bar patronised by the young. Live music every other Thu. Skittle alley for hire; secluded garden. Two guest beers.
❀ ◑ ◗ ♣ ⌓ P

Olde Two Brewers
St James Street (near bottom of Gold Hill) ☎ (0747) 54211
11–3, 6–11
Courage Best Bitter, Directors; Wadworth 6X; guest beers [H]
300-year-old free house with many different drinking areas and superb views of the Blackmoor vale. The landlord wears a different bow tie each eve and exchanges a drink for a tie he hasn't got. Excellent home-cooked food.
❀ ◑ ◗ P

Sherborne

Digby Tap
Cooks Lane
☎ (0935) 813148
11–2.30, 5.30–11
Beer range varies [H]
Unpretentious and unspoilt, side-street tap room, convenient for the abbey. W Dorset CAMRA *Pub of the Year* 1992/3. Five beers usually available.
♨ ♘ ◑ ⇌ ♣ ⌓

Skippers
Horsecastles ☎ (0935) 812753
11.30–2.30, 5.30–11
Draught Bass [H]**; guest beers**
Excellent, one-bar drinkers' pub serving a wide range of good food. Three guest beers plus a house beer.
Q ❀ ◑ ◗ ⇌ ♣ P

Shipton Gorge

New Inn
Off A35 ☎ (0308) 897302
11.30–2, 6.30 (6 summer)–11
Palmers BB, IPA [H]
Pleasant country pub, south of the Bridport to Dorchester road in a good walking area. Large open fireplace and an oak settle in the small bar.
♨ Q ♘ ❀ ◑ ◗ ♿ ▲ ♣ P

Shroton

Cricketers
W of A350 ☎ (0258) 860421
11–3, 7–11
Ringwood Best Bitter; Smiles Best Bitter [H]**; guest beer**
Friendly local with a good restaurant. Near Hod Hill iron age fort.
♨ Q ❀ ◑ ◗ ♣ P

Sixpenny Handley

Roebuck
High Street ☎ (0725) 552002
11.30–3, 6.30–11
Ringwood Best Bitter, XXXX Porter, Old Thumper; guest beer [H]
Upmarket, L-shaped bar with a cosy fireside, resembling someone's front room. Old village pictures; piano for the odd sing-song. No food Mon.
♨ Q ♘ ❀ 🛏 ◑ ◗ ▲ ♣ P

Stalbridge

Stalbridge Arms
Lower Road ☎ (0963) 62447
11.30–2.30, 6–11
Smiles Best Bitter [H]
Basic drinking pub in a large village. No lunches Mon.
♨ ❀ 🛏 ◑ ◗ ♣ P

Dorset

Swanage

Black Swan Inn

High Street ☎ (0929) 422761
12–3, 7–11 (11–11 summer)
Pitfield ESB; Wiltshire Stonehenge Best Bitter [H]
Pretty, traditional building in a hilltop position. Its sign depicts the Purbeck quarry industry; the comfortable bar makes good use of Purbeck stone. Former stables now serve as a children's room; two gardens. ♋ ❀ 🛏 ◐ ◑ ▲ ♣ P

Red Lion

High Street ☎ (0929) 423533
11–11 (may vary winter)
Whitbread Strong Country, Flowers Original [G]; guest beer (summer)
Popular, down-to-earth but friendly pub. The public bar has an open fire and artefacts. The lounge, with an iron stove and a pool table, leads to a large garden. Eve meals Fri and Sat only in winter.
♛ ♋ ❀ ◐ ◑ ⊟ ♣ ☌ P

Sydling St Nicholas

Greyhound Inn

High Street ☎ (0300) 341303
11–3, 6–11
Tetley Bitter; Wadworth 6X [H]; guest beers
Large, one-bar free house and restaurant. Four guest beers are usually served; cider occasionally in summer. Skittle alley. ♛ ♋ ❀ ◐ ◑ ♣ ☌ P

Symondsbury

Ilchester Arms

Off A35 ☎ (0308) 22600
11–2.30, 6.30–11
Palmers BB, IPA [H]
Unspoilt, welcoming country pub offering an extensive menu. Popular with tourists.
♛ Q ❀ 🛏 ◐ ◑ ⊟ ♿ ▲ ♣ P

Tarrant Gunville

Bugle Horn

Off A354, N of Tarrant Hinton
☎ (025 889) 300
11.30–2.30, 6–11
Wadworth 6X; guest beer [H]
Comfortably furnished village local on the edge of Cranborne Chase. Large rear garden and a small front terrace to rest on after long walks in the country. ♛ Q ❀ ◐ ◑ ♣ P

Tarrant Monkton

Langton Arms

☎ (0258) 89225
11–3, 6–11
Marston's Pedigree; Smiles Best Bitter, Exhibition; Wadworth 6X; guest beers [H]
Traditional, 17th-century, thatched country pub with frequently changing guest ales served in the lounge bar and on request in the public bar. Extensive outside play area for children. Skittle alley; excellent food. Q ❀ 🛏 ◐ ◑ ♣ P

Trent

Rose & Crown

Off A30 ☎ (0935) 850776
12–2.30, 7–11
Hook Norton Best Bitter [H]; guest beers
Converted farmhouse, now a fine village local. A warm welcome and delicious cuisine have made it deservedly popular. *Guinness Pub Food* regional award-winner.
♛ Q ♋ ❀ ◐ ◑ ☌ P

Verwood

Albion Inn

Station Road ☎ (0202) 825267
11–2.30, 5 (6 Sat)–11; 12–2.30, 7–10.30 Sun
Gibbs Mew Salisbury, Deacon, Bishop's Tipple [H]
Built in 1866, a lovely pub which once had a ghost called Wesley, exorcized by the local vicar. ♛ Q ❀ ◐ ◑ ⊟ P

Weymouth

Kings Arms

Trinity Road ☎ (0305) 770055
10–11
Devenish Royal Wessex; Fuller's Chiswick; Marston's Pedigree [H]; guest beers
Welcoming harbourside pub with a split-level bar and a wide range of games. Three beers from the Whitbread range. ◐ ◑ ♿ ♣ ☌

Waterloo

Grange Road ☎ (0305) 784488
11.30–2.30 (3 Fri, 4 Sat), 6.30–11
Gibbs Mew Local Line, Salisbury [H]
Friendly corner local, close to the seafront. A third beer may also be available. Wheelchair access is via the back door.
Q ❀ ◐ ◑ ♿ ≡ ♣

Weatherbury

7 Carlton Road North (off Dorchester Rd)
☎ (0305) 786040
11–2.30, 5.30–11; 11–11 Fri & Sat
Draught Bass [H]; guest beers
Large, modern lounge bar in a residential area. Good value food most eves. Friendly staff and the best range of beer in Weymouth: four guests.
❀ 🛏 ◐ ◑ ♿ ≡ ♣ P

Wimborne

Cricketers Arms

Park Lane ☎ (0202) 882846
11–2.30, 6–11; 11–11 Fri & Sat
Eldridge Pope Hardy Country, Royal Oak; Wadworth 6X [H]
Large, one-bar, town-centre pub, opposite the cricket pitch. Three distinct and comfortable drinking areas feature wood panelling and sporting prints. Good food. Beers may vary.
♛ ◐ ◑ ♣

Crown & Anchor

Wimborne Road, Walford (B3078) ☎ (0202) 841405
10.30–3, 6–11
Hall & Woodhouse Badger Best Bitter [H]
Pleasant, friendly, out-of-town local, by the River Allen, near Walford Mill Craft Centre. No food Sun.
♛ Q ❀ ◐ ♿ ▲ ♣ P

Winkton

Fishermans Haunt

Salisbury Road
☎ (0202) 484071
10.30–2.30, 6–11
Draught Bass; Courage Directors; Ringwood XXXX Porter, Fortyniner [H]
17th-century, Avon valley hotel with a welcome as warm as its fire. Good value food. Children welcome in one lounge. ♛ Q ❀ 🛏 ◐ ◑ ♿ P

Lamb Inn

Burley Road ☎ (0425) 72427
11–2.30, 6–11; 11–11 Sat
Beer range varies [H]
Superb popular free house in a green field setting offering six, ever-changing, interesting guest beers and good value bar food with a vegetarian option. ♛ ❀ ◐ ◑ ⊟ ♿ ♣ P

Worth Matravers

Square & Compass

Off B3069 OS977777
☎ (0929) 439229
11–3, 6–11
Marston's Pedigree; Whitbread Strong Country [G]; guest beers
Superb monument to the Purbecks and the Newman family who have run the pub for 87 years. A 14th-century house with two serving hatches, and a stone-flagged corridor and sitting rooms.
♛ Q ♋ ❀ ▲ ♣ ☌ P

Yetminster

White Hart

☎ (0935) 872338
11.30 (11 Sat)–2.30, 7–11
Draught Bass; Ringwood Best Bitter [H]
Splendid, 500-year-old, thatched pub in the village centre. Run on traditional lines, with a lively public bar. The comfortable lounge boasts a magnificent fireplace. Skittle alley. Good value food.
♛ Q ♋ ❀ ◐ ◑ ⊟ ♣ P

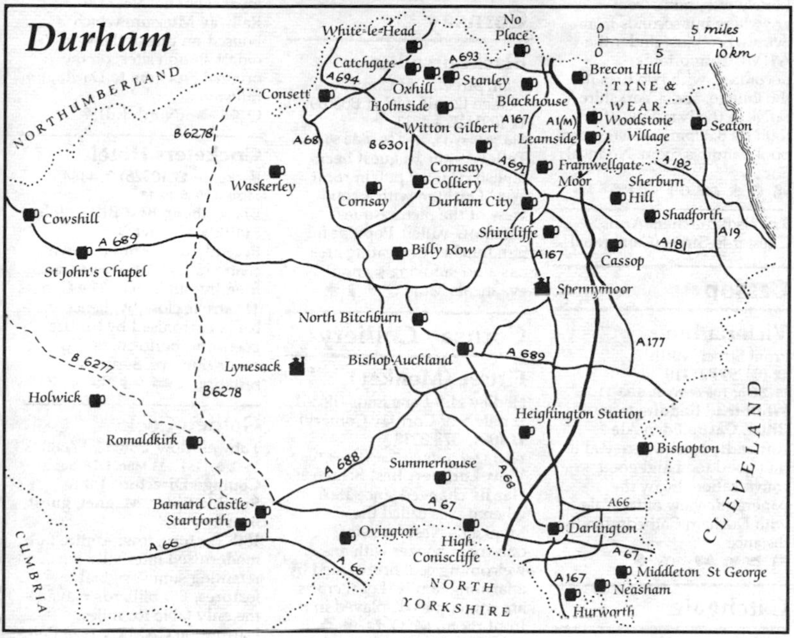

Butterknowle, Lynesack; **Whitworth Hall**, Spennymoor

Barnard Castle

Kings Head
Market Place ☎ (0833) 690333
11–3 (4 Sat), 6–11 (11–11 Sat in summer)
Butterknowle Conciliation Ale; Courage Directors; Marston's Pedigree; John Smith's Bitter Ⓗ
Imposing one-time hotel, now a pub, coffee shop and nursing home. Dickens stayed here in 1838 while researching *Nicholas Nickleby*. Two large, oak-panelled lounge bars.
◐ ◑ ♿ P

Old Well
The Bank ☎ (0833) 690130
12–2.30, 7–11; 12–2.30, 7–10.30 Sun
Courage Directors; John Smith's Bitter; Whitbread Boddingtons Bitter Ⓗ
Cosy, old pub and restaurant with a small front bar and a larger room at the rear.
Q ◐ ◑ ⊟ ♣

Billy Row

Royal George
Well Bank (B6298)
☎ (0388) 764765
7 (12 Sat)–11
Ind Coope Burton Ale; Stones Best Bitter Ⓗ**; guest beers** (occasionally)
Large, two-roomed village inn, with decor based on a railway theme. A collection of engine name plates adorns the lounge, with a replica steam engine cab at one end.
❀ ◐ ◑ ♿ ♣ P

Try also: Cowstail (Free)

Bishop Auckland

Newton Cap
Bank Top (A689)
☎ (0388) 605445
11–2.30, 7–11
Camerons Strongarm Ⓗ
Traditional locals' pub near the town centre: a lively bar with a pool room and an events room. Down-to-earth atmosphere. Excellent view across the Wear valley from the rear of the pub. Ringo played. ♔ Q ❀ ⊟ ⇌ ♣

Bishopton

Talbot
The Green ☎ (0740) 30371
11–3, 6–11
Camerons Strongarm; Ind Coope Burton Ale; Tetley Bitter Ⓗ
Pleasant village local with extra trade from out-of town diners. The centre for various village activities.
♔ Q ❀ ◐ ◑ ♣ P

Blackhouse

Charlaw Inn
On B6532
☎ (0207) 232085
11–3, 6–11
McEwan 80/-; S&N Theakston Best Bitter, XB Ⓗ**; guest beer**
Very large, five-roomed pub, including a restaurant and a conservatory for families. Outside play area for children. Very sociable owners offer regular pub games in the bar which features soccer memorabilia. Guest ales become more available in summer.
Q ⛄ ❀ ◐ ◑ ⊟ ♿ ♣ P

Brecon Hill

Smiths Arms
☎ (091) 385 6915
12–11
Draught Bass; S&N Theakston Best Bitter; Stones Best Bitter Ⓗ

Lonely pub, miles from anywhere but seconds from everywhere, just under the A1(M). Comfortably decorated, with two fires in the lounge, and a Yorkshire range in the bar. Now offers food till 8.30pm and has a neat pool/families room. No meals Sun.
♛ Q ❀ ⛟ ◐ ◑ ⊞ P

Try also: Butchers Arms, Chester-le-Street (Camerons)

Cassop

Victoria Inn
Front Street North
☎ (0429) 821410
11–2 (not Tue or Wed), 6.30–11
Whitbread Boddingtons Bitter, Castle Eden Ale Ⓗ
A friendly local where you'll find good food and good conversation. Enjoy the panoramic view of the vale, with Durham Cathedral in the distance.
♛ ⛟ ❀ ⛟ ◐ ▲ ♣

Catchgate

Smiths Arms
North Road (B6168)
☎ (0207) 234309
11–3, 6–11; 11–11 Sat
S&N Theakston Best Bitter Ⓗ
Corner pub whose large, L-shaped bar room attracts lively pool and darts players. Quiet lounge. Guest beers planned.
Q ⛟ ❀ ⛟ ◐ ◑ ⊞ ♿ ▲ ♣ P

Consett

Bellamys
Newmarket Street (near bus station) ☎ (0207) 503654
11–3, 6–11; 11–11 Sat
John Smith's Bitter; Thwaites Bitter Ⓗ
Pub close to the town's college. The bar is in the centre of the room, and a small annexe doubles as a dining room. General knowledge quiz Thu and music quiz Sun; musical entertainment occasional weekends.
◐ ◑ ♿ ▲ ♣

Grey Horse
Sherburn Terrace (A692)
☎ (0207) 502585
7–11; 1–5, 7–11 Sat
McEwan 80/-; S&N Theakston XB Ⓗ
Cosy, popular pub on the edge of the town centre. The bar and lounge are separated by a small-paned glass partition. Quiz nights Wed; music Thu, Fri and Sat, with folk music or sing-alongs with local singers.
Q ⊞ ♿ ♣ P

Cornsay

Blackhorse Inn
Main Street, Old Cornsay Village (2 miles W of B6301)
☎ (091) 373 4211
7 (6.30 Sat)–11; 12–2.30, 7–10.30 Sun
Tetley Bitter Ⓗ**; guest beers**
Stylish country pub in rural West Durham with a good view of the picturesque Gladdow valley. Popular for Sun lunches (the eating area has a no-smoking section). No eve meals Mon. Q ❀ ◑ ♣ P

Cornsay Colliery

Firtree (Monkey)
Hedley Hill Lane Ends (B6301, ½ mile S of Cornsay Colliery)
☎ (091) 373 3212
7–11; 12–2, 7–10.30 Sun; closed Tue
Vaux Lorimers Best Scotch Ⓗ
Hardly changed since 1868, when it was called the Monkey's Nest: a basic, one-room boozer with a welcoming coal fire, owned by a farming family. Local crafts are sometimes displayed in the front room. ♛ Q ⛟ ❀ ♣ P

Try also: Hamsteels Inn, Quebec (John Smith's)

Cowshill

Cowshill Hotel
On A689 ☎ (0388) 537236
11–3, 7–11
Tetley Bitter Ⓗ
Basic, but comfortable Dales pub at the head of Neardale; convenient for Killhope Lead Mining Museum. Many butter-making implements are on show. Book meals.
♛ Q ❀ ⛟ ◐ ◑ ⊞ P

Darlington

Burns Tavern
Thompson Street East
☎ (0325) 381235
11–3, 5.30–11; 11–11 Fri & Sat
Samuel Smith OBB Ⓗ
Busy, modern pub, very well designed both inside and out, with lots of interesting details. A welcoming lounge and a very popular public bar. Sam Smith's have put much thought into creating this modern 'local'.
❀ ◐ ◑ ⊞ ♿ ♣ P

Central Borough
Hopetown Lane
☎ (0325) 468490
11–11
Camerons Strongarm Ⓗ
Small, street-corner local in an area of terraced housing. Run by the same tenants for over 30 years, who have a very loyal clientele. Near the Railway Museum which is housed on one of the world's oldest station sites, on the original Stockton to Darlington railway.
Q ⊞ ⇌ (North Rd) ♣

Cricketers Hotel
Parkgate ☎ (0325) 384444
11.30–3.30, 5.30–11
Black Sheep Best Bitter; John Smith's Magnet Ⓗ
Recently modernised, town-centre hotel with a warm and friendly public bar. The Civic Theatre is close by, hence the bar is patronised by theatre-goers and performers. No meals Sun eve. Separate restaurant. ⛟ ◐ ◑ ⇌ ♣ P

Golden Cock
Tubwell Row ☎ (0325) 468843
11–3, 6–11; 11–11 Mon, Fri & Sat
Courage Directors; John Smith's Bitter, Magnet; guest beer Ⓗ
18th-century, town-centre pub, modernised internally but retaining some original features. Bar billiards played – the only table for miles. Darlington CAMRA 1993 *Pub of the Year*. ⇌ ♣

Pennyweight
Bakehouse Hill (Market Place)
☎ (0325) 464244
11–11
Vaux Double Maxim; Wards Sheffield Best Bitter Ⓗ**; guest beers**
Attractive, modern pub in an 18th-century building.
◐ ♿ ⇌

Red Lion
Priestgate ☎ (0325) 467619
11–11
Marston's Pedigree; Whitbread Boddingtons Bitter, Castle Eden Ale, Flowers Original, Porter Ⓗ**; guest beers**
A lively, modern public house. The single long bar has two small, secluded areas at one end, and traditional decor. Mini-beer festivals are held regularly. ◐ ♿ ⇌ ♣

Tap & Spile
99 Bondgate ☎ (0325) 381679
11.30–3, 6.30 (4.30 Thu–Sat)–11
Camerons Bitter, Strongarm; guest beers Ⓗ
Popular, town-centre local, after the style of a Victorian alehouse. Offers up to eight real beers and occasional ciders. Regular live jazz and blues nights. ◐ ♿ ⇌ ♣ ⌽

Travellers Rest
West Auckland Road, Cockerton (A68, 1 mile W of centre) ☎ (0325) 468177

11–3, 6–11
John Smith's Bitter, Magnet [H]
Attractive, 1920s, two-roomed local in a now-urbanised village. A comfortable, music-free lounge and a plain public bar. Built for the long-defunct Haughton Road Brewery Co.
Q ⊞ ♣

Try also: Falchion, Blackwellgate; **Turk's Head,** Bondgate (both Camerons)

Durham City

Colpitts Hotel
Hawthorne Terrace (A690, 200 yds from bus station)
☎ (091) 386 9913
11–3, 5.30–11; 11–11 Fri & Sat
Samuel Smith OBB [H]
Bohemian pub with a bar, a small lounge and a pool room. Stages regular folk and trad. jazz, as well as a quiz. Locals and students mix amicably.
⛼ Q ⇌ ♣

Court Inn
Court Lane, Old Elvet (next to gaol) ☎ (091) 384 6536
11–11
Draught Bass [H]
Busy, updated, Victorian pub, recently purchased by a local landlord. No jukebox or pool; just a comfortable, warm interior, popular with students and locals. Very good food.
Q ♉ ◐ ◗ ♿

Elm Tree
Crossgate ☎ (091) 386 4621
12–3, 6–11; 12–11 Sat; 12–2, 7–10.30 Sun
Vaux Samson [H]**; guest beers**
Friendly, regulars' pub which is quiet midweek, but busy and cosmopolitan at the weekend, catering for all. Handy for the bus station. Guest beers are from the Vaux range. Q ⛟ ◐ ⇌ P

Garden House
North Road (5 mins' walk from bus and rail stations)
☎ (091) 384 3460
11–3, 5.30–11
Vaux Samson; Wards Sheffield Best Bitter; guest beer [H]
Traditional-style pub with a large conservatory and a friendly, warm atmosphere. Regular quiz nights and a karaoke night. Home-cooked food includes a traditional Sun lunch and special monthly theme nights.
Q ❀ ◐ ◗ ⇌ ♣ P

Half Moon
New Elvet
☎ (091) 386 4528
11–11
Draught Bass [H]

A *Good Beer Guide* regular, a pub dominated by its crescent-shaped bar. Refurbished since its last entry. Q ⇌

Victoria Hotel
86 Halgarth Street (A177, near Dunelm House)
☎ (091) 386 5269
11–3, 7–11
McEwan 80/-; S&N Theakston Best Bitter [H]**; guest beer**
A listed building: an old, three-roomed pub, popular with locals and students. Collection of Toby jugs in the bar and a large selection of whiskies. ⛼ Q ⛟ ⊞ ⇌

Try also: Bridge, North Rd (S&N); **Dun Cow,** Old Elvet (Whitbread)

Framwellgate Moor

Marquis of Granby
Front Street (just off A167 bypass, on old Great North Road) ☎ (091) 386 9382
11–4, 6–11
Samuel Smith OBB [H]
A *Guide* regular, and a popular local: one large drinking area, a pool/games room and a small snug, with traditional decor. Excellent beer prices.
❀ ♣ P

Tap & Spile
27 Front Street (just off A167)
☎ (091) 386 5451
11.30–3, 6–11
Camerons Bitter [H]**; guest beers**
Third in the Tap & Spile chain, converted in 1988 to a now familiar format with stone walls, plain floors and basic furniture. Three rooms, but the back room can be partitioned and children admitted, except late on busy eves. Up to eight guest beers. Q ♉ ♣ ♁

Try also: Happy Wanderer (Bass); **Lambton Hounds,** Pity Me (Vaux)

Heighington Station

Locomotion One
Heighington Lane, Newton Aycliffe (1 mile W of A167 at Aycliffe) ☎ (0325) 320132
11–11
Butterknowle Conciliation Ale; McEwan 80/-; Marston's Pedigree; S&N Theakston Best Bitter, Old Peculier [H]
Historic, 1860s railway station converted into a pub of character. George Stephenson placed his engine *Locomotion* on the lines of the Stockton and Darlington railway here in Sept 1825. Trains still run to the door. ⛼ ❀ ◐ ♿ ⇌ P

High Coniscliffe

Duke of Wellington
On A67 ☎ (0325) 374283
11–3, 6–11
Camerons Strongarm; Whitbread Flowers Original [H]
Traditional, one-roomed village local, opposite a popular riverside beauty spot. Quoits played.
⛼ Q ❀ ◐ ♿ ♣ P

Holmside

Wardles Bridge Inn
Front Street (¾ mile off B6532)
☎ (091) 371 0926
11–11
McEwan 80/-; S&N Theakston Best Bitter, XB; Younger No. 3 [H]
Village pub: a relaxing place for a drink, with a large, very friendly bar and a smaller lounge. Very popular Thai meals available (only by reservation). The new landlady has a very friendly manner.
⛼ Q ♉ ❀ ◐ ◗ ⊞ ♿ ♣ P

Holwick

Strathmore Arms
Off B6277 ☎ (0833) 40362
11.30–3, 7–11
Butterknowle Bitter; Camerons Bitter; John Smith's Bitter; guest beer [H]
Isolated but welcoming hostelry, three miles along a cul-de-sac near the south bank of the Tees. Worth the journey! Just a stroll away from the Pennine Way. The bar is cosy and warm, arranged in part around an open hearth; small dining room attached. The piano is actually used.
⛼ Q ❀ ⛟ ◐ ◗ ▲ ♣ P

Hurworth

Bay Horse
The Green ☎ (0325) 720663
11–11
John Smith's Magnet [H]
Attractive village pub in 18th-century cottages: a plain bar and a cosier lounge, with a small conservatory/restaurant at the rear. No food Sun. The central archway beneath the sundial of 1738 leads to a small garden.
Q ❀ ◐ ◗ ⊞ ♣ P

Leamside

Three Horse Shoes
Pithouse Lane (off A690, West Rainton–Great Lumley road)
☎ (091) 584 2394

Durham

12-3 (not Mon or Tue), 7-11
S&N Theakston Best Bitter, XB Ⓗ; guest beer
Friendly country inn: a large bar with a lounge at one end and a family room at the other. Regular charity nights.
⌂ ☺ ❀ ◐ ◑ ♿ ▲ ♣ P

Middleton St George

Fighting Cocks

Darlington Road
☎ (0325) 332327
11.30-2.30, 5.30-11; 11-11 Sat
Vaux Double Maxim, Extra Special; Wards Sheffield Best Bitter Ⓗ
Arguably the oldest railway ticket sales office still in existence, being on the original alignment of the Stockton and Darlington railway. Much updated: now a comfortable large room with a bar area and an area set aside for eating. No meals Sun eve. ❀ ◐ ◑ ♣ P

Try also: Havelock (John Smith's)

Neasham

Fox & Hounds

24 Teesway ☎ (0325) 720350
11-3 (4 Sat), 6.30-11
Vaux Samson, Double Maxim; Wards Sheffield Best Bitter Ⓗ
Village pub near a scenic stretch of the Tees: a small bar, a meals-based lounge and a family conservatory. The last overlooks an equipped play area. ☺ ❀ ◐ ◑ ⊟ ♿ ♣ P

No Place

Beamish Mary Inn

600 yds off A693
☎ (091) 370 0237
12-3, 6-11; 12-11 Fri & Sat
McEwan 80/-; S&N Theakston Best Bitter, XB; guest beers Ⓗ
Lounge/diner of Victorian/Edwardian character and a lively bar in an ex-mining community pub. Weekly folk nights; blues music in a converted stables, which also hosts an annual beer festival. No Place Bitter is brewed by Big Lamp. ⌂ Q ❀ 🛏 ◐ ◑ ⊟ ♿ ▲ ♣ P

Try also: Sun Inn, Beamish Museum (S&N)

North Bitchburn

Red Lion

North Bitchburn Terrace (off B6286, towards Howden-le-Wear) ☎ (0388) 763561
12-2.30, 7-11
Courage Directors; John Smith's Bitter, Magnet Ⓗ; guest beers
Warm, welcoming village pub with a comfortable bar, a games room and a lounge, where a good choice of meals is available. Previous winner of Durham CAMRA *Best Pub* award. ⌂ ❀ ◐ ◑ ⊟ ♣ P

Ovington

Four Alls

By the green ☎ (0833) 27302
11.30-2.30, 6.30-11
S&N Theakston Best Bitter, XB Ⓗ
Four-roomed, traditional village local, decorated with sporting memorabilia. Pool and darts area.
⌂ ◐ ◑ ♿ ♣ P

Oxhill

Ox Inn

On A693, ¾ mile W of Stanley
☎ (0207) 233626
12-3 (5 Sat), 7-11; 12-11 Fri
Bass Worthington BB, Draught Bass Ⓗ; guest beer
Large bar with a high ceiling and a small conservatory, leading to a patio and garden/play area. Recently refurbished and under new ownership, hosting live music occasionally.
Q ☺ ❀ ▲ ♣ P

Romaldkirk

Kirk Inn

The Green ☎ (0833) 50260
12-2.30, 6-11
Black Sheep Best Bitter; Butterknowle Conciliation Ale; Whitbread Boddingtons Bitter, Castle Eden Ale Ⓗ; guest beers
Charming, single-room pub, with a warm and welcoming atmosphere, situated on the village green. A small dining room now offers exceptional food prepared by the landlord himself, who also serves no keg beer. ⌂ Q ❀ ◐ ◑ ♣ P

St John's Chapel

Golden Lion

Market Place (A689)
☎ (0388) 537231
11-3, 7-11
Morland Old Speckled Hen Ⓖ; Ruddles County; John Smith's Magnet Ⓗ
Unusual, E-shaped pub which is comfortable and friendly, serving good meals. Children welcome; holiday flats to let.
⌂ Q ❀ 🛏 ◐ ◑ ♿ ▲ ♣ P

Try also: Blue Bell (Tetley)

Seaton

Seaton Lane Inn

Seaton Lane (B1404, just off A19) ☎ (091) 581 2038
12-3, 7-11; 12-2, 7-10.30 Sun
Black Sheep Best Bitter; Butterknowle Bitter; S&N Theakston Best Bitter Ⓗ
Originally a 17th-century blacksmith's cottage, a pub which has been in the same family for 46 years and in the *Guide* since 1977. A basic bar and a comfortable lounge. Families are welcome in the neat garden. See the pictorial history of the village on the bar wall. Described by the local press as an 'oasis in a beer desert'. Q ❀ ♣ P

Shadforth

Plough

South Side ☎ (091) 372 0375
12-2 (not Mon-Wed), 7-11; 11-11 Sat
Draught Bass; Stones Best Bitter; guest beers Ⓗ
Traditional, old-fashioned pub with a touch of class, frequented by village locals and visitors. Good quality guest beers; around 30 have been sold in six months.
⌂ Q ◐ ◑ ♣ P ⚡

Sherburn Hill

Moor Edge

Front Street (outskirts of Durham City)
☎ (091) 372 1618
12-3 (11-4 Fri & Sat), 7-11
Vaux Lorimers Best Scotch, Extra Special; Wards Sheffield Best Bitter Ⓗ
Typical village pub: a bar and lounge with coal fires; a previous Durham CAMRA *Best Pub* award-winner. Quoits played. ⌂ Q ❀ ⊟ ♣ P

Try also: Burley Lodge (S&N)

Shincliffe

Seven Stars

On A177 ☎ (091) 384 8454
11.30-3.30, 6.30-11
Vaux Samson; Wards Sheffield Best Bitter Ⓗ
Coaching inn dating from 1752; now a smart village pub with two, well-furnished rooms and an à la carte restaurant. Note the collection of miners' lamps in the bar.
Q ❀ ◐ ◑ ⊟

Stanley

Blue Boar Tavern

Front Street (off A693)
☎ (0207) 231167

11–3, 7–11; 11–11 Thu–Sat
Butterknowle Conciliation Ale, Black Diamond, High Force; Ind Coope Burton Ale; Tetley Bitter [H]; guest beers
Former coaching inn, popular for lunchtime meals. Blues/rock music every weekend. The guest beer changes every two weeks. A recent Durham CAMRA *Pub of the Year*.
⌂ Q ❀ ◐ ♿ ▲ P

Startforth

Royal Star
Low Startforth Road (A67, facing Barnard Castle)
☎ (0833) 37374
11–11
Ind Coope Burton Ale; S&N Theakston XB; Tetley Bitter; guest beer [H]
Two-roomed local in Startforth, the 'Yorkshire' part of Barnard Castle, across the ancient county bridge. Meals available 11.30–9.30 (12–2 Sun). ❀ ◐ ⊞ ♣ P

Summerhouse

Raby Hunt
On B6279 ☎ (032 574) 604
11.30–3, 6.30–11
Marston's Bitter, Pedigree; guest beers [H]
Neat, welcoming, old stone free house in a pretty whitewashed hamlet: a homely lounge and a bustling locals' bar. Good, home-cooked lunches (not served Sun). Raby Castle is worth a visit, just five miles away.
⌂ ❀ ◑ ⊞ ♣ P

Waskerley

Moorcock
Between Stanhope and Consett
☎ (0207) 508233
11–3, 7–11
S&N Theakston XB [H]
Open-plan, old-fashioned rural pub which enjoys a tourist trade all year round (next to marked walks and fishing). Snacks and sandwiches available. Pool table and a dartboard.
⌂ Q ❀ ⊨ ▲ ♣ P ⚟

White-le-Head

Highlander Inn
On B6311 ☎ (0207) 232416
7–11; 12–3, 7–11 Sat; 12–2.30, 7–10.30 Sun
Belhaven 80/-; Butterknowle Conciliation Ale [H]; guest beer
Popular village pub set on top of a hill near Tantobie: a lively bar and an intimate lounge, with a small dining room off. Weekly folk, jazz and blues Thu. Lunches served Sun only.
Q ☋ ❀ ◗ ⊞ ♿ ▲ ♣ P ⚟

Witton Gilbert

Glendenning Arms
Front Street (A691)
☎ (091) 371 0316
11–4, 7–11
Vaux Samson [H]
After 18 years in the *Guide*, this local remains unspoilt, with the same licensee in charge. Two comfortable rooms in traditional style, with racing and country sports memorabilia in the bar.
⌂ Q ♣ P

Travellers Rest
Front Street (A691)
☎ (091) 371 0458
11–3, 6–11
McEwan 80/-; S&N Theakston Best Bitter, XB, Old Peculier; Younger Scotch, No. 3 [H]
Smart, country-style pub. The open-plan drinking area has a split-level, no-smoking section. The conservatory is ideal for children. Wide variety of meals in the bar or restaurant. Petanque played.
⌂ Q ☋ ❀ ◐ ♣ P ⚟

Try also: Centurion, Langley Park (Vaux)

Woodstone Village

Floaters Mill
1½ miles E of A1(M), 1½ miles SE of A183 ☎ (091) 385 6695
11.30–2.30, 7–11
Camerons Bitter, Strongarm [H]
Very smart pub/restaurant with a conservatory eating area. The single bar is split by a pillar. Popular for family meals. Children's adventure play area (but near a main road with no safety fence).
Q ❀ ◐ ♣ P

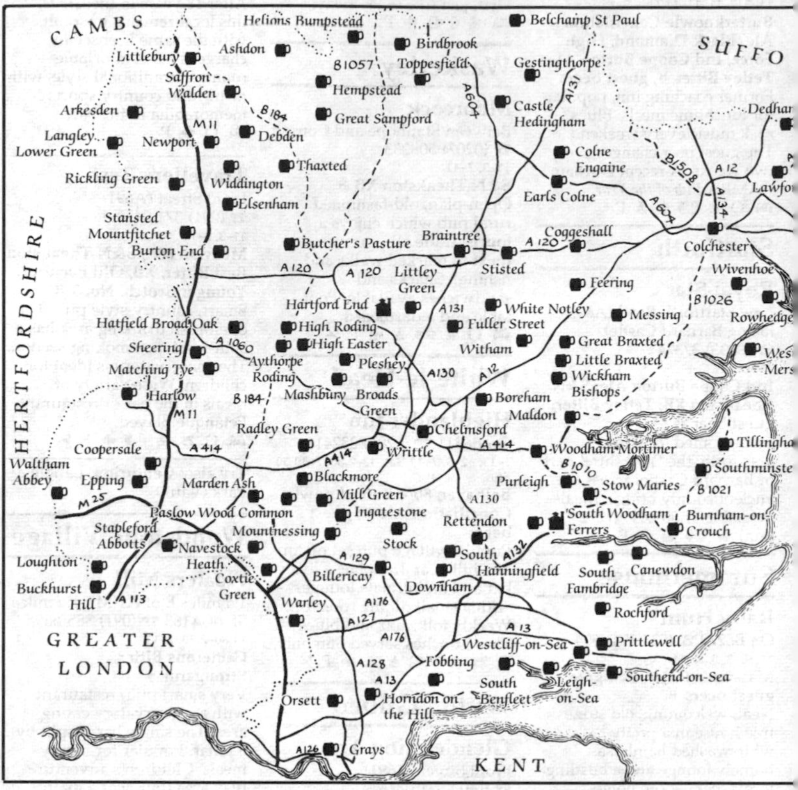

Crouch Vale, *South Woodham Ferrers*; **Ridleys**, *Hartford End*

Ardleigh

Lion

The Street ☎ (0206) 230083
12–3, 7–11
Tolly Cobbold Mild, Original Ⓗ
400-year-old, two-bar village local with lots of oak beams: an old coaching house.
Q ❀ ♣ P

Arkesden

Axe & Compasses

☎ (0799) 550272
12–2.30, 6–11
Greene King IPA, Abbot Ⓗ
Superb, 17th-century, traditional village local with a thriving food trade. A welcoming pub with local characters, in a picturesque village. ♨ Q ❀ ◐ ◑ ♣ P

Ashdon

Bonnet

Steventon End
☎ (0799) 584513
12–3, 6–11
Greene King IPA, Abbot Ⓗ; **Mauldons Squires** Ⓖ
Comfortable, popular, oak-beamed pub, featured in *Reuben's Corner* by Spike Mays. Separate restaurant (no food Tue eve). Q ❀ ◐ ◑ ▲ ♣ P

Aythorpe Roding

Axe & Compasses

On B184 ☎ (0279) 876647
10.30–3, 5.30–11 (10.30–11 summer Sat)
Adnams Broadside; Bateman XXXB; Gibbs Mew Wiltshire; Greene King IPA Ⓗ
Old roadhouse with a long, narrow interior and a good mix of local and passing trades. Fresh food. Phone to confirm accommodation.
♨ Q 🛏 ◐ ◑ ♿ P

Belchamp St Paul

Cherry Tree Inn

Knowl Green OS784413
☎ (0787) 237263
12–3, 7–11; closed Tue
Adnams Bitter, Broadside; Greene King IPA Ⓗ
Cosy, isolated, 16th-century pub, refurbished. Good value beer and food (fresh veg and home cooking). Good play area.
♨ Q ❀ 🛏 ◐ ◑ ▲ ♣ P

Billericay

Coach & Horses

36 Chapel Street (off High St, B1007) ☎ (0277) 622873
10–4, 5.30–11; 10–11 Fri, Sat & when busy
Greene King IPA, Rayments Special, Abbot Ⓗ, **Winter Ale** Ⓖ
Welcoming one-bar local on the site of the former Crown Brewery tap. Collection of jugs on the ceiling and carved elephants behind the bar. Good value meals (no food Sun). Long-standing, friendly landlord. ♨ ❀ ◐ ⇌ ♣ P

Birdbrook

Plough

The Street ☎ (044 085) 336
11–2.30, 6–11

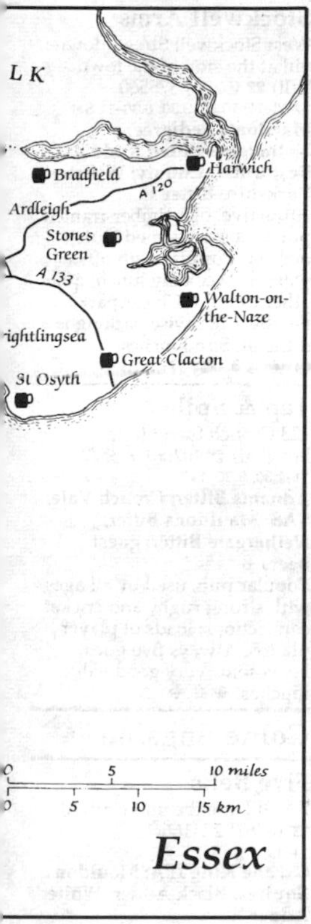

Adnams Bitter; Greene King IPA Ⓖ; guest beer
Traditional, friendly village local. Good value snacks.
⛫ Q ❀ ⊞ ♣ P

Blackmore

Leather Bottle
The Green ☎ (0277) 821891
11–11
Adnams Bitter; Brains Dark; Crouch Vale Woodham IPA; Greene King IPA; Nethergate Bitter Ⓗ; guest beers
Busy, friendly, cosy village pub. ⛫ Q ❀ ◖ ◗ ♣ ⌓ P

Boreham

Queens Head
Church Road ☎ (0245) 467298
10.30–3, 6–11
Greene King IPA, Abbot Ⓗ
Friendly, traditional village local, in the same family for 54 years. Good value. No food Sun. Q ❀ ◖ ⊞ ♣ P

Bradfield

Strangers Home Inn
The Street (B1352 – follow the camping signs)
☎ (0255) 870304
12–3 (extends when busy), 7–11
Tolly Cobbold Original; Whitbread Flowers Original Ⓗ
Fine, busy, one-bar local with a wood-burning open fire and a stove. Good simple food and excellent camping facilities. Garden with Hebridean sheep, Shetland ponies and goats. On the Essex Way. Pool table, but no jukebox.
⛫ Q ❀ ◖ ◗ ♿ ▲ ♣ P

Braintree

Wagon & Horses
South Street ☎ (0376) 553356
11–3, 5.30 (6 Sat)–11
Greene King XX Mild, IPA, Abbot Ⓗ, Winter Ale Ⓖ
Well-renovated pub with a large lounge bar, a raised dining area and a friendly snug. Monthly games nights.
⛟ ❀ ◖ ◗ ⇄ ♣ P

Brightlingsea

Railway Tavern
Station Road (off B1029, near waterfront) ☎ (0206) 302581
11–3 (not Mon–Thu, except bank hols & July–Sept), 5.30–11
Bateman XXXB; Mauldons Bitter; guest beers Ⓗ
Two bars and a family room give an insight into old Brightlingsea. The front bar has railway memorabilia and the larger rear bar has pool and darts. Guests include a mild. ⛫ ⛟ ❀ ▲ ♣

Broads Green

Walnut Tree
½ mile from old A130 at Great Waltham OS694125
☎ (0245) 360222
11.30–2.30, 6.30–11; 12–2.30, 7–10.30 Sun
Ridleys IPA Ⓗ/Ⓖ
Clean, pleasant, three-bar country pub; a well-furnished lounge and a basic public bar with a real fire and a trophy cabinet. Entrance is through a cosy middle snug. Snacks lunchtime. ⛫ Q ❀ ⊞ ♣ P

Buckhurst Hill

Warren Wood
Epping New Road (A104)
☎ (081) 505 3737
11–11
Adnams Broadside; Courage Best Bitter, Directors; Ruddles Best Bitter, County Ⓗ
Busy, thriving pub on the edge of Epping Forest, with a splendid country view at the rear. Courage Best is sold as Webster's Wonderful Wallop. The beer range may vary.
⛫ ❀ ◖ ♿ P

Burnham-on-Crouch

New Welcome Sailor
Station Road ☎ (0621) 784778
11–3, 6–11; 11–11 Sat
Greene King IPA, Abbot Ⓗ
Basic town pub, more popular with men than women. Most pub games played. ⇄ ♣ P

Olde White Harte
The Quay ☎ (0621) 782106
11–3, 6–11; 11–11 Sat
Adnams Bitter; Tolly Cobbold Bitter Ⓗ
Old riverside pub populated by locals and yachtsmen. Can be crowded and noisy in summer. Best to sit on the jetty and watch the sun set over the Crouch. ⛫ Q ❀ ⛼ ◖ ◗ P

Burton End

Ash
1 mile from Stansted OS532237
☎ (0279) 814841
11.30–2.30 (3 Sat), 5.30 (6 Sat)–11
Greene King IPA, Rayments Special, Abbot Ⓗ
15th-century pub extended to provide a lounge bar/dining room and a larger public bar with a quarry-tiled floor, to accommodate country characters and their dogs. Good, wholesome food, reasonably priced (no meals winter Sun). Near the airport but retaining a quiet, rural atmosphere.
⛫ ❀ ◖ ◗ ⊞ ♣ P

Butcher's Pasture

Stag
Duck Street (1 mile W of B184)
☎ (0371) 870214
11–2.30 (extends if busy), 6–11
Ridleys IPA Ⓗ
Friendly village pub with plain wooden benches and tables in the public bar but a refurbished, extended and comfortable saloon bar. Occasional live music. Fine views from the large garden.
⛫ ❀ ◖ ◗ ⊞ ▲ ♣ P

Canewdon

Chequers Inn
High Street ☎ (0702) 258251
12 (11.30 Sat)–3, 7–11
Greene King IPA, Abbot; Wadworth 6X Ⓗ; guest mild
Superb, traditionally furnished inn with a snug family room. Used by the local cricket team; cribbage and dominoes played. A quiet village pub, welcoming to visitors. The Sun roasts are recommended (book) and good bar meals are served (except Sun eve and Mon). Q ⛟ ❀ ◖ ◗ ♣ P

Castle Hedingham

Bell Inn

10 St James Street
☎ (0787) 60350
11.30–3, 6–11
Greene King IPA, Abbot Ⓖ
Excellent, genuine, timbered pub with casks behind the bar. Good value food (not served Mon eve, except bank hols).
♨ Q ꝏ ❀ ◐ ◑ ⊞ ▲ ♣ P

Chelmsford

Endeavour

351 Springfield Road (follow Chelmsford signs from A12 Boreham interchange, 1 mile)
☎ (0245) 257717
11–11; 12–2, 7–10.30 Sun
Greene King IPA, Abbot Ⓗ
Quiet, three-room, suburban pub with a traditional atmosphere. Unusual pub sign: the sailing ship one side and the spacecraft the other. No food Sun. No-smoking dining area. ♨ Q ◐ ◑ ♣

Partners

30 Lower Anchor Street
☎ (0245) 265181
11–3, 5–11; 11–11 Sat
Adnams Bitter; Crouch Vale Best Bitter; Fuller's London Pride; Greene King IPA; Wadworth 6X Ⓗ**; guest beer**
Friendly, often busy, street-corner local. A games room doubles (triples) as a family/ meeting room. The patio is a summer suntrap. Near cricket and football grounds. No food Sun. ꝏ ❀ ◐ ≢ ♣ P

Red Lion

147 New London Road
☎ (0245) 354092
10.30–11
Adnams Extra; Everards Tiger; Ridleys IPA Ⓗ
Popular, traditional, street-corner pub, with a comfortable lounge and a long, basic, often lively, public bar. ❀ ◐ ♣

White Horse

25 Townfield Street (behind station) ☎ (0245) 269556
11–3, 5.30 (7 Sat)–11
Draught Bass; M&B Highgate Mild; S&N Theakston Best Bitter; Stones Best Bitter Ⓗ**; guest beers**
Roomy, friendly, one-bar pub with a good range of games, but no pool or jukebox. Over 500 guest beers in the last two years (up to six available). Snacks weekday lunch. ≢ ♣

Coggeshall

Fleece

West Street ☎ (0376) 561412
11–11
Greene King IPA, Abbot Ⓗ
Handsome, timber-framed and pargetted pub, built in 1503, next to Paycocke's House (NT), in a charming country town. Children welcome (garden with play area). Call first to camp. No food Tue eve.
♨ ❀ ◐ ◑ ♿ ▲ ♣ P

Colchester

British Grenadier

67 Military Road (300 yards SE of station) ☎ (0206) 799654
11–2.30, 6–11; 11–11 Sat
Adnams Mild (not winter), **Bitter, Old; guest beer** Ⓗ
Very popular workingman's pub with traditional games. Pool in the back bar, darts in the front. Happy hour 6–7 Mon–Fri. Q ≢ (Town) ♣

Dog & Pheasant

24 Nayland Road, Mile End (A134) ☎ (0206) 852427
11–2.30, 5.30–11
Greene King XX Mild, IPA, Abbot, Winter Ale (winter) Ⓗ
Large, friendly pub with good service in public and lounge-style areas. An indoor balcony and a restaurant are features. Mixed clientele; darts and pool. ❀ ◐ ◑ ♿ ♣ P

Dragoon

82 Butt Road (just S of centre)
☎ (0206) 573464
11–3 (4 Sat), 5.15 (7 Sat)–11; 11–11 Fri
Adnams Mild, Bitter, Old; Tetley Bitter; guest beer Ⓗ
Very popular pub with a comfortable, quiet saloon, and a public with pool and darts. Good value food Mon–Sat lunch, with specials. At least four, changing guest beers.
❀ ◐ ⊞ ≢ (Town) ♣

Odd One Out

28 Mersea Road (B1025)
☎ (0206) 578140
11–3 (4 Sat; not Mon–Thu), 5.30 (6 Sat)–11
Archers Best Bitter; Mauldons Bitter; Ridleys IPA; guest beers Ⓗ
The basic beer-drinker's pub of Colchester, with a friendly atmosphere, popular with all sorts. Four guest beers, one always a mild. The back bar is no-smoking Fri and Sat eves, and available for meetings during the week. Keen prices.
♨ Q ≢ (Town) ⍥ ⊘

Rose & Crown Hotel

Eastgates, East Hill (bottom of Ipswich Rd) ☎ (0206) 866677
11–2.30, 6–11
Tolly Cobbold Original, Old Strong, Tollyshooter Ⓗ
Pleasant hotel bar in a 15th-century, timber-framed and beamed building. A la carte food in the bar or restaurant.
♨ Q 🛏 ◐ ◑ ≢ (Hythe) P

Stockwell Arms

West Stockwell Street (down hill at the side of the town hall) ☎ (0206) 575560
10.30–11; 10.30–3.30, 6.30–11 Sat
Marston's Pedigree; Nethergate Bitter; Ruddles Best Bitter, County; Webster's Yorkshire Bitter Ⓗ
Attractive, old, timber-framed pub in the acclaimed Dutch quarter. Popular with office workers weekday lunch, quiet other times. NCP car park nearby, otherwise parking is difficult. Sun lunches.
Q ❀ ◐ ◑ ≢ (Town) ♣

Tap & Spile

123 Crouch Street (opp. hospital) ☎ (0206) 573572
11–2.30, 5.30–11
Adnams Bitter; Crouch Vale SAS; Mauldons Bitter; Nethergate Bitter; guest beers Ⓗ
Popular pub, used by all ages, with strong rugby and cricket connections; loads of player photos. Always five guest beers sold. Very good value lunches. ❀ ◐ ♣ ⍥

Colne Engaine

Five Bells

7 Mill Lane (behind church)
☎ (0787) 224166
11–11
Greene King IPA; Mauldons Squires, Black Adder, White Adder Ⓗ
300-year-old, timber-framed, two-bar village pub with wood burning fires. Busy food trade. The attached barn/ family room functions as the village hall. Four pool teams. Restaurant upstairs.
♨ Q ꝏ ❀ 🛏 ◐ ◑ ♣ P

Coopersale

Theydon Oak

Stonard Hill (1 mile SE of Epping) OS474018
☎ (0992) 572618
11–3, 5.30–11
Draught Bass; Charrington IPA; Mauldons Black Adder; Wadworth IPA, 6X; guest beers Ⓗ
Small bar with a white-painted, wood exterior. Very busy particularly at weekends and parking is often a problem. ♨ Q ❀ ◐ ◑ P

Coxtie Green

White Horse

173 Coxtie Green Road (off A128 by Black Horse pub) OS564959 ☎ (0277) 372410
11.30–3, 5.30–11
Bateman XB; Crouch Vale Best Bitter; Linfit Old Eli; Marston's Pedigree; Nethergate Old Growler; Wadworth 6X Ⓗ

Cosy, comfortable country pub with a children's playground in the large garden. Usually six ales, varying seasonally. Occasional beer festivals. A traditional pub with games. No food Sun. ❀ ◖ ◗ ♣ P

Debden

Plough
High Street ☎ (0799) 540396
12–3, 6–11; 12–11 Sat
Greene King IPA, Rayments Special, Abbot Ⓗ
Friendly, 17th-century, locals' pub with a superb garden for children. Deservedly popular, home-cooked food (extensive menu, game the speciality).
♛ Q ❀ ◖ ◗ ▲ ♣ P

Dedham

Anchor Inn
The Heath (1 mile S of village)
☎ (0206) 323131
11–4, 6–11; 11–11 Sat
Greene King IPA Ⓗ
Pleasant, old, oak-beamed village pub with games in a separate room. No meals on Sun eve; book for Sun lunch.
♛ Q ❀ ◖ ◗ ♣ P

Downham

De Beauvoir Arms
Downham Road
☎ (0268) 710571
12–3, 5–11; 11–11 Fri, Sat & when busy
Courage Directors; Greene King IPA; Morland Old Speckled Hen; Moorhouse's Pendle Witches Brew; guest beers
Friendly, one-bar pub, popular with walkers; close to the Essex Wildlife Trust nature reserve. Foreign cuisine and quiz nights are specialities; barbecues in summer. Pendle Witches Brew is sold as Beavers' Lodge house beer. No meals Tue. Occasional cider.
❀ ◖ ◗ ▲ ♣ ⌓ P

Earls Colne

Bird in Hand
Coggeshall Road (B1024)
☎ (0787) 222557
12–2.30 (extends if busy), 6–11; 12–2.30, 7–10.30 Sun
Ridleys Mild Ⓔ**, IPA** Ⓖ
Pleasant pub with two small bars. Pool, darts and shove-ha'penny in the games area. Pictures in the saloon reveal connections with a nearby wartime USAAF base. A family pub, but no under 14s.
♛ Q ❀ ◖ ◗ ⊟ ♣ P

Castle
High Street ☎ (0787) 222694
11–11
Greene King XX Mild, IPA, Abbot Ⓗ
Traditional, beamed country-town pub, with log fires. Two bars: the rear is plain with a fruit machine; the front is comfy and has a piano – pianists welcome. Very reasonably priced B&B. Crib and dominoes.
♛ Q ❀ 🛏 ♣ P

Elsenham

Crown
High Street ☎ (0279) 812827
11–3, 6–11; 12–2.30, 7–10.30 Sun
Nethergate Bitter; Taylor Walker Best Bitter Ⓗ
Deservedly popular, village pub with a pargetted exterior and a good reputation for food (not served Sun). Friendly.
♛ Q ❀ ◖ ◗ ♣ P

Epping

Forest Gate
Bell Common (just off B1393 on Ivy Chimneys road)
OS451011 ☎ (0992) 572312
10–2.30, 5.30–11
Adnams Bitter Ⓗ**, Broadside** Ⓖ**; Greene King Abbot; Ridleys IPA** Ⓗ**; guest beers**
On the edge of Epping Forest, a traditionally decorated, small bar which often gets very busy. ♛ Q ❀ ♣ ⌓ P

Feering

Sun Inn
3 Feering Hill (B1024, near Blackwater bridge)
☎ (0376) 570442
11–3, 6–11; 11–11 some Sats
John Smith's Bitter; Wadworth 6X Ⓗ**; guest beers**
Recently refurbished, charming, timbered pub with exposed beams and a huge, open fire. Bistro-style English and Mediterranean food, all home-cooked. Cider in summer. Families welcome in a separate area of the bar.
♛ Q ❀ ◖ ◗ ♿ ♣ ⌓ P

Fobbing

White Lion
Lion Hill (B1420, 1 mile S of Five Bells interchange on A13)
☎ (0375) 673281
11–2.30 (4.30 Fri & Sat), 5.30–11
Ind Coope Burton Ale; Taylor Walker Best Bitter; Tetley Bitter Ⓗ
Traditional coaching inn which feels like a country pub, despite the proximity of Basildon and the A13. Enjoys a pleasant position on the brow of a hill, overlooking a fine old church. Unspoilt and friendly. No food Sun. ♛ Q ❀ ◖ P

Fuller Street

Square & Compasses
1½ miles off A131, between Terling and Great Leighs
OS748161 ☎ (0245) 361477
11–3 (4 Sat), 6–11
Ridleys IPA Ⓖ
Traditional, welcoming country pub with good food, known locally as the Stoke Hole. Unusual pitch-penny stool in the public bar. Folk first Fri of each month; annual folk weekend in early summer. No eve meals Thu or Sun.
♛ Q ❀ ◖ ◗ ▲ ♣ P

Gestingthorpe

Pheasant
Audley End ☎ (0787) 61196
11–3, 6–11
Adnams Bitter; Greene King IPA, Abbot Ⓗ**; Nethergate Bitter, Old Growler** Ⓖ**; guest beer**
Multi-roomed pub, the focal point of the village. Good food; extensive vegetarian menu (book weekends). Occasional live music. Local cider. ♛ ꝏ ❀ ◖ ◗ ▲ ♣ P

Grays

Wharf
Wharf Road South (off A126)
☎ (0375) 372418
11–3 (4 Sat), 6 (7 Sat)–11
Ind Coope Burton Ale; Tetley Bitter; Young's Bitter Ⓗ
Listed pub next to the Thames: a very popular pub which can get busy (especially the public). The saloon is smaller and quieter. Outdoor seating overlooks the river. Lunches Mon–Sat. ❀ ◖ ⊟ ≋ ♣ P

Great Braxted

Du-Cane Arms
Tiptree Road ☎ (0621) 891697
11.45–2.30, 7 (6.30 Fri & Sat)–11
Adnams Extra; Greene King IPA Ⓗ
Friendly village pub offering a good variety of well-presented food. ♛ Q ❀ ◖ ◗ P

Great Clacton

Robin Hood
211 London Road (A133)
☎ (0255) 421519
11–11 (11–3, 5.30–11 winter)
Adnams Bitter; Draught Bass; Charrington IPA Ⓗ
Spacious, low-ceilinged, comfortable pub with an imaginative menu, ideal for a pause on the way to Clacton-on-Sea. ♛ Q ❀ ◖ ◗ ▲ P ⊘

Essex

Great Sampford

Red Lion Inn
Finchingfield Road (B1053)
☎ (0799) 586325
12–3, 5.30–11
Ridleys Mild [G], IPA [H]
Pleasant, friendly local, with a varied menu in the bar and restaurant. ♛ ❀ 🛏 ◐ ◗ ♣ P

Harlow

Archers Dart
Coppice Hatch, Partridge Road (off Southern Way)
11–3.30, 5.30 (6.30 Sat)–11
Greene King IPA, Abbot [H]
Estate pub with an unusual upstairs cellar. Built in 1979. No food Sun. ◐ ♣ P

Harwich

Alma Inn
25 Kings Head Street (off the quay) ☎ (0255) 503474
11–3 (extends in summer), 7 (6 Fri)–11
Greene King IPA; Tolly Cobbold Mild; guest beer [H]
One large bar with a tiny private bar at the side in an Elizabethan pub refronted by the Georgians. Live trad. jazz monthly. ♛ Q ❀ 🛏 ◐ ≢ ♣

Hanover Inn
65 Church Street
☎ (0255) 502927
10.30–3 (extends busy Sats), 6.30–11
Tolly Cobbold Mild, Bitter, Old Strong; Whitbread Boddingtons Bitter [H]
Cosy, timbered, trawlerman's pub with Admiralty charts in the front bar. The fire burns coal trawled from the sea. Don't miss the mild. Pool and darts in the back bar.
♛ ⊟ ≢ ♣

Hatfield Broad Oak

Cock Inn
High Street ☎ (0279) 718273
11–3, 5.30–11
Adnams Mild, Bitter, Broadside [H]; guest beer
Friendly village local with bare floorboards, a large collection of pictures and ancient beams. Handpainted, 16th-century walls in the Boardroom. Large restaurant. ♛ Q ❀ ◐ ◗ ♣ P

Helions Bumpstead

Three Horseshoes
Water Lane OS650414
☎ (0440) 730298
11.45–2.30, 7–11; 12–2, 7–10.30 Sun
Greene King IPA, Abbot [H]
Fine, friendly, old, remote pub, offering good value food (not served Mon/Tue eves or Sun). Award-winning gardens.
♛ Q ❀ ◐ ◗ ⊟ ▲ ♣ P

Hempstead

Bluebell Inn
High Street ☎ (0799) 599486
11.30–3, 6.30–11
Greene King IPA, Rayments Special [H]; guest beer
Excellent, 16th-century, listed building in a delightful village. Very comfortably furnished, with a dining area and a warm welcome. Comprehensive range of good value food. The birthplace of Dick Turpin.
♛ Q ♉ ❀ ◐ ◗ ♣ P

High Easter

Cock & Bell Inn
The Street ☎ (0245) 31296
12–2.30, 7–11
Crouch Vale Millennium Ale; Gibbs Mew Salisbury, Bishop's Tipple; Ruddles County [H]
14th-century, Grade II-listed building, steeped in history and awarded for its good food. The beer range may change.
♛ Q ❀ ◐ ◗ ♣ P

High Roding

Black Lion
The Street ☎ (0279) 872847
10.30–3, 6–11 (11.30 Sat)
Adnams Extra; Ridleys IPA [G]
15th-century pub with a timber-beamed interior. The home-cooked Italian food is renowned. No jukebox or machines. ♛ Q ❀ ◐ ◗ P

Horndon on the Hill

Bell Inn
High Road ☎ (0375) 672451
11–2.30 (3 Sat), 6–11
Draught Bass [G]; Charrington IPA; guest beers [H]
Popular, 15th-century coaching inn in a picturesque village; an interesting pub with a 93-year-old hot cross bun collection! Quality food in the pub and restaurant. Guest beers changed regularly. Good views from the patio area behind. ♛ Q ❀ ◐ ◗ P

Ingatestone

Star
High Street ☎ (0277) 353618
11–2.30, 6–11
Greene King IPA, Abbot [G]
Old village local with a mellow, cosy interior, little changed over the years. Noted for its huge log fire, over which hangs an old clock permanently showing closing time. Regular live country or folk music. ♛ ♉ ❀ ≢ P

Langley Lower Green

Bull
Park Lane ☎ (0279) 777307
12–2.30, 6–11
Adnams Bitter, Broadside; Greene King IPA [H]
Classic village pub with a loyal local clientele. A pitch-penny game is concealed under a bench seat in the saloon. No food.
♛ Q ❀ ♣ P

Lawford

Manningtree Station Buffet
☎ (0206) 391114
10.30–11
Adnams Bitter, Marston's Pedigree; Mauldons Black Adder; St Austell HSD; Summerskills Best Bitter [H]
Famous station buffet, a listed Victorian building, with decor straight out of *Brief Encounter*. Excellent food: don't miss Sun lunch (book). Eve meals Thu–Sat. Intimate dining room and a patio for train spotters. Beer and food prices are keen.
Q ❀ ◐ ◗ ≢ (Manningtree)

Leigh-on-Sea

Crooked Billet
51 High Street, Old Town
☎ (0702) 714854
11.30–3, 6–11
Adnams Bitter; Crouch Vale Woodham IPA; Hook Norton Best Bitter; Ind Coope Burton Ale; Taylor Walker Best Bitter; Tetley Bitter [H]; guest beers
16th-century, listed building comprising two bars, both with bay window seats giving superb estuary views. A Taylor Walker 'Heritage' pub with a changing selection of quality guest beers and its own house beers (not brewed here). No food Sun. Popular on summer weekends.
♛ Q ❀ ◐ ⊟ ≢ ♣

Little Braxted

Green Man
Kelvedon Road (1½ miles SE of village) OS849130
☎ (0621) 891659
11–3, 6 (6.30 winter)–11
Ridleys IPA [H]
Pleasant, country pub with a cosy, traditional lounge and good value food.
♛ Q ❀ ◐ ◗ ⊟ ♣ P

Littlebury

Queens Head Inn
High Street
☎ (0799) 522251
12–11

Bass Worthington BB; Courage Directors; Marston's Pedigree; Ruddles Best Bitter; Younger IPA [H]**; guest beers**
600-year-old village local with traditional features and ETB three-crown accommodation. Guest beer emphasis on microbreweries. Easter beer festival. Excellent value food.
♛ Q ♉ ❀ ⛟ ◖ ◗ ♣ P

Littley Green

Compasses
2 miles from A130 towards Hartford End OS699172
☎ (0245) 362308
11–3, 6–11
Ridleys Mild, IPA [G]
Picturesque, Victorian, cottage-type pub with open views of countryside. Close to Ridleys brewery and difficult to find, but well worth persevering. Friendly.
♛ Q ❀ ♿ P

Loughton

Royal Standard
126 High Road (A121)
☎ (081) 502 5645
11–11
Adnams Bitter; Draught Bass; Charrington IPA; Young's Bitter [H]
Pub with a tiled Victorian facade, a mock-Tudor interior and a horseshoe-shaped bar.
❀ ◖ ♿ ⊖ ♣

Maldon

Blue Boar Hotel
Silver Street ☎ (0621) 852681
11–2.30 (3 Fri & Sat), 6–11
Adnams Bitter [G]
Splendid, 14th-century coaching inn with character.
♛ Q ❀ ⛟ ◖ ⊟ ♣ P

White Horse
High Street ☎ (0621) 851708
10.30–3, 5.30–11
Courage Best Bitter, Directors; Wadworth 6X [H]**; guest beer**
Friendly High Street pub offering a wide variety of guest beers. ⛟ ◖ ◗ ♣

Marden Ash

Stag
Brentwood Road (A128)
☎ (0277) 362598
11–2.30 (3 Fri & Sat), 5.30–11
McMullen AK, Country, Stronghart [H]
Traditional and welcoming pub, comprising one bar along the front of the building, with an open fire at each end. Friendly landlord; weekly quiz nights. Good value beer and food. ♛ ❀ ◖ ◗ ♿ ♣ P

Mashbury

Fox
Great Waltham Road (between Waltham and Good Easter) OS650127 ☎ (0245) 31573
12–2.30 (not Mon), 6.30–11; 12–2.30, 7–10.30 Sun; closed Tue
Adnams Extra; Ridleys IPA [G]
Difficult-to-find, cottage-style, Victorian pub with rural views and a friendly atmosphere. Busy eves and Sun lunch because of its quality food. Folk singing and morris dancing. ♛ Q ❀ ◖ ◗ ▲ P

Matching Tye

Fox
☎ (0279) 731335
12–3, 6–11
Adnams Bitter; Wadworth 6X; Wells Eagle; Whitbread Boddingtons Bitter [H]
Cosy, village pub with a relaxing atmosphere. The bar is semi-split into three areas and many foxy artefacts are evident. Boules terrain in the garden. ♛ Q ❀ ◖ ◗ ♣ P

Messing

Old Crown
Lodge Road ☎ (0621) 815575
11.30–3, 6–11
Adnams Extra; Ridleys IPA [H]
Charming, typical rural Essex village local with pews and cosy corners. Separate restaurant, sometimes busy. Children welcome.
♛ Q ◖ ◗ ♣ P

Mill Green

Viper
Mill Green Road (2 miles from Ingatestone via Fryerning Lane, towards Highwood) OS641019 ☎ (0277) 352010
10–2.30 (3 Sat), 6–11
Adnams Bitter; Cains Bitter; Fuller's London Pride [H]
Old, timber-framed pub in woodland, with a splendid garden. Three bars: a simple public, a cosy snug, and a lounge. A rare unspoilt survivor in this area. Beer range may vary.
♛ Q ❀ ◖ ⊟ ♿ ♣ ⌒ P

Mountnessing

Prince of Wales
199 Roman Road (B1002, ¾ mile E of A12 jct)
☎ (0277) 353445
11–3, 6–11 (11–11 summer)
Adnams Extra [H]**; Ridleys Mild** (winter) [G]**, IPA** [H]**, Winter Ale** [G]**; guest beer**
Traditional pub with oak beams, mentioned in the *Domesday Book*. Friendly atmosphere, with families encouraged. Popular food.
♛ ❀ ◖ ◗ P

Navestock Heath

Plough
Sabines Road OS538970
☎ (0277) 372296
11–3.30, 6–11
Beer range varies [H]
Superb pub with a friendly atmosphere and 11 ales, including a mild. Good value food and beer. Quiz nights, live C&W and a monthly trad. jazz night. Local CAMRA *Pub of the Year* 1991 and 1992.
♛ Q ♉ ❀ ◖ ◗ ♿ ♣ P

Newport

Coach & Horses
Cambridge Road (B1383)
☎ (0799) 540292
11–3, 6–11
Greene King IPA; Tolly Cobbold Original [H]**; guest beers**
Warm and welcoming, 16th-century coaching inn offering excellent restaurant (no-smoking) and bar food.
♛ Q ❀ ◖ ◗ ▲ ⇌ ♣ P ⊬

Orsett

Foxhound
High Road ☎ (0375) 891295
11–3.30, 6–11
Courage Best Bitter, Directors; Crouch Vale Woodham IPA [H]
Typical village pub, popular with locals, one of whom made the pub sign, which holds a cryptic message. The saloon is full of foxhound memorabilia and its own tree sits in the centre. Basic public bar. Attached restaurant.
♛ Q ❀ ◖ ◗ ⊟ ♣ P

Paslow Wood Common

Black Horse
Stondon Road (off A414, towards Stondon Massey) OS588017 ☎ (0277) 821915
11.30–3.30, 6–11
Adnams Bitter; Bateman XB; Fuller's ESB; Greene King Abbot; Morland Old Speckled Hen; Wadworth 6X [H]**; guest beer**
A good range of beers, including a weekly-changing guest and an occasional real cider, in a popular country pub with a keen landlord. Try the 'leg wobbler' glasses.
♛ ❀ ◖ ◗ ▲ ♣ P ⊬

Pleshey

White Horse
The Street ☎ (0245) 37281
11–3, 7–11
Morland Old Speckled Hen; Nethergate Bitter; Whitbread Boddingtons Bitter [H]

Pleasant, old, timber-framed pub in an historic village, with a number of separate eating and drinking areas. Eclectic menu; families welcome. The beer range may vary. Ask the landlady about the ghosts.
♔ Q ❀ ◖ ◗ ▲ P

Prittlewell

Spread Eagle
267 Victoria Avenue (A127)
☎ (0702) 348383
11–2.30 (3 Sat), 5 (7 Sat)–11
Adnams Bitter; Bass Worthington BB; Charrington IPA; Fuller's London Pride; M&B Highgate Mild; Stones Best Bitter [H]**; guest beers**
A 1923 reconstruction of an 18th-century coaching inn, retaining its original, listed facade. Two bars, with games in the public. Tue quiz; Fri music club (upstairs). Usually eight ales. Regular beer festivals. Function room with real ale. ❀ ⊕ ♿ ≹ ♣ P

Purleigh

Bell
The Street ☎ (0621) 828348
11–3, 6–11
Adnams Bitter; Greene King IPA; Ind Coope Benskins Best Bitter; guest beers [H]
Superb, friendly village pub with a beautiful view of the countryside and a wonderful inglenook. ♔ Q ❀ ◖ ◗ ♣ P

Radley Green

Thatchers Arms
500 yds from A414, between Writtle and Norton Heath OS622054 ☎ (0245) 248356
12–2.30, 6–11
Ridleys Mild, IPA [H]
Secluded, friendly, one-bar local with a large caravan and camping area. Snacks only Sun lunch. ♔ Q ❀ ◖ ◗ ▲ ♣ P

Rettendon

Wheatsheaf
Main Road, Rettendon Common ☎ (0245) 400264
11–3 (may vary), 6–11
Ridleys Mild, IPA [H]**; guest beers** (occasionally)
Very friendly, roadside pub offering an extensive range of home-made food. Live music Sat. ♔ Q ❀ ◖ ◗ ▲ ♣ P

Rickling Green

Cricketers Arms
½ mile W of B1383 OS511298
☎ (079 988) 322/595
11–3, 6–11
Tetley Bitter; guest beers [G]
Enlarged pub in an idyllic setting, overlooking the cricket green. One mild and one strong ale are always available. Excellent, imaginative food. Restaurant open 12–7 Sun.
♔ ⛟ ❀ ⛿ ◖ ◗ ⊕ P

Rochford

Golden Lion
North Street ☎ (0702) 545487
12 (may vary)–11
Fuller's Chiswick, London Pride; Greene King IPA, Abbot [H]**; guest beers**
Deservedly popular free house, serving over 250 guest beers each year, including milds and porters; eight–ten ales at any one time. Lunchtime meals at good prices (no food Sun). A local CAMRA *Pub of the Year* on five occasions. ◖ ≹ ♣ ⌓

Rowhedge

Walnut Tree
Fingringhoe Road
☎ (0206) 728149
12–2.30 (11–3 Sat), 7.30–11
Fuller's Chiswick, Mr Harry; Tolly Cobbold Old Strong; Wadworth 6X [H]
Cosy, friendly pub on the western edge of Rowhedge, with a rock jukebox and pool. Excellent food, including vegetarian dishes, at sensible prices. The beer choice varies seasonally. ❀ ◖ ◗ ♣ P

Saffron Walden

Gate
74 Thaxted Road (B1383)
☎ (0799) 522321
11–3, 6–11 (11–11 summer)
Greene King XX Mild (winter)**, IPA, Rayments Special, Abbot** [H]
Busy, friendly, town local with an excellent, outside play area for children. Good value food. Petanque played; quiz night Sun; keen darts following.
♔ ⛟ ❀ ◖ ◗ ♿ ♣ P

St Osyth

White Hart
Mill Street ☎ (0255) 820318
11–3, 7–11 (restaurant extension)
Adnams Bitter; Courage Directors; John Smith's Bitter; guest beers [H]
Friendly, family-run pub with darts, knick-knacks and old photos. Commitment to guest beers. Speciality Sun lunches.
♔ Q ❀ ◖ ◗ ♣ P

Sheering

Crown
The Street ☎ (027 989) 203
11–3, 5–11; 11–11 Fri & Sat
Adnams Mild (occasionally)**, Bitter; Courage Best Bitter** [H]
Pub with a spacious, cosy interior, furnished with settees. Large, well-laid-out restaurant. ❀ ◖ ◗ ♣ P

South Benfleet

Anchor
1 Essex Way (2 mins uphill from station) ☎ (0268) 756500
12 (11 Sat)–3, 5–11
Courage Directors; Marston's Pedigree; Ruddles Best Bitter; guest beer [H]
Originally the Blue Anchor, built in 1380 and used as the manor court. Photos of old Benfleet and exposed beams enhance the character of this tastefully refurbished, family pub. Function room in former stables. ♔ ❀ ◖ ◗ ≹ ♣ P

Southend-on-Sea

Bakers Bar
15–17 Alexandra Street (50 yds from High St) ☎ (0702) 390403
12–3, 5.30–midnight (1am Fri & Sat); 7–10.30 Sun, closed Sun lunch
Crouch Vale Woodham IPA, Best Bitter [H]**; Shepherd Neame Bishops Finger; Woodforde's Norfolk Nog; guest beers** [G]
Excellent real ale refuge offering guest beers (at a price!) in vaulted cellars of an excavated Georgian bakehouse. Extensive restaurant food menu. Busy at weekends in the atmospheric basement. Special events include festivals and jazz.
❀ ◖ ◗ ≹ (Central) ⌓

Cork & Cheese
363 Chartwell Square, Victoria Circus (lower level of shopping centre) ☎ (0702) 616914
11–11; closed Sun
Marston's Pedigree [H]**; guest beers** [H]/[G]
Large, town-centre free house, offering a wide range of guest ales and occasional mini-beer festivals. Over 170 guests during 1992/93 (see blackboards). Live music Mon and Thu. Satellite TV and games machines; prominent jukebox. Lunches in the upstairs bar/restaurant.
❀ ≹ (Victoria/Central)

Liberty Belle
10–12 Marine Parade
☎ (0702) 466936
10–11
Courage Best Bitter, Directors; Marston's Pedigree [H]; guest beers
Large seafront pub with an olde-worlde character, rather spoilt by games and video machines. One-bar layout but the original lounge and public bars are still apparent. Display of seafaring artefacts. Three pool tables and darts on a raised section. ❀ ◖ ♣

South Fambridge

Anchor Hotel
Fambridge Road
☎ (0702) 203535
11–3, 6–11; 11–11 Sat
Adnams Bitter; Crouch Vale Woodham IPA; Greene King Abbot Ⓗ; guest beers
In an historic village setting, in the Crouch valley, this 1912 hotel combines a warm welcome with good value food in the bar or restaurant (blackboard specials). No meals Sun/Mon eves. Function room. Large garden. Ciders in summer. Q ❀ ◑ ◐ ♿ ♣ ⇔ P

South Hanningfield

Old Windmill
South Hanningfield Road
☎ (0268) 710762
11–11 (midnight Thu–Sat)
Adnams Bitter; Greene King IPA, Abbot; Webster's Yorkshire Bitter Ⓗ
Formerly two cottages from 1703, converted and extended. Original fireplaces and timbers. An old barn now houses a restaurant (carvery and steaks recommended). Blackboard specials in the bar area; no food Sun eve. Discos Tue, Thu and Sun. Seasonal events. ♨ ❀ ◑ ◐ ♣ P

Southminster

Station Arms
Station Road ☎ (0621) 772225
12–3, 5.30–11; 11–11 Sat
Crouch Vale Best Bitter; guest beers Ⓗ
Weatherboarded, high street pub where good beer and conversation are the most important features. Keen dominoes players especially welcome. No eve meals Wed.
♨ Q ☺ ❀ ◑ ◐ ⇌ ♣ ⇔

South Woodham Ferrers

Curlew
80 Gandalf's Ride (from west, follow signs to Country Park; turn left into Gandalf's Ride)
☎ (0245) 321371
12–3, 6–11; 12–11 Fri & Sat
Shepherd Neame Master Brew Bitter, Spitfire; guest beers Ⓗ
Popular, modern, out-of-town-centre pub. Very pleasant atmosphere; something for everyone. Q ❀ ◑ ◐ ♿ ♣ P

Stansted Mountfitchet

Dog & Duck
Lower Street ☎ (0279) 812047
10–2.30, 5.30 (6 Sat)–11
Greene King IPA, Rayments Special, Abbot Ⓗ
Typical Essex timbered village local. Genuinely friendly and professionally run. Snacks Mon–Sat lunchtimes.
Q ❀ ⊞ ⇌ ♣

Stapleford Abbotts

Rabbits
Stapleford Road (B175)
☎ (0708) 688203
11–2.30, 6–11
Adnams Bitter; Ind Coope Benskins Best Bitter, Burton Ale Ⓗ
Friendly local with a children's garden play area. No meals Sun. ♨ Q ❀ ◑ ◐ ♿ P

Stisted

Dolphin
Coggeshall Road (A120)
☎ (0376) 321143
10.30–3, 6–11
Adnams Extra; Ridleys IPA Ⓖ
Unspoilt and welcoming, many-beamed pub with log fires and an excellent garden for children. No eve meals Tue or Sun. ♨ Q ❀ ◑ ◐ P

Onley Arms
The Street ☎ (0376) 325204
11–3 (extends if busy), 7–11
Ridleys IPA Ⓗ
Cosy, one-bar, rural village pub built in 1853 for the Onley Estate workers. Separate dining room open Wed–Sat, with all food home cooked.
Petanque. ♨ Q ❀ ◑ ◐ ♣ P

Stock

Bear
The Square ☎ (0277) 840232
11.30–3, 6–11 (restaurant extension)
Adnams Bitter; Ind Coope Burton Ale; Tetley Bitter; guest beer Ⓗ
Superb, circa 14th-century, snug, two-bar pub with tasteful furnishings, ample seating and various artefacts. Excellent restaurant. Spacious function room upstairs.
Q ☺ ❀ ◑ ◐ ♿ ♣ P

Hoop
High Street ☎ (0277) 841137
10–11
Beer range varies Ⓗ/Ⓖ
Pub offering up to ten ales (mostly gravity-dispensed) and an annual beer festival in May. Large garden; small bar (can be crowded). Good range of meals. Q ❀ ◑ ◐ ♿ ♣ ⇔

Stones Green

Green Swan
Clacton Road ☎ (0255) 870243
12–2.30, 7–11; closed Mon
Mauldons Bitter Ⓗ
Homely, quiet, French restaurant/pub, where the French landlady cooks. Food is good, but not cheap. Families allowed. Dudley's Old Wallop house beer is made by Mauldons (4.2% ABV).
Petanque. ♨ ❀ ◑ ◐ ♣ ⇔ P

Stow Maries

Prince of Wales
Woodham Road
☎ (0621) 828971
11–11
Beer range varies Ⓗ
Friendly atmosphere in a comfortable, unpretentious setting. At least four interesting beers available, including a mild and a strong ale. A traditional gem.
♨ Q ☺ ❀ ◑ ◐ ⛺ ♣ ⇔ P

Thaxted

Rose & Crown
Mill End ☎ (0371) 831152
11 (12 winter)–2.30, 6–11
Adnams Old; Ridleys IPA; guest beer (summer) Ⓗ
Friendly, well-run local in an historic town. Believed to have been built on the site of a monks' hostelry. Cosy dining area. Excellent, home-cooked food. ❀ 🛏 ◑ ◐ ⊞ ⛺ ♣ P

Tillingham

Cap & Feathers
South Street ☎ (0621) 779212
11–3, 6–11
Crouch Vale Woodham IPA, Best Bitter Ⓗ
Unspoilt, 15th-century village inn, now Crouch Vale brewery's only tied house. Home-smoked meat and fish available. Other Crouch Vale beers also served occasionally.
♨ Q ☺ ❀ 🛏 ◑ ◐ ⇔ ⚡

Toppesfield

Green Man
Church Lane ☎ (0787) 237418
11–2.30, 7–11
Greene King IPA, Abbot Ⓗ
Excellent, welcoming and roomy pub in a remote village. Huffers (rolls) only weekdays. Restaurant open weekends.
♨ Q ❀ ◑ ◐ ⊞ ⛺ ♣ P

Waltham Abbey

Welsh Harp
Market Square
☎ (0992) 711113
11–3 (10–4 Tue), 6–11 (11–11 summer); 10–11 Sat
McMullen AK, Country Ⓗ
Olde-worlde-type pub, with beams and leaded windows. Friendly welcome. ◑ ♿

White Lion
11 Sun Street (50 yds from Market Sq) ☎ (0992) 718673
11–2.30, 6–11 (11–11 summer); 10–11 Sat
McMullen AK [H]
Unpretentious, one-bar pub serving no food at all. More of a locals' pub than for visitors, but seek it out. ♿ ♣

Walton-on-the-Naze

Royal Marine ('Barkers')
3 Old Pier Street
☎ (0255) 674000
11–11
Adnams Bitter, Broadside; Greene King Abbot; Marston's Pedigree; Whitbread Boddingtons Bitter [E]/[G]
From the outside it doesn't look like a pub – but inside there is no doubt! Huge leaded windows, three bars and a separate dining area. Unusual electric/gravity-fed dispense from an upstairs cellar.
♨ Q ◐ ◑ ▲ ⇌

Warley

Alexandra
114 Warley Hill (B186)
☎ (0277) 210456
11–2.30 (3.30 Fri & Sat), 6–11
Greene King XX Mild, IPA, Rayments Special, Abbot [H], **Winter Ale** [G]
Superb Victorian house with two traditional bars and an off-sales section; in the landlord's family since 1928, though he plans to retire soon. Greene King are planning the first refurbishment since 1931; hopefully it will retain the rustic feel. Hot snacks at most times.
⊕ ⇌ (Brentwood) ♣ P

Westcliff-on-Sea

Cricketers Inn
228 London Road
☎ (0702) 343168
11.30–2.30, 6–11 (Tudor Bar); 12–11 (Sportsman Bar)
Greene King IPA, Rayments Special, Abbot [H]; **guest beers**
Tudor-style pub rebuilt after a fire in 1922; formerly an hotel and stables. In the same family for about 50 years. The Tudor Bar was refurbished in 1992; the Sportsman Bar has been partly redone and houses dartboards, pool, machines, and Sky TV. ◐ ⇌ ♣ P

Palace Theatre Centre
430 London Road
☎ (0702) 347816
12–2.30, 6–11
Crouch Vale SAS; Greene King IPA, Abbot [H]
Comfortable, friendly theatre bar with a family atmosphere, offering a changing selection of stronger guest beers. Free live music Sun lunch and eve. Courtyard patio. Food from the bistro, except Sun.
Q ❀ ◐ ◑ ♿ ⇌

West Mersea

Fountain
Queens Corner
☎ (0206) 382080
11–3 (4 Sat), 6 (7 Sat)–11
Crouch Vale SAS, Willie Warmer; Greene King IPA; Mauldons Suffolk Punch [H]
Large, comfortable pub on an island popular with watersports enthusiasts. Accommodation at reasonable prices. Pool table. Beers change seasonally but the same brewers are featured all year.
Q ⛍ ❀ 🛏 ◐ ◑ ♿ ▲ ♣ P

White Notley

Cross Keys
The Street ☎ (0376) 83297
11–3, 6.30 (7 Sat)–11
Ridleys Mild, IPA [H]
Unspoilt, 14th-century, village local, formerly Chappells brewery: a public bar and a cosy saloon with an adjoining restaurant area. Rolls only Tue lunchtime; eve meals Fri and Sat. Quiz nights. Interesting mural of local characters.
♨ Q ❀ ◐ ◑ ⇌ P

Wickham Bishops

Mitre
The Street ☎ (0621) 891378
11.30–3.30, 5.30–11; 11.30–11 Sat
Adnams Extra; Everards Tiger; Ridleys IPA [H]
Two-bar village pub: a basic public bar for drinking, and a small saloon bar next to the restaurant. Children welcome in the restaurant. Interesting mitre design on the fire grate.
♨ ❀ ◐ ◑ ⊕ P

Widdington

Fleur de Lys
High Street ☎ (0799) 540659
11–3, 6–11
Adnams Bitter; Draught Bass; Courage Directors; Whitbread Flowers IPA [H]; **guest beers**
Friendly, well-run village local, offering a good choice of ales and an extensive range of good value, home-cooked English and continental dishes. Live folk music Fri eve. Comfortable family room.
♨ Q ⛍ ❀ ◐ ◑ ♿ ▲ ♣ P

Witham

George
36 Newland Street
☎ (0376) 511098
10–2.30, 5.30–11; 10–11 Fri & Sat
Adnams Extra; Everards Tiger; Ridleys Mild, IPA, Winter Ale [H]
Good value, welcoming, town pub with a public bar and a quiet, 16th-century, timber-framed saloon (some beams from the demolished Grays brewery). The function room doubles as a children's room. Disabled access to the saloon planned. Q ⛍ ◐ ⊕ ⇌ ♣ P

Victoria
Faulkbourne Road, Powers Hall End (2 miles from centre)
☎ (0376) 511809
11–3 (3.30 Sat), 6–11
Ridleys IPA [H]/[G]
Spacious, renovated, country house on the edge of town, with a long-serving landlord: a large locals' public bar and a comfortable lounge. No meals Sun. ♨ Q ⛍ ❀ ◐ ◑ ⊕ ♣ P

Wivenhoe

Black Buoy
Black Buoy Hill
☎ (0206) 822425
11–2.30 (3 Sat), 6–11
Tolly Cobbold Bitter, Original; Whitbread Flowers Original; guest beers [H]
Super, nautical pub with a good atmosphere, in the old part of town, with small framed drawings, prints and cartoons on the walls. Family room. Reasonably priced, good food, but beer is not cheap. ♨ Q ⛍ ◐ ◑ ⇌ P

Horse & Groom
The Cross ☎ (0206) 824928
10.30–3, 5.30 (6 Sat)–11
Adnams Mild, Bitter, Old [H]; **guest beer**
Popular local with two bars, but no price difference. If you want to play darts, arrive early. No lunches Sun.
Q ❀ ◐ ♣ P

Woodham Mortimer

Hurdlemakers Arms
Post Office Road
☎ (0245) 225169
11–3, 6–11
Greene King IPA, Abbot [H]
Lovely, old country pub with a large garden and children's play area. Stone-flagged saloon bar. Excellent menu.
♨ Q ❀ ◐ ⊕ ♣ P

Writtle

Wheatsheaf
The Green ☎ (0245) 420695
11–2.30 (3 Fri & Sat), 5.30–11
Greene King IPA, Rayments Special, Abbot [H]
Small, cottage-style, friendly, village pub retaining a public bar and a cosy saloon.
Q ❀ ◐ ♣ P

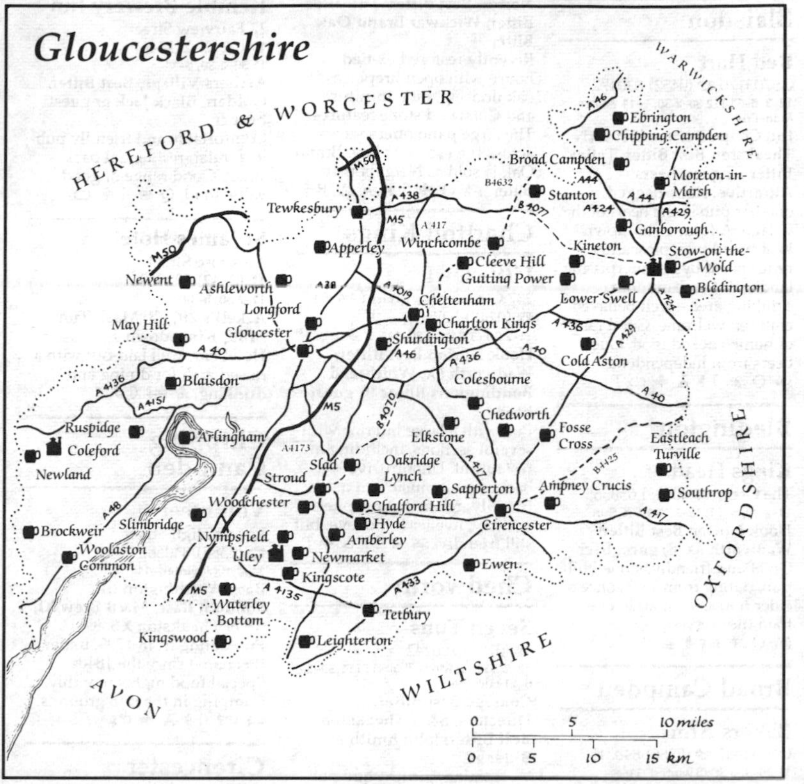

Donnington, *Stow-on-the-Wold*; **Freeminer**, *Coleford*; **Uley**, *Uley*

Amberley

Black Horse

OS849016 ☎ (0453) 872556
12–3 (Sat, Sun & bank hols only), 6.30–11
Archers Best Bitter; Hook Norton Best Bitter, Old Hooky; Tetley Bitter Ⓗ; guest beers
Old village pub of character where a conservatory-style extension overlooks the Nailsworth valley. Has a local clientele and atmosphere, but gets busy at weekends. Families welcome in the restaurant. Note limited lunch opening. ⛫ Q ❀ ◑

Ampney Crucis

Crown of Crucis

On A417 ☎ (0285) 851806
11–11
Archers Village; Ruddles County; Tetley Bitter Ⓗ
Attractive country hotel with a very popular bar and restaurant. Excellent food in both, although the bar can get crowded. Riverside garden. Families welcome.
⛫ ❀ 🛏 ◑ P

Apperley

Farmers Arms

Ledbury Road (B4213, ½ mile from centre) ☎ (0452) 780307
11–2.30, 5 (6 Sat)–11
Mayhem's Oddas Light, Sundowner Ⓗ; guest beers
Thriving roadside pub which opened its own brewery in 1992, complete with a viewing gallery and museum. Own cider also available.
⛫ ❀ ◑ ♿ ▲ ⌓ P

Arlingham

Red Lion

High Street ☎ (0452) 740269
11–3, 7–11; 11–11 Sat
Draught Bass; Hook Norton Best Bitter; Morland Old Speckled Hen; John Smith's Bitter; Uley Bitter Ⓗ; guest beers (occasionally)
Lively local at the village centre, in a remote cul-de-sac created by a long loop of the River Severn.
⛫ ❀ ◑ ▲ ♣ ⌓ P

Ashleworth

Boat Inn

The Quay (beyond the tithe barn on the road to 'The Quay') OS819251
☎ (0452) 700272
11–2.30, 6–11
Arkell's 3B, Kingsdown; Smiles Best Bitter Ⓖ
A miracle of survival, sitting on the bank of the Severn some distance from the village centre. In the same family for over 400 years and the interior has hardly changed in a century. Q ❀ P

Gloucestershire

Blaisdon

Red Hart
OS703170 ☎ (0452) 830472
12–3, 6–11 (12.30–2.30, 7–11 winter Mon–Fri)
Ind Coope Burton Ale; S&N Theakston Best Bitter; Tetley Bitter [H]; guest beers
Attractive, stone-flagged, one-bar pub in the heart of the village. A former run-down Whitbread pub, pleasantly refurbished by an enterprising landlord. Large outdoor drinking area – well-behaved children welcome. Good range of home-cooked food. Guest beers from independents.
♛ Q ❀ ◐ ◑ ▲ ♣ ⌓ P

Bledington

Kings Head
The Green ☎ (0608) 658365
11–2.30, 6–11; 12–2, 7–10.30 Sun
Hook Norton Best Bitter; Wadworth 6X [H]; guest beer
Quiet and friendly, stone-built pub, dating from 1535, once a cider house. Upmarket eve food (not served Sun).
♛ Q ❀ 🛏 ◑ ⊟ P

Broad Campden

Bakers Arms
Off B4081 ☎ (0386) 840515
11.30–3, 5.30 (6 winter)–11
Donnington BB, SBA; Hook Norton Best Bitter [H]; guest beers
Fine old Cotswold pub of character, offering a good selection of bar food, including vegetarian. Folk music third Tue of the month.
♛ Q ❀ ◐ ◑ ♣ P

Brockweir

Brockweir Country Inn
Off A406, over Brockweir Bridge OS539011
☎ (0291) 689548
11.30–3, 6–11; 11.30–11 Sat
Draught Bass; Hook Norton Best Bitter; Wye Valley Hereford Bitter [H]; guest beers
Pub with oak beams from a locally-built ship. Chepstow Racecourse and Tintern Abbey are nearby and Offa's Dyke path runs past the front door. Guest ciders in summer.
♛ Q ❀ 🛏 ◐ ◑ ▲ ♣ ⌓ P

Chalford Hill

Old Neighbourhood Inn
OS896032 ☎ (0453) 883385
11–3, 6–11
Archers Best Bitter; Hook Norton Best Bitter; Thwaites Bitter; Wickwar Brand Oak Bitter [H]
Recently restored ex-tied house with open fireplaces, oak flooring, pine furniture and Cotswold stone features. The large patio offers views across the Frome valley. Brand Oak is sold as Neighbourly Bitter. ♛ Q ❀ ◐ ◑ ♣ ⌓ P

Charlton Kings

Little Owl
237 Cirencester Road (A435)
☎ (0242) 527404
11–2.30 (3 Sat), 5.30–11
Hook Norton Best Bitter; Wadworth 6X; Whitbread Boddingtons Bitter [H]; guest beer
Pub with a large interior with several sections, including a restaurant. Unobtrusive background music and a friendly, relaxed atmosphere midday; livelier in the eve, but still friendly. ♛ ❀ ◐ ◑ ♿ ♣ P

Chedworth

Seven Tuns
☎ (0285) 720242
12–2.30 (not Mon), 6.30–11 (11.30–3, 6–11 summer)
Courage Best Bitter, Directors; S&N Theakston Best Bitter; John Smith's Bitter [H]
Welcoming, picturesque pub in an attractive Cotswold village, within walking distance of the Roman villa. The garden has a stream and waterwheel. The name of the pub refers to a local word for chimneys. ♛ Q ❀ 🛏 ◐ ◑ P

Cheltenham

Bayshill Inn
St Georges Place (behind bus station) ☎ (0242) 524388
11–3, 5–11
Hall & Woodhouse Tanglefoot; Wadworth IPA, 6X [H]; guest beer
Lively, unspoilt town pub, with a very good atmosphere and a regularly changing guest beer. Both beer and food are excellent value.
🛏 ◐ ≷ ♣ ⌓

Beaufort Arms
184 London Road (A40, 1 mile E of centre) ☎ (0242) 526038
11–2.30, 6–11
Hall & Woodhouse Tanglefoot; Wadworth IPA, 6X, Farmer's Glory [H], Old Timer [G]
Very tidy pub and bistro with an à la carte choice; bar menu also available. A large race horses mural covers one wall.
❀ 🛏 ◐ ◑ ♣ ⌓ P

Kemble Brewery Inn
27 Fairview Street
☎ (0242) 243446
11.30–2.30, 6–11
Archers Village, Best Bitter, Golden, Black Jack *or* guest beer [H]
Comfortable and friendly pub in a quiet, residential back street. Good range of good value food. Q ❀ ◐ ♣ ⌓

St James Hotel
Ambrose Street
☎ (0242) 522860
11–2.30, 5–11
Arkell's 2B, 3B, Mash Tun Mild, Kingsdown [H]
Hotel bar, well laid-out with a raised area for dining and drinking. ❀ 🛏 ◐ ◑

Chipping Campden

Volunteer
Lower High Street
☎ (0386) 840688
11–3, 6 (7 winter)–11
Bass Worthington BB, Draught Bass; M&B Brew XI; S&N Theakston XB [H]
Pub dating from 1709, under this name since the 1840s. Special food nights monthly. Camping in the pub grounds.
♛ 🛏 ◐ ◑ ▲ ♣ ⌓

Cirencester

Drillmans Arms
34 Gloucester Road, Stratton (A417) ☎ (0285) 653892
11–3, 5.30–11; 11–11 Sat
Archers Village, Best Bitter; Wadworth 6X [H]
Two-bar pub dating from the 18th century, once Archers's first tied house, but now a friendly free house. Archers Village is sold under a house name. ♛ ❀ ◐ ◑ ♣ P

Oddfellows Arms
10–14 Chester Street (off A417)
☎ (0285) 641540
11 (11.30 Sat)–3, 5 (7 Sat)–11
Courage Best Bitter; Wadworth 6X [H]; guest beers
Sensitively refurbished, back-street pub worth making the effort to find. Now upmarket, with a good range of food and frequently changing guest beers. Large garden at the rear; comfortable family room. ♛ ⛟ ❀ ◐ ◑ ▲

Talbot
Victoria Road (off A417)
☎ (0285) 653760
11.30–2.30 (11–4 Sat), 6.30–11
Arkell's 2B, 3B, Noel Ale [H]
Pleasant local serving good value food (not available Sun).
❀ ◐ ▲ ♣ P

Cleeve Hill

High Roost
On B4632 ☎ (0242) 672010
11.30–2.30 (3 Sat), 7–11
Hook Norton Best Bitter, Old Hooky [H]; guest beer
Pub reached by a flight of steps, set on the highest hill in the county. Expansive views through bay windows across the Vale of Severn. Jukebox and satellite TV. No food Tue eve. ❀ 🛏 ◖ ◗ ▲ ♣ P

Cold Aston

Plough
☎ (0451) 821459
11–2.30, 6.30–11; 12–2.30, 7–10.30 Sun
Wadworth IPA, 6X [H]
Small, unspoilt Cotswold village pub with stone floors and a low-beamed ceiling. Handy for Folly Farm Waterfowl Park. Varied menu.
🔥 Q ❀ ◖ ◗ ▲ ♣ P

Colesbourne

Colesbourne Inn
On A435 ☎ (0242) 870376
11–3, 6–11
Wadworth IPA, 6X, Farmer's Glory [H]; guest beer
Traditional, 200-year-old Cotswold inn in a picturesque village, featuring sedate and comfortable panelled bars, with an emphasis on food in the main bar. The old stables, with rare 'Lunnet' windows, have been converted into bedrooms. 🔥 Q ❀ 🛏 ◖ ◗ P

Eastleach Turville

Victoria Inn
OS198053 ☎ (036 785) 277
10.30–2.30 (3 Sat), 7–11
Arkell's 3B, Kingsdown [H]
16th-century pub overlooking a charming Cotswold village. An L-shaped bar layout, with a restaurant opening off the rear of the lounge section. Good, home-made food.
🔥 Q 🐴 ❀ ◖ ◗ ♣ ⇔ P

Ebrington

Ebrington Arms
Just off B4035 OS186399
☎ (0386) 78223
11–2.30, 6–11
Donnington SBA; Hook Norton Best Bitter [H]
Friendly old pub at the village centre, with a superbly preserved open fireplace in the dining area. A wide selection of hot meals is listed on a beam (not served Sun eve).
🔥 Q 🐴 ❀ 🛏 ◖ ◗ ♣ ⇔ P

Elkstone

Highwayman
Beechpike (A417)
☎ (0285) 821221
11–2.30, 6–11; 12–2.30, 7–10.30 Sun
Arkell's 2B, 3B, Kingsdown [H]
17th-century inn with a wealth of comfortable furnishings, as well as a family room, a restaurant and a back room.
🔥 🐴 ❀ ◖ ◗ ♿ ♣ P

Ewen

Wild Duck Inn
Drakes Island OS006976
☎ (0285) 770310
11–11
Fuller's London Pride; S&N Theakston XB, Old Peculier; Wadworth 6X [H]
Grade II-listed farm building, built in 1563 and licensed since 1936. An Elizabethan fireplace holds a log fire. Very busy local trade as well as tourists. Award-winning garden. House 'Duckpond Bitter' is brewed by Archers.
🔥 Q ❀ 🛏 ◖ ◗ ♣ P

Fosse Cross

Hare & Hounds
On A429 ☎ (0285) 720288
11–3, 6–11
Everards Tiger; Hook Norton Best Bitter; S&N Theakston Old Peculier; Wadworth 6X [H]
300-year-old, Cotswold stone pub on the Fosse Way. Meals include vegetarian and children's. Adjacent caravan site. 🔥 ❀ ◖ ◗ ♿ ▲ ♣ ⇔ P

Ganborough

Coach & Horses
On A424 ☎ (0451) 830208
11–3, 6.30 (6 Fri & Sat)–11
Donnington XXX, BB, SBA [H]
Pleasant country pub on the main road, popular for its beer and food (no meals Sun eve). The nearest pub to the brewery and one of few to keep Mild all year round. Pub games include bottle walking.
🔥 Q ❀ ◖ ◗ ▲ ♣ P ⚡

Gloucester

Dick Whittington
100 Westgate Street
☎ (0452) 502039
11–11
Marston's Pedigree; Wadworth 6X, Old Timer; Whitbread Boddingtons Bitter, Best Bitter [H]
Grade I-listed building with a provincial Georgian facade and a timber-framed interior. Run as an olde-worlde tavern, with a dining room at the front and lounge at the rear. Cellar bar for the young. ❀ ◖

Fountain
53 Westgate Street
☎ (0452) 522562
11–11
Draught Bass; Marston's Pedigree; Wadworth 6X; Whitbread Boddingtons Bitter [H]; guest beer
17th-century inn on the site of an alehouse from 1216. The stone-flagged courtyard acts as a public bar. A ghost haunts the cellar. Popular for food.
❀ ◖ ◗ ⇌ ♣ P

Linden Tree
73–75 Bristol Road (A430, S of centre) ☎ (0452) 527869
11–2.30 (3 Sat), 5.30–11
Draught Bass; Hall & Woodhouse Tanglefoot; Hook Norton Best Bitter; Wadworth 6X [H], Farmer's Glory [G]; guest beers
Excellent Grade II-listed pub, offering good, traditional English food and very comfortable accommodation. No meals Sun eve.
🔥 ❀ 🛏 ◖ ◗

Waterfront
Merchants Road
☎ (0452) 308326
11–11
Oakhill Black Magic; Whitbread Best Bitter [G]; guest beers
Imaginative development of two floors of a former pillar house in the city docks. The emphasis is on cask ales, with nine guests. Games, live music, free peanuts and charitable challenges make it fun for all ages.
❀ ◖ ◗ ♣ ⇔ P

Whitesmiths Arms
81 Southgate Street
☎ (0452) 414770
11–3, 6–11 (11–11 summer)
Arkell's 2B, 3B, Mash Tun Mild, Kingsdown [H]
Named after maritime metal-workers, a pub opposite the historic docks and National Waterways Museum, with fitting decor. 🔥 ◖ ◗ ⇌ ♣

Guiting Power

Farmers Arms
OS096247 ☎ (0451) 850358
11.30–2.30, 5.30–11; 12–2.30, 7–10.30 winter Sun
Donnington BB, SBA [H]
Friendly, lively, popular Cotswold village pub.
🔥 ❀ 🛏 ◖ ◗ ♣ ⇔ P

Hyde

Ragged Cot Inn
On Minchinhampton–Aston Down road OS887012

☎ (0453) 731333
11–2.30, 6–11 (may be 11–11 summer)
Courage Directors; Marston's Pedigree; S&N Theakston Best Bitter; Uley Old Spot Ⓗ; guest beer
Comfortable, 16th-century free house in open country, close to Minchinhampton Common.
Q P

Kineton

Halfway House
OS096266 ☎ (0451) 850344
11–2.30, 6–11
Donnington BB, SBA Ⓗ
Very lively, but not too noisy, inn. The single bar has stools as well as dining tables. Local events on the noticeboard.
P

Kingscote

Hunters Hall
On A4135 ☎ (0453) 860393
11–3, 6.30–11
Draught Bass; Hook Norton Best Bitter; Uley Old Spot; Wadworth 6X Ⓗ
16th-century coaching inn with a chintzy ante-room, a public bar with oak settles, a lounge and a games room with pool; also a jukebox.
Q P

Kingswood

Dinneywicks Inn
High Street ☎ (0453) 843328
10.30–3, 6–11
Wadworth IPA, 6X, Farmer's Glory, Old Timer Ⓗ; guest beer
Three-storey building, matching other properties in the area in age and style, but the interior is much altered. A lively local with food aimed at healthy eaters. The name derives from Dinneywicks Hill, a local burial ground for horses.

Leighterton

Royal Oak Inn
The Street ☎ (0666) 890250
12–2.30, 7–11
Butcombe Bitter; Eldridge Pope Royal Oak; Hook Norton Best Bitter; S&N Theakston Old Peculier Ⓗ
300-year-old free house, much modernised inside: one bar with a restaurant off. Thoughtful range of beers.
Q P

Longford

Queens Head
84 Tewkesbury Road (A38)
☎ (0452) 301882
11–2.30 (3 Sat), 6–11
Marston's Pedigree; Morland Old Speckled Hen; Wadworth 6X; Whitbread WCPA, Boddingtons Bitter, Flowers Original Ⓗ
18th-century inn with original beams and a stone-flagged public bar area. Excellent selection of bar meals. Colourful flower baskets outside reflect a warm welcome inside. P

Lower Swell

Golden Ball
OS175255 ☎ (0451) 830247
11–2.30, 6–11; 12–2.30, 7–10.30 Sun
Donnington BB, SBA Ⓗ
Excellent but unspoilt village local, offering good food and cider. No eve meals Wed or Sat in winter.
Q P

May Hill

Glasshouse Inn
Off A40 W of Huntley
OS709213 ☎ (0452) 830529
11.30–2.30, 6–11; 12–2, 7–10.30 Sun
Butcombe Bitter; Whitbread WCPA Ⓖ; guest beer
Unspoilt, old country pub with a brick-tiled floor. The outdoor drinking area has an old cider press and a bench canopied by a yew hedge. Warm welcome. P

Moreton-in-Marsh

Black Bear
High Street ☎ (0608) 50705
11–3 (10.30–4 Tue), 6–11
Donnington BB, XXX, SBA Ⓗ
Busy, two-bar, town-centre pub, parts of which date back 300 years. Features a poltergeist called Fred. Paved courtyard. Q P

Newent

George Hotel
Church Street ☎ (0531) 820203
11–11
Draught Bass; John Smith's Bitter; Wadworth 6X; Wye Valley Hereford Bitter Ⓗ
Mid-17th-century 'Commercial and Posting house', with a large bar resulting from the removal of some internal walls. The pleasant atmosphere is enlivened at times by the local rugby team. Limited parking. P

Newland

Ostrich
On B4231 ☎ (0594) 833260
12–2.30, 6–11; 12–2.30, 7–10.30 Sun
Exmoor Gold; Marston's Pedigree; Ringwood Old Thumper; Shepherd Neame Spitfire; Whitbread Boddingtons Bitter Ⓗ
Charming and unspoilt, traditional English pub with friendly staff. Wide range of good food; the beer range may vary. Full of character, enhanced by beams and a log fire. Q

Newmarket

George Inn
Off A46 in Nailsworth centre
OS837994 ☎ (0453) 832530
11–2.30, 6–11
Archers Best Bitter; Oakhill Bitter; Tetley Bitter Ⓗ; guest beer
Friendly, well-run local with valley views. Beer festival in July. P

Nympsfield

Rose & Crown
Off B4066 OS801004
☎ (0453) 860240
11.45–2.30, 6–11
S&N Theakston Old Peculier; Uley Bitter, Old Spot; Wadworth 6X; Whitbread Boddingtons Bitter Ⓗ
Large village local with a good range of beer and food. Originally a coaching inn.
P

Oakridge Lynch

Butchers Arms
On northern edge of the village ☎ (0285) 760371
12–3, 6–11
Archers Best Bitter; Draught Bass; Ruddles Best Bitter, County; S&N Theakston Best Bitter; Tetley Bitter Ⓗ
Superb, popular pub, a fine, 18th-century former slaughterhouse and butcher's shop, with three sensitively modernised bars and a restaurant. Eve meals Wed–Sat. Q P

Ruspidge

New Inn
On B4227 ☎ (0594) 824508
7–11; 12–4, 7–11 Sat
Archers Golden Ⓗ; guest beer
Fairly basic but friendly village local. The games room has an interesting range of games. P

Sapperton

Daneway Inn
N of A419, 4 miles W of Cirencester OS939034
☎ (0285) 760297

11–2.30 (3 Sat), 6.30–11
Archers Best Bitter Ⓔ/Ⓗ; **Draught Bass** Ⓗ; **Wadworth 6X** Ⓖ
Excellent pub built in 1784 for canal workers, at one end of the defunct Sapperton tunnel. The comfortable lounge is dominated by a fireplace with a Dutch carving. Daneway Bitter, is reputedly from Archers. Cider in summer.
⌂ Q ♘ ❀ ◑ ◗ ⊞ ♣ ⌓ P

Shurdington

Bell
Main Road ☎ (0242) 862245
11–3, 5–11; 11–11 Fri & Sat
Whitbread WCPA, Boddingtons Bitter Ⓗ; **guest beers**
Once the village bakery, a friendly, two-bar inn serving three guest beers, one from an independent. Extensive menu of value, home-made meals and take-aways. Camping by arrangement.
⌂ Q ❀ ◑ ◗ ▲ ♣ ⌓ P

Slad

Woolpack
On B4070 ☎ (0452) 813429
12–3, 6–11
Marston's Pedigree; Uley Old Spot; Wadworth 6X; Whitbread Flowers IPA, Original Ⓗ
Authentic 16th-century pub, clinging to the side of the Slad valley. Made famous by Laurie Lee in *Cider with Rosie*, signed copies of which are available. The author still uses the pub. Weston's Old Rosie cider, of course. ⌂ Q ❀ ◑ ◗ ♣ ⌓ P

Slimbridge

Tudor Arms
Shepherds Patch OS728042
☎ (0453) 890306
11–2.30, 7–11 (11–11 summer Sat)
Hook Norton Best Bitter; Uley Bitter; Wadworth 6X; Whitbread Boddingtons Bitter Ⓗ; **guest beers**
Well-run, large country pub on the way to the Wildfowl Trust. Restaurant and no-smoking family room; newly refurbished accommodation.
♘ ❀ ⛟ ◑ ◗ ▲ ♣ P ⚟

Southrop

Swan Inn
OS201035 ☎ (036 785) 205
12–2.30, 7–11
Morland Bitter Ⓗ; **guest beers**
Attractive, creeper-covered village pub dating back to the 17th century. Imaginative upmarket food in the dining areas. ⌂ Q ❀ ◑ ◗ ⊞ ▲ ♣

Stanton

Mount Inn
Old Snowshill Road OS072342
☎ (0386) 73316
11–11 (11–3, 6–11 winter)
Donnington BB, SBA Ⓗ
Building dating from 1640, a pub for the last 50 years. Open-plan with two bars, it draws a mix of locals and tourists. A keen sporting pub with good views. No eve meals Sun. ⌂ Q ❀ ◑ ◗ ♣ P

Stow-on-the-Wold

Queens Head
The Square ☎ (0451) 830563
11–2.30, 6 (6.30 Sat)–11
Donnington BB, SBA Ⓗ
Fine old popular Cotswold pub. Occasional live music.
⌂ ❀ ◑ ◗ ♣ ⌓

Stroud

Clothiers Arms
1 Bath Road (A46, S of railway viaduct) ☎ (0453) 763801
11–2.30, 4.30–11; 11–11 Sat
Furgusons Dartmoor Best Bitter; Ind Coope Burton Ale; Smiles Best Bitter; Tetley Bitter; Wadworth 6X Ⓗ
Friendly town free house with a three-quarter circular bar and a games alcove. Note the Stroud brewery memorabilia. Terraced garden. A restaurant extension offers an excellent menu. ❀ ◑ ◗ ≠ P

Tetbury

Trouble House Inn
On A433, 1 mile NE of town
☎ (0666) 502206
11–2.30, 6–11
Wadworth IPA, 6X Ⓗ
Cosy roadside pub with a long and colourful history.
⌂ ♘ ❀ ◑ ◗ ▲ ♣ P

Tewkesbury

Black Bear
High Street ☎ (0684) 292202
11–2.30, 6–11; 11–11 Sat
Whitbread Boddingtons Bitter, Best Bitter Ⓗ; **guest beers** Ⓖ
The oldest pub in Gloucestershire, with a dining area which used to be the stables. Six guest beers from independents. No eve meals Sun or Mon. ❀ ◑ ◗

Waterley Bottom

New Inn
E of N Nibley along 1½ miles of narrow lanes OS758964
☎ (0453) 543659
12–2.30, 7–11
Cotleigh Tawny; Greene King Abbot Ⓗ; **S&N Theakston Old Peculier** Ⓖ; **Smiles Best Bitter** Ⓗ, **Exhibition** Ⓖ; **guest beers**
Large, friendly free house in a beautiful setting, surrounded by steep hills. A house beer (WB) is brewed by Cotleigh. Detailed map required for first-time visitors. CAMRA SW region *Pub of the Year* 1992.
⌂ Q ❀ ⛟ ◑ ◗ ♣ ⌓ P

Winchcombe

Plaisterers Arms
Abbey Terrace
☎ (0242) 602358
11–3, 6–11
Draught Bass; Ind Coope Burton Ale; Tetley Bitter; Wadworth 6X Ⓗ
Cosy two-bar pub with an unusual layout.
❀ ⛟ ◑ ◗ ▲ ♣

White Hart
High Street ☎ (0242) 602359
10–11
Marston's Pedigree; Whitbread WCPA; Boddingtons Bitter Ⓗ; **guest beer**
Pub with a relaxed atmosphere, popular with locals and tourists. Regular live music. Good range of food. Family room in summer only. ♘ ❀ ⛟ ◑ ◗ ▲ ♣ P

Woodchester

Ram Inn
Station Road (up hill from S Woodchester turn off A46) OS839023 ☎ (0453) 873329
11–3, 6–11
Archers Best Bitter; Hardington Best Bitter; Hook Norton Old Hooky; Ruddles County; Uley Bitter, Old Spot Ⓗ; **guest beers**
Large, bustling pub, popular with younger drinkers: a big L-shaped bar with oak beams. Outdoor drinking area with valley views. ⌂ ❀ ◑ ◗ ♣ P

Woolaston Common

Rising Sun
1 mile off A48 through Netherend village OS590009
☎ (0594) 529282
12–2.30 (not Wed), 6.30–11; 12–2.30, 7–10.30 Sun
Hook Norton Best Bitter; S&N Theakston Best Bitter; Thwaites Bitter Ⓗ; **guest beers**
Lovely country pub with excellent views and a friendly landlord. Beautiful floral display in summer. Large collection of whisky bottles.
⌂ Q ❀ ◑ ◗ ▲ ♣ P

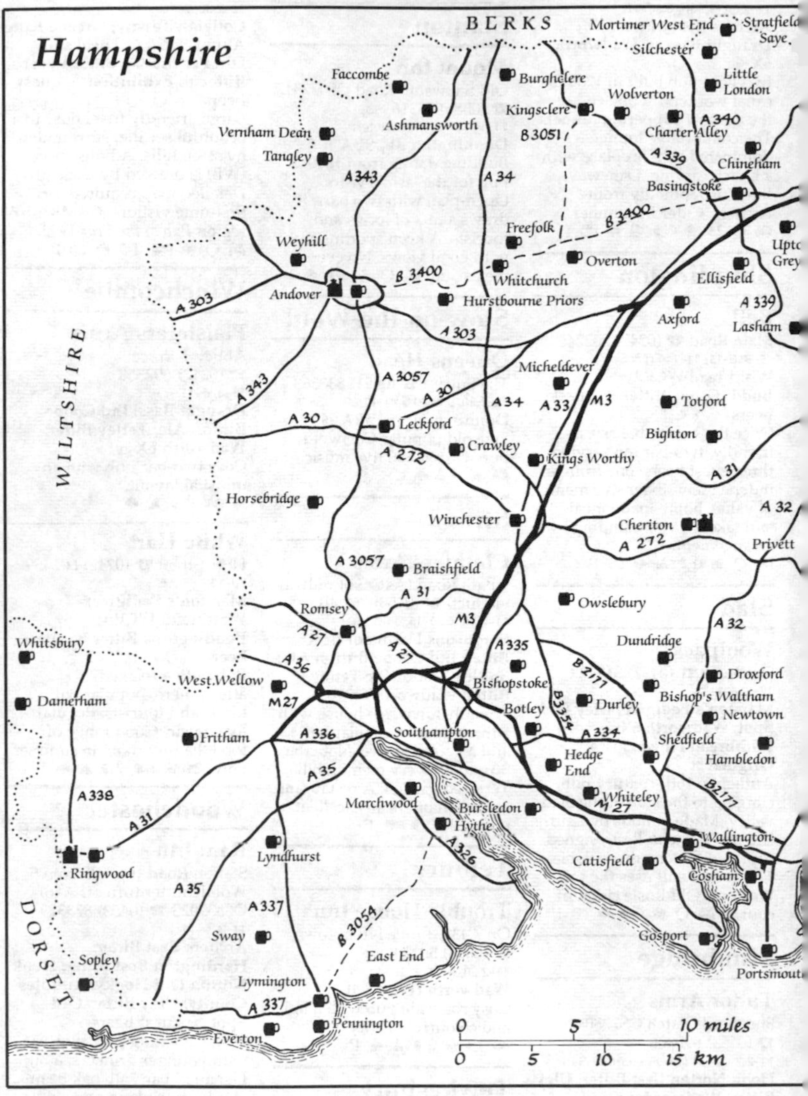

Cheriton, *Cheriton*; **Gale's**, *Horndean*; **Hampshire**, *Andover*; **Ringwood**, *Ringwood*; **Worldham**, *East Worldham*

Aldershot

Albion

Waterloo Road
☎ (0252) 319286
12–3, 5.30–11; 11–11 Fri & Sat
Gale's Best Bitter, 5X, HSB Ⓗ
Good back-street local with a comfortable public bar with pool and satellite TV, and a cosy snug. Small garden. No food Sun. ❀ ◐◑ ≢ ♣

Garden Gate

4 Church Lane East
☎ (0252) 21051
12–2.30 (3 Sat), 6–11
Greene King XX Mild, IPA, Abbot Ⓗ, **Winter Ale** Ⓖ
Another independent brewer's pub, making a superb addition to an otherwise poor choice in town. Basic, friendly and intimate; a small back room is available for families or meetings. A pleasant, quiet retreat, highly recommended.
⚔ ♉ ≢ ♣ P

Red Lion

Ash Road ☎ (0252) 23050
11–11
Ballard's Midhurst Mild; Courage Best Bitter, Directors; Worldham Old Dray Ⓗ
Prominent 1930s roadside pub with two contrasting bars. On

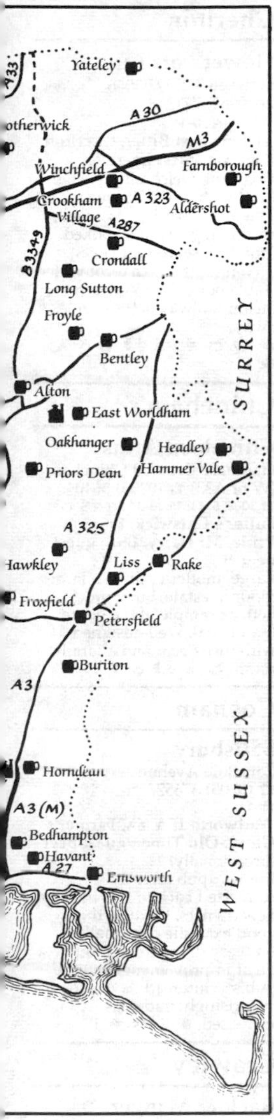

the site of the first Red Lion, one of the original pubs before the military camp arrived in 1854.
Q ❀ 🛏 ◖ ⊟ P

Royal Staff
37a Mount Pleasant Road
☎ (0252) 22932
11-3, 5-11; 12-11 Sat
Fuller's Hock, London Pride, ESB [H]
Beautifully refurbished in the best Victorian style: a 'back-street' local with a very comfortable and lively single bar and a strong community atmosphere. Good children's garden. ❀ ◖ ⇌ ♣

Alton

Eight Bells
Church Street ☎ (0420) 82417
11-3, 6-11; 11-11 Fri & Sat
Draught Bass; Marston's Pedigree; Ringwood Best Bitter; Worldham Old Dray [H]
Cosy, beamed pub with a large collection of chamber pots. Very popular at lunchtimes and can get very crowded. The atmosphere of a village pub only five minutes' from the centre. Alton's only free house. Q ◖ ◗

Wheatsheaf Inn
Market Square ☎ (0420) 83316
11-3, 5-11
Courage Best Bitter, Directors; Ushers Best Bitter, Founders [H]
Much-renovated, comfortable, two-bar pub. Live music on Thu; crowded weekends with a young clientele. 🛏 ◖ ⊟ ♣

Andover

Globe
High Street ☎ (0264) 323415
10.30-2.30, 5-11
Marston's Bitter, Pedigree, Owd Rodger (winter) [H]
Circa 1742: a coaching inn beside the market square (markets Thu and Sat), with a dining room upstairs. Carefully restored; pleasant nooks and corners. A resident lady ghost patrols areas where dogs and cats refuse to enter.
⛫ ◖ ◗ ⇌ ♣

Lardicake
Adelaide Road
☎ (0264) 323447
11-3, 5.30-11; 11-11 Fri, Sat & summer
Archers Best Bitter; Fuller's London Pride; guest beers [H]
Unsophisticated, one-bar pub next to a housing estate but close to the town centre. Popular with workers at lunchtime and a good local trade eves. Three guest beers. No wheelchair access to the ladies' WC.
⛫ ❀ ◖ ◗ ♿ ♣ P

Ashmansworth

Plough
Off A343 ☎ (0635) 253047
12-2.30 (not Mon or Tue, Jan-Easter), 6-11
Archers Village, Best Bitter, Black Jack, Golden; guest beer [G]
Friendly, single-bar village local, close to Highclere Castle, at the highest point in the county. Beer is served from casks behind the bar (cooled in summer). Full of character.
⛫ Q ❀ ◖ ▲ P

Axford

Candover Crown
On B3046 ☎ (0256) 389492
11.30-2.30, 6-11
Hall & Woodhouse Badger Best Bitter, Tanglefoot; Marston's Pedigree; Whitbread Boddingtons Bitter [H]
Attractive, two-bar, country pub with a dining extension. Busy Sun lunchtimes. Note the tapestry of the Last Supper in the restaurant.
⛫ ❀ ◖ ◗ ♣ P

Basingstoke

Bounty
Bounty Road ☎ (0256) 20071
11-2.30 (3 Sat), 5.30 (5 Fri)-11
Courage Best Bitter; Ushers Best Bitter, Founders [H]
Former John Mays pub next to Mays Bounty cricket ground, used by Hampshire CC. One of Basingstoke's few remaining pubs of character, with a friendly landlord. Office workers lunchtime; locals eves. No food Sun.
⛫ Q ❀ ◖ ♣ P

Bedhampton

Golden Lion
54 Bedhampton Road (B2177)
☎ (0705) 614396
10-2.30, 6-11
Ind Coope Friary Meux Best Bitter, Burton Ale [H]
Good, straightforward local in an early 19th-century building, relatively unchanged. The amiable staff serve good value food in the small lounge. Handy for Havant rugby ground. ❀ ◖ ⊟ ♿ ⇌ ♣ P

Bentley

Star Inn
London Road ☎ (0420) 23184
11-3, 6-11
Courage Best Bitter; Ushers Best Bitter, Founders [H]
Single, cosy bar with traditional wood panelling; pleasant and welcoming. Smart casual dress required. The restaurant has a reputation for quality (no eve meals Sun or Mon). Meeting room available; car park across the busy A31. Q ❀ ◖ ◗ P

Bighton

Three Horseshoes
Off A31/B3047 OS616344
☎ (0962) 732859
11-2.30, 6-11; 12-2, 7-10.30 Sun
Gale's XXXD, BBB, Best Bitter (summer), **5X, HSB** [H]

Delightful, rural local, well off the beaten track, with country crafts in the locals' bar. Quiet, relaxing lounge. Note the old pub sign. Handy for Mid-Hants Steam Railway (Ropley station). No food Mon.
⛫ Q ❀ ◑ ⊞ ♿ ♣ P

Bishopstoke

Foresters Arms
1 Stoke Common Road
☎ (0703) 620287
11–3, 6–11; 11–11 Sat
Gibbs Mew Wiltshire, Salisbury, Deacon, Bishop's Tipple Ⓗ
Genuine community pub with a team or society for everyone. A quiet lounge and a lively public bar (prices equal).
⛫ Q ♨ ❀ ⛿ ♣ ⌓ P ⚡

Bishop's Waltham

Bunch of Grapes
St Peter's Street
☎ (0489) 892935
10–2 (2.30 Sat), 6–11; 12–2, 7–10.30
Courage Best Bitter Ⓖ**; Ushers Best Bitter** Ⓗ
Although only yards from the town centre, this is a traditional community local. A *Guide* entry since 1975.
Q ❀ ♣

Botley

Brewery Bar
10 Winchester Street
☎ (0489) 782324
11–3, 5–11; 11–11 Sat
Banks's Mild; Marston's Bitter, Pedigree Ⓗ
Sympathetically refurbished village pub, once the Edwards Brewery tap. A lively public bar with wood flooring and a large, quieter lounge; patio garden. No food Sun.
❀ ◑ ⊞ ▲ ♣ P

Braishfield

Newport Inn
Newport Lane ☎ (0794) 68225
10–3, 6–11
Gale's BBB, Best Bitter, 5X, HSB Ⓗ
Unspoilt Victorian village inn which has a piano and sing-song Sun eve. The sandwiches are famed! Large garden with many animals. ⛫ ❀ ⊞ ♣ P

Burghclere

Queen
Harts Lane (1 mile E of A34, N of village) ☎ (0635) 27350
11–3, 6–11
Adnams Bitter, Broadside; Arkell's 3B Ⓗ
Friendly local with a good atmosphere, especially if you like a flutter on the horses at nearby Newbury. Darts, crib, dominoes and bar billiards. No food Sun. ❀ ◑ ♣ P

Buriton

Five Bells
High Street ☎ (0730) 263584
11–2.30 (3 Fri & Sat), 5.30–11
Ballard's Best Bitter; Ind Coope Friary Meux Best Bitter, Burton Ale; Ringwood XXXX Porter; Tetley Bitter Ⓗ**; guest beers**
Traditional free house: a two-bar pub, with imposing fireplaces. Excellent range of ales and food. Live folk music Wed.
⛫ Q ❀ ◑ ◗ ⊞ ▲ ♣ P

Bursledon

Linden Tree
School Road (off A27/A3025)
☎ (0703) 402356
11–2.30 (3 Sat), 6 (5 Fri)–11
Draught Bass; Wadworth IPA, 6X, Farmer's Glory (summer), **Old Timer** Ⓗ
Excellent, comfortable, one-bar pub with no obtrusive gaming machines. A children's play area makes it ideal in summer. High quality, home-cooked food (not served Sun).
⛫ ❀ ◑ ♣ P

Vine Inn
High Street, Old Bursledon
☎ (0703) 403836
11.30–3, 6–11; 11.30–11 Sat
Marston's Bitter, Merrie Monk, Pedigree Ⓗ
Smart, comfortable local on a narrow lane in *Howard's Way* country. Quiz night Tue; darts Wed. ❀ ◑ ◗ ▲ ⇌ ♣

Catisfield

Limes at Catisfield
34 Catisfield Lane
☎ (0329) 842926
11–2.30, 6 (7 Sat)–11
Gale's Best Bitter, HSB; Gibbs Mew Salisbury, Bishop's Tipple; Ringwood Fortyniner, Old Thumper Ⓗ
Victorian building converted to a pub; a small, quiet lounge and a busier public. Petanque terrain in the garden justifies bar extensions in summer! Children welcome at weekends only.
Q ♨ ❀ ◑ ◗ ⊞ ♿ ♣ P

Charter Alley

White Hart
☎ (0256) 850048
12–3, 7–11
Brakspear Bitter; Fuller's London Pride; guest beers Ⓗ
Cosy village pub with a small front bar and a large back bar with a skittles alley and games area. Quiz nights Mon; live music Thu. A good selection of guests is changed weekly; cider in summer.
⛫ Q ❀ ◑ ◗ ♣ ⌓ P

Cheriton

Flower Pots Inn
Between A272/B3046
☎ (0962) 771318
11.30–2.30, 6–11
Archers Best Bitter; Cheriton Pots Ale; guest beers Ⓖ
Excellent, welcoming village local with its own brewery. The public bar boasts a well; cosy lounge. Home-cooked food (not served Sun eve); accommodation in a converted stable block. The Watercress Steam Railway is three miles away.
⛫ Q ♨ ❀ ⛿ ◑ ◗ ⊞ ♿ ▲ ♣ P

Chineham

Chineham Arms
Hanmore Road, N Chineham (W of A33) ☎ (0256) 56404
11.30–3, 5–11; 11.30–11 Fri & Sat
Fuller's Chiswick, London Pride, Mr Harry, ESB; guest beer Ⓗ
Large, modern pub in a large, modern estate, but a much better example of the genre than usual. Well designed, with nice decor and a family room. ♨ ❀ ◑ ◗ ♿ ♣ P

Cosham

Salisbury
Lonsdale Avenue
☎ (0705) 376577
11–11
Wadworth IPA, 6X, Farmer's Glory, Old Timer; guest beer (occasionally) Ⓗ
Pre-war pub recently converted back to two bars by new owners, Wadworth. A good example of a small brewery doing things right – a great improvement from the pub's Whitbread days. Not surprisingly trade has increased. ❀ ◑ ⇌ ♣ P

Crawley

Rack & Manger
Stockbridge Road (A272)
☎ (0962) 776281
11–3, 5.30–11; 11–11 Sat
Banks's Mild; Marston's Bitter, Pedigree, Owd Rodger Ⓗ
Large pub, midway between Winchester and Stockbridge: a lively public bar and a quiet lounge, due for enlargement. Popular with agricultural students.
⛫ ❀ ◑ ◗ ⊞ ▲ ♣ P

Crondall

Castle
Croft Lane ☎ (0252) 850892
12–2.30, 7 (6 summer)–11
Fuller's Hock, Chiswick, London Pride, Mr Harry, ESB Ⓗ

Refurbished single-bar pub which should appeal to most tastes. A proper village 'local'. The landlord is a trained chef and the food is excellent (no meals Mon eve). Skittle alley for hire. ♛ Q ❀ ◑ ◗ ♣ P

Crookham Village

Black Horse
The Street ☎ (0252) 616434
11–2.30 (3 Fri & Sat), 5.30–11
Courage Best Bitter, Directors; Wadworth 6X Ⓗ
First rate, welcoming, beamed and popular village hostelry. Good value food (not available Sun). The Basingstoke Canal is nearby and the area is good for walks. Excellent garden for children. Q ❀ ◑ P

Damerham

Compasses Inn
On B3078, W of Fordingbridge
☎ (072 53) 231
11–2.30, 6–11; 11–11 Sat
Ringwood Best Bitter; Tetley Bitter; Wadworth 6X; guest beer Ⓗ
Village pub with quiet lounge and lively public bars. The large beer garden has a children's play area. The excellent food includes vegetarian; large restaurant. ♛ Q ❀ ⛟ ◑ ◗ ▲ ♣ P

Droxford

White Horse
South Hill (A32)
☎ (0489) 877490
11–3, 6–11
Burts Nipper, Newport Best Bitter; Morland Old Speckled Hen; Wadworth 6X, Old Timer; guest beers Ⓗ
Traditional, 16th-century coaching inn with contrasting lounge and public bars. The gents' boasts a well. One of the few pubs in the Meon valley that has not become a restaurant that also sells beer. ♛ Q ⛾ ❀ ⛟ ◑ ◗ ⊟ ♣ P

Dundridge

Hampshire Bowman
Dundridge Lane (1 mile off B3035) OS578185
☎ (0489) 892940
11–2.30, 6–11
Archers Village, Golden; King & Barnes Sussex, Festive Ⓖ**; guest beers**
Classic country pub down a classic country lane. A single bar with a brick floor. The serving counter has a cask stillage behind; excellent log burner. Well-regarded food (not served Mon, or Sun eve). Quiz Mon.
♛ Q ❀ ◑ ◗ ▲ ♣ P

Durley

Robin Hood
Durley Street ☎ (0489) 860229
11–2.30, 6–11; 11–11 Sat
Banks's Mild; Marston's Bitter, Pedigree Ⓗ
Ex-17th-century coaching inn, now a good village local with a lounge. Home-made snacks lunchtime and eves; barbecues in summer. ♛ Q ❀ ⊟ ♣ P

East End

East End Arms
Lymington Road (3 miles E of IOW ferry) OS363968
☎ (0590) 65223
11.30–3, 6–11
Cook's Yardarm Ⓖ**; Fuller's London Pride; Poole Dolphin** Ⓗ**; Ringwood Fortyniner, Old Thumper** Ⓖ
Popular country pub used mainly by locals. A basic public and a comfortable lounge with patio doors to the garden. Traditional country game pies; occasional ciders.
♛ Q ❀ ◑ ◗ ⊟ ♿ ♣ ⌓ P

East Worldham

Three Horseshoes
Cakers Lane ☎ (0420) 83211
11–2.30, 6–11
Gale's BBB, Best Bitter, HSB Ⓗ
Pleasant, single-bar, roadside pub with unusual barrel seats, set in a lovely village. Can be very quiet. The dining area offers inexpensive Sun roasts, but no eve meals Sun or Mon.
Q ❀ ◑ ◗ ♣ P

Ellisfield

Fox
Fox Green Lane (off A339)
☎ (0256) 381210
11.30–2.30 (3 Sat), 6.30–11
Fuller's London Pride; Gale's HSB; Hall & Woodhouse Tanglefoot; Hampshire King Alfred's; Marston's Pedigree; S&N Theakston Old Peculier Ⓗ
Very friendly pub with two bars offering a wide range of ales and good food. Darts and dominoes. Hard to find, but a must. ♛ Q ❀ ◑ ◗ ⊟ ♣ P

Emsworth

Coal Exchange
South Street ☎ (0243) 375566
10.30–3, 5.30–11; 10.30–11 Sat
Gale's XXXD, BBB, Best Bitter, 5X, HSB Ⓗ
Small old pub with a tiled front, in the town centre. One comfortable bar with a good atmosphere and a good food menu; eve meals in summer.
♛ Q ❀ ◑ ◗ ♿ ▲ ⇌ ♣

Fairfield
125 New Brighton Road (B2147) ☎ (0243) 373304
11–2.30, 6–11
Gale's BBB, Best Bitter, HSB Ⓗ
Elegant, Regency-style building to the north of town, with two bars, a pool area and restaurant. Live entertainment weekends.
Q ❀ ⛟ ◑ ◗ ⇌ P

Milkmans Arms
North Street ☎ (0243) 373356
11 3, 6–11 (10–11 summer); 11–11 Sat
Gale's BBB, HSB Ⓗ
Excellent, one-bar convivial local. Home-cooked food till 8pm. Q ❀ ◑ ◗ ♿ ⇌ ♣

Everton

Crown Inn
Old Christchurch Road
☎ (0590) 642655
11–2.30, 6–11
Draught Bass; Fuller's London Pride; Whitbread Strong Country, Flowers Original Ⓗ**; guest beers** (summer)
19th-century, two-bar, traditional village inn with smoke-screen windows. The lively public bar has an excellent jukebox; the lounge is quieter. Sun quiz nights in winter (local league). Floral displays in summer. ♛ Q ❀ ◑ ◗ ⊟ ♿ ▲ ♣ ⌓ P

Faccombe

Jack Russell
Off A343 ☎ (0264) 87315
12–2.30, 7–11
Ringwood Best Bitter, Fortyniner Ⓗ**; guest beer**
Pleasant, friendly country pub in good walking country. In the large conservatory (where children over five are allowed), all the tables are set for food; popular with diners.
♛ Q ❀ ⛟ ◑ ◗ ♿ ♣ P

Farnborough

Imperial Arms
12 Farnborough Street
☎ (0252) 542573
11–2.30, 5–11; 11.30–11 Fri & Sat
Courage Best Bitter; John Smith's Bitter; Wadworth 6X; guest beers Ⓗ
Three distinct bars, a pool room, sports room and a saloon, cater for all. No food Sun. Interesting and ever-changing guest beers.
Q ❀ ◑ ⊟ ⇌ (North) ♣ P

Old Ford
Lynchford Road, South Farnborough ☎ (0252) 544840
11–11
Courage Best Bitter; Marston's Pedigree; John Smith's Bitter; Worldham Old Dray Ⓗ

Built in the 1850s and architecturally part of North Camp station, where the platform was extended for General Gordon. Dining area, pool room at the rear, and a large garden with summer barbecues, a playground and a pets corner. ♘ ❀ ◖ ◗ ⇌ (North Camp) ♣ P

Prince of Wales

184 Rectory Road (off A325)
☎ (0252) 545578
11.30–2.30, 6 (5.30 Fri)–11
Brakspear Bitter; Fuller's London Pride; Hall & Woodhouse Badger Best Bitter, Tanglefoot; Hogs Back TEA; Wadworth 6X [H]; guest beers
The best free house for miles, with a wide range of guest beers. A convivial and traditional hostelry which is invariably busy. Stages occasional small brewery promotions, including for mild. Friendly staff and excellent lunches (not served Sun). Q ❀ ◖ ⇌ (North) P

Freefolk

Watership Down

On B3400, Whitchurch–Overton road ☎ (0256) 892254
11.30–3, 7–11
Archers Best Bitter; Brakspear Bitter; guest beers [H]
One-bar house dating back to the 19th century. The very spacious garden has many amenities. Food is home made. Renamed after the Richard Adams book, set locally.
♨ ❀ ◖ ◗ ♣ P

Fritham

Royal Oak

2 miles W of B3078 OS232141
☎ (0703) 812606
11–3, 6–11
Marston's Pedigree; Whitbread Strong Country [G]
In a class of its own – a tiny unspoilt, thatched pub in the heart of the New Forest. Strong support for all country sports. ♨ Q ❀ ▲ ♣

Froxfield

Trooper

OS727273 ☎ (0730) 284293
12–2.30, 5.30–11
Draught Bass; Ringwood Best Bitter [H]; guest beers [H]/[G]
Isolated local which boasts a number of eccentricities. Theme food eves. Well worth the climb up 'Little Switzerland'. ♨ Q ❀ ◖ ◗ ⌓ P

Froyle

Prince of Wales

Lower Froyle ☎ (0420) 23102
11–2.30, 6–11
Fuller's London Pride, ESB; S&N Theakston Old Peculier; Wadworth 6X; guest beers [H]
Edwardian country pub in a scenic village. Originally thatched, but now rebuilt as a single, smart saloon bar with an eating area. Convivial, but can get busy. Family-owned and -run with home-cooked food (not served Sun eve).
♨ Q ♘ ❀ ◖ ◗ ♣ P

Gosport

Manor Hotel

Brewers Lane, Bridgemary (off A32) ☎ (0329) 232946
11–11
Draught Bass; Courage Directors; guest beers [H]
Large, rambling hotel bar with a collection of chamber pots. The two guest beers are sold as house beers, offering the best value. 🛏 ◖ ◗ ♿ ♣ P

Queens Hotel

143 Queens Road (off B3333, Stoke Rd) ☎ (0705) 525518
12–2.30 (11.30–3.30 Fri), 7–11; 11.30–11 Sat
Archers Village; Fuller's London Pride; Greene King Abbot; guest beers [H]
Single-bar beer drinkers' haven, in the back streets. The building has unusual brick and stone finishings, with etched windows; an old open fire with an elegant surround provides the focus inside. Two frequently changing guest beers. ♨ ♣

White Swan

36 Forton Road (A32)
☎ (0705) 584138
11.30–3 (4 Sat), 5.30 (6.30 Sat)–11
Courage Best Bitter, Directors; Ushers Best Bitter [H]
Basic locals' pub with several darts teams. Owned by Ushers although it still looks like a Courage pub. Occasionally has other Ushers beers. ♣ ⌓

Hambledon

New Inn

West Street ☎ (0705) 632466
12–2.30, 7–11
Ballard's Trotton; Eldridge Pope Hardy Country; Ringwood XXXX Porter, Fortyniner, Old Thumper [H]
Pleasant, two-bar pub with no frills, just good drinking and socialising. No food, but reasonable prices and a friendly atmosphere. At over 450 years, the oldest pub in the village. ♨ Q ❀ ♿ ▲ ♣ P

Vine Inn

West Street ☎ (0705) 632419
11.30–2.30 (3 Sat), 6–11
Burts Nipper; Gale's BBB, HSB; Morland Old Speckled Hen; Wells Bombardier [H]; guest beers (occasionally)
Pleasant old pub with two bars and wooden beams. The quiet, welcoming atmosphere is enhanced by an unusual real fire, a well and intimate areas in the lounge. Ideal for cricket country. Eve meals Thu–Sat.
♨ Q ❀ ◖ ◗ ▲ ♣

Hammer Vale

Prince of Wales

Hammer Lane OS867326
☎ (0428) 652600
11–3, 6–11; 11–11 Sat
Gale's BBB, Best Bitter, 5X, HSB [G]
Impressive, red-brick roadhouse built in 1927 to serve the new A3. Fortunately, the road passed elsewhere, leaving the pub in splendid rural isolation. Largely unchanged: one long bar, with jacketed casks on stillage, serves three drinking areas. Live music Sun eve.
♨ Q ❀ ◖ ◗ ▲ ♣ P

Havant

Robin Hood

6 Homewell ☎ (0705) 482779
11–11
Gale's BBB, 5X, HSB [G]
Excellent old pub in the town centre, behind the church, with unspoilt character and a friendly atmosphere. Public car park at the rear.
♨ ❀ ◖ ♿ ⇌ ♣

Hawkley

Hawkley Inn

Pococks Lane OS747291
☎ (0730) 284205
12–2.30 (3 Sat), 6–11
Ballard's Trotton, Best Bitter; Ringwood Fortyniner; guest beers [H]
Busy village free house with a varied clientele. Furnished in a very individual style and popular with walkers, who are made welcome. No food Sun eve. ♨ ❀ ◖ ◗ ♣ ⌓ ⊁

Headley

Holly Bush

High Street ☎ (0428) 712211
11–2.30, 6–11
Courage Best Bitter; Ushers Best Bitter, Founders [H]
Very comfortable, welcoming Victorian local with period decor. Separate eating and drinking areas around a central bar. The original pub is over the road. The garden has a play area.
♨ Q ❀ ◖ ◗ ♣ P

Hedge End

Barleycorn

2 Lower Northam Road
☎ (0489) 784171
11–2.30 (3 Sat), 5.30 (5 Fri)–11; 12–2 (may be 3 summer), 7–10.30 Sun

Banks's Mild; Marston's Bitter, Pedigree Ⓗ
Located in the original village centre, a busy, good value pub with one drinking area divided into several sections. The garden has a barbecue. No food Sun. ❀ ◐ ♣ P

Horndean

Ship & Bell
6 London Road (A3)
☎ (0705) 592107
10–11
Gale's BBB, Best Bitter, 5X, HSB Ⓗ
The Gale's brewery tap. A spacious hotel catering for all with its contrasting lounge and public bars. No food Sun eve. ◐ ◑ ▲ ♣ P

Horsebridge

John O'Gaunt
½ mile W of A3057, S of King's Somborne ☎ (0794) 388394
11.30–2.30 (11–3 Sat), 6–11; 12–2.30, 7–10.30 Sun
Adnams Bitter; Palmers IPA; Ringwood Fortyniner Ⓗ
Fine village pub in the lovely Test valley – superb walking country. A down-to-earth free house offering very good value for money. Guest beers occasionally replace the Adnams. No food Tue eve. Well used shove-ha'penny board. ❀ ◐ ◑ ♣ P

Hurstbourne Priors

Hurstbourne
At B3400/B3048 jct
☎ (0256) 892000
11–11
Wadworth 6X; guest beers Ⓗ
Open-plan, family-run country local with a reputation for beer and food, overlooking a cricket pitch. Three spare handpumps offer an ever-changing choice of guest ales. Watch your step, there is a stud farm next door.
Q ❀ ◐ ◑ ♣ P

Hythe

Lord Nelson
High Street ☎ (0703) 842169
11–11; 11–3, 6–11 Mon & Wed
Ringwood Best Bitter, XXXX Porter; Wadworth 6X; Whitbread Castle Eden Ale, Flowers Original Ⓗ
Small pub with quaint bars and a garden overlooking Southampton Water and yacht marina. Good value lunches. Handy for the Southampton ferry. ❀ ◐ ♣

Kingsclere

Swan Hotel
Swan Street ☎ (0635) 298314
11–2.30, 5.30 (6 Sat)–11
Tetley Bitter; guest beers Ⓗ
Large pub and restaurant, dating back to 1459 in parts, with a gallery. Good mix of clientele. At least four changing beers. No food Sun eve.
◐ ◑ ♣ P

Kings Worthy

Cart & Horses
London Road (A33/A3090 jct, near M3 jct 9)
☎ (0962) 882360
11–3, 6–11 (11–11 bank hols)
Marston's Bitter, Pedigree, Owd Rodger Ⓗ
Large, upmarket and busy roadhouse and restaurant with a good selection of food at all times. Extensions are planned to improve the catering facilities. The bar is a quiet drinker's retreat with bar billiards. Children's playground in the garden.
❀ ◐ ◑ ♣ P

Lasham

Royal Oak
☎ (0256) 381213
11–2.30 (3 Sat), 6–11
Fuller's London Pride; Hampshire King Alfred's; Hogs Back TEA; Hook Norton Old Hooky Ⓗ
Traditional two-bar village local with a friendly atmosphere. Ask for games.
Q ❀ ◐ ◑ ♣ P

Leckford

Leckford Hutt
On A30, 3 miles E of Stockbridge
☎ (0264) 810738
11–2.30, 6–11
Marston's Bitter, Pedigree Ⓗ
Cosy, welcoming main-road pub that caters for all. Numerous traditional games; collections of chamber pots and beer bottles. The landlord will explain the pub name. Occasional live music. Ideal for ramblers.
Q ❀ ◐ ◑ ▲ ♣ P

Liss

Spread Eagle
Farnham Road, West Liss (A325) ☎ (0730) 892088
11–3, 5–11
Ind Coope Benskins Best Bitter; Tetley Bitter; guest beers Ⓗ
Fine, 15th-century pub on a small green. The ancient oak is reputed to have been the local hanging tree. Two bars and a restaurant. Cider in summer.
❀ ◐ ◑ ▲ ♣ P

Little London

Plough Inn
Silchester Road
☎ (0256) 850628
11–2.30 (3 Sat), 6–11
Greene King Abbot; Ringwood Best Bitter; Wadworth 6X; Whitbread Wethered Bitter Ⓗ
Small country pub backing on to open fields, overlooking Pamber Forest; an ideal stop-off on country walks. Bar billiards, darts, etc. A basic, unpretentious, olde-worlde pub. ❀ ♣ P

Long Sutton

Four Horseshoes
The Street OS748471
☎ (0256) 862488
11.30–2.30, 6–11
Gale's XXXD, BBB, Best Bitter, 5X, HSB Ⓗ
Compact, isolated local, superbly situated a mile from the village. A good blend of locals and foodies, who travel miles for the award-winning fare in a friendly, relaxed atmosphere with a log fire. Attractive conservatory open all year. Good value Sun roasts. No food Sun eve.
Q ❀ ◐ ◑ ▲ ♣ P

Lymington

Red Lion
High Street ☎ (0590) 672276
11–11
Marston's Pedigree; Ringwood Best Bitter; Wadworth 6X Ⓗ
Lively, two-bar pub popular with shoppers and locals. Children welcome in an enclosed rear garden. Home-cooked fare (Sun lunches and eve meals in summer only).
❀ ◐ ◑ ♣ P

Lyndhurst

Mailmans Arms
High Street ☎ (0703) 284196
11–2.30, 6–11
Banks's Mild; Marston's Bitter, Pedigree Ⓗ
Friendly, comfortable pub. Occasional live entertainment; barbecues in summer. Good value lunches and extensive eve pizza menus. Free car park nearby. Q ❀ ◐ ◑ ♣

Marchwood

Pilgrim
Hythe Road ☎ (0703) 867752
11–2.30 (3 Sat), 6–11
Draught Bass; Courage Best Bitter, Directors Ⓗ

Hampshire

Beautiful thatched inn with immaculate gardens. Home cooking with a vegetarian option and a children's menu; eve meals in the restaurant.
♛ Q ❀ ◖ P

Micheldever

Dever Arms
Winchester Road (off A33)
☎ (0962) 774339
11.30–3, 6–11
Hall & Woodhouse Badger Best Bitter; Hook Norton Mild, Best Bitter; Hop Back Summer Lightning [H]; guest beers
Extensively refurbished pub in a quiet, pretty village. Well worth a short detour from the A33 or M3 for food and beer. Something for all tastes. No food Sun eve.
♛ ♞ ❀ ◖ ◗ ♿ ▲ ♣ P

Mortimer West End

Red Lion
Church Road ☎ (0734) 700169
11–11
Hall & Woodhouse Badger Best Bitter, Hard Tackle, Tanglefoot; Wadworth 6X [H]; guest beers
Circa 1549 building; nooks and crannies add to its charm. Very much a food-oriented house, rather than a haunt for a quiet pint or two. Quiz Sun eve. ♛ ❀ ◖ ◗ P

Turners Arms
West End Road
☎ (0734) 332961
12–3, 6–11
Brakspear Bitter, Special [H]
Outstanding, Victorian village pub with extensive bar 'specials' and a set menu. Happy, unpretentious atmosphere. Children welcome if well behaved.
♛ ❀ ◖ ◗ P

Newtown

Travellers Rest
Church Road OS613123
☎ (0329) 833263
11–3, 6–11
Gibbs Mew Wiltshire, Salisbury, Bishop's Tipple; guest beers [H]
Popular, two-bar country pub, with an outside gents'. The public bar has a piano and there is now a restaurant.
♛ Q ♞ ❀ ◖ ◗ ▣ ▲ ♣ P

Oakhanger

Red Lion
The Street ☎ (0420) 472232
11–3, 6–11
Courage Best Bitter, Directors; Worldham Old Dray [H]
Pub where the superb public bar is dominated by a 32lb stuffed pike and lively locals. The saloon is more refined and food based, but not without atmosphere. Likely to be crowded for all the right reasons. ♛ Q ❀ ◖ ◗ ▣ P

Overton

Red Lion
High Street ☎ (0256) 770268
11–11
Courage Best Bitter; Gale's HSB; Marston's Pedigree; Ruddles Best Bitter; Webster's Yorkshire Bitter; Young's Special [H]; guest beers
Large, three-room pub with a small skittle alley. Occasional live music. Book for Sun lunch; no food Sun eve.
♛ Q ❀ ◖ ◗ ♣ P

Owslebury

Ship Inn
Off B2177 ☎ (0962) 777358
11–2.30, 6–11
Banks's Mild; Marston's Bitter, Pedigree [H]
Smart, busy, two-bar country inn with a dining area (families welcome). An active village pub with many sports teams and a large garden with children's playground, cricket net and bowls green.
♛ Q ❀ ◖ ◗ ▣ ♿ ▲ ♣ P

Pennington

Musketeer
North Street ☎ (0590) 676527
12 (11.30 Sat)–3, 5.30–11
Brakspear Bitter; Fuller's London Pride; Ringwood Best Bitter [H]; guest beers
Traditional, friendly, one-bar pub in the village centre, mostly used by locals. The pub sign of a musketeer is based on an original sculpture. Three guest beers. ♛ Q ❀ ♣ P

Petersfield

Good Intent
40 College Street (one-way system northbound)
☎ (0730) 63838
11–2.30, 6–11; closed Mon
Draught Bass; Fuller's London Pride; Hall & Woodhouse Tanglefoot; Ringwood Best Bitter; guest beers [G]
16th-century free house with a rambling single bar. All beers are served from the cellar. Popular restaurant (no food Sun eve). ♛ Q ◖ ◗ ⇌ P

Portsmouth

Artillery Arms
Hester Road, Milton
☎ (0705) 733610
11–3, 6–11
Gale's BBB, Best Bitter, HSB; Ind Coope Burton Ale; Ringwood Old Thumper; Tetley Bitter; guest beers [H]
Unchanging corner local, hidden away down a small back street. Two bar areas: a lively public bar with pool and darts, and a quiet lounge with a family room attached. Probably the best value in the city. ♞ ▣ ♣ P

Connaught Arms
119 Guildford Road, Fratton
☎ (0705) 646455
11.30–2.30 (3.30 Fri), 6–11; 11–11 Sat
Marston's Pedigree; Morland Old Speckled Hen; Wadworth 6X; guest beers [H]
Large, friendly, single-bar local tucked away in the back streets. Quiz every other Mon. Constantly changing guest ale. Good food (not served Sun).
❀ ◖ ⇌ (Fratton) ♣

Dolphin
41 High Street, Old Portsmouth (opp. cathedral)
☎ (0705) 823595
11–11
Brakspear Bitter; Gale's HSB; Marston's Pedigree; Morrells College; S&N Theakston Old Peculier; Wadworth 6X [H]
Large, old pub with two distinct areas. The beer range varies weekly, with up to 12 beers. Beer is also available in four-pint jugs. Large groups catered for. Regular beer and cider/perry festivals. ♛ ❀ ◖ ◗ ⇌ (Harbour) ♣ ⌓

Electric Arms
190–192 Fratton Road, Fratton
☎ (0705) 823293
11–3, 6–11; 11–11 Fri & Sat
Ind Coope Burton Ale [H]
Town-centre local with a ready welcome. Many sports teams share this centre of the community. Reputedly haunted by the ghost of a former landlady.
◖ ▣ ⇌ (Fratton) ♣

Florist
324 Fratton Road, Fratton
☎ (0705) 820289
11–3, 6–11; 11–11 Sat
Wadworth IPA, 6X, Farmer's Glory, Old Timer [H]
Small, two-bar pub, acquired by Wadworth in 1991. The front public bar has darts and pool; comfortable lounge at the rear. The exterior has half-timbering and a 'witch's hat' tower.
Q ❀ ▣ ♿ ⇌ (Fratton)

Olde Oyster House
291 Locksway Road, Milton
☎ (0705) 827456
6 (11 Sat)–11 (may vary; closed weekday lunch)
Wadworth 6X; guest beers H
Large pub opposite the Milton locks, with a varied clientele. The lounge is used as a games/ family room. Guest beers change regularly and there is always a bargain ale, plus two real ciders. P

Red White & Blue
150 Fawcett Road, Southsea
☎ (0705) 814470
11–11
Gale's XXXD, BBB, HSB H
Compact local which serves moose's milk on Canada Day! Patriotic decor of two nations. XXXD mild is known as 'Gnome'. Lunches on request. (Fratton)

Squires
60 Queen Street
☎ (0705) 818346
11–2 (not Wed), 7–11; closed Tue
Gibbs Mew Deacon; Ringwood Best Bitter, Old Thumper; guest beers H
Cool and calming restoration of an 18th-century inn with a galleried bar. Good value food at all times (open all day Sun). Close to HMS Victory, Mary Rose and Warrior. (Harbour)

Tap
17 London Road, North End
☎ (0705) 699943
10.30–11
Fuller's London Pride; Gibbs Mew Bishop's Tipple; Hall & Woodhouse Tanglefoot; Mitchell's Best Bitter; Ringwood Old Thumper H**; guest beers**
Opened in 1985 as the brewery tap to the former Southsea Brewery. An enterprising and successful free house with a varying choice of ten ales, usually including a mild; Inch's cider, a perry plus a wide range of Belgian and Dutch bottled beers. Local CAMRA *Pub of the Year* 1992.

Wine Vaults
43–47 Albert Road, Southsea (opp. Kings Theatre)
☎ (0705) 864712
11.30–3.30, 5.30–11; 11–11 Sat
Hampshire King Alfred's; Mitchell's Best Bitter; Otter Bitter, Ale; guest beers H
Free house whose rotating range of up to ten beers has trebled in size since opening in 1987. Its house beers are brewed by Courage. Regular beer festivals. Often crowded despite its beer pricing policy. Eve meals end at 8.30.

Priors Dean

White Horse (Pub With No Name)
OS714290 ☎ (024 058) 387
11–2.30 (3 Fri & Sat), 6–11
Ballard's Best Bitter; Courage Best Bitter, Directors; King & Barnes Sussex; Ringwood Fortyniner; S&N Theakston Mild H**; guest beers** H/G
Famous old pub hidden in a field and difficult to find. A classic country pub with nine real ales, including a house beer brewed by Ringwood. Beware of the pond in the car park. No food Sun lunch or Mon and Tue eves.
Q P

Privett

Pig & Whistle
Gosport Road (A32)
☎ (0730) 88421
11–11
Ballard's Best Bitter; Courage Directors; Fuller's London Pride; Ringwood Best Bitter, Old Thumper H
Large, roadside hostelry, part of the Lawns Hotel complex. The single spacious bar has a games area. Food all day; live music of all sorts at weekends.
P

Rake

Flying Bull
London Road ☎ (0730) 892285
11–2.30 (3 Sat), 6 (5 Fri & Sat)–11
Eldridge Pope Dorchester, Hardy Country, Royal Oak H
Friendly, roadside pub on the old A3. The Hampshire/ Sussex boundary runs through the bar. P

Ringwood

Inn on the Furlong
12 Meeting House Lane
☎ (0425) 475139
11–3, 5–11; 11–11 Wed, Fri, Sat & summer
Ringwood Best Bitter, XXXX Porter, Fortyniner, Old Thumper H**; guest beers**
Superb, thriving local in the centre of town. A central bar serves a multi-roomed pub with flagstones and traditional furnishings. Excellent value meals served in a conservatory; also a games room. Live music Tue. Car park opposite.
Q

Romsey

Tudor Rose
Cornmarket ☎ (0794) 512126
11–11
Courage Best Bitter, Directors H

15th-century alehouse, just 250 square feet in a single bar. A friendly haven from the town-centre bustle. The only pub in the county in every edition of the *Guide*. Yard for summer drinking. Lunchtime snacks. Q

Rotherwick

Coach & Horses
The Street ☎ (0256) 762542
11–11
Hall & Woodhouse Badger Best Bitter, Hard Tackle, Tanglefoot; Gribble Ale, Reg's Tipple, Black Adder II; Wells Eagle H
Beamed pub with wooden floors and red brickwork; a traditional alehouse with a good, varied selection of ales. Varied clientele, young and old. Q P

Shedfield

Sams Hotel
Upper Church Road (off B2177) ☎ (0329) 832213
11.30–2 (3.30 Sat), 4.30 (6.30 Sat)–11
Banks's Mild; Marston's Bitter, Pedigree H
Unspoilt, roadside country inn with three bars, a cosy lounge and a traditional jug and bottle. HQ of Shedfield cricket club (pitch opposite) and reputedly the birthplace of British petanque. Bar billiards.
Q P

Silchester

Calleva Arms
☎ (0734) 700305
11–2.30, 6 (5 Sat)–11
Gale's BBB, Best Bitter, 5X, HSB H
Very spacious pub, split into three sections. Parts date back to the 18th century. Very good outdoor facilities and a good menu with good prices. No food Sun lunch. Silchester has Roman connections. Q
P

Sopley

Woolpack
Ringwood Road (B3347, W side of one-way system)
☎ (0425) 72252
11–11
Marston's Pedigree; Ringwood Best Bitter; Wadworth 6X H
Attractive, thatched pub in the centre of a picturesque village. The patio and conservatory overlook a stream and paddock with ducks and geese. Children's playground. Good range of food at a fair price. P

Hampshire

Southampton

Freemantle Arms
33 Albany Road, Freemantle (near A3057) ☎ (0703) 320759
10.30–3, 6–11; 10.30–11 Sat
Banks's Mild; Marston's Bitter, Pedigree Ⓗ
Friendly local in a quiet cul-de-sac: two bars with plenty of plant and aquatic life! Popular, colourful garden and patio. Good value beers: a good boozer. ❀ ♣

Gate
138–140 Burgess Road, Bassett (A35) ☎ (0703) 678250
11–3, 7–11
Eldridge Pope Hardy Country, Blackdown Porter, Royal Oak Ⓗ
Large, open-plan bar near the university, popular with locals and students. Sky TV for sport. Can be loud and lively but still friendly. Eve meals by arrangement. ❀ ◑ ◗ ♣ P

Hobbit
134 Bevois Valley Road
☎ (0703) 232591
12–3 (not weekdays in winter), 6–11; 12–11 Sat
Brakspear Bitter; Hop Back Summer Lightning; Whitbread Boddingtons Mild, Flowers IPA, Original, Porter Ⓗ**; guest beers**
Thriving young people's pub with live music most nights in the downstairs bar. Can be crowded late eve. Guest beers from small breweries.
❀ ◑ ⇌ (St Denys)

Junction Inn
21 Priory Road, St Denys
☎ (0703) 584486
11.30–3, 5 (7 Sat)–11
Banks's Mild; Marston's Bitter, Pedigree Ⓗ**, Owd Rodger** (winter) Ⓖ
Superbly preserved Victorian-style public and lounge bars and a small snug for non-smokers. National winner of CAMRA *Best Restored Pub* 1990. A busy, friendly local with lots of atmosphere and no music. Children welcome in the garden. Home-cooked lunches (not served Sun).
Q ◑ ⇌ (St Denys) ♣ ⊬

Marsh
42 Canute Road (under A3025 Itchen bridge) ☎ (0703) 635540
11–11; 11–5, 7–11 Sat
Banks's Mild; Marston's Bitter, Pedigree Ⓗ
Unusual-shaped docklands pub of great character. Formerly a lighthouse, which explains the semi-circular bars. The public bar displays prints of the old city centre. Eve meals are popular with nearby Ocean Village residents. Pool room. ❀ ◑ ◗ ⊟ ♿ ♣

New Inn
Bevois Valley Road
☎ (0703) 228437
11.45–3, 6.45–11
Gale's XXXD (summer)**, BBB, Best Bitter, 5X, HSB** Ⓗ**, Prize Old Ale** Ⓖ
Excellent, bustling drinkers' pub with its own rugby union team. Gale's Festival Mild is often available, plus a large range of Belgian beers and over 100 malt whiskies. Good value lunches. ◑ ♣

Park Inn
37 Carlisle Road, Shirley (off A3057, Romsey road)
☎ (0703) 787835
11–3 (3.30 Sat), 5 (6 Sat)–11
Hall & Woodhouse Tanglefoot; Wadworth IPA, 6X, Farmer's Glory, Old Timer Ⓗ
Popular, friendly, side-street local close to the shops. Maintains a two-bar feel and has some interesting mirrors. Slightly more upmarket than most local pubs. ❀ ♣

Richmond Inn
108 Portswood Road, Portswood ☎ (0703) 554523
11–11
Banks's Mild; Marston's Bitter, Pedigree Ⓗ
Welcoming local in a busy shopping district. Standard public bar and comfier lounge with prints of ocean liners. Note the lovely old LSD till. Nice whisky selection. Function room.
❀ ⊟ ⇌ (St Denys) ♣

South Western Arms
38 Adelaide Road, St Denys
☎ (0703) 324542
11.30–2.30 (not Mon), 6–11
Eldridge Pope Dorchester, Hardy Country; Gale's HSB; Hall & Woodhouse Tanglefoot; Hampshire King Alfred's Ⓗ**; guest beers**
One-bar, popular drinking local, deceptively large. An upstairs drinking area retains wooden beams and floorboards. Attracts a wide selection of drinkers. Home-cooked fare (Tue–Sat), no chips; vegetarian option. Five independents' guest beers.
❀ ◑ ⇌ (St Denys) ⇽ P

Waterloo Arms
101 Waterloo Road, Freemantle ☎ (0703) 220022
12–11
Hop Back Mild *or* **Wheat Beer, GFB, Special, Entire Stout, Summer Lightning** Ⓗ
Locals' pub, but with a mixed clientele. Represents half of the Hop Back chain. The beer is cooled by an underground stream. No food Sun.
❀ ◑ ⇌ (Millbrook) ♣

Wellington Arms
56 Park Road, Freemantle
☎ (0703) 227356
11.30–2.30, 6 (7 Sat)–11; 12–2.30, 8–10.30 Sun
Fuller's London Pride; Gibbs Mew Deacon; Palmers IPA; Ringwood Best Bitter, XXXX Porter; Wadworth 6X Ⓗ**; guest beers**
Busy, comfortable, back-street free house with two lounges and a mass of Iron Duke memorabilia. No food Sun.
❀ ◑ ⇌ (Central)

Stratfield Saye

Four Horseshoes
West End Green
☎ (0734) 332320
12–2, 6–11; 11–11 Fri & Sat
Morland Bitter, Old Masters, Old Speckled Hen Ⓗ
Country pub with two bars: a quiet, comfortable lounge bar and a friendly public. Good for games. ♨ Q ❀ ◑ ♣ P

Sway

Forest Heath Hotel
Station Road ☎ (0590) 682287
11–3, 6–11; 11–11 Sat & summer
Gale's HSB; Smiles Best Bitter; Wadworth 6X; Whitbread Boddingtons Mild, Bitter, Flowers Original Ⓗ**; guest beers**
Victorian coaching house, now a village pub with two bars and a restaurant. Children's garden play area. Live music weekday eves and quizzes Sun.
♨ Q ❀ ⊨ ◑ ◗ ▲ ⇌ ♣ P

Tangley

Cricketers Arms
Uphill at the war memorial crossroads ☎ (0264) 70823
11–3, 6–11; 11–11 Sat
Archers Best Bitter; Fuller's ESB; Hampshire King Alfred's, Pendragon; Hop Back Summer Lightning; Ind Coope Burton Ale Ⓗ
Welcoming country pub in a quiet village. Two bars; the front is more atmospheric and features cricketing memorabilia and an open fire. A little hard to find. No food Sun eve.
♨ Q ❀ ◑ ◗ ♿ ▲ ♣ P

Totford

Woolpack Inn
On B3046 ☎ (0962) 732101
11.30–3, 6–11
Eldridge Pope Dorchester, Hardy Country; Gale's HSB; Palmers BB Ⓗ**; guest beer**
16th-century flint building with a pleasant garden, in Hampshire's smallest hamlet, near The Grange (NT). A mix of country pub and small hotel. Worth a visit for food and beer. Warm welcome.
♨ ❀ ⊨ ◑ ◗ ♿ ▲ ♣ P

Upton Grey

Hoddington Arms
☎ (0256) 862371
11 (11.30 Sat)–2.30, 6 (7 Sat)–11
Morland Bitter, Old Speckled Hen; Wells Bombardier Ⓗ
18th-century, listed building in a pretty village. Excellent cuisine. Note the unusual lattice ceiling in the bar billiards room. Good family room. Genuinely friendly.
♔ Q ⛵ ❀ ◐ ◑ ♣ P

Vernham Dean

George
Upton Road ☎ (0264) 87279
11–2.30, 6–11
Marston's Bitter, Pedigree Ⓗ
Beautiful pub in a small village, retaining its original features: two real fires, beams and small nooks. Very welcoming. No eve meals Wed or Sun. ♔ Q ❀ ◐ ◑ ♣ P

Wallington

White Horse
44 North Wallington (off A27/M27 jct 11) ☎ (0329) 235197
11–3, 5–11
Draught Bass; Burts Nipper; London Pride; guest beers Ⓖ
Small village local by the River Wallington which may be reached by footbridge from Fareham High Street. Old village photos in the lounge; excellent dining room (Thu–Sat eves). Q ❀ ◐ ⊞ ♿ ♣ ⌓

West Wellow

Rockingham Arms
Canada Road (off A36, 1 mile from centre) ☎ (0794) 22473
11.45–2.30, 6–11
Beer range varies Ⓗ
Smartly furnished country free house on the northern edge of the New Forest with direct footpath access. Friendly atmosphere, with a games bar, lounge and restaurant. Up to six ales, including house beers declaring their brewer.
♔ ❀ ◐ ◑ ▲ ♣ P

Weyhill

Weyhill Fair
On A342, just N of A303
☎ (0264) 773631
11.30–2.30, 6 (7 Sat)–11; 12–2.30, 7–10.30 Sun
Morrells Bitter, Varsity Graduate Ⓗ**; guest beers**
Popular pub just outside Andover, providing a good range of meals and ales (always three guest beers, including a mild). Friendly, and popular with a wide range of people. No food Sun eve.
♔ Q ⛵ ❀ ◐ ◑ ♿ P ⁄

Whitchurch

Prince Regent
London Road (B3400)
☎ (0256) 892179
11–11
Archers Best Bitter; Hop Back GFB, Summer Lightning Ⓗ**; guest beer** (occasionally)
Basic locals' boozer with a view over the Test valley. Welcoming landlord; excellent value food; very good jukebox.
❀ ◐ ◑ ♣ P

Whiteley

Parsons Collar
Rockery Avenue, Solent Business Park (N of M27 jct 9)
☎ (0489) 880035
11–2.30, 5 (6.30 Sat)–11; 11–11 Fri
Thwaites Bitter, Craftsman Ⓗ
Built in 1990, a refreshing change from most hotel/brewery chains' attempts; a Canadian-style construction, with a flagstone floor. Its name derives from the appearance of a pint with a white head (collar). ♔ ⛵ ❀ ◐ ◑ ♿ P

Whitsbury

Cartwheel
Whitsbury Road (3 miles NNW of Fordingbridge) OS129188 ☎ (072 53) 362
11–2.30, 6–11
Beer range varies Ⓗ
Comfortable, genuine free house in a remote village just outside the New Forest. Previous incarnations were a barn, a bakery and a wheelwright's – hence the name. The beer range changes regularly. Excellent food from an extensive menu (no eve meals Tue). ♔ ❀ ◐ ◑ ♣ P

Winchester

First Inn Last Out
Wales Street ☎ (0962) 865963
11–11
Brains Dark; Courage Best Bitter; Fuller's London Pride Ⓗ**; guest beers**
12th-century riverside inn, alongside the Pilgrims' Way and Itchen Nature Reserve. Barbecues and hog-roasts in summer. Two guest beers, changed fortnightly, are very reasonably priced. Horse racing and rugby themes.
⛵ ❀ 🛏 ◐ ◑ ♿ ▲ ♣ P

Foresters Arms
North Walls ☎ (0962) 861539
11–3 (4.30 Sat), 5.30 (6 Sat)–11
Marston's Bitter, Pedigree Ⓗ
Typical side-street local, close to the sports centre. Comfortable and friendly; everyone is made welcome in a single bar with two drinking areas. Watch out for the darts when leaving the gents'. Limited menu. ◐ ◑ ▲ ⇌ ♣

Fulflood Arms
28 Cheriton Road (300 yds off A272) ☎ (0962) 865356
5–11; 12–2.30, 5–11 Fri; 11–3, 6–11 Sat; closed Mon–Thu lunch
Marston's Bitter, Pedigree Ⓗ
Traditional, quiet, two-bar local behind the station. Its tiled sign still proclaims 'Winchester Brewery'.
Q ⊞ ⇌ ♣

Hyde Tavern
Hyde Street ☎ (0962) 862592
11–2.30 (3 Sat), 5.30 (6 Sat)–11
Marston's Bitter, Pedigree Ⓗ
Double-gable-fronted, two-bar pub below street level; the oldest pub in town. The very homely interior features brass ornaments, low ceilings and painful door frames for people over six-feet tall. Q ⊞ ⇌

Winchfield

Barley Mow
The Hurst ☎ (0252) 617490
11–2.30 (3 Sat), 6–11
Courage Best Bitter, Directors; John Smith's Bitter Ⓗ
Late-1920s village pub near the Basingstoke Canal. The public bar has wooden bench seats, while the lounge is more intimate and comfortable, with a dining area. ♔ ❀ ◐ ◑ ⊞ P

Wolverton

George & Dragon
Towns End (1 mile off A339)
☎ (0635) 298292
12–3, 5.30–11 (all day if busy)
Brakspear Special; Fuller's London Pride; Hampshire King Alfred's; Wadworth IPA, 6X Ⓗ
Cosy country inn with big log fires and oak beams. Good home-made food, including seasonal specials like venison pie. Overlooking open fields, an ideal stop-off on country walks. Large garden.
♔ ❀ ◐ ◑ ⊞ ♣ P

Yateley

Cricketers
Cricket Hill Lane OS824605
☎ (0252) 872105
11–2.30, 5.30–11; 11–11 Sat
Morland Bitter, Old Masters Ⓗ
Fine, old-fashioned pub, set back from the road, next to the village green: a rustic public bar and a large saloon. The garden is popular with families. No food Sun.
Q ❀ ◐ ⊞ ♣ P

BEER FESTIVAL CALENDAR 1994

CAMRA beer festivals provide wonderful opportunities for sampling beers not normally found in the locality. Festivals are staffed by CAMRA members on a voluntary basis and offer a wide range of interesting real ales from breweries all over the country, plus live entertainment and much more. The major event is the *Great British Beer Festival* in August, where over 300 different beers can be enjoyed. For further details of this and the regional events outlined below, together with precise dates and venues, contact CAMRA on (0727) 867201.

JANUARY
Atherton
Bradford
Exeter
York

FEBRUARY
Basingstoke
Battersea
Dorchester
Durham
Fleetwood
Sussex
Truro

MARCH
Bridgwater
Bristol
Camden (London Drinker)
Darlaston
Darlington
Dukeries (N Notts)
Ealing
Eastleigh
Rugby
Wigan

APRIL
Coventry
Farnham
Great North-Western
Luton
Mansfield
Newcastle upon Tyne
Oldham
Portsmouth
Swansea

MAY
Alloa
Barnsley
Boat of Garten
Cambridge
Camden (Cider and Perry Exhibition)
Chester
Chippenham
Cleethorpes
Colchester
Dewsbury
Doncaster
Dudley
Lincoln
Northampton
Ongar
Rhyl
Stockport
Sunderland
Wolverhampton
Woodchurch
Yapton

JUNE
Bury St Edmunds
Catford
Exeter
Grays
St Ives (Cambs)
Salisbury

JULY
Ardingly
Canterbury
Chelmsford
Cornwall
Cotswolds
Derby
Grantham
Heart of England
Southminster
Surrey
Tameside Canals
Woodcote

AUGUST
Great Bntish Beer Festival
Peterborough
Portsmouth
Rochester (Euro-Festival)

SEPTEMBER
Bellefield (Birmingham)
Burton upon Trent
Chappel
Denbigh
Durham
Feltham
Harbury
Ipswich
Letchworth
Maidstone
Newton Abbot
Northampton
Sheffield
Shrewsbury

OCTOBER
Alloa
Bath
Bedford
Cardiff
Darlington
East Lancs
Eastleigh
Edinburgh
Guernsey
Holmfirth
Keighley
Loughborough
Middlesbrough
Norwich
Nottingham
Overton
Stoke-on-Trent
Wakefield

NOVEMBER
Aberdeen
Bury
Dudley
Jersey
Mid Wales
Rochford

DECEMBER
London (Pig's Ear)

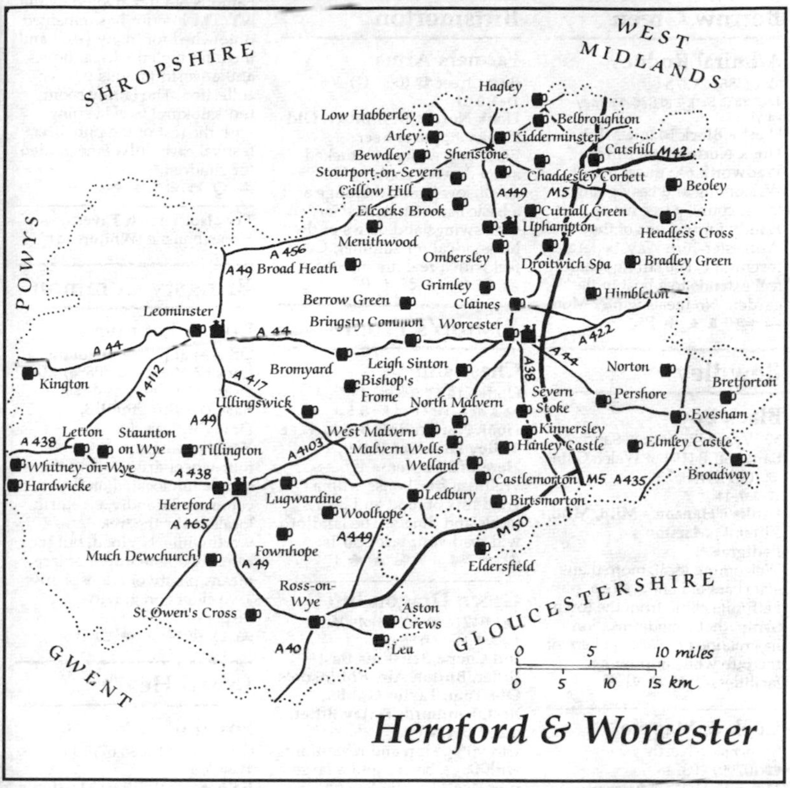

Cannon Royal, *Uphampton*; **Dunn Plowman**, *Leominster*; **Jolly Roger**, *Worcester*; **Wye Valley**, *Hereford*

Arley

Harbour Inn

Signed from B4194 at Button Oak ☎ (0299) 401204

12–3 (4 Sat; not Mon, Tue, Thu & Fri in Jan–Feb), 7–11

Draught Bass; Brains Dark; Whitbread Boddingtons Bitter, Flowers Original (summer), **Wethered Winter Royal; guest beers** Ⓔ

Cosy free house with a restaurant to the rear, and a large garden. Close to the Severn Valley Railway station and River Severn.

♛ ❀ ◐ ◑ ♿ ⇌ (SVR) ♣ P

Aston Crews

White Hart

☎ (0989) 750203

11–3, 7–11

Hook Norton Best Bitter, Old Hooky; guest beer Ⓗ

300-year-old village local with a restaurant, pleasantly refurbished and catering for an older clientele. Marvellous views over farmland.

Q ❀ ◐ ◑ P

Belbroughton

Holly Bush

Stourbridge Road (A491)

☎ (0562) 730207

11–3, 6–11 (11–11 bank hols)

Ansells Mild; HP&D Bitter, Entire; Tetley Bitter Ⓗ

Small, three-roomed, roadside pub with good, home-cooked traditional fare (not served Sun eve). Live entertainment courtesy of Ron, who still tickles the ivories on Wed, Fri and Sat eve. Special beers at Xmas and Easter.

♛ Q ❀ ◐ ◑ ♣ P

Olde Horseshoe

High Street ☎ (0562) 730233

11–3 (4 Sat), 5.30 (6 Sat)–11

S&N Theakston Mild, Best Bitter, XB, Old Peculier; guest beer Ⓗ

Fine old pub in the centre of a pretty village: a large bar area, with a pool table, and a small lounge, which can get very crowded as the home-cooked food is very popular. Barbecues in summer. Good choice of vegetarian meals. The beer range may vary.

❀ ◐ ◑ ⊟ ♿ ♣ ⌓ P

Beoley

Holly Bush Inn

Gorcott Hill (signed from A435/B4095 jct)

☎ (056 44) 2427

11.30–2.30, 5.30–11

Draught Bass; Courage Directors; John Smith's Bitter Ⓗ

Tastefully refurbished, large, one-roomed country pub, found towards the end of the old A435, now a no-through road. Very popular with eaters; families welcome.

❀ ◐ ◑ ♿ P

Berrow Green

Admiral Rodney
☎ (0886) 21375
12–2.30 (3 Sat), 7 (6 Sat)–11 (may vary)
Hanby Black Magic Mild; Hook Norton Best Bitter; Wadworth 6X; guest beer Ⓗ
Welcoming and easy-going, large, country free house. Handy for walkers of the Worcestershire Way. Separate restaurant. The strong nautical feel extends to a boat in the garden. No meals winter Mon.
⛫ ❀ ◑ ◗ ▲ ♣ P

Bewdley

Black Boy
50 Wyre Hill (follow Sandy Bank, off B4194 at Welch Gate)
☎ (0299) 403523
12–3, 7–11
Banks's Hanson's Mild, Mild, Bitter Ⓔ; **Marston's Pedigree** Ⓗ
Welcoming local, more than 400 years old and a steep half-mile climb from the town. Sympathetic modernisation has retained the atmosphere of the pub while improving facilities. Q ♨ ❀ ⊟ ♣

Cock & Magpie
Severnside North
☎ (0299) 403748
11–3, 6–11; 11–11 Sat & summer
Banks's Mild, Bitter Ⓔ
Two-bar local on the former Coles Quay, by the River Severn. Popular with locals, visitors and people of all ages.
Q ⊟ ≠ (SVR) ♣

Hop Pole Inn
Cleobury Road
☎ (0299) 402127
11.30–3, 6–11
Banks's Mild; Marston's Bitter, Pedigree Ⓗ
Situated almost a mile above the town, this pleasant, two-roomed hostelry has earned a place in the *Guide* for many years. The lounge is a welcome area for diners, the bar comfortable and friendly. An additional beer from Marston's is sometimes available. Q ❀ ◑ ◗ ⊟ ♣ P

Little Pack Horse
High Street ☎ (0299) 403762
11–3, 6–11; 11–11 Sat
Ind Coope Burton Ale; Lumphammer; guest beer Ⓗ
16th-century pub that has been restored to reflect tradition, together with a touch of the eccentricity that is the hallmark of the Little Pub Co. chain. No music.
⛫ ♨ ◑ ◗ ≠ (SVR) ♣

Birtsmorton

Farmers Arms
Birts Street ☎ (068 41) 308
11–3, 6–11
Hook Norton Best Bitter, Old Hooky Ⓗ; **guest beer**
Black and white pub tucked away down a country lane; a small, low-beamed lounge and a basic bar with darts. Garden with swings and views of the hills – ideal for summer. Cosy feel with a real fire in winter.
⛫ Q ❀ ◑ ◗ ♿ ♣ P

Bishop's Frome

Chase Inn
On B4214 ☎ (0885) 490234
12–3.30, 6–11; 11–11 Fri & Sat
Hook Norton Best Bitter; Wye Valley Hereford Bitter, Hereford Supreme Ⓗ
Well-run free house with a good mix of food and beer, locals and diners. The landlord will read your tarot cards.
⛫ ❀ 🛏 ◑ ◗ ⊟ ▲ ♣ P

Green Dragon Inn
Off B4214 ☎ (0885) 490607
12–3, 7–11; 11–11 Sat
Ind Coope Benskins Best Bitter, Burton Ale; Robinson's Old Tom; Taylor Golden Best, Landlord; Tetley Bitter; guest beers Ⓗ
Old village inn and restaurant with flags, beams and a large fireplace. Once had a cult following, but is still popular, with up to eight beers and value food. Exudes character, but the games room can dominate at weekends. Focal point for village youngsters.
⛫ ◑ ◗ ⊟ ▲ ♣ P

Try also: Wheatsheaf Inn, Fromes Hill (brew pub)

Bradley Green

Red Lion Rib Room
Droitwich Road (B4090)
☎ (0527) 821376
11–3, 6–11 (11–11 June–Aug & bank hols)
Ansells Mild; Ind Coope Burton Ale; guest beer Ⓗ
Typical Mad O'Rourke pub, full of junk: a diesel engine, oars, pigs' heads, etc. Sawdust on the floor. Skittle alley for hire. ⛫ ❀ ◑ ◗ ♿ ▲ ♣ P

Bretforton

Fleece
The Cross (50 yards S of B4035) ☎ (0386) 831173
11–2.30, 6–11; 12–2.30, 7–10.30 Sun
Everards Beacon; Hook Norton Best Bitter; M&B Brew XI; Mansfield Old Baily; Uley Pig's Ear Ⓗ
Famous old inn, owned by the NT. The interior has remained untouched for many years and includes inglenooks, antiques and a world-famous pewter collection. The family room (no-smoking) is in keeping with the rest of the pub. Beer festival early July. Fine garden for children.
⛫ Q ♨ ❀ ◑ ◗ ♣ ⇔ ⅟

Try also: Thatch Tavern, Honeybourne (Whitbread)

Bringsty Common

Live & Let Live
Off A44 at pub sign, follow track OS699547 ☎ (0886) 21462
11–3 (not Tue), 6–11; 11–11 Sat
Bass Worthington BB, Draught Bass Ⓗ
You'll need a compass and four-wheel drive to find this simple inn located on the common! Friendly, eccentric locals make the trek worthwhile. No food, but the recently opened-up fireplace means plenty of atmosphere. Two ciders on gravity dispense.
⛫ Q ❀ ⊟ ▲ ♣ ⇔ P

Broad Heath

Fox Inn
On B4204 ☎ (088 67) 219
11.30–3, 6–11
Batham Best Bitter; Marston's Bitter; guest beer Ⓗ
Pub with a large lounge bar retaining some beams from its 16th-century past, and a separate public bar with pool and darts. Do not confuse with Broadheath near Worcester. This one is near Tenbury Wells. ⛫ ❀ ◑ ◗ ♿ ▲ ♣ P

Broadway

Crown & Trumpet
Church Street (Snowshill road)
☎ (0386) 853202
11–3 (may extend summer), 5–11
Wadworth 6X; Whitbread Boddingtons Mild, Bitter, Flowers IPA, Original Ⓗ
Fine, 17th-century, Cotswold stone inn complete with oak beams and log fires. The welcoming interior has been bypassed by most of the 20th century. Popular with locals and tourists alike. Food for walking parties by arrangement.
⛫ ❀ 🛏 ◑ ◗ ▲ ♣ ⇔ P

Bromyard

Bay Horse Hotel
High Street ☎ (0885) 482635
11–11

Banks's Bitter; Draught Bass; guest beer Ⓗ
Stalwart town pub, often busy, with a listed bar and wood panelling which has survived a knock-through quite well. Also has a priest hole, a friendly mixed clientele and a restaurant. The guest beer is usually from the Bass range.
♛ ⛟ ◗ ♿ ♣ P

Crown & Sceptre
7 Sherford Street
☎ (0885) 482441
11–2.30 (3 Fri, 3.30 Sat), 6.30–11
Banks's Bitter; Hook Norton Best Bitter; guest beers Ⓗ
Never a dull moment in this ex-Whitbread pub, now a pleasant, keenly-run, free house. Various drinking areas are furnished with maps and old adverts. Popular with locals and visitors to the sports centre. Restaurant and two unusual guest beers available.
♛ ❀ ⛟ ◖ ◗ ♣ P

Callow Hill

Royal Foresters
On A456 ☎ (0299) 266286
11–11
Greene King Abbot; John Smith's Bitter Ⓗ
Pleasant, popular, main-road inn where families are welcome. A cosy lounge with a hot fire, and a recently-opened pool room. Forest Dark Mild is a house beer (brewer unknown).
♛ Q ♉ ❀ ♣ P

Castlemorton

Plume of Feathers
Gloucester Road
☎ (0684) 81554
11–3, 6.30–11
Draught Bass; Whitbread Boddingtons Bitter Ⓗ**; guest beer**
Cosy, village local with lots of character and views of the Malvern Hills. Busy bar with seating around the fire; separate lounge and dartboard areas. Good food with generous portions. ❀ ◖ ◗ P

Catshill

Plough & Harrow
419 Stourbridge Road
☎ (0527) 77355
12–2.30 (3 Sat), 7–11
Ansells Bitter; Ind Coope Burton Ale Ⓗ
Two-roomed roadside inn with a small restaurant serving good fare. Live piano most weekends. No meals Sun–Mon. ♛ ❀ ◖ ◗ ⊟ ♣ P

Chaddesley Corbett

Fox Inn
Lower Chaddesley (A448)
☎ (0562) 777247
11–2.30, 5 (6.30 Sat)–11
S&N Theakston Mild, Best Bitter, XB, Old Peculier Ⓗ
Pleasant roadhouse: a main bar plus an adjoining function room/snug. A restaurant area leads off the lounge (comprehensive menu and a Sun lunchtime carvery). Speciality food nights.
♛ ❀ ◖ ◗ ♿ ▲ ♣ ⌓ P

Swan
High Street ☎ (0562) 777302
11–4.30, 7–11
Batham Mild, Best Bitter, Batham XXX Ⓗ
Spacious, country pub with a garden, a lively, popular bar, a tastefully modernised lounge, a children's room and a restaurant. Jazz Thu. Barbecues in summer.
♛ ♉ ❀ ◖ ◗ ⊟ ♿ ▲ ♣ ⌓ P

Claines

Mug House
Claines Lane ☎ (0905) 56649
12–2.30 (3 Sat), 5–11
Banks's Mild, Bitter Ⓔ
Ancient and unspoilt pub in the village churchyard with pleasant views across fields to Worcester. A large mural in the lounge depicts how it all might have been in 1745. No food Sun/Mon.
♛ Q ♉ ❀ ◖ ▲ ♣

Cutnall Green

New Inn
Kidderminster Road (A442)
☎ (0299) 851202
12–2.30, 5.30 (6 Sat)–11
Banks's Mild; Marston's Bitter, Pedigree Ⓗ
Small and friendly pub with a semi-separate restaurant area. Reasonably priced 'lite bites' at lunchtime. Vegetarian meals available. ♛ ❀ ⛟ ◖ ◗ P

Droitwich Spa

Gardeners Arms
Vines Lane ☎ (0905) 772936
11–3, 5.30–11; 11–11 Fri & Sat
Banks's Hanson's Mild, Bitter Ⓔ
Pub situated beneath Dodderhill church, close to Vines Park and the River Salwarpe in an historic part of a town once famous for salt production. Small and often busy, with the emphasis on the mild. Medium-sized garden with a good view of the church. ❀ ⊟ ⇌ ♣ ⌓ P

Try also: Old Cock, Friar St (Marston's)

Elcocks Brook

Brook Inn
☎ (0527) 543209
12–2.30, 5–11
Banks's Mild; Marston's Bitter, Pedigree Ⓗ
Busy, comfortable pub near Callow Hill, with real fires. Recently extended and refurbished. Ample parking.
♛ ❀ ◖ P

Eldersfield

Greyhound
Lime Street ☎ (0452) 840381
11–3, 6–11
Butcombe Bitter Ⓖ
Wood-panelling, bentwood bench seats and stone flags: a model unspoilt local. Seats outside in summer but beware of the free range chickens. Lunchtime snacks.
♛ Q ❀ ♣ P

Elmley Castle

Queen Elizabeth
Main Street ☎ (0386) 710209
12–3, 7–11
Marston's Bitter Ⓗ
Visited by its namesake in 1575, a traditional village inn which has remained unchanged under the present landlord for 30 years. Handy for walkers on Bredon Hill. Can get rather smoky. Plenty of street parking.
♛ Q ❀ ♣ P

Evesham

Trumpet
Merstow Green (off southern end of main street)
☎ (0386) 446227
11–2.30, 5–11 (11–11 summer Sat)
Bass Worthington BB, Draught Bass; guest beers Ⓗ
Convivial town-centre local, with a small forecourt.
Q ❀ ◖ ▲ ⇌ ♣ ⚡

Try also: Olde Red Horse, Vine St (M&B)

Fownhope

Green Man Inn
On B4224 ☎ (0432) 860243
11–2.30, 6–11; 12–2.30, 7–10.30 Sun
Hook Norton Best Bitter; Marston's Pedigree; Samuel Smith OBB Ⓗ
Classic 500-year-old, black and white coaching inn, very popular with drinkers and diners from Hereford. Known

for good value beer and food (restaurant). Guests have fishing rights on the nearby Wye. The longest running *Guide* entry for Herefordshire.
♨ ❀ 🛏 ◖ ◗ ⊞ ♿ ♣ ⌓ P

Grimley

Camp House
Camp Lane (1½ miles off A443) OS836607
☎ (0905) 640288
11–3, 6–11
Whitbread Flowers IPA, Castle Eden Ale [H]; guest beer
Pleasant, family-run pub in a scenic spot on the riverbank. Original quarry-tiled floors; peacocks, geese and ducks in the garden. Guest beers from Whitbread.
♨ Q ❀ ◖ ◗ ♿ ▲ ♣ P

Hagley

Station Inn
95 Worcester Road (off A456)
☎ (0562) 882549
11–11
Banks's Mild, Bitter [E]
Smart, busy village pub: a comfortable, rambling one-roomer with many separate drinking areas. Warm welcome for locals and visitors alike. ❀ ◖ ⇌ P

Hanley Castle

Three Kings
Off B4211 ☎ (0684) 592686
12–3, 7–11 (may vary)
Butcombe Bitter; Thwaites Bitter [H]; guest beers
Multi-roomed pub next to the church in a sleepy village. A real gem: CAMRA West Midlands *Pub of the Year* 1990 and 1992, and national CAMRA *Best Country Pub* 1993. Up to three guest beers available. Beware erratic opening hours. Music Sun and alternate Thu. No food Sun eve. ♨ Q ❀ 🛏 ◖ ◗ ⌓

Hardwicke

Royal Oak
On B4348, 1 mile from B4352 jct ☎ (0497) 3248
12–2.30, 7–11
Draught Bass; Hook Norton Best Bitter [H]
Beautifully situated, isolated free house convenient for both Hay-on-Wye bookshops and country walks. A pleasant, two-bar pub, with the second bar a restaurant (eve meals).
♨ Q ❀ ⊞ ♣ P

Headless Cross

Gate Hangs Well
98 Evesham Road (off A441)
☎ (0527) 401293
12–3, 5.30–11; 12–11 Sat
Ansells Bitter, Mild; HP&D Entire [H]
Comfortable, lively pub with a welcoming atmosphere: a single room with a bar area. Lunchtime meals. ♨ ❀ ◖ ♿

Seven Stars
75 Birchfield Road (off A441)
☎ (0527) 402138
12–11
Marston's Pedigree; Ruddles Best Bitter; Webster's Yorkshire Bitter [H]
Basic locals' pub. A bar area, a lounge, a games room and a snug all fit into this small roadhouse. Parking close by.
⌓

Hereford

Barrels
69 St Owen Street
☎ (0432) 274968
11–11
Wye Valley Hereford Bitter, HPA, Hereford Supreme, Brew 69 [H]; guest beer
Brash, basic, lively city-centre home of the successful Wye Valley brewery. Frequented by students at weekends, otherwise local banter predominates. Charity beer and music festival, each Aug. CAMRA Hereford's *Pub of the Year* 1992. Not to be missed. No food. ❀ ⊞ ♿ ⇌ ♣ ⌓

Cock of Tupsley
Ledbury Road, Tupsley
☎ (0432) 274911
11.30–3, 5.30–11; 11–11 Sat
Banks's Mild, Bitter [E]; Marston's Pedigree [H]
Pub purpose-built for Banks's in 1967: a public bar, complete with pool and a large, wrought-iron cock horse. The open-plan lounge has a modern feel with stone, old pictures and varied furnishings. ❀ ◖ ⊞ ♣ P

Lancaster
1 St Martin's Street
☎ (0432) 275480
11–3, 6–11; 11–11 Sat & summer
Beer range varies [H]
Basic, but popular free house beside the River Wye, busy on summer eves. The main bar has a down-to-earth locals' feel; the back bar is often quiet. Usually a minimum of three guest ales available.
Q ◖ ◗ ⊞ ♣ ⌓

Sun Inn
71 St Owen Street
☎ (0432) 266403
11–3, 6–11
Draught Bass; Whitbread WCPA; Wye Valley Hereford Bitter [H]; guest beer
City pub delightfully caught in a time warp – how Hereford's pubs used to be. Three bars: the back bar was the last in Hereford to have table service (until 1992). Simple front bar with benches, TV, locals and a superb pewter bar, on which sit wooden cider barrels.
Q ❀ ⊞ ⇌ ♣ ⌓

Three Elms Inn
1 Canon Pyon Road
☎ (0432) 273338
11–11
Draught Bass; Marston's Pedigree; Whitbread Boddingtons Bitter; Flowers Original, Porter [H]; guest beers
Refurbished pub with a large, open-plan lounge bar: not the usual Whitbread house. A very enthusiastic landlord ensures no-one is disappointed. Seven or eight beers and mini-beer fests refresh an otherwise uninspiring area of Hereford for pubs. Good for families.
ᗢ ❀ ◖ ◗ ⊞ ♿ ♣ P

Treacle Mine
83–85 St Martin's Street
☎ (0432) 266022
11–4, 6–11; 11–11 Fri & Sat
Banks's Bitter [E]; Greene King IPA, Abbot [H]; guest beer
Single-bar pub with an unorthodox mix of satellite TV and old timbers mirrored by a mix of young and old clientele. Worthy of a visit on any pub crawl. ❀ ♣

Try also: Castle Pool Hotel, Castle St (Free)

Himbleton

Galton Arms
☎ (090 569) 672
12–2.30, 7–11
Banks's Bitter; Home Mild; S&N Theakston Best Bitter, XB, Old Peculier [H]
Genuine and unpretentious village pub with a warm and welcoming atmosphere. Deep rural setting; attractive garden.
♨ Q ❀ ◖ ◗ ♣ ⌓ P

Kidderminster

Castle Inn
50 Park Lane ☎ (0562) 69406
10–11
John Smith's Bitter; Stones Best Bitter [H]
Pub recently converted to one U-shaped room, with prices to match the local Banks's outlet.
Q ❀ ⇌ ♣

King & Castle
Severn Valley Railway Station, Comberton Hill
☎ (0562) 747505
11–3 (4 summer Sat), 5 (6 summer Sat)–11

Draught Bass; Batham Best Bitter; M&B Highgate Mild; guest beers Ⓗ
1980s-built Great Western Railway refreshment room! Part of the Severn Valley Railway terminus. Good value food (eve meals Thu–Sun). No music. Children welcome until 9pm. ⛰ ◑ ◗ ♿ ⇌ (SVR) ♣ P

Station Inn

Farfield ☎ (0562) 822764
12–3, 6–11; 12–11 Sat
Greenalls Davenports Bitter; Tetley Bitter Ⓗ
Friendly and comfortable, two-roomed local, situated above and behind the BR station. The garden is secure and safe for children.
Q ❀ ◑ ⊟ ⇌ (& SVR) ♣ P

Kington

Olde Tavern

22 Victoria Road
☎ (0544) 231384
11–2.30 (not Mon–Fri), 7.30–11; 12–2.30, 7.30–10.30 Sun
Ansells Bitter Ⓗ
A must for all followers of the old English pub – a true Victorian living relic: two small bars, one with settles, the other wood-panelled, with many curios. Electric lighting is the only interloper in this local. The ornate front tops it off nicely. Q ⊟ ♣

Royal Oak Hotel

Church Street ☎ (0544) 230484
11–3, 5.30–11 (11–11 summer Sat)
Banks's Mild; Marston's Bitter, Pedigree Ⓗ
Straightforward and friendly, two-bar pub, Kington's 'first and last' pub in England. A plain, brightly lit public at the front and a neat, intimate lounge to the rear. Restaurant only open during summer months. No lunches in winter. Eve meals end at 8.30.
⛰ ❀ 🛏 ◑ ◗ ⊟ ♣

Kinnersley

Royal Oak

Off A38 ☎ (0905) 371482
11–3, 6–11 (restaurant supper licence)
Banks's Bitter; Hook Norton Best Bitter; guest beer Ⓗ
Village pub with a number of areas on different levels, including an open-plan 'Oak Bar' at the front and a separate restaurant. A well-run local.
⛰ Q ❀ ◑ ◗ ♿ ▲ ♣ ⌓ P

Lea

Crown Inn

Gloucester Road (A40)
☎ (0989) 750407
12–3, 6.30 (7 winter Mon–Thu)–11
Greene King Abbot; Wadworth 6X Ⓗ**; guest beer**
Ex-Whitbread house now on the up and up as the enthusiastic landlady develops this two-level, two-bar, roadside village pub. More handpumps and redecoration due, but that should not disturb the pub ghost. Unusual wooden fireplace in the public bar. Friendly welcome.
⛰ Q ❀ ⊟ ▲ ♣ P

Ledbury

Brewery Inn

Bye Street ☎ (0531) 634272
11–3, 7–11; 12–2.30, 7–10.30 Sun
Banks's Mild; Marston's Bitter, Pedigree Ⓗ
Back-street pub with plenty of atmosphere: a rare example of a successful refurbishment keeping many original features, including the splendid small snug, the upstairs games room, and even the outside loo. Good buzz. Parking awkward.
⛰ Q 🐴 ❀ ⊟ ♿ ⇌ ♣ ⌓

Try also: Olde Talbot Hotel, New St (Free)

Leigh Sinton

Royal Oak

☎ (0886) 832664
11–3, 6–11
Marston's Bitter, Pedigree Ⓗ
Small, cosy country local with low beams and an impressive collection of implements and brasses. Interesting reading on the walls. ⛰ Q ❀ ◑ ♣ P

Leominster

Black Horse

74 South Street
☎ (0568) 611946
11–2.30, 6–11; 11–11 Sat
Courage Directors; Dunn Plowman BHB, Woody's Crown, Shire Horse Ale, Muletide; Wadworth 6X Ⓗ**; guest beer**
Outstanding free house and brewery tap for the adjacent Dunn Plowman brewery. A plain interior with a lively public, a small lounge and a restaurant. Always friendly.
❀ ◑ ◗ ⊟ ♿ ⇌ ♣ ⌓ P

Grapes Vaults

Broad Street ☎ (0568) 611404
11–3, 7–11
Banks's Mild; Marston's Bitter, Merrie Monk, Pedigree Ⓗ
Behind a plain facade is concealed a superbly restored town pub. Etched-glass and old wooden screens divide it into discrete drinking nooks and corners. Well-run, serving a wholesome menu until 9pm. The Marston's range may vary. ⛰ Q ◑ ◗ ⇌ ♣

Letton

Swan Inn

On A438 ☎ (0544) 327304
11–11
Draught Bass; guest beers Ⓗ
Comfortable and amenable, roadside pub at the heart of the Wye valley. An open plan bar, a small, cosy locals' public and a restaurant. Food always available. Guest beers are usually quite adventurous.
⛰ Q ❀ ◑ ◗ ⊟ ▲ ♣ P

Low Habberley

Fountain Inn

Off B4190, Wolverley–Bewdley road ☎ (0562) 822397
12–2.30, 6.30–11
Draught Bass; M&B Highgate Mild; Stones Best Bitter Ⓗ
Country pub just outside Kidderminster, serving good food. Well worth a visit. Skittles played.
⛰ ◑ ◗ ♿ ♣ P

Lugwardine

Crown & Anchor

Cotts Lane (off A438, by school) ☎ (0432) 851303
11.30–11
Bass Worthington BB, Draught Bass; Hook Norton Best Bitter Ⓗ
Popular pub in a village east of Hereford. An elaborate menu has given it a reputation for food, especially at weekends. Dishes include eel pie (eels from the nearby River Lugg). Some character despite being knocked through.
⛰ Q ❀ ◑ ◗ ⌓ P

Malvern Wells

Malvern Hills Hotel

Wynds Point (B4232/A449 jct)
☎ (0684) 40237
11–11
Draught Bass; Hook Norton Best Bitter; Wood Parish Ⓗ
Comfortable lounge bar in an upmarket weekend retreat on the ridge of the Malvern Hills. Walkers welcomed, but requested to remove muddy boots. ⛰ ❀ 🛏 ◑ ◗ P

Menithwood

Cross Keys Inn

Between A443 and B4202
OS709690 ☎ (058 470) 425
11–3, 6–11
Marston's Bitter, Pedigree; guest beer Ⓗ

Roadside pub in a quiet village, very popular with the local community. Weston's cider in summer. Ask for the famous steak sandwiches.
♨ Q ♘ ❀ 🛏 ♿ ♣ ⌓ P

Much Dewchurch

Black Swan

On B4348 ☎ (0981) 540295
12–2.30, 6.30–11
Crown Buckley Best Bitter, Rev. James [H]; guest beers
Arguably the oldest drinking house in the county. Two main drinking areas subtly divide into several distinct sections, giving much character in a quiet village. Reasonable food. Dewchurch Farmhouse cider; usually five guest beers.
♨ ❀ ◖ ◗ ⊞ ♿ ♣ ⌓ P

North Malvern

Star Inn

59 Cowleigh Road (B4219)
☎ (0684) 574280
12–3 (not winter Mon–Fri), 7–11
S&N Theakston Mild, Best Bitter, XB [H]
Friendly three-roomer with some magnificent Victorian bar furniture. Separate pool room and skittle alley. Folk music Thu. ♣ ⌓ P

Norton

Norton Grange

Evesham Road (A435/B439 jct)
☎ (0386) 871477
11.30–3, 6–11
Marston's Bitter, Pedigree; guest beer [H]
Recently refurbished inn, with something for everybody. Food available at all times; families welcomed. Coaches by appointment only.
♘ ❀ ◖ ◗ ♿ ♣ P ⊘

Ombersley

Cross Keys

Kidderminster road (just N of roundabout) ☎ (0905) 620588
11–3, 6–11
Batham Best Bitter; Marston's Bitter, Pedigree; guest beer [H]
Village local catering for a variety of customers. The entrance to the car park is easily missed but the pub sign is notable: one side depicts a pig and parrot. Small games room separate from the main drinking area. Patio area at the rear. ♨ Q ❀ ◖ ◗ ♣ P

Pershore

Millers Arms

8 Bridge Street
☎ (0386) 553864
11.30–2.30, 7–11
Adnams Extra; Hall & Woodhouse Tanglefoot; Wadworth IPA, 6X, Farmer's Glory; guest beers [H]
Comfortable, olde-worlde, market town pub, lively and popular with young people. Constantly changing guest beers. Eve meals in summer.
♘ ❀ ◖ ◗ ♣

Ross-on-Wye

Crown & Sceptre

Market Place ☎ (0989) 62765
11–3, 7–11; 11–11 Sat
Draught Bass; Morland Old Speckled Hen [H]; guest beer
Medium-sized, one-bar town pub that can get busy at the weekend. An enthusiastic landlord is striving to make this *the* real ale pub in an otherwise disappointing pub town. ❀ ♣

St Owen's Cross

New Inn

At A4137/B4521 jct
☎ (0989) 87274
12–3, 6–11
Draught Bass; Courage Directors; Hook Norton Old Hooky; Smiles Best Bitter [H]; guest beer
Friendly, 16th-century inn with a sensible balance between ale and excellent food (restaurant). Both locals and diners rest at ease amongst settles, benches and fine fireplaces. Herefordshire CAMRA *Pub of the Year* runner-up 1992.
♨ Q ❀ 🛏 ◖ ◗ ▲ ♣ P

Severn Stoke

Boar's Head

☎ (0905) 371484
12–3, 7 (6 summer)–11
Hook Norton Best Bitter, Old Hooky; Taylor Landlord [H]
Pub closed for several years, but now re-opened after extensive renovations. Efficient service in comfortable surroundings, with a food emphasis. ♨ ❀ ◖ ◗ ▲ ♣ P

Rose & Crown

☎ (0905) 371249
11.30–2.30, 6–11; 12–2.30, 7–10.30 Sun
Ansells Bitter; Ruddles Best Bitter [H]; guest beer
Pub dating back to 1490, well noted for its open log fires. The large garden has a play area for children. No food Sun lunch. ♨ ❀ ◖ ◗ ▲ ♣ P ⊘

Shenstone

Plough

Off A450/A448 OS865735
☎ (0562) 777340
11–3, 6.30–11; 12–2.30, 7–10.30 Sun
Batham Best Bitter, XXX [H]
Traditional rural pub in the centre of a small village. Hard to find but worth seeking out. A covered yard may be used by families. A *Guide* regular, with a good range of Weston's bottled cider (one draught). No food. ♨ Q ⊞ ♣ ⌓ P

Staunton on Wye

New Inn

Off A438 ☎ (098 17) 346
12–2.30 (not Mon), 7–11
S&N Theakston Best Bitter, XB [H]
Pleasant, three-bar village pub that has bounced back to life: a real public bar (and real locals), and an area for eating. Superb rural views and an excellent location from which to explore the Wye valley.
♨ Q ❀ ◖ ◗ ⊞ ♿ ▲ ♣ P

Stourport-on-Severn

Holly Bush Inn

53–54 Mitton Street
☎ (0299) 822569
12–3.30, 6.30–11
S&N Theakston Mild, Best Bitter, XB, Old Peculier [H]; guest beer
Friendly local, recently refurbished. One main bar is split into three. Eve meals finish at 9pm. ♘ ❀ ◖ ◗ ♣

Rising Sun

50 Lombard Street
☎ (0299) 822530
10.30–11
Banks's Hanson's Mild, Mild, Bitter [E]; Marston's Pedigree [H]
Friendly, one-room pub with a pleasant outside drinking area overlooking the canal. Meals Tue–Sat lunchtime and early eve. ♨ Q ❀ ◖ ◗ ♣

Wheatsheaf

High Street ☎ (0299) 822316
10.30–11
Banks's Hanson's Mild, Mild, Bitter [E]; Camerons Strongarm [H]
Two-room local, five minutes' walk from the canal basin. Children's meals available, served outside. Snacks all day.
❀ ◖ ⊞ ♣ P

Try also: Tontine, Severnside (Banks's)

Tillington

Bell Inn

Tillington Road
☎ (0432) 760395
11–3, 6–11; 11–11 Sat
Draught Bass; Samuel Smith OBB; Whitbread WCPA, Boddingtons Bitter, Flowers Original [H]

Popular, refurbished village pub. The public bar features pool, darts and TV. The lounge neatly divides into two plush areas, one cosy, one light and airy. Also boasts a restaurant. No meals Sun eve.
🜲 Q ❀ ◐ ◗ ⊟ ▲ ♣ ⌓ P

Ullingswick

Three Crowns

Signed 1½ miles from A417 (½ mile E of village) OS605497
☎ (0432) 820279
12–3 (not Tue), 7–11
Ansells Bitter; Ind Coope Burton Ale; Tetley Bitter H
Superb, isolated, two-bar free house. The centuries-old, candlelit bar has tremendous character and retains many original features. Popular for good food, with an interesting menu – but portions can be on the small side. No meals Tue.
🜲 Q ❀ ◐ ◗ ♣ P

Uphampton

Fruiterers Arms

Off A449 at the Reindeer pub OS839649 ☎ (0905) 620305
12–3, 7–11
Donnington BB; John Smith's Bitter; guest beers H
Rural pub with a plain bar and a cosy lounge. The landlords own the adjacent mobile home site (caravans allowed). A guest mild and a guest bitter are available. No food Sun. Home of Cannon Royal brewery.
🜲 Q ❀ ◐ ⊟ ▲ ♣ ⌓ P

Welland

Hawthorn

Upper Welland Road
☎ (0684) 575340
12–2.30, 6.30–11
Marston's Bitter, Pedigree H**; guest beer**
Recently but sympathetically modernised pub, retaining its local atmosphere, yet friendly and welcoming. The guest beer is often unusual for the area. 🜲 Q ❀ 🛏 ◐ ◗ P

Pheasant

☎ (0684) 310400
12–3, 6.30–11
Ansells Bitter; Ind Coope Burton Ale; Tetley Bitter E
Large pub with a function room. Pleasant for summer visits and good for families (screened no-smoking area and an enclosed play area in the garden). 🜲 ❀ ◐ ◗ P ⊁

West Malvern

Brewers Arms

Lower Dingle (signed off B4232) ☎ (0684) 568147
12–3, 7 (6 summer)–11 (12–11 summer Sat)
Marston's Bitter, Merrie Monk, Pedigree H
Pub tastefully refurbished after a fire, and much of the charm (but all of the locals!) has been retained. Families and Malvern Hills walkers warmly welcomed.
🜲 Q ❀ ◐ ◗ ♣ ⌓

Whitney-on-Wye

Rhydspence Inn

On A438, 1½ miles W of village ☎ (0497) 831262
11–2.30, 7–11
Draught Bass; Marston's Pedigree; Robinson's Best Bitter H
Famous and plush, 14th-century inn that straddles the Welsh border: a typical black and white inn with many original features and splendid fireplaces. Genteel atmosphere. Food ranges from à la carte to bar snacks; extensive wine list. Genuine public bar.
🜲 Q ❀ 🛏 ◐ ◗ ⊟ ♣ ⌓ P

Woolhope

Crown Inn

☎ (0432) 860468
12–2.30, 7 (6.30 Fri & Sat in summer)–11; 12–2.30, 7–10.30 Sun
Draught Bass; Hook Norton Best Bitter; Smiles Best Bitter H
Relaxing rural inn, very busy at weekends and run with enthusiasm. Always popular with diners from town; not a locals' pub, but an area is set aside for drinking at leisure. Countywide reputation for its food. 🜲 Q ❀ ◐ ◗ ♿ ⌓ P

Try also: Butchers Arms (Free)

Worcester

Crown & Anchor

Hylton Road ☎ (0905) 421481
12–2.30 (3 Sat), 6–11
Marston's Bitter, Merrie Monk, Pedigree H
Small, friendly pub on the west side of the river, popular with students and locals.
❀ ◐ ♣

Dragon Inn

The Tything ☎ (0905) 25845
11–11
Marston's Bitter; S&N Theakston XB; guest beers H
Easy-going pub with a strong commitment to real ale: good selection of guest beers. Varied clientele. Live music fairly regularly.
❀ ◐ ⇌ (Foregate St) ♣

Lamb & Flag

The Tything ☎ (0905) 26894
11–2.30, 5.30–11
Marston's Bitter, Pedigree H
Unspoilt, two-roomed pub with a convivial atmosphere. Locally famed for its Draught Guinness (keg) – decanted and left to settle. Cigarette smoke can be a problem.
Q ⇌ (Foregate St) ♣

Virgin Tavern

Tolladine Road ☎ (0905) 23988
Hours vary
Marston's Bitter, Merrie Monk, Pedigree H
Friendly pub with a welcoming atmosphere; quite busy on weekends.
❀ ◐ ◗ ♿ ⇌ (Shrub Hill) P

The Symbols

🜲	real fire	♿	easy wheelchair access
Q	quiet pub (at least one bar)	▲	camping facilities at the pub or nearby
🐴	indoor room for children	⇌	near British Rail station
❀	garden or other outdoor drinking area	⊖	near underground station
🛏	accommodation	♣	pub games
◐	lunchtime meals	⌓	real cider
◗	evening meals	P	pub car park
⊟	public bar	⊁	no-smoking room or area

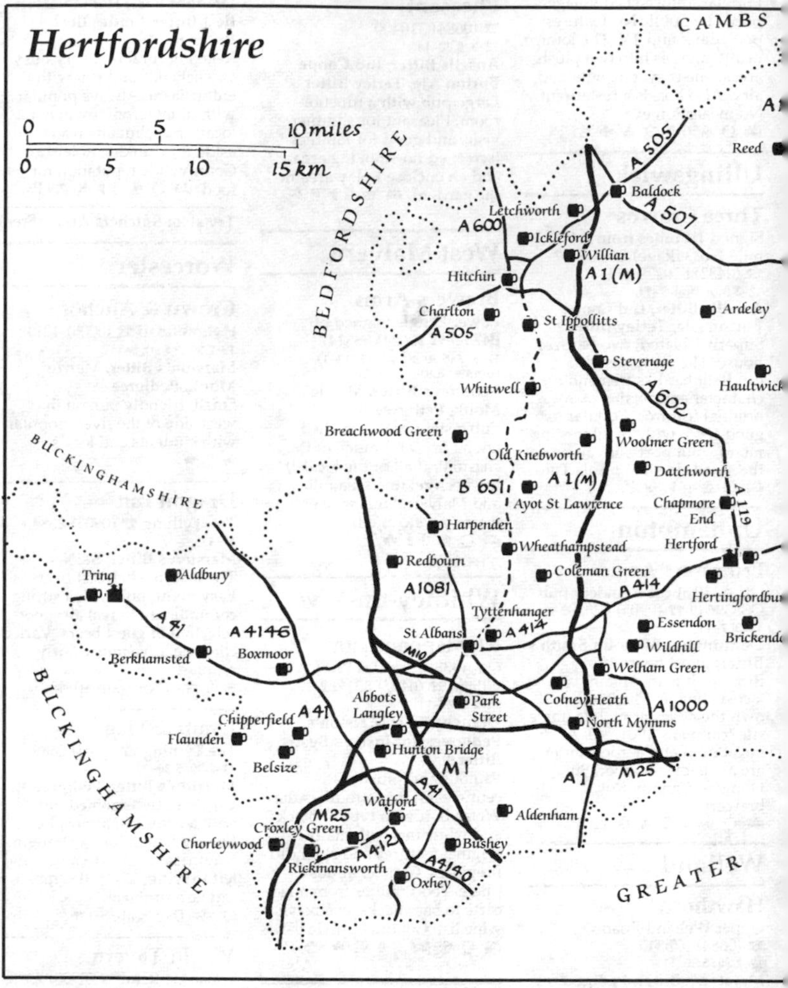

McMullen, Hertford; Tring, Tring

Abbots Langley

Compasses

95 Tibbs Hill Road
☎ (0923) 262870
11–11

Courage Best Bitter, Directors; Ruddles County; guest beers Ⓗ
Traditional locals' pub with a strong food emphasis. Guest beers change regularly. Stocks over 100 whiskies, plus a few whiskeys. Q ❀ ◐ ◑ ♿ P

Aldbury

Greyhound

Stocks Road ☎ (044 285) 228
10.30–11

Tetley Bitter; Tring Ridgeway Ⓗ
Attractive pub in a picturesque village close to the Ashridge Estate (NT). The traditional, unspoilt public bar is dominated by a huge fireplace; the lounge bar is aimed towards diners and has a bistro-like atmosphere. No eve meals Sun or Mon. Happy hour 5–7 Mon–Sat. Burton Ale is available at weekends.
⛰ ❀ ◐ ◑ ⊞ ♿ ♣

Aldenham

Roundbush

Near B462 OS145985
☎ (0923) 857165
11–3 (4 Sat), 5.30–11

Ind Coope Benskins Best Bitter, Burton Ale Ⓗ
Genuine country pub, circa 1800, with two distinctly separate drinking areas catering for all. Shove-ha'penny. ⛰ ❀ ◐ ♣ P

Try also: Three Compasses, Patchetts Green (Benskins)

Ardeley

Jolly Waggoner

OS310272 ☎ (0438) 861350
11.30–3, 6–11

Greene King IPA Ⓖ, **Abbot** Ⓗ
Picturesque, 16th-century former cottages in a charming village setting: one recently enlarged bar, a restaurant and

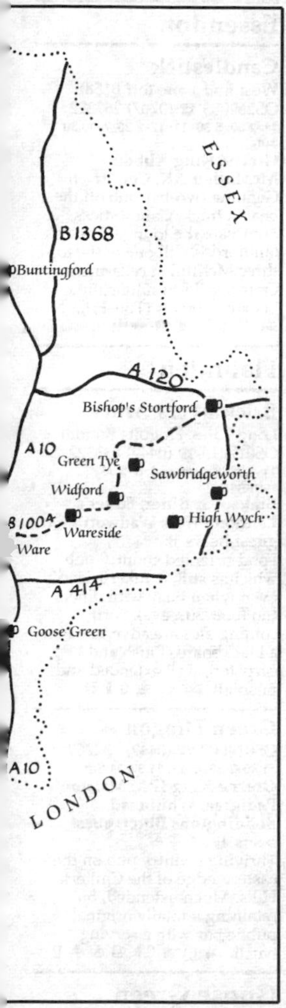

a large garden. No meals Sun, or Mon eve. ♛ ❀ ◐ ◗ P

Ayot St Lawrence

Brocket Arms
Near Shaws Corner OS196168
☎ (0438) 820250
11–2.30, 7–11
Draught Bass; Greene King IPA, Abbot; Marston's Pedigree; Wadworth 6X Ⓗ; guest beers
Splendid, ancient village pub in a quiet setting (except at weekends and bank holidays). Excellent restaurant; good value bar snacks.
♛ ❀ ⊏ ◐ ◗ ⊟ ♣ ⌓ P

Baldock

Boot
High Street ☎ (0462) 893160
11–2.30 (3.30 Sat), 5 (6.30 Sat)–11
Greene King IPA, Abbot Ⓗ
Basic two-bar local, rebuilt in the 1920s, featuring traditional pub games, a quiz team, and less common games. No food Sun. ❀ ⇌ ◐ ♣ P

White Hart
21 Hitchin Street
☎ (0462) 893247
11–3.30 (2.30 Tue & Thu, 4.30 Sat), 5.30 (7 Sat)–11; 11–11 Fri
Greene King XX Mild, IPA, Rayments Special, Abbot Ⓗ
Pleasant, one-bar pub with photographs of old Baldock. A meeting place for the local church campanologists (without their bells). A true drinkers' pub where the darts area does not impose on the bar. Discounts for OAPs on real ales weekday lunchtimes.
❀ ⇌ ♣ P

Belsize

Plough
Between Sarratt and Chipperfield OS035009
☎ (0923) 262800
11–3, 5.30–11 (may vary)
Greene King IPA; Marston's Pedigree; Whitbread Flowers IPA Ⓗ
Out-of-the-way pub worth the effort to find. Popular with horse riders and ramblers. Steaks are a speciality (eve meals Tue–Sat).
♛ ❀ ◐ ◗ ♣ P

Berkhamsted

Boat
Gravel Path, Ravens Lane (off A41) ☎ (0442) 877152
11–3, 5.30–11
Fuller's Hock, Chiswick, London Pride, Mr Harry, ESB Ⓗ
Large, modern canalside pub with a varied clientele. Often crowded but the service is excellent. Home-cooked food prepared by three chefs; extensive wine list. Elegant patio with a well-tended garden (barbecues summer weekends). ❀ ◐ ◗ ⇌ P

Rising Sun
George Street (next to GU Canal lock 55) ☎ (0442) 864913
11–3, 6–11
Greene King IPA; Whitbread Flowers Original Ⓗ
Totally unspoilt, pub tucked away behind houses and fronting onto the canal lock. The walled and gated canalside patio makes it good for families. Small games room behind the bar. ❀ ◐ ◗ ⇌ ♣

Bishop's Stortford

Fox
74 Rye Street (B184)
☎ (027 965) 1623
11–11
Courage Directors; Greene King IPA, Abbot; Wells Eagle Ⓗ; guest beers
Basic local, popular with all ages. ♛ Q ◐ ◗ ⊟ ♣ P

Boxmoor

Post Office Arms
46 Puller Road ☎ (0442) 61235
11–3, 5.30–11; 11–11 Fri & Sat
Fuller's Hock, London Pride, ESB Ⓗ
Friendly town local attracting a mixed clientele to its small public bar and larger, extended lounge. Beware, the Chiswick Bitter is keg. Parking can be difficult in the narrow road. Barbecues in summer. No food Sun. ♛ ❀ ◐ ⊟ ♣

Breachwood Green

Red Lion
16 Chapel Road
☎ (0438) 833123
11–3, 5.30–11
Greene King IPA, Rayments Special, Abbot Ⓗ
Pleasant village pub, popular with airport workers.
♛ ❀ ◐ ◗ P

Brickendon

Farmers Boy
1 Brickendon Lane
☎ (0992) 511610
11–3, 5.30–11
Greene King IPA, Rayments Special, Abbot; guest beers Ⓗ
Pub maintaining two bars albeit with the lounge extended to accommodate diners. New inside loos. The gardens make this just the place for a summertime visit.
❀ ◐ ◗ ♿ ⇌ ♣ P

Buntingford

Crown
High Street ☎ (0763) 271422
12–3, 5.30–11; 12–11 Sat
Banks & Taylor Shefford Bitter; Ruddles County; Wadworth 6X; guest beers Ⓗ
Popular small town pub with a function room. Local CAMRA *Pub of the Year* 1991.
♛ ⌓ ❀ ◐ ◗

Bushey

Stag
134 Merryhill Road (off A411 at war memorial)
☎ (081) 950 3122
12–4, 5.30–11
Greene King IPA; Ind Coope Benskins Best Bitter; Marston's Pedigree Ⓗ
Comfortable free house in a quiet area. Occasional live music. ❀ ♣ P

Swan
25 Park Road (just off A411)
☎ (081) 950 2256
11–11
Ind Coope Benskins Best Bitter, Burton Ale [H]
A single public bar with lots of character. ♨ Q ♣

Chapmore End

Woodman
30 Chapmore End (off B158, ½ mile S of A602 jct) OS328163
☎ (0920) 463143
12–3, 6–11
Greene King IPA, Abbot [G]
A classic, unspoiled village pub where ale is served straight from the cellar. Try a pint of 'Mixed'. Open fires in winter; large garden for families in summer. Lunches served Mon and Wed–Fri. No price difference between the two bars. ♨ Q ❀ ◖ ♣ P

Charlton

Windmill
☎ (0462) 432096
10.30–2.30 (3.30 Sat), 5.30–11
Adnams Broadside; Mansfield Riding Mild; Wells Eagle [H]
Refurbished village pub with a pleasant atmosphere where home-cooked food is served daily. Six resident peacocks and ducks on the stream by the garden. Q ❀ ◖ ◗ ♣ P

Chipperfield

Royal Oak
1 The Street ☎ (0923) 266537
12–2.30, 6 (6.30 Sat)–11; 12–2.30, 7–10.30 Sun
Hook Norton Best Bitter, Old Hooky; Marston's Pedigree [H]**; guest beer** [H]/[G]
Smart, tidy, friendly pub where highly polished wood and brass abound, plus a large collection of matchboxes and ties. No food Sun.
♨ Q ❀ ◖ ♿ ♣ P

Chorleywood

Black Horse
Dog Kennel Lane (off A404)
☎ (0923) 287252
11–11
Adnams Bitter; Greenalls Mild, Bitter, Thomas Greenall's Original; Wadworth 6X [H]
Deceptively large pub on the edge of the common. Home-made food (not served Sun eve); occasional live folk music. Local CAMRA *Pub of the Year* 1992. ♨ ❀ ◖ ◗ P

Coleman Green

John Bunyan
1 mile off B651 OS189128
☎ (058 283) 2037
11–2.30 (3 Sat), 6–11
McMullen AK, Country [H]
Welcoming country pub in a remote hamlet within half a mile of the highest point in Hertfordshire. A jug spotters' paradise. Good, reasonably priced, fast food (not served Sun eve). The large garden has plenty of room for children.
♨ Q ❀ ◖ ◗ ♿ ♣ P

Colney Heath

Crooked Billet
88 High Street
☎ (0727) 822128
11–2.30, 5.30–11; 11–11 Sat
Greene King Abbot; Hook Norton Best Bitter; S&N Theakston Best Bitter; Wadworth 6X [H]
200-year-old, cottage-style village pub with two bars. The large garden, with barbecue area, overlooks a paddock and farmland. All food is home made. ♨ ❀ ◖ ♣ P

Croxley Green

Sportsman
2 Scots Hill (A412)
☎ (0923) 773021
11–3, 5.30–11
Ind Coope Benskins Best Bitter, Burton Ale; Tetley Bitter [H]
Friendly, lively pub, very games oriented. Good lunches.
❀ ◖ ♣ P

Datchworth

Plough
5 Datchworth Green (off B197)
☎ (0438) 813000
11.30–2.30 (3 Sat), 6–11
Greene King XX Mild, IPA, Abbot [H]
Small, welcoming local just off the village green: one room with a large, open wood fire in the centre, a garden to the rear and a car park opposite. Camping for Caravan Club members only. No food Sun.
♨ Q ❀ ♣ P

Tilbury (Inn Off The Green)
Watton Road (off B197)
☎ (0438) 812496
11–3, 5 (6 Sat)–11
Draught Bass; Fuller's London Pride; Palmers IPA; guest beers [H]
Friendly two-room pub with a dining area. Its range of nine beers always includes one mild. Wide selection of home-cooked food. Camping for Caravan Club members only.
Q ❀ ◖ ◗ ♣ ⛺ P

Essendon

Candlestick
West End Lane (off B158)
OS262083 ☎ (0707) 261322
11–2.30, 5.30–11; 12–2.30, 7–10.30 Sun
Greene King Abbot; McMullen AK, Country [H]
Genuine two-bar pub off the beaten track. Candlesticks dominate the lounge. The landlord is still one of the top three McMullen cellarmen. Only snacks Sun lunchtime; book eve meals (Tue–Fri).
♨ Q ❀ ◖ ◗ ⊞ ♣ P

Flaunden

Bricklayers Arms
Long Lane, Hogpits Bottom
OS017013 ☎ (0442) 833322
11–2.30 (3 summer), 6 (5.30 summer)–11
Brakspear Bitter; Fuller's London Pride; Wadworth 6X; guest beers [H]
Food-oriented country pub which is still 'drinker-friendly' even when busy with diners (no food Sun eve). Forth-coming ales are advertised on a blackboard. Plush and carpeted; well extended and unspoilt. ♨ Q ❀ ◖ ◗ P

Green Dragon
OS014007 ☎ (0442) 832269
11.30–2.30, 6–11; 11.30–11 Sat
Greene King IPA; Marston's Pedigree; Whitbread Boddingtons Bitter; guest beers [H]
Thriving country pub on the eastern edge of the Chiltern Hills. Much-extended, but retaining a totally original public bar with a serving hatch. ♨ Q ❀ ◖ ◗ ⊞ ♿ ♣ P

Goose Green

Huntsman
Lord Street (1½ miles from Hoddesdon on the Balls Park, Hertford road) OS352091
☎ (0992) 443294
11–3, 6–11
Courage Directors; Greene King Abbot; Ruddles Best Bitter; Tetley Bitter; Wadworth 6X [H]
Comfortably renovated pub on a back road, set in large grounds and very popular with families in summer. One large bar area falls into several sections. Read *The Times* in the gents' reading room! Eve meals Wed–Sat. ♨ ❀ ◖ ◗ P

Green Tye

Prince of Wales
☎ (027 984) 2513
11.30–3.30, 6.30–11
Courage Directors; McMullen AK, Country [H]

Traditional country pub in a picturesque village. The landlord is a dab hand at playing optics! Eve meals Thu–Sat only. ⛫ ◖ ◗ ♣ P

Try also: Hoops, Perry Green (Free)

Harpenden

Carpenters Arms
14 Cravells Road (off A1081)
☎ (0582) 460311
11–3, 5.30–11
Courage Best Bitter; Ruddles County; Webster's Yorkshire Bitter [H]; guest beers
Small, welcoming pub with a friendly atmosphere, boasting a large collection of celebration ales and American car number plates. No meals Sun or Mon eves, but the food is excellent. Beware the keg Scrumpy Jack on handpump.
⛫ Q ❀ ◖ ◗ ♣ P

Gibraltar Castle
Lower Luton Road, Batford
☎ (0582) 460005
11–3, 5.30–11; 11–11 Sat
Fuller's Chiswick, London Pride, ESB [H]
Well-restored old roadside hostelry. Food is available in all opening hours (including a vegetarian choice). Live music some Sats. ⛫ ❀ ◖ ◗ ♣ P

Haultwick

Rest & Welcome
3 miles off A10, near Dane End
☎ (0920) 438323
12–2, 6.30–11
McMullen AK [H], Country [G]
Not easy to find, but well worth the effort, a small, one-bar pub with a friendly welcome. ⛫ ❀ ◖ ◗ P

Hertford

Great Eastern
29 Railway Place
☎ (0992) 583570
12–2.30, 6 (7 winter Sat)–11
McMullen AK, Country [H]
Friendly two-bar local with decor on a railway theme. Winner of many awards for floral displays and in this guide for many years.
❀ ◖ ♿ ⇌ (East) ♣ P

Millstream
88 Port Vale (vehicle access via A119, North Rd and Beane Rd)
☎ (0992) 582755
11–3.30 (4.30 Sat), 5.30 (7 Sat)–11
Courage Directors; McMullen AK, Country [H]
Comfortably refurbished, lively, friendly, one-bar local in estate agents' 'Lower Bengeo'. Plenty of repartee across the bar, all in good fun.
❀ ⇌ (North) ♣ P

White Horse
33 Castle Street
☎ (0992) 501950
12–2.30, 5.30 (7 Sat & bank hols)–11
Everards Tiger, Old Original; Fuller's London Pride; Greene King IPA; Hook Norton Best Bitter [H]; guest beers [G]/[H]
Once a beerhouse, this old, timber-framed building is now a real ale connoisseur's delight. Guests include all the famous independent brewers. Large range of country wines and real cider, plus a varied lunch menu weekdays. ⛫ Q ♘ ◖ ⇌ (East/North) ⍟ ⊁

Hertingfordbury

Prince of Wales
244 Hertingfordbury Road (off A414) ☎ (0992) 581149
11–2.30, 5.30–11
Fuller's London Pride; McMullen AK; Marston's Pedigree; S&N Theakston XB; Wadworth 6X; Younger IPA [H]; guest beers [G]/[H]
One-bar free house in a now bypassed village, offering a good range of ales. Meals include Greek dishes from the landlord's homeland. No eve meals Sun.
⛫ ❀ ⌂ ◖ ◗ ♿ ♣ P

High Wych

Rising Sun
1 mile W of Sawbridgeworth
☎ (027 972) 4099
11–3, 5–11
Courage Best Bitter, Directors; guest beer [G]
A real gem, basically unchanged since the 1920s. Locally known as Sid's after a previous landlord. Its 20th year in this guide. Parking limited. ⛫ Q ♿ ♣ P

Hitchin

Victoria
1 Ickleford Road
☎ (0462) 432682
12–3, 5.30–11
Greene King IPA, Abbot [H]
Friendly local, just off the town centre. ❀ ◖ ◗ ⇌ P

Hunton Bridge

Kings Head
Bridge Road (off A41)
☎ (0923) 262307
11–3, 5.30–11
Ind Coope Benskins Best Bitter, Burton Ale; Tetley Bitter; guest beer [H]
Old pub, refurbished to a high standard; one rambling bar with a congenial atmosphere plus a balcony. The family-cum-games room in the old stables is open in summer only. The enormous riverside garden has a nature trail and an aerial runway.
⛫ Q ♘ ❀ ◖ ◗ ♣ P

Ickleford

Cricketers
107 Arlesey Road (off A600)
☎ (0462) 432629
11–3, 5.30–11; 11–11 Sat
Draught Bass; Fuller's London Pride; Hall & Woodhouse Tanglefoot; Taylor Landlord; Tetley Bitter; Wadworth 6X [H]; guest beers
Lively village pub which attracts custom from near and far. Drinking here is like a brewery crawl around Britain: as many as ten ales at one time. Very friendly.
❀ ⌂ ◖ ◗ ♣ ⍟ P

Letchworth

Arena Tavern
3 Arena Parade (behind Town Hall) ☎ (0462) 686400
11–11
Nethergate Bitter, Old Growler; S&N Theakston XB, Old Peculier; Wadworth 6X [H]
Cosy, traditional pub among the shops, serving quality home-cooked meals. A welcome relief in an almost dry Quaker town. Live music Tue, Wed and Sun eves; wide-ranging clientele. Three beers at a time. No meals Sun; eves only by arrangement. The car park opposite is free after 6pm. ◖ ⇌

North Mymms

Old Maypole
43 Warrengate Road, Water End (off B197 by bus depot) OS229042 ☎ (0707) 642119
11–2.30, 5.30–11
Greene King IPA, Abbot [H]
16th-century, split-level pub with a no-smoking room where supervised children are welcome. No food Sun.
⛫ Q ♘ ❀ ◖ P ⊁

Woodman
Warrengate Road, Water End (off B197 by bus depot) OS228043 ☎ (0707) 50502
11–3, 5.30–11
Courage Directors; Marston's Pedigree [H]; guest beer [G]/[H]
Old free house, popular with students from the local veterinary college. No food Sun. Woodmans Best house beer is supplied by Courage.
Q ❀ ◖ P

Old Knebworth

Lytton Arms
Park Lane OS230203
☎ (0438) 812312
11–3, 5–11; 11–11 Fri & Sat

Hertfordshire

Banks & Taylor Shefford Bitter, SOS; Draught Bass; Fuller's London Pride; M&B Highgate Mild; S&N Theakston Best Bitter; guest beers Ⓗ
Large Lutyens-designed building on the edge of Knebworth Park. Its wide selection of beers always includes one mild. Also stocks a selection of bottled beers and guest ciders and perry.
🔥 Q ✿ ◐ ◑ ♿
≢ (Knebworth) ♣ ⌓ P

Oxhey

Haydon Arms
76 Upper Paddock Road (off A4008) ☎ (0923) 234834
Ind Coope Benskins Best Bitter; guest beers Ⓗ
Traditional-style community local comprising two drinking areas. Guest beers change regularly. ✿ ◐ ≢ (Bushey) ♣

Park Street

Overdraught
86 Park Street ☎ (0727) 874280
11–11
Marston's Bitter, Pedigree; Tetley Bitter; Wadworth 6X; guest beer Ⓗ
Formerly a keg-only brewery-tied pub, now transformed into a welcoming free house, with two cosy bars. Good value, home-cooked meals.
✿ ◐ ◑ ≢ ♣ P

Redbourn

Cricketers
East Common ☎ (0582) 792410
11–2.30, 5.30–11; 12–2.30, 7–10.30 Sun
Bass Worthington BB, Draught Bass; Charrington IPA Ⓗ
Friendly village pub by the common with two contrasting bars. An African Grey parrot presides over the lounge bar. Food includes a vegetarian choice (no meals Sun).
Q ◐ ◑ ⊟ ♿ ♣ P

Reed

Cabinet
High Street (off A10, opp. transport café, first right, first left) OS364361
☎ (0763) 848366
12–3, 6–11
Adnams Bitter; Banks & Taylor Shefford Bitter; Greene King IPA, Abbot Ⓖ**; guest beers**
Cosy, weatherboarded village pub with a large garden. Difficult to find, but it offers a constantly changing range of additional beers. Eve meals Wed–Sat. 🔥 ⛹ ✿ ◐ ◑ ♣ P

Rickmansworth

Fox & Hounds
High Street ☎ (0923) 772174
11–11
Courage Best Bitter, Directors; Fuller's London Pride Ⓗ
Comfortable two-bar pub in a central position, handy for the Indian restaurants. Small car park but a public one is adjacent. No food Sun.
🔥 ✿ ◐ ♿ ⊖ P

St Albans

Camp
149 Camp Road (off Hatfield Rd) ☎ (0727) 851062
11–2.30, 5.30–11; 11–11 Fri & Sat
Courage Directors; McMullen AK, Country Ⓗ
Large, friendly, two-bar town pub in an area known as the Camp (Romans). The landlord is a winner of McMullen's *Master Cellarman* award.
◐ ⊟ ♿ ≢ (City) ♣ P

Farriers Arms
32 Lower Dagnall Street (off A5183) ☎ (0727) 851025
12–2.30, 5.30–11
McMullen AK, Country; guest beer Ⓗ
A perennial entry in this guide; a thriving local with many sporting activities. ◐ ♣

Garibaldi
61 Albert Street (off Holywell Hill) ☎ (0727) 855046
11–11
Fuller's Hock, Chiswick, London Pride, ESB Ⓗ
Well-run, popular, side-street local with a mixed clientele. Renowned for its varied range of home-made meals, including Mexican specialities. No food Sun eve.
✿ ◐ ◑ ≢ (Abbey) ♣ ⚟

Jolly Sailor
3 Stonecross, Sandridge Road (B651) ☎ (0727) 850481
11–11
Mansfield Riding Mild; Wells Eagle, Bombardier; guest beer Ⓗ
Friendly two-bar pub on the northern side of the city. The large public bar has an emphasis on games; cosy old-fashioned saloon at the front. Beware the keg Scrumpy Jack cider on handpump. No food Sun. 🔥 ◐ ⊟ ♣ P

Lower Red Lion
34–36 Fishpool Street
☎ (0727) 855669
12–2.30 (3 Fri & Sat), 5.30–11
Adnams Bitter; Fuller's London Pride; Greene King IPA, Abbot; Morland Old Speckled Hen Ⓗ**; guest beers**
Unspoilt, two-bar, 17th-century hotel in the conservation area on the road to St Michael's village. The only free house in St Albans. Three varying guest beers. No food Sun. 🔥 Q ✿ 🛏 ◐ P

Try also: Blue Anchor, Fishpool St (McMullen)

St Ippollitts

Greyhound
London Road (B656 outside village) ☎ (0462) 440989
11–11
Morland Old Speckled Hen; Whitbread Boddingtons Bitter; guest beer Ⓗ
Friendly pub serving home-cooked food. Regular folk music sessions. 🔥 ✿ ◐ ◑ P

Sawbridgeworth

Gate
81 London Road (A1184)
☎ (027 972) 2313
11.30–2.30, 5.30–11; 11.30–11 Sat
Brakspear Bitter; Morland Old Speckled Hen; Wadworth 6X; Whitbread Boddingtons Bitter Ⓗ**; guest beer**
Note the unusual inscribed sign on this 150-year-old pub which stands on the site of a former toll gate. Keen darts, pool and football teams. No food Sun. Constantly-changing guest beer. ✿ ◐ P

Three Horseshoes
166 West Road
☎ (027 972) 2485
11.30–2.30 (3 Sat), 5.30 (7 Sat)–11
McMullen AK, Country Ⓗ**, Stronghart** Ⓖ
Relaxed, friendly pub with quiet alcoves, on the edge of town. Good food (not served Mon). ✿ ◐ ◑ ♣ P

Stevenage

Coopers Apprentice
Magpie Crescent (1 mile from A602, off Gresley Way)
☎ (0438) 316337
11–11
Adnams Bitter; Bass Worthington BB, Draught Bass; Fuller's London Pride; Stones Best Bitter Ⓗ**; guest beers**
Large, modern pub on the eastern edge of town. Comfortable, with a pleasant atmosphere and popular with the locals. A games venue. No meals Sun eve. ✿ ◐ ◑ ♿ ♣ P

Tring

Kings Arms
King Street (near Natural History Museum)
☎ (0442) 823318
11.30–2.30, 7–11

Brakspear Special; Tring Ridgeway; Wadworth 6X; guest beers Ⓗ
Excellent back-street local which is hard to find, but impossible to miss! Inventive home-cooking always available. The pub has become the unofficial brewery tap for Tring brewery. No-smoking area at lunchtime only.
🏠 Q ❀ ◖ ◗ ♣ ⚡

Robin Hood
1 Brook Street ☎ (0442) 824912
11.30–2.30 (3 Sat), 5.30 (6.30 Sat)–11
Fuller's Chiswick, London Pride, Mr Harry, ESB Ⓗ
Smart, street-corner pub with a friendly welcome and a relaxed atmosphere. The interior is bedecked with breweriana, old prints, banknotes and horse brasses.
🏠 Q ❀ ◖ ◗

Tyttenhanger

Plough
Tyttenhanger Green (off A414, via Highfield Lane) OS182059
☎ (0727) 857777
11–2.30 (3 Sat), 6–11; 12–2.30, 7–10.30 Sun
Fuller's London Pride; Greene King IPA; Marston's Pedigree; Morland Old Speckled Hen; S&N Theakston Best Bitter; Taylor Landlord; guest beers Ⓗ
Five other beers are regularly available at this very popular free house where good value lunches are also served. Huge collection of bottled beers from all around the world. The garden is very popular in summer. 🏠 Q ❀ ◖ ♿ P

Ware

New Rose & Crown
35 Watton Road
☎ (0920) 462572
11.30–2.30, 5–11; 11–11 Fri & Sat
Greene King XX Mild, IPA, Rayments Special, Abbot Ⓗ
Just off the town centre, a down-to-earth pub with a pine interior in its one L-shaped bar. A cheerful, friendly locals' local. No food weekends.
◖ ⇌ ♣

Wareside

Chequers
On B1004 ☎ (092 046) 7010
12–2.30, 6–11
Adnams Bitter; Bateman XB; Brakspear Bitter; Wadworth 6X; Young's Special; guest beer Ⓗ
Cottage pub with a friendly village atmosphere, offering excellent home-made food and an unusual whisky selection. Herts CAMRA *Pub of the Year* 1992. No food Sun eve.
🏠 Q 🛏 ◖ ◗ ⛺ ♣ P

Watford

Nascot Arms
11 Stamford Road (400 yds from station) ☎ (0923) 224007
11–3, 5.30–11; 11–11 Sat
Greene King IPA, Rayments Special, Abbot Ⓗ, **Winter Ale** Ⓖ
Two-bar, back-street pub where locals prevail but visitors are always welcomed. Cheap lunches (no food Sun). Voted local CAMRA *Pub of the Year* 1991 and hopes to reintroduce mild when cellar work is carried out. A covered area is usually available for children. ❀ ◖ ⇌ (Junction)

White Lion
79 St Albans Road
☎ (0923) 223442
11–11
Courage Best Bitter, Directors; Wadworth 6X Ⓗ
Busy two-bar pub with a basic public bar and a comfortable saloon. Pub games are popular. No food Sun. Small car park. 🚂 ❀ ◖ 🀫
⇌ (Junction) ♣ P

Welham Green

Hope & Anchor
Station Road ☎ (0707) 262935
11–2.30 (3 Sat), 5.30 (6 Sat)–11
Courage Best Bitter, Directors; John Smith's Bitter Ⓗ
Early 18th-century, two-bar pub with games in the public bar. A proper Sunday lunch is served. Large prize-winning garden. ❀ ◖ 🀫 ♿ ⇌ ♣ P

Wheathampstead

Nelson
Marford Road
☎ (0582) 832196
11–3, 5 (6 Sat)–11
Fuller's London Pride; Greene King Abbot; Hook Norton Best Bitter; S&N Theakston Best Bitter; Wadworth 6X; Young's Special Ⓗ; **guest beers**
A single bar with a central open fire, offering reasonably priced, home-cooked meals, and a wide range of beers. Mon is quiz night, open to all.
🏠 ❀ ◖ ◗ ♣ P

Try also: Cross Keys, Gustard Wood (Free)

Whitwell

Maidens Head
High Street ☎ (0438) 871392
11.30–3 (4 Wed), 5.30 (6 Sat)–11
Courage Directors; McMullen AK, Country Ⓗ
Timbered pub of character with friendly locals and bar staff. 🏠 ❀ ◖ ◗ 🀫

Widford

Bell
Main Street, Hunsden Road (B180) ☎ (0279) 842454
11–3, 6–11; 11–11 Sat
Adnams Bitter; Bass Worthington BB, Draught Bass; Fuller's London Pride Ⓗ
Smart free house with a separate dining room and a pool room.
❀ ◖ ◗ P

Wildhill

Woodman
45 Wildhill Lane (between B158 and A1000) OS263068
☎ (0707) 42618
11.30–2.30, 5.30–11; 12–2, 7–10.30 Sun
Greene King IPA, Abbot; McMullen AK Ⓗ
Genuine local with a warm welcome for visitors. Probably one of the lowest-priced pubs in the county. Football fans are advised to check that Barnet have not lost before talking football to the landlord. Good chip-free meals, but not served Sun. Q ❀ ◖ ♣ P

Willian

Three Horseshoes
Baldock Lane (opp. church, up tiny side lane) OS224307
☎ (0462) 685713
11–11
Greene King IPA, Abbot Ⓗ, **Winter Ale** Ⓖ
Regularly in this guide, a cosy, one-roomed country pub in a pretty village on the edge of Letchworth town. A quiet haven where machines and muzak are banned. Home-cooked lunches (not served Sun). Contract bridge players are welcomed. Same landlord for 23 years. Park wisely.
🏠 Q ◖ ♣

Woolmer Green

Fox
21 New Road (200 yds from B197) ☎ (0438) 813179
11–3, 6.30–11
McMullen AK, Country Ⓗ
Small, one-roomed village pub hidden just off the main road, past the village pond. Live music most Sats; strong domino and cribbage teams. No food Tue eve.
Q ❀ ◖ ◗ ⇌ (Knebworth)
♣ P

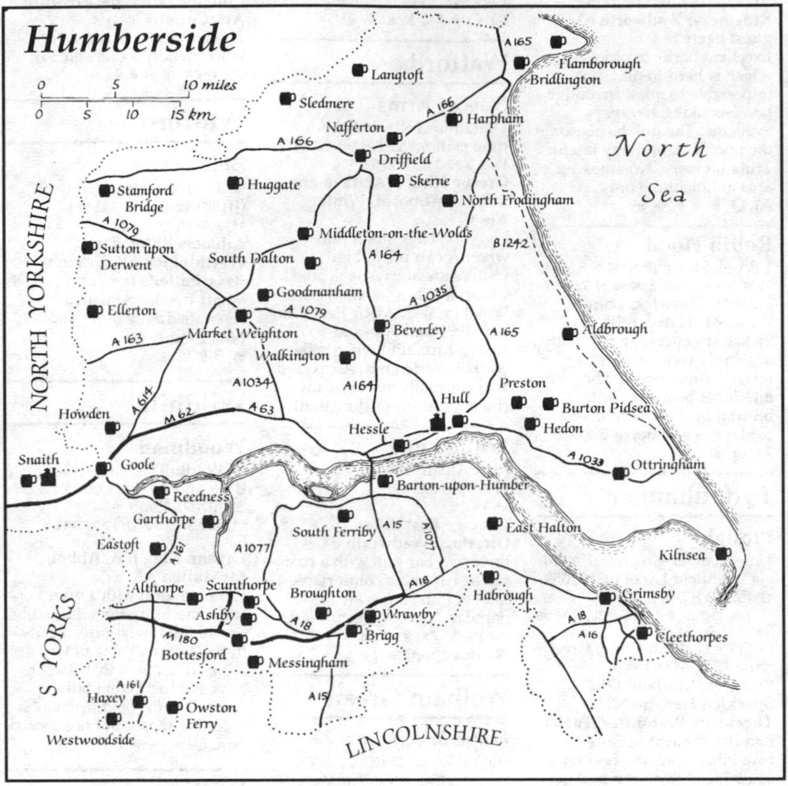

Hull, Hull; Old Mill, Snaith

Aldbrough

Double Dutch

350 Seaside Road (1 mile from village on the coast)
☎ (0964) 527786
12–3 (not Tue–Thu in winter), 7–11; closed Mon
Old Mill Bitter; Tetley Bitter Ⓗ; guest beer
Thirties roadside pub next to a caravan park. Formerly the Royal Hotel, now named after its Dutch owner. An oil painting in the bar depicts the original pub, a victim of coastal erosion. ⌂ ☾ ◗ P

Althorpe

Dolphin

27 Trunk Road (A18)
☎ (0724) 783469
11–3, 6.30–11
Vaux Samson; Wards Sheffield Best Bitter Ⓗ
Roadside pub with an emphasis on, and an excellent reputation for, food. Fully equipped family room.
Q ☺ ☾ ◗ ⇌

Ashby

Crown Hotel

209 Ashby High Street
☎ (0724) 840899
11–11
Mansfield Riding Bitter, Old Baily Ⓗ
Established drinkers' pub dating from 1909. Tastefully refurbished by Mansfield but the 'alehouse' atmosphere remains intact. Eve meals on request. Live music Mon and Sat eves. ☾ ⊞ ♣ P

Open Hearth

Warley Road ☎ (0724) 842318
11.30–3 (12–4 Sat), 7–11
Samuel Smith OBB Ⓗ
Friendly estate pub named after a type of ironmaking furnace: a smart lounge and a bar with snooker, pool and darts. Good value food Mon–Fri lunchtimes. The cheapest Sam Smith's in the area. Q ☾ ⊞ ♣ P

Barton-upon-Humber

Volunteer Arms

13 Whitecross Street (off A1077) ☎ (0652) 32309
11–3, 5.30–11
Burtonwood Mild, Bitter Ⓗ
Pleasant, two-roomed pub. On-street parking. ⌂ Q ☾

Wheatsheaf

5 Holydyke (A1077/B1218 jct)
☎ (0652) 33175
11–3, 5.30–11
Wards Mild, Sheffield Best Bitter Ⓗ
Fine old pub with a lounge bar and a separate snug. Weekday lunches. Q ☾ ⇌ P

Beverley

Mariner's Arms

Flemingate ☎ (0482) 881241
4 (5 Wed, 12.30 Sat)–11
Vaux Bitter; Wards Thorne Best Bitter Ⓗ

Substantial pub near Beverley Beck and the Army Transport Museum. Comfortably furnished, with two distinct drinking areas but few original features. Barbecues. ❀ ♣ P

Queens Head
Wednesday Market
☎ (0482) 867363
11–3, 5–11; 11–11 Fri & Sat
Wards Thorne Best Bitter Ⓗ**; guest beer**
Pub whose Brewers' Tudor exterior overlooks Beverley's smaller market place. Refurbished and extended to the rear, where families are catered for. ◑ ◗ ≠ ♣

Rose & Crown
North Bar Without
☎ (0482) 862532
11–3, 6–11
Wards Mild, Thorne Best Bitter, Sheffield Best Bitter, Kirby Ⓗ**; guest beer**
Substantial Brewers' Tudor pub adjacent to the historic North Bar, Westwood and the racecourse. A comfortably furnished smoke room and a lounge offering home-cooked food: a popular eating establishment. ❀ ◑ ◗ ♣ P

Royal Standard
30 North Bar Within
☎ (0482) 882434
Wards Mild, Thorne Best Bitter Ⓗ
Classic, two-roomed town local. Original twenties bentwood seating adorns the bar, which is popular with the racing fraternity; well-furnished lounge to the rear (Dolly's Bar). Darley motif in the bar window. Q ❀

White Horse Inn (Nellies)
22 Hengate ☎ (0482) 861973
11–11
Samuel Smith OBB, Museum Ⓗ
One of Beverley's landmarks: this famous Georgian inn offers a multi-roomed interior with gas lighting, stone-flagged floors, roaring coal fires and home cooking. Note the rocking horse sign above the main entrance. Folk and jazz upstairs. ⩕ Q ❀ ◑ ♣ P

Woolpack Inn
37 Westwood Road (near Westwood hospital)
☎ (0482) 867095
11.30–2.30, 7–11
Burtonwood Mild, Bitter Ⓗ
Superbly located in a residential street near the Westwood; a pub built circa 1830 from a pair of cottages. History of the building and its former landlords in the small snug. Parking can be difficult. No food Sun. Q ❀ ◑

Bottesford

Black Beauty
Keddington Road
☎ (0724) 867628
11.30–11; 11–11 Sat
Mansfield Riding Mild, Riding Bitter, Old Baily Ⓗ
Welcoming estate pub with a refurbished bar, a small lounge and a large function room, open Fri/Sat eves. Live music weekends. Unusually for the area, serves all three Mansfield beers. ❀ ⊞ ♣ P

Bridlington

Bull & Sun
11 Baylegate ☎ (0262) 676105
11–4.30, 6–11; 11–11 Fri, Sat & summer
Vaux Bitter; Wards Mild, Thorne Best Bitter Ⓗ
Former millinery shop, near the historic Baylegate and priory in Bridlington old town. The basic front room has framed music sheets on the walls. ⛟ ❀ ◑ ◗ ♿ ▲ ♣

Olde Star Inn
17 Westgate, Old Town
☎ (0262) 676039
11–11
S&N Theakston Best Bitter, XB; Younger Scotch, No. 3 Ⓗ
Multi-roomed pub in the old town. The restaurant has a reputation for excellent food. ⩕ ❀ ⛼ ◑ ♣ P

Old Ship Inn
90 St John's Street
☎ (0262) 670466
11–4, 7–11
Wards Mild, Thorne Best Bitter Ⓗ
Thriving local by the old town, with a good, traditional atmosphere. Facilities for children include a covered outdoor play area. ⛟ ❀ ◑ ♣

Pack Horse Inn
Market Place ☎ (0262) 675701
11–3, 7–11
Burtonwood Bitter Ⓗ
Listed building thought to be 300 years old. The upper windows give an impression of three storeys, but the pub is in fact only two – a relic from Daylight Tax days. Comfortable, open-plan lounge with a relaxed atmosphere; separate pool room. ⩕ ❀ ◑ ♣

Brigg

Brocklesby Ox
Bridge Street (A15/A18)
☎ (0652) 650292
12–3 (may extend), 5.30–11; 11–11 Sat
Burtonwood Bitter, Forshaw's Ⓗ
Smallish old pub extensively renovated, with much woodwork, stained-glass and framed pictures in evidence. The lounge contains a small dining area, and the bar a pool table. No food Mon.
⩕ ◑ ◗ ⊞ ≠ ♣ P

White Horse
Wrawby Street (just off new link road, A15/A18)
☎ (0652) 652242
11–2.30, 5–11
Wards Mild, Sheffield Best Bitter Ⓗ
Welcoming old inn popular for its award-winning meals. Recipient of the brewery's cellarmanship award. Vehicular access has been restricted by a new road layout, and requires a detour. Eve meals Thu–Sat only.
◑ ◗ ⊞ ≠ ♣ P

Broughton

Red Lion
High Street ☎ (0652) 652560
11–3, 6–11; 11–11 Fri & Sat
Mansfield Riding Mild, Riding Bitter, Old Baily Ⓗ
Smart pub with a small bar, a medium-sized lounge/dining room and a large games room. Good value, home-cooked meals (no food Sun eve or Mon; book Sun lunch). Own bowling green. Caravan site nearby. Q ❀ ◑ ◗ ⊞ ▲ ♣ P

Burton Pidsea

Nancy
Church Street ☎ (0964) 670330
12–2 (3 Fri & Sat), 7–11
Tetley Mild, Bitter Ⓗ
Old pub in the village centre, next to the church. The lounge used to be a blacksmith's and retains the forge; beamed ceiling in the bar area. Named after a local racehorse from the 1850s. ⩕ ❀ ◑ ◗ ♣ P

Cleethorpes

Crows Nest
Balmoral Road
☎ (0472) 698867
11.30–3.30, 6.30–11
Samuel Smith OBB Ⓗ
Large estate pub with a basic bar and a quiet, comfortable lounge. The only Sam's for miles. Q ⛟ ❀ ⛼ ◑ ⊞ ♣ P

Nottingham House
7 Seaview Street (just off seafront) ☎ (0472) 694368
12 (11 Sat)–11
Tetley Mild, Bitter Ⓗ
Town drinking pub with a superb facade. Unusually for the area, there are three separate rooms, including a snug. Free bread and dripping Sun lunch. Supports many local activities. Highly recommended. Q ♿ ≠ ♣

Humberside

Willys
17 High Cliff Road
☎ (0472) 602145
11–11
Bateman Mild, XB; Willys Original 🄷; guest beers
Pub clearly of wine bar origin, but a great real ale supporter; its own brewery can be seen from the bar. Other Willys brews are usually available, including Old Groyne, the ingredients for which include Tasmanian leatherwood honey! November beer festival. No-smoking upstairs some eves. ❀ ◖ ▲ ≹ ⊬

Driffield

Mariners Arms
47 Eastgate South (near cattle market) ☎ (0377) 43708
12–4 (6 Sat), 7–11; 12–11 Thu
Burtonwood Mild, Bitter 🄷
Traditional, street-corner, two-room local, busy on market day (Thu) and popular for quiz nights. Look out for the entertaining football team noticeboard and the dart-playing dog! ❀ ≹ ♣ P

Old Falcon
Market Place ☎ (0377) 241021
11–3, 7–11; 11–11 Sat
Hull Governor; Ind Coope Burton Ale; Tetley Bitter 🄷
Compact and cosy, welcoming main-street local. Popular for home-made steak and kidney pie lunches (Thu–Sat). Old Hull Brewery sign. ◖ ≹ ♣ P

East Halton

Black Bull
Townside (main street)
☎ (0469) 540207
11.30–3, 5–11; 11–11 Fri & Sat
Bass Mild XXXX, Worthington BB, Draught Bass; Stones Best Bitter 🄷
Deservedly popular village local: a good-sized bar and a comfortable lounge. Above average, good value meals.
Q ❀ ◖ ◗ ⊞ ♣ P

Eastoft

River Don
Sampson Street
☎ (0724) 798225
12–3, 7–11
John Smith's Bitter 🄷
250-year-old village pub offering good food and a warm welcome. Freshwater fishing nearby. Large games room. ♨ ⛐ ❀ ◖ ◗ ♿ ▲ ♣

Ellerton

Boot & Shoe
Main Street ☎ (0757) 288346
11–3, 6–11
John Smith's Bitter; Old Mill Bitter 🄷
Pleasant village pub dating back 400 years, offering three separate drinking areas. Quiet midweek lunch, but popular in the eves with locals. Quiz Wed. ♨ Q ❀ ◖ ◗ P

Flamborough

Royal Dog & Duck
Dog & Duck Square, Tower Street ☎ (0262) 850206
11–11
Draught Bass; John Smith's Bitter; Stones Best Bitter 🄷
Old, village-centre pub with beams, bric-a-brac and a comfortable atmosphere. Good meals (local specialities); separate dining room.
♨ ⛐ ❀ ◖ ◗ ♿ ▲ ♣ P

Garthorpe

Bay Horse
Shore Road ☎ (0724) 798306
12–2, 7–11
Mansfield Riding Mild, Riding Bitter 🄷
Comfortable, traditional pub with a large lounge bar and a pool and games room. Small entrance hall. Previously a John Smith's pub; the new landlord is very popular. Live entertainment weekly.
♨ Q ❀ ◖ ◗ ♣ P

Goodmanham

Goodmanham Arms
Main Street ☎ (0430) 872379
7–11; 12–2, 7–11 Sat (opens weekday lunchtime by arrangement)
Black Sheep Best Bitter; Clark's Traditional Bitter *or* **Old Mill Bitter; S&N Theakston Best Bitter 🄷**
Fine, traditional local opposite a Norman church and run by a friendly, semi-retired couple. A small extra room is opened when busy. On the Wolds Way. ♨ Q ❀ P

Goole

Old George
Market Square
☎ (0405) 763147
11–3, 7–11
Bass Light, Draught Bass; Stones Best Bitter 🄷
Lively town-centre pub with an unusual collection of cigarette lighters. Emphasis on food lunchtimes; popular with a younger clientele in the eve.
❀ ◖ ≹ ♣ P

Woodlands
Rutland Road ☎ (0405) 762738
11–5, 7–11
John Smith's Bitter 🄷
Friendly, three-roomed estate pub with a superb, traditional snug. Popular with all ages.
♨ Q ♣ P

Grimsby

Angel
175 Freeman Street
☎ (0472) 342402
11–11
S&N Theakston Mild; Younger IPA, No. 3 🄷
Busy corner pub with a Scottish-looking exterior. Full of local characters: the quiet back room, known locally as the House of Lords, is highly recommended.
Q ⊞ ≹ (Docks) ♣ P

Corporation
88 Freeman Street
☎ (0472) 356651
11–11
Bass Mild XXXX, Draught Bass 🄷
Traditional, three-roomed pub, very much in keeping with the area. Used by all ages and all walks of life. Don't miss the back room.
◖ ⊞ ≹ (Docks) ♣

Duke of Wellington
Pasture Street
☎ (0472) 356976
11–11
Bass Mild XXXX, Worthington BB, Draught Bass 🄷
Large, one-room, town-centre pub, formerly the Hewitts Tavern, now returned to its previous title after a Victorian-style refurbishment. Food all day (not Sun). Busy weekend eves, with live entertainment Fri. ◖ ◗ ≹ (Town) P

Honest Lawyer
Ladysmith Road (near Bird's Eye) ☎ (0472) 356224
11–11
Bass Mild XXXX, Worthington BB, Draught Bass 🄷
1960s pub on the edge of an industrial estate; popular with factory staff lunchtimes. A games-oriented bar and a comfortable lounge. No food weekends.
❀ ◖ ◗ ⊞ ♿ ♣ P

Hope & Anchor
148 Victoria Street
☎ (0472) 342565
11–11
Ind Coope Burton Ale; Tetley Mild, Bitter 🄷; guest beers
19th-century, town-centre pub: a bar with pub games and music, and a lounge for lively conversation. Good lunches (not served Sun). A three-times local *Pub of the Year* and Ind Coope cellarmanship guild member, offering four guest beers, and a beer festival each March.
◖ ⊞ ♿ ≹ (Town)

Spiders Web
180 Carr Lane ☎ (0472) 692065
12 (11 Sat)–11
Courage Directors; John Smith's Bitter, Magnet; Wilson's Mild Ⓗ
Large, friendly, three-room, estate-type pub: a lively bar and a quiet lounge. Regular quality live music. Q ❀ ⊞ ⇌ (Cleethorpes) ♣ P

Swigs
21 Osborne Street
☎ (0472) 354773
11–11; closed Sun lunch
Bateman XB; Willys Original Ⓗ**; guest beers**
Narrow, town-centre pub popular with office workers at lunchtime and a mainly younger clientele in the eve. Three guest beers. ◐ ♿ ⇌

Habrough

Horse & Hounds
Station Road ☎ (0469) 576940
11–11 (may close 3–7)
McEwan 80/-; S&N Theakston Mild, XB, Old Peculier; Younger IPA, No. 3 Ⓗ
Tastefully converted farmhouse/rectory adjoining the Habrough Hotel, offering beer at reasonable prices and excellent food. Good local trade; quiz night Tue. 80/- and IPA are both sold, even though they are the same beer under different names.
♨ Q ⛿ ◐ ◑ ⊞ ⇌ ♣ P

Harpham

St Quintin Arms
Main Street ☎ (0262) 490329
7–11; 12–3, 7–11 Tue
Courage Directors; John Smith's Bitter Ⓗ
Community pub at the heart of a small village just off the A166. One bar serves two rooms in the listed building. Well laid-out dining area.
♨ ❀ ⛿ ◐ ◑ ♿ ♣ P

Haxey

Loco
31–33 Church Street
☎ (0427) 752879
12–3 (not Mon–Fri), 6–11
John Smith's Bitter, Magnet Ⓗ
Former village Co-op and fish shop, with a prominent railway theme. Memorabilia include an engine smokebox.
♨ Q ☺ ❀ ◐ ◑ ♿ ♣

Hedon

Shakespeare Inn
9 Baxtergate ☎ (0482) 898371
11–11
Vaux Samson; Wards Mild, Thorne Best Bitter, Sheffield Best Bitter, Extra Special Ⓗ
Cosy and popular one-roomer featuring breweriana and Hedon memorabilia. Over 3,000 beer mats adorn the ceiling. Busy food trade lunchtime. Eve meals Fri only, till 7.30. ♨ ❀ ◐ ♣ P

Hessle

George Inn/Top House
Prestongate ☎ (0482) 648698
11–11
Bass Mild XXXX, Draught Bass; Stones Best Bitter Ⓗ
Well-run local with three drinking areas and a large garden. The name Top House comes from days when there were Bottom, Middle and Top Houses in this street.
Q ☺ ❀ ◐ ♣ P

Howden

Wheatsheaf
85 Hailgate ☎ (0430) 430722
11–11
John Smith's Bitter Ⓗ
Traditional public house close to the minster. Welcoming atmosphere; popular with locals. Eve meals finish at 8.30.
Q ☺ ❀ ⛿ ◐ ◑ ⛺ ♣ P

Huggate

Wolds Inn
Driffield Road ☎ (0377) 88217
12–3, 6.30 (7 winter)–11
John Smith's Bitter; Tetley Bitter Ⓗ
Pleasant village pub in the heart of the Wolds; popular eves for meals (booking advisable). Wooden beams and brass. No lunches Mon, when only the bar is open.
Q ❀ ⛿ ◐ ◑ ♿ P

Hull

Bay Horse
113 Wincolmlee (400 yds N of North Bridge, W of river)
☎ (0482) 29227
11–11
Bateman Mild, XB, XXXB, Salem Porter, Victory Ⓗ
Hull CAMRA's *Pub of the Year* 1991, offering the full range of Bateman beers in their only tied house north of the Humber. Tastefully renovated and extended in 1990. Rugby league memorabilia.
Welcomes all. ♨ ◐ ◑ ♿ ♣ P

Duke of Wellington
104 Peel Street (N of Spring Bank, NW of centre)
☎ (0482) 29603
12–3, 6.30–11
Hull Mild; Taylor Landlord; Tetley Bitter Ⓗ**; guest beers**
Back-street, re-styled, Victorian corner local, popular with locals and students and often crowded. Four, usually strong, guest beers.
❀ ♿ ♣ P

East Riding
37 Cannon Street
☎ (0482) 29134
12–5, 7 (6 Sat)–11
Tetley Mild, Bitter Ⓗ
Small, street-corner, two-roomed industrial pub to the north of the city centre. The no-nonsense bar features rugby league memorabilia, whilst the cosy lounge is wood-panelled. Hull CAMRA *Pub of the Year* 1990. ⊞ ♣

King William Hotel
43 Market Place, Old Town
☎ (0482) 23997
11–11
Malton Double Chance; Old Mill Mild, Bitter; Selby Old Tom Ⓗ
Hull's only genuine free house; a former Hull Brewery pub dating from the reign of King William IV, from whom it takes its name (not the statue of William of Orange opposite). House beer from Cropton. Five guest beers. Hull CAMRA *Pub of the Year* 1992. ♨ Q ⌽

Mutiny on the Bounty
1 High Street ☎ (0482) 589280
11–3, 5 (4 Sat)–11; 11–11 Fri
Mansfield Riding Mild, Riding Bitter, Old Baily Ⓗ**; guest beer**
Imposing Georgian building built in 1820 as dock offices. Note the split staircase opposite the entrance. Named after the Hull ship bought by the Admiralty for the expedition to the South Seas. Superb woodwork and Mutiny memorabilia. ◐ ◑ ♣

Oberon Hotel
Queen Street (near Corporation Pier) ☎ (0482) 24886
11–3, 5.30–11
Bass Mild XXXX, Draught Bass Ⓗ
Solid, simple, two-roomed pub close to the marina. Decorated with nautical memorabilia and frequented by Humber pilots.
Q ♿ ♣

Old Blue Bell
Market Place, Old Town
☎ (0482) 24382
11–3, 6–11
Samuel Smith OBB, Museum Ⓗ
Famous old town pub with an original layout of snug, corridor and long, narrow bar; pool room upstairs. A courtyard connects to an adjoining indoor market. Large collection of bells.
Q ☺ ❀ ◐ ♣

Olde Black Boy
150 High Street, Old Town
☎ (0482) 26516
12–3, 7–11
Tetley Bitter Ⓗ; guest beers
The first Tap & Spile Charterhouse pub, a former Tetley Heritage Inn. Its history is explained in the small, wood-panelled front room. Folk music Sun lunchtime.
♨ Q ◖ ⊂⊃

Olde White Harte
25 Silver Street, Old Town (down alley) ☎ (0482) 26363
11–11
S&N Theakston XB, Old Peculier; Younger IPA, No. 3 Ⓗ
Over 400 years old and the venue for the meeting which refused King Charles entry to the city at the start of the Civil War. Wonderful dark timber, stained-glass, and two sit-in fireplaces, plus a courtyard. Varied lunch menu. Upstairs rooms. ♨ Q ❀ ◖ ♣

Plimsoll's Ship Hotel
103 Witham ☎ (0482) 25995
11–3, 6–11
Hull Mild, Bitter, Governor; Tetley Bitter Ⓗ
Small, narrow pub with a fancy Victorian facade. The galley-style interior has a delightful bar surround, a stained-glass dome and light pine fittings, with exposed brick and bare floorboards. On the outskirts of the city centre, just across North Bridge. Busy Fri and Sat nights. ◖ ♣

Royal William
Waterhouse Lane
☎ (0482) 215881
11.30–2.30 (11–4.30 Sat), 5.30 (6.30 Sat)–11
Marston's Pedigree; S&N Theakston Best Bitter, XB; Stones Best Bitter; Whitbread Flowers Original; Younger No. 3 Ⓗ; guest beers
Hull's 'country pub' in the town, situated by the Princes Quay shopping centre car park. One L-shaped room with an old-world atmosphere. Meals till 8pm. ❀ ◖ ◗ ⇌ ♣

Wellington Inn
55 Russell Street (near A1079 Beverley Rd/Freetown Way jct) ☎ (0482) 29486
11.30 (11 Sat)–11
Mansfield Riding Mild, Riding Bitter, Old Baily Ⓗ
Friendly local on the edge of the city centre, with several areas linked around a central bar. Excellent value bar meals. Impressive mobile real ale bar for hire. ❀ ◖ ♣ P

Whalebone Inn
165 Wincolmlee (between Scott St and Sculcoates Bridges, W of river) ☎ (0482) 27980
11.30–3, 5–11; 11.30–11 Fri & Sat
Tetley Mild, Bitter Ⓗ
The old industrial area next to the river used to include whale processing plants which gave this pub its name. A popular, no-frills drinkers' local. ♣

Kilnsea

Crown & Anchor
Main Street ☎ (0964) 650276
11–11
Bass Mild XXXX, Draught Bass; Tetley Bitter Ⓗ
Pub in a prominent and remote location overlooking the Humber estuary and Spurn Point, which has probably never been refurbished but has evolved its own special style. A community pub serving the coastguard station. Busy in summer.
♨ ⛄ ❀ 🛏 ◖ ◗ ▲ ♣ P

Langtoft

Ship Inn
Front Street ☎ (0377) 87243
12–3, 7–11
John Smith's Bitter; Tetley Bitter Ⓗ; guest beer (summer)
Cosy, friendly village local with a reputation for good food. Children welcome in the pool room and restaurant. Caravan site nearby.
♨ ❀ 🛏 ◖ ◗ ▲ ♣ P

Market Weighton

Half Moon
9 High Street ☎ (0430) 872247
12–3, 7–11; 11–11 Fri & Sat (may close 3–7 Sat)
Burtonwood Mild, Bitter Ⓗ
Pub where a single, long room serves as a bar and lounge, one at either end. Photographs of old Hull and trawlers adorn the 'lounge' walls; trophies from team successes are in the 'bar'. Very popular with young and old. ◖ ♿ ♣ P

Messingham

Bird in the Barley
Northfield Road
☎ (0724) 762994
11.30–3 (3.30 Sat, not Mon), 5 (7 Sat)–11
Ruddles Best Bitter, County; John Smith's Bitter; Webster's Yorkshire Bitter; guest beer Ⓗ
Smart, one-roomed, country-style pub between Messingham and Scunthorpe. Good service is a feature and lunchtime meals are very popular. Active guest beer policy, but the availability is sometimes disappointing.
◖ ♣ P

Middleton-on-the-Wolds

Robin Hood
Beverley Road
☎ (0377) 217319
11.30–3, 7–11 (may vary)
Burtonwood Mild, Bitter Ⓗ
Local in the middle of town: one long main room, adorned with Robin Hood memorabilia. A small bar opens when busy. Football, quiz and dart teams. Bar snacks. ❀ ⊟ ♿ ♣ P

Nafferton

Cross Keys
2 North Street (200 yds off A166) ☎ (0377) 44261
12–3 (not Mon), 7–11
Old Mill Bitter; John Smith's Bitter; Younger Scotch Ⓗ
Very friendly and spacious village inn, popular for good bar food (not Mon, Tue or Sun eves); also a separate restaurant and a games/family room. Occasional live music.
⛄ 🛏 ◖ ◗ ⇌ ♣

North Frodingham

Star Inn
Main Street ☎ (0262) 488365
7–11; 12–2.30, 7–10.30 Sun
John Smith's Bitter; Younger Scotch Ⓗ
Pleasant village pub adorned with aircraft pictures and decorative mirrors, and with a relaxed atmosphere. Good food selection (no meals Thu eve). Several malt whiskies; separate games room.
♨ ◖ ◗ ♣ P

Ottringham

Watts Arms
Main Street ☎ (0964) 622034
12–3 (summer only), 7–11
Camerons Bitter; Hull Mild Ⓗ
Village-centre local with pool, a jukebox, satellite TV and games machines in the bar; Brewers' Tudor-style lounge. Originally built by the lord of the manor and then owned by Darleys and the original Hull Brewery. Country and western on Fri eve. Eve meals Thu–Sat in summer only. ◖ ◗ ♣ P

Owston Ferry

Crooked Billet
Silver Street ☎ (042 772) 264
11–3 (not Mon), 7–11
Wards Thorne Best Bitter Ⓗ
Trentside village pub, Wards's *Pub of the Year* 1992. Weekend sing-alongs; boxing club upstairs. Ask for the handpump. ♨ ⛄ ❀ ◖ ♿ P

Preston

Nag's Head
11 Sproatley Road
☎ (0482) 897517
12–3, 7 (5.30 Fri)–11
Bass Mild XXXX; Old Mill Bitter; Stones Best Bitter Ⓗ

Old pub on the edge of the village, extended in 1985 to form a lounge with a beamed ceiling and cottage decor. Separate public bar and a conservatory used by families.
☎ ❀ ◐ ♣ P

Reedness

Half Moon

Main Street ☎ (0405) 704484
12–3, 7–11
Marston's Pedigree; Whitbread Trophy, Castle Eden Ale Ⓗ**; guest beer**
Traditional, very clean and polished local with a campsite behind and Blacktoft Sands RSPB reserve nearby. Whitbread guest beer.
♛ Q ❀ ◐ ▲ ♣ P

Scunthorpe

Queensway

Ashby Road ☎ (0724) 865059
11–3, 5.30–11
Whitbread Boddingtons Bitter, Trophy, Castle Eden Ale Ⓗ
Popular pub adorned with pictures of old Scunthorpe. Guest beers from the Whitbread collection. Separate restaurant. ♛ ❀ ◐ ◑ ≹ P

Riveter

50 Henderson Avenue
☎ (0724) 862701
11–3, 5.30–11; 11–11 Sat
Old Mill Mild, Bitter, Bullion Ⓗ
Pub converted from a workingman's club, noisy and crowded in the eve. Large games area for pool and darts; small car park. ♣ P

Skerne

Eagle

Wansford Road
☎ (0377) 42178
12–2, 7–11
Camerons Bitter, Strongarm (summer) Ⓗ
Remarkable, unspoiled, homely pub with two rooms and no bar. Drinks are brought to your table from a Victorian cash register beer engine in the small cellar off the entrance hall. Children at lunchtime only. ♛ Q ❀ ♣ P

Sledmere

Triton Inn

On B1253 ☎ (0377) 86644
12–3, 7–11
Tetley Bitter; Younger Scotch Ⓗ
Traditional, comfortable and rambling inn, in an interesting and delightful village. Next to Sledmere House in typical Wolds countryside.
♛ ❀ ⛟ ◐ ◑ ♣ P

Snaith

Black Lion

9 Selby Road ☎ (0405) 860282
11–3.30, 7–11
Tetley Mild, Bitter Ⓗ
The antithesis of a theme pub, evolved from the stables of a former coaching inn. The welcoming landlord and loyal regulars tell different tales of the pub's history. ❀ ⊟
≹ (limited service) P

Brewers Arms

10 Pontefract Road (A645)
☎ (0405) 862404
11–3, 6–11 (midnight supper licence)
Old Mill Mild, Bitter, Bullion Ⓗ
Excellent conversion of an impressive country lodge, from 1720. Note the well in the centre of the lounge. A secret tunnel reputedly runs to the local stately home. ❀ ⛟ ◐ ◑
≹ (limited service) P

South Dalton

Pipe & Glass

West End ☎ (0430) 810246
11.30–3, 6.30–11
S&N Theakston Best Bitter; John Smith's Bitter; Whitbread Castle Eden Ale Ⓗ
Comfortable, multi-roomed inn with a restaurant which caters well for vegetarians (no meals Sun eve); also a games room with its own bar for the younger element. Enclosed play area in the garden, under a 500-year-old yew tree.
♛ Q ☎ ❀ ◐ ◑ ♿ ♣ P

South Ferriby

Hope & Anchor

Sluice Road (A1077)
☎ (0652) 635242
12 (11 Sat & summer)–3, 7 (5 Sat, 6 summer Sat)–11
Mansfield Riding Mild, Riding Bitter Ⓗ**; guest beers**
Pub situated at the confluence of the Rivers Ancholme and Humber, with superb views from the large family room at the rear. Children's play equipment in the garden. A small snug leads off the front bar. No eve meals Mon–Thu in winter. ☎ ❀ ◐ ◑ ♣ P

Stamford Bridge

Swordsman Inn

The Square ☎ (0759) 71307
11–3, 6–11; 11–11 Fri & Sat
Samuel Smith OBB Ⓗ
Old coaching inn overlooking the River Derwent, offering a snug, family room, tap room and beer garden. Bar games include pool; quizzes Wed and Sun. Bar meals available lunchtimes, Tue–Sun, and eves, Thu–Sat, in summer only. Fishing at the rear.
♛ ☎ ❀ ◐ ◑ ♿ ♣ P

Sutton upon Derwent

St Vincent's Arms

Main Street ☎ (0904) 608349
11–3, 6–11
Mansfield Riding Bitter; Old Mill Bitter; S&N Theakston XB, Old Peculier; John Smith's Bitter; Taylor Landlord; Tetley Bitter Ⓗ
Picturesque village inn, extended in the front bar but maintaining a cosy atmosphere. Popular with locals and travellers alike. Good reputation for food.
♛ Q ❀ ◐ ◑ ▲ P

Walkington

Barrel Inn

35 East End
☎ (0482) 868494
12–3 (summer), 5.30–11; 11.30–11 Sat; 11–11 bank hols
Courage Directors; Old Mill Bitter; Ruddles Best Bitter; Webster's Yorkshire Bitter Ⓗ
Dual-levelled, one-roomed pub, close to the pond of the village which claims to be the geographical centre of the county. Popular with cricket teams. Bar snacks. ♛ ❀

Westwoodside

Park Drain

400 yds off B1396 OS726988
☎ (0427) 752255
11–11
Mansfield Riding Bitter; John Smith's Bitter; Wilson's Mild Ⓗ
Unusual, remote, Victorian pub built for the proposed mining community. The large bar, comfortable lounge and excellent restaurant are warmed by straw-fired central heating. Note the wells in the car park. Meals all day Sun.
♛ ❀ ◐ ◑ ▲ ♣ P

Wrawby

Jollies

Brigg Road (A15/A18)
☎ (0652) 655658
11–3, 7 (6 summer)–11
Bass Worthington BB, Draught Bass Ⓗ
Small, modernised pub; the single lounge bar has a 'snug' created by partitions. Popular for meals and can be very busy (eve meals Fri–Sun). Children's play area in the garden. ❀ ◐ ◑ P

Isle of Wight

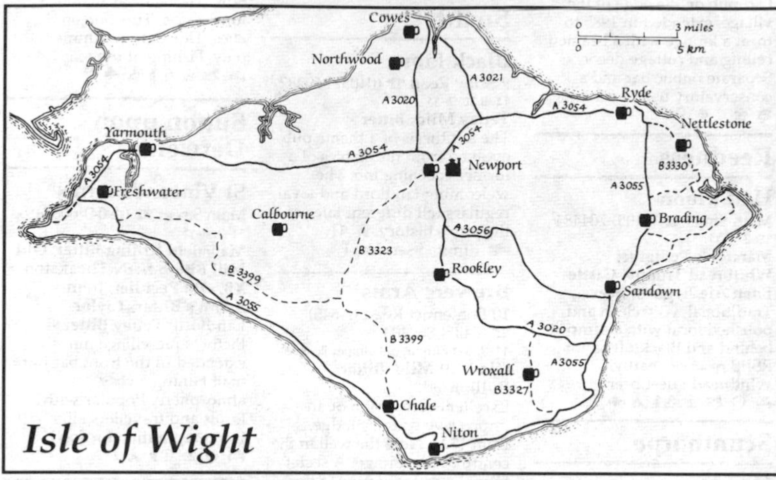

Burts, Newport

Brading

Anglers Inn

Yarbridge (off A3055, E at traffic lights) ☎ (0983) 406212

11–3, 7–11 (11–11 summer)

Gale's XXXD (summer), **Best Bitter, 5X, HSB** Ⓗ

Unusual one-bar pub on the edge of the village, beside the River Yar. ❀ ◐ ◑ ♿ ⇌ ♣ P

Try also: Village Inn, Bembridge (Whitbread)

Calbourne

Sun Inn

On B3041, Newport–Freshwater road

☎ (0983) 78231

11–3, 5–11; 11–11

Courage Best Bitter, Directors Ⓗ

Traditional country pub, 102 years old, with a popular, sometimes noisy public bar, a quieter lounge bar and a dining room (no-smoking). Children are welcome in the small conservatory.

Q ⛾ ❀ ◐ ◑ ♿ ▲ ♣ P

Chale

Wight Mouse

On B3399, 100 yds from A3055

☎ (0983) 730431

11–11 (midnight restaurant)

Fuller's Chiswick; Marston's Pedigree; Wadworth 6X; Whitbread Boddingtons Bitter, Strong Country Ⓗ; **guest beer**

Very busy, old stone pub with an adjoining hotel. An award-winning family pub with a garden play area. Food served all day; live music every night; 365 whiskies (one for every day of the year). Near Blackgang Chine Theme Park.

♛ ⛾ ❀ ⛿ ◐ ◑ ▲ P

Cowes

Anchor

1 High Street ☎ (0983) 292823

11–11

Eldridge Pope Hardy Country; Hall & Woodhouse Tanglefoot; Wadworth 6X; Whitbread Boddingtons Bitter, Flowers Original; guest beers Ⓗ/Ⓖ

Ancient town-centre inn where the former stables have been converted to a games and children's room, with an occasional bar for events. Original home-made food available all day; steak and ale and fish pies are specialities. Fresh vegetarian food; roasts on Sun. Thatcher's cider sometimes stocked.

♛ ⛾ ❀ ◐ ◑ ⊖

Kingston Arms

176 Newport Road, West Cowes (A3020)

☎ (0983) 293393

11–11; 11–2.30, 5–11 Tue–Thu

Gale's BBB, 5X, HSB Ⓗ

Traditional locals' pub with a friendly atmosphere. Home-cooked food with daily menu changes (book for beef and real ale pie!). Live music Sat nights. Stained-glass in the bar proclaims the former Mew Langton brewery ownership.

♛ ❀ ⛿ ◐ ◑ ♣ P

Freshwater

Vine Inn

School Green Road

☎ (0983) 752959

11–3 (may extend summer), 5.30–11

Gale's BBB, Best Bitter, 5X, HSB Ⓗ

Friendly two-bar local, offering interesting menus in the bars and restaurant. Traditional games and occasional fancy dress events. Close to car parks and shops; excellent country walks and Tennyson's home nearby.

♛ Q ⛾ ❀ ◐ ◑ ♿ ♣ P

Try also: Lord Palmerstone, Golden Hill Fort (Free)

Nettlestone

Roadside Inn

Nettlestone Green

☎ (0983) 612381

11–11

Gale's Best Bitter, HSB Ⓗ

Family-run village pub in mock Tudor style. Family atmosphere and reasonable prices. Features a daily specials board (eve meals June–Sept only; no food Wed in summer). Collection of model cars on display in the lounge bar.

Q ⛾ ❀ ⛿ ◐ ◑ ♣ P

Newport

Prince of Wales

36 South Street (opp. bus station) ☎ (0983) 525026

11–3, 6–11 (11–11 summer)

Ushers Best Bitter, Founders [H]
Good, basic street-corner boozer. ♨ ◖ ◗ ♣

Try also: Railway Medina, Sea St (Gale's)

Niton

Buddle Inn

St Catherine's Road, Undercliffe (follow signs to St Catherine's Point)
☎ (0983) 730243
11–3, 6–11; 11–11 Fri, Sat & summer
Draught Bass; Brakspear Bitter; Whitbread Flowers IPA, Original [H]**; guest beers**
Ancient, stone-built pub with strong smuggling connections. Home cooking; family room in summer.
♨ ♘ ❀ ◖ ◗ ♿ ▲ ♣ P

Try also: White Lion, High St (Whitbread)

Northwood

Travellers Joy

85 Pallance Road (off B3325)
☎ (0983) 298024
11–2.30, 5–11 (11–11 summer)
Draught Bass; Burts Nipper; Gibbs Mew Bishop's Tipple; Ringwood Old Thumper; Ruddles County; S&N Theakston Old Peculier [H]
Local CAMRA *Pub of the Year* 1992. One cask-conditioned cider and a real mild always available. The large garden has a play area for children. Always a friendly atmosphere; good value food.
♘ ❀ ◖ ◗ ▲ ♣ ⌓ P

Try also: Horseshoe (Gale's)

Rookley

Chequers

Off A320 ☎ (0983) 840314
11–3, 6–11
Burts Nipper; Courage Best Bitter, Directors; John Smith's Bitter [H]
Superb country roadhouse serving good value food. Extensively refurbished and extended although very much a restaurant with a bar. The stone-flagged public bar remains a haven for drinkers.
♨ Q ♘ ❀ ◖ ◗ ⊞ ▲ ♣ P

Try also: Mallards (Free)

Ryde

Castle

164 High Street (10 mins' walk from ferry) ☎ (0983) 811138
10.30–11
Gale's XXXD (summer)**, BBB, 5X, HSB** [H]
Traditional, two-level, open-plan pub in the town centre, with original etched-glass windows and an open fire. A fine example of an unspoilt pub. ♨ ⇌ ♣

Lake Superior

59 Marlborough Road, Elmfield (Ryde–Sandown road) ☎ (0983) 563519
11–3, 5.30–11
Bass Worthington BB, Draught Bass; Burts Newport Best Bitter; Eldridge Pope Royal Oak; Hall & Woodhouse Tanglefoot; Taylor Landlord [H]
Very friendly local (lovely loos!). The dartboard is always in use. ♨ ♘ ❀ ♿ ♣ P

Yelfs Hotel

Union Street ☎ (0983) 564062
10.30–11
Draught Bass; Burts Newport Best Bitter; Ind Coope Burton Ale; Whitbread Flowers Original [H]
Pleasant bar in a large, plush town-centre hotel with a patio drinking area and a relaxed atmosphere.
♨ Q ❀ 🛏 ◖ ◗ ⇌ ⚟

Sandown

Commercial

15 St Johns Road (off High St)
☎ (0983) 403848
10.30–11
Gale's BBB, Best Bitter, HSB [H]
Pub with a pleasant, subtle decor and a pool table in the lounge. All the Gale's country wines are available; food in summer only.
♨ ♘ ◖ ◗ ⊞ ♿ ⇌ ♣

Try also: Castle, Fitzroy St (Inntrepreneur)

Wroxall

Star Inn

Clarence Road (B3327)
☎ (0983) 854701
11–3, 7–11
Ansells Bitter; Burts Nipper, Newport Best Bitter; Ringwood Best Bitter [H]
Spacious village pub with two bars, in a pleasant country setting. Normally six cask ales on offer; food available at all times. An original Burts brewery pub. ❀ ◖ ◗ ♣ P

Yarmouth

Wheatsheaf Inn

Bridge Road ☎ (0983) 760456
11–3, 7–11
Eldridge Pope Royal Oak; Mitchell's ESB; Whitbread Boddingtons Bitter, Flowers Original [H]**; guest beers** [G]
Deservedly popular two-bar pub in a small harbour town. The public bar is busy all year, and the whole pub can be crowded summer weekends, due to its excellent reputation for food. A recent extension to the lounge provides more dining area and the large conservatory serves as a family room. ♨ Q ♘ ❀ ◖ ◗ ♿

The Symbols

♨	real fire	♿	easy wheelchair access
Q	quiet pub (at least one bar)	▲	camping facilities at the pub or nearby
♘	indoor room for children	⇌	near British Rail station
❀	garden or other outdoor drinking area	⊖	near underground station
🛏	accommodation	♣	pub games
◖	lunchtime meals	⌓	real cider
◗	evening meals	P	pub car park
⊞	public bar	⚟	no-smoking room or area

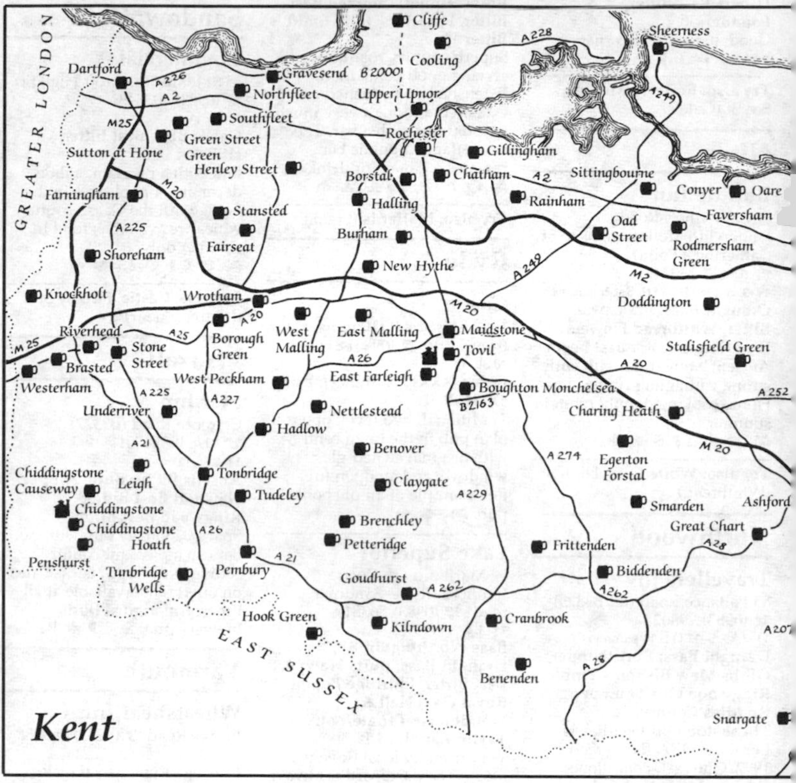

Goacher's, *Tovil;* **Larkins**, *Chiddingstone;* **Shepherd Neame**, *Faversham*

Ashford

Beaver Road Off-Licence

36 Beaver Road (A2070, near station) ☎ (0233) 622904
11 (3 Wed)–10.15; 12–3, 7–10.15 Sun
Beer range varies Ⓖ
Friendly off-licence with at least two beers during the week and four at weekends, from all around the country, on average 20/25% cheaper than pub prices. Taste before you buy. ⇌

Hare & Hounds

Maidstone Road, Potters Corner (A20, 2 miles from centre towards Maidstone)
☎ (0233) 621760
11–3, 5.30–11
Draught Bass; Courage Best Bitter; guest beers Ⓗ
Friendly and busy pub offering the only regular pint of Bass in the area. Popular for its good value, home-cooked food. ❀ ◖◗ P

Benenden

King William IV

The Street ☎ (0580) 240636
11–3, 6–11
Shepherd Neame Master Brew Bitter, Porter Ⓖ**, Bishops Finger** *or* **Spitfire** Ⓗ
Excellent village local with two contrasting bars: the public for those who prefer the jukebox and bandit, the saloon for those who like convivial conversation. No food Sun; eve meals Wed–Sat only.
♨ Q ❀ ◖◗ ♣ P

Try also: Bull, The Street (Free)

Benover

Woolpack Inn

Benover Road (B2162, 1 mile S of Yalding) ☎ (0892) 730356
11–2.30 (3 Sat), 6–11
Shepherd Neame Master Brew Bitter, Porter, Bishops Finger Ⓗ
Comfortable country local where a warm welcome is assured. A 17th-century pub with stone floors and open fires, a good-sized family room and a garden. Generous portions of excellent, home-cooked food (daily specials board); no food Sun eve.
♨ Q ⚇ ❀ ◖◗ ♣ P

Biddenden

Castletons Oak

Cranbrook Road (1 mile S of village; follow signs for Chest Hospital) OS846361
☎ (0580) 291385
11–11; 11–3, 6–11 Mon
Harveys BB; guest beers Ⓗ
Pebble-dashed and weatherboarded building on a crossroads. Look for the strange inn sign (old man sitting on a coffin). The single bar has two split-levels and a small dining area. Large

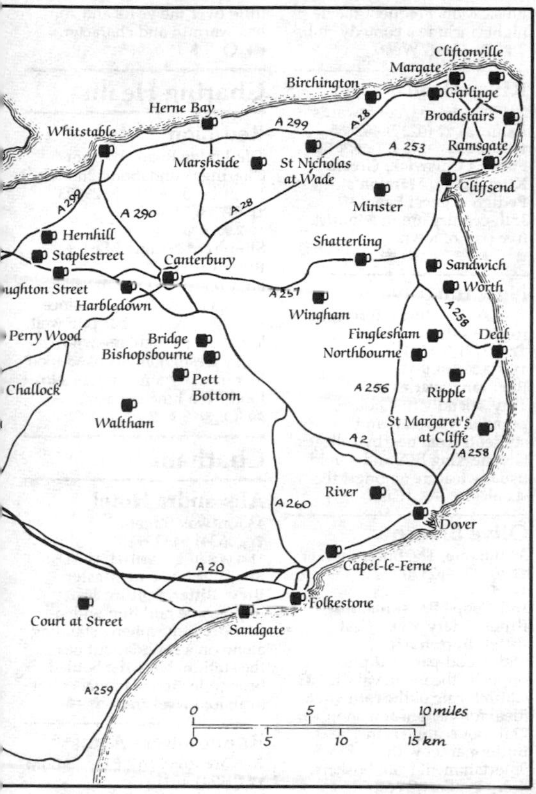

garden for families. Camping for CC members.
♨ ⛵ ❀ ◐ ◑ ⌓ P

Birchington

Seaview Hotel

96 Station Road
☎ (0843) 41702
11–11
Shepherd Neame Master Brew Bitter, Spitfire Ⓗ
Built in 1865 to cater for travellers on the newly-built London, Chatham and Dover railway: a one-bar pub boasting a friendly atmosphere and welcoming to old and young.
♨ ❀ 🛏 ◐ ◑ ▲ ⇌ ♣ P

Bishopsbourne

Mermaid

400 yds off A2
☎ (0227) 830581
11–3, 6–11
Shepherd Neame Master Brew Bitter, Porter Ⓗ
Attractive friendly pub in a typically Kentish village, the former home of author Joseph Conrad. Labour-saving electronic heads and tails tosser by the dartboard.
♨ Q ❀ ◐

Borough Green

Railway

(A227, opp. station)
☎ (0732) 882016
11–11
Mitchell's Best Bitter, Fortress, ESB Ⓗ**; guest beers**
Grand old Victorian pub of many small bars, offering one guest mild at all times, regularly changed. Mild is rare in Kent, as is the Mitchell's range. ♨ ◐ ⊟ ⇌ ♣ P

Borstal

White Horse

86 Borstal Street
☎ (0634) 842801
12–3, 7–11 (maybe 12–11 summer)
Greene King IPA, Rayments Special, Abbot Ⓗ
Smallish, popular village pub, fairly unspoilt. Bar billiards in the bar; separate lounge bar.
♨ ❀ ♣ P

Boughton Monchelsea

Red House

Hermitage Lane (off B2163, down Weirton Rd and East Hall Hill) OS783488
☎ (0622) 743986
12–3, 7–11; 12–11 Sat
Greene King IPA, Abbot; guest beers Ⓗ
Excellent free house well worth making the effort to find. The range of guest beers constantly changes but a minimum of four are usually available; also a wide selection of imported speciality beers (including fruit beer). Beerfest May. ♨ ⛵ ❀ ◐ ◑ ▲ ♣ ⌓ P

Boughton Street

Queen's Head Inn

111 The Street ☎ (0227) 751369
11–4, 6–11; 11–11 Sat
Shepherd Neame Master Brew Bitter, Porter Ⓗ
16th-century pub recently extended into a public bar, a saloon and a restaurant. Good for games.
Q ❀ 🛏 ◐ ◑ ▲ ♣ P

Try also: Woodmans Hall (Free)

Brasted

Bull Inn

High Street ☎ (0959) 562551
10.30–2.30, 5.30–11; 10.30–11 Sat
Shepherd Neame Master Brew Bitter, Spitfire, Porter, Bishops Finger Ⓗ
Busy main-road pub in a village full of antique shops, catering for local and passing trade. Neo-Tudor-style decor; friendly service. The food is popular and often worth booking. ❀ ◐ ◑ ♣ P

Brenchley

Bull

High Street ☎ (0892) 722701
11–3, 5–11
Greene King IPA, Abbot; Shepherd Neame Best Bitter; guest beer Ⓗ
Single-bar Victorian inn attracting mainly regulars, but a very warm welcome is given to strangers. Darts and quiz nights are held weekly. Set at the centre of a village that has won the *Best Kept Village in England* award. Well worth a visit. ♨ Q ❀ 🛏 ◐ ◑ ♿ ♣ P

Bridge

Plough & Harrow

High Street ☎ (0227) 830455
11–3, 6–11
Shepherd Neame Master Brew Bitter, Porter Ⓗ
Friendly village local, good for games. Originally a maltings and brewery, 302 years old.
♨ Q ▲ ♣ P

Try also: White Horse (Free)

Broadstairs

Brown Jug
204 Ramsgate Road, Dumpton (A255) ☎ (0843) 862788
11–3, 6–11 (may be 11–11 summer)
Greene King IPA; King & Barnes Sussex; Whitbread Fremlins Bitter Ⓗ
Reputedly a billet for officers during the Napoleonic wars, this flint-walled pub of real character, run by two sisters, stands out in an area lacking decent real ale. Quiz nights, games and a homely atmosphere in the best sense. Intriguing collection of jugs.
⩩ Q ❀ ⊟ ⇌ (Dumpton Pk) ♣ P

Lord Nelson
11 Nelson Place
☎ (0843) 861210
11–3.30, 6.30–11; 11–11 Sat
Whitbread Fremlins Bitter Ⓗ
Building which began life as a tailor's and draper's, before becoming a pub in 1815. A cosy, intimate pub with a welcoming clientele and full of Nelsonian memorabilia. A short and rewarding walk up from the beach. ❀ ⇌ ♣

Burham

Toastmasters Inn
65–67 Church Street
☎ (0634) 861299
11.45–3.30, 5.30–11; 11.45–11 Thu, Fri & Sat
Beer range varies Ⓗ
Pub tucked out of the way but providing an excellent combination of good food and ale. Seven handpumps usually provide a surprise, with real cider to boot. Separate restaurant. ❀ ◑ ◗ ⌓ P

Windmill
Rochester Road
☎ (0634) 861919
11–3, 6–11
Bass Worthington BB; Fuller's London Pride; S&N Theakston Best Bitter Ⓗ
A recent conversion to a free house, this pub is worth a visit for its bar billiards table and popular back-room restaurant, especially Sun. ◑ ◗ ♣ P

Canterbury

Canterbury Tales
12 The Friars (opp. Marlowe Theatre) ☎ (0227) 768594
11–11
Goacher's Light; Shepherd Neame Master Brew Bitter; guest beers Ⓗ
Lively pub decorated in 1920s pastels, with a marble bar and theatrical memorabilia. Live music Mon. Frequent theme nights include a comedy club.
◑ ◗ ⇌ (East/West)

Kings Head
204 Wincheap (A28 towards Ashford) ☎ (0227) 462885
11–2.30, 6.30–11; 12–2, 7–10.30 Sun
Fuller's Chiswick; Greene King Abbot; Marston's Pedigree; guest beers Ⓗ
15th-century inn in a tourist-free part of town.
❀ ◑ ◗ ⇌ (East) ♣

New Inn
19 Havelock Street (off ring road, E side of city)
☎ (0227) 464584
11–3 (3.30 Sat), 6–11
Beer range varies Ⓗ
Tiny, friendly free house, popular with staff and students from nearby colleges. Greene King IPA and a mild usually feature amongst the six ales. ❀ ⇌ (East)

Olive Branch
39 Burgate, The Buttermarket
☎ (0227) 462170
11–11
Ind Coope Benskins Best Bitter, Friary Meux Best Bitter, Burton Ale Ⓗ
Old, wood-panelled pub opposite the medieval Christ Church gate of the cathedral; ideal for visitors and shoppers. Outdoor seating is in The Buttermarket with entertainment from buskers.
◑ ♿ ⇌ (East/West)

Try also: Canterbury Beer Shop, Northgate (off-licence); **Imperial**, Martyrs Field Rd (Free)

Capel-le-Ferne

Royal Oak
New Dover Road (old A20)
☎ (0303) 244787
11.30–3 (4 Sat), 6 (7 Sat)–11
Morland Old Speckled Hen; Shepherd Neame Master Brew Bitter; Wadworth 6X Ⓗ**; guest beers**
Split-level, two-bar pub next to a camping and caravan park (channel views). Ten minutes' drive from the channel tunnel terminal. The amusement machines and pool table are kept well away from the cosy main bar. ⩩ ◑ ⊟ ▲ ♣ P

Challock

Chequers
Church Lane ☎ (0233) 740672
11–3, 7–11
Adnams Bitter; Courage Best Bitter; Greene King IPA; guest beer Ⓗ
Built in 1629 from ships' timbers and first sold ale in 1635; originally thatched, then tiled with Kent pegs in the 1700s. Once partly used as a shop, but the inn has changed little over the years and still has warmth and character.
⩩ Q ◑ ◗ P

Charing Heath

Red Lion
Tile Lodge Road (W from Charing roundabout, 2nd left, 1½ miles on left) OS929493
☎ (0233) 712418
11–2.30, 6.30–11
Shepherd Neame Master Brew Bitter Ⓗ
First registered in 1709 and known as the Red Lion since 1762: a cosy, two-bar pub well loved by its regulars, who enjoy fresh, home-cooked food in a friendly atmosphere. No food Mon lunch or Sun.
⩩ Q ❀ ◑ ◗ P

Chatham

Alexandra Hotel
43 Railway Street
☎ (0634) 843959
11–3 (4 Sat), 5 (7 Sat)–11; 11–11 Fri
Shepherd Neame Master Brew Bitter, Spitfire Ⓗ
Impressive building with a friendly atmosphere, standing alone on a roundabout near the station. Note the bottled beer collection. Bar snacks not available weekends. ❀ ⇌

Ropemakers Arms
70 New Road (A2 near station)
☎ (0634) 402121
12–3, 7–11
Goacher's Light; Greene King Abbot; guest beers Ⓗ
Friendly locals' pub, peaceful, despite being on the main road. Formerly used by ropery workers from Chatham Dockyard. No food Sat; Sun lunch by arrangement.
◑ ⇌ ♣ P

Chiddingstone Causeway

Little Brown Jug
On B2027 opp. Penshurst station ☎ (0892) 870318
11.30–3, 6.30–11
Harveys BB Ⓗ**; guest beers**
Warm, family-run traditional inn which stocks a good selection of ales (at least three guests). The bar food is well recommended; B&B available.
⩩ Q ❀ 🛏 ◑ ◗ ♿ ▲
⇌ (Penshurst) ♣ ⌓ P

Chiddingstone Hoath

Rock
Midway between Penshurst and Chiddingstone
☎ (0892) 870296
11.30–3, 5.30–11
Larkins Bitter; Shepherd Neame Master Brew Bitter Ⓗ

Set in the middle of the Kent countryside, this old oak-beamed pub has a stone floor in the public bar, with a fire-warmed lounge on a slightly higher level. Well worth the drive to find it.
♨ Q ❀ ◖ ◗ ⊞ ♿ ▲
⇌ (Penshurst) ♣ P

Claygate

White Hart
On B2162 ☎ (0892) 730313
11–3, 6–11
Goacher's Light; Shepherd Neame Master Brew Bitter; Wadworth 6X Ⓗ
Friendly local: a comfortable two-bar house set in open countryside of orchards and hop gardens. Good value bar snacks; separate restaurant.
♨ ❀ 🛏 ◖ ◗ ♿ ⇌ ♣ ⌂ P

Cliffe

Victoria Inn
Church Street ☎ (0634) 220356
11–3, 7–11; 12–11 Sat; 12–3, 7.30–10.30 Sun
Shepherd Neame Master Brew Bitter Ⓗ
Situated in the centre of Cliffe village, near Rochester: a friendly locals' pub offering traditional folk nights and an unusual farmyard in the garden. Beware the keg Scrumpy Jack cider on fake handpump. ♨ ❀ ♣

Cliffsend

Sportsman
123 Sandwich Road (A256, between Ramsgate and Sandwich) ☎ (0843) 592175
11–11
Shepherd Neame Master Brew Bitter, Spitfire Ⓗ
Overlooking Pegwell Bay, a pub dating back to 1750 with strong claims for a smuggling past. Recently changed ownership and now a popular village local as well as a welcoming roadhouse for travellers. ♨ Q ❀ ◖ ♣ P

Cliftonville

Olde Charles Tavern
Northdown Road
☎ (0843) 221817
11–3, 6–11; 11–11 Sat
Courage Best Bitter; Ruddles County; Webster's Yorkshire Bitter Ⓗ
Not as old as it may appear, this pub is Edwardian rather than Tudor. The spacious interior still manages to be cosy, with sofas supplementing the usual pub furniture. Carvery upstairs, although food can be eaten downstairs. Check for eve meals in winter. A good place for a family. ♨ ❀ 🛏 ◖ ◗ P

Conyer

Brunswick Arms
The Street ☎ (0795) 521569
12–2.30 (3 Sat; not Mon); 7–11
Courage Best Bitter; guest beers Ⓗ
Welcoming, two-bar local with a Kentish dartboard and a skittle alley (for hire). Two varying guest beers, one always at a low price. Good value meals, including steak promotions. ♨ ❀ ◖ ◗ ♣

Ship Inn & Smugglers Restaurant
Conyer Quay, Teynham
☎ (0795) 521404
11–3, 6–11
Beer range varies Ⓗ
Enterprising, creekside free house, providing an ever-changing range of five beers, as well as Biddenden cider and 175 malt whiskies. Happy hour until 7pm every eve, except Sat. Noted for food; seafood is a speciality. Annual beer festivals. ❀ ◖ ◗ ♣ ⌂

Cooling

Horseshoe & Castle
Main Road ☎ (0634) 221691
11.30–3, 7–11
Beer range varies Ⓗ
Nestled in the quiet, picturesque village of Cooling (near Rochester), noted for its Dickensian connections, this pub offers three real ales and good food. Said to have a haunted cellar. No food Tue eve. ❀ ◖ ◗ ♣ ⌂ P ⊬

Court at Street

Welcome Stranger
On B2067, 1 mile W of Port Lympne wildlife park
☎ (0233) 720400
12–2 (3 Sat), 6–11
Shepherd Neame Master Brew Bitter Ⓗ**; guest beers**
One-bar locals' pub, but all are welcome. Occasional cider; no lager. One of a dying breed of pubs and a proper watering hole. Q ❀ ⌂ P

Cranbrook

Prince of Wales
High Street ☎ (0580) 713058
11.30–2.30, 6.30–11
Beer range varies Ⓗ
Renowned town-centre free house of two bars: a public with a jukebox, pool, etc. and a split-level, simply furnished saloon. Can get very busy and has a vibrant atmosphere. Always has at least three real ales. Occasional mini-beer festivals. ♨ ❀ ◖ ◗

Try also: All pubs in Cranbrook sell real ale

Dartford

Fulwich
150 St Vincents Road (off A226 E of centre) ☎ (0322) 223683
11–2.30, 6.30–11; 11–11 Fri & Sat; 12–2.30, 7–10.30 Sun
Ind Coope Burton Ale; Tetley Bitter; guest beer Ⓗ
A popular public bar frequented by a younger clientele, and a quieter, plusher saloon. ◖ ⊞ ⇌ ♣

Tiger
28 St Albans Road (off A226, E of centre) ☎ (0322) 293688
11–11
Courage Best Bitter; Shepherd Neame Master Brew Bitter; John Smith's Bitter Ⓗ**; guest beer**
Back-street, one-bar local, with a 'posh' end. The guest beer changes monthly. ❀ ◖ ⇌ ♣

Wat Tyler
High Street ☎ (0322) 272546
11 (10 Thu & Sat)–11
Courage Best Bitter; S&N Theakston Mild; guest beers Ⓗ
Long, narrow 14th-century town pub. A rare outlet for mild. A mystery house beer, Wat Tyler Bitter, is reasonably priced. Two guest beers change all the time; cider varies. Folk music Fri eve and Sun lunch. Q ◖ ⇌ ⌂

Deal

Admiral Keppel
90 Manor Road (off A258)
☎ (0304) 374024
12–11
Draught Bass; Charrington IPA Ⓗ
Welcoming local in Upper Deal, worth the walk to find. A former multi-bar pub but still cosy. Beware the car park's entrance. ❀ ◖ ♣ P

Alma Hotel
126 West Street
☎ (0304) 360244
11–3, 7–11
Courage Directors; Ridleys IPA, Winter Ale Ⓗ
Cosy pub with a horseshoe-shaped bar displaying a collection of naval memorabilia. Selection of mustards sold. The landlord is a former Ridleys employee who collects his own beer. ⇌ ♣

King's Head
9 Beach Street ☎ (0304) 368194
11–3, 6–11; 11–11 Sat
Ruddles County; Shepherd Neame Master Brew Bitter; Wadworth 6X; Webster's Yorkshire Bitter Ⓗ
Lively pub near the seafront, attracting a young clientele.
❀ 🛏 ⇌ P

Saracens Head
Alfred Square ☎ (0304) 381650
11–3 (4 Fri), 6 (6.30 Fri)–11; 11–11 Sat
Shepherd Neame Master Brew Bitter, Spitfire, Porter [H]
Large, single-bar corner pub in an historic part of town.
♨ ◖ ◗ ⇌

Ship Inn
141 Middle Street
☎ (0304) 372222
11–11
Draught Bass; Charrington IPA; Fuller's ESB; Greene King Abbot; Shepherd Neame Master Brew Bitter [H]
Cosy pub in the old part of town near the seafront, with Royal Navy prints and memorabilia in the bar. Live piano Sun. ♨ ◖ ◗ ⊟ ⇌

Doddington

Chequers
The Street
11–3.45, 7–11; 11–11 Fri & Sat
Shepherd Neame Master Brew Bitter, Porter, Bishops Finger [H]
Friendly and welcoming local, over 500 years old, with historic smuggling connections and two ghosts. A rare outlet in the area for Bishops Finger.
♨ ❀ ◖ ♣ P

Dover

Blakes
52 Castle Street (near market square) ☎ (0304) 202194
11–3, 7–11; closed Sun
Draught Bass; Fuller's London Pride; Wadworth IPA [H]**; guest beers**
Popular town-centre wine bar noted for its beer and food. Two bars attract a smart clientele; busy lunchtime with office staff. Usually two guest beers. Q ❀ ◖ ◗ ⇌ (Priory)

Boars Head
46–48 Eaton Road
☎ (0304) 204490
11–3, 6–11; 11–11 Sat
Greene King IPA, Rayments Special, Abbot [H]
Busy local in a residential area, well worth the effort of finding. Formerly a Whitbread tied house (don't be put off by the pub sign), it offers a changing selection of beers. Occasional live music; skittle alley. ♨ ❀ ◖ ⇌ (Priory) ♣

Crown & Sceptre
25 Elms Vale Road
☎ (0304) 201971
11.30–3 (4 Sat), 7–11; 11.30–11 Fri
Shepherd Neame Master Brew Bitter, Spitfire [H]
Two-bar local in a residential area, formerly a Charrington house. The walls are adorned with a collection of ship prints.
❀ ⇌ (Priory) ♣

Eagle Hotel
London Road ☎ (0304) 201543
10–11
Courage Best Bitter, Directors; John Smith's Bitter [H]**; guest beer** (occasionally)
Large, two-bar corner pub surmounted by a golden eagle. Spacious separate games area and occasional live music.
⊟ ⇌ (Priory) ♣

King Lear
Old Folkestone Road, Aycliffe
☎ (0304) 204756
11–3.30, 6.30–11; 11–11 Fri & Sat
Bateman Mild, Salem Porter; Whitbread Fremlins Bitter [H]
Local pub in a scenic part of Dover, now cruelly defaced by the construction of the new A20. ♨ ❀ ⇌ (Western Docks) ⌓ P

East Farleigh

Victory
Farleigh Bridge (by station)
☎ (0622) 726591
11–11
Goacher's Mild, Light (summer), **Dark** (winter); **Tetley Bitter** *or* **Ind Coope Burton Ale** [H]
Small, friendly local overlooking the river; ideal for sunny afternoons in the garden watching the boats.
⊳ ❀ ◖ ◗ ▲ ⇌ ♣

Walnut Tree
Forge Lane ☎ (0622) 726368
12–3, 6–11
Shepherd Neame Master Brew Bitter, Spitfire [H]
Low-beamed country pub with interesting memorabilia. The large beer garden can get quite busy. Home-cooked food includes an extensive vegetarian range.
♨ Q ❀ ◖ ◗ ♿ ▲ P

East Malling

Rising Sun
Mill Street ☎ (0732) 843284
12–11
Goacher's Light; Harveys BB; Shepherd Neame Master Brew Bitter [H]**; guest beer**
Recently refurbished but still retaining village local charm and comfort. A family-run pub attracting friendly regulars with its keenly priced beers and good value food.
❀ ◖ ◗ ♿ ⇌ ♣

Egerton Forstal

Queens Arms
SW from Egerton to T-junction, turn right, then 1st left, 300 yds OS893464
☎ (0233) 76386
11–3, 6–11
King & Barnes Sussex; Palmers IPA; Wadworth IPA [H]**; guest beers** [G]

Comfortable local with timber beams 150 years old. The landlady's father was Bombardier Billy Wells, the boxer, after whom Charles Wells Brewery named Bombardier Bitter. Try the excellent all day breakfasts. No meals Tue. Jazz Sun lunchtime. ♨ ❀ ◖ ◗ ♣ ⌓ P

Fairseat

Vigo
Gravesend Road (A227, 1 mile N of A20) ☎ (0732) 822547
12–2.30 (3 Sat, not Mon), 6–11
Harveys XX Mild, BB; Young's Bitter, Special; guest beers [H]
An ale drinkers' haunt: an ancient drovers' inn which still has a large paddock behind for penning cattle overnight. At least six beers at any time. Can be noisy if the Kentish form of table skittles, Dadlums, is in progress. ♨ Q ♣ P ⊬

Farningham

Chequers
High Street ☎ (0322) 865222
11–11
Fuller's London Pride, ESB; Morland Old Speckled Hen; guest beers [H]
Enterprising free house in a pleasant village just off the A20. At least six beers change weekly. ♨ ❀ ◖ ♣

Faversham

Crown & Anchor
41 The Mall ☎ (0795) 532812
10.30–3 (4 Sat), 5.30 (6 Sat)–11
Shepherd Neame Master Brew Bitter [H]
Unspoilt pub whose engaging Hungarian landlord is proud of his home-cooked food. Specialities include goulash, steaks, omelettes and doorstep sandwiches. No food Sun.
⊳ ◖ ⇌ ♣

Elephant Inn
31 The Mall ☎ (0795) 590157
11.30–2.30 (3 Sat), 5.30–11 (11–11 summer)
Greene King XX Mild, IPA, Rayments Special, Abbot [H]**; guest beers**
Former Fremlins pub which probably has the most extensive range of beers in Kent (up to 22 real ales). Well refurbished, especially the garden/barbecue area, children's room (a former brewhouse) and eating area – a 'Tardis' of delights.
⊳ ❀ ◖ ◗ ⇌ ♣

Finglesham

Crown
The Street ☎ (0304) 612555
11–3, 6–11

Marston's Pedigree; Ruddles County; Shepherd Neame Master Brew Bitter, Porter; Webster's Yorkshire Bitter Ⓗ
Popular village local and restaurant; friendly and welcoming. Food available at all times. 🏔 ◑ ◗ P

Folkestone

Richmond Tavern
1 Margaret Street
☎ (0303) 254857
11–3 (2.30 Mon & Thu, 4 Sat), 6 (7 Sat)–11
Shepherd Neame Master Brew Bitter Ⓗ
Thriving street-corner pub catering for a local trade. Holds regular fund-raising activities in aid of *Guide Dogs for the Blind*.
❀ ⥃ (Harbour) ♣

Frittenden

Knoxbridge Inn
Cranbrook Road (A229 Cranbrook–Staplehurst road)
☎ (0580) 891298
12 (6 Mon)–11
Fuller's London Pride; Harveys Pale Ale; Hook Norton Best Bitter; Larkins Sovereign Ⓗ**; guest beers**
Enterprising and popular roadhouse: a single, long, U-shaped bar (where one end is like a public bar, the other a saloon), plus a small dining area. Occasional live music and mini-beer festivals.
🏔 ❀ ◑ ◗ ♿ ⛺ ♣ P

Garlinge

Hussar
221 Canterbury Road
☎ (0843) 831732
11–11
Charrington IPA Ⓗ
Large roadside pub easily missed on the way into Margate. The large, single-bar interior manages to keep a pleasant atmosphere. Music at weekends. ❀ ◑ ♣ P

Gillingham

Barge
63 Layfield Road
☎ (0634) 850485
12–3.30, 7–11; 11–11 Sat
Wadworth 6X; guest beers Ⓗ
Pub with a recently remodelled interior and a picturesque view of the River Medway. Well worth finding. The three guest beers are frequently changed. ❀ ♣

Cannon
15 Garden Street, Brompton
☎ (0634) 841006
11–11
Webster's Yorkshire Bitter; guest beer Ⓗ
Ex-Truman's pub which retains the original tiled frontage: a busy, two-bar local which is due for extension. Large beer garden. ❀ ⊞ ♣

King George V
1 Prospect Row, Brompton (near Chatham Dockyard)
☎ (0634) 842418
11.30–4, 6 (7 Sat)–11
Draught Bass Ⓗ**; guest beers**
Formerly the King of Prussia, owned by Winch of Chatham: a pub with strong naval connections. No food Sun. Q ◑

Napier Arms
153 Britton Street (off Canterbury St) ☎ (0634) 578219
12–3, 5.30–11; 11–11 Fri & Sat
Beer range varies Ⓗ
Two-bar lively local, where Gillingham FC was formed. Good value snacks available. Open quiz nights Sun. Three handpumps offer an ever-changing choice of ales.
ꝏ ⊞ ⥃ ♣

Roseneath
79 Arden Street (off High St)
☎ (0634) 852553
11.30–11
Beer range varies Ⓗ
Busy back-street local which holds an annual charity beer festival in the garden. Snakehound Ale is a house ale (named after the breed of the pub dog, Golly), brewed by Goacher's. The large garden has a play area. Shirts must be worn in the bar, but a very friendly atmosphere prevails.
❀ ◑ ◗ ⥃ ♣

Try also: Golden Lion, Brompton High St (Courage)

Goudhurst

Green Cross
Station Road (A262, 1 mile W of village) ☎ (0580) 211200
12–2.30, 6.30–11; 12–2.30 Sun, closed Sun eve
Archers Black Jack; Exmoor Ale; Harveys BB Ⓗ
Quiet country pub with a large open bar and a restaurant at the rear. Close to Finchcocks Garden. Good range of malt whiskies. 🏔 Q ❀ ◑ ◗ P

Gravesend

Jolly Drayman
1 Love Lane (off A226 by BP garage) ☎ (0474) 352355
11–2.30, 6–11; 12–3, 7–11 Sat
Draught Bass; Charrington IPA; Fuller's London Pride; guest beers Ⓗ
Low-ceilinged pub in the offices of a former brewery. Handy for central shops and offices, with a good, friendly atmosphere. The entrance is in Wellington St. Lunches served weekdays only. ❀ ◑ ⥃ ♣ P

Kent & Essex
98 Old Road West (B261, ½ mile from station along Darnley Rd)
☎ (0474) 352186
11–11
Brakspear Special; Courage Directors; Webster's Yorkshire Bitter Ⓗ
Lively local with a wide range of customers, in a part of town where good beer is scarce. Highly-rated folk club in the function room on Thu (admission charged). Beware the keg Scrumpy Jack cider on a fake handpump. No food Sun. ꝏ ❀ ◑ ♿ ⥃ ♣ P

Somerset Arms
10 Darnley Road (one-way system near station)
☎ (0474) 533837
11–3.30, 5–11; 11–11 Fri & Sat
Beer range varies Ⓗ
Centrally located, recently refurbished and extended pub where decorations include pictures of old Gravesend. Friendly service with a good mix of customers. Good food and an impressive range of guest beers. Weekend discos. Eve meals Mon–Thu.
🛏 ◑ ◗ ⥃ ♣

Windmill Tavern
45 Shrubbery Road (on Windmill Hill, off Parrock St)
☎ (0474) 352242
11–11
Harveys BB; Ruddles Best Bitter, County; Wadworth 6X; Webster's Yorkshire Bitter; guest beers Ⓗ
A country pub in town, with a prize-winning garden (summer barbecues). Not easy to find: head away from the town centre and climb the east side of the hill. No-smoking area only at lunchtime.
❀ ◑ ◗ ⊞ ♿ ⥃ ♣ P ⚟

Try also: Prince Albert, Wrotham Rd (Shepherd Neame)

Great Chart

Hooden Horse
The Street ☎ (0233) 625583
11–2.30, 6–11
Goacher's Light; Hook Norton Old Hooky; Hop Back Summer Lightning; S&N Theakston Old Peculier; Taylor Landlord; guest beer Ⓗ
Tiled and timbered floors, a hop-decorated ceiling and scattered tables and chairs characterise this pub. Two guests always available (including a mild), plus good, home-cooked food. Jazz nights monthly. ❀ ◑ ◗ ⌓

Try also: Swan (Whitbread)

Kent

Green Street Green

Ship
Green Street Green Road (B260) ☎ (0474) 702279
12–3.30, 6–11
Courage Best Bitter; Wadworth 6X; Young's Bitter Ⓗ
Popular, 17th-century hostelry where the landlord is always ready to discuss the merits – or otherwise – of Kent County Cricket Club. Excellent value lunches – especially the bacon doorsteps. Regular gourmet/curry nights. Families welcome in the converted stables. The beer range may vary. ⛬ ☺ ❀ ◖ ♿ P

Hadlow

Rose Revived
Ashes Lane (A26 Tonbridge road) ☎ (0732) 850382
11–3, 6–11
Harveys BB; King & Barnes Sussex; Wadworth 6X; guest beer Ⓗ
Pleasant old pub, split into three bar areas, with oak beams throughout. Attracts a mixed clientele; mainly regulars but also passing trade. Boasts a collection of old keys. ⛬ Q ❀ ◖ ♿ ⛺ P

Halling

Homeward Bound
High Street ☎ (0634) 240743
12–3, 7–11
Shepherd Neame Master Brew Bitter Ⓗ
Friendly, one-bar village pub with pool and darts. No lunches Sun. ⛬ ❀ ◖ ⇌ ♣ P

Harbledown

Old Coach & Horses
Church Hill ☎ (0227) 761330
11.30–2.30 (3 Sat), 6 (7 Sat)–11
Beer range varies Ⓗ
Pub near the Black Prince's Well. The precipitous garden offers views over orchards and hop gardens. Two or three real ales available, from a list of Young's, Fuller's, Adnams, Courage and Greene King beers. ⛬ ❀ ◖ ◗ P

Henley Street

Cock Inn
Gold Street (1 mile from Sole Street station) OS664672
☎ (0474) 814208
12–2.30 (not Mon), 5–11; 11–11 Sat
Beer range varies Ⓗ/Ⓖ
Deservedly popular country pub where the range of ales is constantly varied (minimum of ten at any time); also up to four real ciders. Well worth the walk from the station.
⛬ Q ❀ ♣ ⌓ P

Herne Bay

Prince of Wales
173 Mortimer Street (near seafront) ☎ (0227) 374205
10–3.30, 6–11
Shepherd Neame Master Brew Bitter Ⓗ
Pub with a high-ceilinged, Victorian interior with some good glass and woodwork. The large games room has two pool tables. Q ♿ ♣

Rose Inn
111 Mortimer Street
☎ (0227) 375081
10–11
Fuller's London Pride; Shepherd Neame Master Brew Bitter; guest beers Ⓗ
Smart, comfortable pub in the pedestrianised area near the seafront. ◖ ♣

Hernhill

Red Lion
Crookham Lane
☎ (0227) 751207
11–3, 6–11; 11–11 Sat
Fuller's London Pride; Shepherd Neame Master Brew Bitter; guest beers Ⓗ
Enterprising one-bar pub and upstairs restaurant, set in an historic village. Originally a 14th-century hall house. Three other varying beers available. The garden features a children's play area, Bat and Trap and petanque.
☺ ❀ ◖ ◗ ♣ P

Hook Green

Elephants Head
On B2169, between Frant and Lamberhurst OS655359
☎ (0892) 890279
11–3, 6–11
Harveys XX Mild, Pale Ale, BB, Old Ale, Armada Ⓗ
Overlooking hopfields, a pub almost astride the county boundary. One of the few Harveys pubs to stock the entire range, including special brews. Lots of inglenooks and beams; highly recommended.
⛬ Q ❀ ◖ ◗ ♣ P

Kilndown

Globe & Rainbow
SW of Lamberhurst; 1st left off A21 OS700353 ☎(0892) 890283
11–2.30, 6–11
Harveys BB; Whitbread Fremlins Bitter, Flowers IPA, Original; Young's Special Ⓗ
Pub with a very large bar area, with basic fitments, plus a spacious garden and a fairly new restaurant. Check out the 30 malt whiskies on a cart-wheel above the bar and try the sandwich steak.
⛬ Q ❀ 🛏 ◖ ◗ ⌓ P

Knockholt

Harrow Inn
Harrow Road ☎ (0959) 532168
11–2.30 (3.30 Sat), 5.30–11
Shepherd Neame Master Brew Bitter, Best Bitter, Spitfire, Porter, Bishops Finger Ⓗ
Edge-of-village pub, popular with office workers at lunchtime and locals in the eve, with pub games and quizzes. Dates back to the 14th century. Families welcome.
⛬ Q ❀ ◖ ◗ ⛺ ♣ P

Leigh

Fleur de Lis
High Street ☎ (0732) 832235
11–2.30 (3 Sat), 6–11
Greene King IPA, Rayments Special, Abbot Ⓗ
Attractive-looking pub with plenty of window boxes in summer. The inside is heavily decorated with old farm implements and darts trophies. Regular events include quiz nights, live bands and a curry club. Eve meals Tue–Sat. ❀ ◖ ◗ ⇌ ♣ P

Maidstone

Fishers Arms
22 Scott Street (off A229 N of town) ☎ (0622) 753632
11–3, 6–11
Morland Bitter, Old Masters, Old Speckled Hen; guest beer Ⓗ
Large, single-bar, ex-Courage house now owned by Morland. The guest beer is usually from Goacher's. No food weekends.
❀ ◖ ⇌ (East) ♣

Greyhound
77 Wheeler Street (near prison)
☎ (0622) 754032
10.45–3.30, 6–11
Shepherd Neame Master Brew Bitter, Porter Ⓗ
Friendly, two-bar, street-corner local in the older part of town, a short step from the centre and worth the effort. Try the landlady's home-made weekday lunches (no food Sun). Q ❀ ◖ ⇌ (East) ♣ P

Pilot
23–25 Upper Stone Street (A229, one-way system, southbound) ☎ (0622) 691162
11–3, 6 (7 Sat)–11
Harveys XX Mild, BB, Old, Armada Ⓗ
400-year-old traditional pub offering a friendly welcome,

the only Harveys house in the Maidstone area. Live music Sun lunchtime (when no meals are served). Harveys seasonal beers when available.
⛫ ❀ ◖ ◗ ⇌ (East) ♣

Margate

Orb
243 Ramsgate Road (A254, 1 mile from centre)
☎ (0843) 220663
11–11
Shepherd Neame Master Brew Bitter [H]
A regular *Guide* entry since 1976: a two-bar local which offers special events and occasional live music by the landlord. ⛫ ⛾ ❀ ◖ ⊞ ♣ P

Princess of Wales
20 Tivoli Road
☎ (0843) 223944
11–3, 6–11; 11–11 Sat
Shepherd Neame Master Brew Bitter [H]
Unspoilt, two-bar, corner beer house, with a popular and friendly atmosphere: a good example of the type of pub which becomes rarer every year. Bar snacks. ⛾ ❀ ⊞ ♣

Quart in a Pint Pot
28 Charlotte Square
☎ (0843) 223672
11.30–3, 5.30–11; 11–11 Sat
S&N Theakston Best Bitter; Smiles Best Bitter; Thwaites Bitter [H]
Pub well worth the walk up the high street into a surprisingly intimate part of town. Look out for the pepperpot folly on the roof. Inside is a very cosy, expanded back-street pub with an intriguing and adventurous range of beers which changes regularly. Summer barbecues.
❀ ◖ ◗ ♿ ▲ ♣

Spread Eagle
25 Victoria Road
☎ (0843) 293396
11.30–11
Fuller's London Pride; Greene King IPA; Mitchell's ESB; Young's Special [H]**; guest beers**
An old reliable amongst Thanet pubs. The Victorian frontage is fixed to Georgian premises and the pub blends well into the village-like locale. Always seven real ales on the bar, and the atmosphere is welcoming and busy. No food Sun. ⛾ ❀ ◖ ◗ ♣

Marshside

Gate Inn
Chislet turn off A28 in Upstreet ☎ (0227) 860498
11–2.30 (3 Sat), 6–11
Shepherd Neame Master Brew Bitter, Spitfire, Porter, Bishops Finger [G]
Splendid country pub with ducks, apple trees, quizzes, rugby and cricket teams and a regular pub pianist. No keg lager in Lent. Pub beer festival in August; mummers at Christmas. The landlord likes to discuss theology. Smoking restrictions apply weekday lunchtimes in one bar.
⛫ Q ⛾ ❀ ◖ ◗ ♿ ▲ ♣
P ⍻

Minster (Thanet)

Saddler
Monkton Road
☎ (0843) 821331
10.30–2.30, 6–11; 11–11 Sat
Shepherd Neame Master Brew Bitter, Spitfire [H]
Very much the village local, but with a warm welcome for casual visitors. Dates back to Victorian times when a saddler occupied the cottage next door. A mainstay of Bat and Trap leagues. No meals Tue or Sun. Q ❀ ◖ ◗ ⇌ ♣

Nettlestead

Hop Pole
Nettlestead Green (B2015)
☎ (0622) 812133
11–3 (not Mon), 6–11
Fuller's London Pride; Harveys BB [H]
Comfortable, single-bar pub with a fine collection of old farm implements and dried hops. Popular at weekends for its good value bar snacks and large garden.
❀ ◖ ◗ ⇌ (Yalding) P

New Hythe

Bricklayers Arms
440 New Hythe Lane (off A228/A20) ☎ (0622) 718151
11–3, 5–11; 11–11 Fri & Sat
Courage Best Bitter; Wadworth 6X; guest beer [H]
Friendly, 18th-century pub with fishing and windsurfing nearby. Opens all day Mon–Sat in the fishing season. Good range of inexpensive pub food (not served Sun).
⛫ ❀ ◖ ◗ ♿ ⇌ ♣ P ⍻

Northbourne

Hare & Hounds
The Street ☎ (0304) 365429
10.30–3, 6–11
Draught Bass; Shepherd Neame Master Brew Bitter; guest beers [H]
Busy country pub in a rural village, popular for its food. Normally stocks two or three varied guest beers. The garden has play equipment. ❀ ◖ ◗ P

Northfleet

Six Bells Inn
Old Perry Street (off B262 near swimming pool)
☎ (0474) 567309
11–3 (4 Sat), 5.30 (6 Sat)–11
Courage Best Bitter, Directors; Wadworth 6X [H]
Old pub, possibly 16th-century in parts, in an out-of-town area where good beer is hard to find. The pub ghost is said to have been seen in the bar. The restaurant is closed Sun eve. ❀ ◖ ◗ ⊞ ♿ ♣ P

Oad Street

Plough & Harrow
Opp. craft centre
☎ (0795) 843351
11–11
Greene King IPA, Abbot; Shepherd Neame Master Brew Bitter; Tolly Cobbold Mild, Bitter; Whitbread Boddingtons Bitter [H]
Friendly, warm and welcoming free house, justly popular with locals and visitors alike. An imaginative, varying beer range makes it a real ale island in a sea of Courage. Beware the keg Scrumpy Jack. Real cider in summer. Swale CAMRA *Pub of the Year* 1992. No eve meals Mon or Tue.
⛫ ⛾ ❀ ◖ ◗ ⊞ ♣ ⌽ P

Oare

Three Mariners
Church Road
☎ (0795) 533633
10.30–3 (5 Sat), 6 (7 winter)–11
Shepherd Neame Master Brew Bitter, Spitfire, Porter [H]
Traditional nautical pub decorated with wooden flotsam and boasting a fine set of handpumps. Children's playhouse and a barbecue in the garden; views of the creek. Good value meals (must book Sun lunch). Bat and Trap played. ⛫ ⛾ ◖ ◗ ♣ P

Pembury

Black Horse
High Street ☎ (0892) 822141
11–11
Harveys BB; Marston's Pedigree; Ruddles Best Bitter; Wadworth 6X; Young's Special [H]
Very busy single bar with a mainly regular, local clientele. The restaurant specialises in fish. The Black Horse Bitter sold is a rebadged beer from an unrevealed brewery. Difficult to park.
⛫ Q ❀ ◖ ◗ ♿ ♣

Kent

Penshurst

Bottle House Inn
Smarts Hill (½ mile N of Smarts Hill on Coldharbour Lane) OS516421
☎ (0892) 870306
11–2.30, 6–11
Ind Coope Burton Ale; King & Barnes Sussex; Young's Bitter Ⓗ
Popular, remote pub dating back to the 15th century, though extensively modernised. Good food in the bar and restaurant (no meals Sun eve). The landlord is a Burton *Master Cellarman*.
♨ ❀ ◖ ◗ ⌓ P

Perry Wood

Rose & Crown
☎ (0227) 752214
12–2.30 (3 Sat), 7–11; closed Mon
Brakspear Special; Shepherd Neame Master Brew Bitter; Wadworth 6X Ⓗ**; guest beers**
16th-century free house, ideal for families, set in pleasant woodland. The large, attractive garden is complete with a children's play area and a Bat and Trap pitch. Live music every Tue eve. Local reputation for quality, freshly prepared meals.
♨ ❀ ◖ ◗ ♣ P ⊭

Pett Bottom

Duck Inn
Follow signs to Pett Bottom from Bridge ☎ (0227) 830354
11.30–3, 6.30–11
Greene King Abbot; guest beer Ⓖ
Long, low building, featured in local boy Ian Fleming's *Moonraker*. A very attractive, classic country pub.
♨ Q ⛇ ❀ ◖ ◗ ♿ ▲ ⌓ P

Petteridge

Hopbine
Petteridge Lane (off A21, ½ mile S of Brenchley)
☎ (0892) 722561
12 (11 Sat)–2.30, 6–11
King & Barnes Mild, Sussex, Broadwood, Festive Ⓗ
One-bar pub set in a picturesque area, with friendly staff and clientele. Also stocks seasonal, old and Christmas ales. Regular folk music nights and appearances in this guide. Still the only K&B house in Kent. No food Wed.
♨ ❀ ◖ ◗ ♣ P

Rainham

Green Lion
High Street (A2)
☎ (0634) 231938
11–11
Courage Best Bitter; John Smith's Bitter; guest beer Ⓗ
Built in 1346, a former coaching inn known simply as the Lion until this century. Pets corner and play area in the garden; families are welcome in the function room. Bar food Mon–Sat, lunchtime and early eve; barbecues. The Scrumpy Jack is not real cider. Prices are equal in all bars.
❀ ◖ ♣ P

Ramsgate

Artillery Arms
36 Westcliff Road
☎ (0843) 853282
11–11
John Smith's Magnet; Webster's Yorkshire Bitter; Young's Special Ⓗ**; guest beers**
Said to have been a brothel in Victorian times, this recently refurbished corner local offers an adventurous and changing roster of beers. Always open to suggestions for new beers. Lively clientele.
Q ◖ ▲ ⇌ ♣ ⌓

Churchill Tavern
The Paragon (overlooking Royal Harbour)
☎ (0843) 587862
11.30–11 (restaurant open all day Sun)
Felinfoel Double Dragon; Fuller's London Pride; Hall & Woodhouse Tanglefoot; Ringwood Old Thumper; Taylor Landlord; guest beers Ⓗ
Beautifully restored, clifftop pub rebuilt inside from old timbers and genuine church pews and now offering nine real ales. Folk club Sun; jazz Wed; quiz night Thu. Good value restaurant. No-smoking areas only at lunchtimes.
♨ Q ◖ ◗ ⌓ ⊭

Wheatsheaf
17 High Street, St Lawrence
☎ (0843) 597937
10.30–2.30 (3 Fri), 5.30–11; 11–11 Sat
Courage Directors Ⓗ**; guest beer** (occasionally)
Farmhouse-style building dating from 1883 and comprising a single bar which manages to preserve its intimacy. Lively clientele; warm welcome.
⛇ ❀ ▲ ⇌ ♣

Ripple

Plough
Church Lane (off A258 at Ringwould) OS346499
☎ (0304) 360209
11–3, 6–11 (may vary)
Draught Bass; Ind Coope Burton Ale; Shepherd Neame Master Brew Bitter; guest beers Ⓗ
Popular, 16th-century, rural local with a restaurant upstairs. A range of guest beers is usually available; occasional beer festivals held.
♨ ⛇ ❀ ◖ ◗ ♣ P

River

Royal Oak
36 Lower Road (off A256, near Dover)
☎ (0304) 822073
11–11 (may close afternoons)
Shepherd Neame Master Brew Bitter, Spitfire Ⓗ
Open-plan pub created from an original flint building and a cottage next door, in a pleasant, residential area. Crabble Mill and Kearsney Abbey gardens are nearby.
◖ ⇌ (Kearsney) ♣ P

Try also: Fox, Temple Ewell (Whitbread)

Riverhead

Beehive
28 Chipstead Lane (150 yds from A25/A2028 jct)
☎ (0732) 742601
12–3, 6–11
Adnams Bitter; Morland Old Speckled Hen; Young's Bitter, Special Ⓗ
Small, low-ceilinged, cosy pub with a relaxed atmosphere, built in 1649. The occasionally used back room contains an old bread oven. The play area in the garden includes a wendy house. Situated in a narrow one-way lane.
♨ Q ❀ ▣ ◖ ◗ ♣

Rochester

Greyhound
68 Rochester Avenue
☎ (0634) 844120
11–3, 6–11; 11–11 Sat
Shepherd Neame Master Brew Bitter, Porter Ⓗ
Late-Victorian terraced local. The public bar is basic but the saloon boasts a real coal range and four chaises-longues. Warm and cosy, with a relaxing atmosphere. No meals Sun. ♨ ❀ ◖ ⊞ ⇌ ♣

Ship Inn
347 High Street
☎ (0634) 844264
11–11
Courage Best Bitter; Wadworth 6X; guest beer Ⓗ
Lively pub, often packed to the gunwales! Live entertainment every night and live modern jazz Sun lunchtimes. Food is good value (not served Sun). ❀ ◖
⇌ (Rochester/Chatham) P

Who'd Ha' Thought It
9 Baker Street (50 yds off Maidstone Rd, B2097)
☎ (0634) 841131
11–11
Beer range varies [H]
As the name implies, a tucked-away, serious ale-drinking pub serving eight ales, usually tending toward the strong side. A real cider is also sold but beware the Scrumpy Jack. Cosy and homely. Snacks at lunchtimes. Try reading the ceiling! ♛ ❀ ⌓

Rodmersham Green

Fruiterers Arms
The Green ☎ (0795) 424198
11–3, 6–11
Courage Best Bitter, Directors; S&N Theakston Best Bitter [H]
Popular village pub with a smart lounge area and a comfortable public bar. A large garden and summer barbecues make it ideal for families. Local reputation for meals, including gourmet nights. ♛ ❀ ◖ ◗ ♣ P

St Margaret's at Cliffe

Hope Inn
High Street
☎ (0304) 852444
10.30–11
Shepherd Neame Master Brew Bitter [H]
18th-century village pub, tastefully refurbished, attracting both local and tourist trade.
♛ ❀ ◖ ◗ ▲ ♣ P

St Nicholas at Wade

Bell Inn
The Street ☎ (0843) 47250
11–2.30, 6–11
King & Barnes Sussex; Wadworth 6X; Whitbread Fremlins Bitter, Flowers IPA [H]
Easily accessible country pub dating from Tudor times, with a post-war extension to the rear. The large number of small rooms helps preserve an intimate atmosphere, especially suitable for families.
♛ Q ❀ ◖ ◗ ▲ ♣ P

Sandgate

Ship Inn
65 High Street
☎ (0303) 248525
11–3, 6–11
Greene King IPA [H]**; Ind Coope Burton Ale; Mauldons Black Adder; S&N Theakston Best Bitter** [G]**; Wadworth 6X** [H]**; Younger No. 3** [G]
Busy two-bar pub, HQ of Sandgate Clog Morris, serving excellent pub food. Caricatures of locals adorn the wall and a friendly welcome is extended to all by the highly energetic landlord, who is now, at long last, the owner. ❀ ◖ ◗ ⊞ ♣

Sandwich

Greyhound
10 New Street ☎ (0304) 612675
10–3, 7–11
Courage Best Bitter; Shepherd Neame Master Brew Bitter; Webster's Yorkshire Bitter [H]
Large, wood-panelled bar near the market. ❀ ▲ ⇌ ♣

Try also: Kings Arms, Strand St (Pubmaster)

Shatterling

Green Man
Pedding Hill (on A257 between Ash and Wingham)
☎ (0304) 812525
11–2.30 (3 Sat), 6.15–11
Shepherd Neame Master Brew Bitter; Young's Bitter, Special [H]
Isolated pub in a very attractive rural setting, drawing local, passing and tourist trade. Ideal for a relaxing stay in Kent.
❀ 🛏 ◖ ◗ ▲ ♣ P

Sheerness

Queen's Head
264 High Street
☎ (0795) 662475
11–11
Courage Best Bitter; Marston's Pedigree; Ruddles County [H]**; guest beers**
Sociable and inviting pub with split-level drinking areas. Pictures of queens past and present adorn the walls. Don't forget to enter the weekly beer raffle. ❀ ⇌ ♣

Red Lion
High Street, Blue Town
☎ (0795) 663165
12–3, 6 (8 Sat)–11; 12–3, 8–10.30 Sun
Greene King Abbot [H]**; guest beers**
Unspoilt, unpretentious beer drinkers' haven, offering the best range on Sheppey, including a Greene King house beer. The range comes specifically from independents only. Q ⊞ ⇌ ♣

Try also: Ship on Shore, Marine Parade (Free)

Shoreham

Crown
High Street ☎ (0959) 522903
11–3, 7–11
Greene King IPA, Rayments Special, Abbot [H]
Friendly, village pub offering good value food, especially the home cooking (no meals Sun eve). The cash register has to be seen. 'The pub where you are only a stranger but once.'
♛ Q ❀ ◖ ◗ ⊞ ♿ ⇌ ♣ P

Royal Oak
High Street ☎ (0959) 522319
10–3, 6–11 (may extend); 10–11 Sat
Adnams Bitter, Broadside; Brakspear Special; guest beers [H]
Very popular and friendly pub, now with Sky TV. Sephams Farm cider is made less than a mile away.
♛ ❀ ◖ ◗ ⇌ ♣ ⌓ ⚟

Sittingbourne

Barge
17 Crown Key Lane
☎ (0795) 423291
11 (11.30 Sat)–3, 5 (7 Sat)–11
Courage Best Bitter; King & Barnes Sussex; S&N Theakston Best Bitter; John Smith's Bitter [H]**; guest beers**
Formerly the White Hart. Popular with local office workers at lunchtime and offers a varying range of guest beers. ❀ ◖ ◗ ♿ ⇌ ♣ ⌓ P

Long Hop
Key Street (A2, 1 mile N of town on main bus route)
☎ (0795) 425957
11–11; 11–2.30, 6–11 Tue
Courage Best Bitter; Ruddles County [H]
Cosy, small pub in a clapboard/brick building. Friendly atmosphere.
♛ ⛄ ◖ ◗ ♿ ♣ P

Park Inn
86 Park Road (near High St)
☎ (0795) 472486
11–2.30 (4 Sat), 7–11
Shepherd Neame Master Brew Bitter, Porter [H]
Quiet corner pub with frosted windows. The saloon is popular in the eves.
♛ Q ❀ ⇌ ♣

Ship Inn
22 East Street (A2)
☎ (0795) 425087
11–3 (4 Fri & Sat), 6.30–11
Courage Best Bitter; guest beers [H]
Nice saloon with a games area; a workers' habitat. The guest beers are changed on a regular basis. No food Sun.
♛ ⛄ ◖ ◗ ⇌ ♣ P

Smarden

Bell

Bell Lane (1 mile from village)
☎ (0233) 770283
11.30–2.30 (3 Sat), 6–11
Fuller's London Pride; Goacher's Light; Harveys Pale Ale; Marston's Pedigree; Ringwood Old Thumper; Shepherd Neame Master Brew Bitter Ⓗ
Excellent, 16th-century country pub, the like of which is increasingly hard to find. A very popular, low-ceilinged, three-bar pub (one bar no-smoking), with a large family room off the main public bar. Biddenden cider. 🏰 Q ♨ ❀ 🛏 ◑ ◗ ▲ ♣ ⌓ P ⅄

Snargate

Red Lion

On B2080, Brenzett–Appledore road OS990286
☎ (0679) 344648
11–3, 7–11
Adnams Bitter; Bateman XB; guest beer Ⓖ
Visiting 'Doris's' is a must: this unspoilt pub is like a step back in time. Stone and timber floors, a marble counter, open fires, unusual pub games and a friendly atmosphere are all to be enjoyed in this three-roomed pub.
🏰 Q ❀ ♣ ⌓ P

Southfleet

Wheatsheaf

8 High Cross Road, Westwood (½ mile W of village)
☎ (0474) 833210
11–11
Courage Best Bitter, Directors; Marston's Pedigree; Ruddles County Ⓗ**; guest beers** (occasionally)
Thatched pub with a pianist/vocalist Thu/Sun nights and morris men on Wed. Note the thatched gents' toilet. The large garden has a pond. 🏰 ❀ ◑ ◗ ♣ P

Stalisfield Green

Plough

☎ (0795) 890256
12–3, 7–11 (closed Mon except bank hol lunchtimes)
Adnams Extra; Harveys BB; Ind Coope Burton Ale; Shepherd Neame Master Brew Bitter; guest beer (occasionally) Ⓗ
Classic, 15th-century, two-bar free house, set in impressive countryside. Noted for its good food – fish is a speciality and booking advisable. Shut the Box and shove-ha'penny played. Caravans welcome.
🏰 Q ❀ ◑ ◗ ▲ ♣ P

Stansted

Black Horse

Tumblefield Road (1 mile from A20, top of Wrotham Hill)
☎ (0732) 822355
11–2.30, 6 (7 winter)–11
Whitbread Fremlins Bitter Ⓗ**; guest beers**
Pub acting as a post office as well as the centre of village life. Now owned by the landlord and the range of up to four guest beers is more adventurous. Two quiz teams; Bat and Trap played. Caravan site a half-mile away.
🏰 ♨ ❀ ◑ ⊟ ▲ ♣ P

Staplestreet

Three Horseshoes

☎ (0227) 750842
11–3 (4.30 Sat), 6–11; 11–11 Thu & Fri
Shepherd Neame Master Brew Bitter, Porter Ⓖ
Typically Kentish building with a list of landlords going back to 1690; also a collection of stone bottles and many table-top games. Food is simple but good value.
🏰 Q ❀ ◑ ◗ ▲ ♣ P

Try also: Dove, Dargate (Shepherd Neame)

Stone Street

Padwell Arms

1 mile S of A25 between Seal and Ightham OS569551
☎ (0732) 61532
12–3, 6–11
Hall & Woodhouse Badger Best Bitter; Harveys Sussex; Hook Norton Old Hooky; Young's Bitter; guest beers Ⓗ
Old pub set at the heart of the Garden of England, with views over orchards. Friendly, welcoming atmosphere; very popular with locals; ideal for summer eves. 🏰 ❀ ◑ ▲ P

Sutton at Hone

Ship

Main Road ☎ (0322) 863387
11–3, 5–11; 11–11 Fri & Sat
Courage Best Bitter Ⓗ**; guest beers**
Popular village pub with an enterprising landlord. Two bars cater for all tastes; two guest beers are constantly changed. 🏰 ❀ ◑ ▲
⇌ (Farningham Rd) ♣ P

Tonbridge

Royal Oak

Lower Hayesden Lane (W off A26 at Shell roundabout, follow signs to L Hayesden) OS569457 ☎ (0732) 350208
11–11
Adnams Bitter Ⓗ**; guest beers**
Friendly, well-frequented pub with a helpful beer guide on a blackboard, and one beer always on special offer. Live music in one bar; annual beer festival in the field opposite. Eve meals Mon–Fri.
🏰 Q ♨ ❀ ◑ ◗ ♿ ▲ ♣ P

Stags Head

Stafford Road (over river from High St, 1st left, 1st left again)
11–3, 6–11; 11–11 Thu–Sat
Whitbread Flowers IPA; Taylor Best Bitter; guest beers Ⓗ
One-bar pub of Victorian origin with a lounge area in front of the bar and games areas at either end. A good range of wines complements the ales. ◑ ◗ ♿ ⇌ ♣ P

Tovil

Royal Paper Mill

39 Tovil Hill ☎ (0622) 752095
11–3, 7–11
Goacher's Mild, Light, Dark, Porter Ⓗ**, Old** Ⓖ**; guest beer** Ⓗ
Genuine, friendly local that also attracts the discerning beer lover. Goacher's first pub, so it nearly always has the full range. Photos of workers at local paper mills, with descriptions of their jobs, adorn the walls.
🏰 ⇌ (Maidstone West) ♣

Tudeley

George & Dragon

Five Oak Green Road (B2161, W of Five Oak Green) OS635448 ☎ (0892) 832521
11–3, 6–11; 11–11 summer Sat
Greene King IPA, Rayments Special, Abbot Ⓗ
Recently taken over by Greene King and refurbished to a decent standard; a smallish saloon bar plus a larger, more spartan public bar with a bar billiards table. A restaurant offers good home-cooked food. Set in the middle of the hop gardens of Kent.
🏰 Q ❀ ◑ ◗ ♣ P

Tunbridge Wells

Crystal Palace

69 Camden Road
☎ (0892) 548412
11–3 (4 Sat), 7–11
Harveys Mild, Pale Ale, BB, Old Ⓗ
A pre-1890 pub, popular with office workers at lunchtime and with regulars for games in the eve. No food Sun. ❀ ◑ ♣

Sir Alf Ramsey
Surrey Close, Showfields Estate (off Eridge Rd)
☎ (0892) 530996
12–3, 6–11; 11.30–4.30, 6.30–11 Sat
Harveys BB; guest beers [H]
Friendly local pub where the two guest beers vary.
❀ ◐ ◑ P

Underriver

White Rock Inn
Off B245 OS557520
☎ (0732) 833112
12–3, 6–11
Harveys BB; Webster's Yorkshire Bitter; guest beers [H]
The only pub in the centre of this pretty village. Popular with office workers who drive out into the country. The large garden houses dovecotes.
♛ Q ☋ ❀ ◐ ◑ ♿ ♣ P

Upper Upnor

Tudor Rose
High Street
☎ (0634) 715305
12–3, 7–11
Young's Bitter, Special; guest beers [H]
Friendly, multi-roomed pub, near Upnor Castle and the River Medway. No food Sun.
♛ ☋ ❀ ◐ ◑ ♣

Waltham

Lord Nelson
Kake Street
☎ (0227) 700628
12–3, 7–11 (supper licence; closed Tue)
Adnams Bitter; Goacher's Light; Harveys BB; guest beer [H]
Gracious Georgian main bar and a small public bar boasting a collection of large metal artefacts. The huge garden has a play area, a horse, and Wiltshire Horns sheep.
♛ ❀ ◐ ◑ ▲ ♣ ⊖ P

Try also: Compasses, Crundale (Free)

Westerham

General Wolfe
High Street
☎ (0959) 562104
11 (12 Sat)–3, 6–11
Greene King IPA, Abbot [H]
Low-ceilinged, weatherboarded house of much character, with a friendly atmosphere. The safest bet in this popular tourist town, it was once the Westerham Brewery tap. Small outside sitting area. No food at weekends. ♛ Q ❀ ◐ P

West Malling

Joiners Arms
High Street
☎ (0732) 840723
11–3, 5–11; 11–11 Fri & Sat
Shepherd Neame Master Brew Bitter, Spitfire, Porter, Bishops Finger [H]
Friendly two-bar local supporting a varied clientele. Spitfire is not always available. No food Sun.
♛ ❀ ◐ ♿ ⇌ ♣

West Peckham

Swan
The Green ☎ (0622) 812271
11–3 (4 Sat), 6–11; 11–11 summer Sat
Courage Best Bitter; Harveys BB; Shepherd Neame Porter; Wadworth 6X; Whitbread Boddingtons Bitter [H]
Country pub of 16th-century origins where the single bar is neatly separated into three areas: a public bar area with darts and skittles, a pleasant saloon/lounge area, and a discrete restaurant. A suitable venue for watching cricket on the village green.
♛ Q ❀ ◐ ◑ ♿ ♣ P

Whitstable

Coach & Horses
37 Oxford Street
☎ (0227) 264732
11–3 (3.30 Sat), 6.30–11
Shepherd Neame Master Brew Bitter, Porter [H]
Popular, lively high street local. ❀ ◐ ◑ ♿ ▲ ⇌ ♣

Noah's Ark
83 Canterbury Road (A290)
☎ (0227) 272332
11–3, 6–11
Shepherd Neame Master Brew Bitter [H]
Basic, friendly local with the same landlord for 30 years. Euchre sessions Sun; also shove-ha'penny.
❀ ◐ ⇌ ♣ P

Smack Inn
Middle Wall (near beach)
☎ (0227) 273056
10.30–3, 7–11
Shepherd Neame Master Brew Bitter [H]
Lively, wood-panelled pub named after the oyster smacks whose crews used to drink here.
Q ❀ ♿ ▲ ⇌ ♣ P

Tankerton Arms
Tower Hill
☎ (0227) 272024
12–11
Fuller's London Pride; Shepherd Neame Master Brew Bitter; guest beers [H]
Built circa 1900, this former hotel and bar attracts locals and students. Extensive panoramic views of the Thames estuary. Live jazz at least one night a week. Look for the carved post on the bar. A friendly pub with a very full menu and up to three guest beers.
♛ Q ☋ ❀ ◐ ◑ ⇌

Try also: Fountain, Bexley St (Free)

Wingham

Dog
Canterbury Road
☎ (0227) 720339
11–3, 6–11
Adnams Bitter; Draught Bass; Bateman XXXB; Shepherd Neame Master Brew Bitter [H]
Historic village pub established in the reign of King John. During the 18th century it was the local assizes, and mail was sorted here until the village PO was established.
♛ ❀ ◐ ⊡ P

Try also: Eight Bells, Wingham Well (Free)

Worth

St Crispin
The Street (off A258 between Deal and Sandwich)
☎ (0304) 612081
11–2.30, 6–11
Gale's HSB; Marston's Pedigree; Shepherd Neame Master Brew Bitter; Whitbread Boddingtons Mild [H]**; guest beers** [G]
Popular old village local, carefully refurbished and extended. Noted for its food in both the bar and restaurant. Varied range of guest beers.
♛ Q ❀ ⊨ ◐ ◑ ▲ ♣ P

Try also: Blue Pigeons, The Street (Free)

Wrotham

George & Dragon
High Street
☎ (0732) 884298
11–3, 6–11
Courage Best Bitter [H]**; guest beer**
Two long, narrow bars with beamed ceilings prove the building is older than it first appears. The history is detailed on a framed text on one wall. A mixed, local clientele contributes to the warm and friendly atmosphere.
♛ ❀ ◐ ◑ ⊡ ♣

Try also: Rose & Crown, High St (Shepherd Neame)

Lancashire

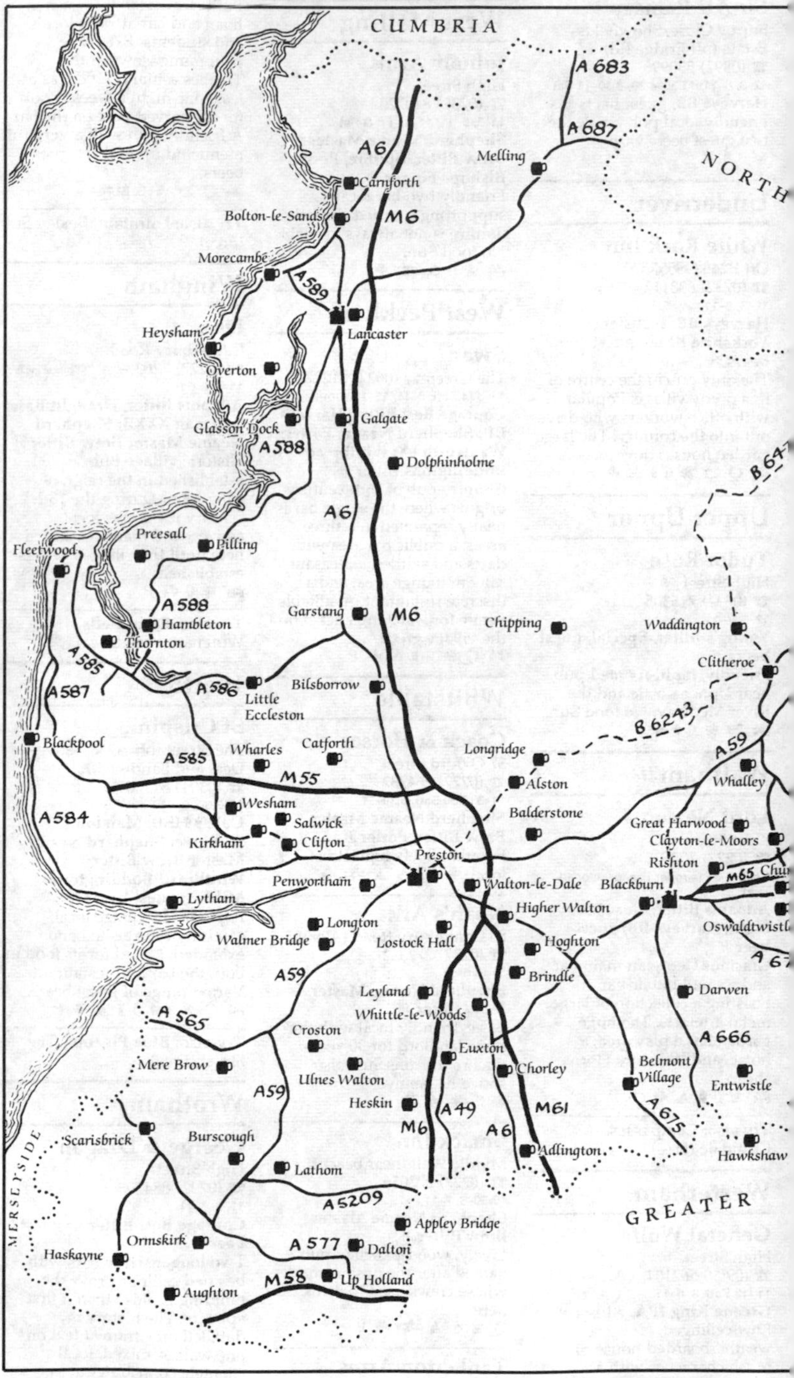

Lion's, *Burnley;* ***Little Avenham,*** *Preston;* ***Mitchell's,*** *Lancaster,* ***Moorhouse's,*** *Burnley;* ***Preston,*** *Preston;* ***Thwaites,*** *Blackburn*

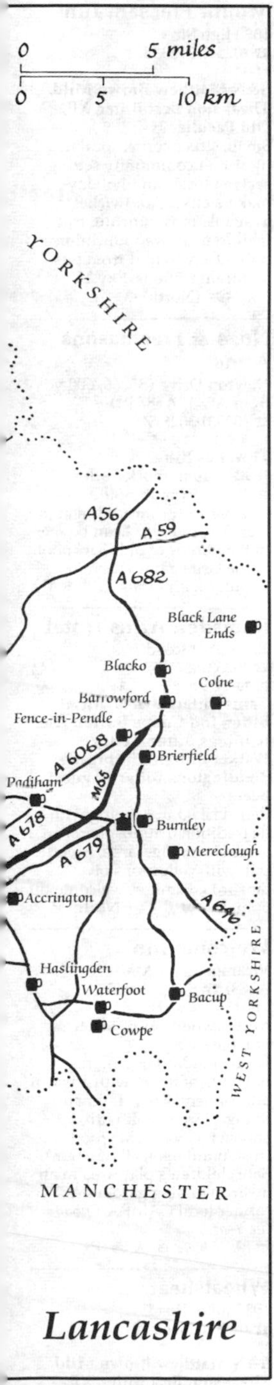

Accrington

Abbey

Bank Street ☎ (0254) 235727
11.30–3.30, 7–11
John Smith's Bitter Ⓗ; guest beer (weekends)
Busy, back-street local with two rooms. Excellent lunches.
❀ ◑ ⇌

George

185 Blackburn Road
☎ (0254) 383441
12–4.30, 7–11; 11–11 Fri & Sat
Beer range varies Ⓗ
Open-plan, friendly local near the college, with a mixed clientele. Six ever-changing ales. ❀ ◑ ◗ ⇌ ♣

Nag's Head

78 Blackburn Road
☎ (0254) 233965
11–11
Thwaites Mild, Bitter Ⓗ
Small, three-roomed local with a varied clientele. ⇌

Adlington

White Bear

Market Street ☎ (0257) 482357
11–11
S&N Matthew Brown Mild, Theakston Best Bitter, XB, Old Peculier Ⓗ
Excellent, three-roomed, stone town pub. Good atmosphere and good value food (all day Sun; till 8pm other eves; no food Mon eve).
❀ ◑ ◗ ⇌ ♣

Alston

White Bull

257 Preston Road
☎ (0772) 784151
11–3, 5.30–11; 11–11 Sat
Thwaites Best Mild, Bitter Ⓗ
Roadside pub with two real fires and two gardens. Noted for good food, at all times (all day Sun). Family room lunchtime. ❀ ◑ ◗ ♣ P

Appley Bridge

Wheatsheaf

287 Miles Lane (B5375)
☎ (0257) 252302
12–3.30, 5.30–11; 12–11 Fri & Sat
Greenalls Mild, Bitter Ⓗ
Immensely popular, comfortable pub in a semi-rural area. Collection of mugs and jugs. Excellent value food (pizzas only eves). ❀ ◑ ◗ ⇌ ♣ P

Aughton

Dog & Gun

233 Long Lane
☎ (0695) 423303
Burtonwood Mild, Bitter, Forshaw's Ⓗ
Excellent village local, a pub for a quiet pint and a good conversation with friendly locals. Two lounges on either side of a central drinking area. Bowling green. Q ❀
⇌ (Aughton Pk) ♣ P

Stanley Arms

St Michaels Road (off A59)
☎ (0695) 423241
11.30–3, 5.30–11
Cains Bitter; Walker Mild, Bitter Ⓗ
Busy, local meeting place. Good value food until 7.30; family room until 8pm. Children's play area outside. Crown green bowling. No food Sun eve. ❀ ◑ ◗
⇌ (Town Green) P

Bacup

New Inn

Rochdale Road
☎ (0706) 873130
11.30–11
Thwaites Best Mild, Bitter Ⓗ
Comfortable, four-roomed local with traditional wood-panelled ceilings and 19th-century murals. ♣

Balderstone

Myerscough

Whalley Road (A59)
☎ (0254) 812222
11.30–3, 5.30–11
Robinson's Best Mild, Best Bitter, Old Tom Ⓗ
Pleasant country pub with a large, wood-panelled lounge and a separate room with a coal fire. Preserved Canberra and Lightning aircraft stand opposite at the BAe factory. Eve meals till 8.30 (not Sun).
Q ❀ ◑ ◗ P

Barrowford

Barrowford Conservative Club

Gisburn Road ☎ (0282) 614002
7–11; 12–4, 7–11 Sat; 7.30–10.30 Sun
John Smith's Bitter; Taylor Golden Best Ⓗ
Three-storey, comfortable, listed building. Snooker tables on the top floor. Show this guide or CAMRA membership for entrance (non-club members must be in half an hour before closing). ♣

Old Bridge Inn

Gisburn Road ☎ (0282) 613983
3–11; 11–4, 7–11 Sat
Robinson's Hartleys XB, Best Bitter Ⓗ
Semi-open-plan, welcoming pub, still retaining Hartley Bell windows. ❀ ♿ ♣ P

Belmont Village

Black Dog

Church Street ☎ (020 481) 218
12–3.30 (4 Sat), 6.15–11

Lancashire

Holt Mild, Bitter [H]
Popular moorland village pub on the Bolton–Preston road. The landlord whistles the classics and invites occasional live orchestras. No jukebox. No food Mon, or Tue eve. The only Holt pub in Lancashire.
🔥 Q 🐴 ❀ 🛏 ◑ ◗ ♣ P

Bilsborrow

Owd Nells
St Michaels Road (off A6)
☎ (0995) 40010
11–11
Jennings Bitter; Preston Pride; Whitbread Fremlins Bitter, Flowers IPA [H]**; guest beers**
Canalside pub with a thatched roof and many attractions. Good outside facilities for children. Guest beers keep changing. Craft shops nearby.
🐴 ❀ 🛏 ◑ ◗ ♿ P

White Bull
Garstang Road (A6)
☎ (0995) 40324
11–11
S&N Matthew Brown Mild, Theakston Best Bitter [H]
Pleasant, unspoilt, friendly, canalside pub. 🔥 Q ◑ P

Blackburn

Florence Hotel
149 Moss Street
☎ (0254) 53100
11–2, 6–11; 11–11 Thu–Sat & summer
Thwaites Best Mild, Bitter, Craftsman [H]
Attractive, large, open-plan pub with separate drinking areas and a games room. Entertainment every weekend and Thu, popular with local couples. ❀ ◑ ♣

Moorgate Arms
168 Livesey Branch Road
☎ (0254) 51408
11–11
Thwaites Mild, Bitter [H]
Popular local with darts, pool and dominoes. Basically L-shaped layout, with a separate vault at the rear. Handy for Ewood Park and the canal. Note the original windows. ❀ ⇌ (Mill Hill) ♣

Navigation Inn
Canal Street, Mill Hill
☎ (0254) 53230
10.30–11
Thwaites Mild, Bitter [H]
Well-patronised, atmospheric local right on the canal, with two distinct sides. Very games-oriented tap room.
⊟ ⇌ (Mill Hill) ♣ P

Park Hotel
85 Montague Street
☎ (0254) 676524
11–11
S&N Matthew Brown Mild, Bitter, Theakston Best Bitter [H]
Very popular pub close to the college. Recently opened out, with a well-designed pool area, but still retains its original Lion Brewery windows. ◑ ♿ ⇌ ♣

Black Lane Ends

Hare & Hounds
3 miles from Colne on Skipton Old Road ☎ (0282) 863070
11–3 (not Tue & Thu), 7–11
Taylor Dark Mild, Golden Best [H]
Small, friendly pub set high in a remote Pennine landscape.
🔥 Q ❀ ◑ ◗ ♿ ▲ ♣ P

Blacko

Cross Gaits
Beverley Road (A682)
☎ (0282) 616312
5.30–11 (12–3, 5.30–11 summer; closed Mon & Tue in summer); 12–3, 6–11 Fri & Sat
Burtonwood Mild, Bitter, Forshaw's [H]
16th-century inn in a rural setting. A popular family pub with a good range of food.
🔥 Q ❀ ◑ ◗ ♣ P

Blackpool

Bispham Hotel
Red Bank Road (off A584)
☎ (0253) 51752
11–3 (4 Sat), 6 (7 Sat)–11
Samuel Smith OBB [H]
Deservedly popular, welcoming house close to the promenade. The smart lounge features statuettes and an illuminated ceiling panel. Live entertainment Thu–Sat. Thriving sports and social club. No food Sun. ◑ ⊟ ♿ ♣

Clarence Hotel
88 Preston New Road (A583)
☎ (0253) 761064
12–3, 6 (7 Sat)–11
Thwaites Best Mild, Bitter [H]
1950s, open-plan, two-level pub with a large, basic public bar. Well-known for good value, local fare; popular Wed/Sun trivia/pop quizzes. Children allowed into the main bar up to 8.30pm.
🐴 ❀ ◑ ◗ ⊟ ♣ P

Empress Hotel
59 Exchange Street (400 yds N of station) ☎ (0253) 20413
11–11 (1am summer Fri & Sat)
Thwaites Best Mild, Bitter [H]
Large, Victorian pub with its own dance floor and Wurlitzer organ. Twenty-one years in this guide. 🛏 ⇌ (North) ♣

Mount Pleasant Inn
103 High Street
☎ (0253) 293335
11–11
S&N Matthew Brown Mild, Theakston Best Bitter, XB, Old Peculier [H]
Small, street-corner local in a tight-knit community setting, serving locals and holiday-makers alike. Sandwiches available most lunchtimes (children allowed lunchtimes only). Easy to find from bus and train stations. Sky TV.
◑ ⊟ ⇌ (North) ♣

No. 4 & Freemasons Arms
Newton Drive (B5266, 600 yds from A583/A587 jct)
☎ (0253) 302877
11–3, 6–11; 11–11 Sat
Thwaites Bitter [H]
1890s pub in mock Tudor style, incorporating the original 18th-century inn at the rear. The old No. 4 can be seen in the photos of old Blackpool, in the large games room. Popular with locals. ❀ ◑ ♣ P

Ramsden Arms Hotel
204 Talbot Road
☎ (0253) 23215
10.30–11
Cains Bitter; Hydes' Anvil Bitter; Ind Coope Burton Ale; Jennings Bitter; Tetley Walker Bitter; Whitbread Boddingtons Bitter [H]**; guest beers**
Refurbished in keeping with its traditional atmosphere: an award-winning, large, friendly pub with collections of tankards. Families welcome till 6pm. 🐴 🛏 ◑ ⇌ (North) P

Welcome Inn
Vicarage Lane, Marton (off A583) ☎ (0253) 765372
11–11
Burtonwood Mild, Bitter, Forshaw's [H]
Large, modern pub on the outskirts of town, with a warm atmosphere. Cosy, intimate lounge; large vault with snooker. Good value food (restaurant open all day Sun). Safe children's play area in an award-winning garden. A former local CAMRA *Pub of the Year*.
🐴 ❀ ◑ ◗ ⊟ ♿ ▲ ♣ P

Wheatsheaf
192 Talbot Road
☎ (0253) 25062
11–11
S&N Matthew Brown Mild, Theakston Best Bitter, XB, Old Peculier [H]
Spartan boozer with a modernised, comfy extension. Frequented by many local characters – an experience not to miss! Q ⇌ (North) ♣

Bolton-le-Sands

Blue Anchor
Main Road ☎ (0524) 823423
11–11
Mitchell's Mild, Best Bitter, ESB Ⓗ
Robust, friendly local at the heart of a large village: a games room, a restaurant and a snug. Parking for residents only, otherwise difficult.
🝊 ❀ 🛏 ◑ ◗ ♣

Brierfield

Waggon & Horses
Colne Road ☎ (0282) 613962
11.30–2.30, 5–11; 11.30–11 Fri & Sat
Thwaites Best Mild, Bitter Ⓗ
Former CAMRA *Best Refurbished Pub*: a popular roadside house which hosts meetings. Antique furniture; genuine Italian marble fire-place in the snug. One room is still gas lit. Resident ghost. Eve meals Thu–Sat. Wheelchair access via garden doors.
🝊 Q ❀ ◑ ◗ ♿ ⇌ ♣ P

Wigglesworth
Burnley Road ☎ (0282) 615720
4 (12 Thu–Sat)–11 (12–11 summer)
Ind Coope Burton Ale; Tetley Walker Dark Mild, Bitter Ⓗ**; guest beers**
Large, multi-roomed pub next to the Unit Four cinema. Excellent value Sun lunches. Occasional eve meals.
Q ◑ ⇌ ♣ P

Brindle

Cavendish Arms
Sandy Lane (B5256)
☎ (0254) 852912
11–3, 5.30–11
Burtonwood Mild, Bitter Ⓗ
Outstanding, traditional village pub with stained-glass and wood carving, near Hoghton Towers. Children welcome at mealtimes.
🝊 Q ❀ ◑ ◗ ⊞ ♣ P

Burnley

Mechanics (Shuttle Bar)
Manchester Road
☎ (0282) 30005
11–3, 5.30–11
Moorhouse's Pendle Witches Brew; John Smith's Bitter; Thwaites Bitter; guest beers Ⓗ
Large council-run arts centre. Real ale is only available in the bottom bar. The only true free house in Burnley centre.
◑ ♿ ⇌ (Manchester Rd) P

Tim Bobbin
319 Padiham Road (near M65 jct 10) ☎ (0282) 424165
11–3, 7–11; 11–11 Fri & Sat
Samuel Smith OBB, Museum Ⓗ
Large, main-road pub with a country pub atmosphere. Games room.
❀ ◑ ⇌ (Barracks) ♣ P

Wheatsheaf
112 Colne Road (1 mile from centre) ☎ (0282) 421120
12–4, 6–11
Moorhouse's Premier; John Smith's Bitter Ⓗ
Friendly welcome in a busy local. Emphasis on games. ♣

Burscough

Martin Inn
Martin Lane (off A570/B5242)
☎ (0704) 895788
11.30–3, 5.30–11
Draught Bass; Courage Directors; Marston's Pedigree; John Smith's Bitter; Wilson's Mild Ⓗ
Remote, welcoming inn, near Martin Mere Wildfowl Trust, with a large, stone-floored bar area. Run by colourful licensees. Good choice of food.
🝊 ❀ 🛏 ◑ ◗ ▲ ♣ P

Carnforth

Cross Keys
Kellet Road ☎ (0524) 732749
12–3, 7–11
Mitchell's Best Bitter Ⓗ
Pub just east of the Lancaster Canal, with a basic vault at the rear and a lounge divided into two distinct areas. Mainly local clientele. Bowls club next door. 🝊 ❀ ◑ ⇌ ♣ P

Catforth

Bay Horse Hotel
Catforth Road (off B5267)
☎ (0772) 690389
11–11
Burtonwood Bitter Ⓗ
Village-centre local, with good, cheap food right up to closing time. Live entertainment Fri.
🝊 ❀ ◑ ◗ ⊞ ♿ ▲ ♣ P

Running Pump
Catforth Road (off B5267)
☎ (0772) 690265
11.30–3, 6–11
Robinson's Best Mild, Best Bitter Ⓗ
Traditional, three-roomed, country-pub, named after the 17th-century village pump outside (depicted in the stained-glass windows). Well-cooked, good value lunches. 🝊 Q ◑ ♣ P

Chipping

Sun Inn
Windy Street ☎ (0995) 61206
11–4, 6–11; 11–11 Sat
Whitbread Boddingtons Mild, Bitter Ⓗ
Deservedly popular, stone pub in a picturesque village, the centre of Lancashire cheese making. Beware the steep stairs at the front. Reputedly haunted. Q ❀ ◑ ♣ P

Chorley

Albion
29 Bolton Street (A6 S of centre) ☎ (0257) 275225
12–11
Ind Coope Burton Ale; Tetley Walker Mild, Bitter Ⓗ
Two-roomed, town-centre pub of character, with a basic bar and a comfortable lounge. Occasional live music at weekends. Public car park to the rear. ❀ ◑ ⊞ ⇌ ♣

Malt'n'Hops
50–52 Friday Street (through railway underpass, left for 100 yds) ☎ (0257) 260967
11–11
Moorhouse's Pendle Witches Brew; Taylor Landlord; Whitbread Boddingtons Bitter; Wilson's Mild, Webster's Yorkshire Bitter; guest beers Ⓗ
Small, comfortable free house, converted from a shop: a single bar with an unusual exterior. Public car park opposite. A local CAMRA award-winner. ❀ ⇌

Railway
20–22 Steeley Lane (through railway underpass)
☎ (0257) 266962
12–11
Draught Bass; S&N Matthew Brown Mild, Theakston Best Bitter; Stones Best Bitter; guest beers Ⓗ
Lots of dark wood and mirrors in a single bar with four alcoves. Boisterous at weekends. 🝊 ❀ ⇌

Shepherds Arms
Eaves Lane ☎ (0257) 275659
12 (11 Sat)–11
S&N Matthew Brown Mild, Bitter, Theakston Best Bitter Ⓗ
Friendly local on the north side of town: a lounge, a front room, a cosy, part-enclosed snug and a separate rear vault. Near Leeds and Liverpool Canal bridge 66. Betting shop at the rear. ⊞ ♣

Church and Oswaldtwistle

Royal Oak Inn
334 Union Road, Oswaldtwistle (left from station) ☎ (0254) 236367
12–4 (4.30 Sat), 7–11
Thwaites Mild, Bitter Ⓗ
Open-plan, village-centre pub. Small games area. ⇌ ♣

Lancashire

Thorn Inn
St James Road, Church
☎ (0254) 237827
12-3 (4 Fri & Sat), 7-11
Thwaites Best Mild, Bitter Ⓗ
Stone-built, rural, friendly local with parts from the 18th century. ❀ ◖ ♿ ⇌ ♣ P

Clayton-le-Moors

Wellington Hotel
Barnes Square ☎ (0254) 235762
1.30-11; 12-5, 7-11 Sat
Thwaites Mild, Bitter Ⓗ
Large, multi-roomed local, semi-open plan but retaining a separate tap room. ♣

Clifton

Windmill Tavern
Station Road ☎ (0772) 687203
11-3, 6.30-11 (11-11 summer Sat)
Mitchell's Best Bitter, Fortress, ESB Ⓗ; **guest beers**
Pub dating from 1700, based on a windmill. The large lounge was once the grain store; the games room is part of the mill and has pool. Good value food; children's farm and play area. Two guest beers. ♨ ♘ ❀ ◖ ♿ ⇌ (Salwick: request) ♣ P

Clitheroe

New Inn
Parsons Lane ☎ (0200) 23312
11 (5 Wed)-11
Moorhouse's Premier; Robinson's Hartleys XB (summer); **Whitbread Boddingtons Mild, Fremlins Bitter, Boddingtons Bitter** Ⓗ
Small, friendly, traditional, beer drinkers' pub opposite the castle. Folk music Tue; jam sessions Sun. ♨ Q ♘ ❀ ▲ ⇌ (summer weekends) ♣ P

Colne

Admiral Lord Rodney
Waterside Road, South Valley
☎ (0282) 864079
12-3, 7-11; 12-11 Fri & Sat
Dent T'Owd Tup; Goose Eye Bitter; S&N Theakston Mild, Best Bitter, XB, Old Peculier Ⓗ
Friendly local with an extensive menu (Sun lunch a speciality; no food Mon eve). Live music Thu: blues, country rockabilly and 60s. Pool, table football and other games. ♨ ❀ ◖ ◗ ♿ ⇌ ♣ 🍎 P ⊘

Red Lion
Market Street ☎ (0282) 863473
11-11
Taylor Dark Mild, Best Bitter Ⓔ
Popular, town-centre pub where satellite TV caters for sports fanatics. Very keen pool team. Toby jugs, brasses and antique plates. ♨ ◖ ♿ ♣ P

Cowpe

Buck
Cowpe Road (off A681 at Waterfoot, ½ mile S of centre)
☎ (0706) 213612
12-4 (not Mon-Fri), 7-11
Tetley Walker Bitter; Thwaites Best Mild, Bitter Ⓗ
Cosy village pub on the edge of the moors. Warm and welcoming. ♨ ❀ ◖ ♣ P

Croston

Black Horse
Westhead Road
☎ (0772) 600338
11.30-11
Banks's Mild, Bitter; Burton Bridge Bridge Bitter; Camerons Strongarm; Jennings Bitter; guest beers Ⓗ
Excellent, large village pub with a restaurant and a bowling green. Three hundred different beers each year. CAMRA regional *Pub of the Year* 1990. Beer festivals. Food extension Sun afternoon. ♨ ♘ ❀ ◖ ◗ ⊟ ⇌ ♣ P

Crown Hotel
Station Road ☎ (0772) 600380
11.30-3 (2.30 Mon & Tue), 5.30 (6 Sat)-11
Tetley Walker Mild, Walker Best Bitter; Thwaites Mild, Bitter, Craftsman; guest beers Ⓗ
Friendly, comfortable pub catering for locals and visitors in two separate drinking areas around a central bar. Weekly guest beer. No food Sun. ♨ Q ♘ ❀ ◖ ⊟ ⇌ P

Dalton

Ashurst Beacon Inn
Beacon Lane (Ashurst Beacon road) ☎ (0695) 632607
11-11
Burtonwood Bitter; S&N Theakston Mild, Best Bitter, XB, Old Peculier; Younger Scotch Ⓗ
Superb, 19th-century, rural pub with excellent facilities for families. Wide range of guest beers. Next to Beacon Country Park. Q ♘ ❀ ◖ ◗ ♿ ▲ ♣ P

Darwen

Entwistle Arms
15 Entwistle Street
☎ (0254) 703575
12.30-3, 6.15-11; 12.30-11 Fri & Sat
Thwaites Best Mild, Bitter Ⓗ
Comfortable local, behind St Peter's church. Games emphasis. ⇌ ♣

Golden Cup
610 Blackburn Road (A666)
☎ (0254) 702337
11.30-3, 5.30-11
Thwaites Mild, Bitter, Craftsman Ⓗ
The oldest pub in town: three small, cosy rooms with low ceilings. Attractive cobbled forecourt. Good value lunches. Q ❀ ◖ P

Sunnyhurst Hotel
Tockholes Road, Sunnyhurst
☎ (0254) 873035
12-3 (not Mon-Thu), 7-11 (extends summer)
Thwaites Mild, Bitter Ⓗ
Small, tidy, two-roomed pub with a games room. Homely atmosphere. Large selection of whiskies. Close to Darwen moors and Tower. Q ❀ ◖ ♣

Dolphinholme

Fleece
½ mile W of village OS509532
☎ (0524) 791233
12-3, 6-11
Mitchell's Mild, Best Bitter, ESB Ⓗ
Former farmhouse on a lonely crossroads, with a cosy, oak-beamed lounge leading to a small games/family room and dining room. Good quality food (no meals Sun eve or Mon). ♨ ♘ ❀ ◖ ◗ ♣ P

Entwistle

Strawbury Duck
Overshaws Road OS727178
☎ (0204) 852013
12-3 (not Mon), 7-11; 12-11 Sat
Marston's Pedigree; Taylor Best Bitter, Landlord; Whitbread Boddingtons Bitter Ⓗ; **guest beers**
Old, isolated but busy, country pub, by the station. A good base for walks in hill country and around reservoirs. Authentic Indian cuisine. Children welcome until 8.30pm. Three guest beers a week. ♨ ♘ ❀ 🛏 ◖ ◗ ⇌ ♣ P ⊘

Euxton

Euxton Mills
Wigan Road (A49/A581 jct)
☎ (0257) 264002
11.30-3, 5.30 (6.15 Sat)-11
Burtonwood Mild, Bitter Ⓔ, **Forshaw's** Ⓗ
Very cosy, comfortable pub: a split-level, two-bar lounge and a small front vault. Children allowed in the rear room for the excellent meals. Q ♘ ❀ ◖ ◗ ⊟ ♣ P

Fence-in-Pendle

Harpers Inn
Harpers Lane (near A6068/B6248 jct) ☎ (0282) 616249
11.30-3, 6.30-11
S&N Theakston Best Bitter, Old Peculier; Thwaites Mild, Bitter, Craftsman Ⓗ
Attractive, split-level pub. Good value food (all day Sun). Families catered for. ❀ ◖ ◗ P

Fleetwood

North Euston Hotel

The Esplanade
☎ (0253) 876525
11–3.30, 6–11; 11–11 Sat
Draught Bass; Ruddles County; John Smith's Bitter; Wilson's Mild, Bitter, Webster's Yorkshire Bitter; guest beers [H]
Imposing, Victorian, stone-fronted building, overlooking the estuary. Impressive views of Morecambe Bay and the Lakeland hills. Close to the pier, tram and bus termini and the Knott-End ferry. Large, elegantly appointed public rooms. ☋ ⛟ ◖ ♿ P

Wyre Lounge Bar

Marine Hall, The Esplanade
☎ (0253) 771141
11–3.30, 7–11
Courage Directors; Moorhouse's Premier, Pendle Witches Brew; guest beers [H]
Extremely popular part of the Marine Hall complex, twice a local CAMRA *Pub of the Year*. A comfortable lounge offers an excellent choice of regularly-changed beers. Q ❀ ◖ ♿ P

Galgate

Plough

Main Road ☎ (0524) 751337
11–11
Whitbread Boddingtons Bitter; guest beers [H]
Old pub at the southern end of the village. Modernised and open-plan, but cosy. Handy for the canal. ♨ ❀ ◖ ♣ P

Garstang

Royal Oak

Market Place
11–3.30, 7–11; 11–11 Thu–Sat
Robinson's Best Mild, Hartleys XB, Best Bitter, Old Tom [H]
Former coaching inn currently under alteration. The intimate, old-fashioned atmosphere is likely to be diminished and a restaurant added. Drinking area outside on the old market square. ❀ ⛟ ◖ ♣ P

Glasson Dock

Victoria

Victoria Terrace
☎ (0524) 751423
11–11 (11–3.30, 6–11 winter)
Mitchell's Mild, Best Bitter, Fortress (summer) [H]
End-of-terrace, built about 1838 and revamped in 1991, with a few nautical features. A large main bar has bays leading to games and dining areas. ♨ ❀ ◖ ◗ ♿ ♣ P

Great Harwood

Royal Hotel

Station Road ☎ (0254) 883541
12–1.30 (3 Sat), 7–11
Thwaites Bitter; guest beers [H]
Cosy pub with a separate bar, lounge and restaurant within an open-plan layout. Food is served while open. Four guest beers; wide selection of continental bottles. No loud music. A CAMRA regional *Pub of the Year*.
☋ ❀ ⛟ ◖ ◗ ▲ ♣

Hambleton

Wardleys Riverside Pub

Wardleys Creek, Kiln Lane (off A588 at the Shovels pub)
☎ (0253) 700203
12–3, 6.30–11
Courage Directors; John Smith's Bitter [H]**; guest beers**
Pub built in 1710 where the wall pictures reflect past connections with the ship-building and cotton trades. Attractive dining area. Beware the poorly lit road with sharp bends. ❀ ◖ ◗ ♿ ▲ ♣ P

Haskayne

Kings Arms

Delf Lane ☎ (0704) 840245
12–3, 5.30–11; 12–11 Fri & Sat
Robinson's Best Bitter; Tetley Walker Mild, Bitter; guest beers [H]
Pub with a growing reputation for good crack in comfortable surroundings. Friendly, community feel. Little touches make it special. A la carte restaurant. Mini-beer festivals.
♨ Q ❀ ◖ ◗ ⊟ ♣ P

Haslingden

Foresters Arms (Th'Owd Tack)

Pleasant Street ☎ (0706) 216079
12–11
Whitbread Boddingtons Bitter; Wilson's Mild, Bitter, Webster's Yorkshire Bitter [H]
Small, busy local near the town centre, with a games room and an unspoilt and friendly atmosphere. ♨ ♣

Hawkshaw

Red Lion

91 Ramsbottom Road (A676)
☎ (0204) 852539
12–3, 7–11 (may vary)
Taylor Golden Best, Best Bitter, Landlord; guest beers [H]
Set in a picturesque area, a pub just in Lancashire with its car park in Gtr Manchester. Completely rebuilt in 1990, with a single very comfortable bar area. ⛟ ◖ P

Heskin

Farmers Arms

Wood Lane (B5250)
☎ (0257) 451276
12–3, 5–11
Whitbread Boddingtons Bitter, Castle Eden Ale, Flowers Original; guest beers [H]
Comfortable and attractive country pub with a split-level lounge and a public bar. Large garden for children. Eve meals till 8. ☋ ❀ ◖ ◗ ⊟ ♣ P

Heysham

Royal

Main Street
11–11; 11–3, 6–11 Mon & Tue
Mitchell's Mild, Best Bitter [H]
Old, rambling, low-beamed building near St Patrick's chapel. Good local trade but also packed with holiday-makers in the season. Children admitted to the games room.
♨ ❀ ◖ ♣ P

Higher Walton

Mill Tavern

15 Cann Bridge Street (A675)
☎ (0772) 38462
11–2, 5.30–11
Burtonwood Bitter [H]
Friendly village local with a comfortable lounge and a separate games area. ◖ ♣ P

Hoghton

Black Horse

Gregson Lane ☎ (0254) 852541
11–11
S&N Matthew Brown Mild, Bitter, Theakston Best Bitter, XB [H]
Large, friendly, open-plan village pub with a separate games area. ❀ ◖ ♣ P

Kirkham

Queens Arms

7 Poulton Street (A585)
☎ (0772) 686705
11 (12 winter, 11.30 winter Thu–Sat)–11
S&N Theakston Mild, Best Bitter, XB, Old Peculier; Younger Scotch *or* **No. 3** (occasionally) [H]
Excellent, well-run, lively, town-centre local, full of character, with a friendly landlord. Hot roast beef sandwiches every Thu eve; barbecues in summer. Children welcome in the designated area; excellent garden. Pool room. Disabled WC. ❀ ◖ ◗ ♿ ⇌ ♣

Lancashire

Lancaster

Fat Scot
2 Gage Street (near Dalton Sq)
☎ (0524) 63438
11–11
Mitchell's Best Bitter, Fortress Ⓗ
Small, dark pub: heavy metal on the jukebox, leather on many of the customers. ⇌ ♣

George & Dragon
24 St George's Quay
☎ (0524) 844739
11.30–11
Vaux Bitter, Samson; Wards Thorne Best Bitter Ⓗ
Single, rather small bar, modernised but eschewing the usual carpet, wall lights, etc. in favour of a more robust style, but still comfortable. Near the maritime museum. ❀ ◐ ⇌ P

Golden Lion
Moor Lane ☎ (0524) 39447
12–3, 7–11
S&N Theakston Mild, Bitter, XB, Old Peculier Ⓗ
Pub since at least 1612, where prisoners on the way to the gallows had a last drink. An L-shaped bar with an adjoining 'Heritage Room' (old photos and ephemera); games room. Wide mix of customers. Folk music Wed. ♘ ♣ ⊬

John O' Gaunt
55 Market Street
☎ (0524) 65356
11.30–3, 6–11; 11–11 Fri; 11–5, 7–11 Sat
Ind Coope Burton Ale; Jennings Bitter; Tetley Walker Bitter; Whitbread Boddingtons Bitter Ⓗ
Pub with a handsome, original frontage: popular with both students and older customers. Newspapers provided. Varied home-cooked food. Eve meals Fri only. Live music Sun lunch, and Sun–Thu eves.
❀ ◐ ⇌

Priory
36 Cable Street
12–3, 6–11; 11–11 Fri & Sat; 7–10.30 Sun, closed Sun lunch
Mitchell's Mild, Best Bitter, ESB, Single Malt Ⓗ**; guest beers**
The leading guest beer pub in N Lancs: an unprepossessing large bar but the landlord creates his own atmosphere. Often packed. Weston's Perry in summer. Next to the bus station. ⇌ ♣ ⌓

Royal
Thurnham Street
☎ (0524) 65007
11.30–3, 6–11
Thwaites Best Mild, Bitter, Craftsman Ⓗ
Pub knocked through in 1992 to make a single, large bar with lots of corners. Quiz Wed; live music Sun. Near the town hall. ❀ ◐ ⇌ P

Sidings Bar
Greaves Road (rear of Greaves Hotel) ☎ (0524) 63943
5–11; 11–11 Sat & bank hols
Mitchell's Best Bitter, ESB Ⓗ**; guest beers**
Recently opened bar in the old pub cellar, under separate management from the hotel above. A single, rather small bar with new woodwork and stained-glass. The TV can be intrusive. ♨ ❀ 🛏 ◑ ♿ ♣ P

Lathom

Railway Tavern
Station Road, Hoscar Moss (¾ mile N of A5209) OS469116
☎ (0704) 892369
11–3, 5.30–11
Jennings Bitter, Oatmeal Stout; John Smith's Bitter; Tetley Walker Mild, Bitter Ⓗ
Changes may be afoot in this unspoilt and unpretentious country pub, so enjoy it while you can. A classic example of our country pub heritage, not far from the canal. Always quiet and relaxing. The beer range varies.
♨ Q ⇌ (Hoscar) ♣ P

Ship Inn
Wheat Lane (off A5209, over swing bridge)
☎ (0704) 893117
12–3, 5.30 (7 Sat)–11
Moorhouse's Pendle Witches Brew; S&N Theakston Mild, Best Bitter, XB; guest beers Ⓗ
Locally known as the Blood Tub and idyllically located on a canal bank in a conservation area. A popular free house with nine handpumps and five guest beers. Annual beer festivals. No food Sun.
Q ♘ ❀ ◐ ▲ ♣ P

Leyland

Dunkirk Hall
Dunkirk Lane (B5248/B5253 jct) ☎ (0772) 422102
11–3, 5–11; 11–11 Fri & Sat
Courage Directors; John Smith's Bitter; Whitbread Boddingtons Bitter Ⓗ
17th-century converted farmhouse, now a listed building. Flag floors, wood-panelled walls and oak beams feature. Children allowed in for meals. ❀ ◐ ◑ ♣ P

Eagle & Child
Church Road
☎ (0772) 433531
11.45–11
Burtonwood Bitter, Forshaw's Ⓗ
One-bar pub with an elongated layout, incorporating separate drinking areas. Children allowed in at lunchtime. ❀ ◐ ⇌ ♣ P

Gables
Hough Lane ☎ (0772) 422032
11.30–3, 7–11
Greenalls Bitter, Thomas Greenall's Original Ⓗ
Handsome, red-bricked ex-doctor's house in the town centre. Handy for the Motor Museum. ◐ ⊞ ⇌ ♣ P

Little Eccleston

Cartford Country Inn & Hotel
Cartford Lane (off A586)
☎ (0995) 670166
11.30–3, 6.30 (7 winter)–11
Whitbread Boddingtons Bitter; guest beers Ⓗ
Delightfully-situated free house by the River Wyre (fishing rights). Extensive bar menu with daily specials and a children's menu. Outdoor play area. Ever-changing guest beers. Local CAMRA *Pub of the Year* 1991. Watch out for George, the friendly ghost.
♨ Q ♘ ❀ 🛏 ◐ ◑ ♿ ♣ P

Longridge

Duke William
Chapel Hill ☎ (0772) 783289
7 (3 Fri, 11 Sat)–11
Whitbread Chester's Mild, Boddingtons Bitter, Flowers IPA Ⓗ
Comfortable, large, open-plan pub with a raised area. Mixed clientele. Live entertainment five nights a week. ❀ ♣ P

Old Oak
111 Preston Road (B6243)
☎ (0772) 783648
5–11; 12–5, 7–11 Sat
S&N Theakston Mild, Best Bitter, XB, Old Peculiar Ⓗ
Stone pub at the entrance to the town: a single, L-shaped room with settles around the fire. Separate (members only) snooker room. ♨ ♣ P

Towneley Arms
Berry Lane ☎ (0772) 782219
11–3.30, 6–11
Tetley Walker Mild, Bitter Ⓗ
Town-centre pub next to a long-closed railway station. Wood-panelled rooms with a roaring fire. ♨ Q ⊞ P

Longton

Dolphin (Flying Fish)
Marsh Lane OS459254
☎ (0772) 612032
12–3 (not Mon–Fri), 7–11

Thwaites Best Mild, Bitter Ⓗ
Remote farmhouse on the edge of Longton Marsh. A small, old-fashioned tap room and a lounge in a modern extension. Those arriving by boat, please sign the visitors' book. Twenty continuous years in this guide.
♔ Q ❀ ⊟ ♣ P

Lostock Hall

Victoria

Watkin Lane ☎ (0772) 35338
11–3, 6–11; 11–11 Sat
Ruddles Best Bitter; John Smith's Bitter Ⓗ
Popular, main-road (A582) pub with a large vault. Home of the local pigeon club and a prize brass band. Bus stop outside. ❀ ◖ ⊟ ⇌ ♣ P

Lytham

Hole in One

Forest Drive (off B5261)
☎ (0253) 730598
11–3, 6–11; 11–11 Fri & Sat
Thwaites Bitter Ⓗ
Busy, friendly, modern local on a new housing development, close to Fairhaven golf course. Full of golfing memorabilia. Large games room; popular quiz nights. Good home-made food (daily specials). Q ❀ ◖ ⊟ ♿ ⇌ (Ansdell) ♣ P

Queens

Central Beach ☎ (0253) 737316
11–11 (11–3.30, 5–11 winter)
S&N Theakston Best Bitter, XB, Old Peculier; Younger No. 3 (occasionally) Ⓗ
Characterful, authentic Victorian pub, in the town centre, overlooking the green and estuary. Good reputation for food. Satellite TV. Car park in winter only (public parking opposite).
♘ ❀ 🛏 ◖ ◗ ⊟ ⇌ ♣ P

Taps

Henry Street (just off Lytham Sq) ☎ (0253) 736226
11–11
Marston's Pedigree, Moorhouse's Black Cat Mild, Pendle Witches Brew; Whitbread Boddingtons Bitter; guest beers Ⓗ
Friendly, popular, traditional alehouse that serves a wide selection of ever-changing guest beers. Award-winning landlord. Free tasties Sun. Difficult parking. ♔ ◖ ♿ ⇌

Melling

Melling Hall

☎ (0524) 221298
12–2.30 (not Wed), 6–11; 12–2, 7–10.30 Sun
Taylor Landlord; Tetley Walker Bitter; Whitbread Boddingtons Bitter Ⓗ**; guest beer**
17th-century manor house converted in the 1940s to a well-appointed hotel. The friendly locals' bar is entered via the left-hand door. Garden play area. ♔ ❀ 🛏 ◖ ◗ ♣ P

Mere Brow

Legh Arms

The Gravel ☎ (0772) 812225
11.30–3, 5–11; 11.30–11 Sat
Tetley Walker Bitter; Whitbread Higsons Mild, Boddingtons Bitter, Higsons Bitter Ⓗ**; guest beer**
Friendly village local with good range of ales and excellent food. Just off the main road, with good passing trade and local characters. Can be busy eves. Try the roast lunches. ♘ ❀ ◖ ⊟ ♿ ♣ P

Mereclough

Kettledrum

302 Red Lees Road
☎ (0282) 424591
11–3, 6–11
Courage Directors; S&N Theakston Best Bitter, XB, Old Peculier; John Smith's Bitter Ⓗ
Attractive roadside inn on the outskirts of Burnley. Very popular for eating, as well as drinking, with a separate dining area and an upstairs restaurant. ♔ Q ◖ ◗ ♣ P

Morecambe

Joiner's Arms

Queen Street ☎ (0524) 418105
11–11
Thwaites Best Mild, Bitter Ⓗ
Lively and unpretentious local attracting a varied clientele. Children admitted to the back (games) room. Sandwiches at all times. ♣

Ormskirk

Greyhound

100 Aughton Street
☎ (0695) 576701
11–11
Walker Mild, Bitter, Winter Warmer Ⓗ
Characteristic market town local. A recent convert to Sky TV but it retains a traditional public bar, separate drinking areas, a corridor serving hatch and a games room. Next to a car park. ♔ Q ⊟ ⇌ ♣

Horse Shoe

24 Southport Road
☎ (0695) 572956
11–11
Tetley Walker Dark Mild, Bitter Ⓗ
Friendly alehouse in a terrace opposite the famous tower-and-steeple parish church. Sky TV (popular football sessions). Next to a car park. ♔ ⇌ ♣

Prince Albert

109 Wigan Road, Westhead (2 miles from centre)
☎ (0695) 573656
12–3 (5 Sat), 5 (7 Sat)–11
Tetley Walker Dark Mild, Bitter; guest beers Ⓗ
Comfortable, friendly village pub with staunch local support. Popular quiz Thu; good value food; serious doms team; beer bottle collection. Attention to detail makes the pub special.
♔ Q ❀ ◖ ▲ ♣ P

Yew Tree

Grimshaw Lane (towards Southport, 1st right after A59/A570 jct) ☎ (0695) 573381
12–3.30, 5–11.30
Cains Bitter Ⓗ
Modern pub, one of the last to be built by Higsons: a spacious lounge, a well-patronised public bar and a genuine snug, with a doms table. Good value food (no meals Sun). Additions to the beer range possible. Q ❀ ◖ ⊟ ⇌ ♣ P

Overton

Globe

Main Street ☎ (0524) 858228
11–4, 7 (6 summer)–11
Mitchell's Mild, Bitter Ⓗ
Pub renovated in 1990 with all modern amenities, including a large conservatory (reinstating an original feature). Child-friendly (play garden, nappy-changing, children's menu). Often full of diners (no eve meals Sun–Thu in winter).
❀ 🛏 ◖ ◗ ♿ ♣ P

Ship

Main Street ☎ (0524) 858231
12–4, 7–11
Thwaites Best Mild, Bitter Ⓗ
Genuine, unspoilt, late-Victorian village inn: a haven of quiet in small rooms. Stuffed birds on display. Try the thick sandwiches. No lunches Tue; eve meals in summer only. Own bowling green. Q ❀ ◖ ◗ ♣ P

Padiham

Alma Inn

36 Alma Street (off Church St)
☎ (0282) 772894
12–3, 5–11; 11–11 Sat
Tetley Walker Bitter; Wilson's Mild, Webster's Green Label, Yorkshire Bitter Ⓗ

Traditional local with a core of regulars. Pool, domino and darts teams. Q ❀ ◐ ◗ ♿ ♣

Penwortham

St Teresa's Parish Centre

Queensway ☎ (0772) 743523
12–4 (not Mon–Fri), 7–11
Burtonwood Mild, Bitter, Forshaw's; Ind Coope Burton Ale; Tetley Walker Mild, Bitter Ⓗ**; guest beers**
Thriving, three-bar Catholic club in a residential area: a comfortable lounge and games and concert rooms, offering live entertainment and two monthly guest beers. CAMRA *Club of the Year* 1990. Entry restrictions: CAMRA members anytime; other visitors six times a year (25p). ♣ P

Pilling

Golden Ball

School Lane ☎ (0253) 790212
6–11; 11–11 Sat & summer
Thwaites Bitter Ⓗ
Pub attractively set in a village on the edge of wildfowl marshes. Quiet in winter, but there is an active social club; busy in summer (two crown greens). Photos of old Pilling include both the current and previous Golden Ball.
❀ ◐ ◗ ♿ ▲ ♣ P

Preesall

Saracens Head

200 Park Lane (B5377)
☎ (0253) 810346
12–3, 5.30–11
Thwaites Best Mild, Bitter Ⓗ
Busy 19th-century pub, well known for good value meals (all day Sun). Often packed with diners: to avoid food, use the refurbished games room.
❀ ◐ ◗ ▲ ♣ P

Preston

Black Horse

166 Friargate
11–11; 11–4, 7.30–11 Sat; 7–10.30 Sun, closed Sun lunch
Robinson's Best Mild, Hartleys XB, Best Bitter, Old Tom Ⓗ
Superb, town-centre pub in a shopping area: a Grade II-listed building with side rooms, an upstairs, 1920s-style bar, an unusual, curved tiled bar, wood-panelling, stained-glass and a mosaic floor. A thriving meeting place.
Q ❀ ◐ ⇌

Fox & Grapes

Fox Street ☎ (0772) 52448
10.30–11
S&N Matthew Brown Mild, Theakston Best Bitter, Old Peculier; Younger Scotch, IPA, No. 3 Ⓗ
Small, one-bar, town-centre pub, refurbished in 1920s style with wooden floors, etc. Popular and often crowded. Twenty years in the *Guide*. No food Sun. ◐ ⇌

Gastons

30 Avenham Street
☎ (0772) 51380
12–3, 6–11; 12–11 Fri & Sat
Little Avenham Pickled Priest, Clog Dancer, Torchlight, Pierrepoints Last Drop Ⓗ**; guest beers**
Multi-level, two-bar, town-centre free house which started brewing in 1992. The upper bar is popular with younger people; downstairs is quieter. Large number of beers; beer festivals. Family room Sun. Public car park nearby. ◐ ◗ ⇌ ♣

Guild Merchant

Tag Lane, Ingol (next to roundabout on Tom Benson Way) ☎ (0772) 760882
11–11
Banks's Mild, Bitter Ⓔ**; Camerons Strongarm** Ⓗ
Modern pub opened in Preston Guild Year 1992 – hence the name: one bar serving a large lounge split into separate drinking areas, including a conservatory.
❀ ◐ ◗ ♿ P

Lamb & Packet

91a Friargate ☎ (0772) 51857
11.30–11; 11.30–3.30, 6.30–11 Sat
Thwaites Best Mild, Bitter, Craftsman Ⓗ
Small, well-run, one-bar pub near the university. Raised drinking area. Good value meals till 6.30 weekdays. Often crowded in term-time. ◐ ◗ ⇌

Mitre Tavern

90 Moor Lane ☎ (0772) 51918
12–2.30, 5.30–11; 12–11 Wed–Sat
Vaux Samson; Wards Sheffield Best Bitter; guest beer Ⓗ
Comfortable, two-room pub just off the town centre. Good vault with pool and darts. Vaux guest beer. ❀ ◐ ♣ P

New Britannia

Heatley Street ☎ (0772) 53424
11–3 (4 Fri & Sat), 6–11
Marston's Pedigree; Whitbread Trophy, Castle Eden Ale Ⓗ**; guest beer**
Small, one-bar pub near the university. Popular with the heavy metal creed, but all are made welcome. Often crowded weekends. No food Sat. Bulmers cider. Whitbread-supplied guest beer. ◐ ⇌ ⌓

New Welcome

15 Cambridge Street
☎ (0772) 53933
12–3 (4 Sat), 7–11
Thwaites Best Mild, Bitter Ⓗ
Small, former back-street local rejuvenated by new housing and a new landlord. A warm welcome in a cosy, central bar serving three areas. ♣ P

Old Black Bull

35 Friargate ☎ (0772) 823397
10.30–11
Whitbread Boddingtons Bitter Ⓗ**; guest beers**
Busy, town-centre pub, a Grade II-listed building with a tiled frontage. One large main room, with a tiny, busy front vault. A local CAMRA award-winner. Three guest beers. No food Sat. Public car park at the rear. ❀ ◐ ⇌ ♣

Old Blue Bell

114 Church Street
☎ (0772) 51280
11–3 (4 Sat), 5 (7 Sat)–11
Samuel Smith OBB Ⓗ
The oldest pub in Preston, with a cosy and intimate atmosphere in a large, busy lounge with two quiet snugs. No food Sun. Handy for curry restaurants. Quiz nights Tue.
❀ ◐ P

Real Ale Shop

Lovat Road ☎ (0772) 201591
11 (12 Sun)–2, 5 (7 Sun)–10
Moorhouse's Premier, Pendle Witches Brew; Taylor Landlord Ⓗ**; guest beers** Ⓗ/Ⓖ
Busy off-licence selling an ever-changing range of guest beers, exotic imported beers and fruit wines. Q ⌓

Stanley Arms

24 Lancaster Road
☎ (0772) 254004
11–11; 7–10.30 Sun, closed Sun lunch
Marston's Pedigree; S&N Theakston Mild, Best Bitter, XB, Old Peculier; Younger IPA Ⓗ**; guest beers**
Wood-panelled, one-bar pub in a Grade II-listed building by the Guild Hall. Foreign bottled beers and Bulmers cider. Can get crowded. ◐ ⇌ ⌓

Unicorn

378 North Road
☎ (0772) 57870
12–3, 6–11; 12–11 Sat
S&N Matthew Brown Mild, Theakston Best Bitter, XB, Old Peculier; Younger No. 3 Ⓗ
Attractive, stone-fronted, listed building, north of the town centre. One-room layout with a separate pool area. Folk club Mon; quiz Thu; live music. Upstairs room for hire.
❀ ◐ ♣

Windsor Castle
8 Egan Street (over footbridge from bus station)
☎ (0772) 53387
11–11
Thwaites Bitter, Craftsman Ⓗ
Homely, medium-sized local on the edge of the town centre. Friendly welcome. Q

Rishton

Rishton Arms
Station Road
12–3, 7–11
Thwaites Best Mild, Bitter, Craftsman Ⓗ
Pleasant, two-roomed pub, handy for the cricket ground. Grandfather clock in the lounge. P

Salwick

Hand & Dagger
Treales Road (off A583 at sign to Salwick & Clifton, past BNFL to canal)
☎ (0772) 690306
11.30–3, 6.30–11
Greenalls Mild, Bitter, Thomas Greenall's Original Ⓗ
Country pub over 200 years old, with a large garden and pets corner. Popular with locals; quality home-cooked food (all day Sun).
Q (request) P

Scarisbrick

Heatons Bridge Inn
2 Heatons Bridge Road (B5242)
☎ (0704) 840549
11–11.30
Tetley Walker Mild, Walker Best Bitter Ⓗ
Very popular, canalside inn, tastefully extended and offering excellent value lunches (no food eve or Sun).
Q P

Thornton

Burn Naze
Gamble Road ☎ (0253) 852954
11–11; 11–3.30, 7–11 Wed
Moorhouse's Premier; Tetley Walker Dark Mild, Bitter Ⓗ
Late-Victorian pub of character, popular with locals. Lively and friendly, with one of the few public bars in the area. Next to ICI. P

Ulnes Walton

Rose & Crown
120 Southport Road (A581)
☎ (0257) 451302
11.30–3, 5.30–11; 11.30–11 Sat
Burtonwood Mild, Bitter, Forshaw's, Top Hat Ⓗ
Attractive country pub with a central bar and a large garden. Parrots are on display inside and out; large aviary.
P

Up Holland

Sandbrook Arms
Sandbrook Road, Tontine (off B5206) ☎ (0695) 625775
11–11
Tetley Walker Dark Mild, Bitter; guest beers Ⓗ
Enterprising local, known as the Queens Arms until recently. Happy hour 5–7 weekdays. Handy for trekkers to Billinge Hill.
(Orrell) P

White Lion
10 Church Street (off A577)
☎ (0695) 622727
12–3, 7–11
Ind Coope Burton Ale; Jennings Bitter; Tetley Walker Bitter Ⓗ
Picturesque village pub opposite the church. Up Holland's oldest inn, probably originating as a monks' brewhouse and said to be the haunt of a notorious local highwayman, George Lyons, hanged at Lancaster Castle in 1815. Q P

Waddington

Lower Buck
Church Road ☎ (0200) 28705
11–3, 6–11; 11–11 Thu–Sat
Robinson's Best Bitter; Taylor Best Bitter; Tetley Walker Bitter Ⓗ
Unaltered Dickensian pub in a Grade I-listed building. A good village local with piano sing-alongs at weekends.
Q P

Walmer Bridge

Longton Arms
2 Liverpool Old Road
☎ (0772) 612335
2 (12 Sat)–11; 12–midnight bank hols
Greenalls Mild, Bitter Ⓗ
Small, village local with a tiny public bar at the front and a cosy lounge with small armchairs. Q P

Walton-le-Dale

Victoria
97 Higher Walton Road
☎ (0772) 204420
11–11
Whitbread Boddingtons Bitter; guest beers Ⓗ
Victorian, main-road local. A central bar serves a lounge and vault. P

Waterfoot

Jolly Sailor
Booth Road, Booth Place (off B6238, ¼ mile N of centre)
☎ (0706) 214863
11–3, 5.30–11; 11–11 Fri & Sat
S&N Theakston Best Bitter; Taylor Landlord; Whitbread Boddingtons Mild, Bitter Ⓗ
Tastefully decorated lounge with a separate dining room. Home-cooked food (all day Sun). Children welcome to eat.

Wesham

Stanley Arms
8 Garstang Road, South Wesham ☎ (0772) 685254
12–5, 7–11
S&N Theakston Best Bitter, XB Ⓗ
Small, friendly, street-corner local near the biscuit factory. Park nearby. Q

Whalley

Swan Hotel
King Street ☎ (0254) 822195
11–11
Lion's Bitter; Whitbread Boddingtons Bitter Ⓗ
Welcome oasis in a quartet of pubs in a village dating back to medieval times. Excellent value meals. Open all day Sun for diners only. Busy in the eve. Lion's Bitter at a low price. Q P

Wharles

Eagle & Child
Church Road (2 miles off B5269 near radar station)
OS448356 ☎ (0772) 690312
12–3 (not Mon–Fri, except bank hols), 7–11
Cains Bitter, FA; Whitbread Boddingtons Bitter Ⓗ
Rural free house with a thatched roof, low-beam ceilings and a collection of antique farm implements. Carved wooden-backed seats and unspoilt decor; no electronic games. Not to be missed. Q P

Whittle-le-Woods

Royal Oak
216 Chorley Old Road
☎ (0254) 76485
2.30–11
S&N Matthew Brown Mild, Bitter, Theakston Mild, Best Bitter Ⓗ
Small, terraced local: a small front room with a fire and a games room. Interesting Nuttalls windows. Full of atmosphere and characters. A meeting place for mature motorcyclists. Q

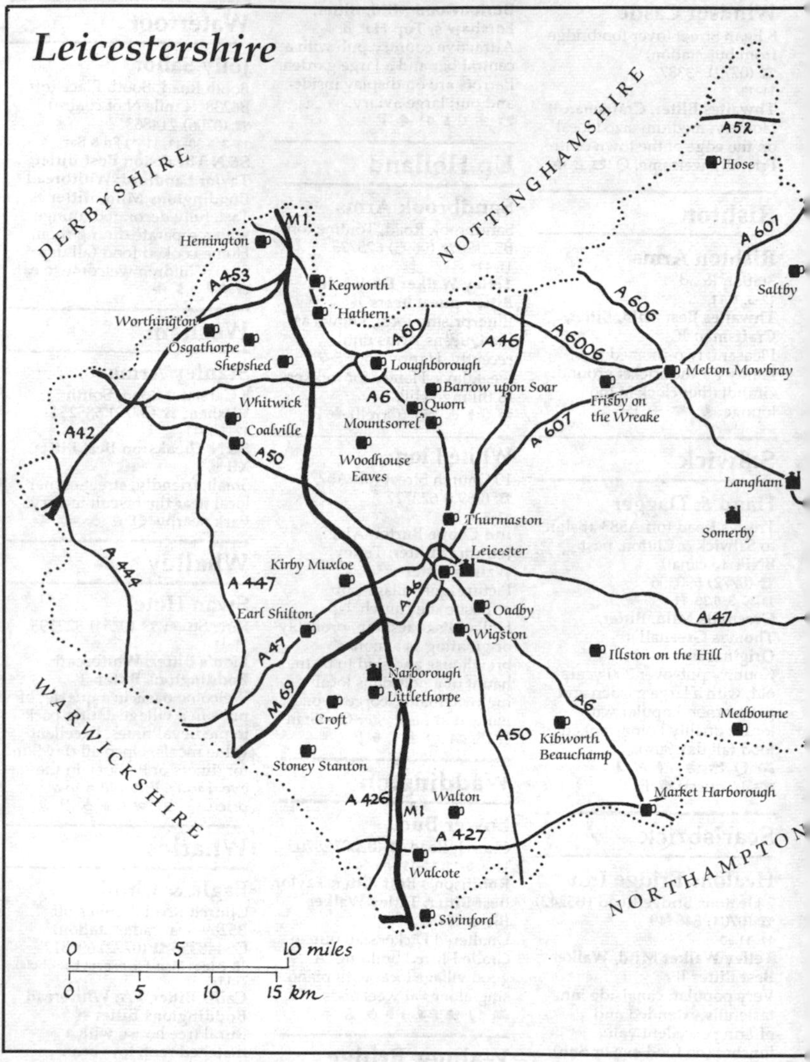

Everards, *Narborough;* **Featherstone, Hoskins, Hoskins & Oldfield,** *Leicester;* **Parish,** *Somerby;* **Ruddles,** *Langham*

Barrow upon Soar

Navigation Inn

Mill Lane ☎ (0509) 412842
11–3, 5.30–11; 11–11 Sat
Draught Bass; Greenalls Shipstone's Mild, Shipstone's Bitter; Marston's Pedigree Ⓗ
Cosy canalside pub with an unusual bar top of old coins. Skittles played regularly (room for functions). No food Sat or Sun. ⛴ ❀ ☾ ♿ ▲ ♣ P

Clipsham

Olive Branch

Main Street ☎ (0780) 410355
12–3, 6–11
Mansfield Riding Bitter, Old Baily Ⓗ**; guest beers** (occasionally) Ⓖ
Attractive old stone building where the small bar is cosy and friendly, although most of the pub is occupied by a restaurant. Beware the obscure car park entrance.
♨ Q ❀ ☾ ◗ ♿ P

Coalville

Bulls Head

Warren Hills Road (B587, 2½ miles NE of centre)
☎ (0530) 810511
11–2.30, 7–11; 12–2.30, 7–10.30 Sun
Ansells Bitter; Ind Coope Burton Ale; Marston's Pedigree; Tetley Bitter Ⓗ

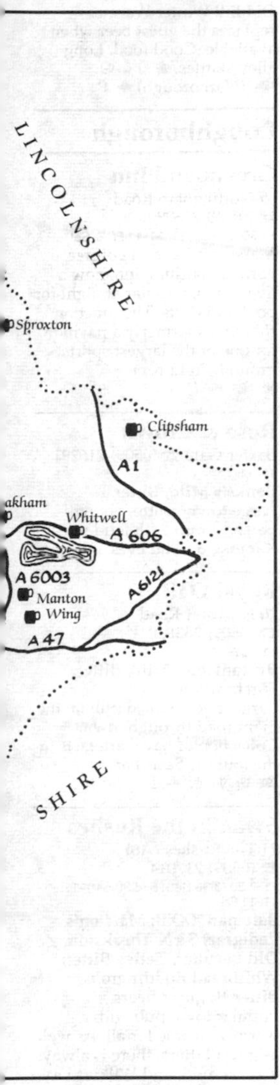

Busy roadside pub on the edge of Charnwood Forest. The lounge is pleasantly divided into several drinking areas and the large beer garden has plenty of seating. No food Sun.
⛫ Q ❀ ◑ P

Croft

Heathcote Arms

Hill Street ☎ (0455) 282439
11.30–2.30, 5.30–11; 11–11 Sat
Adnams Bitter; Everards Mild, Beacon, Tiger, Old Original Ⓗ; guest beers
Unspoilt village pub with three rooms, on a hilltop overlooking the river. Relaxed, friendly atmosphere and home-cooked food. Table and alley skittles.
⛫ Q ❀ ◑ ◗ ⊞ ♣ P

Earl Shilton

Red Lion

High Street ☎ (0455) 840829
11–2.30 (3 Sat), 5.30 (6 Sat)–11
Draught Bass; M&B Mild Ⓗ
Basic beer drinkers' pub on the main A47. Three separate rooms with one central bar.
❀ ⊞ P

Frisby on the Wreake

Bell Inn

2 Main Street ☎ (0664) 434237
12–2.30, 6–11; 12–2.30, 7–10.30 Sun
Ansells Bitter; Draught Bass; Bateman Mild, XXXB; Marston's Pedigree; Tetley Bitter Ⓗ; guest beers
Large village locals' pub with a basic but friendly atmosphere. Dates back to 1759 but extended at the rear to provide a family room. Popular for its good, cheaply-priced food and for its turnover of guest beers. Limited parking.
⛫ Q ☋ ❀ ◑ ♣ ⌓ P

Hathern

Dew Drop Inn

Loughborough Road
☎ (0509) 842438
12–3 (not Mon–Fri), 7–11
Hardys & Hansons Best Mild, Best Bitter Ⓗ
Small, traditional pub with a tiny lounge, but a large selection of malt whiskies. Popular with the locals. Parking for three cars only.
⛫ Q ⊞ ♣ P

Three Crowns

Wide Lane ☎ (0509) 842233
12–2.30, 5.30–11; 12–11 Sat (11–3, 7–11 summer Sat)
Bass Worthington BB, Draught Bass; M&B Mild, Highgate Mild Ⓗ
Lively village local with three separate drinking areas. Home of many local teams. Skittle alley to the rear. ⛫ ❀ ♣ P

Hemington

Jolly Sailor

21 Main Street
☎ (0332) 810448
11–11
Draught Bass; M&B Mild; Marston's Pedigree; guest beers Ⓗ
Friendly two-roomed local set back from the road. Always three guest beers available.
⛫ ❀ ♿ ⛺ ♣ P

Hose

Black Horse

21 Bolton Lane
☎ (0949) 60336
12–2.30, 6.30 (7 Sat)–11
Home Mild, Bitter; S&N Theakston Best Bitter Ⓗ; guest beers
Excellent example of a mid-Victorian village pub: an authentic 1930s tap room plus a cosy snug and lounge/dining room. Skittle alley at the rear. The innovative menu often features oriental meals (with vegetarian option). No food Mon eve or Sun. Always two or three guest beers available.
⛫ Q ☋ ❀ ◑ ◗ ⊞ ♿ ♣ P

Try also: Rose & Crown, Bolton Lane (Free)

Illston on the Hill

Fox & Goose

Main Street ☎ (053 755) 340
12–2 (2.30 Sat), 7–11; 12–2, 7–10.30 Sun
Everards Mild, Beacon, Tiger, Old Original; Ridleys IPA Ⓗ
Two-roomed, basic country pub with a friendly, relaxed atmosphere. Local mementoes in the bar. Worth finding.
⛫ Q ❀ ⊞ ♣

Kegworth

Red Lion

24 High Street (200 yds W of A6) ☎ (0509) 672466
11–3, 5–11
Draught Bass; M&B Mild; Marston's Pedigree; Tetley Bitter; guest beers Ⓗ
Three-roomed village local offering good value for the area. HQ of various village societies, including the Homing Bird Society. Near East Midlands airport and Donington race track. Book camping in advance. Children welcome until 8.30.
⛫ Q ☋ ❀ ⛺ ♣ P

Kibworth Beauchamp

Coach & Horses

2 Leicester Road
☎ (0533) 792247
11.30 (11 Sat)–3, 5 (6 Sat)–11
Ansells Mild, Bitter; Draught Bass; Tetley Bitter Ⓗ
Warm, cosy old coaching inn, on the main A6, with coin-filled beams and horse brasses. Popular with locals and passing custom. Traditional home-cooked food.
⛫ ❀ ◑ ◗ P

Kirby Muxloe

Royal Oak
35 Main Street
☎ (0533) 393166
11–2.30, 6–11
Adnams Bitter; Everards Mild, Beacon, Tiger, Old Original Ⓗ**; guest beers**
The modern exterior conceals a comfortable, traditionally-styled lounge and a separate restaurant, popular for business lunches. Basically a locals' pub, formerly called the Spanish Blade. Bar snacks include large filled baguettes.
◑ ◗ P

Leicester

Black Horse
1 Foxon Street, Braunstone Gate ☎ (0533) 540030
12–2.30, 5.30 (6 Sat)–11
Everards Beacon, Tiger, Old Original Ⓗ**; guest beers**
120-year-old drinkers' pub close to the city centre, popular with students. Friendly atmosphere; untouched by refurbishment. Reckoned to have the longest-running Sun eve quiz. ❀ ♣

Freemans Arms
19 Aylestone Road (A426 near Granby Halls) ☎ (0533) 550923
11.30–2.30, 5.30–11; 11.30–11 Sat (but closes 2.30–5.30 for home soccer matches)
Marston's Pedigree; Tetley Bitter Ⓗ
19th-century house, formerly the Freemans Hotel. One large room split three ways into a quiet area, the main bar with darts, and an area with a pool table. Note the collection of antiquities on the high shelf behind the bar. Q ◑ ♣

Hat & Beaver
60 Highcross Street
☎ (0533) 622157
11–3, 6–11
Hardys & Hansons Best Mild, Best Bitter, Kimberley Classic Ⓔ
Traditional two-roomed local, a former Bass pub. Relaxed atmosphere; TV in the bar. Well-filled cobs usually available. Handy for the Shires shopping centre. ❀ ⊟ ♣

New Road Inn
201 Welford Road
☎ (0533) 707696
12–2.30 (3 Sat), 6 (7 Sat)–11
Ansells Mild, Bitter; Ind Coope Burton Ale; Tetley Bitter Ⓗ
100-year-old pub, close to the university on the main A50. Large, open-plan and popular with students. Petanque played. ❀ ◑ ♣ P

Salmon Inn
19 Butts Close Lane
☎ (0533) 532301
11–2.30, 5–11; 11–11 Thu–Sat
Banks's Mild, Bitter Ⓔ
Small, fully refurbished pub (in typical Banks's style), serving a varied clientele. Close to St Margaret's bus station and the Shires shopping centre. ❀ ◑

Tom Hoskins
131 Beaumanor Road (off A6 Abbey Lane) ☎ (0533) 611008
11.30–3, 5.30 (6 Sat)–11
Hoskins Beaumanor Bitter, Penn's Ale, Premium, Churchill's Pride, Old Nigel Ⓗ**; guest beers**
The Hoskins brewery tap: a lively, friendly bar and a comfortable lounge. Brewery trips can be arranged. Handy for the Great Central Steam Railway. Some beers may change. Book eve meals.
Q ❀ ◑ ◗ ♣ P

Tudor
100 Tudor Road
☎ (0533) 620087
11–2.30 (3 Sat), 6–11; 12–2.30, 7–10.30 Sun
Everards Mild, Beacon, Tiger, Old Original Ⓗ
Corner pub in a terrace with a Victorian exterior. Still has two rooms and a games room upstairs. ❀ ♣

Victoria Jubilee
112 Leire Street (off A46 Melton road) ☎ (0533) 663599
11–2.30 (3.30 Sat), 6–11
Marston's Bitter, Pedigree Ⓗ**, Owd Rodger** (winter) Ⓖ
Friendly two-roomed locals' pub, originally called the Full Moon. The name changed with Queen Victoria's Jubilee in 1887. ❀ ⊟ ♣

Wilkies
29 Market Street
☎ (0533) 556877
11–11; closed Sun
Marston's Pedigree; Whitbread Boddingtons Bitter, Flowers Original Ⓗ**; guest beer**
Lively German-styled bar, popular with younger drinkers. Large selection of imported bottled beers plus continental-style food. Happy hour Mon–Fri, 5–7. ◑

Littlethorpe

Plough Inn
Station Road ☎ (0533) 862383
11–2.30 (3 Sat), 6–11
Everards Beacon, Tiger, Old Original; Ridleys IPA Ⓗ**; guest beer**
Friendly, thatched village local with an unspoilt, cosy interior. Old Bill Winter Warmer replaces the guest beer when available. Good food. Long alley skittles. ❀ ◑ ◗ ⊟
⇌ (Narborough) ♣ P

Loughborough

Greyhound Inn
69 Nottingham Road
☎ (0509) 216080
11.30–2, 5.30–11; 11–11 Fri & Sat
Marston's Bitter, Pedigree Ⓗ
Former coaching inn, now a lively pub, popular at night for pool and darts. The function room was formerly a pavilion for one of the largest sports grounds in Europe.
❀ ⇌ ♣ P

Rose & Crown
Baxter Gate ☎ (0509) 216291
11–11
Banks's Mild, Bitter Ⓔ
Large town-centre, young persons' pub with loud music. Karaoke on Thu eves. ◑

Royal Oak
70 Leicester Road
☎ (0509) 263860
11–3, 7–11
Burtonwood Mild, Bitter, Forshaw's Ⓗ
Large, two-roomed pub on the main road through town. Collection of naval artefacts in the lounge. Basic bar.
♨ ❀ ⊟ ♿ ♣ P

Swan in the Rushes
21 The Rushes (A6)
☎ (0509) 217014
11–2.30 (3.30 Sat), 5 (6.30 Sat)–11; 11–11 Fri
Bateman XXXB; Marston's Pedigree; S&N Theakston Old Peculier; Tetley Bitter; Whitbread Boddingtons Bitter Ⓗ**; guest beers**
Popular town pub with a warm welcome for all. As well as guest bitters, there is always a guest mild, and Wilkins Dry plus guest ciders. Food is of high quality and reasonable price. The upstairs function room is a regular venue for live music.
♨ Q 🛏 ◑ ◗ ⊟ ⌓ P

Windmill Inn
Sparrow Hill ☎ (0509) 216314
11–2.30 (3 Fri & Sat), 5 (7 Sat)–11
Banks's Mild; Marston's Bitter, Merrie Monk, Pedigree Ⓗ
Three-roomed pub near the town centre. The oldest pub in town, recently refurbished.
♨ ❀ ◑ ⇌ ♣ P

Try also: Gate Inn, Meadow Lane (Marston's); **Great Central Hotel,** Gt Central Rd (Free); **Jack O'Lantern,** Clarence St (Burtonwood)

Manton

Horse & Jockey
St Marys Road
☎ (0572) 285335
11–2, 7–11
Mansfield Riding Bitter, Old Baily [H]
Unspoilt 250-year-old village pub near Rutland Water. A popular spot for Sunday lunches. 🔥 ❀ 🛏 ◑ ⊟ ♣

Market Harborough

Red Cow
58–59 High Street
☎ (0858) 463637
11–3 (4 Sat), 6–11
Marston's Bitter, Pedigree [H]
Traditional, one-roomed beer drinkers' pub with limited food. Popular for darts, dominoes and cribbage. Q ♣

Medbourne

Nevill Arms
12 Waterfall Way
☎ (085 883) 288
12–2.30, 6–11
Adnams Bitter; Marston's Pedigree; Ruddles Best Bitter, County [H]
Built in 1876 as a coaching inn, on the village green next to an attractive stream. A popular weekend venue for families, as the ducks on the bank are friendly. Pub games are provided for organised parties.
🔥 Q ♞ ❀ 🛏 ◑ ◐ ♣ P

Melton Mowbray

Boat
57 Burton Street
☎ (0664) 60518
11.30–2.30, 7–11
Burtonwood Bitter, Forshaw's, Top Hat [H]
Popular, cosy town pub, with friendly, welcoming staff. Note the rare photographs of old Melton. 🔥 Q ⇌ ♣

Crown
10 Burton Street
☎ (0664) 64682
11–3 (3.30 Sat), 7–11
Everards Old Original [H]**; guest beers**
Friendly town pub, very lively at night and popular with the younger drinker.
🔥 ♞ ❀ ◑ ⇌ ♣

Mountsorrel

Lindens Hotel
22 Halstead Road
☎ (0533) 302163
12–2.30 (3 Sat), 5.30 (7 Sat)–11
Adnams Bitter; Everards Mild, Beacon, Tiger, Old Original [H]
Situated in a residential area. The locals' bar with cheaper beer contrasts with the comfortable hotel lounge. Large garden and outdoor drinking area.
❀ 🛏 ◑ ⊟ ♣ P

Oadby

Black Dog Inn
London Road
☎ (0533) 712233
11–3, 5.30–11; 11–11 Fri & Sat
Banks's Mild, Bitter [E]
Basic, two-roomed beer drinkers' pub with no frills.
♞ ◑ ⊟ P

Cow & Plough
Stoughton Farm Park, Gartree Road (signed from A6)
☎ (0533) 720852
12–3, 5–7 (12–9 summer); 12–3 Sun, closed Sun eve
Hoskins & Oldfield Mild, Brigadier, HOB Bitter [H]**; guest beers**
An old converted barn with an elegant Victorian bar decorated with breweriana and old advertising signs. Genuine pub atmosphere. Also available for private parties. Hours extended by prior arrangement. Q ❀ ♿ ⊖ P

Oakham

Wheatsheaf
Northgate ☎ (0572) 723458
11.30 (11 Sat)–2.30, 6–11
Adnams Bitter; Everards Beacon, Tiger; Shepherd Neame Bishops Finger [H]
Two-roomed local near the church – popular for wedding parties. 🔥 Q ❀ ◑ ⊟ ⇌

Try also: White Lion, Melton Rd (Free)

Osgathorpe

Royal Oak
20 Main Street
☎ (0530) 222443
12–3 (not Mon–Fri), 7–11
M&B Mild; Marston's Pedigree [H]
Friendly local pub in a farming community. Display of horse brasses and an open fire. 🔥 Q ❀ ♿ ▲ ♣ P

Quorn

Apple Tree
Stoop Lane ☎ (0509) 412296
12–3, 7–11
Draught Bass; M&B Mild [H]
Locals' pub with a small bar and a tiny lounge. Basic but busy. 🔥 ❀ ⊟ ♣ P

Blacksmiths Arms
29 Meeting Street
☎ (0509) 412751
12–2, 5.30–11
Marston's Pedigree [H]
Old, beamed pub in a picturesque village, with a tiny lounge and a comfortable bar. The famous Great Central Railway passes through Quorn – the pub is within a mile of the station.
🔥 Q ♞ ❀ ⊟ ♣ P

White Horse
2 Leicester Road
☎ (0509) 620140
12–2.30 (not Mon), 6–11; 12–11 Sat
Adnams Bitter; Everards Beacon, Tiger, Old Original [H]
Homely village local. Look out for the tropical fish and for the 10,000-year-old deer bones found in the car park. Meals Sat and Sun lunchtime only. Folk club alternate Sun.
🔥 ❀ ◑ ♿ ♣ P

Saltby

Nags Head
1 Back Street ☎ (0476) 860491
12–2.30 (3 Sat), 7–11
Greene King Abbot; Ruddles Best Bitter [H]
Village pub, popular with locals and visitors alike. Note the stone lintel over the front door.
🔥 Q ❀ 🛏 ◑ ◐ ⊟ ♣ P

Shepshed

Britannia Inn
28 Britannia Street
☎ (0509) 502350
10.30–2.30, 7–11; 12–2, 7–10.30 Sun
Hardys & Hansons Best Mild, Best Bitter [E]
Well-established, friendly pub in the town centre. Popular with locals who enjoy a sing-along to the 'old-time' jukebox on Sat eve. Separate lounge. Q ♞ ❀ ◑ ♿ ♣ P

Sproxton

Crown Inn
Coston Road ☎ (0476) 860035
12–2.30, 7 (6.30 summer)–11
Everards Mild, Beacon; Marston's Pedigree [H]
100-year-old, stone-built pub in a conservation village. The tables are made from old Singer sewing machines. Petanque played.
🔥 ❀ ◑ ◐ ♿ ♣ P

Stoney Stanton

Francis Arms
Huncote Road
☎ (0455) 272034
11–2, 5.30–11

Banks's Mild; Marston's Bitter, Pedigree [H]
Basic, village beer-drinkers' pub with a collection of rifles on the ceiling. Two separate rooms. ♨ ⊞ ♣ P

Swinford

Cave Arms
North Street ☎ (0788) 860464
12–3 (may extend), 7–11
Bateman XB; Wadworth 6X; Wards Kirby [H]**; guest beers**
Unspoilt old village local named after the former residents of nearby Stanford Hall. Usually two guest beers. Table skittles and a function room upstairs. Site for caravans only. ♨ ❀ ◐ ◑ ♣

Thurmaston

Unicorn & Star
796 Melton Road
☎ (0533) 692849
11 (10.30 Sat)–3, 6–11
Greenalls Shipstone's Mild, Shipstone's Bitter [H]
Basic beer-drinkers' bar with no frills. Comfortable lounge.
♨ ❀ ⊞ ♣ P

Walcote

Black Horse
Main Street (A427)
☎ (0455) 552684
12–2 (not Mon & Tue), 6.30 (5.30 Fri)–11; 12–2.30, 7–10.30 Sun
Hook Norton Best Bitter, Old Hooky; Taylor Landlord [H]**; guest beer**
Popular free house, famous for its oriental food. Continental bottled beers, country wines and Weston's Old Rosie cider available. Black Horse Bitter is brewed by Judges.
♨ Q ◐ ◑ ⌓ P

Walton

Dog & Gun
Main Street ☎ (0455) 552808
11–3, 5–11; 12–4, 7–11 Sat
Banks's Mild, Bitter [E]
Small, traditional, two-roomed village pub dating back to 1846. Used to be a butcher's shop; meat hanging beams survive in the bar alongside other memorabilia. Limited parking. ♨ Q ❀ ◐ ♣ P

Whitwell

Noel Arms
Main Road ☎ (078 086) 334
11–11
Ind Coope Burton Ale; Ruddles County; Tetley Bitter [H]
Traditional public bar with a plush hotel and restaurant added. Handy for Rutland Water. ❀ 🛏 ◐ ◑ ⊞ P ⅟

Whitwick

Kings Arms
22 Silver Street (follow signs to sports centre) ☎ (0530) 832117
11–2.30, 5.30–11
Banks's Mild; Marston's Pedigree [H]
Welcoming village-centre pub: a meeting place for many local clubs, including brass bands who practise in the club room. Known locally as the 'Geese', because of its goose ornaments from all over the world. Lunchtime snacks. ♿ ♣ P

Three Horseshoes
11 Leicester Road
☎ (0530) 837311
11–3, 6.30–11
Draught Bass; M&B Mild [H]
Traditional two-roomer with a welcoming public bar. A classic locals' pub – no niche marketing or themes to spoil it. ♨ Q ❀ ⊞ ♿ ♣

Wigston

Horse & Trumpet
Bull Head Street (A50)
☎ (0533) 886290
11–2.30, 5 (6 Sat)–11; 12–2.30, 7–10.30 Sun
Everards Mild, Beacon, Tiger, Old Original; Ridleys IPA [H]**; guest beer**
Old coaching inn with a comfortably modernised lounge bar. Popular for business lunches and with younger drinkers in the evening, when it can be busy. Long alley skittles.
❀ ◐ ♿ ♣ P

Meadowbank
Kelmarsh Avenue (off A50 at fire station) ☎ (0533) 811926
11–2.30, 6–11; 11–11 Sat
Banks's Mild, Bitter [E]**; Marston's Pedigree** [H]
Modern estate pub with a basic bar and a large, tastefully decorated lounge. Occasional live music in the lounge, and karaoke on Tue nights, otherwise pleasant and relaxed. Q ❀ ◐ ◑ ⊞ ♿ ♣ P

Wing

Cuckoo
3 Top Street ☎ (0572) 85340
11.30–3, 6.30–11
Cains Bitter; Marston's Pedigree; Shepherd Neame Porter, Bishops Finger; Tetley Bitter [H]
Unspoilt village local, once two cottages. Live music performed twice a month; a steam fair and beer festival held in summer. A winner of local CAMRA's *Pub of the Season* award. Beers may vary.
♨ ❀ ◐ ◑ ▲ ♣ P

Woodhouse Eaves

Curzon Arms
44 Maplewell Road
☎ (0509) 890377
11–2.30, 6–11 (varies in summer)
Courage Directors; John Smith's Bitter [H]
Popular village pub with a strong traditional games following. The lounge is geared towards food, while the bar is basic with a tiled floor. Don't let the neon lights outside put you off.
❀ ◐ ◑ ♿ ♣ P

Wheatsheaf
Brand Hill ☎ (0509) 890320
12–3, 7 (6 summer)–11
Draught Bass; Marston's Pedigree; Ruddles County; Taylor Landlord [H]**; guest beers**
Classy country pub on the outskirts of the village, with an extensive bar and restaurant menu. Three guest beers at all times. Not to be missed.
♨ ❀ ◐ ◑ ♿ ⌓ P

Worthington

Malt Shovel
Main Street ☎ (0530) 222343
12–2, 6.30–11; closed Mon
Marston's Pedigree [H]
Cosy village pub where the garden has a play area and pets. The home-made food is highly recommended and children are welcome in a room off the bar (children's meals if requested). Popular with ramblers.
♨ ❀ ◐ ◑ ⊞ ♣ P

Home and Away

One of the best-known beers in the Midlands is to leave Home. Home Mild is traditionally associated with the Daybrook brewery in Nottingham, but now Scottish & Newcastle has announced that it is to be brewed under contract by Mansfield. Meanwhile, S&N presses on with its promotion of Theakston products. Could this be the beginning of the end for yet another local brewery, squeezed out by the pursuit of national brands?

Lincolnshire

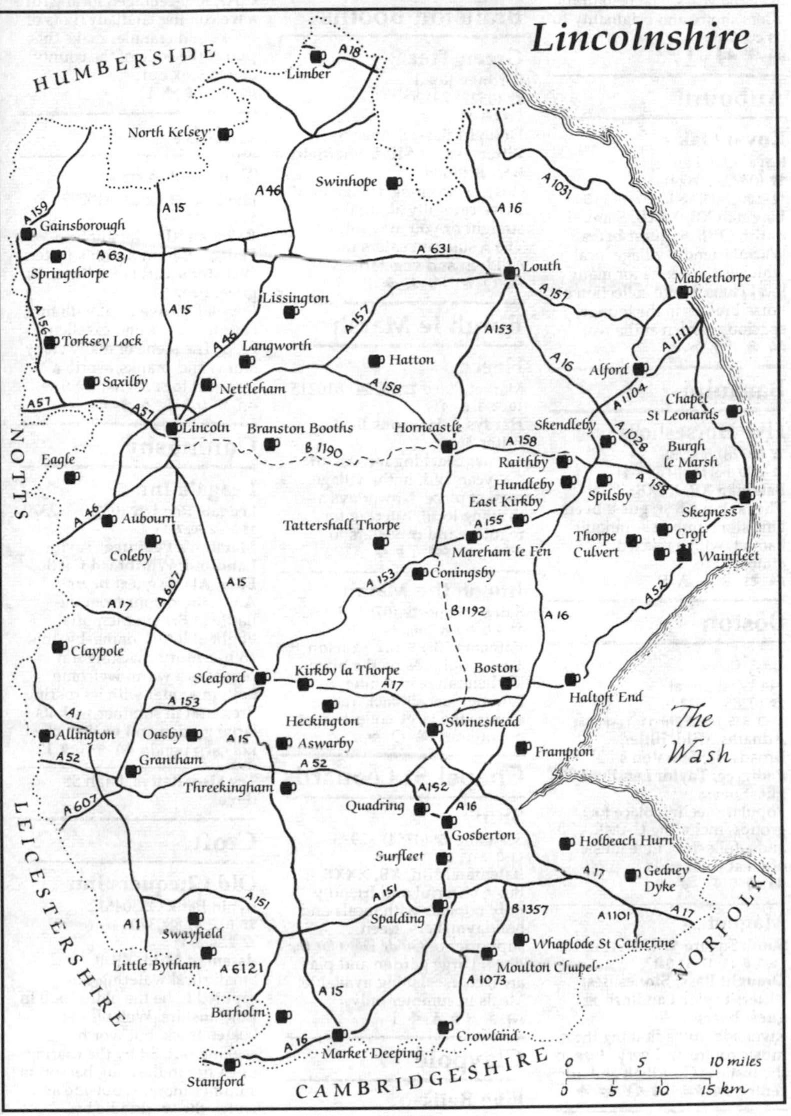

Bateman, Wainfleet

Alford

Half Moon

West Street ☎ (0507) 463477

11–11

Bass Worthington BB, Draught Bass; Vaux Samson Ⓗ

Popular and welcoming market town pub with a cosmopolitan clientele. Expanded into two neighbouring houses to include a comfortable lounge and a restaurant. Host to local clubs and societies. 'Dicko's' house beer (not brewed here).

❀ ◖ ◗ ⊟ ♣ P

Allington

Welby Arms

The Green ☎ (0400) 81361

12–2.30 (3 Sat), 5.30 (6.30 Sat)–11

Draught Bass; John Smith's Bitter; Taylor Landlord Ⓗ**; guest beers**

Situated on the village green, a three-roomed watering-hole worth seeking out. No food Sun eve.

♛ Q ❀ ◖ ◗ ♣ P ⚟

Aswarby

Tally Ho

On A15 ☎ (052 95) 205

12–3, 6–11

Draught Bass; Bateman XB Ⓗ**; guest beers**

A 17th-century property, part of the Aswarby estate; a hostelry and coach stop for

over 100 years. The restaurant offers choice and originality to its customers.
⛰ ❀ 🛏 ◐ ◑ P

Aubourn

Royal Oak
Royal Oak Lane
☎ (0522) 788291
12–2.30, 7–11; 12–2.30, 7–10.30 Sun
Bateman XB, XXXB; Samuel Smith OBB Ⓗ; guest beers
Warm, friendly village local which is the venue for many local clubs. Large collection of horse brasses in the lounge; spacious garden at the rear.
⛰ ❀ ◐ ◑ ♣ P

Barholm

Five Horseshoes
☎ (0778) 560238
12–2.30 (not Mon–Fri), 6–11
Bateman XB, XXXB; S&N Theakston XB Ⓗ; guest beers
Fine stone pub in a tranquil hamlet, with a relaxed atmosphere.
⛰ 🐴 ❀ ♿ ▲ P

Boston

Eagle
144 West Street
☎ (0205) 361116
11–3, 6 (5 Thu & Fri)–11; 11–11 Sat
Adnams Mild, Bitter, Broadside; Marston's Pedigree; Taylor Landlord Ⓗ; guest beers
Popular meeting place for groups, including CAMRA and a folk club. Live music often at weekends.
⛰ ❀ ◐ 🚌 ⇌ ♣

Magnet
South Square ☎ (0205) 369186
11–3, 6–11; 11–11 Sat
Draught Bass; Stones Best Bitter; Taylor Landlord Ⓗ; guest beers
Riverside pub adjoining the music centre and very close to the historic Guildhall and arts centre. ⛰ 🛏 ◐ ◑ 🚌 ⇌ ♣

Mill Inn
Spilsby Road (near Pilgrim Hospital) ☎ (0205) 352784
11–3, 7–11
Draught Bass; Bateman Mild, XB, XXXB Ⓗ
Smart and popular pub renowned for its good value food. ❀ ◐ ◑ ♿ ▲ P

New Castle
Fydell Street ☎ (0205) 361144
11–4, 7–11; 11–11 Fri
Draught Bass; Bateman Mild, XB Ⓗ
Large pub just outside the town centre with boat moorings on the River Witham nearby. Games include bar skittles. ❀ ⇌ P

Branston Booths

Green Tree
Bardney Road
☎ (0522) 791208
11–4, 7–11
Draught Bass; Stones Best Bitter; Wards Mild, Sheffield Best Bitter Ⓗ
Cosy, welcoming village local. Drive carefully along the straight or you may miss it. The restaurant caters for children and vegetarians.
⛰ Q ❀ ◐ ◑ ▲ ♣ P

Burgh le Marsh

Fleece
Market Place ☎ (0754) 810215
10.30–3, 6–11
Hardys & Hansons Best Bitter Ⓔ
Former coaching inn, about 400 years old, in the village market place. Nowadays a thriving local, catering for regulars and travellers to 'Skeggy'. 🛏 ◐ ◑ ♣

Inn on the Marsh
Storeys Lane ☎ (0754) 810582
11–4 (3 Tue & Thu), 6–11
Bateman XB; Vaux Samson Ⓗ
Toast your toes by the open kitchen range in winter; in summer just sit back and admire the large collection of bric-a-brac. ⛰ Q ♣

Chapel St Leonards

Ship
Sea Lane ☎ (0754) 72975
11–3, 7–11
Bateman Mild, XB, XXXB Ⓗ
Busy, cheerful and friendly pub, popular with locals and holidaymakers. Keen supporter of *Guide Dogs for the Blind*. Large garden and play area; coarse fishing available. Meals in summer only.
⛰ ❀ ◐ ◑ ▲ ♣ P

Claypole

Five Bells
Main Street ☎ (0636) 626561
12–3, 7–11
Bateman XB, XXXB; Vaux Samson; Wards Sheffield Best Bitter Ⓗ; guest beers
Good value, home-cooked food is on offer in this plainly refurbished village inn. Catering does not dominate however and dominoes are often in evidence. The accommodation is excellent and there is a garden where children can play.
⛰ Q ❀ 🛏 ◐ ◑ ♿ ▲ ♣ P

Woolpack
Main Street ☎ (0636) 626274
12–11
Marston's Bitter, Pedigree Ⓗ; guest beers

Cosy, low-ceilinged local with a welcoming landlady. Lots of nooks and crannies make this pub at the edge of the county one to seek out.
⛰ ❀ ◐ ◑ ♣ P

Coleby

Tempest Arms
Hill Rise ☎ (0522) 810287
11.30–3, 6.30–11
Bateman XB; Marston's Pedigree; John Smith's Bitter; Webster's Yorkshire Bitter Ⓗ; guest beer
Popular village local with fine country views and excellent food. The scene of many crazy stunts and pranks; worth a visit just to see what's going on. ❀ ◐ ◑ ♿ ▲ ♣ P

Coningsby

Leagate Inn
Leagate Road ☎ (0526) 342370
11.30–2.30, 7–11
Marston's Pedigree; Taylor Landlord; Whitbread Castle Eden Ale Ⓗ; guest beers
A worthy detour from the Battle of Britain Memorial Flight at RAF Coningsby, this 16th-century coaching inn provides a warm welcome, both in winter with its roaring fires, and in summer with its large garden and well-stocked koi carp ponds. ⛰ ❀ ◐ ◑ P

Try also: Rattys, High St (Free)

Croft

Old Chequers Inn
Lymn Bank OS504612
☎ (0754) 880320
12–2.30, 7–11
Bateman Mild, XB Ⓗ
Small rural watering-hole, reputed to be the oldest pub in Lincolnshire. Well off the beaten track, but worth seeking out. Sit by the roaring open fire in the snug bar, or, in summer months, outside and watch the world idle by.
⛰ Q ❀ ◐ ◑ 🚌 ♿ ♣ P

Crowland

George & Angel
2 North Street ☎ (0733) 210550
10.30–3.30, 6–11; 10.30–11 Sat
Draught Bass; Marston's Pedigree; John Smith's Bitter, Magnet; Wilson's Mild Ⓗ
Popular, small town pub built in 1714 with stone from nearby Crowland Abbey and featuring a Collyweston slate roof. A Grade II-listed building, it stands close to the historic Trinity Bridge. Basic bar and comfortable lounge; resident organist on Sat nights.
⛰ ❀ ◐ 🚌 ♣ P

Eagle

Struggler
High Street ☎ (0522) 868676
12–11
John Smith's Bitter, Magnet; Webster's Green Label, Yorkshire Bitter [H]
Village pub with a warm, friendly atmosphere in the oak-beamed bar. Popular with indoor and outdoor games teams. ♛ ♘ ❀ ♣ P

East Kirkby

Red Lion
Main Road ☎ (079 03) 406
11–3, 7–11
Bateman XB; Springhead Bitter [H]**; guest beers**
Popular and friendly village local with a diverse clientele that includes a resident 'collectomaniac' and seasonal 'fungophile'. Situated near the Lincolnshire Air Museum and Henry II's Bolingbroke Castle. Camping and caravanning in the pub grounds.
♛ ♘ ❀ ◗ ▲ P

Frampton

Moores Arms
Church End ☎ (0205) 722408
11–2.30, 7–11
Draught Bass; Bateman XB [H]
Popular pub in a quiet village, located opposite the church.
Q ♘ ❀ ◖ ◗ ♿ ▲ ♣ P ⚟

Gainsborough

Drovers Call
Lea Road ☎ (0427) 612044
11–3, 6–11
Bass Mild XXXX, Special, Draught Bass; John Smith's Bitter [H]
Large locals' pub on the outskirts of town. Recently extensively redecorated.
Q ◖ ⊞ ♿ ⇶ (Lea Rd) P

Gedney Dyke

Chequers
☎ (0406) 362666
11–3, 7–11
Adnams Bitter; Draught Bass; Bateman XXXB; Greene King Abbot; Morland Old Speckled Hen [H]
Comfortable country pub well worth seeking out, especially if hungry as well as thirsty. Bridge played – beginners are welcome; Sun night quizzes. Dates back to circa 1795.
♛ ❀ ◖ ◗ ♣ P

Gosberton

Bell
High Street ☎ (0775) 840186
11–3, 6–11
Draught Bass; Coach House Innkeeper's; Home Bitter; Marston's Pedigree; S&N Theakston XB, Old Peculier [H]
Grade II-listed building dating from 1671, with wood-panelled interior walls and a pleasant, friendly atmosphere.
♛ Q ❀ ⛟ ◖ ◗ ⊞ P

Grantham

Angel & Royal Hotel (Angel Bar)
High Street ☎ (0476) 65816
11.30–2.30 (3 Fri, 4 Sat), 6 (7 Sat)–11
Adnams Bitter; Draught Bass; Bateman XXXB [H]**; guest beers**
Reputedly England's oldest coaching inn, established in the 13th century and commissioned by the Knights Templar. Note the huge inglenook and sculptured stone window. Local CAMRA *Pub of the Year* 1991 and 1992; cosmopolitan clientele.
♛ Q ❀ ⛟ ◖ ◗ ⊞ ⇶ P ⚟

Beehive
10–11 Castlegate
☎ (0476) 67794
11–3, 7–11; 11–11 Fri
Adnams Bitter, Broadside [H]
Renowned for being the only pub in England with a living pub sign. Friendly atmosphere; popular with young people. No food Sun.
♘ ❀ ◖ ⇶

Chequers
Market Place ☎ (0476) 76383
12–3 (4 Sat), 7 (5 Thu)–11; 12–11 Fri
S&N Theakston Mild, Best Bitter, XB; Younger IPA, No. 3 [H]**; guest beers**
Popular town-centre pub with a wide range of real ales which attracts a cross-section of people. ◖ ⇶

Manners Arms
70 London Road
☎ (0476) 63082
11–11
Everards Mild, Beacon, Tiger, Old Original; Morland Old Speckled Hen [H]
Recently refurbished, one-roomed town pub with a pool-playing area to the rear. Wheelchair access is via the rear entrance. ❀ ◖ ♿ ⇶ P

White Lion
53 Bridge End Road
☎ (0476) 62084
11–11
Courage Directors; John Smith's Bitter [H]**; guest beer**
Popular town pub which caters for all ages. The bar centres on games and has pool tables and darts. The lounge is quiet and serves good value lunches Mon–Sat.
♛ Q ❀ ◖ ⊞ ♿ ⇶

Try also: Odd House, Fletcher St (Free)

Haltoft End

Castle Inn
☎ (0205) 760393
11–3, 7–11
Bateman Mild, XB, Salem Porter [H]
Typical, friendly local with a well-balanced mix of clientele. A keen darts and domino pub, with occasional clay pigeon shoots. Excellent adventure playground for children. Reputedly haunted.
♛ ❀ ⛟ ◖ ◗ ♣ P

Hatton

Midge Inn
Main Road ☎ (0507) 578348
11.30–3, 7–11
Draught Bass; Greene King Abbot; Stones Best Bitter [H]
Pleasant roadside inn on the main Lincoln–Skegness route. Good food and a relaxed atmosphere. No meals Mon.
♛ ❀ ◖ ◗ ♿ P

Heckington

Nags Head
34 High Street ☎ (0529) 60218
11–3, 7–11
Vaux Samson; Wards Thorne Best Bitter, Sheffield Best Bitter [H]
17th-century coaching inn with a friendly welcome. The emphasis is on catering, with many home-made dishes. Shut the Box played.
Q ❀ ⛟ ◖ ◗ ⊞ ♿ ⇶ ♣ P

Try also: Royal Oak, High St (Tolly Cobbold)

Holbeach Hurn

Rose & Crown
Marsh Road ☎ (0406) 26085
11–11
Elgood's Cambridge Bitter [H]
Happy rural pub with a mixed clientele. Set in six acres and ideal for picnics and barbecues (barbecues provided – bring your own food). A brand new restaurant is to open in 1994. Camping for tents and caravans. ♛ ❀ ◖ ◗ ▲ ♣ P

Horncastle

Kings Head
Bullring ☎ (0507) 523360
11–3 (4 Sat), 7–11
Bateman Mild, XB, Salem Porter; John Smith's Bitter [H]
Cosy diminutive pub which, with its award-winning, outdoor floral display, affords a warm welcome. Known locally as the Thatch and once popular with petty thieves during the town's fairs and market days, because of the ease of escape through the back door. ♛ ◖ ♣

Lincolnshire

Red Lion
Bullring ☎ (0507) 523338
11–3, 7–11
Greenalls Shipstone's Mild, Bitter; Tetley Bitter 🄷
Pleasant market town pub, with a friendly welcome: a regular meeting place for local clubs and societies. Supports a flourishing theatre in the converted stables, which were regularly used during the famous horse fairs of days gone by.
♛ Q ♉ 🛏 ◖ ♿ ♣ P

Hundleby

Hundleby Inn
Main Road ☎ (0790) 52577
11–3, 6.30–11
Draught Bass; Bateman XB 🄷
Popular, unspoilt village local which continues its links with *Guide Dogs for the Blind*. Whist, darts and domino teams play in local leagues. The more energetic can walk the nearby Franklin Way.
♛ ❀ ◖ ◗ ⊟ ▲ ♣ P

Kirkby la Thorpe

Queens Head
Church Street ☎ (0529) 305743
11.30–3, 6.30–11
Draught Bass 🄷
Large food-oriented pub offering an excellent cold carvery: a welcome oasis off the busy A17. Meals not available Sun and Mon eves.
❀ ◖ ◗ P

Langworth

New Station
Main Road ☎ (0522) 750475
11–3.30, 7–11
Courage Directors; John Smith's Bitter 🄷
Large, modern roadside pub, much extended. The landlord has a long-standing reputation for his fish and chips.
❀ ◖ ◗ ♿ ♣ P

Limber

New Inn
High Street (A18)
☎ (0469) 60257
11–2.30 (4.30 Sat), 7–11
Bass Worthington BB; Bateman XXXB; McEwan 80/- 🄷; guest beer
Deservedly popular pub owned by the Earl of Yarborough, whose name is used to describe a poor bridge hand and also adorns many pubs in the area not owned by him. A magnificent mausoleum can be visited close by.
♛ Q ❀ 🛏 ⊟ ♣ P

Lincoln

Dog & Bone
10 John Street (near E Lincs College) ☎ (0522) 522403
12–3, 7–11
Draught Bass; Bateman XB, XXXB, Salem Porter 🄷; guest beers
Friendly, one-roomed pub, until recently a two-roomer called the Gay Dog. Boasts an array of antiques and old relics with a touch of humour.
♛ ❀ ◖ ♿ ⇌ ♣ P

Golden Eagle
21 High Street
☎ (0522) 521058
11–3, 5.30–11; 11–11 Fri & Sat
Adnams Broadside; Bateman XB; Everards Beacon; Fuller's London Pride; Taylor Golden Best 🄷; guest beers
Traditional, friendly pub at the southern end of the High Street; the second pub in Lincoln to be run by the Small Beer beer agency. Old Lincoln prints and memorabilia adorn the walls. Changing selection of guest beers. No food Sun.
Q ❀ ◖ ♣ ⌓ P

Jolly Brewer
26 Broadgate
☎ (0522) 528583
11–11
Bass Worthington BB, Draught Bass; Everards Tiger; S&N Theakston XB; Younger Scotch, No. 3 🄷; guest beers
Very popular city-centre pub attracting a wide range of customers. Previously known as the Unity. Substantial lunchtime snacks. A perennial entry in this guide.
♛ ❀ ♿ ⇌ ♣ ⌓ P

Peacock Inn
23 Wragby Road
☎ (0522) 524703
11.30–2.30, 5–11; 11–11 Sat
Hardys & Hansons Best Mild, Best Bitter, Kimberley Classic 🄷
Friendly local within easy walking distance of the tourist area and city centre. No food Sun. ♛ ❀ ◖ ♣ P

Portland Arms
50 Portland Street
☎ (0522) 513912
11–11
Draught Bass; Courage Directors; John Smith's Bitter, Magnet 🄷; guest beers
Simple town pub with absolutely no ties. A lively tap room with a pool table and usual pub games, and a cosy, quiet best room with collections of ducks and bar towels. Friendly welcoming atmosphere. Five guest beers from near, far and wide, including a mild.
❀ ⊟ ⇌ ♣ P

Prince of Wales
77a Bailgate
☎ (0522) 528894
11–2.30, 7 (6 summer)–11
Courage Directors; Marston's Pedigree; John Smith's Bitter, Magnet 🄷
Friendly uphill pub in the tourist area; the castle and cathedral are a short walk away. Dominoes and darts popular. Good value lunches.
❀ ◖ ⊟ ♣

Queen in the West
12 Moor Street (50 yds N off A57) ☎ (0522) 526169
11.30–3, 5.30–11; 11–4, 7–11 Sat
Bateman XB; S&N Theakston Best Bitter, XB, Old Peculier; Taylor Landlord; Younger No. 3 🄷; guest beers
Ever-popular street-corner local in the west of the city. Always bustling with people, especially in the evening. Fine lunchtime food and up to eight beers available. Its twelfth consecutive year in this guide says it all.
◖ ⊟ ♿ ♣

Sippers
26 Melville Street
☎ (0522) 527612
11–3, 6 (4 Fri)–11; 7–10.30 Sun, closed Sun lunch
Courage Directors; Marston's Pedigree; John Smith's Bitter, Magnet; Wilson's Mild 🄷; guest beers
Popular and comfortable street-corner pub near the station, with a large display of seafaring memorabilia. Always a warm welcome and a wide range of guest beers.
◖ ◗ ♿ ⇌ ♣

Small Beer (Off-Licence)
91 Newland Street West (off A57) ☎ (0522) 528628
10.30–10.30
Bateman XXXB; Taylor Landlord; Wards Sheffield Best Bitter 🄷; guest beers
Street-corner off-licence which has been in this guide for many years. Sells a wide range of guest beers, bottled beers from around the globe and various ciders. ⌓

Strugglers
83 Westgate
☎ (0522) 524702
11–3, 5.30–11; 11–11 Fri & Sat
Bass Mild XXXX, Draught Bass 🄷
Busy, basic and bursting with people – a little gem. A fine example of Lincoln life and incredibly popular for its size.
Q ❀ ♣

Victoria
6 Union Road (by west gate of castle) ☎ (0522) 536048
11–11
Bateman XB; Everards Old Original; Taylor Landlord Ⓗ; guest beers
The city's most celebrated on-going beer exhibition: the four guest beers include a mild, more are added on special feature nights and there are June and Xmas mini-festivals. Fine collection of blackboards. The genial hosts purvey pints with a patter that must be paid for!
Q ❀ ◖ ♣ ⌓

Try also: City Vaults, Gaunt St (Wards)

Lissington

White Hart
☎ (0673) 885205
11–2.30 (not Mon), 7–11
Bass Worthington BB, Draught Bass Ⓗ; guest beer
Comfortable village inn offering excellent food and occasional speciality eves. Holds an annual pub pentathlon and is a centre for other sports e.g. clay pigeon shooting. ♨ ❀ ◖ ◗ ♿ ♣ P

Little Bytham

Willoughby Arms
Station Road (B1176)
☎ (0780) 410276
12–3 (not Mon–Fri), 6–11
Ruddles County Ⓗ; guest beers
Cosy and welcoming village pub with splendid views over rolling fields from the back room bar. Two guest beers always available.
♨ Q ❀ ◖ ◗ ♿ ♣ P

Louth

Lincolnshire Poacher
211 Eastgate (1 mile E of centre) ☎ (0507) 603657
11–3.30, 5–11; 11–11 Sat
Hardys & Hansons Best Mild, Best Bitter, Kimberley Classic Ⓗ
Georgian-style dwelling-house converted into a two-room pub with accommodation. Extensive refurbishment took place in 1993. Friendly and comfortable atmosphere. Only snacks on Wed, Fri and Sat.
❀ 🛏 ◖ ◗ ♿ ♣ P

Masons Arms
Cornmarket ☎ (0507) 609525
11–11
Draught Bass; Bateman Mild, XB, XXXB, Salem Porter; Marston's Pedigree Ⓗ
Old posting or coaching inn from the 18th century, splendidly restored by the present owners, and providing all the facilities of a small country hotel, including comfortable and spacious bars. Food and coffee are available all day. Q ❀ 🛏 ◖ ◗ ♣

Olde Whyte Swanne
45 Eastgate ☎ (0507) 601312
11–3, 7–11; 11–11 Sat
Bass Mild XXXX, Draught Bass; Stones Best Bitter Ⓗ
Built in 1612, the oldest pub in Louth, with a magnificent public bar at the front and a modern lounge at the rear. The cellars are reputedly haunted. Next to a public car park (free at night). ♨ ◖ ⊟ ♣

Wheatsheaf
62 Westgate ☎ (0507) 606262
11–3, 5–11
Whitbread Boddingtons Bitter, Bentley's Yorkshire Bitter, Flowers Original Ⓗ; guest beer
Situated in a quiet Georgian terrace, this inn, dating from 1625, is equally attractive inside and out. Good pub food served Mon–Fri.
♨ Q ◖ ◗ ♣ P

Woolpack
14 Riverhead Road (1 mile E of centre at the river head of the old canal) ☎ (0507) 606568
11–3 (not Mon), 7–11
Bateman Mild, XB, XXXB Ⓗ
Former 19th-century wool merchant's house, now a traditional, friendly local with three rooms to suit all tastes. The short walk out of town is well rewarded.
♨ Q ❀ ⊟ ♣ P

Mablethorpe

Montalt Arms
George Street (off High St)
☎ (0507) 472794
11–3, 7–11
Draught Bass; Bateman XB; Stones Best Bitter Ⓗ; guest beer
Comfortable, L-shaped lounge bar with a well-appointed restaurant. Named after a local medieval knight who was killed in a duel. Plenty of woodwork and photos of bygone Mablethorpe. Not a typical seaside trippers' pub. Limited parking. ❀ ◖ ◗ P

Mareham le Fen

Royal Oak
Main Street ☎ (0507) 568357
11–3, 7–11
Bateman XB Ⓗ
As featured in *Profile of Mareham le Fen*, this attractive, thatched pub maintains many old traditions of village life. Excellent home-made food includes Bateman XXXB sausages. ♨ ❀ ◖ ◗ P

Market Deeping

Vine
19 Church Street
☎ (0778) 342387
11–3, 5.30–11
Wells Eagle, Bombardier Ⓗ; guest beers
Former 1870s prep school, now a very friendly local with a small lounge and larger busy bar area. The many social nights include quizzes and barn dances. Active charity fundraisers. Eve meals finish early and are not available Sun. ♨ Q ❀ ◖ ◗ ♿ ♣ P

Try also: Coachhouse (Free); Goat, Frognall (Free)

Moulton Chapel

Wheatsheaf
4 Fengate (B1420)
☎ (0406) 380525
11–3 (not Wed), 7–11
Draught Bass; Elgood's Cambridge Bitter; Greene King IPA Ⓗ; guest beer
Friendly pub in an out-of-the-way Fenland village. The public bar area boasts a splendid range and a collection of pottery pigs. Once owned by Bradfords brewery (closed 1928). Eve meals and camping by prior arrangement. Meeting room available.
♨ ⛹ ❀ ◖ ♿ ▲ ♣ P

Nettleham

White Hart
14 High Street
☎ (0522) 751976
11.30–3, 7–11
Draught Bass; Bateman Mild, XB, XXXB; Marston's Pedigree Ⓗ
Friendly pub in a commuter village. Internally renovated following a fire in 1992 and now as welcoming as ever. Good food from an extensive menu.
♨ ⛹ ❀ ◖ ◗ ⊟ ♿ ♣ P

Try also: All pubs in Nettleham serve real ale

North Kelsey

Royal Oak
High Street ☎ (0652) 678544
12–3, 7–11
Stones Best Bitter; Vaux Samson; Wards Sheffield Best Bitter Ⓗ
Fine village pub with a friendly atmosphere. The lounge bar has a wood burning stove, and there is also a games room and a small snug. Quiz nights Tue; music quiz alternate Sats. Popular for meals. ♨ Q ❀ ◖ ◗ ⊟ ♣ P

Lincolnshire

Oasby

Houblon Arms
Main Street ☎ (052 95) 215
12–3 (not Mon–Fri), 7–11
Ind Coope Burton Ale; Tetley Bitter Ⓗ; guest beers
Built of local stone, this old village pub is a rural gem. The beamed interior, real fires, abundant ornamentation and friendly atmosphere create a popular country inn.
♔ Q ❀ 🛏 ◐ ◗ P

Quadring

White Hart
7 Town Drove
☎ (0775) 821135
11–3 (not Mon), 6.45–11
Bateman Mild, XB, XXXB Ⓗ
Comfortable, popular village local with a welcoming atmosphere, catering for all ages. At one time the back of the pub was a bakery. Challenge the pub dog to a beer-mat flipping contest. Wheelchair access is via the car park. ♔ ❀ ♿ ♣ P

Raithby

Red Lion
Main Street ☎ (0790) 53727
11–3 (not Mon–Fri), 7–11
Home Bitter; S&N Theakston XB Ⓗ
Excellent cuisine complements the fine cellarmanship at this inviting village pub with an intimate restaurant (eve meals Wed–Sat only). Freshly madc pizzas. ♔ ❀ 🛏 ◐ ♣ P

Saxilby

Ship
Bridge Street ☎ (0522) 702259
11.30–2.30 (3 Fri & Sat), 7–11
John Smith's Bitter Ⓗ
Sporting pub, popular with locals and boaters; by England's oldest canal. Good simple food. Caravans can park by prior arrangement. Eve meals Fri and Sat only.
❀ ◐ ◗ ♿ ▲ ⇌ ♣ P

Skegness

Vine Hotel
Vine Road, Seacroft (1 mile S of centre, off Drummond Rd)
☎ (0754) 763018
11–11
Draught Bass; Bateman XB, XXXB, Salem Porter Ⓗ
An oasis of peace and calm in a secluded wooded setting away from the hurly-burly of the resort: leafy gardens in summer, a roaring fire in winter. Possibly visited by Tennyson and reputedly haunted by a murdered excise man. ♔ ❀ 🛏 ◐ ◗ ⊟ ▲ ♣ P

Skendleby

Blacksmiths Arms
Main Street
☎ (075 485) 662
11–3, 6–11
Bateman Mild, XB, XXXB Ⓗ
Pub where a cosy bar has an open view of the cellar. The large restaurant houses a well dating back to 1650 – no one has been down but the water remains crystal clear. The pump is still in working order, but has been disabled to prevent curious customers flooding the pub.
♔ Q ❀ 🛏 ◐ ◗ ♿ ▲ P

Sleaford

Marquis of Granby
65 Westgate
☎ (0529) 303223
11.30–3, 5.30–11; 11.30–11 Fri & Sat
Tetley Bitter; Whitbread Flowers Original Ⓗ
Small but comfortable local, well worth finding. The real fire in the winter months is a rare find in Sleaford. The covered courtyard is ideal for children when it is raining.
♔ ❀ ◐ ⇌ ♣

Nags Head
64 Southgate
☎ (0529) 413916
11–3, 7–11; 11–11 Fri & Sat
Draught Bass; Bateman XB, XXXB Ⓗ
Friendly, no-frills town pub serving an excellent range of filled rolls. The upstairs function room has live music at weekends with a late licence. ❀ ◐ ◗ ⇌ ♣ P

Rose & Crown
2 Watergate
☎ (0529) 303350
11–2.30, 7–11; 10.30–3, 6.30–11 Fri & Sat
Mansfield Riding Bitter, Old Baily Ⓗ
Popular, busy town-centre pub; always friendly, with helpful bar staff. Large, enclosed outdoor drinking area. No food Sat or Sun.
❀ ◐ ⇌ ♣ P

Spalding

Lincolnshire Poacher
11 Double Street
☎ (0775) 766490
11–3, 5–11
S&N Theakston Best Bitter, XB, Old Peculier Ⓗ; guest beers
Busy and lively pub which always serves at least four guest beers. The enterprising landlord has created a cosmopolitan atmosphere. Pleasant riverside frontage.
❀ 🛏 ◐ ◗ ♿ ⇌

Spilsby

Nelson Butt
10 Market Street
☎ (0790) 52258
10.30–2.30, 6–11
Draught Bass; Bateman XB Ⓗ
Basic, no-frills, small market town pub with a friendly welcome. Q ♣

White Hart
Cornhill, Market Square
☎ (0790) 52244
11–11
Hardys & Hansons Best Bitter, Kimberley Classic Ⓗ
Large, comfortable market town coaching inn with its own 150-year-old posting box – possibly the oldest in the country. A taxi service and mini bus serves the community and customers alike. Snooker and pool in separate rooms.
♔ ♞ ❀ 🛏 ◐ ◗ ⊟ ♣ P

Springthorpe

New Inn
14–16 Hill Road
☎ (042 783) 254
12–2, 7–11; 12–2, 7–10.30 Sun
Bateman XXXB; Marston's Pedigree Ⓗ
Excellent village local with superb food and a genial host who is always ready with a song for his appreciative clientele.
♔ Q ❀ ◐ ◗ ⊟ ♣ P

Stamford

St Peters Inn
St Peters Street ☎ (0780) 63298
11–2.30 (not Mon), 7–11; 11–11 Sat
Marston's Bitter, Pedigree Ⓗ; guest beers
A small lounge bar with exposed stone walls, and the Friars restaurant upstairs; downstairs the cave-like Cloisters Bar is a mecca for real ale lovers with two handpumps and up to five casks on the bar. No food Mon, or Tue and Wed eves.
❀ ◐ ◗ ⇌ ♣ P

White Swan
Scotgate ☎ (0780) 52834
11–3, 5 (6 Sat)–11
Bateman Mild, XB, XXXB, Salem Porter, Victory Ⓗ
Former Manns pub taken over in 1988. The only Bateman tied house to offer the full range of beers. A one-roomed pub, with a mixed clientele, which acts as a pre-dinner bar for the restaurant opposite.
♔ ⇌ ♣

Try also: Dolphin, East St (Wells)

Surfleet

Mermaid

Main Road ☎ (0775) 85275
11.30–3, 6.30–11
Adnams Broadside; Bateman XXXB; Courage Directors; Greenalls Shipstone's Bitter Ⓗ
Pub once a brewery, situated by the side of the River Glen and now popular for meals. Pleasant atmosphere, large garden and a play area. 🔥 Q 🐎 ❀ 🛏 ◖ ◗ ⊟ ♿ ▲ ♣ P

Swayfield

Royal Oak

27 High Street
☎ (0476) 550247
11–2.30, 6–11
Bass Worthington BB, Draught Bass Ⓗ**; guest beers**
Large, open-plan pub, popular with locals and those in search of good food: a long bar, a discrete pool room, and a rugby-playing landlord.
🔥 ❀ ◖ ◗ ♿ ♣ P

Swineshead

Wheatsheaf Hotel

Market Place ☎ (0205) 820349
12–2.30, 6–11; 12–11 Sat
Draught Bass; Bateman XB; Tetley Bitter Ⓗ
Traditional village pub with a good selection of bar and restaurant meals. Trad. jazz live on alternate Thus. Strong football ties and home of the Lincs Junior Cup winners for the last two seasons. No food Tue or Sun.
🔥 Q ❀ 🛏 ◖ ◗ ⊟ ♿ ♣ P

Try also: Wheatsheaf, Hubberts Bridge (Free)

Swinhope

Click'em Inn

On B1203 ☎ (0472) 398253
11–2.30 (3 Sat; not Mon), 7–11
S&N Theakston XB, Old Peculier; Taylor Best Bitter Ⓗ**; guest beer**
Isolated but popular Wolds pub: a genuine free house, well worth the find. Its name derives from the click of the gate to the opposite field, into which farmers drove flocks whilst drinking at the pub.
🔥 Q ❀ ◖ ◗ ♣ P

Tattershall Thorpe

Blue Bell

☎ (0526) 342206
12–3, 7 (6 summer)–11
Courage Directors; John Smith's Bitter; Tetley Bitter Ⓗ**; guest beers**
Picturesque, thatched pub which was the Dambusters' local and dates from 1250, when the priest hole was popular with the clergy. Nowadays the warm welcome, the restaurant and the two acres of ground, attract both locals and visitors.
🔥 🐎 ❀ ◖ ◗ ♿ ▲ ♣ P

Thorpe Culvert

Three Tuns

Culvert Road OS471603
☎ (0754) 880495
11–2.30, 7–11
Tetley Bitter Ⓗ**; guest beers**
250-year-old riverside pub with a large garden handy for fishing. Regularly lit with old gas lamps to enhance the atmosphere. A warm welcome is provided by Oscar, the pub's small dog. Steaks (36 oz) and traditional Irish cuisine are served.
🔥 Q ❀ ◖ ◗ ▲ ⇌ ♣ P

Threekingham

Three Kings Inn

Salters Way ☎ (0529) 240249
11–11
Bass Worthington BB, Draught Bass; Stones Best Bitter Ⓗ
Welcoming, 17th-century coaching inn. The interesting collection of handpumps includes an original swan neck pump.
🐎 ❀ ◖ ◗ ♿ ▲ ♣ P

Torksey Lock

White Swan

1 Newark Road
☎ (0427) 71653
11–11
Bass Worthington BB, Draught Bass; Stones Best Bitter Ⓗ
Welcoming pub, offering wholesome food, at the entry to Foss Dyke from the River Trent and convenient for boaters. Good for families with its family room, play area in the garden and kids' menu.
🔥 🐎 ❀ ◖ ◗ ▲ ♣ P

Wainfleet

Red Lion

High Street
☎ (0754) 880301
11–3, 7–11
Bateman Mild, XB, XXXB Ⓗ
A large bar and a comfortable lounge, with a growing waddle of ducks nesting around the fireplace. The nearest Bateman pub to the brewery. Camping is in the grounds so Bateman's pilgrims can wake to the sight and aroma of the brewery. Book for Sun lunch. 🔥 ❀ 🛏 ◖ ◗ ⊟ ♿ ▲ ⇌ ♣ P

Whaplode St Catherine

Blue Bell

Cranesgate
☎ (0406) 34300
12–2 (not Mon–Thu), 6–11
Bateman XB; Vaux Samson Ⓗ
Lively village local with a fun-loving landlord. Built in the 17th century and under the same ownership for 25 years.
🔥 ❀ ▲ ♣ P

The Symbols

🔥	real fire	♿	easy wheelchair access
Q	quiet pub (at least one bar)	▲	camping facilities at the pub or nearby
🐎	indoor room for children	⇌	near British Rail station
❀	garden or other outdoor drinking area	⊖	near underground station
🛏	accommodation	♣	pub games
◖	lunchtime meals	ᗝ	real cider
◗	evening meals	P	pub car park
⊟	public bar	⊬	no-smoking room or area

Greater London

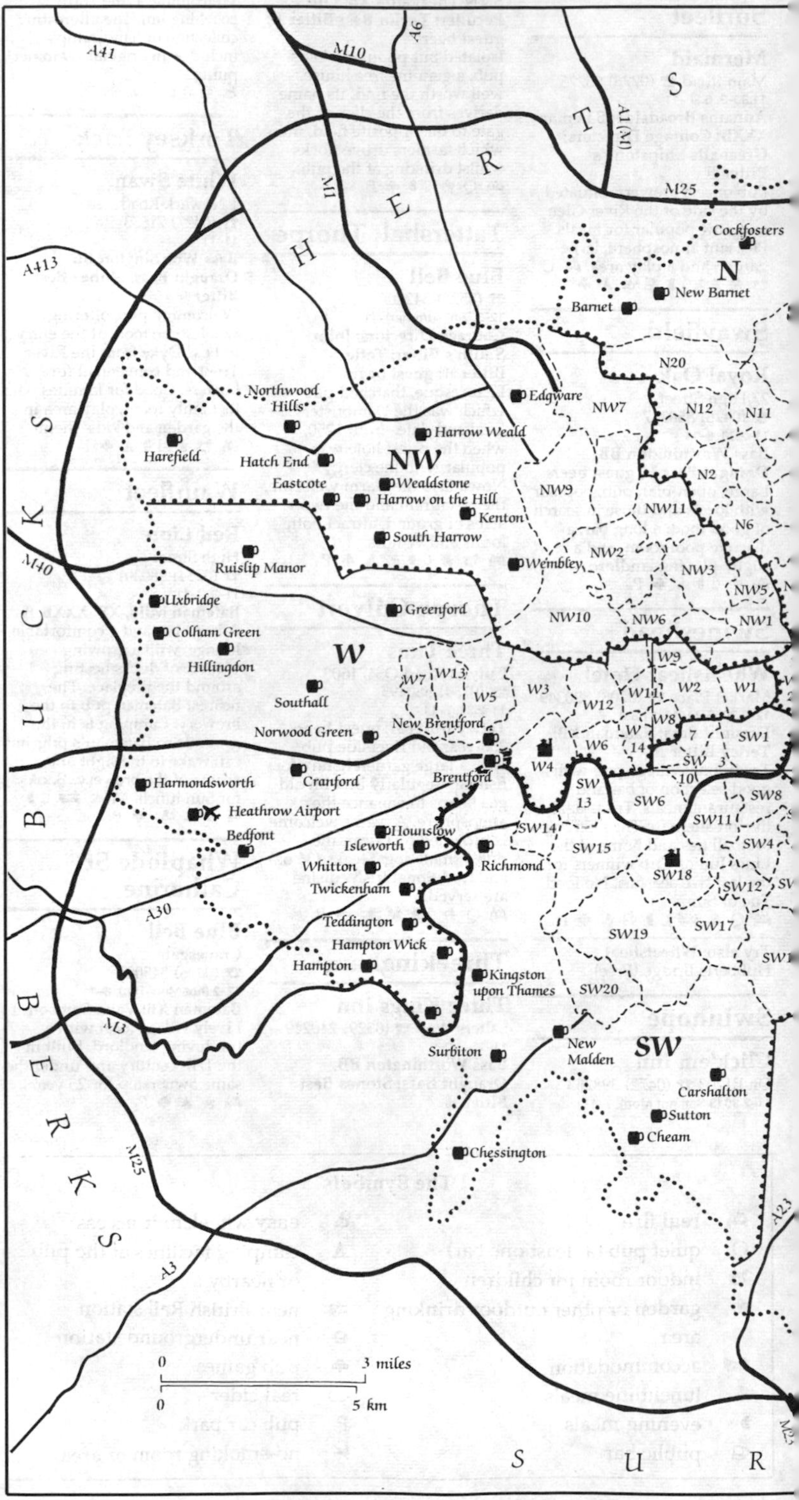

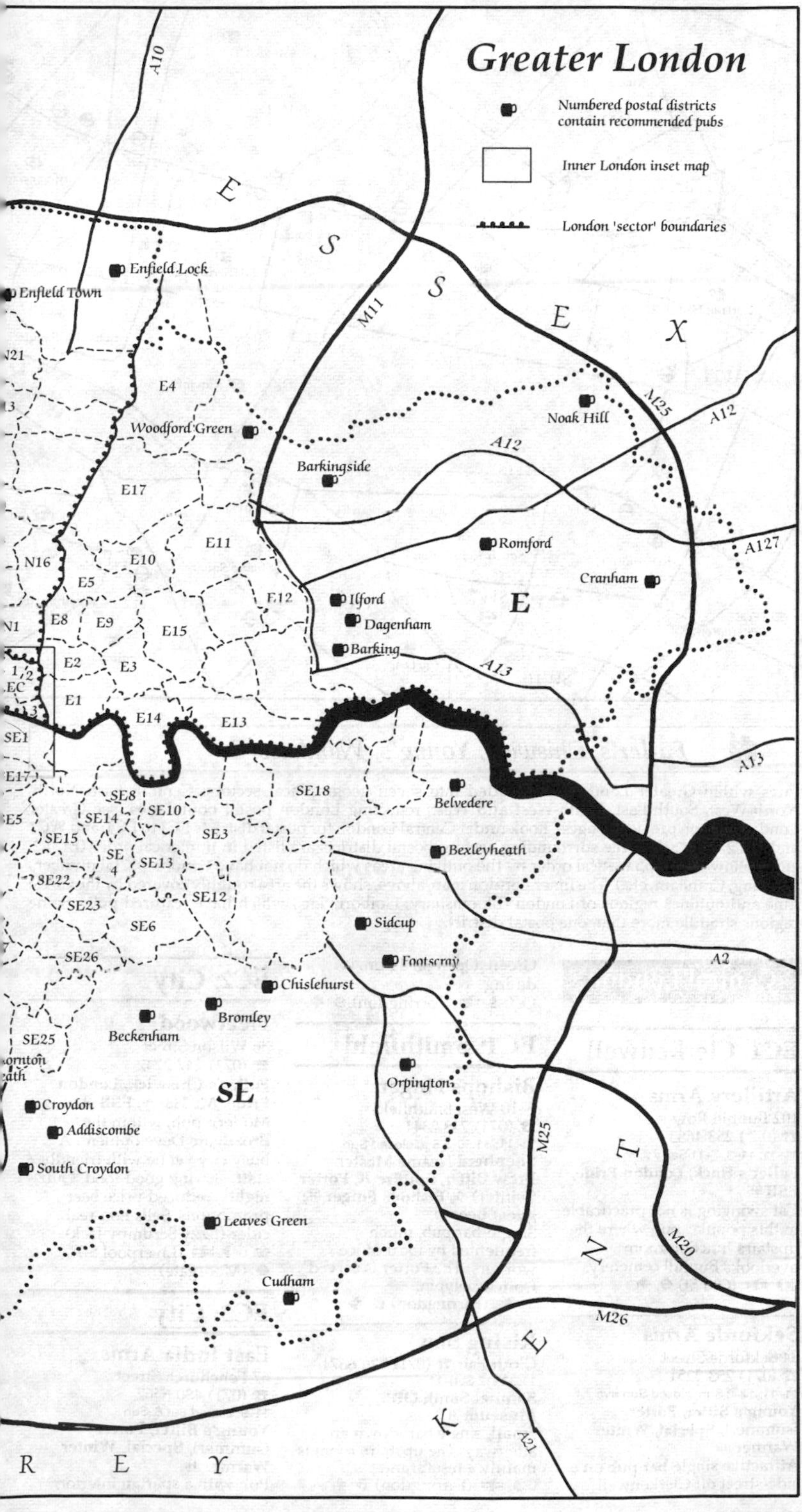
Greater London
Numbered postal districts contain recommended pubs
Inner London inset map
London 'sector' boundaries
ESSEX
KENT
REY
E
SE
A10
M11
M25
A12
A127
A13
A2
M20
M26
A21
Enfield Lock
Enfield Town
Woodford Green
Barkingside
Noak Hill
Romford
Cranham
Ilford
Dagenham
Barking
Belvedere
Bexleyheath
Sidcup
Footscray
Chislehurst
Bromley
Beckenham
Orpington
Croydon
Addiscombe
South Croydon
Leaves Green
Cudham
N21
N16
N1
E4
E17
E11
E10
E5
E12
E8
E9
E15
E2
E3
E1
E14
E13
EC
SE1
SE17
SE5
SE8
SE10
SE14
SE15
SE3
SE4
SE13
SE18
SE22
SE12
SE23
SE6
SE26
SE25

Greater London

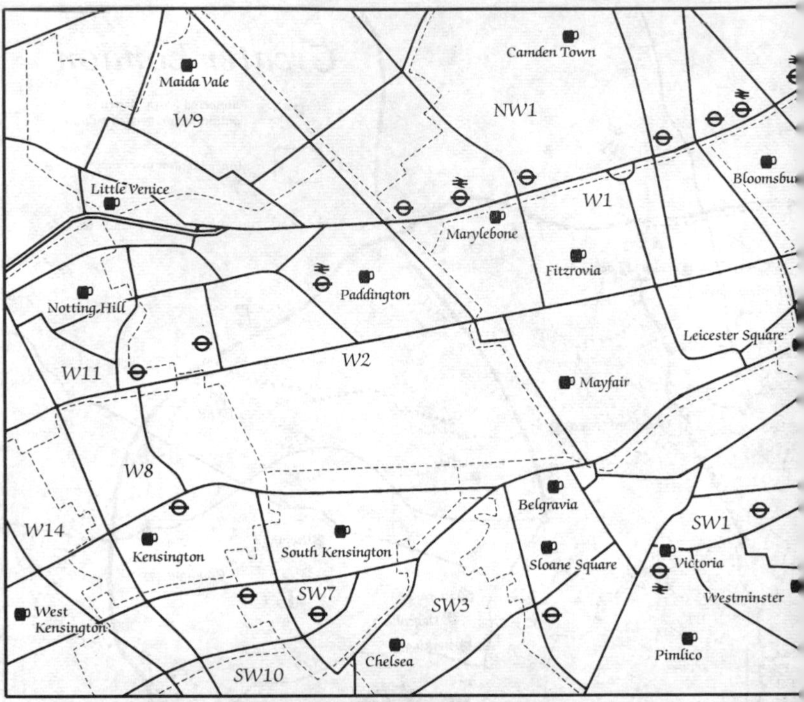

Fuller's, *Chiswick*; **Young's**, *Wandsworth*

Pubs within Greater London are divided into seven geographical sectors: Central, East, North, North-West, South-East, South-West and West, reflecting London postal boundaries (see Greater London map on previous pages). Look under Central London for postal districts EC1 to EC4, and WC1 and WC2. For each of the surrounding sectors, postal districts are listed in numerical order (E1, E2, etc.), followed in alphabetical order by the outlying areas which do not have London postal numbers (Barking, Cranham, etc.). The Inner London map, above, shows the area roughly covered by the Circle Line and outlines regions of London (Bloomsbury, Holborn, etc.) which have featured pubs. Some regions straddle more than one postal district.

Central London

EC1: Clerkenwell

Artillery Arms
102 Bunhill Row
☎ (071) 253 4683
11–11; 11–3, 7–11 Sat
Fuller's Hock, London Pride, ESB Ⓗ
Cat swinging is not practicable in this popular pub where the upstairs function room overlooks Bunhill cemetery.
◑ ◗ ⇌ (Old St) ⊖ ♣

Sekforde Arms
34 Sekforde Street
☎ (071) 253 3251
11–11; 12–3 Sun, closed Sun eve
Young's Bitter, Porter (summer), **Special, Winter Warmer** Ⓗ
Attractive single-bar pub on a side-street off Clerkenwell Green. Open till 4 Sun, if dining.
Q ◑ ◗ ⇌ (Farringdon) ⊖ ♣

EC1: Smithfield

Bishops Finger
9–10 West Smithfield
☎ (071) 248 2341
11–11; 11.30–3 Sat; closed Sun
Shepherd Neame Master Brew Bitter, Spitfire Ⓗ, **Porter** (winter) Ⓖ, **Bishops Finger** Ⓗ; **guest beer**
Single-bar pub, much frequented by local office workers. The Porter is served from a polypin.
◑ ⇌ (Farringdon) ⊖ ♣

Rising Sun
Cloth Fair ☎ (071) 726 6671
11.30 (12 Sat)–11
Samuel Smith OBB, Museum Ⓗ
Small, single bar, down an alleyway. The upstairs room is mainly a restaurant.
◑ ◗ ⇌ (Farringdon) ⊖ ♣

EC2: City

Fleetwood
36 Wilson Street
☎ (071) 247 2242
Fuller's Chiswick, London Pride, Mr Harry, ESB Ⓗ
Modern pub, within the Broadgate Development. A busy city venue with friendly staff, serving good food. Quiz nights; reduced-price beer promotions. Sells non-real cider (fizzy Scrumpy Jack).
❀ ◑ ◗ ⇌ (Liverpool St) ⊖ (Moorgate)

EC3: City

East India Arms
67 Fenchurch Street
☎ (071) 480 6562
11–9; closed Sat & Sun
Young's Bitter, Porter (summer), **Special, Winter Warmer** Ⓗ
Pub with a spartan interior;

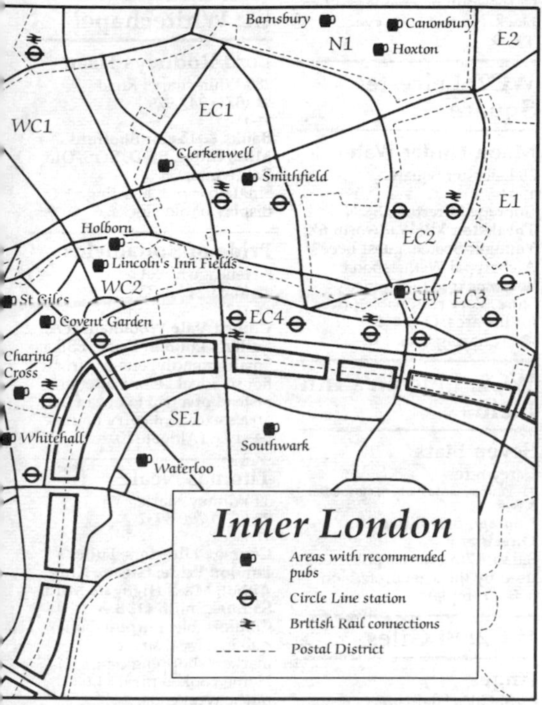

often crowded. Note the unusual handpumps. No dirty clothing admitted. Watch for happy hours.
Q ⇌ (Fenchurch St)
⊖ (Tower Hill)

Lamb Tavern
10–12 Leadenhall Market
☎ (071) 626 2454
11–9 (may close earlier); closed Sat & Sun
Young's Bitter, Special, Winter Warmer Ⓗ
Pub in the heart of the Victorian covered market, with bars on three levels. The no-smoking area closes at 3pm. Q ◐ ⇌ (Fenchurch St)
⊖ (Monument/Bank) ⊬

Swan
Ship Tavern Passage
☎ (071) 283 7712
11–9; closed Sat & Sun
Fuller's Hock, Chiswick, London Pride, ESB Ⓗ
Former Whitbread pub reopened by Fuller's in 1992. A tiny beer-only bar on the ground floor, and a full bar upstairs. Q ⇌ (Bank)
⊖ (Monument)

Three Lords
47 Minories
11–11 (may close earlier)
Young's Bitter, Special, Winter Warmer Ⓗ
Rebuilt in 1986 as an exact external copy of the old pub. The name refers to the 1745 Jacobite Rebellion. The no-smoking cellar bar closes at 7pm. Q ◐ ⇌ (Fenchurch St)
⊖ (Tower Gateway DLR) ⊬

EC4: City

Banker
Cousin Lane ☎ (071) 283 5206
11–9; closed Sat & Sun
Fuller's Chiswick, London Pride, ESB Ⓗ
Split-level pub overlooking the Thames, beneath Cannon Street station. ◐ ◑ ♿
⇌ (Cannon St) ⊖

City Retreat
Shoe Lane ☎ (071) 353 7904
11–9 (may vary); 11–11 Fri; closed Sat & Sun
Young's Bitter, Porter (summer), **Special, Winter Warmer** Ⓗ
Small, single bar at the bottom of an office block.
Q ◐ ⇌ (Farringdon/ Blackfriars) ⊖ ♣

Olde Cheshire Cheese
145 Fleet Street
☎ (071) 353 6170
11.30–11 (10 Sat; may vary)
Samuel Smith OBB, Museum Ⓗ
Famous city pub consisting of several bars and restaurants. A recent renovation has extended the pub without destroying its olde-worlde charm. The OBB represents good value for the city. The main bars are in Wine Office Court; the back bar is in Peterborough Court. ♨ Q
◐ ◑ ⇌ (Blackfriars) ⊖ ♣

WC1: Bloomsbury

Calthorpe Arms
252 Grays Inn Road
☎ (071) 278 4732
11–3, 5.30–11; 11–11 Thu–Sat
Young's Bitter, Porter, Special, Winter Warmer Ⓗ
Relaxed, welcoming local near the ITN building. The upstairs dining room is open lunchtimes; eve meals on request. Q ❀ ◐ ♿ ⇌ (King's Cross) ⊖ (Russell Sq)

Queens Head
66 Acton Street
☎ (071) 837 4491
11–11
Draught Bass; Charrington IPA; Fuller's London Pride Ⓗ**; guest beers**
Pleasant, long-roomed bar with large mirrors and quality tiling. Cider sometimes available. ❀ ◐ ♿ ⇌ (King's Cross/St Pancras) ⊖ ♣ 🍏

WC1: Holborn

Cittie of Yorke
22 High Holborn
☎ (071) 242 7670
11–11; 11.30–3, 5.30–11 Sat; closed Sun
Samuel Smith OBB, Museum Ⓗ
Very distinctive, Gothic building on the site of a 15th-century inn and coffee house. The magnificent baronial hall at the rear boasts huge vats, screened compartments and a triangular stove. Comfortable front bar; a maze of vaulted cellars. ♨ Q
◐ ◑ ♿ ⇌ (Farringdon)
⊖ (Chancery Lane) ♣

Princess Louise
208 High Holborn
☎ (071) 405 8816
11–11; 12–3, 6–11 Sat; 12–2, 7–10.30 Sun
Brakspear Bitter, Special; Wadworth IPA; Wards Thorne Best Bitter, Sheffield Best Bitter Ⓗ
Large, single-bar pub with an exquisite interior featuring an ornate ceiling, brass fittings, beautiful tiling and large, decorated mirrors. A Victorian architectural gem; even the toilets are worth a visit! The extensive range of beers includes a house beer. Busy weekdays; quiet at weekends.
⊖

Three Cups
21–22 Sandland Street
☎ (071) 831 4302
11–11 (open weekends in summer only)
Young's Bitter, Special, Winter Warmer Ⓗ
One-bar pub, attracting office workers. Range of good malt whiskies. Q ❀ ◖ ◗ ♿ ⊖ ♣

WC2: Charing Cross

Marquis of Granby
51 Chandos Place
☎ (071) 836 7657
11–11
Adnams Bitter; Ind Coope Burton Ale; Tetley Bitter Ⓗ
Narrow, friendly pub near St Martin-in-the-Fields.
◖ ◗ ⇌ ⊖

WC2: Covent Garden

Freemasons Arms
Long Acre ☎ (071) 836 3115
11.30–11
Greene King IPA, Rayments Special, Abbot Ⓗ
Large, comfortable pub. The Football Association was formed here. Upstairs bar.
◖ ⊖

Hogshead Ale House
Drury Lane
11–11
Whitbread Boddingtons Bitter Ⓗ**; guest beers** Ⓗ/Ⓖ
One of Whitbread's chain of semi-free houses which has an air-cooled gravity dispense stillage. Formerly the Sun.
⊖ (Holborn)

Marquess of Anglesea
Bow Street ☎ (071) 240 3216
11–11
Young's Bitter, Porter, Special, Winter Warmer Ⓗ
Comfortable, corner pub with a first-floor restaurant.
◖ ◗ ⇌ (Charing Cross) ⊖

Roundhouse
1 Garrick Street
☎ (071) 836 9838
11–11
S&N Theakston Best Bitter, Old Peculier; Wadworth 6X; Younger IPA; guest beers Ⓗ
Corner pub with adventurous guest beers and foreign bottled beers. Somewhat pricey but by no means the most expensive in this area. ◖ ◗ ⊖ ⌓

WC2: Holborn

Newton Arms
31 Newton Street
11–11; 11–3, 7–11 Sat; closed Sun
Greene King IPA; Ind Coope Burton Ale; Tetley Bitter Ⓗ
Corner pub in a modern office block. No meals Fri eve.
◖ ◗ ⊖

WC2: Leicester Square

Moon Under Water
28 Leicester Square
11–11
Courage Directors; S&N Theakston XB; Wadworth 6X; Younger Scotch; guest beer Ⓗ
Archetypal Wetherspoon house next to the Comedy Store. Very reasonable prices for the area. Q ◖ ◗ ♿
⇌ (Charing Cross) ⊖

WC2: Lincoln's Inn Fields

Seven Stars
Carey Street
11–11 (may close earlier); closed Sat & Sun
Courage Best Bitter, Directors Ⓗ
Small, 17th-century pub, much used by the legal profession.
◖ ⊖ (Temple)

WC2: St Giles

Angel
61 St Giles High Street
12–11; 12–3.30, 6–11 Sat; closed Sun
Courage Best Bitter, Directors Ⓗ
Old, reputedly haunted pub near Centrepoint. Handy for Oxford Street shops.
◖ ⊖ (Tottenham Ct Rd) ♣

East London

E1: Stepney

Colet Arms
94 White Horse Road
11–11; 11–5, 8–11 Sat; 12–3, 8–10.30 Sun
Pitfield Bitter, ESB Ⓗ
Traditional, semi-island bar in a comfortable, quiet pub, very much a local. Live music (piano and singer) Sat and Tue eves. Named after the founder of St Paul's School, John Colet, who lived nearby.
Q ♿ ⇌ (Limehouse)
⊖ (Stepney Green) ♣

Hollands
Brayford Square
☎ (071) 790 3057
11–11
Young's Bitter, Special, Winter Warmer Ⓗ
A treasure house of Victoriana, breweriana and press cuttings. A Grade II-listed building for its original interior, with boarded ceiling, pine panelling and glasswork.
⇌ (Limehouse)
⊖ (Whitechapel/Shadwell)

E1: Whitechapel

Lord Rodneys Head
285 Whitechapel Road
☎ (071) 247 9795
11–11
Banks & Taylor Shefford Mild, Bitter, SOD, SOS, Old Bat (winter) Ⓗ
Single-bar pub boasting a display of old clocks. ♿ ⊖ ♣

Pride of Spitalfields
3 Heneage Street
☎ (071) 247 8933
11–11
Crouch Vale Woodham IPA; Fuller's London Pride, ESB Ⓗ
Small, friendly, one-bar free house. Ideal before, after or instead of a trip to one of the area's excellent curry houses.
🛏 ◖ ⊖ (Aldgate E)

Thomas Neale
39 Watney Market
☎ (071) 790 8932
11–11
Courage Directors; Fuller's London Pride; Greene King Abbot; M&B Highgate Mild; Samuel Smith OBB Ⓗ
Comfortable, purpose-built pub in a local street market/shopping centre. Home-cooked meals. Live music weekends.
❀ ◖ ⊖ (Shadwell)

White Hart
1 Mile End Road
☎ (071) 790 2894
11–11
Marston's Pedigree; Wadworth 6X; Young's Bitter, Special Ⓗ
Basic boozers' pub with a superb glass partition and mirrors. The only pub left of the once-large Murphy's chain. The beer range may change.
⊞ ⇌ (Bethnal Green) ⊖

E2: Bethnal Green

Camdens Head
456 Bethnal Green Road
11–11
Courage Directors; Greene King IPA, Abbot; S&N Theakston XB; Younger Scotch; guest beers Ⓗ
An oasis in a 'fizz' area, converted from a disco-style dive to a pleasant, traditional-style pub. Occasional beer festivals and special promotions offer a range of ales. No food Sun eve.
◖ ◗ ⇌ ⊖

Nelson's Head
32 Horatio Street
☎ (071) 739 6054
11–11
Bateman Mild, XB, XXXB Ⓗ
Bateman's only London tied house. Live music most Thu eves. ♣

E2: Bow

Owl & Pussycat
34 Redchurch Street
☎ (071) 739 2808
11-11; 11-3, 7-11 Sat
Arkell's 3B; Courage Directors; Eldridge Pope Hardy Country; Fuller's London Pride; Hook Norton Best Bitter; Wadworth 6X Ⓗ
Beers from some 12 different breweries, with occasional milds, and a convivial atmosphere in a Grade II-listed pub. ❀ ◐ ⇌ (Liverpool St) ⊖

E3: Bow

Unicorn
27 Vivian Road
11-11
Fuller's Hock, London Pride, Mr Harry; Whitbread Flowers Original Ⓗ
Friendly, back-street local. Lunchtime snacks. ❀ ♣

E4: Chingford

Royal Oak
219 Kings Head Hill
☎ (081) 529 1492
11-3, 5.30-11; 11-11 Sat (public bar)
Courage Directors; McMullen AK, Country, Stronghart Ⓗ**; guest beer**
Large, brick-built suburban local with a plush lounge where much food is served, and a plain public bar where much beer is drunk, and games are played.
❀ ◐ ◑ ⊟ ♿ ♣ P

E5: Clapton

Anchor & Hope
15 High Hill Ferry
☎ (081) 806 1730
11-3, 5.30 (6 Sat)-11
Fuller's London Pride, ESB Ⓗ
Small, one-bar, riverside pub unchanged for many years.
❀ ♣

Prince of Wales
146 Lea Bridge Road
☎ (081) 533 3463
11.30-11
Young's Bitter, Porter (summer), **Special, Winter Warmer** Ⓗ
Large, riverside, two-bar pub with a selection of photos and paintings of the Prince of Wales (past and present).
❀ ◐ ◑ ⊟ ♿ P

E8: Hackney

Lady Diana
95 Forest Road
11.30 (11 Sat)-3, 5 (7 Sat)-11
Fuller's Chiswick, London Pride; Greene King Abbot; guest beers Ⓗ
Photos of old Hackney adorn the walls of this friendly, comfortable pub where pizzas are a speciality. ❀ ◐ ◑

E9: Hackney

Falcon & Firkin
274 Victoria Park Road
☎ (081) 985 0693
11-3, 6-11 (11-11 summer)
Falcon Bitter, Hackney Best Bitter, Dogbolter Ⓗ**; guest beers**
One-bar, Victorian brew pub with a room for families. View the mash tuns through a window (brewery tour available). Live music Thu–Sun eves. Good food and friendly staff. Two guest beers a week. Eve meals summer only. Wheelchair WC.
✱ ❀ ◐ ◑ ♿ ⇌ ⊖ ○ P

E9: Homerton

Chesham Arms
15 Mehetabel Road
☎ (081) 985 2919
11-3.30, 5.30 (7 Sat)-11
Adnams Broadside; Courage Best Bitter; Crouch Vale Woodham IPA; Wadworth 6X Ⓗ**; guest beers**
One-bar pub backing onto the North London line.
❀ ◐ ⇌ (Hackney Central)

E9: Victoria Park

Royal Standard
84 Victoria Park Road
12-11
Courage Best Bitter, Directors; Marston's Pedigree; guest beers Ⓗ
Two-bar local; Imperial Russian Stout sold. ◐ ♣

E10: Leyton

Drum
557 Lea Bridge Road
11-11
Courage Directors; Greene King IPA, Abbot; S&N Theakston XB; Younger Scotch Ⓗ
Enlarged during the last 12 months, a typical Wetherspoon house and a very friendly local, decorated with drums.
Q ❀ ◐ ◑ ⇌ (Walthamstow Central) ⊖

Hollybush
Grange Road ☎ (081) 539 3709
11.45-3 (11-3.30 Sat), 7-11
Greene King IPA, Abbot Ⓗ
Small, smart house near Leyton Orient FC.
❀ ⇌ (Leyton Midland) ⊖ ♣

E11: Leytonstone

Birkbeck
45 Langthorne Road
☎ (081) 539 2584
11-11
Bass Worthington BB, Draught Bass; Nethergate Bitter; Tetley Bitter; guest beers Ⓗ
Every person deserves a local like this; tastily restored to its former glory with a friendly atmosphere. Easily the best real ale pub in the area. Regularly changed guest beers. ❀ ⊟ ⊖ (Leyton) ♣

Woodhouse Tavern
119 Harrow Road
11-3 (4 Sat), 5 (7 Sat)-11; 11-11 Fri
Adnams Bitter Ⓗ**; guest beer**
Tidy, two-bar local with a club room. ♔ ❀ ⊟ ♣

E12: Manor Park

Blakesley Arms
53 Station Road
☎ (081) 478 6023
11-11
Draught Bass; Charrington IPA Ⓗ
Large, friendly pub with an L-shaped saloon bar and a small public bar. Old prints and posters (also shove-ha'penny) feature in the saloon. ❀ ⊟ ⇌ ♣

E13: Plaistow

Black Lion
59 Plaistow High Street
☎ (081) 472 2351
11-3, 5-11; 11-11 Sat
Courage Best Bitter, Directors; guest beer Ⓗ
Large pub with two contrasting bars, bar billiards and Sky TV. The restaurant is open weekday lunchtimes, Sat eve and Sun lunch. Bar meals till 7.30 Mon–Fri. Imperial Russian Stout is usually available. Boxing gym attached. ❀ ◐ ◑ ⊖ ♣ P

E14: Stepney

Queens Head
8 Flamborough Street
☎ (071) 790 6481
11-3, 5 (7.30 Sat)-11
Young's Bitter, Special, Winter Warmer Ⓗ
Friendly local, with three drinking areas, in a conservation area. Weekday lunches. ◐ ⇌ (Limehouse) ⊖ ♣

E15: Stratford

Theatre Royal
Gerry Raffles Square
☎ (081) 534 3124
11-3, 5-11 (closes earlier if no production at the theatre); closed Sun

Adnams Broadside; Wadworth 6X; Wells Eagle Ⓗ
Theatre bar, open to the public. Very busy at times.
⇌ ⊖

E17: Walthamstow

Coppermill
Coppermill Lane
11–11
Fuller's London Pride, ESB; Greene King IPA; Marston's Pedigree; Morland Bitter; Tetley Bitter Ⓗ
Small, popular local near an old coppermill, now used by the water authorities. ⇌ (St James's St) ⊖ (Blackhorse Rd) ♣

Grove Tavern
Grove Road ☎ (081) 509 0230
11–11
Draught Bass; Charrington IPA; M&B Highgate Mild; Tetley Bitter Ⓗ
Old Charrington house bought from the brewery by the present owner. Snacks lunchtime.
♨ ♞ ❀ ⇌ ⊖ ♣

Village
31 Orford Road
☎ (081) 521 9982
11–11
Bass Worthington BB, Draught Bass; Fuller's London Pride; guest beers Ⓗ
One-bar pub displaying a large selection of cameras and whisky bottles. Families welcome. No food Sun eve (other eves till 8).
♞ ❀ ◖ ◗ ♿ ⇌ ⊖

Barking

Britannia
1 Church Road (near A123)
☎ (081) 594 1305
11–3, 5–11; 11–11 Sat
Young's Bitter, Porter (summer), **Special, Winter Warmer** Ⓗ
Young's only pub in Essex offers a friendly, relaxing atmosphere. A large pub with a plush saloon and a more basic public. Occasional themed music nights. The lunches (weekdays) are good value. Q ❀ ◖ ⊟ ⇌ ⊖ ♣ P

Barkingside

New Fairlop Oak
Fencepiece Road, Fulwell Cross (A123) ☎ (081) 500 2217
11–11
Courage Directors; Greene King IPA, Abbot; S&N Theakston XB; Younger Scotch Ⓗ**; guest beer**
Fairly large, typical Wetherspoon pub, with food available midday–10pm. Usually a guest beer; several beer festivals each year.
❀ ◖ ◗ ♿ ⊖ (Fairlop) P ⊘

Cranham

Thatched House
348 St Mary's Lane (B187)
☎ (0708) 228080
11–3, 5.30–11
Adnams Bitter; Draught Bass; Charrington IPA; Fuller's London Pride; guest beers (weekends) Ⓗ
Good, convivial pub on the edge of the countryside. The family room has children's toilet facilities. Local CAMRA *Pub of the Year* 1992. In every edition of the *Guide*.
♞ ❀ ◖ P

Dagenham

Eastbrook
Dagenham Road (A1112)
☎ (081) 592 1873
11–3 (4 Sat), 5 (6 Sat)–11
Bass Worthington BB, Draught Bass; Courage Best Bitter, Directors; Fuller's London Pride, ESB; guest beers Ⓗ
Large, comfortable wood-panelled pub with a friendly landlord. Occasional beer festivals. The range of beers may vary. Food is available at all times (book eves). Beer is a bit pricey, but B&B is good value. ❀ 🛏 ◖ ◗ ⊟ ♿ ⊖ (East) ♣ P

Ilford

Prince of Wales
63 Green Lane (A1083)
☎ (081) 478 1326
11–3, 5.30–11; 11–11 Fri & Sat
Ind Coope Burton Ale; Tetley Bitter Ⓗ
Small, friendly, two-bar local on the eastern side of the town centre. Sky TV for football. Weekday lunches.
❀ ◖ ⊟ ♣ P

Rose & Crown
16 Ilford Hill (A118)
☎ (081) 478 7104
11–11
Adnams Bitter; Everards Tiger; Ind Coope Benskins Best Bitter, Burton Ale; Nethergate Bitter; Tetley Bitter Ⓗ**; guest beers**
Comfortable and friendly, town pub with one large bar and the best choice of beers in Ilford. Always three or four guest beers; occasional beer festivals. ◖ ⇌

Noak Hill

Bear
Noak Hill Road
11–3.30 (4 Sat), 5.30 (6 Sat)–11
Draught Bass; Charrington IPA; Fuller's London Pride; Greene King IPA Ⓗ**; guest beers** (occasionally)
Comfortable and popular pub with a good menu. The large garden has a games area for children. Wheelchair WC.
♞ ❀ ◖ ♿ P

Romford

Durham Arms
101 Brentwood Road (near A125) ☎ (0708) 748601
12 (11 Sat)–3.30, 5 (6 Sat)–11
Adnams Bitter; Marston's Pedigree; Tetley Bitter Ⓗ**; guest beers**
Pub situated away from the town centre, but within walking distance of the station. Quiz and karaoke nights; barbecues in summer. Safe garden for children.
❀ ◖ ♿ ⇌ P

Woodford Green

Cricketers
299–301 High Road
☎ (081) 504 2734
11–3 (4 Sat), 5.30–11
Courage Directors; McMullen AK, Country, Stronghart Ⓗ
Friendly, traditional-style pub with good value beers. CAMRA's *London Pub of the Year* 1991. ❀ ◖ ⊟ ♣ P

Travellers Friend
496–498 High Road
11–11
Adnams Broadside; Courage Best Bitter, Directors; Ridleys IPA; Wadworth 6X Ⓗ
A gem of a pub with wood panelling and snob screens. Friendly and cosy, with a good range of beers (the range may change). ♨ Q ❀ ◖ ♿ P

North London

N1: Barnsbury

Crown
116 Cloudesley Road
☎ (071) 837 7107
11–11
Fuller's Chiswick, London Pride, ESB Ⓗ**; guest beer**
Large, welcoming, one-bar pub with a central island bar. Its exquisite Victorian interior has been recently refurbished. Varied clientele; popular with locals. No food Sun eve.
♨ Q ♞ ❀ ◖ ◗

N1: Canonbury

Compton Arms
4 Compton Avenue
☎ (071) 359 6883
11–11
Greene King IPA, Rayments Special, Abbot Ⓗ**, Winter Ale** Ⓖ

Small, cottage-style building in a side-street near Highbury Corner. Busy early eve (meals till 8). TV for sport. A good pub for a chat. Q (Highbury & Islington)

Earl of Radnor
106 Mildmay Grove
(071) 241 0318
11–11
Fuller's London Pride, ESB H
Lovingly restored Victorian pub enjoying a village atmosphere. Home-cooked food weekdays, and a roast on Sun. Proudly lacks fruit machines and a jukebox.
Q

Marquess Tavern
32 Canonbury Street
(071) 354 2975
11–11
Young's Bitter, Porter (summer), Special, Winter Warmer H
Excellent pub in a fine Georgian building. The single bar, with distinct saloon and public areas, is traditional and comfortable. An example of what a good London pub can be like. Q (Essex Rd) (Highbury & Islington)

N1: Hoxton

George & Vulture
63 Pitfield Street
(071) 253 3988
11–3 (4 Sat), 5 (7 Sat)–11
Fuller's London Pride, ESB H
Friendly, family-run pub offering good value food. Separate pool and darts bar. Do not be deterred by Hoxton's shabbiness.
(Old St)

Prince Arthur
49 Brunswick Place, Charles Square (071) 253 3187
11–11; 11–5, 8–11 Sat; 12–3.30, 8.30–10.30 Sun
Shepherd Neame Master Brew Bitter, Spitfire H
Small, single-bar local, established over 300 years ago. Possibility of real cider in summer. Q (Old St)

N2: East Finchley

Welch's Ale House
High Road (081) 444 7444
11–3, 5.30–11; 11–11 Sat
Brakspear Special; Fuller's London Pride; Greene King Abbot; Ruddles County; Wadworth 6X; Webster's Yorkshire Bitter H**; guest beers**
An unassuming shop frontage masks a thriving, genuine free house. The five guest beers usually include a mild or porter. Good range of country wines.

N4: Crouch End

Tap & Spile
29 Crouch Hill
(071) 272 4748
11–3, 5–11, 11–11 Fri & Sat
Bateman Mild; Cains FA; Clark's Burglar Bill; Nethergate IPA, Old Growler; S&N Theakston XB H**; guest beers**
Free house with an ever-changing rota of 200-plus guest beers, and Crone's cider occasionally. Pavement tables, bar billiards, toasted sandwiches and sometimes accordion music complete the picture. (Crouch Hill)

N6: Highgate

Bull
North Hill (081) 340 4412
12–11
Adnams Bitter; Ind Coope Burton Ale; Tetley Bitter H
Genuinely old pub, modified slightly over the years. Good, warm feel. Most pubs in Highgate are worth a visit.

N7: Holloway

Admiral Mann
9 Hargrave Place
(071) 485 4739
11–3 (4 Sat), 6 (7 Sat)–11; 11–11 Fri
McMullen AK, Country, Stronghart H
Small, friendly, two-bar country pub in the town, very much a local. Formerly three cottages, which opened as a pub in 1920. Children and dogs allowed. Home-cooked food. Q

Holloway
295 Holloway Road
(071) 607 9207
11–11
Archers Old Cobleigh's; Fuller's London Pride, ESB; Taylor Landlord; Wadworth 6X; Whitbread Boddingtons Bitter H**; guest beers**
Genuine free house next to the tube station and attracting students. Separate pool and electronic games area; live rock music Sat night. The menu includes roast Sun lunches.
(Holloway Rd)

N11: New Southgate

Banker's Draft
36–38 Friern Barnet Road
(081) 361 7115
11–11
Courage Directors; S&N Theakston Best Bitter, XB; Wadworth 6X; Younger Scotch H**; guest beer**
Outstanding conversion of a former bank. A much needed oasis for the area. No food Sun eve. Q (Arnos Grove)

N12: North Finchley

Moss Hall Tavern
283 Ballards Lane
(081) 445 0356
11–11
Fuller's Chiswick, London Pride, ESB H
Large, busy pub opposite a bus garage. Cosmopolitan clientele in the public bar; the lounge is divided into two drinking areas. No food Sun eve.
(Woodside Pk)

Tally Ho
749 High Road
(081) 445 4390
11–11
Courage Directors; Greene King IPA, Abbot; S&N Theakston XB; Younger Scotch H**; guest beer**
Imposing, prominently-sited pub, in typical Wetherspoon style. The upstairs bar is no-smoking. No food Sun eve.
Q (Woodside Pk)

N13: Palmers Green

Whole Hog
430–434 Green Lanes
(081) 882 3597
11–11
Courage Directors; Greene King IPA, Abbot; S&N Theakston XB; Younger Scotch H**; guest beer**
A welcome addition to this under-pubbed area. A shop premises converted to the specification and standard expected from Wetherspoon. No food Sun eve.
Q

N16: Stoke Newington

Shakespeare
Allen Road (071) 254 4190
12–2.30, 5–11; 11–11 Sat
Draught Bass; Brakspear Bitter; Greene King Abbot; S&N Theakston Old Peculier; Taylor Landlord; Whitbread Boddingtons Bitter H
Recently restored, Victorian pub with a large, wooden wall figurine, French posters and

Shakespearian paintings. Young, friendly clientele; bluesy jukebox. Summer barbecues. Large selection of foreign bottled beers.
❀ 🛏 ♿ ⇌ ♣

Tanners Hall
145 Stoke Newington High Street (one-way system)
☎ (071) 249 6016
11–11
Courage Directors; Greene King Abbot; S&N Theakston Best Bitter, XB; Wadworth 6X; Younger Scotch 🄷
Very large, Victorian, single-bar pub, with a conservatory. A mixed clientele; at least six beers. Q ❀ ◖ ◗ ⇌ ♣ ⌓ ⚟

N20: Whetstone

Cavalier
67 Russell Lane
☎ (081) 368 2708
11–3, 5.30–11 (11–11 summer)
Courage Best Bitter, Directors 🄷
Large, well-appointed, two-bar, 1930s estate pub in mock Tudor style, with wood panelling, a large patio and a garden. Weekday lunches.
❀ ◖ ⊟ ♣ P

N21: Winchmore Hill

Dog & Duck
76 Hoppers Road
☎ (081) 886 1987
12–11
Brakspear Bitter; McMullen AK; Morland Old Speckled Hen; Whitbread Boddingtons Bitter; guest beers 🄷
Welcoming, tucked-away local, affectionately known as the Woof & Kwak. Although tied to Whitbread, two other ales are available.
♔ Q ❀ ♿ ♣

Green Dragon
889 Green Lanes (A105)
☎ (081) 360 3725
11–11
Courage Best Bitter, Directors; Wadworth 6X 🄷
Fine, main-road pub with two large, wood-panelled bars and a pool room off the public bar. Access to the large patio and garden is from the lounge. Always busy.
Q ❀ ◖ ⊟ ♿ ⇌ ♣ P

Half Moon
749 Green Lanes
☎ (081) 360 5410
11–11
Courage Directors; Greene King IPA, Abbot; S&N Theakston XB; Younger Scotch 🄷**; guest beer**
One of Wetherspoon's smaller shop conversions, but still with all the expected facilities. Comfortable and popular. No food Sun eve. Q ◖ ◗ ♿ ⇌ ⚟

Barnet

King George
High Street ☎ (081) 449 4563
11–3, 5.30–11; 11–11 Sat
Draught Bass; Charrington IPA; Fuller's London Pride 🄷
Large, bustling, town-centre pub. An island bar serves three distinct drinking areas.
Q ❀ ◖ ◗ ♿ ⊖ (High Barnet) ♣ P

Olde Mitre Inn
High Street
11–11; 11–3, 7–11 Sat
Ind Coope Benskins Best Bitter, Burton Ale; Tetley Bitter; Wadworth 6X 🄷
Traditional coaching inn, renovated with care. An oasis of tranquillity in comparison with some of its neighbours. No food Sun.
Q ◖ ⊖ (High Barnet) P

Moon Under Water
High Street ☎ (081) 441 9476
11–11
Courage Directors; Greene King IPA, Abbot; S&N Theakston XB; Younger Scotch 🄷**; guest beer**
One of Wetherspoon's more mature outlets. A long single bar opens on to a large rear drinking area, which belies the narrow street frontage. Very crowded weekend eves. No food Sun eve. Q ❀ ◖ ◗ ♿ ⊖ (High Barnet) ⚟

Cockfosters

Cock & Dragon
Chalk Lane ☎ (081) 449 7160
11–3, 5–11 (11–11 summer)
Ind Coope Burton Ale; Tetley Bitter; Wadworth 6X 🄷**; guest beer**
Imaginatively restored 1930s Art Deco-style pub behind the cricket ground. Outstanding Thai and Malay cuisine, at the bar or in the well-appointed restaurant. Handy for the M25 (jct 24). ❀ ◖ ◗ ♿ ⊖ P

Trent Tavern
20 Cockfosters Road
☎ (081) 449 5888
11–11
Courage Best Bitter, Directors; John Smith's Bitter 🄷
Substantial, 1950s roadhouse with two fine, wood-panelled bars. Popular with locals and students. Prize-winning gardens. ❀ ◖ ◗ ⊟ ♿ ⊖ P

Enfield Lock

Greyhound
425 Ordnance Road
☎ (0992) 764612
11–2.30 (3.30 Sat), 6.30 (7 Sat)–11
McMullen AK, Country 🄷
Fine, unspoilt, two-bar local on the River Lea Navigation, overlooking the former royal small arms factory. A large, traditional public bar and a cosy, welcoming saloon.
♔ Q ❀ ◖ ◗ ⊟ ⇌ ♣ P

Enfield Town

Cricketers
17–19 Chase Side Place
☎ (081) 363 5218
11–3, 5.30–11; 11–11 Sat
Courage Directors; McMullen AK, Country 🄷
Pub tucked away off the town centre. The well-appointed public bar has bar billiards. The spacious lounge has a part set aside for lunches and booked eve meals. Large patio.
Q ❀ ◖ ◗ ⊟ ♿ ⇌ (Enfield Chase) ♣ P ⚟

Old Wheatsheaf
3 Windmill Hill
☎ (081) 363 0516
11–3, 5–11; 11–11 Fri & Sat
Adnams Bitter; Ind Coope Burton Ale; Taylor Walker Best Bitter; Tetley Bitter 🄷
Former CAMRA *London Pub of the Year*, now under new management but retaining high standards. Patronised by office workers and locals. Eve meals on request. ❀ ◖ ♿ ⇌ (Enfield Chase) ♣ P

New Barnet

Hadley Hotel
Hadley Road ☎ (081) 449 0161
11–11
Fuller's London Pride; Ruddles County; Webster's Yorkshire Bitter 🄷
Not at all what one expects to find in leafy suburbia: a single bar with three distinct drinking areas. Accommodation is a rarity for this part of London. ❀ 🛏 ◖ ◗ ♣

Railway Bell
13 East Barnet Road
☎ (081) 449 1369
11–11
Courage Directors; Greene King IPA, Abbot; S&N Theakston XB; Younger Scotch 🄷**; guest beer**
Large, one-bar pub where the convivial surroundings are undisturbed by the passing of high speed trains. No food Sun eve. Q ❀ ◖ ◗ ♿ ⇌ ⌓ P ⚟

North-West London

NW1: Camden Town

Lord Nelson
48 Stanhope Street
☎ (071) 387 1147
11–11
Courage Best Bitter, Directors; Young's Bitter, Special, Winter Warmer Ⓗ
Narrow, one-bar pub rebuilt in 1830. Popular lunchtimes; occasional piano music.
❀ ◐ ◑ ⇌ (Euston) ⊖ (Warren St)

Neptune
51 Werrington Street
☎ (071) 380 1390
11–11
Wells Eagle, Bombardier Ⓗ
Comfortable, corner pub, recently redecorated. Popular with BR staff. Snacks available.
⇌ (Euston) ⊖ ♣

Quinns
65 Kentish Town Road
☎ (071) 267 8240
11–11
Bateman Mild; Everards Tiger; Gale's HSB; Greene King IPA, Abbot; Marston's Pedigree Ⓗ
Well-refurbished free house. Apart from the ales, there is a menu of Bavarian beers that is highly recommended – as is the food. Slightly expensive but worth it. ❀ ◐ ◑
⇌ (Camden Rd) ⊖

Spread Eagle
141 Albert Street
☎ (071) 267 1410
11–3, 5–11; 11–11 Fri & Sat
Young's Bitter, Special, Winter Warmer Ⓗ
Large, multi-bar pub in central Camden. Popular with the younger crowd, including students. Q ❀ ◐ ◑
⇌ (Camden Rd) ⊖

Square Tavern
26 Tolmers Square
☎ (071) 387 3959
11–11; closed Sat & Sun
Young's Bitter, Special, Winter Warmer Ⓗ**; guest beers**
Modern pub, purpose-built in 1981, in a square near Euston station. Adjoining wine bar and restaurant, where real ale is available by the jug. Guest beers sometimes include a mild. Not cheap for the area.
❀ ◐ ◑ ♿ ⇌ (Euston)
⊖ (Warren St/Euston Sq) ♣

NW1: Marylebone

Perseverence
11 Shroton Street
☎ (071) 723 7469
11–3, 4.30–11; 11–11 Fri & Sat
Draught Bass; Fuller's London Pride Ⓗ
Small and friendly pub with one horseshoe bar and a large open skylight. Sky TV.
❀ ◐ ◑ ♿ ⇌ ⊖ ♣

NW2: Cricklewood

Beaten Docket
50–56 Cricklewood Broadway
☎ (081) 450 2972
11–11
Courage Directors; Greene King IPA, Abbot; S&N Theakston XB; Younger Scotch Ⓗ**; guest beer**
Large pub, typically Wetherspoon's, in an area not known for real ale. Guest beer Fri and Sat.
Q ❀ ◐ ◑ ♿ ⇌ ⊖ ⍻

NW3: Hampstead

Duke of Hamilton
New End ☎ (071) 794 0258
11–11
Fuller's London Pride, ESB Ⓗ
Traditionally-run Victorian pub, with a horseshoe bar and a cellar bar for functions. Popular with rugby and cricket followers. Other Fuller's beers are frequently on sale. ❀ ⊖ ♣

Flask
14 Flask Walk
☎ (071) 435 4580
11–11
Young's Bitter, Porter (summer), Special, Winter Warmer Ⓗ
A real friendly local: a fine public bar where the high Edwardian windows make it irresistible on summer eves. Also a well-established lounge and a new conservatory. Occasional jazz midweek. N London CAMRA *Pub of the Year* 1993. Q ◐ ⊟ ♿ ⊖ ♣

Holly Bush
Holly Mount, Heath Street
☎ (071) 435 2892
11–3, 5.30 (6 Sat)–11
Greenalls Bitter; Ind Coope Benskins Best Bitter, Burton Ale; guest beers Ⓗ
Pleasant, traditional pub with several bars and alcoves, just off the busy main street. Gas-lit, it features Benskins memorabilia. Once the haunt of local artist George Romney and prints of his work are displayed. Q ❀ ◐ ◑ ⊖

Spaniards Inn
Spaniards Road
☎ (081) 455 3276
11–11
Bass Worthington BB, Draught Bass; Fuller's London Pride; Greene King IPA; M&B Mild Ⓗ**; guest beer**
Built in 1701, the only genuine Georgian facade on any Hampstead pub. A haunt of Dick Turpin, and used by Keats, Goldsmith and Karl Marx. The private quarters are reputedly haunted. Near Kenwood House.
♛ Q ☋ ❀ ◐ ◑ ♿
⇌ (Hampstead Heath) P

Washington
50 Englands Lane
☎ (071) 722 6118
11–11
Ind Coope Burton Ale; Tetley Bitter; Young's Bitter
Well-preserved, Victorian, street-corner pub: ornate mirrors and woodwork abound. Cricket club; quiz night Tue. Weekday lunches.
◐ ⊖ (Belsize Pk) ♣

NW5: Kentish Town

Pineapple
51 Leverton Street
☎ (071) 485 6422
12 (11 Sat)–11
Brakspear Bitter; Marston's Pedigree; Whitbread Boddingtons Bitter Ⓗ
Small, cosy, back-street, Victorian gem, with fantastically nicotine-stained paintwork and superb brewery mirrors. May not always open on time.
⇌ ⊖ ♣

NW5: Maitland Park

Lord Southampton
2 Southampton Road
☎ (071) 485 3106
11–4 (5.30 Sat), 5.30 (7.30 Sat)–11
Courage Best Bitter; John Smith's Bitter; Wadworth IPA Ⓗ
Back-street, Victorian, corner local named after the landowner. Karl Marx lived nearby in Grafton Terrace and is said to have been a customer. Handy for Queens Crescent market.
♿ ⇌ (Gospel Oak) ⊖ (Chalk Farm) ♣

NW6: Kilburn

Queen's Arms
1 Kilburn High Road
☎ (071) 624 5735
11–11

Greater London

Young's Bitter, Special, Winter Warmer Ⓗ
Large, 1950s corner pub with lots of wood and old prints. Retains a public bar, plus a roof garden. Q ❀ ◐ ◑ ⊟ ♿ ⛺ ⇌ (Kilburn High Rd) ⊖ (Kilburn Pk) ♣ P

NW7: Mill Hill

Rising Sun
137 Marsh Lane
☎ (081) 959 3755
12 (11 Sat)–3, 5.30 (6 Sat)–11
Ind Coope Burton Ale; Tetley Bitter; Young's Bitter Ⓗ**; guest beer**
A Taylor Walker Heritage Inn; a delightful, rural pub which has served travellers for some 400 years. A tiny bar plus three rooms, where children are welcome up to 9pm. An additional lounge opens at busy times. Popular with families in summer. No eve meals Sun or Mon.
Q ⛵ ❀ ◐ ◑ ♣ P

NW9: Kingsbury

Green Man
125 Slough Lane
☎ (081) 204 6014
11–11
Courage Best Bitter; Marston's Pedigree; Ruddles County; John Smith's Bitter; Webster's Yorkshire Bitter Ⓗ**; guest beer**
Large, attractive, 1930s, local, occupied by the same tenant since 1936. One horseshoe bar serves three rooms. Two quizzes weekly. TV for sport only. Families welcome. The restaurant opens for lunch and functions. No food Sun.
❀ ◐ ♿ ♣ P ⊬

JJ Moon's
553 Kingsbury Road
☎ (081) 204 9675
11–11
Courage Directors; Greene King IPA, Abbot; S&N Theakston XB; Younger Scotch Ⓗ**; guest beer**
Former shop, now a small, busy Wetherspoon local, which holds occasional beer festivals. Six specials daily (one is vegetarian), plus good value Sun roasts. The guest beer changes weekly.
Q ◐ ◑ ⊖

NW10: Harlesden

Grand Junction Arms
Acton Lane ☎ (081) 965 5670
11–11
Young's Bitter, Porter, Special, Winter Warmer Ⓗ
Large, comfortable, three-bar pub with moorings on the canal. The garden contains children's play equipment; barbecues in summer. Good value food all day, including vegetarian (no meals Sun).
Q ❀ ◐ ◑ ⊟ ♿ ⇌ ⊖ P

NW11: Golders Green

White Swan
243 Golders Green Road
☎ (081) 458 2036
11–11
Ind Coope Burton Ale; Tetley Bitter Ⓗ
Lively, welcoming, main-road pub with lots of character and a superb, large garden. Good, home-cooked food.
❀ ◐ ◑ ⊖ ♣

Eastcote

Case Is Altered
High Road ☎ (081) 866 0476
11–3, 5.30–11; 11–11 Sat
Ind Coope ABC Best Bitter, Benskins Best Bitter, Burton Ale; Tetley Bitter; Wadworth 6X; Young's Special Ⓗ
Grade I-listed ex-farmhouse with a stone-flagged floor in the 'old' public bar, which used to be the stables. Restaurant in the barn behind. Very popular.
♛ Q ⛵ ❀ ◐ ◑ ♣ P

Edgware

Change of Hart
High Street ☎ (081) 952 0039
11–11
Greene King IPA; Ind Coope Burton Ale; Taylor Walker Best Bitter; Tetley Bitter; Wadworth 6X; Young's Bitter Ⓗ
Formerly the White Hart, and once a coaching inn where Dick Turpin reputedly stayed. The doorstep sandwiches are a meal in themselves. Wheelchair WC.
Q ❀ ◐ ◑ ♿ ♣ ⌓ P

Harefield

Plough
Hill End Road
☎ (0895) 822129
11–3, 5.30–11; 11–11 Sat
Brakspear Bitter, Special, Old; Fuller's London Pride; Hook Norton Best Bitter; M&B Highgate Mild Ⓗ**; guest beers**
Excellent, one-bar free house near the hospital; busy in summer. Good value food (not served Sun). Up to three guest beers. ❀ ◐ ♿ P

White Horse
Church Hill ☎ (0895) 822144
11.30–3.30, 6–11; 11–11 Fri & Sat
Greenalls Mild, Bitter; Greene King Abbot; Tetley Bitter; Wadworth 6X Ⓗ**; guest beer**
Excellent, lively, traditional local on the south side of the village: a Grade II-listed building from the 17th century.
⛵ ❀ ◐ ◑ ⊟ ♿ ♣ ⌓ P

Harrow on the Hill

Castle
West Street ☎ (081) 422 3155
11–11
Fuller's London Pride, Mr Harry, ESB Ⓗ
Well-run pub, full of atmosphere, with a large, comfortable lounge to the rear.
Q ❀ ◐ ⊟ ⇌ ⊖ (S Harrow) ♣

Harrow Weald

Seven Balls
749 Kenton Lane
☎ (081) 954 0261
11.30–3, 5.30 (6 Sat)–11
Ansells Mild; Ind Coope Benskins Best Bitter, Burton Ale; Tetley Bitter Ⓗ**; guest beers**
250-year-old pub with a country feel: horse brasses and beams abound. The mild is rare for the area. Occasional beer festivals. No food Sun.
⛵ ❀ ◐ ♣ P

Hatch End

Moon & Sixpence
250 Uxbridge Road
☎ (081) 420 1074
11–11
Courage Directors; Greene King IPA, Abbot; S&N Theakston XB; Younger Scotch Ⓗ**; guest beers** (weekends)
Tasteful conversion of a bank, and deservedly popular. Can get crowded, especially weekend eves. A welcome change in an area dominated by Carlsberg-Tetley pubs. Occasional beer festivals.
Q ❀ ◐ ◑ ⇌

Kenton

New Moon
25–26 Kenton Park Parade, Kenton Road ☎ (081) 909 1103
11–11
Courage Directors; Greene King IPA, Abbot; S&N Theakston XB; Younger Scotch Ⓗ**; guest beers** (weekends)
Now established as Kenton's favourite watering-hole, putting its Taylor Walker neighbour to shame. Occasional beer festivals.
Q ◐ ◑

Northwood Hills

Northwood Hills Hotel

Joel Street ☎ (0923) 835857
11–11
Ind Coope Benskins Best Bitter, Burton Ale; Tetley Bitter Ⓗ; guest beers
Large, one-bar pub which has retained separate drinking areas. Local lad Elton John began his career here. Quiz Wed night. No food Sun.
❀ ◖ ⊖ ♣ P

South Harrow

JJ Moon's

Shaftsbury Parade, Shaftsbury Circle ☎ (081) 423 5056
11–11
Courage Directors; Greene King IPA, Abbot; S&N Theakston XB; Younger Scotch Ⓗ; guest beers
Small, but friendly Wetherspoon pub. Good food.
Q ◖ ◗ ⊖ ⅟

Wealdstone

Royal Oak

Peel Road ☎ (081) 427 3122
11–11
Ind Coope Benskins Best Bitter, Burton Ale; Tetley Bitter; Young's Bitter Ⓗ; guest beer
Imposing, 1930s pub with a conservatory. The public bar has the same prices as the lounge, which is divided into separate drinking areas. No food Sun. ❀ ◖ ⇌ ⊖ ♣

Wembley

JJ Moon's

397 High Road
☎ (081) 903 4923
11–11
Courage Directors; Greene King IPA, Abbot; S&N Theakston XB; Younger Scotch Ⓗ; guest beers (weekends)
Cavernous pub, popular with office workers and handy for Wembley Stadium. Occasional beer festivals. No food Sun eve.
Q ◖ ◗ ⇌ (Central) ⊖ ⌓

South-East London

SE1: Southwark

Founders Arms

52 Hopton Street (via footpath from Blackfriars Bridge)
☎ (071) 528 1899
11–11
Young's Bitter, Special, Winter Warmer Ⓗ
Riverside pub and restaurant affording grand views across the Thames to St Paul's. Popular with business people.
❀ ◖ ◗ ♿ ⇌ (Blackfriars) ⊖

Lord Clyde

27 Clenham Street
☎ (071) 407 3397
11–11; 11–3, 7–11 Sat
Ruddles Best Bitter, County; Webster's Yorkshire Bitter; guest beer Ⓗ
Very comfortable and traditional, two-roomed pub, in the same family for 35 years. Superb tiled exterior, once typical of Truman's house style. ◖ ⇌ (London Bridge) ⊖ (Borough) ⌓

Market Porter

9 Stoney Street
☎ (071) 407 2495
11–11; 11–3, 7–11 Sat
Fuller's London Pride; Greene King Abbot; Harveys BB; Young's Bitter Ⓗ
Popular, old free house next to the Borough market, with secluded alcoves in a spacious downstairs bar. Restaurant and bar upstairs. One of the few pubs in the area to serve eve and weekend meals. ◖ ◗
⇌ (London Bridge) ⊖ ♣

Ship

68 Borough High Street
☎ (071) 403 7059
11–11
Fuller's Chiswick, London Pride, ESB Ⓗ
One long, comfortable bar, busy lunchtimes and early eves. Attractive garden. The upstairs function room, a smoke-free zone, is used for dining at lunchtime.
◖ ◗ ⇌ (London Bridge) ⊖ (Borough) ♣

Ship Aground

33 Wolseley Street
☎ (071) 237 3314
11–11; 11–4, 8–11 Sat
Courage Best Bitter, Directors Ⓗ
Friendly, back-street pub, unspoilt by the nearby upmarket development. Next to Dockhead, alias 'Blackwall' fire station from TV's *London's Burning*. ❀ ◖

Wheatsheaf

6 Stoney Street
☎ (071) 407 1514
11–11
Courage Best Bitter; Wadworth 6X Ⓗ; guest beers
Classic market pub with a real public bar; always busy. A mild or porter is always amongst the guests. Weekday lunches. ❀ ◖ ⇌ (London Bridge) ⊖ ♣ ⌓

SE1: Waterloo

Kings Arms

25 Roupell Street
☎ (071) 928 5745
11–3 (3.30 Sat), 5 (8 Sat)–11; 11–11 Fri; 12–2.30, 7–10.30 Sun
Ind Coope Burton Ale; Taylor Walker Best Bitter; Tetley Bitter; Young's Special Ⓗ
Tucked right next to Waterloo station, the best two-bar pub in the area, boasting a large miniatures collection. Occasional quiz nights. The landlord holds the *Guild of Master Cellarmen* award. No meals at weekends. Parking a problem.
Q ❀ ◖ ◗ ⇌ ⊖

Prince William Henry

218 Blackfriars Road
☎ (071) 928 2474
11–11; 12–3, 7–11 Sat
Young's Bitter, Porter, Special, Winter Warmer Ⓗ
Modern pub, named after King Henry IV, frequented by musicians from the South Bank concert halls and local business people.
❀ ◖ ♿ ⇌ ⊖

SE3: Blackheath

Bitter Experience Off-Licence

129 Lee Road, Lee
☎ (081) 852 8819
11 (10 Sat)–9.30; 12–2, 7–9 (Sun)
Fuller's London Pride; Shepherd Neame Master Brew Bitter; guest beers Ⓖ
Off-licence with an excellent range of beers and ciders, plus British and foreign bottled beers. The beers above are usually stocked, plus at least four others. ⇌ ⌓

British Oak

109 Old Dover Road
☎ (081) 858 1082
12–3 (4 Sat), 5 (6.30 Sat)–11; 11–11 Fri
Courage Best Bitter, Directors; John Smith's Bitter; Wadworth 6X Ⓗ
Two-bar pub just off the main road. The saloon is panelled in standard Courage style; the other bar is more basic. ❀ ♣

Hare & Billet Alehouse

1a Elliot Cottages, Hare & Billet Road
☎ (081) 852 2352
11–11
Brakspear Bitter; Fuller's London Pride; Morland Old Speckled Hen; guest beers Ⓗ
Recently 'themed', a friendly pub on the heath. Also sells Whitbread cask beers.
❀ ◖ ♿ ⇌

SE4: Brockley

Wickham Arms
69 Upper Brockley Road
11–11
Courage Best Bitter, Directors Ⓗ
Former two-bar pub, turned open-plan but retaining wood panelling in the 'saloon'. Decorated with photographs of bygone Brockley and New Cross. Attracts locals and students from Goldsmiths College. The TV is inescapable. Weekday lunches.
❀ ◖ ⇌ ⊖ (New Cross)

SE5: Camberwell

Duke of Clarence
181 Camberwell Road
☎ (071) 703 4007
11–11
Draught Bass; Charrington IPA; M&B Highgate Mild Ⓗ
A rare treat for the area: the narrow, unassuming frontage belies the character and size of this staunch family local. The public bar fronts the main road and the comfortable saloon is at the rear, with a cosy snug in-between. ◖ ♿ ♣

SE6: Catford

Catford Ram
9 Winslade Way
☎ (081) 690 6206
11–3.30 (4 Sat), 5.30 (6.30 Sat)–11; 11–11 Fri
Young's Bitter, Special, Winter Warmer Ⓗ
Comfortable, split-level pub in a shopping precinct, catering for local custom. Q ◖ ⇌ ♣

Tigers Head
350 Bromley Road
11–11
Courage Directors; Greene King IPA, Abbot; S&N Theakston XB; Younger Scotch Ⓗ**; guest beers** (weekends)
Large Wetherspoon pub on a busy crossroads. Occasional beer festivals. Unusual collection of wooden shoe inserts. No food Sun eve.
Q ❀ ◖ ◗ ♿ ⇌ (Beckenham Hill) ⌓ ⚟

SE8: Deptford

Dog & Bell
116 Prince Street
☎ (081) 692 5664
11–11
Fuller's London Pride, ESB Ⓗ**; guest beers**
Friendly, back-street local stocking a wide range of malt whiskies, and regularly changing guest beers from independents.
Q ❀ ◖ ◗ ⇌ ♣

Royal George
85 Tanners Hill
☎ (081) 692 2594
11–3, 5.30–11; 11–11 Fri & Sat
Samuel Smith OBB; Museum Ⓗ
Quiz nights Wed in this popular, back-street local; pool room upstairs. Eve meals finish early.
❀ ⇌ (New Cross) ⊖ ♣

SE10: Greenwich

Admiral Hardy
7 College Approach, Greenwich Market
☎ (081) 858 6452
11–11
Ind Coope Burton Ale; Shepherd Neame Master Brew Bitter, Best Bitter, Porter; Tetley Bitter Ⓗ**; guest beer**
Busy town-centre pub with good local and seasonal tourist trades. The wood-panelled walls bear nautical pictures. Meals till 6pm (later in summer). ◖ ◗ ⇌ ♣

Ashburnham Arms
25 Ashburnham Grove
☎ (081) 692 2007
12–3, 6–11
Shepherd Neame Master Brew Bitter, Spitfire, Porter, Bishops Finger Ⓗ
Popular, back-street pub with live music alternate Mons. The small backroom is used to display works by local artists. Food includes a range of vegetarian meals (last food orders 8.45pm; no meals Sun and Mon eves).
❀ ◖ ◗ ⇌ ♣

Cricketers
22 King William Walk
☎ (081) 858 3630
11–11; 11–5, 7–11 Sat
Draught Bass; Charrington IPA Ⓗ
Comfortable pub near the National Maritime Museum. Can get very crowded on market days. Collection of banknotes in the saloon, pictures of cricketers in both bars. ⇌

Fox & Hounds (McGowan's Free House)
56 Royal Hill
☎ (081) 692 6147
11–11
Fuller's London Pride; Greene King Abbot; Young's Bitter Ⓗ**; guest beer**
Long, narrow, comfortable pub in an upmarket area. The guest ale changes fortnightly. No meals Sun.
❀ ◖ ◗ ⇌

SE12: Lee

Crown
117 Burnt Ash Hill
11–3, 5.30–11; 11–11 Fri & Sat
Young's Bitter, Porter, Special, Winter Warmer Ⓗ
Large, village-type pub with a small, compact public bar. Near Grove Park Hospital.
Q ❀ ◖ 🛏 ⇌ ♣ P

SE13: Lewisham

Joiners Arms
66 Lewisham High Street
☎ (081) 852 9245
11–11
Draught Bass; Fuller's London Pride Ⓗ
Long, narrow pub attracting a youthful trade. Handy for the shopping centre. ⇌ ♣

SE14: New Cross

Rose Inn
272 New Cross Road
☎ (081) 692 3193
11–4, 5.30 (7 Sat)–11
Courage Best Bitter, Directors; Young's Special Ⓗ
Large, one-bar pub divided into separate drinking areas by wooden screens. Can get crowded when Millwall are at home. ⇌ ⊖ ♣

SE15: Nunhead

Railway Tavern
66 Gibbon Road, Peckham
☎ (071) 639 3608
11–11
Courage Best Bitter; Greene King IPA Ⓗ
Basic, three-bar, corner local by Nunhead station. The back bar is dominated by a pool table, but the absence of muzak, TV and machines in the saloon attracts many regulars. No price differential between the bars. ⇌ ♣

SE17: Walworth

Crown
115 Brandon Street
☎ (071) 703 3580
11–11
Draught Bass; Fuller's London Pride; Young's Special Ⓗ
Victorian pub with a recently renovated original facade of a Wenlock alehouse. Warm and friendly. ❀ ⇌ (Elephant & Castle) ⊖

SE18: Plumstead Common

Star Inn
158 Plumstead Common Road
☎ (081) 854 1524
11–11; 11–4, 7–11 Sat

Courage Best Bitter, Directors; Wadworth 6X; guest beer Ⓗ
Spacious, three-bar local near Plumstead Common. The guest beer changes regularly.
Q ❀ ◑ ◗ ♣

SE18: Woolwich

Bull
151 Shooters Hill
☎ (081) 856 0691
11–3, 5.15 (7 Sat)–11
Courage Best Bitter, Directors Ⓗ
Grade II-listed pub, built in 1881 to replace the original Bull, which dated back to the early 1700s. Near the top of Shooters Hill, the old Roman road from London to Dover. No food Sun. Q ❀ ◑ ♣

Prince Albert (Roses)
Hare Street ☎ (081) 854 1538
11–11; closed Sun eve & bank hol eves
Archers Village; Greene King Abbot; Morland Old Speckled Hen; Shepherd Neame Master Brew Bitter, Porter; Wadworth 6X Ⓗ; guest beers
Friendly, town local, handy for the shops. A sporting pub, with teams for football, cricket, darts and pool. No food Sun eve. ◑ ◗ ♿ ≈ (Arsenal) ♣

Red Lion
6 Red Lion Place, Shooters Hill
☎ (081) 856 0333
11–11
Courage Best Bitter, Directors Ⓗ
Formerly a Beasley's house. There has been a pub on this site for centuries. The jukebox can sometimes get quite loud.
❀ ♣ P

SE22: East Dulwich

Clock House
196a Peckham Rye
☎ (081) 693 2901
11–11
Young's Bitter, Porter, Special, Winter Warmer Ⓗ
Opposite Peckham Rye Common: a pub with a raised seating area at the front and a room at the back furnished in club-room style. Large collection of interesting time pieces. ❀ ≈ (Peckham Rye)

Crystal Palace Tavern
193 Crystal Palace Road
☎ (081) 693 4968
12–11
Ind Coope Burton Ale; Taylor Walker Best Bitter; Tetley Bitter Ⓗ; guest beers (occasionally)
CAMRA SE London's *Pub of the Year* for two years running. A local institution. Pictures of the Crystal Palace exhibition adorn the walls in the saloon. Quiz nights and other events. Note the etched-glass panels behind the bar. Q ❀ ≈

SE23: Forest Hill

Bird in Hand
35 Dartmouth Road
☎ (081) 699 7417
11–11
Courage Directors; Greene King IPA, Abbot; S&N Theakston XB; Younger Scotch Ⓗ; guest beers (weekends)
Local history photographs decorate the walls of this Wetherspoon house which enjoys a quiet, relaxing atmosphere and a mainly local trade. No food Sun eve.
Q ◑ ◗ ≈ ⌓

Railway Telegraph
112 Stanstead Road
☎ (081) 699 6644
11–3, 5.30–11; 11–11 Fri & Sat
Shepherd Neame Master Brew Bitter, Best Bitter, Spitfire, Porter, Bishops Finger Ⓗ
Large, popular pub on the South Circular, selling the full range of Shepherd Neame beers. Railway memorabilia.
☺ ❀ ◑ ≈ ♣

SE25: South Norwood

Albion
High Street ☎ (081) 653 0558
11–11
Courage Best Bitter, Directors; Wadworth 6X; Young's Special Ⓗ
Busy, friendly, crossroads pub offering good value beer. Live music Fri and Sun eves. No food Sat or Sun.
◑ ≈ (Norwood Jct) ♣

Alliance
High Street ☎ (081) 653 3604
11–11
Courage Best Bitter, Directors; Marston's Pedigree; Wadworth 6X Ⓗ; guest beers
Welcoming, one-bar local with a country-style decor. Weekday home-cooked lunches include vegetarian and vegan options. Worthington White Shield and Imperial Russian Stout are stocked.
◑ ♿ ≈ (Norwood Jct) ♣

SE26: Sydenham

Bricklayers Arms
189 Dartmouth Road
☎ (081) 699 1260
11–11
Young's Bitter, Special, Winter Warmer Ⓗ
Large, friendly pub whose back room houses many interesting artefacts. Purpose-built children's room.
☺ ❀ ◑ ♿ ≈ (Forest Hill)

Dulwich Wood House
39 Sydenham Road
☎ (081) 693 5666
11–11
Young's Bitter, Special, Winter Warmer Ⓗ
Country-style pub in the middle of town. The back bar displays rare pictures of the motor racing circuit in Crystal Palace Park. The large garden has petanque, a children's area, a garden and a bar.
♔ ❀ ◑ ≈ (Sydenham Hill) ♣ P ⊭

SE27: West Norwood

Hope
49 Norwood High Street
☎ (081) 670 2035
11–11
Young's Bitter, Porter, Special, Winter Warmer Ⓗ
Small and friendly, one-bar local with a five-pump beer engine on the island bar. Pictures of ships and old advertisements. Regular fund-raising events. Q ❀ ≈

Horns
40 Knights Hill
☎ (081) 670 2231
11–11
Courage Best Bitter, Directors Ⓗ
Two-bar pub with typical Courage panelled decor. One quiet bar; the other is equipped with Sky TV.
❀ ≈ ♣

Addiscombe

Claret Wine Bar
5a Bingham Corner, Lower Addiscombe Road (A222)
☎ (081) 656 7452
11.30–11
Eldridge Pope Royal Oak; Palmers IPA Ⓗ; guest beers
Despite the name, an ale drinkers' bar in a shopping parade. Recent improvements include a new beer cellar. Usually five ales are served. No food weekends. ◑ ≈

Beckenham

Coach & Horses
Bunhill Road (off A222)
11–3, 5.30 (7 Sat)–11
Courage Best Bitter, Directors Ⓗ
Busy, back-street pub handy for Safeway.
❀ ◑ ≈ (Junction) ♣ P

Greater London

Jolly Woodman
Chancery Lane (off A222)
11–3, 5–11; 11–11 Fri & Sat
Draught Bass; Charrington IPA; Fuller's London Pride Ⓗ
Bustling, side-street local with a village atmosphere. Plenty of sporting teams, plus a motorcycling club. Very warm welcome. Occasional live music Sun eves. The cheapest pub in Beckenham.
⛫ Q ❀ ◑ ≹ (Junction) ♣

Belvedere

Royal Standard
39 Nuxley Road
11–11; 11–3, 5.30–11 Tue–Thu
Draught Bass; Charrington IPA Ⓗ**; guest beers**
Popular local with a maritime flavour. No food Sun.
♉ ❀ ◑ ◗ P

Bexleyheath

Bitter Experience (Off-Licence)
Broadway ☎ (081) 304 2039
11–2, 6–9; 10.30–9.30 Thu–Sat; 7–9 Sun
Beer range varies Ⓖ
Real ale off-licence with a continuously changing range of beers.

Robin Hood & Little John
Lion Road
☎ (081) 303 1128
11–2.30, 6–11
Courage Best Bitter, Directors; John Smith's Bitter; Wadworth 6X Ⓗ**; guest beers**
Popular local featuring many guest beers rarely seen in the South-East. ❀

Royal Oak (Polly Clean Stairs)
Mount Road
☎ (081) 303 4454
11.30–3, 6–11; 12–2.30, 7–10.30 Sun
Courage Best Bitter; Ruddles County; Wadworth 6X Ⓗ**; guest beers**
Excellent, historic, village-style local, surviving in the midst of suburbia. Hot and cold lunchtime snacks. Q ❀ P

Bromley

Arkwrights Wheel
10 Widmore Road
☎ (081) 460 4828
11 (10.30 Thu–Sat)–11
Adnams Bitter; Ind Coope Burton Ale; Tetley Bitter; Wadworth 6X Ⓗ
Refurbished pub by the new shopping centre, popular at lunchtime for its excellent value meals. Arkwrights Ale is brewed for the pub by the Falcon & Firkin, and sold at a bargain price during happy hour. ⛫ ◑ ≹ (North)

Bitter End (Off-Licence)
139 Masons Hill
☎ (081) 466 6083
12–3 (not Mon), 5–10 (9 Mon); 11–10 Sat; 12–2, 7–9 Sun
Beer range varies Ⓖ
Enterprising off-licence with an ever-changing range of ales, and often up to nine beers at weekends. Bottled beers and cider. ≹ (South) ⌔

Freelands Tavern
31 Freelands Road (off A222)
☎ (081) 464 2296
11–3, 5.30–11
Courage Best Bitter, Directors Ⓗ
Comfortable, suburban, corner pub, well-known locally for its charity fund-raising. Friendly atmosphere; quizzes held.
❀ ◑ ♿ ≹ (North) ♣

Chislehurst

Queens Head
High Street ☎ (081) 467 3490
11–3 (3.30 Sat), 5.30–11
Ind Coope Burton Ale; Tetley Bitter; Wadworth 6X; Young's Special; guest beer Ⓗ
Spacious, congenial pub next to the village pond. A large forecourt is used as a pavement drinking area. Occasional barbecues and live music in the sizeable garden in summer. ❀ ◑ ♣ P

Rambler's Rest
Mill Place ☎ (081) 467 1734
11–3, 5.30–11
Adnams Bitter; Courage Best Bitter, Directors; Wadworth 6X; guest beer Ⓗ
Split-level bar where the upper level is normally bustling. Pleasantly set at the edge of the common, ideal for commuters after the trek up the hill. No food Sun.
Q ❀ ◑ ≹ P

Croydon

Builders Arms
65 Leslie Park Road (off A222)
11.30–3, 5 (6.30 Sat)–11; 11.30–11 Fri
Fuller's Hock, Chiswick, London Pride, Mr Harry, ESB Ⓗ
Attractive, friendly, back-street pub with two cosy, saloon-standard bars. The former public bar now houses the food counter and the other gives access to a surprisingly large garden. Quiz night Mon. No eve food Fri–Sun (till 8.30 other eves). Q ❀ ◑ ◗ ≹ (E Croydon/Addiscombe)

Crown
90 Stanley Road
11–11
Ruddles County; Webster's Yorkshire Bitter Ⓗ
Excellent, street-corner local with bar walls adorned with a collection of plates. Large range of pub games (ask). Live music Tue (modern jazz) and Sat. ♣

Dog & Bull
24 Surrey Street (off A235)
☎ (081) 688 3664
11–11
Young's Bitter, Porter, Special, Winter Warmer Ⓗ
Lively, street-market pub offering good value lunches (Mon–Fri). Soon to be extended into the butcher's shop next door, when a garden will also be developed.
Q ❀ ◑ ≹ (E/W Croydon)

Golden Lion
144 Stanley Road
☎ (081) 684 1395
11–11
Courage Best Bitter, Directors; King & Barnes Sussex Ⓗ
Friendly local fielding ten darts teams. Regular charity fund-raising activities. ❀ ♣

Porter & Sorter
Station Road (off A222)
☎ (081) 688 4296
11–11; 12–3 Sun, closed Sun eve
Courage Best Bitter, Directors; Young's Special Ⓗ**; guest beer**
A rare survivor of old Croydon, amidst the glass and concrete: a comfortable and welcoming pub serving commuters and office workers. Food until 6pm (except Sun).
❀ ◑ ≹ (E Croydon) P

Cudham

Blacksmiths Arms
Cudham Lane OS446598
☎ (095 95) 72678
11–2.30, 6–11
Courage Best Bitter, Directors; King & Barnes Sussex; Wadworth 6X Ⓗ
Popular village local, within the Cudham conservation area, retaining much olde-worlde charm. Classic car meet first Sun of the month; barbecues in summer. No meals Mon eve. No-smoking area lunchtime only.
⛫ Q ❀ ◑ ◗ P ⊁

Footscray

Seven Stars
High Street ☎ (081) 300 2059
11.30–3.30, 5–11

Draught Bass; Charrington IPA; Fuller's London Pride, ESB; Greene King IPA; M&B Highgate Mild Ⓗ**; guest beers**
16th-century pub retaining many original features and offering outstanding value for the area. Wide range of guest beers. No food Sun. ❀ ◐

Leaves Green

Crown Inn
Leaves Green Road
☎ (0959) 572920
11–2.30 (3 Sat), 5 (6 Sat)–11
Shepherd Neame Master Brew Bitter, Best Bitter, Spitfire, Porter, Bishops Finger Ⓗ
Parts of this friendly pub date back to 1600 and recent refurbishment has maintained its character. Busy in summer.
Q ❀ ◐ ◑ ▲

Orpington

Cricketers
93 Chislehurst Road (off A208)
☎ (0689) 820164
11–3, 5–11; 11–11 Sat
Courage Best Bitter, Directors; guest beers Ⓗ
Comfortable, one-bar pub by Broomhill Common. Guest beers are chosen from a survey of pub regulars. Take-away Vietnamese and Chinese meals available to order, Mon–Sat, 6–11. ❀ ◐ ◑ ♣ P

Sidcup

Alma
Alma Road ☎ (081) 300 3208
11–2.30, 5.30 (7 Sat)–11
Courage Best Bitter; Young's Bitter, Special Ⓗ
Deservedly popular, back-street local retaining some of its Victorian-style interior.
❀ ♿ ⇌

Bitter Experience (Off-Licence)
High Street
11–2, 6–9; 10.30–9.30 Thu–Sat; 7–9 Sun
Beer range varies Ⓖ
Off-licence with a continuously changing range of real ales.

South Croydon

Rail View
188 Selsdon Road (B275)
☎ (081) 688 2315
11–3, 5.30–11; 12–11 Sat
Draught Bass; Charrington IPA; Fuller's London Pride Ⓗ
Popular local with a lively public bar and a comfortable lounge, decorated on a railway theme. Quiz alternate Sun eves. ❀ ◐ ⊟ ♿ ⇌ ♣ P

Thornton Heath

Horseshoe
745 London Road (at Thornton Heath pond) ☎ (081) 684 1956
11–3, 5.30 (7 Sat)–11; 11–11 Fri
Courage Best Bitter, Directors Ⓗ
Welcoming, two-bar pub fielding pool and darts teams. The public bar can be loud; the saloon is comfortable, and the seating area at the rear of the pub is usually quiet and relaxing. Weekday lunches.
◐ P

South-West London

SW1: Belgravia

Grouse & Claret
14 Little Chester Street
☎ (071) 235 3438
11–11
Beer range varies Ⓗ
Split-level, two-bar pub with a wine bar below and a Thai restaurant above (no food Sat).
◐ ◑ ⇌ (Victoria) ⊖

Star Tavern
6 Belgrave Mews West
☎ (071) 235 3019
11.30–3, 5 (7 Sat)–11; 11.30–11 Fri
Fuller's Chiswick, London Pride, ESB Ⓗ
Unspoilt and unchanging mews pub, an original entry in this guide. *Evening Standard Pub of the Year* 1992.
⩩ Q ◐ ⊖ (Hyde Pk Cnr)

SW1: Pimlico

Rising Sun
44 Ebury Bridge Road
11–11
Young's Bitter, Special, Winter Warmer Ⓗ
Popular local near Victoria coach station.
Q ❀ ◐ ⇌ (Victoria) ⊖

SW1: Sloane Square

Fox & Hounds
29 Passmore Street
11–3, 5.30–11; 12–2, 7.30–10.30 Sun
Draught Bass; Charrington IPA; Greene King IPA Ⓗ
Tiny, busy pub with a beer and wine licence. A well-deserved 21-year entry. ◐ ⊖

SW1: Victoria

Cardinal
23 Francis Street
11–3.30 (3 Sat), 5 (8 Sat)–11
Draught Bass; Charrington IPA; M&B Highgate Mild Ⓗ
Large ex-Finch's pub with a wine and food bar at the rear and a restaurant upstairs.
◐ ⇌ ⊖

SW1: Westminster

Buckingham Arms
62 Petty France
☎ (071) 222 3386
11–11; 11–3, 5.30–11 Sat
Young's Bitter, Porter, Special, Winter Warmer Ⓗ
Popular pub near the Passport Office, with a corridor drinking area behind the bar.
Q ◐ ◑ ⇌ (Victoria) ⊖ (St James's Pk)

Morpeth Arms
58 Millbank ☎ (071) 834 6442
11–11
Young's Bitter, Special, Winter Warmer Ⓗ
Pleasant pub near Vauxhall Bridge, overlooking the Thames. Handy for the Tate Gallery. ◐ ◑ ⇌ (Vauxhall) ⊖ (Pimlico)

Paviours Arms
Page Street
11–11
Fuller's Chiswick, London Pride, ESB Ⓗ
Three-bar, Art Deco pub, serving Thai food, in addition to a traditional menu. ◐ ◑ ⊟

Royal Oak
2 Regency Street
11–11; 11–3, 7–11 Sat
Young's Bitter, Porter, Special, Winter Warmer Ⓗ
One-bar, corner pub near the horticultural halls. Q ◐ ◑

Westminster Arms
9 Storeys Gate
☎ (071) 222 8520
11.30–11; 12–3 Sun, closed Sun eve
Beer range varies Ⓗ
Small pub which used to have a superb view of Big Ben until a large building was put in the way. Wine bar downstairs. Weekday lunches.
◐ ⊖ (St James's Pk)

SW1: Whitehall

Old Shades
37 Whitehall
11–11; 11–3, 7–11 Sat; 12–3 Sun, closed Sun eve
Draught Bass; Charrington IPA; Fuller's London Pride Ⓗ
Long, wood-panelled bar with a lounge at the rear. ⩩ ◐ ◑
⇌ (Charing Cross) ⊖

SW2: Brixton

Hope & Anchor
123 Acre Lane
☎ (071) 274 1787
11–11

Young's Bitter, Porter, Special, Winter Warmer Ⓗ
One-bar, roadside pub that caters for a varied clientele. Recent redevelopment of the garden makes this easily the best pub in the area.
♛ Q ❀ ◖ ◗ ♿ ⇌ ⊖

SW3: Chelsea

Coopers Arms
87 Flood Street
11–11
Young's Bitter, Special, Winter Warmer Ⓗ
Busy café-bar-style pub offering an extensive menu.
◖ ◗

Princess of Wales
145 Dovehouse Street
☎ (071) 351 5502
11–11
Courage Best Bitter, Directors; Wadworth 6X Ⓗ
Locals' pub behind the Royal Marsden Hospital.
◖ ⊖ (S Kensington)

Rose
86 Fulham Road
☎ (071) 589 6672
11–11
Fuller's London Pride, Mr Harry, ESB Ⓗ
Ornate, friendly pub with much wood and tilework. Upstairs theatre.
◖ ◗ ⊖ (S Kensington)

Surprise
6 Christchurch Terrace
☎ (071) 352 4699
11–11
Draught Bass; Charrington IPA; guest beers Ⓗ
Popular, back-street pub: one bar but two distinct drinking areas. Q ◖ ◗

SW4: Clapham

Rose & Crown
2 The Polygon, Old Town
☎ (071) 720 8265
11–11
Fuller's London Pride; Harveys BB; guest beers Ⓗ
Cosy, one-bar pub with homely features, fresh flowers and good food. Meals till 8pm.
Q ❀ ◖ ◗ ⊖ (Common) ♣

SW6: Fulham

Jolly Brewer
308–310 North End Road
11–11
Courage Best Bitter; Ruddles County; Webster's Yorkshire Bitter Ⓗ
Busy, popular, street market pub. ◖ ⊖ (Broadway) ♣

SW6: Parsons Green

Duke of Cumberland
235 New Kings Road
11–11
Young's Bitter, Porter, Special, Winter Warmer Ⓗ
Large pub, originally called Ponds End Tavern, established 1657 and rebuilt in 1893 on this site. ♛ ◖ ⊟ ⊖

White Horse
1 Parsons Green
☎ (071) 736 2115
11–3, 5 (7 Sat)–11
Draught Bass; Charrington IPA; M&B Highgate Mild, Old; Traquair House Ale (winter); **guest beers** Ⓗ
Large, busy pub, facing Parsons Green, with a large outside terrace. Mini-beer festivals several times a year.
◖ ◗ ⊖

SW7: South Kensington

Anglesea Arms
15 Selwood Terrace
11–3, 5.30 (7 Sat)–11
Adnams Bitter; Brakspear Special; Eldridge Pope Hardy Country; Young's Special; guest beer Ⓗ
One of the first free houses to sell independent brewers' beers in London. Twenty-one years in this guide. ◖ ◗ ⊖

SW8: Battersea

Old Red House
133 Battersea Park Road
☎ (071) 622 1664
11–11
Courage Best Bitter, Directors; Marston's Pedigree; Wadworth 6X Ⓗ
Warm and friendly pub, the longest held licence in Battersea. Darts and quizzes weekdays; entertainment Fri–Sun includes discos, live music and karaoke. ❀ ◖ ◗
⇌ (Battersea Pk Rd) ♣ P

SW8: Kennington

Roebuck
84 Ashmole Street (off Claylands Rd; can be reached through housing estate opp. Oval west gates)
☎ (071) 820 9793
11–11
Bass Worthington BB, Draught Bass; guest beer Ⓗ
Very tasteful pub with a conservatory at the rear and a small garden. Darts, dominoes and football teams. Vegetarian meals on request; book Sun lunch. Not easy to find.
❀ ◖ ♿ ⊖ (Oval) ♣ ⊭

SW8: Stockwell

Priory Arms
83 Lansdowne Way
☎ (071) 622 1884
11–11
Young's Bitter, Special; Wadworth 6X Ⓗ; **guest beers**
Small, one-bar pub, popular with students. Voted CAMRA SW London *Pub of the Year* 1992. Warm welcome. Meals until 7pm, except Sun.
❀ ◖ ⊖ ♣ ⌓

SW8: South Lambeth

Surprise
16 Southville ☎ (071) 622 4623
11–3, 5–11 (11–11 summer)
Young's Bitter, Special, Winter Warmer Ⓗ
Small pub at the side of Larkhall Park; ideal for children in summer. Pinball in the back room. ♛ Q ❀ ◖ ◗
⇌ (Wandsworth Rd)
⊖ (Stockwell) ♣

SW9: Stockwell

Old White Horse
261 Brixton Road
11–11
Ind Coope Burton Ale; Tetley Bitter Ⓗ
Very old, traditional pub, attracting mainly locals with its friendly and warm atmosphere. Sandwiches and rolls. ❀ ◖ ♿ ⇌ (Brixton)
⊖ ♣ P

SW10: West Brompton

Fox & Pheasant
1 Billing Road
☎ (071) 352 2943
11–3, 5.30–11
Draught Bass; Charrington IPA; guest beer Ⓗ
Tiny, two-bar pub used by locals, near Chelsea FC. Parking difficult.
❀ ◖ ⊖ (Fulham Broadway)

SW10: West Chelsea

Chelsea Ram
32 Burnaby Street
☎ (071) 351 4008
11–3, 5.30–11; 11–11 Fri
Young's Bitter, Porter, Special, Winter Warmer Ⓗ
Comfortable, back-street pub near Lots Road power station and Chelsea Wharf. No jukebox or piped music.
Q ◖

SW11: Battersea

Raven
140 Westbridge Road
☎ (071) 228 1657
11–11
Courage Best Bitter; Fuller's London Pride, Mr Harry; Wadworth 6X; Young's Bitter Ⓗ
Interesting, Dutch-gabled, corner pub, the oldest in Battersea.
❀ 🛏 ◐ ◗ ⇌ (Clapham Jct)

SW11: Clapham

Beehive
197 St John's Hill
☎ (071) 228 0198
11–3, 5–11; 11–11 Fri & Sat
Fuller's Chiswick, London Pride, ESB Ⓗ
Small, welcoming local.
Q ◐ ⇌ (Junction)

Falcon
2 St Johns Hill
☎ (071) 228 4077
11–11
Draught Bass; Charrington IPA; Fuller's London Pride Ⓗ**; guest beers**
Large pub near the station, featuring wood panelling, mirrors and a massive bar. An air of faded elegance prevails. Two beer festivals annually.
♨ ◐ ◗ ♿ ⇌ (Junction)

SW12: Balham

Grove
39 Oldridge Road
☎ (081) 673 6531
11–11
Young's Bitter, Special Ⓗ
Pub with a large, ornate Victorian exterior and an original interior in the saloon. The lively public bar has darts and bar billiards. The saloon bar is decorous, but with music – live Sat. Generous portions of good food.
❀ ◐ ▲ ⇌ (Clapham South) ♣

Nightingale
97 Nightingale Lane
☎ (081) 673 1637
11–3, 5.30–11; 11–11 Fri & Sat
Young's Bitter, Special, Winter Warmer Ⓗ
Bustling, friendly pub where recent refurbishments have enhanced the bar. Local CAMRA *Pub of the Year* 1992. A massive fundraiser for local charities via its famous annual walk. No food Sun.
Q ⛾ ❀ ◐ ◗ ♿
⇌ (Wandsworth Common)
⊖ (Clapham South)

SW13: Barnes

Bulls Head
373 Lonsdale Road
☎ (081) 876 5241
11–11
Young's Bitter, Porter, Special, Winter Warmer Ⓗ
World-famous music pub on the south bank of the Thames, specialising in jazz and jazz-fusion. ❀ ◐ ◗ ⇌ (Barnes Bridge) ♣

Coach & Horses
27 Barnes High Street (A3003)
☎ (081) 876 2695
11–11
Young's Bitter, Special, Winter Warmer Ⓗ
Superbly welcoming, conversational local. Quiz nights (Mon); barbecues in summer. Garden play area for children. ♨ ❀ ◐ ◗
⇌ (Barnes Bridge)

Red Lion
2 Castlenau (A306)
☎ (081) 748 2984
11–11
Fuller's Chiswick, London Pride, Mr Harry, ESB Ⓗ
Large, family pub with a spacious and ornate restaurant. Popular at weekends. ❀ ◐ ◗ ⇌

SW14: Mortlake

Hare & Hounds
216 Upper Richmond Road, East Sheen ☎ (081) 876 4304
11–11
Young's Bitter, Special, Winter Warmer Ⓗ
A change of management has transformed this large roadside pub into one of the best bets for miles. Excellent garden. Q ❀ ◐ ◗

SW15: Putney

Fox & Hounds
167 Upper Richmond Road
☎ (081) 788 1912
11–11
Fuller's London Pride Ⓗ**; Greene King Abbot** Ⓖ**; Wadworth 6X; Whitbread Boddingtons Bitter, Flowers Original; guest beer** Ⓗ
Comfortable and spacious, one-bar pub; busy, with a younger clientele. Occasional festivals of ales served by gravity on the enclosed patio. Eve meals till 7.30. ❀ ◐ ◗
♿ ⇌ ⊖ (E Putney) ♣

Green Man
Putney Heath
☎ (081) 788 8096
11–11
Young's Bitter, Special, Winter Warmer Ⓗ
Unspoilt pub dating back to 1700, offering a warm welcome to its many regulars and guests. A busy, cosy public bar; outdoor bar, barbecue and meals all day in summer (no eve meals in winter). Q ❀ ◐ ◗ ⊞ ♣

Half Moon
93 Lower Richmond Road
☎ (081) 780 9383
11–11
Young's Bitter, Special Ⓗ
Famous live music venue with folk, jazz, blues or rock every night in a separate room. The saloon displays pictures of old Putney and musicians.
❀ ⊞ ♣

SW16: Streatham

Pied Bull
498 Streatham High Road
☎ (081) 764 4003
11–3.30, 5.30–11; 11–11 Sat
Young's Bitter, Special, Winter Warmer Ⓗ
Two-bar pub with many drinking areas in the saloon. The back bar is especially recommended, popular with all ages. ♨ Q ◐ ◗ ⊞ ⇌ P

SW17: Earlsfield

Leather Bottle
538 Garret Lane
☎ (081) 946 2309
11–11
Young's Bitter, Special, Winter Warmer Ⓗ
Pleasant, old pub with a warm atmosphere. Large garden, a lively public bar and a new family room. Popular in summer. More rural than urban.
♨ ⛾ ❀ ◐ ◗ ⊞ ♣ P

SW18: Wandsworth

Old Sergeant
104 Garratt Lane
☎ (081) 874 4099
11–3, 5–11; 11–11 Mon, Fri & Sat
Young's Bitter, Special, Winter Warmer Ⓗ
Welcoming and friendly local, an essential part of the Wandsworth tour.
❀ ◐ ⇌ (Town)

Spread Eagle
High Street
☎ (081) 874 1326
11–11
Young's Bitter, Special, Winter Warmer Ⓗ
Pub with magnificent glass screens in a large saloon bar, a smaller back room for diners, and a popular public bar.
♨ Q ◐ ◗ ⊞ ⇌ (Town)

Greater London

SW19: Merton

Princess Royal
25 Abbey Road
☎ (081) 542 3273
11–3, 5.30 (5 Fri, 6 Sat)–11
Courage Best Bitter, Directors; Marston's Pedigree; John Smith's Bitter; Wadworth 6X Ⓗ
Friendly locals' corner pub comprising a small public bar and a larger saloon. Once part of the Hodgson's of Kingston estate. ❀ ◖ ◗ ⊞
⊖ (S Wimbledon) ♣

SW19: Wimbledon

Broadway
141 The Broadway
☎ (081) 542 1293
11–11
Courage Best Bitter, Directors; John Smith's Bitter Ⓗ**; guest beer**
Large, main-road pub next to Wimbledon's only cinema, boasting some original Art Deco styling. Hodgson's brewery detail is also still intact. Dress restrictions eves.
♉ ❀ ◖ ⇌ ⊖

Hand in Hand
6 Crooked Billet, Wimbledon Common (off A281)
☎ (081) 946 5720
11–11
Young's Bitter, Porter, Special, Winter Warmer Ⓗ
Large pub which a horseshoe bar divides into public bar and saloon areas. Originally a bakehouse, and a beerhouse until 1974. Often very busy in summer. The family room may be used for darts in the eve.
♨ Q ♉ ❀ ◖ ◗ ♣ ⚡

SW20: Raynes Park

Cavern
100–102 Coombe Lane
☎ (081) 944 8211
11–11
Fuller's London Pride; Whitbread Boddingtons Bitter; Young's Bitter, Special Ⓗ
New pub converted from a restaurant. Its decor includes a red telephone box and Beatles/Stones posters. A major contributor to the widening beer range in SW20's four pubs. The CD jukebox is loud when appropriate.
❀ ◖ ⇌

Carshalton

Racehorse
17 West Street (off A232)
☎ (081) 647 1296
11–3, 5–11; 11–11 Sat
Courage Best Bitter, Directors; King & Barnes Sussex, Old, Festive Ⓗ**; guest beers**
Well-run, comfortable, two-bar pub with a formal eating area in the lounge, serving a wide range of meals. At least two guest beers every week (one always low-priced). No food Sun eve. Q ❀ ◖ ◗ ⇌ ♣ P

Railway Tavern
47 North Street (off A232)
☎ (081) 669 8016
12–3, 5.30–11; 12–11 Sat
Fuller's Hock, London Pride, Mr Harry, ESB Ⓗ
Small, street-corner local with ornate windows and mirrors. A home for many teams from marbles to morris dancing. Afternoon hours are flexible; if locked, knock. Crusty bread sandwiches at all times.
⇌ ♣

Cheam

Railway
32 Station Way (off A217/A213) ☎ (081) 642 7416
11–3, 5–11; 11–11 Thu–Sat
Courage Best Bitter, Directors Ⓗ
Detached, 19th-century building housing a comfortable single bar with 'Lords' and 'Commons' ends. Very much a local where the emphasis is on beer and conversation. Quiz nights in winter. No food Sun.
Q ◖ ◗ ⇌ ♣

Chessington

North Star
271 Hook Road, Hook (A243)
☎ (081) 397 4227
12 (11 Sat)–11
Draught Bass; Fuller's London Pride; M&B Highgate Mild, Old; Young's Bitter Ⓗ
The only regular outlet for mild in the Royal Borough. No food weekends. Q ❀ ◖ ♣ P

Kingston upon Thames

Boaters Inn
Lower Ham Road, Canbury Gardens ☎ (081) 541 4672
11–3, 5–11; 11–11 Fri, Sat & summer
Brakspear Bitter; Everards Tiger; S&N Theakston XB; John Smith's Bitter; Wadworth 6X Ⓗ
Attractive, modern pub in riverside gardens with its own moorings. Popular with all; crowded in summer. No eve meals Mon or Sun. ♉ ❀ ◖ ◗

Bricklayers Arms
53 Hawks Road (off A2043)
☎ (081) 546 0393
11–11
Morland Bitter, Old Masters, Old Speckled Hen Ⓗ
Busy pub with a vast food menu (a carry-out service is available). Eve meals till 8pm (6pm Sat, no eve meals Sun).
Q ♉ ❀ ◖ ◗ ♣

Canbury Arms
49 Canbury Park Road
☎ (081) 546 1822
11–11
Courage Best Bitter, Directors; guest beers Ⓗ
Busy local near the Crown Court, with a huge reference library behind the bar. No eve meals Sun.
Q ♉ ❀ ◖ ◗ ⇌ ♣ P

Cocoanut
Mill Street ☎ (081) 546 3978
11–3, 5.30–11; 11–11 Sat
Fuller's Hock, Chiswick, London Pride, ESB Ⓗ
Part of the local community, with occasional special nights. No food Sun. CAMRA Greater London *Pub of the Year* 1992. No food Sun. Q ❀ ◖ ♣

Park Tavern
19 New Road
11–11
Brakspear Special; Young's Bitter, Special; guest beers Ⓗ
Welcoming local near Richmond Park, stocking a varied range of guest beers. Parking difficult. ♨ ❀

Wych Elm
Elm Road ☎ (081) 546 3271
11–3, 5–11; 11–11 Sat
Fuller's Hock, Chiswick, London Pride, Mr Harry, ESB Ⓗ
Friendly pub with a large regular following. Ornately decorated lounge and a basic, but tidy public. Impressive floral displays. No food Sun.
❀ ◖ ⊞ ♣

New Malden

Royal Oak
90 Coombe Road (B283)
☎ (081) 942 0837
11–11
Ind Coope Benskins Best Bitter, Burton Ale; Tetley Bitter; Young's Bitter, guest beer Ⓗ
Large corner local given a sympathetic refurbishment and retaining a public bar. Quizzes; karaoke; live comedy Thu nights. No food Sun eve. Beware Addlestones cider on fake handpump.
♉ ❀ ◖ ◗ ⇌ ♣ P ⚡

Richmond

Orange Tree
Kew Road ☎ (081) 940 0944
11–11

Young's Bitter, Porter, Special, Winter Warmer [H]
Fine, popular pub in a large Victorian building with a fringe theatre upstairs and a bistro/wine bar downstairs. Good variety of meals; food counter in the lounge (no food Sun eve). ♛ Q ❀ ◐ ◗ ⇌ ⊖

Princes Head
The Green ☎ (081) 940 1572
11–11
Fuller's Chiswick, London Pride, ESB [H]
Attractive pub, established circa 1740. The lounge bar is in traditional style, enhanced with prints of old Richmond. Good, home-cooked bar food. Enjoy a stroll around Richmond Green and its adjoining lanes. ❀ ◐ ◗ ⇌ ⊖

Shaftesbury Arms
Kew Road ☎ (081) 948 4782
12 (11 Sat)–11
Young's Bitter, Special, Winter Warmer [H]
Comfortable local just outside the main town, near the rugby grounds. Handy for Kew Gardens. Q ❀ ⇌ ⊖ ♣

White Cross Hotel
Water Lane ☎ (081) 940 6844
11–11
Young's Bitter, Porter, Special, Winter Warmer [H]
Extremely popular, Thames-side pub in a splendid, picturesque setting. Excellent bar food and service. The function room, up from the bar, provides extra space at busy times. Riverside terrace bar in summer. Local CAMRA *Pub of the Year* 1992.
♛ Q ❀ ◐ ◗ ⇌ ⊖

Surbiton

Bun Shop
22–26 Berrylands Road (off A240) ☎ (081) 399 3124
11–11
Adnams Bitter; guest beers [H]
Pub offering a range of varying guest beers (usually three) and holding occasional beer festivals. A two-bar pub, but no price difference. Skittles by arrangement in the function room, which also has regular live music. No food weekends.
Q ♞ ◐ ⇌ ♣

Waggon & Horses
1 Surbiton Hill Road (A240)
11–2.30, 5–11; 11–11 Fri & Sat
Young's Bitter, Porter (summer), Special, Winter Warmer [H]
The only Young's pub in the Royal Borough with a public bar. The landlord celebrated his 25th anniversary at the pub in 1992. Summer barbecues; no food weekends.
Q ❀ ◐ ⊞ ⇌ ♣

Sutton

New Town
7 Lind Road (off A232)
☎ (081) 642 0567
11–3, 5–11; 11–11 Sat
Young's Bitter, Porter, Special, Winter Warmer [H]
Popular, friendly, street-corner pub. The public bar has an adjoining games room and there is a contrasting, three-level saloon bar. Good food (not served Sun eve).
Q ❀ ◐ ◗ ⊞ ⇌ ♣

West London

W1: Fitzrovia

Bricklayers Arms
31 Gresse Street
11–11
Samuel Smith OBB, Museum [H]
Small, pleasant pub on two floors. A previous winner of CAMRA's *Pub Refurbishment Award.*
◐ ◗ ⊖ (Tottenham Ct Rd) ♣

Duke of York
47 Rathbone Street
11–11 (5 Sat); closed Sun
Draught Bass; Charrington IPA; Fuller's London Pride [H]
Locals' pub with a horseshoe bar, at the end of a pedestrianised street of small shops. Happy hours weekdays. Snacks Mon–Fri lunchtimes. ⊖ (Goodge St)

George & Dragon
151 Cleveland Street
12–11; 12–3, 7–11 Sat
Draught Bass; Charrington IPA; Fuller's London Pride [H]
Locals' pub serving weekday lunches. ◐ ⊖ (Gt Portland St)

King & Queen
1 Foley Street
11–11; 11–3, 7–11 Sat
Fuller's London Pride; Ruddles Best Bitter, County [H]
Red-brick, Gothic-style pub, near Middlesex Hospital. ◐

W1: Marylebone

Beehive
7 Homer Street
11–3, 5.30 (7 Sat)–11; 11–11 Fri
Brakspear Bitter; Whitbread Boddingtons Bitter, Wethered Bitter [H]
Small, neat, side-street local.
◐ ⇌ ⊖

Golden Eagle
59 Marylebone Lane
☎ (071) 935 3228
11–11; 11–3, 7–11 Sat
Draught Bass; Brakspear Bitter; guest beers [H]
Tiny, corner pub with live piano music at weekends. ◐

Turners Arms
26 Crawford Street
11–11
Shepherd Neame Master Brew Bitter, Spitfire [H]
Unusual brewer for this area. The pub houses a large display of antique weapons.
◐ ◗ ⇌ ⊖

Wargrave Arms
40 Brendon Street
☎ (071) 723 0559
11–11; 11–3, 7–11 Sat
Young's Bitter, Special, Winter Warmer [H]
Ex-Finch's corner pub.
◐ ◗ ⇌ (Paddington)
⊖ (Edgware Rd)

Worcester Arms
89 George Street
11 (12 Sat)–11
Marston's Pedigree; S&N Theakston XB; John Smith's Bitter; Whitbread Boddingtons Bitter; guest beers [H]
Small, friendly pub boasting an Alton Brewery mirror. The beer range varies. ◐ ⇌ ⊖ ♣

W1: Mayfair

Guinea
30 Bruton Place
☎ (071) 409 1728
11–11; 11–3, 7–11 Sat; closed Sun
Young's Bitter, Porter, Special, Winter Warmer [H]
Small mews pub dating back to the 15th century. First mentioned as the Guinea in 1755, leased by Young's in 1888. No lunches Sat. ◐ ◗ ⮌

Windmill
Mill Street ☎ (071) 491 8050
11–11; 11–3 Sat; closed Sun
Young's Bitter, Porter, Special, Winter Warmer [H]
Split-level pub with a food counter in the lower bar and a restaurant upstairs.
◐ ◗ ⊖ (Oxford Circus)

W2: Paddington

White Hart
31 Brook Mews North (off Craven Rd) ☎ (071) 402 4417
12–11
Courage Best Bitter, Directors; Wadworth 6X [H]
Well-hidden pub at the end of a mews. ◐ ⇌ ⊖ ♣

W3: Acton

Castle
140 Victoria Road
☎ (081) 992 2027

Greater London

11–11
Fuller's London Pride, ESB Ⓗ
An oasis on the edge of an industrial area. Can be busy at lunchtime, when you may spot a famous face from the nearby BBC studios. Ideal for a quiet eve drink.
❀ ◖ ◗ ⊟ ⊖ (North) ♣ P

Kings Head
214 High Street
☎ (081) 992 0282
11–11
Fuller's Chiswick, London Pride, ESB Ⓗ
Recently redecorated coaching inn displaying photographs of old Acton and the pub. Jasper, the Parrot, is as sharp as ever. No food Sun.
❀ ◖ ⊖ (Town) ♣

W4: Chiswick

Bell & Crown
72 Strand-on-Green
☎ (081) 994 4164
11–11
Fuller's Chiswick, London Pride, Mr Harry, ESB Ⓗ
Pub overlooking the Thames, with a conservatory giving a view of Kew Bridge. Handy for the Engine Museum.
◖ ◗ ⇌ (Kew Bridge)

George & Devonshire
8 Burlington Lane
☎ (081) 994 1854
11–11
Fuller's Chiswick, London Pride, Mr Harry, ESB Ⓗ
Large, multi-roomed pub near Fuller's brewery, overlooking the notorious Hogarth roundabout. Eve meals Mon–Fri. ◖ ◗ ⊟

George IV
185 Chiswick High Road
☎ (081) 994 4624
11–11
Fuller's London Pride, ESB Ⓗ
Large, two-bar pub, where the lounge is broken up into alcoves.
❀ ◖ ⊟ ⊖ (Turnham Green)

Windmill
214 Chiswick High Road
11–11
Fuller's Chiswick, London Pride, ESB Ⓗ
Popular pub which gets very busy at times. No food Sun eve.
◖ ◗ ⊖ (Turnham Green) ♣

W5: Ealing

Castle Inn
36 St Mary's Road
☎ (081) 567 3285
11–11
Fuller's London Pride, ESB Ⓗ
Friendly family pub, drawing some custom from Thames Valley University opposite, especially American academics. The patio wins prizes every year.
❀ ◖ ⊟ ♿ ⊖ (South) ♣

Fox & Goose
Hanger Lane ☎ (081) 997 2441
11.30–11
Fuller's Chiswick, London Pride, ESB Ⓗ
Small public bar, a large saloon and a pleasant garden, all acting as a welcome refuge from the infamous Hanger Lane gyratory system. ❀ ◖ ◗ ⊟ ♿ ⊖ (Hanger Lane) P

Red Lion
13 St Mary's Road
☎ (081) 567 2541
11–11
Fuller's Chiswick, London Pride, ESB Ⓗ
Also known as Stage Six due to its proximity to the Ealing film studios, this gem of a pub has its walls lined with photographs from films and TV. Deservedly popular; try the garden in summer.
Q ❀ ◖ ⇌ (Broadway) ⊖

Rose & Crown
Church Place, St Mary's Road
☎ (081) 567 2811
11.30–3 (4.30 Sat), 5.30 (7 Sat)–11; 11–11 Fri
Fuller's Chiswick, London Pride, ESB Ⓗ
Popular local with a genuine public bar and a large saloon, which includes a 'greenhouse' annexe. Tucked away behind St Mary's church. Very pleasant garden.
Q ❀ ◖ ◗ ⊟ ⊖ (South)

Wheatsheaf
41 Haven Lane
☎ (081) 997 5240
11–11
Fuller's Chiswick, London Pride, ESB Ⓗ
Single-bar local which has retained its character and its well-defined drinking areas. Infinitely preferable to the nearby Chef & Brewer emporium. Q ❀ ◖ ◗ ⇌ (Broadway) ⊖ ♣

W6: Hammersmith

Builders
King Street ☎ (081) 748 4511
11–11
Young's Bitter, Porter, Special, Winter Warmer Ⓗ
Two-bar pub close to Hammersmith's shopping centre. Very busy before and after concerts at Hammersmith Apollo. ❀ ◖ ⊖

Cross Keys
57 Black Lion Lane
☎ (081) 748 3541
11–11
Fuller's Chiswick, London Pride, ESB Ⓗ
Popular pub, halfway between King Street and the Thames. Food served all day. ❀ ◖ ◗ ⊖ (Stamford Brook) ♣

Dove
19 Upper Mall
☎ (081) 748 5405
11–11
Fuller's London Pride, ESB Ⓗ
Historic, 17th-century, riverside pub, originally called the Dove Coffee House. Listed in the *Guinness Book of Records* as having the smallest public bar. *Rule Britannia* was composed upstairs. Eve meals in summer only.
❀ ◖ ◗ ⊖ (Ravenscourt Pk)

Salutation
King Street ☎ (081) 748 3668
11–11
Fuller's Chiswick, London Pride, ESB Ⓗ
Large pub with an interesting tiled frontage.
◖ ⊖ (Stamford Brook)

Thatched House
115 Dalling Road
☎ (081) 748 6174
11–11
Young's Bitter, Porter, Special, Winter Warmer Ⓗ
Popular local, near Brackenbury village. Occasional barbecues. Q ❀ ◖ ◗ ⊖ (Ravenscourt Pk)

W7: Hanwell

White Hart
324 Greenford Avenue
☎ (081) 578 1708
11–11
Fuller's London Pride, ESB Ⓗ
Corner pub featuring three bars, an off-licence and a quiet 'private' bar. Antique handpumps on the saloon wall. ♛ Q ⊟ ⇌ (Castle Bar Pk) P

W8: Kensington

Britannia
1 Allen Street ☎ (071) 937 1864
11–11
Young's Bitter, Porter, Special, Winter Warmer Ⓗ
Busy, wood-panelled pub close to Kensington's shops. A split-level lounge has two bars and a conservatory (no-smoking lunchtimes). No food Sun. Q ◖ ⊟ ⊖ (High St) ⚡

Churchill
119 Kensington Church Street
☎ (071) 727 4242
11–11
Fuller's Chiswick, London Pride, Mr Harry, ESB Ⓗ

Extremely busy pub hung about with a plethora of bric-a-brac. Q ◖ ◗ ⊖ (Notting Hill Gate)

Windsor Castle

114 Campden Hill Road
☎ (071) 727 8491
11–11
Draught Bass; Charrington IPA; Young's Bitter 🄷
Cosy, three-bar pub built in 1835. Garden bar in good weather. Food all day. Q ❀ ◖ ◗ ⊖ (Notting Hill Gate)

W9: Little Venice

Warwick Castle

6 Warwick Place
☎ (071) 286 6868
11–11
Bass Worthington BB, Draught Bass; Charrington IPA; Fuller's London Pride; Wadworth 6X; Young's Bitter; guest beer 🄷
Busy pub near a canal basin. ♛ ◖ ⊖ (Warwick Ave)

W9: Maida Vale

Warrington Hotel

93 Warrington Crescent
☎ (071) 286 2929
11–11
Brakspear Special; Fuller's London Pride, ESB; Ruddles County; Young's Special 🄷
Large, ornate Victorian 'gin palace', with florid decor and a semi-circular marble bar. Thai food eves
◖ ◗ ⊟ ⊖ (Warwick Ave)

W11: Notting Hill

Hoop

83 Notting Hill Gate
☎ (071) 229 6755
11–11
Young's Bitter, Porter, Special 🄷, Winter Warmer 🄶
Ex-Finch's pub facing a busy road junction.
◖ ⊖ (Notting Hill Gate)

Portobello Star

171 Portobello Road
☎ (071) 229 8016
11–11
Whitbread Castle Eden Ale, Flowers Original 🄷
Small, one-bar pub in the market.
◖ ⊖ (Notting Hill Gate)

W12: Shepherd's Bush

Crown & Sceptre

57 Melina Road
☎ (081) 743 6414
11–11 (may close Sat afternoon if QPR are at home)
Fuller's Chiswick, London Pride, ESB 🄷
Popular, back-street pub. ◖

Moon on the Green

172–174 Uxbridge Road
☎ (081) 749 5709
11–11 (may close Sat afternoon if QPR are at home)
Courage Directors; Greene King IPA; S&N Theakston XB; Younger Scotch; guest beer 🄷
Typical Wetherspoon pub which has brought welcome variety to the area. ◖ ◗ ⊖

W13: West Ealing

Forester

2 Leighton Road
☎ (081) 567 1654
11–3, 5.30–11; 11.30–11 Fri & Sat
Courage Best Bitter, Directors; Ruddles County; John Smith's Bitter 🄷; guest beers
Imposing, Edwardian structure, with many original features unaffected by recent refurbishment. The conservatory leads to the garden. Imperial Russian Stout has returned following efforts by the guv'nor and customers.
Q ❀ ♿ ≢ ⊖ (Northfield) ♣

Kent

2 Scotch Common (B455)
☎ (081) 997 5911
11–11
Fuller's London Pride, ESB 🄷
Recently refurbished pub retaining the split-level main saloon and a public bar. Small children's room. The large garden backs on to a park.
Q ♘ ◖ ♿ ≢ (Castle Pk Halt) ⊖ (Ealing Broadway) ♣ P

W14: West Kensington

Britannia Tap

150 Warwick Road
☎ (071) 602 1649
11–11
Young's Bitter, Porter, Special, Winter Warmer 🄷
Claimed to be the smallest pub in London, before it was enlarged in 1969. Still small, but a genuine local. Weekday lunches. ◖ ≢ (Kensington Olympia) ⊖ (Earl's Crt)

Seven Stars

253 North End Road
11–11
Fuller's London Pride, ESB 🄷
Large, two-bar pub rebuilt in 1938 in Art Deco style.
❀ ◖ ⊟ ⊖

Warwick Arms

160 Warwick Road
☎ (071) 603 3560
11–11
Fuller's Chiswick, London Pride, Mr Harry, ESB 🄷
Busy local dating from 1828. The rear section has exposed brickwork and a fireplace. Note the attractive Wedgwood handpumps. Handy for Olympia. No food weekends.
❀ ◖ ◗ ≢ (Kensington Olympia) ⊖ (Earl's Crt) ♣

Bedfont

Beehive

333 Staines Road
☎ (081) 890 8086
12–4, 5.30–11 (may vary)
Fuller's London Pride, ESB 🄷
Excellent pub with a friendly, lively atmosphere, an attractive lounge and a well-kept garden. Good value food (not served Sun). Barbecues in summer.
❀ ◖ ◗ P

Brentford

Express

Kew Bridge ☎ (081) 560 8484
11–3, 5.30–11
Draught Bass; Young's Bitter, Special, Winter Warmer 🄷
Popular, family-owned pub near Kew Bridge Steam Museum. Roomy and comfortable. No food Sun.
Q ❀ ◖ ≢ (Kew Bridge) ⊖ (Gunnersbury)

Colham Green

Crown

Colham Green Road
☎ (0895) 442303
11–3 (5 Sat), 5 (6 Sat)–11; 11–11 Fri
Fuller's London Pride, ESB 🄷
Busy pub in a rural setting with a fine garden for children and summer barbecues served from an adjoining barn.
Q ❀ ◖ ◗ ⊟ ♣ P

Cranford

Queens Head

High Street ☎ (081) 897 0722
11–11
Fuller's Chiswick, London Pride, Mr Harry, ESB 🄷
Tudor-style pub: one bar but two distinct drinking areas. A lounge to one side is used for dining (home-cooked food; not served weekend eves). Award-winning garden.
♛ ♘ ❀ ◖ ◗ ♣ P

Greenford

Bridge Hotel

Western Avenue (A40/A4127 jct) ☎ (081) 566 6246
11–3, 5.30–11; 11–11 Sat
Young's Bitter, Special, Winter Warmer 🄷

Greater London

Large, 1930s roadhouse, now part of a modern hotel. The bar has retained its original character, with wood panelling and cosy window alcoves.
Q ❀ 🛏 ◐ ♿ ≠ ⊖ P

Hampton

White Hart

High Street (A304)
☎ (081) 979 5352
11–3, 5.30–11; 11–11 Fri & Sat
Brakspear Old; Greene King Abbot; Ringwood Fortyniner; Whitbread Boddingtons Bitter; Woodforde's Nelson's Revenge Ⓗ
Comfortable, traditional pub with a friendly, relaxed atmosphere. Eight handpumps serve a selection from over 100 regularly-changing beers; a true free house. Very good lunches.
⛼ Q ❀ ◐ ♿ ≠ ♣ P

Hampton Wick

White Hart

High Street
☎ (081) 977 1786
11–3.30, 5.30–11; 11–11 Thu, Fri & Sat
Fuller's Chiswick, London Pride, Mr Harry, ESB Ⓗ
Large, mock-Tudor pub at the foot of Kingston Bridge. A spacious, oak-panelled lounge has a friendly atmosphere. Excellent, good value food (Tue–Sat eve till 8.30).
⛼ ❀ ◐ ◑ ≠ P

Harmondsworth

Crown

High Street
☎ (081) 759 1007
11–11; 12–3, 7.30–10.30 Sun
Brakspear Bitter; Courage Best Bitter, Directors Ⓗ
Village-centre pub with one large bar divided into several drinking areas. A small plough stands on one roof. Excellent, varied menu, reasonable food prices and a good vegetarian selection.
⛼ ❀ 🛏 ◐ ◑ ♿ ♣

Heathrow Airport

Tap & Spile

Upper Concourse, Terminal 1
☎ (081) 897 8418
11–11
Marston's Pedigree; Mitchell's Best Bitter; Whitbread Castle Eden Ale Ⓗ**; guest beers**
Formerly the Pilots Arms bar, on a balcony overlooking the check-in desks. The beer range constantly changes but can be a bit pricey. Selection of foreign beers. Q ⊖ ⌂

Hillingdon

Turks Head

47 Harlington Road
☎ (0895) 232720
11–11
Courage Best Bitter, Directors; Webster's Yorkshire Bitter Ⓗ**; guest beer**
Ex-Harman's pub with one guest beer always available, plus real pork scratchings. Very cosy and highly recommended. ❀ ◐ ◑ ♿ ♣ P

Hounslow

Earl Russell

274 Hanworth Road (A314)
☎ (081) 570 1560
11–11
Fuller's London Pride, ESB Ⓗ
Traditional, friendly, Victorian local. Good value weekday lunches. ❀ ◐ ⊟ ≠
⊖ (Central) P

Jolly Farmer

177 Lampton Road (off A4)
☎ (081) 570 1276
11–11
Courage Best Bitter, Directors; Wadworth 6X Ⓗ
Popular, cosy local. Friendly licensees offer very good weekday lunches.
❀ ◐ ⊟ ⊖ (Central) P

Lord Clyde

77 Inwood Road (opp. Inwood Park) ☎ (081) 572 9019
11–11
Courage Best Bitter; Hall & Woodhouse Badger Best Bitter, Tanglefoot; Morland Bitter, Old Masters Ⓗ
Pleasant, side-street local, recently extensively refurbished. Fields a leading darts team. Occasional live entertainment.
❀ ◐ ◑ ⊟ ♿ ≠ ⊖ (East) ♣

Moon Under Water

84–86 Staines Road
☎ (081) 572 7506
11–11
Courage Directors; Greene King IPA, Abbot; S&N Theakston XB; Younger Scotch Ⓗ**; guest beers**
Deservedly popular Wetherspoon house, offering up to four guest beers a week. Good value food at all hours, except Sun eve. Beer festivals.
Q ❀ ◐ ◑ ♿ ≠ ⊖ (Central) ⚲

Isleworth

Castle

18 Upper Square, Old Isleworth ☎ (081) 560 3615
11–11
Young's Bitter, Porter, Special, Winter Warmer Ⓗ
Popular pub, close to the Thames, serving good value lunches. The conservatory, away from the bar, is suitable for families.
⛼ Q ♘ ❀ ◐ ⊟ ≠ ♣ P ⚲

County Arms

Hall Road ☎ (081) 560 3971
11–11
Exmoor Beast; Taylor Landlord; Wadworth 6X; Webster's Yorkshire Bitter Ⓗ**; guest beers**
Former Watney house, recently released from the tie. Original 1930s decor; live music. A constantly-changing range of beers always includes a mild. No food Sun.
⛼ Q ♘ ❀ ◐ ⊟
≠ (Hounslow) ♣ ⌂ P

Town Wharf

Swan Street, Lower Square, Old Isleworth (off A300)
☎ (081) 847 2287
11.30–3, 5.30–11 (11.30–11 summer)
Samuel Smith OBB, Museum Ⓗ
Riverside pub on an old wharf: a comfortable upstairs lounge and an outside drinking area overlooking the Thames. Live jazz Thu; quiz Mon and Wed. Children welcome downstairs.
♘ ❀ ◐ ◑ ⊟ ♣ P

New Brentford

Globe

104 Windmill Road
☎ (081) 560 8932
11–11
Fuller's London Pride, ESB Ⓗ
One-bar pub with an attractive garden. Adorned with old photographs of local landmarks. No food Sun eve.
❀ ◐ ◑ ♣

Lord Nelson

Enfield Road
☎ (081) 568 1877
11–11
Fuller's London Pride, ESB Ⓗ
A strong Antipodean flavour rules in this friendly, sports-oriented local. Its wide range of food is often featured in the press. No meals Sun eve.
❀ ◐ ◑ ≠ (Brentford) ♣

Norwood Green

Plough

Tentelow Lane (A4127)
☎ (081) 571 1945
11–11
Fuller's Chiswick, London Pride, ESB Ⓗ
Lots of nooks and crannies for quiet drinking in this 17th-century, low-beamed building. Sports clubs meet here. No food Sun. ⛼ Q ❀ ◐ ♣ P

Ruislip Manor

JJ Moon's
12 Victoria Road
☎ (0895) 622373
11–11
Courage Directors; Greene King IPA, Abbot; S&N Theakston XB; Younger Scotch Ⓗ; guest beer
Traditional-style, mock Victorian alehouse converted from an old Woolworth's store. Always busy.
Q ❀ ◖ ◗ ⊖ ⌓

Southall

Scotsman
96 Scotts Road (off A3005)
☎ (081) 574 1506
11–3.30, 5.15–11; 12–4.30, 7–11 Sat
Fuller's London Pride, ESB Ⓗ
Hard-to-find, back-street local, comprising two very contrasting bars: a boisterous public and a quiet, relaxed saloon. ♛ Q ◖ ⊟ ♣

Teddington

Builders Arms
Field Lane ☎ (081) 977 4710
11–3, 5.30–11 (11–11 summer)
Brakspear Bitter; Courage Best Bitter, Directors; Gale's HSB; King & Barnes Sussex; Marston's Pedigree Ⓗ
Back-street Victorian local off the high street, offering a good range of beers at reasonable prices. ❀ ◖ ⊟ ⇌ ♣

Queen Dowager
North Lane ☎ (081) 977 2583
11–3, 5.30–11; 11–11 Fri & Sat
Young's Bitter, Special, Winter Warmer Ⓗ
Small, comfortable local off the main street, with a fine garden. Named after Queen Adelaide, the widow of William IV. No food Sun.
Q ❀ ◖ ⊟ ⇌ ♣

Twickenham

Albany
Station Yard ☎ (081) 892 1554
11–3.30, 5.30–11; 11–11 Fri & Sat
Bass Worthington BB, Draught Bass; Fuller's London Pride; M&B Highgate Mild; Wadworth 6X; Young's Bitter Ⓗ
Large, comfortable pub serving excellent, good value food. Look out for the beer festivals. Popular on rugby days. ◖ ◗ ⇌ ♣ P

Eel Pie
9–11 Church Street (off A305)
☎ (081) 891 1717
11–11
Gribble Ale; Hall & Woodhouse Badger Best Bitter, Tanglefoot; Pilgrim Porter; Wadworth 6X; Wells Eagle Ⓗ
Ex-wine bar in Twickenham's oldest shopping street, offering traditional and continental lunches (not Sun). Popular with rugby fans.
◖ ⇌ ♣

Prince Albert
30 Hampton Road (A311)
☎ (081) 894 3963
11–11
Fuller's Hock, Chiswick, London Pride, ESB Ⓗ
Friendly, Victorian local, little changed from when it had been in the same family for three generations. Occasional live music (mainly blues); regular quizzes. Q ❀ ◖ ⇌ (Strawberry Hill) ♣

Uxbridge

Crown & Sceptre
High Street ☎ (0895) 236308
11–11
Courage Best Bitter, Directors; Wadworth 6X Ⓗ
Grade II-listed building, dating from 1759. Home-cooked food – try the award-winning steak and kidney pies and seafood. This oasis in a shopping area has also won a floral display award. Children welcome afternoons. No food Sun. ♞ ❀ ◖ ⊟ ⊖ ♣

Load of Hay
33 Villier Street
☎ (0895) 234676
11–3, 5.30 (7 Sat)–11
Courage Best Bitter; John Smith's Bitter Ⓗ; guest beers
Cosy local with two bars, 15 minutes' walk from the town centre (near Brunel University). Originally built as the Officers' Mess for Elthorne Light Militia. An ever-changing range of guest beers makes it popular.
Q ❀ ◖ ◗ P ⊬

Whitton

Admiral Nelson
Nelson Road ☎ (081) 894 9998
11.30–11
Fuller's Chiswick, London Pride, ESB Ⓗ
Busy, high street pub, popular with Harlequins RFC. Varied menu Mon–Sat. ♛ ❀ ◖ ◗ ⇌

White Hart
121 Kneller Road
☎ (081) 863 3646
11–11
Greene King IPA; Smiles Best Bitter; Wadworth 6X; Webster's Yorkshire Bitter Ⓗ
17th-century coaching inn purchased as a free house in 1991 after closure in 1989 following a fire. Sympathetically restored, with 300-year-old roof timbers inlaid in the brick walls of the bar servery. Good value food.
❀ ◖ ◗ ⇌ ♣ P

The Symbols

♛	real fire	♿	easy wheelchair access
Q	quiet pub (at least one bar)	▲	camping facilities at the pub or nearby
♞	indoor room for children	⇌	near British Rail station
❀	garden or other outdoor drinking area	⊖	near underground station
🛏	accommodation	♣	pub games
◖	lunchtime meals	⌓	real cider
◗	evening meals	P	pub car park
⊟	public bar	⊬	no-smoking room or area

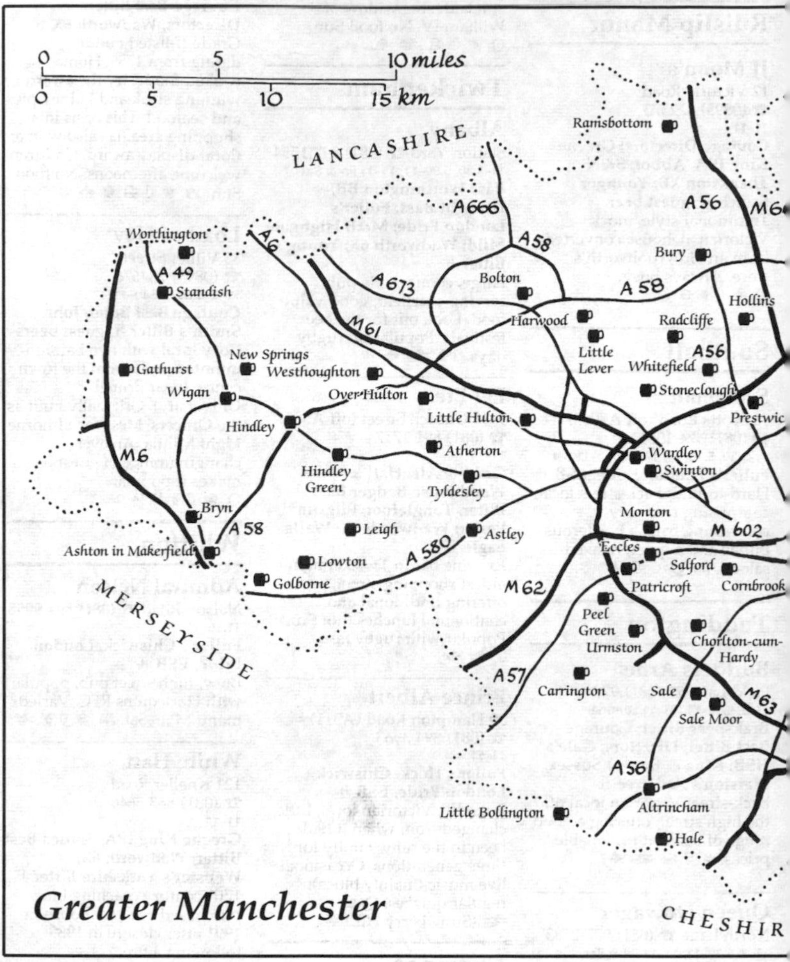

Hydes' Anvil, *Manchester*; **Holt**, *Cheetham*; **Lees**, *Middleton Junction*; **Thomas McGuinness**, *Rochdale*; **Oak**, *Heywood*; **Robinson's**, *Stockport*; **West Coast**, *Chorlton-on-Medlock*

Altrincham

Grapes Inn

Regent Road
☎ (061) 928 8714
11.30–11
Taylor Landlord; Whitbread Boddingtons Mild, Bitter; guest beer Ⓗ
Recent refurbishment to a two-room alehouse, with contrasting bars popular with all ages. Good, home-cooked food.
☾ ⊞ ≢ ⊖ ♣ P

Malt Shovels

Stamford Street
☎ (061) 928 2053
11.30–3, 5–11; 11–11 Fri & Sat
Samuel Smith OBB, Museum Ⓗ
Friendly, multi-roomed town-centre pub with live jazz almost every night; pool room upstairs. Near the former site of the Richardson & Goodall brewery. No food Sun.
❀ ☾ ♿ ≢ ⊖ ♣

Orange Tree

Old Market Place
☎ (061) 928 2600
11–11
Courage Directors; Marston's Pedigree; Webster's Green Label, Wilson's Bitter; guest beer Ⓗ
Winner of the local CAMRA *Pub of the Year* award, with a courageous guest beer policy. The present building, dating from 1880, was once the smallest pub in town. Records show a man sold his wife here in 1823 for 1/6. The snug/family room is no-smoking.
♉ ❀ ☾ ◗ ≢ ⊖ ♣ ⚟

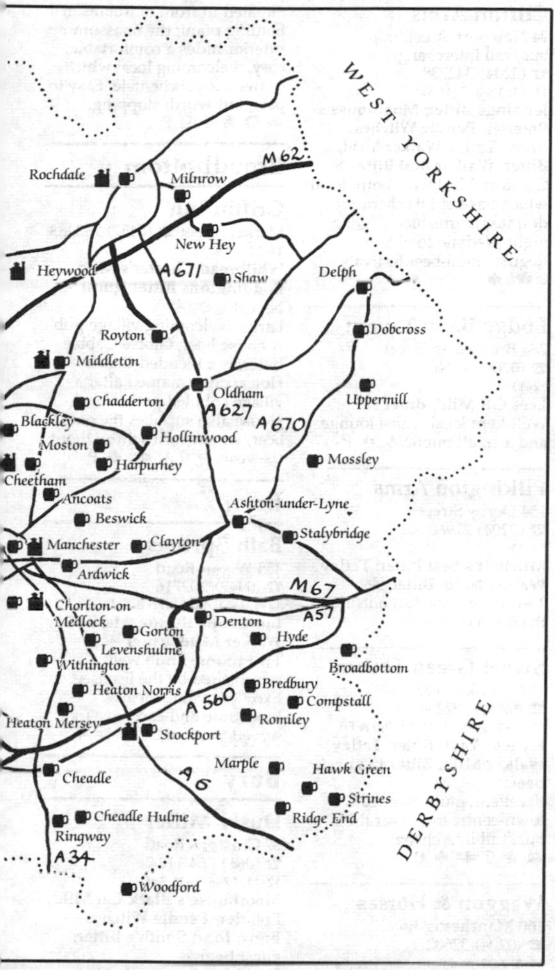

Tatton Arms
Tipping Street
☎ (061) 941 2502
11–11
Whitbread Boddingtons Bitter Ⓗ
Thriving two-room local where the pictures reflect the landlord's nautical background and the locals' interest in the two Manchester football teams. The pub has four teams of its own. No food Sun. ❀ ◐ ≹ ⊖ ♣ P

Ancoats

Jolly Angler
Ducie Street (behind Piccadilly station) ☎ (061) 236 5307
12–3, 5.30–11; 12–11 Sat
Hydes' Anvil Light, Bitter Ⓗ
Tiny and basic hidden gem with a welcoming, friendly atmosphere. Live folk music Mon and Thu.
⛫ ≹ (Piccadilly) ⊖ ♣

White House
Great Ancoats Street (A665)
☎ (061) 228 3231
12–3, 5 (7 Sat)–11
Holt Bitter; guest beers Ⓗ
Friendly, two-room free house near the Rochdale and Ashton Canals, and opposite the new superstores complex. Lunches on request.
❀ ≹ (Piccadilly) ⊖ ♣

Ardwick

Union
Higher Ardwick (off A6 at Apollo) ☎ (061) 273 2186
11–11
Burtonwood Mild, Bitter Ⓗ
One of several welcome gains for Burtonwood in Manchester. Long one of the city's unsung gems, it now at last has beer to match its special atmosphere.
⎙ ≹ (Mon–Fri rush hours only) ♣

Ashton in Makerfield

Eagle & Child
233 Heath Road (½ mile from centre)
☎ (0942) 726421
12–3.30, 7–11; 11–11 Fri & Sat
Greenalls Mild, Bitter, Thomas Greenall's Original Ⓗ
Pub with friendly staff and a mixed clientele, close to Haydock Park racecourse. Note the collection of plates on a mining theme. The public bar has games and the landlord sponsors sporting activities. ❀ ♿ ♣

Ashton-under-Lyne

Dog & Pheasant
528 Oldham Road
☎ (061) 330 4894
12–5 (6 Sat), 7.30–11
Banks's Mild; Marston's Bitter, Pedigree Ⓗ
Hospitable and comfortable pub close to Daisy Nook Country Park. Tempting menu. ❀ ◐ ◑ P

Heroes of Waterloo
3 Mossley Road
☎ (061) 530 2181
11–3, 5–11
John Smith's Bitter; guest beers Ⓗ
Single-room conversion of a terrace used to build stage-coaches, converted in 1854 to a pub serving Ashton army barracks. ⌂ ❀ ◐ P

Oddfellows Arms
Kings Road, Hurst
☎ (061) 330 6356
12–11
Robinson's Best Mild, Best Bitter Ⓗ
In the same family since 1914, a cosy, many-roomed pub with traditional features. Occasional barbecues in the walled garden. Reputed to be where the NUM was started.
Q ❀ ◐ ♣ ⚟

Witchwood
Old Street ☎ (061) 344 0321
12–3 (4 Sat), 5 (7 Sat)–11; 12–11 Fri (Venue Bar open till midnight Thu–Sat)
S&N Theakston Best Bitter, XB, Old Peculier; Whitbread Boddingtons Bitter; guest beers Ⓗ
Popular pub in a quiet part of town. The thriving concert room with its late bar makes it a premier suburban venue. Nine handpumps in the front bar provide a wide range of beers, many of which are also served in the rear bar.
≹ ♣

Greater Manchester

Astley

Cart & Horses
Manchester Road
☎ (0942) 870751
12–11
Holt Mild, Bitter Ⓗ
Pub with a large, well-decorated lounge, a standing area in front of the bar, a tap room and a raised no-smoking room. ❀ ◖ ♣ P ⅟

Atherton

Atherton Arms
6 Tyldesley Road
☎ (0942) 882885
11–11
Holt Mild, Bitter Ⓗ
A large, bright, comfortable lounge and a well-used tap room with pool and snooker tables. Also a hall served by a small bar. ♿ ⇌ ♣ P

Beswick

Britannia
2 Rowsley Street (off A662)
☎ (061) 223 1604
11–11
Lees GB Mild, Bitter Ⓗ
Side-street gem poised for stardom as Manchester's new stadium takes shape nearby. Two rooms: a busy vault with darts, TV and bench seating, and a quieter lounge with a pool table. Friendly regulars; live entertainment most Sat eves. Food Mon–Fri. ◖ ⊞ ♣

Blackley

Pleasant Inn
390 Chapel Lane (off A6104)
☎ (061) 740 3391
1–11
Robinson's Best Mild, Best Bitter Ⓗ, **Old Tom** (winter) Ⓖ
Small community pub in an 18th-century Crab village. Lively, sporting vault, lounge and snug/golf society club room. Q ❀ ⊞ ♣

Bolton

Anchor Inn
Union Buildings (off Bradshawgate) ☎ (0204) 26467
11–11; 12–5, 7–11 Sat
Draught Bass Ⓗ
Pleasant pub decorated with nautical prints. Quiz nights Tue. ◖ ⇌ ♣

Bolton Castle
520 Tonge Moor Road
☎ (0204) 301763
11.30–11
Holt Bitter Ⓗ
Large, multi-roomed local with a friendly atmosphere. Holt's only tied house in town. ⇌ (Hall 'th' Wood) ♣ P

Clifton Arms
94 Newport Street (opp. bus/rail interchange)
☎ (0204) 342738
11–11; 11–3, 7–11 Sat
Jennings Bitter; Moorhouse's Premier, Pendle Witches Brew; Tetley Walker Mild, Bitter, Walker Best Bitter Ⓗ
Comfortable, town-centre local which has kept its character despite refurbishment. Quiz night Wed; no food Sun. Regular mini-beer festivals. ◖ ⇌ ♣

Lodge Bank Tavern
264 Bridgeman Street
☎ (0204) 31946
12–11
Lees GB Mild, Bitter Ⓗ
Well-kept local with a lounge and a small public. ♿ ♣ P

Pilkington Arms
154 Derby Street
☎ (0204) 27960
11–11
Mitchell's Best Bitter; Tetley Walker Mild, Bitter Ⓗ
Two-room local just outside the town centre. ♣

Sweet Green Tavern
127 Crook Street
☎ (0204) 392258
11.30–3, 6.30–11; 11–11 Thu & Fri
Hydes' Anvil Bitter; Tetley Walker Mild, Bitter Ⓗ; **guest beers**
Excellent, multi-roomed, town-centre local near the bus/rail interchange.
⛫ ❀ ◖ ⇌ ♣ P

Waggon & Horses
160 Manchester Road
☎ (0204) 32602
11–3, 7.30–midnight (1am Thu, 2am Fri & Sat)
Tetley Walker Mild, Bitter; Whitbread Boddingtons Bitter Ⓗ; **guest beers**
Friendly, young people's pub near the football ground.
◖ ⇌ ♣

Bredbury

Arden Arms
Ashton Road
11.30–3 (4 if busy), 5.30–11
Robinson's Best Mild, Best Bitter Ⓔ
One of the few traditional Robinson's pubs left. Small individual rooms contribute to the comfortable and intimate atmosphere, in a semi-rural location. Q ❀ P

Horsfield Arms
Ashton Road ☎ (061) 430 6390
11.45–11; 11.45–3, 7–11 Sat
Robinson's Best Mild, Best Bitter Ⓔ
Situated in front of Robinson's bottling plant; the unassuming exterior hides a comfortable, cosy, welcoming local which draws a loyal clientele. Easy to pass, but worth stopping.
⛫ Q ❀ ◖ ⊞ P

Broadbottom

Griffin Inn
Market Street ☎ (0457) 763383
11–11
Whitbread Chester's Mild, Boddingtons Bitter; guest beer Ⓗ
Large, welcoming village pub. A house beer, Gibble Gabble Bitter, is a blended Coach House brew, named after a village cobbled path. Coach House also supplies the guest beer, which varies throughout the year. ❀ ◖ ♿ ⇌ ♣ P

Bryn

Bath Springs
455 Wigan Road
☎ (0942) 202716
12–5, 7–11; 12–11 (Fri & Sat)
Ind Coope Burton Ale; Tetley Walker Mild, Bitter Ⓗ
Two-roomed pub well refurbished by the licensee. Excellent value meals lunchtime and early eve (not served Sun eve). ◖ ◗ ⇌ ♣

Bury

Dusty Miller
87 Crostons Road
☎ (061) 764 1124
12–11; 12–4, 7–11 Sat
Moorhouse's Black Cat Mild, Premier, Pendle Witches Brew; John Smith's Bitter; guest beer Ⓗ
Rare Moorhouse's tied house, refurbished in 1992, yet retaining its traditional two-roomed layout, with a new, enclosed courtyard.
❀ ◖ ⊖ ♣

Famous Gamecock Inn
455 Rochdale Old Road, Jericho (B6222, opp. Fairfield hospital) ☎ (061) 764 4784
11–4, 6–11
Moorhouse's Premier; Whitbread Boddingtons Bitter; guest beers Ⓗ
Friendly, traditional house with an increasing range of beers; Gamecock Strong Ale is brewed by Oak. Free quiz night Tue. Excellent range of home-cooked foods, curries a speciality.
⛫ Q ☎ ❀ ◖ ◗ ♣ P

Old Blue Bell
Bell Lane ☎ (061) 761 3674
12–11; 12–4.30, 7–11 Sat
Holt Mild, Bitter Ⓗ

Extensive, multi-roomed pub, acquired by Holt and well refurbished. Live music Thu eve and some Sun eves. Note the splendid weather vane and a star carved in stone, symbolising the old Star Brewery. ♉ ⊖ ♣

Tap & Spile
36 Manchester Old Road
☎ (061) 764 6461
12–3, 5–11; 11–11 Fri & Sat
Ruddles Best Bitter; Thwaites Bitter; guest beers [H]
Recently refurbished as a Tap & Spile, with a railway theme. Spot the pub's previous name hidden in the new decor. Six, ever-changing guest beers. Family room till 8pm.
♉ ☾ ♿ ⊖ ♣ ⌂

Carrington

Windmill Inn
Manchester Road
☎ (061) 775 2251
11.30–11
Samuel Smith OBB, Museum [H]
Low-ceilinged, former coaching house, with wooden settle seating. The large garden is popular with families on summer eves. ❀ ☾ ⊡ ♣ P

Chadderton

Horton Arms
Streetbridge ☎ (061) 624 7793
11.30–11
Lees GB Mild, Bitter [H]
Comfortable, modernised house retaining a number of separate drinking areas and a country pub feel. Weekday lunches 12–2. Q ❀ ☾ ♣ P

Sun Mill Inn
505 Middleton Road
☎ (061) 624 6232
12–3, 7–11; 12–11 Fri
Whitbread Chester's Mild, Boddingtons OB Bitter; guest beers [H]
Busy, cheerful pub opposite a sports centre, named after a local cotton mill. A working pianola, an unusual fountain in the lounge, and fine etched windows of the Oldham Brewery all feature. ☾ ♣ P

Cheadle

Queens Arms
220 Stockport Road (A560)
☎ (061) 428 3081
12–11; 12–4, 6–11 Sat
Robinson's Best Mild, Bitter, Best Bitter [H]
Stockport's only outlet for the rare Robinson's ordinary bitter: a multi-roomed, traditional pub that can be busy at lunchtimes. The large garden has a children's play area; family room until 7.30pm. No food weekends.
⛫ ♉ ❀ ☾ ♣ P ⚡

Cheadle Hulme

Cheadle Hulme
47 Station Road (A5149)
☎ (061) 485 4706
11–11; 11–3, 7–11 Sat
Holt Mild, Bitter [H]
Upmarket pub, a typical Holt house in that the beer prices are low. A rare chance to have a restaurant meal with Holt's beers (weekday bar lunches).
❀ ☾ ♿ ⇌ P

Church Inn
90 Ravenoak Road (A5149)
☎ (061) 485 1897
11–3, 5.30–11; 11–11 Fri, Sat & bank hols
Robinson's Best Mild, Best Bitter [H]
Attractive, cottage-style pub, with an unspoilt, multi-roomed interior and a lively atmosphere. Service is excellent, even when very busy. Meals until 7.30.
⛫ Q ❀ ☾ ◗ ⇌ ♣ P

Cheetham

Derby Brewery Arms
95 Cheetham Hill Road
11–11
Holt Mild, Bitter [H]
Holt's brewery tap: a large, roomy pub.
☾ ⇌ (Victoria) ⊖

Queens Arms
Honey Street ☎ (061) 834 4239
12–4, 7–11; 12–11 Wed–Fri
Bateman Mild, XB, XXXB; Taylor Best Bitter, Landlord [H]**; guest beers**
A rare example of an Empress Brewery tiled facade, on a pub with a large garden overlooking the Irk valley. Seven guest ales and a range of continental beers available. Eve meals by arrangement.
⛫ ❀ ☾ ⇌ (Victoria) ⊖ ♣ ⌂

Chorlton-cum-Hardy

Beech
Beech Road ☎ (061) 881 1180
11–11; 11–4, 7–11 Sat
S&N Theakston XB; Taylor Landlord; Whitbread Chester's Best Bitter, Flowers Original [H]
Thriving, three-roomed pub, just off the village green.
❀ ⊡ ♣

Chorlton-on-Medlock

King's Arms
4a Helmshore Walk (off A6 at Ardwick Green, via Cale St/ Skerry Close) ☎ (061) 273 1053
11–11
West Coast Mild, Best Bitter, Yakima Grande Porter, Yakima Grande PA, Ginger Beer, Extra Special [H]**; guest beers** (occasionally)
Still the spiritual home of West Coast's splendid beers – now the brewery's moved – attracting a wide clientele to its two contrasting rooms. The homely front bar has a pianist Sat/Sun/Mon eves; live music in the carpeted back room last Tue of the month. No food Sun.
☾ ⇌ (Piccadilly) ⊖ ⌂ P

Clayton

Strawberry Duck
Crabtree Lane (off A662)
☎ (061) 223 4415
11.30–11; 11.30–4.30, 7–11 Sat
Holt Mild, Bitter; Whitbread Boddingtons Bitter; guest beers [H]
Welcoming, bustling free house, by lock 13 of the Ashton Canal. Refurbished and extended in a manner to put most brewery schemes to shame. The house beer is brewed by Coach House. No food weekends. ⛫ ☾ ♣ P

Compstall

Andrew Arms
George Street ☎ (061) 427 2281
11–11
Robinson's Best Mild, Best Bitter [H]
Pub which pleases all who visit: an open fire in winter in the comfortable lounge, and a vault for TV fans and card players. Handy for Etherow Country Park. ⛫ ❀ ☾ ♣ P

Cornbrook

Hope Inn
297 Chester Road
☎ (061) 848 0638
11–4, 7–11
Hydes' Anvil Light, Bitter [E]
Basic, two-room, street-corner local in an area which once boasted a multitude of pubs and breweries. Q ♣

Delph

Royal Oak (Th' Heights)
Broad Lane, Heights (1 mile above Denshaw Rd) OS982090
☎ (0457) 874460
7–11
Whitbread Chester's Mild, Boddingtons Bitter; guest beers [H]
Isolated, 250-year-old stone pub on an historic packhorse route overlooking the Tame valley. A cosy bar and three rooms. Good, home-cooked food (eve meals Fri–Sun). Ask to see Glenville!
⛫ Q ❀ ◗ ♿ P

Greater Manchester

Denton

Dog & Partridge

148 Ashton Road
☎ (061) 336 3954
12.30–11
Robinson's Best Mild, Bitter [H]
Comfortable and welcoming, multi-roomed, community pub out of the town centre with a mixed clientele, mostly stalwart regulars. A rare outlet for Robinson's ordinary bitter.
Q ⊕ ♣

Red Lion

1 Stockport Road, Crown Point
☎ (061) 336 2066
11–11; 11–4, 7–11 Sat
Hydes' Anvil Mild, Light, Bitter [E]
Victorian, red-brick crossroads pub with four spacious rooms and a friendly, local clientele. Can be busy, especially at weekends. Lunches weekdays.
Q ◖ ⇌

Dobcross

Navigation Inn

Wool Road (A670)
☎ (0457) 872418
11.30–3, 5 (7 Sat)–11
Banks's Hanson's Mild, Bitter; Marston's Pedigree [H]
Next to the Huddersfield narrow canal, a stone pub built in 1806 to slake the thirst of navvies cutting the Standedge tunnel. The open-plan interior is a shrine to brass band music. Popular with visitors and locals. Eve meals weekdays 5–7.30.
❀ ◖ ◗ ♿ P

Eccles

Crown & Volunteer

Church Street (A57)
☎ (061) 789 4809
11.30–5, 7–11
Holt Mild, Bitter [H]
Popular community pub with a busy social scene. Boasts an attractive 1930s interior with most of its original features intact. ⊕ ⇌ ♣

Lamb

Regent Street (A57)
☎ (061) 789 3882
11–11; 11–5, 7–11 Sat
Holt Mild, Bitter [H]
Recently redecorated but unchanged, four-roomed Edwardian pub of great character. Note the superb, curved mahogany bar with cut glass. Full-size snooker table in the billiard room. Children welcome at lunchtime.
Q ♘ ⊕ ⇌ ♣ P

Gathurst

Gathurst Station Inn

Gathurst Lane
☎ (0257) 252690
12–4 (not Mon), 7–11; 12–11 Thu–Sat
Taylor Landlord; guest beers [H]
Former station buildings on the Wigan–Southport line, brought back to life as an excellent free house offering a wide range of beers, mainly from independent breweries. Handy for the Douglas Valley Way and the Leeds–Liverpool Canal. Meals in summer and all day Sun.
♜ ❀ ◖ ◗ ♿ ⇌ ♣ P

Golborne

Millstone Inn

Harvey Lane ☎ (0925) 728031
12–4, 7–11; 12–11 Fri & Sat
Greenalls Mild, Bitter; Stones Best Bitter [H]
Friendly, sporting local off the town centre, close to Haydock Park racecourse: a drinking area in front of the bar, two comfortable lounges (vast brass collection), and a tap room. Lunches 12–2.30; children welcome until 8.
♘ ❀ ◖ ♣ P

Gorton

Coach & Horses

227 Belle Vue Street (A57/6010 jct, opp. Showcase cinema)
☎ (061) 223 0440
12–4 (not Mon–Fri), 7–11
Robinson's Best Mild, Best Bitter, Old Tom (winter) [H]
Unspoilt local, recently saved from a road scheme and much old tiling and leaded-glass survives. The traditional atmosphere attracts mainly a mature clientele. Pianist Sat eve. ⊕ ⇌ (Belle Vue) ♣ P

Hare & Hounds

187 Abbey Hey Lane (off A635) ☎ (061) 231 3070
12–11
Whitbread Boddingtons Bitter; guest beer [H]
Splendid, unchanged, much-loved side-street pub with three contrasting rooms: a busy vault, delightful smoke room, and extended lounge, all with a friendly atmosphere. Guest beer Fri eve and Sat.
❀ ⊕ ⇌ ♣

Waggon & Horses

738 Hyde Road (A57, Far Lane corner) ☎ (061) 231 6262
11–11
Holt Mild, Bitter [H]
Low prices are far from being the only attraction at this perennially popular drinkers' haunt, which has been modernised into four linked, but contrasting, areas. Local morris dancers call for the mid-Sept Rushcart procession.
⇌ (Ryder Brow) ♣ P

Hale

Railway

Ashley Road ☎ (061) 941 5367
11–11
Robinson's Best Mild, Hartleys XB, Best Bitter, Old Tom (winter) [H]
A beer house since Victorian times, the present 1930s building is a comfortable multi-roomed village local in an affluent suburb. No food Sun. Children welcome until 9.
Q ♘ ❀ ◖ ⊕ ♿ ⇌
⊖ (Altrincham) ♣

Harpurhey

Junction

Queen's Road
☎ (061) 202 5808
11–11
Holt Bitter; Lees Bitter; Whitbread Boddingtons Bitter [H]
Friendly, unspoilt, three-roomed free house, popular with the Irish community. Boasts an unusual, circular exterior and the deepest cellar in Manchester – ask the landlord for a tour! Reasonably-priced range of Mancunian beers. ♘ ❀ ⊕
⊖ (Woodlands Rd) ♣

Harwood

House Without a Name

75–77 Leagate ☎ (0204) 300063
12.30 (12 Wed–Sat)–11
Holt Bitter; Whitbread Boddingtons Bitter [H]
Small, Tudor-style pub: a lounge and a public bar. Built in 1832 and once a pub brewery. ❀

Hawk Green

Crown Inn

Hawk Green Road
☎ (061) 427 2678
11–3, 5.30–11
Robinson's Best Mild, Best Bitter [H]
Originally a farmers' pub, now mostly a haunt of the young. The accent on food of the past few years seems to be declining. ❀ ◖ ◗ ♿ P

Heaton Mersey

Griffin

552 Didsbury Road (A5145)
☎ (061) 432 2824
12–11
Holt Mild, Bitter [H]

Fine, multi-roomed local, benefiting from a recent extension which managed to maintain both the pub's atmosphere and its superb mahogany bar. Usually busy.
Q ❀ ◑ ⇌ (E Didsbury) P ⊬

Heaton Norris

Nursery
Green Lane (off A6)
☎ (061) 432 2044
11.30–3, 5.30–11; 11.30–11 Sat & bank hols
Hydes' Anvil Mild, Bitter Ⓔ
Comfortable, unspoilt, 1930s pub with its own bowling green. Well hidden in a pleasant suburban area. A good choice of rooms includes a superb, wood-panelled lounge. Excellent bar food (limited menu Sat; set lunches only Sun). Q ❀ ◑ ⊞ ♣ P

Hindley

Edington Arms
186 Ladies Lane (½ mile N of A58) ☎ (0942) 59229
12–11
Holt Mild, Bitter; Tetley Walker Bitter; Whitbread Boddingtons Bitter Ⓗ**; guest beers**
Good atmosphere in a pub with a large function room. Two house beers, Edington Mild and Savage Head Bitter, come from an undisclosed brewery. ❀ ♿ ⇌ ♣ ⌓ P

Ellesmere Inn
32 Lancaster Road (100 yds S of A58) ☎ (0942) 56922
11.30–4.30, 6.45–11
Burtonwood Mild, Bitter Ⓗ
Friendly, two-roomed local with a very good atmosphere.
⇌ ♣

Hindley Green

Alexandra
621 Swan Lane (off A577)
☎ (0925) 55219
11–11
Burtonwood Mild, Bitter, Forshaw's Ⓗ
Recently renovated, two-roomed local on the edge of historic Westhoughton; a welcome oasis. Quiz night Sun. The beer range may vary.
⛫ ❀ ⛿ ◑ ◗ ♿ ♣ P

Hollins

Hollins Bush Inn
257 Hollins Lane (via Hollins Brow, off A56 at Blackford Bridge) ☎ (061) 766 5692
12–3, 6–11; 12–11 Fri & Sat
Lees GB Mild, Bitter Ⓔ
Friendly, three-roomed local, reputed to be 200 years old. Very popular with families at weekends. Good selection of bar snacks (not served Sun).
Q ❀ ♿ ♣ P

Hollinwood

Bridgewater
197 Manchester Road
☎ (061) 628 8464
11.30–11; 11.30–3, 7–11 Sat
Holt Mild, Bitter Ⓗ
Holt's 'rebuilt' house which will soon be its only outlet in the locality: an open-plan lounge and an extremely busy vault. ❀ ◑ ⊞ ♿ ♣ P

Hyde

White Lion
Market Place ☎ (061) 368 2948
12–3 (4 Sat), 6.30 (6 Sat)–11
Robinson's Best Mild, Best Bitter Ⓔ**, Old Tom** Ⓗ
Recovering well after a bad dose of 'Robinsonisation' in the main room, and the painting over of the superlative bronze tiling. The regulars' tap room, with its long bar, remains, and the pub is deservedly popular. Right by the market and full Sat. ◑ ⊞ ⇌ (Central/Newton) ♣

Try also: Oddfellows, Ridling Lane (Vaux)

Leigh

Tamar
416 Wigan Road
☎ (0942) 679459
12–11
Holt Mild, Bitter Ⓗ
A recent Holt convert: a comfortable lounge and a tap room. Its bowling green is depicted in stained-glass in the passage. Meals 12–4.
⛫ ❀ ◑ ♣ P

Victoria
Kirkhall Lane ☎ (0942) 606114
12–4, 7–11; 12–11 Sat
Tetley Walker Mild, Bitter Ⓗ
Recently refurbished pub with a small tap room, served via a hatch, a darts room and a lounge; new lounge and pool room to the rear. The friendly locals are keen on sport; handy for Leigh RLFC. Q ♣

Levenshulme

Sidings
Broom Lane ☎ (061) 257 2084
12–11
Holt Mild, Bitter Ⓗ
Recently refurbished, two-room pub: a large, two-part lounge, and a vault with pool and a choice of three types of dartboard. Vegetarian option always on the menu (no food Sat). Busy, friendly and cheap.
❀ ◑ ♿ ⇌ ♣ P

Little Bollington

Swan With Two Nicks
Park Lane (off A56 by Stamford Arms)
☎ (061) 926 9570
11.30–3, 5.30–11
Marston's Pedigree; Whitbread Boddingtons Bitter, Flowers IPA, Castle Eden Ale Ⓗ
A picturesque walk from the NT property of Dunham Hall takes you across the River Bollin to this typical Cheshire country pub. Walk back along the embankment of the Bridgewater Canal for superb panoramas of Cheshire. No eve meals Mon. ⛫ ❀ ◑ ◗ P

Little Hulton

Dukes Gate
Cleggs Lane (A5082)
☎ (061) 790 1893
11.30–11; 11.30–3, 6–11 Sat
Holt Mild, Bitter Ⓗ
Pub opened in 1986, and very popular with the locals. Close to the M61 (no access).
Q ❀ ♣ P

Little Lever

Horseshoe Inn
Lever Street (off A6053)
☎ (0204) 72081
12–4, 7–11; 11–11 Sat
Hydes' Anvil Mild, Bitter Ⓔ
Traditional, two-roomed pub with a lounge and vault. Lots of teams; quite a village atmosphere. Q ⊞ ♣

Jolly Carter
168 Church Street (A6053)
☎ (0204) 71344
12–11
Taylor Landlord; Whitbread Chester's Mild, Boddingtons Bitter Ⓗ
Bright, friendly pub with a good welcome. The lounge and vault are served from a central bar. One of the few in the area to offer hot early eve meals. Mini-beer festivals.
❀ ◑ ◗ ♿ ⇌ (Moses Gate) ♣ P

Lowton

Hare & Hounds
Golborne Road
☎ (0942) 728387
12–11
Ind Coope Burton Ale; Tetley Walker Mild, Bitter Ⓗ**; guest beers**
Large, open-plan pub with low ceiling beams, a sunken lounge area for tall people, and a tap room, all served from a central bar. Appeals to all ages. Eve meals till 8.30.
⛫ ❀ ◑ ◗ ♿ ♣ P

Greater Manchester

Red Lion

324 Newton Road
☎ (0942) 671429
12–3.30, 5.30–11; 12–11 Fri & Sat
Greenalls Mild, Bitter, Thomas Greenall's Original; Stones Best Bitter; Young's Bitter Ⓗ
Large, open-plan pub with a pool room with its own bar. The pleasant lounge, away from the bar, leads to a bowling green and the landlord's war games centre. The beer range may vary.
❀ 🛏 ◐ ◑ ♣ P

Manchester City Centre

Beerhouse

Angel Street (off A664, NE of city) ☎ (061) 839 7019
11.30–11
Courage Directors; Marston's Pedigree; Moorhouse's Pendle Witches Brew; S&N Theakston Old Peculier; West Coast Best Bitter, Extra Special Ⓗ
Cheerful, basic, free house. An astonishing number of functional handpumps adorns the triangular bar which dominates the ground floor.
◐ ⇌ (Victoria) ⊖ ♣ ⌓ P

Castle

66 Oldham Street (A62 near Piccadilly Gardens)
☎ (061) 236 2945
11.30–5.30 (4.30 Sat), 7.30 (8 Sat)–11; 12–3, 7.30–10.30 Sun
Robinson's Best Mild, Bitter, Best Bitter, Old Tom Ⓗ
All that a city-centre pub should be: busy, friendly and well run. A largely untouched, Victorian beerhouse with a front bar, tiny parlour and a pool/concert room (live blues Thu eve). The only Robinson's house in the centre, unusually selling all four beers year-round. Q ♿ ⇌ (Piccadilly) ⊖ (High St/Market St) ♣

Circus

86 Portland Street
☎ (061) 236 5818
11–3, 5–11 (may vary)
Tetley Walker Bitter Ⓗ
The smallest pub in the city, two rooms with a tiny, one-person bar. No draught lager, no music; a gem of former times defying 'progress'. Very busy lunchtimes. Must be seen. ♨ Q ⇌ (Piccadilly) ⊖ (Oxford Rd)

City Arms

48 Kennedy Street
☎ (061) 236 4610
11.30–11; closed Sun
Jennings Bitter; Moorhouse's Premier, Pendle Witches Brew; Tetley Walker Bitter; guest beers Ⓗ
Two-roomed pub, very busy at lunchtimes, when good value meals are available. A true 'local' at the business heart of the city. ◐ ⇌ (Oxford Rd) ⊖ (St Peter's Sq) ♣

Peveril of the Peak

127 Great Bridgwater Street
12–3 (not Sat), 5.30 (7 Sat)–11; 7–10.30 Sun, closed Sun lunch
Courage Directors; Ruddles Best Bitter; Webster's Yorkshire Bitter, Wilson's Bitter Ⓗ
Named after a famous stagecoach, a classic pub, triangular in shape. Note the exterior tiling and the stained-glass and wood interior. Holds a ceilidh night during the week; popular with students. Open Sat lunch when Man Utd are at home. ♨ ⊟
⇌ (Oxford Rd) ⊖ (St Peter's Sq) ♣ P

Unicorn Hotel

26 Church Street
☎ (061) 832 7938
11.30–10.30 (11 Fri); 11.30–3, 5.30–11 Sat; 12–2, 7–10.30 Sun
Bass Light, Worthington BB, Draught Bass; Stones Best Bitter; guest beer Ⓗ
Large, oak-panelled pub, opposite the street market. Popular with older customers.
⇌ (Victoria/Piccadilly)
⊖ (High St/Market St)

Vine

38 Kennedy Street
☎ (061) 236 3943
11.30–11; 11.30–3, 7–11 Sat; 12–3 Sun, closed Sun eve
Courage Directors; John Smith's Bitter; Whitbread Boddingtons Bitter Ⓗ
A busy pub, especially at lunchtime, with a listed tiled exterior. The bars are on three levels with varying music and noise levels. Food Mon–Fri.
◐ ⇌ (Oxford Rd) ⊖ (St Peter's Sq)

Marple

Bowling Green

Stockport Road
☎ (061) 427 7918
11–11
Holt Bitter; John Smith's Magnet; Wilson's Mild, Webster's Yorkshire Bitter Ⓗ
Not a place for fainthearts, shrinking violets or aesthetes: busy, down to earth and raucous. A basic local.
❀ ⇌ ♣ P

Hatters Arms

Church Lane
☎ (061) 427 1529
11–3, 5.30–11
Robinson's Best Mild, Best Bitter Ⓗ
One of the last local refuges for traditional pub lovers: a tiny terrace-end house with a legendary landlady, lovely bar panelling and separate rooms, including a particularly good vault. ♣

Middleton

Brunswick Hotel

122 Oldham Road
☎ (061) 643 2125
12–3 (not Wed), 7–11; 12–11 Fri & Sat
Coach House Gunpowder Strong Mild; Ind Coope Burton Ale; Tetley Walker Bitter; West Coast Best Bitter Ⓗ**; guest beers**
Basic, street-corner local with boisterous clientele. Two distinct drinking areas and a superb (loud) jukebox. Imaginative guest beers.
❀ ⌓

Oddfellows Arms

191 Oldham Road
☎ (061) 643 2906
12–3 (4 Sat), 5 (7 Sat)–11; 12–11 Fri
Holt Bitter; John Smith's Bitter; Wilson's Mild, Bitter Ⓗ
Popular local, with a friendly atmosphere and pool, darts and football teams. Photographs of old Manchester and Rochdale add a nostalgic air.
⊟ ♿ ⇌ (Mills Hill) ♣ P

Tandle Hill Tavern

14 Thornham Lane (unmetalled road 1 mile off A671/A664)
☎ (0706) 345297
12–3 (not Mon–Fri winter, & sometimes summer), 7 (7.30 winter)–11
Lees Bitter, Moonraker (winter) Ⓗ
Welcoming, two-roomed pub at the heart of a small farming community in the Thornham Woodland Trust conservation area. A good place to finish a walk on the nearby Oldham Way. Informal quiz nights. Snacks at weekends. Children welcome in the darts room.
♨ ❀ ♣

Milnrow

Free Trade Tavern

115 New Hey Road
☎ (0706) 847056
12–3.30, 7–11
Lees GB Mild, Bitter Ⓗ
Friendly pub on the edge of town. ❀ ⇌ ♣ P

Waggon Inn

Butterworth Hall
☎ (0706) 48313
11–11
Burtonwood Mild, Bitter Ⓗ
Attractive, friendly 18th-century local just off the main street. ꙮ ⇌ ♣ P

Monton

Park Hotel
142 Monton Road
☎ (061) 788 9045
11–11; 11–4, 7–11 Sat
Holt Mild, Bitter Ⓗ
Popular 1950s pub in the posher part of Eccles. With its large vault, lounge and pleasant snug, it is unusual for pubs of this era.
Q ⊞ ♣ P

Mossley

Tollemache
415 Manchester Road
☎ (0457) 832354
11–3, 5–11
Robinson's Best Mild, Best Bitter Ⓗ
Popular, cosy and sociable, stone local close to the countryside on the edge of Mossley. The garden overlooks the Huddersfield Narrow Canal. Small, oak-panelled rooms, a polished wood bar and lively conversation.
♨ Q ❀ ♣ P

Moston

Blue Bell
493 Moston Lane
☎ (061) 683 4096
11–11; 11–4, 7–11 Sat
Holt Mild, Bitter Ⓗ
Classic, Edwardian Holt pub with a vault, lounge and other drinking areas, recently refurbished. Note the corbels with painted bluebells in the back lounge. Always busy.
Q ⚘ ❀ ♣ P

New Hey

Bird in the Hand (Top Bird)
113 Huddersfield Road (A640)
☎ (0706) 847978
11.30–3, 5–11; 11.30–11 Sat
Samuel Smith OBB Ⓗ
Small, friendly pub, one of the few traditional Sam's pubs in the area. Note the almost identically named pub (also Sam's) just down the hill.
⇌ ♣ P

New Springs

Colliers Arms
Wigan Road (B5238, NE of Wigan) ☎ (0942) 831171
1.30–5 (not Thu), 7.30–11
Burtonwood Mild, Bitter Ⓗ
Unspoilt, 18th-century alehouse – a gem. Always a warm welcome; sing-along Sat. Rural crafts displayed.
♨ Q ♣ P

Oldham

Bridge Inn
Moorhey Street
☎ (061) 624 8626
11–11
Lees GB Mild, Bitter Ⓔ
Very popular, three-roomed pub with a friendly atmosphere and pleasant surroundings; busy at weekends. Look for the stained-glass window depicting the pub's name.
❀ ⊞ ♣ P

Dog & Duck
25 St Domingo Street (opp. Civic Centre) ☎ (061) 624 3328
11.30–11
Banks's Mild, Bitter Ⓔ
Detached, red-brick, three-storey, town-centre pub, well refurbished despite a mainly open-plan layout. Irish music dominates the jukebox. The pool room has a dartboard.
⇌ (Werneth) ♣

Dog & Partridge
376 Roundthorn Road
☎ (061) 624 3335
11.30–3 (not Mon–Thu), 7–11; 11–11 Fri
Lees GB Mild, Bitter Ⓔ
Popular, detached pub in a semi-rural setting, with low-beamed ceilings. Pleasantly and comfortably furnished. ♨ ❀ ♣ P

Royal Oak
178 Union Street, Rhodes Bank
☎ (061) 624 1031
11–11; 11–3, 4.45–11 Tue & Thu; 11–4, 7–11 Sat
Robinson's Best Mild, Best Bitter Ⓔ, **Old Tom** (winter) Ⓖ
Friendly town-centre local which concentrates on beer. The impressive horseshoe-shaped bar dates from 1928.
Q ⚘ ⇌ (Mumps) ♣

Over Hulton

Watergate Toll
421 Watergate Drive (near M61 jct 4) ☎ (0204) 64989
11–11
Whitbread Boddingtons Mild, Bitter, Flowers Original Ⓗ; **guest beer**
Former private house, changed to pub and restaurant in 1991. Good restaurant food (all day Sun) or bar snacks. A different guest ale each week, sometimes two.
♨ ⚘ ❀ ◖ ◗ ♿ P

Patricroft

Stanley Arms
295 Liverpool Road (A57)
☎ (061) 788 8801
11–11
Holt Mild, Bitter Ⓗ
Lively, street-corner local with a small front vault, a lounge with a piano and a games room at the back.
♨ ⊞ ⇌ ♣

Peel Green

Grapes
431 Liverpool Road (near M63 jct 2) ☎ (061) 789 6971
11–11; 11–4.30, 7–11 Sat
Holt Mild, Bitter Ⓗ
Excellent, Edwardian Holt pub with four large rooms and all its original features, including splendid mahogany, cut-glass, tiling and fireplaces. Recent redecorations have enhanced its appeal. Children welcome at lunchtime. Q ⚘ ◖ ⊞ ♣ P

Prestwich

Royal Oak
Whittaker Lane, Heaton Park
☎ (061) 773 8663
12–11
Hydes' Anvil Light, Bitter Ⓔ
Comfortable and friendly local, tucked away just off Bury Old Road. The only Hydes' pub in town. Q ❀ ⊞ ⇌ (Heaton Pk) ♣ P

Radcliffe

Wilton Arms
Coronation Road (off Turks Rd, off B6292)
☎ (061) 724 7068
11–11
Holt Mild, Bitter Ⓔ
Modern Holt estate pub with a good, friendly atmosphere. Its proximity to the town's football and cricket grounds reflects the pub's enthusiasm for sport. The Wilton Room is the domain of the senior citizens. Q ❀ ⊞ ♿ ⇌ ♣ P

Ramsbottom

Royal Oak
39 Bridge Street
☎ (0706) 822786
12–11
Thwaites Best Mild, Bitter, Craftsman Ⓗ
Friendly village-centre pub near the East Lancs Railway. Recently renovated and extended but retains three rooms. Thriving pub games teams add to the atmosphere. Meals Wed–Sun. ⚘ ❀ ◖

Ridge End

Romper
☎ (061) 427 1354
12–2.30 (3 Sat), 6–11
S&N Theakston Old Peculier; Taylor Landlord; Wadworth 6X Ⓗ

Longtime haunt of the Cheshire set, now giving beer the same prominence as its well-known food. Tucked on the bend of the road, with the Dark Peak on one side, its neon sign illuminates the Cheshire plain on the other; a setting now threatened by a new road. ❀ ◖ ◗ P

Ringway

Romper
Sunbank Lane (off A538)
☎ (061) 980 6806
11.30–11; 11.30–3, 5.30–11 Sat
Draught Bass; S&N Theakston Best Bitter; Whitbread Boddingtons Mild, Bitter; guest beers H
Multi-roomed country pub next to the massive sprawl of the airport. Low ceilings, wooden beams and a real fire add to the atmosphere. Good value lunches for the area (cold meals only Sun). The large garden can be noisy due to aircraft. ♨ Q ❀ ◖ ♣ P

Rochdale

Albert Hotel
62 Spotland Road (A608)
☎ (0706) 45666
11–11
Burtonwood Mild, Bitter H
Popular local with a good early eve atmosphere in its open-plan bar, games, TV and quiet rooms. Free 'golden oldies' jukebox. Q ♣

Dog & Partridge Inn
370 Oldham Road
☎ (0706) 45858
11–3 (4 Fri & Sat), 5–11
Vaux Bitter, Samson H**; guest beers**
One of a number of pubs Vaux has acquired in the area, refurbished to a high standard. A regular guest beer is very competitively priced.
❀ ◖ ♿ P

Flying Horse Hotel
37 Town Hall Square
☎ (0706) 46412
11–11
Holt Mild; Lees Bitter; Marston's Pedigree; Taylor Landlord; Whitbread Boddingtons Bitter; guest beers H
Impressive stone edifice facing the town hall. A tasteful refurbishment has created a relaxing atmosphere, which, together with good, home-cooked food, attracts a varied clientele. Dress restrictions Fri and Sat eves. 🛏 ◖ ◗

Healey Hotel
172 Shawclough Road
☎ (0706) 45453
12–3 (4 Sat), 5 (7 Sat)–11
Robinson's Best Mild, Best Bitter H**, Old Tom** (winter) G
Welcoming, out-of-town pub, recently extended without losing character. Nice tilework. Eve meals Tue–Thu.
🐴 ❀ ◖ ◗ ♣

Merry Monk
234 College Road (near A6060/B6222 jct)
☎ (0706) 46919
12–11
Marston's Bitter, Pedigree; Thwaites Best Mild; guest beers H
Friendly, unpretentious local with an uncommon Ring the Bull game. ♣ P

Spring Inn
183 Broad Lane (¼ mile off A671) ☎ (0706) 33529
11–11
Lees GB Mild, Bitter H
Popular, traditional house with a friendly atmosphere and good facilities, including an outdoor children's activity centre and menagerie.
Q 🐴 ❀ ◖ ◗ 🀫 ♿ ▲ ♣ P

Two Ships
Hope Street (off A671)
☎ (0706) 47171
12–3 (may extend Fri & Sat), 7–11
Ind Coope Burton Ale; Stones Best Bitter; Thwaites Mild, Bitter, Craftsman; Tetley Walker Bitter H
Spacious, lively pub, rightly popular. Note the splendid war memorial plaque in the no-smoking front room. Folk night Tue. Children welcome at lunchtime.
🐴 ◖ ♣ P ⊬

Romiley

Duke of York
Stockport Road
☎ (061) 430 2806
11.30–11
Courage Directors; John Smith's Bitter; Whitbread Boddingtons Bitter H
Long, low, white building of harmonious proportions. Just as pleasing inside, with a beamed lounge and a big, active public bar.
Q ❀ ◖ ◗ ⇌ ♣ P

Royton

Dog & Partridge Inn
148 Middleton Road
☎ (061) 620 6403
11–11
Lees GB Mild, Bitter H
Just out of Royton centre, a popular local, often very busy. Fine collection of malt whiskies.
🐴 ◖ 🀫

Puckersley Inn
Narrowgate Brow (via Dogford Rd, off A671)
☎ (061) 624 4973
5 (4.30 Fri, 12 Sat)–11
Lees GB Mild, Bitter H
Popular, detached, stone-fronted pub on the edge of the green belt, with panoramic views from the car park. The pleasantly and comfortably furnished lounge bar has mirrors, horsebrasses and beams. Lively vault.
Q 🀫 ♣ P

Sale

Railway Inn
Chapel Road (behind Town Hall)
11.30–3 (4 Fri & Sat), 5.30 (7 Sat)–11
Robinson's Best Mild, Best Bitter H
Rendered unimaginatively open-plan in the mid-70s but comfortably furnished and still very much a local. Access to the Bridgewater Canal across the road. Quiz night Tue. No food Sun. ❀ ◖ ⊖ ♣ P

Sale Moor

Legh Arms
Northenden Road (A6144/B5166 jct)
11.30–11; 11.30–4, 7–11 Sat
Holt Mild, Bitter H
Large, multi-roomed local, acquired from Taylor's Eagle brewery in 1924, with many original features, including a revolving door. An island bar serves a large vault, lounge, snug, lobby and smoke room. Round bowling green. Live music Fri–Sun nights.
Q ❀ ♣ P

Salford

Ashley Brook
517 Liverpool Street
☎ (061) 737 0988
11.30–11; 11.30–4, 7–11 Sat
Holt Mild, Bitter H
Built in 1990, after a Methodist minister helped secure the licence, first applied for in the 1920s. Great community atmosphere; friendly bar staff. Very good lunches. Take care in the car park. Q ◖ ♿ ♣ P

Crescent
20 Crescent (A6)
☎ (061) 736 5600
12 (7.30 Sat)–11; 12–2.30, 7.30–10.30 Sun
Beer range varies H
Friendly, multi-roomed, rambling independent free house. A good selection of home cooking includes curries. Popular with students from the nearby university.
♨ Q ❀ ◖ ⇌ (Crescent) ♣ ⌓ P

Kings Arms
Bloom Street
☎ (061) 839 4338
12–11
Cains Bitter; Holt Bitter; S&N Theakston Best Bitter; Taylor Landlord Ⓗ
Former Groves & Whitnall pub, in a Grade II-listed building, now a Boddington Pub Co free house. Selection of Belgian and German bottled beers.
◖ ⇌ ⊖ (Victoria) ♣ ⌓

Olde Nelson
Chapel Street (opp. cathedral)
☎ (061) 832 6189
11–3.30, 5.30 (7 Sat)–11
Whitbread Chester's Mild, Boddingtons Bitter, Trophy Ⓗ
Unaltered Victorian local complete with etched-glass, a screen and a sliding door to the vault. Regulars and CAMRA are fighting its demolition for a wider road.
⇌

Peel Park Inn
Chapel Street (A6, next to hospital)
☎ (061) 832 2654
11–11
Courage Directors; John Smith's Bitter Ⓗ
Smart, single-room pub with a tiny frontage.
⇌ ◖ ⇌ ♣

Star
Back Hope Street
1–4, 7–11
Robinson's Best Mild, Best Bitter Ⓔ**, Old Tom** (winter) Ⓗ
Popularly known as 'One-armed Wally's', this character-filled pub has been in the family for decades. Its idiosyncracies include one tiny bar, outside ladies' and inside gents'. Home of Manchester's oldest established folk club (Wed).
Q ❀ ♿ ♣

Union Tavern
105 Liverpool Street
11–4.30 (5.30 Sat), 7–11
Holt Mild, Bitter Ⓗ
Good, honest, two-roomed boozer which keeps busy in a run-down area, partly due to an active sports and social club. Log-end darts is a speciality.
⊞ ⇌ (Crescent) ♣ P

Welcome
Robert Hall Street (off A5066)
11.30–4, 7–11
Lees GB Mild, Bitter Ⓗ/Ⓔ
Immaculate pub in an area where much of the surrounding housing is now empty, awaiting refurbishment. The handpulls are electrically assisted.
Q ⊞ ♣ P

Shaw

Black Horse
203a Rochdale Road
☎ (0706) 847173
2 (11 Sat)–11
Lees GB Mild, Bitter Ⓗ
Stone-built, roadside pub with a cosy, timber-beamed lounge and a friendly vault. Lees's beer is the cheapest in the locality. ❀ ⊞ P

Blue Bell Hotel
Market Street ☎ (0706) 847856
11.30–11; 11.30–4, 7–11 Sat
Robinson's Best Mild, Best Bitter Ⓔ**, Old Tom** Ⓗ
Detached, stone-built, three-storey pub with mullioned windows, dating from 1763. The top floor was originally used for weaving. Several distinct rooms/areas, including alcoves either side of the fireplace. A meeting place for the local motorcycle club.
❀ ◖ ⇌ ♣ P

Stalybridge

Stalybridge Station Buffet Bar
Rassbottom Street
12–3.30, 5.30–11 (may vary)
Beer range varies Ⓗ
Largely untouched gem which is threatened by BR with closure again. An original Victorian buffet with real character. Local folk club (Sat).
♨ ◖ ◗ ⇌ ⌓ P

White House
Water Street ☎ (061) 303 2288
11–11
Banks's Mild Ⓔ**; Marston's Bitter; S&N Theakston Best Bitter, XB** Ⓗ**, guest beers**
Bustling, town-centre pub, well used by locals; modernised, but retaining separate rooms and the elusive quality of 'pubiness' at its best. Folk club Thu. Good range of foreign bottled beers and single malt whiskies.
◖ ⇌ ♣ P

Standish

Dog & Partridge
School Lane ☎ (0257) 421413
12–5.30, 7–11
Tetley Walker Dark Mild, Mild, Walker Bitter, Walker Best Bitter; Whitbread Boddingtons Bitter Ⓗ
Pub with a warm, friendly atmosphere, attracting a mixed trade. Quiz mad. Q ♿ P

Horseshoe Inn
1 Wigan Road (A49)
☎ (0257) 421240
12–11
Burtonwood Mild, Bitter Ⓗ
Large, open-plan pub offering live music, darts, dominoes, pool and quizzes. ◖ ♣ P

Stockport

Arden Arms
Millgate ☎ (061) 480 2185
11.30–3, 5–11; 11.30–11 Fri & Sat
Robinson's Best Mild, Best Bitter, Old Tom Ⓗ
Outstanding, town-centre, old-fashioned pub with a collection of grandfather clocks. Recent changes (an extension) are in keeping with the rest of the pub, which boasts a fine bar snug. No food Sun. Q ⇌ ◖ ♣ P

Armoury
Shaw Heath, Edgeley (down Greek St from A6)
☎ (061) 480 5055
11–11; 11–4, 7.30–11 Sat
Robinson's Best Mild, Best Bitter Ⓔ
Multi-roomed, ex-Bell's pub. Choose from a bright lounge, back darts room, and a fine vault. Public parking nearby. Handy for Edgeley Park.
Q ⇌ ♣

Blossoms
2 Buxton Road, Heaviley (A6)
☎ (061) 480 2246
11.30–4, 5.30–11
Robinson's Best Mild, Best Bitter, Old Tom Ⓗ
Multi-roomed gem successfully refurbished in 1992. Three rooms and a bar area attract a varied clientele. Long-established folk club upstairs Sat eve. Local CAMRA *Pub of the Year* 1992.
Q ◖ ⇌ (Davenport) ♣ P

Boar's Head
Market Place
☎ (061) 480 3978
11.30 (11 Sat)–4, 6 (7 Sat)–11; 11.30–11 Fri; closed Sun
Samuel Smith OBB, Museum Ⓗ
Vibrant market local appealing to all tastes. Live music Wed–Sat. ◖ ⇌

Grapes
Castle Street, Edgeley
☎ (061) 480 3027
11–11
Robinson's Best Mild, Best Bitter, Old Tom (winter) Ⓗ
Lively, down-to-earth boozer in Edgeley shopping precinct. Often busy and can be smoky. Handy for County FC.
⇌ ♣

Manchester Arms
25 Wellington Road South (A6) ☎ (061) 480 2852
11–11

Greater Manchester

Robinson's Best Mild, Best Bitter, Old Tom (winter) Ⓗ
Totally cosmopolitan – even to the 'biker-friendly' sticker. Very much a local institution, the 'MA' caters for rock music lovers, but also has a very comfortable back room. Often very noisy, but a fine welcome.
₼ ◖ ≹

Olde Woolpack
Brinksway (A560)
☎ (061) 429 6621
11.30–3, 7.30–11; 11.30–11 Fri
Marston's Pedigree; S&N Theakston Best Bitter; Tetley Walker Bitter Ⓗ**; guest beers**
Once abandoned by the big brewers, now a thriving free house selling a rotating guest mild and bitter. Active darts team and can be busy on Fri and Sat eves. Sun lunch is a set meal. Parking difficult. Close to the giant blue pyramid.
❀ ◖ ♿ ≹ ♣ P

Queens Head (Turners Vaults)
Little Underbank (almost under the iron bridge)
☎ (061) 480 1545
11.30 (11 Sat)–3.30, 7–11; 11–11 Fri; 7–10.30 Sun, closed Sun lunch
Samuel Smith OBB, Museum Ⓗ
Award-winning renovation at a smashing, feature-packed pub, originally a tasting room for the wine merchant next door. Small front bar and two back rooms (one no-smoking). Good cosmopolitan atmosphere.
Q ◖ ≹ ⚟

Stanley Arms
40 Newbridge Lane
☎ (061) 480 5713
12–3 (not Mon–Thu), 5–11; 12–11 Sat
Ryburn Bitter, Rydale Bitter, Stabbers Ⓗ**; guest beers**
Large, split-level pub divided into four areas, popular with all ages. Up to 16 beers at one time, including two house milds from Ryburn. Note the Laurel and Hardy prints in the back bar area. Live music/DJ weekends, a big screen TV and two pool tables. Lunches Fri and Sat. Occasional cider.
❀ 🛏 ◖ ♣ ⌓ P

Stoneclough

Lord Nelson
Kearsley Hall Road (off A667)
☎ (0204) 794563
12–3, 7–11
Thwaites Mild, Bitter Ⓗ
Basic, multi-roomed pub facing a former power station, with a large games room at the rear. Live folk band in the Railway Room Tue and Thu.
₼ Q ❀ ≹ (Kearsley) ♣ P

Strines

Sportsman
105 Strines Road (B6101)
☎ (061) 427 2888
12–3, 5.30–11
Mitchell's Dark Mild, Best Bitter, Fortress (occasionally)**; guest beers** Ⓗ
Comfortable pub with a vault and a large lounge where simple, home-cooked food is served. Recently acquired free house status, serving two interesting guest beers. Superb views across the valley.
Q ❀ ◖ ◗ ▲ ≹ P

Swinton

Cricketers Arms
227 Manchester Road
☎ (061) 794 2008
11.45–3.30 (4 Sat), 7–11
Holt Mild, Bitter Ⓔ
Basic local with two rooms, attracting the more mature drinker. ⊞ ♣

Farmers Arms
160 Manchester Road (A6, opp. Victoria Park)
☎ (061) 794 5599
11–11
S&N Theakston Best Bitter, Old Peculier; Whitbread Boddingtons Bitter; guest beers Ⓗ
1830s beerhouse extended in 1990, with a large vault and an alcoved lounge. Good value lunches. Varied eve entertainment. ❀ ◖ ⊞ ♣ P

Tyldesley

Colliers Arms
105 Sale Lane (A577)
☎ (061) 790 2065
2 (1 Fri, 12 Sat)–11
Courage Best Bitter; Holt Bitter; Wilson's Mild, Bitter Ⓗ
Good, traditional roadside local with a comfortable lounge and a tap room.
❀ ♣ P

Half Moon
115 Elliot Street
☎ (0942) 873206
11–4 (5 Sat), 7–11
Holt Mild, Bitter Ⓗ**; guest beer**
Large, low-roofed lounge and a pool room, drawing a mixed clientele; busy at weekends. The house beer is Bongs Bitter, Bongs being an old local name for Tyldesley. ❀ ♣

Mort Arms
235 Elliot Street
☎ (0942) 883481
12–11
Holt Mild, Bitter Ⓗ
Busy, town-centre local comprising a wood-panelled lounge bar and a tap room. Caters for all ages. ♣

Uppermill

Cross Keys
Off Running Hill Gate (off A670) ☎ (0457) 874626
11–3, 6.30–11; 11–11 Sat & summer
Lees GB Mild, Bitter Ⓗ
Attractive, 18th-century, stone building overlooking Saddleworth church. The public bar has a stone-flagged floor and a Yorkshire range. The hub of many activities, including mountain rescue. Folk night Wed.
₼ Q ❀ ◖ ♿ ▲ ♣ P

Urmston

Lord Nelson Hotel
Stretford Road
☎ (061) 747 7685
11–11
Holt Mild, Bitter Ⓗ
Built shortly after Nelson's death at Trafalgar (1805); rebuilt and extended in 1877 and once an hotel. The first floor rear windows depict Nelson's battles. Refurbished but retains a multi-roomed layout. Popular with all ages.
⊞ ≹ ♣ P

Wardley

Morning Star
520 Manchester Road (A6)
☎ (061) 794 4927
12–11
Holt Mild, Bitter Ⓗ
Isolated, friendly outlet with a strong local following. Live music weekends.
❀ ⊞ ≹ (Moorside) ♣ P

Westhoughton

Hartcommon
490 Wigan Road (A58)
☎ (0942) 813356
12–3.30 (4 Sat), 7–11
S&N Theakston Mild, Best Bitter, XB, Old Peculier Ⓗ
Small local of character in a former mining village. Warm welcome. ♣ P

White Lion
Market Street ☎ (0942) 813120
11–11
Holt Mild, Bitter Ⓗ
Good town-centre local with a distinctive Holt character. Note the geyser and fine etched windows above the bar. ❀ ♣ P

Whitefield

Coach & Horses
71 Bury Old Road (A665)
☎ (061) 798 8897
11–11
Holt Mild, Bitter Ⓗ
Built in 1830 and virtually unchanged; once a staging

post for the Burnley–Manchester mail coach. Now one of a declining number of tenanted Holt pubs. Q ⊞ ♿ ⊖ (Besses o' th' Barn) ♣ P

Eagle & Child

Higher Lane (A667)
☎ (061) 766 3024
12–11
Holt Mild, Bitter Ⓗ
Imposing 1930s Holt pub with a mock Tudor exterior but a genuine, friendly interior. Recently refurbished and enlarged. Superb bowling green and garden. Cheap food.
Q ♘ ◖ ⊞ ♿ ≠ (Besses o' th' Barn) ♣ P

Wigan

Beer Engine

69 Poolstock Lane (B5238, off A49) ☎ (0942) 42497
12–11
Beer range varies Ⓗ
A true free house: a comfortable lounge, vault and a large function room, offering a wide variety of music. Annual 'Beer, Pie & Music' festival. At least seven beers always available. Full-size snooker table; own bowling green. ❀ ◖ ⊞ ♿
≠ (NW/Wallgate) ♣ P

Bird i' th' Hand (Th 'en 'ole)

Gidlow Lane (off B5375)
☎ (0942) 41004
12–11
S&N Theakston Best Bitter; Tetley Walker Mild, Bitter Ⓗ
The apotheosis of the two-roomed local. Admire the Walker's mosaic and ironwork over the door.
❀ ◖ ◗ ⊞ ♿ ♣ P

Bold Hotel

Poolstock Lane, Worsley Mesnes (B5238, off A49)
☎ (0942) 41095
12–4.30 (5 Sat), 7–11
Burtonwood Mild, Bitter Ⓗ
Small, unchanged boozer on the edge of town, popular with RL supporters. Collection of walking sticks. ❀ ♣

Millstone

Wigan Lane (old A49)
☎ (0942) 45999
12–4, 7.30–11
Thwaites Best Mild, Bitter Ⓗ
Comfortable local near Central Park, selling the cheapest beer in town. Lunches 12–2.
❀ ◖ ♿ ≠ (Wallgate) ♣ P

Orwell

Wigan Pier, Wallgate
☎ (0942) 323034
11–11
Cains Bitter; Greenalls Thomas Greenall's Original; Tetley Walker Mild, Bitter; Whitbread Boddingtons Bitter; guest beers Ⓗ
Large, modern pub at the heart of the Pier complex, drawing a daytime tourist trade; more lively eves with a younger clientele. An outlet for West Coast brewery beers.
◖ ◗ ≠ (NW/Wallgate) P

Raven

Wallgate ☎ (0942) 43865
11–11
Tetley Walker Mild, Best Bitter, Winter Warmer Ⓗ
Ornate Victorian pub with many original features.
❀ ◖ ≠ (NW/Wallgate)

Springfield Hotel

47 Springfield Road (off B5375)
☎ (0942) 42072
12–3.30, 7–11; 12–11 Sat
Walker Mild, Best Bitter, Winter Warmer Ⓗ
Large, friendly pub near Wigan Athletic FC, featuring the usual excellent Walker's decor and admirable woodwork. 1992 Wigan CAMRA *Pub of the Year*. Can be busy match days. ⊞ P

Swan & Railway

Wallgate ☎ (0942) 495032
11–3.30, 5.30–11; 12–2.30, 7–10.30 Sun
Banks's Mild, Bitter; Bass Mild XXXX, Worthington BB, Draught Bass; Courage Directors Ⓗ
Friendly pub with an Edwardian, urban atmosphere. Excellent selection of eight ales. Weekday lunches.
🛏 ◖ ≠ (NW/Wallgate)

Withington

Red Lion

Wilmslow Road (B5093)
11–11
Banks's Mild; Marston's Bitter, Pedigree, Owd Rodger; guest beer Ⓗ
Large multi-roomer, served from one U-shaped, very long bar. Parts of the pub, including the vault, are old, with waves of extensions at the back. The famous bowling green and garden are very popular with both students and locals. No children eve. Eve meals Mon–Thu. ♘ ❀ ◖ ◗ ⊞ ♣ P

Woodford

Davenport Arms (Thief's Neck)

550 Chester Road (A5102)
11–3.30, 5.15 (5.30 Sat)–11
Robinson's Best Mild, Best Bitter Ⓗ**, Old Tom** Ⓔ
Classic country pub, multi-roomed and unspoilt, on the edge of prosperous suburbs. In the same family for 60 years. Unusual mix of aviation and farming memorabilia.
♨ Q ❀ ◖ ⊞ ♣ P ⚟

Worthington

Crown

Platt Lane, Standish (between A5106 and A49, end of Bradley Lane) ☎ (0257) 421354
11–11
S&N Theakston Mild, Best Bitter, XB; Whitbread Boddingtons Bitter; guest beers Ⓗ
Not to be missed: a country pub and restaurant with antique furniture and a wide variety of good value meals.
♨ Q ◖ P

The Symbols

♨	real fire	♿	easy wheelchair access
Q	quiet pub (at least one bar)	▲	camping facilities at the pub or nearby
♘	indoor room for children	≠	near British Rail station
❀	garden or other outdoor drinking area	⊖	near underground station
🛏	accommodation	♣	pub games
◖	lunchtime meals	⍥	real cider
◗	evening meals	P	pub car park
⊞	public bar	⚟	no-smoking room or area

Merseyside

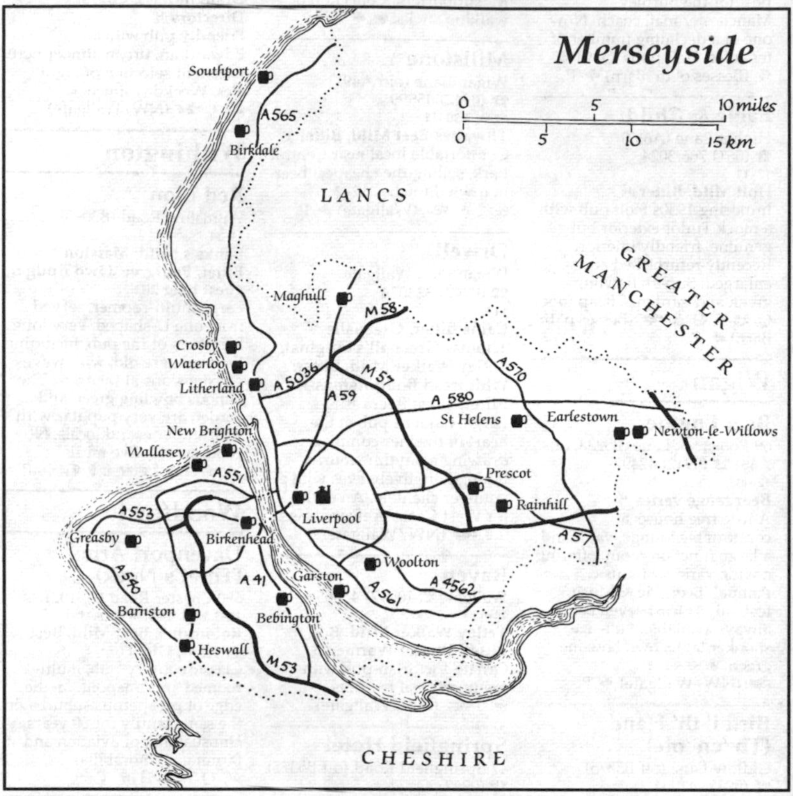

Cains, Liverpool

Barnston

Fox & Hounds
107 Barnston Road (A551, between Arrowe Park and Gayton) ☎ (051) 648 7685
11.30–3, 5.30–11
Courage Directors; Marston's Pedigree; Ruddles Best Bitter, County; Webster's Yorkshire Bitter Ⓗ
Cosy, three-roomed converted coach house with real fires. Excellent value food (not Sun), but beer is a bit pricey. Darts on Mon. ♨ Q ❀ ◖ ♿ ♣ P

Bebington

Cleveland Arms
31 Bebington Road, New Ferry
☎ (051) 645 2847
11–11
Thwaites Best Mild, Bitter, Craftsman Ⓗ
Lively, open-plan pub in a pedestrian area. A previous local CAMRA *Pub of the Year* whose standards remain high.
⇌ ♣

Rose & Crown
57 The Village
☎ (051) 643 1312
11.30–3, 5.30–11; 11.30–11 Fri & Sat
Thwaites Best Mild, Bitter Ⓗ
Bustling, friendly, multi-room local in the centre of an old village. No food Sun.
Q ◖ ⇌ ♣ P

Three Stags
Church Road ☎ (051) 334 3428
11–3, 5.30 (5 Fri)–11; 11.30–11 Sat
Cains Bitter; Tetley Walker Mild, Bitter, Winter Warmer; guest beers Ⓗ
Large pub with an adjoining Porterhouse restaurant. The huge lounge was recently split into a smoke room (with satellite TV), a comfortable lounge and a family room.
⛄ ❀ ◖ ◗ ♿ ⇌ (Spital) P

Birkdale

Upsteps
20 Upper Aughton Road (off A526 Eastbourne Rd)
☎ (0704) 69931
11.30–11
S&N Matthew Brown Bitter, Theakston Mild, Best Bitter, XB Ⓗ
Cosy, traditional pub with a friendly licensee. The name comes from the flight of stairs up to the door. Once known as Bankfield House. ⊟ ⇌ ♣

Birkenhead

Commodore
25 Lord Street (off Cleveland St) ☎ (051) 647 6558
12–11
Oak Wobbly Bob; S&N Theakston Best Bitter, XB, Old Peculier; Younger Scotch, IPA; guest beers Ⓗ
Traditional local in the back streets of old docklands. With its rock music, a bikers' and younger persons' bolt hole, although not exclusively. Two pool tables, Sky TV and a pinball; four or five constantly changing guest beers from independent brewers. A Whitbread-free zone!
◖ ⇌ (Hamilton Sq) P

Crown
128 Conway Street (opp. market) ☎ (051) 647 9108
11.30–11
Cains Mild, Bitter, FA; Eldridge Pope Dorchester; Jennings Mild, Sneck Lifter; guest beers Ⓗ
Town-centre alehouse with the best choice of beers for miles – 16 at the last count. A single bar serves three rooms and a varied clientele. Recently saved from demolition and well worth a visit. Family room till 6pm.
⇌ (Central/Hamilton Sq) ♣ P

Lord Napier
St Pauls Road, Rock Ferry (off A41) ☎ (051) 645 3659
11–11
Cains Mild; Mansfield Old Shilling; Whitbread Boddingtons Bitter Ⓗ
Friendly, comfortable, two-room pub with a family atmosphere. Keen darts and, particularly, bowls teams (unfortunately no green of its own). ⇌ (Rock Ferry) ♣

Old House at Home
30 Queen Street, Tranmere
☎ (051) 666 1578
11–11
Banks's Mild, Bitter Ⓔ
Local CAMRA *Pub of the Year* 1992, serving drinkers of all ages. The bar and lounge are serviced from one area; the cosy, compact garden has swings. The landlord seldom misses a chance to speak to customers and cares well for local pensioners.
⇌ (Green Lane) ♣

Shrewsbury Arms
38 Claughton Firs, Oxton
☎ (051) 652 1775
11.30–3, 5–11; 11.30–11 Sat
Cains Mild, Bitter, FA; S&N Theakston Best Bitter; Whitbread Boddingtons Bitter Ⓗ
Traditional, very popular pub with beamed ceilings, attracting a cosmopolitan clientele. No food Sun. Sit in the rose garden. Q P

Crosby

Crow's Nest
Victoria Road
☎ (051) 931 3081
11.30–3, 5.30–11; 11.30–11 Fri & Sat
Cains Bitter Ⓗ
Well-established local preserving its separate bar, snug and lounge. Regulars' spirited opposition prevented the intrusion of a jukebox and a fruit machine, thus retaining the pub's lively conversational character. Deservedly popular.
Q ⇌ (Blundellsands) P

Earlestown

Wellington
Earle Street ☎ (0925) 290850
Burtonwood Mild, Bitter Ⓗ
One of Earlestown's smaller pubs, with a comfortable L-shaped lounge, with divided seating areas, and a well-used tap room. ⇌ ♣

Garston

Dealers Arms
79–81 St Mary's Road
☎ (051) 427 5877
11–11
Cains Mild, Bitter Ⓗ
Popular locals' pub with three small rooms. Q ⇌ ♣

King Street Vaults
King Street ☎ (051) 427 5850
11–11
Walker Mild, Bitter Ⓗ
Typical Peter Walker pub close to the docks, underneath the bridge from Garston centre. Sporting trophies galore. ♣

Swan Inn
James Street ☎ (051) 427 2032
11–11
Tetley Walker Mild, Bitter Ⓗ
Small, side-street local off the main shopping street. ⇌ ♣

Greasby

Irby Mill
Mill Lane ☎ (051) 604 0194
11.30–3, 5–11; 11.30–11 Sat
Cains Mild, Bitter; Jennings Bitter; S&N Theakston Best Bitter; Tetley Walker Bitter; Whitbread Boddingtons Bitter Ⓗ**; guest beers**
Unspoilt, traditional country pub, with three rooms. No background music or slot machines. Q ♣ P

Heswall

Black Horse
Village Road, Lower Heswall (off A540 towards River Dee)
☎ (051) 342 2254
11.30–11
Bass Mild XXXX, Special, Draught Bass; guest beers Ⓗ
Village local appealing to all age groups, opposite the church. Darts and dominoes played in the bar; the lounge has a snug and a sunken conservatory. Tiny car park but plenty of space nearby. No food Sun. ♣ P

Litherland

Priory
64 Sefton Road (off A5036)
☎ (051) 928 1110
11.30–11
Ind Coope Burton Ale; Walker Mild, Bitter, Best Bitter, Winter Warmer Ⓗ
A large, multi-level, comfortable lounge and a fair-sized public bar, situated in the residential area of Litherland, where real ale is a rarity. Good food at lunchtime. ⇌ (Seaforth/Litherland) ♣ P

Liverpool: *City Centre*

Everyman Bistro
Hope Street, L1 (opp. Catholic cathedral) ☎ (051) 708 9545
12–midnight; closed Sun
Brakspear Bitter; Fuller's Chiswick; guest beers Ⓗ
Cellar bar/bistro with a relaxed continental-style atmosphere. Busy lunchtime and after 11pm; popular with students and theatre-goers to the upstairs Everyman Theatre. Very good selection of home-cooked, reasonably priced food, with many vegetarian dishes. Q
⇌ (Lime St) ⊖ (Central)

Flying Picket
24 Hardman Street, L1 (in courtyard of unemployed resources centre)
☎ (051) 709 3995
11–11; closed Sun
Coach House Coachman's Ⓗ
Popular bar frequented by trade unionists and public alike, handy for the numerous restaurants in the area. Regular live music upstairs but the keg bar means a trek downstairs for your ale.
⇌ (Lime St) ⊖ (Central) P

Globe
Cases Street, L1 (opp. Central station)
11–11
Cains Mild, Bitter; guest beers Ⓗ
A local in the city centre, with a tiny back lounge. The floor is inclined to exaggerate the feeling of inebriation.
⇌ (Lime St) ⊖ (Central)

Grapes
60 Roscoe Street, L1 (off Berry St, near Chinatown)
☎ (051) 709 8617
11–11
Cains Bitter; guest beers Ⓗ
Cosy, friendly pub which caters for both locals and visitors alike. Always welcoming. Free food Sun lunch; quiz night Mon; Fri eve Cajun music. ⇌ (Lime St) ⊖ (Central)

Lord Warden
21 London Road, L3 (close to Empire Theatre)
☎ (051) 207 1719
11.30–11
Cains Bitter; Tetley Walker Mild, Bitter Ⓗ

Comfortable, refurbished pub handy for theatres and cinemas. Busy late eves.
⇌ ⊖ (Lime St)

Peter Kavanagh's
2–6 Egerton Street, L8 (last road off Catherine St before Toxteth) ☎ (051) 709 3443
11–11
Cains Bitter; Ind Coope Burton Ale; Tetley Walker Bitter Ⓗ
Splendid old pub in a row of cottage-style houses. The original bar has two separate (and usually) quiet rooms on either side, with another two rooms off. Bric-a-brac abounds in the bar area. Q ◖ ◗

Poste House
23 Cumberland Street, L1
☎ (051) 236 4130
11–11
Cains Mild, Bitter Ⓗ**; guest beer**
Small, cosy pub, sometimes still known by its nickname of the Muck Midden. The upstairs room is used during busy periods. Friendly atmosphere but can be very smoky. Lunches weekdays only. Q ◖ ⇌ (Lime St) ⊖ (Moorfields)

Railway
18 Tithebarn Street, L2
☎ (051) 236 7210
11.30–11; 12–3, 7.30–10.30 Sun
Cains Mild, Bitter, FA; guest beers Ⓗ
Former Mellors pub opposite the now-closed Exchange station, popular for its good value lunches. Also serves breakfast from 9.15 – if the door is closed, knock! No food Sun. ◖ ⇌ (Lime St) ⊖ (Moorfields)

Roscoe Head
Roscoe Street, L1 (opp. bombed church)
☎ (051) 709 4490
11–11
Ind Coope Burton Ale; Jennings Bitter; Tetley Walker Mild, Bitter Ⓗ
Classic, traditional, city-centre pub that's been in every edition of this guide. Four small rooms: the back lounge can only just accommodate the many awards won and the unique tie collection. Quiz on Tue; no food Sun. A welcome for all. Q ◖ ⇌ (Lime St) ⊖ (Central)

Ship & Mitre
133 Dale Street, L2 (near Birkenhead tunnel entrance)
☎ (051) 236 0859
11–11 (8 Mon–Tue); 7–11 Sat; closed Sun
Cains Mild, Bitter; Oak Wobbly Bob; guest beers Ⓗ
Gas-lit pub, popular with students at lunchtime. Good value weekday lunches and the best range of beers in Liverpool. Live music Fri teatime. Function room.
◖ ⇌ ⊖ (Lime St) ⌓

Swan
86 Wood Street, L1 (behind Bold St) ☎ (051) 709 5281
11.30–11
Marston's Pedigree; Oak Wobbly Bob; guest beers Ⓗ
Lively ex-bikers' pub with an upstairs bar. Occasional house beers sold; regular charity events; the best jukebox in the city. Live music upstairs Mon and Wed. Good value, home-cooked food, plus a vegetarian option, till 7pm. ◖ ◗ ⇌ (Lime St) ⊖ (Central) ⌓

United Powers
66–68 Tithebarn Street, L2
☎ (051) 236 5205
11.30–11; closed Sun
Guest beers Ⓗ
Popular, well-run, ex-Threlfalls pub on the fringe of a business area. Good value lunches (not served Sat); trad. jazz Wed nights. Always a guest beer available, usually from an independent brewery.
◖ ⇌ (Lime St) ⊖ (Moorfields)

White House
185 Duke Street, L1
11–11
Walker Mild, Bitter Ⓗ
Two-roomed pub, split by a corridor, situated on the corner of Berry Street in the heart of Chinatown. Happy hours and occasional free food. ⊞ ⇌ (Lime St) ⊖ (Central)

White Star (Quinns)
24 Rainford Gardens, L2
☎ (051) 236 8520
11.30–11
Bass Worthington BB, Draught Bass; guest beers Ⓗ
Pub near the site of the Cavern, of Beatles fame, catering for shoppers and business people alongside a strong regular trade. Bass maintain the pub sympathetically and supply the guest beers. ⇌ (Lime St) ⊖ (Moorfields)

Liverpool: *East*

Albany
40–42 Albany Road, L13
☎ (051) 228 8597
11–11
Cains Mild, Bitter Ⓗ
Friendly, two-room local: bar to the left, snug to the right. Food Mon–Fri. ◖

Claremont
70 Lower Breck Road, L6
☎ (051) 263 7656
12–11
Cains Bitter; Tetley Walker Dark Mild, Mild, Bitter Ⓗ
Basic, no-nonsense, two-room pub in a building of architectural interest. Food is limited to snacks, but the daily home-made soups are great value. No food Sun. ⊞ ♿ ♣

Clock
110 High Street, Wavertree, L15
2 (12 Mon & Sat)–11
Cains Bitter Ⓗ
Pub close to Picton Clock, a local landmark. Much expanded from the tiny, cosy pub of the 70s. Wheelchair users can arrange for the door at the rear to be opened. ♿

Clubmoor
119 Townsend Lane, L6
☎ (051) 263 4220
11–11
Cains Mild, Bitter Ⓗ
Handsome, detached building: a large, open-plan lounge and a bar with Sky TV and darts. Quiz Tue and Thu, live music Wed. Within walking distance of Liverpool FC. Q ❀ ⊞ ♣

Durning Arms
149 Wavertree Road, L7
11.30–11
Cains Bitter; Tetley Walker Bitter Ⓗ
Pub rebuilt during the 1960s, with a well-used bar and a comfortable lounge. Occasional live music. Opposite a proposed shopping complex.
◖ ⊞ ♿ ⇌ (Edge Hill) ♣ P

Edinburgh
4 Sandown Lane, L15 (100 yds off Wavertree High St)
12–11
Cains Bitter; Walker Mild, Bitter Ⓗ
Tiny local hidden away from the busy High Street. Separate bar, but the same prices as in the lounge. Friendly welcome. Well worth a visit.

Falstaff
110 Gateacre Park Drive, L25
☎ (051) 428 5116
11–11
Jennings Bitter; Tetley Walker Mild, Bitter, Winter Warmer Ⓗ
Now reverted to its original name and real ale, after a few years as the Boulevard restaurant. Live music Sun eve; cheap day Thu. ⊞ ♣ P

Rocket
2 Bowring Park Road, L14
☎ (051) 220 8821
11–11
Cains Bitter Ⓗ
Excellent, modern pub at the end of the M62 and close to the site of a former pub of the same name. Named after the pioneer loco, which is depicted in relief on the side of the pub. No food Sat.
❀ ◖ ♿ ⇌ (Broad Green) P

Royal Standard
Deysbrook Lane, L12
☎ (051) 228 2777
11.30–11
Cains Bitter; Greenalls Mild, Bitter, Thomas Greenalls Original [H]
Suburban pub, pleasantly modernised. The single lounge bar has alcoves and subdued lighting. Soft background music. ❀ P

Wheatsheaf
186 East Prescot Road, L14 (A57) ☎ (051) 228 5080
11.30–11
Cains Bitter; guest beer [H]
Hospitable, traditional pub, offering waitress service in the two lounges. Busy bar.
Q ⊞ P

Liverpool: *North*

Abbey
153 Walton Lane, L4
☎ (051) 207 0086
11–11
Walker Mild, Bitter [H]
Splendid, three-storey pub, handy for Everton FC. A real local, with a separate bar and a snug. Quiz nights. 🏰 ⊞ ♣

Bull
Dublin Street, L3 (corner of Gt Howard St) ☎ (051) 207 1422
11–11
Tetley Walker Mild, Bitter [H]
Street-corner local with one bar and a distinctly Irish flavour. Always packed at lunchtimes with office workers, manual workers and executives. Good value sandwiches and pies. A gem of a pub where a warm welcome is guaranteed. ≠ (Sandhills)

Clock
167 Walton Road, L4
☎ (051) 207 3594
11–11
Walker Mild, Bitter [H]
Busy, two-roomed, street-corner local, incorporating a comfortable lounge and a lively bar area. A truly classic Liverpool pub, well worth a visit for the friendly atmosphere and the licensee's exuberant personality.
🏰 ⊞ ≠ (Kirkdale) ♣

Melrose Abbey
331 Westminster Road, L4
☎ (051) 922 3637
11.30–11
Tetley Walker Dark Mild, Mild, Bitter [H]
Deservedly popular, three-roomed pub. The friendly atmosphere is complemented by the real fire in the main lounge, giving this pub real character. Popular with rail workers and football fans.
🏰 ⊞ ≠ (Kirkdale) ♣

Prince Arthur
93 Rice Lane, L9 (A59)
☎ (051) 525 4508
11–11
Walker Mild, Bitter, Winter Warmer [H]
Former CAMRA *Pub Preservation Award*-winner: a feast of original woodwork, etched-glass and mosaic in an L-shaped bar, corridor drinking area and cosy lounge. A well-used pub, always lively; not just a showpiece.
⊞ ≠ (Rice Lane/Walton) ↺ P

Sefton Arms
2 Ormskirk Road, L9 (A59)
☎ (051) 525 8787
11.30–11
Cains Mild, Bitter [H]
Modern pub near Aintree Racecourse. The large lounge has a jukebox; the bar is quiet. Disabled toilet facilities at the rear of the pub: ask barstaff for help. Popular Sun market nearby. No food Sun.
Q ⛵ ❀ ◐ ⊞ ♿ ≠ (Aintree) ♣ P

Selwyn
106 Selwyn Street, L4
☎ (051) 525 0747
11–11
Tetley Walker Mild, Bitter [H]
Large, three-roomed pub with a small, peaceful snug, a lively lounge with pool and TV, and a boisterous public bar with darts. Q ⊞ ≠ (Kirkdale) ♣

Liverpool: *South*

Anglesea Arms
36 Beresford Road, L8 (off the Dingle end of Park Rd)
☎ (051) 727 4874
11–11
Tetley Walker Mild, Bitter [H]
Nice, comfortable pub, with a good atmosphere, and friendly customers and staff. Opposite Toxteth market and in a good shopping area. Well worth travelling the short distance from town. ⊞

Masonic
19 Lodge Lane, L8 (100 yds from Smithdown Rd jct)
11.30–11
Tetley Walker Mild, Bitter [H]
Small, friendly, characterful pub on the edge of Toxteth. Has a public bar, but one price (very reasonable) is charged throughout. The lounge has two distinct areas.
🏰 ≠ (Edge Hill)

Royal George
99 Park Road, L8
☎ (051) 708 9277
11–11
Tetley Walker Mild, Bitter; guest beers [H]
Friendly alehouse, locally known as Black's. Sells the cheapest guest beers in the city. Often noisy but the enthusiasm with which it's run is very inviting. Popular karaoke; Sky TV. Home-made soup daily. Free food is a regular eve feature. ◐ ♣

Willowbank
329 Smithdown Road, L15 (A562 opp. Sefton General Hospital)
11.45–11
Ind Coope Burton Ale; Walker Mild, Bitter, Winter Warmer [H]
Recently extended, imposing pub set back from the main road. Popular with students and can get very busy. No food Sun. ❀ ◐ ⊞ ♣ P

Maghull

Red House
31 Foxhouse Lane
☎ (051) 526 1376
11–3, 5–11; 11–11 Fri & Sat
Jennings Bitter (summer); **Tetley Walker Dark Mild, Mild, Bitter, Winter Warmer** [H]
Friendly suburban local renowned for its modestly priced lunches. Liverpool buses stop outside. No food Sun. ❀ ◐ ⊞ ≠ ♣ P

New Brighton

Commercial
Hope Street ☎ (051) 639 2105
11.30–11
Cains Bitter; Walker Mild, Bitter, Best Bitter, Winter Warmer [H]
Traditional, two-roomed, street-corner local with a basic bar and a cosy lounge (table service). A peaceful haven for older people. Note the black and white pictures of Victorian New Brighton. Q ♿ ≠ ♣

Newton-le-Willows

Old Crow Inn
Crow Lane East (A572, 1 mile from centre) ☎ (0925) 225337
12–3.30, 7–11; 12–11 Fri & Sat
Tetley Walker Mild, Bitter [H]
Popular roadside local with a large, divided lounge, catering for all ages, and a popular tap room. ❀ ◐ ⊞ ♣ P

Prescot

Clock Face
Derby Street ☎ (051) 430 0701
11–11
Thwaites Bitter, Craftsman [H]

Attractive pub on the edge of the town centre, with a relaxed and friendly atmosphere. The gentle ripple of conversation is rarely broken by other noises. An oasis for the quiet drinker. Quiz Mon. 🝙 Q ☾ P

Rainhill

Commercial (Comic)

Station Road (off A57)
☎ (051) 426 6446
11–11
Cains Mild, Bitter; S&N Theakston Best Bitter; Tetley Walker Bitter Ⓗ
Large Victorian pub, locally known as the Comic, resplendent with Joseph Jones Knotty Ash Ales windows. Very much a characterful, busy local. ❀ ⊞ ⇌ ♣ P

St Helens

Duke of Cambridge

27 Duke Street (A570)
☎ (0744) 613281
11–11
Vaux Bitter, Samson; Wards Mild; guest beer Ⓗ
Compact pub with a lively bar and a noisy lounge. Handy for the town centre.
⊞ ⇌ (Central) ♣

Hope & Anchor

194 City Road ☎ (0744) 24199
12–11
Tetley Walker Mild, Bitter Ⓗ
Well-run local with special events and discos on some nights (very loud). ⊞ ♣

Phoenix

Canal Street (off A53 near glass works) ☎ (0744) 21953
11–11
Cains Bitter; S&N Theakston Best Bitter; guest beers Ⓗ
Friendly alehouse, popular with students at weekends. The well-patronised bar is very busy on darts nights, and has a rugby league theme, with international touring team photos. Happy hours. Lunchtime snacks.
⊞ ⇌ (Shaw St) ♣

Royal Alfred

Shaw Street ☎ (0744) 26786
11–11
Cains Bitter Ⓗ
Large, town-centre pub with cosmopolitan drinkers. Quizzes, live music and discos. 🛏 ☾ ⊞ ⇌ (Central) ⊖ ♣ P

Turks Head

Cooper Street ☎ (0744) 26949
11–11
Cains Bitter; Tetley Walker Mild, Bitter Ⓗ
Interesting, lively half-timbered pub, unusual for the area. Live music, karaoke and quizzes.
🝙 ⊞ ⇌ (Central) ♣

Wheatsheaf

36 Westfield Street (A58)
☎ (0744) 37453
11–11
Tetley Walker Dark Mild, Bitter Ⓗ
Small, one-roomed pub with a mixed clientele. ⇌ (Central)

Southport

Berkeley Hotel

Queens Road ☎ (0704) 530163
12–11
Courage Directors; Marston's Pedigree; Moorhouse's Pendle Witches Brew; Ruddles Best Bitter, County; guest beers Ⓗ
Family-run, 12-bed hotel close to the town centre. Nine cask beers, including two guests plus Berkeley Bitter, brewed for the hotel by Moorhouse's. George, the pet Vietnamese pot-bellied pig, often frequents the bar! ❀ 🛏 ☾ ◗ ⇌ (Chapel St) ♣ P

Legendary Lancashire Heroes

101 Shakespeare Street
☎ (0704) 533668
12–10.30
Moorhouse's Pendle Witches Brew; Oak Best Bitter; Taylor Landlord; guest beers Ⓗ
Enterprising off-licence with an ever-changing range of real ales and an impressive choice of bottled beers from around the world.

Zetland Hotel

Zetland Street ☎ (0704) 544541
11.30–11
Burtonwood Mild, Bitter, Forshaw's, Top Hat Ⓗ
Large Victorian pub with its own bowling green. Public bar prices are the same as in other parts of the pub. Family room till 8.30. 🝙 ⛴ ❀ ⇌ ♣ P

Wallasey

Brighton

133 Brighton Street, Seacombe (A554 opp. town hall)
☎ (051) 638 1163
11.30–3, 5.30–11; 11.30–11 Fri & Sat
Cains Bitter Ⓗ
Very friendly pub, thanks to the licensee. Popular with locals, town councillors and wedding parties. Architecturally, one of the best buildings in the area, over 100 years old, and has sold beer since 1883. ⊞ ♿ ♣

Farmers Arms

225 Wallasey Village
☎ (051) 638 2110
11.30–3, 5–11; 11.30–11 Fri & Sat
Cains Mild, Bitter; S&N Theakston Best Bitter; Tetley Walker Bitter Ⓗ
Well-furnished, popular, regulars' pub with a front bar, side snug and back lounge to cater for all tastes. Bandit in the bar but no jukebox. Seventy years old.
☾ ⊞ ⇌ (Grove Rd)

Ferry

Tobin Street ☎ (051) 639 1753
11–11
Cains Bitter Ⓗ
Very popular pub, known locally as the Eggy. Situated on a bank of the Mersey, it affords good views across the river. One of the oldest pubs in the area, within walking distance of the ferries. No food Sun. ⛴ ❀ ☾ ◗ ♣ P

Primrose Hotel

Withens Lane, Liscard (off Manor Rd) ☎ (051) 637 1340
12–3, 5–11 (12–11 March–Oct)
Cains Bitter; S&N Theakston Best Bitter Ⓗ
Unmistakable half-timbered pub with wood-panelled walls, an ornate ceiling and a mixed clientele. ❀ ♣ P

Prince Alfred

3 Church Road, Seacombe
☎ (051) 638 1674
11–11
Cains Bitter; Whitbread Boddingtons Mild, Bitter Ⓗ
Superb, small, community pub with a friendly atmosphere, almost lost amidst a sea of keg pubs, close to the famous Mersey ferry terminal (Seacombe). ☾ ♿ ♣

Waterloo

Marine

3–5 South Road (end of busy shopping road, off A565 close to seafront) ☎ (051) 928 3358
12–11
Cains Bitter Ⓗ
Spacious, multi-roomed, 1930s-type pub, recently refurbished. Comfortable, but not plush – appeals to an older clientele and others who enjoy conversation. Close to the sea and marina. 🝙 Q ⊞ ⇌ ♣

Woolton

Cobden Vaults

Quarry Street
☎ (051) 428 2978
11.30–11
Courage Directors; Ruddles County; John Smith's Bitter Ⓗ
Busy pub full of bric-a-brac. Quiz night Mon. A rare outlet for these beers in Liverpool.
♣

GOOD BEER GUIDE BEERS OF THE YEAR

Chosen by CAMRA tasting panels, by votes from the public at CAMRA beer festivals, and by a poll of CAMRA members, these are the *Good Beer Guide Beers of the Year*. Each took its place as a finalist in the *Champion Beer of Britain* competition at the Great British Beer Festival at Olympia. These aren't the only good beers in the country, but they were found to be consistently outstanding in their categories. They have also been awarded a tankard symbol in the breweries section of this book.

DARK AND LIGHT MILDS

Adnams Mild
Bateman Mild
Coach House Gunpowder Strong Mild
St Austell XXXX Mild
Tetley Mild
Woodforde's Mardler's Mild

BITTERS

Caledonian Deuchars IPA
Hanby Drawwell Bitter
Nethergate Bitter
Otter Bitter
Plassey Bitter
Taylor Best Bitter

BEST BITTERS

Adnams Extra
Batham Best Bitter
Cropton Two Pints Best Bitter
Exmoor Gold
Reepham Rapier Pale Ale
Taylor Landlord

STRONG BITTERS

Exe Valley Exeter Old Bitter
Felinfoel Double Dragon
Hop Back Summer Lightning
Mauldons White Adder
Pilgrim Crusader Premium Bitter
Rooster's Rooster's

OLD ALES AND STRONG MILDS

Adnams Old
Hardington Old Ale
Sarah Hughes Original Dark Ruby Mild
King & Barnes Old Ale
Malton Owd Bob
Woodforde's Norfolk Nog

BARLEY WINES

Ballard's Wassail
Gibbs Mew Bishop's Tipple
Marston's Owd Rodger
Robinson's Old Tom
Woodforde's Headcracker

PORTERS AND STOUTS

Bateman Salem Porter
Coach House Blunderbus Old Porter
Malton Pickwick's Porter
Oakhill Black Magic
Reepham Velvet Stout
Young's Porter

BOTTLE-CONDITIONED BEERS

Bass Worthington White Shield
Burton Bridge Burton Porter
Courage Imperial Russian Stout
Eldridge Pope Thomas Hardy's Ale
Gale's Prize Old Ale
Harveys 1859 Porter

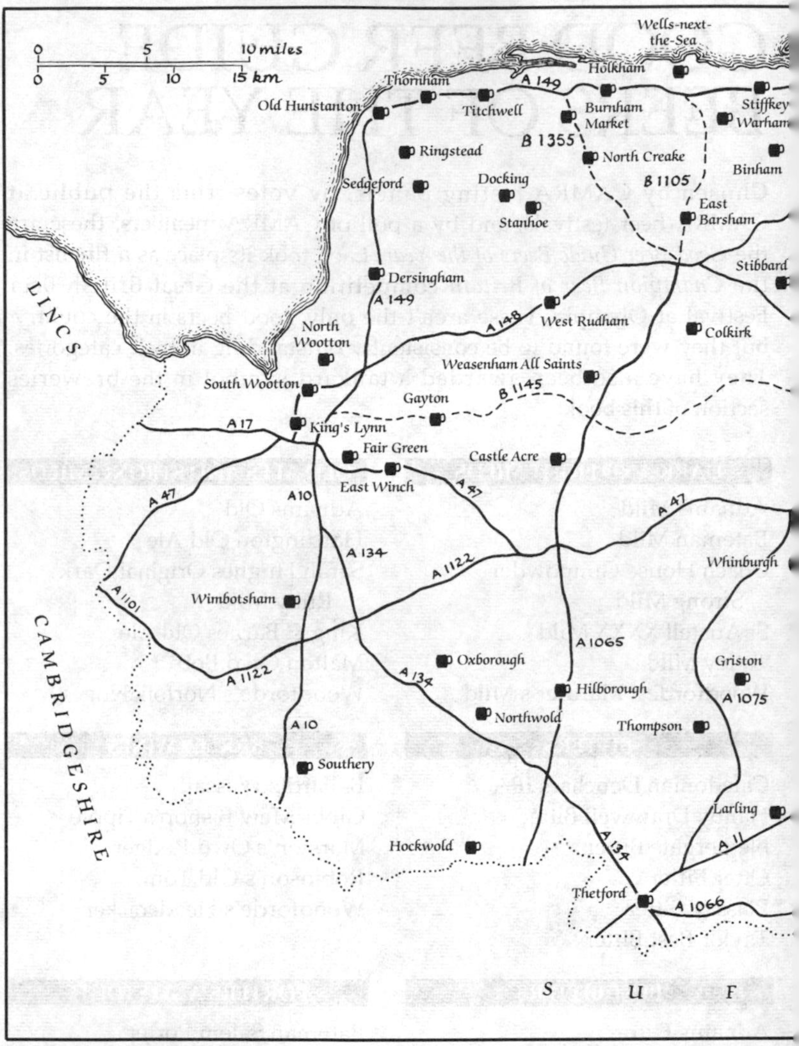

***Reepham**, Reepham; **Reindeer**, Norwich; **Woodforde's**, Woodbastwick*

Attleborough

Griffin Hotel

Church Street ☎ (0953) 452149
10.30–2.30, 5.30–11
Brakspear Bitter; Greene King Abbot; Whitbread Wethered Bitter; guest beers Ⓗ
Comfortable, 16th-century coaching inn at the centre of this market town, with a reputation for the quality and variety of its West Country ales. A good menu includes vegetarian dishes.
Q ❀ ◖◗ ⇌ ♣ ⌂ P

Binham

Chequers

Front Street ☎ (0328) 830297
11–11
Adnams Bitter; Draught Bass; M&B Highgate Mild; Woodforde's Wherry Ⓗ**; guest beers**
17th-century, cosy, comfortable inn with genuine beams and an old inglenook with original built-in cupboards on either side. A more popular pub of late, and this is reflected in a wider choice of ales. Quiet campsite at the rear. All day breakfasts served.
♛ Q ☕ ❀ ⛿ ◖◗ ▲ ♣ P

Briston

Green Man

Hall Street ☎ (0263) 860993
11–11
Greene King IPA, Abbot Ⓗ
Long-established, popular village pub which serves reasonably priced food. Note the original inglenook.
♛ ❀ ◖◗ ♣ P

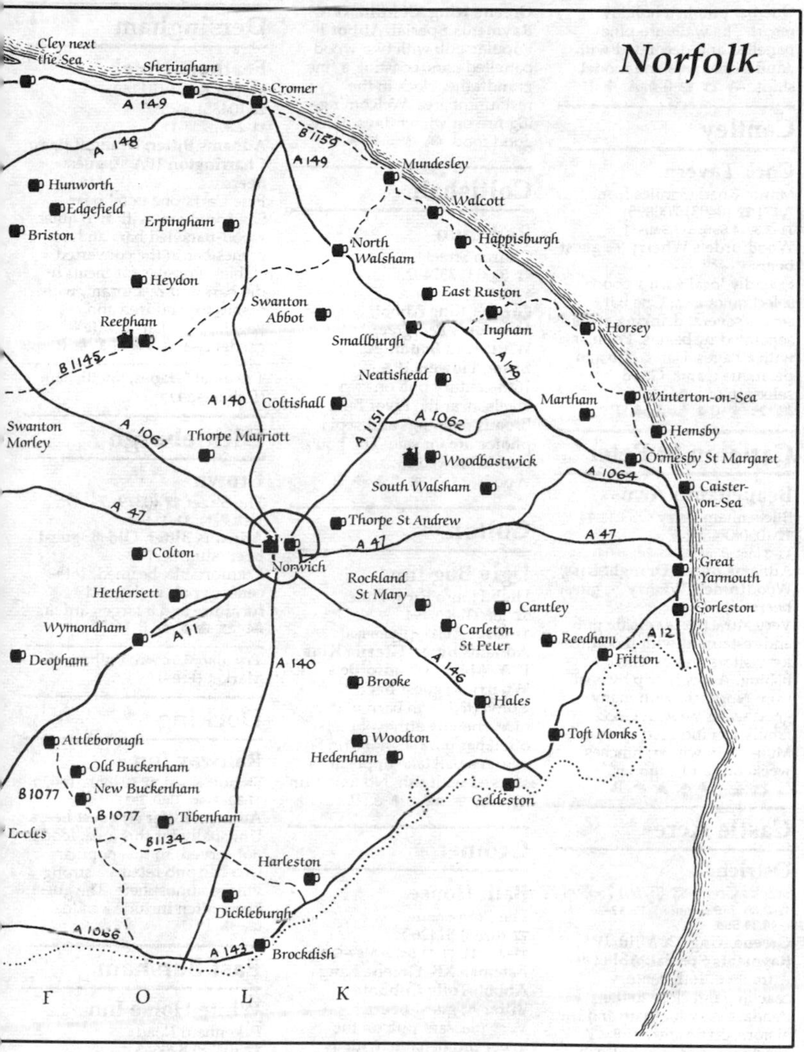

Brockdish

Greyhound Inn

The Street ☎ (037 975) 775
12–2.30, 7–11
Greene King IPA, Abbot; Woodforde's Wherry Ⓖ
17th-century pub with a small bar where beer is served from the cellar. An assortment of goods, including eggs, is also sold. The background classical music adds to the relaxed atmosphere. Lunches Wed–Sun; eve meals Wed–Sat.
♛ ❀ ⛟ ◐ ◑ ♣ P ⅄

Try also: King's Head (Adnams)

Brooke

White Lion

The Street ☎ (0508) 50443
12–3, 5.30–11; 12–11 Sat
Adnams Bitter; Draught Bass; Fuller's London Pride; M&B Highgate Mild; Stones Best Bitter Ⓗ
Attractive pub, just off the main Norwich road, facing the meres in the village centre, well populated by ducks.
♛ ❀ ◐ ◑ ♿ ♣ P

Burnham Market

Hoste Arms

The Green ☎ (0328) 738257
11–3, 5–11
Adnams Bitter; Ruddles Best Bitter, County; Webster's Yorkshire Bitter; Woodforde's Wherry Ⓗ**; guest beer**
17th-century inn full of interest, offering regular live entertainment, i.e. jazz and classical eves. Accommodation includes two rooms with four-poster beds.
♛ Q ❀ ⛟ ◐ ◑ P

Caister-on-Sea

Ship

Victoria Street ☎ (0493) 728008
11–11
Greene King IPA; Whitbread Flowers Original Ⓗ**; guest beer**

One-bar pub in a holiday resort. The walls are pine panelled and decorated with nautical pictures and model ships. 🏰 ♞ ❀ ◖ ◗ ▲ ♣ P

Cantley

Cock Tavern
Manor Road (3 miles from A47) ☎ (0493) 700895
11–3.30 (4 Sat), 6 (7 Sat)–11
Woodforde's Wherry Ⓗ**; guest beers**
Friendly local with a good selection of ales. One bar serves several drinking areas separated by beams. Popular with all ages. Darts, crib and petanque teams. Good selection of food.
🏰 ♞ ❀ ◖ ◗ ♿ ▲ ♣ P

Carleton St Peter

Beauchamp Arms
Buckenham Ferry OS350044
☎ (0508) 480247
11–3 (not winter Mon–Fri), 6–11
Adnams Bitter; Draught Bass; Woodforde's Wherry Ⓗ**; guest beers**
Very attractive riverside pub and restaurant with moorings for visitors and excellent fishing. A lovely trip by boat from Norwich, with many good walks nearby. Good family facilities. No eve meals Mon–Fri in winter; lunches weekends and summer.
Q ♞ ❀ ◖ ◗ ♿ ▲ ♣ P

Castle Acre

Ostrich
Stocks Green ☎ (0760) 755398
12–2.30, 7 (6 summer)–11; 12–2, 7–10.30 Sun
Greene King XX Mild, IPA, Rayments Special, Abbot Ⓗ
Attractive, 16th-century coaching inn close to the Peddars Way footpath and the historic castle and priory. A constant *Guide* entry, also in CAMRA's *Good Pub Food*.
🏰 Q ♞ ❀ 🛏 ◖ ◗ ▲ ♣ P

Cley next the Sea

George & Dragon
High Street ☎ (0263) 740652
11–3, 6–11; 12–2, 7–10.30 Sun
Greene King IPA, Rayments Special, Abbot Ⓗ
Pub with much to interest bird watchers. A hide in an attic room overlooks a 'scrape' and has a telescope. Quality food in the bar, where St George and the Dragon artefacts are displayed. 🏰 ❀ 🛏 ◖ ◗ P

Colkirk

Crown
Crown Road ☎ (0328) 862172
11–2.30, 6–11; 12–2.30, 7–10.30 Sun
Greene King XX Mild, IPA, Rayments Special, Abbot Ⓗ
Popular pub with two wood-panelled bars, boasting a fine grandfather clock in the restaurant area. Welcoming log fire on winter days. Very good food. 🏰 ❀ ◖ ◗ ♣ P

Coltishall

Red Lion
Church Street
☎ (0603) 737402
11–3, 5–11
Greene King Abbot; Marston's Pedigree; Whitbread Boddingtons Bitter, Flowers IPA Ⓗ
16th-century pub on two levels, near the River Bure. Broads paintings and sepia photos are for sale. The house beer is brewed by Woodforde's. ❀ ◖ ◗ ♣ P

Colton

Ugly Bug Inn
High House Farm Lane
☎ (0603) 880794
11–3, 5.30–11 (11–11 summer)
Adnams Bitter; Greene King IPA, Abbot; Woodforde's Wherry Ⓗ**; guest beer**
Converted farm barn with a nice, friendly atmosphere; often has quiz sessions on Sun eve. A small lake opposite is stocked with fish. No food Sun eve. 🏰 ❀ 🛏 ◖ ◗ ♿ P

Cromer

Bath House
The Promenade
☎ (0263) 514260
11–3, 7–11; 11–11 Sat & May–Oct
Bateman XB; Greene King Abbot; Tolly Cobbold Bitter Ⓗ**; guest beers**
Very pleasant pub on the lower promenade, with a friendly landlord.
Q ❀ 🛏 ◖ ◗

Try also: Red Lion, Brooke St (Free)

Deopham

Victoria
Church Road
☎ (0953) 850783
12–2.30 (not Mon & Tue), 7–11
Adnams Bitter; Draught Bass; Greene King Abbot; Woodforde's Wherry Ⓗ**; guest beer**
Quiet, friendly village pub with a single bar and original wooden beams. Very good food includes vegetarian and children's dishes. Fields quiz and petanque teams.
🏰 ◖ ◗ ▲ ♣ P

Dersingham

Feathers Hotel
Manor Road (B1140)
☎ (0485) 540207
11–2.30, 5.30–11
Adnams Bitter; Draught Bass; Charrington IPA Ⓗ**; guest beers**
Fine Carrstone hotel near Sandringham, with two quiet, wood-panelled bars and a games bar in the converted stables. Popular for meals in the bars and restaurant, with dishes for children and vegetarians. Large, safe garden. 🏰 ❀ 🛏 ◖ ◗ ♣ P

Try also: Grapes, Snettisham (Pubmaster)

Dickleburgh

Crown
The Street ☎ (0379) 741475
12–3, 7–11; 11–11 Sat
Adnams Bitter, Old Ⓗ**; guest beer** (summer)
Comfortable, beamed, 16th-century pub with good furniture and a large garden.
🏰 ♞ ❀ ◗ ♣ P ⚡

Try also: Crown, Pulham Market (Free)

Docking

Railway Inn
Station Road ☎ (0485) 518620
11.30–3 (not Thu), 7–11
Adnams Bitter Ⓗ**; guest beers**
Unusually for this area, food is not served, so this popular, two-bar pub retains a strong village atmosphere. The guest beers often include a mild.
🏰 ♣ P

East Barsham

White Horse Inn
Fakenham Road
☎ (0328) 820645
11–3, 7–11 (11–11 summer)
Greene King Abbot; Whitbread Boddingtons Bitter; Woodforde's Wherry Ⓗ
Comfortable, 17th-century inn, next to historic East Barsham Manor. Displays collections of baseball caps and banknotes.
🏰 ❀ 🛏 ◖ ◗ ♣ P

East Ruston

Butchers Arms
Oak Street ☎ (0692) 650237
12–3, 7–11
Adnams Bitter; Draught Bass; M&B Highgate Mild; guest beers Ⓗ
Comfortable, refurbished rural pub and restaurant with ornate windows and a very friendly atmosphere. Superb food, unbelievable value.
Q ♞ ❀ ◖ ◗ 🚂 ♿ ♣ P

East Winch

Carpenters Arms
Lynn Road ☎ (0553) 841228
11–3, 5.30–11 (11–11 summer)
Greene King IPA, Abbot [H]**; guest beers**
A welcome pub, with a homely olde-worlde interior, on an otherwise dry stretch of the A47. Good food; children welcome. ❀ ◖ ◗ ♣ P

Eccles

Old Railway Tavern
Station Road
12–2.30, 5.30–11
Adnams Bitter [G]**; Greene King IPA** [H]**, Abbot; guest beers** (occasionally) [G]
Better known as the Eccles Tap; a peaceful haven from the rat race. A great pub for conversation. ♨ Q ❀ ◖ ◗ ⇌ (Eccles Rd) ♣ P

Edgefield

Three Pigs
Norwich Road ☎ (026 367) 634
11–2.30, 7 (6 summer)–11
Adnams Bitter; Woodforde's Wherry [H]
Village pub over 200 years old and thought to have had smuggling connections. No food Mon eve. Worthington White Shield available.
❀ ◖ ◗ ▲ ♣ P ⊁

Erpingham

Spread Eagle Inn
☎ (0263) 761591
11–3, 6.30–11
Woodforde's Wherry, Nelson's Revenge, Norfolk Nog, Baldric, Headcracker [H]
Pub with a long bar and separate games and family rooms. The extensive gardens offer camping. The house beer is brewed by Woodforde's.
♨ Q ⊃ ❀ ◖ ◗ ♿ ▲ ♣ P

Fair Green

Gate Inn
Hill Road ☎ (0553) 840518
12–3, 7–11
Greene King IPA, Abbot; Whitbread Flowers Original [H]
Small local, just off the A47 near Middleton. ♨ ❀ ◖ ◗

Fritton

Decoy Tavern
Beccles Road ☎ (0493) 488277
11.30–3, 7–11
Ind Coope Burton Ale; Tolly Cobbold Original; Whitbread Flowers Original [H]
Small, comfortable roadside pub with a dining area; close to Fritton Woods and riverside walks. ♨ ❀ ◖ ◗ ♣ P

Gayton

Crown
Lynn Road ☎ (0553) 636252
11–3, 6.30–11; 12–2, 7–10.30 Sun
Greene King XX Mild, IPA, Rayments Special, Abbot [H]
Comfortable and welcoming pub with a roaring fire. Despite the restaurant's good reputation, which attracts many visitors, the pub is very much part of village life.
♨ Q ⊃ ❀ ◖ ◗ ♣ P

Geldeston

Lock Inn
Station Road OS391908
☎ (050 845) 414
12–3 (not Mon–Fri), 7–11 (11–11 summer)
Reindeer Bitter; Woodforde's Wherry, Baldric, Headcracker; guest beers [G]/[H]
Pub where the original front bar is still only lit by candles and the fire, located in a pleasant riverside setting, with ghosts and live music. Three or more guest beers.
♨ ⊃ ❀ ◖ ◗ ▲ ♣ ⌓ P

Gorleston

Cliff Hotel
Cliff Hill ☎ (0493) 662179
11–11
Ind Coope Burton Ale; Scotts Golden Best; Tetley Bitter [H]
Clifftop hotel with views over the harbour and coast. Two comfortable bars; the large garden is very popular in summer with locals and holidaymakers.
Q ❀ 🛏 ◖ ◗ ♿ P

Dock Tavern
Dock Tavern Lane
☎ (0493) 442255
11–11
Adnams Bitter; Woodforde's Wherry; guest beers [H]
Single-bar pub split into areas; close to the main street and riverside. ♨ ⊃ ❀ ◖ ◗

Links Hotel
Marine Parade
☎ (0493) 662550
11–11
Adnams Mild, Extra, Broadside; guest beer [H]
Large seafront hotel boasting many original Lacons Brewery features. The lounge has an adjoining restaurant; pool room. ⊃ ❀ ◖ ◗ P

Great Yarmouth

Allens
Greyfriars Way (just SE of town hall) ☎ (0493) 856758
11–3, 6–11
Adnams Mild, Bitter, Old, Broadside; Wadworth 6X [H]
Lively, town-centre pub with a smart, wood-panelled interior.
▲ ⇌ (Vauxhall)

Clipper Schooner
Friars Lane (off South Quay)
☎ (0493) 854926
11–11
Adnams Mild, Bitter, Old, Broadside [H]**, Tally Ho** [G]**; guest beers** [H]
This 1930s pub, close to the old town wall, offers hot food all day. Comfortable atmosphere and a warm welcome. Look for the map of the 'Rows' to see how many pubs have disappeared over the years.
Q ⊃ ❀ ◖ ◗ ♿ ♣ P

Ship Inn
Greyfriars Way (just SE of town hall) ☎ (0493) 855533
11–11
Adnams Mild, Bitter, Old, Broadside [H]**; guest beer**
Comfortable, two-bar pub split into different areas, close to the docks. A large, table-size chessboard is regularly in use. Once visited you will want to return; popular with all ages.
♨ Q 🛏 ◖ ◗ ▲ ⇌ ♣

Griston

Waggon & Horses
Church Road ☎ (0953) 883847
11–3, 6.30–11
Greene King IPA, Rayments Special, Abbot [H]**, Winter Ale** [G]
Classic Norfolk village local with wooden beams, a welcoming atmosphere and good food. Q ❀ ◖ ◗ ▲ ♣

Hales

Chequered Flag
Yarmouth Road
☎ (0508) 46468
11.30–3, 7–11
Tetley Bitter; Tolly Cobbold Mild, Original [H]
Long, two-bar pub with collections of cigarette cards, and old photos of the pub. The garden features aviaries and a bowling green.
⊃ ❀ ◖ ◗ ♣ P

Happisburgh

Hill House
☎ (0692) 650004
11–2.30, 7–11 (11–11 summer)
Adnams Bitter; Greene King Abbot; Woodforde's Wherry [H]
Built in the 15th-century and extended in the 17th-century, this beamed, single-bar pub with an inglenook offers accommodation in a converted signal box, built for a railway that never happened. Sir Arthur Conan Doyle wrote, drank and stayed here. No food Sun or Mon eves.
♨ ⊃ ❀ 🛏 ◖ ◗ ♿ ▲ ♣ P

Norfolk

Harleston

Cherry Tree
London Road ☎ (0379) 852345
11–2.30, 6–11
Adnams Mild, Bitter, Old, Broadside, Tally Ho H
Still one of the very best in Norfolk. The quaint heating system enhances the bouquet of the ales in winter. Petanque played. ⚘ Q ❀ ♿ ♣ P

Hedenham

Mermaid
Norwich Road (B1332)
☎ (050 844) 480
11–3, 5 (7 Sat)–11
Adnams Bitter; Draught Bass; Greene King IPA G
Comfortable, refurbished country pub, which has retained much of its original character, with large open fires offering a warm welcome.
⚘ ❀ ◖◗ ▲ ♣ P

Hemsby

King's Head
North Road ☎ (0943) 730568
11–3, 6 (7 winter)–11
Courage Directors; John Smith's Bitter H**; Woodforde's Wherry, Nelson's Revenge** G
Pleasant, one-bar pub with real fires in both the bar and lounge. Occasional folk music.
⚘ Q ❀ ◖◗ ▲ P ⚡

Hethersett

King's Head
Norwich Road
☎ (0603) 810206
11–2.30, 5.30 (5 Fri, 6 Sat)–11
Courage Directors; Marston's Pedigree; Ruddles Best Bitter; Wadworth 6X; Webster's Yorkshire Bitter H**; guest beer**
Old, beamed village pub, parts of which date from 1620. The small bar is comfortable and features a 1950s brick inglenook and an old bottle collection; also a larger lounge and a dining area. Eve meals Fri and Sat only.
⚘ Q ❀ ◖◗ ♣ P

Heydon

Earle Arms
☎ (026 387) 376
11–3, 6.30–11
Adnams Bitter, Broadside; Greene King Abbot G
Unspoilt pub in a picturesque village. ⚘ ✿ ❀ ◖ ♣ P

Hilborough

Swan
On A1065 ☎ (076 06) 380
11 (10.30 Sat)–2.30, 6–11
Draught Bass; Greene King IPA, Abbot H**; guest beers**
Friendly roadside free house six miles south of Swaffham. The regularly changing guest beers usually include a mild.
⚘ Q ❀ 🛏 ◖◗ ♣ P

Try also: Windmill, Great Cressingham (Free)

Hockwold

New Inn
Station Road (B1112)
☎ (0842) 828668
11–3, 6–11; 11–11 Sat
Greene King IPA, Abbot H
17th-century coaching inn offering a relaxed atmosphere and a friendly welcome, plus good food. Traditional games include bar billiards. Active in local charities. No meals Sun eve. ⚘ ❀ 🛏 ◖◗ ▲ ♣ P

Holkham

Victoria
Park Road ☎ (0328) 710469
11–3, 7–11 (11–11 summer)
Greene King IPA; Marston's Pedigree H
Children are welcome in this circa 1820 pub on the edge of the Holkham Estate. Popular with tourists, the restaurant has a fine view over the marshes. Luxurious fireside seating. A bar area adjoins the restaurant and there is another small bar.
⚘ Q ❀ 🛏 ◖◗ ♣ P

Horsey

Nelson Head
The Street (just off B1159)
☎ (0493) 393378
11–2.30 (3 Sat), 7 (6 summer)–11
Adnams Bitter (summer)**; Woodforde's Wherry** H
Friendly, one-bar country pub with nautical artefacts. Popular with visitors to the marshes and Horsey Mill, and within walking distance of the Broads and beach. Austrian food is a speciality.
⚘ Q ✿ ❀ ◖◗ ♣ P

Hunworth

Hunny Bell
The Green ☎ (0263) 712300
10.30–3, 5.30–11
Adnams Bitter; Greene King Abbot; Woodforde's Wherry H
Long-established, welcoming free house on the green of a picturesque village. Good food. ⚘ ✿ ❀ ◖◗ P

Ingham

Swan
Sea Palling Road
☎ (0692) 581099
11–3, 6–11
Adnams Bitter; Mitchell's ESB; Woodforde's Wherry H**; guest beers**
Heavily restored, 14th-century, thatched country pub with exposed beams and old brickwork. Good local trade. No food Sun eve or Mon in winter.
⚘ Q ✿ 🛏 ◖◗ ♣ P

Try also: Kingfisher, Stalham (Free)

King's Lynn

Crossways
Valingers Road
☎ (0553) 771947
11–3, 7–11
Greene King XX Mild, IPA, Abbot H
Good example of a traditional street-corner local with a friendly welcome. ◖◗ ♣

Dukes Head Hotel (Lynn Bar)
Tuesday Market Place
☎ (0553) 774996
11–2.30, 6–11; closed Sun
Adnams Bitter; Draught Bass; Greene King Abbot H**; guest beer**
Friendly, small bar within an imposing Forte hotel overlooking the market place. Snacks, meals and accommodation in the hotel.
Q 🛏 ⇌

London Porterhouse
London Road ☎ (0553) 766842
11.30–2.30, 6–11
Greene King IPA, Abbot G
Small, popular town pub, close to the South Gate. The only gravity dispense in the area.
Q ❀ ♣

Tudor Rose
St Nicholas Street
☎ (0553) 762824
11–11
Adnams Bitter, Broadside; Draught Bass; Fuller's London Pride; Woodforde's Wherry H**; guest beers**
15th-century pub with panelled walls and oak beams, just off the historic Tuesday Market Place. The quiet front bar and more lively back bar often have different beers, including interesting guest ales. Q ❀ 🛏 ◖◗ ⇌

White Horse
9 Wootton Road, Gaywood
☎ (0553) 763258
11–3 (3.30 Sat), 6–11
Greene King IPA; John Smith's Bitter; Webster's Yorkshire Bitter H**; guest beers**
Busy, two-roomed town pub near the Gaywood Clock. No food, no frills, but lots of activity. ♣ P

Try also: Jolly Farmers, Wisbech Rd (Free); **Seven Sisters**, Extons Rd (Free)

Larling

Angel

On A11 ☎ (0953) 717963
11–2.30, 5–11; 11–11 Fri, Sat & when busy
Adnams Bitter; Charrington IPA; guest beer [H]
Outside appearances can be deceptive, for inside is an excellent local with a strong farming flavour. The beer range often offers surprises.
♛ Q ❀ 🛏 ◐
⇌ (Harling Rd) ♣ P

Martham

King's Arms

The Green ☎ (0493) 740204
11–11
Adnams Bitter, Broadside, Old [H]; guest beer
Large village local overlooking the green and duckpond; two bars and a pool room. Entertainment some Sat eves. Own bowling green. ☋ ❀ ♣ P

Mundesley

Royal Hotel

Paston Road ☎ (0263) 720096
11–2.30, 6–11
Adnams Bitter; Greene King IPA, Abbot [H]; guest beer
Dark, comfortable, beamed bar with an inglenook, plus a better lit lounge. The hotel itself has Nelson connections and has had royal patronage in the past. Worthington White Shield is available.
♛ ☋ ❀ 🛏 ◐ ◑ P

Try also: Manor Hotel (Free)

Neatishead

White Horse

The Street ☎ (0692) 630828
12–2.30 (11–3 summer), 6–11
Greene King IPA, Abbot; Tolly Cobbold Mild, Original [H]
Pub where the lower bar features wartime memorabilia. Restaurant at street level and chairs and tables at the front. A children's room is behind the pub. Friendly local atmosphere at the heart of a quiet village.
♛ ☋ ❀ 🛏 ◐ ◑ ♣ P

New Buckenham

King's Head

Market Place ☎ (0953) 860487
11.30–2.30, 7–11
Wadworth 6X; Whitbread Boddingtons Bitter [H]; guest beer
Welcoming, two-roomed pub on the village green. Good food (not served Mon).
♛ Q ❀ ◐ ◑ ♣

Try also: George (Pubmaster)

North Creake

Jolly Farmers

Burnham Road
☎ (0328) 738185
11–2.30 (3 Sat), 6–11
Greene King IPA [H], Abbot; Ind Coope Burton Ale [G]
A two-bar establishment with a big fireplace; the only surviving pub in the village. Home to an unusual artefact, namely a Max Bygraves gold disc! Worthington White Shield available. No food Mon. Family room open in summer.
♛ Q ☋ ❀ ◐ ◑ ♣ P

Try also: Ostrich, South Creake (Free)

North Walsham

Scarborough Hill House Hotel

Yarmouth Road
☎ (0692) 402151
11–3, 7–11
Bateman XB [G]; guest beer (occasionally)
Hotel with a bar and dining area, set in large grounds in rural surroundings on the outskirts of town.
Q ☋ ❀ 🛏 ◐ ◑ ▲ ♣ P

White Swan

Church Street ☎ (0692) 402354
10.30–3, 7–11
Courage Best Bitter; Webster's Yorkshire Bitter; Woodforde's Nelson's Revenge [H]
Busy local. Although the bar has been extended and opened out a little, the original style of decor has been retained.
❀ ▲ ⇌ ♣ P

Northwold

Crown

High Street ☎ (0366) 727317
12–2.30, 6–11; 11–11 Sat
Greene King IPA, Abbot [H]; guest beers
Recently opened, well-restored village local providing a variety of drinking areas, good food and guest ales.
❀ ◐ ◑ ♣ P

Try also: Crown, Mundford (Free)

North Wootton

Red Cat Hotel

Station Road ☎ (0553) 631244
11–2.30, 6–11
Adnams Bitter, Old; Draught Bass [H]
Refurbished village hotel with character; look out for the mummified cat. The house beer is brewed by Woodforde's. ♛ ❀ 🛏 ◐ ◑ ♣ P

Norwich

Catherine Wheel

St Augustines Street (between inner ring and Norwich pool)
☎ (0603) 627852
11–11
Adnams Bitter; Draught Bass; Ind Coope Burton Ale; Tetley Bitter [H]; guest beers
A drab exterior hides a bright and busy corner local with an attractive brick and beam interior; mind the well! Upstairs restaurant and bar meals. One mild amongst the guests. ◐ ◑

Champion

101 Chapelfield Road (near St Stephen's roundabout)
11–3, 7–11; 12–2, 7.30–10.30 Sun
Adnams Bitter, Old, Broadside, Tally Ho [H]; guest beer (summer)
Basic, three-bar, city-centre pub, popular with office workers at lunchtime. ⇌ ♣

Eaton Cottage

Mount Pleasant
☎ (0603) 53048
11–3, 5.30–11; 11–11 Sat
Courage Best Bitter; Marston's Pedigree; Samuel Smith OBB; Webster's Yorkshire Bitter [H]; guest beer
With probably the last snug in Norwich, this pub is rare in not being knocked-through. Live music Thu eve. ❀ ♣ P

Fat Cat

West End Street (100 yds from A47) ☎ (0603) 624364
12–3, 4.45–11; 11–11 Fri & Sat
Adnams Bitter; Fuller's London Pride; Wells Bombardier; Woodforde's Norfolk Nog [H]; guest beers
No frills, no jukebox, no food – just beer: 12 ales on offer, from all over the country, four on gravity. A blast from the past not to be missed. Live piano twice a week; folk night Thu.
❀ ♣ ⌓

Freemason's Arms

Hall Road (near inner ring)
☎ (0603) 623768
11–3 (4.30 Sat), 6 (7.30 Sat)–11
Woodforde's Mardler's Mild, Wherry, Nelson's Revenge, Norfolk Nog [H]
Busy single bar in a good drinking area, very popular at lunchtime. Good games. ♣

Gatehouse

Dereham Road (just outside ring) ☎ (0603) 620340
11.30–11
Bass Worthington BB, Draught Bass; M&B Highgate Mild; S&N Theakston Best Bitter, Old Peculier [H]; guest beers
Excellent riverside pub with a large garden, ideal in summer for families and barbecues.

Norfolk

Rebuilt from an old coaching house, burnt down in 1930, with much wood panelling in evidence. 🔥 Q ❀ ◖ ♿ ♣ P

Horse & Dray

137 Ber Street ☎ (0603) 624741

11–11

Adnams Mild, Bitter, Old, Broadside; guest beers Ⓗ

Comfortable, one-bar pub, close to the city shopping centre, offering two or three regularly changing guest beers. 🔥 ❀ ◖ ♣

Plasterers Arms

Cowgate (near Anglia Sq)

10.30–11; 12–2.30, 7–10.30 Sun

Adnams Mild, Bitter, Broadside; Everards Old Original; Ind Coope Burton Ale; Tetley Bitter Ⓗ

A dark scruffy interior freckled with star-like fairy lights sets the tone for this long-standing free house, recently acquired and unchanged by Adnams. Frequented by Norwich's more colourful inhabitants, attracted by the excellent ale and cheap food (not served Sun). Q ◖

Pottergate Tavern

Pottergate (200 yds N of City Hall) ☎ (0603) 614589

10.30–11

Draught Bass; Fuller's London Pride; Greene King XX Mild, IPA, Rayments Special, Abbot Ⓗ

City-centre, corner pub with an interesting 1930s exterior. The split-level interior features a semi-circular bar.
🐴 ◖ ♣ ⌓

Rosary Tavern

Rosary Road (near yacht and rail stations) ☎ (0603) 666287

11–3, 5.30–11

Adnams Bitter; Bateman XXXB; Marston's Pedigree; Woodforde's Wherry Ⓗ; **guest beers** Ⓗ/Ⓖ

Small but friendly pub with a new extension fronting the enclosed rear garden. Crib is very popular, so is darts. Some ten or so real ales are usually on offer, many drawn from cellar casks.
🐴 ❀ ◖ ≢ ♣ ⌓ P

St Andrew's Tavern

St Andrew's Street (250 yds N of market place)
☎ (0603) 614858

11–11; closed Sun

Adnams Mild, Bitter, Broadside, Tally Ho; Robinson's Best Bitter; Wadworth 6X Ⓗ; **guest beer**

Popular city-centre pub near St Andrew's Hall, decorated with pub signs and other breweriana. Public car park opposite. Q 🐴 ❀ ◖ ♣

Tap & Spile (White Lion)

Oak Street ☎ (0603) 620630

11–11

Beer range varies Ⓗ

Pub focusing on beer, with a changing selection of up to 11 and probably the best value in the city. Bar billiards and live music. 🔥 ♣ ⌓ P

Windmill

Knox Road (off B1140, near prison) ☎ (0603) 34531

11–2.30, 6–11

Greene King XX Mild, IPA, Rayments Special, Abbot Ⓗ

Two-bar local built in 1921, with a 1930s extension that houses the large, well-lit public bar. The lounge is smaller but comfortable. Barbecues summer weekends.
❀ ◖ ⊟ ♿ ≢ ♣ P

Old Buckenham

Ox & Plough

The Green ☎ (0953) 860004

12–2.30, 5–11; 11–11 Sat

Adnams Bitter; Greene King IPA Ⓗ; **guest beers** (summer)

Friendly free house in a picturesque setting on the green. Up to five guest beers.
🔥 🐴 ❀ ◖ ◗ ♿ ▲ ♣ P

Old Hunstanton

Ancient Mariner

Golf Course Road (off A149)
☎ (0485) 534411

11–3, 6–11; 11–11 Sat

Adnams Bitter, Broadside; Draught Bass Ⓗ; **guest beers**

Large bar attached to the Le Strange Arms Hotel. Sensitive division of the drinking area helps retain a pub-like atmosphere. Large garden and well-equipped family room, plus good food.
🔥 🐴 ❀ 🛏 ◖ ◗ ♣ P

Try also: Lodge, Cromer Rd; **Neptune**, Cromer Rd (both Free)

Ormesby St Margaret

Grange Hotel

On Caister bypass (A149)
☎ (0493) 731877

12–11

Adnams Bitter; Bateman XXXB; Charrington IPA Ⓗ; **guest beers**

Former 18th-century country house, now a hotel. Families are well catered for, with a pets corner and good-sized garden. Pool area off the lounge; children's pool table in the family room.
🔥 Q 🐴 ❀ 🛏 ◖ ◗ ▲ ♣ P

Jolly Farmers

West Road (off crossroads in village centre) ☎ (0493) 730471

11.30–11

Adnams Bitter; Ruddles Best Bitter, County; Webster's Yorkshire Bitter Ⓗ

Not easy to find, but worth seeking out. A popular village local with a single bar divided into areas; comfortable seating. The garden has a children's play area. ❀ ◖ ◗ ♣ P

Try also: First & Last, Caister bypass (Whitbread)

Oxborough

Bedingfield Arms

☎ (0366) 21300

12–3, 5 (7 Sat)–11

Beer range varies Ⓗ

Village free house opposite the historic Oxborough Hall, serving an ever-changing range of guest beers. No food Mon eve. ❀ ◖ ◗ ♣ P

Reedham

Railway Tavern

Havaker
☎ (0493) 700340

12–3, 7–11; 11–11 Sat

Greene King IPA Ⓗ; **guest beers**

Two-bar pub and restaurant by the Norwich/Yarmouth line at Reedham station. Comfortable family accommodation, and a secluded garden. Kingfisher cider in summer.
🔥 ❀ 🛏 ◖ ◗ ≢ ♣ ⌓ P

Reepham

Old Brewery House

Market Square
☎ (0603) 870881

11–3, 6 (may vary)–11

Adnams Bitter, Old; Greene King Abbot; Reepham Rapier; Whitbread Boddingtons Bitter Ⓗ; **guest beers**

Fine old building overlooking the market square with genuine beams and wood-panelled rooms. The food is well recommended. Popular with locals and visitors.
Q 🐴 ❀ 🛏 ◖ ◗

Try also: Kings Arms, Market Sq (Free)

Ringstead

Gin Trap

High Street ☎ (048 525) 264

11.30–2.30, 7 (6 summer)–11

Adnams Bitter; Draught Bass; Greene King Abbot; Woodforde's Norfolk Nog Ⓗ; **guest beers**

Village pub with a split-level bar and a pleasant garden. The decor reflects the pub name. A house beer is also available.
🔥 ❀ ◖ ◗ ♣ P

Rockland St Mary

New Inn
New Inn Hill ☎ (050 88) 395
12 (11 summer)–3, 7.30 (6 summer)–11
Greene King Abbot; Tetley Bitter; Whitbread Flowers IPA; guest beers Ⓗ
Comfortable, friendly local on the eastern edge of the village with boat moorings opposite and good walks for ramblers.
🏰 Q ☺ ❀ ◑ ◗ ♣ P

Sedgeford

King William IV
Heacham Road (B1454)
☎ (0485) 71765
11–3, 5.30 (7 winter)–11
Draught Bass; M&B Highgate Mild Ⓗ; guest beers
Never a dull moment in this lively village local which caters for most tastes. Good value food and a wide range of guest beers make it worth a detour from the coast or the nearby Peddars Way footpath. Cider in summer.
🏰 ❀ ◑ ◗ ♣ ⌓ P

Sheringham

Two Lifeboats Hotel
High Street ☎ (0263) 822401
10–11
Greene King IPA, Rayments Special, Abbot Ⓗ
Two-bar hotel which is comfortable, slightly rambling and reputedly haunted. Good view of the sea from the outside drinking area. Worthington White Shield available. ❀ 🛏 ◑ ◗ ⇌ ♣

Try also: Sea View Hotel, High St (Free)

Smallburgh

Crown
North Walsham Road
☎ (0692) 536314
11.30–2.30, 5.30–11; 12–4, 7–11 Sat
Greene King IPA, Abbot; Tetley Bitter; Tolly Cobbold Mild Ⓗ
Thatched, beamed building which dates from the 15th century and features a large open fire, and tables and chairs made from wooden barrels and firkins. A friendly local, offering good food. Attractive dining room (no food Sun eve).
🏰 Q ☺ ❀ 🛏 ◑ ◗ ⊟ ♣ P

Southery

Jolly Farmers
Feltwell Road (B1386)
☎ (036 66) 327
11–2.30, 6–11
Adnams Bitter; Greene King IPA, Abbot Ⓗ
Welcoming, 1960s family pub with excellent bar and restaurant meals always available at very reasonable prices. Beware the precipitous entrance to the car park!
❀ ◑ ◗ P

South Walsham

Ship Inn
The Street ☎ (060 549) 553
11–3, 6–11; 11–11 Sat
Ruddles Best Bitter; Woodforde's Wherry Ⓗ
Cosy village pub with a traditional brick and beam interior in both bars. Good imaginative food.
🏰 ☺ ❀ ◑ ◗ ▲ ♣ P

South Wootton

Farmers Arms
Knights Hill Village (A148)
☎ (0553) 675566
11–11
Adnams Bitter, Broadside; Draught Bass; Ruddles County; Samuel Smith OBB Ⓗ; guest beers
Well-executed barn conversion at Knights Hill Village complex on the King's Lynn ring road. The sports complex, hotel and conference centre (which stage many special events) ensure the large bar is often very busy. 🏰 Q ☺ ❀ 🛏 ◑ ◗ ♿ ▲ P

Stanhoe

Crown
On B1155 ☎ (0485) 518330
11–3, 6–11
Elgood's Cambridge Bitter Ⓗ, GSB Ⓖ
Small, friendly village local, frequented by the farming community, and popular with visitors to the area, especially birdwatchers. Eve meals to order only. Camping for CC members. 🏰 Q ❀ ◑ ♣

Stibbard

Ordnance Arms
Guist Bottom (A1067, 1 mile NW of Guist) ☎ (032 878) 471
11–2.30, 5.30–11
Greene King IPA Ⓗ; guest beer
Two-bar pub hosted by a friendly landlord. Snacks lunchtimes and Thai food in the restaurant eves. A good country local. 🏰 ❀ P

Stiffkey

Red Lion
Wells Road ☎ (0328) 830552
11–2.30 (3 Sat & winter), 6–11
Greene King IPA, Abbot Ⓗ; Woodforde's Wherry Ⓗ/Ⓖ; guest beers
Superb pub with open fires and separate bars, in an unspoilt village which attracts ramblers on the coastal walks. Re-opened in 1990 after 20 years as a private house – one of three former pubs in the village which were victims of the Watney revolution. 🏰 Q ☺ ❀ ◑ ◗ ⊟ ♿ ▲ ♣ P

Swanton Abbot

Weavers Arms
Aylsham Road
☎ (069 269) 655
11–3 (5 Sat), 7–11
Adnams Bitter, Old, Broadside Ⓗ
Quiet, unspoilt country pub with beams and an open fire. Old agricultural implements adorn the walls.
🏰 Q ☺ ❀ ◑ ◗ ⊟ ♣ P

Swanton Morley

Darby's
Elsing Road ☎ (0362) 637647
11–2.30, 6–11
Adnams Bitter, Broadside; Woodforde's Mardler's Mild, Wherry Ⓗ; guest beers
Friendly village pub converted from two cottages, with a farming theme. Four guest beers.
🏰 Q ☺ ❀ 🛏 ◑ ◗ ♿ ▲ ♣ P

Thetford

Albion
Castle Street ☎ (0842) 752796
11–2.30, 6–11; 11–11 Fri; 12–2, 7–10.30 Sun
Greene King IPA, Abbot Ⓗ
Small, friendly local set amongst flint-faced cottages in the older part of town, near the Castle Hill monument. This no-frills pub has consistently offered a low-priced bitter. Q ❀ ◑ P

Try also: Bell Hotel, King St (Free); **Black Horse,** Magdalen St (Inntrepreneur)

Thompson

Chequers
Griston Road OS922969
☎ (095 383) 360
11–3, 6–11
Adnams Bitter; Draught Bass; Fuller's London Pride Ⓗ; guest beers
Friendly, 16th-century, thatched pub boasting an ancient inn sign. Close to the Peddars Way long distance path; excellent reputation for good value food. Kingfisher cider in summer. The family room is very small.
☺ ❀ ◑ ◗ ♿ ♣ ⌓ P

Thornham

Lifeboat Inn
Ship Lane (off A149)
☎ (048 526) 236
11–11

Adnams Bitter, Broadside [H]; **Greene King XX Mild** [G], **IPA, Abbot** [H]; **guest beers**
Although much extended in recent years, this old smugglers' inn retains much of its atmosphere, partly due to the oil lamp lighting. Popular for food and accommodation, and often very busy in summer. Ask for the mild.
♨ Q ♉ ❀ ⊟ ◖ ◗ ♣ P

Thorpe Marriott

Otter
Acres Way ☎ (0603) 260455
11.30–3, 5.30–11
Greene King XX Mild, IPA, Rayments Special, Abbot [H]
New, multi-level pub with an Edwardian decor, built as part of the Thorpe Marriott development. Theme nights once a month; quiz nights Tue; bar billiards. No eve meals Sun. ❀ ◖ ◗ ♣ P ⊬

Thorpe St Andrew

Gordon
Gordon Avenue
☎ (0603) 34658
11–2.30, 7–11
Greene King IPA, Abbot; Ind Coope Burton Ale; Tetley Bitter [H]
Friendly local with a long, curved single bar. ❀ ♣ P

Tibenham

Greyhound
The Street ☎ (037 977) 676
12–3 (not Mon–Fri), 7–11
Beer range varies [H]
Two-bar village pub which is worth finding. The pub games are plentiful and varied and the family room is open in summer. Camping in the pub grounds. ♨ ♉ ❀ ▲ ♣ P

Titchwell

Three Horseshoes
Main Road ☎ (0485) 210202
11–3, 6–11
Adnams Bitter; Draught Bass [H]; **guest beers**
Situated on the north Norfolk coastal road and a welcome stop for travellers, with accommodation, good food and a welcome for families to complement the guest beers.
♨ Q ♉ ❀ ⊟ ◖ ◗ ♣ P

Toft Monks

Toft Lion
Beccles Road (A143)
☎ (050 277) 702
11.30–2.30, 6.30–11
Adnams Bitter; Draught Bass [H]; **guest beers**
Comfortable, friendly local with many agricultural implements on the walls. A good country pub offering reasonably-priced, home-cooked food and comfortable accommodation.
No food Tue eve in winter.
♨ Q ♉ ❀ ⊟ ◖ ◗ ♿ ▲ ♣ P

Walcott

Lighthouse
Coast Road ☎ (0692) 650371
11–3, 6.30–11
Adnams Bitter; Ind Coope Burton Ale; Tetley Bitter [H]; **guest beer** (occasionally)
Very popular pub with locals and holidaymakers: barbecue and children's disco Tue eve in summer. Good value food; separate dining area.
♨ ♉ ❀ ◖ ◗ ▲ ♣ P

Warham

Three Horseshoes
The Street ☎ (0328) 701547
11–2.30 (3 summer), 6–11; 11–11 Sat
Greene King IPA, Abbot; Woodforde's Wherry, Nelson's Revenge (summer) [G]
Old village pub with basic decor and some unusual artefacts, including a 1921 electric pianola (played Sat). Food made with local produce.
♨ Q ♉ ❀ ⊟ ◖ ◗ ▲ ♣ P

Weasenham All Saints

Ostrich
On A1065 ☎ (032 874) 221
11–3, 7–11
Adnams Bitter, Broadside [H]
Cosy pub with a large fireplace. Worthington White Shield and fruit and veg are also sold. ♨ Q ❀ ♣ P

Wells-next-the-Sea

Crown Hotel
The Buttlands ☎ (0328) 710209
11–2.30, 6–11; 12–2.30, 7–10.30 Sun
Adnams Bitter; Marston's Pedigree; Tetley Bitter (summer) [H]
A coaching inn since the 18th century; a fine hotel, facing a tree-lined green. The Tudor building has a Georgian facade. ♨ ♉ ❀ ⊟ ◖ ◗ ♿ P

West Rudham

Dukes Head
Lynn Road ☎ (0485) 528540
11–3, 6.30–11; 12–2.30, 7–10.30 Sun
Adnams Bitter; Woodforde's Wherry [H]; **guest beer**
Old pub which was extended (upwards) in the 17th century, giving rise to an unusual flint, brick and Carrstone facade. The interior is cosy, with a half-panelled back bar.
♨ Q ❀ ◖ ◗ ♿ ♣ P

Whinburgh

Mustard Pot
The Street ☎ (0362) 692179
11–3, 6.30–11
Woodforde's Wherry [H]; **guest beer**
Converted 17th-century houses and shop, making a long, narrow bar. A nice, friendly local. ♨ ❀ ◖ ◗ ♣ P

Wimbotsham

Chequers
Church Road ☎ (0366) 387704
11.45–2.30, 6–11
Greene King XX Mild, IPA, Abbot [H]
Friendly local off the A10, just north of Downham Market.
Q ♉ ❀ ◖ ◗ ▲ ♣ P

Winterton-on-Sea

Fishermans Return
The Lane ☎ (0493) 393305
11–2.30, 6 (7 winter)–11
Adnams Bitter; Webster's Yorkshire Bitter [H]; **guest beers** [H]/[G]
Popular two-bar local near the beach, serving good value food. The lounge bar has a cosy feel with lots of beams (mind the headcracker) and brasses. Wood panelling and local photographs in the bar. House beer from Adnams.
♨ Q ♉ ❀ ◖ ◗ ♣ P

Woodbastwick

Fur & Feather
½ mile from Salhouse village, off B1140 ☎ (0603) 720003
11–3, 6–11
Woodforde's Mardler's Mild, Broadsman, Wherry, Porter, Nelson's Revenge, Norfolk Nog, Headcracker [G]
Brewery tap in an idyllic setting with views across to the bowling green. A pub converted from thatched cottages with a traditional brick, beam and plaster interior. Excellent food. Spring water from the brewery borehole is on sale. ◖ ◗ ♿ P

Woodton

King's Head
Hempnall Road
☎ (050 844) 329
11–3, 6–11; 11–11 Sat
Greene King IPA [H]
Single-bar pub in a row of converted cottages.
Q ❀ ◖ ◗ ▲ ♣ P

Wymondham

Feathers
Town Green ☎ (0953) 605675
11–2.30, 7 (6 Fri & Sat)–11
Adnams Bitter; Draught Bass; Greene King Abbot [H]; **guest beer**
Busy, friendly local with one, beamed bar and a good atmosphere, serving a good selection of home-cooked food. House beer from Reepham. Decorated with old farming implements. ❀ ◖ ⇶ ♁

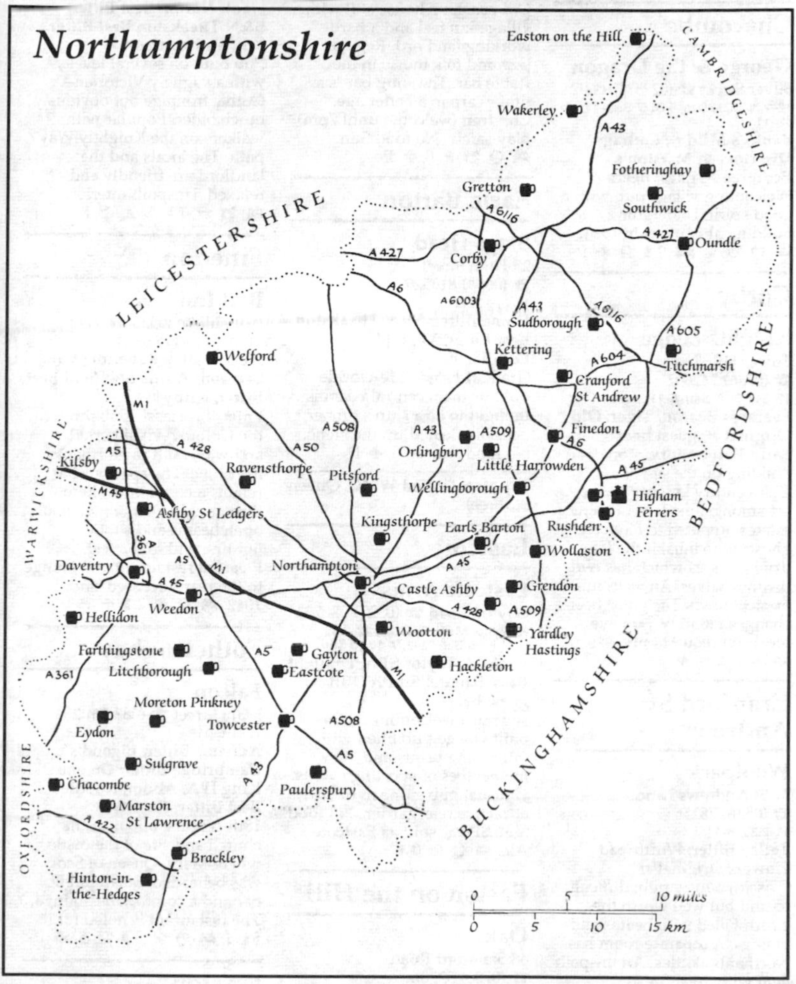

Nene Valley, Higham Ferrers

Ashby St Ledgers

Old Coach House Inn

☎ (0788) 890349
12–2.30, 6–11

Everards Old Original; Holden's Special; Maclay Scotch Ale; Sarah Hughes Ruby Mild; Whitbread Flowers Original Ⓗ; guest beers

The quintessential country pub, with real fires, wood-panelling and a large, attractive garden. A pub with real character, winter or summer. Month-long beer festival twice a year. Prices are the same in both bars.
♛ Q ♞ ❀ ⛿ ◐ ◑ ♣ P

Try also: White Horse, Welton (Free)

Brackley

Red Lion

11 Market Place
☎ (0280) 702225
11–3, 5.30–11; 11–11 Fri & Sat

Wells Eagle, Bombardier Ⓗ; guest beers

Stone-built pub dating from the 16th century, situated on a corner of the market square. A public bar with pool table leads on to a rear lounge and snug. The Red Lion golf society meets regularly. Live music most Fris. Licensed garden for summer parties. ♛ ❀ ◐ ▣ ♣

Try also: Greyhound & Bell, High St (Courage)

Castle Ashby

Falcon

☎ (0604) 696200
12–3, 7–11

Adnams Bitter; Hook Norton Old Hooky; Nix Wincott Two Henrys Ⓗ

Smart country hotel and restaurant in a preserved village on the Marquess of Northampton's estate. The attractive bar has exposed beams, stone walls and an open fire; on the ground floor there is a restaurant. Also a cellar bar. Q ❀ ⛿ ◐ ◑ P

Northamptonshire

Chacombe

George & the Dragon

Silver Street ☎ (0295) 710602
12–2.30 (3.30 Sat), 5.30 (7 Sat)–11; 12–11 Fri
Banks's Mild [H]; Courage Directors [G]; Marston's Pedigree [H]; guest beers
Welcoming village pub with a good spirit. Undergoing building alterations in 1994.
♛ Q ♞ ❀ 🛏 ◐ ◑ ⊟ ♣ P

Corby

Knights Lodge

Tower Hill Road
☎ (0536) 742602
12–3 (4 Fri & Sat), 6–11
Everards Beacon, Tiger, Old Original [H]; guest beer
Early 17th-century, stone building on the site of a 12th-century knights' lodge, set amongst modern housing estates. Reputed to have eight ghosts who inhabit the long drinking area which has two distinct halves. An oasis in an ex-steel town. The guest beer changes monthly. Sun eve meals on request only.
♛ ❀ ◐ ◑ ♿ ♣ P

Cranford St Andrew

Woolpack

17 St Andrews Lane
☎ (0536) 78256
11–2.30, 6–11
Tetley Bitter; Whitbread Flowers Original [H]
Classic country pub; difficult to find but well worth the effort. Filled with beams and brasses. A separate room has Northants skittles. An unspoilt gem with open fires.
♛ Q ❀ ⊟ ♣ P

Daventry

Coach & Horses

Warwick Street
☎ (0327) 76692
11–2.30 (12–3 Sat), 5 (4.30 Fri, 5 Sat)–11
Ind Coope Burton Ale; Marston's Pedigree; Tetley Bitter [H]
Old coaching inn close to the town centre, with a friendly atmosphere, more like a village local. Open quiz night on Sun; live jazz in the stable bar every other Thu. No food Sat or Sun. ♛ Q ❀ ◐ ♣

Dun Cow

Brook Street ☎ (0327) 71545
10.30–2.30 (5 Sat), 5.30 (7 Sat)–11; 10.30–11 Fri
Greenalls Davenports Bitter, Thomas Greenall's Original [H]
Old coaching house still with a village inn feel and a hard-working landlord. Regular jazz and folk music in the stable bar. The snug bar is a time-warp to a better age. Children (welcome until 7pm) play safely. No food Sun.
♛ Q ♞ ❀ ◐ ♣ P

Earls Barton

Stags Head

25 High Street
☎ (0604) 810520
11–3, 6.30–11
Home Bitter; S&N Theakston Best Bitter, XB, Old Peculier [H]
Grade II-listed olde-worlde pub. Its main central beam is thought to be a ship's timber, possibly floated up the Nene. No food Sun. ❀ ◐ ♣ P

Try also: United WMC, Queen St (Free)

Eastcote

Eastcote Arms

Gayton Road ☎ (0327) 830731
12–2 (not Mon), 6–10.30; 12–2.30, 6–11 Fri & Sat; 12–2, 7–10.30 Sun
Banks & Taylor SPA; Draught Bass; Samuel Smith OBB [H]; guest beers
A gem: a welcoming, stone-built village pub filled with interesting prints and mementoes of sporting events. Unusual pub game in the bar; attractive rear garden. No food Sun. SPA is sold as Eastcote Ale. ♛ Q ❀ ◐ P

Easton on the Hill

Oak

48 Stamford Road
☎ (0780) 52286
11–3, 7–11
Greene King IPA, Abbot [H]; guest beer
One-bar pub on the A43, with a popular restaurant. Features a Collyweston slate roof.
Q ❀ ◐ ◑ ♿ ▲ P

Eydon

Royal Oak

Lime Avenue ☎ (0327) 60470
11–2.30, 6.30–11
Hook Norton Best Bitter [H]; guest beer
Small village pub, basically unchanged for the last 30–40 years. Several small rooms, all different. Northants skittles played. ♛ Q ♞ ❀ ⊟ ♣ P

Farthingstone

Kings Arms

☎ (032 736) 604
11–3, 6–11
Hook Norton Best Bitter; S&N Theakston Best Bitter, XB; Wadworth 6X [H]
Pub built on several levels, with a vaguely Victorian–Gothic frontage but obviously much older. Popular with walkers on the Knightly Way path. The locals and the landlord are friendly and relaxed. Unspoilt interior.
♛ ♞ ❀ ◐ ◑ ♿ ▲ ♣ P

Finedon

Bell Inn

Bell Hill ☎ (0933) 680332
11.30–3, 5.30 (6 Sat)–11
Nene Valley Rawhide; Vaux Samson; Wards Sheffield Best Bitter, Kirby [H]
Enter this classic pub through the Gothic-revival period archway, built in Northants ironstone. The spacious bar retains a cosy atmosphere throughout; a large inglenook, open beams and subtle lighting add to the feel. Pleasant restaurant and lounge to the rear. Licensed since 1042. ♛ Q ❀ ◐ ◑ ♣ P

Fotheringhay

Falcon

Main Street ☎ (083 26) 254
10–3, 6–11
Adnams Bitter; Elgood's Cambridge Bitter; Greene King IPA, Abbot; Ruddles Best Bitter, County [H]
18th-century pub near the church and site of the castle where Mary, Queen of Scots, was beheaded. Small public bar and a comfortable lounge. The restaurant is noted for its food. ♛ Q ❀ ◐ ◑ ⊟ ♿ ♣ P

Gayton

Eykyn Arms

20 High Street
☎ (0604) 858361
11–2 (3 Sat), 5.30 (7 Oct–Apr)–11; 12–2.30, 7–10.30 Sun
Wells Eagle [H]; guest beer
Village local. The small front lounge has a nautical and aviation theme. The long bar has Northants skittles. Covered patio with a small room adjacent for families.
♛ Q ♞ ❀ ◐ ♿ ♣ P

Grendon

Half Moon

42 Main Road ☎ (0933) 663263
12–3 (4 Sat), 6 (6.30 Sat)–11
Adnams Broadside; Hall & Woodhouse Tanglefoot; Wells Eagle, Bombardier [H]
Comfortable, 18th-century thatched pub with exposed original beams: a friendly

village local offering a warm welcome. No food Sun.
♨ ⚲ ❀ ◑ ♿ ♣ P

Gretton

Talbot

33 High Street
☎ (0536) 771609
11.30–2.30, 7–11
Adnams Bitter; Everards Tiger Ⓗ
17th-century, stone-built former farmhouse with a very friendly atmosphere. Northants skittles match every Sat eve.
♨ ❀ ⛟ ◑ ⊟ ♿ ♣ P

Hackleton

White Hart

80 Main Road
☎ (0604) 870271
11–3, 6–11
Ruddles Best Bitter; S&N Theakston XB; Webster's Yorkshire Bitter Ⓗ
Stone-built pub whose history goes back to 1739. The two-tier lounge has a 40-ft well built into the bar. The public bar has an inglenook and Northants skittles. Excellent food (not served Sun); large garden at the rear. Children welcome in the lounge.
Q ❀ ◑ ◗ ♣ P

Hellidon

Red Lion

On the Catesby road
☎ (0327) 61200
12–3, 7–11
Courage Directors; Hook Norton Best Bitter; Ruddles Best Bitter Ⓗ
A city-dweller's idea of what a country pub ought to be, but none the worse for that. A smart, dimly-lit lounge with an inglenook, a large bar and a restaurant serving four types of good English sausage. Looks out over pleasant countryside. Friendly but professional service.
♨ ❀ ⛟ ◑ ◗ ⊟ ▲ ♣ P

Higham Ferrers

Green Dragon Hotel

4 College Street
☎ (0933) 312088
11.30–11
Fuller's London Pride, ESB; Ruddles Best Bitter, County; Thwaites Bitter Ⓗ**; guest beers**
Typical small market town hotel with 12 real ales permanently available. The quiet back room overlooks the garden. The upstairs function room is to be converted into a gallery bar. No food Sun eve.
♨ Q ⚲ ❀ ⛟ ◑ ◗ P

Hinton-in-the-Hedges

Crewe Arms

☎ (0280) 703314
11.30–2.30, 6.30–11
Hook Norton Best Bitter; Marston's Pedigree; Morland Old Speckled Hen Ⓗ**; guest beer**
Stone-built pub tucked away at the centre of a remote village. Three bars, all with their own character, one featuring a tank of terrapins. Selection of fruit and country wines. A lovely pub with open fires and wood beams.
♨ Q ❀ ◗ ⊟ ♣ P

Kettering

Old Market Inn

Market Place ☎ (0536) 310311
11–2.30 (3 market days), 5–11
S&N Theakston Old Peculier; Younger IPA Ⓗ**; guest beers**
Modernised old pub and restaurant opposite the market place. The enterprising landlord holds occasional mini-beer festivals. Popular with younger drinkers. No food Sun. ◑ ◗ ♿ ⇌

Try also: Cherry Tree, Sheep St (Wells)

Kilsby

Red Lion

Main Road ☎ (0788) 822265
12–3, 7–11
Adnams Bitter; Hook Norton Best Bitter; Marston's Pedigree; Morland Old Speckled Hen; Wadworth 6X Ⓗ**; guest beers**
Around 150 years old, this building replaced an original thatched pub destroyed by fire. Popular with locals in the evening for pool, skittles and games; also with diners. Regular beer festivals often have a theme, e.g. Black Country (with food to match).
♨ ❀ ◑ ◗ ♿ ♣ P ⊬

Kingsthorpe

Queen Adelaide

50 Manor Road
☎ (0604) 714524
11–2.30 (3 Sat), 5.30–11; 12–2.30, 7–10.30 Sun
Banks's Bitter; Morland Old Speckled Hen; Ruddles Best Bitter; Wadworth 6X Ⓗ
Cosy, popular pub in old Kingsthorpe village; a Grade II-listed building dating back to 1640. The public bar retains its original ceiling and panelling with photographs of the old village. Separate Northants skittles room. Home-cooked lunches Mon–Sat; Sandra's omelettes are a speciality. Q ❀ ◑ ♣ P

Litchborough

Old Red Lion

4 Banbury Road
☎ (0327) 830250
11.30–2.30 (3 Sat; not Mon), 6.30–11
Banks's Bitter Ⓔ
Small country pub where the main room is dominated by a large inglenook and the huge Great Dane whose rosettes hang behind the bar. Pool and Northants skittles. No food Sun or Mon.
♨ Q ❀ ◑ ◗ ♣ P

Little Harrowden

Lamb

Orlingbury Road
☎ (0933) 673300
11–2.30 (3 Sat), 6–11
Wells Eagle, Bombardier Ⓗ**; guest beers**
Pleasant village pub with a cosy, oak-beamed lounge and a good bar with Northants skittles. Advance booking is required for the popular menu; traditional roast only for Sun lunch; no food Sun eve. Live jazz on first Sat of summer months.
♨ ❀ ◑ ◗ ⊟ ♣ P

Try also: Ten O'Clock, Main St (Wells)

Marston St Lawrence

Marston Inn

☎ (0295) 711906
12–2.30 (not Mon Oct–Easter), 7–11
Hook Norton Best Bitter, Old Hooky Ⓗ
Small, friendly out-of-the-way village pub converted from a row of cottages. Three rooms, one serving as a dining room; good home cooking. No food Sun or Mon eves.
♨ Q ❀ ◑ ◗ ♣ ⌓ P

Moreton Pinkney

Old House at Home

The Green ☎ (0295) 760353
11–11
Draught Bass; Morrells Bitter; Tetley Bitter; Wychwood Best Ⓗ
Typical local in a 17th-century farmhouse: until recently a rather scruffy and run-down village pub now being developed by the cheerful landlady and her family. Much money being spent but no harm done yet – rather the opposite. Outside drinking is on the village green.
♨ ⚲ ❀ ⛟ ◑ ◗ ♿ ▲ ♣ P

Northamptonshire

Northampton

Barn Owl
Olden Road, Rectory Farm
☎ (0604) 416483
12–3, 6–11
Greene King IPA, Abbot [H]
A great estate pub, the only Greene King pub in Northampton. Winner of CAMRA's *Best New Pub* award in 1986. One large bar on two levels. ❀ ☾ ♿ ♣ ⌓ P

Cricketers
43 Hervey Street
☎ (0604) 35009
6 (11 Fri & Sat)–11
Hall & Woodhouse Tanglefoot; Wells Eagle [H]**; guest beer**
Back-street local near the racecourse. Live music Fri and Sun, plus quizzes and comedy acts. Cricketers FC has been linked to the pub for 25 years. Fri night curries. Note: lunch opening Fri–Sun only.
♛ ❀ ♣

Crown & Cushion
276 Wellingborough Road
☎ (0604) 33937
11–11
Banks's Bitter; Ruddles Best Bitter [H]**; Webster's Yorkshire Bitter** [G]
Friendly town pub: a large U-shaped bar with a well-used games area to one side. Always busy, particularly weekends, and popular with all ages. Safe, well-equipped play garden. ❀ ♿ ♣

Victoria Inn
2 Poole Street
☎ (0604) 33660
11–2.30, 5.30–11; 11–11 Sat
Draught Bass; Fuller's London Pride; Hook Norton Best Bitter [H]**; guest beers**
Street-corner local (re-opened in 1989), with traditional wood panelling. Close ties with local rugby clubs and handy for after-game drinks. The premier real ale outlet for Northampton. The Bass and Hook Norton alternate; six guest beers. ☾ ♣

Try also: Pioneer, Hazeldene Rd (Courage)

Orlingbury

Queen's Arms
11 Isham Road
☎ (0933) 678258
11.30–2.30, 5.30–11
Draught Bass; Fuller's London Pride; Hook Norton Best Bitter; Marston's Pedigree; Morland Old Speckled Hen; S&N Theakston XB [H]**; guest beers**
Expanding rural local which concentrates on pleasing the real ale aficionado. A mild is always included amongst the three guest beers. Gravity dispense is sometimes available for beers not advertised. Quiet, sheltered garden. Meals Mon–Fri.
♛ Q ❀ ☾ ♣ P

Oundle

Ship Inn
West Street
☎ (0832) 273918
11–3, 6–11; 11–11 Sat
Draught Bass; Marston's Pedigree; Morrells Varsity [H]**; guest beers**
Large, multi-roomed pub, a stone-built former tea room with a low-beamed ceiling.
♛ ❀ 🛏 ☾ ◗ ⊞ ♿ P

Paulerspury

Barley Mow
53 High Street
☎ (0327) 33260
12–3, 7–11
Everards Tiger; Marston's Pedigree; Ruddles Best Bitter; Webster's Yorkshire Bitter [H]**; guest beers**
Open-plan pub and restaurant with lots of wood and stone. The L-shaped bar has plenty of atmosphere; games room upstairs. A large inglenook in the bar is frequently in use. Rebecca, the ghost, is rumoured to appear on occasions.
♛ ❀ 🛏 ☾ ◗ ♣ P

Pitsford

Griffin
High Street ☎ (0604) 880346
12–2.30 (3 Sat; not Mon), 6–11
S&N Theakston Best Bitter, XB, Old Peculier [H]
Listed, stone-built village local; friendly, pleasant and relaxing. ❀ ⊞ P

Ravensthorpe

Chequers
Church Lane
☎ (0604) 770379
11–3, 6–11
Bateman XB; Fuller's London Pride; Samuel Smith OBB; Thwaites Bitter [H]**; guest beers**
One of the county's few free houses, set in rolling countryside and well worth finding. The beamed, single, L-shaped bar is adorned with a vast collection of bric-a-brac creating a warm, cosy atmosphere. Excellent value food and beer.
Q ⛍ ❀ ☾ ◗ ♣ P

Rushden

Feathers
High Street
☎ (0933) 50251
11.30–3, 6–11; 11–11 Sat
Adnams Broadside; Hall & Woodhouse Tanglefoot; Wells Eagle, Bombardier [H]
Typical town-centre pub. The rear lounge overlooks a large patio and garden; smart wood-panelled bar. Sun eve quiz. No food Sun.
♛ ❀ ☾ ♣ P

Try also: King Edward VII, Queen St (Wells)

Southwick

Shuckburgh Arms
☎ (0832) 27400
11–2.30, 6–11
Adnams Bitter; Hook Norton Best Bitter, Old Hooky; Taylor Landlord [G]**; guest beers**
Classic, unspoilt 16th-century village local: a basic bar and a cosy lounge, with bar billiards in the passage.
♛ Q ❀ ⊞ ▲ ♣ P

Sudborough

Vane Arms
Main Street
☎ (0832) 733223
11.30–3 (not Mon), 5.30 (6 Sat)–11
Draught Bass [H]**; guest beers**
Deservedly popular, old thatched village free house with stonework and beams throughout the basic bar and plusher lounge. Small upstairs restaurant. Eight changing guest beers with Belgian fruit beers always on draught, plus Old Rosie cider. Sample tray for tastes. Local CAMRA *Pub of the Year* 1992.
♛ ❀ 🛏 ☾ ◗ ⊞ ♣ ⌓ P

Sulgrave

Star
Manor Road (follow signs to Sulgrave Manor)
☎ (0295) 760389
11–2.30, 6–11
Hook Norton Mild, Best Bitter, Old Hooky [H]
Single-room village pub with stone floors and beams. Framed newspapers adorn the wall, along with chalked-up competitions and the historic events of the day from the landlord. The thinnest customer is George – the skeleton in the corner. No food Sun eve.
♛ Q ❀ 🛏 ☾ ◗ ♿ P

Titchmarsh

Dog & Partridge

6 High Street ☎ (0832) 732546
11.30–2.30, 6–11
Adnams Broadside; Wells Eagle, Bombardier Ⓗ; guest beers
18th-century pub, much improved by the recent addition of a public bar. Two real fires keep the local quiz fanatics warm. Northants skittles. ♨ ❀ ⊞ ♣ P

Towcester

Plough

Market Square ☎ (0327) 50738
11–3, 5–11; 11–11 Sat
Adnams Broadside; Wells Eagle Ⓗ
A long bar to the rear of the pub complements the smaller lounge which fronts onto the market square. Excellent value food at all times. ♨ ◖ ◗

Try also: Sun, Watling St East (Free)

Wakerley

Exeter Arms

High Street ☎ (0572) 87817
12–3 (not Mon), 6–11
Bateman XB; Marston's Pedigree; Morland Old Speckled Hen Ⓗ
Old pub, reputedly haunted, featuring a wood-burning stove in the lounge and a selection of books to read. No food Mon.
♨ ❀ ◖ ◗ ⊞ ▲ ♣ P

Weedon

Heart of England

High Street ☎ (0327) 40335
11–2.30, 5–11 (11–11 summer)
S&N Theakston Best Bitter, XB; Whitbread Boddingtons Bitter Ⓗ; guest beer
Large, rambling pub on the A45 next to the Grand Union Canal. A quiet wood-panelled annexe can be booked for meetings, whilst the spacious garden has play equipment for children. The bar at the back of the pub is for younger drinkers and games.
♞ ❀ 🛏 ◖ ◗ ♣ P

Try also: Globe Hotel, High St (Free); **Wheatsheaf,** High St (Banks's)

Welford

Shoulder of Mutton

12 High Street
☎ (0858) 575375
12–2.30, 7–11
Bass Worthington BB, Draught Bass Ⓗ
Welcoming, 17th-century local with a single bar divided by arches. The games room doubles as a family room when the weather prevents use of the extensive play facilities in the garden. The good value menu caters for children's and vegetarian tastes. No food Thu.
♨ ♞ ❀ ◖ ◗ ♣ P

Wellingborough

Cannon

Cannon Street ☎ (0933) 279629
11–11
Banks & Taylor SOS; Cannon Pride; Fuller's ESB; Wells Eagle Ⓗ; guest beers
Home-brew pub on the edge of town with a large U-shaped bar. Popular with all local drinkers for its welcoming open fires and private corners. A games room stands to the side of the bar and the brewery, in an out-building, supplies the tasty ales.
♨ ❀ ◖ ♣ P

Vivian Arms

153 Knox Road
☎ (0933) 223660
11–2.30 (3 Sat), 6 (7 Sat)–11
Mansfield Riding Mild; Wells Eagle Ⓗ; guest beers
Superb, friendly back-street local: a cosy lounge with a real fire, a wood-panelled bar, plus a large games room.
♨ ❀ ⊞ ♿ ⇌ ♣ P

Wollaston

Boot

35 High Street
☎ (0933) 664270
11.30–2.30 (3 Sat), 6–11
Marston's Pedigree; Tetley Bitter; Tolly Cobbold Original Ⓗ
Listed, whitewashed, thatched pub with a restful atmosphere: always a warm welcome, and a fire in winter. Its two front rooms and skittle room are well worth seeking out. Chip-free menu.
♨ Q ♞ ❀ ◖ ◗ ♣ P

Wootton

Wootton WMC

23 High Street
☎ (0604) 761863
12–2 (2.30 Fri & Sat), 7–11; 12–2.30, 7–10.30 Sun
Greene King IPA; Mansfield Riding Mild; Wells Eagle Ⓗ; guest beers
Formerly the Red Lion, this club retains the atmosphere of a village local. A comfortable bar has a games room to the rear; original stone walls are exposed in both rooms. The concert room doubles as a lounge. CIU entry restrictions apply. Regular unusual guest beers. CAMRA East Midlands *Club of the Year* 1992.
Q ♞ ⊞ ♣ P

Yardley Hastings

Red Lion

189 High Street
☎ (0604) 696210
11–2.30 (3 Fri & Sat), 6–11
Adnams Broadside; Wells Eagle Ⓗ
Popular village local, featuring a low-beamed lounge with exposed stonework and a collection of brasses, a traditional public bar and a games room with Northants skittles. No food Sun.
♨ Q ❀ ◖ ⊞ ♣ P

The Symbols

♨	real fire	♿	easy wheelchair access
Q	quiet pub (at least one bar)	▲	camping facilities at the pub or nearby
♞	indoor room for children	⇌	near British Rail station
❀	garden or other outdoor drinking area	⊖	near underground station
🛏	accommodation	♣	pub games
◖	lunchtime meals	⌓	real cider
◗	evening meals	P	pub car park
⊞	public bar	⊬	no-smoking room or area

Northumberland

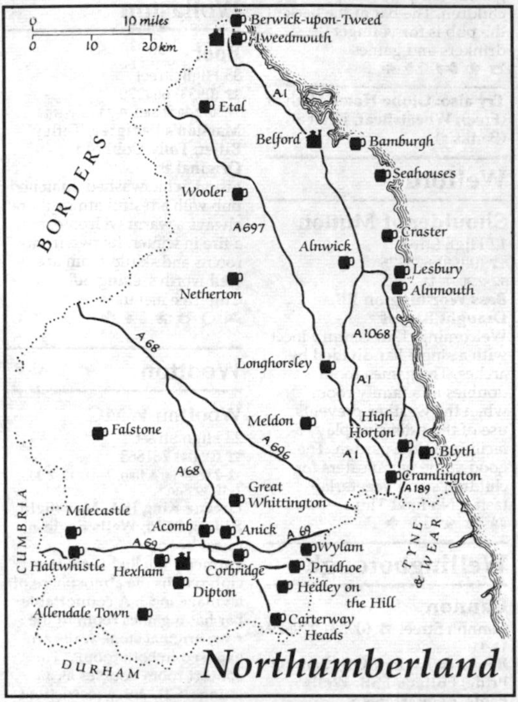

Border, Tweedmouth; Hexhamshire, Hexham; Longstone, Belford

Acomb

Miners Arms
Main Street
☎ (0434) 603909
11–11 (11.30–3, 5.30–11 Mon–Thu, Nov–May)
Big Lamp Bitter; Courage Directors; Federation Best Bitter, Buchanan's Original; Morrells Varsity; Robinson's Bitter H; guest beers
Traditional village pub with real fire, beams, stone walls and welcome, dating from 1745. Good food.
Q

Allendale Town

Golden Lion
Market Place (B6303)
☎ (0434) 683225
11–11
Butterknowle Bitter; Camerons Strongarm H; guest beers
Pleasant, friendly, town-centre pub with good food at affordable prices.
P

Kings Head Hotel
Market Square (B6303)
☎ (0434) 683681
11–11
S&N Theakston Best Bitter, XB, Old Peculier; Younger Scotch H; guest beers
Welcoming pub in a pleasant town high in the Pennines.
Q P

Alnmouth

Schooner Hotel
Northumberland Street
☎ (0665) 830216
11–11
Beer range varies H
17th-century coaching inn right by the sea. A resident ghost has a taste for Belhaven beers.
P

Alnwick

Oddfellows Arms
Narrowgate ☎ (0665) 602695
11–11
Vaux Samson, Extra Special H
Traditional local with a country atmosphere in the town centre. Q

Queens Head Hotel
Market Street ☎ (0665) 602422
11–11
Vaux Lorimers Best Scotch, Extra Special; Wards Sheffield Best Bitter H
Comfortable hotel bar in a busy market town.

Shepherd's Rest
Alnwick Moor (½ mile N of town) ☎ (0665) 510809
11–3, 6–11 (may vary)
Courage Directors; Hadrian Gladiator; guest beer H
Comfortable, friendly pub with a small restaurant and two real fires. Families welcome.
Q P

Tanners Arms
Hotspur Street
☎ (0665) 602553
12–3 (not Mon or Tue), 7–11
Belhaven 80/-, St Andrew's Ale H; guest beers
Interesting local with a welcoming licensee. The bright exterior belies its traditional furnishings.

Anick

Rat Inn
☎ (0434) 602814
11–3, 6–11
Courage Directors; Ruddles Best Bitter, County; Webster's Yorkshire Bitter; Whitbread Boddingtons Mild; guest beer H
Quaint, old country inn with beamed ceilings and an extensive food range. Runs a boules league.
Q P

Bamburgh

Castle Hotel
Front Street ☎ (066 84) 351
12–3, 6–11
Vaux Lorimers Best Scotch, Samson H
Friendly seaside local with a fine atmosphere and modern facilities.

Victoria Hotel
Front Street ☎ (066 84) 431
11–11
Longstone Bitter; Stones Best Bitter; Tetley Bitter H; guest beer
Historic hotel with a comfortable bar, close to the castle and a superb beach. The hotel is an imposing Gothic building; the bar is the haunt of the local brewer whose beer is on sale. Pool room and restaurant.
Q

Berwick-upon-Tweed

Barrels
59 Bridge Street
☎ (0289) 308013
12–2 (not Thu), 7–11
S&N Theakston Best Bitter [H]; guest beers
A varied selection of guest beers is served in this modern bar beside the historic Elizabethan bridge across the Tweed. A subterranean disco bar is open eves only. ≋

Pilot Inn
Low Greens ☎ (0289) 304214
11–3, 7–11
Broughton Greenmantle Ale [A]
Cosy local with a nautical theme, adjacent to the historic town's ramparts. ⊟ ≋

Blyth

Oddfellows Arms
91 Bridge Street
☎ (0670) 356535
11–11
Stones Best Bitter [H]; guest beers
Colourful local with two rooms and much polished woodwork.

Carterway Heads

Manor House Inn
On A68 ☎ (0207) 55268
12–3, 6–11
Butterknowle Bitter [H]; guest beers
Popular hostelry on the major north–south route, with pleasant views over the Derwent valley. Make time to enjoy the excellent home-cooked food. Thatcher's cider and Weston's perry also available. ⛼ Q ❀ ◖ ◗ ⌓ P

Corbridge

Black Bull Inn
☎ (0434) 632261
11–11
Fuller's Chiswick; Whitbread Fremlins Bitter, Boddingtons Bitter, Castle Eden Ale [H]; guest beers
Recently renovated pub with stone floors. Several drinking and dining areas lead off the main bar. Note the lists of future guest beers (some served straight from the cask). ◖ ◗

Dyvels
Station Road ☎ (0434) 633566
12–3 (not Mon–Fri), 7–11 (may vary winter)
Draught Bass; Stones Best Bitter [H]; guest beers
Welcoming pub, close to Hadrian's Wall. Visit the pub's shop next door and stock up with antiques.
⛼ Q ♨ ❀ ⛟ ♿ ≋ ⌓ P

Golden Lion Hotel
☎ (0434) 632216
12–11 (may vary winter)
S&N Theakston Best Bitter [H]
Basic locals' pub in this historic town. ◖

Lion of Corbridge
Bridge End ☎ (0434) 632504
11–3, 6–11
Tetley Bitter [H]; guest beers
Hotel with a public bar and a restaurant area. Admire the handsome ship pictures and various clocks.
⛼ Q ❀ ⛟ ◖ ◗ ≋ P

Tynedale Hotel
Market Place ☎ (0434) 712149
12–3, 7–11
S&N Theakston Best Bitter, XB [H]; guest beers
Popular local, a good base for exploring Northumberland's Roman history. The pub has its own fish and chip take-away service. ⛟ ◖

Wheatsheaf Hotel
St Helens Street
☎ (0434) 632020
11–11
Wards Sheffield Best Bitter [H]
Imposing pub just off the Market Square; a locals' bar and a restaurant.
⛼ ❀ ⛟ ◖ ◗ ⊟ ♿ P

Cramlington

Plough
Middle Farm ☎ (0670) 737633
11–3, 6–11; 11–11 Fri & Sat
S&N Theakston XB [H]; guest beers
A fine conversion of former agricultural buildings in the heart of the old village, with some notable architectural features. Good food and company make this a very popular meeting place.
❀ ◖ ⊟ ♿ ≋ P

Craster

Jolly Fisherman
Haven Hill ☎ (0665) 576218
11–3, 6–11
Wards Sheffield Best Bitter [H]
Welcoming pub in a tiny village famous for seafood. Enjoy the splendid view.
⛼ ❀ ♿ ♣ P

Dipton

Dipton Mill Inn
Dipton Mill Road (S of Hexham, off B6306)
☎ (0434) 606577
12–3, 6–11
Hadrian Gladiator; Hexhamshire Low Quarter, Bitter, Devil's Water [H]; guest beer
Warm and comfortable pub serving fine food in lovely countryside.
⛼ Q ♨ ❀ ◖ ♣

Etal

Black Bull
Off B6354 ☎ (0890) 820200
12–3, 6–11 (may vary)
Vaux Lorimers Best Scotch [H]
Northumberland's only thatched pub, set in an isolated but historic village with a castle. The updated interior belies the age of the building. Q ◖ ◗ ♿ P

Falstone

Blackcock Inn
☎ (0434) 240200
11–3, 6–11 (may vary)
Whitbread Boddingtons Bitter, Castle Eden Ale [H]; guest beers
Originating in 1600, an excellent, three-roomed inn which used to have a thatched roof, now sadly replaced. Original beams and real fires in each room; warm welcome assured. Handy for Kielder Reservoir.
⛼ Q ❀ ⛟ ◖ ◗ ⊟ ♿ ▲ P

Great Whittington

Queens Head Inn
☎ (0434) 672267
12–3, 6–11
Taylor Landlord; Whitbread Boddingtons Bitter [H]; guest beers
One of the oldest inns in the country, dating from 1615 and set in lovely countryside near Hadrian's Wall. The newly-built restaurant serves excellent meals.
⛼ Q ❀ ◖ ◗ ♿ P

Haltwhistle

Black Bull
Main Street ☎ (0434) 320463
11–11
Stones Best Bitter; Tetley Bitter [H]
Busy, town-centre pub which can get very crowded in the eve. ⛼ ≋

Railway Hotel
Station Road ☎ (0434) 320269
11–3, 6–11
Whitbread Boddingtons Bitter, Castle Eden Ale [H]
Friendly pub near Hadrian's Wall and Roman remains.
⛼ ◖ ◗ ≋

Northumberland

Spotted Cow Inn
Castle Street ☎ (0434) 320327
11–3, 6–11
Courage Directors; Marston's Pedigree; Ruddles Best Bitter, County; Webster's Yorkshire Bitter [H]; guest beers
Friendly pub in a pleasant town, ideal for walking.
♛ ❀ ◖ ◗ ⇌ P

Hedley on the Hill

Feathers Inn
On minor road, off B6309 OS078592 ☎ (0661) 843268
12–3 (not Mon–Fri), 6–11
Whitbread Boddingtons Bitter [H]; guest beers
Friendly pub in a small hilltop village. Food is available at weekends only.
♛ Q ❀ ◖ ◗ P

Hexham

Globe
Battle Hill ☎ (0434) 603742
11–11
S&N Theakston Best Bitter [H]
Fine, unspoilt, traditional bar with a local atmosphere in a busy market town. ♛ ♿ ⇌

Tap & Spile
Battle Hill ☎ (0434) 602039
11–11
Beer range varies [H]
One of the Tap & Spile chain, with an excellent reputation throughout the North-East. A quiet, comfortable pub.
Q ◖ ⇌

High Horton

Three Horse Shoes
Hathery Lane ☎ (0607) 822410
11–11
Draught Bass; Courage Directors; Marston's Pedigree; Tetley Bitter [H]; guest beers
Spacious, popular pub with six handpumps. Occasional beer festivals are held. Children welcome in the large conservatory. ⚇ ❀ ◖ ♿ ♣ P

Lesbury

Coach Inn
☎ (0665) 830865
12–2.30, 7–11
Longstone Bitter [H]; guest beers
Low-ceilinged old pub, comfortable and friendly.
♛ ❀ ◖ ◗ ♿ ♣ P

Longhorsley

Linden Pub
Linden Hall Hotel
☎ (0670) 516611
11–3, 6–11 (11–11 summer Sat)
Hook Norton Best Bitter; Marston's Pedigree; Whitbread Boddingtons Bitter [H]
Pleasant pub in the grounds of Linden Hall Hotel. Excellent food is served in comfortable surroundings. Children welcome. The courtyard features a giant chessboard.
❀ ◖ ◗ ♿ ♣ P

Meldon

Dyke Neuk
☎ (0670) 72662
11–11
Courage Directors; Ruddles Best Bitter, County [H]; guest beer (spring–autumn)
Large free house which has recently been extensively modernised. ♛ Q ◖ ◗ ⊞ P

Milecastle

Milecastle Inn
Military Road (B6318)
☎ (0434) 320682
12–3, 7–11
S&N Theakston Best Bitter; Webster's Yorkshire Bitter [H]; guest beers
Small, cosy pub with a restaurant renowned for its game dishes. It lies in a popular rambling area within striking distance of Hadrian's Wall and its forts. Walkers are requested to remove their boots. ♛ Q ❀ ◖ ◗ P

Netherton

Star Inn
On B634 ☎ (0669) 80238
11–2, 7–11 (may vary winter)
Whitbread Castle Eden Ale [G]
Remote, unspoilt, marvellous pub in beautiful countryside. A disused cock-fighting pit stands on a hill opposite. Beer is served straight from the cellar. ♛ Q ❀ ⊞ P

Prudhoe

Halfway House
Edgewell ☎ (0661) 832688
11–3, 6–11; 11–11 Fri & Sat
S&N Theakston Best Bitter [H]; guest beers
Constantly improving roadhouse with a long bar and two rooms. ◖ P

Seahouses

Olde Ship Hotel
Main Street ☎ (0665) 720200
11–3, 6–11
Longstone Bitter; S&N Theakston Best Bitter, XB (summer) **[H]**
Built as a farmhouse in 1745, now an excellent, small, family-owned hotel. The bar is a treasurehouse of nautical and antique pieces: ships' figureheads, navigating instruments, model boats, etc.
♛ Q ❀ ⛼ ◖ ♿ ▲ ♣ P

Tweedmouth

Angel Inn
Brewery Bank (A1167, off A1)
☎ (0289) 306273
11–3, 7–11; 11–11 Sat
Border Old Kiln Bitter [H]; guest beers
Original Border Brewery tied house circa 1780; now a warm, welcoming hostelry stocking beers brewed locally by women brewsters. The starting point for brewery tours.
Q ❀ ▲ P

Harrow
96 Main Street
☎ (0289) 305451
11–3, 6.30–11
Vaux Lorimers Best Scotch [H]
No frills in a bustling, traditional local with two rooms. It stands on land which changed hands between England and Scotland 14 times in the Middle Ages. Can still produce a culture shock!

Wooler

Anchor
2 Cheviot Street
☎ (0668) 81412
11–4, 7–11
Vaux Lorimers Best Scotch, Samson [H]
Friendly, country pub, cosy and comfortable. Set in fine countryside, with a warm welcome assured.
♛ Q ❀ ⛼ ◖

Wylam

Boathouse
Station Road ☎ (0661) 853431
12–3 (not Mon), 6–11; 11–11 Sat
Draught Bass; Butterknowle Conciliation Ale; S&N Theakston XB; Taylor Landlord; Whitbread Boddingtons Bitter; Younger No. 3 [H]; guest beers
Friendly pub with six regular beers on handpumps, plus guests. Lunches served weekends only in winter. Bar billiards played.
♛ ❀ ◖ ⇌ ♣ P

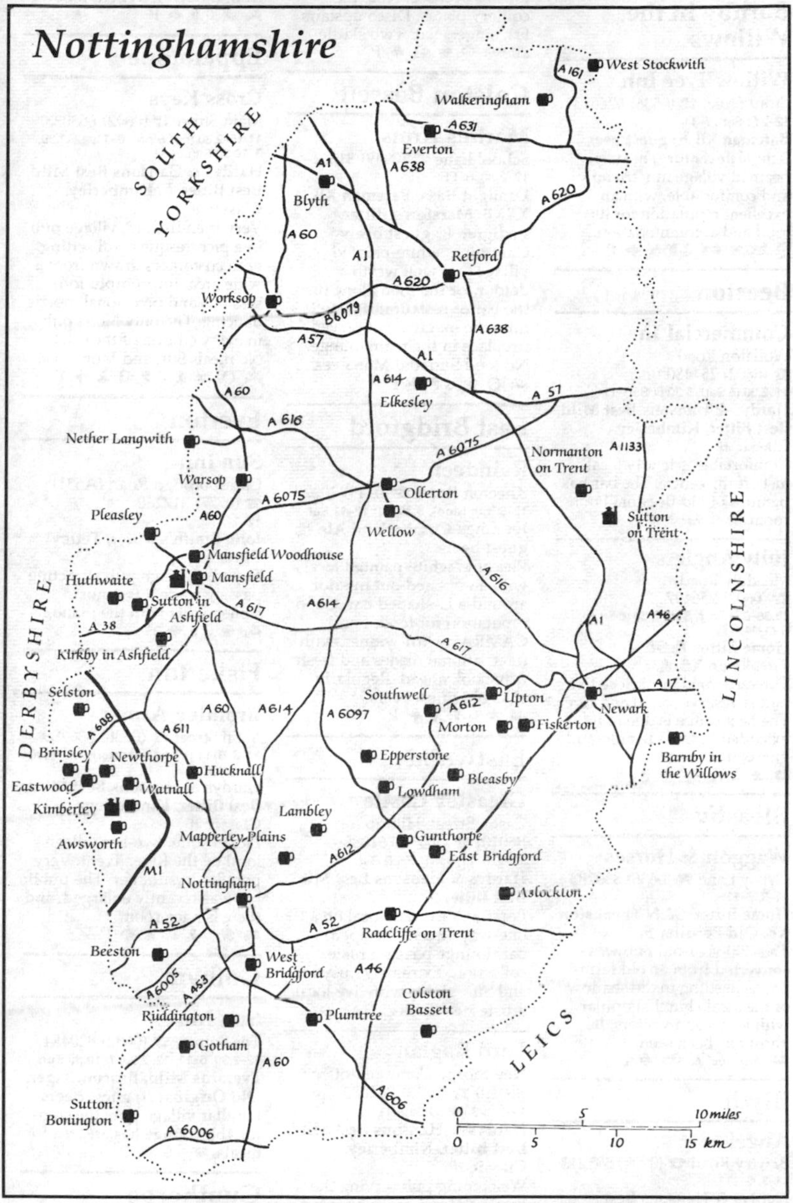

Hardys & Hansons, *Kimberley;* **Mansfield**, *Mansfield;* **Springhead**, *Sutton on Trent*

Aslockton

Cranmer Arms

Main Street ☎ (0949) 50362
11–3.30, 5.30–11; 11–11 Sat
Home Bitter [H]; guest beer
Friendly local named after Thomas Cranmer, a native of the village. Children's garden play area. S&N guest beer.
♨ ❀ ◖ ▲ ⇌ ♣ P

Awsworth

Gate Inn

Main Street ☎ (0602) 329821
12–3 (4 Sat), 7–11
Hardys & Hansons Best Mild, Best Bitter [E]
Superb, old traditional pub once owned by Offilers of Derby (closed 1966). Near the site of the once-famous Forty Bridges – see photos in the passage. Pool room.
Q ❀ ◖ ⊟ ♣ P

Barnby in the Willows

Willow Tree Inn
Front Street ☎ (0636) 626613
12–2 (3 Sat), 7–11
Bateman XB [H]; guest beer
Late 17th-century, heavily-beamed village inn; friendly and comfortable, with an excellent reputation for its food and accommodation.
Q 🐎 ❀ 🛏 ◐ ◑ ♿ ♣ P

Beeston

Commercial Inn
Wollaton Road
☎ (0602) 254480
11–2.30 (5 Sat), 5.30 (7 Sat)–11
Hardys & Hansons Best Mild, Best Bitter, Kimberley Classic [H]
Comfortable, friendly local, just off the centre. The bar has pictures of old Beeston. Pool room. ❀ ◐ ⊟ ♣ P

Jolly Anglers
Meadow Road
☎ (0602) 256497
11.30–3 (4 Fri & Sat), 6.30 (6 Fri & Sat)–11
Home Bitter [E]; S&N Theakston XB [H]
Three-roomed local close to a nature reserve, canal and river. The beer range is due to be extended to include mild and guests from S&N.
🐎 ❀ ◐ ⊟ ⇌ ♣ P

Bleasby

Waggon & Horses
Gypsy Lane ☎ (0636) 830283
11–3, 6–11
Home Bitter; S&N Theakston XB, Old Peculier [H]
This 200-year-old pub was converted from an old farm-house nestling in the shadow of the local church. Popular with locals and visitors. Its ghost has been seen.
⛫ ❀ ◐ ♿ ▲ ⇌ ♣ P

Blyth

Angel
Bawtry Road ☎ (0909) 591213
11–3, 6–11
Hardys & Hansons Best Bitter [H]
A long-standing *Guide* entry. Huge fires; large garden.
⛫ Q 🐎 ❀ 🛏 ◐ ◑ ⊟ ♣ P

Brinsley

Robin Hood
Hall Lane ☎ (0773) 713604
12–3, 6.30 (7 winter)–11
Hardys & Hansons Best Mild, Best Bitter [E]
Characterful village pub in DH Lawrence country, rumoured to be haunted upstairs by a former licensee. Note the colliery plates. Disco upstairs Fri; singers Sat. Two skittle alleys. Q ❀ ⊟ ♣ P

Colston Bassett

Martins Arms
School Lane ☎ (0949) 81361
12–2.30, 6–11
Draught Bass; Bateman XB, XXXB; Marston's Bitter, Pedigree [H]; guest beers
Charming, white-painted village inn; well worth a detour for the food alone (in the bar or restaurant). Don't miss the magnificent carved fireplace in the main lounge. No food Sun and Mon eves.
⛫ Q ❀ ◐ ◑ ♣ P

East Bridgford

Reindeer
Kneeton Road ☎ (0949) 20227
12–3 (not Mon), 5.30–11; 12–11 Sat
Jennings Cumberland Ale [H]; guest beers
Pleasing, white-painted local with an opened-out interior around a U-shaped bar. Good reputation for food. Local CAMRA award-winner, with international dishes and fresh fish; book ahead. Regularly changed guest beers.
⛫ ❀ ◐ ◑ ▲ ♣ P

Eastwood

Greasley Castle
Castle Street, Hilltop (off B6010) ☎ (0773) 761086
11–4, 6–11; 11–11 Fri & Sat
Hardys & Hansons Best Mild, Best Bitter [E]
Popular Victorian local on a one-way street. The open bar/lounge boasts a plate collection. Extremely busy Fri and Sun nights with live local artistes. ❀ ⊟ ♣

Lord Raglan
Newthorpe Common (off B6010) ☎ (0773) 712683
11–3, 5.30 (6.30 Sat)–11
Hardys & Hansons Best Mild, Best Bitter, Kimberley Classic [H]
Welcoming pub serving the local estates. Games-oriented bar; weekend sing-along in the olde-worlde lounge. Wed night quiz. Good quality food.
⛫ ❀ ◐ ⊟ ♣ P

Elkesley

Robin Hood
High Street ☎ (077 783) 259
11.30–3.30, 6.30–11; 11.30–11 Sat
Whitbread Boddingtons Bitter; Trophy [H]; guest beers
Popular village local which also attracts passing trade from the A1. Excellent food.
⛫ ❀ ◐ ◑ ♣ P

Epperstone

Cross Keys
Main Street ☎ (0602) 663033
11.45–2.30 (not Mon), 6–11; 12–2.30, 7–10.30 Sun
Hardys & Hansons Best Mild, Best Bitter [E], Kimberley Classic [H]
Very friendly, old, village pub in a picturesque rural setting, with customers drawn from a wide area. Impromptu folk sessions and occasional morris dancing. The only Notts pub in every edition of the *Guide*. No meals Sun and Mon eves.
⛫ Q 🐎 ❀ ◐ ◑ ⊟ ▲ ♣ P

Everton

Sun Inn
Gainsborough Road (A631)
☎ (0777) 817260
12–11
John Smith's Bitter; Tetley Bitter [H]
Friendly village pub attracting passing trade. Live music some nights with the piano.
⛫ ❀ ◐ ◑ ♣ P

Fiskerton

Bromley Arms
Main Street ☎ (0636) 830789
11–3, 6–11 (11–11 summer); 12–10.30 Sun for meals
Hardys & Hansons Best Mild, Best Bitter, Kimberley Classic [H]
Picturesque, two-bar village local by the River Trent. Very popular in summer. The public bar was recently enlarged, and there is a tea room.
⛫ ❀ ◐ ◑ ⊟ ▲ ♣ P ⚡

Gotham

Sun Inn
The Square ☎ (0602) 830484
12–2.30, 6–11; 12–2.30, 7–10.30 Sun
Everards Mild, Beacon, Tiger, Old Original [H]; guest beers
Popular village pub; the comfortable lounge has an area for meals. ❀ ◐ ◑ ♣ P

Gunthorpe

Tom Browns
Trentside ☎ (0602) 663642
11–3, 6–11; 11–11 Sat & summer
Home Bitter; S&N Theakston Best Bitter, XB, Old Peculier [H]; guest beers
Converted former schoolhouse on the riverside. Excellent food (no chips) is served in the bar and restaurant. A low-priced ale is always on offer. Good overnight moorings for boaters. No food service in the bar Sat/Sun eves. ❀ ◐ ◑ ▲ P

Hucknall

Red Lion
High Street
10.30–2.30, 6–11
Home Mild, Bitter 🄴
Traditional town local with a through passage and four interconnecting rooms. Can be crowded weekends. ⊞ ♣ P

Huthwaite

Godfrey's Freehouse
222 Blackwell Road (B6026)
☎ (0623) 550087
11–3, 7–11 (11–11 summer)
S&N Theakston Mild, Best Bitter, XB, Old Peculier 🄷; **guest beer** (weekends)
Pub nicely refurbished into a one-room bar with a conservatory eating area.
♔ Q ᘎ ❀ ◐ ◑ ♣ P ⁄

Kimberley

Cricketers Rest
Chapel Street ☎ (0602) 380894
11–3.30 (4 Sat), 6.30–11
Hardys & Hansons Best Mild, Best Bitter 🄷
Comfortable, well-appointed, open-plan pub with a discrete dartboard area. Reputedly haunted by a former landlady. Attracts young people: Mon night disco; Thu night quiz.
❀ ♣

Nelson & Railway
Station Road ☎ (0602) 382177
10.30–3, 5–11; 10.30–11 Fri, Sat & bank hols
Hardys & Hansons Best Mild, Best Bitter, Kimberley Classic 🄷/🄴
Unspoilt village pub in a pleasant location, just across from the brewery. A wood-panelled bar and an attractively restored, beamed lounge with an adjoining dining area. Budget B&B. Excellent food. Cheap beer 5–7 Mon–Fri. Its 19th year in the *Guide*. ❀ 🛏 ◐ ◑ ⊞ ♣ P

Queens Head
Main Street ☎ (0602) 382117
10.30–4, 6–11
Hardys & Hansons Best Mild, Best Bitter 🄴
Prominent, street-corner local, busy with young people at weekends. A quiet, small snug in the top corner; upstairs lounge featuring live music from local artistes. ❀ ◐ ⊞ ♣

Kirkby in Ashfield

Countryman
Park Lane ☎ (0623) 752314
12–4, 7–11
S&N Theakston Best Bitter, XB, Old Peculier; Younger No. 3 (occasionally) 🄷
18th-century inn with numerous beamed alcoves. Decorated by a wandering sculptor in the late 1970s: his work can still be admired in the bar area. Irish folk band most Fri nights. ᘎ ❀ ◐ ◑ P

Wild Orchid
Southwell Lane
☎ (0623) 721283
11.30–3, 6.30–11
Hardys & Hansons Best Mild, Best Bitter, Kimberley Classic 🄷
New pub catering for the local estate trade. One well-furnished, large room is divided into smaller drinking areas. Separate games areas.
❀ ◐ ♿ ♣ P

Lambley

Robin Hood
Main Street ☎ (0602) 312531
11–3, 6–11
Home Bitter; S&N Theakston XB, Old Peculier (summer) 🄷
In the middle of a linear village, this pub has a local trade, although it is also known for its beer and skittles parties. Originally a WH Hutchinson & Sons house.
Q ❀ ⊞ ♣ P

Lowdham

Old Ship
Main Street ☎ (0602) 663049
11.30–2.30, 5.30–11; 11.30–11 Sat
Courage Best Bitter; Marston's Pedigree; John Smith's Bitter 🄷
Warm and friendly atmosphere in a lively pub, originally a coaching house, well renovated. Eating area at the end of the lounge (waitress service); pool table in the bar.
♔ Q ᘎ ❀ ◐ ◑ ⊞ ⇶ ♣ P

Mansfield

Plough
Nottingham Road
☎ (0623) 23031
11–11
Marston's Pedigree; Whitbread Boddingtons Bitter, Trophy 🄷; **guest beers**
Large, one-roomed pub with six ales always available. Mon night quiz; live music Thu. Good value food. Handy for the football ground. ❀ ◐

Westfield Hotel
Westfield Lane ☎ (0623) 25090
11–11
Mansfield Riding Mild, Riding Bitter 🄷
Lively, friendly town pub hosting frequent games nights. No food Sun. Specify handpumped beer if ordering in the lounge. ❀ ◐ ⊞ ♣ P

William IV
208 Stockwell Gate
☎ (0623) 21283
11–11
Mansfield Riding Mild, Riding Bitter, Old Baily 🄷
Well-decorated pub with separate areas for the locals' bar, lounge, family room and two pool tables. Quizzes Fri and Sun nights. Range of pinball and video machines.
ᘎ ❀ ◐ P

Mansfield Woodhouse

Greyhound Inn
High Street ☎ (0623) 643005
12–4 (5 Sat), 7–11 (may vary summer)
Home Mild, Bitter; S&N Theakston Mild, Best Bitter, XB, Old Peculier 🄷
Typical village local, popular with all ages. A lounge bar and a tap room, with a welcoming atmosphere.
❀ ⊞ ♣ P

Mapperley Plains

Travellers Rest
On B684 ☎ (0602) 264412
11–11
Home Mild, Bitter; S&N Theakston Best Bitter, XB, Old Peculier; Younger IPA, No. 3 🄷
Friendly pub on the outskirts of Nottingham, in an elevated position. Children's play area and 'Pop Inn' family room. Varied menu, including vegetarian and children's options, available 12–8 (12–2 Sun and Mon)
♔ ᘎ ❀ ◐ ◑ ♿ ▲ ♣ P ⁄

Morton

Full Moon Inn
Main Street ☎ (0636) 830251
11–3, 6–11
S&N Theakston Best Bitter, XB, Old Peculier 🄷; **guest beers**
Traditional, oak-beamed village local, popular with all ages. Note the rhyme above the entrance. The excellent food means it can get crowded with diners. Handy for Southwell Racecourse.
♔ ◐ ◑ ⇶ (Fiskerton) P

Nether Langwith

Jug & Glass
Queens Walk ☎ (0623) 742283
11.30–3, 7–11 (11–11 summer)
Hardys & Hansons Best Bitter 🄴, **Kimberley Classic** 🄷
Long, stone-built pub in an old village. Popular in summer for its pleasant setting by the River Poulter.
♔ Q ❀ ◐ ◑ ⊞ ♣ P

Nottinghamshire

Newark

Crown & Mitre
Castle Gate
☎ (0636) 703131
11.30–3, 6.30–11; 11.30–11 Fri & Sat
Draught Bass; John Smith's Bitter; Wards Sheffield Best Bitter [H]; guest beer
Pleasant town pub with a single bar, built in the late 19th century; very popular. Its upstairs pool room is used by a number of teams. Bar meals are served Mon to Fri; special Sun lunches in the function room. 🏰 ꝏ ✿ ◐ ♿ ⇌ (Castle) ♣ P

Mail Coach
London Road
☎ (0636) 605164
11–2.30 (3 Wed & Fri, 4 Sat), 5.30 (7 Sat)–11
Hoskins & Oldfield Tom Kelly's Stout; Ind Coope Burton Ale; Marston's Pedigree; Tetley Bitter [H]; guest beers
Very busy, pleasant town pub; a mainly Georgian building but some parts are older. The cellar reputedly houses part of the old town wall. Various board games, plus an infuriating ball-round-a-maze game. 🏰 ✿ 🛏 ◐ ♿ ⇌ (Castle) ⌓ P

Malt Shovel
Northgate ☎ (0636) 702036
11.30–3, 7 (5 Fri)–11
Taylor Landlord; Wards Sheffield Best Bitter [H]; guest beers
A pub for all ages; office workers predominate at lunchtimes. A cheerful, welcoming place where the emphasis is on convivial conversation. Dates from the 16th century and was originally a bakery. At least four beers always available. 🏰 ✿ ◐ ♿ ⇌ (Castle/ Northgate)

Wing Tavern
Bridge Street
☎ (0636) 702689
11–3 (2.30 Tue & Thu), 7–11
S&N Theakston Best Bitter, XB, Old Peculier; Younger No. 3 [H]
Small, single-bar, town local with a pool room. Hidden away in a corner of the market place, next to the parish church, but well worth seeking out. ꝏ ✿ ⇌ (Castle/ Northgate) ♣

Newthorpe

Ram Inn
Beauvale (off B600 via Dovecote Rd) ☎ (0773) 713312
11–4, 6–11; 11–11 Sat
Hardys & Hansons Best Mild, Best Bitter [E], Kimberley Classic [H]
Friendly roadside pub, very popular with the local community. Excellent value food. 🏰 ✿ ◐ ◑ ⊞ ♣ P

Normanton on Trent

Square & Compass
Eastgate ☎ (0636) 821439
12–3, 6–11
Adnams Bitter, Broadside; Stones Best Bitter [H]; guest beers
Popular, low-beamed pub and small restaurant (the Gun Room), specialising in game. The landlord once kept a cask of Adnams Tally Ho for 12 months before tapping it – the result was nectar!
🏰 ✿ 🛏 ◐ ◑ ▲ ♣ P

Nottingham

Bell Inn
Angel Row, Old Market Square ☎ (0602) 475241
10.30–11; 10.30–2.30, 5.30–11 Sat; 12–2, 7–10.30 Sun
Draught Bass; Eldridge Pope Royal Oak; Jennings Bitter; Marston's Pedigree; S&N Theakston XB, Old Peculier [H]; guest beers
Busy, city-centre inn dating back to the 15th century, with a varied clientele. Cellar tours and history talks by appointment. Trad. jazz Sun lunch and Mon and Tue eves. Up to three guest beers a week. No food Sun. Q ✿ ◐

Boat Inn
Priory Street, Old Lenton
☎ (0602) 786482
11–2.30 (3 Sat), 6 (6.30 Sat)–11
Home Mild, Bitter [E]; S&N Theakston XB; Younger Scotch [H]
One-roomed local with a friendly atmosphere and attractive wood panelling with inlaid mirrors. Close to the Queen's Medical Centre.
✿ ◐ ♣

Coopers Arms
Porchester Road, Thorneywood ☎ (0602) 502433
11 (11.30 Sat)–2.30 (3.30 Mon & Fri, 4.30 Sat; not Wed), 6 (5.30 Fri, 6.30 Sat)–11
Home Mild, Bitter [E]
1890s pub with four rooms, including a pool room and a skittle alley. Q ꝏ ⊞ ♿ ♣ P

Fox at Sneinton
Dale Street, Sneinton
☎ (0602) 504736
11–3 (4 Sat), 6–11
Ansells Bitter; Ind Coope Burton Ale; Taylor Landlord; Tetley Bitter [H]; guest beers
Comfortable, popular pub close to Green's Windmill. A drinker's pub with a lively bar, a quiet lounge and a games room upstairs. ✿ ♣

Grove
273 Castle Boulevard, Lenton
☎ (0602) 410637
11.30–3, 5.30 (6 Sat)–11
Home Bitter; Marston's Pedigree; S&N Theakston XB, Old Peculier; Younger IPA, No. 3 [H]; guest beers
Prominent Victorian pub: one multi-level room refurbished with bare floorboards and bric-a-brac. Popular with students; handy for the local marina. Weston's cider. Eve meals until 7pm.
◐ ◑ ⌓ P

Limelight
Wellington Circus
☎ (0602) 418467
11–11
Adnams Bitter; Courage Directors; Marston's Pedigree; S&N Theakston XB, Old Peculier; Whitbread Boddingtons Bitter [H]; guest beers
Part of the Nottingham Playhouse theatre complex, but has its own individual character. Usually very busy. Fortnightly Sun lunchtime jazz sessions. A regularly changing range of guest beers usually includes a mild. ✿ ◐ ◑

Lincolnshire Poacher
161 Mansfield Road (400 yds N of Victoria centre)
☎ (0602) 411584
11–3, 5 (6 Sat)–11
Draught Bass; Bateman Mild, XB, XXXB, Salem Porter, Victory; Marston's Pedigree [H]; guest beers
Drinkers' house offering a good range of ales, with changing guests, draught Weston's perry and over 70 malt whiskies. Daily menu of freshly-produced meals and snacks (till 8.30pm). Unusual pub memorabilia. No food Sun eve. Q ✿ ◐ ◑ ⌓

Magpies
Meadow Lane
☎ (0602) 863851
11–3, 5–11; 11–11 Fri
Home Mild, Bitter [E]
Pub at the eastern edge of the city, ideally located for the racecourse, Trent Bridge cricket ground and both football clubs. Pool table in the bar. ✿ ◐ ◑ ⊞ ♣ P

March Hare
248 Carlton Road, Sneinton
☎ (0602) 504328
11.30–2.30, 6–11; 12–2.30, 7–10.30 Sun
Courage Directors; John Smith's Bitter [H]

Pub where a post-war brick exterior leads to a welcoming interior with a functional bar and a comfortable lounge. Pool table in the bar.
Q ◑ ⊟ ♿ ♣ P

New Market Inn

38 Lower Parliament Street
☎ (0602) 411532
11–4, 5.30 (7 Sat)–11; 12–2.30, 7–10.30 Sun
Home Mild, Bitter; S&N Theakston Best Bitter, XB; Younger IPA [H]; guest beers
Three quiet and comfortable lounge areas and a bar filled with railway items. Quiz, table skittles, darts and domino teams. Renowned for low prices. Sun lunch to order only. Q ☺ ◑ ⊟ ♣ P

Plainsman

149 Woodthorpe Drive, Mapperley ☎ (0602) 622020
10.30–2.30, 6–11
Hardys & Hansons Best Mild, Best Bitter [E], Kimberley Classic [H]
Two houses knocked together, with the lounge and bar on different levels – both equally welcoming and unpretentious.
⊟ ♣ P

Portland Arms

24 Portland Road (N of centre, off A610) ☎ (0602) 782429
11.30–3, 7–11
Hardys & Hansons Best Bitter, Kimberley Classic [H]
Friendly, back-street, Victorian local; now open-plan but still with defined drinking areas. Bar snacks are both good and cheap. ❀ ♣

Queens Hotel

2 Arkwright Street (opp. station) ☎ (0602) 864685
11–2.30, 5.30–11; 11–11 Fri
Greenalls Shipstone's Mild, Bitter, Thomas Greenall's Original; Stones Best Bitter; Tetley Bitter [H]
Traditional town pub with a Victorian-style bar and a comfortable lounge.
🛏 ◑ ⊟ ≹ ♣ P

Red Cow

Windmill Lane, Sneinton
☎ (0602) 501632
11.30–3, 6–11
Courage Directors; Mansfield Riding Bitter; Marston's Pedigree; John Smith's Bitter; Wilson's Mild [H]
Deceptively large, two-bar pub: a plain drinkers' bar and a very plush lounge, plus a large concert room and games area to the rear. Q ❀ ◑ ⊟ ♣

Tom Hoskins

12–14 Queens Bridge Road
☎ (0602) 850611
11.30–3, 5.30–11; 11.30–11 Fri & Sat
Bateman Mild; Hoskins Beaumanor Bitter, Penn's Ale, Old Nigel [H]; guest beers
Impressive restoration of a former Whitbread theme pub. Sky TV is screened, but conversation is the order of the day. Q ❀ ◑ ≹ ♣ P

Trip to Jerusalem

Brewhouse Yard, Castle Road
☎ (0602) 473171
11–3 (4 Sat), 5.30 (may be 7, 6 Sat)–11
Hardys & Hansons Best Mild, Best Bitter, Kimberley Classic; Marston's Pedigree [H]
Dated 1189 and laying claim to being the oldest pub in England, the Trip is a must for visitors. Three rooms: the 'Front' (at the back), the 'Ward' and the 'Rock Lounge' with its 60-ft chimney, from the days when it was the maltings for the castle into whose rock the pub is cut.
♨ Q ❀ ◑ ≹ ♣

Ollerton

White Hart

Station Road ☎ (0623) 822410
11.30–4, 7–11
Samuel Smith OBB [H]
Tucked away in the centre of the old village, a pub popular with locals and visitors to nearby Sherwood Forest.
◑ ⊟ ♿ ⛺ ♣ P

Pleasley

Plough

669 Chesterfield Road North (A617) ☎ (0623) 810386
11–11
Ansells Mild; Ind Coope Burton Ale; Mansfield Old Baily; Tetley Bitter [H]; guest beers
One-roomed pub recently gutted and refurbished with beams, etc. Noted for its food (not served Sun eve). At least two guest beers.
❀ ◑ ◗ ♿ P ⅄

Plumtree

Griffin

Main Road ☎ (0602) 375743
11–2.30, 5.30–11; 12–2, 7–10.30 Sun
Hardys & Hansons Best Mild, Best Bitter [E], Kimberley Classic [H]
150 years old and well modernised, the Griffin affords a welcome to all. Very good food (not served Sun). Folk club Tue eve. Families are welcome (play area).
Q ◑ ◗ ♣ P

Radcliffe on Trent

Royal Oak

Main Road ☎ (0602) 333798
11–11
Fuller's Chiswick; Marston's Pedigree; Whitbread Boddingtons Bitter, Castle Eden Ale, Flowers Original, Pompey Royal [H]; guest beers
Cosy and convivial, village local serving an extensive and varying range of beers. The food menu includes authentic Italian dishes.
♨ ◑ ◗ ⊟ ≹ ♣ P

Retford

Clinton Arms

Albert Road (S of centre, off A638) ☎ (0777) 702703
11–11
Courage Directors; John Smith's Bitter; Webster's Green Label, Yorkshire Bitter [H]; guest beers
Splendid pub, popular with all ages: a social centre for sports clubs and other organisations. Enterprising guest beer policy.
☺ ❀ ◑ ♿ ≹ ♣ P

Market Hotel

West Carr Road, Ordsall
☎ (0777) 703278
11–3, 6–11; 11–11 Sat
Draught Bass; Fuller's Chiswick; Marston's Pedigree; S&N Theakston Old Peculier; Stones Best Bitter; Taylor Landlord [H]; guest beers
Pub with usually around 14 real ales, plus a separate restaurant and a large function room. Q ❀ ◑ ◗ ♿ ≹ P

Turks Head

Grove Street ☎ (0777) 702742
11–3, 7–11; 11–11 Sat
Vaux Samson; Wards Sheffield Best Bitter [H]
Possibly Retford's most attractive pub, with its panelled interior and homely atmosphere. Good lunchtime food trade. ❀ ◑ ♿ ♣

Ruddington

Red Lion

1 Easthorpe Street
☎ (0602) 844654
11–2.30, 5.30–11; 11–11 Fri & Sat
Home Mild, Bitter; S&N Theakston XB [H]; guest beers
Excellent village pub, very popular with the locals. Cosy lounge. Two guest beers each week. ❀ ⊟ ♿ ♣ P

Selston

Bull at Selston

Alfreton Road
☎ (0773) 810591
12–4, 7–11
Courage Directors; Marston's Pedigree; Ruddles Best Bitter, County; John Smith's Bitter; Wilson's Mild [H]; guest beers

Nottinghamshire

Detached, red-brick, late-Victorian pub with a circular bar. A raised stage area hosts varied, regular live entertainment. Sun night quiz.
♛ ❀ ◐ ◑ ♣ P

Horse & Jockey
Church Lane
☎ (0773) 863022
4.30 (11 Thu–Sat)–11
Ruddles Best Bitter Ⓗ; guest beers
The oldest pub in Selston: a basic three-roomed local that time has forgotten. Ever-changing guest beers. ❀ ♣

Southwell

Saracens Head
Market Place
☎ (0636) 812701
11–3, 6–11 (11–11 summer)
Draught Bass; John Smith's Bitter Ⓗ
Historic, 12th-century coaching inn, originally the Kings Arms and much visited by royalty over the years. Charles I spent his last night of freedom here. Byron was also a regular visitor. Two welcoming hotel lounge bars, close to Southwell Minster.
♛ Q ❀ 🛏 ◐ ◑ P

Sutton Bonington

Anchor Inn
Bollards Lane
☎ (0509) 673648
12–3 (not Mon–Thu), 7–11; 12–11 Sat
Banks's Mild Ⓗ; Marston's Merrie Monk Ⓖ, Pedigree Ⓗ
Family-run, very welcoming, single-room pub on two levels. Reputed to be haunted by a previous landlord. Barbecues on Fri eves in summer.
♛ ❀ ♣ P

Sutton in Ashfield

Mapplewells Inn
Alfreton Road
☎ (0623) 552314
11–11
Mansfield Riding Mild, Riding Bitter, Old Baily Ⓗ
Large, two-roomed pub on the outskirts of town, with two pool tables in the tap room. The lounge has been refurbished. ❀ ◐ ◑ ⊟ ♿ ♣ P

Upton

Cross Keys
Main Street
☎ (0636) 813269
11.30–2.30, 5.30 (6 Sat)–11; 12–2.30, 7–10.30 Sun
Bateman XXXB; Brakspear Bitter; Marston's Pedigree; Whitbread Boddingtons Bitter Ⓗ; guest beers
Warm and friendly old pub in a conservation area. The upstairs restaurant is open Fri and Sat eves, and Sun lunch; bar meals at all times. Guest ales are changed two or three times a week. Quality folk groups play on Sun eves Sept–May; piano sing-alongs Wed eve. ♛ ❀ ◐ ◑ ♣ P

Walkeringham

Three Horseshoes
High Street
☎ (0427) 890959
11.30–3, 7–11
Draught Bass; Stones Best Bitter Ⓗ; guest beer
Comfortable village pub with a large lounge and a restaurant offering home-cooked food.
♛ ❀ ◐ ◑ ♣ P

Warsop

Hare & Hounds
Church Street
☎ (0623) 842440
11–3, 6–11
Hardys & Hansons Best Mild, Best Bitter Ⓗ
Traditional and lively, mock-Tudor pub in the town centre, with a busy tap room.
♛ Q ⚭ ❀ ◐ ◑ ♣ P

Watnall

Queens Head
Main Road
☎ (0602) 383148
11–2.30 (3 Fri & Sat), 5.30–11
Home Mild, Bitter; S&N Theakston XB, Old Peculier Ⓗ
Lovely, old village inn with an exposed, long, low wood-panelled bar, unspoilt tap room and a small, quiet, intimate snug. Very relaxed midweek. Q ❀ ◐ ♣ P

Royal Oak
Main Road
☎ (0602) 383110
11–3.30, 5 (7 Sat)–11
Hardys & Hansons Best Mild, Best Bitter Ⓗ/Ⓔ
Old village pub of quality with a comfortable, friendly atmosphere. Upstairs lounge; a log cabin at the back of the pub caters for entertainment and functions. Lunches Tue–Fri.
Q ❀ ◐ ⊟ ♿ ♣ P

Wellow

Red Lion
The Green ☎ (0623) 860001
11–3, 5.30–11
Courage Directors; Ruddles Best Bitter, County; Whitbread Boddingtons Bitter Ⓗ
Old pub opposite the village maypole. Q ❀ ◐ ◑ P ⊬

West Bridgford

Bridgford Wines (Off-Licence)
116 Melton Road
☎ (0602) 816181
5 (7 Mon, 11 Thu–Sat)–11; 12–2, 7–10.30 Sun
Springhead Bitter Ⓖ; guest beers
Off-licence with usually four–six real ales on draught, plus around 100 bottled beers from Britain and Europe. Supplies cask beer for parties.
⫏ P

West Stockwith

Waterfront Inn
☎ (0427) 891223
12–3, 7–11
Adnams Bitter; S&N Theakston XB; John Smith's Bitter Ⓗ; guest beer
Village pub overlooking a marina on the River Trent; popular with boating enthusiasts, especially in summer. Good range of food.
⚭ ❀ ◐ ◑ ♣ P

Worksop

Greendale Oak
Norfolk Street (near market, off B6034) ☎ (0909) 489680
12–4.30, 7–11; 11–11 Fri & Sat
Bass Worthington BB; Stones Best Bitter Ⓗ
Small, cosy, mid-terrace pub built in 1790, offering a friendly welcome. Keen darts and dominoes teams.
Q ❀ ◐ ▲ ♣ P

Manor Lodge
Mansfield Road (signed off A60) ☎ (0909) 474177
11–3, 5–11; 12–2.30, 7–10.30 Sun
Adnams Broadside; Draught Bass; Hull Governor; Springhead Bitter; Stones Best Bitter Ⓗ; guest beers
Unusual, five-storey, Elizabethan manor house, built in 1593 for the Earl of Shrewsbury with many original features still intact. Set in extensive grounds, it has a children's play area. Fri night folk club with live music.
♛ Q ❀ 🛏 ◐ ◑ ♣ P ⊬

Newcastle Arms
Carlton Road ☎ (0909) 485384
11.30–3, 5.30–11
Courage Directors; Marston's Pedigree; Ruddles County; Webster's Green Label, Yorkshire Bitter Ⓗ; guest beers
Popular free house catering for all ages. Comfortable and friendly atmosphere. Busy at weekends.
⚭ ❀ ◐ ◑ ♿ ⇌ ♣

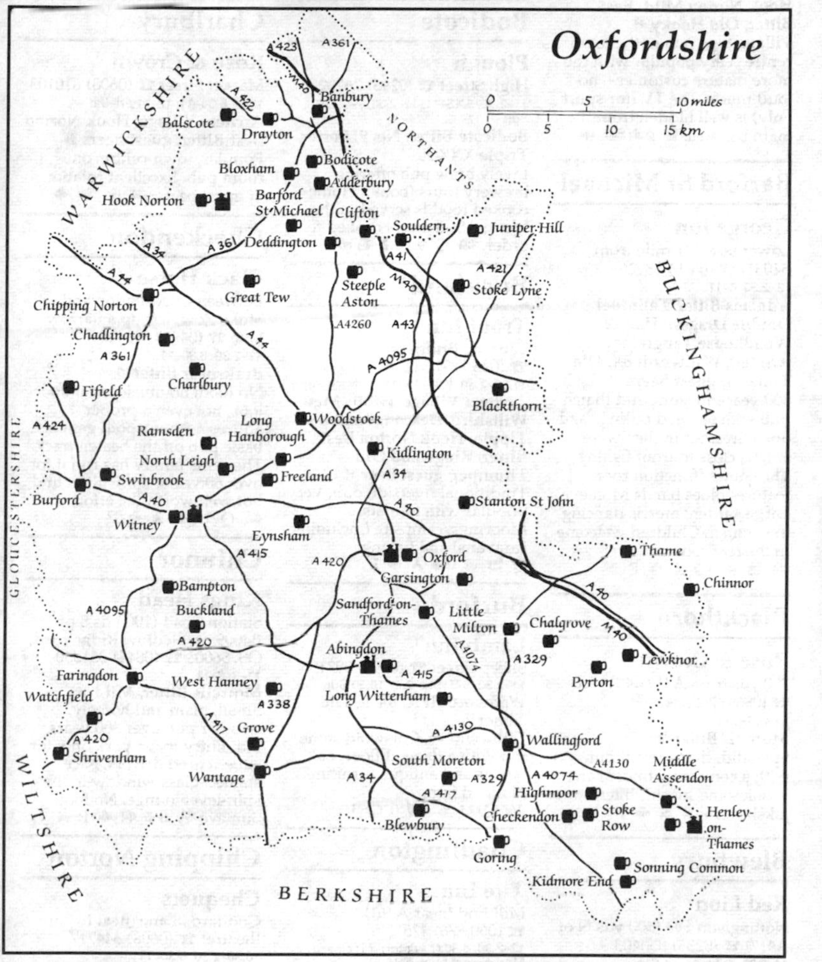

Brakspear, *Henley-on-Thames;* **Hook Norton,** *Hook Norton;* **Morland,** *Abingdon;* **Morrells,** *Oxford;* **Wychwood,** *Witney*

Abingdon

College Oak

Peachcroft Road, Peachcroft
☎ (0235) 554937
12 (11 Sat)–3, 5.30 (6 Sat)–11
Bass Worthington BB, Draught Bass Ⓗ
Unusual estate pub; one large bar with many artefacts. Named after St Peter's College (Radley) which used to own the land that Peachcroft was built on. Satellite TV is popular on football and fight nights. P

Adderbury

White Hart

Tanners Lane ☎ (0295) 810406
11–2.30, 5–11
Marston's Pedigree; Whitbread Boddingtons Bitter; guest beers Ⓗ
Tastefully refurbished 17th-century inn; quiet and friendly.
Q P

Try also: Bell, High St (Free)

Balscote

Butchers Arms

Shutford Road (off A422)
☎ (0295) 730750
12–3, 6–11
Hook Norton Best Bitter Ⓗ
Classic, one-roomed village pub, popular with hikers and locals. Conversation rules!
Q P

Bampton

Romany

Bridge Street ☎ (0993) 850237
11–11
Archers Village, Best Bitter; Hook Norton Mild, Best Bitter; guest beers Ⓗ
Very friendly, pleasant village inn, popular with locals and diners alike. Three guest beers. The extensive menu has a vegetarian option.
P

Banbury

Coach & Horses

Butchers Row ☎ (0295) 273552
10.30–3, 7–11

Hook Norton Mild, Best Bitter, Old Hooky Ⓗ
Village-type pub in the town centre. Very popular with the more mature customer – no loud music. The TV (for sport only) is well hidden from the main bar area. ❀ 🛏 ≢ ♣

Barford St Michael

George Inn
Lower Street (1 mile from B4031) ☎ (0869) 38226
12–2.30, 6–11
Adnams Bitter; Felinfoel Double Dragon; Hall & Woodhouse Tanglefoot (winter); **Wadworth 6X, Old Timer** Ⓗ; **guest beers**
300-year-old stone and thatch pub with beamed ceilings and open fires. Set in the Swere valley, close to trout fishing. The games/function room features blues bands Mon eve. Large garden; morris dancing in summer. Children welcome in the rear room.
🔥 ⛄ ❀ ◐ ◑ ▲ ♣ P

Blackthorn

Rose & Crown
300 yds from A41/B4011 jct ☎ (0869) 252534
12–3, 7–11
Morrells Bitter Ⓗ
Splendid, characterful pub with a convivial atmosphere. Wholesome snacks, interesting jukebox. 🔥 ❀ ♿ ♣ P

Blewbury

Red Lion
Nottingham Fee (300 yds N of A417) ☎ (0235) 850403
11–2.30, 6–11; 11–11 Sat
Brakspear Bitter, Old, Special Ⓗ
Picturesque pub, dating from 1785, in a village to the north of the Berkshire downs. An emphasis on food means daily specials and vegetarian choices, also a separate restaurant (no food Sun eve). The village is noted for its cob and thatched walls. Wheelchair access to the new extension. 🔥 Q ❀ ◐ ◑ ♿ P

Bloxham

Red Lion Inn
High Street ☎ (0295) 720352
11–2.30, 7–11
Adnams Bitter; Wadworth 6X; guest beers Ⓗ
Pleasant, friendly country pub with two bars and a large garden. Food served daily (roast Sun lunch Oct–Apr; barbecues Sun in summer).
🔥 Q ❀ ◐ ◑ ♿ ▲ ♣ P

Bodicote

Plough
High Street ☎ (0295) 262327
11–2.30, 5.45–11; 12–2.30, 7–10.30 Sun
Bodicote Bitter, No. 9, Porter, Triple XXX Ⓗ
Lively brew pub offering brewery tours (book). Home-cooked food is served in the lounge. Sun meals cooked to order. 🔥 Q ❀ ◐ ◑ ⊟ ♣

Buckland

Trout Inn
Tadpole Bridge
☎ (036 787) 382
11.30–2.30, 5.30–11 (11–11 May–Sept)
Archers Village; Gibbs Mew Wiltshire, Deacon, Bishop's Tipple; Hook Norton Best Bitter; Ringwood Old Thumper; guest beer Ⓗ
Traditional riverside pub. Very popular with tourists. Moorings, campsite (including caravans) and fishing.
Q ⛄ ❀ ◐ ◑ ▲ ♣ P

Burford

Lamb Inn
Sheep Street ☎ (0993) 823155
11–2.30, 6–11; 12–2, 7–10.30 Sun
Wadworth IPA, 6X Ⓗ, **Old Timer** Ⓖ
14th-century, Cotswold stone inn with a flagged floor, oak beams and antique furniture. No food Sun.
🔥 Q ⛄ ❀ 🛏 ◐ ◌ P

Chadlington

Tite Inn
Mill End (near A361)
☎ (060 876) 475
12–2.30, 6.30 (7 winter)–11; closed Mon except bank hols
Hall & Woodhouse Badger Best Bitter; Wychwood Hobgoblin Ⓗ; **guest beers**
16th-century free house and restaurant. The delightful garden has country views and allows disabled access. No jukebox, slot machines or games. Children welcome.
🔥 Q ❀ 🛏 ◐ ◑ ♿ P

Chalgrove

Red Lion
High Street ☎ (0865) 890625
11.30–3, 6–11
Brakspear Bitter; Fuller's London Pride; Greene King Abbot; guest beers Ⓗ
Popular, attractive village pub, 350 years old: a Grade II-listed building, recently renovated to create several drinking areas. Families are welcome. Two guest beers; wide range of good value, home-cooked food, including vegetarian. No-smoking dining room. No food Sun eve. 🔥 ❀ ◐ ◑ ♿ ♣

Charlbury

Rose & Crown
Market Street ☎ (0608) 810103
12–3, 5.30–11; 12–11 Fri–Sat
Archers Village; Hook Norton Best Bitter; guest beers Ⓗ
Popular, town-centre, one-room pub. Excellent rotation of guest beers. 🔥 ❀ ≢ ♣

Checkendon

Black Horse
Between Checkendon and Stoke Row, left up a narrow lane ☎ (0491) 680418
11–2.30, 6.30–11
Brakspear Bitter Ⓖ
No food, no music, no indoor loos, not even a proper address! An unspoilt gem of a basic pub off the beaten track. The same family has run it for over 60 years. Difficult to find, but well worth the effort.
🔥 Q ⛄ ❀ ▲ ♣ P

Chinnor

Kings Head
Station Road (100 yds S of B4009 on Bledlow Ridge road) OS756008 ☎ (0844) 351530
11–3, 6–11
Morrells Bitter, Mild Ⓗ
Small, plain and homely, two-bar pub over 300 years old. Entry to car park only for experienced drivers. Nice stained-glass window in the split-level lounge. No food Sun eve. ❀ ◐ ◑ ⊟ ♣ P

Chipping Norton

Chequers
Goddards Lane (next to theatre) ☎ (0608) 644717
10.30–2.30, 5.30–11
Fuller's Chiswick, London Pride, Mr Harry, ESB Ⓗ
Well-renovated real local with a friendly atmosphere. Aunt Sally played. Eve meals till 8.30. 🔥 Q ❀ ◐ ◑ ♿ ♣

Clifton

Duke of Cumberland's Head
On B4031 ☎ (0869) 38534
12–2.30, 6.30–11
Adnams Bitter; Exmoor Gold; Hook Norton Best Bitter; Smiles Best Bitter; Wadworth 6X Ⓗ; **guest beers**
Thatched, 17th-century stone pub with beams, inglenook and restaurant. Vibrant atmosphere! No food Sun eve in winter. 🔥 Q ❀ 🛏 ◐ ◑ ♿ P

Deddington

Crown & Tuns
New Street (A4260, Oxford road) ☎ (0869) 37371

11–4, 6–11
Hook Norton Mild, Best Bitter, Old Hooky Ⓗ
Fine Georgian coaching inn, a friendly, unpretentious little one-bar local. Conversation and dominoes rule; 21st year in this guide. 🜲 Q ❀ ♣

Drayton

Roebuck
Stratford Road
☎ (0295) 730542
11–2.30, 6–11
Fuller's London Pride; Hook Norton Best Bitter; Marston's Pedigree; Ruddles County; Whitbread Boddingtons Bitter Ⓗ
17th-century, picturesque village inn with a reputation for food.
🜲 Q ❀ ⛟ ◖◗ ⊟ P

Try also: Roebuck, N Newington (Free)

Eynsham

Queens Head
Queen Street ☎ (0865) 881229
12–2.30, 6.30–11
Morland Bitter, Old Masters, Old Speckled Hen Ⓗ**; guest beer**
18th-century, basic, two-bar village pub. The public bar has darts; both the lounge and bar contain railway memorabilia. Wheelchair access at the rear.
🜲 ❀ ⛟ ⊟ ♿ ♣

Faringdon

Bell Hotel
Market Place ☎ (0367) 240534
11–11
Hall & Woodhouse Tanglefoot; Wadworth 6X, Farmer's Glory, Old Timer Ⓗ**; guest beers**
16th-century inn where the bar retains some original features. Pleasant courtyard.
🜲 ♉ ❀ ⛟ ◖◗ ♣ P

Folly
London Street ☎ (0367) 240620
10.30–2.30, 5.30–11
Morrells Bitter, Varsity Ⓗ
Charming little town pub with no frills. 🜲 Q ❀ ⊟ ♣

Fifield

Merrymouth Inn
Stow Road (A424)
☎ (0993) 831652
11–2.30, 6–11; 12–2.30, 7–10.30 Sun
Donnington BB, SBA Ⓗ
Historic 13th-century inn with a beamed bar and a stone floor. Extensive renovations have been well done. Home cooking on an open log grill.
🜲 Q ♉ ❀ ⛟ ◖◗ ▲ ♣ P

Freeland

Oxfordshire Yeoman
Wroslyn Road
☎ (0993) 882051
11–2.30, 6–11
Morrells Bitter, Mild Ⓗ
Cotswold stone pub with a low ceiling and exposed beams. The stone floor area used to be a cart shed; a tethering post with rings is still visible. No eve meals Sun, and only till 8pm Mon.
🜲 ❀ ◖◗ ♣

Garsington

Three Horseshoes
16 The Green ☎ (086 736) 395
11–3, 6.30–11 (11–11 summer)
Draught Bass; Morrells Bitter, Varsity Ⓗ
A pub since 1801, where a magnificent ship's keel supports the bar ceiling. Food is cooked to order by a French chef for the large lounge/restaurant. Huge garden (children's play area). No meals Sun and Mon eves.
🜲 ❀ ◖◗ ♣ P

Goring

Catherine Wheel
Station Road (off B4009)
☎ (0491) 872379
11–2.30, 6–11
Brakspear Mild, Bitter Ⓗ**, Old** Ⓖ**, Special** Ⓗ
Over 500 years old and extended into an old blacksmith's shop; the oldest pub in one of the most picturesque villages on the Thames. The split-level bar is L-shaped, with a public bar end. The gents' is well hidden behind a secret panel. No food Sun eve. 🜲 ❀ ◖◗ ⇌ ♣ P

John Barleycorn
Manor Road (off B4009)
☎ (0491) 872509
10–2.30, 6–11
Brakspear Bitter, Special Ⓗ
Attractive, 16th-century, low-beamed inn with a cosy saloon and good food. Close to the Thames and the Ridgeway path. Q ❀ ⛟ ◖◗ ⊟ ⇌ ♣

Great Tew

Falkland Arms
Off B4022 ☎ (0608) 83653
11.30–2.30 (not Mon), 6–11; 12–2, 7–10.30 Sun
Donnington BB; Hook Norton Best Bitter; Taylor Landlord; Wadworth 6X; guest beers Ⓗ
Outstanding, 16th-century, classic, thatched pub in a preserved village. Oak panels, settles and flagstoned floors; malts, fruit wines, snuff, oil lamps, clay pipes and walking sticks sold. Numerous guest beers – a gem! No food Sun.
🜲 Q ❀ ⛟ ◖ ▲ ♣ ⌽

Grove

Volunteer
Station Road ☎ (0235) 769557
11–11
Archers Village; Draught Bass; Hook Norton Best Bitter; Morland Bitter; Wadworth 6X Ⓗ**; guest beer**
Friendly local on the edge of Wantage, popular for its Bangladeshi food (best to book). Free mini-bus nightly from Grove centre, returning at closing time. ◖◗ ♣

Henley-on-Thames

Saracen's Head
129 Greys Road (off A4155, up hill half a mile SW of A4130/A4155 jct)
☎ (0491) 575929
11–2.30 (3 Sat), 5.30–11
Brakspear Mild, Bitter, Old, Special Ⓗ
A friendly welcome in a popular and busy local which has an emphasis on games. Fields teams for crib, darts, pool and quizzes. Home-cooked snacks always available.
🜲 ❀ ⛟ ▲ ⇌ (not winter Sun) ♣ P

Highmoor

Dog & Duck
On B481, S of Nettlebed
☎ (0491) 641261
12–3, 6–11
Brakspear Bitter, Old, Special Ⓗ
Cosy, two-bar, roadside pub in Chiltern woodland, a popular area for walkers and cyclists. A small, no-smoking dining room offers good value, home-made food, including vegetarian (no food Mon). Classic car night, third Mon of the month. 🜲 Q ❀ ◖◗ ♣ P

Hook Norton

Gate Hangs High
1 mile N of village
☎ (0608) 737387
11–3, 6.30–11
Hook Norton Best Bitter Ⓗ
Pleasant, isolated country pub, with a bricked bar area. The restaurant has meal appeal; no food Sun eve, booking advisable for the set Sun lunch. 🜲 Q ❀ ◖◗ ▲ ♣ P

Pear Tree
Scotland End ☎ (0608) 737482
12–2.30 (3 Sat), 6–11

Oxfordshire

Hook Norton Mild, Best Bitter, Old Hooky, Twelve Days [H]
Charming, refurbished, one-room brewery tap. No food Tue eve; other eves meals till 8.
♛ Q ❀ ⛟ ◐ ◑ ▲ ♣ P

Juniper Hill

Fox

☎ (0869) 810616
12–2, 7–11
Hook Norton Best Bitter [H], **Old Hooky** [G]
Friendly pub in the centre of this hamlet: the Waggon & Horses in *Lark Rise to Candleford*. ♛ Q ❀ ♣ ⌓ P

Kidlington

Kings Arms

The Moors ☎ (086 75) 3004
11–3, 6–11
Ind Coope ABC Best Bitter, Burton Ale; guest beer [H]
Small busy, traditional, two-bar locals' pub.
Q ◐ ◑ ⊟ P

Kidmore End

New Inn

Chalkhouse Green Road (off B481, at Sonning Common)
☎ (0734) 723115
11–2.30, 6–11
Brakspear Bitter [H], **Old** [G], **Special** [H]
Comfortable, two-bar pub with beams, wood panelling and a large garden, opposite the village pond and near the church. Good cooking, with an imaginative menu (vegetarian choices). ♘ ❀ ◐ ◑ P ⅟

Lewknor

Olde Leathern Bottel

1 High Street (off B4009, near M40 jct 6) ☎ (0844) 351482
11–2.30, 6–11
Brakspear Bitter, Old, Special [H]
Comfortable and inviting, family-run village pub with a friendly atmosphere and a large, well-kept garden. The food is good quality, home-made and reasonably priced (vegetarian options). The unusual game of 'Spoof' is played.
♛ ♘ ❀ ◐ ◑ ⊟ ♿ ♣ P

Little Milton

Plough

Stadhampton Road (A329)
☎ (0844) 278180
11–11
Morrells Bitter, Mild, Varsity, Graduate; guest beer [H]
17th-century, stone-walled and timber-beamed pub with a village atmosphere. Good value food available all day with vegetarian choices. Large, enclosed play area and garden with a pets corner and Aunt Sally. Discount for senior citizens on beer and spirits.
♛ ♘ ❀ ◐ ◑ ▲ ♣ P ⅟

Long Hanborough

Bell

Main Road ☎ (0993) 881324
10.30–3 (varies), 6–11
Morrells Bitter, Varsity [H]
Cosy, old, two-bar stone and slate pub with a beamed function room and a children's play room.
♘ ❀ ◐ ◑ ⇌ ♣ P

Long Wittenham

Machine Man Inn

Fieldside (1 mile off A415, follow signs) ☎ (086 730) 7835
11–3, 6.30–11
Eldridge Pope Dorchester, Hardy Country, Royal Oak; guest beers [H]
Genuine village local which used to belong to the machine mender – hence the name. ETB-approved accommodation. One mile from Clifton lock on the Thames. Good value, home-made food includes a vegetarian option. Families welcome. Four guest beers.
♛ ❀ ⛟ ◐ ◑ ♿ ♣ ⌓ P

Middle Assendon

Rainbow

On B480, 1 mile N of A4130 jct
☎ (0491) 574879
11.30–2.30, 6–11; 12–2.30, 7–10.30 Sun
Brakspear Bitter [E], **Old** [G], **Special** [E]
Friendly, old, low-beamed local in a beautiful Chiltern dry valley. Popular with walkers and cyclists. Bar snacks only Sun lunch. The handpumps operate electric pumps. ❀ ◐ ⊟ ▲ ♣ P

North Leigh

Woodman

New Yatt Road (off A4095)
☎ (0993) 881790
12–3, 6–11; 12–11 Sat
Hook Norton Best Bitter; Wadworth 6X; Wychwood Shires [H]**; guest beers**
Small village pub offering a large terrace, a garden and home-made food. Twice-yearly beer festivals. Aunt Sally. Jazz and cider in summer. ♛ ♘ ❀ ⛟ ◐ ◑ ♿ ▲ ♣ ⌓ P ⅟

Oxford

Anchor

2 Hayfield Road, Walton Manor (off Woodstock Rd)
☎ (0865) 510282
11.30–3, 7 (earlier in summer)–11
Adnams Broadside; Hall & Woodhouse Tanglefoot; Wadworth IPA, 6X, Farmer's Glory [H]**; guest beers**
Spacious pub, not far from the centre. Awarded CAMRA *Best Pub Refurbishment* 1992 for its well restored 1930s decor. Known locally as Dolly's Hut. Good, changing selection of food, usually including a fish dish. Handy for canal boats (bridge 240 on the Oxford Canal). ♛ ❀ ◐ ◑ ♣ P

Black Boy

91 Old High Street, Headington (off A420)
☎ (0865) 63234
11–3, 6–11; 11–11 Sat
Morrells Bitter, Mild, Varsity, Graduate, College [H]
Large local, appealing to all. The small saloon is a quiet retreat. Award-winning garden. Q ❀ ◐ ◑ ⊟ ♿ ♣ P

Bookbinders Arms

17–18 Victor Street, Jericho
☎ (0865) 53549
10.30–3, 7–11; 10.30–11 Sat
Morrells Bitter, Mild [H]
Friendly, single-bar locals' pub with two distinct areas. Very popular for pub games. ◐ ♣

Butchers Arms

5 Wilberforce Street, Headington (past the Shark, first left, first right) ☎ (0865) 61252
11.30–2.30 (11–3 Sat), 6 (4.30 Fri, 5.30 Sat)–11
Fuller's Hock, London Pride, Mr Harry, ESB [H]
Locals' pub with a warm, friendly atmosphere. Families welcome lunchtime and early eve. Hard to find but worth the effort. ♛ ❀ ◐ ♿ ♣

Cricketers Arms

43 Iffley Road (A4158)
☎ (0865) 726264
12–3, 6.30–11
Morland Bitter, Old Masters, Old Speckled Hen; guest beer [H]
Traditional, two-bar local. The lively public bar hosts jazz every Tue eve, and blues alternate Sun lunch. The lounge bar has a relaxed atmosphere. Good range of vegetarian meals; no food Sun eve. ❀ ◐ ◑ ⊟ ♣

Eagle & Child

49 St Giles ☎ (0865) 58085
11–2.30, 5–11
Ind Coope Burton Ale; Tetley Bitter; Wadworth 6X [H]

Excellently restored pub of character, once frequented by CS Lewis and Tolkien. Retains many intimate alcoves and is ideal for a quiet chat. The unobtrusive extension leads onto a pleasant outdoor drinking area. Q ❀ ◖ ◗

Fir Tree Tavern
163 Iffley Road (A4158)
☎ (0865) 247373
12–3, 5.30–11
Morrells Bitter, Mild, Varsity, Graduate [H]
Small, split-level Victorian pub with an intimate atmosphere; popular with locals and students. Piano player Wed and Sun eve; quiz Thu. Freshly-made pizzas. Children welcome until 8pm.
❀ ◖ ◗ ♣

Gloucester Arms
Friars Entry (off Magdalen St)
☎ (0865) 241177
11–11
Ind Coope Burton Ale; Tetley Bitter; Wadworth 6X; guest beers [H]
City-centre pub with a lively atmosphere; popular with students and rock enthusiasts. Close to the Oxford Playhouse and signed photos of actors are displayed. The decor is unfussy, with much wood and snob screens. ◖ ⇌

Marlborough House
60 Western Road, Grandpont (off A4144) ☎ (0865) 243617
11.30–2.30, 6–11; 11.30–11 Sat
Ind Coope ABC Best Bitter, Burton Ale; Tetley Bitter [H]
Built on the site of the city's first station, a friendly, back-street local long popular with students and locals alike. Pool room upstairs. ❀ ◖ ⇌ ♣

Old Tom
101 St Aldates (A420)
☎ (0865) 243034
10.30–3, 5 (5.30 Fri & Sat)–11
Morrells Bitter, Mild, Varsity [H]
Small, comfortable, 17th-century city-centre pub, popular with locals, students and tourists, with a lively but friendly atmosphere. Takes its name from the bell at Christ Church College. No-smoking area lunchtime only; eve meals finish early. Q ❀ ◖ ◗ ⇌ ⊬

Osney Arms
45 Botley Road, Osney (A420)
☎ (0865) 247103
11–2.30, 6–11; 11–11 Sat
Greene King IPA, Rayments Special, Abbot [H]
Basic community local with an established clientele, successful in local pool, cricket and quiz leagues. Can get a bit smoky in the eves. ⊞ ⇌

Quarry Gate
19 Wharton Road, Headington
☎ (0865) 62593
11–3, 6–11
Courage Best Bitter, Directors; Marston's Pedigree; John Smith's Bitter [H]**; guest beers**
Friendly suburban local with a lounge/family room and a busy public bar. Ever-changing range of guest beers and ciders.
Q ❀ ◖ ◗ ⊞ ♣ ⌓ P

Victoria Arms
Mill Lane, Old Marston
☎ (0865) 241382
11.30–2.30, 6–11 (11.30–11 summer)
Draught Bass; Hall & Woodhouse Tanglefoot; Wadworth 6X, Farmer's Glory, Old Timer [H]**; guest beer**
Popular, attractive riverside pub where the surrounding grounds include a children's play area. A frequent destination for those punting upriver. Can be crowded Sun lunch. ♛ ❀ ◖ ◗ ♿ P

Pyrton

Plough
Off B4009 N of Watlington
☎ (0491) 612003
11.30–2.30, 6 (7 Tue)–11; closed Mon eve
Adnams Bitter; Brakspear Bitter; Fuller's ESB [H]
Attractive, 17th-century, thatched pub in a quiet country village. Popular for its extensive menu of home-made food in the bar or restaurant (where families are welcome at lunchtime).
♛ ❀ ◖ ◗ ▲ ♣ P

Ramsden

Royal Oak
High Street ☎ (0993) 868213
11–2.30, 6.30–11
Banks's Bitter; Hook Norton Best Bitter, Old Hooky [H]**; guest beers**
17th-century inn with a courtyard. The restaurant serves high quality food using local produce. Long-serving staff create an efficient, friendly atmosphere.
♛ Q ❀ ⛟ ◖ ◗ ♿ ▲
⇌ (Finstock Halt) ♣ P

Sandford-on-Thames

Fox
☎ (0865) 777803
12–2.30, 7 (6 summer)–11
Morrells Bitter, Mild (weekends), **Varsity** (summer) [G]
Popular, unspoilt local offering the cheapest beer in the Oxford area. In this guide for 16 consecutive years.
♛ Q ❀ ⊞ ♣ P

Shrivenham

Prince of Wales
High Street ☎ (0793) 782268
11–3, 6–11
Hall & Woodhouse Tanglefoot; Wadworth IPA, 6X [H]**, Old Timer** [G]**; guest beer**
Cosy, stone-built country pub; a 17th-century coaching inn. Good food (no meals Sun eve). Regularly changed guest beers. ♛ Q ❀ ◖ ◗ ♣ P

Victoria Tavern
Station Road ☎ (0793) 783443
11.45–2.20, 5.30 (6 Sat)–11
Archers Village; Arkell's 2B; Wadworth 6X [H]
Unpretentious, friendly local. Good variety of wholesome food. ♛ ❀ ◖ ◗ ♣ P

Sonning Common

Bird in Hand
Peppard Road (B481)
☎ (0734) 723230
11–2.30, 6–11
Courage Best Bitter; Fuller's London Pride; Ruddles County [H]
Low-beamed, 16th-century pub with a large inglenook. Very popular restaurant (standard pub menu); also bar meals. Vegetarian options. No meals Sun eve. The attractive, enclosed garden is ideal for children. Q ❀ ◖ ◗ P

Souldern

Fox
Off B4100 ☎ (0869) 345284
11–3, 5 (6 Sat)–11
Draught Bass; Fuller's London Pride; Hook Norton Best Bitter; guest beers [H]
Friendly, Cotswold stone pub in the village centre. A small restaurant offers good food (not served Sun eve).
♛ Q ❀ ◖ ◗ ♿ ♣ P

South Moreton

Crown
High Street (off A417 and A4130) ☎ (0235) 812262
11–3, 5.30–11
Adnams Bitter; Hall & Woodhouse Tanglefoot; Wadworth IPA [H]**, 6X** [G]**; guest beer** [G]/[H]
Popular, traditional village local with a spacious single bar. The floorboards, rugs, deep red walls and ceiling generate a warm, cosy atmosphere. Good value, home-cooked food with

vegetarian choices and daily specials. Interesting games.
⛼ Q ⛍ ❀ ◐ ◗ ♣ P

Stanton St John

Star Inn

Middle Road ☎ (0865) 351277
11–2.30, 6.30–11; 12–2.30, 7–10.30 Sun
Hall & Woodhouse Tanglefoot; Wadworth IPA, 6X, Farmer's Glory, Old Timer H
17th-century inn retaining some original features. Tasty, home-cooked food, including a vegetarian option, at reasonable prices. Children may bring well-behaved parents to the no-smoking family room and garden.
⛼ Q ⛍ ❀ ◐ ◗ ⊞ ♣ P ⚟

Steeple Aston

Red Lion

South Street (E of A4260)
☎ (0869) 40225
11–3, 6–11
Hall & Woodhouse Tanglefoot G**; Hook Norton Best Bitter; Wadworth 6X** H
Friendly, discerning pub where the cosy bar has a library. Bar lunches, except Sun, and a dining room for eve meals, Tue–Sat.
⛼ Q ❀ ◐ ◗ P

Stoke Lyne

Peyton Arms

Off B4100 ☎ (0869) 345285
10.30–2.30 (not Mon), 6–11
Hook Norton Mild, Best Bitter, Old Hooky (winter) G
Small, basic village local unchanged by time – a real rural gem. ⛼ Q ❀ ⊞ ♣

Stoke Row

Cherry Tree

Off B481 ☎ (0491) 680430
10–3, 6–11
Brakspear Mild, Bitter, Old, Special G
Picturesque, low-beamed village local. Families are welcome in the lounge and the games room, which has a pool table. The garden has swings and a slide. Snacks available lunchtimes (not Mon). Plays host to a Velocette owners' club. ⛼ ⛍ ❀ ⊞ ♣ P

Swinbrook

Swan

2½ miles E of Burford
☎ (0993) 822165
11.30–2.30, 6–11
Morland Bitter; Wadworth 6X H
Characterful, 16th-century, riverside country inn, offering good home-cooked food (not served Sun eve). Darts, cards and shove-ha'penny in the flagstoned tap room.
⛼ Q ◐ ◗ ♿ ♣ ⛢ P

Thame

Rising Sun

High Street ☎ (084 421) 4206
11–2.30, 6–11
Hall & Woodhouse Tanglefoot; Hook Norton Best Bitter; Wadworth 6X H**; guest beers**
Attractive, 16th-century, oak-beamed building with an overhanging first floor and low ceilings. Excellent home-cooked menu. Board games.
⛼ ❀ ◐ ◗ ♣

Six Bells

44 Lower High Street
☎ (084 421) 2088
11–3, 6–11; 11–11 Sat
Fuller's Hock, Chiswick, London Pride, Mr Harry, ESB H
Warm and comfortable, old two-bar pub; much improved under Fuller's management. All six bells are rung at closing time! Keg cider on a fake handpump. No meals Sun eve.
Q ⛍ ❀ ◐ ◗ ♣ P

Wallingford

Cross Keys

48 High Street (A4130)
☎ (0491) 837173
11–3, 6–11
Brakspear Mild, Bitter, Old, Special H
Unspoilt, three-roomed, 17th-century town pub: a small, comfortable lounge and a public bar with steps up to a darts room. Children's play area in the garden. Reputedly haunted. Eve meals till 8.30. No food Sun.
Q ❀ ◐ ◗ ⊞ ♣ P

Wantage

Royal Oak

Newbury Street
☎ (023 57) 3129
12–2.30 (not Mon–Thu), 5.30–11
Adnams Bitter; Fuller's London Pride; Hall & Woodhouse Badger Best Bitter, Tanglefoot; Wadworth 6X; Wychwood Shires; guest beers H
Pleasant, slightly dog-eared pub with two large bars, attracting people from all walks of life. Beware the fake Scrumpy Jack handpumps. Food Fri and Sat lunchtimes only. 🛏 ◐ ♿

Watchfield

Royal Oak

Oak Road ☎ (0793) 782668
11.30–2.30, 6.30–11
Ushers Best Bitter H**; guest beer**
Friendly, ivy-covered local, dating back to the 18th century. Boasts a skittle alley and satellite TV. ❀ ◐ ◗ ♣ P

West Hanney

Lamb Inn

School Road ☎ (0235) 868917
11–2.30, 6.30–11; 12–2.30, 7–10.30 Sun
Hall & Woodhouse Badger Best Bitter; Morland Bitter; Wadworth 6X; guest beers H
Quiet country pub refurbished in a 19th-century style, with antique furniture, pictures and Chinese rugs on an old wood-block floor. No food Sun eve. Q ⛍ ❀ ◐ ◗ ♣ P ⚟

Witney

Carpenters Arms

132 Newland ☎ (0993) 702206
10.30–2.30, 6–11
Morrells Bitter H
Comfortable pub with one bar, and a small games room, popular with all ages. Ideal for a quiet drink. Worthington White Shield stocked. ❀ P

Court Inn

Bridge Street ☎ (0993) 703228
10.30–3, 6–11; 12.30–3, 7–10.30 Sun
Courage Best Bitter; John Smith's Bitter H
17th-century coaching inn, with a large, comfortable lounge and a small bar/games room. Probably the best pint of John Smith's in the county, served by a Yorkshire landlord. 🛏 ◐ ◗ ⊞ ♣ P

House of Windsor

31 West End ☎ (0993) 704277
12–3.30 (not Mon), 6 (7 Sat)–11
Hook Norton Best Bitter; Marston's Pedigree; Wadworth 6X H**; guest beers**
Popular local featuring aeronautical memorabilia. A comfortable single bar, but beware of the proximity of the doors to the bar when entering. ⛼ ◐ ◗ ♣

Try also: Red Lion, Corn St (Morrells)

Woodstock

Black Prince

2 Manor Road (A34)
☎ (0993) 811530
12–2.30 (3 Sat), 6.30–11
Archers Village; S&N Theakston XB, Old Peculier; guest beer H
Comfortable, 16th-century pub of character, situated in Old Woodstock. Note the suit of armour in the bar. Good meals, with Mexican food a speciality. ⛼ ❀ ◐ ◗ P

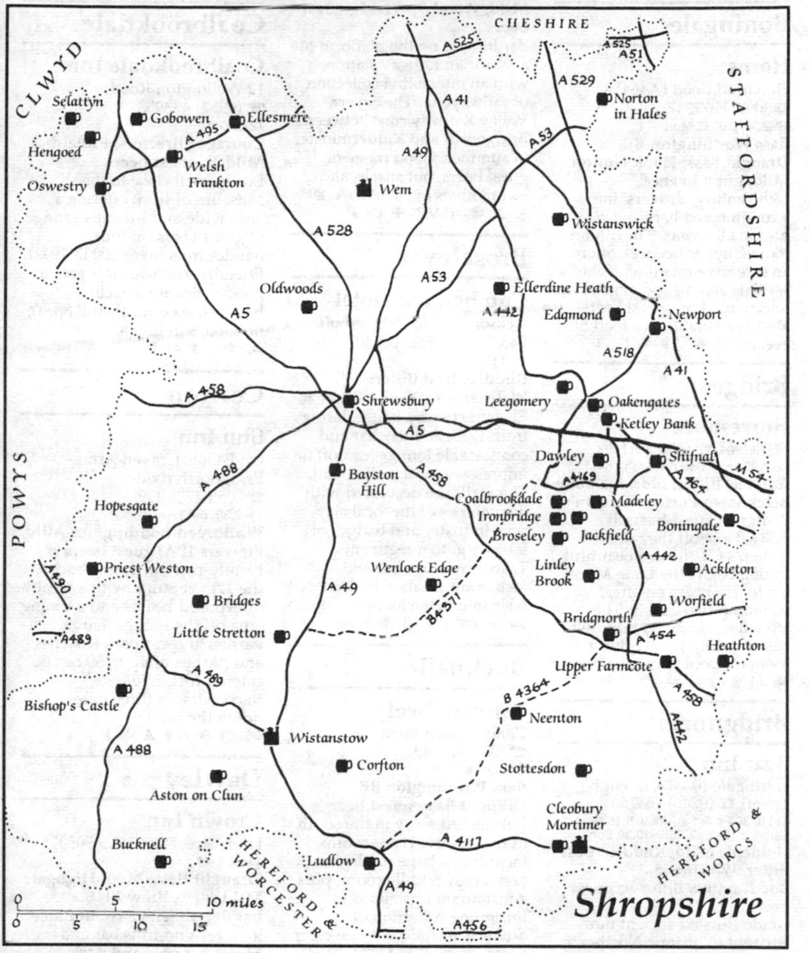

Hanby, Wem; Hobsons, Cleobury Mortimer; Wood, Wistanstow

Ackleton

Folley Inn

Stableford (B4176, 6 miles S of Telford) ☎ (074 65) 225
12–3, 7 (6.30 Sat)–11
Banks's Mild, Bitter Ⓔ
Open-plan, roadside inn in a rural location. No dogs allowed. Q ❀ ♣ P

Aston on Clun

Kangaroo Inn

Near Craven Arms
☎ (058 87) 263
12–3, 7–11
Bass Worthington BB, Draught Bass; M&B Highgate Mild Ⓗ**; guest beers**
Roadside pub with a lounge and a large public bar where woodwork and Australian mementoes abound. The large garden has a children's play area. Caravans and campers welcome. The village is famous for its Arbor tree.
♨ ◐ ▲ ⇌ ♣ P

Try also: Engine & Tender, Broome (Free)

Bayston Hill

Compasses

Hereford Road (A49)
☎ (0743) 872921
12–3 (not Mon–Fri in winter), 5–11; 12–11 Fri & Sat
Draught Bass; M&B Highgate Mild, Brew XI Ⓗ**; guest beer** (weekends)
Friendly local on the main road, with a snug and a public bar with decor that reflects its name. Collection of carved wooden elephants. Shove-ha'penny and bar skittles. Snacks. Q ❀ ⊟ ♿ ♣ P

Bishop's Castle

Castle Hotel

Market Square
☎ (0588) 638403
12–3, 6.30–11
Wadworth 6X; Whitbread Boddingtons Bitter; guest beers Ⓗ
Fine country town hotel whose entrance leads into a snug front bar with much original woodwork in evidence; larger through room off. Good selection of games. A venue for various activities.
♨ Q ⛟ ◐ ♣ P

Boningale

Horns
Holyhead Road (A464)
☎ (0902) 372347
12–2.30, 6.30 (7 Mon)–11
Bass Worthington BB, Draught Bass; Hook Norton Mild; guest beers Ⓗ
18th-century, drovers' inn with timbered bars and real fires in all rooms. The dining room (supper licence), offers an extensive menu with chef's specials and a good vegetarian selection. Three guest beers always available. No food Sun eve. Q P

Bridges

Horseshoes
OS394964 ☎ (058 861) 260
12–2.30 (later Sat; not Mon), 6–11
Adnams Bitter; Eldridge Pope Blackdown Porter; Marston's Pedigree; guest beers Ⓗ
Pub set just off the road to Bishop's Castle, in a beautiful setting below the Long Mynd. Up to five beers on offer, including two guests. The attractive, rendered building has one main room, plus a room for pool without a bar.
Q P

Bridgnorth

Bear Inn
Northgate (B4373, in High Town) ☎ (0746) 763250
11 (10.30 Fri & Sat)–2.30, 5.15 (6 Sat)–11; 12–2.30, 7.30–10.30 Sun
Holden's Mild; Ruddles Best Bitter; Whitbread Boddingtons Bitter Ⓗ**; guest beers**
Grade II-listed ancient inn, adjacent to historic Northgate. Up to six real ales, plus cider, served to wash down the excellent lunches (not served Sun). A gourmet night is held in the lounge each Thu (booking essential). Note the old brewery in the garden.
Q (SVR) P

Bell & Talbot
2 Salop Street (B4364, old A458) ☎ (0746) 763233
11.30–3, 6 (7 winter)–11
Batham Best Bitter; Hook Norton Best Bitter; S&N Theakston XB; guest beers Ⓗ
Grade II-listed free house with two character-laden rooms. The rear courtyard contains the old brewery building, reached through a passage decorated with a real ale mural. (SVR)

Railwaymans Arms
SVR Station, Hollybush Road (off B4364) ☎ (0746) 764361
11–11 (11–2.30, 7–11 winter)
Bass Worthington BB; Batham Best Bitter; M&B Highgate Mild; Wood Special Ⓗ**; guest beers**
Bar located on the platform of a Victorian railway station, with an interesting collection of railwayana. The Severn Valley Railway runs between Bridgnorth and Kidderminster in summer. Good range of guest beers, hot snacks and locomotives available.
(SVR) P

Broseley

Cumberland Hotel
Jackson Avenue (signed off B4375) ☎ (0952) 882301
10–11
Ruddles Best Bitter; Webster's Yorkshire Bitter Ⓗ
Elegant country house dating from 1715. A lively bar and comfortable lounge lead off an impressive mosaic-tiled hall. The walls are decorated with mementoes of the local clay pipe industry and badges of long-forgotten regiments. Tasty, inventive bar and restaurant meals. Children welcome in the lounge.
P

Bucknell

Baron of Beef
Chapel Lawn Road
☎ (054 74) 549
12–2.30, 6.30–11
Bass Worthington BB, Draught Bass; guest beer Ⓗ
Pub tucked away in the south of the county. Three rooms, including a large public bar and a cosy middle room, plus a restaurant upstairs. An intriguing collection of artefacts includes a huge cider press. P

Cleobury Mortimer

Bell Inn
Lower Street ☎ (0299) 270305
11–3, 7 (6 Sat)–11
Banks's Mild, Bitter Ⓔ
Pub with a multi-level lounge and an old-fashioned bar, plus a pool room and a private snooker club room at the rear (day membership available).

Kings Arms Hotel
Church Street ☎ (0299) 270252
11.30–11
Greene King Abbot; Hook Norton Best Bitter; Taylor Landlord; guest beers Ⓗ
Large, single-roomed inn dating back to 1530, with a central fireplace and a choice of tables and chairs or comfy sofas. The restaurant serves a wide choice of reasonably-priced meals (no food Sun eve).

Coalbrookdale

Coalbrookdale Inn
12 Wellington Road
☎ (0952) 433953
12–3, 6–11
Courage Directors; Pitfield Mild Ⓗ**; guest beers**
Lively local close to the Museum of Iron, offering a very wide and inventive range of guest beers on four handpumps (over 200 in 1992). Friendly locals always give a good welcome. Excellent, home-cooked meals (till 8pm); no food Sun lunch.
P

Corfton

Sun Inn
On B4368, Craven Arms–Bridgnorth road
☎ (058 473) 239
11–2.30, 6–11
Whitbread Boddingtons Mild, Flowers IPA; guest beers Ⓗ
Family-run inn dating back to the 17th century, with a wealth of exposed beams and a dining area off the lounge. Large garden and car park (coaches and parties of up to 50 can be catered for). Ludlow Racecourse is three miles down the road.
Q P

Dawley

Crown Inn
High Street ☎ (0952) 505015
11–4, 7–11
Draught Bass; M&B Highgate Mild Ⓗ/Ⓔ**, Brew XI** Ⓔ
Large pub with a comfortable lounge, a no-frills bar and rooms for pool and darts. A good, friendly pub for all ages in a pedestrianised part of town. Very good jukebox.

Three Crowns Inn
Hinkshay Road (off B4373 at Finger Rd garage)
☎ (0952) 590868
11–3 (4 Fri & Sat), 6.30–11
Marston's Bitter, Pedigree Ⓗ
Small, town pub with a U-shaped lounge, part of which is given over to darts and pool. A good, friendly, relaxed atmosphere prevails.
P

Edgmond

Lamb Inn
Shrewsbury Road (B5062, 1½ miles from Newport)
☎ (0952) 810421
12–2.30 (3 Sat), 7–11
Greenalls Mild, Davenports Bitter, Thomas Greenall's Original; Tetley Bitter Ⓗ

Large country pub with three bars, a dining room, a pool room and a function room (karaoke every Mon). Frequented by all ages and local agricultural college students. Good value food (not served Sun or Mon eves).
♛ ❀ ⛼ ◖ ◗ ♿ ▲ ♣ P

Ellerdine Heath

Royal Oak
1 mile off A53 OS603226
☎ (0939) 250300
11–3, 5 11; 11 11 Sat
Draught Bass; Brains SA; Hanby Drawwell; Mansfield Riding Mild; Wood Parish [H]; guest beers
1992 local CAMRA *Pub of the Year*. A popular, friendly, rural pub set in a farming community. Locally nicknamed the Tiddly, because of its small bar. No food Tue. Camping by prior arrangement. Cider in summer.
♛ ⛟ ❀ ◖ ◗ ▲ ♣ ⌓ P

Ellesmere

White Hart
Birch Road
☎ (0691) 622333
12–3 (varies summer), 7–11
Banks's Mild; Marston's Bitter [H]
Interesting old pub, Grade II-listed, which is popular with users of the nearby Llangollen Canal, at the centre of Shropshire's Lake District.
❀ ⊡ ▲ ♣

Gobowen

Cross Foxes
The Cross
☎ (0691) 670827
11–11
Banks's Mild; Marston's Bitter, Pedigree [H]
Welcoming village local with a bar and a comfortable lounge. Adjacent to the railway station.
⊡ ♿ ⇌ P

Heathton

Old Gate
Between Bobbington and Claverley ☎ (0746) 710431
12–2.30, 7–11; 12–2.30, 7–10.30 Sun
HP&D Entire; Taylor Landlord; Tetley Bitter [H]
This 16th-century country inn is very much a family house, with a patio, beautiful gardens and a children's play area. Food, served at all sessions, includes a child's menu. The chargrilled steaks and gammon are well-known.
♛ ❀ ◖ ◗ ♿ ▲ P

Hengoed

Last Inn
Off B4579, 3 miles N of Oswestry ☎ (0691) 659747
7–11; closed Mon–Sat lunch
Draught Bass; Whitbread Boddingtons Bitter; Wood Special [H]; guest beers
Country pub with separate games and family rooms. No meals Tue eve; Sun lunch served. Eleven years in this guide. ♛ Q ⛟ ◗ ⊡ ♿ P

Hopesgate

Stables Inn
Off A488 ☎ (0743) 891344
11.30–2.30, 7–11; closed Mon
Felinfoel Double Dragon; Marston's Pedigree; Tetley Bitter; Wood Special [H]
Outstanding pub on the drovers' road in the South Shropshire hills, warm and welcoming. The cosy, L-shaped bar boasts a massive log fire. First class, home-cooked cuisine is served in a small dining room; eve meals Wed–Sat. Boules played.
♛ Q ❀ ◖ ◗ ⌓

Ironbridge

Crown
10 Hodge Bower (off A4169, Madeley Hill; follow Belmont Rd) ☎ (0952) 433128
12–3, 7–11
Banks's Mild, Bitter [E]
Traditional local situated in a scenic spot above the historic Ironbridge gorge, and offering good food. The games room has a dartboard and a pool table. Eve meals Wed–Sat (plus Tue in summer).
❀ ◖ ◗ ♣ P

Jackfield

Boat
Ferry Road (across river via a footbridge at the foot of the inclined plain) ☎ (0952) 882178
12–3 (2.30 winter), 6 (7 winter)–11
Banks's Mild, Bitter [E]
Cosy, compact, riverside pub. Note the original Coalbrookdale range and the flood level markers on the door. Good value food.
♛ Q ❀ ◖ ◗ ♣ ⌓

Ketley Bank

Lord Hill Inn
Main Road (off A5, near Oakengates) ☎ (0952) 613070
12–2.30 (3 Sat), 7 (5 Thu & Fri)–11; 12–2.30, 7–10.30 Sun
Hook Norton Best Bitter; M&B Highgate Mild; Stones Best Bitter [H]; guest beers
Popular real ale Mecca frequented by drinkers from all over Telford. Strong pub games teams and both bars can get crowded. A regular winner of the local CAMRA *Pub of the Year* award.
♛ ⛟ ❀ ⊡ ⇌ ♣ P

Leegomery

Malt Shovel
Hadley Park Road (off A442)
☎ (0952) 242963
12–3, 5–11
Banks's Mild; Marston's Bitter, Pedigree [H]
Friendly local with a small bar and a lounge adorned with brass. Bar lunches Mon–Fri.
♛ Q ◖ ⊡ ♣ P

Linley Brook

Pheasant Inn
Britons Lane (off B4373, Broseley–Bridgnorth road)
☎ (0746) 762260
12–2.30, 6.30 (7 winter)–11
Hook Norton Mild; Mitchell's Best Bitter; guest beers [H]
Two-roomed pub in an attractive, rural setting, well worth finding. A cosy lounge; bar billiards in the bar and good food. Two guest beers always available. Children are only allowed in the garden.
♛ Q ❀ ◖ ◗ ♣ P

Little Stretton

Green Dragon
☎ (0694) 722925
11–3 (extends summer weekends), 6–11
Ansells Mild; Tetley Bitter; Wadworth 6X; Wood Parish; guest beer [H]
Well-appointed pub in idyllic surroundings at the start of Ashes Hollow – a valley which leads up to the Long Mynd, and one of the many walks in the area.
♛ Q ❀ ◖ ◗ ▲ P

Ludlow

Bull Hotel
Bull Ring
☎ (0584) 873611
11–11
Banks's Mild; Marston's Bitter, Pedigree; guest beer [H]
Coaching inn of classic proportions. Do not be fooled by the plain front that was destroyed by fire in 1795. Go through the coaching arch to admire the timbered Tudor part around the yard. One long bar with various corners and levels. Hosts Ludlow's fringe festival. Marston's guest beer. ♛ ❀ ◖ ◗ ⇌

Church Inn
Buttercross ☎ (0584) 872174
11–11
Ruddles County; Webster's Yorkshire Bitter 🄷; guest beers (summer)
Tucked in the heart of Ludlow, behind Buttercross and away from the traffic on one of the town's most ancient sites: an upmarket inn close to St Laurence's church, the largest and most majestic in Shropshire. A house beer, Bellringer, is not brewed here.
Q 🛏 ◖ ◗ ⇌

Madeley

All Nations
Coalport Road
☎ (0952) 585747
12–3 (4 Sat), 7–11
All Nations Pale Ale 🄷
Popular, one-bar pub overlooking Blists Hill Museum. One of four brew pubs left before the modern resurgence. Always popular, not least because of its prices. Accessed by the road opposite the museum, or via a warren of roads from Madeley centre.
❀ ▲ ♣ P

Neenton

Pheasant Inn
On B4364, 6 miles from Bridgnorth
12.30–2.30 (not Mon–Fri), 7–11; 12–3, 7.30–10.30 Sun
Marston's Bitter, Pedigree 🄷
Characterful 17th-century, black and white village pub; a panelled lounge bar/snug and a locals' bar with log fires. Small restaurant where booking is essential. No food Sun eve. 🔥 ❀ ◖ ◗ 🍽 ♣ P

Newport

Shakespeare Inn
Upper Bar ☎ (0952) 811924
11–11
Banks's Mild; Draught Bass; S&N Theakston Best Bitter, XB, Old Peculier 🄷; guest beer
Old, single-bar market town pub, frequented by all ages. Excellent floral display every spring and summer. Pool room. 🔥 ❀ ♿ ♣ P

Try also: New Inn, Stafford St (Free)

Norton in Hales

Hinds Head
Main Road (1½ miles W of B5415, Woore–Market Drayton road) OS703387
☎ (0630) 653014
12–3, 5–11; 11–11 Sat
Bass Worthington BB, Draught Bass; M&B Springfield Bitter 🄷
Large, village inn with a small, cosy bar, a lounge and a restaurant. Note the entrance window advertising Joule's Stone Ales.
❀ ◖ ◗ 🍽 ♿ ▲ ♣ P

Oakengates

Compasses Inn
Beverley ☎ (0952) 616176
12–3, 7–11
Draught Bass; M&B Springfield Bitter; guest beers 🄷
Popular pub with an emphasis on guest beers, and food in an L-shaped dining room. Hosts occasional beer festivals for charity. The garden has children's play equipment.
❀ ◖ ◗ ⇌ P

Duke of York
Market Street ☎ (0952) 612741
11–11
Banks's Mild, Bitter; Draught Bass; Whitbread Boddingtons Bitter 🄷
Busy, lively, two-bar, main-street pub. ❀ 🍽 ⇌ P

Try also: Rose & Crown Inn, Holyhead Rd (Ansells)

Oldwoods

Romping Cat
Near Bomere Heath
☎ (0939) 290273
12–3 (2.30 Tue & Wed; not Fri), 7–11
Whitbread Castle Eden Ale; guest beers 🄷
Always a genuine welcome at this homely country pub, well known for its charitable efforts. Three guest beers.
Q ❀ ♣ P

Oswestry

Black Gate
Salop Road ☎ (0691) 653168
11–11
Banks's Bitter; Fuller's ESB; guest beers 🄷
Black and white, timber building dating from 1621, named after the south entrance to the town. Weston's cider available. Q ☕ ◖ ◗ ♿ ⌓

Golden Lion
Upper Church Street
☎ (0691) 653747
12–3, 6.30–11
Banks's Mild; Marston's Bitter, Merrie Monk, Pedigree 🄷
Cosy, long-established, edge-of-town pub, with an attractive garden. No food Mon. Q ❀ ◖ ◗ ♣ P

Sun Inn
Church Street ☎ (0691) 653433
7–11; 12–2.30, 7–11 Wed; 12–3, 7–11 Sat
Draught Bass 🄷; guest beer
Street-corner pub, sympathetically renovated as a genuine free house. The dining area serves home-cooked food. Note the original Walker windows. A house beer, Clog Iron Bitter, is not brewed here.
Q ◖ ◗ 🍽 ♿ ♣

Priest Weston

Miners Arms
OS293973 ☎ (093 872) 352
11–3, 6–11
Bass Worthington BB, Draught Bass 🄷
Classic country pub whose name reflects the history of the area. These industrial reminders of the past, and the nearby stone circle, more than justify a diversion to find this remote pub. Holds its own folk festival.
🔥 Q ❀ ◖ ◗ ♣ ⌓ P

Selattyn

Cross Keys
Ceiriog Road (B4579)
☎ (0691) 650247
11.30–closing varies (11–4 Sat; not Wed), 6–11
Banks's Mild, Bitter 🄷
17th-century gem of a village pub which incorporates the village shop (being redeveloped). Just off Offa's Dyke. 🔥 Q ❀ ♿ ♣ P

Shifnal

White Hart
High Street ☎ (0952) 461161
12–3, 6–11; 12–11 Fri & Sat
Draught Bass; Holden's Mild, Bitter; Ind Coope Burton Ale 🄷; guest beers
Historic, friendly, highly regarded hostelry. Good food includes home-made specials. Three guest beers. ❀ ◖ ⇌ P

Shrewsbury

Castle Vaults
Castle Gates ☎ (0743) 358807
11.30–3, 6–11; 11–11 Fri & Sat; 12–3 Sun, closed Sun eve
Courage Directors; Crown Buckley Dark; Marston's Pedigree; Ruddles Best Bitter; Wood Special 🄷; guest beers
Free house in the shadow of the castle, specialising in Mexican food. Its eight handpumps underline the increased choice of beers. Roof garden. No lunches Sun.
🔥 Q ❀ 🛏 ◖ ◗ ⇌

Coach & Horses
Swan Hill ☎ (0743) 365661
10–11
Draught Bass; guest beers Ⓗ
Unspoilt Victorian pub in a quiet part of the town, attracting customers from all walks of life. The bar is wood panelled, with a partitioned area at the side; the lounge is used as a restaurant 12–3 daily. Two guest beers are constantly changing.

Dog & Pheasant
20 Severn Street, Castle Fields
☎ (0743) 352835
12–3 (5 Fri & Sat), 7–11
Burtonwood Mild, Bitter, Forshaw's, Top Hat Ⓗ
Pub with a lively bar at the front, and a quieter lounge displaying wartime RAF memorabilia. The outside seating faces the world's first iron-framed houses. Just a stone's throw from the River Severn. Q

Dolphin
48 St Michaels Street
☎ (0743) 350419
12–3, 5.30–11; 12–11 Fri & Sat
Beer range varies Ⓗ
Late Georgian pub with a porticoed entrance. No keg beers or lager, but a choice of up to five guest beers from a constantly changing range. No under 21s admitted. Q

Dun Cow Pie Shop
171 Abbey Foregate
☎ (0743) 356408
11–3, 6–11; 11–11 Fri & Sat
Ansells Mild; Marston's Pedigree; Tetley Bitter Ⓗ
Black and white building, one of the more picturesque of Shrewsbury's pubs. While the inside has been opened up, the feeling of age (under all the ornaments) still prevails. The pies here are Desperate Dan's! Lumphammer house beer is from Carlsberg-Tetley.
P

Loggerheads
Church Street ☎ (0743) 355457
11–11
Draught Bass; M&B Mild, Brew XI; Stones Best Bitter Ⓗ
Cosy, side-street pub with four rooms, one with a shove-ha'penny board and strong sporting links. Don't miss the room on the left, with its scrubbed-topped tables and high-backed settles.
Q

Nags Head
Wyle Cop ☎ (0743) 362455
11–11
Beer range varies Ⓗ
Historic house of considerable architectural interest, with lots of wood mouldings. Reputed to be haunted and has a jetty at the rear. Three of the four beers come from the Carlsberg-Tetley range, the other is a guest. Can be lively.

Proud Salopian
Smithfield Road (50 yds from Welsh Bridge)
☎ (0743) 236887
11–11
Draught Bass; Brains Bitter; Wadworth 6X; Whitbread Boddingtons Mild, Bitter Ⓗ
Pub set across a busy road from the River Severn, which has the beer floating at times of high flood. Thomas Southam was the Proud Salopian in the name.

Station Hotel
Castle Foregate
☎ (0743) 344716
11–3 (3.30 Mon; 4 Fri & Sat), 7–11
Draught Bass; M&B Mild, Brew XI Ⓔ
Large, traditional bar with a small lounge at the front and a pool room at the rear, all linked by a corridor.
Q

Stottesdon

Fox & Hounds
High Street (3 miles off B4363 at Billingsley)
☎ (074 632) 222
12–3 (not Mon–Fri), 7–11
Fox & Hounds Wust, Bostin, Gobstopper; guest beers Ⓗ
Small home-brew pub at the heart of Shropshire. Skittle alley at the rear for hire; quoits also played. Camping possible. Well worth finding. Lunches served Sat.
Q P

Upper Farmcote

Red Lion O'Morfe
Off Bridgnorth–Stourbridge road, follow signs for Claverley ☎ (0746) 710678
11.30–2.30 (4 Sat), 7–11
Banks's Mild, Bitter; Bass Worthington BB, Draught Bass Ⓔ**; guest beers** Ⓗ
Large country pub with a lounge, conservatory, a no-smoking restaurant (children welcome), a bar and a pool room. A large, separate function room only serves keg beer. Eve meals Mon–Thu.
Q P

Welsh Frankton

Narrowboat Inn
Ellesmere Road (A495)
☎ (0691) 661051
11–3, 7–11
Beer range varies Ⓗ
Modern pub at the side of the Shropshire Union (Llangollen) Canal. Always three real ales available. P

Wenlock Edge

Wenlock Edge Inn
Hilltop (B4371) OS570963
☎ (074 656) 403
11.30–2.30 (3 Sat; not Mon), 6–11
Robinson's Bitter; Webster's Yorkshire Bitter; guest beer Ⓗ
Good atmosphere in a welcoming, family-run pub on top of the beautiful Wenlock Edge. Children welcome if eating. All food is freshly prepared and home-cooked.
Q P

Wistanswick

Red Lion
Off A41, Tern Hill–Hinstock road ☎ (0630) 638304
12–3 (4 Sat), 7–11
Banks's Mild; Marston's Bitter Ⓗ
Small country pub with a lounge and bar. The landlady uses only local products in her home-cooked meals. Well worth finding. Small family room off the lounge.
P

Worfield

Davenport Arms (Dog)
Main Street ☎ (074 64) 320
11–2 (not Mon), 7–11; 12–11 Sat
Banks's Mild, Bitter; Draught Bass; Marston's Pedigree; Wood Special Ⓗ
Locals' pub with a low ceiling and much timber, set in a gem of a village with very little traffic. Folk eve every other Thu. Quoits played. Well worth hunting out.
Q P

Updates to entries in the *Good Beer Guide* are published in CAMRA's newspaper, *What's Brewing*. Join CAMRA and receive a free copy each month.

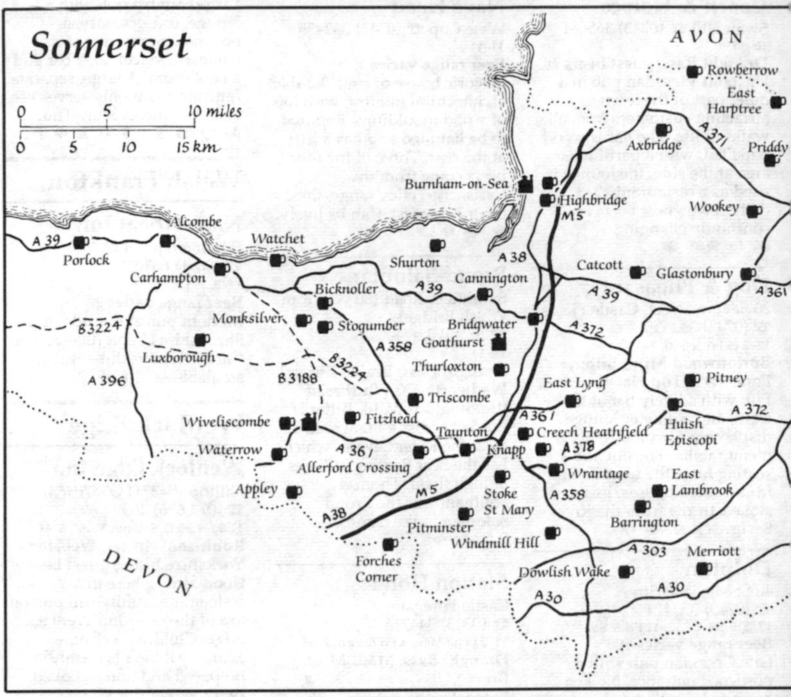

🏭	***Ash Vine,** Trudoxhill; **Berrow,** Burnham-on-Sea; **Bridgwater,** Goathurst; **Cotleigh, Exmoor,** Wiveliscombe; **Oakhill,** Oakhill; **RCH,** Burnham-on-Sea*

Alcombe

Britannia

Manor Road ☎ (0643) 702384
11.30–3, 6.30–11
Ushers Best Bitter; Wadworth 6X; guest beer Ⓗ
Traditional local founded in 1701. The panelled lounge boasts a 1931 mural of Exmoor on one beam. Good value, home-made food.
♨ ❀ 🛏 ◖ ◗ ⊟ ▲ ≢ (W Somerset Railway) ♣ ⛾

Allerford Crossing

Victory Inn

1st left past Norton Fitzwarren on road to Wiveliscombe
☎ (0823) 461282
11–3, 6–11
Draught Bass; Cotleigh Tawny; Exmoor Ale; Fuller's London Pride; Hall & Woodhouse Tanglefoot; Wadworth 6X Ⓗ
Excellent family pub with a good reputation for meals, offering up to 11 real ales plus the odd guest beer. The excellent garden has its own menagerie, plus a play area and a family room.
♨ Q ☋ ❀ ♣ P ⚡

Appley

Globe Inn

Off A38 ☎ (0823) 672327
11–2.30 (not Mon), 6.30–11
Cotleigh Tawny; guest beer Ⓗ
Unspoilt country pub with a traditional corridor serving area and a variety of rooms, including a dining room and a skittle alley. In a remote area but worth finding.
♨ Q ☋ ❀ ◖ ◗ ♣ P

Axbridge

Lamb Inn

The Square ☎ (0934) 732253
11–2.30 (3 Sat), 6.30–11
Draught Bass; Butcombe Bitter; Wadworth 6X; guest beers Ⓗ
Rambling pub now owned by Butcombe, opposite King John's hunting lodge. Large, terraced garden. The unusual bar is made of bottles. Q ❀
🛏 ◖ ◗ ⊟ ♿ ▲ ♣ ⛾ ⚡

Barrington

Royal Oak

Off B3168 ☎ (0460) 53455
12–2.30, 6.30–11; 12–11 Sat
Berrow 4Bs; guest beers Ⓗ
Old stone pub in a pretty village, a couple of miles from the A303, with up to six guest beers on at any one time. Good range of continental bottled beers and malt whiskies. Good value, tasty bar food. Popular with locals and visitors alike.
♨ Q ❀ ◖ ◗ ⊟ ♿ ♣ ⛾ P

Bicknoller

Bicknoller Inn

Church Lane (off A358)
☎ (0984) 56234
12–2.30, 5.30 (6 Sat)–11
Draught Bass; Charrington IPA; Whitbread Boddingtons Bitter Ⓗ
Late-14th-century, thatched country inn, nestling below the western slopes of the Quantock Hills. Ideal for walkers and riders. Skittle alley and games room.
♨ Q ☋ ❀ ◖ ◗ ⊟ ♿ ♣ P

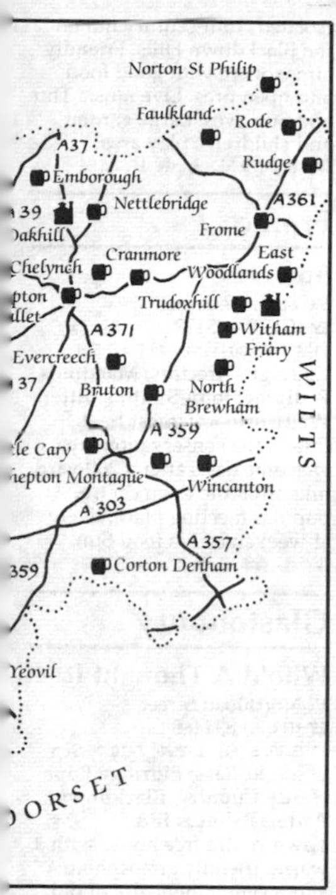

Bridgwater

Commercial Inn

Redgate Street (near station)
☎ (0278) 426989
11–2.30 (3.30 Sat), 7 (6.30 Sat)–11
Butcombe Bitter; guest beers Ⓗ
Modernised, popular local with a bar area (pool table), plus a lounge and a skittle alley. Guest beers from Whitbread. ♣ P

Fountain Inn

1 West Quay (near town bridge) ☎ (0278) 424115
11.30 (11 Sat)–3, 6.30–11
Butcombe Bitter; Wadworth 6X, Farmer's Glory, Old Timer Ⓗ**; guest beers**
Enlarged, one-bar local with enamel signs on the walls, attracting a good mix of clientele. Table skittles and darts. ♣

Bruton

Blue Ball

2 Coombe Street (A359)
☎ (0749) 812315
11.30–3, 5.30–11
Draught Bass; Fuller's London Pride; guest beer Ⓗ
Basic public bar with character, and a quiet, comfortable lounge. John Steinbeck reputedly wrote parts of *The Grapes of Wrath* in the traditional forge bar. Occasional ciders.
Q ♣

Burnham-on-Sea

Royal Clarence Hotel

The Esplanade
☎ (0278) 783138
11–11
Butcombe Bitter; RCH Clarence Pride, Pitchfork, Old Slug Porter Ⓗ**, Regent** Ⓖ**; Wadworth 6X** Ⓗ**; guest beers**
Large seafront hotel with its own brewery supplying an increasing range of beers. Hosts the largest beer festival in Somerset (last weekend in Feb) and offers a regular list of guest beers.
Q ♣ P

Cannington

Malt Shovel

Blackmoor Lane (off A39)
☎ (0278) 653432
11–3, 7 (6.30 summer)–11
Butcombe Bitter; John Smith's Bitter Ⓗ**; guest beers**
Quiet country pub on a road at the back of the village. A warm and friendly atmosphere in a wood-panelled bar and a lounge. Free of machines and music.
Q ♣ P

Carhampton

Butchers Arms

Main Road ☎ (0984) 821333
11–3, 7–11; 11–11 Sat
Cotleigh Tawny; Ushers Best Bitter; Wadworth 6X Ⓗ
Village local with a good range of games and activities. The only pub in West Somerset that carries on the ancient tradition of wassailing apples for cider making. Rich's cider sold. Recommended for families, with good children's activities.
♣ P

Castle Cary

Horse Pond

The Triangle ☎ (0963) 50318
10.30–2.30, 5.30–11
Courage Best Bitter; John Smith's Bitter; Marston's Pedigree; guest beers Ⓗ
Large, simply furnished, town pub with several rooms, including a games room. Live music Sat nights. No food Mon eve.
♣ P

Catcott

King William

Off A39 ☎ (0278) 722374
11.30–3, 6–11
Eldridge Pope Dorchester, Hardy Country, Royal Oak; Palmers IPA Ⓗ
Village pub with a modern restaurant extension, a small public bar with a dartboard and a traditional lounge bar with a glass-covered old well in the centre, discovered when an extension added the family room and skittle alley.
Q ♣ P

Chelynch

Poacher's Pocket

½ mile N of A361 at Doulting
☎ (0749) 880220
11–2.30, 6.15 (6 Fri & Sat)–11
Butcombe Bitter; Wadworth 6X Ⓗ
Part-14th-century pub in a small village some way from the A361. Mostly given over to food, but it remains popular as a locals' drinking pub. The large garden is well patronised on summer weekends.
♣ P

Corton Denham

Queens Arms Inn

3 miles S of A303
☎ (0963) 220317
12–2.30, 7–11 (11.30–3, 6.30–11 summer)
Brakspear Bitter; Tetley Bitter; Wells Bombardier Ⓗ**; guest beers**
Comfortable, rural pub in superb walking country, offering guest traditional ciders and a chalkboard listing guest ales of the month.
Q ♣ P

Cranmore

Strode Arms

Off A361, follow signs to E Somerset Railway
☎ (0749) 880450
11.30–2.30, 6.30–11; 12–3 Sun, closed Sun eve
Draught Bass; Wadworth IPA, 6X; guest beers Ⓗ
Substantial, upmarket, 14th-century inn overlooking the village duck pond. A large main bar; separate restaurant, but excellent food is available throughout the pub (no food Sun eve). A popular weekend rendezvous for visitors to the East Somerset Railway.
Q P

Creech Heathfield

Crown

Off A361 ☎ (0823) 412444
11–2.30 (3 Sat), 6–11
Cotleigh Tawny; Ruddles County; Ushers Best Bitter Ⓗ
Cosy, two-roomed, thatched pub where unusual traditional pub games are played. Good fresh food.
Q ♣ P

Somerset

Dowlish Wake

New Inn

☎ (0460) 52413
11–3, 6–11
Butcombe Bitter; S&N Theakston Old Peculier; Wadworth 6X [H]
Popular village pub with two bars and a good-sized garden which caters for families. A good range of home-cooked food includes Swiss specialities. Near Perry's Cider farm.
♛ Q ♞ ❀ 🛏 ◐ ◑ ⊟ ♣ ⌓ P

East Harptree

Castle of Comfort

On B3134, ½ mile N of B3135 jct ☎ (0761) 221321
12–2.30, 7–11
Draught Bass; Butcombe Bitter [H]**; guest beers** (weekends)
Stone-built coaching inn on the former Roman road. Two bars serve up to four ales, including two guests at the weekend – often unusual brews. Also noted for its food. Live music Fri. Ask the landlord about the real ale ghost!
Q ❀ ◐ ◑ ♿ ♣ P

East Lambrook

Rose & Crown

Off A303 ☎ (0460) 40433
11.30–2.30 (3 Sat), 7.30–11 (11.30–3, 6–11 summer)
Bass Worthington BB, Draught Bass; Otter Ale; guest beer [H]
Cosy, oak-beamed, two-bar village pub. Burrowhill cider.
♛ Q ♞ ❀ ◐ ◑ ⊟ ♿ ▲ ♣ ⌓ P

East Lyng

Rose & Crown

On A361 ☎ (0823) 698235
11–2.30, 6.30–11
Butcombe Bitter; Eldridge Pope Hardy Country, Royal Oak [H]
Comfortable, civilised old whitewashed pub with a timeless feel. A small restaurant leads off the main bar area, which abounds with antique furniture, sofas and old prints. Attractive garden with pleasant views across the Somerset Levels.
♛ Q ❀ 🛏 ◐ ◑ ♣ P

East Woodlands

Horse & Groom

1 mile SE of A361/B3092 jct
☎ (0373) 462802
12–2.30 (not Mon), 6–11
Bateman XB; Brakspear Special; Butcombe Bitter; Hook Norton Best Bitter; Wadworth 6X; guest beer [G]
17th-century inn on the western edge of Longleat estate: a cosy bar with an open fireplace and a flagstone floor, plus a small dining room and an extension for families. Specialises in seafood (over 30 varieties).
♛ Q ♞ ❀ ◐ ◑ ⊟ ▲ ♣ P

Emborough

Old Down Inn

At A37/B3139 crossroads
☎ (0761) 232398
11.30–3, 7–11
Draught Bass [G]
Atmospheric coaching inn with a diversity of rooms and old furniture. Burnt down in 1886. No food Sun.
♛ Q 🛏 ◐ ⊟ ▲ ♣ P

Evercreech

Bell Inn

Bruton Road ☎ (0749) 830287
12–3, 6 (5.30 Fri)–11; 11–11 Sat
Butcombe Bitter; Courage Best Bitter; Wadworth 6X; guest beer [H]
17th-century inn with roaring fires in the single bar. Restaurant area and a games room. ♛ Q ◐ ◑ ♣ ⌓ P

Faulkland

Tucker's Grave Inn

On A366, 1 mile E of village
☎ (0373) 834230
11–2.30, 6–11
Draught Bass; Butcombe Bitter [G]
The burial place of a 1747 suicide; a former cottage that has doubled as an inn for over 200 years. Three old-fashioned rooms; no bar counter. Renowned locally for its cider. The story of Tucker can be found above the parlour fire.
♛ Q ❀ ⊟ ♣ ⌓ P

Fitzhead

Fitzhead Inn

Off B3227 ☎ (0823) 400667
12–3, 7–11
Cotleigh Tawny [H]**; guest beers**
Rejuvenated, cosy village pub with oak beams. Much of the furniture was hand-made by the present landlord.
♛ ♞ ❀ ◐ ◑ ⊟ ♣

Forches Corner

Merry Harriers

OS182171 ☎ (082 342) 270
11.30–2.30, 6.30–11
Exmoor Ale; Hall & Woodhouse Tanglefoot; Smiles Best Bitter; Thompson's Best Bitter [H]**; guest beer**
Isolated, 15th-century inn on the Blackdown Hills. Friendly atmosphere with good food and open fires. Live music Thu and Sun eves. Large garden and children's play area.
♛ ❀ ◐ ◑ ♿ ▲ ♣ P

Frome

Sun

6 Catherine Street
☎ (0373) 473123
11–2.30, 5.30–11; 11–11 Fri & Sat
Courage Directors; Marston's Pedigree; John Smith's Bitter; Wadworth 6X; guest beer [H]
Pub in the conservation area, a welcome oasis after a 200-yard hike from the town centre. A popular meeting place, lively at weekends. No food Sun.
♛ ❀ 🛏 ◐ ♣ ⌓

Glastonbury

Who'd A Thought It

17 Northload Street
☎ (0458) 834460
11–2.30, 6–11; 12–2.30, 7–10.30 Sun
Draught Bass; Eldridge Pope Hardy Country, Blackdown Porter; Palmers IPA [H]
Town-centre free house with a warm, friendly atmosphere and a sympathetic use of old wood, decorated with pre-war paraphernalia and railway and country artefacts. Live music fortnightly. No pool tables, jukebox or gaming machines. Good food.
♛ Q ❀ 🛏 ◐ ◑ ♿ ▲ P

Highbridge

Coopers Arms

Market Street ☎ (0278) 783562
11–3, 5.30–11; 12–3, 7.30–10.30 Sun
Palmers IPA [E]**; guest beers**
Modernised pub with two lounge bars and a public bar with skittle alley and darts. A blackboard lists the beers in stock (including three guests); check which are on with staff. Coopers Brue and Best are house beers (not brewed here).
Q ❀ ⊟ ▲ ⇌ ♣ P

Huish Episcopi

Rose & Crown (Eli's)

☎ (0458) 250494
11–2.30, 5.30–11; 11.30–11 Fri & Sat; 12.30–2.30, 7–10.30 Sun
Draught Bass; Butcombe Bitter; Whitbread Boddingtons Bitter [H]**; guest beer**
Old thatched cottage inn which never got around to installing a bar! A quiet, multi-roomed local with real cider. Well worth a visit. Snacks available.
Q ♞ ❀ ♣ ⌓ P

Knapp

Rising Sun Inn
Off A361 OS301254
☎ (0823) 490436
11–2.30, 6.30–11 (restaurant licence)
Draught Bass; Exmoor Ale; Whitbread Boddingtons Bitter Ⓗ
Country pub with a plush bar, close to the walking routes on the Somerset Levels. A meeting/children's room is to the side of the bar area. A recent award-winner for its extensive fish menu. Eve meals in the restaurant. Cider in summer. Busy at weekends.
⛼ Q ⛭ ❀ ◖ ♿ ▲ ⌓ P

Luxborough

Royal Oak of Luxborough
OS006292 ☎ (0984) 40319
11–2.30, 6–11
Bateman XXXB; Cotleigh Tawny; Exmoor Gold Ⓖ**; Whitbread Flowers IPA** Ⓗ**; guest beers**
Rural gem set deep in a fold of the Brendon Hills, known locally as the Blazing Stump. Folk club Fri; quiz Tue. Good home-made food.
⛼ Q ❀ 🛏 ◖ ◗ ▲ ♣ ⌓ P

Merriott

Swan Inn
44 Lower Street
☎ (0460) 73302
11–3, 6–11
John Smith's Bitter Ⓗ**; guest beers**
Comfortable, one-bar village pub serving local Burrow Hill cider. No food Sun eve.
Q ❀ ◖ ◗ ♣ ⌓

Monksilver

Notley Arms
On B3288 ☎ (0984) 56217
11–2.30, 6–11; 12–2.30, 7–10.30 Sun
Ruddles County; S&N Theakston Best Bitter; Ushers Best Bitter; Wadworth 6X Ⓗ
Village pub in a very rural spot; a centre for walking over the Brendon Hills, and locally noted for its award-winning food. Large, child-friendly garden. Cider in summer.
⛼ Q ⛭ ❀ ◖ ◗ ♣ ⌓ P

Nettlebridge

Nettlebridge Inn
On A367 ☎ (0749) 841360
11.30–2.30, 6–11
Oakhill Best Bitter, Black Magic, Yeoman Ⓗ
Big roadside pub in a pretty valley on the edge of the Mendips; the 'tap' for the nearby Old Brewery at Oakhill. Friendly, welcoming staff give priority to food (very good value) in the spacious main bar. ❀ 🛏 ◖ ◗ P

North Brewham

Old Red Lion
On Maiden Bradley–Bruton road ☎ (0749) 850287
12–2.30, 6–11
Butcombe Bitter; Oakhill Best Bitter; Whitbread Flowers Original; guest beer Ⓗ
Stone-built former farmhouse in an isolated, rural setting. The bar is the old dairy, with flagged floors. No food Mon.
⛼ Q ❀ ◖ ◗ ♣ ⌓ P

Norton St Philip

Fleur de Lys
High Street ☎ (0373) 834333
11–2.30, 6–11
Draught Bass; Charrington IPA; Oakhill Best Bitter; Wadworth 6X Ⓗ
Ancient stone building, parts of which may date from the 13th century. Recent extensive, but mainly sympathetic, refurbishment means the re-sited bar now blocks the old passageway through which the pub ghost was said to pass on his way to the gallows.
⛼ Q ⛭ ❀ ♣ P

Pitminster

Queens Arms
Off B3170 at Corfe
☎ (0823) 42529
11–11
Draught Bass; Cotleigh Tawny; Eldridge Pope Blackdown Porter; Exmoor Ale Ⓗ**; guest beers**
Very popular village pub, with two bars and a function room/bar. Usually four guest beers available, normally strong ones. Regular folk and jazz eves.
⛼ Q ⛭ ❀ 🛏 ◖ ◗ ⊟ ▲ ♣ ⌓ P

Pitney

Halfway House
On B3153 ☎ (0458) 252513
11.30–3, 5.30–11
Ash Vine Bitter Ⓖ**; Cotleigh Tawny; Exmoor Ale; Oakhill Best Bitter** Ⓗ**; guest beers**
Small, one-bar village pub, tastefully refurbished in country pine style. Frequent guest beers. Chess played Tue night. ⛼ Q ❀ ◖ ◗ ♣ P

Porlock

Ship Inn
High Street ☎ (0643) 862507
10.30–3, 5.30–11
Draught Bass; Courage Best Bitter; Cotleigh Old Buzzard Ⓗ**; guest beer** (summer)
13th-century, thatched inn within walking distance of the sea and moor: an old bar with a stone floor and a log fire. A pub for conversation (no piped music), with a separate games room. Mentioned in *Lorna Doone*. Vegetarian meals.
⛼ Q ⛭ ❀ 🛏 ◖ ◗ ♿ ▲ ♣ ⌓ P

Priddy

New Inn
☎ (0749) 676465
11.30–2.30, 7–11; 12–2.30, 7–10.30 Sun
Eldridge Pope Hardy Country; Marston's Pedigree; Wadworth 6X Ⓗ
15th-century farmhouse on the village green with flagged bars. A warm and friendly pub with a reputation for good food, including a choice of vegetarian meals. Popular at weekends.
⛼ ❀ 🛏 ◖ ◗ ⊟ ▲ ♣ ⌓ P

Rode

Cross Keys
High Street ☎ (0373) 830354
11–2.30, 6–11
Bass Worthington BB, Draught Bass Ⓗ
Traditional, two-bar village pub, formerly the Fussell's brewery tap. Extensive range of single malt whiskies.
Q ⊟ ▲ ♣

Try also: Bell Inn, Frome Rd (Nethergate)

Rowberrow

Swan Inn
From Churchill on A38, fork left after ½ mile OS451583
☎ (0934) 852371
12–2.30, 6–11
Draught Bass; Butcombe Bitter; Wadworth 6X; guest beers Ⓗ
Former cider house, converted from three stone cottages. Two bars, with fake beams and a big fireplace. ⛼ Q ❀ ◖ ♿ P

Rudge

Full Moon
1 mile N of A36 at Standerwick OS829518
☎ (0373) 830936
12–3 (not Mon), 6–11
Draught Bass; Butcombe Bitter; Wadworth 6X Ⓗ
Splendid, 300-year-old inn, greatly extended in recent years but retaining most of its original features. The emphasis is on the eve food trade; bar snacks only lunchtime. No food Sun eve.
⛼ Q ⛭ ❀ 🛏 ◗ ▲ P

Somerset

Shepton Mallet

Horseshoe Inn
Bowlish (A371, ½ mile E of centre) ☎ (0749) 342209
12–2.30, 6–11
Draught Bass; Pitfield Wiltshire Stonehenge Bitter, ESB H
Stone pub on the outskirts of town. Much of the lounge is now set up as a restaurant. However, there is also a popular and splendidly well-equipped public bar.
🏨 ❀ ◖ ▶ ⊞ ♣

Shepton Montague

Montague Inn
Off A359, S of Bruton OS675316
☎ (0749) 813213
12–3 (not Mon–Fri), 5.30–11
Butcombe Bitter; Marston's Pedigree; guest beer (summer) G
Remote, but convivial country pub.
🏨 Q ❀ ⌂ P

Shurton

Shurton Inn
Follow signs to Hinckley Point power station
☎ (0278) 732695
11–3, 6–11; 12–3, 7.30–10.30 Sun
Exmoor Ale; Hall & Woodhouse Badger Best Bitter H; **guest beers**
Lively village pub with regular and varied music eves.
🏨 Q ❀ ◖ ▶ ♣ ⌂ P

Stogumber

White Horse Inn
☎ (0984) 56277
11–2.30, 6–11
Cotleigh Tawny; Exmoor Ale H
Traditional pub opposite the 12th-century church in a pretty village. Restaurant and accommodation are in an old market house, now joined to the pub.
🏨 Q ❀ ◖ ▶ ⊞ ♣ ⌂ P

Stoke St Mary

Half Moon
Off A358 at Henlade
☎ (0823) 442271
11 (11.30 Wed–Sat)–2.30, 6–11
S&N Theakston Best Bitter; Wadworth 6X; Whitbread Boddingtons Bitter H
Popular, renovated country pub with a stone-flagged bar and a no-smoking dining area (children's menu).
Q ☺ ❀ ◖ ▶ ▲ P

Taunton

Black Horse
36 Bridge Street
☎ (0823) 272151
11–3, 7–11
Marston's Pedigree; Whitbread Boddingtons Bitter, Flowers IPA; guest beer H
Lively, modernised, one-bar pub with interconnecting areas which extend a surprisingly long way. Popular with all ages. Guest beers from the Whitbread range.
❀ ◖ ▶ ⚊ ⇌ ⊞

Mason's Arms
Magdalene Street
☎ (0823) 288916
10.30–3, 6–11
Draught Bass; Exe Valley Dob's Best Bitter H; **guest beers**
Comfortable, one-bar pub with a relaxing atmosphere, situated off the main streets. Fresh food always available. Limited parking. Q 🚃 ◖ ▶ P

Pen & Quill
Shuttern (opp. law courts)
☎ (0823) 256982
11–11
Draught Bass; Butcombe Bitter; Marston's Pedigree; Whitbread Flowers IPA H
Friendly, popular town pub with olde-worlde decor. Lunchtime live jazz first Sun in the month; annual weekend jazz festival. 🏨 Q ◖ ▶ ⚊

Thurloxton

Green Dragon
Off A38, Taunton–Bridgwater road OS275298
☎ (0823) 413115
12–2.30, 7 (4.30 Fri)–11.30
Cotleigh Tawny; Eldridge Pope Hardy Country; guest beer H
Historic coaching inn, small and uncommercial. The huge inglenook displays a collection of old cider barrel miniatures. Horse riding by arrangement in the surrounding countryside. No food Sun eve.
🏨 ❀ 🚃 ◖ ▶ ▲ ♣ ⌂ P

Triscombe

Blue Ball
1 mile off A358 ☎ (098 48) 242
11 (10.30 summer)–2.30, 7 (6.30 summer)–11
Cotleigh Tawny; Exmoor Ale; Wadworth 6X H
17th-century, thatched pub at the foot of the Quantock Hills, ideally situated for walkers. Extensive picturesque garden; dominoes and skittles played; good food. Generally busy at weekends, especially in summer.
Q ☺ ❀ ◖ ▶ ▲ ♣ P

Trudoxhill

White Hart
½ mile S of A361 at Nunney Catch OS749438
☎ (0373) 836324
12–2.30 (3 Sat), 7 (6.30 Fri & Sat)–11
Ash Vine Trudoxhill, Bitter, Challenger, Black Bess Porter, Tanker; Butcombe Bitter; guest beer H
Comfortable, open-plan village pub with exposed beams and a large fireplace. The Ash Vine brewery is at the rear.
🏨 ❀ ◖ ▶ ⌂ P

Watchet

West Somerset Hotel
Swain Street ☎ (0984) 34434
11–11
Courage Directors; Ushers Best Bitter H; **guest beers**
Enterprising, friendly, family-run, former coaching inn serving the local community as well as tourists. Activity holidays are arranged. Situated near the West Somerset Railway station and the harbour.
☺ ❀ 🚃 ◖ ▶ ⊞ ▲ ♣

Waterrow

Rock Inn
On B3227 ☎ (0984) 23293
11–2.30, 6–11
Cotleigh Tawny; Exmoor Gold H
Old pub set against a rock face (which forms part of the rear wall), in a small valley. One bar, with a public area at one end and a lounge at the other, leading to a restaurant.
🏨 Q ❀ 🚃 ◖ ▶ ▲ ♣ ⌂ P

Wincanton

Bear Inn
12 Market Place
☎ (0963) 32581
11–2.30, 5.30–11; 11–11 Sat
Draught Bass; Fuller's London Pride; Marston's Pedigree; guest beers H
Large former coaching inn with several drinking areas, plus a substantial games and function room. Weekly archery in the skittle alley. No food Sun eve. 🏨 🚃 ◖ ▶ ▲ ♣ P

Windmill Hill

Square & Compass
Off A358 at Stewley Cross OS310165 ☎ (0823) 480467
11.30–2.30, 6.30–11
Draught Bass; Exmoor Ale; Whitbread Boddingtons Bitter, Flowers Original H
Pleasant pub, a bit off the beaten track, with nice views. Interesting range of bar food, with vegetarian options; also a

dining room, which welcomes children. Play area in the garden. Parking for caravans next to the pub.
🜲 Q ♞ ❀ ◖ ◗ ♣ P

Witham Friary

Seymour Arms
Off B3092, by old station OS745410 ☎ (0749) 850742
11–3, 6–11
Ushers Best Bitter 🄷
Old village local, unspoilt by progress, with a central serving hatch and a fine garden. Richards cider on gravity dispense.
🜲 Q ❀ ⊞ ▲ ♣ ⌓

Wiveliscombe

Courtyard
High Street ☎ (0984) 23737
11.30–3, 7–11
Exe Valley Exeter Old; Exmoor Ale; Morrells Varsity 🄷/🄶
Small, quiet bar with household furnishings. The new cellar bar has the beers on gravity dispense. Q ◖ ◗ ▲ ⌓

Wookey

Burcott Inn
On B3139 ☎ (0749) 673874
11–2.30 (3 Sat), 6–11
Butcombe Bitter 🄷**; guest beers**
Deservedly popular roadside pub with a friendly atmosphere. Over 40 different guest beers per year (always two available) in an L-shaped bar with a copper serving top and a small games room. The good-sized garden boasts an old cider press. Good quality food; no eve meals Sun or Mon 🜲 Q ❀ ◖ ◗ ♣ P

Wrantage

Canal Inn
On A372 ☎ (0823) 480210
12–3, 7–11
Exmoor Ale; Whitbread Boddingtons Bitter, Flowers Original 🄷
Friendly local with good food and an outdoor children's play area. Skittles and darts played. Lane's local cider.
🜲 ❀ ◖ ◗ ♿ ▲ ♣ ⌓ P

Yeovil

Armoury
The Park ☎ (0935) 71047
11–3, 6–11
Adnams Broadside; Butcombe Bitter; Wadworth 6X, Farmer's Glory 🄷
Lively, simply furnished, town pub, converted from an old armoury. Q ❀ ◖ ♿ ♣ P

Staffordshire

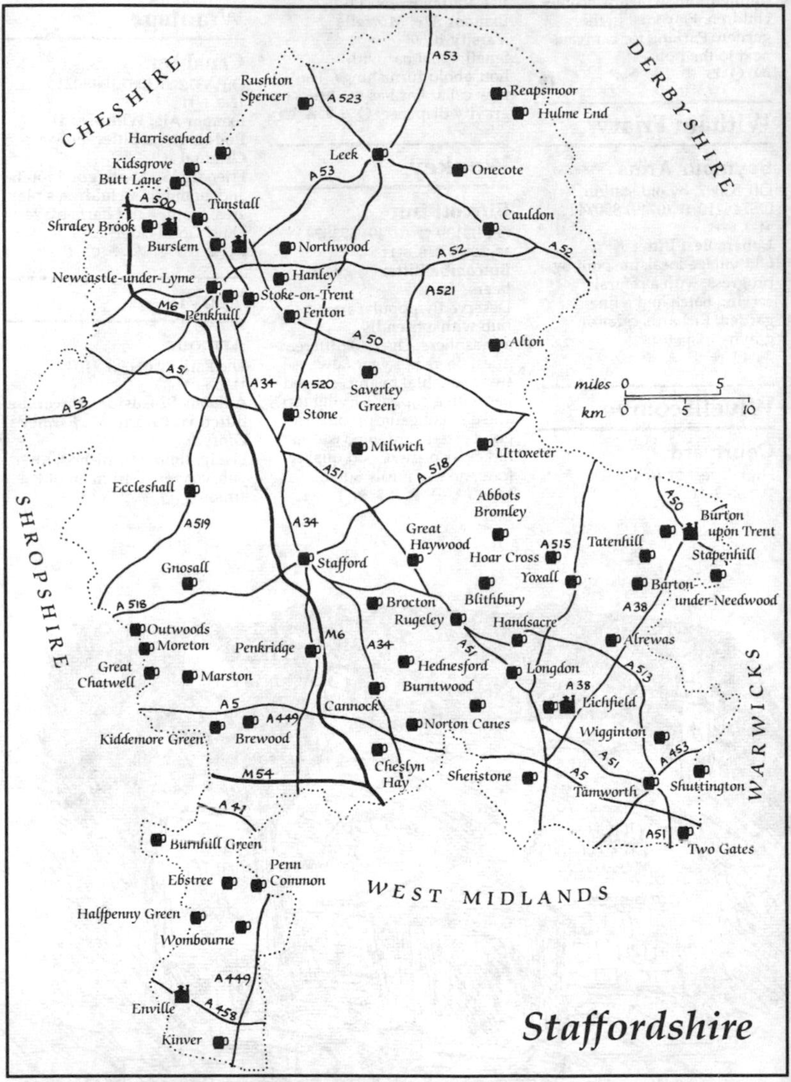

Burton Bridge, Burton upon Trent; Enville, Enville; Heritage, Burton upon Trent; Lichfield, Lichfield; Marston's, Mundane, Burton upon Trent; Rising Sun, Shraley Brook; Titanic, Burslem

Abbots Bromley

Bagot Arms

Bagot Street (B5234)
☎ (0283) 840371
11–2.30, 5.30–11; 12–2.30, 7–10.30 Sun
Marston's Bitter, Pedigree [H]
18th-century coaching inn: a meeting place for Blithfield Reservoir enthusiasts.
P

Alrewas

George & Dragon

Main Street ☎ (0283) 790202
11–2.30 (3 Sat), 6–11; 12–2.30, 7–10.30 Sun
Marston's Pedigree [H]
Busy village-centre pub.
P

Alton

Talbot Inn

Red Road ☎ (0538) 702767
12–2.30 (not winter Mon), 6.30 (7 winter)–11
Ansells Bitter; Ind Coope Burton Ale [H]

An 18th-century pub in the beautiful Churnet valley, with an emphasis on food. Very handy for Alton Towers.
❀ 🛏 ◐ ◗ ♿ P

Barton-under-Needwood

Top Bell
Barton Gate ☎ (0283) 712510
12–3, 6 (7 Sat)–11
Burtonwood Bitter, Forshaw's Ⓗ
Typical, oak-beamed country pub which encourages live music (Wed, Fri and Sun) and raises money for charity.
🏰 ⛵ ❀ ◐ ◗ ♿ ♣ P

Blithbury

Bull & Spectacles
Uttoxeter Road (B5014)
☎ (0889) 22201
12–3, 6–11
Ind Coope Burton Ale; Marston's Pedigree; guest beer Ⓗ
15th-century country pub close to Blithfield Reservoir. No food Mon. 🏰 ❀ ◐ ◗ 🀫 ♣ P

Brewood

Admiral Rodney
Dean Street ☎ (0902) 850853
11–2.30 (3 Sat), 5.30–11
HP&D Entire; Tetley Bitter Ⓗ
Typical HP&D-style pub, but with a Staffordshire rather than a Black Country theme, including a collection of pottery. Best to book for meals; no food Sun. 🏰 ◐ ◗ P

Swan
Market Square
☎ (0902) 850330
11–3, 7–11
Draught Bass; M&B Highgate Mild; Stones Best Bitter; S&N Theakston XB; guest beers Ⓗ
One-roomed lounge pub with mostly original wooden beams and two snug areas. Skittle alley upstairs. 🏰 ♣ P

Brocton

Chetwynd Arms
Cannock Road
☎ (0785) 661089
11.30–3, 5.45–11; 11–11 Sat
Banks's Mild, Bitter Ⓔ**; Camerons Strongarm; Marston's Pedigree** Ⓗ
Bustling main-road pub at the north-western boundary of Cannock Chase. No meals Sat eve or Sun. ❀ ◐ ◗ 🀫 ♿ ♣ P

Burnhill Green

Dartmouth Arms
Snowden Road ☎ (074 65) 268
12–2.30 (not Mon summer; not Mon–Wed winter), 7 (6 summer)–11
Ansells Bitter, Mild; Ind Coope ABC Best Bitter, Burton Ale Ⓗ**; guest beers**

Comfortable, beamed village pub with a deserved reputation for food (not served Sun eve). 🏰 Q ❀ ◐ ◗ P

Burntwood

Trident
166 Chase Road (off B5190)
☎ (0543) 689720
12–3 (4 Sat), 7–11
Marston's Pedigree Ⓗ
Friendly local with a lounge full of pictures and model planes, and a traditional bar with pool tables. Q 🀫 ♣ P

Burton upon Trent

Beacon Hotel
277 Tutbury Road (off A50)
☎ (0283) 68968
11–3, 6–11
Draught Bass Ⓔ**; guest beer**
Spacious, family-run three-roomer. Extensive food menu (children's and vegetarian options). Purpose-built family room; safe garden.
Q ⛵ ❀ 🛏 ◐ ◗ 🀫 ♣ P

Burton Bridge Inn
24 Bridge Street (A50 by Trent Bridge) ☎ (0283) 36596
11.30–2.15, 5.30–11; 12–2, 7–10.30 Sun
Burton Bridge Summer Ale, XL, Bridge Bitter, Porter, Festival, Old Expensive Ⓗ**; guest beer** (Sun)
Small, friendly brewery tap where no music or machines detract from the fine beers brewed here. Wooden pews, award-covered walls and good conversation. Q ◐ ♣

Derby Inn
Derby Road ☎ (0283) 43674
10.30–3, 5.30–11
Marston's Pedigree Ⓗ
Pub with a small lounge and a basic bar. Buy your veg from a corner of the bar. 🀫 ♣ P

Duke of York
Victoria Street (off Albert St, off Derby St) ☎ (0283) 68118
10.30–11
Marston's Pedigree Ⓗ**, Owd Rodger** (winter) Ⓖ
Small locals' bar with an extended lounge in Marston's Victoriana style. Food weekdays till 8.30. ◐ ◗ 🀫 ⇌

Roebuck Hotel
Station Street ☎ (0283) 68660
11–11; 11–3, 6–11 Sat
Ansells Mild, Bitter; Ind Coope ABC Best Bitter, Burton Ale, Tetley Bitter Ⓗ**; guest beer**
Popular one-roomer which can get busy Fri and Sat eves. Over 200, mostly independent, beers have been pulled through the guest beer pump. Good value bar meals (eves till 8, except Sun). ❀ 🛏 ◐ ◗ ⇌ ♣

Cannock

Shoal Hill Tavern
Sandy Lane (B5012)
☎ (0543) 503302
12–2.30 (3 Sat), 6–11
S&N Theakston Mild, Best Bitter, XB, Old Peculier Ⓗ
Pleasant, two-roomed pub, from the 18th century. On the edge of a good walking area.
Q ❀ ◐ ◗ 🀫 ▲ P

Cauldon

Yew Tree
Off A523 ☎ (0538) 308348
11–3, 6–11
Draught Bass; Burton Bridge XL; M&B Mild Ⓗ
Charming rural pub adorned with a superb collection of working antique polyphones, a pianola and grandfather clocks. Q ❀ ▲ ♣ P

Cheslyn Hay

Woodman Inn
Little Wood Lane, Littlewood (off A354) ☎ (0922) 413686
12–3, 7–11; 11–11 Sat
S&N Theakston Mild, Best Bitter, XB, Old Peculier Ⓗ
Formerly a Victorian brewhouse, now a good pub, well stocked outdoors.
Q ❀ ◐ 🀫 ⇌ (Landywood) ♣ P

Ebstree

Hollybush
Ebstree Road OS854959
☎ (0902) 895587
12.30–2.30 (11.30–3 Sat), 6–11; 12–2.30, 7–10.30 Sun
Ansells Bitter, Mild; Ind Coope Burton Ale; Tetley Bitter Ⓗ
Pleasant country pub, just west of the Staffs and Worcester Canal.
🏰 ❀ ◐ ◗ 🀫 ♣ P

Eccleshall

Royal Oak
High Street ☎ (0785) 850230
11.30–3, 6.30–11
Burtonwood Bitter, Forshaw's; Morland Old Speckled Hen Ⓗ
Large, town-centre free house with a restaurant, a lounge and a small, cosy snug, plus an impressive upstairs function room. Imposing mock Tudor, arched frontage.
⛵ ❀ ◐ ◗ ♣ P

St George Hotel
Castle Street ☎ (0785) 850300
11–11
Ind Coope Burton Ale; Tetley Bitter; Whitbread Boddingtons Bitter; guest beer Ⓗ

Enterprising hotel which may soon start brewing. The site has been occupied at various times by a coaching inn, a draper's shop and an undertaker's. ♨ ♘ ❀ 🛏 ◐ ◑ ♣ P

Gnosall

Boat
Wharf Road ☎ (0785) 822208
11 (11.30 winter)–11
Marston's Bitter, Pedigree [H]; guest beer (summer)
Popular pub, next to bridge 34 on the Shropshire Union Canal. Meals served Easter-end Sept. ♨ ❀ ◐ ◑ ♿ ♣ P

Royal Oak
Newport Road (A518)
☎ (0785) 822362
12–3, 6–11
Ansells Bitter; Ind Coope Burton Ale; Tetley Bitter [H]
Hospitable, two-roomed village local with a narrow, basic bar and a comfortable lounge. ♨ ❀ ◐ ◑ ⊞ ♣ P

Great Chatwell

Red Lion
2 miles E of A41 OS792143
☎ (0952) 70366
12–3 (not Mon), 6 (7 winter, 5 summer Sat)–11
Draught Bass; Tetley Bitter [H]; guest beers
Recently renovated country pub. Excellent children's play area. ♨ ♘ ❀ ◐ ◑ ♣ P

Great Haywood

Clifford Arms
Main Road ☎ (0889) 881321
12–4, 7–11; 11–11 Sat
Banks's Bitter; Draught Bass [H]
Former coaching house rebuilt in 1934, close to the Trent and Mersey Canal, the Shugborough Estate, Cannock Chase and the Staffordshire Way. Eve meals Tue–Sat.
♨ Q ❀ ◐ ◑ ⊞ ♣ P

Halfpenny Green

Royal Oak
Off B4176 OS825920
☎ (0384) 221318
11–2.30 (3 Sat), 6–11
Banks's Mild, Bitter [E]
Popular, old country local on a crossroads near the aerodrome and Halfpenny Green Vineyard. ♨ ❀ ◐ ◑ ⊞ ♣ P

Handsacre

Crown Inn
The Green ☎ (0543) 490239
11–3, 6–11
M&B Highgate Mild; Stones Best Bitter [H]
Picturesque and friendly pub on the canal. Games room.
Q ♘ ❀ ◐ ⊞ ♣ P

Harriseahead

Royal Oak
High Street ☎ (0782) 513362
7–11; 12–3, 7–11 Sat; 12–2.30, 7–10.30 Sun
Courage Directors; Marston's Bitter; John Smith's Bitter [H]; guest beers
Busy, two-roomed local with a smallish bar and a larger lounge. The widest choice of ales in the area. Handy for Mow Cop. ❀ ♣ P

Hednesford

Queens Arms
Hill Street ☎ (0543) 878437
12–3, 6.30 (7 Sat)–11
Bass Worthington BB, Draught Bass; M&B Highgate Mild [E]
Two-roomed, traditional pub with a strong local following.
Q ◐ ⊞ ⇌ ♣ P

Hoar Cross

Meynell Ingram Arms
1 mile W of A515 at Newchurch ☎ (0283) 75202
12–3, 6–11; 12–11 Sat
Marston's Pedigree; Whitbread Boddingtons Bitter [H]
Former estate pub in a rural setting. No food Sun eve.
♨ Q ❀ ◐ ◑ ⊞ P

Hulme End

Manifold Hotel
Hulme End (B5054)
☎ (028 84) 537
12–2.30, 7–11
Wards Mild, Thorne Best Bitter [H]; guest beer (summer)
Impressive, welcoming stone hotel in open countryside by the River Manifold. Occasional live music.
♨ ❀ 🛏 ◐ ◑ ♿ ▲ ♣ P

Kiddemore Green

New Inns
Between Brewood and Bishops Wood OS859089
☎ (0902) 850614
12–3, 7–11
Burtonwood Mild, Bitter, Forshaw's [H]
Pleasant, isolated, country inn with wooden beams and brass. Burtonwood is new to the area. No food Sun.
♨ ❀ ◐ ♣ P

Kinver

Plough & Harrow
High Street ☎ (0384) 872659
12–3 (not Mon–Thu, Oct–Mar), 7–11
Batham Mild, Best Bitter [H]
Three-roomed pub, known locally as the Steps. No food Sun eve. ♨ ♘ ❀ ◐ ◑ ⊞ ♣ P

Leek

Abbey Inn
Abbey Green Road
☎ (0538) 382865
11–2.30 (3 Sat), 6.30–11
Draught Bass; guest beer [H]
Idyllic country pub where the bar meals are popular with the locals. Near Alton Towers.
♨ ❀ 🛏 ◐ ◑ ♣ P

Roebuck
Derby Street ☎ (0538) 372179
10–3, 7–11
Draught Bass; M&B Highgate Mild [H]
Wood-panelled, town-centre pub, frequented by members of the Leek RFC. Activities include quizzes, angling and clay pigeon shooting. ❀ ◐

Swan
2 St Edward Street
☎ (0538) 382081
11–3, 7–11
Draught Bass; M&B Highgate Mild [H]; guest beers
Three-roomed pub whose function room is much used by local societies. Weekly guest beer. ♨ ❀ ◐ ⊞ ♣ P

Lichfield

George & Dragon
Beacon Street ☎ (0543) 263554
11–3, 5.30–11; 11–11 Sat
Banks's Mild, Bitter [E]; Marston's Pedigree [H]
Smart, yet traditional Banks's house. ⊞ ♣ P

George IV
28 Bore Street (next to Guildhall) ☎ (0543) 263032
11–3 (4 Thu–Sat), 7–11
Draught Bass; M&B Highgate Mild [H]
Popular and busy, city-centre drinking house: three rooms, plus a function room.
♘ ◐ ◑ ⊞ ♿ ⇌ (City) ♣ P

Greyhound Inn
Upper St John Street
☎ (0543) 262303
12–3, 5–11; 11–11 Fri & Sat
Ansells Bitter; Draught Bass [H]; guest beer
The first pub in the city to serve a guest premium beer. A busy local with an extended lounge area. Quiz nights.
◐ ◑ ⊞ ⇌ (City) ♣ P

Scales
Market Street ☎ (0543) 264526
11–3, 7–11
Draught Bass; Stones Best Bitter [H]
Friendly, old-time pub: a bar, a panelled lounge and a dining room, recently refurbished. Paved outdoor drinking area. Keen darts following.
♘ ❀ ◐ ⊞ ⇌ (City) ♣

Longdon

Swan with Two Necks
Brook End (off A51)
☎ (0543) 490251
12–2.30, 7–11; 12–2, 7–10.30 Sun
Ansells Bitter, Mild; Burton Bridge Bridge Bitter; Ind Coope Burton Ale [H]
Four hundred-year-old pub run by a French landlord, in an award-winning village. No food Sun. ♨ Q ❀ ◖ ◗ ⊞ P

Longsdon

New Inn
Leek Road (A53)
☎ (0538) 385356
12–3, 7–11
Banks's Mild; Marston's Bitter, Pedigree [H]
Imposing, white roadside building: one room with a split-level arrangement; good atmosphere. ♨ Q ♣ P

Marston

Fox
1 mile NW of Wheaton Aston OS935140 ☎ (0785) 840729
12–3, 7 (6 summer)–11
Lloyds Derby Bitter; Mansfield Old Baily; Wadworth 6X; Wells Eagle; Wood Special; guest beers [H]
Quiet, country free house, especially popular with cyclists. No gimmicks. The beer range may vary.
♨ Q ❀ ⊞ ♿ ▲ ♣ ⌓ P

Milwich

Green Man
On B5027 ☎ (0889) 505310
12–3, 6 (5 Sat)–11
Bass Worthington BB, Draught Bass [H]**; guest beers** (weekends)
Friendly village pub by a tiny 1833 schoolhouse. List of landlords since 1792 in the bar.
♨ ❀ ◖ ▲ ♣ P

Moreton

Rising Sun
2 miles E of A41 OS799168
☎ (0952) 70251
12–5, 7–11; 12–11 Sat
Banks's Mild; Marston's Bitter, Pedigree [H]
Friendly, rather isolated, country pub. Bar billiards in the snug, which also serves as a family room.
♨ ♉ ❀ ◖ ◗ ♣ P

Newcastle-under-Lyme

Crossways
Ironmarket ☎ (0782) 616953
11–11; 11–4, 7–11 Sat
Vaux Samson; Wards Sheffield Best Bitter; guest beers [H]
Active local which caters for a cross-section of customers. Chess board on request. The house beer is brewed by Coach House. ⇄ ◖ ♣ ⌓

Old Brown Jug
Bridge Street ☎ (0782) 616767
12–2.30 (3 Fri, 4 Sat), 6–11
Marston's Bitter, Merrie Monk, Pedigree, Owd Rodger [H]
Town-centre local, dating back to 1790: a bar area with wooden floorboards and a cosier lounge area. ❀ ♣ P

Victoria Inn
King Street (A53)
☎ (0782) 615569
11–3 (4 Sat), 5 (7 Sat)–11
Bass Worthington BB, Draught Bass [E]**; Whitbread Boddingtons Bitter** [H]
Victorian, two-roomed local, convenient for the town centre and the New Victoria Theatre. Bar snacks and morning coffee. Sun eve quiz.
Q ❀ ⊞ ♣

Norton Canes

Railway Tavern
Norton Green Lane (off A5, ¾ mile along Norton Hall Lane)
☎ (0543) 279579
12–2 (3 Sat), 7–11
Ansells Bitter, Mild; Ind Coope Burton Ale; Tetley Bitter [H]
Village pub with one room and a keenly supported bowls club (bowling green at the rear). ❀ ◖ ♣ P

Onecote

Jervis Arms
On B5054 ☎ (0538) 304206
12–3, 7–11
Draught Bass; Ruddles County; S&N Theakston Mild, XB, Old Peculier [H]
Popular country inn noted for its hospitality, food and large garden; good for families. Takes its name from Nelson's lieutenant, Admiral Jervis.
Q ♉ ❀ ◖ ◗ ⊞ ♿ ▲ ♣ P

Outwoods

Village Tavern
Signed from A518 OS788182
☎ (095 270) 216
12–3 (2 winter), 6 (7.30 winter)–11
Hanby Drawwell; Marston's Bitter [H]**; guest beers**
Small country inn, off the beaten track, but worth finding. Noted for its extensive curry menu. Children welcome.
♨ Q ❀ ◖ ◗ ▲ ♣ P

Penkridge

Cross Keys
Filance Lane (by bridge 86 of Staffs and Worcs Canal) OS925134 ☎ (0785) 712826
11–3 (4 Sat), 6.30 (5 Fri)–11
Bass Worthington BB [E]**, Draught Bass** [H]**; M&B Highgate Mild; Stones Best Bitter** [E]
Modernised pub, attracting much canal trade. Barbecue in the garden. No food Sun lunch. ❀ ◖ ◗ ♿ ♣ P

Penn Common

Barley Mow
Penwood Lane (off Wakeley Hill, off A449) OS949902
☎ (0902) 333510
12–2.30, 6.30–11; 11–11 Sat
Banks's Mild; Ind Coope Burton Ale; Marston's Pedigree; guest beer [H]
Hidden gem, circa 1630, with a warm welcome. Near Penn golf course. Bulmers cider available. ♨ ❀ ◖ ◗ ⌓ P

Reapsmoor

Butchers Arms
8 miles E of Leek on Longnor road ☎ (029 88) 4477
12–3, 7–11
Marston's Pedigree [H]**; guest beers**
Welcoming, rural pub, popular with locals. Can be isolated in winter. ♨ Q ▲ P

Rugeley

Prince of Wales
Church Street ☎ (0889) 586421
12–3, 6–11
Draught Bass; M&B Highgate Mild [H]
Friendly local with pleasant company. ❀ ◖ ⊞ ♣ P

Rushton Spencer

Crown Inn
Bent Lane (off A523)
☎ (0260) 226231
11–3, 6–11
S&N Theakston Best Bitter, XB, Old Peculier; Younger IPA [H]
Small, rural local with three rooms. Popular with walkers from Cloud End. Good value Greek food. Q ❀ ◖ ◗ ▲ P

Saverley Green

Hunter
Sandon Road OS970385
☎ (0782) 392067
12–3, 7–11
Burtonwood Mild, Bitter, Forshaw's, Top Hat [H]**; guest beers**
Cosy, country pub with great hospitality. Occasional beer festivals. ♨ ♉ ❀ ◖ ▲ ♣ P

Staffordshire

Shenstone

Bulls Head
Birmingham Road
☎ (0543) 480214
11.30–11 (11.30–2.30, 5.30–11 Oct–Mar)
Draught Bass; M&B Brew XI; Stones Best Bitter [H]; guest beers [H]/[G]
In part a former courthouse: a pub on the edge of the village, popular with office workers at lunchtime, and diners eves. Developing bar area where drinkers are being encouraged. Good free house feel for a managed pub.
Q P

Shraley Brook

Rising Sun
Knowlebank Road (B5500, 1½ miles W of Audley)
☎ (0782) 720600
12–3, 6.30–11; 12–11 Sat
Rising Sun Sunlight, Rising, Setting, Sunstroke, Total Eclipse (winter), **Solar Flare [H]; guest beers**
Free house with its own brewery, in the shadow of the M6. Wide range of foreign beers and malt whiskies. Two ciders. P

Shuttington

Wolferstan Arms
Main Road ☎ (0827) 892238
11–2.30 (3 Sat), 6–11
Banks's Mild; Marston's Pedigree [H]
Large, popular country pub on top of a hill with an outdoor children's play area. Elevated views over fields from the restaurant and Scenic Lounge.
P

Stafford

Bird in Hand
Victoria Square, Mill Street
☎ (0785) 52198
11–11; 11–4, 7–11 Sat
Courage Best Bitter, Directors; John Smith's Bitter; guest beers [H]
Popular and enterprising, town-centre pub with a bar, snug, lounge and a games room.

Castle Tavern
Doxey Road, Castletown
☎ (0785) 47719
11–11 (restaurant licence Sun afternoon)
Banks's Mild, Bitter [E]; Marston's Pedigree [H]
Recently refurbished, busy pub opposite the new Sainsbury's. Wheelchair WC.

Coach & Horses
Mill Bank ☎ (0785) 223376
11.30–3.30 (4 Fri, 4.30 Sat), 7 (6 Fri)–11
Bass Worthington BB, Draught Bass; S&N Theakston Best Bitter, XB [H]
Straightforward pub near the main post office and Victoria Park. In the *Guide* for 19 consecutive years.

Cottage by the Brook
Peel Terrace ☎ (0785) 223563
12–3, 7–11; 12–11 Fri & Sat
Ansells Mild; Ind Coope Burton Ale; Marston's Pedigree; Tetley Bitter; guest beer [H]
Large, lively, four-roomed pub warmed by real fires in the lounge and club room, where children are welcome. Bar snacks.

Nags Head
Mill Street ☎ (0785) 223513
12–3, 5–11
Draught Bass; M&B Highgate Mild [H]
Extended town-centre pub with a menu including speciality sausages (till 8pm).

Stafford Arms
Railway Street ☎ (0785) 53313
5.30 (7.30 Sat)–11; closed lunchtimes
Beer range varies [H]
Fine one-roomer, opposite the station, whose beers have attracted a strong following – always five guests. P

Sun
Lichfield Road ☎ (0785) 42208
11.30–2.30, 6.30 (6 summer)–11
Bass Worthington BB, Draught Bass; guest beer [H]
Pleasant, multi-roomed, town-centre pub and olde-worlde restaurant. Reference library for crosswords/quizzes.
P

Telegraph Inn
Wolverhampton Road (A449)
☎ (0785) 58858
11–11
Draught Bass; M&B Highgate Mild; Stones Best Bitter; guest beer [H]
Good, honest local with a lounge and a back bar. Next to the railway, just out of the town centre. Good value meals. P

Stapenhill

Boathouse Inn
The Dingle (off A444)
☎ (0283) 38831
12–3, 7–11
Marston's Pedigree; Ruddles County; S&N Theakston Old Peculier; guest beer [H]
Pub on a bank of the Trent, beside the ferry bridge, with a garden play area for children. Families welcome. Trad. jazz Thu eve. Q P

Stoke on Trent: *Burslem*

Bulls Head
St John Square
☎ (0782) 834153
11.30–3 (3.30 Sat), 5.30 (6.30 Sat)–11; 11.30–11 Fri
Titanic Best Bitter, Lifeboat, Premium, Capt. Smith's, Wreckage [H]; guest beers
Town-centre house recently bought by Titanic. Popular with young and old. At least two guest beers, always from an independent.
Q (Longport) P

Post Office Vaults
☎ (0782) 811027
11–11
Bass Worthington BB, Draught Bass; M&B Highgate Mild; Marston's Pedigree; Ruddles County [H]
Small, friendly and cosy pub, re-opened under its original name, after several years of closure. (Longport)

Butt Lane

Crown Inn
Chapel Street (300 yds off A34)
☎ (0782) 783634
12–3, 7–11
Burtonwood Mild, Bitter, Forshaw's, Top Hat [H]
Cosy, traditional corner pub with 1900s decor, appealing to all ages. Ten minutes' walk from the canal. P

Fenton

Malt 'n' Hops
295 King Street (A50)
☎ (0782) 313406
12–3, 7–11
Burtonwood Mild; guest beers [H]
A former local CAMRA *Pub of the Year*, where the welcoming hosts always offer a range of guest beers. (Longton)

Hanley

Coachmakers Arms
65 Lichfield Street (next to bus station) ☎ (0782) 262158
11.30–4, 7–11
Bass Worthington BB, Draught Bass; M&B Highgate Mild [H]
Classic, small, mid-terraced town pub: three rooms and a corridor, with a tiny public bar. A very friendly local.
Q

Golden Cup
65 Old Town Road
☎ (0782) 212405
11–5, 7.30–11
Draught Bass [H]

Convivial, small local with a splendid bar and fittings. Its ornate Edwardian exterior proudly proclaims 'Bass only'. The interior is divided into three distinct areas: games, bar and snug. Handy for Hanley Forest Park. ❀ ♣

Kidsgrove

Clough Hall Hotel

Clough Hall Road (from A50, or A34, follow signs to ski slope) ☎ (0782) 777131
12–3, 5.30–11; 12–11 Fri & Sat
Banks's Mild, Bitter; Marston's Pedigree Ⓔ
Pub built in 1938, now one large, rambling lounge where the music is not too intrusive. Lively, event-organising managers. Book Sun lunch; no food Mon, or on Sat and Sun eves; other eves till 7pm. Lakeside garden.
❀ ◐ ≠ (Kidsgrove) ♣ P

Northwood

Cross Guns

19 Vincent Street
☎ (0782) 268520
12–4 (not Mon–Wed), 7–11
Bass Worthington BB, Draught Bass; M&B Mild Ⓗ
Smart, comfortable lounge and a traditional bar in a side-street gem. ❀ ♣

Penkhull

Terrace Inn

148 Penkhull New Road
☎ (0782) 47631
11–3.30 (4 Thu & Sat), 6–11; 11–11 Fri
Draught Bass Ⓗ
Modern village pub where the lounge is very popular with older people, and the busy public bar has an emphasis on games. On a steep hill within walking distance of the town centre. Q ❀ ◐ ⊞ ♿ ♣ P

Stoke

Blacks Head

North Street (just off A500)
☎ (0782) 415594
12–3 (4 Fri & Sat), 5.30 (7 Sat)–11
Draught Bass; guest beers Ⓗ
Originally a terraced pub, now standing on its own, and extended. Six beers, including the house beer, Roaches Best Ale (not brewed here). Always a good atmosphere; popular with students and locals alike. Weekday lunches. ◐ ≠ ♣

Staff of Life

Hill Street ☎ (0782) 48680
11–4, 7–11
Draught Bass Ⓔ
Unmodernised, popular, corner town pub, with three rooms off a central corridor. Note the fine, locally made tiled floor in the back room. Bags of character in a typical Potteries local. Q ⊞ ≠ ♣

Tunstall

Globe

High Street ☎ (0782) 839816
11–3, 4.30 (6.30 Sat)–11; 12–2.30, 7–10.30 Sun
Draught Bass Ⓗ
No-nonsense, street-corner local at the lower end of town, on the main bus route. A long, narrowish bar is used for games; the smaller smoke room has a serving hatch. Retains a 1930s feel. ⊞ ♣

White Hart

Rowndwell Street
☎ (0782) 835817
11–5, 7–11; 11–11 Fri & Sat
Banks's Mild; Marston's Bitter, Pedigree Ⓗ
Friendly, well-kept, street-corner drinkers' pub on the edge of the town centre. The only Marston's pub in town: one room divided into two. Lunches weekdays.
Q ❀ ◐ ⇔

Stone

Pheasant

Old Road ☎ (0785) 814603
11.30–4, 6–11; 11.30–11 Fri & Sat
Bass Worthington BB, Draught Bass Ⓗ
Friendly local, immaculately maintained and improved by the present landlord. Eve meals Fri–Sat; no food Sun.
🏰 ⛟ ❀ ◐ ◗ ⊞ ≠

Tamworth

Hamlets Wine Bar

Lower Gungate
☎ (0827) 52277
10.30–2.30, 7 (6.30 Fri)–11
Marston's Pedigree; Samuel Smith OBB Ⓗ**; guest beers** Ⓗ/Ⓖ
Lively, town-centre free house that sells considerably more beer than the wine its name suggests. Popular with students and gets loud weekends. Occasional mini-beer festivals. Not to be missed. ◐ ≠ ♣

Market Vaults

Market Street ☎ (0827) 69653
11–11
Banks's Mild, Bitter Ⓔ
Modernised, popular, town-centre pub with sociable hosts. Book for eve meals (not served Fri or Sat). ❀ ◐ ◗ ≠ ♣

Tatenhill

Horseshoe

Main Street ☎ (0283) 64913
11.30–3, 5.30–11 (11–11 bank hols)
Marston's Pedigree Ⓗ
18th-century village pub which has been internally altered to provide drinking and dining areas, but which has retained its simple, beamed features. Highly regarded food (not served Mon eve). Q ❀ ◐ ◗ P

Two Gates

Bull's Head

Watling Street (A5/A51 jct)
☎ (0827) 287820
11.30–2.30, 7–11
Banks's Mild; Marston's Pedigree Ⓗ
Popular, well-frequented local. Darts, doms, football and golf are all supported. No jukebox. Good passing trade. Q ❀ ◐
⊞ ♿ ≠ (Wilnecote) ♣ P

Uttoxeter

Black Swan

Market Street ☎ (0889) 564657
11–3.30, 5.30–11; 11–11 Wed, Fri & Sat
Draught Bass Ⓗ
Welcoming, 17th-century listed local. ⊞ ≠ ♣ P

Vaults

Market Place ☎ (0889) 562997
11–2.30 (3 Sat), 5.30 (5 Fri & Sat)–11
Draught Bass Ⓗ
Busy, old pub of character.
⊞ ≠ ♣

Wigginton

Old Crown

120 Main Road (off A513, 1 mile N of Tamworth)
☎ (0827) 64588
11.30–3, 6–11; 12–2.30, 7–10.30 Sun
S&N Theakston Mild, Best Bitter, XB, Old Peculier Ⓗ
Modernised pub with views from the lounge and gardens.
Q ❀ ◐ ◗ ⊞ ♿ ♣ P

Wombourne

Old Bush

High Street ☎ (0902) 893509
11.30–3, 6–11; 11–11 Sat
Banks's Mild, Bitter Ⓔ
Three-roomed, refurbished 1930s pub, noted for its family atmosphere and home-cooked food (not served Sun eve or after 8pm). Q ◐ ◗ ⊞ ♿ ♣ P

Yoxall

Crown Inn

Main Street ☎ (0543) 472551
12–3, 6.30–11
Marston's Pedigree Ⓗ
Attractive village pub with a conservatory for families. The lounge dining area serves good quality food. Traditional bar. ⛟ ❀ ◐ ◗ ⊞ ♿ ♣ P

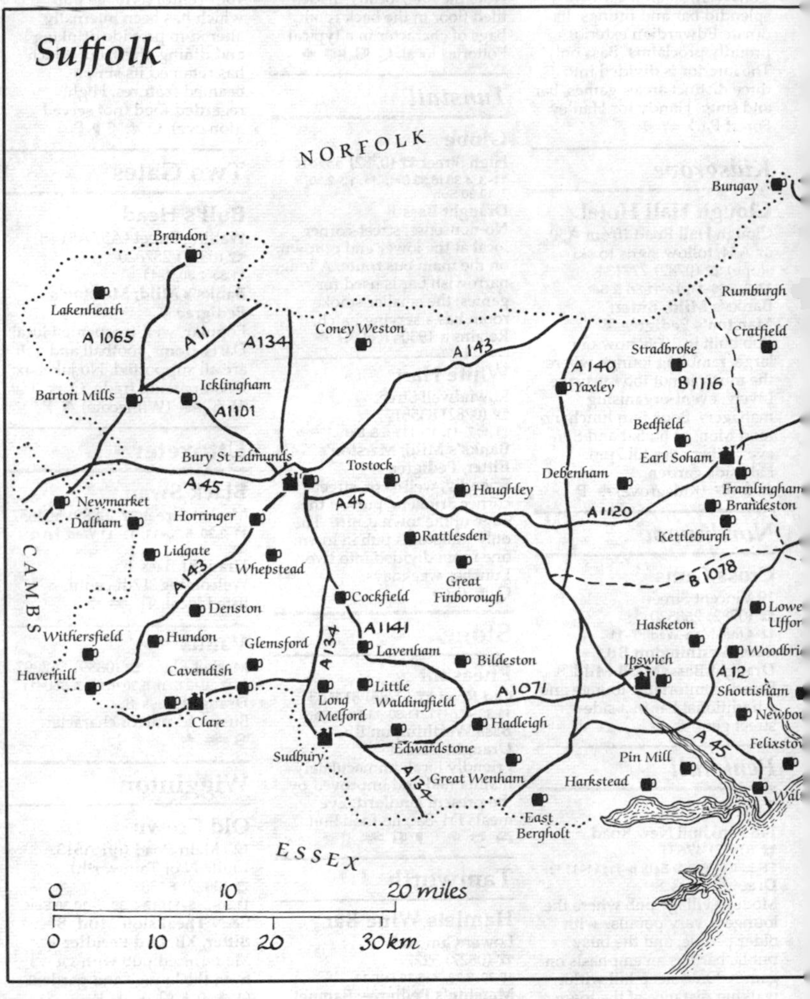

Adnams, Southwold; **Earl Soham,** Earl Soham; **Greene King,** Bury St Edmunds; **Mauldons,** Sudbury; **Nethergate,** Clare; **Scott's,** Lowestoft; **Tolly Cobbold,** Ipswich

Aldeburgh

White Hart

High Street ☎ (0728) 453205
11–3 (may extend), 6–11; 11–11 Sat
Adnams Bitter, Old, Broadside Ⓗ
Pub where the compact, wood-panelled bar provides an ideal setting for locals and visitors to meet. Very busy on bank hols and summer weekends.

Try also: Cross Keys; Crabbe St (Adnams)

Barton Mills

Bell

Bell Lane ☎ (0638) 713625
11–3, 5–11
Greene King IPA, Abbot Ⓗ
Friendly village local with enthusiastic games teams. Note the old photographs of village life.

Bedfield

Crown

Church Lane (leave A1120 in Earl Soham) ☎ (072 876) 431
11.30–3, 6–11; 11–11 Sat
Greene King IPA; guest beer Ⓗ
Village local with a friendly welcome; usually has a guest beer. P

Try also: Victoria, Earl Soham (Earl Soham)

Bildeston

Kings Head

High Street ☎ (0449) 741434
11–3, 5–11; 11–11 Sat (12–2.30, 6.30–11; 11–11 Sat winter)

Greene King IPA [H]**; guest beers**
Large, timber-framed pub on the market square, opened out into one rambling bar area, with a restaurant. Relaxed atmosphere. Live music (Sat); annual beer festival in the garden. The Bildeston Bitter is brewed by Mauldons.
♛ 🛏 ◐ ◑ ▲ ⌓ P

Blaxhall

Ship
☎ (072 888) 316
11–3 (not Mon), 7–11
Adnams Bitter; Tolly Cobbold Mild [H]
Traditional pub, well known for its local folk singers who often spontaneously perform. Very good value meals. Chalet accommodation.
❀ 🛏 ◐ ◑ ▲ ♣ P

Bramfield

Bell
The Street (beside A144)
☎ (098 684) 395
11–2.30, 6.30–11
Adnams Mild, Bitter [G]
Basic, down-to-earth, two-bar pub with a Ring the Bull game in the public bar. Note the thatched church with a detached round tower.
Q ❀ ⊟ ▲ ♣ P

Brandeston

Queens Head
The Street ☎ (0728) 685307
11.30–2.30, 5.30 (6 Mon & Sat)–11
Adnams Mild, Bitter, Old Broadside [H]
Excellent country pub with a large family room. Good value home-cooked food, especially the puddings.
♛ ♨ ❀ 🛏 ◐ ◑ ⊟ ▲ P

Brandon

Five Bells
Market Hill ☎ (0842) 813472
11–2.30, 5–11; 11–11 Fri & Sat
Greene King XX Mild, IPA [H]
Busy pub where the patio gives a good view of the market. Eve meals finish at 8.30. Q ❀ ◐ ◑ ⊟ ⇌ ♣ P

Bungay

Chequers
Bridge Street ☎ (0986) 893579
12–3, 5.30–11; 12–11 Sat
Adnams Bitter; Greene King IPA [H]**; guest beers**
17th-century drinkers' pub in a fine old market town, well worth a visit. At least four ever-changing guest beers.
❀ ◐ ▲ ♣

Green Dragon
Broad Street ☎ (0986) 892681
11–11 (may close weekday afternoons)
Adnams Bitter; Green Dragon Chaucer Ale, Bridge Street Bitter, Dragon [H]**; guest beer**
Formerly the Horse & Groom, a pub closed for several years, then refurbished, renamed and reopened in 1991. Warm and friendly atmosphere; caters for all tastes. Wholesome, inventive good value food. The Green Dragon Brewery is behind the pub.
♛ Q ♨ ❀ ◐ ◑ ▲ ♣ P

Bury St Edmunds

Black Boy
69 Guildhall Street
☎ (0284) 752723
11–3 (2.30 Sat), 5–11
Greene King XX Mild, IPA, Abbot [H]
15th-century pub near the town centre, popular lunchtime with workers and shoppers. Good value food. Occasional pub theatre upstairs. Q ◐ ⇌

Dog & Partridge
Crown Street (near St Mary's church) ☎ (0284) 764792
11–2.30, 5–11; 12–3, 7–11 Sat; 12–2.30, 7–11 Sun
Greene King IPA, Rayments Special, Abbot [H]
Full of olde-worlde charm, a Grade II-listed pub near the cathedral and church where Mary Tudor is buried. It featured in TV's *Lovejoy* and adjoins Greene King's brewery. No food Sun.
❀ 🛏 ◐ ⊟ ⇌ P

Elephant & Castle
21 Hospital Road (Parkway/ Westgate St jct)
☎ (0284) 755570
11–2.30 (3 Sat), 5 (7 Sat)–11; 12–2.30, 7–10.30 Sun
Greene King XX Mild, IPA, Abbot [H]
Homely, two-bar pub with a garden and terrace suitable for children. Family atmosphere. No food Sun eve. ❀ ◐ ◑ P

Flying Fortress
Thurston Road (2 miles from centre) ☎ (028 487) 665
12–2.30, 5 (6 Sat)–11
Adnams Bitter; Charrington IPA; Mauldons Bitter, Black Adder; Nethergate Bitter; Whitbread Flowers IPA [E]
Pub with displays and artefacts connected with the former local WWII airfield. The garden, with an old fire engine, is safe for children; petanque played.
❀ ◐ ◑ ♿ ♣ P

Ipswich Arms
Tayfen Road (400 yds from station towards centre)
☎ (0284) 703623
12–2.30, 6.30–11
Greene King IPA, Abbot [H]
Victorian pub originally called the Segment because of its curved shape. The photograph (1871) in the lounge was taken from the nearby church spire – the highest in Suffolk. No food Sun eve. ❀ ◐ ◑ P

Butley

Oyster
The Street ☎ (0394) 450790
11–3, 5.30–11
Adnams Mild, Bitter, Old, Broadside [H]
Pub on the site of a 12th-century building, modernised in recent years to include a lounge area. Excellent folk night Sun, when no food is served.
♛ Q ♨ ❀ ◐ ◑ ▲ ♣ P

Suffolk

Cavendish

Bull Inn

High Street
☎ (0787) 280245
11–3, 6–11
Adnams XX Mild, Bitter, Old, Broadside Ⓗ
Warm, friendly, timber-framed inn, dating from 1530; now one bar with a dining area. Daily specials are cooked by the proprietor, using fresh ingredients, including fish. No eve meals winter Mon. A rare Adnams pub for the area.
♛ Q ❀ 🛏 ◑ ◗

Clare

Cock

Callis Street
☎ (0787) 277391
11–2.30, 6–11; 11–11 Sat
Adnams Bitter, Old, Broadside (summer), **Tally Ho** Ⓗ
Two-bar pub specialising in high quality, home-cooked food without a restaurant atmosphere. Award-winning garden. No food Sun eve in winter.
♛ Q ❀ ◑ ◗ ⊞ ♣ P

Try also: Bell Hotel, Market Hill (Nethergate)

Cockfield

Three Horseshoes

Stowes Hill (A1141)
☎ (0284) 828177
12–2.30, 6–11
Greene King XX Mild, IPA, Abbot Ⓗ
Thatched, 14th-century former hall house and court. The striking lounge bar boasts an exposed crown post and tie beam, circa 1350; good, lively, locals' public bar. The excellent selection of home-made food includes traditional puddings. No food Tue eve.
♛ Q ☋ ❀ ◑ ◗ ♣ P

Coney Weston

Swan

Thetford Road
☎ (0359) 21295
12–2.30, 5–11
Greene King IPA, Abbot Ⓗ
Simple, Edwardian village pub with a good regular trade. Off the beaten track but worth finding. Q ❀ ♣ P

Cratfield

Poacher

Bell Green ☎ (0986) 798206
12–3, 6–11; 12–11 Sat
Adnams Bitter; Greene King IPA, Abbot Ⓗ
Open-plan bar with many curios, including miniature bottles. Children welcome. Various events throughout the year, especially in summer.
♛ ❀ ◑ ◗ ♿ ▲ ♣ ⌓ P

Dalham

Affleck Arms

☎ (0638) 500306
11–2.30, 6.30–11
Greene King IPA, Abbot Ⓗ
Elizabethan, thatched pub beside the River Kennet; a popular refreshment stop for walkers. ♛ Q ❀ ◑ P

Try also: Ousden Fox, Front St (Greene King)

Debenham

Woolpack

High Street ☎ (0728) 860516
11–3, 5.30–11; 11–11 Fri & Sat
Tolly Cobbold Bitter, Old Strong; Whitbread Flowers IPA; guest beers Ⓗ
Traditional village alehouse, the regimental pub for the Sealed Knot and the English Civil War societies. ♛ Q ♣

Denston

Plumbers Arms

Wickham Street
☎ (0440) 820350
11–2.30, 5–11
Greene King XX Mild, IPA, Abbot Ⓗ
Pub dating from the 1700s, and once the stopping-point for horse traffic between Haverhill and Bury St Edmunds. Book for eve meals.
♛ ❀ ◑ ◗ ♣ P

Dunwich

Ship

St James Street
☎ (072 873) 219
11–3, 6–11 (11–11 summer)
Adnams Bitter, Old, Broadside; Greene King Abbot Ⓗ
Old smugglers' inn of character, in an historic village; sells fresh local fish. Unusually the handpumps are on the back of the bar. Large garden; close to the beach and bird reserves. Cider in summer.
♛ Q ☋ ❀ 🛏 ◑ ◗ ▲ ♣ ⌓ P

East Bergholt

Royal Oak (Dicky)

East End Lane OS099353
☎ (0206) 298221
11.30–2.30, 6–11
Greene King IPA, Abbot Ⓗ
Basic, but friendly public bar on the outskirts of the village, near a large campsite. National-standard dominoes team. ♛ Q ❀ ▲ ♣ P

Eastbridge

Eels Foot

☎ (0728) 830154
11–3, 6–11; 11–11 Fri & Sat
Adnams Mild (summer), **Bitter, Old, Tally Ho** Ⓗ
Good, friendly local, overlooking the marshes and the RSPB Minsmere Reserve. The single public bar is crammed with memorabilia about the pub's name and smuggling. Very busy in summer. No food Wed eve; till 8.30 other eves.
♛ Q ❀ ◑ ◗ ▲ ♣ P

Edwardstone

White Horse

Mill Green (off A1071)
☎ (0787) 211211
11.30–2, 6.30–11
Greene King XX Mild, IPA, Bitter Ⓗ, **Abbot** Ⓖ
Traditional pub where the games include steel quoits, shove-ha'penny and dice. Good value meals Thu–Sat (book for Sun lunch). Try the local cider, if you dare.
♛ Q ❀ ◑ ◗ ⊞ ♣ ⌓ P

Felixstowe

Ferryboat

Felixstowe Ferry
☎ (0394) 284203
11–2.30, 6–11
Tetley Bitter; Tolly Cobbold Bitter, Original; Whitbread Flowers IPA Ⓗ
Very popular, traditional pub, frequented by the local sailing fraternity. Handy for the nearby golf links.
♛ Q ☋ ❀ ◑ ◗ ♣ P

Framlingham

Railway Inn

9 Station Road
☎ (0728) 723693
12 (11 Sat)–3, 6 (7 Sat)–11
Adnams Bitter, Old, Extra Ⓗ
Pub where the public bar, though basic, always offers a friendly welcome. The plush lounge boasts a Victorian fireplace and fine decor.
♛ Q ❀ ⊞ ▲ ♣ P

Glemsford

Crown

Brooke Street ☎ (0787) 281111
11–2, 5–11
Greene King IPA Ⓗ
Friendly village local, a former brew pub full of history, with a well-kept, enclosed garden. Function room over an old stable block. ♛ ❀

Great Finborough

Chestnut Horse
High Road (B1115)
☎ (0449) 612298
11–3, 6–11
Greene King XX Mild, IPA, Abbot Ⓗ
Good, friendly village local attracting a wide range of people with its excellent food, including good curries. It features sewing machine table bases, a collection of cigarette lighters and a large, open brick fireplace. No eve meals Tue or Sun.

Great Wenham

Queens Head
The Row ☎ (0473) 310590
12–2.30, 6 (6.30 Sat)–11
Adnams Bitter; Greene King IPA, Abbot; guest beers Ⓗ
Victorian cottage-style pub with a no-smoking restaurant, offering well over 20 home-made, authentic Indian dishes (not served Mon).
P

Hadleigh

George
High Street ☎ (0473) 322151
11–3, 7–11
Greene King XX Mild, IPA, Abbot Ⓗ
Traditional, beamed pub with a large front public bar and a comfortable lounge. Home of many of Hadleigh's clubs, including its own golf society. A good, unspoilt, friendly, rural pub. Q P

Try also: Four Horseshoes, Whatfield (Free)

Harkstead

Bakers Arms
The Street ☎ (0473) 328595
11.30–2.30, 7–11
Greene King IPA; Tolly Cobbold Bitter, Old Strong Ⓗ
Excellent all-round pub, close to the Stour estuary, offering home-made food. A friendly and basic bar with etched windows is off set by a comfortable lounge and restaurant (booking essential).
Q P

Hasketon

Turks Head
Low Road ☎ (0394) 382584
11–3, 5.30 (6 Sat)–11
Tolly Cobbold Mild, Bitter, Original, Old Strong Ⓗ
16th-century salt house, converted to a pub in the 17th century; now two cosy bars containing much memorabilia and antiques. Large bowling green and a putting green. No food Mon.
Q P

Haughley

Railway Tavern
Station Road (1 mile E of centre) ☎ (0449) 673577
11–2.30, 5.30 (6.30 Sat)–11
Greene King XX Mild, IPA, Abbot; guest beer Ⓗ
19th-century, friendly local near the former station. No food Mon eve.
P

Try also: White Horse (Greene King)

Haverhill

Queen's Head
Queen Street
☎ (0440) 702026
11–11
Courage Best Bitter; Nethergate Bitter; Ruddles Best Bitter, County; Webster's Yorkshire Bitter Ⓗ
Old, town-centre pub serving reasonably-priced food. Retains an etched window from the defunct Wards brewery at Foxearth.
P

Try also: Australian Arms, Hamlet Rd (Greene King)

Horringer

Six Bells
On A143, 2 miles SW of Bury
☎ (0284) 735551
11–2.30, 5.30 (6.15 Sat)–11
Greene King XX Mild, IPA, Rayments Special Ⓗ, **Abbot** Ⓖ
Red-brick, traditional local in a picturesque village, recently refurbished to the landlord's design, and retaining a public bar with bay window seating and cosy corners. The good value food includes speciality pies. Close to Ickworth Park (NT). Q P

Hundon

Plough
☎ (044 086) 789
12–3, 7–11 (11–11 summer)
Greene King IPA; Mauldons Bitter; Nethergate Bitter Ⓗ
Traditional country inn offering a full hotel service. Extensive grounds include a garden terrace and pool. Excellent food, with a vegetarian choice. Disabled WC. Caravan Club site.
P

Icklingham

Red Lion
The Street ☎ (0638) 717802
12–3, 6–11
Greene King IPA, Rayments Special, Abbot Ⓗ
Well-situated, smart, thatched 16th-century inn. Increasingly food oriented, it has acquired a fine reputation.
Q P

Ipswich

County
24 St Helen's Street
☎ (0473) 255153
11–3, 4 (6.30 Sat)–11
Adnams Mild, Bitter, Old, Extra, Broadside, Tally Ho Ⓗ
Large, imposing building near the town centre, with a contrasting boisterous bar and quieter lounge/dining area. The only Adnams pub to offer the complete range. An ideal local for live theatre and cinema, one of only ten pubs in town serving eve meals.

Greyhound
Henley Road (near Christchurch Park)
☎ (0473) 252105
11–2.30, 5–11; 11–11 Sat (closed Xmas day)
Adnams Mild (summer), **Bitter, Old, Broadside; Morland Old Speckled Hen; S&N Theakston XB; guest beer** Ⓗ
Very popular local which always seems busy; the public bar is normally quieter than the lounge. Guest beers always available. P

Lord Nelson
Fore Street ☎ (0473) 254072
11–4, 7–11; 11–11 Fri & Sat
Adnams Mild, Bitter, Old, Broadside Ⓗ
Lively bar, but the lounge is subdued – the ideal place for a quiet chat. A vibrant dockside local dating back to 1663.

Woolpack
Tuddenham Road
☎ (0473) 253059
11.30–2.30, 5.30–11; 12–2.30, 7–10.30 Sun
Tolly Cobbold Mild, Bitter, Original, Old Strong Ⓗ
Reputedly the oldest brick-built pub in town, taking its name from an old wool yard which stood next door. Retains four rooms, including a games room and a tiny front public bar. The cosy lounge is warmed by a huge log fire.
Q P

Try also: Brewery Tap (Tolly Cobbold)

Kettleburgh

Chequers
Easton Road ☎ (0728) 723760
11–2.30, 6–11
Tolly Cobbold Mild; Greene King IPA; Marston's Pedigree [H]
A good all-round venue dating from 1912, after a previous pub was destroyed by fire. Alterations are planned to create a third (snug) bar. The garden extends down to the River Deben.
🔥 Q 🚼 ❀ ◐ ◑ ▲ P

Lakenheath

Plough
Mill Road ☎ (0842) 860285
11–2.30, 6–11
Greene King XX Mild, IPA [H]
Popular pub at the centre of a busy village. The fine flint exterior is typical of the locality, and conceals a spacious bar and a pool room.
❀ ♣ P

Try also: Half Moon, High St (Greene King)

Lavenham

Angel
Market Place ☎ (0787) 247388
11–2.30 (3 Sat), 6–11
Courage Directors; Nethergate Bitter [H]**, Old Growler** (winter) [G]**; Ruddles County; Webster's Yorkshire Bitter** [H]
Impressive, 14th-century coaching inn overlooking the market cross and Guildhall. Pick a quiet time and ask to see the medieval vaulted cellars. Good, home-cooked food using fresh local ingredients; the menu changes daily. 🔥 Q ❀ 🛏 ◐ ◑ P

Lidgate

Star
The Street ☎ (0638) 500275
11–2.30, 7–11
Greene King IPA, Abbot [H]
The centre of activity in an unspoilt village. Spit roast beef is a speciality; barbecues every summer weekend. Note the unusual handpumps.
🔥 ❀ ◐ ◑ ♣ P

Try also: Fox, Ousden (Greene King)

Little Waldingfield

Swan
The Street ☎ (0787) 248584
11–3, 6–11
Courage Directors; Mauldons Bitter; Ruddles Best Bitter; Wadworth 6X [H]**; guest beer**
300-year-old, Grade II-listed building which re-opened, free of tie, in July 1992, after closure by Greene King in 1991. A good local with a wealth of exposed timbers, at the heart of a pretty village. No eve meals Sun.
🔥 Q 🚼 ◐ ◑

Long Melford

George & Dragon
Hall Street ☎ (0787) 371285
11–11
Greene King IPA, Rayments Special, Abbot [H]
Recently refurbished, family-run inn with a lounge-style single bar and a restaurant. A good choice of home-cooked food is always available.
🔥 ❀ 🛏 ◐ ◑ P

Lower Ufford

White Lion
The Street ☎ (0394) 460770
11.30–2.30, 6.30–11
Tolly Cobbold Mild, Bitter, Old Strong; Whitbread Flowers Original [G]
Excellent rural pub with a large open fireplace and gravity beer behind the bar. The setting is almost idyllic, with grazing meadows at the rear leading to the River Deben. Food includes daily specials; no meals Sun eve or Mon. 🔥 Q ❀ ◐ ◑ ♣ P

Lowestoft

Prince Albert
Park Road ☎ (0502) 573424
11–3, 5–11; 11–11 Fri, Sat & summer
Adnams Mild, Bitter, Old, Broadside [H]
Friendly, 1960s, back-street local, away from the town centre. Food is home-made, but not served Sun.
🚼 ❀ ◐ ▲ P

Triangle Tavern
St Peters Street
☎ (0502) 582711
10.30–11
Greene King IPA, Rayments Special, Abbot [H]**; guest beers**
Good, basic, high street pub offering the town's widest choice of beer, with five guest ales at any time. Regular live music Sun, Mon and Thu.
🔥 ▲ ⇌ ♣ ○

Newbourn

Fox
The Street ☎ (0473) 36307
11–3, 6–11 (11–11 summer)
Tolly Cobbold Mild, Bitter, Old Strong; Whitbread Flowers IPA [G]
Busy, 14th-century village inn providing a large range of home-cooked food. The skittle alley in the garden is very popular on summer weekends.
🔥 Q 🚼 ❀ ◐ ◑ ♣ P

Try also: White Horse, Kirton (Pubmaster)

Newmarket

Bushel
Market Street (Rookery shopping centre)
☎ (0638) 663967
10.30–3, 6–11; 10–4.30, 7–11 Sat
Greene King XX Mild, IPA, Rayments Special, Abbot [H]
17th-century public house, once owned by King Charles II. Popular with families and people of all ages; steeped in history. Equal prices throughout the pub.
🔥 Q ❀ ◐ ◑ ♿ ♣

Five Bells
16 St Marys Square
☎ (0638) 664961
11–3 (4 Sat), 6–11
Greene King XX Mild, IPA, Abbot [H]
One-bar, traditional pub with a friendly atmosphere. The enclosed garden has a children's play area and a good petanque pitch.
🔥 ❀ ◐ ♿ ♣

Pin Mill

Butt & Oyster
Off B1456 ☎ (0473) 780764
11–3, 7–11 (11–11 summer)
Tetley Bitter; Tolly Cobbold Mild, Bitter, Original, Old Strong [H]/[G]
Timeless pub of great character, overlooking the River Orwell. The only Suffolk pub to have been in every *Good Beer Guide*. The distinct bar area is adorned with wooden fixtures and memorabilia; large lounge/dining area. CAMRA regional *Pub of the Year* 1992. No eve meals winter Sun.
🔥 Q ◐ ◑ ♣ P

Rattlesden

Five Bells
High Street ☎ (0449) 737373
11–11
Adnams Bitter; Mansfield Riding Bitter; Ridleys IPA; Wadworth 6X; Whitbread Boddingtons Bitter; guest beers [H]
Tiny pub which re-opened, free of tie, in 1991 after several years' closure. One bar, rotating a good range of beers. A good, basic drinking pub, next to the church, overlooking the village.
🔥 Q ❀ ♣

Rumburgh

Buck
Mill Road ☎ (098 685) 257
11–2, 5.30–11
Adnams Bitter; Greene King IPA, Rayments Special [H]
Historic inn, well refurbished and extended to give a number of interlinked areas, including dining and games rooms. The parish church was formerly part of a Benedictine priory and has a 13th-century tower, unusual for Suffolk.
⛫ ❀ ◐ ◑ ⊞ ▲ ♣ P

Try also: White Hart, Halesworth (Free)

Shottisham

Sorrell Horse
☎ (0394) 411617
11–3, 6.30–11
Tolly Cobbold Mild, Bitter, Old Strong [G]
Picturesque, thatched pub of great character. Two bars offer contrast: a quiet public bar with an open fire and bar billiard table, and a lounge, which may be noisy, attracting a younger trade. Good food.
⛫ Q ⛴ ❀ ◐ ◑ ▲ ♣ P

Try also: Ramsholt Arms, Ramsholt Quay (Free)

Sibton

White Horse
Halesworth Road (off A1120, at Peasenhall garage)
☎ (072 879) 337
11.30–2.30, 7–11
Adnams Bitter, Broadside [H]
16th-century inn with a raised gallery. Well-behaved children welcome; large garden/play area. Bar snacks or restaurant meals (winter: no food Sun eve or Mon.)
⛫ ⛴ ❀ 🛏 ◐ ◑ ♣ P

Southwold

Kings Head
High Street ☎ (0502) 723829
11–3, 6–11 (maybe 11–11 summer)
Adnams Bitter, Old, Extra, Broadside [H]
Impressive, split-level lounge and public bars in a most unusual building. The size of the original pub is impossible to imagine as it now rambles into two former shops next door and cottages at the rear. Excellent food.
⛫ Q ⛴ 🛏 ◐ ◑ ▲ ♣ ⊁

Lord Nelson
East Street ☎ (0502) 722079
10.30–11
Adnams Mild, Bitter, Old, Broadside, Tally Ho [H]
Lively bar in a 17th-century inn near coastal cliffs. Over 250 soda syphons are displayed around the bar.
⛫ ❀ ◐ ◑

Stradbroke

Queens Head
Queen Street ☎ (0379) 384384
11–3, 6.30–11
Adnams Mild, Bitter; Greene King IPA, Abbot [H]
Pub with a large interior broken up by a brick fireplace. Barbecues in summer.
⛫ ❀ ◐ ◑ ♿ ▲ ♣ P

Tostock

Gardeners Arms
Church Road (2 miles from A45/A1088 roundabout)
☎ (0359) 70460
11–2.30, 7–11
Greene King IPA, Rayments Special, Abbot [H]
Old building with original beams, near the village green. The basic public bar has church pews and a tiled floor; the comfortable lounge has a large open fireplace. Good food, with a vegetarian option, in the restaurant (no food Sun lunch or Mon/Tue eves). Quoits played.
⛫ ❀ ◐ ◑ ⊞ ♣ P

Walberswick

Bell
Ferry Road ☎ (0502) 723109
11–4, 6–11
Adnams Bitter, Old, Extra, Broadside [H]
Lovely, 600-year-old seaside inn with open fires, beamed ceilings, worn stone and brick floors and high-backed settles. Views to the River Blyth and the sea. Essentially unchanged for years. Eve meals in the restaurant.
⛫ Q ⛴ ❀ 🛏 ◐ ♿ ♣ P

Walton

Tap & Spile
High Road ☎ (0394) 282130
11–4, 5.30–11; 11–11 Fri & Sat
Adnams Bitter; guest beers [H]
Formerly the Half Moon, a very friendly pub with an excellent play area for children. Good bar snacks always available. Numerous interesting guest beers.
⛫ Q ❀ ♣ P

Whepstead

White Horse
Rede Road (use B1066 off A143, turn right at church, ½ mile) ☎ (0284) 735542
11.30–3, 6.30–11
Greene King IPA, Rayments Special, Abbot [H]
Pub with two very different bars: the tap room remains traditional while the lounge offers home-cooked specials with an oriental theme. Hard to find but worthwhile.
⛫ Q ❀ ◐ ◑ ⊞ ♣

Withersfield

Fox
Thurlow Road
☎ (0440) 702426
12–2.30, 5–11; 11–11 Sat
Greene King IPA, Rayments Special, Abbot; Old Mill Bitter [H]**; guest beers**
Friendly pub, currently providing over 100 guest beers a year, in company with good food. No meals Sun eve.
❀ ◐ ◑ P

Try also: White Horse, Hollow Hill (Free)

Woodbridge

Seckford Arms
Seckford Street
☎ (0394) 384446
11–11
Adnams Bitter, Broadside; Draught Bass; guest beers [H]
Family-run free house featuring superb Mayan wood carvings throughout. Note the exposed beams in the lounge and the heated foot rail in the bar. ⛴ ◐ ◑ ⊞ ⇌ ♣ ⌓

Tap & Spile
New Street ☎ (0394) 382679
11.30–2.30, 5.30–11; 11–11 Sat
Adnams Bitter; Marston's Pedigree; Wells Eagle [H]**; guest beers**
Formerly the Mariners Arms, a compact town pub normally offering three guest ales weekdays and five at the weekend. The traditional interior is decorated in the usual Tap & Spile colour scheme. Jazz Mon eve.
⛫ Q ❀ ⊞ ⇌ ♣ ⌓ P

Try also: Olde Bell & Steelyard, New St (Greene King)

Yaxley

Bull
Ipswich Road (A140/B1117 jct)
☎ (0379) 783604
11–3, 5.30–11; 11–11 Fri, Sat & bank hols
Adnams Bitter, Broadside; Woodforde's Wherry [H]**; guest beers**
Genuine free house dating from the 16th century, with plenty of character beneath a high-beamed roof. Large garden and children's play area. Home-cooked food. Very relaxed, rural atmosphere, despite its busy location.
Q ❀ 🛏 ◐ ◑ ▲ ♣ P

Surrey

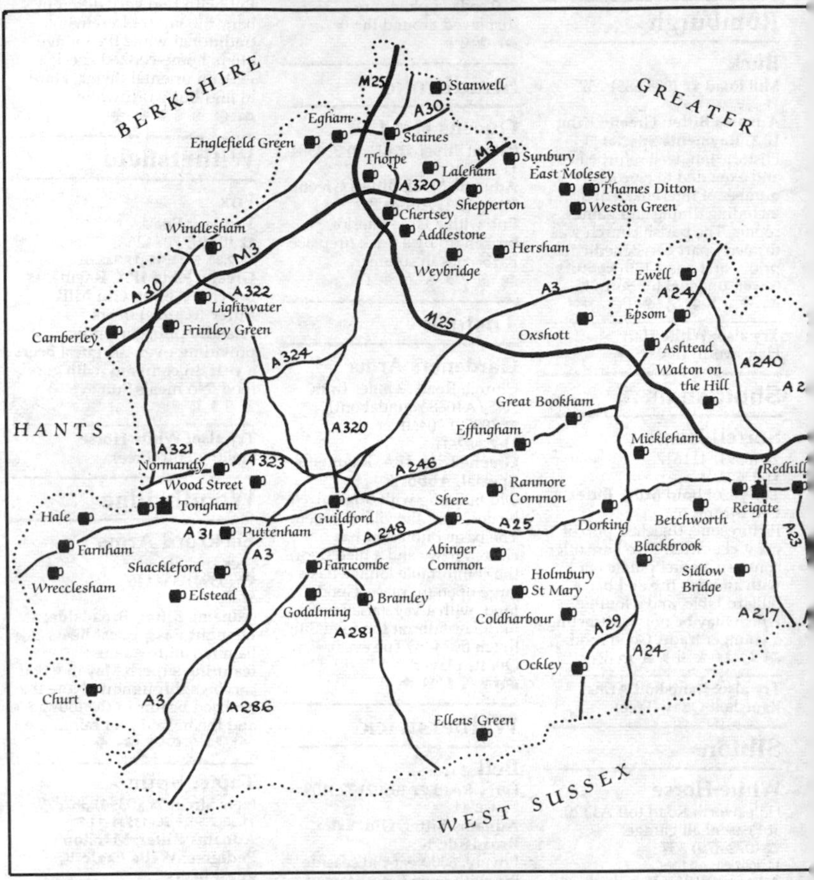

Hogs Back, Tongham; **Pilgrim**, Reigate

Abinger Common

Abinger Hatch
Abinger Lane ☎ (0306) 730737
11–2.30, 6–11
Gibbs Mew Bishop's Tipple; Hall & Woodhouse Badger Best Bitter, Tanglefoot; Ringwood Fortyniner; Wadworth 6X; guest beer Ⓗ
Pub opposite the church, green and duckpond. A single, flagstoned bar with fires and pew seating. ♨ ❀ ◐ ◗ ♣ P

Addlestone

Magnet
Station Road ☎ (0932) 847908
11–11
Greene King IPA, Abbot Ⓗ
Small, plainly decorated, corner local, much improved in recent years. Originally the pub's name alluded to its supposed ability to attract custom, but it is now named after the famous boys' comic.
♨ Q ❀ ◐ ⇌ ♣

Ashtead

Brewery Inn
The Street ☎ (0372) 272405
11–3, 5.30–11
Gale's HSB; Greene King Abbot; Ind Coope Friary Meux Best Bitter, Burton Ale; King & Barnes Sussex; Tetley Bitter Ⓗ
Pub where brewing ceased around 1910. The area surrounding the bar gets quite hectic, whilst the raised lounge area is more sedate. No food Sun eve. Happy hour 5.30–7 weekdays. ❀ ◐ ◗ ⇌ ♣ P

Betchworth

Dolphin
The Street ☎ (0737) 842288
11–3, 5.30–11
Young's Bitter, Porter (summer), Special, Winter Warmer Ⓗ
Attractive country inn with a 16th-century solid flagstone floor and inglenooks. Good food. Popular in summer with motorised locals and walkers.
♨ Q ❀ ◐ ◗ ♣ P

Blackbrook

Plough at Blackbrook
Blackbrook Road OS181466
☎ (0306) 886603
11–2.30, 6–11; 12–2.30, 7–10.30 Sun
King & Barnes Sussex, Broadwood, Old, Festive Ⓗ
Twenty years in this guide and the standards are as high as ever. A country pub with a justifiable reputation for food (no meals Mon eve). The Blackbrook Bar has a collection of ties, and saws on the ceiling.
Q ❀ ◐ ◗ ⊟ P ⚟

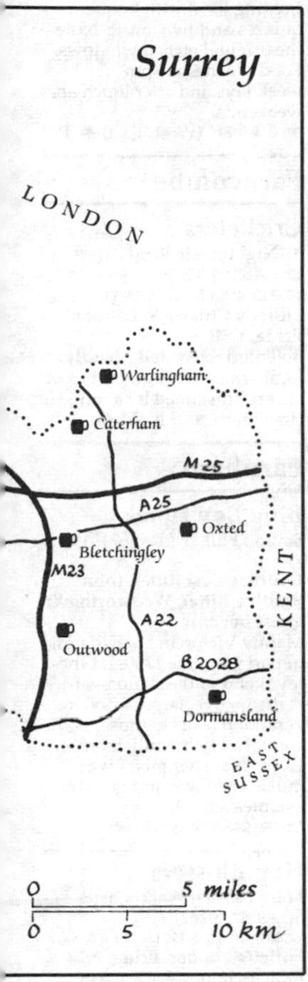

Bletchingley

William IV

Little Common Lane (off A25)
☎ (0883) 743278
11–3, 6–11
Bass Worthington BB, Draught Bass; Fuller's London Pride; Harveys BB; Pilgrim Progress Ⓗ
Fine traditional inn away from the village centre. Originally two 1850s cottages, unaltered for decades. The two small bars at the front are alive with conversation, whereas the back dining room is known for its good value food. Q ❀ ◐◑ P

Bramley

Jolly Farmer

High Street ☎ (0483) 893355
10.30–3, 6–11
Hall & Woodhouse Badger Best Bitter; S&N Theakston Best Bitter, Old Peculier; guest beers Ⓗ
Pleasant, smart pub from the 1500s, featuring good food, a wide range of beers and accommodation. Popular with locals and car-based customers (car park at the rear). The restaurant is in a 400-year-old barn. Q ❀ ⛟ ◐ ◑ ♣ ⌓

Camberley

Bridgers

299 London Road (A30)
☎ (0276) 21534
11.30–3, 5–11
Gibbs Mew Local Line, Salisbury, Bishop's Tipple Ⓗ
Completely refurbished town pub with an attractive, solid, balustraded bar. Victorian pottery, prints and brasses abound. A brisk lunchtime and eve business trade gives way to a younger crowd mid-eve. Named after one of Gibbs Mew brewery's founders. No food Sun eve. ❀ ◐ ◑ ♣

Caterham

Clifton Arms

110 Chaldon Road (B2031)
☎ (0883) 343525
11.30–2.30 (3 Sat), 5.30 (6 Sat)–11
Bass Worthington BB, Draught Bass; Charrington IPA; Fuller's London Pride; Pilgrim Progress; Stones Best Bitter Ⓗ
Pub where the main bar features local photos and old musical instruments. The smaller back bar area is used every Thu by a country and western film club. Live music some Sat nights. No food weekends. Fenced garden. ❀ ◐ P

Chertsey

Golden Grove

St Anns Hill ☎ (0932) 562132
11.30–3, 5.30–11
Adnams Bitter; Ind Coope Burton Ale; Tetley Bitter Ⓗ
Heavily-beamed, low-ceilinged coaching inn on the old stage route to Windsor. The old wooden stables survive. Enjoy the pretty garden, but mind the goat! Eve meals Tue–Fri. Q ❀ ◐◑ ♣ P

Vine

Bridge Road ☎ (0932) 563010
11–3, 5–11 (11–11 summer Sat)
Courage Best Bitter, Directors; Morland Old Speckled Hen Ⓗ
Popular, well-run local dating back 400 years and adorned with cameras, mugs, old records and stuffed birds. Aviary in the garden. Quiz night; interesting live music. Q ❀ ◐ ◑ ♿ ▲ ♣ P

Churt

Crossways Inn

On A287 ☎ (0428) 714323
11–3, 6 (5.30 summer)–11
Courage Best Bitter; guest beers Ⓗ
First class, genuine village local with a strong following for its wide range of ales (three guests). Darts and bar billiards; many games behind the bar. No food Sun. Q ❀ ◐ ⊞ ♣

Coldharbour

Plough

Coldharbour Lane OS152441
☎ (0306) 711793
11.30–3, 6 (7 winter)–11
Adnams Broadside; Gibbs Mew Bishop's Tipple; Hall & Woodhouse Badger Best Bitter; Ringwood Old Thumper; S&N Theakston Old Peculier; Wadworth 6X Ⓗ
Family-run free house in good walking country on the slopes of Leith Hill. Nine ales, including an old ale in winter. Good, traditional home-cooking. Family room lunchtime.
♨ ⛾ ❀ ⛟ ◐ ◑ ♣ ⌓

Dorking

Bush

10 Horsham Road (A2003, 400 yds S of one-way system)
☎ (0306) 889830
11–2.30 (3 Sat), 6–11
Brakspear Bitter; Fuller's London Pride; Harveys BB; guest beer Ⓗ
Friendly, well-run local which hosts an annual marbles competition. Occasional quiz nights. Good value, interesting food (no meals Sun/Mon eves); occasional barbecues.
❀ ◐ ◑ ♣

Queens Head

Horsham Road (A25 one-way system) ☎ (0306) 883041
11–11
Fuller's Chiswick, London Pride, Mr Harry, ESB Ⓗ
Busy, family-run pub with five darts and two pool teams. Happy hour 6–8. Surprisingly large back garden. Beware of the landlord's pickled onions! No food Sun. ❀ ◐ ♣ P

Dormansland

Old House at Home

West Street ☎ (0342) 832117
11–3, 6–11; 11–11 Fri & Sat
Shepherd Neame Master Brew Bitter, Best Bitter, Spitfire, Bishops Finger Ⓗ

Lively pub away from the village centre. Very keen on pub games; board games also available. ⛫ ❀ ◑ ◗ ⇌ ♣ P

East Molesey

Europa

171 Walton Road (B369)
☎ (081) 979 8838
11–11
Courage Best Bitter, Directors; John Smith's Bitter; guest beer 🄷
Pub with three distinctive bars: the lively public has pool and darts. Live music last Sat in the month (usually folk); quiz night every other Thu. Happy hour 5–7, Mon–Sat, and 12–1, 7–8 Sun.
Q ❀ ◑ ⊞ ♣

Effingham

Plough Inn

Orestan Lane ☎ (0372) 458121
11–2.45, 6–11
Young's Bitter, Porter, Special, Winter Warmer 🄷
Good beer does travel – from Wandsworth to the stock-broker belt. An oasis of quality, which also applies to the food. In the eve, meals quickly give way to conversation. Always busy.
Q ❀ ◑ ◗ ♿

Egham

Eclipse

Egham Hill ☎ (0784) 432989
11–3, 5.30–11
Courage Best Bitter; Morland Old Speckled Hen; John Smith's Bitter; Wadworth 6X 🄷
Large, one-bar pub at the foot of Egham Hill. Refurbished in early 1993, resulting in the loss of the public bar to a separate dining area. ❀ ◑ ◗ ♿ ⇌ P

Ellens Green

Wheatsheaf Inn

Off A281, signed Hooks Green (near Bucks Green)
☎ (0403) 822155
11–3, 6–11
King & Barnes Sussex, Broadwood, Old, Festive 🄷
Traditional, low-beamed, 17th-century country pub with a restaurant area. Brasses and wooden seating; reasonable prices. Children's garden.
⛫ Q ❀ ◑ ◗ ♿

Elstead

Star Inn

Milford Road (B3001)
☎ (0252) 703305
11–2.30 (4 Sat), 5.30 (7 Sat)–11
Courage Best Bitter 🄷
Proper village pub – plenty of local atmosphere in the public; cosy and comfy saloon. Convenient for Thursley Common nature reserve. Reasonably priced. Courage Best at its best. Q ❀ ◑ ⊞ ♣

Englefield Green

Beehive

34 Middle Hill (off A30)
☎ (0784) 431621
11–3, 5.30–11; 11–11 Sat
Gale's XXXD (summer), **Best Bitter, 5X, HSB; guest beers** 🄷
Small pub offering an excellent range of beers (three guests and a house beer from Gale's). A beer festival on late May and Aug Bank Hols gives even more choice. ❀ ◑ ◗ ⊖

Epsom

Barley Mow

Pikes Hill (off Upper High St)
☎ (0372) 721044
11–3, 5.30–11
Fuller's Hock, Chiswick, London Pride, Mr Harry, ESB 🄷
Ever-popular local where a rear conservatory backs onto a pleasant garden featuring parakeets, cockateels, rabbits and guinea pigs. Barbecues every summer eve. A porthole as you enter gives a view of the cellar. Q ❀ ◑ ◗

Jolly Coopers

84 Wheelers Lane (off Stamford Green Rd, off B280)
☎ (0372) 723222
11.30–2.30 (3.30 Sat), 5.30 (6 Sat)–11
Ind Coope Friary Meux Best Bitter, Burton Ale; guest beer 🄷
Pub tucked away in the backstreets near Epsom Common. Three separate areas, the public being the largest. The guest beer changes every few months. Q ◑ P

Kings Arms

144 East Street (A24)
☎ (0372) 723892
11–3, 5.30–11; 11–11 Sat
Young's Bitter, Porter (summer), **Special, Winter Warmer** 🄷
Large, roadside inn with a separate public bar. The lounge area backs onto the landscaped garden. Barbecues summer weekends.
❀ ◑ ⊞ ♣ P

Ewell

King William IV

High Street ☎ (081) 393 2063
11–11
Ind Coope Friary Meux Best Bitter, Burton Ale; Tetley Bitter 🄷
Inviting local with frequent quizzes and live music. Note the original etched windows. Food finishes at 7pm weekdays and after lunch at weekends.
❀ ◑ ◗ ⇌ (West/East) ♣ P

Farncombe

Cricketers

37 Nightingale Road
☎ (0483) 420273
12–3 (3.30 Fri & Sat), 5.30–11
Fuller's Chiswick, London Pride, ESB 🄷
Splendid, busy and friendly local where large quantities of ale are consumed by a range of customers. ❀ ◑ ◗ ⇌ ♣

Farnham

Blue Boy Hotel

Station Hill ☎ (0252) 715198
11–11
Courage Best Bitter; John Smith's Bitter; Wadworth 6X; guest beers 🄷
Mainly Victorian hotel, dating in part from the 1700s, at the town end of the station yard. A distinctive, large, wooden verandah leads to the comfortably friendly interior. Good customer mix. Live music weekly. Sun roasts (no eve meals Sun).
⛀ ❀ 🛏 ◑ ◗ ▲ ⇌ ♣

Hop Blossom

Long Garden Walk, Castle Street ☎ (0252) 710770
12.30–2.30, 5.30–11; 11–11 Fri & Sat
Fuller's London Pride, ESB 🄷
Rather cliquey, back-street 'drinking club'. Small and upmarket, with occasional live jazz. ⇌

Lamb

43 Abbey Street
☎ (0252) 714133
11–3, 6–11
Shepherd Neame Master Brew Bitter, Best Bitter, Porter, Bishops Finger 🄷
Good, no-nonsense, cosy, back-street local with good value food (no meals Sun lunch or Tue eve). A *Guide* regular. ❀ ◑ ◗ ⇌ ♣

Frimley Green

Old Wheatsheaf

205 Frimley Green Road (A321) ☎ (0252) 835074
11–3 (4 Sat), 5.30 (6 Sat)–11
Morland Bitter, Old Masters, Old Speckled Hen; guest beer 🄷
100-year-old village local, now refurbished into a single bar with wood-panelled alcoves. Good lunch trade, with locals and passing business drinkers. No meals Sun. ❀ ◑ ♣

Godalming

Aitch's Bar Café
1 Angel Court, High Street
☎ (0483) 861052
11–11
Hogs Back TEA; guest beer Ⓗ
Modern wine bar featuring a good range of beers, including interesting Belgian bottles. Worth a visit. ❀ ◖ ▲ ≹

Red Lion
1 Mill Lane ☎ (0483) 415207
11–11; 11–3, 6.30–11 Sat
Courage Best Bitter, Directors; Wadworth 6X; guest beer Ⓗ
Large, lively, two-bar, town-centre pub formed from several old properties, including the Mayor's residence and the courthouse. Features of the latter can be seen in the public bar. The cellar used to house prisoners. Imaginative guest beers. No food Sun eve.
❀ ◖ ◗ ⊞ ▲ ≹ ♣

Great Bookham

Anchor
161 Lower Road (off A246, via Eastwick Rd) ☎ (0372) 452429
11–2.30 (4 Sat), 5.30–11
Courage Best Bitter, Directors; guest beer Ⓗ
500-year-old local with oak beams, exposed brickwork and two fires. Rustic feel despite its location in a dormitory town. The guest beer changes every couple of months. No food Sun. ♨ Q ❀ ◖ P

Guildford

Kings Head
27 Kings Road (A320)
☎ (0483) 68957
11–11
Fuller's Hock, Chiswick, London Pride, ESB Ⓗ
Good, three-bar local, dating from the 1860s. Regular games eves; can be busy lunchtimes with students. No food Sun eve. ❀ ◖ ◗ ⊞ ♣

Live & Let Live
57 Haydon Place
☎ (0483) 64372
11–3, 5.30–11; 11–11 Sat
Morland Bitter, Old Masters, Old Speckled Hen; guest beer Ⓗ
Friendly pub, refurbished into a comfortable, popular single bar. Wed is curry night.
Q ❀ ◖ ◗ ≹

Sanford Arms
58 Epsom Road (A246)
☎ (0483) 572551
11–3, 5.30–11; 11.30–3.30, 6–11 Sat
Courage Best Bitter, Directors; guest beer Ⓗ
Friendly, wood-panelled local with well-separated bars. The garden has an aviary and a conservatory. The guest beer, from independent breweries, changes regularly. Q ❀ ◖ ◗ ⊞ ≹ (London Rd) ♣ ⅄

Spread Eagle
46 Chertsey Street (A320)
☎ (0483) 35018
10.30–2.30 (3 Fri, 3.30 Sat), 5–11
Courage Best Bitter, Directors; John Smith's Bitter; Young's Special; guest beer Ⓗ
Popular pub, for the last few years the best in Guildford. The range of independent guest beers is outstanding. Though tending towards the young on Fri nights, there is a good mix of customers. Excellent food (no meals Sun).
❀ ◖ ≹ (London Rd) ♣ P

Hale

Black Prince
174 Upper Hale Road, Upper Hale (A3016) ☎ (0252) 714530
12–11
Fuller's Chiswick, London Pride, ESB Ⓗ
Friendly, traditional, two-bar local. ❀ ◖ ⊞ ♣ P

Hersham

Bricklayers Arms
6 Queens Road (off A317)
☎ (0932) 220936
11–2.30, 5.30–11; 11–11 Sat
Courage Best Bitter; Fuller's London Pride; Hall & Woodhouse Tanglefoot; Marston's Pedigree; Wadworth 6X; Webster's Yorkshire Bitter Ⓗ
Cosy Victorian pub retaining two bars. Busy lunchtimes (excellent, home-cooked food; not served weekend eves). Spectacular floral displays in summer. ❀ 🛏 ◖ ◗ ⊞ ♿ ♣

Holmbury St Mary

Kings Head
Pitland Street (off B2126, follow signs to MSSL) OS112442 ☎ (0306) 730282
11–3, 6–11; 11–11 Sat
Fuller's London Pride; Ringwood Best Bitter, Old Thumper; Young's Bitter Ⓗ
Not easy to find, but worth it: a pub featuring a large garden with good views, wooden pews and unusual church-like, arched doors. A friendly backwater in a picturesque environment. ♨ ❀ ◖ P

Laleham

Turks Head
The Broadway ☎ (0784) 469078
11–11
Courage Best Bitter, Directors; Gale's HSB; Marston's Pedigree; Wadworth 6X Ⓗ
Busy pub in an attractive, riverside, suburban village. Extensive food. Q ◖ ◗ ▲

Lightwater

Red Lion
114 Guildford Road
☎ (0276) 72236
11–11
Courage Best Bitter, Directors; John Smith's Bitter; guest beer Ⓗ
Basic, large, one-bar boozer in a pretty village. Strong local following. Interesting guest beers. ❀ ◖ ◗ ♣

Mickleham

King William IV
4 Byttom Hill (off A24 southbound) OS174538
☎ (0372) 372590
11–3, 6–11
Adnams Bitter; Hall & Woodhouse Badger Best Bitter; Whitbread Boddingtons Bitter; guest beer Ⓗ
Pub charmingly perched on a hillside, opposite Norbury Park and overlooking the River Mole. Five vegetarian meals on the extensive menu (no meals Mon eve). Beautiful garden. ♨ Q ❀ ◖ ◗

Normandy

Anchor
Guildford Road (A323)
☎ (0483) 235195
11–3, 4.30–11
Hall & Woodhouse Badger Best Bitter, Hard Tackle, Tanglefoot; Harveys XX Mild; guest beers Ⓗ
Pleasant, well-run pub with interesting beers. Special food events, including barbecues in summer. Good Sun lunches, children welcome. No meals Sun eve. Skittle alley for hire.
♨ Q ❀ ◖ ◗ ♣ P

Duke of Normandy
Guildford Road (A323)
☎ (0483) 235157
11.30–3, 6–11
Greene King XX Mild, IPA, Abbot, Winter Ale Ⓗ
Good local known for beer and good value food (till 8pm; no food Sun eve) – steak and kidney pie recommended. Friendly. ❀ ◖ ◗ ⊞ ♣ P

Ockley

Cricketers Arms
Stane Street (A29)
☎ (0306) 627205
11–3, 6–11
Fuller's London Pride; Pilgrim Progress; Ringwood Best Bitter Ⓗ

Pub dating from the 16th century where the flagstoned bar has a large inglenook. Patio in front; garden with fish pond to the side. Good value food. 🏰 ❀ ◖ ◗ ♣ P

Outwood

Dog & Duck
Prince of Wales Road
OS313460 ☎ (0342) 842964
11–11
Everards Old Original; Gribble Black Adder II; Hall & Woodhouse Badger Best Bitter, Hard Tackle, Tanglefoot; Wadworth 6X Ⓗ
Very friendly local serving good food with daily specials. Quiz night Sun. Games include Ring the Bull.
🏰 ❀ ◖ ◗ ♣ P

Oxshott

Bear
Leatherhead Road (A244)
☎ (0372) 842747
11–3, 5.30–11
Young's Bitter, Porter (summer)**, Special, Winter Warmer** Ⓗ
Comfortably appointed pub with a good, friendly atmosphere. Children allowed in the large conservatory. Extensive menu of home-cooked food at reasonable prices, which changes daily.
🏰 Q ♘ ❀ ◖ ◗ ♣ P

Oxted

George Inn
52 High Street, Old Oxted (off A25) ☎ (0883) 713453
11–11
Adnams Bitter; Draught Bass; Fuller's London Pride; Harveys BB; Morland Old Speckled Hen; Wadworth 6X Ⓗ
Well-renovated, 500-year-old pub serving excellent and good value food at all times. The pleasant atmosphere is enhanced by the absence of music and electronic games.
🏰 Q ❀ ◖ ◗ P

Puttenham

Good Intent
The Street (off B3000 near church) ☎ (0483) 810387
11–2.30, 6–11
Courage Best Bitter; Wadworth 6X; guest beer Ⓗ
Village pub with a public bar, a games area and a comfortable saloon. The last has old beams, a large log fire and a snug eating area. Both the guest beers and the bar meals are interesting and varied. Popular with locals, walkers and diners. 🏰 ❀ ◖ ◗ ♣ P

Ranmore Common

Ranmore Arms
OS112501 ☎ (0483) 283783
11–11 (may close winter afternoons)
Cotleigh Tawny; Fuller's London Pride; Hall & Woodhouse Badger Best Bitter, Hard Tackle; Hogs Back TEA; Pilgrim Progress; guest beer Ⓗ
One-bar pub with a large fireplace and an extensive garden. The guest beer, from an independent brewer, changes monthly. Barbecues and other events in summer; live music Fri. No eve meals Mon–Wed. 🏰 ❀ ◖ ◗ ▲ ♣ P

Redhill

Hatch
Shaws Corner, Hatchlands Road (A25 by war memorial)
☎ (0737) 764593
11–2.30, 5.30–11; 12–3, 6.30–11 Sat
Greene King IPA, Rayments Special, Abbot; guest beers Ⓗ
17th-century forge renovated to expose original beams. The Edwardian theme is more tasteful than most. Over 160 guest beers in two years (eight always available), plus Belgian beers. ❀ ◖ ♣

Home Cottage
Redstone Hill (A25 behind station) ☎ (0737) 762771
10.30–11
Young's Bitter, Porter, Special, Winter Warmer Ⓗ
Victorian coaching house with Victorian handpumps. A family pub with food always available. Friendly restaurant. A former CAMRA Surrey *Pub of the Year*.
🏰 Q ♘ ◖ ◗ ⇌ P

Reigate

Nutley Hall
8 Nutley Lane (rear of car park on the one-way system)
☎ (0737) 241741
11–11
King & Barnes Sussex, Broadwood, Old, Festive Ⓗ
Basic, one-bar pub with a dining room. Although hidden away, it can get very busy in the eve with serious beer drinkers. ❀ ◖ ◗ ⊞ ⇌ ♣ P

Yew Tree
99 Reigate Hill (A217)
☎ (0737) 244944
11–11
Courage Best Bitter, Directors; John Smith's Bitter; Wadworth 6X Ⓗ
Comfortable, panelled pub halfway up Reigate Hill. Good value food all day. Popular with people working late in the office. 🏰 Q ❀ ◖ ◗ P

Shackleford

Cyder House Inn
Peperharow Lane OS935453
☎ (0483) 810360
11–3, 5.30–11
Cyder House Piston Broke, Old Shackle; Wadworth 6X; guest beers Ⓗ
Surrey's only pub brewery, in good walking country. A popular, well-run pub that attracts a range of customers. Can be crowded on Sun and in summer with diners. Worth trekking through lanes to find. Six beers. 🏰 ❀ ◖ ◗ ♣

Shepperton

Barley Mow
67 Watersplash Road (off B376) ☎ (0932) 225580
11–11
Courage Best Bitter; Gale's HSB; Wadworth 6X; Webster's Yorkshire Bitter; guest beer Ⓗ
Lively local on a side road – well worth seeking out. A traditional village pub with atmosphere. Warm welcome.
🏰 ❀ 🛏 ◖ ♿ ⇌ P

Shere

Prince of Wales
Shere Lane ☎ (0483) 202313
11–2.30, 6–11
Young's Bitter, Porter, Special, Winter Warmer Ⓗ
Pub in a delightful village with a pretty stream, ideal for an afternoon stroll. A small public dominated by pool contrasts with a more sedate lounge often used by diners. Excellent children's facilities.
🏰 Q ♘ ❀ ◖ ◗ ⊞ ♣

Sidlow Bridge

Three Horseshoes
Ironsbottom (off A217)
OS249463 ☎ (0293) 862315
12–2.30 (3 Sat), 7 (6 Fri)–11
Fuller's London Pride, Mr Harry; Harveys BB; Morland Old Speckled Hen; guest beer Ⓗ
Small, rural pub: no motorbikes, but helicopters very welcome. Originally a coaching stop on the London to Brighton run. Q ❀ ◖ ♣ P

Staines

Blue Anchor
High Street ☎ (0784) 452622
11–11
Ruddles Best Bitter; Wadworth 6X; Webster's Yorkshire Bitter Ⓗ
Ever-popular pub offering live music most eves, from heavy metal to jazz. A listed building with a preserved window-tax frontage.
🏰 ❀ 🛏 ◖ ♿ ⇌ ♣ P

Hobgoblin
Church Street ☎ (0784) 452012
11–11
Wychwood Shires, Best, Dr Thirsty's Draught, Hobgoblin; guest beers H
An unbelievable transformation from the old Clarence. Expect a warm welcome, and then enjoy your drink in a most attractive, traditional pub. Although only a single bar, the public and lounge areas are well defined.
Q

Stanwell

Wheatsheaf
Town Lane ☎ (0784) 253372
11–11; 11–4, 7–11 Sat
Courage Best Bitter, Directors; guest beer H
Splendid, traditional pub which offers a low-beamed, cosy interior to locals and visitors alike. The benches at the front are popular in summer. Q P

Sunbury

Flower Pot Hotel
Thames Street ☎ (0932) 780741
11–11
Draught Bass; Brakspear Bitter; Greene King IPA; Tetley Bitter; Young's Porter, Special H
Small, quiet and friendly pub, by the Thames.
Q P

Thames Ditton

Angel
Portsmouth Road (A307)
☎ (081) 398 4511
10.30–3.30, 5.30–11; 11–11 Sat
Courage Best Bitter, Directors; Wadworth 6X; Young's Bitter H
Corner pub and restaurant on the main road near the green. At one time a coroner's court sat here (the mortuary was next door). Q

Thorpe

Rose & Crown
Green Road ☎ (0344) 842338
11–3, 5.30–11 (11–11 summer Fri & Sat)
Courage Best Bitter, Directors H
Former hunting lodge, by the green: plenty of beams, dark wood, and comfortable seats. In summer, sit in the large garden and let the children attack the bouncy castle.
Q P

Tongham

White Hart
76 The Street (A3014)
☎ (0252) 782419
11–3, 5.30–11; 11–11 Fri & Sat
Courage Best Bitter; Hogs Back TEA; John Smith's Bitter H
Attractive, rambling local, busy and convivial. Mixed clientele: local societies use the distinct bars. Eve meals by arrangement.

Walton on the Hill

Fox & Hounds
Walton Street ☎ (0737) 812090
11–11
Draught Bass; Charrington IPA; Fuller's London Pride; M&B Highgate Mild; guest beers H
Cosy one-bar pub with a low ceiling, originally two cottages. Four regular ales plus four guests, two of which change weekly. An unusual horizontal handpump dispenses the IPA. Excellent range of food.
Q P

Warlingham

Hare & Hounds
Limpsfield Road (B269, E of centre) ☎ (0883) 623952
11–3, 5–11; 11–11 Fri & Sat
Draught Bass; Charrington IPA; Fuller's London Pride; M&B Highgate Mild H
Lively local with many societies and charity fund-raising events. One horseshoe-shaped bar with games on one side. The enclosed back garden has a children's play area. No food Sun. P

Weston Green

Alma Arms
Alma Road (off A309)
☎ (081) 398 4444
11–2.30 (3 Fri & Sat), 6–11
Courage Best Bitter, Directors; Marston's Pedigree H
Former hunting lodge with an oak-beamed interior, overlooking a picturesque green and pond. A regular *Guide* entry. Q (Esher) P

Weybridge

Old Crown
83 Thames Street (off A317)
☎ (0932) 842844
10.30–11
Courage Best Bitter, Directors; King & Barnes Sussex H
16th-century, weatherboarded pub close to the junction of the Rivers Thames and Wey. Several rooms with differing atmospheres. Home-cooked food, with daily specials, at all times. Q P

Prince of Wales
Anderson Road (off A3050)
☎ (0932) 852082
11–11
Adnams Bitter; Fuller's London Pride; Tetley Bitter; Wadworth 6X; Whitbread Boddingtons Bitter H
Popular, cosy pub with traditional decor and no noisy machines. The restaurant is used for bar lunches and a full menu eves (not Sun). Good value food. Q P

Windlesham

Windmill Inn
London Road (A30)
☎ (0276) 72281
11–3, 5–11; 11–11 Fri & Sat
Brakspear Bitter; Courage Best Bitter; Fuller's London Pride; Marston's Pedigree; Ruddles County H**; guest beer** G/H
Pub with an enterprising range of beers and up to five others on gravity dispense. Worth visiting just to see what is available. A cosy single bar with a pleasant atmosphere, split into two: the handpump section and the cask section.
Q

Wood Street

White Hart
White Hart Lane
☎ (0483) 235939
11–3, 6–11
Brains SA; King & Barnes Broadwood; Palmers IPA, Tally Ho!; Ringwood Old Thumper; Ruddles Best Bitter H
Picturesque village pub with a beamed interior and a resident ghost. One large, square bar with an adjacent restaurant. Exotic ales with regular mini beer festivals (except in winter). Occasional live music.
Q

Wrecclesham

Bat & Ball
Bat & Ball Lane, Boundstone OS833445 ☎ (0252) 792108
12–11
Brakspear Bitter; Fuller's London Pride; Marston's Pedigree; Young's Bitter, Special; guest beers H
Out-of-the-way free house with good family facilities. Excellent meals (no food Sun eve). The range of beers varies. Worth finding.

Sandrock
Sandrock Hill Road OS831444
☎ (0252) 715865
11–11
Batham Mild, Best Bitter; Brakspear Bitter; guest beers H
Unsurpassed for quality and selection; a beer festival in a functional but comfortable, no-frills pub with bar billiards. Black Country beers feature (usually eight). No food Sun.
Q

East Sussex

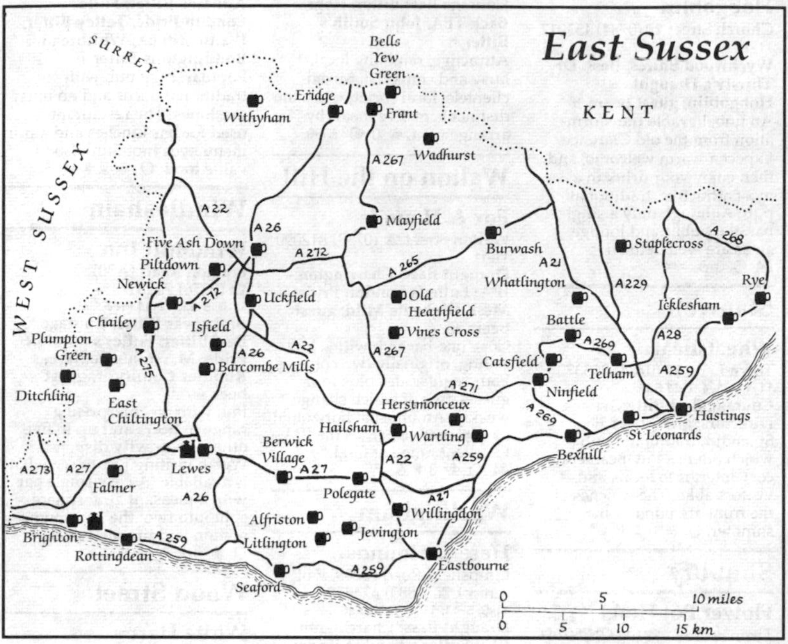

Harveys, Lewes; **Kemptown**, Brighton

Alfriston

Market Cross/ Smugglers

Waterloo Square
☎ (0323) 870241
11–3, 6.30–11
Courage Best Bitter, Directors; Harveys BB, Old Ⓗ
Pub in a picturesque village, with a warm atmosphere. The huge sit-in inglenook unfortunately has gas-powered logs. A pub with two names, allegedly two ghosts, and a large collection of early kitchen implements. Attractive (no-smoking) conservatory.
Q ❀ ◐ ◑ ⊁

Barcombe Mills

Angler's Rest

Mill Road (1 mile W of A26, N of Lewes) OS428150
☎ (0273) 400270
11.30–2.30 (3 Sat; not Mon), 6–11 (may vary)
Arkell's 3B; Fuller's ESB; Harveys BB, Old; Wadworth 6X Ⓗ**; guest beer**
Single-bar pub in a rural location next to the old SR railway station and near the River Ouse. Children are catered for in a separate dining area and a garden play area. Note the extensive collection of miniatures. The beer range may vary. ♨ ❀ ◐ ◑ ▲ ♣ P

Battle

Chequers

Lower Lake (A2100)
☎ (0424) 772088
11–3, 6–11; 11–11 Sat
Whitbread Fremlins Bitter, Boddingtons Bitter, Flowers Original Ⓗ
Smart, beamed pub, very close to the site of the Battle of Hastings and the abbey. Dates back to the 15th century.
♨ ❀ ⊨ ◐ ◑ ▲ ≥ P

1066

High Street (A2100)
☎ (0424) 773224
10–3, 5–11; 10–11 Fri, Sat & summer
Morland Old Speckled Hen; Wadworth 6X; Whitbread Fremlins Bitter, Flowers Original Ⓗ
Busy, lively, split-level pub near the abbey. Folk club Sun eve, often featuring big names. Restaurant upstairs.
♨ ❀ ⊨ ◐ ◑ ▲ ≥ ♣

Bells Yew Green

Brecknock Arms

☎ (0892) 750237
11.30–2.30, 6 (7 winter)–11
Harveys XX Mild, Pale Ale, BB, Old Ⓗ
Pub where hop memorabilia and a collection of bottles decorate the public bar. Note the little handpumps in the saloon, which offers a view of a defunct brewery. ♨ Q ❀ ◐ ⊞ ♿ ≥ (Frant) ♣ P

Berwick Village

Cricketers Arms

In lane 100 yds S of A27, near Alfriston OS519053
☎ (0323) 870469
11–3, 6–11
Harveys BB, Old Ⓖ
Highly recommended, genuinely rustic village pub; totally unspoilt, with stone floors in the main bars. Beer comes from casks behind the bar. Eve meals in winter are restricted to Thu–Sat.
♨ Q ❀ ◐ ◑ ♿ ♣ P

Bexhill

Sportsman

15 Sackville Road
☎ (0424) 214214
10.30–11
Harveys BB; King & Barnes Festive; Ruddles County; Webster's Yorkshire Bitter; guest beer Ⓗ
Small, cosy pub in the town centre with an outgoing landlady and sociable locals. Suntrap garden. The only pub

in town offering a decent range of beers. ❀ ◐ ⇌ ♣

Try also: Bell Hotel, Old Town (Courage)

Brighton

Albion

28 Albion Hill (behind the former Tamplins Brewery) ☎ (0273) 604439
11–11
Brakspear Bitter; Marston's Pedigree; Whitbread Boddingtons Mild, Bitter; guest beer Ⓗ
Friendly, unspoilt corner local situated on a steep hill, causing an unusual split-level bar. The host uses his guest beer rights to the full benefit of his varied clientele. ❀ ♣ ⊂

Basketmakers Arms

12 Gloucester Road (300 yds SE of station) ☎ (0273) 689006
11–3, 5.30–11; 11–11 Fri & Sat
Gale's XXXD, BBB, Best Bitter, 5X, HSB Ⓗ
Very popular back-street pub noted for live music on Sun night and piped music at other times. The interior is a cornucopia of tins and other ephemera. Over 70 malt whiskies available. ◐ ⇌ ♣

Bugle Inn

24 St Martins Street (N of 'The Level', off Lewes Road, behind the church) ☎ (0273) 607753
11–3, 6–11; 11–11 Fri & Sat
Courage Best Bitter, Directors; Harveys BB; Young's Special Ⓗ
Difficult to find but worth the effort, this small, intimate local has one of the few island bars in the area. A mixed range of customers ensures a lively atmosphere; often crowded in the eve. Parking not so much difficult as impossible. ⛀ ❀

Evening Star

55 Surrey Street (200 yds S of station) ☎ (0273) 328931
11–11
Beer range varies Ⓗ
Basic, almost spartan, single-bar pub named after the last steam loco built by BR at Swindon. No electronic gadgetry, just a selection of taped blues/jazz/rock played at a volume which permits easy conversation. Up to nine beers sold, some of the more uncommon at premium prices; ciders vary. Q ❀ ⇌ ♣ ⊂

George Beard

125 Gloucester Road (300 yds SE of station) ☎ (0273) 607765
11–3, 5–11
Adnams Broadside; Fuller's London Pride; Greene King Abbot; Harveys BB, Old Ⓗ**; guest beers**
Spacious town pub effectively refurbished in Victorian style. Formerly the Eagle – see the history on the wall as you enter. Quiz Sun night; beer festivals April and October. The house beer is brewed by Adnams. No food weekends. ◐ ⇌ ♣

Greys

105 Southover Street (up steep hill, E of 'The Level') ☎ (0273) 680734
11–3, 5.30–11; 11–11 Sat
Whitbread Flowers Original Ⓗ**; guest beers**
Very much a part of the local music scene, the small single bar is adorned with posters for local events. Live bands somehow manage to squeeze in Sun lunch and Mon eve. Food is often unusual, including a vegetarian option; no meals Sun. ❀ ◐

Hand in Hand

33 Upper St James Street, Kemptown ☎ (0273) 602521
11–11
Hall & Woodhouse Badger Best Bitter, Tanglefoot; Kemptown Bitter, Celebrated Staggering Ale, SID Ⓗ
Brighton's only brewery is situated in this corner pub with unusual decor. Good selection of food (eve meals finish at 6.30). Regular mild and winter ales also sold. ◐ ◗

Lamb & Flag

9 Cranbourne Street (near Churchill Sq) ☎ (0273) 326415
10.30–11; closed Sun
Fuller's London Pride; King & Barnes Sussex Ⓗ
Close to both shops and offices, a busy town local, attracting much passing trade. Friendly landlord, keen to please; good snacks. Q

Lion & Lobster

24 Sillwood Street (100 yds S of Norfolk Sq) ☎ (0273) 776961
11–3, 7–11; 11–11 Fri & Sat
Beer range varies Ⓗ
An ever-changing range of five beers is offered in this large, single-bar corner pub and restaurant. Regular music at weekends. ◐ ◗

Lion & Unicorn

26 Sussex Street (E of St Peter's church) ☎ (0273) 625555
11–11
Ind Coope Burton Ale; Tetley Bitter Ⓗ**; guest beers**
Also known as the Blue House, this elevated corner local commands a fine view over the town. The decor is dominated by a growing collection of breweriana. Filling bar snacks available all day. Occasional live music and unusual guest beers. Limited parking. ❀ ♣ P

Lord Nelson

36 Trafalgar Street (200 yds E of station) ☎ (0273) 682150
10.30–3, 5.30–11
Harveys XX Mild (summer), **Pale Ale, BB, Old, Armada** Ⓗ
Two-bar pub renowned for its good food. Busy at most times. Q ❀ ◐ ⇌ ♣

Preston Brewery Tap

197 Preston Road (A27) ☎ (0273) 508700
11–11
Courage Best Bitter; Harveys BB; Ruddles County; Wadworth 6X; Young's Special Ⓗ
Popular, friendly pub on the main road to London. Cheap beer during happy hour on Fri and Sat nights and Sun lunchtime. Pool table in an alcove; music at an acceptable volume. Good range of food (not served Sun eve). ⛀ ❀ ◐ ◗ ⇌ (Preston Pk)

Robin Hood

2–3 Norfolk Place
10.30–11
Draught Bass; Hall & Woodhouse Badger Best Bitter; Harveys BB Ⓗ**; guest beers**
A good selection of guest beers (sometimes at premium prices), at a popular local with decor based on Sherwood Forest. ◐

Royal Oak

46 St James's Street ☎ (0273) 699248
10.30–11
Courage Best Bitter, Directors; Marston's Pedigree Ⓗ
Unrenovated, two-bar pub east of the town centre. The public bar is dominated by a pool table; the saloon is wood-panelled and traditional. Live folk music Fri eve, when no food is served. Q ❀ ◐ ◗ ♣

Sir Charles Napier

50 Southover Street (up steep hill, E of 'The Level') ☎ (0273) 601413
11–3, 6–11
Gale's XXXD, BBB, Best Bitter, 5X, HSB Ⓗ
Traditional corner local which is often busy. The single wood-panelled bar, however, has several cosy corners for a quiet chat. Used as HQ by the local cycling club who meet on Tue eve. ⛀ ❀ ◐ ◗ ♣ ⊂

East Sussex

Sussex Yeoman
7 Guildford Street (150 yds W of station) ☎ (0273) 327985
10.30–11
Fuller's London Pride; Greene King Abbot; Harveys BB; Mansfield Riding Bitter; Mitchell's Best Bitter; Thwaites Bitter [H]
Single-bar, popular pub with a good selection of ten real ales. Features a speciality sausage and mash menu. ◐ ◑ ⇌

Burwash

Bell
High Street (A265)
☎ (0435) 882304
11–2.30, 6–11
Burts Nipper; Harveys BB; Morland Old Speckled Hen [H]
Historic pub with an unusual collection of mulling irons and barometers. A superb house, in this guide for all 21 years. No food Sun eve.
♛ Q ♞ ❀ ⛟ ◐ ◑ ♣ ⌓ P

Catsfield

White Hart
On A261 ☎ (0424) 892650
10–3, 6–11
Draught Bass; Charrington IPA; Harveys BB [H]
Village local, weatherboarded in true Sussex style. Its big fireplace is ideal for drying off after a walk in 1066 country. Snacks only Sun.
♛ ♞ ❀ ◐ ◑ ▲ ♣ P

Chailey

Horns Lodge
South Chailey (A275)
☎ (0273) 400422
11–3, 6–11
Greene King IPA; Harveys BB; John Smith's Bitter [H]
Family-run, single-bar pub with dining and children's areas, plus a large garden. Winner of many pub games trophies. No eve meals Sun.
♛ ❀ ◐ ◑ ♣ P

Try also: Kings Head, A275/A272 crossroads (Beards chain)

Ditchling

Bull Hotel
2 High Street (B2116/B2112 jct) ☎ (0273) 843147
11–3, 6–11 (may vary)
Brakspear Bitter; Whitbread Boddingtons Bitter, Pompey Royal, Flowers Original, Porter [H]; guest beers
Unspoilt, 16th-century village pub with many outbuildings. A large open fire, low beams and antique furnishings create a good atmosphere, with a tiny snug bar making a good contrast. Despite the sign, the pub is named after a Papal edict – not the animal. Guest beers are from the Whitbread range. ♛ Q ❀ ⛟ ◐ P

White Horse Inn
16 West Street (20 yds W of B2116/B2112 jct)
☎ (0273) 842006
11–11
Harveys BB [H], Old [G]; guest beers
Single-bar village pub which is striving to be the local: a free house, reputedly haunted and close to Anne of Cleves's house. The games room hosts occasional beer festivals. Good value food. ♛ ❀ ◐ ◑ ♣

Eastbourne

Arlington Arms
360 Seaside (A259)
☎ (0323) 724365
11–11
Harveys XX Mild, BB, Old [H]
Recently refurbished local, a mile-and-a-half east of the town centre; an excellent example of a cottage conversion swallowed up in the town's expansion. Eve meals Fri and Sat. Children welcome at lunchtime. The public bar is no cheaper. ♞ ❀ ◐ ◑ ♿ ♣ P

Hogshead
South Street (400 yds S of station) (0323) 723017
11–11
Harveys BB; Wadworth 6X; Whitbread Boddingtons Bitter, Flowers Original [H]; guest beers [G]
Pub renovated to recreate a pre-war atmosphere, with bare boards and pine. Very popular with the young and noisy crowd, but welcoming. Beer available in four-pint jugs (often at a discount). Frequent mini-beer festivals.
◐ ⇌ ♣ ⌓

Hurst Arms
76 Willingdon Road (A22, 1½ miles N of centre)
☎ (0323) 712762
11–11
Harveys Pale Ale, BB, Old, Armada [H]
Popular, traditional red-brick local with a games-oriented public and a quiet saloon. A continuous *Good Beer Guide* entry since 1978. Increased range of hot and cold snacks (the steak and kidney pies are recommended). Stocks Harveys commemorative brews when available. Q ❀

Lamb
High Street, Old Town (A259)
☎ (0323) 720545
10.30–3, 5.30–11
Harveys XX Mild (summer), **Old, Armada [H]**
Harveys' showpiece house, dating in part from 1290, with a timbered frontage and beams. Three bars, all on different levels of the same floor. The passage from the church next door was used for hiding clergy in the Middle Ages. Excellent. Q ♞ ❀ ◐ ◑

East Chiltington

Jolly Sportsman
Chapel Lane (off B2116)
OS372153 ☎ (0273) 890400
11.30–2.30, 6 (7 winter)–11; closed Mon
Harveys BB; John Smith's Bitter [H]; guest beers (summer)
A true centre of rural life; a pub well off the beaten track, with good views of the South Downs and Sussex Weald. Popular with ramblers and, on summer Suns, families. Separate areas for dining and pool. Note the use of the 'ancient' Beards pump clip. No food Mon or Tue, or Sun eve.
❀ ◐ ◑ ♣ P

Eridge

Huntsman
Eridge Station (just off A26)
☎ (0892) 864258
11.30–2.30, 6–11
King & Barnes Mild (summer) **[G], Sussex, Broadwood, Festive [H], Old [G]**
Pub situated off the newly reconstructed A26, near the quiet station. A cheerful greeting is guaranteed as you enter the L-shaped saloon; the public bar has darts and bar billiards. Large rolls tempt you at the bar. Eve meals at weekends only.
Q ❀ ◐ ◑ ⊞ ♿ ⇌ ♣ ⌓ P

Falmer

Swan
Middle Street, North Falmer (A27) ☎ (0273) 681842
11–2.30, 6–11
Gibbs Mew Bishop's Tipple; King & Barnes Broadwood; Palmers BB; Shepherd Neame Master Brew Bitter, Bishops Finger [H]
Traditional, L-shaped, two-bar local. The landlord's family has been here for three generations, since 1903. A winter ale or another dark beer is also available. No food Sun.
♛ ❀ ◐ ⇌ ♣

Five Ash Down

Firemans Arms
☎ (0825) 732191
11.30–2.30, 6–11; 11.30–11 Sat

Harveys BB; Younger IPA; guest beers Ⓗ
Well-established, friendly local with a good cross-section of regulars. Strong interest in steam locomotives and associated machinery; a lively annual steam enthusiasts' rally is held on New Year's Day. The good selection of guest beers changes regularly; various ciders.
♔ Q ❀ ◖ ◗ ⊟ ♿ ▲
⇶ (Buxted) ♣ ⌓ P ⊬

Frant

Abergavenny Arms
On A267 ☎ (0892) 750233
11–11
Harveys BB; King & Barnes Mild; Ringwood Fortyniner Ⓗ**; guest beers**
Large country pub on two levels with lots of beams. There has been an alehouse on this site since 1450. The lounge was used as a court room in the 18th century (cells in the cellar). Constantly changing range of beers. Q ❀ ◖ ◗ ♣ P

Hailsham

Grenadier
High Street ☎ (0323) 842152
11–3, 6–11; 11–11 Fri
Harveys XX Mild, BB, Old, Armada Ⓗ
Popular, two-bar town pub with a well renovated interior. In the same family for over 40 years. ❀ ◖ ♿ ♣ P

Hastings

First In, Last Out
14–15 High Street, Old Town (off the Bourne)
☎ (0424) 425079
11–11
Adnams Broadside; FILO Crofter, Cardinal; Wadworth 6X Ⓗ
Small, friendly brew pub; a window in the bar overlooks the full mash brewery and alcove seating gives privacy. Note the impressive, open central fireplace. The home-brewed ales are among the cheapest in the area – not to be missed. Lunches Tue–Sat.
♔ Q ⛟ ◖ ▲

Old Pump House
64 George Street, Old Town (off A259) ☎ (0424) 422016
11–3, 6 (7 winter)–11
Shepherd Neame Master Brew Bitter, Best Bitter, Spitfire, Bishops Finger Ⓗ
Originally housing a water pump, this timbered building dates from the 15th century and, situated in a pedestrianised street, attracts tourists and locals alike. If you enter by the front door, the bar is upstairs! Eve meals till 8.30.
⛀ ❀ ◖ ◗

Stag Inn
14 All Saints Street, Old Town (off the Bourne)
☎ (0424) 425734
12–3, 6 (7 Mon)–11; 12–11 Sat
Shepherd Neame Best Bitter, Spitfire, Porter, Bishops Finger (summer) Ⓗ
Ancient smugglers' pub with a warm welcome for everyone, in the Old Town's most picturesque area. Features include its own game (Loggits) and a collection of mummified cats. Offers a malt whisky of the week and cheap beer early eve. Sussex CAMRA *Pub of the Year* 1993.
♔ Q ⛀ ❀ ⛟ ◖ ◗ ⊟ ▲ ♣

Try also: Royal Standard, E Beach St, Old Town (Shepherd Neame)

Herstmonceux

Welcome Stranger
Chapel Row (½ mile E of village, S off A271) OS639122
☎ (0323) 832119
12–3 (not Mon–Fri), 7–11
Harveys XX Mild (summer), **BB, Old; Smiles Bitter** Ⓗ
Almost defying description: a superb example of a very old country pub, very small and very low. Beer is served through a hatch into the bar room. Highly recommended and well worth the search. Opening days vary! ♔ Q

Icklesham

Queens Head
Parsonage Lane (off A259, Hastings–Rye road)
☎ (0424) 814552
11–3, 6–11; 11–11 Sat
Cotleigh Tawny; Fuller's London Pride; Greene King Abbot; Harveys Pale Ale Ⓗ**; guest beers**
Tile-hung country pub in a quiet, rural setting, with a magnificent mahogany public bar. Superb views from the garden; warm, friendly atmosphere. A large collection of old farming implements adorns the walls. Boules pitch outside. The beer range changes.
♔ Q ❀ ◖ ◗ ♿ ▲ ♣ ⌓ P ⊬

Isfield

Laughing Fish
Off A26 ☎ (0829) 750349
11–3, 6–11; 12–3, 7.30–10.30 Sun
Harveys Pale Ale, BB, Old Ⓗ**; guest beer**
Friendly Victorian village pub, next to the station (Lavender Line) and two miles from Bentley Wildfowl Park. A centre for folk music, pub games, quizzes, etc. The cellar is cooled by an underground stream. No food Mon eve.
♔ ⛀ ❀ ⛟ ◖ ◗ ▲ ♣ P

Try also: Halfway House, A26 (Harveys)

Jevington

Eight Bells
High Street ☎ (0323) 484442
11–2.30, 6–11; 12–2, 7–10.30 Sun
Adnams Broadside; Courage Best Bitter; Harveys BB; Wadworth 6X Ⓗ**; guest beers**
Nestling in the Downs, an ex-Courage pub in the hands of the same landlord for over 20 years. Inglenook, beams, etc., in one bar; the other is more modern but fits in well. An ideal watering hole if walking on the Downs.
♔ Q ❀ ◖ ◗ ♣ P

Lewes

Black Horse
Western Road (old A27, opp. County Hall) ☎ (0273) 473653
11–2.30, 6–11
Brakspear Special; Fuller's London Pride; Harveys BB Ⓗ**; guest beer**
Two-bar local selling a good selection of ales, generally including one guest beer. Originally a coaching inn, built in 1810, it boasts numerous pictures of old Lewes.
Q ❀ ⛟ ◖ P

Gardeners Arms
46 Cliffe High Street
☎ (0273) 474808
11–11
Beer range varies Ⓗ
Friendly free house nearly opposite the Harveys brewery, offering up to eight, ever-changing real ales. Pew-style seating in a barn-like interior. Occasional live music.
◖ ◗ ⇶ ♣ ⌓

Lewes Arms
1 Mount Place (off High St)
☎ (0273) 473152
11–11
Harveys BB Ⓗ
Good selection of guest beers in a pub located in the castle's shadow. Three bars, including one devoted to games.
♔ ◖ ⇶ ♣

Litlington

Plough & Harrow
OS523018 ☎ (0323) 870632
11–2.30, 6–11

East Sussex

Gribble Reg's Tipple; Hall & Woodhouse Badger Best Bitter, Hard Tackle; Wells Eagle Ⓗ; guest beers
Pub where a good choice of beers is guaranteed – many unusual for the area. An ideal venue for summer Sun lunches, but gets very busy. Railways are one of the landlord's passions – hence the Southern Railway memorabilia. Q ❀ ◐ ◑ ♿

Mayfield

Middle House

High Street ☎ (0435) 872146
11–11
Greene King Abbot; Harveys BB; Wadworth 6X Ⓗ
Grade I-listed Elizabethan building, built in 1575. Now the main road has been diverted away from the village, peace has enhanced the setting. Note the inglenook. Comfy chesterfields provide seating. Live music Sun. 🔥 Q ❀ 🛏 ◐ ◑ ♣ P

Rose & Crown

Fletching Street (¼ mile E of village) ☎ (0435) 872200
11–2.30, 5.30–11
Fuller's Chiswick; Greene King Abbot; Harveys BB Ⓗ; guest beers
Country inn with varying levels and a different character in each area. The large inglenook has seats – very hot in winter! The excellent beer choice for the area includes frequent rare guest beers. High quality food.
🔥 Q 🚸 ❀ 🛏 ◐ ◑ ▲ ♣ P

Newick

Crown

Church Road (off A272, S of village green) ☎ (0825) 723293
11–11
Adnams Bitter; Brakspear Special; Greene King Abbot; Harveys BB Ⓗ
One-bar village local, once a hotel and retaining an archway for coaches. Popular with the rugby club. A venue for pub games, discos and eccentric competitions. No food Sun. 🔥 ❀ ◐ ♣ P

Try also: Royal Oak, Church Rd (Whitbread)

Ninfield

United Friends

The Green (A271)
☎ (0424) 892462
11–2.30, 6–11
Charrington IPA; Fuller's London Pride; Harveys BB; Morland Old Speckled Hen Ⓗ
Genuine free house offering a good range of beers; a blackboard lists what's due and when. Warm and friendly welcome.
🔥 Q 🚸 ❀ 🛏 ◐ ◑ ♿ ▲ ♣ P

Old Heathfield

Star Inn

Church Street (off B2096)
OS599203 ☎ (0435) 863570
11–3, 6–11
S&N Theakston XB, Old Peculier; Younger Scotch, IPA Ⓗ; guest beer Ⓖ
14th-century village local, actually in the churchyard. Comfortable saloon; superb views from the garden. The beer range is unusual for the area. No eve meals Sun or Mon. 🔥 Q ❀ ◐ ◑ ♣ P

Piltdown

Peacock

Shortbridge (B2102)
☎ (0825) 762463
11–2.30, 5.30–11
Courage Directors; Harveys BB; Whitbread Boddingtons Bitter, Flowers Original Ⓗ
Picturesque, oak-beamed pub with an inglenook, and gardens front and rear. A popular young people's meeting place. Near the site of the Piltdown Man hoax.
🔥 ❀ ◐ ◑ P

Plumpton Green

Fountain Inn

Station Road ☎ (0273) 890294
10.30–2.30, 6–11 (may vary)
Young's Bitter, Special, Winter Warmer *or* Porter Ⓗ
Young's most southerly tied house, which has appeared in every *Good Beer Guide*. The landlord, who has been at the pub for over 25 years, has received many awards for the pub, which originated as a bakehouse.
🔥 ◐ ◑ ⇌ (Plumpton) ♣ P

Polegate

Dinkum

54 High Street
☎ (0323) 482029
11–11
Harveys BB, Old, Armada Ⓗ
A town pub, originally the Polegate Inn, but named by Aussies stationed nearby during WWI who considered the place to be 'fair dinkum'. The public and saloon bars have different characters: one work-a-day, the other plush.
Q 🚸 ❀ ◐ ⇌ ♣ P

Rottingdean

Black Horse

65 High Street
☎ (0273) 302581
10.30–2.30, 6–11
Adnams Bitter; Charrington IPA; Harveys BB; Young's Special Ⓗ
Traditional, three-bar popular local: a cosy snug, a public bar offering a selection of pub games, and a large saloon.
🔥 ◐ ♣

Rye

Ypres Castle

Gun Gardens
☎ (0797) 223248
11–11
Hook Norton Best Bitter, Old Hooky; King & Barnes Sussex; Pitfield Mild Ⓗ; guest beers
Not immediately obvious, this unspoilt pub is well worth seeking out. Access is on foot only. Superb views of the harbour, plus a safe garden. Good food all day – fresh fish a speciality – and a warm welcome guaranteed.
🔥 Q 🚸 ❀ ◐ ◑ ⇌ ♣

St Leonards

Horse & Groom

Mercatoria (off A259)
☎ (0424) 420612
11–3, 5.30–11
Courage Best Bitter, Directors; Harveys Pale Ale, BB; Wadworth 6X; Wells Bombardier Ⓗ
Smart, well-kept pub decorated with sporting prints. Not far from the seafront but well tucked away in the heart of old St Leonards. Worth seeking out for its pleasant, comfortable atmosphere.
Q 🚸 ◐ ⇌ (Warrior Sq) ♣

New George & Dragon

Tower Road (off A21)
☎ (0424) 434055
11–3, 6–11; 11–11 Fri & Sat
Arkell's 3B; Fuller's London Pride, ESB; Greene King Abbot; Harveys BB; Thwaites Craftsman Ⓗ; guest beers
Renamed and revitalized, back-street pub, off the main shopping area. Six or more beers are always available in this oasis of choice. A real locals' pub which makes everyone welcome.
Q ❀ ♿ ♣

Seaford

Wellington

Steyne Road
☎ (0323) 890032
11–2.30 (3 Sat), 5.30–11
Harveys BB, Old; Wadworth 6X; guest beers Ⓗ
Large, two-bar pub adorned with all manner of breweriana and bric-a-brac, including a display of photos of old

Seaford. The brewer of Old Welly, the house beer, is a state secret! See the blackboard in the saloon bar for guest beer details. No food Sun.
Q ♨ ❀ ◖ ⊟ ≢ ♣

White Lion Hotel
74 Claremont Road
☎ (0323) 892473
11–2.30, 6–11
Fuller's London Pride; Harveys BB, Old [H]; guest beers
Spacious bar within a hotel, much modernised but comfortable. Blackboards display both the extensive range of food and guest beers (no food Sun eve). Set in a holiday accommodation area; note the photograph of the *Fawlty Towers* cast! Good base for walkers on the South Downs.
❀ ⛟ ◖ ◗ ≢ ♣ P

Try also: Beachcomber, Marine Drive (Free); **Lord Admiral**, Pelham Rd (Free)

Staplecross

Cross Inn
On B2165
☎ (0580) 830217
11–2.30, 6–11
Harveys BB; Ruddles Best Bitter; Wadworth 6X [H]
Another fine village local, full of beams, inglenook, etc.; this one has a ghost, too. Good, wide beer choice.
♛ Q ♨ ♿ ▲ ♣ P

Telham

Black Horse
Hastings Road (A2100, Battle–Hastings road)
☎ (0424) 773109
11–3, 5.30–11
Shepherd Neame Master Brew Bitter, Best Bitter, Spitfire, Bishops Finger [H]
Attractive, weatherboarded roadside pub, recently acquired by Shepherd Neame. Warm welcome, lots of beams, good food. Games room on the first floor; skittle alley in the attic; boules played in summer. Annual music weekend in a marquee every Spring Bank Holiday.
♛ Q ❀ ◖ ◗ ♿ ▲ ♣ P

Uckfield

Alma Arms
Framfield Road (B2102, E of centre) ☎ (0825) 762232
11–2.30, 6–11; 12–2, 7–10.30 Sun
Harveys XX Mild, Pale Ale, BB, Old, Armada [H]
Pub with a traditional public bar, plus a comfortable saloon, a family room and a small garden area. In the same family for generations. A rare opportunity to sample the full Harveys range. No food Sun.
Q ♨ ❀ ◖ ⊟ ♿ ≢ ♣ P ⊬

Try also: Brickmakers Arms, Ridgewood Estate (Free)

Vines Cross

Brewers Arms
OS594179 ☎ (043 53) 2288
11–2.30, 6–11
Adnams Bitter; Fuller's London Pride; Harveys BB; guest beers [H]
Welcoming country pub in a hamlet near Horam: a comfortable public bar and a cosy saloon. The genuine home cooking is excellent value. Home of a past world champion Tug of War team. Well worth finding.
♛ ♨ ❀ ◖ ◗ ♿ ♣ P

Wadhurst

Greyhound
St James Square (B2099)
☎ (0892) 783224
11–2.30, 6–11; 11–11 Sat
Draught Bass; Charrington IPA; Fuller's London Pride; Ruddles County [H]; guest beer
Tastefully refurbished house with a warm welcome; spacious, comfortable and homely. Once the meeting place of the Hawkhurst Gang – a band of local thieves now long gone. Boasts a quality restaurant and an impressive inglenook. Small brewery guest beer.
♛ Q ❀ ◖ ◗ ♿ ♣ P

Wartling

Lamb at Wartling
On minor road N of roundabout, E of Pevensey
OS658092 ☎ (0323) 832116
11–2.30 (3 Sat & summer), 7 (6.30 Sat & summer)–11
Draught Bass; Charrington IPA; Fuller's London Pride [H]
Pub and restaurant, next to the church, featuring two real fires and a pool room.
♛ Q ♨ ❀ ◖ ◗ ♣ P

Whatlington

Royal Oak
OS763193
☎ (0424) 870492
11–3, 6–11; closed Tue
Harveys Pale Ale; Marston's Pedigree; Young's Special; guest beer [H]
Magnificent country inn dating from 1490. Its classic interior includes an 80-ft well. Welcoming atmosphere and high quality food – the landlord owns a butcher's shop.
♛ Q ❀ ◖ ◗ ♣ P

Willingdon

Red Lion
99 Wish Hill (just off A22)
☎ (0323) 502062
11–2.30, 5.30–11; 12–2.30, 7–10.30 Sun
King & Barnes Sussex, Broadwood, Old, Festive [H]
Single-bar village local at the foot of the South Downs. Warm atmosphere; good quality food (no meals Sun). It was the model for the pub in George Orwell's *Animal Farm*.
❀ ◖ ◗ ♣ P

Withyham

Dorset Arms
On B2110, Groombridge–Hartfield road
☎ (0892) 770278
11–3, 5.30 (6 Sat)–11
Harveys XX Mild, Pale Ale, BB [H]
Originally a 16th-century farmhouse, but an inn since the early 18th century. A fine example of a Sussex local, with a good cross-section of regulars and an excellent choice of fine food cooked on the premises. A good rustic location with al fresco eating and drinking in the summer.
♛ Q ❀ ◖ ◗ ♣ ⌓ P

West Sussex

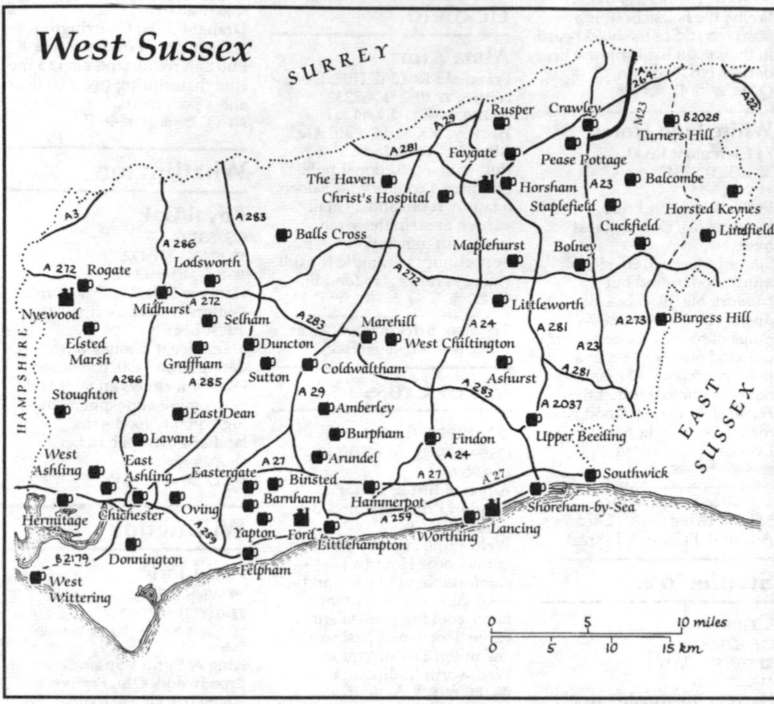

Arundel, *Ford*; **Ballard's**, *Nyewood*; **Brewery on Sea**, *Lancing*; **King & Barnes**, *Horsham*

Amberley

Black Horse

High Street (off B2139)
☎ (0798) 831552
11–3, 6–11
Greene King IPA; Ind Coope Burton Ale; Whitbread Flowers Original Ⓗ
Fine example of an unspoilt village local, near the South Downs Way and the Chalkpits Industrial Museum.
ሸ ❀ ◖◗ ⊟ ♣

Arundel

Eagle

41 Tarrant Street (100 yds up High St hill, left, left again after 200 yds) ☎ (0903) 882304
11–3, 5.30–11; 11–11 Fri & Sat
Fuller's London Pride; Wadworth 6X Ⓗ**; guest beers**
Once the Eagle brewery of Lambert & Norris, but ceased brewing for them in the late 1920s. Look for the eagle above the door. One bar, with wood flooring, always extremely popular. Four guest beers. ሸ Q ◖ ▲ ⇌

Try also: White Hart, High St (Free)

Ashurst

Fountain

On B2135, S of Partridge Green
☎ (0403) 710219
11–2.30, 6–11
Courage Best Bitter Ⓗ**; Fuller's London Pride; King & Barnes Broadwood** Ⓖ**; John Smith's Bitter** Ⓗ
Splendid 16th-century pub next to a duck pond. The recently opened skittle alley doubles as a function room. The pub rugby team occasionally plays in the adjacent field.
ሸ Q ❀ ◖ ♣ P

Balcombe

Cowdray Arms

London Road (B2036/B2110 jct) ☎ (0444) 811280
11–3, 5.30–11 (11–11 Sat in May–Sept)
Harveys BB; guest beers Ⓗ
Comfortable, traditional house which always has a good selection of real ales and an excellent range of food. Yearly beer festival in April. The conservatory is no-smoking.
Q ❀ ◖◗ P ⊭

Balls Cross

Stag

Kirdford Road OS987263
☎ (0403) 77241
11–3, 6–11
King & Barnes Mild, Sussex, Broadwood, Old, Festive (occasionally) Ⓗ
Delightful 16th-century country pub with a stone floor, and a cosy bar with an inglenook. Friendly locals and landlord. No food Sun eve.
ሸ Q ☋ ❀ ◖◗ ♿ ♣ P

Barnham

Murrell Arms

Yapton Road ☎ (0243) 553320
11–2.30, 6–11; 11–11 Sat
Gale's BBB, Best Bitter Ⓖ**, HSB** Ⓗ**, 5X** Ⓖ
Three-bar pub of great character next to a tiny village green. The interior is filled with local history and breweriana. Antique auctions held alternate Suns. The landlord and landlady celebrate 30 years here this year.
ሸ Q ☋ ❀ ◖◗ ⊟ ⇌ ♣ P

Binsted

Black Horse

Binsted Lane (off A27/B2132) OS980064
☎ (0243) 551213
11–3, 6–11
Gale's HSB Ⓖ; Ruddles County Ⓗ; guest beers Ⓖ
Off the beaten track, but worth finding: a pub offering up to ten guest beers, all from independents, including some rare finds. Fine views across the valley from the garden. Food in the bar or the conservatory/restaurant. Regular theme nights.
Q P

Bolney

Eight Bells

The Street (near A272/A23 jct)
☎ (0444) 881396
11.30–3, 6–11; 11.30–11 Sat
King & Barnes Sussex, Festive; S&N Theakston Best Bitter, Old Peculier; Younger IPA Ⓗ; guest beers
400-year-old village pub near the South Downs. The only pub known to play Javelot. Popular with families at weekends.
Q P

Burgess Hill

Brewers Arms

251 London Road (A273)
☎ (0444) 232153
11–2.30, 6–11; 11–11 Fri & Sat
Charrington IPA; guest beers Ⓗ
True locals' pub where the old Kemptown (Brighton) Brewery logo can still be found on the front wall. A 1928 replacement for a much older building next to a ginger beer brewery, hence the name. Two bars, the back one an occasional venue for music.

Burpham

George & Dragon

2½ miles N of A27, E of Arundel OS039089
☎ (0903) 883131
11–2.30, 6–11
Arundel Stronghold; Courage Directors; Harveys BB Ⓗ; guest beers
Popular free house in a pleasant village, offering regular changes to the menu and beer range. A good base for walks on the Downs or in the Arun valley. No food Sun eve.
Q P

Chichester

Mainline Tavern

Whyke Road
☎ (0243) 782238
11–11
Courage Directors; Gale's HSB; Ruddles Best Bitter; Wadworth 6X; Whitbread Flowers Original; Young's Special Ⓗ
Large, modern local by a level-crossing, with a novel concept in interior decor. Popular with fans of discos and loud music. Happy hours 5–7 and occasional price promotions. P

Rainbow Inn

St Pauls Road (B2178, ½ mile N of centre)
☎ (0243) 785867
10–11
Ind Coope Friary Meux Best Bitter, Burton Ale; Tetley Bitter; guest beer Ⓗ
Friendly local offering good value meals most of the day, with monthly special food eves. Well worth the walk from the city centre. Continually changing and unusual guest beers.
Q P

Try also: Hope Inn, Spitalfield Lane (Carlsberg-Tetley)

Christ's Hospital

Bax Castle

On Barns Green road from Christ's Hospital
☎ (0403) 730369
11.30–2.30, 6–11
Adnams Bitter; Draught Bass; Courage Directors; Fuller's London Pride Ⓗ; guest beers
Friendly, one-roomed pub off the beaten track but worth finding. Close to a famous public school and the trackbed of an old railway, now the Downs Link footpath.
P

Coldwaltham

Labouring Man

Old London Road (off A29 S of Pulborough)
☎ (079 887) 2215
11.30–3, 6–11
Eldridge Pope Hardy Country, Royal Oak Ⓗ; guest beers
Friendly village pub on the western edge of the Wild Brooks. The original thatched building burnt down in 1905 and the current pub opened in 1907. A good location for country walks. Eve meals Fri–Sat only.
P

Crawley

Maid of Sussex

89 Gales Drive
☎ (0293) 525404
11–3 (3.30 Sat), 6–11
Courage Best Bitter, Directors; Webster's Yorkshire Bitter Ⓗ
Large, friendly, well-run estate pub, popular with business people at lunchtime and locals eves. The landlord has been here 20 years, over half of them in the *Guide*!
(Three Bridges) P

Plough

Ifield Street, Ifield
☎ (0293) 524292
11–3 (4 Sat), 6–11
King & Barnes Sussex, Broadwood, Old, Festive Ⓗ
Traditional village local on the edge of town, next to the church and Ifield Barn Theatre. No food Sun lunch.
Q (Ifield)

White Hart

High Street ☎ (0293) 520033
11–11
Harveys XX Mild (summer), **BB, Old, Armada, Tom Paine Ⓗ**
Popular, town-centre, two-bar pub whose frontage reminds you that Crawley was once a small country town on the way to Brighton. No food weekends. P

Cuckfield

White Harte

South Street ☎ (0444) 413454
11–3, 6–11
King & Barnes Sussex, Broadwood, Old, Festive Ⓗ
Friendly, two-bar pub with an olde-worlde atmosphere; genuine oak beams and an inglenook in the saloon. Note the paintings of the pub amongst the horse brasses. Mind the log pile outside the back door. Family room only open in summer. No food Sun.
Q P

Donnington

Blacksmiths Arms

Selsey Road (B2201, 2 miles S of Chichester) ☎ (0243) 783999
11–2.30, 6–11
Arundel Best Bitter; Draught Bass; Fuller's London Pride; Hall & Woodhouse Badger Best Bitter; Hook Norton Old Hooky; Ringwood Best Bitter Ⓗ
An intriguing collection of antique bric-a-brac festoons the interior of this free house,

noted for its food (not served Sun eve). Nice garden with play equipment. Ringwood Best is sold as 'Blacksmiths Bitter'. ♛ 🚼 ❀ ◖ ◗ ♣ ⌓ P

Duncton

Cricketers

On A285, 3½ miles S of Petworth ☎ (0798) 42473
11–3, 6–11
Hop Back Summer Lightning; Ind Coope Friary Meux Best Bitter, Burton Ale; guest beer [H]
Friendly, Grade II-listed country pub, built in 1600 as a brewery. The single bar features cricketing memorabilia and a pianola. The attractive garden offers weekend barbecues in summer, occasionally with music. No eve meals Sun or Mon in winter. Cider varies.
♛ ❀ ◖ ◗ ♿ ⌓ P

East Ashling

Horse & Groom

On B2178 ☎ (0243) 575339
11–3, 5.30–11
Ind Coope Friary Meux Best Bitter, Burton Ale; guest beer [H]
Attractive, listed, 18th-century, small village pub popular with the locals and for its restaurant (children welcome). Fine enclosed garden. The guest beer is usually an ordinary bitter; cider in summer.
♛ ❀ ◖ ◗ ⌓ P

East Dean

Hurdlemakers

1½ miles E of A286 at Singleton ☎ (024 363) 318
11–2.30 (3 Sat), 6–11
Adnams Bitter [H]**; Ballard's Wassail** [G]**; King & Barnes Mild; Ruddles County; Webster's Yorkshire Bitter** [H]**; guest beers**
Friendly, well-run free house in the centre of this South Downs village; walkers welcome. Excellent garden with a covered patio. Good range of food and good access to Goodwood Racecourse and country park. Mind the duck crossing nearby. Wheelchair access is via the garden.
♛ Q 🚼 ❀ ◖ ◗ ♿ ♣

Eastergate

Wilkes Head

Church Lane (400 yds off A29/B2233 jct)
☎ (0243) 543380
11–2.30 (3 Sat), 5.30 (6 Sat)–11; 11–11 Fri
Ind Coope Benskins Best Bitter, Burton Ale; guest beer [H]
Friendly, 18th-century, red-brick village pub. Flagstones and an open log fire enhance the lounge bar, which has a 'nookey corner'! Caravans welcome at the campsite.
♛ Q ❀ 🚐 ▲ ♣ P

Elsted Marsh

Elsted Inn

SW of Midhurst, off A272 OS834207 ☎ (0730) 813662
11–3, 5.30–11
Ballard's Trotton, Best Bitter, Wassail; Draught Bass; Fuller's London Pride [H]**; guest beers**
Welcoming, well-refurbished Victorian pub, the former home of Ballard's Brewery. Excellent food with imaginative dishes, as well as traditional fare. Up to three guest beers. Highly recommended.
♛ Q ❀ ◖ ◗ ♿ ♣ P

Faygate

Holmbush

Faygate Lane ☎ (0293) 851539
12–2.30, 5–11
Morland Old Speckled Hen; Whitbread Boddingtons Bitter, Flowers Original [H]**; guest beers** (occasionally)
Comfortable, welcoming village local with a central bar serving a games area at one end and a split-level lounge area and restaurant at the other. Agricultural implements adorn the walls. Occasional live music. Children welcome in the restaurant. ♛ ❀ ◖ ◗ ♿ ⇌ (peak times only) ♣ P

Felpham

Old Barn

Felpham Road (off A259)
☎ (0243) 821564
11–11
Arundel Best Bitter, Stronghold; Greene King Abbot; guest beers [H]
Thatched, single-bar pub at the northern end of the village, close to the sea and Butlin's. At least three guest beers usually available.
♛ ❀ ♿ ♣ P

Findon

Findon Manor Hotel (Snooty Fox Bar)

High Street ☎ (0903) 872733
11–2.30 (3 Sat), 6–11
Fuller's London Pride, ESB [H]**; guest beer**
Cosy, independent bar attached to a country house hotel in a converted Victorian manor house.
♛ ❀ 🛏 ◖ ◗ P

Graffham

White Horse

Heyshott Road OS926176
☎ (079 86) 331
11–3, 6–11
Bateman XXXB; Eldridge Pope Dorchester, Blackdown Porter; Palmers IPA; guest beers [H]
Popular family and walkers' pub at the foot of the South Downs. Book for Sun lunch. Downland views from the restaurant and large garden.
♛ Q 🚼 ❀ ◖ ◗ ♿ ▲ ♣ P ⊬

Hammerpot

Woodmans

On A27, Arundel–Worthing road ☎ (090 674) 240
11–3, 6–11
Gale's BBB, Best Bitter, HSB [H]
16th-century, thatched roadside pub with low beams, inglenook and a well-trodden brick and oak floor. Good pub food. Mature gardens.
♛ Q ❀ ◖ ◗ ♿ ♣ P

The Haven

Blue Ship

Midway between A281 at Bucks Green and A29 OS084306 ☎ (0403) 822709
11–3, 6–11
King & Barnes Mild (occasionally)**, Sussex, Broadwood, Old** [G]
One of the classic pubs of Great Britain: four small rooms, the front one having a stone slab floor and inglenook. No bar as such, drinks are served through a hatch in the top half of two doors. No eve meals Sun or Mon.
♛ Q 🚼 ❀ ◖ ◗ ♿ ♣ P

Try also: Queens Head, Bucks Green (Courage)

Hermitage

Sussex Brewery

36 Main Road (A259)
☎ (0243) 371533
11–11
Eldridge Pope Blackdown Porter; Everards Old Original; Hall & Woodhouse Badger Best Bitter, Hard Tackle, Tanglefoot [H]
Friendly, busy pub with plenty of atmosphere, near Emsworth, on the Sussex/Hants border. Speciality sausage menu with over 30 varieties. The brewery is no longer in production and

a house beer, Hermitage Best, is actually Charles Wells Eagle. (Emsworth) P

Horsham

Black Jug
31 North Street
(0403) 253526
11–3, 5 (6 Sat)–11
Bateman XB; Courage Directors; Marston's Pedigree; Wadworth 6X; Webster's Yorkshire Bitter H
Gimmick-free pub with traditional values, which used to be run by local gaolers. Good fresh food is prepared on the premises. Range of 27 malt whiskies and eight authentic Polish/Russian flavoured vodkas.
Q P

Dog & Bacon
North Parade (0403) 252176
11–2.30, 6–11
King & Barnes Mild, Sussex, Broadwood, Old, Festive H
Refurbished, popular pub on the edge of town. Eve meals Wed–Sat.
P

Kings Arms
Bishopric (Guildford road)
(0403) 253588
11–2.30 (3 Fri & Sat), 5.30–11
King & Barnes Sussex, Broadwood, Old, Festive H
Situated 100 yards from the brewery and used by its staff: a basic, two-bar drinking pub in an 18th-century coaching house.

Stout House
29 Carfax (0403) 267777
10–4, 7.30–11; closed Tue eve
King & Barnes Mild (summer), **Sussex, Broadwood, Festive, Old** H
Small, friendly, traditional pub in the newly pedestrianised area by the bandstand. Has now been in this guide for 11 years; one of King & Barnes's finest. Can get smoky at times.

Tanners Arms
78 Brighton Road
(0403) 250527
11–2.30 (3.30 Sat), 6–11
King & Barnes Mild, Sussex, Old H
Small drinkers' local with an emphasis on beer rather than food: a public bar and small snug bar. A recently erected pub sign now makes it easier to locate. Snacks lunchtimes.
Q

Try also: Bedford, Station Rd (Whitbread)

Horsted Keynes

Green Man
The Green (0825) 790656
11–3, 6–11
Harveys BB H**; guest beers**
Railway-oriented, two-roomed pub, just a mile from the famous Bluebell Railway and perfectly set on the village green.
P

Lavant

Earl of March
Lavant Road (A286, 2 miles N of Chichester) (0243) 774751
10.30–2.30, 6–11
Arundel Stronghold; Ballard's Best Bitter; Maclay Oat Malt Stout; Otter Ale; Ringwood Old Thumper; Ruddles Best Bitter H**; guest beers**
Roomy, oak-panelled pub with a Downs view from the garden. Regular live music includes jazz every Sun eve. Popular with all and often lively. Game is prominent amongst the home cooking (quiet dining area). Consistently the best value pub in the area. Dogs welcome.
Q P

Try also: Royal Oak, E Lavant (Gale's)

Lindfield

Linden Tree
47 High Street
(0444) 482995
11–3, 6–11
Arundel Stronghold; Greene King Rayments Special; Marston's Pedigree; Palmers Tally Ho!; Ringwood Old Thumper; Wadworth 6X H
Small, friendly free house with shop-like bay windows, situated in a picturesque village. Can get very busy and rather smoky in winter. Popular with younger drinkers late on weekend eves. Remains of a long-defunct brewery can be seen in the back garden. No food Sun. Beer range varies.

Snowdrop
Snowdrop Lane (via Lyoth Lane, off A272)
(0444) 412259
11–2.30 (3 Fri & Sat), 6–11
King & Barnes Sussex, Broadwood, Old, Festive H
Former farm cottages in an appropriate rural location. The saloon bar has been much extended to provide a large area for diners indulging from an extensive menu. The public bar provides genuine 'local' facilities, including games. No food Sun or Mon eves.
Q P

Try also: Witch, Sunte Ave (Grand Met)

Littlehampton

Dewdrop
96 Wick Street
(0903) 716459
10.30–3, 5.30–11
Gale's BBB, 5X H
Small, friendly town house with games.

New Inn
5 Norfolk Road (near seafront)
(0903) 713112
Arundel Best Bitter, Stronghold, Old Knucker H**; guest beers**
Former coaching inn from the 1760s, once part of the Norfolk Estate, now a friendly local with two bars, plus a games room, maintaining the inn-keeping traditions. Food always available.

Littleworth

Windmill
Littleworth Lane, Partridge Green OS193205
(0403) 710308
11–3, 5–11
King & Barnes Mild, Sussex H**, Festive, Old** G
A fine, friendly local with a comfortable saloon bar and a public bar with a strong rustic theme. Q P

Lodsworth

Hollist Arms
Off A272, halfway between Midhurst and Petworth
(079 85) 310/471
11–3, 6–11
Ballard's Midhurst Mild, Trotton, Best Bitter, Wassail H
Quiet village pub and restaurant, popular with diners: a narrow public bar and two smaller rooms. Large, pleasant garden.
Q P

Maplehurst

White Horse
Park Lane (between A281 and A272 S of Nuthurst)
(0403) 891208
12–2.30 (11–3 Sat), 6–11
Adnams Broadside; Brakspear Bitter; Fuller's London Pride; King & Barnes Sussex H**; guest beers** (weekends)
Quiet pub without intrusive music, popular with locals and families at weekends. No smoking in the conservatory at

lunchtimes. Two bars with real fires, one has the widest bar top in Sussex. Pleasant garden with a rural outlook. Children welcome at lunchtimes.
♛ Q ♘ ❀ ◐ ◑ ♣ ◯ P ⊬

Marehill

White Horse Inn
On A283, just E of Pulborough
☎ (0798) 872189
11.30–3, 6–11
Draught Bass; Morland Old Speckled Hen; Young's Bitter, Special; guest beers [H]
Successfully re-licensed since disposal by Whitbread, this enterprising free house has seen a variety of uses in its 300-year history, as evidenced by the various buildings in the garden. Reputedly haunted. No food Sun eve.
♛ Q ♘ ❀ ◐ ◑

Midhurst

Crown Inn
Edinburgh Square
☎ (0730) 813462
11–11
Draught Bass; Fuller's London Pride, ESB; Shepherd Neame Master Brew Bitter [H]**; Taylor Landlord; guest beers** [G]
Welcoming, traditional old pub and restaurant. Superb hospitality and quality fare make it justifiably popular. The ever-changing range of beers on gravity dispense in the cellar and out the back give the staff plenty of exercise! Two annual beer festivals. ♛ Q ❀ 🛏 ◐ ◑ ♣

Royal Oak
Chichester Road (A285)
☎ (0730) 814611
11–11
Ballard's Midhurst Mild, Best Bitter; Ringwood Best Bitter, Old Thumper; Whitbread Flowers IPA, Original [H]
Spacious, single-bar pub with low partitions forming individual areas. Live music two nights a week. Large (32 oz) steaks and grills. The large car park is surrounded by a long, sloping lawn. Look out for Dwile Flonking days in July. ♛ ❀ ◐ ◑ ♣ P

Swan Inn
Red Lion Street
☎ (0730) 812853
11–11 (food licence Sun afternoon)
Harveys XX Mild, Pale Ale, BB, Armada [H]
15th-century, split-level inn in the middle of the market square. A restaurant, where children are welcome, offers food all day (except 4–5pm Mon–Sat), including vegetarian options. Opens at 8am for breakfast. Note the mural in the upper bar.
♛ ❀ 🛏 ◐ ◑ ♣

Try also: Wheatsheaf, Rumbolds Hill (King & Barnes)

Oving

Gribble Inn
Gribble Lane OS900050
☎ (0243) 786893
11–2.30, 6–11
Gribble Harvest Pale, Gribble Ale, Reg's Tipple, Black Adder II; Hall & Woodhouse Badger Best Bitter, Tanglefoot [H]
Impressive village inn, housed in a 16th-century thatched building. Home-brewed ales are produced in a compact brewhouse (where patrons can view the process), adjoining the skittle alley. Fine garden. Good bar food (not served Sun eve). Inch's cider.
♛ Q ♘ ❀ ◐ ◑ ♿ ♣ ◯ P ⊬

Pease Pottage

James King
Horsham Road (just off A23/M23 jct) ☎ (0293) 612261
11–2.30 (3 Sat), 6–11
King & Barnes Sussex, Broadwood, Old, Festive [H]
Large, roadside pub whose newer exterior contrasts with past photos displayed inside. Separate restaurant and also a dining area which allows children. ❀ ◐ ◑ ♿ P

Rogate

Wyndham Arms
North Street (A272)
☎ (0730) 821315
11–3, 6–11
King & Barnes Sussex; Ringwood Best Bitter, Fortyniner, Old Thumper [G]**; guest beer** [H]
Unspoilt, two-bar, 16th-century village local with very good home-cooked food. Reputedly haunted. B&B accommodation includes a family room. Tiny car park. Dogs welcome.
♛ Q 🛏 ◐ ◑ ⊞ ♣ P

Try also: White Horse (Free)

Rusper

Plough Inn
High Street ☎ (0293) 871215
11–3, 6–11
Courage Directors; Fuller's London Pride; Mitchell's ESB [H]**; guest beers**
Welcoming village pub with low beams, offering a wide range of guest ales at all times. Excellent value home-cooked meals – try the steak and kidney braised in the ale of the day; children's menu on request. Large garden.
♛ ❀ ◐ ◑ ♣ P

Selham

Three Moles
1 mile S of A272, halfway between Petworth and Midhurst OS935206
☎ (079 85) 303
11–2.30, 5.30–11; 11–11 Fri & Sat
King & Barnes Mild, Sussex, Broadwood, Old [H]
Small, isolated country pub, definitely worth seeking out. Traditional pub games and hospitality are features, as are regular sing-song and folk nights. Snacks available lunchtimes. A highly recommended boozer.
♛ Q ❀ ▲ ♣ P

Shoreham-by-Sea

Royal Sovereign
Middle Street
☎ (0273) 453518
11–4, 5.30–11
Hall & Woodhouse Badger Best Bitter; Morland Old Speckled Hen; Whitbread Pompey Royal [H]**; guest beers** (occasionally)
Small town pub, very popular and friendly: a listed building decorated outside with old United Brewery green tiles, and flowers in season.
Q ◐ ⇌

Southwick

Kings Head
Fishersgate Terrace (A259)
☎ (0273) 419156
11–11
Eldridge Pope Hardy Country; Hall & Woodhouse Badger Best Bitter, Hard Tackle, Tanglefoot; Harveys BB; Kemptown SID [H]
Free house on the main coast road in an area not too rich in real ale. Good food is available at all times. Small outside patio upstairs. The views of the harbour make it handy for ship spotting. Reasonable prices but parking difficult.
❀ ◐ ◑ ⇌ (Fishersgate) ♣

Staplefield

Jolly Tanners
Handcross Road
☎ (0444) 400335
11–3, 5.30–11
Fuller's Chiswick, London Pride; Thwaites Mild; Wadworth 6X [H]**; guest beers**

Welcoming, inglenooked village pub opposite the green, with a popular restaurant area.
♨ Q ❀ ◖ ◗ P

Stoughton

Hare & Hounds

Off B2146, through Walderton OS791107 ☎ (0705) 631433
11–3, 6–11
Adnams Broadside; Gale's HSB; Gibbs Mew Bishop's Tipple; Taylor Landlord; Whitbread Boddingtons Bitter [H]; **guest beers**
Fine example of a Sussex flint-faced building in a secluded South Downs setting. Popular and lively, with a good local trade. Humorous posters advertise the guest beers. Good value food, with fresh local seafood a speciality. Nineteenth year in the *Guide*.
♨ Q ❀ ◖ ◗ ♣ P

Sutton

White Horse

OS979152 ☎ (079 87) 221
11–2.30 (3 Sat), 6–11
Bateman XB; Courage Best Bitter, Directors; Young's Bitter [H]; **guest beer**
Characterful Georgian village inn: a comfortably furnished saloon but bare boards feature in the village bar. Popular in summer with walkers and visitors to the Roman villa at Bignor. ♨ Q ❀ 🛏 ◖ ◗ ♣ P

Turners Hill

Red Lion

Lion Lane ☎ (0342) 715416
11–3, 6–11
Harveys XX Mild, Pale Ale, BB, Old [H]
Unchanging village pub, popular with followers of country pursuits. Organises an annual pram race. Draught Harveys Armada and Elizabethan sometimes available. No food Sun.
♨ ❀ ◖ P

Try also: Crown (Friary Meux)

Upper Beeding

Bridge

High Street ☎ (0903) 812773
11–2.30 (3 Sat), 5.30–11
King & Barnes Mild (summer), **Sussex, Old, Festive** [H]
Friendly local with three drinking areas, situated on the bank of the River Adur. Hikers welcome to bring their own lunches to the garden. N.B. Traffic calming measures and the proximity to a narrow bridge make parking difficult.
❀ ◖ ♣

West Ashling

Richmond Arms

Mill Lane (400 yds W of B2146) OS807074
☎ (0243) 575730
11–3, 5.30–11; 11–11 Sat in summer (food licence Sun afternoon)
Brakspear Bitter; Fuller's Chiswick; Greene King Abbot; Marston's Pedigree; Taylor Landlord; guest beers [H]
Excellent ten-pump, small village free house, near the duck pond, catering for locals and visitors. Four guest beers include a mild. Good food; bar billiards and a skittle alley. Children welcome until 9pm. Cider in summer.
♨ ❀ ◖ ◗ ▲ ♣ ⊖ P

West Chiltington

Five Bells

Smock Alley OS091172
☎ (0798) 812143
11–3, 6–11
King & Barnes Sussex; guest beers [H]
Spacious one-bar pub near the village, with an imaginative selection of four guest ales (211 different ales in the past three years). A rare outlet in this area for real mild and cider. No food Sun or Mon eves. ♨ Q ❀ ◖ ◗ ⊖ P

Queens Head

The Hollows (2 miles SW of B2139/B2133 jct) OS090185
☎ (0798) 813413
11–3, 6–11
King & Barnes Sussex; Wadworth 6X; Whitbread Boddingtons Bitter, Castle Eden Ale, Flowers Original [H]
400-year-old, two-bar pub at the village centre, run by a former King & Barnes brewhouse manager. Collections of coins, banknotes and bottles everywhere. Clog and morris dancing.
♨ Q ❀ ◖ ◗ ⊟ ♣ P

West Wittering

Lamb Inn

Chichester Road (B2179, 1½ miles NE of centre) OS804992
☎ (0243) 511105
11–2.30, 6–11
Arundel Stronghold; Ballard's Best Bitter [H], **Wassail** [G]; **Bunces Benchmark, Best Bitter; Ringwood Fortyniner** [H]; **guest beers**
Handy for the local sailing centre and beaches, an old, convivial roadside inn, with a wide range of good, home-made food and room for drinkers in the eve. Local small breweries are well represented. No meals Sun eve in winter.
♨ Q ❀ ◖ ◗ ♿ ▲ P ⊬

Worthing

Alexandra

28 Lyndhurst Road (near hospital) ☎ (0903) 234833
11–3, 6–11
Draught Bass; Charrington IPA; Harveys BB; guest beer [H]
Friendly, two-bar corner local with a games room. So far the Alex has avoided being 'improved' out of recognition: the accent is on the beer and service rather than modern gimmicks. ❀ ◖ ◗ ⊟ ♿ ♣

Cricketers

66 Broadwater Street West (close to Broadwater Green)
☎ (0903) 233369
11–3.30, 6–11; 11–11 Fri & Sat
Bass Worthington BB, Draught Bass; Charrington IPA; Fuller's London Pride [H]
Georgian-fronted, comfortably appointed pub with a popular restaurant. Home to the local cricket team. No meals Sun and Mon eves. Q ❀ ◖ ◗ ♣

Vine

27–29 High Street, Tarring
☎ (0903) 202891
11–2.30 (3 Sat), 6–11
Arundel Best Bitter; Hall & Woodhouse Badger Best Bitter; Harveys BB; Hop Back Summer Lightning [H]; **guest beers**
Popular local in a well preserved village street. The former Parsons Brewery stands at the rear. Occasional live music. No food Sun. Q ❀ ◖ ♿ 🚉 (W Worthing) P

Wheatsheaf

Richmond Road
☎ (0903) 207395
10.30–3, 5.30–11
Draught Bass; Charrington IPA; Fuller's London Pride; Harveys BB [H]
Comfortable, town-centre pub that fortunately escaped the 1960s redevelopment of the Civic Centre. ❀ ◖ ◗ ♿ 🚉 ♣

Yapton

Maypole Inn

Maypole Lane (off B2132, ½ mile N of B2233 jct) OS977042
☎ (0243) 551417
11–2.30, 5.30–11
Mansfield Riding Mild; Ringwood Best Bitter; Whitbread Flowers Original; Younger IPA; guest beers [H]
Excellent, welcoming pub. At least three guest beers (all from independent breweries), continually changing; regular mini-beer festivals. Meals are good value (not served Sun or Tue eves).
♨ Q ❀ ◖ ◗ ⊟ ♿ ♣ P

Tyne & Wear

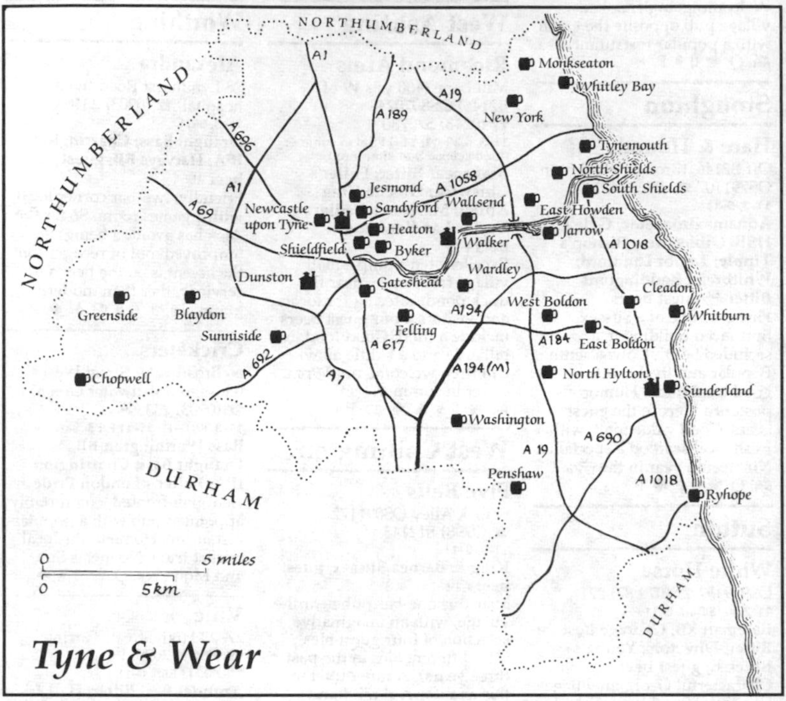

***Big Lamp**, Newcastle upon Tyne; **Federation**, Dunston; **Hadrian**, Walker; **Vaux**, Sunderland*

Blaydon

Black Bull
Bridge Street ☎ (091) 414 2846
11.30–3, 6–11
Camerons Bitter, Strongarm; guest beers Ⓗ
Splendid, traditional two-roomed pub. Its warm, friendly and comfortable interior is characterised by polished wood and brass.
⛼ Q ❀ ⊟ ≢ ♣

Byker

Free Trade Inn
St Lawrence Road (off A186, near Glasshouse Bridge)
☎ (091) 265 5764
11–11
McEwan 80/-; S&N Theakston Best Bitter, XB; Younger No. 3 Ⓗ
Split-level, very popular pub overlooking the river, offering companionship in a basic, homely establishment. Live music each Tue; random displays of art produced by the regular crowd. Can be very busy. Garden across the road. ⛼ ❀

Glendale
Potts Street ☎ (091) 265 5174
11–11
Draught Bass; Stones Best Bitter Ⓗ**; guest beer**
The large number of personal tankards hanging in the bar demonstrates that this very popular pub has a loyal group of regulars. Small bar and a comfortable back lounge. Interesting selection of guest beers for a Bass house.
◐ ⊖ (Byker/Chillingham Rd)

Ship Inn
Stepney Bank
☎ (091) 232 4030
11–11
Whitbread Boddingtons Bitter, Castle Eden Ale, Flowers Original Ⓗ
Unspoilt, basic pub, popular with a wide range of customers. Live music from an interesting collection of players most weekends. Next to Byker City Farm and near the music and crafts centre. Friendly and comfortable. ❀ ⊖

Tap & Spile
Shields Road ☎ (091) 276 1440
12–3, 6–11; 11–11 Fri & Sat
Hadrian Gladiator; Marston's Pedigree; Thwaites Craftsman Ⓗ**; guest beers**
The first of the Tap & Spile chain. Very friendly staff and customers ensure a warm welcome. Constantly changing list of up to ten beers. Live jazz from time to time. ♿ ⊖ ⌓

Chopwell

West Farm Hotel
Hall Road ☎ (0207) 563133
11 (12 Fri & Sat)–3, 6–11
Beer range varies Ⓗ
Imaginative conversion of farm buildings, pleasantly free from brewers' corporate refurbishments. The first building in Chopwell on the approach from High Spen, sitting on the hilltop giving splendid views of the Derwent valley. Q ◐ ◑ P

Cleadon

Cottage Tavern
North Street (A1018)
☎ (091) 536 7883
11–3, 5.30–11
Vaux Samson, Extra Special Ⓗ
A Vaux farmhouse-style interior in a small roadside village pub. Pleasant walks on nearby hills. ❀ ♣

Try also: New Ship, Sunderland Rd (Vaux)

East Boldon

Grey Horse
Front Street ☎ (091) 536 4186
11–11
Vaux Samson; guest beer Ⓗ
Large roadside pub which dominates the street scene with its impressive exterior. Two contrasting rooms with a food-oriented lounge make it popular. ◐ ◗ ♣ P

East Howdon

Duke of Wellington
Northumberland Dock Road
☎ (091) 262 3079
11–11
Jennings Mild; Ruddles County; guest beers Ⓗ
Impressive roadside pub in a depressed shipbuilding area. Built to last, with solid woodwork and strong masonry. ⊖ (Howdon)

Felling

Wheatsheaf
26 Carlisle Street
☎ (091) 438 6633
12–3, 7–11; 12–11 Fri & Sat
Big Lamp Bitter, Prince Bishop Ale, Summerhill Stout, ESB, Blackout; guest beer Ⓗ
Big Lamp brewery's only tied house. Basic but very friendly and renowned for some of the cheapest beer in the North-East. One bar opens on to a small room which can accommodate any overspill and houses photographs of the brewery and brewing process.
⚘ ⊖

Gateshead

Borough Arms
80–82 Bensham Road
☎ (091) 478 1323
11.30 (11 Sat)–3 (4 Fri & Sat), 6–11
Ruddles Best Bitter; guest beers Ⓗ
Two-roomed local with a thriving bar and a quiet side room adjacent to the bar hatch. No frills, but an exceptionally friendly pub. Ever-changing selection of ales. Q ⊖ P

Station Hotel
Hills Street (beside High Level bridge) ☎ (091) 478 3721
11–11
Jennings Mild; Ruddles Best Bitter; guest beers Ⓗ
Small, basic, comfortable bar with a small adjoining room known affectionately as 'The Coffin'. Good collection of breweriana and replica skulls in a friendly, uninhibited atmosphere. ⚘ ⊖ ⌓

Greenside

White Swan
Main Street ☎ (091) 413 4255
11–4, 6–11
Banks's Bitter; Camerons Bitter, Strongarm Ⓗ
Many-roomed village pub where the staff and landlord offer a friendly welcome to all.
⚘ Q ♉ ❀ ⊞ P ⚟

Heaton

Chillingham Hotel
Chillingham Road
☎ (091) 265 5915
11–11
Bass Worthington BB, Draught Bass; S&N Theakston Best Bitter, XB; Taylor Landlord Ⓗ**; guest beer**
Imposing roadside pub with two rooms, very well fitted out with woodwork from an elegant ocean liner. Interesting back bar and mirrors. Popular with a wide cross-section of customers. Live music upstairs.
❀ ♿ ⊖ (Chillingham Rd)

Jarrow

Jarrow Lad
Western Road
☎ (091) 489 8039
1 (12 Fri & Sat)–4, 7–11
Vaux Samson, Extra Special Ⓗ
Basic, no-frills drinkers' pub, but friendly. Another Vaux beer is sometimes on sale instead of Extra Special.
❀ ⊖ P

Try also: Dougies Tavern, Blackett St (Vaux)

Jesmond

Lonsdale
Lonsdale Terrace
☎ (091) 281 0039
11–11
McEwan 80/-; S&N Theakston Best Bitter, XB Ⓗ
Very popular pub, recently refurbished to a high standard. The plush lounge has old maps of the area whilst there is a sporting theme in the cosy bar. Live music upstairs every Tue. Can be very busy at weekends.
◐ ⊞ ⊖ (W Jesmond)

Monkseaton

Shieling
Hepscott Drive, Beaumont Park ☎ (091) 251 3408
11.30–3, 5–11; 11–11 Fri & Sat
Ind Coope Burton Ale; Tetley Bitter Ⓗ
Large, comfortable two-roomed pub with several distinct areas served from a central bar. Extensive range of meals, including vegetarian options. No food Sun eve.
◐ ◗ ♿ ⊖ (W Monkseaton) P

Newcastle upon Tyne

Armstrong Hydraulic Crane
Scotswood Road
☎ (091) 272 3261
11–11
Beer range varies Ⓗ
A welcome oasis in the cask ale desert of West Newcastle, offering constantly changing ales and value for money food. Interesting mirrored ceiling in the lounge. ⚘ ❀ ⛟ ◐ P

Bridge Hotel
Castle Garth ☎ (091) 232 7780
11–3, 5.30 (5 Sat)–11; 12–2.40, 7–10.30 Sun
Bass Worthington BB; S&N Theakston Best Bitter, XB; guest beer Ⓗ
Large pub at the Newcastle end of the High Level bridge. Two large rooms: the lounge has a huge fireplace and some fine mirrors. Very popular live music venue downstairs.
❀ ⊞ ≋ (Central) ⊖ P

Broken Doll
Blenheim Street
☎ (091) 232 1047
11–11
S&N Theakston Best Bitter, XB, Old Peculier Ⓗ
Imposing and impressive venue for live entertainment with a loud but distinctive jukebox and good company. Evocative of other eras with its Victorian architecture, unspoilt 1960s interior and the old Matthew Brown sign above the bar. The brewery's gone but the Doll lives on.
≋ (Central) ⊖

Chapel Park
Greenway, Chapel Park (in small shopping precinct, off B6324) ☎ (091) 267 6887
11–3, 6–11; 11–11 Sat
Camerons Bitter, Strongarm Ⓗ
Modern L-shaped lounge doing its best to irrigate the beer desert in the west of the city. Q ♣

Cooperage
32 Close, Quayside
☎ (091) 232 8286
11–11
Ind Coope Burton Ale; Marston's Owd Rodger; Tetley Bitter; guest beers Ⓗ
Former cooperage, one of Newcastle's oldest buildings, dating back to the 14th century. Beamed ceilings add to the character. Restaurant and function room (discos held regularly). Can get busy eves. ◐ ◗ ≋ (Central) ⊖ ⌓

Tyne & Wear

Crown Posada
37 Side ☎ (091) 232 1269
11–3 (4 Sat), 5.30 (7 Sat)–11; 11–11 Thu & Fri
Butterknowle Conciliation Ale; Hadrian Gladiator; S&N Theakston Best Bitter; Whitbread Boddingtons Bitter; guest beers H
Exceptionally beautiful and well-maintained city-centre pub with a long, narrow room and a snug beside the entrance. Stained-glass windows, wooden bar fittings and an impressive bar dominate. Spanish murals lurk behind the wallpaper and are surprisingly rediscovered every decade.
Q ♿ ⇌(Central) ⊖

Duke of Wellington
High Bridge ☎ (091) 261 8852
11–11
Alloa Arrol's 80/-; Ind Coope Burton Ale; Marston's Pedigree; Taylor Landlord; Tetley Bitter H
Bustling city pub where the central bar is almost completely surrounded by a single room affording three distinct areas. Redolent of old Newcastle, from the photographs on the walls to the wood and brass fittings. Can get busy on weekend eves. ⇌(Central) ⊖(Monument)

Frog & Nightgown
3 Waterloo Street
☎ (091) 232 2014
11–11
Draught Bass; Stones Best Bitter H
Froggy knick-knacks abound in this cosy and intimate ground-floor bar where you can watch the world go by. Regular live music upstairs, where the ale is also available.
⇌(Central) ⊖

Newcastle Arms
57 St. Andrews Street
☎ (091) 232 3567
11–11
Ind Coope Burton Ale; Taylor Landlord; Tetley Bitter H
Architecturally pleasing, street-corner local in the city centre. L-shaped, with a small snug and a varied clientele. Happy hour prices make this one of the cheapest places to drink in the city. ⊖ (St James)

Old George Inn
Old George Yard
☎ (091) 232 3956
11–11
Bass Worthington BB, Draught Bass; Stones Best Bitter H
The oldest continually-licensed pub in Newcastle, split-level in design with a function room and another separate room open at busy times. This does not prevent occasional overcrowding, nor does the three-tier price list. A down-to-earth pub with a varied clientele. ◐ ⇌(Central) ⊖(Monument/Central)

Rose & Crown
164–166 City Road
☎ (091) 232 4724
11–11; 12–2, 7–10.30 Sun
Draught Bass; Butterknowle Conciliation Ale; S&N Theakston Best Bitter, XB H
So far unspoilt pub in two main rooms near the quayside area. Friendly staff and a keen landlord ensure a cheerful welcome. Local amateur musicians practise here on alternate Mons. ⊖ (Manors)

Try also: Quayside, Close (Vaux)

New York

Shiremoor House Farm
Middle Engine Lane
☎ (091) 257 6302
11–11
Draught Bass; S&N Theakston Best Bitter, Old Peculier; Stones Best Bitter; guest beers H
Attractively renovated old farm buildings retaining a natural rustic appearance. Highly commended in CAMRA's 1990 *Pub Design Awards*. Runs mini-beer festivals. Q ❀ ◐ ◑ ♿ ⛺ P

North Hylton

Shipwrights
Ferryboat Lane
☎ (091) 549 5139
11–3, 7–11
Vaux Samson; Wards Sheffield Best Bitter H
Low-ceilinged, riverside pub with a good local reputation for food. Brass dominates the interior. ♨ ◐ ◑ ♣ P

North Shields

Chainlocker
Duke Street, New Quay (opp. ferry landing)
☎ (091) 258 0147
11.30–4, 6–11; 11–11 Fri & Sat
Draught Bass; Ind Coope Burton Ale; Marston's Pedigree; Taylor Landlord; Tetley Bitter H**; guest beers**
Rebuilt early this century, with glazed tiles outside, good food and a real fire inside. Quiz Wed, folk Fri. Chainlocker Ale is brewed by Marston Moor.
♨ ◐ ◑ ⊖ ♣

Magnesia Bank
1 Camden Street
☎ (091) 257 4831
11–11
Butterknowle Conciliation Ale; Taylor Landlord; Tetley Bitter; Yates Bitter; guest beers H
Popular pub, in an area famed for good ale. Tastefully converted from a former club. Happy hours 5–7.
♨ ❀ ◐ ◑ ⊖ ♣ P

Porthole
11 New Quay (100 yds from ferry landing)
☎ (091) 257 6645
11.30–4, 6–11
S&N Theakston Best Bitter; guest beers H
Interesting old pub (1834), a free house with a nautical feel to its bar. Stocks three guest beers in winter, five in summer. Q ⛄ ❀ ◐ ◑ ♿ ⊖ P

Prince of Wales
2 Liddle Street
☎ (091) 296 2816
11–3, 7–11 (may vary; 11–11 summer)
Samuel Smith OBB, Museum H
Newly reopened after 27 years of lying idle. Previously the Old Wooden Dolly, now refurbished in traditional style with real fires in all three rooms (plus two ghosts). A huge wooden doll stands outside (copy of a ship's figurehead).
♨ Q ⛄ ❀ ◐ ◑ ⊞ ♿ ⊖ ♣

Stag Line
11 Howard Street
☎ (091) 296 4491
11–11 (11–3, 6–11 winter)
Longstone Bitter; Vaux Double Maxim; Whitbread Boddingtons Bitter; guest beers H
Attractively renovated, historic building, high above the River Tyne, serving good food in comfortable surroundings.
Q ❀ ◐ ◑ ⊖ P

Tap & Spile
184 Tynemouth Road
☎ (091) 257 2523
11–11
Hadrian Gladiator; S&N Theakston Old Peculier; guest beers H
A good example of the Tap & Spile chain: a pleasant, comfortable pub with ten handpumps, always offering interesting ales. ◐ ◑ ⊖ ♣ ⍥

Wooden Doll
103 Hudson Street
☎ (091) 257 3747
11–3, 6–11
Courage Directors; Ind Coope Burton Ale; Marston's Pedigree; S&N Theakston Old Peculier; Taylor

Landlord; Tetley Bitter; guest beer Ⓗ
Good views over the river mouth, at a pub with a permanent art exhibition. Live music every night; quiz Wed. Good food (not served Sun eve). Recently extended and refurbished to a high standard.
Q ◐ ◑ ⊞ ♿ ⊖ P

Penshaw

Grey Horse
Village Green, Old Penshaw
☎ (091) 584 4882
11–3 (4 Sat), 6 (5.30 Sat)–11
Tetley Bitter Ⓗ
Comfortable village pub in the shadow of a local folly, the 'Penshaw Monument', built for the famous Lambton family. A *Guide* regular for over ten years. No food Sun.
❀ ◐

Ryhope

Prince of Wales
Ryhope Street
☎ (091) 521 3480
11–4.30, 6–11
Vaux Extra Special Ⓗ
Cosy local in a former pit village, serving a mainly local clientele, but with a warm welcome assured. ❀ ◐ ◑ ♣

Sandyford

Legendary Yorkshire Heroes
Archbold Terrace
☎ (091) 281 3010
11–11
McEwan 70/-; Ruddles County; Samuel Smith OBB; guest beers Ⓗ
An oasis in Newcastle's glass and concrete commercial heartland. Twelve handpumps are supplemented by regular beer festivals. Three rooms cater for all tastes, although live music events can dominate the whole building. Still popularly known as 'The Archer'. ◐ ♿ ⊖ (Jesmond) ⊬

Shieldfield

Globe Inn
2 Barker Street
☎ (091) 232 0901
11–11
Draught Bass; Stones Best Bitter Ⓗ
Estate pub near the new multi-screen cinema. A busy bar and a smaller, comfortable lounge with displays of paintings by a local artist.
❀ ⊖ (Jesmond/Manors) P

South Shields

Alum House
Ferry Street ☎ (091) 427 7245
11–11
Beer range varies Ⓗ
Cosy alehouse by the ferry landing, the former William Woods brewery tap, with a relaxed atmosphere and six ever-changing guest beers. Good value meals (till 7pm) and traditional music nights.
Q ❀ ◐ ◑ ⊖ P

Chichester Arms
Laygate (A194/B1298 jct)
☎ (091) 456 1711
11–3, 5–11; 11–11 Sat
Ind Coope Burton Ale; Tetley Bitter; guest beers Ⓗ
Two-roomed corner pub next to the Metro station, with a basic bar/games area and a more relaxed lounge. A function room doubles as a food area at lunchtimes.
Q ◐ ⊞ ⊖ (Chichester) ♣

Dolly Peel
137 Commercial Road
☎ (091) 427 1441
11–11
Courage Directors; S&N Theakston XB; Taylor Landlord; Younger No. 3; guest beers Ⓗ
Established, award-winning free house with a welcoming atmosphere, noted for its individuality. Two guest beers and an extensive malt whisky selection; fresh sandwiches always available.
Q ⊖ (Chichester) ♣

Holborn Rose & Crown
East Holborn (opp. middle dock gates) ☎ (091) 455 2379
11–11
Bass Worthington BB, Draught Bass; S&N Theakston XB; Younger No. 3; guest beer Ⓗ
L-shaped, riverside pub with a dockside atmosphere and occasional live entertainment. Well worth finding. ❀ ⊖ ♣

Scotia
Mile End Road
☎ (091) 455 3495
11–11; 7–10.30 Sun, closed Sun lunch
McEwan 80/-; S&N Theakston Best Bitter, XB, Old Peculier; Younger No. 3; guest beer Ⓗ
Refurbished, town-centre corner pub operating a no-keg beer policy. Lively and popular. ⊖

Try also: Stag's Head, Fowler St (Bass)

Sunderland: *North*

Harbour View
Harbour View, Roker (A183)
☎ (091) 567 1402
11–11
Bass Worthington BB, Draught Bass; guest beer Ⓗ
Pleasant pub overlooking the marina and mouth of the Wear. Always busy and, with its close proximity to Roker Park, hectic on match days.
⛺ ❀ ◐ ◑

St Hilda's Parish Centre
Beaumont Street, Southwick
☎ (091) 549 4999
11–3 (not Mon–Fri), 7–10.30; closed Tue
S&N beers in rotation; guest beer (occasionally) Ⓗ
Large community centre in a former labour exchange, catering for a number of local groups. Local CAMRA branch *Club of the Year*. All profits are ploughed into charity.
☕ ♿ ♣ ⊬

Try also: Flying Boat, Sea Rd, Seaburn (Tetley)

Sunderland: *South*

Brewery Tap
Dunning Street
☎ (091) 567 7472
11–11
Vaux Samson, Double Maxim, Extra Special Ⓗ
Small, two-roomed pub in the Vaux brewery car park, with a plethora of photos of the old town. Can get busy at weekends. Car park eves and weekends only.
◐ ⊞ ♿ ⇌ ♣ P

Coopers Tavern
Deptford Road, Millfield (off Hylton Rd) ☎ (091) 567 1886
11–11
Vaux Lorimers Best Scotch, Samson, Double Maxim, Extra Special Ⓗ
Former rundown pub on the city outskirts, revamped by the brewery as a cask-only management training pub. Excellent comfortable interior decorated in typical Vaux style. ♣

Museum Vaults
33 Silksworth Row (near Vaux brewery) ☎ (091) 565 9443
12–11
Vaux Samson; Wards Sheffield Best Bitter Ⓗ
One of the oldest pubs in the city, small and unspoilt. Popular with students, so can get noisy (no quiet room at weekends!). Other Vaux group ales appear on a rota basis.
⛺ Q ❀ ⇌ ♣

Saltgrass
36 Ayres Quay, Hanover Place, Deptford
☎ (091) 526 7229
11.45–3, 5.30–11; 11.30–11 Fri & Sat
Vaux Samson, Double Maxim, Extra Special; Wards Sheffield Best Bitter Ⓗ

1993 CAMRA NE region *Pub of the Year*: a splendid traditional pub with a warm and welcoming atmosphere. The crowded bar is always busy, but the lounge is quieter. Over ten years in this guide.
⛫ ❀ ◖

Tap & Spile
Salem Street, Hendon
☎ (091) 514 2810
12–3, 6–11; 12–11 Wed–Fri; 11–11 Sat
Camerons Bitter; Hadrian Gladiator; Marston's Pedigree; Mitchell's ESB; S&N Theakston Old Peculier; guest beers Ⓗ
Out of the way but definitely not to be missed: a bare brick and floorboard alehouse, popular with students but still full of local character. Live music most Mon nights. The only pub in the area with real cider (a range).
⛫ ⊕ ⇌ ♣ ⌓

Try also: Victoria Gardens, off Villette Rd (S&N)

Sunniside

Potters Wheel
Front Street (A6076/A692 jct)
☎ (091) 488 3628
11.30–3, 5.30–11
Draught Bass; S&N Theakston Best Bitter, XB; guest beers Ⓗ
Recently reopened and refurbished by the Fitzgerald's chain and featuring a large, partitioned lounge. The guest beers bring much needed choice to the area. 100 yards from the terminus of the Tanfield Railway for steam train trips through pleasant countryside on summer Sundays. ❀ ◖ ◗ P

Tynemouth

Tynemouth Lodge Hotel
Correction House Bank, Tynemouth Road
☎ (091) 257 7565
11–11
Draught Bass; Belhaven 80/-; Butterknowle Conciliation Ale; S&N Theakston Best Bitter; guest beers Ⓗ
Cosy, friendly, genuine free house. A warm welcome is assured from staff, regulars and the licensee.
⛫ Q ◖ ⊖ ⌓ P

Wallsend

Hadrian Lodge Hotel
Hadrian Road
☎ (091) 262 7733
11–3, 6–11
S&N Theakston Best Bitter; Tetley Bitter Ⓗ**; guest beer**
Peaceful hotel bar in a modern building, adjacent to the Metro line. Comfortably furnished, friendly and airy. Q ❀ ⛟
◖ ◗ ♿ ⊖ (Hadrian Rd)

Rose Inn
Rose Hill Bank
☎ (091) 263 4545
11–11
Banks's Bitter; Camerons Bitter, Strongarm Ⓗ
Interesting one-roomed pub which stands alongside a busy main road linking Newcastle to the coast. Pine, wallpaper and draped curtains belie the original architecture. Thu is quiz night.
Q ◖ ◗ ⊖ (Hadrian Rd)

Wardley

Green
Whitemare Pool
☎ (091) 495 0171
11.30–3, 5.30–11; 11–11 Sat
Draught Bass; Ruddles County Ⓗ**; guest beers**
Large roadside pub beside a golf course. The bar, large lounge and restaurant are all in modern style. Q ❀ ◖ ◗ P

Washington

Three Horse Shoes
Washington Road, Usworth
☎ (091) 536 4183
12–3, 5–11; 11–11 Fri & Sat
Vaux Lorimers Best Scotch, Samson; Wards Sheffield Best Bitter; guest beer Ⓗ
Known locally as the 'Nip Inn', now an isolated pub with a reputation for good value food. Put to numerous uses over the years including as an officers' mess and a watch tower. Handy for the local aircraft museum. Can get busy during factory lunch-hour.
❀ ◖ ◗ ⊕ ♣ P

West Boldon

Black Horse Inn
Rectory Bank ☎ (091) 536 1814
11–3, 7–11
Marston's Pedigree; Whitbread Fremlins Bitter, Boddingtons Bitter, Porter, Flowers Original Ⓗ
Food-oriented hostelry near a parish church, steeped in local history. Busy at weekends and favoured by the younger drinker. Very popular for its good value meals (book).
❀ ◖ ◗ P

Whitburn

Jolly Sailor
1 East Street ☎ (091) 529 3221
11–11
Bass Light, Draught Bass Ⓗ
Multi-roomed pub next to an award-winning village green. Good value lunches. The Bass Light handpump has no pump clip – ask. ⛫ ◖ ♣

Try also: Whitburn Lodge, Mill Lane (Bass)

Whitley Bay

Briar Dene
The Links ☎ (091) 252 0926
11–11
Bass Worthington BB; S&N Theakston Best Bitter, XB; Stones Best Bitter; guest beers Ⓗ
Renewed and revitalised, large Fitzgerald's pub with sea views over the links. Deservedly very popular.
Q ⛹ ❀ ◖ ◗ ⊕ ♿ ♣ P

The Symbols

⛫	real fire	♿	easy wheelchair access
Q	quiet pub (at least one bar)	▲	camping facilities at the pub or nearby
⛹	indoor room for children	⇌	near British Rail station
❀	garden or other outdoor drinking area	⊖	near underground station
⛟	accommodation	♣	pub games
◖	lunchtime meals	⌓	real cider
◗	evening meals	P	pub car park
⊕	public bar	⚟	no-smoking room or area

Warwickshire

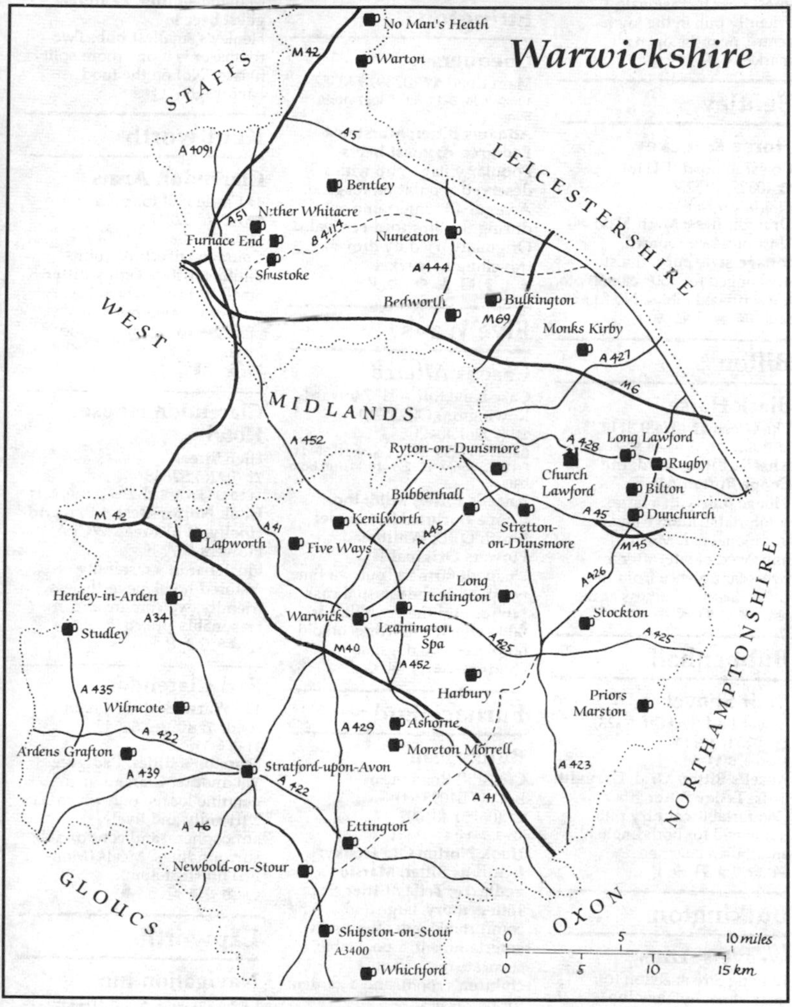

Judges, Church Lawford

Ardens Grafton

Golden Cross

Wixford Road, Bidford-on-Avon OS104538
☎ (0789) 772420
11–2.30, 6–11
Draught Bass; Highgate Mild; Ruddles County; Tetley Bitter; Webster's Yorkshire Bitter; guest beer H
Fine views over the Vale of Evesham to the Cotswolds from this old stone-built pub which has collections of old dolls and toys. Reputation for good food.
Q ❀ ◐ ◗ ♿ ▲ ♣ P

Ashorne

Cottage

☎ (0926) 651410
12–3 (not Mon–Fri), 7–11
Ansells Bitter, Mild H
Quiet, brick-built, Victorian country pub, noticeably green inside and out. One large room, with an open fire at one end and a woodburning stove at the other, serves as a pool room and bar. Can be busy in summer with cricketers. Sun lunches served. ❀ ◗ ♣

Bedworth

Prince of Wales

Bulkington Road
☎ (0203) 313202
12–2.30 (4.30 Mon & Fri, 5 Sat), 7–11
Mansfield Riding Mild; Wells Eagle, Bombardier H**; guest beer** (occasionally)
Small local with a lively bar. Quieter lounge. ❀ ♣ P

White Swan

All Saints Square
☎ (0203) 312164
11–11
Wells Eagle, Bombardier H**;**

guest beer (occasionally)
Friendly pub in the town centre, near the open air market. ◖ ⊞ ≋ ♣

Bentley

Horse & Jockey
Coleshill Road (B4116)
☎ (0827) 715236
12–3, 5.30 (7 Sat)–11
Draught Bass; M&B Mild [H]
Unspoilt, two-roomed, cottage-style pub, almost unchanged for 150 years. Note the scrubbed tables. No food Sun. ♛ ❀ ◖ ⊞ ♣ P

Bilton

Black Horse
The Green ☎ (0788) 811473
11–3, 5.30–11; 11–11 Fri & Sat
Ansells Bitter, Mild; Ind Coope Burton Ale [H]
Village pub with a large, comfortable lounge and a traditional bar. Much improved of late, after a two-year absence from the *Guide*. Disabled access at the rear. ❀ ◖ ⊞ ♿ ♣ P

Bubbenhall

Malt Shovel
Lower End (just off A423)
☎ (0203) 301141
11.30–3, 6–11
Ansells Bitter, Mild; Draught Bass; Tetley Bitter [H]
Comfortable country pub renowned for both English and Italian cuisine.
♛ ❀ ◖ ◗ ⊞ ♣ P

Bulkington

Weavers Arms
12 Long Street, Ryton (off main street by New Inn)
☎ (0203) 314415
12–4, 6–11 (may close earlier afternoons)
Draught Bass; M&B Mild; guest beers [H]
Friendly village pub tucked up a quiet, dead-end road.
♛ Q ❀ ◖ ⊞ ♣ ⌓

Dunchurch

Greenman
14 Daventry Road (A45)
☎ (0788) 810210
11–2.30, 6–11; 11–11 Sat
Ansells Mild; Marston's Pedigree; Morland Old Speckled Hen; S&N Theakston XB; John Smith's Bitter [H]
Traditional village pub with a cosy atmosphere and good food. Popular with tourists because of the village's history.
♛ Q ❀ 🛏 ◖ ◗ ♣ P

Ettington

Chequers
Main Road ☎ (0789) 740387
10.30–2.30, 6–11; 12–2.30, 7–10.30 Sun
Adnams Bitter; Marston's Pedigree [H]**; guest beers**
Popular village pub with a deserved reputation for food. A venue for entertainment during the Stratford Festival. Originally used by drovers travelling to market.
❀ ◖ ◗ ⊞ ▲ ♣ ⌓ P

Five Ways

Case is Altered
Case Lane (off A4177 towards Rowington) OS225701
☎ (0926) 484206
Bar 11.30–2.30, 6–11; Lounge 8.30–11 Fri & Sat only; 12–2, 7–10.30 Sun both bars
Ansells Bitter, Mild; Ind Coope Burton Ale; Samuel Smith OBB; Whitbread Flowers Original [H]
Unspoilt farmers' pub – a time warp. Note the unusual cask pumps and the bar billiards table which still works on old 6d pieces. No dogs; no children. ♛ Q ⊞ ♣ P

Furnace End

Bulls Head
Coleshill Road (near B4114/B4098 jct)
☎ (0675) 481602
12–3, 7–11; 11–11 Sat
Hook Norton Old Hooky; Jennings Bitter; Marston's Pedigree; Tetley Bitter [H]
16th-century, large and comfortable pub offering live entertainment, a pool table, a separate restaurant, a children's room, and a garden for barbecues.
♛ ᘓ ❀ ◖ ◗ ♿ P

Harbury

Gamecock
Chapel Street ☎ (0926) 612374
11.30–3, 7–11
Banks's Mild, Bitter [H]
Unpretentious, one-roomed country pub, down-to-earth, with friendly locals. Can be busy when the darts or crib team is at home. Good value lunchtime meals. The regulars are well known for elaborate carnival floats. Jigsaws and quiz nights are the latest crazes. ♛ Q ❀ ◖ ♣

Henley-in-Arden

Three Tuns
High Street ☎ (0564) 792723
11–3, 5.30–11; 11–11 Mon & Sat
Marston's Bitter, Pedigree; guest beer [H]
Henley's smallest pub. Two rooms, or is it one room split in two? Not on the food bandwagon. Q ❀

Kenilworth

Clarendon Arms
44 Castle Hill (opp. castle)
☎ (0926) 52017
11–3, 5.30–11
Courage Directors; John Smith's Bitter; Tetley Bitter [H]
Small, old pub which is very food orientated but still manages to remain a good local.
ᘓ ❀ ◖ ◗

Clarendon House Hotel
High Street
☎ (0926) 57668
11.30 (11 Fri & Sat)–2.30 (3 Sat), 6–11
Hook Norton Best Bitter, Old Hooky; Whitbread WCPA, Flowers IPA [H]
Plush bar in a tastefully restored hotel: nevertheless, friendly, welcoming and reasonably priced.
Q 🛏 ◖ ◗ P

Earl Clarendon
127 Warwick Road (main road) ☎ (0926) 54643
11–3, 6–11
Marston's Bitter, Pedigree [H]
Yet another Clarendon: a genuine locals' pub which has a friendly and lively atmosphere, and comfortable surroundings. Meals (Mon–Fri) finish at 8pm.
Q ❀ ◖ ◗ ⊞ ♿ ♣

Lapworth

Navigation Inn
Old Warwick Road (B4439)
☎ (0564) 783337
11–2.30, 5.30–11; 11–11 Sat
Draught Bass; M&B Mild, Brew XI; guest beer [H]
Busy, canalside pub which offers more unusual guest beers. A must.
♛ Q ❀ ◖ ◗ ⊞ ♿ ≋ ♣ P

Leamington Spa

Avenue
Spencer Street
☎ (0926) 425601
12–3, 6–11; 11–11 Fri & Sat
Ansells Bitter, Mild; Tetley Bitter [H]**; guest beers**
Friendly, traditional town pub in Victorian style, with a warm atmosphere. Meals not available Sun but the bar nibbles are excellent. Friendly hosts and staff. The guest beers change weekly.
◖ ≋ ♣

Hope & Anchor
Hill Street ☎ (0926) 423031
11–11
Ansells Bitter, Mild [H]
Small, single, L-shaped bar with a friendly atmosphere, situated on the end of a terrace just out of town. A popular pub for locals. Beware of the dummy keg cider handpump.
♣

Railway
12 Clemens Street (left from station, 2nd right)
☎ (0926) 888958
10.30–11
Banks's Mild, Bitter [E]; Marston's Pedigree [H]
Old-fashioned, Victorian pub with regular live music: country and western, Irish folk and 60s music. Soup and sandwiches available.
❀ ⊞ ≋ ♣ ⌓

Somerville Arms
4 Campion Terrace
☎ (0926) 426746
11–2.30 (3 Fri & Sat), 5.30 (6 Sat)–11
Ansells Bitter, Mild; Ind Coope Burton Ale; Marston's Pedigree; Tetley Bitter [H]
Traditional, two-room, Victorian local with great atmosphere. Busy bar at the front, intimate lounge at the rear. Examples of the landlord's humour abound.
Q ⊞ ♣

Long Itchington

Harvester
Church Road ☎ (0926) 812698
11–3, 6–11
Hook Norton Best Bitter, Old Hooky; guest beer [H]
Welcoming pub in the village centre. Fine food in a traditional country inn. The guest beer is changed weekly.
( ) ⊞ ♣ P

Long Lawford

Sheaf & Sickle
1 Coventry Road
☎ (0788) 544622
12–3, 6.30–11; 11–11 Sat
Ansells Bitter, Mild; Tetley Bitter; guest beer [H]
Roadside local with many unusual features: a small, comfy lounge and a bar leading into a games/family area. Over 200 guest ales have been sold. Own cricket pitch at the rear. ❀ ( ) ▲ ♣ P

Monks Kirby

Denbigh Arms
Main Street ☎ (0788) 832303
12–2.30 (not Mon), 7–11; 12–2.30, 7–10.30 Sun
S&N Theakston Best Bitter, XB, Old Peculier; Younger IPA, No. 3 [H]
17th-century pub opposite a 14th-century church. Formerly a farmhouse-cum-inn, part of the Earl of Denbigh's estate. Bought from Bass in 1992. Folk club every Fri night.
Q ❀ ⊨ ( ) ♣ P ⚟

Moreton Morrell

Black Horse
2 miles from M40 jct 12
☎ (0926) 651231
11.30–2.30 (3 Sat), 7 (6.30 summer)–11
Hook Norton Best Bitter; Shepherd Neame Bishops Finger [H]
Friendly village local with a games area in the back bar. Popular with students from the local agricultural college. Peaceful garden to the rear.
Q ❀

Nether Whitacre

Dog Inn
Dog Lane ☎ (0675) 481318
12–2.30, 6–11
Draught Bass; M&B Mild, Brew XI [H]
400-year-old, black and white country inn with beams and horse brasses. Very popular in summer, when children can use the garden. Q ❀ ( ) ♿ P

Newbold-on-Stour

Bird in Hand
☎ (0789) 450253
12–2.30, 6–11; 12–11 Sat
Hook Norton Mild, Best Bitter, Old Hooky [H]
Roadside village local. Originally two bars, now one, with a games area on one side. Bought by Hook Norton from Whitbread.
⛫ ❀ ⊨ ( ) ♣ P

No Man's Heath

Four Counties
Ashby Road (B5493)
☎ (0827) 830243
11–2.30, 6–11
Ind Coope Burton Ale; Marston's Pedigree; Tetley Bitter; guest beers [H]
Former coaching inn, yet a safe refuge for highwaymen on the border between four counties. Beamed ceilings and three real winter fires – very cosy. Guest beers change regularly. Cheap pub fare.
⛫ ❀ ( ) ♣ P

Nuneaton

Fox
11a The Square, Attleborough
☎ (0203) 383290
11–3.30, 5–11
Draught Bass; M&B Mild; guest beers [H]
Traditionally refurbished local run by a landlord who really cares about his customers. Cheap beer for the locality. Lunchtime snacks.
Q ❀ ⊞ ♿ ♣ ⌓

Griffin Inn
Coventry Road (300 yds from Griff Island towards Bedworth) ☎ (0203) 312149
11.30–3, 5–11
Banks's Bitter [E]; S&N Theakston XB [H]
300-year-old miners' pub with olde-worlde bars, a pool room and large family gardens. Customers are welcome to view the medieval cellars.
⛫ Q ❀ ( ) ⊞ ▲ ♣ P

Punch Bowl
Tuttle Hill ☎ (0203) 383809
11.30–3, 7–11
Mansfield Riding Mild; Wells Eagle [H]
Three-roomed, roadside pub, an ex-M&B house. A handy stop on the A47. Limited menu choice (more in summer).
) ⊞ ♣ P

Railway Tavern
Bond Street ☎ (0203) 382015
11–11
Brains Dark; Marston's Pedigree; Whitbread Boddingtons Bitter, Flowers Original [H]; guest beer
Solid, basic pub where railway pictures and ephemera decorate the walls. Splendid lunches; bar nibbles Sun lunchtimes (when no meals are served). ❀ (≋ ♣

Priors Marston

Falcon Inn
Hellidon Road ☎ (0327) 60562
12–3, 6 (7 winter)–11
Beer range varies [H]
Comfortable country pub with low ceilings and a feature inglenook. Rich in olde-worlde character. Strong food trade and can get busy at weekends. Slightly up-market clientele. Four ales always available.
⛫ Q ( ) P

Rugby

Alexandra Arms
72–73 James Street
11–2.30, 5.30 (7 Sat)–11; 7–10.30 Sun, closed Sun lunch
Home Bitter; S&N Theakston Best Bitter, XB; Younger IPA; guest beers [H]
Cosy, town-centre pub near a multi-storey car park and theatre. A large, well-equipped games room and an L-shaped bar. Disabled facilities.
❀ (♿ ≋ ♣

Warwickshire

Half Moon
Lawford Road
☎ (0788) 574420
11–4, 5.30–11; 11–11 Fri; 10–11 Sat
Ansells Bitter, Mild; Ind Coope Burton Ale; guest beer [H]
Single-roomed, mid-terrace, basic local boozer, decorated with old prints of Rugby. Attracts a wide section of society in one of the few remaining 'beer only' hostelries. The landlord's varied music selection is unobtrusive. 🔥 ♿ ♣

Raglan Arms
50 Dunchurch Road
☎ (0788) 544441
12–3, 7–11; 12–2.30, 7–10.30 Sun
Banks's Mild; Marston's Bitter, Merrie Monk, Pedigree; [H]; guest beers
Deceptively large, terraced pub, very close to Rugby's famous public school. A pub simply to sit and drink in. Beers very reasonably priced. No food and no music.
Q ♣ P

Victoria Inn
1 Lower Hillmorton Road
☎ (0788) 544374
12–2.30 (4 Sat), 6 (7 Sat)–11
Draught Bass; M&B Highgate Mild, Brew XI [H]; guest beer
Victorian corner pub with original fittings, near the town centre. Pool and darts in the bar; friendly lounge. Trad. jazz Mon eve. No weekend food.
◐ ⊟ ⇌ ♣

Ryton-on-Dunsmore

Blacksmiths Arms
High Street ☎ (0203) 301818
12–3, 6–11
Banks's Bitter; Draught Bass; M&B Brew XI [H]
Popular village pub with a large display of brasses. Good, home-cooked food a speciality (not served Sun eve).
🐎 ❀ ◐ ◑ P

Shipston-on-Stour

Black Horse
Station Road ☎ (0608) 661617
12–2, 7–11
Home Bitter; Ruddles Best Bitter; S&N Theakston XB; Webster's Yorkshire Bitter [H]; guest beers
Thatched pub dating back to the 12th century; originally a row of cottages for Cotswold sheep farmers. Interesting interior, with an excellent family room leading to a garden. Good value food.
🔥 🐎 ❀ ◐ ◑ ⊟ ♿ ♣ P

Shustoke

Griffin
Church Road (B4114, on sharp bend) ☎ (0675) 481205
12–2.30 (2.15 Sat), 7–11 (10.30 Sat)
M&B Mild; Marston's Pedigree; S&N Theakston Old Peculier; Wadworth 6X; guest beers [H]
350-year-old, cosy coaching inn, very popular with people from far afield. Guest beers change every two days. No meals Sun.
🔥 Q 🐎 ❀ ◐ ♿ ⌓ P

Plough Inn
The Green ☎ (0675) 481557
12–2.30 (3 Sat), 7 (6.30 Thu–Sat)–11
M&B Highgate Mild, Brew XI [H]
Quiet village pub with friendly staff and clientele. Local CAMRA *Pub of the Year* 1992. No food Sun.
🔥 Q ❀ ◐ ◑ ♿ ♣ P

Stockton

Barley Mow
School Street ☎ (0926) 812713
12–2.30, 6.45 (6.30 Fri & Sat)–11
M&B Highgate Mild [H], Brew XI [E]; guest beer [H]
Traditional village pub with a separate bar and lounge. The restaurant upstairs is noted for steaks. ❀ ◐ ◑ ♣ P

Stratford-upon-Avon

Queens Head
Ely Street ☎ (0789) 204914
11.30–11; 12–2.30, 7–10.30 Sun
Draught Bass; M&B Highgate Mild, Brew XI [H]; guest beers
Popular town-centre pub, dating back to the 16th century: an L-shaped bar with a lively atmosphere. No food Sun eve. 🔥 ❀ ◐ ◑ ⇌ ⌓

Shakespeare Hotel
Chapel Street ☎ (0789) 294771
11–2.30, 6–11
Draught Bass; Donnington SBA; Hook Norton Best Bitter, Old Hooky [H]
Beautiful, half-timbered, Tudor hotel serving real ale in the Froth & Elbow bars, which have their own entrance. Two relaxing bars, a refuge from the Shakespeare industry.
🔥 Q 🐎 ❀ 🛏 ◐ ⇌ ♣

Stretton-on-Dunsmore

Shoulder of Mutton
Brookside (dead-end road by phone box) ☎ (0203) 542601
12–3 (not Mon–Thu), 8–11; 12–3, 8–10.30 Sun
M&B Mild, Brew XI [H]
Superbly unspoilt, 19th-century village local with a small, wood-panelled snug and a tiled bar. Crumpets are toasted on the real fire Mon eve. A 75-year-old air rifle club meets and shoots in the bar. Jazz last Wed of month.
🔥 Q ⊟ ♿ ▲ ♣ ⌓ P

Studley

Little Lark
108 Alcester Road (A435)
☎ (0527) 853105
12–2.30 (3 Sat), 6–11
Ind Coope Burton Ale; Lumphammer [H]; guest beer
Typically wacky Mad O'Rourke-style pub with a printing theme and sawdust on the floor. Alligator is always on the menu; also look out for emu, kangaroo and buffalo. 🔥 ◐ ◑

Warton

Hatters Arms
Church Road ☎ (0827) 892408
12–3, 6–11; 11–11 Fri & Sat
Ansells Mild; Draught Bass; Marston's Pedigree; Tetley Bitter [H]
Friendly village local with a comfortable, cosy lounge where a real fire burns in winter. 'Stones' restaurant – where you cook your own food on a hot stone. No food Sun. 🔥 ❀ ◐ ◑ P

Warwick

Kings Head
39 Saltisford (A425)
☎ (0926) 493096
10.30–3, 5.30–11
Ansells Bitter, Mild; guest beer [H]
Henry VIII is the king on this fine Georgian pub which has a reputation for good value lunches – try the cholesterol special! No food Sun.
🔥 ❀ ◐ ⊟ P

New Bowling Green
13 St Nicholas Church Street
☎ (0926) 493642
12–2.30, 5–11; 12–11 Fri & Sat
Wells Eagle, Bombardier [H]
Excellent, old, timbered pub, complete with low ceilings and exposed beams: two small bars and a games room. The passage through the pub leads to a large, secluded, walled garden. Beware the Scrumpy Jack keg cider served through a fake handpump. ❀ ⇌ ♣

Old Fourpenny Shop Hotel
27 Crompton Street (off A429 & A4189) ☎ (0926) 491360
12–2.30, 5.30–11; 11.30–3, 7–11 Fri & Sat

M&B Brew XI; guest beers H
Fine Georgian building close to the racecourse and famous for its varied guest beers which change almost daily. A well-furnished, split-level bar with a separate dining area. Enclosed garden at the rear. No meals Sun.
❀ 🛏 ◖ ◗ ♣ P

Tilted Wig

11 The Market Place
☎ (0926) 410466
12–3, 5–11; 11–11 Fri, Sat & summer; 12–3, 8–10.30 Sun
Ansells Bitter; Judges Barristers *or* Old Gavel Bender; Tetley Bitter H
Grade II-listed building in the centre of town. The spacious bar has a part-stone-flagged floor, large inglenooks and pine furniture. Aimed at the more sophisticated drinker. Function room. No meals Sun eve. ❀ ◖ ◗ ≋

Whichford

Norman Knight

☎ (060 884) 621
12–2.30 (3 Sat), 7–11
Hook Norton Best Bitter; Whitbread Flowers Original H
Undeveloped little village local, facing the green.
♔ Q ❀ ♣ P

Wilmcote

Swan House Hotel

The Green ☎ (0789) 267030
11–11
Hook Norton Best Bitter; S&N Theakston XB H
Listed building, dating back to the 18th century, with a natural well and beamed ceilings. Very close to Mary Arden's House. Friendly atmosphere; excellent food.
♔ ❀ 🛏 ◖ ◗ ♿ ≋ ♣ P

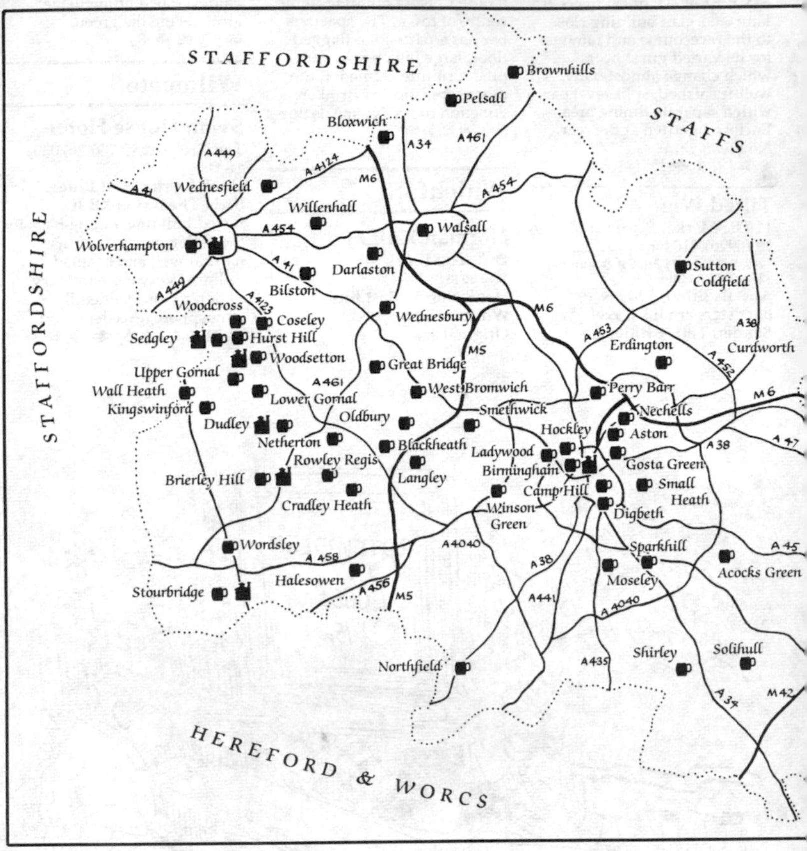

Aston Manor, *Birmingham;* ***Banks's,*** *Wolverhampton;* ***Batham,*** *Brierley Hill;* ***British Oak,*** *Dudley;* ***Holden's,*** *Woodsetton;* ***Sarah Hughes,*** *Sedgley;* ***Pitfield,*** *Stourbridge*

Barston

Bulls Head

Barston Lane ☎ (067 544) 2830
11–2.30, 5.30 (6 Sat)–11
Draught Bass; M&B Brew XI H
Traditional country pub and centre of village life, partly dating back to 1490, with oak beams and log fires. No meals Wed or Sun eves.
Q P

Bilston

Spread Eagle

Lichfield Street (A41)
☎ (0902) 403801
11–3.30, 7–11
British Oak Eve'ill Bitter, Dungeon Draught, Old Jones; Tetley Bitter H
Three-roomed urban pub, including a basic bar with wooden floorboards. British Oak's second pub. The beer range may vary.
P

Trumpet

High Street (A4039)
☎ (0902) 43723
12–3, 8–11; 12–3, 8–10.30 Sun
Holden's Mild, Bitter, Special H
Popular, one-roomed jazz centre, hosting live acts nightly and Sun lunchtime. Lunches Mon–Fri. P

Birmingham: *Acocks Green*

Bernie's Off-Licence

908 Warwick Road
☎ (021) 708 1664
12–2 (not Mon or Wed), 5.30–10; 12–2, 7–10 Sun
Beer range varies H
Off-licence offering a varied choice of ales.

Aston

Manor Tavern

Portland Street
☎ (021) 326 8780
11–2.30 (3 Sat), 5.30 (7 Sat)–11; 11–11 Fri
Ansells Bitter, Mild;

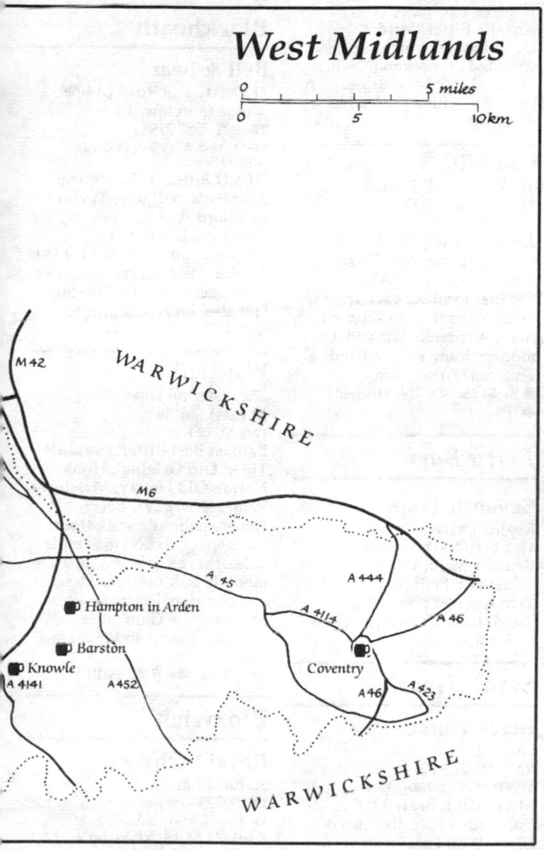

Marston's Pedigree; Tetley Bitter H
Friendly, well-refurbished corner local not far from the site of the old Ansells brewery. Good value eve meals Sat. ☾ ⊞

Camp Hill

Brewer & Baker

Old Camp Hill
☎ (021) 772 8185
11–11
Banks's Mild, Bitter E**; Marston's Pedigree** H
Popular pub with a mixed clientele and a welcoming landlady. ❀ ☾ ♿ ♣ P

City Centre

Atkinsons Real Ale Bar

Stephenson Street (rear of Midland Hotel)
☎ (021) 643 2601
11–2.30, 5–11; closed Sun
Hook Norton Old Hooky G**; Marston's Pedigree; Ruddles County** H**; S&N Theakston Old Peculier** G**; Whitbread Boddingtons Bitter** H
Small, popular bar situated at the rear of a large city-centre hotel, used by local shop and office workers at lunchtime. Q ⛟ ☾ ⥃ (New St) ⌂

Old Contemptibles

Edmund Street
☎ (021) 236 5264
12–11 (9 Sat); closed Sun
Draught Bass, M&B Highgate Mild, Brew XI; guest beers H
Built in the 1800s as a hotel, but never opened as such. Note the very high ceiling in the right-hand room. Usually two guest beers.
Q ☾ ◗ ⥃ (Snow Hill)

Prince of Wales

Cambridge Street
☎ (021) 643 9460
11–3.30, 5–11; 11–11 Sat
Ansells Bitter, Mild; Ind Coope Burton Ale; Marston's Pedigree; Tetley Bitter H
One of the very few old buildings in the area, set between the convention centre and the indoor arena. Eve meals until 8pm.
☾ ◗ ⥃ (New St) ♣

Digbeth

Adam & Eve

201 Bradford Street
☎ (021) 772 8390
12–11; 12–4, 7–11 Sat
HP&D Mild, Entire; Marston's Pedigree; Wadworth 6X; guest beers H
Friendly corner pub staging regular live music in the lounge. Upstairs function room. ☾ ♿ ♣

Forge Tavern

Fazeley Street
☎ (021) 773 5747
12–3, 5.30–11; 11–11 Thu & Fri
Banks's Mild; Marston's Pedigree H
Pub next to the Grand Union Canal, popular with industrial workers. Pool room; disco every Sat eve. ❀ ☾ ♿ ♣

Spotted Dog

104 Warwick Street
☎ (021) 772 3822
7–11; 12–3, 7–10 Sun
Ansells Bitter, Mild; HP&D Entire H
Friendly pub catering for all. Lovely stained-glass windows.
Q ❀ ⥃ (New St)

White Swan

Bradford Street
☎ (021) 622 2586
11–3, 6–11
Ansells Mild; Tetley Bitter H
Unspoilt, late-Victorian corner pub with decorated exterior tiled walls and an ornate tiled ceiling in the bar. Q ♿
⥃ (New St/Moor St) ♣

Erdington

Beer Shop

New Street (50 yds off A38)
☎ (021) 384 3636
5.30 (7 Sun)–10
Beer range varies H
Off-licence with an excellent range of up to six ever-changing real ales, plus a wide choice of British and foreign bottled beers. ⥃ (Erdington)

Safe Harbour

Moor Lane (A4040/A453)
☎ (021) 356 4257
11–2.30 (3 Fri & Sat), 5 (6 Sat)–11
Ansells Bitter, Mild; Tetley Bitter H
Comfortable lounge and a basic bar, known as the Grave Diggers (opposite a cemetery). Friendly staff. ❀ ☾ ⊞ P

Gosta Green

Old Union Mill

Holt Street (near Aston University) ☎ (021) 359 1716
12 (11.30 Fri & Sat)–3, 5 (5.30 Sat)–11

Ansells Bitter; HP&D Entire; Marston's Pedigree; Tetley Bitter; guest beer (occasionally) H
Popular student pub, crowded at weekends.
❀ ◐ ◑ ⇌ (New St/Moor St)

Hockley

Black Eagle
Factory Road (near A41/B144 jct) ☎ (021) 523 4008
11–3 (4 Sat), 5.30 (7 Sat)–11; 11–11 Fri
Ansells Bitter, Mild; HP&D Entire H
A gem: Birmingham CAMRA's 1993 *Pub of the Year*. Friendly staff and good food.
Q ❀ ◐ ◑

Church Inn
Hockley Hill ☎ (021) 515 1851
12 (7 Sat)–11
Ansells Bitter, Mild; Batham Best Bitter; Ind Coope Burton Ale H
Welcoming pub, where the food is excellent. Q ◐ ◑ ⊞ ♣

Ladywood

Cross Keys
81 Steward Street (off A457)
☎ (021) 454 3058
12–2.30, 5.30–11
Ansells Mild H
This L-shaped pub must be the smallest in Birmingham. Strong domino theme in the one room which has black and white timbers. ◐ ♣

Moseley

Prince of Wales
118 Alcester Road
☎ (021) 449 4198
11–3 (3.30 Sat), 5.30 (6 Sat)–11
Ansells Bitter, Mild; Ind Coope Burton Ale H
Two-roomed pub, where the back room is served through a small hatch. Popular with locals at lunchtime. Q ⊞ ♿

Nechells

Villa Tavern
307 Nechells Park Road
☎ (021) 328 9831
11–3 (4 Sat), 6.30–11; 11–11 Fri
Ansells Bitter, Mild; HP&D Entire; Marston's Pedigree; Tetley Bitter H
Refurbished Victorian tavern with two bars, plus a pool room. Popular with locals and draymen. Q ◐ ⊞ ♿
⇌ (Aston) ♣ P

Northfield

Cavalier
214 Fairfax Road
☎ (021) 475 4083
11–11; 11–3, 6–11 Sat
Ansells Bitter, Mild H
Quiet lounge which can be crowded at weekends, when the local folk band appears. A basic bar with a pool table.
❀ ⊞ ⇌ P

Old Mill
31 West Heath Road
☎ (021) 475 1337
12–3, 6–11
Ansells Bitter, Mild; Ind Coope Burton Ale; Tetley Bitter H
Popular local set back from the main Northfield to West Heath road. A friendly bar and a modern lounge. Live band Thu; quiz/disco Sun.
❀ ◐ ⊞ ♿ ⇌ (Northfield)
♣ P

Perry Barr

Seventh Trap
Regina Drive
11–3, 5–11; 11–11 Fri & Sat
Banks's Mild, Bitter E**; Marston's Pedigree** H
Two-roomed pub in the standard Banks's style. Used by local students.

Small Heath

Black Horse
Green Lane
☎ (021) 773 7271
11–11; 11–3.30, 7.30–11 Sat
M&B Mild, Brew XI E
Pub with a friendly, mixed clientele and atmosphere; a games venue for locals. Near the disused, Victorian terracotta swimming baths.
⊞ ♣

Sparkhill

Cherry Arbour
66 Stratford Street (150 yds from A41)
☎ (021) 766 8452
11–11; 11–4, 7–11 Sat
M&B Mild, Springfield Bitter E
Turn-of-the-century, three-roomed pub. There used to be a cherry orchard at the rear.
❀ ⊞ ♿ ⇌ (Small Heath) P

Winson Green

Bellefield
Winson Street (off A457)
☎ (021) 558 0647
12–3, 6–11
Everards Mild, Tiger, Old Bill; Morland Old Speckled Hen; guest beers H
Unspoilt, beautifully tiled pub with a notable ceiling in the bar. The lounge has tile-framed pictures.
Q ❀ ◐ ♣ P

Blackheath

Bell & Bear
71 Gorsty Hill Road (A4099, ¾ mile from town)
☎ (021) 561 2196
11–11; 11–3, 6–11 Sat; 12–2.30, 7–10.30 Sun
HP&D Bitter, Mild, Entire; Marston's Pedigree; Taylor Landlord H
Comfortable, rambling, one-room pub, popular for bar snacks. The restaurant (Cantonese) is open Tue–Sun, and also offers Sun lunches.
❀ ◐ ◑ P

Waterfall
132 Waterfall Lane
☎ (021) 561 3499
12–2.30, 5.30–11
Batham Best Bitter; Everards Tiger, Old Original; Hook Norton Old Hooky; Marston's Pedigree H**; guest beers**
A mere half-mile walk from the town or station to sample at least seven fine ales. Regular monthly quizzes (first Mon) and occasional karaoke eves. The 'Bow Tie Club' offers brewery, racing and breakfast trips.
❀ ◐ ◑ ⊞ ⇌ (Old Hill) P

Bloxwich

Royal Exchange
Stafford Road (A34)
☎ (0922) 479618
12–3, 5–11; 11–11 Sat
Banks's Mild; Marston's Bitter, Pedigree H
Characterful, popular local featuring sporting memorabilia.
⚔ Q ❀ ◐ ⊞ ♣ P

Brierley Hill

Bell
172 Delph Road (B4172, off A461) ☎ (0384) 72376
12–3, 5 (6 Sat)–11; 11–11 Fri
HP&D Bitter, Mild, Entire, Deakin's Downfall; Tetley Bitter H
Popular Victorian pub at the foot of the famous Delph Nine locks. Note the collection of bells in the bar and lounge. Regular quiz night with a free buffet; barbecues in summer. No food Sun.
⚔ ❀ ◐ ⊞ ♣ P

New Talbot
Brettell Lane (A461)
☎ (0384) 79993
11–3, 6–11
Holden's Mild; Ruddles County; Webster's Yorkshire Bitter H**; guest beer**
Tastefully restored old pub, decorated with interesting artefacts. Q ❀ ◐ ◑ P

Roebuck
Amblecote Road
☎ (0384) 79137
12–3, 5.30–11
HP&D Mild, Entire; Tetley Bitter 🄷
Former Ansells house, refurbished and reopened as a smart HP&D pub with extremely friendly service. Near the giant Merry Hill shopping centre. Vegetarian dishes. ◖ ◗ ⊟ ♣ P

Try also: Vine (Bull & Bladder), Delph Rd (Batham)

Brownhills

Hussey Arms
Chester Road North
☎ (0543) 373198
12–2.30 (3 Fri), 5.30–11; 12–11 Sat
HP&D Mild, Entire; Tetley Bitter 🄷**; guest beers** (occasionally)
Typical Brummie pub, recently converted from Ansells. The only HP&D pub in the area, it has a welcoming feel despite its large size. ❀ ◖ ◗ ⊟ ♣ P

Coseley

Painter's Arms
Avenue Road (off B4483)
☎ (0902) 883095
12–3, 5–11; 11–11 Fri & Sat
Holden's Mild, Bitter 🄴
Former private house, acquired by Holden's in 1939, with a long, narrow lounge bar and a small back room. Children welcome in the lounge. Eve meals Thu–Sat; no lunches Sun. ❀ ◖ ◗ ⇌ P

White House
Daisy Street, Daisy Bank (B4163) ☎ (0902) 402703
11–3, 6–11
HP&D Bitter, Mild, Entire, Deakin's Downfall 🄷**; guest beers**
Lively Black Country local: a basic bar and a cosy lounge. Good value food. Quizzes Wed/Sun. 🔥 ◖ ◗ ⇌ ♣ P

Try also: Old Bush, Skidmore Rd (Holden's)

Coventry

Biggin Hall Hotel
214 Binley Road, Copsewood
☎ (0203) 457046
10.30–11
Banks's Mild; Marston's Bitter, Pedigree, Owd Rodger 🄷
Pub with a mock Tudor exterior, a smart bar and a plush, wood-panelled lounge, boasting a large, central oak table. Virtually unchanged since 1923. Children welcome in the games room.
Q ☺ ❀ ◖ ⊟ ♿ ♣ P

Black Horse
Spon End ☎ (0203) 677360
10.30–3, 4.30–11
Draught Bass; M&B Mild, Brew XI 🄷
Pub in a popular part of pre-war Coventry (there isn't much left). Plans to flatten the pub caused a furore.
🔥 Q 🛏 ⊟ ♣ P

Boat Inn
188 Black Horse Road, Exhall
☎ (0203) 361438
12–3, 7 (may be earlier)–11
Ansells Bitter, Mild; Ind Coope Burton Ale; S&N Theakston XB; Tetley Bitter 🄷
Single-bar local with distinct drinking areas. Very handy for the canal. One of the original Heritage Inns, but refurbishment lends it a more modern and spacious interior. Meals Mon–Fri. 🔥 Q ❀ ◖ ♣ P

Elastic Inn
Ford Street (opp. sports centre)
☎ (0203) 227039
11–3, 5.30–11
Ansells Bitter, Mild; Tetley Bitter 🄷
Over 150-year-old city pub on the very edge of the centre. Varied clientele but mainly locals at night. Q ◖ ♣

Greyhound
118 Much Park Street
☎ (0203) 221274
12–3, 6–11
Mansfield Riding Mild; Wells Eagle, Bombardier 🄷
Pub close to law courts, and frequented by lawyers and university students. No food Sun. ❀ ◖ ♣

Greyhound Inn
Sutton Stop, Black Horse Road
☎ (0203) 363046
11–2.30, 6–11
Banks's Bitter; Bass Worthington BB, Draught Bass; M&B Highgate Mild 🄷
Popular pub at Hawksbury canal junction: an old three-roomer full of bric-a-brac. The outdoor drinking area is on the canal bank. Famous for its food (pies). No meals Sun lunch. 🔥 Q ❀ ◖ ◗ P

Malt Shovel
Spon End ☎ (0203) 220204
12 (12.30 Fri & Sat)–2.30, 7–11; 12.30–2.30, 7–10.30 Sun
Ansells Bitter, Mild; Tetley Bitter; guest beer 🄷
One of the original Heritage Inns, a small, cosy one-roomer with nooks and crannies. A convivial, popular watering hole. 🔥 Q ❀ ◖ ♿ ♣ P

Old Windmill
Spon Street ☎ (0203) 252183
11.30–2.30, 6 (7 Sat)–11; 12–2, 7–10.30 Sun
Ansells Mild; Courage Directors; Ruddles Best Bitter, County; Webster's Yorkshire Bitter 🄷**; guest beer**
16th-century olde-worlde pub offering cheap lunches (not served Sun).
🔥 Q ◖ ♿ ⛀

Peacock Inn
94 Gosford Street (near University) ☎ (0203) 220327
10–11
Ansells Bitter; Draught Bass; S&N Theakston Old Peculier; Tetley Bitter 🄷
Popular student pub serving very cheap lunches.
❀ ◖ ⛀

Rainbow Inn
73 Birmingham Road, Allesley
☎ (0203) 402888
11–11
Ansells Mild; Courage Best Bitter, Directors; John Smith's Bitter 🄷**; guest beer**
17th-century coaching house which retains the feel of a village pub: a busy bar, plus a quiet lounge for meals (lunches Mon–Sat; eve meals Tue–Fri, till 8.30).
Q ❀ ◖ ◗ ⊟ ♣ P

Royal Oak
22 Earlsdon Street, Earlsdon
☎ (0203) 674140
5–11
Ansells Bitter, Mild; Draught Bass; Tetley Bitter 🄷
Recently re-opened after a total redesign, a pub whose convivial atmosphere is enhanced by large, communal drinking tables and a civilised clientele. Waiter service at the rear of the bar. 🔥 Q

Town Wall Tavern
Bond Street ☎ (0203) 220963
11–3, 5–11
Draught Bass; M&B Mild, Brew XI 🄷**; guest beer**
Old pub in the city centre, the haunt of artistes from the Begrade Theatre nearby, and journalists from the newspaper offices. A small but comfortable lounge, and a bar with a snug. 🔥 Q ◖ ⊟ ♣

Cradley Heath

Waggon & Horses
100 Reddal Hill Road (A4100)
☎ (0384) 636035
11 (11.30 Sat)–3, 7–11
Banks's Mild, Bitter 🄴
Boisterous, two-roomed, Black Country local.
❀ ⊟ ⇌ ♣ P

Curdworth

Beehive
Beehive Lane
☎ (0675) 470223
11.30–11; 11.30–2.30, 6–11 Sat

Ansells Bitter, Mild; Ind Coope Burton Ale; Tetley Bitter Ⓗ
Friendly village local with a traditional bar. The lounge has been extended into a number of open-plan drinking and eating areas.
Q ❀ ◑ ◗ ⊟ ♿ ♣ P

Darlaston

Fallings Heath Tavern
Walsall Road (A4038)
☎ (021) 526 3403
12–2.30 (3 if busy), 7–11
Ansells Bitter, Mild; HP&D Deakin's Downfall; Tetley Bitter Ⓗ
Traditional local: a busy bar and a quieter lounge. Mild is the best-selling beer.
❀ ⊟ ♣ P

Dudley

Lamp Tavern
116 High Street (A459)
☎ (0384) 254129
11–11
Batham Mild, Best Bitter, XXX Ⓗ
Lively, welcoming local with a plain bar, a comfortable lounge and an adjacent eating area (meals till 8pm).
Q ❀ ◑ ◗ ⊟ ♿ ♣ P

Maltshovel
Tower Street ☎ (0384) 252735
11–3, 5.30–11; 11–11 Sat
Banks's Mild, Bitter Ⓔ
Cosy, one-roomed pub near the market place, overlooked by the castle and the zoo, and within easy reach of the bus station. No food Sun.
Q ❀ ◑ ♣ P

Old Priory
New Street ☎ (0384) 455810
12–11
HP&D Bitter, Mild, Entire Ⓗ
Originally an early 19th-century home-brew house known as the Britannia, now refurbished in comfortable Victorian style with chaises longues in the U-shaped drinking area. Near the market place. ◑ ♣

Try also: British Oak, Salop St (Free); **Old Vic,** King St (S&N)

Great Bridge

Royal Oak
261 Whitehall Road (B4166)
☎ (021) 520 7096
12–3, 6.30–11
Banks's Mild Ⓔ**; Lichfield Xpired; Marston's Pedigree; Morrells Graduate; Wadworth 6X** Ⓗ**; guest beers**
Cosy, one-roomed pub serving good value food at all times, except Sun. ❀ ◑ ◗ ♿ P

Halesowen

Fairfield Inn
Fairfield Road, Hurst Green
11–3, 5.30–11
Banks's Hanson's Mild, Bitter Ⓔ**; Marston's Pedigree** Ⓗ
Large, two-roomed roadside local: a traditional bar and a busy, smart lounge, with a collection of miniatures.
❀ ◑ ⊟ ⇌ (Rowley Regis) ♣ P

Loyal Lodge
15 Furnace Hill (just off A459)
☎ (021) 585 5863
11–2.30, 5 (6 Sat)–11; 12–2.30, 7–10.30 Sun
HP&D Bitter, Mild, Entire, Deakin's Downfall Ⓗ
Old building refurbished to provide various seating areas around the bar. Traditional Sun lunches (no food Sun eve). Quizzes alternate Sun eves.
❀ ◑ ◗ ♿ P

Queens Head
Birmingham Street
☎ (021) 550 1548
12–2.30, 5.30 (7 Sat)–11
Greenalls Davenports Bitter, Thomas Greenall's Original Ⓗ
Comfortable town-centre hotel, opposite the local leisure centre. Popular with office workers, students and shoppers alike. Eve meals Mon–Thu till 8.45: a good value, home-cooked choice.
Q ❀ ◑ ◗ P

Rose & Crown
Hagley Road, Hasbury (B4183)
☎ (021) 550 2757
12–2.30 (3 Sat), 6–11
HP&D Mild, Entire; Tetley Bitter Ⓗ
Well frequented, large, open-roomed establishment with various drinking areas served from a central bar. Many interesting artefacts, including a kitchen range. Warm welcome. ◑ ♣ P

Hampton in Arden

White Lion
High Street ☎ (0675) 442833
12–2.30, 5.30 (6 Sat)–11
Draught Bass; M&B Brew XI; John Smith's Bitter Ⓗ
Homely, welcoming pub with a basic bar that has remained unchanged for 50 years.
Q ◑ ◗ ⊟ ⇌ P

Hurst Hill

Hurst Hill Tavern
Caddick Street (off A463)
☎ (0902) 880318
12–4, 7–11
Banks's Hanson's Mild, Mild, Bitter Ⓔ
Very friendly, popular local, a former brew pub, opposite the 'Strict and Particular' Baptist church. Summer barbecues.
❀ ⊟ ♣ P

Kingswinford

Park Tavern
182 Cot Lane (500 yds from A4101) ☎ (0384) 287178
12–11
Ansells Bitter; Batham Best Bitter; Ind Coope Burton Ale; Tetley Bitter Ⓗ
Pleasant, friendly local near Broadfield House Glass Museum. ❀ ⊟ ♣ P

Union
Water Street (off A4101)
☎ (0384) 295698
12–2.30 (4 Sat), 6 (7 Sat)–11
Banks's Mild, Bitter Ⓔ
Small, traditional local in the same family for 60 years. Family oriented in summer.
❀ ♣ P

Knowle

Vaults
St John's Close
☎ (0564) 773656
12–2.30, 5 (6 Sat)–11
Ansells Mild; Elgood's GSB; HP&D Bitter; Ind Coope Burton Ale; Tetley Bitter; guest beers Ⓗ
Basement pub with seating on two levels. Home-made soup is a speciality (no food Sat eve). ◑ ◗ ♣

Langley

Crosswells
High Street ☎ (021) 552 2629
12–2.30 (3 Fri & Sat), 6 (7 Sat)–11
HP&D Bitter, Mild, Entire; Tetley Bitter Ⓗ
Friendly, comfortable, two-roomed pub near the HP&D brewery. No food Sun.
◑ ⊟ ♿ ⇌ (Langley Green) ♣ P

New Navigation
Titford Road (off A4123)
☎ (021) 552 2525
11.30–3, 6–11
HP&D Bitter, Mild, Entire; Tetley Bitter Ⓗ
Friendly, welcoming pub almost at the end of the Titford Canal. Eve meals if booked. ❀ ◑ ♣ P

Lower Gornal

Red Cow
84 Grosvenor Road (300 yds from B4176) ☎ (0384) 253760
12–4.30, 6.30 (7 Sat)–11

Banks's Hanson's Mild, Bitter Ⓔ
Old Black Country local of character; a pub since 1835 and a traditional oasis in an area of redevelopment. Comfortable snug lounge. Hot pork sandwiches available Fri and Sat. ❀ ⊞ ♣ P

Netherton

White Swan (Tommy Turner's)
45 Baptist End Road (400 yds off A459) ☎ (0384) 256101
12–2.30 (3.30 Fri & Sat), 7–11
Banks's Mild; HP&D Entire; guest beers Ⓗ
Welcoming, 18th-century former home-brew house (Roe's), with a contrasting bar and lounge. Good value home cooking features locally-made faggots and prize-winning sausages. ♔ ❀ ◐ ◑ ⊞ ♣ P

Oldbury

Waggon & Horses
Church Street (off A4034, near bus station) ☎ (021) 552 5467
12–2.30 (3 Fri), 5 (6 Sat)–11; 12–2.30, 7–10.30 Sun
Draught Bass; Batham Best Bitter; Everards Old Original; Marston's Pedigree; Whitbread Boddingtons Bitter Ⓗ**; guest beers**
Friendly, two-roomed, Black Country hostelry with original tiled walls, a copper ceiling and other fittings. Excellent, home-cooked food in the bars and function room (book Sun lunch). Popular with office workers at lunchtime. ♔ ❀ ◐ ◑ ⇌ (Sandwell & Dudley)

Pelsall

Royal Oak
Yorks Bridge, Norton Road
☎ (0922) 691811
11.30–3, 5.30–11
Ansells Bitter, Mild; Banks's Mild; Ind Coope Benskins Best Bitter, Burton Ale Ⓗ
Pleasant canalside pub. Good food. ♔ ❀ ◐ ◑ ⊞ ♿ ♣ P

Rowley Regis

Cock Inn
75 Dudley Road (B4171)
☎ (021) 561 4273
12–3, 5–11
HP&D Bitter, Mild, Entire Ⓗ
Popular, friendly pub in the HP&D Victoriana style. Quizzes Thu; no food Sun eve. ♔ Q ❀ ◐ ◑ ♿ ♣ P

Sir Robert Peel
1 Rowley Village (B4171)
☎ (021) 559 2835
12–4.30, 7–11
Ansells Bitter, Mild; Draught Bass; Tetley Bitter; guest beers (occasionally) Ⓗ
The oldest building in Rowley Village, formerly a police station, now a traditional, three-roomed pub, licensed since 1840. Servery in the entrance passageway. Warm welcome. ♔ Q ❀ ⊞ ⇌ ♣

Sedgley

Beacon Hotel
129 Bilston Street (A463)
☎ (0902) 883380
12–2.30, 5.30–10.45 (11 Fri); 11.30–3, 6–11 Sat
M&B Mild, Springfield Bitter; Sarah Hughes Sedgley Surprise, Ruby Mild Ⓗ**; guest beers**
Pub boasting a prize-winning Victorian interior, following gradual and loving refurbishment. The original tower brewery can be visited by appointment.
Q ⛟ ❀ ◐ ♣ P

Bull's Head
Bilston Street (A463)
☎ (0902) 679606
12–3 (4 Sat), 6–11
Holden's Mild, Bitter Ⓔ
Locals' pub with a strong darts following and an interesting photo collection in the lively bar; cosy lounge at the rear. The house beer is known as Lucy B (not brewed here).
Q ❀ ◐ ⊞ ♣ ⚲

Shirley

Bernie's Real Ale Off-Licence
266 Cranmore Boulevard (off A34) ☎ (021) 744 2827
12–2 (not Mon), 5.30–10
Adnams Extra; Batham Best Bitter; Hook Norton Best Bitter; Smiles Exhibition; Titanic Premium; Wadworth 6X Ⓗ
Six beers are always available from hundreds supplied by breweries large and small each year. Try before you buy system. ♿ ⚲

Red Lion
Stratford Road
☎ (021) 744 1030
11–2.30 (3 Sat), 6.30–11
Ansells Bitter, Mild; Marston's Pedigree; Tetley Bitter Ⓗ
Main-road pub in a shopping square: a large lounge with three areas. The old bar area is now a pool room. ◐ ♣

Smethwick

Ivy Bush
218 St Paul's Road (B4169)
☎ (021) 565 0929
10–11
Holden's Mild, Bitter, Special Ⓗ
Recently renovated, former M&B pub with a friendly atmosphere. No food Sun.
⛟ ◐ ♿ ⇌ (West) ♣

Solihull

Hobs Meadow
Ulleries Road (near ice rink)
☎ (021) 743 2201
11.30–2.30, 5.30 (6 Sat)–11; 12–2.30, 7–10.30 Sun
Ansells Bitter, Mild; Ind Coope Burton Ale; Tetley Bitter Ⓗ
Ansells Big Steak house: a large, split-level lounge and a basic bar. Unique two-pocket pool table. The garden has play equipment.
❀ ◐ ◑ ⊞ ♿ ♣ P ⚟

Old Colonial
Damson Lane (800 yds from A45 along Damson Parkway)
☎ (021) 705 9054
11.30–11; 11–3, 6.30–11 Sat
Draught Bass; Fuller's ESB; M&B Mild Ⓗ**, Brew XI** Ⓔ**; guest beer** Ⓗ
One-roomed pub divided into seven areas. Live music, karaoke and theme nights staged. Children welcome at lunchtime. Eve meals if booked. ⛟ ❀ ◐ ♿ ♣ P

Stourbridge

Longlands Tavern
Western Road
☎ (0384) 392073
11–3, 6–11
Banks's Mild, Bitter Ⓔ
Smart, popular, back-street pub. Q ⊞ ♣ P

Moorings Tavern
High Street, Amblecote (A491)
☎ (0384) 374124
12–3, 5–11
Draught Bass; Enville Ale; Pitfield Mild, Bitter; S&N Theakston XB; Whitbread Boddingtons Bitter Ⓗ**; guest beer**
Lively one-roomer near the Grade II-listed Stourbridge bonded warehouse and canal basin, sporting a canal-influenced decor and serving good value food (no meals Sun eve). Wide selection of ales.
❀ 🛏 ◐ ◑ ♿ ⇌ P

Old White Horse
South Road
☎ (0384) 394258
12–3, 5–11
Draught Bass; Courage Directors Ⓗ**; guest beers**
Harvester pub/restaurant with a rediscovered commitment to local drinkers and real ale. Wheelchair WC.
❀ ◐ ◑ ♿ ♣ P

West Midlands

Plough
154 Bridgnorth Road, Wollaston (A458)
☎ (0384) 393414
12–2.30 (3 Fri & Sat), 7 (6.30 Sat)–11; 12–2.30, 7–10.30 Sun
Draught Bass; M&B Mild; Stones Best Bitter Ⓗ
Highly decorated old house, with its original windows still intact. A keen sporting pub, with darts and pool in the bar; the lounge is mainly used for eating and by older customers. Folk club Tue eve. Warm and friendly. ❀ ◐ ◑ ♿ ♣ P

Robin Hood
196 Collis Street, Amblecote (one-way street)
☎ (0384) 440286
12–3, 6–11
Banks's Mild Ⓔ**; Batham Best Bitter; Enville Ale; Everards Tiger; Hook Norton Old Hooky; guest beers** Ⓗ
Well-established, popular free house which offers varied vegetarian and à la carte meals. ⛫ ❀ 🛏 ◐ ◑ ♿ P

Seven Stars
Brook Road, Oldswinford (B4186) ☎ (0384) 394483
11–11
S&N Theakston Mild, Best Bitter, XB, Old Peculier; guest beer Ⓗ
Free house, full of character with ornate tiling and a beautiful carved-wood back bar fitting. Two large rooms plus a restaurant area.
◐ ◑ ⇌ (Junction)

Shrubbery Cottage
28 Heath Lane, Oldswinford
☎ (0384) 377598
12–2.30, 6–11; 12–2.30, 7–10.30 Sun
Holden's Mild, Bitter, Special Ⓗ
Popular, one-roomed local on a busy road near Oldswinford Cross. A welcome retreat for staff from the local college at lunchtime.
❀ ◐ ⇌ (Junction) P

Sutton Coldfield

Blake Barn Inn
Blake Street ☎ (021) 308 8421
11–3, 5.30–11; 11–11 Sat
Banks's Mild, Bitter Ⓔ**; Marston's Pedigree** Ⓗ
Smart, popular, estate pub with rural decor. Same manager for ten years.
❀ ◐ ♿ ⇌ (Blake St) P

Crown
Walsall Road, Four Oaks
☎ (021) 308 1258
11–11
Ansells Bitter, Mild; Ind Coope Burton Ale; Marston's Pedigree; Tetley Bitter Ⓗ
Very large, suburban pub with a real ale bar. The extensive lounge has Indian, Mexican and Greek food franchises. Popular with all ages. ◐ ◑ 🗗 ♿ ⇌ (Butler's Lane) P

Duke
Duke Street ☎ (021) 355 1767
11.30–3, 5.30–11; 12–2.30, 7–10.30 Sun
Ansells Bitter, Mild; Ind Coope Burton Ale; Tetley Bitter Ⓗ
Unspoilt, friendly and traditional local. Note the fine, carved-wood bar shelves with engraved mirrors. The small lounge is quiet and homely.
Q ❀ 🗗 ⇌ ♣ P

Laurel Wines Off-Licence
63 Westwood Road (off A452)
☎ (021) 353 0399
12–2, 5.30 (5 Sat)–10.30; 12–2, 7–10.30 Sun
Batham Best Bitter; Burton Bridge Festival; Marston's Pedigree; guest beers Ⓖ
Popular off-licence offering a large range of real ales.

Station
Station Street ☎ (021) 355 3640
11–11
Draught Bass; Marston's Pedigree; Stones Best Bitter Ⓗ
Busy, multi-roomed pub, right next to the station and near the town centre. Frequent entertainment. Beware the sloping floor in the main public bar. No food Sun.
❀ ◐ 🗗 ⇌ ♣

White Lion
Hill Village Road, Four Oaks
☎ (021) 308 5353
11–3, 5.30–11; 11–11 Sat
Draught Bass; M&B Mild, Brew XI Ⓗ
Pub recently refurbished in rural style. Good food. ❀ ◐ ◑ ⇌ (Butler's Lane) ♣ P

Upper Gornal

Britannia (Sally's)
109 Kent Street
☎ (0902) 883253
12–3, 7–11
Courage Directors; Marston's Pedigree; S&N Theakston XB; John Smith's Bitter Ⓗ**; guest beers**
Former brew pub (built in 1780) which boasts an untouched late-19th-century tap room. Beer is served from handpumps against the wall. The former butcher's shop at the front has been converted to a lounge bar. The original brewhouse at the rear is still intact and there are plans to brew again. ⛫ Q ❀ 🗗 P

Try also: Old Mill, Windmill St (Holden's)

Wall Heath

Wall Heath Tavern
High Street (A449)
☎ (0384) 287319
11–3, 6–11
HP&D Mild, Entire; Tetley Bitter Ⓗ
Busy roadside pub with a reputation for good food.
❀ ◐ ◑ 🗗 ♿ ♣ P

Walsall

Butts Tavern
Butts Road
☎ (0922) 29332
12–3.30, 7–11
Ansells Bitter, Mild Ⓗ
Large, pre-war pub with a friendly bar and a quieter lounge where dress restrictions apply.
⛫ ❀ 🗗 ♣

Duke of York
Lumley Road, Chuckery (off A34) ☎ (0922) 27593
12–3, 6–11
Draught Bass; M&B Highgate Mild, Brew XI Ⓗ**; guest beer**
Large, comfortable bar and a plush lounge. Quiz nights. Close to the Highgate Brewery.
❀ 🗗 ♣

Hamemaker's Arms
87 Blue Lane West (A454)
☎ (0922) 28083
11.30–3, 6–11; 11–11 Sat
Banks's Mild, Bitter Ⓔ
Pleasantly modernised, 1930s pub with a well laid-out bar, and a warm, bright, comfortable lounge. Handy for the town centre. No food Sun.
Q ❀ ◐ ◑ 🗗 ⇌ ♣ P

Katz
23 Lower Rushall Street (off A34) ☎ (0922) 725848
12–2.30, 5.30 (7 Sat)–11; closed Sun
Ansells Bitter; Burton Bridge Bridge Bitter; HP&D Entire; Ind Coope Burton Ale, Marston's Pedigree; guest beer Ⓗ
Lively, two-roomed pub with an upstairs pool room catering for the younger element. Katz is an old nickname for this Victorian pub. Note the tiny defunct tower brewery at the rear. ❀ ◐ ◑ ⇌

King Arthur
Liskeard Road, Park Hall (off A34, 2 miles S of centre)
☎ (0922) 31400
12–2.30, 5.30–11; 12–11 Sat
Courage Best Bitter; M&B Highgate Mild; Ruddles Best Bitter, County; John Smith's Bitter Ⓗ
Friendly pub with two

substantial rooms in which families are welcome. Superb food (no meals Sun). Not easy to find, but worth the effort.
❀ ◐ ◑ ♣ P

New Fullbrook
West Bromwich Road (A4031/A4148 jct)
☎ (0922) 21761
11.30–11
Banks's Mild; M&B Highgate Mild, Springfield Bitter, Brew XI Ⓔ
1930s roadhouse with a large bar, a games room and a pleasant lounge. It boasts record sales for Highgate Mild. ⛟ ❀ ◐ ⊟ ⇌ (Bescot Stadium) ♣ P

New Inn
113 Wednesbury Road
☎ (0922) 23301
12–3, 6–11; 12–11 Fri
Banks's Mild, Bitter Ⓔ
One-roomed local where a Sun quiz and Fri night folk music enhance the friendly atmosphere. ♣ P

New Inns
John Street
☎ (0922) 27660
12–3, 5.30 (7 Sat)–11; 12–3, 8–10.30 Sun
Ansells Bitter, Mild; Ind Coope Burton Ale; guest beer Ⓗ
Traditional, small-roomed, Victorian back-street local with a cosy lounge and a passageway drinking area. A rare haven from jukebox and fruit machines. Beautifully-cooked, interesting food (not served Sun, or Mon eve).
⛫ Q ❀ ◐ ◑ ⊟ ♣

Oak Inn
336 Green Lane (A34, near cinema) ☎ (0922) 645758
12–2.30 (11.30–3 Sat), 7–11; 7–10.30 Sun, closed Sun lunch
Pitfield Mild, Bitter, Wiltshire Stonehenge Bitter; guest beers Ⓗ
Much-improved pub with an island bar. Its relaxing and pleasant atmosphere makes it popular with office and factory workers at lunchtime, and locals and lorry drivers eves. Walsall CAMRA *Pub of the Year* 1992. No food Sat eve or Sun. ⛫ ❀ ◐ ◑ ⇌ ♣ P

White Lion
150 Sandwell Street
☎ (0922) 28542
12–3, 7 (6 Sat)–11
Ansells Bitter, Mild; Burton Bridge Porter; HP&D Bitter, Entire; Ind Coope Burton Ale Ⓗ
Large, three-roomed pub in a residential area, not far from the town centre. No food Sun.
❀ ◐ ⊟ ♣

Wednesbury

Cottage Spring
106 Franchise Street (off B4200 behind Ikea store)
☎ (021) 526 6354
11–2.30 (5 Sat), 6 (7 Sat)–11; 12–11 Fri
Holden's Stout (occasionally) Ⓗ**, Mild, Bitter** Ⓔ**, XB, Special, XL** Ⓗ
Small, friendly local, popular with pub games and sports enthusiasts. Reasonably-priced food (not served Sun, or Mon eve). Quiz night Thu. Satellite TV in the bar. ◐ ◑ ⊟ ♣ P

Woodman
74 Wood Green Road (A461, opp. Sandwell College)
☎ (021) 556 1637
12–11; 12–4, 6.30–11 Sat
Banks's Mild; Courage Best Bitter Ⓔ**, Directors; Ruddles County** Ⓗ
Large, roadside pub, continually under threat of demolition for road improvement. The bar is basic, the smoke room more comfortable.
⛟ ⊟ ♿ ⇌ (Bescot) ♣

Wednesfield

Broadway
Lichfield Road (A4124)
☎ (0922) 405872
12–3, 5 (6 Sat)–11
Ansells Mild; Ind Coope Burton Ale; Tetley Bitter Ⓗ
Large, roadside hostelry with rooms of different styles. No food Sun. ◐ ⊟ ♿ ♣ P

Pheasant
Wood End Road
☎ (0902) 725548
11–3, 5.30–11
HP&D Bitter, Mild, Entire; Tetley Bitter Ⓗ
Large, suburban pub with an island bar, serving a varied clientele. No food weekends.
⛫ ❀ ◐ ♣ P

Pyle Cock
Rookery Street (A4124)
☎ (0902) 732125
10.30–11
Banks's Mild, Bitter Ⓔ
Locals' boozer with lovely etched windows depicting a pyle cock. Q ♣ P

West Bromwich

Churchfield Tavern
18 Little Lane (next to Sandwell General Hospital)
11–11
Banks's Hanson's Mild, Mild, Bitter Ⓔ
Three-roomed pub: a small bar, a pleasant lounge and a games room. Livestock and children's play area in the garden. ⛟ ❀ ◐ ⊟ ♿ ♣

Sow & Pigs
Hill Top (A41)
☎ (021) 553 3127
12–11
Banks's Hanson's Mild, Bitter Ⓔ
Popular, two-roomed local where the decor celebrates the role of pigs in Black Country culture. Q ❀ ◐ ◑ ♣ ⌓

Wheatsheaf
High Street, Carter's Green (off A41) ☎ (021) 553 4221
11–11; 12–2.30, 7–10.30 Sun
Holden's Mild, Bitter Ⓗ/Ⓔ**, Special** Ⓗ
Two-roomed pub with a lively bar and a quieter lounge at the rear. Eve meals Sat.
❀ ◐ ◑ ♣ ⌓

Try also: Nelson, New St (M&B); **Vine,** Roebuck St (Free)

Willenhall

Brewers Droop
44 Wolverhampton Street (behind Lock Museum)
☎ (0902) 607827
12–3 (4 Sat), 6–11
Batham Best Bitter; Everards Old Original; Hook Norton Old Hooky; S&N Theakston Old Peculier Ⓗ**; guest beers**
Comfortable, two-roomed former coaching house which holds a mini-beer festival every two months. Folk club Thu, quiz alternate Tue and regular 'Black Country Nites Out'.
◐ ◑ ♣

Falcon
Gomer Street West
☎ (0902) 633378
12–11
Banks's Mild, Bitter Ⓔ**; Ruddles County; Samuel Smith OBB** Ⓗ**; guest beers**
Well-hidden, two-roomed local with a strong darts following. Guest beers vary widely. ❀ ⊟ ♣ ⌓

Robin Hood
54 The Crescent
☎ (0902) 608006
12–3 (3.30 Sat), 5.30 (7 Sat)–11; 12–2.30, 7–10.30 Sun
Ansells Mild; Ind Coope Burton Ale; Tetley Bitter; guest beers Ⓗ
Eleventh consecutive year in the *Guide*: everything a small pub should be. The guest beers are changed regularly.
❀ ♣ P

Wolverhampton

Brewery Tap
Dudley Road ☎ (0902) 351417
12–11

HP&D Bitter, Mild, Entire, Deakin's Downfall; Tetley Bitter H
Multi-alcoved hostelry with a viewing gallery to the brewery at the rear. HP&D's Victorian Black Country alehouse style of decor. No food Sun.
P

Clarendon Hotel
38 Chapel Ash (A41, off ring road) ☎ (0902) 20587
11–11
Banks's Mild, Bitter E**; Camerons Strongarm** H
Banks's brewery tap, recently spoiled by progress, with the loss of the public and corridor bars. Weekday lunches. P

Combermere Arms
On A41, at Chapel Ash
☎ (0902) 21880
11–2.30, 6–11
Draught Bass; M&B Highgate Mild; Stones Best Bitter H
Cunningly disguised as a terraced house: a small lounge, a smoke room, a games room and a corridor, all served by one bar. Note the tree growing in the gents'.

Feathers
Molineux Street
☎ (0902) 26924
11–3, 5–11; 12–11 Fri; 11–11 Sat (closes Sat afternoon when Wolves are at home)
Banks's Mild, Bitter E
Small, friendly local, handy for the university and football ground. Award-winning garden. Weekday lunches.

Fox & Goose
430 Penn Road
☎ (0902) 332191
12–3, 5.30–11
HP&D Bitter, Mild, Entire H
One-roomed, typical HP&D pub in a timber-framed building with steps to the entrance. P

Great Western
Sun Street ☎ (0902) 351090
11–11; 11–2.30, 5.15–11 Sat; 12–2.30, 7–10.30 Sun
Batham Best Bitter; Holden's Mild, Bitter, Special H
CAMRA national *Pub of the Year* 1991; a revitalised pub next to the old low level station, displaying railway memorabilia. Excellent value Black Country food. A Grade II-listed building with a pleasant lounge extension.
P

Homestead
Lodge Road, Oxley (off A449; vehicle access through housing estate) ☎ (0902) 787357
11–2.30 (3 Sat), 6–11

Ansells Bitter, Mild; Ind Coope Burton Ale; Marston's Pedigree H
Large, pleasant suburban pub with an excellent children's playground, a plush lounge and a roomy bar. P

Lewisham Arms
69 Prosser Street, Park Village (off A460) ☎ (0902) 53505
11.30–3, 6–11; 11–11 Sat
Banks's Mild, Bitter E
Glorious Victorian alehouse with etched windows and iron balconies. A large, unspoilt bar caters for all; small smoke room.

Newhampton Inn
Riches Street (off A41)
☎ (0902) 745773
11–11
Courage Best Bitter, Directors; Marston's Pedigree; Ruddles County; John Smith's Bitter; guest beers H
Surprisingly large, street-corner local with an extensive garden and a bowling green. Three rooms draw a diverse clientele. Daily changes in the guest beer and cider.
Q

Paget Arms
Park Lane (off A460)
☎ (0902) 731136
12–3 (3.30 Sat), 6 (7 Sat)–11
Home Mild, Bitter; S&N Theakston Mild, XB, Old Peculier H**; guest beers**
Large estate pub with three rooms of different character. Note the clock built into the outside wall. Weekday lunches. P

Parkfield Tavern
Parkfield Road (A4039)
☎ (0902) 342996
12–4, 6–11; 12–11 Fri & Sat
Banks's Hanson's Mild, Bitter E
Turn-of-the-century town pub, recently well-refurbished.
Q P

Posada
Lichfield Street
☎ (0902) 710738
11–2.30, 5–10.30; 11–10.30 Fri & Sat (closes Sat afternoon when Wolves are at home)
HP&D Mild, Entire, Deakin's Downfall, Plant's Progress; Tetley Bitter H
Victorian pub with its original bar, fittings and tiled front. The only HP&D outlet in the town centre; popular with students. Weekday lunches.

Stamford Arms
Lime Street (off Lea Rd)
☎ (0902) 24172
12–3, 6–11; 12–11 Sat

Banks's Mild, Bitter E
Street-corner, Victorian local comprising several rooms. Notable exterior tiling.
Q

Swan
Bridgnorth Road, Compton
☎ (0902) 754736
11–3, 5–11; 11–11 Sat
Banks's Mild, Bitter H
Mostly Victorian pub with a lounge, bar and snug, on a busy corner. Q P

Westacres
Finchfield Hill
☎ (0902) 757922
12–2.30, 5.30–11
HP&D Bitter, Mild, Entire; Tetley Bitter H
Popular one-roomer: a typical HP&D pub, recently altered internally to provide alcoves.
P

Woodcross

Horse & Jockey
Robert Wynd ☎ (0902) 884552
12–3, 7–11
Banks's Mild, Bitter E**; Marston's Pedigree; Tetley Bitter** H**; guest beers**
Well-renovated local with keen darts and dominoes teams. Near Sedgley Beacon. No food Sun (till 8.30 other eves). P

Woodsetton

Park Inn
George Street (off A457/A4123) ☎ (0902) 882843
11–11
Holden's Stout, Mild, Bitter, Special H
Friendly, comfortable brewery tap which holds regular all-weather barbecues in a large conservatory. Holden's XB is sold as Lucy B Bitter. Popular with office workers at lunchtime. No food Sun.
(Tipton) P

Try also: Swan, Sedgley Rd (Free)

Wordsley

Samson & Lion
140 Brierley Hill Road (B4180)
☎ (0384) 77796
11.30–11
Banks's Mild; Batham Best Bitter; Enville Ale H**; guest beers**
Sympathetically restored hostelry next to lock 4 on the Stourbridge Canal. Facilities for boaters; skittle alley; barbecues in summer. No meals Sun eve.
P

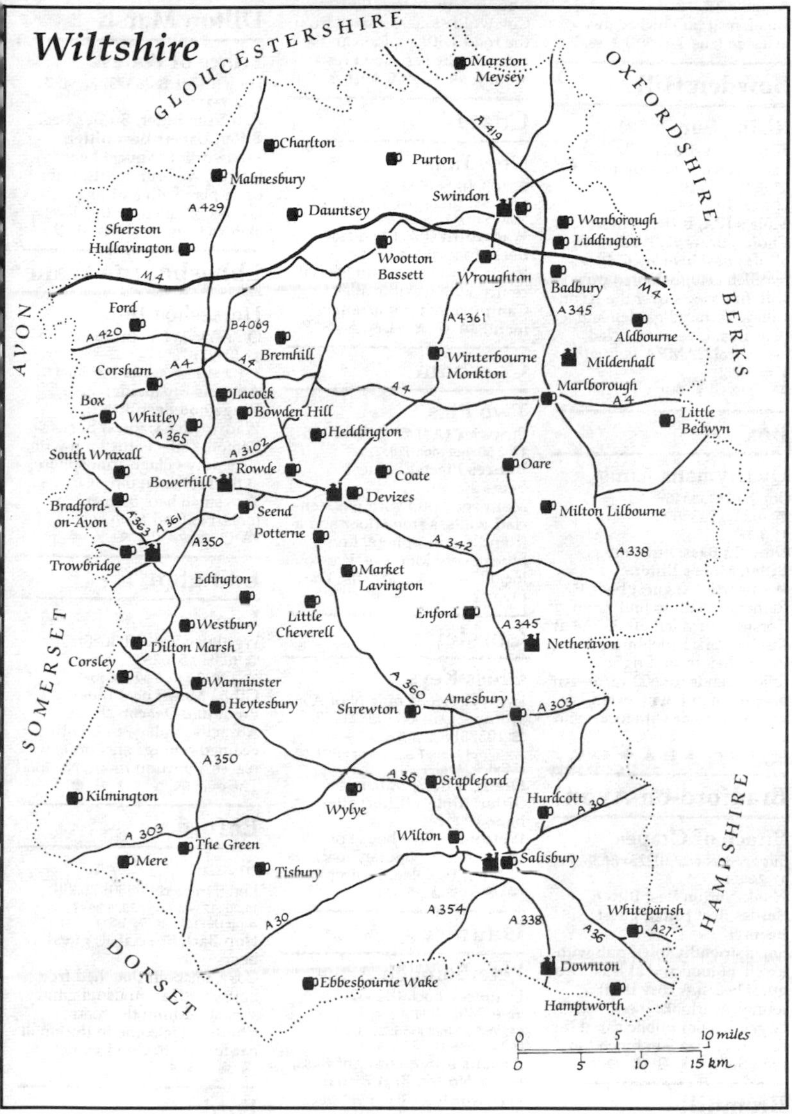

Archers, Arkell's, *Swindon;* **Bunces,** *Netheravon;* **Foxley,** *Mildenhall;* **Gibbs Mew,** *Salisbury;* **Hop Back,** *Downton/Salisbury;* **Mole's,** *Bowerhill;* **Ushers,** *Trowbridge;* **Wadworth,** *Devizes*

Aldbourne

Blue Boar

The Green ☎ (0672) 40237
11–3, 6–11
Wadworth IPA, 6X Ⓗ
Old, picturesque pub overlooking an idyllic village green. No food Sun eve.
Q P

Amesbury

Antrobus Arms Hotel

Church Street ☎ (0980) 623163
10.30–2.30, 6–11
Draught Bass; Wadworth IPA (summer), **6X, Old Timer** Ⓗ
Georgian three-star hotel near Stonehenge. A pleasant high-ceilinged bar with coaching memorabilia and a secluded, walled rear garden.
Q P

Badbury

Bakers Arms

Off A346, near M4 jct 15
☎ (0793) 740313
11–3, 6–11

Arkell's 2B, 3B [H]
Small, neat pub tucked away in a side lane. ♔ ❀ ◖ ◗ ♣ P

Bowden Hill

Rising Sun
32 Bowden Hill (1 mile E of Lacock past abbey, up hill)
☎ (0249) 730363
11–2.30, 6–11
Mole's IPA, Bitter, Landlord's Choice, Brew 97; Wadworth 6X [H]**; guest beer** [H]/[G]
Excellent, stone-floored pub with fine views over the Avon valley. Terraced garden and play area. Live music Wed eve. Local CAMRA *Pub of the Year* 1992.
♔ Q ❀ ◖ ◗ ♣ ⌓ P

Box

Quarrymans Arms
Box Hill OS834693
☎ (0225) 743569
11–3, 7–11
Draught Bass; Butcombe Bitter; Mole's Bitter, Wadworth 6X; guest beer [H]
Rather difficult to find: from Corsham turn left off the A4 at Rudloe Park Hotel into Beech Road, then second right; follow bends for 600 yards. An open-plan pub with extensive views, popular with locals and visitors.
♔ ❀ 🛏 ◖ ◗ ⊟ ▲ ♣ ⌓ P

Bradford-on-Avon

Bunch of Grapes
Silver Street ☎ (0225) 863877
11–2.30, 6.30–11
Hook Norton Best Bitter; Smiles Best Bitter; guest beers [H]
Small, friendly town pub with excellent food and at least two guest beers. A cosy front lounge overlooks the street; larger, livelier public bar at the rear. Live jazz Sun lunch (no food Sun). ◖ ◗ ⊟ ⇌ ♣ ⌓

Bremhill

Dumb Post
Dumb Post Hill (signed from A4) OS975727 ☎ (0249) 813192
11.30–2.30 (not Wed), 7–11
Archers Best Bitter; Wadworth IPA, 6X, Old Timer [H]**; guest beers**
Comfortable, friendly free house, offering the best value beer in the area. A parrot is in residence. ♔ ❀ ◖ ⊟ ♣ P

Charlton

Horse & Groom
On B4040 ☎ (0666) 823904
12–2.30, 7–11
Archers Village; Mole's Bitter; Wadworth 6X [H]
Country inn in traditional Cotswold stone, set back from the road with a saloon and a large public bar. Good restaurant. ♔ Q ❀ ◖ ◗ ⊟ ♿ P

Coate

New Inn
☎ (0380) 860644
12–2 (not Tue or Thu; 11–3.30 Sat), 5 (6.30 Sat)–11
Wadworth IPA, 6X; guest beers (occasionally) [G]
Village local, a thriving social centre with a skittle alley. Camping by prior arrangement. ♔ Q ❀ ⊟ ♿ ▲ ♣ P

Corsham

Two Pigs
Pickwick (A4) ☎ (0249) 712515
12–2.30 (not Mon–Fri), 7–11
Bunces Pigswill; guest beers [H]
Main-road pub with wooden-clad walls, a stone floor and a friendly atmosphere. Live blues every Mon eve. Previous local CAMRA *Pub of the Year*. Over 21s only. ♔ ❀ ⌓

Corsley

Cross Keys
Lye's Green (½ mile N of A362 at Royal Oak jct) OS821462
☎ (0373) 832406
12–3 (not Mon, Tue, Thu or Fri), 6.30 (7 Sat & Mon)–11
Draught Bass; Butcombe Bitter; Mole's Bitter; guest beer [H]
Welcoming free house of character. A popular, spacious pub with a splendid fireplace.
♔ ❀ ◖ ◗ ▲ ♣ ⌓ P

Dauntsey

Peterborough Arms
Dauntsey Lock (B4069)
☎ (0249) 890409
11.30–2.30 (not Mon; 11–3 Sat), 6 (7.30 Mon)–11
Ansells Bitter; Draught Bass; Hook Norton Best Bitter; Wadworth 6X [H]**; guest beer**
Friendly pub where the comfortable lounge has a display of foreign currency. Children welcome in the skittle alley. Good range of food (no food Mon). Campsite for caravans.
♔ Q 🚼 ❀ ◖ ◗ P

Devizes

Hare & Hounds
Hare & Hounds Street
☎ (0380) 723231
11–2.30 (3 Sat), 7–11
Wadworth IPA, 6X [H]
Friendly local, slightly away from the centre. Parts are over 300 years old, but there have been additions over the years. Pub games strongly featured. No food Sun. ♔ ❀ ◖ ♣ P

Dilton Marsh

Prince of Wales
High Street ☎ (0373) 865487
11–3, 7–11
Ash Vine Bitter; Smiles Best Bitter; Ushers Best Bitter; Wadworth 6X; guest beer [H]
Simple, well-run locals' pub: open-plan with a dining area. Games-oriented, with a lively skittles team. ❀ ◖ ⇌ ♣ P

Ebbesbourne Wake

Horseshoe Inn
Off A30 via Fovant
☎ (0722) 780474
11 (12 Mon)–2.30, 6.30 (7 Mon)–11
Adnams Broadside; Ringwood Best Bitter; Wadworth 6X; guest beers [G]
Remote 18th-century inn with a friendly village atmosphere, at the foot of an old ox drove. Two small bars displaying old tools. No food Mon eve.
♔ Q ❀ 🛏 ◖ ◗ ⊟ ▲ ♣ P

Edington

Lamb
Westbury Road (B3098)
☎ (0380) 830263
11–2.30 (3 Sat), 5.30 (6 Sat)–11
Gibbs Mew Local Line, Premium, Deacon [H]
Attractive village pub with beamed ceilings and stone fireplaces. Function room. No food Tue eve. ♔ ❀ ◖ ◗ ⊟ ♣ P

Enford

Swan
Longstreet ☎ (0980) 70338
11.30 (12 winter)–2.30, 6.30 (7 winter)–11; 11–6, 7–11 Sat
Hop Back Special [H]**; guest beers**
Cosy, unspoilt thatched free house with an unusual gantry sign straddling the road. Children welcome in the small bar for lunch. Good value.
♔ ❀ ◖ ◗ ♣ P

Ford

White Hart
Off A420 ☎ (0249) 782213
11–3, 5–11
Draught Bass; Hall & Woodhouse Badger Best Bitter, Tanglefoot; Marston's Pedigree; Smiles Exhibition; Wadworth 6X [H]**; guest beers**
Superb old country pub beside a stream. Its restaurant has a good reputation.
♔ Q 🚼 ❀ 🛏 ◖ ◗ ♿ ⌓ P

The Green

Fox & Hounds
Off A30 at Whillby Hedge OS807932 ☎ (0747) 830573
11–2.30, 6–11

Marston's Pedigree; Smiles Bitter; Wadworth 6X Ⓗ; guest beers
Remote 14th-century, thatched, hillside inn with views of the Blackmore vale. The cosy, rambling interior has three bars, a children's room and a skittle alley. Popular with walkers and cyclists.
♛ Q ☋ ❀ ◖ ◗ ⊟ ▲ ♣ ⌂ P ⊬

Hamptworth

Cuckoo Inn
Off A36, onto B3079, 1st right, then ½ mile OS243197
☎ (0794) 390302
11.30–2.30, 6–11; 11.30–11 Sat
Draught Bass; Bunces Best Bitter; Hall & Woodhouse Badger Best Bitter, Tanglefoot; Wadworth 6X; guest beers Ⓖ
Popular pub in a rural setting: four small, interlinked rooms of public bar standard in a 300-year-old, unspoilt thatched cottage. Good garden for children; snacks available.
♛ Q ☋ ❀ ♿ ▲ ♣ ⌂ P

Heddington

Ivy
Off A3102/A4
☎ (0380) 850276
11–3, 6.30–11
Wadworth IPA, 6X, Old Timer Ⓖ
Old, stone, thatched pub with one bar and a garden.
♛ Q ☋ ❀ ▲ ♣ ⌂ P

Heytesbury

Angel Inn
High Street ☎ (0985) 40330
11–3, 6 (6.30 winter)–11
Fuller's London Pride; Marston's Bitter, Pedigree; Ringwood Best Bitter; guest beer Ⓗ
17th-century coaching inn with a highly regarded restaurant and accommodation. Strong local trade from the friendly village, now bypassed. ♛ ❀ 🛏 ◖ ◗ ♣ P

Hullavington

Queens Head
24 The Street ☎ (0666) 837221
11.30–2, 7–11
Archers Village; Wadworth 6X Ⓗ; guest beer
Homely village local where the open fires and recent refurbishment generate a warm atmosphere. Small function room and skittle alley. No food Sun; weekly guest beer. ♛ Q ❀ 🛏 ♿ P

Hurdcott

Black Horse
Black Horse Lane (off A338)
☎ (0980) 611565
11–2.30, 6–11; 11–11 Sat; 12–2.30, 7–10.30 Sun
Gibbs Mew Salisbury, Deacon Ⓗ
Old building at the end of a country lane, formerly three cottages and a forge. Wattle and daub upstairs; beamed bar below. Became a pub around the turn of the century. Good company. No food Mon, except bank hols. Q ❀ ◖ ◗ P

Kilmington

Red Lion
On B3092 ☎ (0985) 844263
11–3, 6.30–11
Butcombe Bitter; Marston's Pedigree; guest beers Ⓗ
Unspoilt, NT-owned pub near Stourhead Gardens. The single bar has a curtained-off area. Good choice of food (not served Fri/Sat eves).
♛ Q ❀ 🛏 ◖ ◗ ♣ ⌂ P

Lacock

George Inn
4 West Street ☎ (0249) 730263
11–3, 5.30–11
Wadworth IPA, 6X, Farmer's Glory Ⓗ
Traditional, cosy inn at the centre of a charming NT village. ♛ Q ☋ ❀ 🛏 ◖ ◗ ⊟ ♣ P ⊬

Liddington

Village Inn
Ham Road ☎ (0793) 790314
12–2.30, 6–11
Draught Bass; Fuller's ESB; Wadworth 6X; Whitbread Flowers Original Ⓗ; guest beers
Cosy, carpeted, split-level lounge bar with red-brick facings and fireplace. No food Sun eve. ♛ Q ❀ 🛏 ◖ ◗ P

Little Bedwyn

Harrow
Off A4 ☎ (0672) 870871
11–2.30 (not Mon), 5.30–11
Hook Norton Best Bitter; guest beers Ⓗ
Pub saved and owned by a village co-operative; smart, intimate and cosy. No food Sun eve. ♛ Q ❀ 🛏 ◖ ◗ ♣

Little Cheverell

Owl
Lower Road ☎ (0380) 812263
12–3 (not Mon–Fri), 7–11
Wadworth IPA, 6X; guest beers Ⓗ
Welcoming village pub with a pleasant garden. Occasional ciders. No meals Mon.
♛ Q ❀ ◖ ◗ ♿ ▲ ♣ ⌂ P

Malmesbury

Red Bull
Sherston Road (B4040, W of town) ☎ (0666) 822108
11–2.30 (3.30 Sat; not Tue), 7 (6 summer)–11
Draught Bass; Whitbread WCPA, Boddingtons Bitter Ⓗ; guest beers
Popular family pub with a children's room/skittle alley.
♛ Q ☋ ❀ ◖ ♿ P

Whole Hog
Market Cross ☎ (0666) 825845
11–11
Archers Best Bitter; Wadworth 6X; guest beer Ⓗ
Former genteel restaurant adjacent to an ancient market cross, now a lively pub/wine bar with a restaurant. The house beer, Pigswill (not Bunces), is very economically priced. Newspapers. Q ◖ ◗

Market Lavington

Drummer Boy
25 Church Street
☎ (0380) 812329
12–2.30 (not Mon), 6–11
Fuller's London Pride; John Smith's Bitter; Wadworth IPA, 6X Ⓗ
Popular village-centre local. Interesting story behind the name. ♛ ❀ ♿ ♣ P

Marlborough

Green Dragon
High Street ☎ (0672) 512366
11–2.30, 7–11
Wadworth IPA, 6X Ⓗ
Old building with a busy bar and rooms below. Popular with the younger set eves.
❀ 🛏 ◖ ◗ ♣

Marston Meysey

Spotted Cow
2½ miles from A419 OS129969
☎ (0285) 810264
11–3 (later Fri & Sat), 6–11
Marston's Pedigree; John Smith's Bitter; Wadworth 6X Ⓗ; guest beer
Cotswold stone building, originally a farmhouse. A popular local, with six darts teams and a quiz Sun. Low-price guest beer usually.
♛ ☋ ❀ 🛏 ◖ ◗ ▲ ♣ P

Mere

Butt of Sherry
Castle Street (B3095)
☎ (0747) 860352
11.30 (11 Sat)–3, 5–11
Gibbs Mew Premium, Deacon, Bishop's Tipple; Ind Coope Burton Ale Ⓗ
Traditional bar with a lively local trade. Public car park opposite. ♛ ◖ ◗ ♣

Milton Lilbourne

Three Horseshoes
On B3087 ☎ (0672) 62323
11.30–2.30 (not Mon), 6.30–11
Adnams Bitter; Wadworth 6X; guest beer Ⓗ

Smart, open-plan bar featuring a 30-ft well. No food Sun eve/Mon.
🔥 Q 🚼 ❀ ◖ ◗ ▲ ♣ P

Oare

White Hart

On A345 ☎ (0672) 62273
11–2.30 (3 Sat), 7–11
Wadworth IPA, 6X; guest beer Ⓗ
Genuine village local. No meals Mon lunch or Tue eve.
🔥 ❀ 🛏 ◖ ◗ ⊟ ♣ P

Potterne

George & Dragon

High Street ☎ (0380) 722139
12–2.30 (not winter Mon), 6.30–11
Wadworth IPA, 6X; guest beers Ⓗ
Thatched, 15th-century roadside inn. The interior has been altered over the years, but is comfortable and retains some early features. Dining room and a skittle alley.
🚼 ❀ 🛏 ◖ ◗ ♣ P

Purton

Home From Home

Pavenhill ☎ (0793) 770077
12–3 (not Mon–Fri), 7–11
Oakhill Bitter; Wadworth 6X Ⓗ**; guest beer**
Very friendly pub with live music on Fri or Sat nights and good value food (not served Sun lunch). ❀ ◖ ◗ ♿

Rowde

Cross Keys

High Street ☎ (0380) 722368
11.30–3, 7–11
Wadworth IPA, 6X, Old Timer Ⓗ
Big, busy pub, rebuilt in 1938.
🔥 Q ❀ ◖ ◗ ♿ ▲ ♣ P

George & Dragon

High Street ☎ (0380) 723053
12–3 (not Mon), 7–11
Wadworth IPA, 6X, Old Timer Ⓖ
Friendly old pub set high above the road, offering good food: fish dishes a speciality.
🔥 Q ❀ ◖ ▲ ♣ P

Salisbury

Anchor Inn

Gigant Street ☎ (0722) 330680
11–3, 5–11
Gibbs Mew Wiltshire, Premium, Salisbury, Deacon Ⓗ
16th-century listed building, which used to be the brewery tap. A popular venue for locals at lunchtime. ◖ ♿ ♣

Avon Brewery Inn

Castle Street ☎ (0722) 327280
11–11
Eldridge Pope Dorchester Ⓗ**, Hardy Country, Blackdown Porter** (winter) Ⓔ**, Royal Oak** Ⓗ
Victorian city-centre pub with a lively clientele, a riverside garden and a splendid, frosted bow window. Excellent value traditional food – try the hot beef sandwiches. ❀ ◖ ♣

Haunch of Venison

Minster Street ☎ (0722) 322024
11–11
Courage Best Bitter, Directors Ⓗ
Old English chop house (circa 1320), now a busy city-centre pub with many historic and unusual features, including a mummified hand, a pewter-topped bar and rows of taps. No meals Sun eve. 21st year in this guide. 🔥 Q ◖ ◗ ≠

Village Inn

33 Wilton Road (A30/A36 W of centre) ☎ (0722) 329707
11–11 (11–3.30, 5.30–11 winter)
Hampshire King Alfred's, Lionheart; Oakhill Bitter; Taylor Landlord; St Austell XXXX Mild Ⓗ**; guest beers**
Convivial pub with a cosy atmosphere. The cellar bar has a piano. Popular with railway enthusiasts. ≠ ♣

Wyndham Arms

27 Estcourt Road (½ mile NE of centre) ☎ (0722) 328594
4.30 (4 Fri, 12 Sat)–11
Hop Back Mild, GFB, Special, Summer Lightning, Wheat Beer Ⓗ
Small, back-street brew pub. Good atmosphere and excellent value. ♣

Seend

Bell

Bell Hill (A361)
☎ (0380) 828338
11–3, 6–11; 11–11 Sat
Wadworth IPA, 6X Ⓗ
Cosy lounge and larger public bar in a well-run inn. The imposing former brewery at the rear is now used for cream teas in summer. Sweeping views. No food Sun.
🔥 Q 🚼 ❀ ◖ ⊟ ♣ P

Sherston

Rattlebone Inn

Church Street ☎ (0666) 840871
12–3, 5.30–11; 12–11 Sat
Smiles Best Bitter; Wadworth 6X Ⓗ**; guest beer**
Lively 16th-century free house with a comfortable, foody lounge and a public bar with games. Restaurant; garden with boules.
🔥 Q ❀ ◖ ◗ ♿ ▲ ♣ P

Shrewton

George Inn

London Road (B3086)
☎ (0980) 620341
11–3 (not Wed), 6–11
Ushers Best Bitter; Wadworth 6X; guest beer Ⓗ
Part-15th-century chalk, flint and stone inn, which once housed a brewery. Excellent food. 🔥 🚼 ❀ ◖ ◗ ▲ ♣ P

South Wraxall

Longs Arms

Upper South Wraxall (off B3109) ☎ (0225) 864450
12–2.30 (3 Sat), 5.30 (7 Sat)–11
Wadworth IPA, 6X Ⓗ
Relaxed, friendly village pub with a spacious, comfortable lounge and a snug locals' public bar. A popular venue for skittles. No food Sun eve or Mon. 🔥 Q ❀ ◖ ◗ ⊟ ♣ P

Stapleford

Pelican Inn

Warminster Road (A36)
☎ (0722) 790241
11–2.30 (3 Sat), 6–11
Otter Bitter; Ringwood Best Bitter, Fortyniner Ⓗ**; guest beer**
18th-century inn, a former stables and mortuary, with a River Til frontage. Excellent value: the cheapest ale in Wilts and large helpings of good food. Pitchers of ale at bargain prices; unusual guest beers. The safe garden has children's games. 🔥 ❀ 🛏 ◖ ◗ ♣ P

Swindon

Clifton Inn

Clifton Street ☎ (0793) 523162
11–2.30, 6–11; 12–2, 7–10.30 Sun
Arkell's 2B, 3B, Kingsdown Ⓗ
Cheerful, airy open-plan bar; hard to find. Lunchtime snacks. ❀ ♿ ♣ P

Glue Pot

Emlyn Square ☎ (0793) 523935
11–11
Archers Village, Best Bitter, Golden, Black Jack, Old Cobleigh's Ⓗ**; guest beer**
Listed stone building in Swindon's railway village, a local CAMRA *Pub of the Season*. No food Sun. ◖ ≠ ♣

Kings Arms Hotel

Wood Street, Old Town
☎ (0793) 522156
11–3, 6–11
Arkell's 2B, Mash Tun Mild, 3B, Kingsdown Ⓗ
Large hotel bar in the old town. No food Sun eve.
🚼 🛏 ◖ ◗ ♿ P

Rising Sun
Albert Street, Old Town
☎ (0793) 529916
11–11
Courage Best Bitter; Ushers Best Bitter, Founders Ⓗ
Busy, back-street pub, referred to as the Roaring Donkey. Bulmers cider. Q ⊞ ♣ ⌓

Swiss Chalet
Chapel Street ☎ (0793) 535610
11–3, 5.30–11
Arkell's 2B, Mash Tun Mild, 3B, Kingsdown Ⓗ
Large single bar with bands several nights a week. ❀ ◐ P

Wheatsheaf
Newport Street, Old Town
☎ (0793) 523188
11–2.30, 5.30 (6 Sat)–11
Wadworth IPA, 6X, Farmer's Glory, Old Timer Ⓗ**; guest beers**
Popular two-bar pub: a lively rear lounge with a quieter front bar. Very crowded weekends. Q ❀ 🛏 ◐ ◑ ⊞ ♿ ♣

Tisbury

Crown
Church Street ☎ (0747) 870221
11–2.30, 7–11
Gibbs Mew Local Line, Salisbury, Deacon Ⓗ
Recently refurbished coaching inn; a listed building playing quiet background music. Good food (special price lunch for OAPs); a skittle alley, darts and a family room.
🏰 ⛾ ◐ ◑ ⊞ ♿ ⇶ ♣ ⌓ P

Trowbridge

Rose & Crown
36 Stallard Street (opp. station)
☎ (0225) 752862
12–3 (5 Sat), 7–11
Courage Directors *or* **Morland Old Speckled Hen; Ushers Best Bitter; Wadworth 6X** Ⓗ
Small, two-bar pub; the public bar features sporting memorabilia. 🏰 Q ◐ ◑ ⊞ ⇶ ♣ ⌓

Wanborough

Black Horse
Callas Hill (at crossroads S end of village) ☎ (0793) 790305
11–3, 5.30–11; 11–11 Sat
Arkell's 2B, Mash Tun Mild *or* **Noel Ale, 3B, Kingsdown** (occasionally) Ⓗ
Classic, classless village alehouse. Garden with goats; bar with backchat. CAMRA regional *Pub of the Year* 1992. No food Sun. ❀ ◐ ⊞ ▲ ♣ P

Plough
High Street ☎ (0793) 790523
11–2.30, 5–11; 11–11 Fri & Sat
Archers Village; Draught Bass; Morland Old Speckled Hen; Wadworth 6X; Whitbread Boddingtons Bitter Ⓗ**; guest beer**
Pretty, thatched pub with long, beamed, stone-walled bars. Weekday lunches.
🏰 Q ❀ ◐ ⊞ ♣ P

Warminster

Masons Arms
East Street ☎ (0985) 212894
11–2.30, 6–11; 11–11 games bar
Draught Bass Ⓗ
Popular locals' pub with a cosy lounge bar and a games room.
Q ◐ ⊞ ⇶ ♣ ⌓ P

Westbury

Oak Inn
Warminster Road (A350)
☎ (0373) 823169
12–3 (not Mon–Fri), 5 (6 Sat)–11
Draught Bass; Ringwood Best Bitter, XXXX Porter, Fortyniner Ⓗ
A mock Tudor exterior conceals a 16th-century inn with more recent additions. A former brewery at the rear is used as offices. ❀ ⊞ ♣ P

Whiteparish

Kings Head
The Street ☎ (0794) 884287
11–2.30 (3 Sat), 6–11
Ringwood Best Bitter Ⓗ/Ⓖ**; Whitbread Strong Country; guest beers** Ⓗ
Friendly, one (public)-bar local with a convivial atmosphere. No food Mon or Tue lunchtime. Caters for all tastes.
🏰 Q ❀ ◐ ◑ ▲ ♣ ⌓ P

Whitley

Pear Tree
Top Lane ☎ (0225) 709131
12–3, 7–11
Eldridge Pope Dorchester, Hardy Country; Hall & Woodhouse Badger Best Bitter; Wadworth 6X Ⓗ**; guest beer**
Delightful pub in an unspoilt village setting, with a half-acre garden and children's play area, duck pond and animals. Regular skittles nights. Barbecues in summer; restaurant upstairs. At least four ales.
Q ⛾ ❀ ◐ ◑ ♣ P

Wilton

Bear Inn
West Street
☎ (0722) 742398
11–3 (4 Sat), 5 (6 Sat)–11
Hall & Woodhouse Badger Best Bitter Ⓗ
16th-century roadside inn with a warm welcome. A one-bar pub, once known as the Drum & Monkey. 🏰 ❀ ♣

Winterbourne Monkton

New Inn
Off A4361 ☎ (067 23) 240
11–3, 6–11
Adnams Bitter; Wadworth 6X; guest beer Ⓗ
Small, friendly local and restaurant, close to Avebury stone circle. 🏰 ❀ 🛏 ◐ ◑ ♿ ♣ P

Wootton Bassett

Old Nick
Station Road ☎ (0793) 848102
11–11
Courage Bitter Ale; Berrow 4Bs, Topsy Turvy; John Smith's Bitter; Wadworth 6X Ⓗ**; guest beer**
Formerly the police station, now an extensive bar. The adjoining courthouse is now a disco bar. Regular beer exhibitions. Scrumpy is cheap. Children welcome.
❀ ◐ ◑ ⊞ ♿ ♣ ⌓ P

Waggon & Horses
High Street ☎ (0793) 852326
10.30–11
Archers Village, Best Bitter; Draught Bass; Ind Coope Burton Ale; Tetley Bitter Ⓗ**; guest beer**
Very old building offering three guest beers. Children welcome. No food Sun eve. Small car park. ◐ ◑ ⊞ ♣ P

Wroughton

Carters Rest
High Street ☎ (0793) 812288
11.30–2.30, 5.30–11; 11.30–11 Sat
Archers Village, Best Bitter, Golden; Marston's Owd Rodger; Morland Old Speckled Hen; Ushers Founders Ⓗ**; guest beers**
Built in 1904, a former Courage house with two busy bars. Usually ten beers (four guests). 🏰 ❀ ◐ ⊞ ♣ P

Wylye

Bell
High Street ☎ (098 56) 338
11 (11.30 winter)–2.30, 6–11
Hall & Woodhouse Badger Best Bitter; Wadworth 6X; Wells Eagle; guest beer Ⓗ
14th-century inn in a quiet setting, with beamed bars featuring exposed stone and an inglenook.
🏰 Q ❀ 🛏 ◐ ◑ ♣ P

North Yorkshire

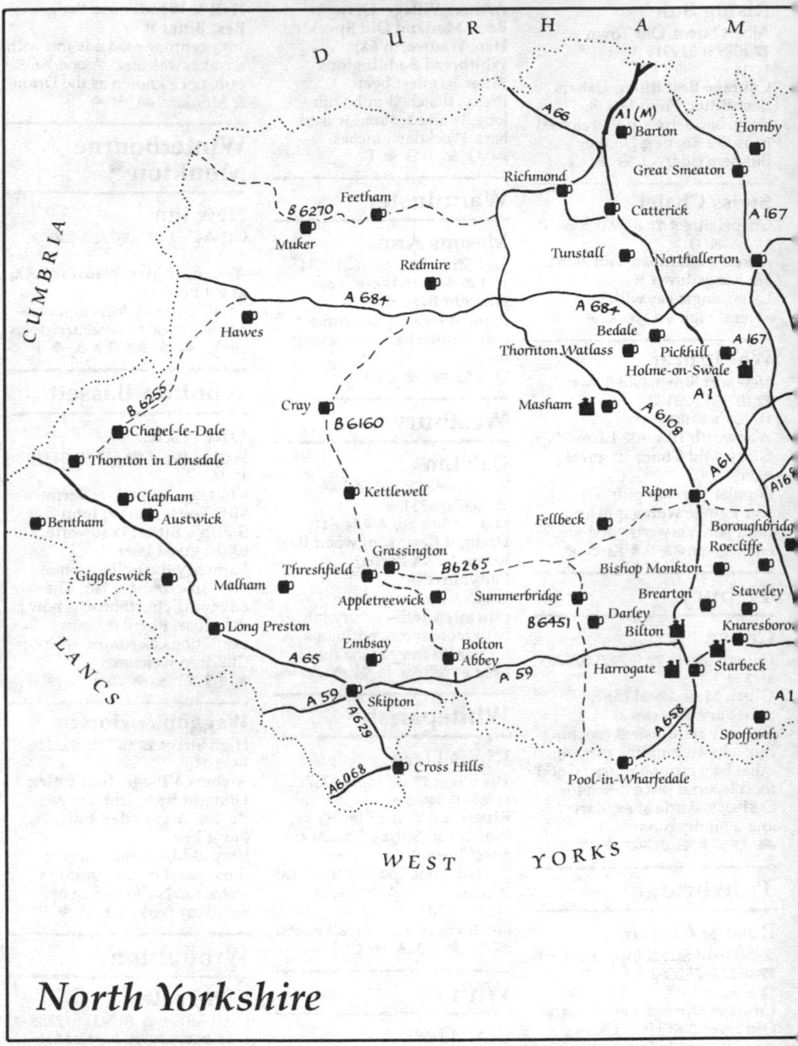

Black Sheep, *Masham;* **Cropton,** *Cropton;* **Daleside,** *Starbeck;* **Franklin's,** *Bilton;* **Hambleton,** *Holme-on-Swale;* **Lastingham,** *Lastingham;* **Malton,** *Malton;* **Marston Moor,** *Kirk Hammerton;* **Rooster's,** *Harrogate;* **Rudgate,** *Tockwith;* **Selby,** *Selby;* **Samuel Smith,** *Tadcaster;* **Whitby's,** *Whitby*

Acaster Malbis

Ship Inn

Moor End ☎ (0904) 705609
11–3, 6.30–11 (11–11 summer)
Taylor Landlord; Tetley Bitter Ⓗ
17th-century coaching inn right beside the river. Once an inn for bargees who plied their trade on the river, now popular with boaters and campers alike. Children's play area. P

Appletreewick

New Inn

Main Street ☎ (0756) 720252
12–3 (not Mon), 7–11
John Smith's Bitter; Younger Scotch, No. 3 (winter) Ⓗ
Friendly inn where the emphasis is on drink. The bar is L-shaped, with a room across the hall. A gated garden is over the road. The large range of foreign beers includes Liefmans Kriek on tap.
Q P

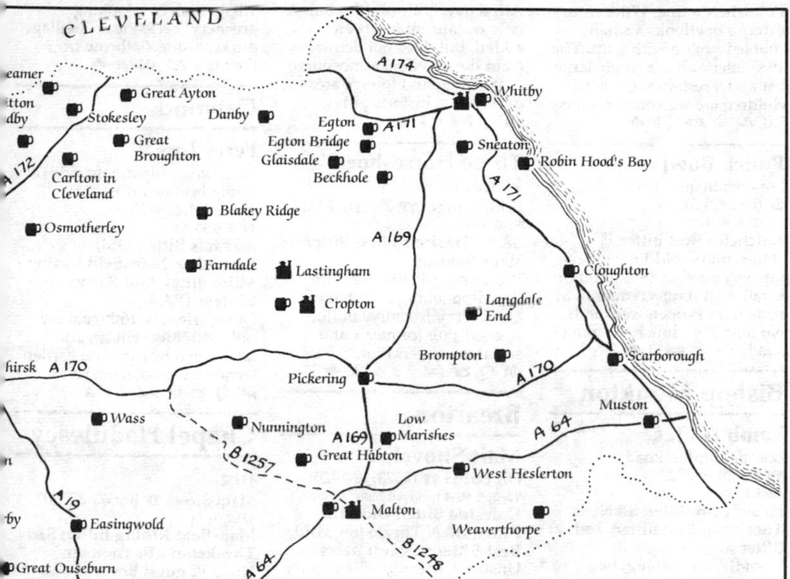

Austwick

Game Cock

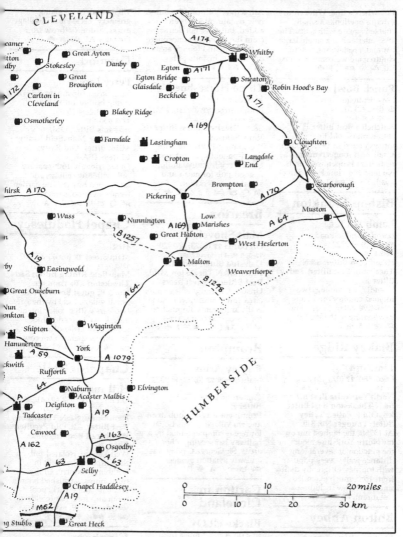

☎ (052 42) 51226
11–2.30, 6.30–11
Thwaites Bitter [H]
Pub with a pristine bar, with Yates & Jackson memorabilia, and a busy dining room overlooking the attractive main street.
❀ ◐ ◑ P

Barton

King William IV

Silver Street
☎ (0325) 377256
11.30–3 (4 Sat; not winter Mon–Fri), 6.30 (4.30 winter Wed–Fri)–11
John Smith's Bitter, Magnet [H]
Roadside local with one large bar and a couple of snugs. The excellent screened garden has play equipment. Local CAMRA *Pub of the Year* 1992.
❀ ◑ ♣ P

Beckhole

Birch Hall Inn

☎ (0947) 86245
11–3, 7–11 (11–11 summer)
S&N Theakston Mild, Best Bitter, XB [H]
Rural gem, originally two cottages now combining a pub, PO and general store: a small front bar and a larger room to the rear. The garden is on a terrace above the pub.
Q ❀ ♣

Bedale

Waggon & Horses

Market Place
☎ (0677) 422747
11–11
Camerons Strongarm [E]; **John Smith's Bitter; Tetley Bitter** [H]
Pub originally two rooms now converted into one, with a convivial atmosphere. Very popular with the locals.
❀ ♿ ♣ P

Bentham

Coach House

Main Street ☎ (052 42) 62305
11–3, 6.30–11
Robinson's Hartleys XB, Best Bitter, Old Tom [H]

Pub where a fine, 17th-century exterior overlooks a small cobbled square with seats. The 1985 interior has a single large bar and a restaurant, where children are welcome. Karaoke Sat. ♛ ❀ 🛏 ◖ ◗ ♣

Punch Bowl

Low Bentham
☎ (052 42) 61344
11.30–2.30, 6–11
Mitchell's Best Bitter Ⓗ
18th-century, old-time village inn, extended in 1986, though small, neat rooms remain. The restaurant is open weekends. No food Mon lunch. Angling available. ❀ 🛏 ◖ ♣ P

Bishop Monkton

Lamb & Flag

Boroughbridge Road
☎ (0765) 677322
12–3, 5.30–11
Hambleton Bitter; S&N Theakston Best Bitter; Tetley Bitter Ⓗ
Friendly, welcoming, two-roomed country inn in an attractive village, featuring pew seating in the lounge.
♛ ❀ ◖ ◗ ♣ P

Blakey Ridge

Lion Inn

OS679997 ☎ (075 15) 320
11–11
North Yorkshire Best Bitter; S&N Theakston Best Bitter, XB, Old Peculier; Tetley Bitter; Younger No. 3 Ⓗ
At 1325ft, the highest inn on the North Yorkshire moors, at the junction of several long distance walks: very popular with tourists. Originally dating from 1552, much extended since, and now including a restaurant. ♛ ❀ 🛏 ◖ ◗ P

Bolton Abbey

Devonshire Arms Hotel (Dukes Bar)

☎ (0756) 710441
11–11
Franklin's Bitter; Tetley Bitter; Whitbread Boddingtons Bitter Ⓗ**; guest beers** (summer)
Comfortable public bar, with sporting memorabilia, attracting a wide variety of clientele, from trippers, hikers and anglers to locals.
♛ 🐎 ❀ 🛏 ◖ ♿ ♣ P

Boroughbridge

Black Bull Inn

St James Square
☎ (0423) 322413
11–3, 6.30–11; 11–11 Fri
Black Sheep Best Bitter; S&N Theakston Best Bitter; John Smith's Bitter Ⓗ
Attractive, 13th-century inn. A new restaurant has been added, but does not detract from the excellent atmosphere of the snug and lounge areas of this fine, historic pub.
♛ Q 🛏 ◖ ◗ ▲

Three Horseshoes Hotel

Bridge Street ☎ (0423) 322314
11–3, 5–11
S&N Theakston Best Bitter Ⓗ**; Vaux Samson** Ⓔ
Welcoming 1930s pub with wood-panelling and stained-glass. Very friendly landlord. A good pub for meals and sociable conversation.
♛ Q 🐎 🛏 ◖ ◗ ♿ ▲ ♣ P

Brearton

Malt Shovel

Off B6165 ☎ (0423) 862929
12–3, 6.45–11; closed Mon
Daleside Bitter; Old Mill Bitter; S&N Theakston Mild, Best Bitter Ⓗ**; guest beers**
Unspoilt, friendly village pub, circa 16th century, with stone walls and beams. Reputation for good food (not served Mon). ♛ Q 🐎 ❀ ◖ ◗ ♣ P

Brompton

Cayley Arms

Main Street ☎ (0723) 859372
11–11
Camerons Bitter; Tetley Bitter Ⓗ
Prominent wayside pub in an ancient village. A functional lounge is complemented by a hallway bar serving other areas. Sir George Cayley was an early aviation pioneer.
♛ 🐎 ❀ ◖ ▲ ♣ P

Carlton in Cleveland

Blackwell Ox

Just off A172, 3 miles from Stokesley ☎ (0642) 712287
12–3, 7–11
Bass Worthington BB, Draught Bass Ⓗ**; guest beers**
Old village local with numerous rooms off a central bar; families welcome. The Thai meals are a speciality. Popular in summer with walkers and campers. The only pub in the village.
♛ Q 🐎 ❀ 🛏 ◖ ◗ ▲ ♣ P

Catterick

Bay Horse Inn

Low Green ☎ (0748) 811383
12–3 (4 Sat; may extend summer), 7–11
S&N Theakston Best Bitter; John Smith's Bitter, Magnet; guest beers Ⓗ
Comfortably refurbished, 100-year-old, traditional village pub overlooking greenery, beckside and village ducks, a stone's throw from the busy A1. ♛ ❀ ♣ P

Cawood

Ferry Inn

King Street (upstream side of swing bridge, off B1222)
☎ (0757) 268515
11–5, 6.30–11
Adnams Bitter, Old, Broadside; Mansfield Riding Mild, Bitter, Old Baily; Ridleys IPA Ⓗ
Quiet, friendly 16th-century pub with low ceilings and a large open hearth. The garden terrace overlooks the river.
♛ Q 🐎 ❀ 🛏 ◖ ◗ ▲ P

Chapel Haddlesey

Jug

Main Street ☎ (0957) 270307
12–3, 7–11
Mansfield Riding Bitter; S&N Theakston XB; Younger No. 3 Ⓗ**; guest beers**
Small village local by the Aire: two bars with a collection of jugs, keen darts/dominoes teams and a friendly ghost. Try the Desperate Dan cow pie. ♛ Q ❀ ◖ ◗ ⊟ ▲ ♣ P

Chapel-le-Dale

Hill Inn

On B6255 ☎ (052 42) 41256
11.30–3, 6.30–11; 11–11 Sat
Dent Bitter; S&N Theakston Best Bitter, XB, Old Peculier; Whitbread Boddingtons Bitter Ⓗ
Well-known, isolated pub on the Three Peaks Walk in potholing country. Utility furnishings, varnished boards and bare stonework; pool room and food bar (children welcome). Folk every Sat.
♛ ❀ 🛏 ◖ ◗ ▲ ♣ P

Clapham

New Inn

☎ (052 42) 51203
11–3, 7–11; 11–11 Sat (sometimes 11–11 summer)
Dent Bitter; McEwan 80/-; Tetley Bitter; Younger No. 3 Ⓗ
Large coaching inn, dated 1776. One bar has leather bench seats and stucco-decorated walls. The other has oak panelling (1990 vintage). Children are welcome in the restaurant (no-smoking).
♛ ❀ 🛏 ◖ ◗ ▲ ♣ P

Cloughton

Bryherstones Inn

Newlands Road (Ravenscar road, 1 mile N of village)
☎ (0723) 870744

11.30–3, 7–11
Camerons Bitter; Younger Scotch, No. 3 Ⓗ
Popular, country inn where families are welcome in the lower room, especially during the day. Lively in the eve and popular for food.
♨ ♞ ❀ ◖ ◗ ⊟ ▲ ♣ P

Cray

White Lion

On B6160, above Buckden
☎ (0756) 760252
11–3, 6–11; 11–11 Sat & summer
Moorhouse's Premier, Pendle Witches Brew; Tetley Mild (summer), Bitter Ⓗ
Cosy, stone-flagged inn nestling in Cray Gill, which cuts into the side of the main valley towards the head of the dale. With the bar back in its former position, the inn has gained space and character.
♨ Q ♞ ❀ 🛏 ◖ ◗ ▲ ♣ P ⊬

Cridling Stubbs

Ancient Shepherd

Weights Lane
☎ (0977) 673316
12–3 (not Sat), 7–11
Marston's Pedigree; Whitbread Trophy Ⓗ
Pub where a daunting exterior belies a welcoming Victorian interior. Separate restaurant.
❀ ◖ ◗ ⊟ ♣ P ⊬

Cropton

New Inn

Rosedale turn off A170 at Wrelton ☎ (075 15) 330
11–3, 5.30–11 (12–2.30, 7–11 winter)
Cropton Two Pints, Scoresby Stout, Special Strong Ⓗ
Free house with its own brewery, situated in an attractive village near Cropton Forest and Rosedale. Popular with walkers and tourists, and the focal point of the village. Tetley beers usually available.
♨ ♞ ❀ 🛏 ◖ ◗ ⊟ ▲ ♣ P

Cross Hills

Old White Bear

Keighley Road
☎ (0535) 632115
11.30–3, 5–11; 11–11 Sat
Goose Eye Bitter; Whitbread Chester's Mild, Boddingtons Bitter, Trophy Ⓗ
Old inn (1735) undergoing sensitive refurbishment and retaining separate rooms. Leased by the owners of the Goose Eye brewery who may soon brew on site. New recipes are tried out on willing locals. Families welcome at lunchtime.
♨ ❀ ◖ ♿ ♣ P

Dalton

Jolly Farmers of Olden Times

Between A19 & A1, just S of A168 OS431762
☎ (0845) 577359
7.30 (8.30 Mon)–11; 12–2 (not winter), 7.30–11 Sat; 12–2, 7–10.30 Sun; closed Mon–Fri lunch
Courage Directors; John Smith's Bitter Ⓗ**; guest beers**
Well-modernised, 200-year-old, beamed village pub with a comfortable lounge and a quiet games room. Good value bar meals.
♨ ❀ 🛏 ◖ ◗ ♿ ▲ ♣ P

Danby

Duke of Wellington

West Lane ☎ (0287) 660351
12–3 (may extend in summer, if busy), 7–11
Banks's Bitter; Camerons Strongarm; John Smith's Magnet Ⓗ
Prominent cluster of 18th-century stone and pantile buildings at a sloping crossroads. Several small, cosy rooms with a recently-opened restaurant.
♨ Q ♞ ❀ 🛏 ◖ ◗ ⇌ P

Darley

Wellington Inn

Darley Head (B5451)
☎ (0423) 780362
11–11
Taylor Best Bitter; Tetley Mild, Bitter Ⓗ
Rebuilt pub and restaurant in a delightful Dales setting.
♨ ♞ ❀ 🛏 ◖ ⊟ ♣ P

Deighton

White Swan Inn

On A19 ☎ (0904) 728287
11.30–2 (3 Sat), 7 (6.30 Sat)–11
S&N Theakston Best Bitter, XB, Old Peculier; Younger Scotch, No. 3 Ⓗ
Country inn and restaurant on a busy main road, popular with visitors in summer.
Q ❀ ◖ ◗ ▲ ♣ P

Easingwold

Station Hotel

Knott Lane (off Raskelf Rd)
☎ (0347) 22635
11–11
Hambleton Bitter; Tetley Bitter; guest beers Ⓗ
Historic Victorian relic of Britain's shortest standard gauge railway. Always stocks two guest beers and one cider. The comprehensive beer list includes Belgian cherry beer on draught. Freshly cooked bar meals and a restaurant.
♨ ❀ 🛏 ◖ ◗ ♣ ⌓

Egton

Horseshoe Inn

From A171 follow Egton or Grosmont signs
☎ (0947) 85274
12–3, 6 (6.30 winter)–11
S&N Theakston Best Bitter, XB, Old Peculier; Tetley Bitter Ⓗ
Grade II-listed pub with a low, oak-beamed ceiling, church settles and a rural atmosphere. Near the NYM railway; don't confuse with the Horseshoe at Egton Bridge.
♨ Q ♞ ❀ 🛏 ◖ ◗ ⊟ ♣ P

Egton Bridge

Postgate Inn

Off A171 OS805054
☎ (0947) 85241
11–11
Camerons Bitter, Strongarm; Everards Old Original (summer) Ⓗ
Attractive hotel overlooking a rustic railway station. Quoits played. Children welcome (children's and vegetarian menus offered). Named after Friar Postgate, a local martyr.
♨ Q ♞ ❀ 🛏 ◖ ◗ ⊟ ⇌ ♣ P

Elvington

Grey Horse

Main Street ☎ (0904) 608335
12–2.30 (3 Sat), 5.30 (7 Sat)–11
Courage Directors; John Smith's Bitter Ⓗ**; guest beer**
Traditional, two-roomed village pub overlooking the green. The superb tap room has log fires, and the good value pub food has a good reputation. Regularly changed guest beers. Note the unusual collection of old wirelesses in the lounge, with its now all too rare bar billiards and skittles.
♨ Q ❀ ◖ ◗ ⊟ ▲ ♣ P

Embsay

Elm Tree

Elm Tree Square
☎ (0756) 790717
11.30–3 (3.30 Sat), 5.30–11 (11–11 summer)
Whitbread Boddingtons Bitter, Bentley's Yorkshire Bitter, Castle Eden Ale; guest beer Ⓗ
Sizeable pub in a square facing the eponymous tree (which may not be an elm!): a large main bar, where meals are served, and a small public bar with old-fashioned seating. Good food includes a 'bargain' Sun lunch and the speciality, Jäger Schnitzel. Trough guest beer. ❀ 🛏 ◖ ◗ ♿ ▲ ♣ P ⊬

North Yorkshire

Farndale

Feversham Arms
Church Houses
☎ (0751) 33206
7 (6.30 summer Sat)–11
Tetley Bitter Ⓗ
Small inn in a remote hamlet in Farndale, popular with walkers. The bar has a stone-flagged floor and a cast iron range. New separate restaurant. Note: closed lunchtime, except Sun.
Q ❀ ◑ ▲ ♣ P

Feetham

Punch Bowl Inn
On B6270, 3½ miles W of Reeth ☎ (0748) 86233
11–3, 6–11; 11–11 Sat & summer
S&N Theakston Mild, Best Bitter, XB, Old Peculier; Younger No. 3; guest beer Ⓗ
Village inn, built in 1638, offering warm hospitality, with traditional music in the bar. Beer festivals Easter and Aug Bank Hol. Over 100 different single malt whiskies. Mountain bikes for hire.
❀ ◑ ♿ ▲ ♣ P

Fellbeck

Half Moon
On B6265, 3 miles E of Pateley Bridge ☎ (0423) 711560
12–3, 6.30–11
S&N Theakston Best Bitter; Taylor Landlord; Younger Scotch Ⓗ
Pleasant roadside inn, close to a local beauty spot, Brimham Rocks: a large, sunny lounge and a small bar. Self-catering cottages to let.
Q ❀ ◑ ▲ ♣ P

Giggleswick

Black Horse
Church Street ☎ (0729) 822506
12–3, 6.30–11
S&N Theakston Best Bitter; Taylor Best Bitter; Tetley Bitter; Younger Scotch Ⓗ
17th-century pub next to the church in the centre of an old village. It boasts mullioned windows and a wood-panelled interior. Roaring fire in winter. Separate dining room.
❀ ◑ ▲ ♣ P

Glaisdale

Anglers Rest
Off A171 ☎ (0947) 87261
11–3, 6–11 (varies summer)
Camerons Strongarm; S&N Theakston Best Bitter; Tetley Bitter Ⓗ
Very friendly, old hilltop pub, formerly called the Three Blast Furnaces but known locally as the Middle House. Popular with walkers and campers. The beer range may vary.
Q ❀ ◑ ▲ ≷ ♣

Arncliffe Arms
☎ (0947) 87209
11–3.30, 6.30–11; 11–11 Fri, Sat & summer
Camerons Bitter, Strongarm Ⓗ
Large hotel near Glaisdale station; known locally as the Bottom House. Karaoke in the eve.
◑ ≷ ♣ P

Grassington

Black Horse Hotel
Garrs Lane ☎ (0756) 752770
11–11
Black Sheep Best Bitter; Ruddles Best Bitter; S&N Theakston Best Bitter, XB, Old Peculier; Tetley Bitter Ⓗ
Comfortable, welcoming hotel bar with a large open fire. Separate dining room.
Q ❀ ◑ ▲

Great Ayton

Buck
West Terrace
☎ (0642) 722242
11–11
Whitbread Boddingtons Bitter, Trophy Ⓗ**; guest beer**
Originally a coaching inn in the 1700s, in Captain Cook's village; now a friendly, cosy pub, furnished in cottage style with divided areas around a central bar. Very good bar meals. Q ❀ ◑ ♣ P

Great Broughton

Wainstones Hotel
High Street ☎ (0642) 712268
11–3, 5–11
Ind Coope Burton Ale; Tetley Bitter Ⓗ
Originally a farmhouse, now the only hotel in the village. The lounge bar has a strong local patronage. Winner of the *Cellarman* award for its Burton Ale. All the village pubs serve real ale.
Q ❀ ◑ ▲ ♣ P

Great Habton

Grapes Inn
4 miles NW of Malton OS759764 ☎ (0653) 86606
12–3 (not Mon), 7–11
Tetley Bitter; John Smith's Bitter Ⓗ**; guest beer**
Stone-built pub in an isolated village in the Vale of Pickering, catering for the local farming community. No-smoking area in the dining room. ❀ ◑ ♣ P

Great Heck

Bay Horse Inn
Main Street ☎ (0977) 661125
12–3, 7–11; 12–11 Sat (may vary)
Tetley Bitter; Whitbread Boddingtons Bitter Ⓗ
Pleasant country pub occupying three old cottages, close to the marina on the Aire and Calder Canal. ❀ ◑ P

Great Ouseburn

Crown
Main Street ☎ (0423) 330430
11–3, 5–11
Ruddles Best Bitter; S&N Theakston Best Bitter; John Smith's Bitter Ⓗ
Village pub opened up, but retaining many original features. Reputedly haunted. Restaurant attached.
Q ❀ ◑ ♿ ♣ P

Great Smeaton

Bay Horse
On A167 ☎ (060 981) 466
12–3, 6.30–11
Courage Directors; John Smith's Bitter; guest beers Ⓗ
Small free house in the middle of a row of cottages, with two linked rooms: a functional bar and a soft-furnished lounge.
❀ ◑ ♿ ♣ P

Harrogate

Hales Bar
Crescent Road
☎ (0423) 569861
11–11
Bass Worthington BB, Draught Bass; Stones Best Bitter Ⓗ
Superb, welcoming, town-centre pub with a small, friendly public bar. The large, atmospheric lounge features gas lighting, stuffed birds, old barrels and unusual gas cigar lighters on the bar. Good food; quiz nights. ◑ ♿ ≷

Muckles
West Park (A61)
☎ (0423) 504463
11–11
Tetley Bitter Ⓗ
U-shaped bar which attracts a mixed clientele, overlooks West Park Stray and serves excellent lunches. ◑ ≷ ♣ P

Tap & Spile
Tower Street (400 yds from West Park Stray)
☎ (0423) 526785
11.30–3, 5–11; 11.30–11 Sat
Beer range varies Ⓗ
Up to ten changing beers in this three-roomed pub. Typical Tap & Spile style: exposed brick and no carpets. Varied clientele. Q ❀ ◑ ≷ ♣

Woodlands
Wetherby Road (A59)
☎ (0423) 883396
11.30–3, 5.30–11
Courage Directors; Ruddles Best Bitter; John Smith's Bitter; Webster's Yorkshire Bitter [H]
Pub with a spacious, open-plan bar and a conservatory, close to the Yorkshire Show Ground. Q ⚇ ◖ ⊟ ♿ P

Hawes

Crown Hotel
Main Street ☎ (0969) 667212
11–11
S&N Theakston Best Bitter, XB, Old Peculier [H]
Early 19th-century pub with two bars, open fires and comfortable surroundings. The garden offers a beautiful view of Wensleydale.
♨ Q ⚇ ❀ ◖ ◗ ♿ ⌓

Helperby

Golden Lion
Main Street ☎ (0423) 360870
12–3 (not Mon), 6–11
Taylor Best Bitter; Tetley Bitter; guest beers [H]
Friendly, inviting village local, formerly a coaching inn. Ever-changing guest beers.
♨ ◖ ◗ ♣

Hornby

Grange Arms
☎ (060 981) 249
11.30–3, 7–11
McEwan 80/-; S&N Theakston XB; guest beers [H]
Pleasant, whitewashed and pantiled village pub, with a snug little bar and a lounge-diner. ♨ Q ❀ ◖ ◗ ⊟ ♣ P

Hutton Rudby

Bay Horse
North Side ☎ (0642) 700252
11–3, 5.30–11; 11–11 Sat
Bass Worthington BB, Draught Bass [H]
Deceptively spacious pub with a low-beamed bar, large lounge and a restaurant (no meals Sun eve).
Q ⚇ ❀ ◖ ◗ ⊟ ♣ P

Kettlewell

Race Horses Hotel
On B6160 ☎ (0756) 760233
11–11
Goose Eye Bitter; S&N Theakston XB, Old Peculier; Webster's Yorkshire Bitter [H]
Ex-coaching inn where a central bar serves the front room (note the open fire dated 1740), a larger back room and a pool room.
♨ Q ❀ ⛟ ◖ ◗ ▲ ♣ P

Kirk Hammerton

Crown Inn
Station Road ☎ (0423) 330341
7.30–11; 12–3, 7.30–10.30 Sun; closed Mon–Sat lunch
Marston Moor Cromwell [H]; **guest beer** (occasionally)
Straightforward village pub, the home of Marston Moor Brewery. Operates extensions for fishermen: 8–10am and 4–7pm summer Sun. One other Marston Moor beer is always available, plus cider in summer. ♨ Q ❀ ⛟ ⊟ ▲ ⇌ (Hammerton) ⌓ P

Knaresborough

Blind Jack's
Market Place ☎ (0423) 869148
11.30–3, 6–11; 11.30–11 Wed–Sat
Beer range varies [H]
Intimate gem created in 1991 in a Georgian listed building; winner of the 1992 CAMRA *New Pub Design Award*. Named after a local hero, it retains many original features and has a single bar, a small snug and upstairs dining rooms. No music or distractions at all. Six beers are constantly changed, usually including a mild.
Q ◖ ◗ ⇌ ♣

Groves
Market Place ☎ (0423) 863022
11–11; 12–3, 7.30–10.30 Sun
S&N Theakston Best Bitter; Younger Scotch, No. 3 [H]
On the corner of the historic market place, a warm and friendly, twin-roomed pub, Yorkshire's only ever-present *Guide* entry. ◖ ⇌ ♣

Half Moon
Abbey Road ☎ (0423) 862663
11.30–3 (not Mon–Thu), 5.30 (7.30 Fri & Sat)–11
Mansfield Riding Bitter; John Smith's Bitter [H]
Small but comfortable, one-roomed lounge with a pool table in an alcove. Holds a tug-of-war each Christmas with a rival pub across the River Nidd. ▲ ♣

Marquis of Granby
York Place (A59)
☎ (0423) 862207
11–3, 6–11
Samuel Smith OBB [H]
Twin-roomed, Victorian-styled pub opposite the swimming baths. ⊟ ▲

Langdale End

Moorcock Inn
OS938913 ☎ (0723) 882268
11–2.30 (2 Sat; not Mon–Thu in winter), 8 (7 Fri & Sat)–11
Beer range varies [H]
Rural gem, rescued from oblivion with a sympathetic renovation. Somewhat remote, it can be either quiet or packed, but is well worth seeking out. ♨ Q ❀ ◖ ▲ ♣

Long Preston

Maypole
☎ (0729) 840219
11–3, 6 (5.30 Sat)–11
Taylor Best Bitter; Whitbread Boddingtons Bitter, Castle Eden Ale; guest beer [H]
Large, main-road local facing the maypole on the green; very much the heart of village life. Two large bars and a dining room. Cider in summer.
♨ Q ❀ ⛟ ◖ ◗ ⇌ ♣ ⌓ P

Low Marishes

School House Inn
3 miles N of A64/A169 jct
☎ (0653) 86247
11–3, 6.30–11
Malton Double Chance; Mansfield Riding Bitter, Old Baily; Tetley Bitter [H]; **guest beers**
Tidy pub with good food and excellent facilities for all the family, both inside and out. Ukers, a violent form of ludo, is a local favourite.
♨ ⚇ ❀ ◖ ◗ ⊟ ▲ ♣ P

Malham

Listers Arms
☎ (0729) 830330
12–3 (2 winter; not winter Tue), 7–11
Ind Coope Burton Ale; Younger Scotch [H]; **guest beers**
Comfortable, three-roomed pub from 1702, just over the bridge on the road to Goredale Scar. Hikers welcome. Bottle-conditioned Belgian beers, a good range of malts and at least two guest beers always available. Cider in summer.
♨ ❀ ⛟ ◖ ◗ ▲ ♣ ⌓ P

Malton

Crown Hotel (Suddaby's)
Wheelgate ☎ (0653) 692038
11–3 (4 Sat), 5.30–11; 11–11 Fri
Malton Pale Ale, Double Chance, Pickwick's Porter, Owd Bob [H]; **guest beers**
Neat hotel offering a full range of local beers. The functional bar is complemented by a conservatory-style extension where children are welcome. The menu includes three vegetarian options.
♨ Q ⚇ ⛟ ◖ ⇌ ♣ P

Kings Head Hotel
Market Square
☎ (0653) 692289
11–3 (extends market days), 6–11
Wards Sheffield Best Bitter; Webster's Yorkshire Bitter; Whitbread Boddingtons Bitter [H]; **guest beers**

Pub whose impressive, ivy-clad facade overlooks the market square. A comfortable front bar and a farmer's bar at the rear.

Masham

Bay Horse
Silver Street ☎ (0765) 689236
11–3, 7–11 (11–11 summer)
Black Sheep Best Bitter, Special Strong; S&N Theakston Best Bitter, XB, Old Peculier Ⓗ
Comfortable, market town pub – the only one in Masham selling both local brews. The lounge has a raised dining area. Bottled Black Sheep also available.

White Bear
Wellgarth ☎ (0765) 689319
11–11
S&N Theakston Mild, Best Bitter, XB, Old Peculier Ⓗ
Friendly, two-roomed village pub serving excellent home-made food (no chips); eve meals Mon–Fri. Live music Sat eve. Theakston's brewery tap, sympathetically refurbished.
♣ P

Muker

Farmers Arms
On B6270 ☎ (0748) 86297
11–3, 7–11
Butterknowle Bitter; S&N Theakston Best Bitter, XB, Old Peculier Ⓗ
Village-centre pub, handy for local footpaths, the Pennine Way and Coast to Coast walks. The inside is opened up, but quite unspoilt, with wooden seating and flagged floors.
Q ♣

Muston

Ship Inn
☎ (0723) 512722
11–2.30, 6–11
Camerons Bitter; Ind Coope Burton Ale; Marston's Pedigree; Tetley Bitter; Whitbread Castle Eden Ale Ⓗ
Village pub with one spacious room serving wholesome food.
▲ ♣ P

Naburn

Blacksmiths Arms
☎ (0904) 623464
12–3.30, 7–11; 11–11 Fri, Sat & summer
S&N Theakston Mild, Best Bitter, XB; Younger Scotch Ⓗ; **guest beers** (occasionally)
Fine example of a village pub, opened up, but still keeping the homely feel with four distinct areas, including a small 'snug'. Near the York–Selby cycleway.
▲ P

Northallerton

Nags Head
High Street ☎ (0609) 772305
11–3, 7–11
John Smith's Bitter Ⓗ
Pub where a modest old facade hides an extended interior. Football and quoits teams; quiz Sun. Friendly atmosphere. No eve meals Sun–Tue.
♣ P

Nun Monkton

Alice Hawthorn
☎ (0423) 330303
12–2, 7–11
Camerons Bitter; Marston's Pedigree; Tetley Bitter Ⓗ
Large, warm and welcoming pub overlooking a typical village scene, with duck pond and maypole. A bit off the beaten track but worth the search. Booking is essential to camp at the pub. Wheelchair access via the rear entrance.
Q ▲ P

Nunnington

Royal Oak
Main Street
11.45–2.30, 6.30–10.30 (11 Fri & Sat); 12–2, 7–10.30 Sun; closed Mon
Ind Coope Burton Ale; S&N Theakston Old Peculier; Tetley Bitter Ⓗ
Pub catering almost exclusively for diners, but also serving a good pint. Note the large collection of old keys and agricultural tools. Relaxed and friendly.
P

Osgodby

Wadkin Arms
Main Street ☎ (0757) 702391
11–3, 6–11
Vaux Bitter, Samson Ⓗ
Typical village pub with three coal fires, real beams and no jukebox.
Q ♣ P

Osmotherley

Golden Lion
West End ☎ (0609) 883526
11–3 (not Mon, except bank hols), 6–11
Courage Directors; John Smith's Bitter, Magnet Ⓗ
Attractive old pub in the village centre. Tables with fresh flowers and candles underline the food emphasis. Children welcome lunchtime. The original starting point for the Lyke Wake long distance walk.
▲ ♣

Pickering

Black Swan Hotel
Birdgate ☎ (0751) 72286
10.30–3, 6–11; 10.30–11 Mon & summer
Courage Directors; Ruddles County; John Smith's Bitter Ⓗ
Former coaching inn, still popular with travellers as well as locals.
♣ P

Pickhill

Nags Head
1 mile from A1
☎ (0845) 567391
11–11
Hambleton Bitter; S&N Theakston Best Bitter, XB, Old Peculier; Younger Scotch Ⓗ
Country inn and restaurant, offering superb food in excellent surroundings. Tap room for the serious drinker.
P

Pool-in-Wharfedale

Hunters Inn
Riffa (A658) ☎ (0532) 841090
11–11
Beer range varies Ⓗ
Formerly a café before a complete refurbishment; now a thriving free house with up to nine beers. Kitchen planned (check for food).
♣ P

Redmire

Kings Arms
☎ (0969) 22316
11–3, 6–11 (11–11 bank hols)
S&N Theakston Best Bitter, XB, Old Peculier; John Smith's Magnet; guest beer Ⓗ
Cosy pub, brimming with atmosphere and good conversation. The patio boasts views of Wensleydale.
Q ▲ ♣ P

Richmond

Black Lion Hotel
Finkle Street ☎ (0748) 823121
10.30–11
Camerons Strongarm; Marston's Pedigree; Tetley Bitter; Whitbread Flowers Original Ⓗ
Old, residential coaching inn off the market place, with traditional bars, serving a good local trade.
Q ♣ P

Holly Hill Inn
Holly Hill (top of Sleagill)
☎ (0748) 825171
12–2, 4.30–11 (12–11 bank hols)
S&N Theakston Best Bitter, XB, Old Peculier; guest beers Ⓗ
True drinkers' pub with an excellent range of beers served in two rooms. Pool, darts and dominoes.
Q ♣ P

Ripon

Golden Lion
Allhallowgate ☎ (0765) 602598
11–3, 7–11

Marston Moor Cromwell; S&N Theakston Best Bitter; John Smith's Bitter Ⓗ**; guest beers**
Friendly, 16th-century town pub and restaurant, partly modernised. Eve meals finish at 8.30. 🅂 ❀ 🛏 ◑ ◗ ♣

One Eyed Rat
Allhallowgate ☎ (0765) 607704
12–3 (not Mon–Thu), 6–11
Daleside Bitter; Taylor Landlord; Whitbread Boddingtons Bitter Ⓗ**; guest beers**
Very popular, terraced pub offering three guest beers and a wide range of bottle-conditioned beers.
⛰ Q ❀ ♣

Wheatsheaf
Harrogate Road (A61, S of centre) ☎ (0765) 602410
12–3, 6–11; 11–11 Sat (may vary summer)
Vaux Lorimers Best Scotch, Samson; Wards Sheffield Best Bitter Ⓗ
Friendly, roadside pub on the edge of the historic city, with a rural feel. ⛰ ❀ ◑ ◗ ♣ P

Robin Hood's Bay

Laurel Inn
☎ (0947) 880400
11–11
Courage Directors; Ruddles Best Bitter; S&N Theakston Old Peculier; John Smith's Bitter; guest beer (winter) Ⓗ
Small, friendly local in a picturesque cliffside village.
⛰ Q 🅂 ❀ ♣

Victoria Hotel
Station Road ☎ (0947) 880205
11.30–3, 6.30–11 (11–11 summer)
Camerons Bitter, Strongarm; S&N Theakston XB; guest beer Ⓗ
Large hotel, built in 1897, with imposing garden views over the village and bay. The modern family room has a pool table. Local artists' work is displayed for sale in the bar.
⛰ 🅂 ❀ 🛏 ◑ ◗ ⊞ ▲ ♣ P

Roecliffe

Crown Inn
☎ (0423) 322578
11.30–3, 6.30–11 (supper licence till 12)
Bass Special; S&N Theakston Best Bitter; Tetley Bitter Ⓗ**; guest beers** (occasionally)
A rather spartan tap room contrasts with the comfortable lounge of this friendly, family-run inn. Handpumps are on the lounge bar only, with a hatch to the tap.
⛰ Q ❀ 🛏 ◑ ◗ ⊞ ♿ ▲ ♣ P

Rufforth

Tankard Inn
Wetherby Road (B1224)
☎ (0904) 83621
11–3, 6–11; 11–11 Sat
Samuel Smith OBB, Museum Ⓗ
Neat and tidy, two-roomed village pub. The 1930s-style bar features old prints of the village. Large children's play area. ⛰ Q ❀ 🛏 ◑ ◗ ⊞ P

Scarborough

Aberdeen Hotel
Victoria Road ☎ (0723) 373030
11–11
Bass Worthington BB, Draught Bass Ⓗ
Comfortable pub. Meals are served until 5.30pm. ◑ ⇌ ♣

Angel Inn
North Street ☎ (0723) 365504
11–3, 5.30–11; 11–11 Fri & Sat
Camerons Bitter; Tetley Bitter Ⓗ
Cosy local, very crowded at weekends. Games-oriented, with photographic mementoes of the landlord's international rugby league career. ⇌ ♣

Cask
Cambridge Terrace
☎ (0723) 500570
11.45–2.30 (3 Fri), 6–11; 11–11 Sat
Ind Coope Burton Ale; S&N Theakston Best Bitter; Tetley Bitter; Younger Scotch, No. 3 Ⓗ**; guest beers**
Popular pub, especially with the young, but welcoming to all, with a dark, bric-a-brac-hung interior. Eve meals finish early. 🅂 ❀ 🛏 ◑ ◗ ⇌

Golden Ball
Sandside ☎ (0723) 353899
11–3, 7–11
Samuel Smith OBB Ⓗ
Harbourside pub with views of the South Bay from the front bar. 🅂 ❀ ◑ ◗ ⊞

Highlander
Stresa Hotel, The Esplanade
☎ (0723) 365627
11–11
Wm Clark's Mild, EXB, No. 68, Thistle Bitter; Tetley Bitter Ⓗ**; guest beers**
Overlooking the South Bay, a bar-brewery with a Scottish flavour. Huge whisky collection. ⛰ Q ❀ 🛏 ⇌

Hole in the Wall
Vernon Road ☎ (0723) 373746
11.30–2.30 (3 Sat), 7–11
Malton Double Chance; S&N Theakston Best Bitter, XB, Old Peculier Ⓗ**; guest beers**
Thriving alehouse just off the town centre. Vegetarian option on the menu (no food Sun). Handy for the spa.
Q ◑ ⇌ ♣

Tennyson Arms
Dean Road ☎ (0723) 363912
11–11
Tetley Mild, Bitter Ⓗ
Friendly two-roomer with a lively, games-oriented bar and a lounge. Regular live entertainment. Snacks always available. ❀ 🛏 ⊞ ♣

Trafalgar Hotel
Trafalgar Street West
☎ (0723) 372054
11–11
Camerons Bitter; Tetley Bitter Ⓗ
Smart, busy, games-oriented local, attracting a varied clientele, especially at weekends. Note the picture of the famous battle hanging in the lounge. ⊞ ⇌ ♣

Seamer (Stokesley)

Kings Head
Hilton Road ☎ (0642) 710397
12–3 (not Mon–Fri), 7–11
McEwan 80/-; S&N Theakston XB Ⓗ
Four cosy rooms around a central bar. No jukebox – a pub for a quiet drink and chat, with a strong regular patronage. A collection of brasses and real fires make this a haven in winter, unchanged for years.
⛰ Q ▲ ♣ P

Selby

Albion Vaults
New Street ☎ (0757) 213817
11–4.30, 7–11
Old Mill Bitter Ⓗ
Former Darley's keg pub, now an Old Mill tied house with friendly staff and a plush modern decor. ◑ ⇌

Brewery Tap
Hillgate ☎ (0757) 702826
10–2, 6–10.40; 12–2, 7–10 Sun
Selby Strong Ale, Old Tom Ⓗ
Off-licence attached to Selby brewery, selling one or other of its two ales for out sales only, available in jars or polypins. ⇌ P

Cricketers Arms
Market Place ☎ (0757) 702120
11–3.30, 5.30–11; 11–11 Mon, Fri & Sat
Samuel Smith OBB Ⓗ
Long, narrow, open-plan lounge bar, divided by alcoves into varied seating areas. Cricketing theme. ◑ ⇌

Shipton

Dawnay Arms
Main Street ☎ (0904) 470334
12–2.30, 6 (6.30 Sat)–11; 12–2.30, 7–10.30 Sun
Camerons Bitter, Strongarm; Tetley Bitter Ⓗ

Roomy, roadside pub, four miles north of York: a large, comfortable lounge, with a more basic bar to the rear. The dining room can be booked for functions. Good local reputation for bar meals. Wheelchair access at the rear.
🔥 Q ❀ 🛏 ◐ ◑ ♿ ▲ ♣ P

Skipton

Royal Shepherd
Canal Street (via alley from High St) ☎ (0756) 793178
11–4, 5–11; 11–11 Fri & Sat
Marston's Pedigree; Robinson's Hartleys XB; Whitbread Boddingtons Bitter, Trophy, Castle Eden Ale Ⓗ
Well-regarded, regular *Guide* entry in a quiet canalside location: a small back bar, a larger main front bar, and a quiet room overlooking an award-winning garden to the side. Lots of photos of old Skipton and a novel stained-glass window. Q ❀ ◐ ⇌ ♣

Sneaton

Wilsons Arms
Beacon Way (2 miles from Ruswarp on B1416)
☎ (0947) 602552
12–3, 7–11 (11–11 summer)
S&N Theakston Best Bitter, XB; John Smith's Bitter Ⓗ
Grade II-listed: a large, extended pub catering for families. Trad. Sun lunch.
🔥 Q 🐴 ❀ ◐ ◑ ▲ ♣ P

Spofforth

Railway Inn
High Street ☎ (0937) 590257
11.30–3, 5.30–11
Samuel Smith OBB, Museum Ⓗ
Victorian village pub next to a long-gone railway station. Always warm and friendly.
🔥 ❀ ◐ ◑ ♣ P

Staveley

Royal Oak
Main Street ☎ (0423) 340267
11.30–3, 5.30–11
Ind Coope Burton Ale; Rudgate Viking; Tetley Bitter Ⓗ
A pretty setting, back from the road, for an old pub with improvements very much in keeping. Cosy feel to the bar. Keen darts team; strong support for the village cricketers. Eve meals Tue–Sat.
🔥 Q ❀ ◐ ◑ ♿ ♣ P

Stokesley

Station
Station Road ☎ (0642) 710436
12–4, 7–11
S&N Theakston Mild, Best Bitter, XB, Old Peculier Ⓗ
Built in 1861 to serve a now-defunct railway; a pub with a light, airy front bar, a small snug and a large bar/function room at the rear. Blues night Thu. Meals only by prior arrangement. 🔥 Q ❀ ♣ P

Summerbridge

Flying Dutchman
Hartwith Bank (B6165)
☎ (0423) 780321
11.30–2.30 (3 summer), 6.30 (5.30 summer)–11
Samuel Smith OBB Ⓗ
Stone-built village inn, ideal for touring the Dales. Good, home-cooked food at reasonable prices.
🔥 ❀ 🛏 ◐ ◑ ♣ P

Tadcaster

Angel & White Horse
On A659 ☎ (0937) 835470
11–2.30, 5 (6 Sat)–11
Samuel Smith OBB, Museum Ⓗ
Large town pub attached to the brewery, with brewery photos in the wood-panelled bar. The brewery shire horses are stabled in the coachyard which also serves as an outdoor drinking area.
🔥 Q ❀ ◐ ▲ ♣

Thirsk

Cross Keys
Kirkgate ☎ (0845) 552250
11–11
John Smith's Bitter, Magnet Ⓗ
No-frills drinkers' pub; an L-shaped bar plus a pool room. ♣ P

Thornton in Lonsdale

Marton Arms
☎ (052 42) 41281
11–11
Dent Bitter; S&N Theakston Best Bitter; Thwaites Bitter; Younger Scotch Ⓗ**; guest beers**
Pre-turnpike coaching inn, dated 1679 but reputedly older. A large, comfortable oak-beamed lounge and a restaurant offering good home cooking. Eleven guest beers and Weston's cider.
🔥 ❀ 🛏 ◐ ◑ ♣ 🍏 P

Thornton Watlass

Buck Inn
1 mile off B6268, Masham–Bedale road ☎ (0677) 422461
11–2.30, 6–11
S&N Theakston Best Bitter; John Smith's Bitter; Tetley Bitter; guest beers Ⓗ
A picturesque village green setting for this bar, lounge, restaurant and function rooms. Caters for all tastes in food. Hambleton beers are regular guests. 🔥 🐴 ❀ 🛏 ◐ ◑ ♣ P

Threshfield

Long Ashes Inn
Just off B6160 ☎ (0756) 752434
11.30–3, 5.30 (6.30 winter)–11
Moorhouse's Pendle Witches Brew; S&N Theakston Mild, Best Bitter, XB (summer); Tetley Bitter Ⓗ**; guest beer** (summer)
Higgledy-piggledy pub on different levels, with stone walls and beamed ceilings. This former lodge stands next to a chalet/caravan park and leisure centre. Full menu with daily specials.
🔥 Q 🐴 ❀ ◐ ◑ ♿ ▲ ♣ P

Old Hall Inn
On B6160, Grassington–Skipton road ☎ (0756) 752441
11–3, 6–11
Moorhouse's Pendle Witches Brew; S&N Theakston Best Bitter; Taylor Best Bitter, Landlord; Younger Scotch Ⓗ
Country inn, popular with locals and visitors alike; stone-flagged, with scatter rugs in the family room and games room. The open lounge has a large coal-fired range and the dining room offers top quality, wide-ranging food. Charming holiday cottage to let. No meals Sun eve or Mon, Christmas–Easter. 🔥 Q 🐴 ❀ 🛏 ◐ ◑ ♿ ▲ ♣ 🍏 P

Tunstall

Bay Horse Inn
Off A1 ☎ (0748) 818564
12–3.30, 7–11.30
Samuel Smith OBB Ⓗ
A welcome return to the *Guide* for this little local inn, tastefully refurbished to provide a natural, open-beamed, homely pub. Village entertainment and the introduction of food, along with a small caravan site, make it an inviting stop for visitors exploring the Dales.
🔥 Q ❀ ◐ ◑ ▲ ♣ P

Wass

Wombwell Arms
2 miles from Coxwold
☎ (0347) 868280
12–2.30, 7–11; closed Mon
Camerons Bitter; Taylor Landlord Ⓗ
18th-century inn with a relaxed, country atmosphere and welcoming log fires. Warm and inviting.
🔥 Q 🛏 ◐ ◑ ♣ P

Weaverthorpe

Star Inn

☎ (094 43) 273
12–3 (not Mon & Tue), 7–11
Taylor Landlord; Tetley Bitter; Webster's Yorkshire Bitter [H]
Country inn with a bar for everyone. The front lounge is comfortable and popular with diners, while the more functional bar is used by the locals.
♨ ⛵ ❀ 🛏 ◖ ◗ ⊟ ▲ ♣ P

West Heslerton

Dawnay Arms

☎ (094 45) 203
11–2.30, 6–11
Younger Scotch, No. 3 [H]
A haven, just off the hectic A64, with several rooms served from one central bar. Nasi Goreng is a speciality dish. ❀ ◖ ◗ ▲ ♣

Whitby

Buck Inn

11 St Annes Staithe
☎ (0947) 601378
11–3, 7–11 (11–11 summer)
John Smith's Bitter, Magnet [H]
Busy quayside pub, popular with locals and visitors. The family room is also used for functions. ⛵ 🛏 ◖ ◗ ≠ ♣

Dolphin Hotel

Bridge Street ☎ (0947) 602197
11.30–3, 7–11 (11–11 summer)
Camerons Strongarm; Ind Coope Burton Ale; Tetley Bitter [H]
Roomy, Edwardian town pub next to the swing bridge, overlooking the harbour.
⛵ 🛏 ◖ ◗ ⊟ ≠ ♣

Duke of York

Church Street ☎ (0947) 600324
11–3, 7–11; 11–11 Sat & summer
Courage Directors; John Smith's Bitter, Magnet [H]
Harbourside pub with a magnificent view, situated at the foot of 199 steps leading up to the abbey and church. Popular in folk week.
🛏 ◖ ◗ ≠ ♣

Wigginton

Cottage Inn

115 The Village
☎ (0904) 763949
11.30–2 (3 Sat), 6–11
S&N Theakston Best Bitter; John Smith's Bitter; Tetley Bitter [H]
Large pub on the border of Haxby and Wigginton, popular with diners. The oversized lounge features discreet alcoves; the conservatory also serves as a family room. No eve meals Sun. ⛵ ❀ ◖ ◗ ⊟ P ⁄

York

Blue Bell

Fossgate ☎ (0904) 654904
12–3, 7–11 (may vary)
Vaux Bitter, Samson; Wards Sheffield Best Bitter [H]
Not York's oldest pub, but unique in its late-Victorian atmosphere where no modern gimmicks divert attention from the beer and conversation. Two cosy rooms and a drinking corridor. Give Jorvik a miss next time and come here instead for some real history. Q ♣

Brown Cow

Hope Street (off Walmgate)
☎ (0904) 634010
11–11; 11–4, 6–11 Tue
Taylor Best Bitter, Landlord [H]
Small, friendly, two-roomed local just within the city walls and surrounded by modern housing. Two large aquaria house a colourful variety of fish. Frequented by the local Ebor Morrismen, as well as several games teams.
Q ❀ ♣

Corner Pin

Tanner Row (narrow lane between the river and the bus station) ☎ (0904) 629946
11–11
Mansfield Riding Mild, Riding Bitter, Old Baily [H]
Large, open-plan town pub and restaurant (used by families when there is no food service). Popular at weekends with younger people.
⛵ ❀ ◖ ≠ ♣

Grapes Hotel

King Street ☎ (0904) 670696
11–11
Thwaites Bitter, Craftsman [H]
Small, city-centre pub, catering mainly for locals; a former Bass pub, now one of four Thwaites pubs in York.
◖ ≠

John Bull

Layerthorpe
☎ (0904) 621593
11.30–3, 5.30–11; 11–11 Fri & Sat
Malton Double Chance; Marston Moor Cromwell; Taylor Landlord [H]**; guest beers**
Still ploughing its own idiosyncratic furrow; the original 1930s interior and memorabilia are of much interest. Guest beers are usually from characterful Yorkshire breweries or notable independents.
♨ Q ❀ ⌓

Minster Inn

Marygate ☎ (0904) 624499
11.30–3, 6–11
Bass Worthington BB, Draught Bass; Ruddles Best Bitter; Stones Best Bitter [H]
Traditional, terraced, multi-roomed pub where the sympathetic interior decor now enhances the tilework behind the bar and in the passageway. The locals always have time for visitors.
Q ◖ ⊟ ≠ ⁄

Other Tap & Spile

North Street ☎ (0904) 656097
11.30–11
Daleside Bitter [H]**; guest beers**
Multi-roomed pub, usually offering eight real ales, a range of German bottled beers, and a varied selection of fruit wines. Bar snacks include vegetarian options. Q ⛵ ◖ ◗ ≠ ⁄

Royal Oak

Goodramgate ☎ (0904) 653856
11–11
Ind Coope Burton Ale; Tetley Bitter [H]
Excellent, three-roomed pub specialising in home cooking (including the bread). Children are welcome in the no-smoking snug, which doubles as a meeting room. Meals 11.30–7.30. Q ⛵ ◖ ◗ ⊟ ⁄

Spread Eagle

Walmgate ☎ (0904) 635868
11–11
S&N Theakston Best Bitter, XB, Old Peculier; Taylor Landlord [H]**; guest beers** (occasionally)
Pub where the regular beer menu is augmented by guest beers, particularly from local microbreweries. Gargantuan chip butties, an extensive range of bar snacks and a gourmet restaurant enhance the reputation. ❀ ◖ ◗ P

Wellington Inn

Alma Terrace, Fulford Road
☎ (0904) 645642
11–3, 7–11; 11–11 Sat
Samuel Smith OBB [H]
Unspoilt, attractive inn, set in a row of terraced houses, with a public bar, games room and a snug. ♨ Q ⛵ ❀ ♣

York Beer Shop

Sandringham Street (off A19/ Fishergate) ☎ (0904) 647136
11 (4.15 Mon, 10 Sat)–10; 12–2, 7–10 Sun
Bateman XXXB; Old Mill Bitter; Taylor Landlord [H]**; guest beers**
Draught beer to take home in any quantity, and a vast range of bottles – foreign and indigenous. Throw in the mouthwatering cheeses and you have an irresistible combination. ⌓

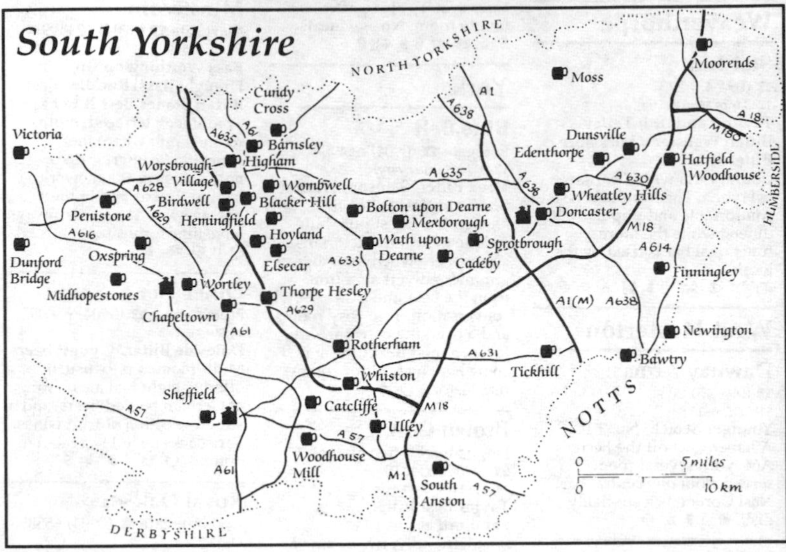

Kelham Island, *Sheffield;* **Stocks,** *Doncaster;* **Wards,** *Sheffield;* **Wortley,** *Wortley*

Barnsley

Old White Bear

150 Pontefract Road, Hoyle Mill (A628, ¾ mile from centre) ☎ (0226) 284947

12–3 (Wed–Sat only), 6.30–11

Courage Directors; Ruddles County; Taylor Landlord; Whitbread Boddingtons Bitter; guest beers H

Popular free house and twice local CAMRA award-winner which offers up to six guest beers. Overlooks a country park and is handy for the football ground. Beer festivals at bank hols; quiz Wed and Sat. Guest cider. ❀ ◖ ◗ P

Bawtry

Turnpike

High Street ☎ (0302) 711960

11–3, 6–11

Stocks Best Bitter, Select, Old Horizontal; guest beers H

Pub converted from a wine bar to cater for all tastes. The interior is of wood, glass and brick, with a part-concrete floor – mind the step! Good value, varied menu (eve meals Tue–Thu). Families welcome. Weekly guest beers. ❀ ◖ ◗

Birdwell

Cock Inn

Pilley Hill (off A61 towards Pilley) ☎ (0226) 742155

12–3, 7–11

Draught Bass; Whitbread Boddingtons Bitter H

200-year-old, popular village local boasting a superb fire range, with much brass. Extensive play area next to the family room under the pub. Fri barbecues in summer; quiz Thu, and an occasional organist. No food Sun eve.

Q ❀ ◖ ◗ ♣ P

Blacker Hill

Royal Albert

Wentworth Road (800 yds off B6096) ☎ (0226) 742193

12 (11 Sat)–4, 7–11

Wards Sheffield Best Bitter E

Attractive pub on a bend in the road – the hub of village life. Splendid wood-panelled snug, a larger games-oriented bar and a pool room upstairs.

Q ❀ ♣ P

Try also: Pheasant; Royal Oak, Barnsley Rd (Wards)

Bolton upon Dearne

Cross Daggers Inn

Church Street (150 yds off B6098) ☎ (0709) 892299

12–4, 7–11

John Smith's Bitter H

Built 1923 and virtually unspoiled, a pub with many rooms including a games room with snooker. The corridor drinking area has early photos of the village. Gents' hairdressing Sat and Sun lunch; quiz Tue, Thu and Sun lunch.

Q ❀ ♣ P

Cadeby

Cadeby Inn

Main Street ☎ (0709) 864009

11–3, 5–11 (may extend summer); 11–11 Sat

Courage Directors; Ind Coope Burton Ale; John Smith's Bitter, Magnet; Samuel Smith OBB; Tetley Bitter H

Converted farmhouse, in a rural village, which has retained its character and atmosphere; large lounge and a cosy public bar. Good bar meals and traditional Sun lunch. The pleasant garden is popular with families.

Q ❀ ◖ ◗ P

Catcliffe

Waverley

Brinsworth Road (B6067) ☎ (0709) 360906

12–4, 6–11

John Smith's Magnet; Taylor Landlord; guest beers H

Large, modern pub where the extensive family room doubles as a concert room (regular entertainment for children and adults). Many playthings outside. The beer range changes regularly.

Q ❀ ◖ ♣ P

Chapeltown

Norfolk Arms
White Lane (A6135, near M1 jct 35A) ☎ (0742) 468414
12–11
Wards Sheffield Best Bitter [E]
Old pub with newer extensions and an active club scene, from pool to pigeons (separate pool room). No food Sun, or eve meals Sat.
❀ ◖ ◗ ⇌ ♣ P

Prince of Wales
80 Burncross Road (1 mile from M1 jct 35)
☎ (0742) 467725
11–3 (4 Sat), 5.30 (5 Fri, 6.30 Sat)–11; 12–2.30, 7–10.30 Sun
Wards Sheffield Best Bitter [H]/[E]
Friendly and comfortable local with a traditional tap room and a wood-panelled lounge. Lunches served Tue–Sat.
Q ❀ ◖ ⇌ ♣ P

Cundy Cross

Mill of the Black Monks
Grange Lane (A633)
☎ (0226) 242244
12–3, 7–11
S&N Theakston Best Bitter, XB, Old Peculier; guest beer [H]
A CAMRA *Conservation Award*-winner, a Grade II-listed, former 12th-century monastic watermill displaying interesting artefacts unearthed during restoration. Increasingly popular with a younger clientele. Occasional live jazz/blues/folk and a weekly quiz. Superb garden.
❀ ◖ P

Doncaster

Corner Pin
145 St Sepulchre Gate West
☎ (0302) 323142
11–3.30, 4.45–11; 11–11 Sat
John Smith's Bitter, Magnet; Stones Best Bitter [H]
Comfortable and friendly street-corner local serving a wide variety of good value home-cooked meals (eve meals finish early). ◖ ◗ ⇌ ♣

Corporation Brewery Taps
135 Cleveland Street
☎ (0302) 363715
12–2 (4 Sat), 7–11
Samuel Smith OBB [H]
Popular and friendly local with a large concert room. Close to the town centre and home to local clubs. The Corporation Brewery itself was demolished around 1959.
Q ♿ ⇌ ♣

Hallcross
Hallgate ☎ (0302) 328213
11–11; 11–4, 6.30–11 Sat
Stocks Best Bitter, Select, Old Horizontal; guest beer [H]
Pub on the edge of the town centre, by the Odeon cinema. Sit in the yard and watch the next brew being prepared in the brewery. ❀ ◖

Masons Arms
Market Place ☎ (0302) 364391
10.30 (11 Mon & Wed)–4, 7.30–11; 12–3, 7.30–10.30 Sun
Tetley Bitter [H]
200-year-old Tetley Heritage Inn, displaying photos of old Doncaster and a history of the pub. Opening hours vary with market days: quieter on Mon and Wed. Q ❀ ⇌

Plough
8 West Laith Gate
☎ (0302) 738310
11–4, 6–11
Draught Bass; Stones Best Bitter; Taylor Landlord [H]
Increasingly popular, 1930s town-centre pub. A busy front bar has an emphasis on pub games. The small rear lounge is decorated with vintage farming photographs. A complete contrast from Whitbread's Tut 'n' Shive 'real ale emporium' next door.
Q ❀ ⇌ ♣

Railway
West Street ☎ (0302) 349700
11 (10.30 Sat)–11
John Smith's Bitter, Magnet; Stones Best Bitter [H]
Bustling town pub with an enormous bar and a tiny lounge. Popular with postal and railway workers. ◖ ⇌ ♣

White Swan
34 Frenchgate ☎ (0302) 366573
11–11
Wards Thorne Best Bitter [H], **Sheffield Best Bitter** [H]/[E]
The last of many pubs which once adorned Frenchgate, this friendly town-centre pub boasts the highest bar in Britain (5ft 3in) in the front tap room, and photos of old Doncaster in the comfortable lounge. No food Sun. ◖ ⇌ ♣

Try also: Regent Hotel, Regent Sq (Free)

Dunford Bridge

Stanhope Arms
Off A628 ☎ (0226) 763104
11–3 (not Mon), 7–11
Tetley Mild, Bitter; guest beer [H]
Five-roomed pub, originally a shooting lodge. Situated in a picturesque valley, next to the Woodhead tunnel. Children welcome. Camping in the grounds. An alternative Pennine Way passes the front door. Q ❀ ◖ ◗ ♿ ▲ ♣ P

Dunsville

Flarepath
High Street
☎ (0302) 887350
11–3, 7–11
Ruddles County; John Smith's Bitter, Magnet; guest beers (occasionally) [H]
Friendly, popular, modern and comfortable pub on the main road. ♣ P

Edenthorpe

Ridgewood
Thorne Road (A18)
☎ (0302) 882841
11–3 (4.30 Fri & Sat), 5.30–11
Samuel Smith OBB [H]
Pub named after a famous racehorse: a comfortable, spacious lounge and a tap room, catering for local and passing trade. The extensive beer garden has a children's playground.
❀ ◖ ♣ P

Elsecar

Fitzwilliam Arms
42 Hill Street (off B6097)
☎ (0226) 742461
12–3.30, 7–11
Vaux Samson; Wards Sheffield Best Bitter [E]
Leaning roadside pub set in an ex-mining village near the Elsecar Heritage Centre. Won cellar awards in 1991/2. Live organ music; barbecues in summer; quiz night Thu.
Q ❀ ▲ ⇌ ♣ P

Try also: Market Hotel, Wentworth Rd (Free)

Finningley

Harvey Arms
Old Bawtry Road (off A614)
☎ (0302) 770200
11–3, 7–11; 11–11 Sat
Draught Bass; John Smith's Bitter [H]
Village pub near the green and duck pond and close to an RAF base famous for its air display. The busy traditional bar has a collection of Robert Taylor aircraft prints; the large lounge boasts leaded windows. Good lunchtime carvery; eve meals Sat only.
❀ ◖ ◗ ♿ ♣ P

Hatfield Woodhouse

Green Tree
Bearswood Green (1 mile from M18 jct 5; at A18/A614 jct)
☎ (0302) 840305

South Yorkshire

11-3, 6-11
Vaux Samson; Wards Thorne Best Bitter Ⓗ
Very popular and comfortable 17th-century inn, offering good and reasonably priced food in a carvery and a separate restaurant; children welcome in eating areas.
♔ Q ❀ 🛏 ◑ ◗ ♿ P

Robin Hood & Little John
Main Street ☎ (0302) 840213
10.30-4, 6-11
Draught Bass; Stones Best Bitter Ⓗ
Friendly village local, busy at weekends. The large garden attracts families. ❀ ◑ ⊟ ♣ P

Hemingfield

Lundhill Tavern
Beech House Road (off A633, ½ mile along Lundhill Rd)
☎ (0226) 752283
12-5, 7-11
Bass Special; John Smith's Bitter, Magnet; Stones Best Bitter; Taylor Landlord; guest beers Ⓗ
Off the beaten track and steeped in local coal mining history. Unusual brass blow lamps hang from beams. Meals served in the bar or restaurant (no food Sun eve or Mon). Competitively priced guest beers. Q ❀ ◑ ◗ ♣ P

Higham

Engineers Arms
Higham Common Lane (off A635) ☎ (0226) 384204
11.30-3, 7 (7.30 Mon & Tue)-11
Samuel Smith OBB Ⓗ
Village local with a superb tap room and a plush lounge. The lawned beer garden is next to a cricket field. A local CAMRA *Pub of the Season*. Q ❀ ◑ P

Hoyland

Furnace Inn
163 Milton Road (off B6097)
☎ (0226) 742000
12-3 (11.30-3.30 Sat), 6.30-11; 12-2.15, 7-10.30 Sun
Vaux Samson Ⓗ**; Wards Thorne Best Bitter, Sheffield Best Bitter** Ⓔ**, Kirby** Ⓗ
Welcoming, stone-built pub by an old forge pond. Local CAMRA *Pub of the Season* 1987–89 and winner of a Kimberley-Clarke Superloo award. Collection of coal mining souvenir plates; floral displays in summer. Winning quiz team. Q ❀ ⇌ ♣ P

Mexborough

Concertina Band Club
9a Dolcliffe Road
☎ (0709) 580841
12-4, 7-11; 12-2, 7-10.30 Sun
Concertina Club Bitter; Mansfield Riding Bitter; John Smith's Bitter; Samuel Smith OBB; Wards Sheffield Best Bitter; guest beers Ⓗ
Visitors are welcomed at this small, friendly private club which is steeped in history. Started brewing on the premises in late 1992. ⇌ ♣

Falcon
Main Street ☎ (0709) 571170
11.30-4 (4.30 Fri, 5 Sat), 7-11
Old Mill Bitter, Bullion Ⓗ
Pub where the large lounge has raised drinking areas; traditional games and pool feature in the tap room. Wheelchair access is via the outside passage.
❀ ◑ ♿ ⇌ ♣

George & Dragon
81 Church Street
☎ (0709) 584375
12-3.30 (4 summer), 7 (6.30 summer)-11 (12-2.30, 7-10.30 winter Sun)
Vaux Samson; Wards Sheffield Best Bitter, Kirby Ⓗ
Welcoming, cosy one-roomed pub with a central bar with many prints of old Mexborough. Children's playground. ❀ ⇌ P

Midhopestones

Midhopestones Arms
Mortimer Road (off A616)
☎ (0226) 762305
12-3, 6-11
Courage Directors; John Smith's Bitter; Taylor Landlord; Wards Sheffield Best Bitter; guest beer Ⓗ
Recently renovated but retaining its original character and cosy, welcoming atmosphere. One bar serves four rooms and a 'cartshed' (barn/restaurant). No food Sun eve; meals finish at 8 other eves. ♔ Q ❀ ◑ ◗ ♣ P ⊬

Moorends

Moorends Hotel
156 Marshland Road
☎ (0405) 812170
11-3, 7-11
Wards Thorne Best Bitter Ⓗ
Substantial 1920s building known as 'Uncle Arthur's'. The landlord regularly wins a Wards *Cellar Award*. Eves are usually lively – country and western or karaoke nights, and very serious dominoes matches. No-smoking family room. ♔ ☋ ❀ ◑ ⊟ ♣ P ⊬

Moss

Star
Moss Road OS589143
☎ (0302) 700497
12-3, 6.30-11
Vaux Bitter, Samson Ⓗ
Warm and friendly inn with three small drinking areas, beside the East Coast main railway line. ♔ ❀ ◑ ⛺ P

Newington

Ship Inn
Misson Road (200 yds from A614) ☎ (0302) 710334
12-3, 7-11
S&N Theakston Best Bitter, XB, Old Peculier Ⓗ
Friendly village local from the 1700s. Traditional Sun lunches but no food Mon. Families welcome.
❀ ◑ ◗ ⊟ ♿ ⛺ ♣ P

Oxspring

Waggon & Horses
Sheffield Road (B6462/B6449 jct) ☎ (0226) 763259
12-3 (summer only), 7 (7.30 winter)-11; 12-11 Sat all year
Bass Worthington BB, Draught Bass; Stones Best Bitter Ⓗ
Warm, welcoming, 150-year-old country pub, originally a Pennine farmhouse, with low, beamed ceilings and nook and cranny rooms; full of character. Holds the village duck race on Gala day, and the Trunce Fell race in summer. Good value meals in the bar or restaurant. ♔ ❀ ◑ ◗ ♣ P

Penistone

Cubley Hall
Mortimer Road, Cubley
☎ (0226) 766086
11-3, 6-11
Ind Coope Burton Ale; Marston's Pedigree; Tetley Bitter Ⓗ
Former country house, multi-roomed and retaining much of the fine, original decor. Occasional bottled beer festivals. Q ☋ ❀ ◑ ◗ P ⊬

Rotherham

Bridge
Greasbrough Road (opp. station) ☎ (0709) 363683
10.30-3 (3.30 Sat), 6-11
Draught Bass; John Smith's Bitter Ⓗ**; Stones Best Bitter** Ⓔ
Many-roomed pub next to the Chapel-on-the-Bridge, with meeting rooms used by local groups. Maps and photographs of turn-of-the-century Rotherham. ◑ ⊟ ⇌ ♣

Effingham
Effingham Street (opp. bus station) ☎ (0709) 363653
11-11
Bass Worthington BB; Stones Best Bitter Ⓗ

Typical town-centre pub with four rooms. Stained-glass windows depict Sir Francis Drake, whose round the world trip was sponsored by the Duke of Effingham. ≹ ♣

Kingfisher
Mary Street ☎ (0709) 838422
11–11
Old Mill Bitter, Bullion H
First licensed in 1882, this pub was carefully renovated when taken over by Old Mill in 1991. Kingfishers depicted around the pub. ❀ ⛟ ☾ ♿ ≹ ♣ P

Turners Arms
Psalters Lane, Holmes
☎ (0709) 558937
12–3, 6–11; 12–3.30, 7.30–11 Sat
Wards Sheffield Best Bitter H
Smart, compact pub modernised in 1992 but retaining three separate areas and lots of pub memorabilia. Known locally as 'T' Green Bricks' after its distinct external tiling. ❀ ♣ P

Tut'n'Shive
9 Wellgate ☎ (0709) 364562
11–11; 7–10.30 Sun, closed Sun lunch
Whitbread Boddingtons Bitter; guest beers H
Large town-centre pub with unusual decor, offering the widest range of traditional beers in Rotherham (up to seven guests). The family room has a four-lane bowling alley. ☺ ☾ ≹

Woodman
Midland Road, Masbrough
☎ (0709) 561486
12–3, 7–11
Stones Best Bitter H
Solid, two-roomed former Bentley's pub. Pool table and dartboard in the games room; snooker table upstairs. Quieter lounge. Q ❀ ⊞ ♣

Sheffield: *Central*

Bath Hotel
66 Victoria Street (off Glossop Rd) ☎ (0742) 729017
12–3, 6 (5 Fri, 7.30 Sat)–11; 12–2, 7.30–10.30 Sun
Ind Coope Burton Ale; Tetley Bitter; Wards Sheffield Best Bitter H
A Tetley Heritage pub converted from Victorian cottages to a small, friendly, two-roomed local. The original ground lease prohibits the use of the site as an alehouse or for other noxious activities! Lunches Mon–Fri. ☾ ♣

Brown Bear
109 Norfolk Street
☎ (0742) 727744
11–11
Courage Directors; John Smith's Bitter, Magnet; Marston's Pedigree; Ruddles County; guest beers H
Rare, traditional-style, two-roomed pub in the city centre. A meeting place, patronised by the cast and audience from the Crucible and Lyceum theatres. Thespian memorabilia. ❀ ☾ ≹

Fagan's
69 Broad Lane
☎ (0742) 728430
11.30–3, 5.30–11; 11–11 Fri & Sat
Ind Coope Burton Ale; Tetley Bitter H
Lively, popular pub with a small snug. Impromptu folk music sessions. Q ❀ ☾ ♣

Fat Cat
23 Alma Street
☎ (0742) 728195
12–3, 5.30–11
Kelham Island Bitter; Marston's Pedigree, Owd Rodger; S&N Theakston Old Peculier; Taylor Landlord; guest beers H
Sheffield's first real ale free house, opened in 1981. Two comfortable rooms, a corridor drinking area and an upstairs function room for overspill. Kelham Island brewery operates from the grounds. Handy for the Industrial Museum. ⛰ Q ❀ ☾ ⌂ ⊬

Lord Nelson
166 Arundel Street
☎ (0742) 722650
11–11; 11.30–5, 8–11 Sat; 12–3, 7.30–10.30 Sun
Hardys & Hansons Best Bitter H
Recently refurbished, street-corner local in an area of small workshops at the edge of the city centre. ☾ ≹ ♣

Moseley's Arms
West Bar ☎ (0742) 721591
11–11; 11–3, 7–11 Sat
Draught Bass; Stones Best Bitter H
Superbly renovated pub just off the city centre: three comfortably furnished rooms, with a friendly atmosphere. A function room upstairs houses a full-sized snooker table. ☾ ⊞ ♿ ≹ (Midland) ♣

Norfolk Arms
26 Dixon Lane
☎ (0742) 761139
11–11; 11–4.30, 7–11 Sat; 12–3, 8–10.30 Sun
Stones Best Bitter E
Popular, traditional street-corner alehouse, in the markets area. Friendly. ≹ ♣

Red Deer
18 Pitt Street (off West St)
☎ (0742) 722890
11.30–3, 5–11; 11.30–11 Fri; 12–3, 7.30–11 Sat; 7.30–10.30 Sun, closed Sun lunch
Ind Coope Burton Ale; Tetley Mild, Bitter; Wards Sheffield Best Bitter H
Friendly, one-roomed local close to the university. Excellent home-cooked meals (children allowed in the function room lunchtime). Quiz Sun. Display of paintings by local artists. ❀ ☾ ♣

Roebuck
72 Charles Street
☎ (0742) 721756
11–3.30, 5 (7 Sat)–11; 12–2.30, 7–10.30 Sun
Wards Sheffield Best Bitter; guest beer H/E
Comfortable, single-roomed pub with an L-shaped lounge bar and a pool/darts area. Extensively renovated but retaining original Wards windows. ☾ ≹ ♣ P

Rutland Arms
86 Brown Street
☎ (0742) 729003
12–3, 5 (7.30 Sat)–11
Ind Coope Burton Ale; Marston's Pedigree; Tetley Bitter; Younger No. 3 H
City-centre gem in a resurgent cultural corner of the city. Behind the distinctive Gilmour's frontage lies a comfortable lounge. Restaurant in an upstairs function room, open Thu–Sat; eve bar meals Mon–Fri till 7pm. Q ❀ ⛟ ☾ ◗ ≹ P

Tap & Spile
42 Waingate ☎ (0742) 726270
11.30–3, 5.30–11; 11.30–11 Sat
Beer range varies H
Large, recently refurbished, ex-Gilmour's street-corner pub. Exposed brickwork and bare floorboards in the large bar and smaller side room with its raised darts area. No-smoking area lunchtime only. Up to ten ales in a constantly changing range. Q ☾ ≹ ♣ ⌂ ⊬

Washington
79 Fitzwilliam Street (off West St) ☎ (0742) 754937
11.30–3, 6.30–11; 12–2, 7–10.30 Sun
Ind Coope Burton Ale; Tetley Mild, Bitter H
Pub where two comfortably furnished rooms feature an extensive display of teapots. Popular meeting place for numerous groups. Lunches Mon–Fri. ☾ ⊞ ♣

Sheffield: *East*

Alma Inn
76 South Street, Mosborough (behind Eckington Hall)
☎ (0742) 484781
11.30–3.30, 7 (6.30 summer)–11
Wards Thorne Best Bitter H, **Sheffield Best Bitter** H/E
Traditional, two-roomed local, split by a central bar. Off the beaten track, but worth seeking out; a friendly welcome is assured. Small play area for children in the rear garden. Q ❀ ⊞ ♣ P

South Yorkshire

Cocked Hat
75 Worksop Road, Attercliffe
☎ (0742) 448332
11–11; 11–3, 7–11 Sat
Marston's Bitter, Pedigree [H]
Excellent Victorian pub by the Don Valley Stadium. Attracts custom from all parts of the city. Good value weekday lunches. Display of bottled beers. ♨ Q ❀ ◖ ♣

Cross Keys
400 Handsworth Road (A57)
☎ (0742) 694413
11–11
Stones Best Bitter [E]
Popular, three-roomed local next to Handsworth church. An outstanding example of an historic, unspoilt pub. ⊟ ♣

Enfield Arms
95 Broughton Lane, Attercliffe
☎ (0742) 425134
11.30–11
Bass Worthington BB, Draught Bass; Stones Best Bitter; Tetley Bitter [H]
Three-roomed free house, including a large games room. Opposite Sheffield Arena and popular with concert-goers. Keenly-priced ale. ◖ ♣

Milestone
12 Peaks Mount, Waterthorpe
☎ (0742) 471614
11–11
Banks's Mild, Bitter [E]**; Camerons Strongarm** [H]
Modern but appealing pub, serving Crystal Peaks shopping centre. The large lounge adjoins a conservatory and the tap room has a viewing glass into the cellar. Good value food. ♨ ❀ ◖ ◗ ⊟ ♿ ♣ P

Sheffield: *North*

Mill Tavern
2–4 Earsham Street, Burngreave ☎ (0742) 756461
11–4, 7–11
Old Mill Mild, Bitter, Bullion [H]
A mock-Tudor frontage leads into a single bar which serves all areas of the pub. A big charity fund-raiser. Regular entertainment. ❀ ◖ ♿ ♣

Railway
299 Holywell Road, Brightside
☎ (0742) 433067
11–11
Tetley Bitter [H]
Friendly and comfortable, two-roomed local near Meadowhall shopping complex. Good value lunches, Mon–Sat. ❀ ◖ ⊟ ♣ P

Robin Hood
Greaves Lane, Little Matlock, Stannington ☎ (0742) 344565
11.30–2.30 (3 Sat & summer), 7–11
Stones Best Bitter [E]
Old, large country pub on the site of a failed spa. Children's play area. Eve meals Thu–Sat, other days by arrangement. Walkers and hikers welcome. ❀ ◖ ◗ ⊟ ♣ P

Staffordshire Arms
40 Sorby Street (300 yds from A6135/B6082 fork)
☎ (0742) 721381
11–11
Stones Best Bitter [E]
Small, convivial back-street local. One bar serves both the main drinking area and a small snug. ♣

Sheffield: *South*

Earl of Arundel & Surrey
Queens Road (A61 1 mile from centre) ☎ (0742) 551006
11–11
Taylor Landlord; Vaux Lorimers Best Scotch; Wards Sheffield Best Bitter [H]
Pub on its own near Bramall Lane football ground. A games venue for locals, with a mixed clientele. Entertainment Sun–Thu. No food Sun. ◖ P

Fleur de Lys
Totley Hall Lane, Totley (A621) ☎ (0742) 361476
11–11
Bass Worthington BB, Draught Bass; Stones Best Bitter [H]
Large, two-roomed pub built in mock-Tudor style with oak panelling. Handy for the Derbyshire moors and popular with a wide cross-section of the public. ❀ ◖ P

Mount Pleasant
293 Derbyshire Lane, Norton
☎ (0742) 554997
11.30–4 (6 Sat), 6 (7 Sat)–11
Banks's Bitter; Tetley Bitter [H]
Stone-built two-roomer, with a community atmosphere: regular outings. ❀ P

Old Mother Redcap
Prospect Road, Bradway
☎ (0742) 360179
11–3, 5.30–11; 11–11 Sat
Samuel Smith OBB [H]
Modern, stone-built estate pub where a single L-shaped room is served by a central bar. A friendly atmosphere makes it popular with all ages, but motorcycle club members are recommended not to attend. Bus terminus outside. ❀ ◖ P

Shakespeare
106 Well Road (off A61 at Heeley Bridge)
☎ (0742) 553935
12–3.30 (4.30 Sat), 5.30 (7 Sat)–11
Ind Coope Burton Ale; Stones Best Bitter; Tetley Bitter [H]
Open-plan pub with three distinct drinking areas; cosy and friendly. Close to Heeley City Farm, with a magnificent valley view. ❀ ♣

Small Beer Off-Licence
57 Archer Road (off A621)
☎ (0742) 551356
12 (10.30 Sat)–10.30; 12–2, 7–10.30 Sun
Bateman XXXB; Taylor Landlord [H]**; guest beers**
Small but well stocked back-street off-licence with a wide range of foreign bottled beers. ♿ ⛀

Sheffield: *West*

Banner Cross
971 Ecclesall Road (A625)
☎ (0742) 661479
11.30–11
Ind Coope Burton Ale; Tetley Bitter; guest beer [H]
Busy suburban local with a wood-panelled lounge and a large, well-decorated tap room. Upstairs games room (snooker and pool). ❀ ◖ ⊟ ♣

Bull's Head
396 Fulwood Road
☎ (0742) 303629
11–11
Bass Worthington BB, Draught Bass; Stones Best Bitter [H]
One-roomed lounge with a tap room atmosphere on one side. Comfortably furnished with ash woodwork. ❀ ◖ ♣ P

Fox & Duck
223–227 Fulwood Road (A57)
☎ (0742) 663422
11–11
Courage Directors; John Smith's Bitter, Magnet [H]
Busy pub in the middle of Broomhill shopping centre. A large bar serves several distinct areas, all traditionally furnished. ❀ ◖ ♣

Lescar
303 Sharrowvale Road
☎ (0742) 663857
12–4, 6 (7 Sat)–11
Draught Bass; Stones Best Bitter [H]
Pub split into two bars. The public has a cosy cheerfulness, while the lounge is quiet. A large back room has a stage; music, comedy and quiz nights are held. The food is good value – Sun lunches a speciality. Q ❀ ◖ ♣ P

Norfolk Arms
Manchester Road, Rivelin Dams, Hollow Meadows (A57)
☎ (0742) 309253
11.30–3.30, 6.30–11; 11–11 Sat
Vaux Samson; Wards Thorne Best Bitter [H]
Roadside inn with an aquarium in the bar. The large, plush lounge boasts a grand piano. Folk music Fri nights. ♨ Q 🛏 ❀ ◖ ◗ ▲ ♣ P

Old Grindstone
3 Crookes ☎ (0742) 660322
11–11
Taylor Landlord; Vaux Samson H; Wards Sheffield Best Bitter H/E, Kirby; guest beer H
Spacious, busy pub. The Victorian design lounge has a raised area; the oak-panelled games room is based on a gentleman's club, offering snooker, pool and darts. Jazz night Mon; quiz Thu. The guest beer changes weekly. Eve meals finish at 7.30.
❀ ◐ ◗ ♿ ▲ ♣

Old Heavygate
114 Matlock Road
☎ (0742) 340003
12–3.30, 7–11
Hardys & Hansons Best Bitter, Kimberley Classic H
Pub dating from 1696 with some original beams in the Oak Room. The lounge has high bar stools and lovingly cared-for potted plants.
Q ❀ ♣ P

South Anston

Loyal Trooper
Sheffield Road
☎ (0909) 562203
12–3, 6–11; 12–11 Sat
Tetley Bitter H
Old village pub with two cosy rooms at the front. The larger back room has a pool table and a darts area. ❀ ◐ ⊞ ♿ P

Sprotbrough

Boat Inn
Nursery Lane, Lower Sprotbrough ☎ (0302) 857188
11–3, 6–11 (11–11 summer)
Courage Directors; John Smith's Bitter, Magnet H
17th-century former coaching house where Sir Walter Scott wrote *Ivanhoe*. Refurbished in 1985: exposed beams, a stone floor and ornamental china give a farmhouse feel. Set in a deep gorge by the River Don (beware twisty roads). Bar meals (no food Sat lunch or Sun eve) and restaurant.
❀ ◐ ◗ ♿ P

Thorpe Hesley

Horse & Tiger
Brook Hill (B6086, near M1 jct 35) ☎ (0742) 468072
11–3, 6–11; 11–11 Sat
Stones Best Bitter; Tetley Bitter H
Restored to its former glory, a pub on the site of an earlier one. Named after an incident involving a travelling circus many years ago. ❀ ♣ P

Tickhill

Scarbrough Arms
Sunderland Street
☎ (0302) 742977
11–3, 6–11
Courage Directors; Ruddles County; John Smith's Bitter, Magnet; guest beers H
Three very different rooms plus an extensive beer garden. Guest beers from independent brewers vary weekly. Good value, home-cooked lunches (not served Sun) include vegetarian options. Smoking restriction mealtimes only.
⌂ Q ❀ ◐ ⊞ ♣ P ⊁

Three Crowns
Northgate ☎ (0302) 745191
11–2.30, 7–11
Tetley Bitter; guest beers H
Formerly the Buttercross: a quiet, comfortable lounge and a low-ceilinged tap room. Usually two guest beers from independent brewers. Family room under construction. Garden chess played.
Q ❀ ⊞ ♣

Ulley

Royal Oak
Turnshaw Road
☎ (0742) 872464
11–3, 6–11
Samuel Smith OBB, Museum H
Popular country inn in a classic village setting. The emphasis is on catering, with home-cooked meals and a vegetarian dish. ⛟ ❀ ◐ ◗ P

Victoria

Victoria Inn
On A616, near pipe works
☎ (0484) 682785
12–2 (Fri, Sat & Sun only), 7–11
Tetley Bitter; Younger IPA H
Step back to 1956: nothing has changed since the present licensees took over this old roadside pub. As in 1956, children are not allowed under any circumstances. ⌂ Q P

Wath upon Dearne

Sandygate
☎ (0709) 877827
11–3, 5 (7 Sat)–11
S&N Theakston Best Bitter; Younger IPA, No. 3 H
Imposing former hospital overlooking the picturesque Dearne valley. Decorated and furnished to a high standard to include a hotel and restaurant. No meals Sun eve.
⌂ ❀ 🛏 ◐ ◗ ♿ ♣ P

Wheatley Hills

Wheatley Hotel
Thorne Road ☎ (0302) 364092
10.30–11
Courage Directors; John Smith's Bitter, Magnet H
Large, well-appointed hotel where the lounge is divided by impressive sliding doors. Well-equipped play area for children outside. Quiz Thu; traditional sing-along Sun.
⛟ ❀ 🛏 ◐ ◗ ⊞ ♣ P

Whiston

Golden Ball
7 Turner Lane ☎ (0709) 378200
11.45–3, 5–11; 11.45–11 Fri & Sat
Ind Coope Burton Ale; Marston's Pedigree; Tetley Bitter H
Typical picture-postcard English pub offering a pleasant outside drinking area and eating facilities. Full of olde-worlde charm with an extensive bar menu and à la carte restaurant. ❀ ◐ ◗ P

Wombwell

Wat Tyler Inn
134 Station Road (B6035)
☎ (0226) 340307
11.30–3, 7–11
John Smith's Bitter, Magnet; Stones Best Bitter; guest beers H
Named after the original poll tax protester; a roadside pub with a pleasant lawned garden. Holds barbecues in summer and regular beer festivals. No food Mon eve or Sun. ⌂ ❀ ◐ ◗ ♣ P

Woodhouse Mill

Princess Royal
680 Retford Road
☎ (0742) 692615
11.30–3.30, 7–11
Ind Coope Burton Ale; Marston's Pedigree; Tetley Bitter H
Large roadhouse which straddles the border between Sheffield and Rotherham. The function room is used by local groups. ⛟ ❀ ◐ ⊞ ⇌ ♣ P

Worsbrough Village

Edmunds Arms
Off A61 ☎ (0226) 206865
11.30–3, 7–11
Samuel Smith OBB H
Splendid village inn opposite a picturesque church: a lounge, tap room and a restaurant (no meals Mon or Sun eves). Good value food. Near a country park and historic watermill.
Q ❀ ◐ ◗ ♿ ♣ P

Wortley

Wortley Arms
Halifax Road (A629)
☎ (0742) 882245
12–11
Tetley Bitter; Wortley Bitter, Earls Ale; guest beers H
16th-century coaching house in a picturesque village, opposite the church. Ideally placed for walkers, it has a comfortable lounge bar with a large open fire, a tap room, a no-smoking snug, and a restaurant. Frequent folk and music nights. Wortley beers brewed in the cellar. ⌂ Q
⛟ ❀ 🛏 ◐ ◗ ♿ ▲ ♣ P ⊁

West Yorkshire

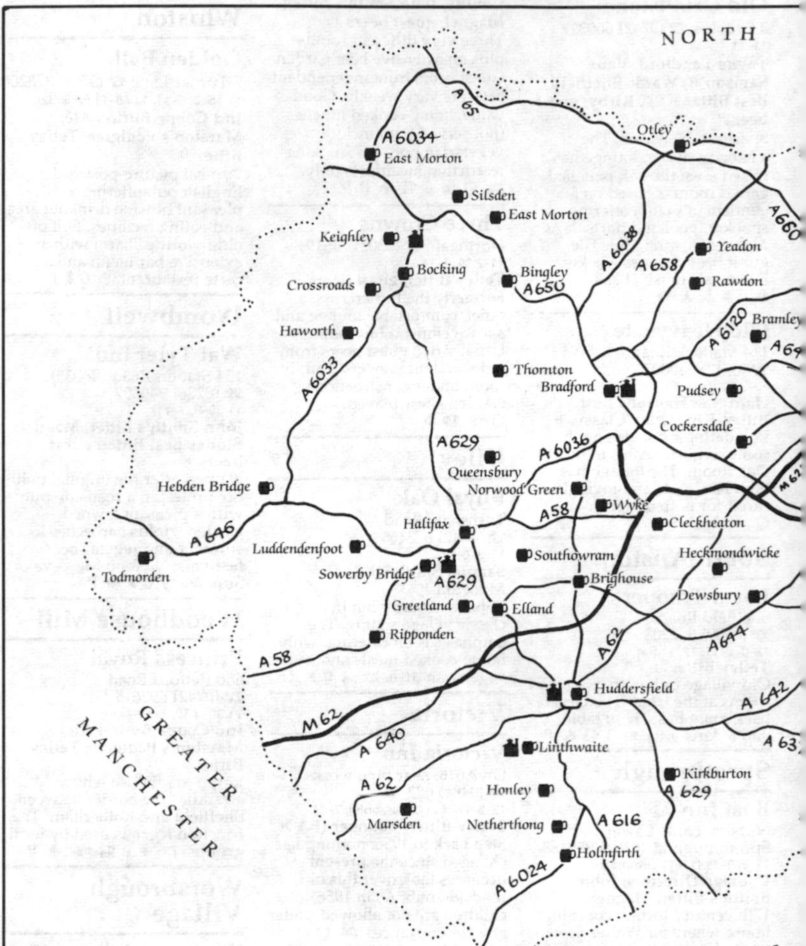

***Clark's,** Wakefield; **Commercial,** Keighley; **Eastwood's,** Huddersfield; **Goose Eye,** Keighley; **Linfit,** Linthwaite; **Ryburn,** Sowerby Bridge; **Steam Packet,** Knottingley; **Taylor,** Keighley; **Trough,** Bradford*

Aberford

Arabian Horse
Main Street
☎ (0532) 813312
11–2.30, 5–11; 11–11 Sat
S&N Theakston Best Bitter; Younger Scotch, No. 3 Ⓗ
18th-century inn on the green of one of Leeds's most attractive villages. Friendly, with a warm welcome. Large open fire. ♣ P

Barwick in Elmet

New Inn
Main Street ☎ (0532) 812289
11.30–3, 5.30–11; 11–4, 6–11 Sat
John Smith's Bitter Ⓗ
Friendly, roadside village inn; a real locals' pub with service from a tiny bar and hatchway.
Q

Bingley

Ferrands Arms
Queen Street ☎ (0274) 563949
11.30–11
Taylor Golden Best, Best Bitter, Landlord, Porter (winter), **Ram Tam** Ⓗ

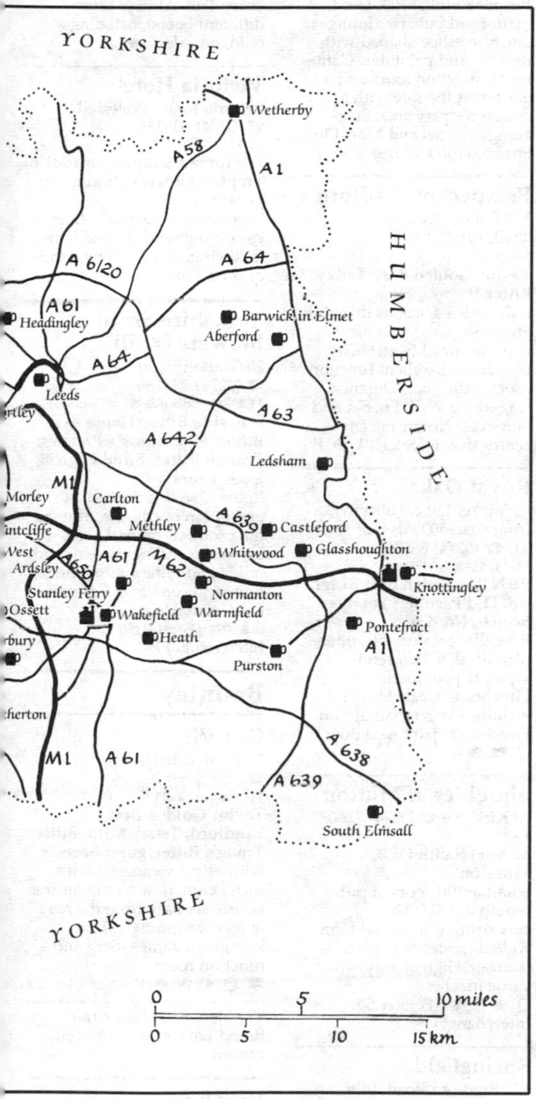

Open-plan pub, now split into three areas, near Bingley arts centre. Enjoys a good view of Bradford & Bingley building society HQ, which has been voted one of the worst buildings ever. Good upstairs function room. Quiz Tue. Easy parking.
☾ ≠ ♣

Bocking

New Inn

Halifax Road (A629 near A6033 jct)
☎ (0535) 643191
11 (4 winter)–11
Mansfield Riding Bitter (H); Taylor Golden Best (E);

Whitbread Boddingtons Bitter, Castle Eden Ale (H)
Popular two-room local, recently refurbished using stained-wood and Yorkshire stone. Pub games team; live music.
♿ ≠ ♣ P

Bradford

Blue Pig Inn

Fagley Lane, Lower Fagley (down track at the end of Fagley Rd) OS193351
☎ (0532) 562738
11–11
S&N Theakston Best Bitter, XB; Taylor Landlord, Tetley Bitter (H); guest beers
Split-level pub on the Leeds Country Way, within a slice of a golf course. Flooding necessitated the building of the low front wall and tortuous entrance route. DJ and quiz most eves. Lunches in summer only.
❀ ☾ ♣ P

Brewery Arms

Louisa Street, Idle
☎ (0274) 610546
11–11
Trough Bitter, Wild Boar, Festival, Blind Pugh (winter) **(H)**
Former Liberal club situated next to Trough brewery, featuring a large lounge with a separate area for pool. The newly-created snug is a retreat during the regular disco nights. ☾ ♣ P

Brewery Tap

51 Albion Road, Idle
☎ (0274) 613936
11.30–3 (4 Sat), 6.30–11
Trough Bitter, Wild Boar (H); guest beer
Previously a public house, then a bakery: one room with a large central bar. Regular live rock music. Own golfing society. Dominoes played with real enthusiasm. ❀ ♣

Brown Cow Inn

886 Little Horton Lane (A6177 jct) ☎ (0274) 574040
12–3, 7–11
Samuel Smith OBB (H)
Pub with a comfortable, split-level lounge and a popular, separate tap room. Live music Fri and Sun. ♣

Corn Dolly

110 Bolton Road
☎ (0274) 720219
11.30–11
Moorhouse's Premier; S&N Theakston Best Bitter, XB; Stones Best Bitter (H); guest beers
Oak beams, open fire, huge lunchtime sandwiches and four constantly-changing guest beers make this popular pub a worthy winner of many awards. Home-cooked meals Mon–Fri. Country and western Wed and Sun. Classic jukebox. Small beer garden. Can get very busy.
♨ ❀ ☾ ♿ ≠ (Forster Sq) ♣ P

Gaping Goose

5–6 Slack Bottom Road, Wibsey
☎ (0274) 601701
12–3, 7–11
S&N Theakston Old Peculier; Taylor Landlord; Tetley Bitter; Whitbread Boddingtons Bitter, Trophy (H)

Friendly, intimate, two-roomed local, opposite the filming location of TV's *Flying Lady*. ❀ ♿ ♣ P

Idle Cock
1190 Bolton Road (A6176/Idle Rd jct, 2 miles from centre)
☎ (0274) 639491
11.30–11
Marston's Pedigree; Old Mill Bitter; S&N Theakston Old Peculier; Taylor Landlord; Tetley Bitter; Whitbread Boddingtons Bitter Ⓗ; guest beers
Large, traditional alehouse including a recently-opened extension and a bottle and jug bar. Live music Tue; jazz club Sun lunch. Friendly welcome guaranteed. Good off-road parking. ❀ ◖ ⊏

Lower Globe
3 Globe Fold, Whetley Hill (B6144, 1 mile from centre)
☎ (0274) 493142
12–11
Vaux Bitter, Samson, Double Maxim Ⓗ; guest beer
Superb old coaching inn dating back to the 18th century. Friendly atmosphere and a good mix of clientele. Collection of miniatures displayed. Karaoke Fri eve. Vaux guest beer. ❀ ◖ ♣ P

New Beehive Inn
171 Westgate
☎ (0274) 721784
11–11
Coach House Coachman's; Moorhouse's Pendle Witches Brew; Old Mill Bitter; Taylor Golden Best, Landlord; Tetley Bitter Ⓗ; guest beers
Genuine, gas-lit inn with five rooms and a new cellar bar, offering live music. Wide range of malt whiskies. Up to four guest beers.
♨ Q ⚇ ❀ 🛏 ◖ ♿ ⇌ (Forster Sq/Interchange) ♣ P

Oddfellows Arms
696 Harrogate Road, Greengates
☎ (0274) 611944
12–4, 6–11; 11–11 Thu–Sat
John Smith's Bitter Ⓗ; guest beer
Large, refurbished pub on the edge of an estate, with two pool tables and a snooker table in the games room. Rotating Courage brand guest beer. Quiz Wed, disco Thu.
❀ ♿ ♣ P

Prince of Wales
91 Harrogate Road, Eccleshill
☎ (0274) 638729
11.30–11
John Smith's Bitter; Tetley Bitter Ⓗ
Purpose-built, brick-faced, main-road pub: two lounges, one horseshoe-shaped with mirrors and paintings. Games room, function room and a garden at the side with a children's play area. Sing-alongs Fri, Sat and Mon. Quiz Sun. No food Sun. ❀ ◖ ♣ P

Prospect of Bradford
527 Bolton Road
☎ (0274) 727018
1–4, 7–11
Taylor Golden Best; Tetley Bitter Ⓗ
Pub with a spacious drinking area and panoramic views over Bradford (watch City play free). Excellent function room with a bar. Organist sing-along Wed, Fri, Sat and Sun eves. Nearer the city centre than it looks. ♨ ♣ P

Royal Oak
32 Sticker Lane, Laisterdyke (ring road 500 yds S of A647 jct) ☎ (0274) 665265
11–11; 11–3, 7–11 Sat
S&N Theakston Best Bitter, XB, Old Peculier; Younger Scotch, No. 3 Ⓗ
Friendly, comfortable, open-plan local, with a semi-separate pool room. Lunchtime meals Mon–Fri include a vegetarian option. Floodlit car park next door.
Q ⚇ ❀ ◖

Shoulder of Mutton
28 Kirkgate ☎ (0274) 726038
11–11
Samuel Smith OBB, Museum Ⓗ
Small, multi-roomed pub rebuilt in 1825. The surprisingly large and high-walled garden is a quiet suntrap. High quality, good value lunches.
Q ❀ ◖ ⇌ (Forster Sq/Interchange) ♣

Springfield
179 Bradford Road, Idle
☎ (0274) 612710
11–11
Vaux Samson Ⓗ
Roadside local on the edge of a housing estate: a small lounge with a pool table, and a lively tap room. Popular with darts players. ♣ P

Tut 'n' Shive
49 Duckworth Lane
☎ (0274) 547372
11–11
Old Mill Bitter; Whitbread Boddingtons Bitter, Flowers Original Ⓗ; guest beers
Part of a growing chain of real ale-oriented pubs. Erratic floors and walls; uniformed staff, but a variety of clientele. Occasional live music. Quiz every Tue. Always seven different beers, including a mild, on sale. ◖ ♣

Victoria Hotel
Victoria Road, Eccleshill
☎ (0274) 639186
11–11
Whitbread Boddingtons Mild, Trophy, Flowers Original Ⓗ; guest beer
Pleasantly-renovated, street-corner pub with a good local following. 50s–70s music and quiz on Sun. Piano. ❀ ♣

Yorkshire Small Brewers (YSB)
20 Grattan Road
☎ (0274) 393166
11.30–11; closed Sun
Daleside Bitter; Goose Eye Bitter; Moorhouse's Premier; Trough Bitter, Blind Pugh Ⓗ; guest beers
Roomy, well-furbished, open-plan beerhouse, offering the products of local small breweries. All normal-strength milds and bitters at low prices. Eve meals end at 8. Car park only available eves.
◖ ◗ ⇌ (Forster Sq/Interchange) P

Bramley

Old Vic
17 Whitecote Hill (A657)
☎ (0532) 561207
11–3 (4 Sat), 7–11
Taylor Golden Best, Landlord; Tetley Mild, Bitter; Trough Bitter; guest beers Ⓗ
Formerly a vicarage, then a social club, now a popular free house, set back from the road in its own grounds. Two lounges, a games room and a function room.
♨ Q ⊞ ♿ ♣ P

Try also: Sandford Arms, Broad Lane (Tom Cobleigh group)

Brighouse

Crown
6 Lightcliffe Road (off A644 at the Albion) ☎ (0484) 715436
11.30–11
Tetley Bitter; guest beer Ⓗ
Genuine, multi-roomed, Victorian locals' pub which survived redevelopment in a residential area up the hill from the town centre. Unusual collections on display, including plates. ❀ ♿ ♣ P

Red Rooster
123 Elland Road, Brookfoot (A6025, ½ mile from centre)
☎ (0484) 713737
12–2 (3 Sat; not Mon & Tue), 5 (6 Sat)–11

Old Mill Bitter; Marston's Pedigree; Moorhouse's Pendle Witches Brew; Rooster's Yankee; Taylor Landlord [H]; guest beers
Compact and friendly, stone-built, genuine free house on a sharp bend 400 yards from canal locks. Limited car parking but nevertheless very popular so, if you want a seat, arrive early. Bikers welcome. Four guest beers.
♨ ⛴ ❀ ◯ P

Bruntcliffe

Shoulder of Mutton
Howden Clough Road (off A650 towards Morley, near M62 jct 27)
☎ (0532) 535085
12–11
Vaux Bitter, Samson [H]
Open-plan lounge and a separate tap room with a friendly atmosphere, in a 19th-century building. Great emphasis on quizzes and music, with something happening every night, except Mon. Ask the landlord about the pub's unusual history and say hello to the cockatiel called Samson! ♨ ❀ ♿ ♣ P

Carlton

Rosebud
Westfield Road (off Leadwell Lane) ☎ (0532) 822236
12–2.30 (4 Sat), 5.30 (7 Sat)–11; 12–11 Fri
John Smith's Bitter; Vaux Samson; Wards Mild [H]
Friendly, two-roomed village local which despite the Webster's signs is actually a Vaux pub. Traditional tap room and good conversation in the lounge. The enthusiastic young landlord has ideas for the future, given the opportunity. No food weekends.
♨ Q ❀ ◐ ♣ P

Castleford

Garden House
Wheldon Road (off A656)
☎ (0977) 552934
11–11
Vaux Samson, Extra Special; Wards Mild, Thorne Best Bitter [H]
Large, friendly local on the edge of town, overlooking the River Aire. The well-patronised tap room features a local artist's drawings of RL players. Busy on RL match days, when visiting supporters are welcome. Good value, home-cooked food.
♨ Q ❀ ◐ ◑ ⊞ ≋ ♣ P

White Lion
Pottery Street (off Methley Rd, A6032, ½ mile W of town)
☎ (0977) 554045
12–11
John Smith's Bitter; Tetley Bitter; Webster's Green Label; Whitbread Flowers IPA, Trophy; guest beer [H]
Friendly, edge-of-town local, built to service the once-thriving Castleford potteries. Warm welcome guaranteed, in comfortable surroundings.
❀ ◐ ◑ ≋ ♣

Cleckheaton

Marsh
28 Bradford Road (A638, 500 yds S of bus station)
☎ (0274) 872104
11.30–3, 7–11; 11.30–11 Fri & Sat
Old Mill Mild, Bitter, Bullion [H]
The colour coordination might not have mellowed but the pub has – into a nice and friendly one! A lively mixture of customers creates a spirited atmosphere, especially on the Wed quiz nights. The crinkly wall now has creaky floorboards for company.
❀ ◐ ♣ P

Try also: West End, Latham Lane, Gomersal (Courage)

Cockersdale

Valley
68 Whitehall Road (A58)
☎ (0532) 852483
11.30–3, 5.30–11; 11.30–11 Sat
Samuel Smith OBB [H]
Tastefully decorated, comfortable roadside inn with a good view over Leeds; close to the Leeds Country Way walk. Four separate areas include pool and meeting rooms. Value for money menu.
♨ ❀ ◐ ◑ ♣ P

Crossroads

Quarry House Inn
1 mile from A629, on Bingley road
☎ (0535) 642239
12–3, 7–11 (11.30 supper licence)
Ind Coope Burton Ale; Taylor Landlord; Tetley Bitter [H]
Family-run converted farmhouse in open countryside with views. The bar is a former church pulpit, set in a small, cosy area. Good quality, home-made food served, especially soups, with a carvery each weekday lunchtime. The mixed grill, served Wed night only, is good value.
♨ Q ⛴ ❀ ◐ ◑ ♿ ▲ P

Dewsbury

John F Kennedy
2 Webster Hill (A644, near bus and railway stations)
☎ (0924) 455828
1–4 (not Mon–Fri), 7–11
Taylor Landlord; Tetley Bitter; Trough Wild Boar [H]; guest beer
Pub which has retained its character, thanks to the longest-serving local licensee. The customer mix is varied but the jukebox is enjoyed by all. ♿ ≋ ♣

Market House
8 Church Street (200 yds N of bus station)
☎ (0924) 457310
11–11
S&N Theakston Best Bitter; Tetley Mild, Bitter [H]
A haven for those who like to chat and drink; a pub with a character of its own, that is respected by customers and landlords alike. A small front room with a bank of five handpumps, a large back room with a serving hatch, and an overflow corridor. Wheelchair access at the rear.
♨ Q ◐ ♿ ≋ ♣

East Morton

Busfeild Arms
Main Road ☎ (0274) 564453
11.30–3 (4 Sat), 5.30 (6 Sat)–11
Bass Light, Worthington BB, Draught Bass; Stones Best Bitter [H]
18th-century, stone-built ex-schoolhouse in an attractive village nestling under Rombalds Moor. Tastefully modernised in wood and stone, with two separate rooms and prints of the old village. Well-behaved children welcome at lunchtime.
❀ ◐ ♣ P

Elland

Colliers Arms
66 Park Road (A6025)
☎ (0422) 372007
11.30–3, 5–11; 11–11 Sat
Samuel Smith OBB, Museum [H]
Smart, roadside cottage pub with two low-ceilinged rooms, plus a conservatory to the rear. Own moorings on the canal behind the pub. Eve meals Wed–Sat in summer, Fri–Sat in winter. ♨ ◐ ◑ P

Oddfellows Arms
12 Elland Lane (off A629, behind Haworth Timber)
☎ (0422) 373605
12–11

Hambleton Best Bitter, Stallion; Tetley Bitter Ⓗ; guest beers
Small, back-street boozer with a comfortable lounge and a small tap room.
◖◗ ♣ P

Glasshoughton

Rock Inn
Rock Hill (off Front St, B6136)
☎ (0977) 552985
11–11
Vaux Extra Special; Wards Mild, Thorne Best Bitter Ⓗ
Popular, friendly, traditional locals' pub, comprising a lounge, a tap room and a snug, all with open fires, making it very cosy on cold nights. Pool room upstairs. Winner of several pub awards. Parking far from easy.
Q ◖◗ ♣ P

Greetland

Star Inn
1 Lindwell (off B6113)
☎ (0422) 373164
12–3 (not Tue), 7–11
Wards Thorne Best Bitter, Sheffield Best Bitter Ⓗ
Popular local: a well-lit busy tap room, and a cosy lounge with subdued lighting. The Calderdale Way footpath starts nearby. ❀ ♣

Halifax

Brown Cow
569 Gibbet Street, Highroad Well (1½ miles from centre)
☎ (0422) 361640
11.30–3, 5–11; 11.30–11 Fri & Sat
Whitbread Trophy, Castle Eden Ale Ⓗ
Unpretentious and friendly pub with sporting connections. Lunches weekdays.
◖ ♿ ♣

Duke of York
West Street, Stone Chair, Shelf (A644, near A6036 jct)
☎ (0422) 202056
11.30–11
Taylor Best Bitter; Whitbread Boddingtons Mild, Bitter, Trophy, Castle Eden Ale, Flowers Original; guest beer Ⓗ
Ancient inn with a remarkable roof-scape. Refurbished within, but still cosy and comfortable. Very popular for food (including vegetarian) till 9pm. Quiz night Wed.
❀ ◖◗ ♣ P

Pump Room
35 New Road (200 yds left from station)
☎ (0422) 381465
11–11
Old Mill Bitter; Taylor Landlord; Tetley Bitter; Whitbread Boddingtons Bitter Ⓗ; guest beers
Superior, traditional alehouse displaying a collection of taps and breweriana: note the Hey's sign over the bar. Home to a golfing society, football club and a quiz team. Up to seven guest beers. Pump Room Bitter is brewed by Coach House.
◖ ≥ ♣ P

Shears Inn
Paris Gates, Boys Lane (behind flats, between mills and down into the mill yard)
☎ (0422) 362936
11.45–4, 7–11; 11.45–11 Sat
Taylor Golden Best, Best Bitter, Landlord; Younger Scotch, No. 3; guest beer Ⓗ
Tiny, popular house, secreted in a narrow, wooded valley and overshadowed by towering mill buildings. A convenient stopping point on the new Hebble Valley Trail. No food weekends.
❀ ◖ ≥ ♣ P

Sportsman
Bradford Old Road, Ploughcroft (¼ mile E of A647, 1 mile N of centre)
☎ (0422) 367000
12–3, 6–11; 12–11 Sat
Ind Coope Burton Ale; Old Mill Bitter; S&N Theakston Old Peculier; Taylor Landlord; Tetley Bitter; guest beer Ⓗ
Popular, hill-top free house with expansive views. Squash, solarium and sauna all available; all-weather ski-slope attached. Folk club Thu; quiz nights Mon–Fri. No eve meals Mon.
❀ ◖◗ ♿ ♣ P

Sportsman Hotel
48–50 Crown Street
☎ (0422) 355704
11–11
Tetley Bitter; guest beer Ⓗ
Lively town local with a fine Edwardian frontage. Well used rooms adjoin the bar. The pool room wall has rugby league scarves and a cabinet displaying pump clips. The jukebox favours rock music. Separate lounge off the bar area.
≥ ♣

Three Pigeons
1 Sun Fold, South Parade (400 yds left from station)
☎ (0422) 347001
12–2 (3 Sat), 7–11
Bass Worthington BB; Ryburn Bitter, Rydale Bitter; Stones Best Bitter; Trough Wild Boar Ⓗ
Fine Art Deco building, designed by Jackson & Fox in 1932. Note the octagonal lobby with its painted ceiling.
Q ♿ ▲ ≥ ♣

Try also: **Clarence**, Lister Lane (Free)

Haworth

Haworth Old Hall
Sun Street (bottom of Main St, opp. park)
☎ (0535) 642709
11–11
Draught Bass; Stones Best Bitter; Taylor Golden Best; Tetley Mild, Bitter Ⓗ
Three-room, 17th-century, Tudor-style building with open stonework, oak beams and mullioned windows. Friendly atmosphere. Large garden; children welcome (ask for the Tudor room). Bar snacks and à la carte restaurant. The en suite accommodation includes a family room.
Q ❀ ◖◗ ▲ ≥ (KWVLR) P

Headingley

Woodies
104 Otley Road (A660)
☎ (0532) 757838
11–11
Marston's Pedigree; S&N Theakston XB; Taylor Landlord; Whitbread Boddingtons Bitter, Trophy, Castle Eden Ale; guest beers Ⓗ
Old-style, back-to-basics pub with lots of bare wood. Open-plan, split-level and popular with all types, especially students. Beware the Scrumpy Jack handpump (keg cider). No food Sun.
❀ ◖ ♣ P

Heath

King's Arms
½ mile off A655
☎ (0924) 377527
11.30–3, 6–11 (11–11 July & Aug)
Clark's Bitter; Taylor Landlord; Tetley Bitter; guest beers Ⓗ
Historic, multi-roomed, 18th-century country inn in an attractive, conserved 'Village of Mansions' near Wakefield. Wood panelling, gas lighting and real fires give a cosy atmosphere. The restaurant also has cask ale. Children's room until 8.30. No bar meals Sun eve, but barbecues Sun eve in summer.
Q ❀ ◖◗ P

Hebden Bridge

Fox & Goose
9 Heptonstall Road (A646 jct)
☎ (0422) 842649
11.30–3, 7.30–11
John Smith's Bitter; guest beers 🄷
Arched, ground floor cellars form this small but cosy local where the keen landlord offers three, constantly changing guest beers, usually from independent breweries.
❀ ◐ ◑ ⇌ ♣

Mount Skip Inn
Wadsworth (via Birchcliffe Rd from Hebden Bridge)
OS007272 ☎ (0422) 842765
12–3 (2 winter; 5 summer Sat; not Mon & Tue in winter), 7–11
Taylor Golden Best, Best Bitter, Landlord; Tetley Bitter 🄷
Pub perched 600 feet above Hebden Bridge, with extensive views over Cragg Vale and Mytholmroyd; popular outside seating in summer. A friendly beamed lounge, a small tap room, and an upstairs restaurant. A golf club and the Calderdale Way footpath are at the rear. No lunches Mon or Tue. ♨ ❀ ◐ ◑ P

Nutclough House Hotel
Keighley Road (A6033, ¼ mile from centre)
☎ (0422) 844361
12–3, 6–11; 11–11 Sat
S&N Theakston Best Bitter; Taylor Landlord; Thwaites Bitter 🄷**; guest beers**
Roomy and comfortable pub which attracts a varied clientele. Regular live music Thu eves. Up to three guest beers. ♨ ❀ ◐ ◑ ⇌ ♣ P

Shoulder of Mutton
38 New Road, Mytholmroyd (B6138) ☎ (0422) 883165
11.30–3, 7–11; 11.30–11 Sat
Whitbread Boddingtons Bitter, Flowers IPA, Trophy, Castle Eden Ale 🄷**; guest beer**
Popular roadside local with a display of toby jugs and china. No meals Tue eve. ♨ ◐ ◑ ▲ ⇌ (Mytholmroyd) ♣ P

Heckmondwike

Old Hall
New North Road (400 yds NW of The Green)
☎ (0924) 404774
11.30–3, 6.30–11
Samuel Smith OBB 🄷
Once the home of Joseph Priestley, discoverer of oxygen, a pub with original 1470 timbers and 1500s stonework. Delightfully restored, with a minstrel's gallery-like function room for hire. Joseph's portrait hangs on a wall and sways in the wind! Q ❀ ◐ ◑ P

Try also: Black Bull, Halifax Rd, Liversedge (Free)

Holmfirth

Elephant & Castle
Hollowgate
☎ (0484) 683178
11.30–5, 7–11
Bass Mild, Worthington BB; Stones Best Bitter 🄷
Simple and restful oasis in a tourist town, despite being on Nora Batty's doorstep. The landlord and landlady intend to keep it this way.
Q 🐎 ❀ ♿ ♣ P

Rose & Crown (Nook)
7 Victoria Square (behind Barclays Bank, down alley off Hollowgate) ☎ (0484) 683960
11.30–11
Samuel Smith OBB; Stones Best Bitter; Taylor Landlord, Ram Tam; Tetley Mild; Younger No. 3 🄷**; guest beer**
Basic, no-frills boozer in the heart of *Summer Wine* country. The landlord (man not beer!) has been chosen as his luxury item on the proverbial desert island by at least one noted journalist! Occasional folk music sessions are well attended.
♨ 🐎 ❀ ▲ ♣

Try also: Shoulder of Mutton, Dunford Rd (Bass)

Honley

Railway
1 Huddersfield Road (at A616/A6024 jct)
☎ (0484) 661309
11–3, 5–11; 11–11 Fri & Sat
Ind Coope Burton Ale; Taylor Landlord; Tetley Mild, Bitter 🄷
Free house, justly proud of its cellarmanship awards, which now serves lunches by popular demand. There are rooms beyond the obvious in this deceptively large Holme valley pub. ◐ ▲ ⇌ ♣ P

Horbury

Caldervale Hotel
Millfield Road, Horbury Junction (signed from A642 bypass) ☎ (0924) 275351
12–3.30, 6.15–11
John Smith's Bitter 🄷**; guest beer**
Large, Victorian, three-roomed local built in 1884 by Fernandes brewery and recently renovated in traditional fashion. Comfortable, friendly and full of local characters. Away from the town centre but well worth the trouble to find.
Q ❀ ♣ P

Huddersfield

Albert Hotel
38 Victoria Lane (near town hall) ☎ (0484) 421065
11–11
Bass Light, Draught Bass; Stones Best Bitter; Taylor Landlord 🄷**; guest beer**
Split-level, Victorian building tastefully refurbished around the original, fine, etched-glass and mahogany bar. A town-centre pub whose customer mix varies throughout the day. Function room. ◐ ⇌

Ale Shoppe
205 Lockwood Road (A616, 1 mile S of centre)
☎ (0484) 432479
10–8 (6 Sat); closed Sun
Taylor Best Bitter *or* **Landlord** 🄷**; guest beer**
Off-licence that sells at least one draught beer at all times. Also has an extensive range of British and European bottled beers, plus all home-brewing requisites. A rare local outlet for real draught cider.
⇌ (Lockwood) ⚲

Berry Brow Liberal Club
6 Parkgate (A616, 2½ miles S of centre)
☎ (0484) 662549
12–2, 7.30–11; 11.30–2.30, 8–11 Sat (11.30–11 Sat in soccer season); 12–2.30, 8–10.30 Sun
Taylor Golden Best, Best Bitter; Tetley Bitter 🄷**; guest beers**
Small and friendly club on a corner site. Show this guide or CAMRA membership at the bar to be signed in; CIU affiliated. Car parking can be difficult but don't let this deter a visit. Snooker table upstairs.
♿ ⇌ (Berry Brow) ♣

Black Horse
107 Occupation Road, Lindley (2½ miles NW of centre)
☎ (0484) 425816
12–3.30 (not Mon–Thu), 7–11; 12–11 Sat
Mansfield Riding Bitter, Old Baily 🄷
In the shadow of Sykes's Victorian clock tower, a homely local boasting a doorway full of original Seth Senior green tiles. Enjoying a

new lease of life under its enthusiastic young landlord.
♿ ♣

Dusty Miller Inn
2 Gilead Road, Longwood (3½ miles W of centre)
☎ (0484) 651763
12–3 (not Mon–Fri), 7–11
Black Sheep Best Bitter; Oak Best Bitter; Old Mill Bitter; S&N Theakston Best Bitter; Taylor Golden Best, Landlord Ⓗ; guest beers
Ivy-clad, stone-built pub set into hillside, with striking views towards the Pole Moor radio masts. Soft furnishings in the rear lounge; pool rooms around the corner. Parking can be difficult but there is a bus terminus close by!
🜲 ❀ ♣

Rat & Ratchet
40 Chapel Hill (A616, just S of ring road jct, towards Holmfirth)
☎ (0484) 516734
12 (11.30 Fri & Sat)–11
Bateman Mild; Mansfield Riding Bitter, Old Baily; Taylor Landlord Ⓗ; guest beers
A huge blackboard proclaims the prices above the bar; bare floorboards lie in front of the bar; amiable staff work behind the bar, and often 14 different beers are served across it. Both the music and clientele can be lively at night. ❀ ☾ ⇌ P

Shoulder of Mutton
11 Neale Road, Lockwood (off B6108, near A616 jct, 1 mile S of centre)
☎ (0484) 424835
7 (3 Sat)–11
Taylor Best Bitter, Landlord; Tetley Mild, Bitter; Thwaites Bitter Ⓗ; guest beers
Pub where recent sympathetic refurbishment has retained individual rooms, panelling and a jukebox! A pool room is tucked away upstairs, out of sight, rather like the pub itself (hidden at the end of a quiet cobbled street).
❀ ⇌ (Lockwood) ♣

Slubbers Arms
1 Halifax Old Road, Hillhouse (just off A641, ¾ mile from centre) ☎ (0484) 429032
11.30–3.30, 6.30 (7 Fri)–11
Marston's Pedigree; Taylor Best Bitter Ⓗ; guest beers
150-year-old beer house which has grown into an odd-shaped pub by absorbing adjoining cottages. Recent alterations, ably assisted by the landlord and customers, give it a genuine period feel: much better than the big brewers' Victorian efforts. 🜲 Q ☾ ♣

Woolpack
19 Westgate, Almondbury (2 miles SE of centre)
☎ (0484) 435702
12–2 (not Mon & Tue), 5–11; 12–11 Sat
Courage Directors; John Smith's Bitter; Webster's Green Label Ⓗ
Open-plan village local that still has character; next to Wormald Hall (1631) and opposite a perpendicular period church. Castle Hill iron age fort (fine views) is nearby. No lunches Sun.
❀ ☾ ♣ P

Zeneca Recreation Club (formerly ICI)
509 Leeds Road (A62, 3 miles NE of centre)
☎ (0484) 514367
12–11
Taylor Best Bitter; Tetley Mild, Bitter Ⓗ; guest beer
Twice winner of CAMRA's *Club of the Year* award: a large club with three lounges, two bars, eight snooker tables, bowls, tennis, hockey, croquet, etc. Can be hired for functions. Show this guide or CAMRA membership to the doorman to be signed in. N.B. The club name might be changed again.
❀ ☾ ♣ P

Try also: Slip Inn, Longwood Gate (Burtonwood)

Keighley

Boltmakers Arms
East Parade
☎ (0535) 661936
11.30–11; 11–4.30, 7–11 Sat
Taylor Golden Best, Best Bitter, Landlord Ⓗ
Very popular, one-room, split-level local, which can get very busy, especially at weekends. Close to BR and Worth Valley railways. Good selection of malt whiskies.
⇌ ♣

Cricketers Arms
Coney Lane (off Worth Way)
☎ (0535) 669912
11–11
Taylor Golden Best, Best Bitter, Ram Tam Ⓗ
Small, one-room, friendly local, nestling between two mills. Tastefully renovated by the present licensee. Try the traditional northern snacks Sun lunchtime. ♿ ⇌ ♣

Eastwood Tavern
Bradford Road (right from station)
☎ (0535) 604849
11.45 (11.30 Fri & Sat)–11
Taylor Golden Best, Best Bitter Ⓗ
Friendly local comprising a main bar, a front snug and a large pool and games room. The rear of the main room has interesting old brewery prints and photographs. Handy for BR and Worth Valley railways.
🜲 ❀ ☾ ⇌ ♣

Grinning Rat/Rat Trap
2 Church Street
☎ (0535) 609747
Grinning Rat 11–11; Rat Trap 8–midnight (2am Thu–Sat, 11 Sun)
Mitchell's ESB; Old Mill Bitter; Taylor Golden Best, Landlord; Tetley Bitter; Whitbread Boddingtons Bitter Ⓗ; guest beers
Centrally placed pub, very popular with all types. Around five regularly changing guest beers give the widest range for miles; always a guest mild, plus a cider or perry. Frequent live music. The Rat Trap is the adjoining night club, with two bars and late-night extensions.
♿ ⇌ ⌓

Red Pig
Church Green
☎ (0535) 605383
12–3, 7–11; 11–11 Fri & Sat
Taylor Golden Best, Landlord; guest beers Ⓗ
Centrally located and popular Bohemian town pub. Local artists' exhibits are often on display; cavers frequently meet here. The interesting beer range often features locally brewed beers, including one beer from either Commercial or Trough. Good range of Belgian bottles and malt whiskies. No dogs. No lunches Wed or Sun. 🜲 ☾ ⇌ ♣

Volunteer Arms
Lawkholme Lane (behind the Cavendish pub in Cavendish St) ☎ (0535) 600173
11–11
Taylor Golden Best, Best Bitter, Ram Tam (winter) Ⓗ
Compact locals' pub with two rooms, the smaller mainly for pub games. Function room.
⇌ ♣

Try also: Vine, Greengate Rd (Taylor)

Keighley to Oxenhope and Back

Keighley & Worth Valley Railway Buffet Car
Stations at Keighley, Ingrow West, Oakworth, Haworth and Oxenhope ☎ (0535) 645214 (talking timetable 647777)
Sat & Sun only, March–Oct

Beer range varies
Volunteer-run railway buffet car giving changing views of the Worth valley. Usually one or two beers available, refilled several times a day. The train is available for hire for weddings, etc., with beer to your own requirements.
▲ (Oxenhope) ⇌ (Keighley) P (Keighley/Ingrow West/ Oxenhope) ⅔

Kirkburton

Royal
64 North Road (½ mile E of A629/B6116 jct)
☎ (0484) 602521
11.30–3 (not Mon), 5–11
Ind Coope Burton Ale; Taylor Landlord; Tetley Mild, Bitter Ⓗ
Large, two-roomed, Victorian pub with a comfortable lounge, a separate games room and a function room. Children welcome. Interesting collection of local decorative plates. Refurbishment planned.
♛ ❀ ◖ ◗ ♣ P

Try also: Windmill, Busker Lane, Skelmanthorpe (Courage)

Knottingley

Steam Packet Inn
2 Racca Green (off A645, ¾ mile E of town)
☎ (0977) 677266
11–11
Steam Packet Mellors Gamekeeper, Chatterley, Bitter Black, Bargee, Poacher's Swag, Giddy Ass; guest beers Ⓗ
Large, multi-roomed brew pub by the canal. Brewery tours by prior arrangement.
♛ ❀ ♣ P

Ledsham

Chequers
Claypit Lane (off A1)
☎ (0977) 683135
11–3, 5.30–11; 11–11 Sat; closed Sun
S&N Theakston Best Bitter; John Smith's Bitter; Younger Scotch, No. 3 Ⓗ
Beautiful, unspoilt village inn with ivy-covered walls and a maze of small rooms. Genuine oak beams, real fires and conversation. Excellent restaurant upstairs. A real gem. ♛ Q ⛵ ❀ ◖ ◗ ♣ P

Leeds

Ale House
79 Raglan Road (near main entrance to University, off A660) ☎ (0532) 455447
12 (4 Mon, 10 Sat)–10.30
Ale House Monster Mash, XB, No. 9, White Rose Ale, Housewarmer; guest beers Ⓗ
Off-licence which commenced brewing in 1987, under *Reinheitsgebot* rules for brews up to and including XB's gravity. Up to six guest beers, plus four real ciders, worldwide bottled beers and unusual wines. ⌓

Chemic Tavern
9 Johnston Street, Woodhouse (½ mile from University campus, near A660)
☎ (0532) 440092
11–3, 5.30–11; 11–11 Sat
Ind Coope Burton Ale; Tetley Bitter Ⓗ
Attractive, stone-fronted house which gives way to two relaxing, low-ceilinged, wood-panelled bars. No electronic diversions, just good banter. Note the tap room tables with inlaid '5s and 3s' boards. A rare mix of student and local clientele gelling together. Q ♣ P

Duck & Drake
Lower Kirkgate
☎ (0532) 465806
11–11
Old Mill Bitter; S&N Theakston Best Bitter, XB, Old Peculier; Taylor Landlord; Younger No. 3; guest beers Ⓗ
A 'real' alehouse situated between the parish church and Kirkgate market. Popular with all walks of life. Live music Tue, Thu and Sun. A pub not to be missed. No meals weekends. ♛ ◖ ⇌ ♣ ⌓

Eagle Tavern
North Street, Sheepscar Junction (A61)
☎ (0532) 457146
11–3, 5.30–11
Taylor Mild, Golden Best, Best Bitter, Landlord, Ram Tam; guest beers Ⓗ
White-painted Georgian building with a large tap room and a friendly lounge. Live music Fri, Sat and Sun, lunch and eve. Local CAMRA *Pub of the Year* 1989, 1990 and 1992. Book your beer, bed and breakfast now. ❀ 🛏 ◖ ♣ ⌓

Grove
Back Row, Holbeck (between M1 and Hilton hotel)
☎ (0532) 439254
11.30–11; 11.30–4, 7–11 Sat
Courage Directors; Ruddles Best Bitter, County; John Smith's Bitter, Magnet; guest beer Ⓗ
Typical Yorkshire corridor pub now into its 32nd year as the home of acoustic music in Leeds – rock, blues, jazz and folk. Saved from the planners by campaigning and the property trend.
♛ ❀ ◖ ⇌ ♣

Jester
Harrogate Road, Alwoodley (A61) ☎ (0532) 682738
11–11
Mansfield Riding Bitter, Old Baily Ⓗ
Large, 1930s roadhouse on the main Leeds–Harrogate road. An open-plan, L-shaped bar has wood-panelling and many artefacts around the walls. A quieter area to one side has raised alcove seating and exposed brick. Large function room (with real ale) on a lower level. ◖ P

Mulberry
Hunslet Road (A61)
☎ (0532) 457621
11.30–11
S&N Theakston Mild, Best Bitter, XB, Old Peculier; Younger Scotch, No. 3 Ⓗ
Small, roadside pub near the Tetley Brewery, popular at lunchtime with local workers. Given the landlord's record of attracting trade through a good range of guest beers, it's a shame that S&N do not let him realise his potential. Limited parking. ◖ P

Nags Head
20 Town Street, Harrogate Road (by police station)
☎ (0532) 624938
11–3, 5.30–11; 11–11 Fri & Sat
Samuel Smith OBB, Museum Ⓗ
Old pub just off the main road in a village suburb: a lively public bar and a pleasantly revamped lounge, with a separate no-smoking room. Darts and doms played enthusiastically; very successful RL team. Quiz nights Tue and Sun. No meals weekends. Q ❀ ◖ ♣ P ⅔

New Roscoe
Bristol Street, Sheepscar (between Roseville Rd and Sheepscar St South)
☎ (0532) 460778
11–11
Tetley Mild, Bitter Ⓗ**; guest beers**
The home of Irish music in Leeds: the well-decorated lounge is venue to bands several times a week. Filled with brass and other antiques. The facade of the old Roscoe leads to a quiet snug and notice the fine model of the old Roscoe in the lounge. The games room (pool) is boisterous. No meals weekends. A Moorhouse's house beer is also served. ◖ P

West Yorkshire

Prince of Wales
Mill Hill ☎ (0532) 452434
11–11
Courage Directors; John Smith's Bitter; guest beers Ⓗ
Bustling city-centre 'local', popular with workers and travellers from the nearby station. A local CAMRA *Pub of the Season* award-winner.
⛟ ◐ ⇌

Viaduct
Lower Briggate (under railway by Swinegate)
☎ (0532) 454863
11–3, 5.30 (7 Sat)–10.30; 11–10.30 Thu & Fri; 12–2, 7–10.30 Sun
Tetley Mild, Bitter Ⓗ
Long, one-room bar, divided from a games area by an impressive oak-panelled hallway, sadly not now used as an entrance. Frequented by a mature clientele of dedicated Tetley drinkers. Mild reigns supreme! Do not be deterred by the outside appearance and location. ⇌ ♣

Victoria Family & Commercial
Great George Street (rear of town hall) ☎ (0532) 451386
11–11; 12–2, 7–10.30 Sun
Tetley Mild, Bitter Ⓗ
19th-century hotel, originally built for visiting judges and lawyers. A splendid, large, genuine Victorian lounge and three smaller, comfy rooms, deservedly popular with locals, office staff and students. Buoyant atmosphere. No food Sun. Q ◐ ⊟ ♿ ⇌

West Yorkshire Playhouse
Quarry Hill Mount (opp. central bus station)
☎ (0532) 442141
12–2.30, 6.30–11 (may vary); closed Sun
Ind Coope Burton Ale; Tetley Bitter Ⓗ
New theatre and bar built on the former Quarry Hill flats complex. An award winner for the theatre with the best disability facilities. The Huntsman Bar serves a large lounge, with a theatre buff clientele paying prices which reflect the lack of an adequate grant. Q ⚲ ◐ ◗ ♿ ⇌ P

Whitelocks
Turks Head Yard, Briggate (N of Marks & Spencer)
☎ (0532) 453950
11–11
McEwan 80/-; Younger Scotch, No. 3 Ⓗ
Unchanged luncheon bar overwhelmed with brass, old mirrors and featuring a marble bar. The tiny lower bar has a small restaurant attached; a newer upper bar has flagged floors and is only open eve. Barrel tables outside (sheltered in winter).
⛰ Q ❀ ◐ ⇌

Wrens
61a New Briggate
☎ (0532) 458888
11–11
Ansells Mild; Ind Coope Benskins Best Bitter, Burton Ale; Tetley Mild, Bitter Ⓗ
Three bars and the 'Charity Corridor' make up this pleasant pub, with a proper public bar and a no-smoking room. Popular with theatre-goers and close to restaurants. Winner of *Leeds in Bloom* contests for its imaginative floral displays.
◐ ⊟ ⇌ ⊬

Linthwaite

Sair Inn
Lane Top, Hoyle Ing, off A62 (up a steep hill)
☎ (0484) 842370
12–3 (not Mon–Fri), 7–11
Linfit Mild, Bitter, Special, English Guineas Stout, Old Eli, Leadboiler Ⓗ**; guest beer**
Multi-roomed, home-brew pub with fine views across the Colne valley. Stone-flagged floors, attractive real fires and animals add to the atmosphere. Wall displays feature the Huddersfield Narrow Canal and the history of brewing. ⛰ ♣ ⌓

Luddendenfoot

Coach & Horses
Burnley Road (A646)
☎ (0422) 884102
11–3, 6.30–11
S&N Theakston Best Bitter, XB, Old Peculier; Younger Scotch Ⓗ
Large, imposing roadside pub, sumptuously furnished, with lots of brassware. Quiz night Thu. ◐ ◗ ♣ P

Marsden

Tunnel End Inn
Reddisher Road (400 yds S of station)
☎ (0484) 844636
12–2 (3 Sat, not Mon–Fri in winter) 7–11
Ind Coope Burton Ale; Tetley Mild, Bitter Ⓗ
Close to the point where the Huddersfield Canal enters the Pennines, with its visitor centre and picnic area, a pub boasting a piano surrounded by books and guides.
⛰ ⚲ ❀ ◐ ⇌ ♣

Methley

New Bay Horse
Main Street
☎ (0977) 553557
11–11
Tetley Bitter Ⓗ**; guest beers**
A real local, the focus of village life. Recently refurbished but keeping a small tap room. Guest beers at a reasonable price.
⚲ ❀ ◐ ⊟ ♿ ♣ P

Morley

Gardeners Arms
Wide Lane (A6123)
☎ (0532) 534261
12–3 (4 Sat), 7 (6.30 summer, 6.45 Sat)–11
Tetley Mild, Bitter Ⓗ
Large, smart pub with pictures of old Morley. A winner of Tetley's *Master of Mild* contest and *Cellarman of the Year*. No meals weekends. ❀ ◐ P

Netherthong

Clothiers Arms
106 School Street (off B6107)
☎ (0484) 683480
12–3.30 (4 Thu; not Mon), 7–11; 12–11 Fri & Sat, & Thu in summer
Ryburn Mild; Stones Best Bitter; Tetley Mild, Bitter; Trough Wild Boar Ⓗ**; guest beers**
Renovated village local, now attracting a wider clientele who admire the beer mat, bottle and jug collections. Ample car parking close by. Ryburn Mild is sold as Ammbleton Ale. No food Sun or Mon. ⚲ ❀ ◐ ♣

Netherton

Star Inn
211 Netherton Lane (B6117, 1 mile from A642)
☎ (0924) 274496
11.30–3 (4 Fri & Sat), 6.30–11
Samuel Smith OBB Ⓔ
Friendly, unspoilt and well-kept village local with a lively tap room, a lounge and a function room. Spacious beer garden overlooking open countryside. Q ❀ ♣ P

Normanton

Junction Inn
Market Place
☎ (0924) 893021
11–4.30, 7–11; 12–2.30, 7–10.30 Sun
Wards Thorne Best Bitter; guest beer (occasionally) Ⓗ
Busy town-centre pub, frequented by a younger clientele in the eve. Children especially welcome at lunchtime, when an extensive

menu of good value bar meals is served (baby's meals are free). Piano sing-along in the tap room Sat night.
❀ ◐ ♿ ⇌ ♣ P

Norwood Green

Old White Beare

Village Street (½ mile NW of A58/A641) ☎ (0274) 676645
11.30–3 (5 Fri), 6–11
Whitbread Trophy, Castle Eden Ale Ⓗ
16th-century village inn named after an English ship which sailed against the Spanish Armada. Modernised and extended, but retaining many of its oldest features. No meals Sun. ♉ ❀ ◐ ♿ ♣ P

Ossett

Brewer's Pride

Low Mill Road, Healey Road (1 mile S of centre)
☎ (0924) 273865
12–3, 5.30–11; 11–11 Fri & Sat
Taylor Landlord; guest beers Ⓗ
Attractive, stone-fronted free house, very popular despite its location, hidden away near the river and railway. The Edwardian-style, three-roomed interior has added breweriana and open fires. Imaginative menu of good, home-cooked food (eve meals end at 8; no eve meals Wed or Sat). Barbecues with live bands held monthly in summer. Four guest beers. ♔ ❀ ◐ ◗ ♣ ⌓

George

Bank Street ☎ (0924) 264754
11–3, 7–11; 11–11 Fri & Sat
Taylor Landlord; Tetley Mild, Bitter Ⓗ
Recently extended and refurbished pub next to a new police station. Mixed clientele in a large, open-plan bar, but still a locals' tap room, too.
❀ ◐ ⊟ P

Little Bull

99 Teall Street (¼ mile from Queens Drive)
☎ (0924) 273569
12–3 (4 Sat), 6 (7 Sat)–11
Thwaites Bitter, Craftsman Ⓗ
Very friendly, working-class local with regular quiz and games nights. A comfortable, L-shaped lounge and a small but lively tap room.
♔ ⊟ ♣ P

Otley

Bay Horse

20 Market Place (B6451)
☎ (0943) 461122
11–11
Tetley Mild, Bitter; guest beers Ⓗ
Small alehouse with a mixed clientele and a friendly atmosphere. Guest beers from independent breweries. Sandwiches lunchtime. ❀

Junction

44 Bondgate (old A660 through town)
☎ (0943) 463233
11–3, 5.30–11; 11–11 Fri & Sat
S&N Theakston XB, Old Peculier; Taylor Best Bitter, Landlord; Tetley Bitter Ⓗ
Very busy, one-roomed, stone corner pub with a tiled floor, panelled walls and a wooden-beamed ceiling. Bric-a-brac abounds. Popular with all types. A Tetley house selling a range of other beers. ♔ ◐

Red Lion

Kirkgate (old A660 through town) ☎ (0943) 462226
11–11
Courage Directors; John Smith's Bitter, Magnet Ⓗ
Very well-kept pub near the market square. Small, with three semi-open-plan drinking areas and a single bar. Large whisky collection. Eve meals till 8, Mon–Thu. Q ◐ ◗

Pontefract

Greyhound

Front Street ☎ (0977) 791571
12–4, 7–11
Marston's Pedigree; Ruddles Best Bitter; S&N Theakston XB; guest beers Ⓗ
Popular, lively, three-roomed pub at the edge of town. Traditional bar; regular live music. Watch out for bank holidays with all-day live music. ♔ ⇌ (Tanshelf) ♣

Liquorice Bush

8 Market Place
☎ (0977) 703843
11–4, 6 (7 Sat)–11
Taylor Landlord Ⓗ; **Vaux Samson** Ⓔ, **Double Maxim** (occasionally) Ⓗ; **Wards Sheffield Best Bitter** Ⓔ; **guest beer** Ⓗ
Town-centre pub, formerly an hotel, as its frontage suggests. Its one large room has recently been refurbished and split into three drinking areas in an imaginative way. No food Sun. ◐ ♿ ⇌ (Baghill) ♣

Tap & Spile

28 Horsefair ☎ (0977) 793468
11–2.30, 4.30–11; 11–11 Fri, Sat & summer
Beer range varies Ⓗ
Typical conversion to a Victorian-style alehouse. Three separate drinking areas (one lounge style) and 12 guest beers make this a Mecca for fans of independents' ales. Wakefield CAMRA *Pub of the Year* 1992. No meals Sun. Occasional cider.
❀ ◐ ♿ ⇌ (Baghill/Monkhill) ♣ ⌓ P

Pudsey

Butchers Arms

30 Church Lane (next to market place) ☎ (0532) 564313
11–3 (3.30 Sat), 5.30 (5 Fri, 7 Sat)–11
Samuel Smith OBB Ⓗ
Typical Yorkshire stone pub providing a warm and friendly welcome. A mainly local clientele, fiercely competitive, whether at darts, dominoes or quizzes. Watch out for the specials nights. No lunches Sun; eve meals Thu and Fri only. ❀ ◐ ◗ ♣

Purston

White House

Pontefract Road (A645)
☎ (0977) 791878
11–4, 7–11
Samuel Smith OBB Ⓗ
Small, friendly, open-plan pub, popular with locals. Interesting collection of local rugby photographs.
❀ ◐ ♿ ♣ P

Queensbury

Pineberry

Brighouse and Denholme Road (½ mile NW of Queensbury lights on Denholme Rd, A644)
☎ (0274) 882168
11.30–3, 5–11; 11–11 Fri & Sat
Ruddles Best Bitter; S&N Theakston XB; Webster's Green Label, Yorkshire Bitter Ⓗ
Friendly and popular pub with extensive views over surrounding farmland. A seating area away from the main bar, and a separate dining room, make the emphasis of the pub its good-value and wide-ranging, home-cooked food, including excellent vegetarian options.
♔ Q ♉ ❀ ◐ ◗ ♿ P

Rawdon

Emmott Arms

Town Street (200 yds up Well Lane from A65)
☎ (0532) 506036
11–3, 5.30–11; 11–11 Sat
Samuel Smith OBB Ⓗ
Busy, low-ceilinged pub with a separate restaurant. Bare stonework and panelled beams give a cosy atmosphere. Mixed clientele in both bars. Restaurant closed Sun eve and Mon. Q ❀ ◐ ◗ ⊟ ♣ P

Ripponden

Blue Ball Inn
Blue Ball Lane, Soyland (off A58, near Baitings reservoir) OS011192 ☎ (0422) 823603
12–2 (not Tue), 7–11
Bass Special, Draught Bass; S&N Theakston Old Peculier; Stones Best Bitter; Taylor Golden Best, Landlord Ⓗ**; guest beer**
Moorland inn dating from 1672, with panoramic views of the surrounding moors and Baitings reservoir. Cosy and welcoming. Folk music/sing-alongs feature regularly. Upstairs restaurant. Wheelchair ramp at car park entrance.
♉ ❀ ⛟ ◖ ◗ ♿ P

Old Bridge Inn
Priest Lane
☎ (0422) 822595
11.30–3.30, 5.30–11; 11–11 Sat
Black Sheep Best Bitter, Special Strong; Taylor Golden Best, Best Bitter Ⓗ
Ancient hostelry with a splendid, timbered structure, in a picturesque setting beside a pack horse bridge. The landlord promotes independent breweries, particularly from Yorkshire, so the range may vary. Pumps are mostly unlabelled. No under-18s or dogs permitted. No food Sun or Sat eve.
♛ Q ❀ ◖ ◗ P

Silsden

Bridge Inn
Keighley Road
☎ (0535) 653144
12–3, 5–11; 11–11 Fri, Sat & sometimes summer
Black Sheep Best Bitter; John Smith's Bitter; Webster's Green Label Ⓗ
Canalside pub which predates the canal, being first recorded in 1660. The original drinking rooms are now the cellars and toilets. The outside drinking area was the original main road. Parking for boats only. Meals mainly in summer.
♉ ❀ ◖ ◗ ≹ (Steeton & Silsden) ♣

South Elmsall

Barnsley Oak
Mill Lane (B6474, ½ mile off A638) ☎ (0977) 643427
12–3.30 (5 Sat), 7–11
John Smith's Bitter Ⓗ
Sixties estate pub on the edge of a mining village, offering panoramic views of the Elms valley from the conservatory. Free sausages and scallops on Sun eve. Q ❀ ◖ ≹ ♣ P

Southowram

Pack Horse
1 Cain Lane ☎ (0422) 365620
12–2, 5–11
Vaux Bitter, Samson; Wards Thorne Best Bitter Ⓗ
Stone-built, traditional local, in the centre of a hilltop village, with a separate tap room for games, including Bull Ring. Copperware collection in the lounge. Plain, value-for-money food at most times. Folk singers Wed eve. ◖ ◗ ♣ P

Sowerby Bridge

Brothers Grimm
17 Causeway Head, Burnley Road (A646) ☎ (0422) 831352
12–11
Ryburn Bitter, Stabbers; Tetley Mild, Bitter Ⓗ
Small Victorian local on a main road bend. Has its own social club and games teams which reflect its strong, friendly, local following. Eve meals on request. ♉ ◖ ♣ P

William IV
80 Wharf Street (A58)
☎ (0422) 833584
11.30–11
Old Mill Bitter; Ryburn Mild, Bitter; Tetley Bitter; Whitbread Boddingtons Bitter; guest beer Ⓗ
Comfortable free house in the main street, concentrating on beer. A loyal outlet for the town's brewery (Ryburn).
❀ ≹ ♣ P

Stanley Ferry

Ferry Boat
Ferry Lane (1 mile W of A642)
☎ (0924) 290596
11–3, 6–11 (11–11 summer)
Ind Coope Burton Ale; S&N Theakston Best Bitter; Tetley Mild, Bitter Ⓗ
Large, canalside pub with nautical decor, by the historic aqueduct over the River Calder. Ideal for families, with a safe outdoor playground and an indoor children's bar. Very popular at weekends (open all day Sun for food). Boat trips from the pub in summer.
♉ ❀ ◖ ◗ ♿ P

Thornton

Blue Boar
354 Thornton Road (B6145)
☎ (0274) 833298
4 (1.30 Fri, 12 Sat)–11
Taylor Best Bitter, Landlord; Trough Bitter Ⓗ
Pub with an open-plan main bar and a separate pool/darts room. Collection of miniatures behind the bar. ❀ ♣

School Green
1549 Thornton Road (B6145, 3 miles from Bradford centre)
☎ (0274) 881345
12–3 (5 Sat), 5.30 (7 Sat)–11
Webster's Green Label, Yorkshire Bitter Ⓗ
Comfortable, well-furbished inn with an open-plan main bar and a traditional tap room. Pictures of old Thornton are displayed. ❀ ◖ ⊕ ♣ P

Todmorden

Masons Arms
1 Bacup Road, Gauxholme (at A6033/A681 jct)
☎ (0706) 812180
7–11; 12.30–3, 7.30–11 Sat; 12–3, 7.30–10.30 Sun
John Smith's Bitter, Magnet; Thwaites Bitter Ⓗ
Cosy pub nestling under a railway bridge. The unusual snug has sycamore-topped tables, reputedly once used for post-mortems. Easy access from the canal towpath.
♛ ❀ ◖ ♿ ≹ (Walsden)

White Hart
White Hart Fold
☎ (0706) 812198
11.30–3, 7–11; 11.30–11 Fri & Sat
Tetley Mild, Bitter; Whitbread Boddingtons Bitter Ⓗ
Former Ramsden's pub with a Brewers' Tudor-style exterior. A typical town-centre pub, popular and spacious. Good for lunches. ❀ ◖ ≹ ♣ P

Woodpecker
224 Rochdale Road, Shade (A6033, towards Littleborough)
☎ (0706) 816088
12–2.30, 5–11; 11.30–11 Sat
Lees GB Mild, Bitter Ⓗ
Busy, main-road locals' pub where a single L-shaped room accommodates both lounge and games areas. The only Lees pub in Yorkshire.
❀ ◖ ♿ ≹ ♣

Wakefield

Albion
94 Stanley Road (follow Peterson Rd from Kirkgate roundabout) ☎ (0924) 376206
11–4, 7–11; 11–11 Sat, & Fri in summer
Samuel Smith OBB Ⓗ
Impressive 1920s estate pub at the edge of the town centre, very popular lunchtimes for the landlady's daily-changing, fresh, home-cooked food. An unusual collection of coloured glassware adorns the lounge. Friendly local clientele.
❀ ◖ ⊕ ≹ (Kirkgate) ♣ P

Beer Engine

77 Westgate End (A642/A638, ½ mile W of centre)
☎ (0924) 375887
12–11
Taylor Landlord; guest beers Ⓗ
Popular, traditional alehouse with a stone-flagged floor, gas lighting and brewery memorabilia. Wakefield's only true free house, with usually four independents' guest beers, which change almost daily. Quiz night Mon. ♛ ❀ ◖ ≹ (Westgate) ♣ ⌓

College

138 Northgate (A61, ¼ mile N of town) ☎ (0924) 374392
11–11
Mansfield Riding Bitter, Old Baily; guest beer Ⓗ
Pub with a large, mock Tudor exterior and an open-plan interior, retaining small drinking niches. Guest beers rotate on a monthly basis. No food Sat/Sun.
❀ ◖ ≹ (Westgate) P

Elephant & Castle

Westgate (opp. Westgate station) ☎ (0924) 376610
11–11
Courage Directors; John Smith's Bitter, Magnet Ⓗ
A beautiful, old Warwick's Boroughbridge Ales tiled frontage conceals a partially opened-out interior, with a separate pool room and a public bar area. Well-priced food and accommodation. A very good place to stay when visiting Wakefield. ♛ 🛏 ◖ ◗ ♿ ≹ (Westgate) ♣

Inns of Court

22 King Street (behind town hall) ☎ (0924) 375560
11–11; 11–4, 7–11 Sat
S&N Theakston XB; John Smith's Magnet Ⓗ
Imposing, three-storey, town-centre hotel, tucked away among narrow streets housing solicitors' practices, offices and law courts. The long, open-plan lounge bar is divided into small drinking areas. Popular with members of the legal profession, their clients and students. No weekend meals.
Q ◖ ♿ ≹ (Westgate) ⌓

Warmfield

Plough Inn

45 Warmfield Lane (400 yds from A655) ☎ (0924) 892007
11–2.30, 7–11 (11.30–11 summer)
S&N Theakston Mild, Best Bitter, XB, Old Peculier; guest beer Ⓗ
Unspoilt, 18th-century country inn overlooking the lower Calder valley, with low, beamed ceilings and a small corner bar. Lively piano sing-alongs Sat nights. Good bar meals (dining licence Sun) – try the Old Peculier Pie. Barbecues in summer.
❀ ◖ ◗ ♣ P

West Ardsley

British Oak

407 Westerton Road (off A653)
☎ (0532) 534792
12–3, 6–11
Whitbread Boddingtons Bitter, Castle Eden Ale, Flowers Original Ⓗ**; guest beers**
Estate pub with an island bar, featuring quizzes on Sun, Mon and Wed, and live music on Sat. The landlord knows as many jokes as there are beers in Britain (many of which have been on sale in the pub already!). Sandwiches lunchtime. Cider in summer.
❀ ♿ ♣ ⌓ P

Wetherby

George & Dragon

8 High Street
☎ (0937) 582888
11–4, 5–11; 11–11 Fri
John Smith's Bitter, Magnet; Tetley Bitter Ⓗ
Stone-built, three-roomed coaching inn with a safe garden overlooking the River Wharfe. Renowned for charity events and popular with cycle clubs, walkers and the nearby racing stables. Eve meals till 8, Mon–Thu.
Q ❀ ◖ ◗ ⊟ ♿ ▲ ♣ P

Royal Oak

North Street
☎ (0937) 580508
11–3, 5.30–11; 11–11 Fri & Sat
McEwan 80/-; S&N Theakston Mild, Best Bitter; John Smith's Bitter; Tetley Bitter; guest beers Ⓗ
White-painted pub with an open, L-shaped interior, a stone-fronted bar with a pantiled roof, and a large tree trunk in the lounge. Quiz Sun; jazz Tue. No food Sun eve. Cider in summer.
❀ ◖ ◗ ♿ ▲ ♣ ⌓ P

Whitwood

Bridge Inn

Altofts Lane (½ mile from A655 at the Rising Sun)
☎ (0977) 551915
11–11; 11–3.30, 7–11 Sat
Black Sheep Bitter, Special Strong; S&N Theakston Mild, XB, Old Peculier; Tetley Bitter Ⓗ
Modern pub/hotel built in old style, using red brick and pantiles. An unusual interior features reclaimed beams, exposed brickwork and flagged floors in several drinking areas on various levels. Food- and business-orientated.
❀ 🛏 ◖ ◗ ♿ P ⚟

Wortley

Wheatsheaf

Gelderd Road (at A62/A6110, ring road, jct)
☎ (0532) 637070
11–11
Mansfield Riding Bitter, Old Baily Ⓗ
Busy, roadside pub serving good food in pleasant surroundings. Near Elland Road football ground, so especially busy on match days. Quiz Thu and Fri. Live music. Eve meals on request.
❀ ◖ ♣ P

Try also: Brick, Tong Rd (Tetley)

Wyke

Junction

459 Huddersfield Road
☎ (0274) 679809
12–11
Thwaites Bitter Ⓗ
Two-roomed pub with a split lounge and a separate pool room. Good, friendly atmosphere. ♣

Yeadon

New Inn

Cemetery Road
☎ (0532) 503220
11.30–3.30, 5.30–11; 11–11 Sat
John Smith's Bitter, Magnet; guest beer Ⓗ
Pub near Yeadon Tarn with an 18th-century exterior, but extensively altered inside. A public bar and a pleasant, rustic-style lounge with a log fire. Good value bar meals (vegetarian option). Pie and peas only eves.
♛ ❀ ◖ ◗ ⊟ P

Tut 'n' Shive

11 The Green (off A65)
☎ (0532) 506052
11–11
Whitbread Boddingtons Bitter Ⓗ**; guest beers**
Built in 1728, an imposing stone pub recently refurbished in the Whitbread Tut 'n' Shive company style. You'll either love it or hate it! Leeds CAMRA *Pub of the Season*, winter 1992/93. ❀ ◖ ◗ ♣ P

Clwyd

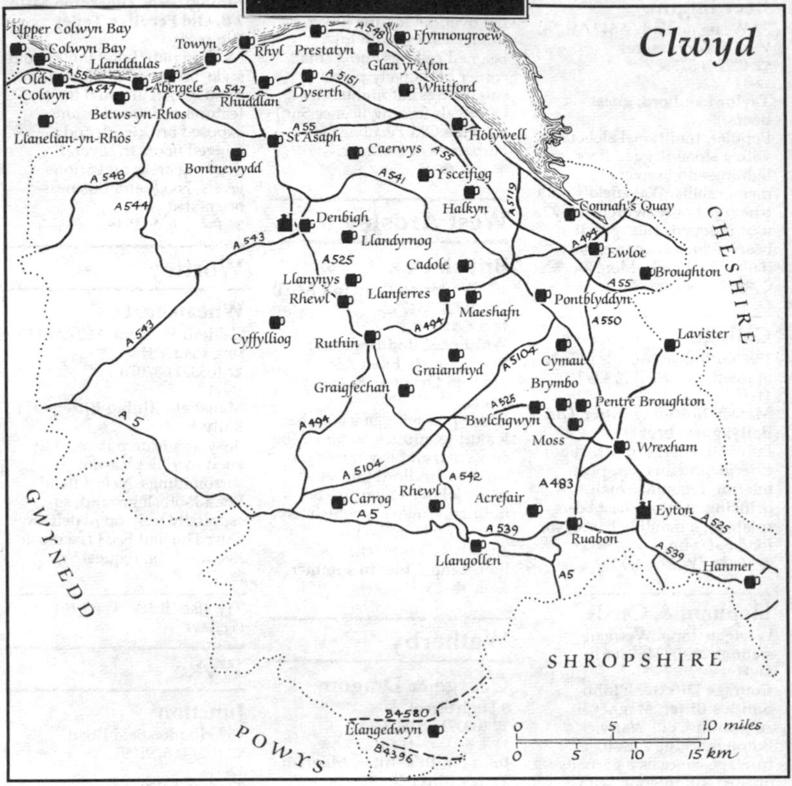

Dyffryn Clwyd, Denbigh; **Plassey**, Eyton

Abergele

Pen-y-Bont
Bridge Street ☎ (0745) 833905
11–11
S&N Matthew Brown Mild, Theakston Best Bitter, XB, Old Peculier H
Large single-bar, comfortable local.
⛰ ☕ ❀ 🛏 ◐ ◗ ▲ ⇄ ♣ P

Acrefair

Duke of Wellington
Llangollen Road, Tref-y-nant (A483) ☎ (0978) 820169
11–3, 7–11
Banks's Mild; Marston's Bitter H
Popular, open-plan pub near the famed Pontcysyllte aqueduct. Garden at front, with swings and a tractor, popular with families. ⛰ ❀

Hampden Arms
Llangollen Road
☎ (0978) 821734
11–4, 7–11 (11–11 summer)
Banks's Mild, Bitter E
Friendly, main-road pub near Plas Madoc leisure centre. Large, lively public bar; quieter lounge. ⊞ ♣ P

Betws-yn-Rhos

Wheatsheaf
☎ (0492) 60218
12–3, 6–11
Crown Buckley Best Bitter; Fuller's Chiswick; John Smith's Bitter H
Old village pub extended to the rear on split levels but still retaining a pleasant bar area at the front. The choice of beers constantly changes.
Q ❀ 🛏 ◐ ◗ P

Bontnewydd

Dolben Arms
W of Trefnant OS015705
☎ (0745) 582207
7–11; 12–3, 7–10.30 Sun
S&N Theakston Mild, XB H
16th-century country inn in a picturesque valley accessible only by lanes. One long room separated into restaurant, lounge and games areas. Lunches on Sun.
Q ❀ ◗ ♣ P

Broughton

Offa's Dyke
Broughton Hall Road (off A5104)
12–3.30, 5–11; 12–11 Fri & Sat
Cains Bitter; Whitbread Higsons Mild, Bitter H
Comfortable, modern estate pub, with a busy bar but quieter lounge. No food Tue, Sat or Sun. ❀ ◐ ♿ ♣ P

Brymbo

Black Lion
Railway Road ☎ (0978) 758307
12 (5 Mon)–11
Burtonwood Mild, Bitter H
Cosy pub in a hollow, with the patina of time enhanced by soft golden lighting. Bar snacks always available.
⛰ ❀ ⊞ ▲ ♣ P

Bwlchgwyn

Westminster Arms
Ruthin Road ☎ (0978) 753875
12–4.30 (not Mon), 7–11
Tetley Walker Dark Mild, Bitter [H]; guest beers
Friendly, bustling village local: a sports-oriented bar and a quieter lounge. No food Sun.
♛ ❀ ◖ ◗ ▲ ♣ P

Cadole

Colomendy Arms
Gwernaffield Road (off A494)
☎ (0352) 85217
12–3, 7–11; 11–11 Sat (closed winter lunchtimes)
Burtonwood Bitter [H]
Village local which welcomes children in the lounge. A footpath leads to Loggerheads country park. A caving society visiting Parris lead mines are regulars. The beer range is to be extended.
♛ Q ♉ ❀ ◖ ◗ ▲ ♣ P

Caerwys

Piccadilly
North Street (B5381 S of A55)
☎ (0352) 720284
12–3, 7 (5 Fri & Sat)–11
Draught Bass; Cains Mild; S&N Theakston Best Bitter; Whitbread Boddingtons Bitter [H]
Four-roomed, unspoilt village pub which still has a tiled floor in the public bar. Suits all ages.
♛ Q ❀ ◖ ◗ ⊞ ♿ ♣ P ⚡

Carrog

Grouse
On B5437, ½ mile off A5
☎ (049 083) 272
12–4, 7–11 (may vary)
Lees GB Mild, Bitter [H]
Homely pub in the Dee valley above Llangollen, affording delightful views. Three drinking areas with old photos. ♛ ❀ ⛟ ◖ ◗ ♣ P

Colwyn Bay

Platform 3
Colwyn Bay Station, Princes Drive ☎ (0492) 533161
11–11
Tetley Walker Bitter [H]
Renovated part of a station, overlooking the bay. Railway carriage restaurant; lounge bar; function room; enclosed gardens and a covered mall. House beer. ♉ ❀ ◖ ◗ ⇌

RAF Club
Imperial Hotel Building, Princes Drive ☎ (0492) 530682
12–2 (11–3 Fri & Sat), 7–11
Lees GB Mild, Bitter [E]
Typical, friendly club; a largish lounge with a small dance floor. Separate snooker/games and TV rooms. Visitors made welcome and can be signed in by members present. ⇌

Toad Hall
West Promenade
☎ (0492) 532726
11.30–3, 6–11
Banks's Mild; Marston's Bitter, Pedigree [H]
Seafront, first-floor bar with a restaurant. Large collection of bottles.
♛ ♉ ❀ ◖ ◗ ⇌ ♣ P

Connah's Quay

Sir Gawain & The Green Knight
Golftyn Lane ☎ (0244) 812623
11.30–3, 5.30–11; 12–11 Fri & Sat; 12–3, 7.30–10.30 Sun
Samuel Smith OBB, Museum [H]
Converted farmhouse local used by students lunchtimes. Close to Dee Estuary Bird Sanctuary. ❀ ◖ ♣ P

Cyffylliog

Red Lion
Off B5105 at Llanfwrog
☎ (0824) 716664
12–3 (summer only), 6.30–11; 12–3.30, 6.30–11 Sat
Lees GB Mild, Bitter [H]
Attractive, unspoilt, rural village inn with bar, pool room and lounge, offering good value food and accommodation.
♛ Q ❀ ⛟ ◖ ◗ ⊞ ▲ ♣ P

Cymau

Talbot Inne
Cymau Road (off A541)
OS297562 ☎ (0978) 761410
12–3, 7–11
Hydes' Anvil Mild, Bitter [E]
Quiet pub with spectacular views. The bar is popular with darts and domino players; more sedate lounge. Q ♣ P

Denbigh

Masons Arms
Rhyl Road ☎ (0745) 812463
11.30–3, 5.30–11
Vaux Lorimers Best Scotch; Wards Mild, Sheffield Best Bitter, Kirby [H]
Local, popular with the young set as well as the discerning drinker. One room divided by a modernised bar. Simple pub fare. ♛ ⛟ ⊞ ▲ ♣

Dyserth

New Inn
Waterfall Road
☎ (0745) 570482
11–3, 5–11; 11–11 Fri & Sat
Marston's Bitter, Pedigree [H]
Typical village pub catering for locals and summer trade: several small, busy rooms.
♛ ❀ ◖ ♿ ▲ ♣ P

Ewloe

Boars Head
Holywell Road (just off A55)
☎ (0244) 531665
11.30–3, 5.30–11
Greenalls Mild, Bitter [H]
Pub with low ceilings, beams and brasses. Plush but very comfortable. Q ❀ ◖ P

Ffynnongroew

Railway Tavern
Main Road ☎ (0745) 560447
12–4, 7–11
Vaux Bitter, Samson; Wards Mild [H]
Busy village pub popular with locals, particularly sporting types. ♛ ❀ ◖ ◗ ⊞ ▲ ♣ P

Glan yr Afon

White Lion
Glan yr Afon Road (S of A548 at Ffynnongroew) OS118817
☎ (0745) 560280
11.30–3 (not Mon), 6–11
Ruddles Best Bitter, County [H]; guest beers
Old-fashioned pub enjoying a lively local trade. Somewhat isolated but worth the visit.
♛ Q ❀ ◖ ◗ ⊞ ♣ ⌓ P

Graianrhyd

Rose & Crown
1 mile off A5104
☎ (082 43) 727
12–3, 5.30–11; 11–11 Fri & Sat
Marston's Pedigree; Whitbread Boddingtons Bitter, Flowers IPA [H]
Cosy out-of-the-way pub, popular with horse riders. Home-made food with a good vegetarian choice. Beware fake handpump for Scrumpy Jack keg cider. ♛ ❀ ◖ ◗ ♣ P

Graigfechan

Three Pigeons
On B5429 ☎ (0824) 703178
6.30–11; 12–3, 7–10.30 Sun
Draught Bass; guest beers [G]
17th-century pub affording fine views over the Vale of Clwyd. Good food (Thu–Sat only); children welcome; regular Welsh nights. Caravan site. ♛ Q ♉ ❀ ◗ ▲ ♣ P

Halkyn

Britannia
Pentre Road (just off A55)
OS211711 ☎ (0352) 780272
11–3, 5.30–11; 11–11 Sat (supper licence)
Lees GB Mild, Bitter [H], Moonraker [G]

500-year-old stone pub with four rooms, popular with the local community. The conservatory restaurant overlooks the Dee estuary. ♨ ⛹ ❀ ◖ ◗ ⊟ ♿ ▲ ♣ P

Hanmer

Hanmer Arms
Off A539 ☎ (094 874) 532
11–11
Ind Coope Burton Ale; Tetley Walker Bitter 🄷
Country hotel with a friendly atmosphere and good facilities. Slightly off the beaten track but a visit will reward all. ♨ Q ⛹ ❀ 🛏 ◖ ◗ ⊟ ♿ ♣ P

Holywell

Glan yr Afon
Milwr (300 yds from old A55)
☎ (0352) 710052
11.30–2.30, 6–11
Courage Directors; Ruddles Best Bitter; Webster's Yorkshire Bitter 🄷
17th-century inn with a deer antler collection in the public bar. Growing reputation for its restaurant and wines. No eve meals Mon. ⛹ ❀ ◖ ◗ ⊟ P

Red Lion
High Street ☎ (0352) 710097
11.30–11
Ansells Mild; Ind Coope Burton Ale; Tetley Walker Bitter 🄷
Basic, unspoilt town pub brimming with atmosphere. The bar divides the games and small lounge areas. ♣

Lavister

Nags Head
Old Chester Road (B5445)
☎ (0244) 570486
11.30–3, 5.30–11
Thwaites Bitter; Whitbread Boddingtons Mild, Bitter 🄷**; guest beers**
The first pub in Wales: an unassuming, friendly roadside pub with a bowling green. Guest beers are usually from Whitbread. ♨ ❀ ◖ ♣ P

Llanddulas

Dulas Arms Hotel
Abergele Road
☎ (0492) 515747
12–2.30 (3 summer), 7 (6 summer)–11 (12–3, 6–11 winter Sat; 11–11 summer Sat; closed Mon lunch in winter)
Lees GB Mild, Bitter, Moonraker 🄷
Pub with a large lounge, an adjoining bar, a snug and a large family room. Spacious garden with a children's adventure playground. Beer festival Aug Bank Hol.
Q ⛹ ❀ 🛏 ◖ ◗ ⊟ ▲ ♣ P ⚡

Valentine Inn
Mill Street ☎ (0492) 518189
12–3, 5.30–11 (may vary); 12–2, 7–10.30 Sun
Draught Bass; M&B Mild 🄷
Small village inn: the lounge features an inviting fire; tiny public bar. Popular with holidaymakers. Eve meals in summer only (till 8pm).
♨ Q ⛹ ❀ ◖ ◗ ⊟ ▲ ♣

Llandyrnog

White Horse Inn
☎ (0824) 790582
11–3, 5.30–11; 11–11 Thu–Sat
Draught Bass; Crown Buckley Best Bitter 🄷
Well-situated village pub with a lively local trade. Regular entertainment; weekly bingo session for OAPs. ◖ ◗ ⊟ ♣ P

Llanelian-yn-Rhôs

White Lion Inn
☎ (0492) 515807
11–3, 6–11
John Smith's Bitter, Magnet; Wilson's Mild 🄷**; guest beer**
Olde-worlde village pub with a tasteful extension for diners. Bar, snug and lounge, to suit all visitors. Friendly landlord.
♨ Q 🛏 ◖ ◗ ♿ ▲ ♣ P

Llanferres

Druid Inn
Ruthin Road (A494)
☎ (035 285) 225
11.30–3, 5.30–11
Burtonwood Bitter 🄷
Extended 300-year-old village inn in a gap in the Clwydian Hills. Extensive views at the front; local churchyard at the rear. Real ale in the top bar only. Near Offa's Dyke path.
♨ ❀ 🛏 ◖ ◗ ▲ P

Llangedwyn

Green Inn
On B4396 ☎ (0691) 828234
11–3 (may extend in summer), 6–11
Whitbread Boddingtons Bitter 🄷**; guest beers**
17th-century former drovers' pub in a picturesque valley: an open lounge and a cosy, slate-flagged area, with an inglenook. Extensive, good value menu. Fly fishing. Cider in summer.
♨ ❀ 🛏 ◖ ◗ ♣ ⌓ P

Llangollen

Cambrian Hotel
Berwyn Street (A5)
☎ (0978) 860686
1.30 (12 summer)–4.30, 7–11
Younger Scotch 🄷
Friendly, grey-rendered, family-run hotel: an unspoilt back bar, popular with locals, a games room and a quiet lounge. Old-fashioned without being olde-worlde. Enjoy while you can. Eve meals in summer only. 🛏 ◗ ⊟ ♣ P

Wynnstay Arms
Bridge Street ☎ (0978) 860710
11–11 (may close winter weekday afternoons)
Ind Coope Burton Ale 🄷
Food-oriented pub with a cosy bar. Popular with tourists in summer. Close to the steam railway. ♨ ❀ ◖ ◗

Llanynys

Cerrigllwydion Arms
2 miles E of A525 OS102677
☎ (0745) 578247
11.30–3, 5.30–11
Crown Buckley Dark, Best Bitter; guest beers (occasionally) 🄷
Out-of-the-way, food-oriented house boasting a collection of teapots and jugs. Garden opposite. The only regular outlet for Buckley's Dark in N Wales. ❀ ◖ ◗ ⊟ ♣ P

Maeshafn

Miners Arms
☎ (0352) 85464
12–3, 5–11
S&N Theakston Best Bitter 🄷
Popular village local in a former lead mining area. Impressive log fire. Popular with walkers. Beware fake handpump for Scrumpy Jack cider. ♨ Q ❀ ◖ ◗ ▲ P

Moss

Bird in Hand
Woodland Road (track off B5433) OS303538
☎ (0978) 755809
12–3 (not Mon–Fri), 7–11
Hydes' Anvil Bitter 🄴
Distinctive pub that is not easy to find. Splendid views; close to Moss Valley Country Park. Three-quarter size snooker table. Lunches on Sun only.
Q ❀ ◗ ♣ P

Old Colwyn

Marine Hotel
Abergele Road
☎ (0492) 515484
11.30–11
Draught Bass; M&B Mild 🄷
Large pub with three bars, a pool room and a restaurant.
Q 🛏 ◖ ◗ ⊟ ♣ P

Pentre Broughton

Cross Foxes
High Street ☎ (0978) 755973
11–3, 7–11
Burtonwood Bitter 🄷
Comfortable local which welcomes children. Summer barbecues. The real fire and games make the public bar friendly. ♨ ❀ ◖ ⊟ ♣ P

Pontblyddyn

Bridge Inn
Wrexham Road (at A541/
A5104 jct) ☎ (0352) 770475
12–3, 7–11 (11–11 summer); dining
licence Sun
Cains Bitter; Courage
Directors Ⓗ; guest beers
Stone-built pub with a log fire
in winter. Patio and garden
with a stream. Separate
restaurant. ♨ ☎ ❀ ◖ ● & P

Prestatyn

Cross Foxes
Meliden Road ☎ (0745) 854984
11.30–3, 6–11; 11–11 Fri & Sat
Banks's Mild; Marston's
Bitter, Pedigree Ⓗ
Modernised pub with an
emphasis on food, and dress
restrictions at weekends
(busy). ❀ ◖ ● A ≈ P

Rhewl (Llangollen)

Sun Inn
Off B5103 OS178448
☎ (0978) 861043
12–3, 6–11
Bass Worthington BB;
Felinfoel Double Dragon Ⓗ
14th-century drovers' pub in
the beautiful Dee valley
featuring stone floors, low
ceilings and small rooms. Busy
weekends with hill walkers
and the local farming
fraternity. ♨ Q ☎ ❀
◖ ● ⊟ & A ♣ P

Rhewl (Ruthin)

Drovers Arms
On A525 ☎ (0824) 703163
11.30–3, 6.30–11
Crown Buckley Best Bitter;
Ruddles Best Bitter Ⓗ
Roadside pub popular with
locals. Growing reputation for
good value food. Welcoming
and roomy. ❀ ◖ ● ⊟ ♣ P

Rhuddlan

New Inn
High Street ☎ (0745) 591305
12–3, 6–11; 12–11 Fri & Sat
S&N Theakston Best Bitter,
XB, Old Peculier Ⓗ
Modernised town pub with a
good local feel. Separate
restaurant, serving good
quality Sun lunches at
affordable prices. Popular with
all ages. ❀ ⊨ ◖ ● & A ♣ P

Rhyl

White Horse
Bedford Street
☎ (0745) 334927
11.30–11
John Smith's Bitter Ⓗ; guest
beers
Town-centre pub frequented
by all ages. Guest mild in
summer; real cider most

weeks. Over 60 guest beers in
the last year (three at a time,
including a Welsh indep-
endent). Local CAMRA *Pub of
the Year 1992.* & A ≈ ♣ ◌

Ruabon

Duke of Wellington
Duke Street (B5606, 50 yds off
High St) ☎ (0978) 820381
12–3, 7–11; 12–11 Thu–Sat
Marston's Bitter, Pedigree Ⓗ
Old, low-ceilinged pub; a
comfortable lounge and a bar
with a jukebox and games. No
eve meals Sun/Mon.
❀ ⊨ ◖ ● ⊟ A ≈ ♣ P

Great Western
Church Street ☎ (0978) 822335
6.30–11; 12–3, 7–10.30 Sun
Burtonwood Bitter Ⓗ
Smart public bar with pool
and electronic games; large
lounge. Q ● ♣ P

Ruthin

Wynnstay Arms
Well Street ☎ (0824) 707215
11.30–3, 6–11; 11.30–11 Fri & Sat
Cains Bitter; Whitbread
Boddingtons Mild, Bitter;
guest beer Ⓗ
Modernised pub with an
eating area. Two bars retain a
local feel. ❀ ◖ ● ⊟ ♣ P

St Asaph

Bryn Dinas
Chester Street (opp. cathedral)
☎ (0745) 582128
11.30–11
Bass Worthington BB,
Draught Bass; M&B Mild;
Thwaites Bitter Ⓗ
Distinctive town pub with a
small lounge. No eve meals
Sat/Sun. ❀ ◖ ● ⊟ A ♣ P

Towyn

Morton Arms
Sandbank Road (200 yds from
A548) ☎ (0745) 330211
11–11
M&B Mild; Whitbread
Boddingtons Bitter Ⓗ
Modern seaside pub with
pleasant decor. The only pub
in the village with the real
thing. The regular entertainment can be noisy. Separate
restaurant. ❀ ◖ ● A ♣ P

Upper Colwyn Bay

Taylors
Pen-y-Bryn Road (½ mile from
West End) ☎ (0492) 533360
11–3, 5.30–11
Courage Directors; Marston's
Pedigree; John Smith's
Bitter Ⓗ
Free house and restaurant,
built ten years ago in old brick,
with a natural wood interior.

Panoramic views from the
lounge; downstairs bar.
Furnished to a high standard.
♨ Q ☎ ❀ ◖ ● & A P

Whitford

Huntsman
Whitford Road OS147780
☎ (0745) 360232
11.30–3, 6.30–11
Bass Worthington BB; S&N
Theakston XB Ⓗ
Unspoilt village local with a
lively public bar, good value
food, and a restaurant.
Popular with all ages. Cask
mild is to be added.
♨ ❀ ◖ ● ⊟ ♣ P

Wrexham

Golden Lion
High Street ☎ (0978) 364964
11.30–11
Bass Worthington BB,
Draught Bass; Stones Best
Bitter Ⓗ
Noisy pub where a jukebox
competes with a TV. A typical
town-centre pub, popular with
the young. ◖ ≈ (Central)

Horse & Jockey
Hope Street ☎ (0978) 351081
11.30–11
Tetley Walker Dark Mild,
Bitter Ⓗ
Interesting, thatched pub in
the centre of town. The front
part was built about 1720.
Q ◖ ≈ (Central/General)

Oak Tree Tavern
Ruabon Road (A5152)
☎ (0978) 261450
12–5, 6.30–11
Marston's Bitter, Pedigree Ⓗ
Traditional local, believed to
take its name from an oak tree
in a nearby burial ground
Much bric-a-brac.
Q ◖ ⊟ ≈ (Central) ♣ P

Railway Inn
17 Railway Road, Rhosddu
☎ (0978) 311172
12–3 (11.30–5 Sat), 7–11
Banks's Mild; Marston's
Bitter, Pedigree Ⓗ
Well-run pub on the outskirts
of town. The comfortable
lounge opens into a lively
public bar. The landlord is a
keen supporter of pub teams.
❀ ◖ ● ≈ (General) ♣ P

Ysceifiog

Fox
N of A541, W of Mold
OS152715 ☎ (0352) 720241
7–11; 12–3, 7–11 Sat
Ansells Mild; Tetley Walker
Bitter; Thwaites Bitter Ⓗ
Real traditional pub, not easy
to find but a little gem.
Lunchtime opening weekends
only. ♨ Q ⊟ P

Dyfed

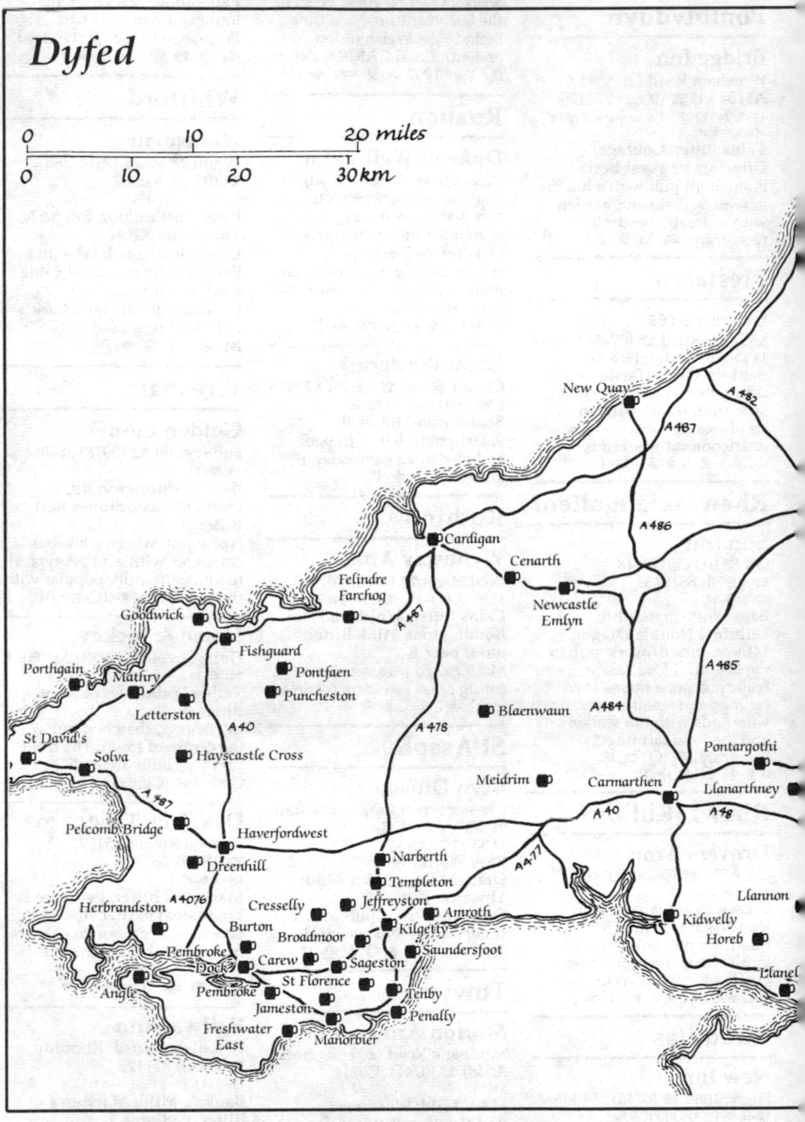

Crown Buckley, Felinfoel, Llanelli

Aberystwyth

Castle

South Road ☎ (0970) 612188
12–3, 5.30–11; 12–11 Sat
Draught Bass H
Large, former Roberts' pub built in imitation of a London gin palace. The closest pub to South Marine beach and harbour – hence many seafaring connections.

Pier Hotel

Pier Street
☎ (0970) 615126
11–4, 5.30–11
Banks's Mild, Bitter E
Pub slightly uphill from the promenade. A large public bar fronts the street while the tiny lounge has its own entrance up a side alley.

Try also: Nag's Head, Bridge St (Banks's)

Ammanford

Wernoleu

Off Pontaman Road (signed off A474)
☎ (0269) 592598
11–11
Beer range varies H
Interesting pub set in a grand house once owned by an industrial magnate. Six guest beers each week.
P

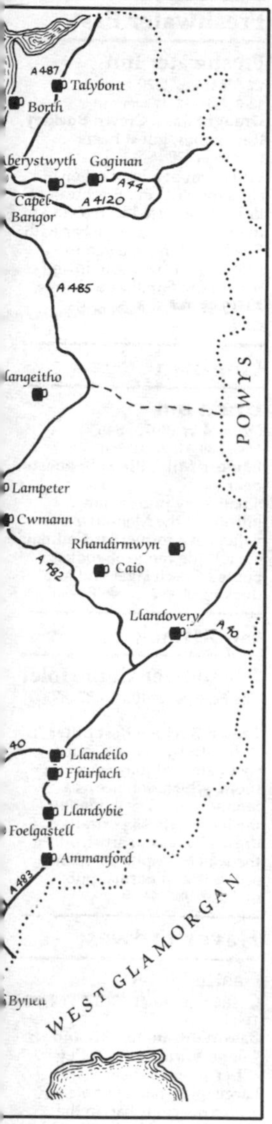

Amroth

New Inn
E end of village
☎ (0834) 812368
11–3 (may extend), 6.30–11
Ind Coope Burton Ale (summer); **Tetley Bitter** Ⓗ; **guest beers** (summer)
400-year-old inn of great character, with a Flemish inglenook fireplace, an enclosed garden and a restaurant upstairs. Superb location, just yards from the beach but can get very crowded in summer. Food served Apr–Oct. ⛫ Q ⛴ ❀ ⛟ ◑ ◗ ⊟ ▲ ♣ P

Angle

Hibernia Inn
Main Street ☎ (0646) 641517
11–3, 6.30–11
Bass Worthington BB; Hancock's HB; guest beer (summer) Ⓗ
Large, cosy local run by one of the Angle lifeboat crew, hence the strong naval theme. A good family pub, near the beach. Good pub grub and snacks available most times.
⛫ Q ⛴ ❀ ◑ ◗ ♿ ▲ ♣ P

Blaenwaun

Lamb Inn
OS237271 ☎ (0994) 448440
Hours vary
Wadworth 6X Ⓗ; **guest beer**
In an isolated hilltop hamlet, a traditional country local with some unusual beers. ❀ ♣ P

Borth

Friendship
High Street ☎ (0970) 871213
12 (11 summer)–3, 6.30 (6 summer)–11
Ansells Bitter; Tetley Bitter Ⓗ
Welcoming, cottage-style pub below road level in this resort village. The same family has held the licence for over 70 years. The corridor and lounge serve as an art gallery. Lunchtime snacks.
⛫ Q ❀ ⊟ ♿ ▲ ⇌ ♣

Broadmoor

Cross Inn
On A477, 2 miles from Kilgetty
☎ (0834) 812287
11–11
Bass Worthington BB Ⓗ; **guest beer** (summer)
Busy, well-kept local catering for the holiday trade and handy for the ferry to Ireland, the Sunday market and beaches. Large playground area. Two bars; snacks and meals served all day.
⛫ Q ⛴ ❀ ◑ ▲ ♣ P

Burton

Jolly Sailor
Burton Ferry (Haverfordwest side of Cleddau Bridge)
☎ (0646) 600378
11–3, 6–11 (11–11 summer)
Ind Coope Burton Ale; Tetley Bitter Ⓗ
If you're into water sports, this is the pub for you, with views of the Cleddau estuary and Milford Haven waterway. Parking for boats, too. Large waterside garden with an adventure playground.
⛫ Q ❀ ◑ ◗ ♿ ▲ ♣ P

Bynea

Lewis Arms
Yspitty Road ☎ (0554) 772878
12–3, 6–11
Felinfoel Dark, Bitter Ⓗ
Village pub also serving an industrial estate. ❀ ◑ ⇌ P

New Plough
76 Cwmfelin Road
☎ (0554) 777187
11.30–3.30, 6.30–11
Crown Buckley Dark, Best Bitter; guest beer Ⓗ
Pleasant village pub with an adjoining restaurant. Supper licence until midnight. Children's play area in the garden. ❀ ◑ ◗ ⇌ ♣

Caio

Brunant Inn
1 mile NE of A482
☎ (055 85) 483
12–3, 7 (6 summer)–11 (may be 12–11 summer)
Hook Norton Best Bitter, Old Hooky Ⓗ; **guest beers**
Friendly pub, full of character, in the centre of the UK's second largest parish. Vast number of pub games; Sun eve debating sessions. Close to the Dolicothi Roman gold mines.
⛫ ❀ ⛟ ◑ ◗ ♿ ▲ ♣ P

Capel Bangor

Tynllidiart Arms
On A44 ☎ (0970) 82428
11–2.30, 6–11 (closed winter Sun eve)
Whitbread Boddingtons Bitter, Flowers Original Ⓗ; **guest beer**
304-year-old cottage inn, formerly connected with the mailcoach trade. Two small bars both have real fires. The guest beer is usually from an independent brewer. Range of bottled-conditioned beers also available. Cider in summer.
⛫ Q ◑ ◗ ⊟ ▲ ♣ ⌓

Cardigan

Red Lion
Pwll Hai (off A484, behind Finch Sq) ☎ (0239) 612782
11–11; 12–3 Sun, closed Sun eve
Crown Buckley Best Bitter, Rev. James Ⓗ
Ancient back-street pub where the large front bar has various drinking areas. Pool room at the rear. Live music Fri. Skittles played. ⛴ ❀ ◑ ◗ ♣

Carew

Carew Inn
☎ (0646) 651267
12–3, 5–11; 11–11 Sat & summer

Dyfed

Bass Worthington BB; Ind Coope Burton Ale [H]
Large, rambling family pub with a local clientele. The Sealed Knot meets here in summer to fight a battle at the castle opposite.
♔ Q ❀ 🛏 ◐ ◑ ▲ ♣ P

Carmarthen

Boars Head
Lammas Street
☎ (0267) 222789
11–11
Felinfoel Dark, Bitter, Double Dragon; guest beer [H]
18th-century coaching inn refurbished. Excellent food.
Q 🛏 ◐ ◑ ⇌ P

Queens Arms
Queen Street ☎ (0267) 231800
11–11
Bass Worthington BB, Draught Bass; guest beer [H]
Comfortable and traditional, two-bar, town-centre hostelry. Snacks lunchtime. Q ❀ ⇌

Cenarth

Three Horseshoes
☎ (0239) 710119
11–11
Draught Bass [G]**; Crown Buckley Dark, Best Bitter** [H]**, Rev. James** [G]**; guest beers**
Busy, traditional inn with a thatched brewhouse at the rear. The garden overlooks Cenarth Falls. Good food.
♔ Q ❀ ◐ ♣ P

Cresselly

Cresselly Arms
Cresswell Quay
☎ (0646) 651210
11–3, 5–11 (may vary)
Bass Worthington BB; Hancock's HB [G]
An oasis in a sea of keg beers. A timeless little gem that has not changed much since 1900, when sail boats unloaded their cargoes here. Hunting and cricket dominate. Beer is served via the four-pint jug. Very busy in summer. Barbecues in hot weather.
♔ Q ❀ ♿ ▲ ♣ P

Cwmann

Ram Inn
On A482, 1 mile from Lampeter ☎ (0570) 422556
11–11
Draught Bass; Fuller's London Pride; guest beer [H]
Originally a drovers' pub, dating back to the 16th century. Now very much a traditional pub with a superb display of Welsh love spoons. Warm welcome. In an area short of real ale pubs, this is a must. ♔ ❀ ◐ ◑ ♿ P

Dreenhill

Denant Mill Inn
Off Dale Road, 2½ miles from Haverfordwest on B4327
☎ (0437) 766569
12–3, 6–11 (hours vary winter)
Beer range varies [H]
A holy grail for ale connoisseurs, set in an old water mill. No house or regular draught beers but a merry-go-round of wonderful ales from all over the UK. Excellent food and accommodation. Live jazz. ♔ Q 🐎 ❀ 🛏 ◐ ◑ ♿ ▲ ♣ P ⊁

Felindre Farchog

Salutation Inn
On A487 ☎ (0239) 820564
11–3 (12–2 winter), 5.30–11
Ind Coope Burton Ale [H]
Village pub which has expanded to become a reasonably-sized hotel. A comfortable lounge, where the emphasis is on meals, and a traditional village bar.
🐎 ❀ 🛏 ◐ ◑ ⊟ ♿ P

Ffairfach

Torbay
Heol Cennen (A483)
☎ (0558) 822029
11–3, 6.30–11 (11–11 summer Sat)
Crown Buckley Dark, Best Bitter [H]
Pretty, one-bar pub, largely given over to an attractive restaurant. Close to historic sites. ♔ ❀ ◐ ◑ ⊟ ⇌ P

Fishguard

Ship Inn
Newport Road, Lower Town (A487) ☎ (0348) 874033
11–3, 7–11; 12–2, 7–10.30 Sun
Bass Worthington Dark, BB [G]/[H]
Excellent haven by the original harbour. Marine knick-knacks dominate this low-ceilinged, beamed pub, famous for hosting film crews from *Moby Dick* and *Under Milk Wood*. Snacks served. ♔ ♣

Try also: Old Coach House, High St (Free)

Foelgastell

Smiths Arms
Off A48 ☎ (0269) 842213
11–11
Crown Buckley Best Bitter; Whitbread Boddingtons Mild, Flowers Original [H]**; guest beer** [G]
Cosy, friendly pub in a quiet village a minute or so off the main holiday route. Interesting menu. ♔ ❀ ◐ ◑ ♣ ⌓ P

Freshwater East

Freshwater Inn
☎ (0646) 672329
12–3, 7–11 (12–11 summer)
Draught Bass; Crown Buckley Rev. James; guest beers (summer) [H]
Little gem of a local set on cliffs overlooking Freshwater Bay. Modernised in 1988 to a high standard: a large bar with five handpumps, a games room and a large-windowed restaurant. Families welcome.
♔ Q ❀ 🛏 ◐ ◑ ♿ ▲ ♣ ⌓ P

Goginan

Druid Inn
On A44 ☎ (0970) 84650
11–3, 5.30–11; closed Sun
Banks's Mild, Bitter [H]**; guest beer**
Small, cosy pub set into a hillside of the Melindwr valley, in a former lead-mining area. Wide range of vodkas, bottled Czech lager and local duck eggs. ◐ ◑ ♿ ♣ P

Goodwick

Glendower Club Hotel
The Square ☎ (0348) 872873
11–11
Crown Buckley Best Bitter [H]
Pub with two bars, a games room and a dining/meeting room, which doubles as a family room. Try to identify the locals whose portraits, drawn by a local artist, adorn the walls. Despite the name, access is as a normal pub.
Q 🐎 ❀ 🛏 ⊟ ♣

Haverfordwest

Castle Hotel
Castle Square ☎ (0437) 769322
11–11
Bass Worthington BB; Ind Coope Burton Ale; Tetley Bitter [H]**; guest beer**
Large, pink-painted hotel, with a spacious bar, in the town centre. Filled with shoppers in the daytime. Good atmosphere; very comfortable (no overalls allowed). Can be noisy Fri and Sat. Guest beers vary in summer. Sun lunches served.
🛏 ◐ ◑ ♿ ▲ ⇌ ♣ ⌓ P

Hayscastle Cross

Cross Inn
On B4330 ☎ (0348) 840216
11.30–3, 6–11 (may extend)
Bass Worthington BB; Felinfoel Bitter [H]
Traditional country pub in a quiet village, with attractive bar fittings and a flagged floor.
♔ Q 🐎 ❀ ◐ ◑ ⊟ ▲ ♣ P

Herbrandston

Taberna Inn
☎ (0646) 693498
11–3, 6–11; 11–11 Fri & Sat
Bass Worthington BB; Felinfoel Double Dragon; Ind Coope Burton Ale Ⓗ; guest beer (summer)
Traditional pub with a good restaurant. The locally-caught seafood is a speciality. Three guest beers in summer.
♨ ❀ 🛏 ◐ ◑ ♿ ♣ P

Horeb

Waun-Wyllt
Off B4309 ☎ (0269) 860209
12–3, 7 (6 Fri, 5.30 Sat)–11
Felinfoel Double Dragon; S&N Theakston Best Bitter Ⓗ; guest beers
Excellent free house set in idyllic countryside. Well worth finding. Q ❀ ◐ ◑ ⊞ P

Jameston

Tudor Lodge
Just outside village on Tenby road ☎ (0834) 871978
3 (12 Sat)–11 (11–11 summer)
Bass Worthington BB, Draught Bass (summer) Ⓗ
Interesting old gem, set in beautiful grounds with a large, shaded lawn in front and a marvellous children's garden behind. A comfortable bar, a separate restaurant and a large family room. Welcoming staff.
♨ Q ♘ ❀ 🛏 ◐ ◑ ⊞ ▲ ♣ P

Jeffreyston

Jeffreyston Inn
Sharp turn off B4586 OS065088
☎ (0646) 651394
11–11
Bass Worthington BB; Crown Buckley Best Bitter; John Smith's Bitter; guest beers Ⓗ
Large pub in a small village, justly famous for its convivial atmosphere. Good food, snooker, garden play house (plus goat), and a minibus service around the neighbourhood. Cider in summer.
Q ♘ ❀ ◐ ◑ ⊞ ♿ ▲ ♣ ⌓ P

Kidwelly

Boot & Shoe
2 Castle Street ☎ (0554) 891341
11–3.30, 6.30–11
Felinfoel Dark, Bitter, Double Dragon Ⓗ
Small, friendly village local.
◐ ◑ ♣

Kilgetty

Kilgetty Arms
☎ (0834) 813219
11–11 (11–3, 6–11 winter)
Felinfoel Dark, Bitter Ⓗ
Traditional local with two small bars and a warm Welsh welcome. Snacks on request.
♨ Q ❀ ◐ ◑ ⇌ ♣ P

Lampeter

Kings Head
14 Bridge Street (A482/A485)
☎ (0570) 422598
11–3.30 (may extend), 5.30–11 (supper licence)
Crown Buckley Best Bitter Ⓗ
Pleasant, little university town local, recently modernised with a small front bar and a larger rear lounge. Aviary in the garden. The menu caters for children and vegetarians.
♨ ❀ ◐ ◑ ♿ ▲ ♣ P

Letterston

Harp Inn
Haverfordwest Road (A40, S end of village)
☎ (0348) 840061
11–3, 5.30–11
Ansells Bitter; Ind Coope Burton Ale; Tetley Bitter Ⓗ
Well-modernised village pub with a popular public bar and a comfortable, well-furnished lounge. ♨ Q ❀ ◐ ◑ ⊞ ♿ P

Llanarthney

Paxton Inn
On B4300 ☎ (0558) 668705
4–11
Bass Worthington BB; Crown Buckley Best Bitter; Tetley Bitter Ⓗ; guest beers
Highly individual, traditional, 250-year-old pub, full of character and curios. Regular jazz, and do-it-yourself music sessions. Folk music and Elizabethan festival in summer. Up to seven guest beers. ◑ ♿ ▲ ♣ ⌓ P

Try also: Golden Grove (Crown Buckley)

Llandeilo

Three Tuns
Market Street ☎ (0558) 823978
2 (1 Sat)–11; closed Sun
Brains Dark; Ind Coope Burton Ale; Tetley Bitter; Wadworth 6X; guest beers Ⓗ
Friendly, back-street local with a reputed customer of the supernatural kind. Situated in the oldest part of town, dating back to the 1770s. Popular with a cross-section of drinkers, young and old.
🛏 ⇌ (not winter Sun) ♣

White Horse
125 Rhosmaen Street (A483, through archway at top of main street) ☎ (0558) 822424
12–3, 5.30–11; 12–2.30, 7–10.30 Sun
Bass Worthington BB; Brains Dark; Wadworth 6X Ⓗ; guest beers
17th-century coaching inn with a courtyard, and railway photos in the snug. A regulars' pub with a welcome for all. Two guest beers. No food Sun.
♨ Q ❀ ◐ ⇌ (not winter Sun) ⌓ P

Try also: Farmers Arms, Rhosmaen St (Crown Buckley)

Llandovery

Red Lion
Market Square ☎ (0550) 20813
11–3 (not Wed), 5.30–11 (may close early); closed Sun
Crown Buckley Dark, Best Bitter Ⓖ
Ancient, friendly and hard to find pub – look for the red pillars. One basic drinking room with no bar. In the same family for over a century.
♨ Q ▲ ⇌ (not winter Sun)

White Hart Inn
60 Stone Street (400 yds from A40) ☎ (0550) 20152
11 (6 Mon)–11
Bass Worthington BB, Draught Bass Ⓗ
17th-century town pub on the former main street – one of only four remaining where there were once 16 pubs.
❀ ◐ ◑ ▲ ⇌ ♣

Try also: Whitehall Hotel, High St (Bass)

Llandybie

Red Lion
The Square ☎ (0269) 851202
11.30–3, 6–11; 12–3 Sun, closed Sun eve
Draught Bass; Whitbread Boddingtons Bitter, Flowers Original Ⓗ
Attractive, stylish pub offering a good welcome to families. Pleasant bilingual atmosphere.
Q ♘ ❀ 🛏 ◐ ◑ ⇌ P ⚡

Llanelli

Bull Inn
Ann Street ☎ (0554) 756283
11–11
Crown Buckley Dark, Best Bitter Ⓗ
Locals' pub with a good atmosphere. ◐ ⊞ ⇌

Halfway Hotel
Swansea Road
☎ (0554) 773571
12–3, 6–11
Bass Worthington BB, Draught Bass Ⓗ
Impressive, original oak bar. Well kept, spacious and comfortable. Q ♘ ❀ ◐ ⊞ P

Masons
Thomas Street
☎ (0554) 775121
12–11
Felinfoel Dark, Bitter; Fuller's London Pride Ⓗ

Pub with a small locals' bar and a well-appointed, spacious lounge. ♨ ⊟

Thomas Arms Hotel
Thomas Street
☎ (0554) 772043
12–11
Crown Buckley Best Bitter, Rev. James [H]
Plush, showpiece pub for Crown Buckley. Various function rooms and a relaxed, roomy lounge bar. 🛏 ◖ ◗ P

Llangeitho

Three Horseshoes
The Square ☎ (0974) 821244
12–3, 5.30–11; closed Sun, except bank hol weekends
Tetley Bitter [H]**; guest beer** (occasionally)
Traditional local in a quiet village, which doubles as a fish and chip shop on Fri nights. Self-catering accommodation available by summer 1994.
♨ Q ❀ ◖ ◗ ⊟ ♿ ▲ ♣ P

Llannon

Red Lion
3 Heol-y-Plas (A476)
☎ (0269) 841276
5 (12 Sat)–11
Felinfoel Dark, Bitter, Double Dragon [H]
Pub dating back to at least the 17th century. Rumoured to have a secret tunnel leading to the neighbouring church, a ghost and to have been visited by Cromwell. Does have a well and a toby jug collection.
♨ Q ♞ ❀ ◗ P

Manorbier

Castle Inn
☎ (0834) 871268
11–11
Bass Worthington BB; guest beers [H]
Beamed, low ceilings trap unwary giants in this interestingly shaped old pub, full of nooks. Opposite a Norman castle and near a beach and cliff walks. Folk music, country and western, and special nights throughout the week. Good surfing.
♨ Q ♞ ❀ ◖ ◗ ▲ ♣

Mathry

Farmers Arms
Off A487 ☎ (0348) 831284
11–11
Bass Worthington BB, Draught Bass [H]
Pub with an old, timbered interior liberally adorned with Guinness cartoons and rural bric-a-brac. A former monks' brewhouse, built in 1291 atop an ancient hill settlement. Local artists' works on show. Families welcome. ❀ 🛏 ◖ ⊟ P

Meidrim

Maenllwyd Inn
¾ mile W of village OS278212
6–11; closed Sun
Crown Buckley Best Bitter [H]
Utterly traditional, country local with a whitewashed parlour with a black-leaded range and a cottage-style sitting room. Beer is served straight from the cellar. No keg at all. ♨ Q ⊟ ♿ ♣

Narberth

Castle Inn
High Street ☎ (0834) 860729
12–3, 7–11
Bass Worthington BB [H]**; guest beers**
Welcoming local opposite what is left of the castle. Keen pool-players; strong musical emphasis; nostalgic jukebox.
♨ ◖ ◗ ♿ ♣

Kirkland Arms
St James Street
☎ (0834) 860423
11–11
Felinfoel Dark, Bitter, Double Dragon [H]
Lively local near the rugby ground, with plenty of character, reflected in the wide variety of exhibits around the walls. An excellent stop on the trek to or from the station.
♞ ❀ ⊟ ♿ ▲ ♣ P

Try also: Dragon Inn, High St (Bass); **Eagle**, High St (Free)

Newcastle Emlyn

Bunch of Grapes
Bridge Street (A475)
☎ (0239) 711185
11.30–11
Courage Best Bitter, Directors [H]**; guest beers**
17th-century building now opened-out, its pine floors giving a café-bar atmosphere.
♨ ❀ ▲ ♣

New Quay

Dolau Inn
Church Street (A486)
☎ (0545) 560881
11–4, 5.30–11; 11–11 Fri, Sat & summer
Hancock's HB [H]
Extended, early 19th-century cottage inn, one of the oldest buildings in the town. Traditional settle seating amongst shipping mementoes. Snacks in summer.
❀ ⊟ ♿ ▲ ♣

Seahorse
Margaret Street (B4342)
☎ (0545) 560736
11–11
Crown Buckley Best Bitter; Hancock's HB [H]
Welcoming, Victorian, one-bar pub in the town centre, high above the fishing harbour. Fine reputation for accommodation. Snacks available. 🛏 ♿ ▲ ♣

Pelcomb Bridge

Rising Sun Inn
Just off A487 ☎ (0437) 765171
11.30–3, 7 (6 summer)–11
Ind Coope Burton Ale; Tetley Bitter [H]
Old country inn tastefully rebuilt and retaining its original character. A family business offering a warm welcome. Good value meals.
Q ❀ 🛏 ◖ ◗ ⊟ ♿ ▲ ♣ P

Pembroke

Old Cross Saws Inn
109 Main Street
☎ (0646) 682475
11–11
Draught Bass; Crown Buckley Best Bitter, Rev. James [H]
Rugby followers' local, larger inside than it looks from the outside. Well-placed for sight-seeing. Bar meals and rolls. ❀ 🛏 ◖ ◗ ♿ ⇌ ♣

Pembroke Dock

Ferry Inn
Pembroke Ferry (underneath Cleddau Bridge)
☎ (0646) 682947
11.30–2.45 (3.45 Mon), 6.30 (7 Mon)–11
Draught Bass; Hancock's HB [H]
Pub at the landing point of the Cleddau river ferry before the bridge was built. A nautical pub, popular with yachtsmen, water skiers and holiday-makers alike. Large menu; carvery Sun.
♨ Q ❀ ◖ ◗ ▲ ♣ P

First & Last
London Road (A477)
☎ (0646) 682687
11–11
Bass Worthington BB [H]**; guest beer**
Keen real ale pub in which you can be served by the oldest licensee in Wales. A lively local with live music Sat; some real characters sup here. Still has gas lighting. Guest beers change regularly. No food Sun. ❀ ◖ ⇌ ♣ P

Penally

Cross Inn
Opp. station ☎ (0834) 844465
11–11
Bass Worthington BB [H]**; guest beer** [G]
Beautifully-situated, sensitively restored village pub, enjoying panoramic views over a golf course to the

sea. The nucleus for the carnival and other local events. An excellent centre for cliff walks or train journeys.
Q ❀ 🛏 ◐ ◑ ▲ ⇌ ♣

Pontargothi

Cresselly Arms
On A40 ☎ (0267) 290221
11–3, 6.30–11
Marston's Pedigree; Whitbread Flowers Original [H]
Handsomely furnished, pretty main-road pub near lovely river walks. Beautiful waterscape from the restaurant. ♛ ♉ ❀ ◐ ◑ P

Pontfaen

Dyffryn Arms
1 mile off B4313
Hours vary
Draught Bass *or* **Ind Coope Burton Ale** [G]
Popularly known as Bessie's, a 1920s time warp in a wooded valley between Mynydd Preseli and Fishguard. Beer is served by jug and conversation is obligatory in this tiny one-roomer. ♛ Q ❀

Porthgain

Sloop Inn
☎ (0348) 831449
12–3, 6–11; 12–11 Fri & Sat
Bass Worthington BB *or* **Hancock's HB** [H]
Seafarers' pub of great character, established in 1743 in an historic harbour and quarrying village on the coastal path in the National Park. The menu includes locally-caught seafood. ♛ ❀ ◐ ◑ ♣ P

Puncheston

Drovers Arms
Off A40, E of Letterston
☎ (0348) 881469
11–11
Bass Worthington BB [H]
Family-run, conversational pub with a flag-floored public bar, rear dining rooms, a lounge bar and a large function room. Lots of outside space, safe for kids. Very warm welcome.
Q ♉ ❀ ◐ ◑ ♿ ♣ P

Rhandirmwyn

Royal Oak Inn
☎ (055 06) 201
11–3, 6–11
Ruddles Best Bitter; Wadworth 6X [H]
Former 15th-century mansion on an old drovers' road, with good views of the Tywi valley. Popular with walkers, campers and ornithologists (RSPB reserve nearby).
♛ Q ❀ 🛏 ◐ ◑ ▲ ♣ P

Sageston

Plough Inn
On main road ☎ (0646) 651557
11–3, 5–11; 11–11 Sat
Bass Worthington BB, Draught Bass; guest beer [H]
Busy, family local, especially in summer, near a popular Sunday market. Good food seven days a week. Convenient for beaches and Irish ferry travellers. Varied guest beer. ♛ ♉ ❀ 🛏
◐ ◑ ♿ ▲ ♣ ⌓ P

St David's

Farmers Arms
Goat Street (A477)
☎ (0437) 720328
11–3, 5.30–11 (11–11 summer)
Whitbread Boddingtons Bitter, Flowers Original [H]**; guest beers** (summer)
19th-century, stone pub with beams, flagstoned floors and an original fireplace. Popular with local fishermen, farmers and rugby followers. Fair range of meals and bar snacks. Large games room with a pool table. ♛ Q ♉ ❀ ◐ ◑ ▲ ♣

St Florence

New Inn
High Street ☎ (0834) 871315
11–3, 5.30–11
Brains Bitter [H] (summer)/ [G] (winter)
Sympathetically enlarged pub in a picturesque village, centred on an old Flemish chimney. Large garden at the rear; patio in front.
♛ Q ❀ ◐ ◑ ⊟ ♿ ▲ ♣ P

Saundersfoot

Old Chemist Inn
The Strand ☎ (0834) 813982
11–11
Bass Worthington BB, Draught Bass; guest beers (summer) [H]
Lively, friendly, two-bar local overlooking the beach. Steps lead down to the paved garden, which leads to the sands. No wheelchair access to the family room.
♛ ♉ ❀ ◐ ◑ ⊟ ♿ ▲ ♣

Try also: Saundersfoot Sport & Social Club, St George's Field (Crown Buckley)

Solva

Ship Inn
Main Street ☎ (0437) 721247
11–11
Bass Worthington BB, Draught Bass; Felinfoel Double Dragon [H]
Small, 300-year-old pub, popular with locals and holidaymakers, in a lovely Pembrokeshire fishing village. On the quay, used as the pub's car park, are the remains and story of the first lighthouse. Daily specials and Sun lunches. ♛ Q ❀ ◐ ◑ ▲ ♣

Talybont

White Lion
The Square ☎ (0970) 832245
11–11
Banks's Mild, Bitter [E]
Large, warm, slate-flagged bar, providing everything from cribbage to bus timetables. Tidy lounge at the rear and a small dining room. Renowned for accommodation and meals. Children admitted.
Q ❀ 🛏 ◐ ◑ ⊟ ♿ ♣ P

Templeton

Boars Head
On A478 ☎ (0834) 860286
11–3, 5.30–11; 11–11 Sat & bank hols
Ruddles Best Bitter; Webster's Yorkshire Bitter [H]
Rural, beamed pub with a large restaurant and a larger menu. A fox hunting theme and hanging hops give a country feel. Beware low door frames. Q ❀ ◐ ◑ ▲ ♣ P

Tenby

Coach & Horses
Upper Frog Street
☎ (0834) 842704
11–11
Whitbread Boddingtons Bitter, Flowers IPA, Original [H]
Old, two-bar pub with a well-earned reputation for home-cooked food. Tigger, the tailless cat, makes occasional appearances. Quiet lunchtimes; crowded late eves.
♛ ❀ ◐ ◑ ⊟ ⇌ ♣

Hope & Anchor
St Julian Street
☎ (0834) 842131
11–3, 7–11 (11–11 summer)
Bass Worthington BB; Crown Buckley Rev. James [H]
Pub near the harbour, with strong nautical influences. Plenty to entertain, with pool and darts teams, quiz nights and dominoes. Always friendly. Meals in summer only. ♛ Q ❀ ◐ ◑ ⇌ ♣

Tenby & District Ex-Servicemen's Club
Ruabon House, South Parade
☎ (0834) 842258
11–3, 6–11; 12–2, 7–10.30 Sun
Bass Worthington Dark, BB [E]
Temporary members are welcomed in this large club boasting two snooker tables and an upstairs function room, which specialises in summer bingo, sing-songs, etc. Children's room lunchtimes only. Q ♉ ⇌ ♣

Mid Glamorgan

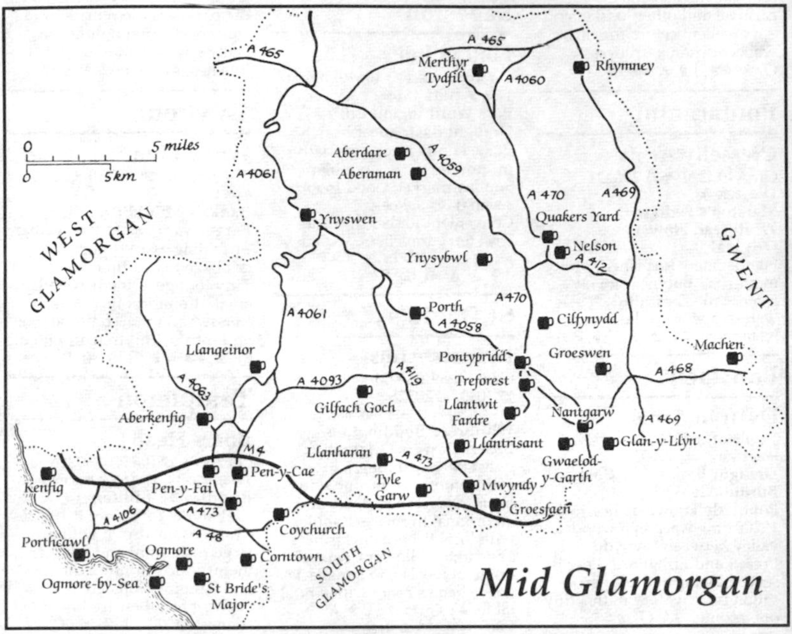

Aberaman

Temple Bar Vaults
Cardiff Road (B4275)
☎ (0685) 876137
12–4, 7–11 (may vary)
Brains SA; Crown Buckley Rev. James; Felinfoel Bitter; Wadworth Farmer's Glory 🄷
Homely local kept by the same family for 106 years. The bar is full of bric-a-brac and has a 'library'. Separate, unobtrusive games room. Beer range may vary. 🔥 Q ❀ ⊟ ♣ P

Aberdare

Glandover Arms
Gadlys Road (B4275, old Hirwaun road)
☎ (0685) 872923
12–4.30, 7–11
Bass Worthington BB; Brains Bitter *or* SA 🄷
Convivial house with a cellar restaurant; eve meals Thu–Sat. ◗ ⊟ ⇌ ♣

Aberkenfig

Swan
128 Bridgend Road
☎ (0656) 725612
11–3.30 (4 Sat), 6–11; 12–2.30, 7–10.30 Sun
Brains Dark, Bitter, SA 🄷
Pleasant, comfortable village pub. Good meals (no food Mon eve or Sun).
◖ ◗ ♿ ⇌ (Sarn) P

Cilfynydd

Commercial Hotel
Cilfynydd Road (1½ miles N of Pontypridd on A4054)
☎ (0443) 402486
11–11
Bass Worthington BB; Brains Bitter; Hancock's HB 🄷
Large, bustling village pub. Pub games and live music most nights. Comfortable lounge areas, and a restaurant (no eve meals Mon). ◖ ◗ ♿ ♣

Corntown

Golden Mile
☎ (0656) 654884
11.30–3, 5 (5.30 Sat)–11
Bass Worthington BB, Draught Bass; Hancock's HB 🄷
Old converted farmhouse with a stone fireplace and exposed beams. Separate restaurant area. Good views from the garden. 🔥 Q ❀ ◖ ◗ ♣ P

Coychurch

Prince of Wales
Main Road ☎ (0656) 860600
12–11
Banks's Mild, Bitter; Marston's Pedigree 🄷
Pleasant, unpretentious village local with a friendly atmosphere. Exposed stone walls both inside and outside. A rare Banks's outlet for the area. Q ◖ ⊟ P

White Horse
Main Road ☎ (0656) 652583
11.30–4, 5.30–11; 11.30–11 Fri & Sat
Brains Dark, Bitter, SA 🄷
A plush restaurant-style lounge, with a heavy emphasis on meals, and a comfortable public bar with rugby memorabilia. Q ❀ ◖ ◗ ⊟ P

Gilfach Goch

Griffin
Hendreforgan (600 yds S of A4093, 1½ miles W of Tonyrefail) OS988875
12–11 (may close afternoons)
Brains SA 🄷
Exceptional, traditional local remotely situated in a small valley bottom and featuring old bric-a-brac and furniture. Hard to find, at the end of a half-surfaced lane and not signposted from the main road, but well worth the effort. Cosy and friendly. Q ❀ ♣ P

Glan-y-Llyn

Fagin's Ale & Chop House
8 Cardiff Road (A4054)
☎ (0222) 811800
11–11
Brains Bitter; Butcombe Bitter; Felinfoel Double Dragon; Hardington Best Bitter; Wadworth 6X;

Whitbread Boddingtons Bitter Ⓗ**; guest beers** Ⓖ
Old terraced cottage with loads of atmosphere, beams and a flagstone floor, converted from a restaurant. A welcoming local with enthusiastic staff. Ever-changing range of ales (up to eight guests), and a restaurant (no meals Sun eve).
❀ ◐ ◑ ⇌ (Taff's Well)

Groesfaen

Dynevor Arms
Llantrisant Road
☎ (0222) 890530
11–3, 5.30–11; 11–11 Fri & Sat
Draught Bass; Hancock's HB; guest beer Ⓗ
Smart village local, popular with all ages. One bar provides separate areas for regular live music or conversation. The guest beer is changed fortnightly.
❀ ◐ ◑ ♣ P

Groeswen

White Cross Inn
On hillside, 1 mile N of A468 OS128870 ☎ (0222) 851332
12–3.30, 6–12; 12–12 Sat; 12–10.30 Sun (supper licence)
S&N Theakston Mild, Best Bitter, XB, Old Peculier Ⓗ
Deceptively large pub with a small bar and two additional rooms. The larger room allows for live entertainment. The patio has a view of Caerphilly castle. Children welcome.
⌂ Q ❀ ◐ ◑ ▲ ♣ P

Gwaelod-y-Garth

Gwaelod-y-Garth Inn
600 yds off Taff's Well–Pentyrch road ☎ (0222) 810408
12–11
Draught Bass; Hancock's HB; guest beers Ⓗ
Ever-popular village local with valley views from the patio. Further refurbishment has created a second bar with stairs to a restaurant. Sun lunches in the restaurant only.
❀ ◐ ◑ P

Kenfig

Prince of Wales
Ton Kenfig (off B4283)
☎ (0656) 740356
11.30–4, 6–11
Bass Worthington BB, Draught Bass Ⓗ**; Marston's Pedigree** Ⓖ**; guest beers**
Old pub with exposed stone walls that have many a tale to tell. Linked with historic Kenfig which lies buried under the sand dunes. Home cooking.
⌂ Q ❀ ◐ ◑ ♿ ▲ ♣ P

Llangeinor

Llangeinor Arms
Off A4093 ☎ (0656) 870268
11–11
Bass Worthington BB; Hancock's HB Ⓗ
Isolated hilltop pub with superb views, oak beams and antique artefacts and furniture. Large conservatory.
⌂ Q ⚭ ❀ ◐ ◑ P

Llanharan

High Corner House
The Square ☎ (0443) 238056
11–11
Brains SA; Marston's Pedigree; Whitbread Boddingtons Bitter, Castle Eden Ale Ⓗ
Large, plush village pub given the Whitbread 'Brewers Fayre' treatment. Bar billiards table.
❀ ◐ ◑ ♣ P

Llantrisant

Penny Farthing
Cardiff Road, Southgate
☎ (0443) 228838
12–3, 6–11
Beer range varies Ⓗ
Single-roomed, open-plan estate pub with a long bar, always offering three real ales. No meals Sun. Q ❀ ◐ ◑ P

Llantwit Fardre

Bush Inn
Main Road ☎ (0443) 203958
12–4.30, 6.30–11; 12–2, 7–10.30 Sun
Draught Bass; Hancock's HB Ⓗ
Quiet, cosy village local with exposed stone walls. Limited parking. Q ⊟ ♣ P

Machen

White Hart
Nant y Ceisiad (100 yds N of A468, under railway bridge, to the right) ☎ (0633) 441005
12–2 (may vary), 6.30–11
Bass Worthington BB; Brains SA Ⓗ**; guest beers**
Mid Glam CAMRA *Pub of the Year* 1992: a rambling pub with extensive wood panelling, some saved from a luxury liner. Excellent guest beer list – one or two mini-beer festivals per year. Small restaurant (no lunches Sat). ⌂ Q ◐ ◑ P

Merthyr Tydfil

Lantern
Bethesda Street, Georgetown
☎ (0685) 383683
12–3, 7–11 (may be 12–11 summer); 12–11 Sat
Crown Buckley Best Bitter, Rev. James Ⓗ**; guest beer**
Formerly a brewery tap, this Grade II-listed building is over 200 years old and features a very comfortable horseshoe-shaped bar with a raised dining area. Live music Thu and Sat. The steak sandwiches come highly recommended. Book Sun lunch. ❀ ◐ ◑ ▲ ⇌

Mwyndy

Barn at Mwyndy
100 yds E of A4119
☎ (0443) 222333
12–2.30, 5.30/6 (7 Sat)–11; 12–2.30, 7–10.30 Sun
Felinfoel Double Dragon; Hancock's HB; Wadworth 6X Ⓗ**; guest beer**
A conversion from an old barn: a restaurant on the upper level, two bars on the lower. Stone walls, beams and agricultural artefacts abound. Mixed couples and families only Sat eve. No eve meals Sun. A house beer is also sold.
⌂ Q ⚭ ❀ ◐ ◑ ♿ P

Castell Mynach Inn
Llantrisant Road (A4119, 800 yds N of M4 jct 34)
☎ (0443) 222298
11–11
Worthington BB, Draught Bass; Hancock's HB Ⓗ
Ever-popular meeting, eating and drinking house. No food Sun. Q ❀ ◐ P

Nantgarw

Cross Keys
Cardiff Road ☎ (0443) 843262
11–11
Bass Worthington BB; Brains Bitter Ⓗ
Comfortable, open-plan house with a small dining area. Serves both as a lunchtime business retreat and an evening local. ❀ ◐ ◑ ♣ P

Nelson

Dynevor
Commercial Street (near bus station) ☎ (0443) 450295
11–11
Bass Worthington BB, Draught Bass; Hancock's HB Ⓗ
Over 200 years old and used by local farmers for a drink after market. Formerly a brew pub. ❀ ◑ ⊟ ♣ P

Ogmore

Pelican
Ewenny Road (B4524, opp. castle) ☎ (0656) 880049
11.30–4, 6.30–11 (varies in summer); 11.30–11 Fri & Sat
Brains Dark, SA; Courage Best Bitter; John Smith's Bitter; Wadworth 6X Ⓗ
Smart, comfortable country pub with a restaurant. Excellent and varied range of pub fare. ❀ ◐ ◑ ▲ ♣ P

Mid Glamorgan

Ogmore-by-Sea

Sea Lawns Hotel

Slon Lane ☎ (0656) 880311
11–11 (12–3, 6–11 winter)
Bass Worthington BB, Draught Bass; guest beers [H]
Large hotel on the Heritage Coastal Path, popular with ale buffs and holidaymakers alike. The smart lounge/restaurant, comfortable bar and function room all have terrific sea views. Over 50 different guest beers served in 1992. No children in the bar. Occasional eve meals. ♨ ❀ 🛏 ◖ ⛺ P

Pen-y-Cae

Ty'r Isha

Off A4061 or A4063, Bridgend side of M4 services OS903827
☎ (0656) 725287
11–4 or later, 6–11; 11–11 Sat
Draught Bass; Hancock's HB [H]
Popular, converted 15th-century farmhouse, once a courthouse.
♨ ❀ ◖ ◗ ♿ ⇌ (Sarn) ♣ P

Pen-y-Fai

Pheasant

Heol-yr-Eglwys (off A4063)
☎ (0656) 653614
11.30–4, 6–11; 11–11 Fri & Sat
Courage Best Bitter; Ruddles Best Bitter, County; Wadworth 6X; Webster's Yorkshire Bitter [H]
Large village pub with a luxurious lounge. Eve meals Thu–Sat. The beer range may vary but there is always one real ale at a special price.
❀ ◖ ◗ 🗔 ♿ ♣ P

Pontypridd

Bunch of Grapes

Ynysangharad Road (behind B&Q, off A4054/A470)
☎ (0443) 402934
11–11
Bass Worthington BB; Brains Bitter, SA; Hancock's HB; John Smith's Bitter; guest beer [H]
Comfortable pub with a sun trap patio and a restaurant.
🐎 ❀ ◖ ◗ ⇌ ♣ P

Greyhound

1 The Broadway (opp. station)
☎ (0443) 402350
11–11
Bass Worthington BB, Draught Bass; Brains SA [H]
Small town pub, invariably bustling. ❀ 🗔 ⇌ ♣

Llanover Arms

Bridge Street (at Ynysybwl jct of A470) ☎ (0443) 403215
11–11
Bass Worthington BB; Brains Dark, Bitter, SA; Wadworth 6X [H]
Bustling town pub with three small bars. ❀ 🗔 ⇌ ♣ P

Porth

Lodge

Eirw Road ☎ (0443) 685393
11–11
Brains SA; Courage Best Bitter; John Smith's Bitter [H]
Comfortable roadside house, handy for Rhondda Heritage Centre. ❀ ◖ ◗ 🗔 ♣ P

Porthcawl

Lorelei Hotel

36–38 Esplanade Avenue
☎ (0656) 782683
12–3, 6–11
Ind Coope Benskins Best Bitter, Burton Ale [H]**; guest beers** [G]
Traditionally-built Victorian hotel near the seafront: a smart comfortable bar and a brasserie-style restaurant. Up to three guest beers. Occasional beer tasting nights with special accommodation rates. ❀ 🛏 ◖ ◗ ⛺

Royal Oak Inn

South Road (B4283, 100 yds from police station)
☎ (0656) 782684
11.30–11
Bass Worthington BB, Draught Bass [H]
Town pub with a basic bar, a comfortable lounge and a dining room. No meals Sun eve. Q ❀ ◖ ◗ ⛺ ♣ P

Quakers Yard

Glantaff Inn

Cardiff Road ☎ (0443) 410822
11–11
Courage Best Bitter, Directors; Marston's Pedigree; Ruddles Best Bitter; John Smith's Bitter [H]
Comfortable, popular inn with a warm, friendly atmosphere. Upstairs restaurant. Interesting collection of water jugs.
Q ❀ ◖ ◗ 🗔 ⇌ P

Rhymney

Farmers Arms

Brewery Row (off B4257)
☎ (0685) 840257
12–5, 7–11; 12–11 Fri & Sat
Brains Bitter [H]**; guest beer**
Basic, friendly local. No lunches Sun. ❀ ◖ 🗔 ⇌ ♣ P

St Bride's Major

Farmers Arms

Wick Road (B4265)
☎ (0656) 880224
12–3, 6–11 (sometimes 12–11)
Courage Best Bitter, Directors; John Smith's Bitter; Ushers Best Bitter, Founders [H]
Large, roadside country pub, opposite the village pond. Two very comfortable rooms: the larger reverts to restaurant use in the eve. Safe garden for children. ♨ Q ❀ ◖ ◗ ♿ P

Fox & Hounds

Wick Road (B4265)
☎ (0656) 880285
12–3, 5.30–11; 12–11 Fri, Sat & summer
Wadworth 6X; Webster's Yorkshire Bitter; guest beer [H]
Comfortable, friendly village local, dating back to the 16th century. No eve meals Sun.
❀ ◖ ◗ P

Treforest

Otley Arms

Forest Road ☎ (0443) 402033
11–11
Bass Worthington BB; Brains SA; Crown Buckley SBB, Rev. James; guest beer [H]
Bustling suburban pub, popular with students and locals. Beware Scrumpy Jack keg cider on fake handpump.
◖ ◗ ⇌ ♣ P

Tyle Garw

Boar's Head

Coed Cae Lane (½ mile off A473) ☎ (0443) 225400
12–4, 7–11
Beer range varies [H]
Small, simply furnished, unspoilt local with a friendly atmosphere. Normally two guest beers. Forest walks opposite. Q ❀ ♣

Ynyswen

Crown Hotel

Ynyswen Road (A4061)
☎ (0443) 772805
11–11
Courage Best Bitter; Marston's Pedigree; Ruddles Best Bitter, County; John Smith's Bitter [H]**; guest beer** [G]
Popular local featuring a red telephone box in the public bar and a comfortable lounge across the hall. Friendly atmosphere. ♨ 🗔 ⇌ ♣

Ynysybwl

Roberttown Hotel

The Square, Robert Street
☎ (0443) 791574
11–11
Brains Dark, Bitter, SA [H]
Valley local with a cavernous bar and a smarter lounge. Pool and snooker tables; live entertainment. Sun lunches served. ❀ ♿ ♣ P

South Glamorgan

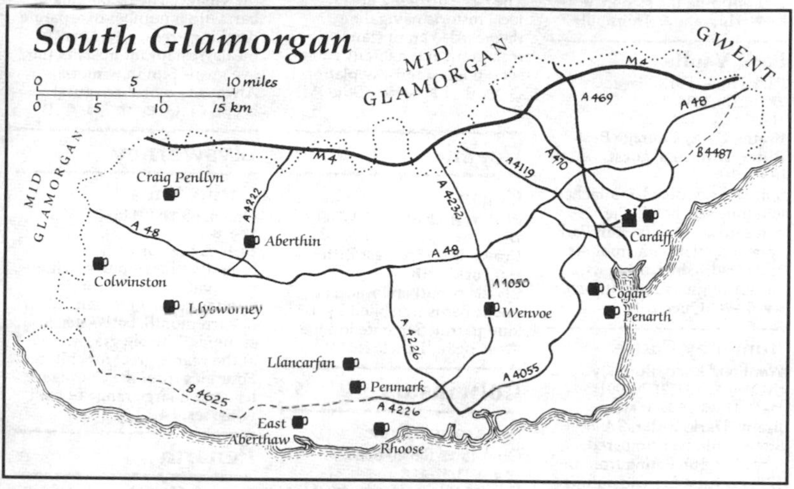

Brains, Bullmastiff, Cardiff

Aberthin

Hare & Hounds
On A4222 ☎ (0446) 774892
11.30–11
Bass Worthington BB Ⓖ, Draught Bass; Hancock's HB Ⓗ
Superb village local with a low ceiling, beams and a family room. The beer garden has a children's play area. Limited parking. Meals in summer only Q 🛏 ❀ ◖ ♿ ▲ ♣ P

Cardiff

Albert
St Mary Street
☎ (0222) 383032
11–11
Brains Dark, Bitter, SA; guest beer Ⓗ
Regarded as the Brains brewery tap although two other pubs also adjoin the brewery. Public bar downstairs, lounge and skittle alley upstairs, both bars refurbished. No food Sun.
◖ ⊞ ≠ (Central)

Black Lion
High Street, Llandaff (A4119)
11-3, 5–11; 11–11 Fri & Sat
Brains Dark, Bitter, SA Ⓗ
Typical Brains town pub: a large, comfortable lounge and a traditional bar. Very popular with locals. Children welcome in the lounge at lunchtime. Eve meals on request.
Q ◖ ⊞ ≠ (Fairwater) ♣

Fox & Hounds
Chapel Row, St Mellons (off B4487) ☎ (0222) 777046
11–11
Brains Dark, Bitter, SA Ⓗ
Popular local which now serves evening meals in a restaurant converted from an old bar. Children's play area in the garden. ❀ ◖ P

Halfway
247 Cathedral Road, Riverside (A4119) ☎ (0222) 345259
11–11
Brains Dark, Bitter, SA Ⓗ
Spacious, tastefully refurbished pub close to parks and the cricket ground. No food Sun. ❀ ◖ ⊞ ♿ ▲ ♣

Kiwis
Wyndham Arcade, St Mary Street ☎ (0222) 229876
12–2am
John Smith's Bitter; guest beers Ⓗ
Pub accessed via an arcade. Admission charge after 10pm, Thu–Sat, when it becomes busy. Two guest beers and some 60 bottled beers from around the globe.
◖ ≠ (Central)

Maltsters Arms
75 Merthyr Road, Whitchurch
☎ (0222) 624326
11–11
Brains Dark, Bitter Ⓗ
Small, real local with a piano sing-song Sat night and skittles matches Thu and Fri in winter. Many charity activities.
Q ❀ ◖ ◗ ⊞ ♿ ♣

Millers Mate
Thornhill Road, Thornhill (A469) ☎ (0222) 626794
11–3, 5.30–11; 11–11 Sat
Banks's Bitter Ⓗ
Old farmhouse converted to a pub, surrounded by a new housing estate. ❀ ♣ P

Ninian Park
Leckwith Road (1 mile W of centre, near football ground)
☎ (0222) 371386
11–11
Brains Dark, Bitter, SA Ⓗ
Modern two-bar pub with a comfortable lounge. A replacement for the original pub demolished for road improvement some 20 years ago.
❀ ⊞ ≠ (Ninian Pk)

Old Arcade
Church Street ☎ (0222) 231740
11–11; 7–10.30 Sun, closed Sun lunch
Brains Dark, Bitter, SA Ⓗ
Famous pub handy for the central market. Basic, but comfortable public bar; the lounge serves excellent hot weekday lunches, but is open Fri and Sat eves only. Rugby memorabilia.
◖ ⊞ ≠ (Central) ♣

Old Cottage
Cherry Orchard Road, Lisvane (E of A469) ☎ (0222) 747582
11–3, 6–11; 12–11 Fri & Sat
Ind Coope Burton Ale; Tetley Bitter Ⓗ
Converted 200-year-old farmhouse in a semi-rural area. Close to Parc Cefn Onn

and opposite the station. ❀ ◖ ◗ ⇌ (Lisvane & Thornhill) P

Park Vaults
Park Hotel, Park Place
☎ (0222) 383471
11–11
Brains Dark; Courage Best Bitter, Directors; guest beers [H]
Spit and sawdust bar attached to a four-star hotel. The entrance is at the back in Park Lane. Popular with students and steadily increasing its variety of guest beers (three).
🛏 ◖ ⇌ (Queen St)

Rompney Castle
Wentloog Road, Rumney (B4239) ☎ (0222) 793991
11–11; 11–3.30, 5.30–11 Mon
Brains Dark, Bitter, SA [H]/[E]
Stone-built, half-timbered, three-bar pub dating from the 17th century. Electric pumps serve the beer in the upper lounge. Indian food can be ordered at the bar and is delivered to the pub by a local take-away. ❀ ⊟ ♣ P

Royal Oak Hotel
200 Broadway (A4161, at Newport Rd) ☎ (0222) 473984
11–11
Brains Dark, Bitter [H]**, SA** [G]
Stylish old pub with sporting trophies in the public bar matched only by splendid stained-glass windows. Boxing fans will feel at home. Live bands in the back bar. The only Brains house serving SA on gravity. Q ❀ ⊟ ♿ ♣

Three Arches
Heathwood Road, Llanishen
☎ (0222) 752395
11–11
Brains Dark, Bitter, SA [H]
One of Brains's largest pubs: three bars and an upstairs function room. Wheelchair access to the lounge.
Q ❀ ◖ ⊟ ♿ ⇌ (Heath High/Low Level) ♣ P

Ty Mawr Arms
Graig Road, Lisvane OS184842
☎ (0222) 754456
12–3, 6–11; 12 (11 summer)–11 Fri & Sat (11–11 Thu in summer)
Courage Directors; John Smith's Bitter; Wadworth 6X [H]**; guest beers**
Large, rambling pub in the countryside, with extensive grounds. Over-21s only served. ♨ ఠ ❀ ◖ ◗ P

Wharf
Schooner Way, Atlantic Wharf
☎ (0222) 480700
11–3, 5–11; 11–11 Sat and May–Oct
Brains Dark, Bitter, SA; guest beer (occasionally) [H]
Newly-built waterside pub in the reclaimed dockland area. The basic drinking area has a local historic navigation theme. Also an upstairs restaurant and a family room set out like a railway platform.
Q ఠ ❀ ◖ ◗ ♿ ⇌ (Bute Rd) P

Cogan

Cogan
Pill Street ☎ (0222) 704280
12–11
Crown Buckley Best Bitter; Hancock's HB [H]
Classic suburban local. The public bar is inhabited by a loud parrot! Separate lounge.
⇌ (Cogan/Dingle Rd)

Colwinston

Sycamore Tree
Off A48 ☎ (0656) 652827
12–3, 6–11; 12–11 Sat
Draught Bass; Hancock's HB; guest beer [H]
Welcoming village pub offering good meals (no lunches Mon in winter). Live music (folk based) some eves.
♨ ❀ ◖ ◗ ♿ ▲ ♣ P

Craig Penllyn

Barley Mow
Off A48 OS978773
☎ (0446) 772558
12–3, 6.30–11
Bass Worthington BB, Draught Bass; Hancock's HB; guest beer [H]
Cosy, three-room pub, very popular for its good-value food (no meals Sun eve or Mon lunch). Popular with families. ♨ Q ❀ ◖ ◗ ♣ P

East Aberthaw

Blue Anchor
Off B4265 ☎ (0446) 750329
11–11
Crown Buckley Best Bitter; Marston's Pedigree; S&N Theakston Old Peculier; Wadworth 6X; Whitbread Boddingtons Bitter, Flowers IPA; guest beer [H]
Award-winning, 14th-century thatched inn: six inter-connecting rooms around a central bar. Be careful with the low oak beams and narrow corridors. Excellent pub food, and a restaurant upstairs.
♨ Q ఠ ❀ ◖ ◗ P

Llancarfan

Fox & Hounds
☎ (0446) 781297
11–3, 6–30–11; 11–11 Fri & Sat
Brains Bitter; Ruddles Best Bitter; John Smith's Bitter; guest beers [H]
CAMRA regional *Pub of the Year* 1992: the focal point of the village. The rectangular bar, with a number of separate drinking areas, offers bar meals; restaurant upstairs (no eve meals Sun in winter). Always two or three guest beers. ♨ Q ఠ ❀ ◖ ◗ ♣ P

Llysworney

Carne Arms
On B4268 ☎ (0446) 773553
12–3, 6–11
Beer range varies [H]
Friendly village pub serving good value food, including a Sunday roast. Quiz third Wed of each month; barbecues in summer. The big grassy area at the rear is great for children. Four ales from the Courage list, and a large range of malt whiskies. ♨ Q ❀ ◖ ◗ P

Penarth

Royal Hotel
1 Queens Road (off A4160)
☎ (0222) 708048
11.30–11
Brains Bitter; Bullmastiff Bitter [H]
Pub boasting the cheapest beer in the area, with a restaurant upstairs. Occasional noisy discos. 🛏 ◖ ◗ ⇌ (Dingle Rd)

Penmark

Six Bells
☎ (0446) 710229
12–11
Hancock's HB [H]
Friendly, traditional country pub: a public bar with a darts area, and a lounge. The bar features Hancock's memorabilia. No eve meals Sun. ♨ Q ❀ ◖ ◗ ♣ P

Rhoose

Highwayman
Fon-mon (west of the airport, at the end of a country lane) OS058673 ☎ (0446) 710205
6.30–11
Brains Dark, Bitter [H]
Large, rambling country pub popular for good value food. Stocks Dublin Guinness. Try the Condemned Man's Meal – but only if very hungry!
♨ Q ❀ ◖ ◗ P

Wenvoe

Wenvoe Arms
Old Port Road (off A4050)
☎ (0222) 591129
11.30–3.30, 5.30–11; 11–11 Fri & Sat
Brains Dark, Bitter, SA [H]
Thriving village pub attracting a good cross-section of the community. A meeting place for the sportier types. Take-aways are offered, in addition to the bar meals and restaurant service.
♨ ఠ ❀ ◖ ◗ ⊟ ♿ ♣ P

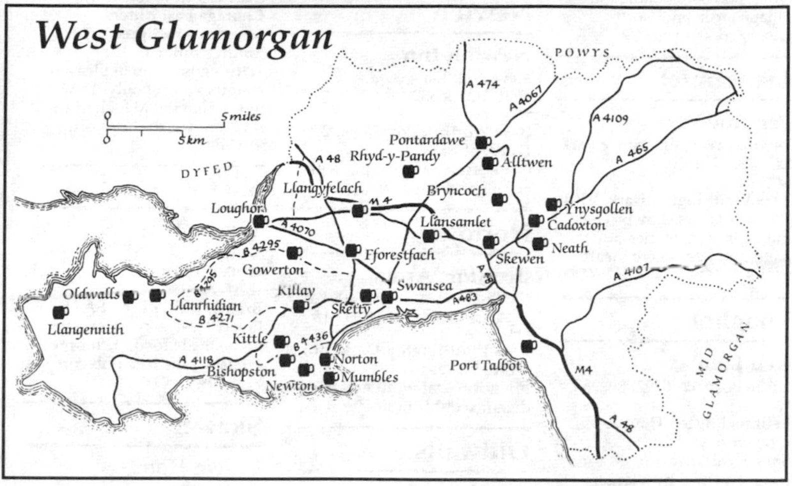

Alltwen

Butchers Arms

☎ (0792) 863100

12–3, 6.30–11

Courage Directors; Everards Old Original; John Smith's Bitter; Wadworth 6X [H]; guest beers

Well-appointed pub at the top of Alltwen Hill. Excellent food; the restaurant overlooks the Swansea valley. Wide selection of single malt whiskies.

♛ Q ❀ ◐ ◑ P

Bishopston

Joiners Arms

50 Bishopston Road (off B4436)

☎ (0792) 232658

11 11

Brains Dark; Courage Best Bitter; John Smith's Bitter; guest beers [H]

Attractive village pub offering a wide range of guest beers; annual beer months (up to 30 beers consecutively). Good food; amiable clientele.

♛ Q ❀ ◐ P

Bryncoch

Dyffryn Arms

Neath Road ☎ (0639) 636184

12–3, 7–11

Whitbread Boddingtons Mild, Bitter, Flowers IPA [H]

Pleasant rural pub. Meals in the bar and restaurant.

❀ ◐ ◑ P

Cadoxton

Crown & Sceptre

Main Road ☎ (0639) 642145

12–11

Whitbread Boddingtons Bitter [H]

Locals' bar and restaurant. Ten minutes' walk from Neath town centre.

❀ ◐ ◑ ⊞ P

Fforestfach

Star Inn

1070 Carmarthen Road

☎ (0792) 586910

11–11

Crown Buckley Dark, Best Bitter [E]

Well-established local serving an industrial estate. Friendly hosts and a rare outlet for Buckley's on electric dispense. Bar snacks lunchtime.

⊞ ♣ P

Gowerton

Welcome to Gower

Mount Street

☎ (0792) 872611

12–4; 7–11; 12–11 Fri & Sat

Crown Buckley Dark, Best Bitter, Rev. James [H]

Comfortable pub, offering good cuisine in a relaxed atmosphere. ◐ ⇌ P

Killay

Railway Inn

Gower Road

☎ (0792) 203946

11.30–3.30, 5.30–11; 11.30–11 Fri & Sat

Crown Buckley Dark, Best Bitter, Rev. James [H]

Pub recently acquired by Crown Buckley. Three rooms contain railway memorabilia. Handy for the Clyne Valley Walk. Snacks available.

❀ ⊞ P

Kittle

Beaufort Arms

18 Pennard Road (B4436)

☎ (0792) 234521

11–11

Crown Buckley Dark, Best Bitter, Rev. James [H]

Friendly country pub, with a large outdoor area. Families welcome. A separate restaurant offers excellent, home-cooked meals.

❀ ◐ ◑ ♣ P

Llangennith

Kings Head Hotel

☎ (0792) 386212

11–11

Crown Buckley Best Bitter, Rev. James [H]

Friendly pub offering magnificent views of Rhossili Bay. Popular with a local campsite.

♛ ❀ ⛟ ◐ ◑ ⊞ ▲ ♣ P

Llangyfelach

Plough & Harrow

Llangyfelach Road (off M4 jct 46) ☎ (0792) 771816

11.30–4, 6–11; 11–11 Fri & Sat

Courage Best Bitter, Directors; John Smith's Bitter [H]

Spacious lounge bar overlooking Penllergaer Woods. ♛ ❀ ◐ ◑ ♣ P

Llanrhidian

Welcome to Town

Off B4295 ☎ (0792) 390015

12–3, 6–11

Younger IPA [H]

Quiet pub overlooking the village green and North Gower coast. Q ❀ ◖ ◗

Llansamlet

Fendrod
Fendrod Way, Enterprise Park
☎ (0792) 701950
11.30–11
Bass Worthington Dark, BB Ⓗ
Welsh Brewers showpiece pub, busy lunchtimes due to its location. Excellent meals.
❀ ◖ ◗ P ⊁

Loughor

Red Lion
Glebe Road ☎ (0792) 892983
12–11
Felinfoel Bitter, Double Dragon Ⓗ
Snug locals' bar complemented by a large, spacious lounge. No food Mon or Tue. ♨ ◖ ⊟ P

Reverend James
180 Borough Road (just off A484) ☎ (0792) 892943
11–11
Crown Buckley Dark, Best Bitter, Rev. James Ⓗ
One of the first outlets for Rev. James. A history of Buckley's brewery is depicted in the excellent adjoining restaurant.
♨ ❀ ◖ ◗ ⊟ ♿ ♣ P

Mumbles

Mumbles Rugby Club
588 Mumbles Road
☎ (0792) 368989
8–11; 11–11 Sat
Bass Worthington Dark Ⓔ**; Brains SA; S&N Theakston Mild, Best Bitter** Ⓗ
Friendly little club where temporary membership is always available. Rugby paraphernalia throughout.

Vincents
580 Mumbles Road
☎ (0792) 368308
12–11
Bass Worthington BB, Draught Bass; guest beer Ⓗ
Loosely based on a Spanish bar, displaying pictures by local artists. Regularly changed guest beer. ◖

Neath

Greyhound
Water Street
☎ (0639) 637793
12–11
Ruddles County; John Smith's Bitter; Webster's Yorkshire Bitter Ⓗ
Lively, friendly one-roomer.
◖ ⇌

Newton

Newton Inn
New Well Lane
☎ (0792) 368329
11.30–11
Bass Worthington Dark, BB, Draught Bass Ⓗ
Comfortable village inn with excellent cuisine. ❀ ◖

Norton

Beaufort Arms
Castle Road ☎ (0792) 406420
11.30–3.30, 5.30–11; 11.30–11 Fri & Sat
Bass Worthington Dark, BB, Draught Bass Ⓗ
Friendly local within walking distance of Mumbles. ❀ ◖ ⊟

Oldwalls

Greyhound
☎ (0792) 390146
12–11
Draught Bass; Hancock's HB Ⓗ**; guest beers**
Excellent free house at the heart of Gower. Renowned for its cuisine, especially local fish.
♨ ❀ ◖ ◗ ⊟ P

Pontardawe

Ivy Bush Hotel
High Street ☎ (0792) 862370
2.30–11
Bass Worthington BB, Draught Bass Ⓗ
Large bar sporting rugby memorabilia. A folk club meets upstairs. ⊟ P

Port Talbot

St Oswalds
Station Road
☎ (0639) 899200
11–3, 6–11
Crown Buckley Best Bitter Ⓗ
Town-centre local with a restaurant. Reasonable value meals. ◖ ⇌

Twelve Knights Hotel
Margam Road (A48)
☎ (0639) 882381
11–11
Marston's Pedigree; John Smith's Bitter; Whitbread Boddingtons Bitter, Flowers IPA, Original Ⓗ
Very well-appointed pub with a relaxed atmosphere. Handy for Margam Park. Food all day Sun. ❀ 🛏 ◖ ◗ P

Rhyd-y-Pandy

Masons Arms
Rhyd-y-Pandy Road OS667020
☎ (0792) 842535
12–11
Bass Worthington Dark; Courage Best Bitter; Marston's Pedigree; John Smith's Bitter Ⓗ
17th-century pub in pleasant countryside yet only three miles from the M4. Hard to find, but worth the effort.
❀ ◖ P

Sketty

Vivian Arms
Sketty Cross
☎ (0792) 203015
12–11
Brains Dark, Bitter, SA Ⓗ
Lively local, serving excellent home-made food, including, arguably, the best pub curry in Wales! ❀ ◖ ⊟

Skewen

Crown Hotel
216 New Road
☎ (0792) 813309
11–11
Brains Dark, Bitter, MA, SA Ⓗ
Locals' bar and a comfortable lounge – the only pub to sell four draught Brains beers. MA is a brewery mix of Bitter and Dark. ⊟ ♣

Swansea

Adam & Eve
High Street
☎ (0792) 655913
11.30–4, 5.30–11; 11–11 Fri & Sat; 12–2.30, 7–10.30 Sun
Brains Dark, Bitter, SA Ⓗ
Traditional, three-roomed local, popular with a varied clientele. Good value lunches.
◖ ⊟ ⇌ ♣

Bryn-y-Mor Hotel
Bryn-y-Mor Road
☎ (0792) 466650
11.30–11
Ansells Bitter, Mild; Ind Coope Burton Ale; Tetley Bitter Ⓗ
Lively, side-street bar with a comfortable lounge. Live music Suns and Weds.
❀ ◖ ⊟ ♣

Builders Arms
36–38 Oxford Street
☎ (0792) 476189
11–11; closed Sun
Crown Buckley Dark, Best Bitter, Rev. James Ⓗ
Smart, split-level pub on the edge of the city centre. Upstairs function room.
Q ◖ ♿ ⇌

Cockett Inn
Waunarlwydd Road, Cockett
☎ (0792) 582083
11–11
Crown Buckley Dark, Best Bitter Ⓗ

Village local with a large bar containing a pool table at one end. Comfortable lounge.
❀ ◖ ⊞ ♣ P

Commercial Inn

Neath Road, Plasmarl
☎ (0792) 771120
12–11
Brains Dark; Courage Best Bitter; John Smith's Bitter; guest beer (weekends) H
Friendly, cosy local. Exotic fish look at customers from within a large tank in the lounge.
❀ Q ⊞

Duke of York

Princess Way ☎ (0792) 653830
11–11
Bass Worthington Dark, BB, Draught Bass H
Comfortable lounge and bar downstairs; Ellington's blues/jazz venue upstairs (live acts Tue–Sat). ◖ ⊞ ⇌ ♣

Queens Hotel

Gloucester Place (near the museum)
☎ (0792) 643460
12–2.30, 6–11
Crown Buckley Best Bitter; S&N Theakston Mild, Best Bitter, Old Peculier H
Airy, one-room bar with pictures of old Swansea, a short walk from the new marina.
❀ ⛿ ◖ ⇌

Singleton Hotel

1 Dillwyn Street (opp. Grand Theatre) ☎ (0792) 655987
11.30–3, 6.30–11
Brains Dark; Courage Directors; Ruddles Best Bitter; John Smith's Bitter; guest beer H
Pub with a theatre theme. Live entertainment seven nights a week (usually free).
⛿ ◖ ⇌ ⊂⊃

Westbourne Hotel

1 Bryn-y-Mor Road
☎ (0792) 459054
12–3, 6–11; 12–11 Fri & Sat
Bass Worthington Dark, Draught Bass; Hancock's HB H
Striking street-corner pub, noted for its Bass.
Q ❀ ◖ ⊞

Ynysgollen

Rock & Fountain Inn

Aberdulais (A465)
☎ (0639) 642681
12–3, 6–11 (may vary)
Crown Buckley Best Bitter; S&N Theakston XB; Wadworth 6X; guest beers H
Comfortable, relaxing pub with a restaurant. The beer range varies. Excellent menu.
Q ❀ ◖ ◗ P

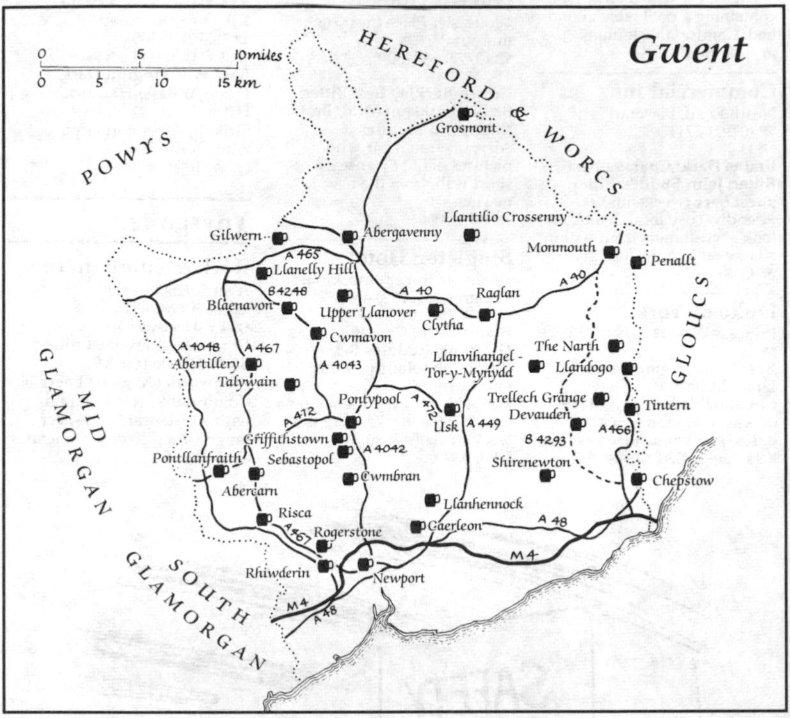

Abercarn

Old Swan
58 Commercial Road
☎ (0495) 243161
12–4.30, 7–11; 12–11 Fri & Sat
Courage Best Bitter; Ushers Best Bitter, Founders 🄷
An old CAMRA plaque by the entrance announces the real ale inside this friendly pub where a cosy lounge area adjoins the public bar. Separate pool room. Past links with the coal industry are evident in the local memorabilia. ♨ ⊟ ♣

Abergavenny

Hen & Chickens
Flannel Street (off High St)
☎ (0873) 853613
10.30–4, 7–11; 10–11 Tue; 10.30–11 Fri & Sat
Bass Worthington BB, Draught Bass 🄷**; guest beer**
Renowned local, long known for the quality of its Bass but now also offering an adventurous range of guest ales on a rota basis. A wide ranging clientele is assured of a warm welcome. Q ♉ ◐ ♣

Somerset Arms
Victoria Street (Merthyr Rd jct)
☎ (0873) 852158
12–3, 7–11
Draught Bass; Felinfoel Bitter 🄷**; guest beer**
Family run pub with a warm welcome for all. Good value meals are served in the lounge; the public bar is particularly cosy and popular. A few minutes' walk from the town centre.
♨ Q ⛟ ◐ ⊟ ♣

Try also: Station, Brecon Rd (Free)

Abertillery

Clynmawr Hotel
Ty Bryn Road (off Gladstone St/A467)
☎ (0495) 212323
12–5, 7–11; 12–11 Sat & summer
Crown Buckley Dark, Best Bitter, Rev. James 🄷
Known locally as the 'Glyn', a traditional inn with a public bar featuring pictures of past darts and skittles teams; also a lounge and an upstairs family room. Handy for Abertillery RFC. ♉ ❀ ⊟ ♣

Blaenavon

Cambrian Inn
Cambrian Road
☎ (0495) 790327
6 (12 Sat)–11
Brains Dark, Bitter, SA 🄷
Traditional locals' pub with a good following: a basic public bar, a separate pool room and a comfortable lounge. A stalwart of this guide.
Q ⊟ ♣

Riflemans Arms
Rifle Street ☎ (0495) 792297
12–11
S&N Theakston Best Bitter; Wadworth 6X; Whitbread Flowers IPA 🄷
Small but well laid-out pub only half a mile from Big Pit Mining Museum. Good food and facilities for children.
♉ ❀ ◐ P

Caerleon

Goldcroft Inn
Goldcroft Common
☎ (0633) 420504
11–11
Courage Best Bitter; Crown Buckley SBB; John Smith's Bitter; Wadworth 6X 🄷

Situated at the end of the village green: a large, open-plan lounge with an adjoining tiny bar. Lovely beer garden, great for children; popular Sun night karaoke. A good place to start a crawl of the many local outlets. Eve meals Wed–Sat.
⌂ ❀ ◖ ◗ ⊞ ♣

Tabard Brasserie

9 High Street ☎ (0633) 422822
12–3 (summer only), 6 (7 Mon)–11; 7–10.30 Sun
Beer range varies Ⓗ
Well-patronised restaurant/bistro serving a regularly changing range of independent guest beers. Excellent quality meals served in the friendly two-bar area; function room upstairs. Real ale dishes often available. Not to be missed. No meals Sun eve. Q ❀ ◖ ◗ P ⊬

Chepstow

Coach & Horses Inn

Welsh Street (near town arch)
☎ (0291) 622626
11–3, 6–11
Brains SA; Crown Buckley Best Bitter, Rev. James; Ushers Best Bitter Ⓗ
Gwent CAMRA *Pub of the Year* 1992: a popular split-level bar with a fireplace at one end. The ales are served from an attractive copper-topped bar. Venue of the Chepstow beer festival in mid-July. Lunches on weekdays only.
❀ ⛾ ◖ ⇌ ♣

Try also: Bridge Inn, Bridge St (Free)

Clytha

Clytha Arms

On old Raglan/Abergavenny road, off B4598
☎ (0873) 840206
11.30–3.30 (not Mon), 6–11; 11–11 Sat
John Smith's Bitter; Wadworth 6X Ⓗ**; guest beers**
Superb recent conversion from a country hotel: a large main bar with an adjoining smaller bar and a separate restaurant. The former Beaufort Arms licensee/chef maintains his excellent standards in food and drink. Cider is usually from Weston's.
⌂ Q ❀ ⛾ ◖ ◗ ♿ ♣ ⌓ P

Cwmavon

Westlakes Arms

On A4043 between Pontypool and Blaenavon
☎ (0495) 772571
12–11
Draught Bass; Hancock's HB Ⓗ**; guest beers** (summer)
Comfortable local in good walking country, two miles from Big Pit Mining Museum. Named after the Westlakes Brewery, once sited just north of the pub. Excellent food (book eves). Q ❀ ◖ ◗ ⊞ P

Cwmbran

Blinkin' Owl

The Oxtens, Henllys Way
☎ (0633) 484749
12–4 (5 Sat), 6 (6.30 Sat)–11
Brains Dark, Bitter, SA Ⓗ
Friendly estate pub long-known for quality beer. Sells take-away as well as in-house meals. A hatch between the lounge and bar keeps the local children's sweet teeth happy.
Q ❀ ◖ ◗ ⊞ ♣ P

Bush Inn

Graig Road, Upper Cwmbran (off Upper Cwmbran Rd)
☎ (0633) 483764
11–3, 7 (6 Fri & Sat)–11
Courage Best Bitter; Webster's Yorkshire Bitter Ⓗ**; guest beer**
Attractive hillside pub with discos every weekend. The small main bar has a comfortable side room where excellent value for money food can be enjoyed. The home-made curries surpass local take-aways, but ring for eve meals at weekends. Parking limited. ⌂ ❀ ◖ ◗ P

Rose & Crown

Victoria Street ☎ (0633) 866700
11–11
Brains SA; Courage Best Bitter; John Smith's Bitter Ⓗ**; guest beer**
Lively local in Cwmbran village, not far from the sports stadium. The split-level lounge hosts popular karaoke eves (Thu and Sun), whilst the bar is a haunt of sports-minded drinkers and HQ of pool and soccer teams. Lunchtime snacks (Mon–Sat). Bulmers cider. ❀ ⊞ ♣ ⌓ P

Try also: Commodore Hotel, Llanyravon (Free)

Devauden

Masons Arms

On B4293 ☎ (029 15) 315
11–11
Draught Bass Ⓗ
Old, unspoilt pub with three rooms served by a small bar – a basic environment with friendly locals and a good warm fire. Pool played.
⌂ ❀ ♣ P

Gilwern

Bridgend Inn

49 Main Road ☎ (0873) 830939
12–3, 7–11; 12–11 Fri, Sat & summer
Morland Old Speckled Hen Ⓗ**; guest beers**
Canalside pub with an open-plan bar which includes a dining area. Popular with locals and passing trade, the latter often visitors to the beautiful Clydach Gorge. Canalbank drinking area.
❀ ⛾ ◖ ◗ ⛺ ♣

Griffithstown

Hanbury Hotel

Windsor Road
☎ (0495) 763620
12–11
Bass Worthington BB, Draught Bass Ⓗ
Popular, good old-fashioned street-corner local with a comfortable lounge and an unspoilt bar. ☋ ❀ ⊞ P

Grosmont

Angel Inn

Main Street ☎ (0981) 240646
12–3, 7–11
Draught Bass; Crown Buckley Best Bitter, Rev. James Ⓗ
Cosy pub in a charming village with an impressive castle, church and tiny town hall. Good walking country. Simple, good value meals always available.
⌂ ❀ ⛾ ◖ ◗ ♣

Llandogo

Sloop Inn

On A466 ☎ (0594) 530291
12–2.30 (3 summer), 6 (5 summer)–11; 12–11 Sat
Draught Bass; Hook Norton Best Bitter Ⓗ**; guest beer** (summer)
Roadside inn with a pleasant lounge, popular with diners, and a cosy public bar. Outdoor play area for children; very comfortable accommodation. An excellent base from which to explore the beautiful Wye valley. ⌂ ❀ ⛾ ◖ ◗ ⊞ ♣ P

Llanelly Hill

Jolly Collier

OS221123 ☎ (0873) 830408
12–4 (not Mon), 6.30–11
Wadworth 6X Ⓗ**; guest beer**
Excellent value food and a warm welcome await you in this hard-to-find village pub near Clydach. The guest beer is regularly changed. Small, comfortable and popular with all sorts. Sun lunches served but booking is necessary.
⌂ ❀ ◗ ⊞ ⛺ ♣ P

Llanhennock

Wheatsheaf Inn

1 mile off Caerleon–Usk road
OS353929 ☎ (0633) 420468
12–11

Gwent

Bass Worthington BB, Draught Bass; guest beer Ⓗ
Beautifully situated old country inn, just a few miles from Newport, with a delightful beer garden where ducks and chickens provide entertainment. Bubbly local atmosphere in the bar. Don't miss the doorstep sandwiches (no food Sun). Note: the Scrumpy Jack cider is keg.
♛ ❀ ◖ ⊟ ♣ P

Llantilio Crossenny

Hostry Inn
On B4233, between Monmouth and Abergavenny
☎ (060 085) 278
12–3, 6–11
Wye Valley Hereford Bitter, Brew 69; guest beers Ⓗ
Welcoming, 15th-century village pub with a large hall/function room. A friendly resident ghost is seen occasionally. Fortnightly folk music on Thu. Good range of food, with lots of vegetarian options.
❀ 🛏 ◖ ◗ ⊟ ▲ ♣ P ⅄

Llanvihangel-Tor-y-Mynydd

Star Inn
1 mile E of Llansoy, off B4293
OS460023 ☎ (029 15) 256
11–3, 6.30–11
Ind Coope Burton Ale; Tetley Bitter Ⓗ
Enjoy the welcoming atmosphere of this isolated country pub, with its excellent log fire in winter and occasional live music. Good food. Boules played.
♛ ᘔ ❀ ◖ ◗ ⊟ ▲ ♣ P

Monmouth

Green Dragon Inn
St Thomas Square
☎ (0600) 712561
11–11
Draught Bass; Hancock's HB; Marston's Bitter, Pedigree; guest beer Ⓗ
Traditional pub opposite the fortified bridge. Popular with visitors and locals alike, both lounge and bar offer pleasant surroundings. Cartoon lovers will appreciate a visit to the gents'. Very good value lunches. ◖ ⊟ ♣

Punch House
Agincourt Square
☎ (0600) 713855
11–3, 5–11; 11–11 Fri & Sat
Bass Worthington BB, Draught Bass; Hancock's HB; Wadworth 6X Ⓗ
Historic pub noted for its home-produced food and summer floral displays. The open-plan bar is adorned with a range of interesting artefacts, including old bound volumes of *Punch* magazine. ❀ ◖ ◗

The Narth

Trekkers
OS525064 ☎ (0600) 860367
11–3.30, 6–11
Draught Bass; Felinfoel Bitter; Freeminer Bitter Ⓗ
Genuine, log cabin-style pub, built in the 1920s and doubling as the village post office. Hard to find but worth the effort. The fireplace is the central focus, with the dining area, and nearby tables and chairs, positioned around it. A community rendezvous with skittles. ♛ Q ❀ ◖ ◗ ♣ P

Newport

Golden Hart
20 Cardiff Road
☎ (0633) 222466
11–11
Ansells Bitter; Tetley Bitter; guest beer Ⓗ
A good example of an unspoilt downtown local, close to the new police HQ and the Royal Gwent Hospital. Fine collection of brass and copperware above the fireplaces. Cheap B&B. Lunches served Sun.
♛ 🛏 ⇌ ♣

Hornblower
126 Commercial Street
☎ (0633) 267575
11–11
Ansells Bitter, Mild; Ind Coope Burton Ale; Tetley Bitter; guest beer Ⓗ
Small, friendly and loud, one-bar bikers' pub, resembling the inside of a galleon. Photos of motorbikes and other related info adorn the walls. Wide range of music on the jukebox, rock disco Thu, and live music planned. Over 70 spirits. 🛏 ⇌

Ivy Bush
65 Clarence Place (near cenotaph) ☎ (0633) 267571
11–11
John Smith's Bitter Ⓗ**; guest beer** (weekends)
Thriving local not far from Newport Castle (late home of the Castle brewery). The front bar has popular karaoke eves (Wed and Fri), while the public bar doubles as a games room. Handy for Newport RFC. ❀ 🛏 ⊟ ⇌ ♣

Queen's Hotel
Bridge Street ☎ (0633) 262992
11–11 (Tudor Bar); 12–2.30, 7–11 (Queen's Bar)
Draught Bass; Brains Dark, Bitter, SA; Hancock's HB Ⓗ
Town-centre hotel with the large 'Queen's Bar' at the front, popular with a younger clientele and a venue for live music. The rear 'Tudor Bar' offers quieter surroundings and a chance to sup one or two ales at bargain prices. Good bar meals.
🛏 ◖ ◗ ⇌ ♣

St Julians
Caerleon Road
☎ (0633) 258663
11.30–11
Courage Best Bitter; Marston's Pedigree; Ruddles Best Bitter; John Smith's Bitter; guest beers Ⓗ
Pub which has rapidly become the best outlet for a top quality pint in the area. Recently expanded in traditional style to make further use of the views across the River Usk. The outdoor balcony makes a beautiful setting for summer drinking. Good value meals (not served Sun eve). Occasional cider. Well worth finding. ♛ ❀ ◖ ◗ ⊟ ♣ ⌓ P

Penallt

Boat Inn
Lone Lane (off A466; access by footbridge from Redbrook)
☎ (0600) 712615
11–3, 6–11
Draught Bass; Hook Norton Best Bitter, Old Hooky; S&N Theakston Best Bitter, Old Peculier; Wadworth 6X Ⓖ**; guest beers**
Small, highly popular pub on the banks of the River Wye, offering the largest choice of cask ales in Gwent (ten in summer). A scenic music venue, with folk on Tue, and jazz or blues on Thu. Excellent value home-made meals. Cider in summer.
♛ ᘔ ❀ ◖ ◗ ⌓

Pontllanfraith

Crown Inn
The Bryn (near A472/A4049 jct) ☎ (0495) 223404
12–3, 5–11; 12–11 Fri & Sat
Courage Best Bitter; Felinfoel Double Dragon; Marston's Pedigree; John Smith's Bitter Ⓗ**; guest beer** (summer)
Two-roomed pub with a basic public bar and a spacious lounge, which is popular with diners. A haven for local golfers. Good, varied menu and outdoor amusements for children. ❀ ◖ ◗ ⊟ ♣ P ⅄

Pontypool

Prince of Wales
Prince of Wales Terrace, Lower Cwmynyscoy
☎ (0495) 756737

11.30–4, 6.30–11
John Smith's Bitter Ⓗ; guest beers
Friendly locals' pub with a genuine welcome for all: a cosy single bar with a separate room for darts, meetings, etc., a short stroll from Pontypool Park. The threat of demolition will hopefully soon be removed. ♨ ❀ ⇶ ♣

Try also: George, Commercial St (Courage)

Raglan

Ship Inn

High Street ☎ (0291) 690635
11–3, 5.30–11
Draught Bass Ⓗ; guest beers
Old country town coaching inn with lots of character, a half-mile from Raglan Castle. Separate dining area.
♨ Q ❀ ◐ ◗ ⊞ ♣

Rhiwderin

Rhiwderin Inn

Caerphilly Road
☎ (0633) 893234
12–3, 5.30 (5 Fri)–11; 12–11 Sat
Draught Bass; Brains Dark; Hancock's HB Ⓗ
Recently renovated, roadside inn with a small public bar and a plush lounge. Good food with vegetarian options
❀ ◐ ◗ ⊞ ♣ P

Risca

Exchange Inn

52 St Mary Street
☎ (0633) 612706
12–5, 7–11
Crown Buckley Best Bitter, SBB, Rev. James Ⓗ
Smart, roadside pub with a spruce interior. Two rooms: a comfortable lounge and a traditional public bar. Sales of cask ales have soared since it became a free house and it is now a useful refreshment stop for visitors taking the local scenic mountain drive. Tasty lunches. ❀ ◐ ⊞ ♣ P

Rogerstone

Tredegar Arms

Cefn Road ☎ (0633) 893417
12–3, 6–11; 12–2, 7–10.30 Sun
Courage Best Bitter Ⓗ; guest beers
Pleasant, roadside pub comprising a small public bar and a roomy lounge with plenty of seating and some standing room. Good range of lunchtime food which extends to include a number of foreign dishes in the evening. A regular entry and deservedly so. ❀ ◐ ◗ ⊞ ♣ P

Sebastopol

Open Hearth

Wern Road (off B4244)
☎ (0495) 763752
11–3, 6–11
Archers Golden; Draught Bass Ⓗ; guest beers
Very popular canalside pub, complete with an adopted waddle of ducks. Tricky to find, but ask any local. The large range of guest ales – competitively priced – usually includes beers from Welsh independents. Good value and varied range of food.
♨ ❀ ◐ ◗ ⊞ ♣ P

Shirenewton

Carpenters Arms

On B4235 Usk–Chepstow road, N of the village ☎ (029 17) 231
11–2.30, 7–11
Marston's Pedigree, Owd Rodger; Ruddles County; Wadworth 6X; Whitbread Boddingtons Bitter, Flowers IPA Ⓗ; guest beer
Fine country pub attracting visitors from miles around. Several rooms feature a variety of items, including a blacksmith's bellows and many chamber pots. Blackboard menus of tasty dishes. ♨ Q ❀ ◐ ◗ P

Talywain

Globe Inn

Commercial Road (Abersychan–Varteg road)
☎ (0495) 772053
6 (11 Sat)–11
Brains Dark; Crown Buckley Dark, Best Bitter; Hancock's HB Ⓗ
Typical valleys pub, friendly and busy. Separate pool room at the rear of the lounge; characterful bar. The beer range is steadily increasing. Cider in summer. ♨ ⊞ ♣ ⌓

Tintern

Cherry Tree

Devauden Road (off A466) OS526001 ☎ (0291) 689292
11–3, 6–11
Hancock's HB Ⓖ
Remote pub in the beautiful Wye valley. The intimate bar has beer brought up from the cellar. Proudly displays CAMRA 10- and 20-year *Good Beer Guide* certificates. Rare old Hancock's toastmaster sign outside. ♨ Q ❀ ♣ ⌓ P

Rose & Crown

On A466 ☎ (0291) 689254
12–2 (not Mon), 6–11 (12–11 Apr–Oct)
Courage Best Bitter; Ushers Best Bitter, Founders Ⓗ
Popular, welcoming pub on the bank of the River Wye. Live entertainment Wed. Vegetarian options on the menu. Bulmers cider.
♨ ❀ 🛏 ◐ ◗ ⊞ ♣ ⌓ P

Trellech Grange

Fountain Inn

Off B4293 OS503011
☎ (0291) 689303
12–3, 6–11
Wadworth 6X; guest beers Ⓗ
Built in the 17th century: a friendly pub with a stream running underneath. Displays an unusual 100-year-old carved Chinese cabinet. The variety of meals includes vegetarian, Sun lunch, child portions and Fri eve fish and chips. ♨ ❀ 🛏 ◐ ◗ ▲ ♣ P

Upper Llanover

Goose & Cuckoo

Off A4042 OS293073
☎ (0873) 880277
11.30–3, 7–11
Bullmastiff Best Bitter; Wadworth 6X Ⓗ; guest beer
Small rural pub on the outskirts of the village, ideal for country walkers. Vegetarian home-made meals a speciality. Large range of malts. ♨ Q ❀ ◐ ◗ ♣ P

Usk

Greyhound

1 Chepstow Road
☎ (0291) 672074
11–3, 7–11
Ind Coope Burton Ale; Tetley Bitter Ⓗ; guest beers
Recently refurbished, comfortable, open-plan pub with a friendly atmosphere. ❀ ◐ ◗ P

Kings Head Hotel

Old Market Street
☎ (0291) 672963
11–11
Fuller's London Pride; Marston's Pedigree; Whitbread Flowers Original Ⓗ; guest beers
Spacious pub with contrasting bars: a traditional public, popular with the young, and a comfortable lounge with an impressive fireplace, popular with the local fire brigade!
♨ Q 🛏 ◐ ◗ ⊞ ♣ P

Royal Hotel

New Market Street
☎ (0291) 672931
11–3, 7–11
Draught Bass; Felinfoel Double Dragon; Hancock's HB Ⓗ
Splendid and very popular, traditional, Victorian-style local, full of character and memorabilia. Excellent food – especially noted for its Sun lunches. ♨ ◐ ◗

Gwynedd

Snowdonia, Gellilydan

Aberdovey

Dovey Inn
Towyn Road ☎ (0654) 767332
11–11 (11–3, 6–11 winter)
Banks's Mild, Bitter Ⓔ**; Marston's Pedigree** Ⓗ
Large local overlooking the estuary, with three drinking areas attracting all ages.
♘ ❀ ◖ ◗ ⊟ ♿ ▲ ≠

Abergwyngregyn

Aber Falls Motel
☎ (0248) 680579
11–11 (12 Thu–Sat)
S&N Theakston Mild, Best Bitter, XB Ⓗ
Large pub in a small village. A large lounge, comfortably furnished, also a conservatory where meals are served and families welcomed. A locals' bar is planned.
♨ Q ❀ ⊨ ◖ ◗ ♣ P

Bangor

Ffriddoedd Bar
Menai Avenue
☎ (0248) 364131
12–2, 6–10.30 (11 Fri); 12–11 Sat
Ansells Mild; Courage Directors; Ind Coope Friary Meux Best Bitter; McEwan 80/- Ⓗ**; guest beers**
University bar, open to the public most eves. Lunches termtime. Closed for student functions. ◖ ▲ ≠ ♣ ⌓ P

Union Hotel
Garth Road ☎ (0248) 362462
11–11
Burtonwood Bitter, Forshaw's Ⓗ
A number of rooms, packed with interesting artefacts, all served by one bar. Adjoins the local boatyard. Good food.
Q ♘ ❀ ⊨ ◖ ◗ ♿ ≠ P

Barmouth

Tal y Don
High Street ☎ (0341) 280508
11–11
Burtonwood Mild, Bitter Ⓗ
Typical town-centre pub, adorned with brass, in a poorly-served seaside town.
♨ ⊟ ≠ ♣

Beaumaris

Olde Bulls Head
Castle Street ☎ (0248) 810329
11–11
Bass Worthington BB, Draught Bass; M&B Mild Ⓗ
Historic Grade II-listed inn, commandeered by Cromwell's troops in 1645: a small China bar, and a main bar with an array of antique weaponry, the town's ancient ducking stool, and a brass water clock. Not to be missed. No bar food Sun.
♨ Q ⊨ ◖ P

Betwys-y-Coed

Glan Aber Hotel
Holyhead Road
☎ (0690) 710325
11–11
Felinfoel Double Dragon; Tetley Walker Bitter Ⓔ
Three rooms, very popular with locals. Different bars for different tastes. ♨ Q ♘
❀ ⊨ ◖ ◗ ▲ ≠ ♣ P

Miners Bridge Inn
Holyhead Road
☎ (0960) 710386
12–5, 6–11
S&N Theakston Mild, Best Bitter; Younger IPA Ⓗ
Friendly, three-roomed village pub. Pool table/darts in the bar; meals in the well-furnished lounge. Also an additional lounge for summer crowds, opening onto the garden. Highly recommended.
❀ ⊨ ◖ ◗ ♿ ▲ ≠ ♣ P

Blaenau Ffestiniog

Manod
Manod Road ☎ (0766) 830346
12–3, 6–11
S&N Theakston Mild, Best Bitter Ⓗ
Traditional, old town pub with a small smoke room and a pleasant lounge. A brewing plant is planned. Q ≠ ♣ P

Bodedern

Crown Hotel
☎ (0407) 740734
12–3.30, 6–11; 11–11 Sat & bank hols
Burtonwood Bitter Ⓗ
Popular, village pub with a comfortable lounge, fairly spartan bar, and a pool/children's room. A useful base when touring Anglesey. ♨ ❀ ⊨ ◖ ◗ ♣ P

Bontnewydd

Newborough Arms
On A487 ☎ (0286) 673126
11–3, 6–11
Draught Bass; Ind Coope ABC Best Bitter, Burton Ale; Tetley Walker Mild, Bitter Ⓗ
Four-roomed local brimming with atmosphere. A centre for village activities.
♨ ❀ ◖ ◗ ⊟ ▲ ♣ P

Caernarfon

Yr Gordon Fach
Hole in the Wall Street
☎ (0248) 673338
11–11 public bar; 11.30–3, 6–11 lounge

Draught Bass; Tetley Walker Bitter; guest beer Ⓗ
Modernised pub with a superb public bar and a plush lounge. Friendly locals.
Q ❀ ◗ ◗ ⊞ ⛺ ♣

Capel Curig

Bryn Tyrch Hotel
☎ (069 04) 223
12–3, 6–11; 12–11 Sat
Marston's Pedigree; Whitbread Flowers IPA, Castle Eden Ale Ⓗ
Old pub ideally located for Snowdonia – very popular with climbers. Good, varied meals. Lounge, bar, quiet room and a TV room.
⛫ Q ❀ 🛏 ◗ ◗ ⛺ ♣ P

Cobden's Hotel
☎ (069 04) 243
11–3, 6–11; 11–11 Sat
Courage Directors; John Smith's Bitter; Webster's Yorkshire Bitter Ⓗ
Informal, family-run hotel in the heart of Snowdonia, with a large lounge, a climbers' bar with a feature rock face, and a restaurant. Freshly prepared local food (mainly British); warm welcome.
⛫ Q ❀ 🛏 ◗ ◗ ♿ ⛺ ♣ P

Cemaes Bay

Stag
High Street ☎ (0407) 710281
11–3.30, 6 (7 winter)–11; 11–11 Sat & summer
Burtonwood Bitter Ⓗ
Good village pub with a small lounge, a larger bar/darts room and a pool room. Good mix of locals and visitors, including yachtsmen. The most northerly pub in Wales.
⛫ Q ❀ ◗ ◗ ♣

Criccieth

Castle
Station Road ☎ (0766) 522624
11–11; closed Sun
Draught Bass Ⓗ
Small, terraced pub where the public bar is full of old GWR pictures. Separate lounge with no real ale.
⛫ ❀ ⊞ ⛺ ⇌ ♣

Dinas Mawddwy

Red Lion
Off A470 ☎ (0650) 531247
11–3, 6–11; 11–11 Sat & summer
Bass Worthington BB, Draught Bass; Felinfoel Double Dragon Ⓗ**; guest beers** (summer)
Friendly local with a large lounge, popular with hill walkers and fishermen. See the brass in the public bar. ⛫ Q 🍼 ❀ 🛏 ◗ ◗ ⊞ ♿ ⛺ ♣ P

Dolgellau

Cross Keys
Mill Street ☎ (0341) 423342
11–11
Bass Worthington BB, Draught Bass Ⓗ
Unspoilt town pub with a friendly landlady who hopes to expand the beer range.
⊞ ⛺ ♣

Fairbourne

Fairbourne Hotel
Station Road
☎ (0341) 250203
11–3, 6–11
McEwan 70/-; Younger IPA Ⓗ
Large, well-appointed, 300-year-old hotel. Excellent food in the lounge; separate restaurant. Breathtaking views of the estuary. Q 🍼 ❀ 🛏 ◗ ◗ ⊞ ♿ ⛺ ⇌ P

Ganllwyd

Tyn y Groes
On A470 ☎ (0341) 402775
11–3, 7–11 (11–11 summer)
Marston's Pedigree; Whitbread Flowers IPA, Boddingtons Bitter (summer) Ⓗ
Valley inn set in a hillside forest, its decor in keeping with the situation. Good value fare.
⛫ 🍼 🛏 ◗ ◗ ⊞ ⛺ ♣ P

Glanwydden

Queens Head
Between Llandudno and Colwyn Bay ☎ (0492) 546570
11–3, 6–11
Ind Coope Benskins Best Bitter, Burton Ale; Tetley Walker Bitter Ⓗ
Quaint village pub, with a pleasant bar, and a rather select lounge. Warm welcome.
⛫ Q ❀ ◗ ◗ ⛺ ♣ P

Holyhead

Boston
London Road
☎ (0407) 762449
12–4, 7–11
Burtonwood Mild, Bitter Ⓗ
Friendly local run by the same family for almost 40 years. A central bar, with separate pool, darts and lounge areas. ⇌ ♣

Llanbedrog

Ship Inn
Pig Street ☎ (0758) 740270
11–3.30, 5.30–11 (11–11 summer); closed Sun
Burtonwood Mild, Bitter Ⓗ
Cosy, friendly pub with a restaurant (seafood). Unusually-shaped, no-smoking family room.
⛫ Q 🍼 ❀ ◗ ◗ ⊞ ♿ ⛺ ♣ P ⚟

Llandudno

London Hotel
121 Upper Mostyn Street
☎ (0492) 876740
12–4, 7–11
Burtonwood Mild, Bitter, Forshaw's Ⓗ
Pub with an interior based on a London theme, including an old red phone box. Folk club Sun; quiz Tue. Family room lunchtime. Q 🍼 🛏 ◗ ♣

Rhoslan
21–22 Great Ormes Road, West Shore
11–3, 6–11
Ansells Bitter; Tetley Walker Bitter Ⓗ
Large roomy pub with separate public and lounge bars. Quiz Sun. Q ◗ ⊞ ♿ ♣

Llanengan

Sun Inn
☎ (075 881) 2260
11–11; closed Sun
Ind Coope Burton Ale; Tetley Walker Bitter Ⓗ**; guest beers** (summer)
Popular pub near Hells Mouth beach. Excellent food; safe gardens.
⛫ ❀ 🛏 ◗ ◗ ⊞ ⛺ ♣ P

Llanfachraeth

Holland Hotel
On A5025 ☎ (0407) 740252
11–3.30 (4 Sat), 7–11 (11–11 summer)
Lees GB Mild, Bitter Ⓗ
Pleasant village local. Traditional layout with several different rooms and a passage, all served from the same small bar. An ideal base for exploring Anglesey.
Q ❀ 🛏 ◗ ◗ ♣ P

Llanfairfechan

Llanfair Arms
Mill Road ☎ (0248) 680521
11–11
Draught Bass; M&B Mild Ⓗ
Busy, basic local (especially eves). ⛫ ❀ ♿ ⇌ ♣

Pen y Bryn
Pen y Bryn Road
☎ (0248) 680017
11–11
Tetley Walker Dark Mild, Bitter Ⓗ
Old village pub with welcoming owners. Can get smoky. 🍼 ⇌

Gwynedd

Llangefni

Railway

High Street ☎ (0248) 722166
11–3.30 (5 Sat), 6.30–11 (12–2, 7–11 Mon–Wed winter)
Lees GB Mild, Bitter, Moonraker Ⓗ
Friendly town pub, now partly opened out and refurbished, but with separate drinking areas and a pool room. Close to the now-defunct station, and retaining a railway theme.
Q ♣

Llanrwst

New Inn

12 Denbigh Street
☎ (0492) 640476
11–11
Banks's Mild; Marston's Bitter, Pedigree Ⓗ
Busy, friendly, one-roomed pub opposite the market.
♨ ❀ ▲ ≠ ♣

Llanwnda

Goat Hotel

☎ (0286) 830256
11.30–3, 7–11; closed Sun
Draught Bass; Whitbread Boddingtons Bitter Ⓗ
Friendly, roadside pub enjoying a busy lunchtime trade (buffet). Extensive garden. Beware Scrumpy Jack keg cider on a fake handpump. ❀ ◖ ◗ ▲ P

Maentwrog

Grapes Hotel

☎ (0766) 85208
11–11
Bass Worthington BB, Draught Bass Ⓗ**; guest beer**
Family-run, 13th-century hotel, overlooking the Vale of Ffestiniog. A la carte basement restaurant.
♨ ❀ ⛟ ◖ ◗ ⊟ ▲ P

Menai Bridge

Liverpool Arms

St Georges Pier
☎ (0248) 712453
11–3.30, 5.30–11
Greenalls Bitter, Thomas Greenall's Original Ⓗ
Interesting old pub with two cosy bars, full of old prints and nautical artefacts. Several other areas include a lounge, a conservatory, and a dining room (children accommodated). Good food.
Q ❀ ◖ ◗

Morfa Nefyn

Y Bryncynan

☎ (0758) 720879
11–3.30, 6.30–11; closed Sun
Whitbread Flowers Original; Tetley Walker Bitter Ⓗ
Modernised country pub and restaurant, with good value country fare. Very busy bank hols. ♨ ♘ ❀ ◖ ◗ ▲ ♣ P

Nefyn

Sportsmans

Stryd Fawr ☎ (0758) 720205
11–11; closed Sun
Draught Bass; Tetley Walker Bitter Ⓗ
Friendly pub, popular with locals and tourists. Snacks available. ♨ Q ❀ ▲ ♣

Penmaenmawr

Bron Eryri

Bangor Road ☎ (0492) 623978
12–11
Banks's Mild; Marston's Bitter, Pedigree Ⓗ
Small two-room pub with an interest in classic bikes (motorcyclists welcomed).
❀ ▲ ≠ ♣

Pentir

Vaynol Arms

☎ (0248) 362896
12–3, 6–11; 11–11 Sat
Ind Coope Burton Ale; S&N Theakston Old Peculier; Tetley Walker Bitter Ⓗ**; guest beers** (summer)
Old village pub, with a public bar, a pleasant, well-furnished lounge, and a dining room.
♨ Q ◖ ◗ ♿ ▲ ♣ P

Porthmadog

Ship

Lombard Street (150 yds from High St) ☎ (0766) 512990
11–11
Ind Coope Burton Ale; Tetley Walker Dark Mild, Bitter Ⓗ**; guest beer**
Popular town pub overlooking a park, and near the Ffestiniog railway. Known for the oriental cuisine in its upstairs restaurant. ♨ ♘ ❀ ◖ ◗ ⊟ ♿ ▲ ≠ ♣ P

Red Wharf Bay

Ship

Off A5025 ☎ (0248) 852568
11.30–3.30, 7–11 (11–11 summer)
Marston's Pedigree; Tetley Walker Dark Mild, Bitter Ⓗ
Interesting, old pub, full of character, almost on the beach. Two main bars, with partly flagged floors, beamed ceilings, stone walls and huge fireplaces; naval artefacts and china. A pub food award-winner. ♨ Q ♘ ❀ ◖ ◗ ♣ P

Rhosgoch

Rhosgoch Hotel (Ring)

1 mile off B5111 OS409892
☎ (0407) 830720
12–3 (not Mon–Thu winter), 6–11; 11–11 Fri & Sat
Bass Worthington BB, Draught Bass; Stones Best Bitter Ⓗ
Not easy to find, but worth the effort: a much improved pub with a small bar serving a pool room, lounge, and a snug. Live entertainment. Caravan Club site. ♨ Q ❀ ◖ ◗ ♣ P

Roewen

Tŷ Gwyn Hotel

☎ (0492) 650232
12–11 (12–2, 5–11 winter)
Lees GB Mild, Bitter Ⓗ
Village pub in an idyllic setting, much changed internally but keeping its atmosphere. Good riverside garden.
♨ Q ♘ ❀ ◖ ◗ ⊟ ▲ ♣ P

Towyn

Corbett Arms Hotel

High Street
☎ (0654) 710264
11–11
Draught Bass; Hancock's HB; Thwaites Bitter (summer) Ⓗ
Hotel bar with a pleasant lounge. Its dress code encourages older clients.
Q ❀ ⛟ ◖ ◗ ♿ ≠ P

Trofarth

Holland Arms

On B5113 ☎ (0492) 650777
Hours vary
Ansells Mild; Tetley Walker Bitter Ⓗ
18th-century coaching house, with a warm welcome, amidst country landscapes. Families welcome till 9pm. Meals served in the lounge or restaurant.
Q ❀ ◖ ◗ ♣ P

Tudweiliog

Lion Hotel

On B4417
☎ (075 887) 244
12–2, 7–11 (11–3, 6–11 summer); 11–11 Sat all year; closed Sun
S&N Matthew Brown Mild, Theakston Best Bitter, XB; Whitbread Boddingtons Bitter Ⓗ
300-year-old inn close to sandy beaches and popular with holidaymakers. Comfortable and friendly. Vegetarian dishes. Q ♘ ❀ ⛟ ◖ ◗ ⊟ ♿ ▲ ♣ P

Powys

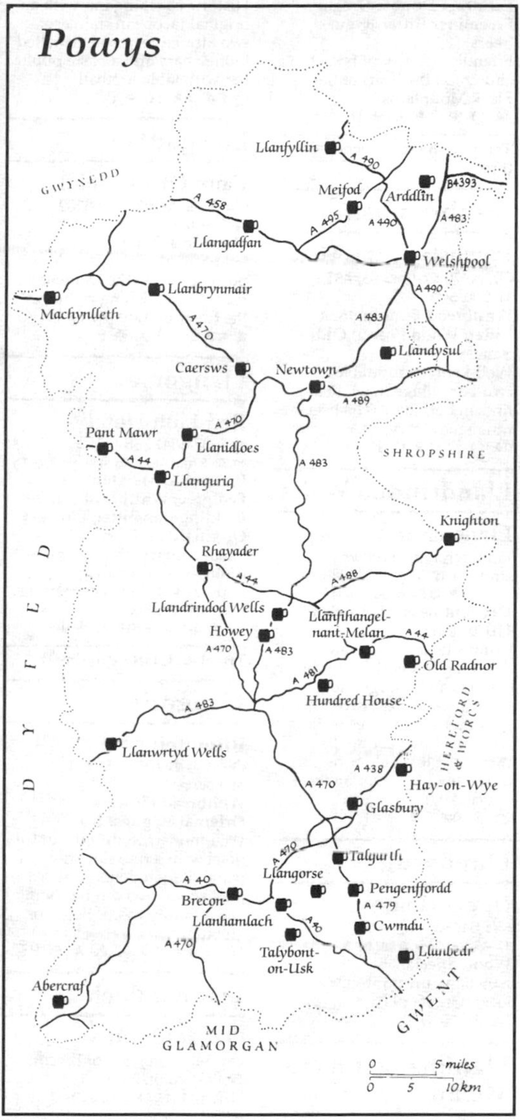

Abercraf

Copper Beech
133 Heol Tawe (off A4067)
☎ (0639) 730269
12–4, 7–11; 12–11 Fri & Sat
Courage Best Bitter, Directors; Ruddles County; Whitbread Flowers IPA 🄷; guest beers
Pub in a very picturesque area, close to the famous Dan yr Ogof caves. Good food always available. Once the home of the owners of Abercraf colliery.
🕮 Q ❀ 🛏 ◖◗ ⊟ ⌓ P

Arddlîn

Horseshoe
On A483/B4392
☎ (0938) 75318
12–3, 5.30–11
Bass Worthington BB; Marston's Pedigree 🄷
Attractive pub on the main road, Offa's Dyke and the old canal. Children's adventure playground in the garden; table football in the bar. Weston's traditional cider available. 🕮 Q ⛾ ❀ 🛏 ◖◗ ⊟ ♣ ⌓ P

Brecon

Gremlin Hotel
The Watton (B4601)
☎ (0874) 623829
12–3, 7–11
Draught Bass; Brains Bitter 🄷
Pleasant old pub with its origins in the Middle Ages. Both the public bar and the lounge are comfortably furnished, while the menu offers a range of highly competitively priced dishes. No eve meals Sun/Mon.
❀ 🛏 ◖◗ ⊟ ♣ P

Old Boar's Head
Ship Street ☎ (0874) 622856
11–3, 5.30–11; 11–11 Tue, Fri & Sat
Brains SA; Fuller's ESB; Holden's Bitter; Hook Norton Best Bitter 🄷; guest beers
Old pub near the bridge over the River Usk. The old boar himself presides over activities in the characterful bar. The spacious rear room has a pool table. Monthly live music. Bar snacks always available, but meals only in summer. Cider also in summer.
❀ ◖ ⊟ ♣ ⌓ P

Try also: Bull's Head Hotel, The Struet (Free)

Caersws

Red Lion
Main Street ☎ (0686) 688606
11.30–3.30, 7–11
Banks's Mild; Marston's Bitter, Pedigree 🄷
Traditional, friendly village local. Q ♿ ⇌ ♣ P

Cwmdu

Farmers Arms
On A479, 6 miles S of Talgarth
☎ (0874) 730464
11–3, 6–11
Draught Bass; Brains Bitter 🄷; guest beers
Friendly country pub. Large, wholesome meals are this hostelry's forté.
🕮 Q ❀ 🛏 ◖◗ ⊟ ⛺ P

Glasbury

Harp
On Hay road ☎ (0497) 847373
11–3, 6–11
Draught Bass; Robinson's Best Bitter; Whitbread Boddingtons Bitter, Flowers Original 🄷
Welcoming riverside inn on the Wye: a 17th-century cider house.
🕮 Q ❀ 🛏 ◖◗ ⊟ ♣ P

Try also: Maesllwch Arms, N of Wye bridge (Bass)

Hay-on-Wye

Blue Boar
Castle Street ☎ (0497) 820884
11–11
Draught Bass; Wadworth 6X; Whitbread Flowers IPA, Original 🄷; guest beers
Traditional pub next to the main gate of the castle, with an inviting wood-panelled public bar. An ideal place to read the books you may have unearthed in the world-famous local bookshops. Eve meals in summer only.
🔥 Q ◐ ◑ ⊞

Howey

Drovers Arms
Off A483 ☎ (0597) 822508
12–2.30 (not Tue), 7–11
Whitbread Boddingtons Bitter, Castle Eden Ale 🄷
Late 19th-century pub just off the main road, featuring a popular, attractively furnished public bar with a piano, and a lounge bar with ornate wood carvings.
🔥 Q 🐴 ❀ 🛏 ◐ ◑ ♣

Hundred House

Hundred House Inn
On A481, 5 miles E of Builth Wells ☎ (0982) 570231
11–3.30 (may extend), 6.30–11
Draught Bass (summer); **Hancock's HB 🄷; guest beer**
Spotless, former drovers' pub set among fine upland scenery. No fewer than five rooms: pool room, farmers' bar, lounge, dining room and garden bar. The interesting menu contains some traditional dishes now infrequently found. Families welcome in the pool room.
🔥 ❀ 🛏 ◐ ◑ ▲ ♣ P ⊬

Knighton

Central Wales Hotel
Station Road (A488)
☎ (0547) 520065
12–3, 5.30–11; 11–11 Sat & summer
Marston's Pedigree; Tetley Bitter 🄷
Small, country town hotel-cum-pub with a lounge, public bar and games room. Conveniently close to the Offa's Dyke footpath. Once owned by the railway and hence the name.
🔥 Q ❀ 🛏 ◐ ◑ ⊞ ▲ ⇌ ♣

Llanbedr

Red Lion
☎ (0873) 810754
12–2.30, 7–11; 12–11 Sat
Felinfoel Double Dragon; Freeminer Bitter 🄷; guest beers
Friendly country pub next to a church, in the heart of the Black Mountains.
🔥 Q ❀ ◐ ◑ ▲ ♣ P ⊬

Try also: Bear, Crickhowell (Free)

Llanbrynmair

Wynnstay Arms Hotel
On A470 ☎ (065 03) 431
11–2.30, 6–11
Whitbread Boddingtons Bitter; Wood Powell Old Sam 🄷
Well-kept, comfortable, two-bar village hotel. Real fires in both bars. The beer range may vary.
🔥 Q ❀ ◐ ◑ ♣ P

Llandrindod Wells

Llanerch Inn
Llanerch Lane (100 yds W of station) ☎ (0597) 822086
11.30–2.30 (3 Fri & Sat), 6–11
Draught Bass; Hancock's HB 🄷; guest beer
Comfortable, 16th-century coaching inn with low-beamed ceilings and a large, stone hearth, set in extensive grounds only a short walk from the town centre. Its mini-beer festival forms part of the town's Victorian week every Aug.
🐴 ❀ 🛏 ◐ ◑ ⇌ P

Llandysul

Upper House
Off B4386
12–3 (not Wed), 6.30–11
Wood Special 🄷
Excellent, unspoilt village local. Quoits played.
🔥 ❀ ⊞ ♣ P

Llanfihangel-nant-Melan

Red Lion
On A44 ☎ (054 421) 220
11–3, 6–11
Hook Norton Best Bitter 🄷
Comfortable and peaceful pub – an excellent refreshment halt on the A44. Radnor Forest provides a backdrop and the pub is popular with hillwalkers.
🔥 Q 🐴 ❀ 🛏 ◐ ◑ ▲ ♣ P

Llanfyllin

Cain Valley Hotel
On A490 ☎ (0691) 648366
11–11
Ansells Bitter; Draught Bass 🄷
Historic coaching inn with an original Jacobean staircase, two attractive, wood-panelled lounge bars and a basic public bar with table football.
Q 🛏 ◐ ◑ ⊞ ♣ P

Llangadfan

Cann Office Hotel
On A458 ☎ (0938) 88202
12–2.30, 6–11
Marston's Bitter 🄷
Six-roomed, attractive old posting inn on the Dolgellau road. Owns fishing rights on the River Banwy. 🔥 Q 🐴 ❀ 🛏 ◐ ◑ ⊞ ▲ ♣ P

Llangorse

Red Lion Hotel
☎ (087 484) 238
11.30–3 (not Mon–Fri in winter), 6–11
Brains SA; Marston's Pedigree; Whitbread Boddingtons Bitter, Flowers Original 🄷
Small country hotel in the centre of a little village. Popular with tourists visiting Llangorse lake.
🔥 ❀ 🛏 ◐ ◑ ⊞ ▲ ♣ P

Try also: Castle Inn (Free)

Llangurig

Blue Bell
On A44 ☎ (055 15) 254
11–2.30, 6–11
Whitbread Flowers Original 🄷; guest beer
Well-modernised, 16th-century hotel with a fine slate-floored bar and an inglenook; also a pool room, two dining rooms and a family room. Book for Sun lunch.
🔥 🐴 🛏 ◐ ◑ ⊞ ♿ ▲ ♣ P

Llanhamlach

Old Ford Inn
On A40, 3 miles E of Brecon
☎ (087 486) 220
11–3, 6–11 (11.30–2.30, 6.30–11 winter)
Marston's Pedigree; Whitbread Boddingtons Bitter 🄷; guest beer (summer)
Roadside pub with a fine view of the Brecon Beacons. A pub since the mid-19th century, when it was a coaching inn. A small public bar and a spacious lounge with a vine and a display of 150 old bottled beers. Families welcome.
❀ 🛏 ◐ ◑ ⊞ ▲ ♣ P

Llanidloes

Mount Inn
China Street (off A470)
☎ (055 12) 2247
11–2.30, 5.30–11; 11–11 Sat

Bass Worthington Dark, BB H
Many-roomed, 17th-century
pub with a cast iron stove.
One of few pubs with a listed
floor! ⚑ Q ◑ ◖ ▶ ⬜ ♣ P

Llanwrtyd Wells

Neuadd Arms Hotel
The Square (A483)
☎ (059 13) 236
11.30–11 (may close afternoons)
**Bass Worthington Dark,
Draught Bass; Felinfoel
Double Dragon; Hancock's
HB** H; **guest beer**
Imposing hotel in the centre of
Britain's smallest town. The
enterprising landlord
organises the mid-Wales beer
festival each Nov and
'Saturnalia' – a winter ales
festival with a Roman theme –
in Jan. The former includes
real ale rambles around the
surrounding mountains and
forests. ⚑ Q ⬜ ◑ ◖ ◖
⬜ ▲ ⇌ ♣ P ⎘

Machynlleth

Skinners Arms
Main Street (A487)
☎ (0654) 702354
11–11
Burtonwood Bitter H
Wooden-beamed, town-centre
pub with a welcoming
atmosphere: a comfortable
lounge and a long, narrow
public bar. ⚑ ◑ ▶ ⬜ ♣

Meifod

Kings Head
On A495 ☎ (0938) 884256
12 (11 summer)–3, 6–11
Burtonwood Bitter H
Impressive, stone-built inn in
the centre of the village. A
traditional public bar with a
pool table, and a plush lounge.
❀ ⛟ ◑ ▶ ⬜ ♣ P

Newtown

Pheasant
Market Street (off A483)
☎ (0686) 625966
11–11
Burtonwood Bitter H
Friendly, timbered pub with a
separate games room. The
public bar has a collection of
walking sticks. ⛟ ⬜ ⇌ ♣

Sportsman
Severn Street (off A483)
☎ (0686) 625885
11–2.30, 5–11
**Ansells Mild; Ind Coope
Burton Ale; Tetley Bitter** H

Excellent, friendly town-centre
pub, popular with a wide
range of customers. Games
area; live traditional music
alternate Tues.
Q ❀ ◑ ⇌ ♣

Old Radnor

Harp Inn
1 mile W of A44/B4362 jct
☎ (054 421) 655
12–2.30 (not Tue), 7–11
Beer range varies H
15th-century inn beautifully
restored by the Landmark
Trust and featuring a stone-
flagged floor, stone walls,
beamed ceiling, antique
furniture and bric-a-brac.
Outside, noisy geese and a
memorable view of Radnor
Forest complete the picture.
Families welcome. Beers
usually come from Wood or
Wye Valley.
⚑ Q ❀ ⛟ ◑ ▶ ⬜ ▲ ♣ P

**Try also: Royal Oak,
Gladestry (Bass)**

Pant Mawr

Glan Severn Arms
Hotel
On A44, 1 miles W of
Llangurig ☎ (055 15) 240
11–2, 6.30–11 (closed Sun before
Xmas–New Year's Eve)
**Bass Worthington Dark,
Draught Bass** H
Two impeccable, quiet,
comfortable bars in a hotel
high in the Wye valley.
Restaurant meals only (book
eves and Sun lunch; no food
Sun eve). ⚑ Q ⛟ P

Pengenffordd

Castle Inn
☎ (0874) 711353
11–3, 6–11
**Wadworth 6X; Whitbread
Boddingtons Bitter** H; **guest
beers**
Friendly country local,
popular with trekkers and
walkers. Located on the
summit of the mountain road
between Talgarth and
Crickhowell, with the highest
hill fort in England and Wales,
Castle Dinas, rising up behind.
⚑ ❀ ⛟ ◑ ▶ ⬜ ▲ ♣ P

Rhayader

Cornhill Inn
West Street (B4518)
☎ (0597) 810869
11–3 (may extend), 6–11
**Marston's Pedigree;
Mitchell's ESB; Wells Eagle** H

Friendly, low-beamed, 400-
year-old pub, reputedly
haunted: a single L-shaped
bar. ⚑ ⛟ ◑ ▲ ♣ ◔

Triangle Inn
Cwmdauddwr (off B4518)
☎ (0597) 810537
11–3, 6.30–11
**Draught Bass; Hancock's
HB** H
Beautiful, little weatherboarded gem overlooking the
River Wye. The ceilings are so
low that customers have to
stand in a hole in the floor to
play darts! Constant
entertainment is provided by
the fish in the aquarium.
❀ ◑ ▲ ♣

Talgarth

New Inn
Bronllys Road ☎ (0874) 711581
11–11
**Tetley Bitter; Whitbread
Flowers Original** H
Very busy pub offering a
warm welcome to locals and
tourists alike. Beer and food
are both very reasonably
priced. Caravans allowed at
the site. ⛟ ◑ ▶ ⬜ ▲ ♣ ◔ P

Talybont-on-Usk

Star Inn
On B4558, ¾ mile from A40
☎ (087 487) 635
11–3, 6–11; 11–11 Sat
**Draught Bass; Brains SA;
Felinfoel Double Dragon;
Marston's Pedigree; S&N
Theakston Old Peculier;
Wadworth 6X** H; **guest beers**
Popular canalside pub which
is a great draw for visitors to
the area. The array of
handpumps is a welcoming
sight, with about 12 beers
available most times. The
above list is a representative
sample of the regular guest
ales. Good bar food.
⚑ ❀ ⛟ ◑ ▶ ⬜ ▲ ♣ ◔

Welshpool

Green Dragon
Mount Street ☎ (0938) 552531
12–11
Burtonwood Bitter H
Pleasant, large, comfortable
pub, known locally as the Top
Hat. ⬜ ⇌ ♣

Pheasant
High Street ☎ (0938) 553104
12–3, 7–11
**Ind Coope Burton Ale; Tetley
Bitter** H
Popular, long, narrow pub
with an outdoor drinking area.
⚑ ❀ ◑ ⇌ ♣

Protect your pleasure — join CAMRA (see page 512)

Borders

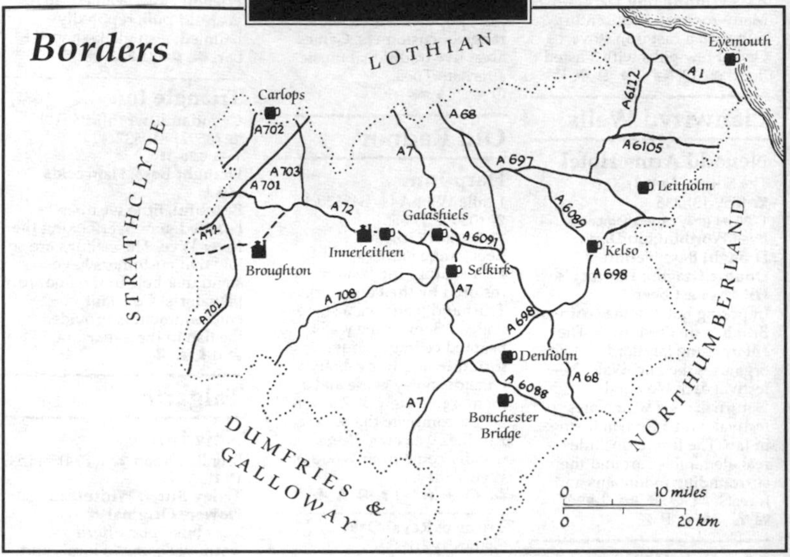

Broughton, *Broughton;* **Traquair House,** *Innerleithen*

Bonchester Bridge

Horse & Hound Country Inn

On A6088 ☎ (045 086) 645
12–2.30, 6.30–11; 11.30–3.30, 5.30–midnight Sat; closed winter Tue. Summer opening: 11 (12.30 Sun)–11 (midnight Sat & Sun)
Orkney Dark Island [H]
18th-century coaching inn with a cosy bar, lounge and restaurant. Ideal for hillwalking, fishing or golfing. Meals include a 72 oz steak – free if eaten within the hour! (Order 24 hours in advance.) Worthington White Shield.
♨ ❀ 🛏 ◐ ◗ ⊞ ▲ ♣ P

Carlops

Allan Ramsay Hotel

On A702 ☎ (0968) 60258
11 (12.30 Sun)–midnight
Belhaven 80/- [H]; guest beer
Friendly, country inn now one large room with two log fires. The bartop is inset with old pennies. Meals all day.
♨ Q ❀ 🛏 ◐ ◗ ⊞ P

Denholm

Auld Cross Keys Inn

On A698 ☎ (045 087) 305
11–2.30 (not Mon), 5–11; 11–midnight Thu & Sat; 11–1 am Fri; 12.30–11 Sun
Broughton Greenmantle Ale; guest beer [H]
Picturesque, 17th-century pub in a conservation village. The low-ceilinged bar has a coal fire. The restaurant is worth booking, especially weekends. Winner of a *Best High Teas* award. ♨ Q ◐ ◗ ⊞ ♣ P

Eyemouth

Ship Hotel

Harbour Road
☎ (089 07) 50224
11 (12.30 Sun)–midnight
Caledonian 80/- [A]; guest beer
Small, family-run hotel on the harbour. Vast selection of rums, as befits a fisherman's haunt.
♨ ⛴ ❀ 🛏 ◐ ◗ ⊞ ▲ ♣ P

Galashiels

Ladhope Inn

33 High Buckholmside (A7, ½ mile N of centre)
☎ (0896) 2446
11–2.30, 5–11 (11–11 summer; 11–midnight summer Fri & Sat; 12.30–11 summer Sun)
Caledonian 80/- [H]; guest beer
Established in 1792, although much altered; a vibrant local, comfortably appointed. ♣

Innerleithen

Traquair Arms Hotel

Traquair Road (B709, off A72)
☎ (0896) 830229
11 (12.30 Sun)–11
Broughton Greenmantle Ale; Traquair House Bear Ale [H]
Family-run, 18th-century hotel with a plush lounge warmed by a log fire. Good home-cooked food from local produce. ♨ Q ❀ 🛏 ◐ ◗ P

Kelso

Red Lion Inn

Crawford Street
☎ (0573) 224817
11–midnight (1 am Fri); 12.30–11 Sun
Belhaven 80/-, St Andrew's Ale; Courage Directors [H]
Superb traditional pub with a surprisingly ornate interior and a fine bar-back. The bar is made from a single piece of mahogany and may be the longest in Scotland. ♨ ⊞ ♣

Leitholm

Plough Hotel

Main Street (A699, off A697, 6 miles N of Coldstream)
☎ (089 084) 252
11.30 (12.30 Sun)–2.30, 5 (6.30 Sun)–11 (7–11 only winter)
Broughton Greenmantle Ale [H]
Unspoilt village local in a rural setting. A rug in the public is a reminder of when the pub, now free, was owned by Vaux.
♨ Q 🛏 ⊞ ♣ P

Selkirk

Cross Keys Inn

Market Place ☎ (0750) 21283
11 (12.30 Sun)–11 (midnight Thu–Sat)
Caledonian 80/- [H]
Vibrant, wee, wood-panelled public bar which leads up to a comfortable lounge. Often-packed, causing congestion in the boy's room, which is interesting, if claustrophobic. Award-winning meals (not served Sat eve). ◐ ◗ ⊞

Central

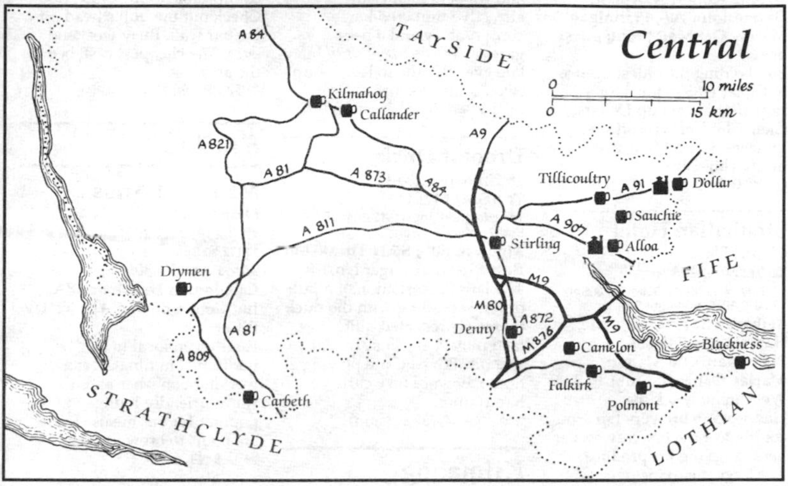

Harviestoun, Dollar; Maclay, Alloa

Alloa

Crams Bar

8 Candleriggs ☎ (0259) 722019
11 (12.30 Sun)–11 (midnight Fri & Sat)
Maclay 80/- [A]
Friendly workingman's bar in a central location. Cheap beer.

Thistle

1 Junction Place
☎ (0259) 723933
11–midnight (including Sun, 1 am Sat)
Maclay 80/-, Kane's Amber Ale, Oat Malt Stout [A]; guest beers
Town-centre pub attached to Maclay's Brewery. A popular lounge and a sociable bar with a games room. Patio open in summer. No food Sun.

Blackness

Blackness Inn

The Square (B903, off A904)
☎ (0506) 834252
11–3, 6–11.30; 12.30–11 Sun
Alloa Arrol's 80/-; Ind Coope Burton Ale; guest beers [E]
Typical country inn, nicely situated on the edge of the River Forth, near Blackness Castle. A warm welcome is assured, with real fires in both bars and award-winning, home-cooked food.

Callander

Waverley Hotel (Claymore Lounge Bar)

88–92 Main Street
☎ (0877) 30245
11–midnight (1am Fri & Sat)
Draught Bass [H]; Belhaven 80/- [A]; Harviestoun 70/-, Old Manor [H]
Comfortable lounge bar in the main street of this popular tourist spot.

Camelon

Rosebank

Main Street
☎ (0324) 611842
11–midnight (11.30 Sun, 1am Fri & Sat)
Whitbread Castle Eden Ale [H]
Pub opened in 1988, a £1.5 million renovation of the former Rosebank Distillery's bonded warehouse on the Forth and Clyde Canal. The Sun eve quiz is very popular.
P

Carbeth

Carbeth Inn

Stockiemuir Road, Blanefield (A809, near Strathblane turn-off) ☎ (0360) 70002
12 (12.30 Sun)–11 (1am Fri & Sat)
Belhaven 80/-, St Andrew's Ale [H]
Old, established country inn where the wood-panelled public bar is heated by a blazing log fire. The lounge serves eve meals until 8.30.
P

Denny

Royal Oak Hotel

169 Stirling Street
☎ (0324) 823768
11–2.30, 5 (6.30 Sun)–11
Younger No 3 [A]
Built in 1794 as a coaching inn, and run by the same family since 1925. The comfortable, quiet bar provides a pleasant atmosphere. Q P

Dollar

Castle Campbell Hotel

11 Bridge Street
☎ (0259) 42519
11–2.30, 5–11 (11.45 Fri & Sat); 12.30–2.30, 6–11 Sun
Alloa Arrol's 80/-; Jennings Bitter [H]; guest beers
Well-kept, family-run hotel, named after the nearby NT property. One beer only in the cellar-style bar; all beers in the well-appointed upstairs lounge. The landlord runs a sloe gin competition every 27th February.
Q P

Kings Seat

19 Bridge Street
☎ (0259) 42515
11–2.30, 5–midnight
Caledonian 80/-; Ind Coope Benskins Best Bitter; Robinson's Bitter; John Smith's Magnet; Stones Best Bitter [H]
Comfortable pub on the main street, offering a wide range of food which can be eaten either in the spacious restaurant or in the cosy bar. Families welcome. Q

Lorne Tavern

17 Argyll Street
☎ (0259) 43423
11–2.30 (Mon only), 5 (3 Wed)–11; 3–midnight Thu; 11–1am Fri & Sat; 12.30–11 Sun

Greene King IPA, Abbot; Harviestoun 70/-, Ptarmigan; Maclay Oat Malt Stout; guest beer Ⓗ
Pub holding the oldest licence in Dollar (1850). Ideal for a stop after a walk up Dollar Glen. Children's certificate. Lunches Sat and Sun; eve meals Thu–Sun.
Q ☋ ◖ ◗ ⊟ ♿ ▲ P

Strathallan Hotel
Chapel Place
☎ (0259) 42205
11–2.30, 5–11.30 (12.30am Fri & Sat); 12.30–2.30, 6–midnight Sun
Belhaven St Andrew's Ale; Harviestoun 70/- 80/-, Ptarmigan, Old Manor; Maclay Oat Malt Stout Ⓗ
Welcoming hotel, the Harviestoun brewery tap. You could meet the brewery owner here sampling his produce. The large menu includes children's specials.
Q ☋ ❀ 🛏 ◖ ◗ ♿ ▲ P ⚟

Drymen

Winnock Hotel
The Square
☎ (0360) 60245
11 (12 Sun)–midnight (1am Fri & Sat)
Broughton Greenmantle Ale; Courage Directors; John Smith's Magnet; Webster's Yorkshire Bitter Ⓗ
Large, 18th-century hotel at the centre of an attractive village. Ceilidhs held on summer Suns; petanque played.
♨ Q ❀ 🛏 ◖ ◗ ⊟ ▲ ♣ P

Falkirk

Behind the Wall
14 Melville Street
☎ (0324) 33338
11–11.30 (midnight Wed & Thu, 12.45am Fri & Sat); 12–midnight Sun
McEwan 80/-; Whitbread Boddingtons Bitter Ⓗ
Housed in a former Playtex bra factory, a pub with a cops and robbers theme: an attractive timbered bar, a conservatory and a beer garden. Tends to get very busy late eve. NB: the toilets are up two flights of stairs.
❀ ◖ ◗ ⇌ (Grahamston)

Drookit Duck
18 Grahams Road
☎ (0324) 613644
11–3, 5–midnight; 11–12.30am Fri & Sat; 7–midnight Sun
McEwan 80/-; S&N Theakston Best Bitter; Younger No.3 Ⓗ
The latest incarnation of a pub of long standing with the duck theme represented quite tastefully. Very busy on Sat when Falkirk FC are playing at home. Beware fake cider handpump.
◖ ♿ ⇌ (Grahamston)

Kilmahog

Lade Inn
At A84/A821 jct, 1 mile from Callander
☎ (0877) 30152
12–2.30, 6–11 (midnight Fri & Sat); 12.30–11 Sun; closed Mon & Tue in Feb
Courage Directors; Ruddles County; Webster's Yorkshire Bitter Ⓗ
A real gem, situated in an area of outstanding beauty. The warm welcome and excellent meals make this inn extremely popular with hill walkers, especially at weekends. The landlord's son runs a brewery in Canada – enthusiasm for good beer runs in the family.
Q ❀ 🛏 ◖ ◗ ♿ ▲ P

Polmont

Black Bull
Main Street
☎ (0324) 716110
11–midnight (1am Fri & Sat); 12.30–11 Sun
Maclay 80/- Ⓐ
Proper village local with a genuine public bar and a comfortable lounge next door. Check out the bull's head on the bar wall. Busy weekend eves. The cheapest cask beer in the area.
◖ ⊟ ⇌ ♣ P

Sauchie

Mansfield Arms
Main Street
☎ (0259) 722020
11 (12.30 Sun)–midnight
Alloa Arrol's 80/- Ⓔ; **Caledonian Deuchars IPA; Ind Coope Burton Ale; Tetley Bitter** Ⓗ
Family-run local in a traditional mining area: a workingmen's bar and a warm, friendly lounge, popular for bar meals. There are plans to brew at the pub.
❀ ◖ ◗ ⊟ ♿ ♣ P

Stirling

Settle Inn
91 St Mary's Wynd (top of Irvine Place)
☎ (0786) 74609
12–11 (midnight Wed–Fri); 11–midnight Sat; 12.30–4, 6.30–11 Sun
Maclay 80/-, Oat Malt Stout Ⓐ
The oldest coaching inn in Stirling, dating back to 1733: a comfortable, unspoilt bar and an informal back room. A must for the price-conscious ale drinker. ♿ ⇌

Tillicoultry

Woolpack
Glassford Square (foot of Tillicoultry Glen, follow signs from main road)
☎ (0259) 750332
11–midnight (1am Fri & Sat); 12.30–11 Sun
Beer range varies Ⓗ
Welcoming bar, handy for walkers returning from a trek around the glen. Good value bar lunches. Q ◖ ◗ ♣

The Symbols

♨	real fire	♿	easy wheelchair access
Q	quiet pub (at least one bar)	▲	camping facilities at the pub or nearby
☋	indoor room for children	⇌	near British Rail station
❀	garden or other outdoor drinking area	⊖	near underground station
🛏	accommodation	♣	pub games
◖	lunchtime meals	⊂⊃	real cider
◗	evening meals	P	pub car park
⊟	public bar	⚟	no-smoking room or area

Dumfries & Galloway

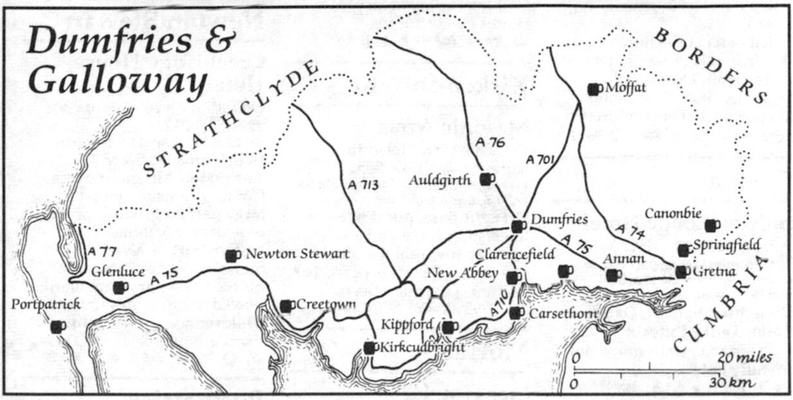

Annan

Blue Bell Inn
High Street ☎ (0461) 202385
11 (12.30 Sun)–11 (midnight Thu–Sat)
S&N Theakston Best Bitter; guest beer [H]
Excellent, traditional boozer with impressive panelling. Very friendly – worth a detour. Q ❀ ⊞ ⛺ ⇌ ♣

Auldgirth

Auldgirth Inn
Off A76, 7 miles N of Dumfries ☎ (0387) 74250
11–2.30, 5–11 (midnight Fri); 11–midnight Sat; 12.30–11 Sun
Draught Bass; Maclay 80/-; guest beer [H]
Quaint country inn bypassed by a road diversion. The comfortable lounge bar is decorated in Tudor style.
⛰ Q 🛏 ◐ ◑ ⊞ P

Canonbie

Riverside Inn
☎ (0387) 71512
11.30–2.30, 6.30–11 (midnight Thu–Sat); 6.30–11 Sun
Yates Bitter; guest beer [H]
Excellent, two-level bar, with a regularly changing guest beer. Good quality food. Well worth finding. ⛰ Q ❀ 🛏 ◐ ◑ P

Carsethorn

Steamboat Inn
Off A710 at Kirkbean
☎ (038 788) 631
11 (11.30 winter)–2.30, 5.30 (6.30 winter)–11 (midnight Fri & Sat)
Belhaven St Andrew's Ale; Whitbread Boddingtons Bitter; guest beer [H]
Small, comfortable bar with a conservatory overlooking the Solway Firth. Good selection of malt whiskies. Real ale is not available in winter.
⛰ Q ♉ ❀ ◐ ◑ ⊞ ♣ P

Clarencefield

Farmers Inn
Main Street ☎ (0387) 87675
11–2.30, 6–11 (midnight Fri); 11–midnight Sat; 12.30–11 Sun; 11–11 bank hols
Caledonian 70/-, 80/-; guest beer [H]
Welcoming, 18th-century inn, formerly the village shop. Cider in summer only. ⛰ ❀
🛏 ◐ ◑ ⊞ ♿ ⛺ ♣ 🍏 P

Creetown

Barholm Arms Hotel
St John Street (off A75)
☎ (067 182) 553
11–3, 6–11; 12.30–11 Sun
Caledonian 80/-; guest beers [H]
Very friendly local in a village bypassed by the main Dumfries–Stranraer road. Close to the shore of Wigtown Bay and opposite a working farrier's. Children's certificate. Two guest beers. ♉ ◐ ◑ ⛺ P

Dumfries

Douglas Arms
Friars Vennel ☎ (0387) 56002
11 (12.30 Sun)–11 (midnight Thu–Sat)
Broughton Greenmantle Ale, Special, Oatmeal Stout, Old Jock; Jennings Cumberland Ale; guest beer [H]
Grand wee pub with a snug.
⊞ ⇌ ♣

Globe Inn
High Street ☎ (0387) 52335
11 (12.30 Sun)–11
McEwan 80/-; Maclay 80/- [H]
17th-century howff in a narrow alley. Superb wood-panelled snug. A favourite haunt of Rabbie Burns. Eve meals in summer only.
◐ ◑ ⊞ ⇌ ♣

New Bazaar
38 White Sands
☎ (0387) 68776
11–11 (midnight Thu–Sat)
Belhaven 80/-; Broughton Greenmantle Ale; McEwan 80/-; Maclay Scotch Ale [H]**; guest beer**
Marvellous, old bar with Victorian fittings. Wheelchair access via the rear door.
♉ ⊞ ♿ ⇌ ♣

Ship Inn
97 St Michael Street
☎ (0387) 55189
11–2.30, 5–11
Courage Directors; Fuller's London Pride; Greene King Abbot [H]**; McEwan 70/-, 80/-** [A]**; Marston's Pedigree** [H]**; S&N Theakston XB** [A]**; guest beer** [H]
Very traditional, two-roomed pub – a gem which should never be missed. ⊞ ♿ ⇌ ♣

Station Hotel (Somewhere Else Bar)
Lovers Walk ☎ (0387) 54316
12–2.30, 5–11; 11.30–2.30, 6–11 Sun
John Smith's Magnet [H]
Pleasant, café-style, basement bar. Wheelchair access is via the hotel.
❀ 🛏 ◐ ◑ ♿ ⇌ P ⚡

Tam O'Shanter
117 Queensberry Street
11–2.30, 5–11; closed Sun
Caledonian 70/-, Deuchars IPA, 80/-; McEwan 80/- [A]
Excellent, cosy bar with several rooms. Q ⊞ ⇌ ♣

Troqueer Arms
Troqueer Road ☎ (0387) 54518
11–11 (midnight Tue & Thu, 1am Fri & Sat); 12.30–midnight Sun
Belhaven 80/-; Caledonian 70/-, 80/-; Maclay 60/- [H]
Friendly local near the Camera Obscura. ❀ ⊞ ♣ P

Glenluce

Kelvin House Hotel
53 Main Street (off A75)
☎ (058 13) 303
11–11 (midnight Fri & Sat)

Dumfries & Galloway

Alloa Arrol's 80/-; guest beer H
Small hotel at the head of Luce Bay in a village now bypassed by the main Dumfries–Stranraer road. Real ale not available Jan–Feb. Children's certificate.

Gretna

Solway Lodge Hotel
Annan Road ☎ (0461) 38266
11 (12 Sun)–11 (midnight Fri & Sat); closed Sun eve & Mon lunch mid-Oct–Easter
Broughton Special, Oatmeal Stout; Tetley Bitter H
Comfortable, welcoming and friendly hotel.
P

Kippford

Anchor Hotel
☎ (0556) 62205
10.30–midnight (10.30–2.30, 6–11 winter)
McEwan 80/- A**; S&N Theakston Best Bitter** H
Magnificent wood-panelled bar with a seafaring flavour. Overlooks the harbour and peaceful hills beyond.
Q P

Mariner Hotel
☎ (0556) 62206
12–2.30, 6–11.30 (11.30–11 Sat & Sun in summer)
Draught Bass; Belhaven 80/-; guest beer H
Comfortable lounge bar with beautiful views over the estuary to hills (breathtaking sunsets!). Split-level bar. Children's play area, plus a children's certificate.
P

Kirkcudbright

Masonic Arms
19 Castle Street (near the harbour) ☎ (0557) 30517
11–2.30, 5–midnight; 11–midnight Sat; 12.30–5, 6–midnight Sun
Draught Bass; guest beers H
Interesting bar with barrels used for the frontage, stools and tables. Selection of old bar mirrors. Two guest beers.
Q

Moffat

Star Hotel
44 High Street
☎ (0683) 20156
11–11 (11–2.30, 5–11 winter); 11–midnight Fri–Sun all year
S&N Theakston Best Bitter H
Welcoming, family-run hotel, the narrowest detached hotel in Britain. The real ale is in the bar but can be ordered from the lounge. High teas served.

New Abbey

Criffel Inn
On A710 ☎ (0387) 85305
11.30 (12.30 Sun)–2.30, 5.30 (6.30 Sun)–11
Broughton Special A
Traditional bar in a small hotel set in a picturesque village near the ruins of Sweetheart Abbey. Old photos and posters of local interest are displayed. Children's certificate.
Q P

Newton Stewart

Creebridge House Hotel
On old main road, E of river
☎ (0671) 2121
12–2.30, 6 (7 Sun)–11 (11.30 Sat)
Belhaven 80/-; S&N Theakston XB; guest beers H
Country house hotel set in large garden grounds on the outskirts of Minnigaff (the eastern part of Newton Stewart). Various rooms lead off the main bar. Bar billiards played; croquet in summer. Children welcome (certificate). Excellent menu.
Q P

Portpatrick

Harbour House Hotel
53 Main Street (on the harbour) ☎ (0776) 81456
11 (12 Sun)–11.30 (12.30 am Fri & Sat)
Alloa Arrol's 80/- A
Open-plan lounge bar in a hotel looking onto a picturesque fishing port. Children's certificate.
P

Springfield

Queens Head
Main Street
☎ (0461) 37173
12–2.30, 7–11 (midnight Thu–Sat)
McEwan 70/-, 80/-; S&N Theakston Mild, Best Bitter H
Refurbished, single-room, village local. The landlady is a very keen domino player. Snacks available.
P

Traditional, wood-floored pub full of interesting bric-a-brac. Live music most nights; popular with office workers at lunchtime. All major sporting events are shown on a big screen TV. Popular with all ages. ◖ ♿

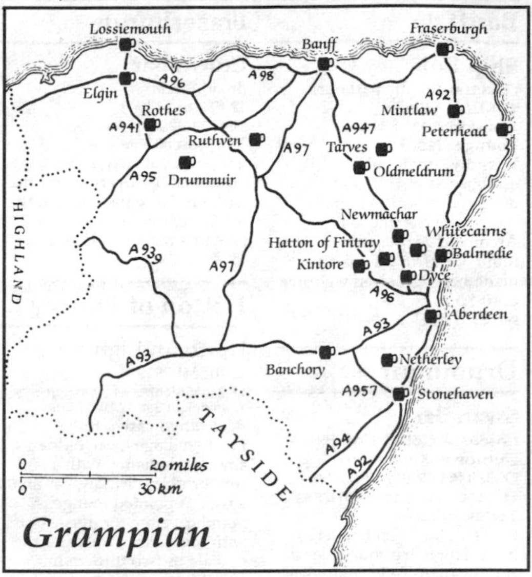

Aberdeen

Ale Cellar
114 Rosemount Viaduct (near His Majesty's Theatre)
☎ (0224) 624700
10–9; closed Sun & Mon
Beer range varies Ⓗ
Specialist beer shop carrying a wide variety of bottled beers and two draught take-away ales, plus an extensive range of German and Belgian beer.

Betty Burke's
45 Langstane Place
☎ (0224) 210359
10–midnight; 5–11 Sun
Alloa Arrol's 80/-; Caledonian 80/-; Ind Coope Burton Ale; Tetley Bitter Ⓗ
Well-established, city-centre bar; lively and popular with a warm welcome for all. Its 'Drink the World' competition features some unusual bottled beers. Fine food available throughout the day. Children's certificate till 8pm.
◖ ◗ ⇌

Blue Lamp
121 Gallowgate (near Marischal College)
☎ (0224) 647472
11–midnight; 6.30–11 Sun
McEwan 80/-; S&N Theakston Best Bitter Ⓗ; Younger No. 3 Ⓐ; guest beers Ⓗ
Small, dark but distinctive bar with a modern, stone-floored lounge which hosts the occasional live band. Visits are enhanced by a free jukebox with an excellent choice of music. ⊞ ♿ ⇌ ♣

Camerons Inn
6 Little Belmont Street (off Union St beside churchyard)
☎ (0224) 644487
11–11.45
Draught Bass; Orkney Dark Island; S&N Theakston Best Bitter Ⓗ; Younger No. 3 Ⓐ; guest beer Ⓗ
Old coaching inn whose tiny, listed snug remains unchanged but can be very claustrophobic at busy times. There's also a modern extension at the back. Occasional impromptu sessions by passing fiddlers, etc. Meals served in the lounge (not Sun). The guest beer is from Caledonian.
◖ ◗ ⊞ ⇌ ♣

Carriages
101 Crown Street
☎ (0224) 595440
11–2.30, 5–midnight; 6–11.30 Sun
Caledonian Deuchars IPA; Marston's Pedigree; S&N Theakston Best Bitter; Whitbread Boddingtons Bitter, Castle Eden Ale, Flowers Original Ⓗ; guest beers
Outstanding bar and lounge with a warm, welcoming atmosphere. Busy trade midweek; regular charity quiz Sun. Excellent service.
Q 🛏 ◖ ◗ ⇌ P

Cocky Hunters
504 Union Street
☎ (0224) 626720
11–midnight; 2.30–11 Sun
Whitbread Boddingtons Bitter, Castle Eden Ale, Flowers Original Ⓗ; guest beers

Filthy McNasty's
37 Summer Street
☎ (0224) 625588
11–midnight; 6.30–11 Sun
Draught Bass; Whitbread Flowers IPA Ⓗ
Traditional, spacious city-centre local; a family-run pub where the bar staff make you feel welcome. Wood features in the decor. Live bands Tue.
◖ ◗ ♿ ⇌

Grill
213 Union Street
11 (7.30 Sun)–11
Draught Bass Ⓗ; McEwan 80/- Ⓐ; guest beer Ⓗ
Superb example of a Scottish bar with magnificent wood panels and a bar gantry. Classic toilets (men only). A friendly welcome; popular with all. ◖ ⇌

Mains of Scotstown Inn
1 Jesmond Square East, Bridge of Don
☎ (0224) 825222
11 (12.30 Sun)–11 (midnight Thu–Sat)
Draught Bass Ⓗ
Former farm, converted to a comfortable suburban lounge bar/restaurant and a lively public bar. Popular for good meals. No under 21s in the bar. ◖ ◗ ⊞ P

Malt Mill
82 Holburn Street
☎ (0224) 573830
12–2, 7–midnight; 7–11 Sun
Courage Directors Ⓗ
Lively bar hosting a wide range of live music every night and drawing a mixed clientele.
◖

Moorings
Trinity Quay
☎ (0224) 587602
11–midnight; 12.30–11 Sun
Draught Bass; Stones Best Bitter; guest beer Ⓗ
The place to tie up for hard rock and real ale. A quaint fishing village bar this ain't.
♿ ⇌ ♣

No. 10 Wine Bar
10 Queens Terrace
☎ (0224) 631928
9.30–midnight
Courage Directors; Whitbread Boddingtons Bitter; guest beers Ⓗ
Lively but friendly bar, open for coffee and breakfast early

in the morning: read all the newspapers and wait in comfort till you can enjoy the good range of beers.
♨ ◖

Prince of Wales
5 St Nicholas Lane
☎ (0224) 640597
11 (12.30 Sun)–10.45 (11.45 Thu–Sat)
Draught Bass; Caledonian 80/-; Orkney Dark Island; S&N Theakston Old Peculier H; **Younger No. 3** A; **guest beers** H
Popular, long bar where a quiet lounge area provides seclusion from the crowds during the frequent busy spells. Good, wholesome lunches Mon–Sat. Live music most Sun afternoons and occasional impromptu sessions.
Q ◖ ≠ ♣

Tilted Wig
55 Castle Street (opp. Court House)
☎ (0224) 583248
12–midnight; 7–11 Sun
Alloa Arrol's 80/-; Caledonian 80/-; Ind Coope Burton Ale; Marston's Pedigree; Robinson's Best Bitter; Tetley Bitter H
Bright, bustling bar, very popular with students and the staff of the Sheriff's Court. Decorated with a legal theme.
◖ ◗ ≠

Balmedie

Coach & Horses
Next to A92, 1 mile N of Balmedie OS966194
☎ (0358) 43249
12–2.30, 5–1am (11.45 Sat, 11 Sun)
Beer range varies H
Compact, active yet tranquil, former roadside coaching inn with a pleasant, well-appointed, olde-worlde-style lounge bar serving well-prepared food. Guest beers on rotation.
♨ Q ◖ ◗ P

Banchory

Tor Na Coille Hotel
Inchmarlo Road (A93, W side of town)
☎ (033 02) 2242
11.30–2.30, 5–11.30
Whitbread Boddingtons Bitter H
Lovely, imposing hotel enjoying a quiet yet friendly atmosphere, on the edge of all Royal Deeside has to offer. Very welcoming staff. Large selection of malt whiskies. A former haunt of Charlie Chaplin. Croquet played. Q 🐴
❀ 🛏 ◖ ◗ ⊞ ♿ ▲ ♣ P

Banff

Ship Inn
Deveronside (by harbour)
☎ (0261) 812620
11–midnight; 12.30–11 Sun
Younger No. 3 H
Friendly, small pub, established in 1710 and designed as a clinker-built boat. Note the unusual Archibald Arrol's mirror. The film *Local Hero* was partly made here. Children welcome until 8pm.
♨ 🐴 ◖ ◗ ⊞ ▲ ♣

Drummuir

Swan Bar
Rosebank Cottage (off B9104, Dufftown–Keith road) OS383444 ☎ (054 281) 230
11 (12.30 Sun)–11 (11.45 Fri & Sat)
Tetley Bitter H
Isolated, but friendly, very basic, single-bar village local, run by an ex-Tetley employee.
◖ ◗ ♿ ♣ P

Dyce

Greentrees
Victoria Street (off A947, Oldmeldrum road) OS887135
☎ (0224) 722283
11 (12.30 Sun)–11 (midnight Thu–Sat)
Beer range varies H
Large, lively village local with a busy meal trade. The bar is decorated with football memorabilia and the lounge is nicely appointed. Vegetarian food. Guest ales are served on rotation.
Q ◖ ◗ ⊞ ♿ ≠ ♣ P

Elgin

Sunninghill Hotel
Hay Street
☎ (0343) 547799
11 (12.30 Sun)–2.30, 5 (6.30 Sun)–11 (midnight Fri & Sat)
Tetley Bitter; guest beer H
Quiet, comfortable hotel lounge near the college.
❀ 🛏 ◖ ≠ ♣ P

Thunderton House
Thunderton Place (off High St)
☎ (0343) 548767
11.30–11 (11.45 Fri & Sat); 12.30–2.30, 6.30–11 Sun
Draught Bass; Courage Directors; Whitbread Boddingtons Bitter, Flowers Original; guest beer H
Busy bar in a carefully renovated, historic building with connections to Bonnie Prince Charlie. A former Temperance hotel. Meals served all day until 7pm.
🐴 ◖ ◗ ♿ ≠

Fraserburgh

Crown Bar
Broad Street
☎ (0346) 514941
11–11.30; 12.30–11 Sun
McEwan 80/- A
Unspoilt, but cosy, old-fashioned bar overlooking the harbour. Note the interesting old Guinness fount. A real gem in a real beer desert.
⊞ ♣

Hatton of Fintray

Northern Lights
☎ (0224) 791261
12–2 (not Mon), 5–11 (1am Fri); 12–midnight Sat; 12.30–11 Sun
Beer range varies H
Lively, village local, hidden amongst housing, with a comfortable, pleasant bar and a well-appointed lounge. A popular venue for music buffs, with regular festivals and the odd ale or two thrown in. Guest beer on rotation.
♨ Q ❀ ⊞ ♿ ♣ P

Kintore

Kintore Arms
The Square (by A96) OS793163
☎ (0467) 32216
11–2.30, 5–11 (midnight Fri); 7–11 Sun
Courage Directors A
Immaculate and honest example of a Scottish snug-type bar, delightfully furnished in light wood, glass and polished metals. A convivial spot.
Q 🐴 🛏 ◖ ◗ ♣ P

Lossiemouth

Clifton
Clifton Road
☎ (0343) 812100
11–2.30, 5–11 (11.45 Fri & Sat)
McEwan 80/-; S&N Theakston Best Bitter; guest beer E
Comfortable bar on the road to the harbour. The walls reflect the nautical and aeronautical connections of the local community. ♨ ▲ ♣ P

Mintlaw

Country Park Inn
Station Road (off A950, New Pitsligo road) OS990485
☎ (0771) 22622
11–11.30 (including Sun)
Courage Directors H
Pleasant, well-appointed lounge with a summer outdoor area. An ideal lunchtime retreat (serving good vegetarian food), near the Aden Country Park and Heritage Centre. Children welcome. ♨ Q ❀ ◖ ◗ ♿ P

Netherley

Lairhillock Inn

On B979 ☎ (0596) 30001
11–2.30, 5.30–11; 11–11 Sat; 12.30–2.30, 6.30–10.30 Sun
Courage Directors; McEwan 80/-; Thwaites Craftsman [H]; **guest beer** [A]
Look for the building with 'inn' on the roof. The Romans would have stopped on their way to Mons Grampus if it had been around then. The large lounge boasts a central fire and an unusual conservatory. The public bar has two fires and a welcoming atmosphere.
Q P

Newmachar

Beekies Neuk

Station Road (by A947) OS885195
☎ (0651) 862740
11–midnight (1am Fri, 11.45 Sat); 12.30–11.30 Sun
Draught Bass; Courage Directors [H]
Congenial snug bar with a bay window, real coal fire and an intimate, friendly atmosphere. The exceptional, large lounge bar provides excellent, inexpensive food.
Q P

Oldmeldrum

Redgarth

Kirk Brae (off A947, Aberdeen–Banff road) OS812273
☎ (0651) 872353
11 (12.30 Sun)–2.30, 5 (5.30 Sun)–11 (11.45 Fri & Sat)
Draught Bass; guest beers [H]
Very popular, pleasant bar whose garden enjoys a magnificent panoramic view. Good value fresh, home-cooked food from a varied menu, including a vegetarian choice. The host is a previous national CAMRA *Pub of the Year* winner. Ever-changing, good guest ales and Redgarth house ale (brewer unspecified).
Q P

Peterhead

Grange Inn

West Road (A950)
☎ (0779) 73472
11–2.30, 5–11 (midnight Wed); 11–midnight Thu; 11–1am Fri & Sat; 12.30–2.30, 6.30–midnight Sun
Younger No. 3; guest beer [H]
Friendly pub on the outskirts of town: a comfortable lounge and a small, plain public bar with bucket seats. Entertainment at weekends.
P

Rothes

Station Hotel

New Street
☎ (034 03) 240
11 (12.30 Sun)–11 (midnight Fri & Sat)
Courage Directors [H]
Solid Scottish howff apparently barely touched by the 1960s and 70s.
P

Ruthven

Borve Brew House

Off A96, Aberdeen–Keith road, NE of Huntly OS506469
☎ (046 687) 343
12.30–11 (including Sun, 11.45 Fri & Sat)
Borve Ale, Bishop Elphinstone Ale, Tall Ships IPA, Cairm Porter [H]
Happiness is hand-pulled at this one-bar, one-stove, full mash brew pub in a rural converted school. The respectable and distinctive ales are brewed by a master brewer and available on rotation. If deserted, call next door!
Q P

Stonehaven

Marine Hotel

Shorehead
☎ (0569) 62155
11–midnight; 12–11 Sun
Draught Bass; guest beers [H]
Popular hotel beside a small, picturesque harbour. Crowded in summer, but you can sit on the harbour wall and relax in the sun. Two guest beers.
Q

Tarves

Globe Inn

Millbank (by B999)
☎ (065 15) 623
11–2.30, 5–midnight (1am Fri); 11–11.45 Sat
Beer range varies [H]
Small, friendly village pub with a lively, compact bar and a multi-purpose meals/pool lounge adjacent. Note: real ale is available in winter only.
Q P

Whitecairns

Whitecairns Hotel

Off B999, Aberdeen–Tarves road OS922183
☎ (0651) 862218
11–midnight (1am Fri); 11–11.45 Sat; 12–11 Sun
Broughton Greenmantle Ale; Maclay 80/- [H]
Straightforward, roadside inn with a busy, friendly, earthy bar and a popular, relaxed lounge. Attentive staff and superb value, fresh, home-cooked food, which includes a vegetarian choice. Live entertainment Fri eve. A racked (filtered) version of Orkney Dark Island is also sold.
Q P

Highland

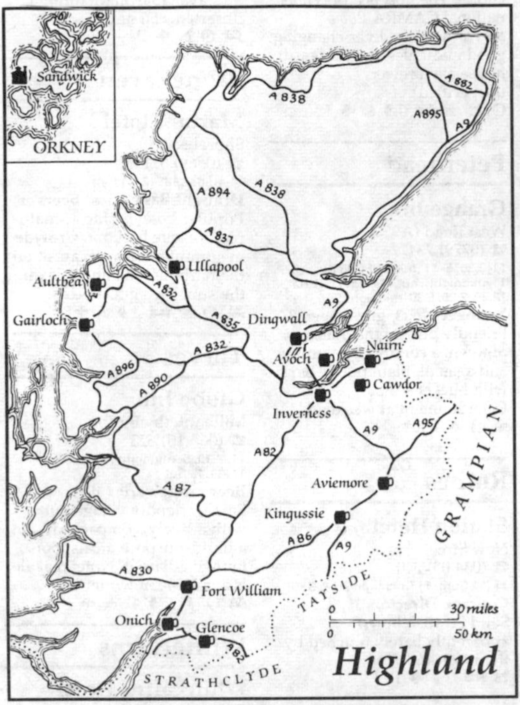

Orkney, Sandwick, Orkney

Aultbea

Drumchork Lodge Hotel

Off A832 OS879885
☎ (0445) 731242
11–11 (including Sun); closed Nov–Feb
Bateman XXXB; guest beer (H)
Splendid, well-situated hotel and idyllic Victorian retreat, enjoying spectacular coastal views (and enchanting sunsets), ideally complemented by a warm, friendly public bar and attentive hosts. Q P

Aviemore

Winking Owl

Grampian Road
☎ (0479) 810646
10.30–midnight; 12.30–11 Sun
Caledonian 70/-; Ind Coope Burton Ale; Jennings Bitter; Marston's Pedigree (H)**; guest beers**
Conversion from a farm building about 30 years ago, much patronised by skiers, hillwalkers and locals. Friendly atmosphere; families and dogs welcomed.
P

Avoch

Station Hotel

Main Street ☎ (0381) 20246
11–2.30, 5–11; 11–11.45 Sat; 12.30–11 Sun
Beer range varies (H)
Popular local in a pleasant fishing village. The hotel arrived with the railway. Good golfing and sailing nearby. Children's play area in the garden. Food all day Sat and Sun (large helpings).
P

Cawdor

Cawdor Tavern

The Lane ☎ (066 77) 316
11–2.30, 5–11; 11–11 Sun
McEwan 80/-; S&N Theakston Best Bitter; Whitbread Flowers Original; guest beer (H)
Pub close to the castle made famous by Shakespeare's *Macbeth*. The lounge bar is oak panelled, with a log fire on chilly days. Sit out on the patio in summer and enjoy the peace and tranquillity of a beautiful village. No eve meals weekdays in winter.
Q P

Dingwall

National Hotel

High Street
☎ (0349) 62166
11–midnight (1am Fri); 12.30–11.30 Sun
Caledonian 80/-; Ind Coope Burton Ale; Tetley Bitter (H)**; guest beers**
Comfortable but utilitarian bar offering four guest beers. Pot plants dominate the decor. The welcome is encouraging in this 1930s-style hotel.
P

Fort William

Alexandra Hotel

The Parade
☎ (0397) 702241
11 (12.30 Sun)–11
Caledonian Deuchars IPA, 80/- (H)
Bright, friendly bar in the town's main hotel. Whilst the hotel was built in the last century, the bar is modern but tasteful. Traditional live music from time to time. Various holiday deals available. AA three-star accommodation.
Q P

Gairloch

Old Inn

The Harbour (A832, S end of village)
☎ (0445) 2006
11–midnight (11.30 Sat); 12.30–11 Sun
Draught Bass; Younger No. 3 (H)
Old West Highland coaching inn, set by a footbridge in a quiet glen, with views of loch and mountain. A warm and friendly, family-run, country inn. Food served noon to 10pm.
P

Glencoe

Clachaig Inn

On old riverside road to rear of NT centre
☎ (085 52) 252
11 (12.30 Sun)–11 (midnight Fri, 11.30 Sat)
Alloa Arrol's 80/-; Caledonian 80/-; Ind Coope Burton Ale (H)**; guest beers**
Legendary pub which is reputedly the biggest seller of real ale in the Highlands. With limited local custom, it attracts climbers, walkers and sundry others from all over Britain and beyond. A vibrant public bar with live folk and other music.
Q P

Inverness

Gellions

10 Bridge Street (between pedestrian precinct and main bridge) ☎ (0463) 233648
9 (12.30 Sun)–11 (1am Wed–Fri, 11.45 Sat)
Courage Directors; McEwan 80/-; Whitbread Flowers Original; guest beer Ⓗ
Previously a small, town-centre hotel, now two bars and an upstairs wine bar. The cellar was the original town jail and old photographs of Inverness are on display in the lounge. No real ale in the public bar. Traditional, home-cooked meals in the wine bar; bar food in the lounge. ◖ ⊞ ♿ ▲ ≠ ♣

Glenmhor Hotel (Nicky Tams)

10 Ness Bank (riverside below castle) ☎ (0463) 234308
11–2.30, 5–11 (1am Thu & Fri, 11.45 Sat; 11–11 summer); 12.30–11 Sun
Ind Coope Burton Ale; McEwan 80/- Ⓗ
Pub in a converted stable at the rear of a busy riverside hotel. Many interesting artefacts, relating to farming and the countryside, adorn the walls. Jazz in the adjoining bistro Tue eve. Popular at weekends with the young set. Excellent bar food.
♛ ❀ ⛟ ◖ ◗ ⊞ ▲ ≠ ♣ P

Heathmount Hotel

Kingsmills Road (up hill from Marks & Spencer)
☎ (0463) 235877
11 (12 Sun)–11 (12.30am Thu & Fri, 11.30 Sat)
McEwan 80/-; S&N Theakston Best Bitter; guest beer Ⓗ
Busy lounge and public bar in the midst of a B&B area. Distinctive decor; imaginative, good value menu. Friendly and efficient service.
⛟ ◖ ◗ ⊞ ♿ ▲ ≠ ♣ P

Phoenix

108 Academy Street (right from station)
☎ (0463) 231335
11–11 (12.30am Thu & Fri)
Bass Worthington BB, Draught Bass; Maclay 80/-; Stones Best Bitter; guest beers Ⓗ
Traditional pub, 100 years old in 1994, featuring sawdust on the floor and white-aproned staff. Friendly, traditional welcome. A rare example of an island bar.
Q ☎ ◖ ◗ ⊞ ♿ ≠ ♣

Kingussie

Royal Hotel

High Street
☎ (0540) 661868
11 (12.30 Sun)–midnight (1am Thu–Sat)
Draught Bass; Ind Coope Burton Ale; Robinson's Bitter; Tetley Bitter Ⓗ**; guest beers**
Large, extended hotel which used to be a coaching house. Friendly staff; large lounge bar; food very good value. Often music at weekends. Up to nine guest beers on sale, regularly at special prices.
☎ ❀ ⛟ ◖ ◗ ♿ ▲ ≠
♣ P ⊭

Nairn

Invernairne Hotel

Thurlow Road ☎ (0667) 52039
11–11 (12.30am Fri)
McEwan 80/- *or* S&N Theakston Best Bitter *or* Younger No. 3 Ⓐ
Nice, friendly bar in a Victorian seaside hotel, with lovely wooden-panelling and a superb fireplace. The beer garden has a path leading to the promenade and beach. Children's certificate till 8.
♛ Q ☎ ❀ ⛟ ◖ ◗ P

Onich

Nether Lochaber

At E terminus of the Corran ferry
11–2.30, 5–11
Draught Bass Ⓗ
Smashing wee public bar tucked behind a hotel on the slipway to the ferry. Owned by the family for 70 years.
Q ☎ ❀ ⛟ ◖ ◗ ⊞ ▲ P

Ullapool

Ferry Boat Inn

Shore Street (overlooking Loch Broom) OS130940
☎ (0854) 612366
11–11 (including Sun)
Beer varies Ⓗ
Small, friendly lounge bar on the village waterfront, with open inland views over a sea loch. Busy throughout the summer months, with food and accommodation available if required, Mar–Oct.
♛ Q ⛟ ◖ ◗ ▲

Lothian

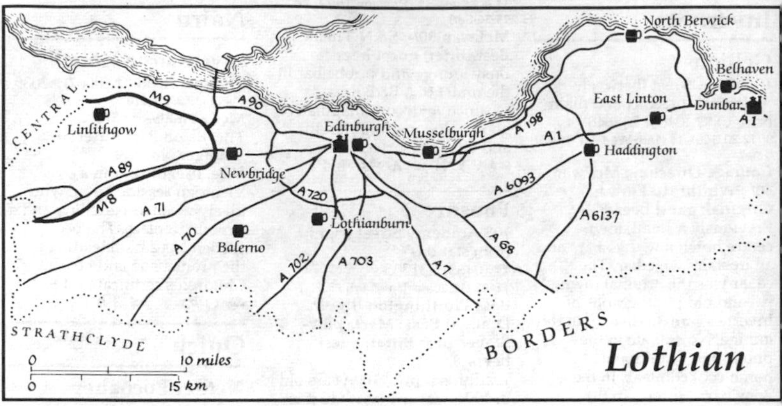

***Belhaven**, Dunbar; **Caledonian**, Edinburgh*

Balerno

Grey Horse
22 Main Street (off A70)
☎ (031) 449 3092
11–2.30, 5–11; closed Sun
Belhaven 80/-, St Andrew's Ale Ⓗ
Traditionally-run, wood-panelled gem set in a village increasingly encroached upon by the city suburbs. A fine bank of handpumps dispenses the delicious (and cheap) beer. A busy local with a number of rare brewery mirrors.
Q ⊞ ♣

Johnsburn House (Stables Bar)
64 Johnsburn Road (off A70)
☎ (031) 449 3877
12–midnight; closed Mon; 12.30–11 Sun
S&N Theakston Best Bitter Ⓗ**; guest beers**
Historic baronial mansion dating from 1760 and now Grade B-listed. The proprietor/chef has earned a well-deserved reputation for his meals. The cosy bar has a convivial atmosphere and three constantly changing guest beers; Worthington White Shield available, too.
♨ Q ♉ ❀ ◖ ◗ P

Belhaven

Mason's Arms
8 High Street (A1087, ½ mile W of Dunbar) ☎ (0368) 63700
11–2.30, 5–11 (1am Thu & Fri); 11–midnight Sat; 12.30– 6 Sun
Belhaven 80/- Ⓗ
Friendly locals' bar just up the lane from the brewery. Lovely beaches nearby in this hamlet on the outskirts of Dunbar. Eve meals Thu–Sat. Q ◖ ◗ ⊞ ♣

East Linton

Crown Hotel
27 Bridge Street (B1377)
☎ (0620) 860335
11–2.30, 5–11 (midnight Thu, 1am Fri); 11–midnight Sat; 12.30–midnight Sun
Belhaven 80/- Ⓗ
Cosy, wood-panelled, locals' bar with a large lounge to the rear. A pair of rare Dudgeon & Co windows remains as a reminder of Belhaven Brewery's past. The games room has a pool table.
♨ 🛏 ◖ ⊞ ♣

Drover's Inn
5 Bridge Street (B1377)
☎ (0620) 860298
11–2.30, 5–11; 12.30–11 Sun (11–11 summer)
Beer range varies Ⓗ
Wood-panelled lounge with a marble-topped bar and a distinct 1930s atmosphere. The service is friendly and courteous with fruit and mints provided for customers. Four, often very unusual, guest beers (but at a price!). Highly recommended food.
♨ Q ◖ ◗

Edinburgh

Bert's Bar
27 William Street
☎ (031) 225 5748
11–11 (midnight Thu–Sat); closed Sun
Alloa Arrol's 80/-; Caledonian 80/-; Greenalls Davenports Bitter; Ind Coope Burton Ale; Maclay 70/-; Taylor Landlord Ⓗ**; guest beer**
Public bar with a snug and sitting room off, and a very fine, ornate old brewery mirror. A good example of modern pub architecture, using quality wood and tiling. Seven beers, plus a guest, always available.
Q ◖ ⊞ ⇌ (Haymarket)

Bow Bar
80 West Bow (between High Street and Grassmarket)
☎ (031) 220 1823
11–11.15; closed Sun
Draught Bass; Caledonian 70/-, ERA, 80/-; Courage Directors; Taylor Landlord Ⓐ**; guest beers**
Traditional Scots, one-room, stand-up bar with efficient, friendly service. Several, long-extinct, brewery mirrors and old cigarette ephemera cover the walls. Large selection of malts, 11 cask ales (including three guest beers), and Worthington White Shield available. Q ⊞

Cumberland Bar
1–3 Cumberland Street (New Town, off Dundas St)
☎ (031) 556 9409
12–11.30; closed Sun
Draught Bass; Caledonian Deuchars IPA, 80/-; Courage Directors Ⓐ**; guest beers** Ⓗ
Completely rebuilt New Town bar, turned into a superb public bar with some peripheral seating and a cosy sitting room. Half wood-panelled and decorated with rare old brewery mirrors. Often extremely busy, but the service is fast and efficient. Fourteen beers, including eight guests on tap. ♨ Q ❀ ◖ ⊞

Drew Nicol's (Coppers)
19 Cockburn Street (near Waverley station)
☎ (031) 225 1441
11–11.45; closed Sun

Ind Coope Burton Ale; Mitchell's Best Bitter Ⓗ; guest beers
One-roomed pub for discerning beer drinkers. Two guest beers and Worthington White Shield available. The house beer is Alloa Arrol's 80/-. Can get extremely smoky and stuffy when busy.
Q ◖ ⊞ ⇌ (Waverley)

Golden Rule
30 Yeaman Place, Fountainbridge (off Dundee St, near the S&N factory)
☎ (031) 229 3413
11–11.30 (11 Mon & Tue); 12.30–11 Sun
Draught Bass; Caledonian Deuchars IPA, 80/-; Courage Directors; Harviestoun 80/-; Orkney Raven Ⓗ; guest beers
Comfortable, split-level lounge bar, with a thriving local trade, housed in a Victorian tenement building. Hot and unpleasantly smoky when busy. Live jazz Wed. Two guest beers.
⊞ ⇌ (Haymarket)

Greenmantle
133 Nicolson Street (near Odeon cinema)
☎ (031) 667 3749
11–midnight (1am Thu & Fri, 11.45 Sat); 12.30–2.30, 7–11 Sun
Broughton Greenmantle Ale; Caledonian 80/-; Ind Coope Benskins Best Bitter, Burton Ale; Tetley Bitter Ⓗ
Friendly, well-run pub with a good, mixed clientele of locals and students. Old photos show the area before planning blight smote the Southside 20 years ago. The Burton Ale *Master Cellarman* award was presented to the licensee in 1993. ◖ ⇌ (Waverley)

Halfway House
24 Fleshmarket Close (between Cockburn St and Waverley station rear entrance)
☎ (031) 225 7101
11–midnight (1am Fri & Sat); 12.30–2.30, 6.30–11 Sun
Belhaven 80/-, St Andrew's Ale; guest beer Ⓗ
Cosy, friendly, wee L-shaped howff tucked away down an Old Town close. Often crowded with newspaper workers and off-duty railwaymen.
⊞ ⇌ (Waverley)

Hampton Hotel
14 Corstorphine Road (A8, opp. Murrayfield Ice Rink)
☎ (031) 337 1130
12–2.30, 5–11.30; 12.30–3, 6.30–11.30 Sun
Belhaven 80/-, St Andrew's Ale; Caledonian 80/- Ⓐ
Family-run hotel with a split-level lounge bar. Often crowded with ice hockey and rugby supporters. Worthington White Shield available. Recommended bar lunches. Limited parking.
Q ⛟ ◖ P

Holyrood Tavern
9 Holyrood Road
☎ (031) 556 5044
12–midnight (1am Thu–Sat); 12.30–11 Sun
Alloa Arrol's 80/-; Caledonian 80/-; Ind Coope Burton Ale Ⓗ; guest beers
Deceptively large, traditional Scots bar with a long unspoilt bar and gantry. Two sitting rooms; the one at the rear has a large, but crumbling, Ushers mirror. Live music Tue–Thu. Three guest beers. Popular with students.
◖ ⊞ ⇌ (Waverley) ♣

Leslie's Bar
45 Ratcliffe Terrace
☎ (031) 667 5957
11 (12.30 Sun)–11 (12.30am Fri, 11.45 Sat)
Draught Bass; Belhaven 80/-; Caledonian 70/-, 80/- Ⓗ; guest beer
A real gem of a Victorian pub, complete with a snob screen which divides the saloon from the public bar. Architecturally one of the best of the city's pubs. ♨ Q ⊞ ♣

Malt & Hops
45 The Shore, Leith
☎ (031) 555 0083
12 (12.30 Sun)–11 (midnight Thu, 1am Fri & Sat)
Alloa Arrol's 80/-; Ansells Mild; Ind Coope Burton Ale; Marston's Pedigree; Tetley Bitter Ⓗ; guest beers
Facing onto the Water of Leith, one of the port's oldest pubs, dating from 1749 and reputed to be haunted. A one-roomed public bar with a welcoming coal fire and three guest beers.
♨ Q ◖ ⊞

Oxford Bar
8 Young Street (near Charlotte Sq) ☎ (031) 225 4262
11 (12.30 Sun)–1am
Belhaven 80/- Ⓐ, St Andrew's Ale; Courage Directors Ⓗ
Tiny yet vibrant New Town drinking shop, retaining signs of its original, early 19th-century parlour arrangement. Traditional pub music.
Q ⊞ ⇌ (Waverley)

Robbie's Bar
367 Leith Walk (A900)
☎ (031) 554 6850
12–midnight (11 Sat); 12.30–11 Sun
Draught Bass; Caledonian Deuchars IPA; Traquair House Bear Ale Ⓗ; guest beers
Victorian-style workingman's bar with interesting woodwork and gantry and rare brewery and whisky mirrors. Worthington White Shield available. Three guest beers. ⊞ ♿ ♣

Royal Ettrick Hotel
13 Ettrick Road (behind Merchiston Bowling and Tennis Club) ☎ (031) 228 6413
11 (12.30 Sun)–midnight
Draught Bass; Broughton Greenmantle Ale; Caledonian 80/- Ⓗ; guest beers
Built as a substantial town house in 1875 and now a splendid hotel set in the leafy Merchiston suburbs. The lounge bar is comfortably appointed and the restaurant/conservatory bright and airy. A good wine list and five guest beers complement the excellent meals. Jazz on Sun afternoon.
Q ❀ ⛟ ◖ ◗ P

Smithie's Ale House
49–51 Eyre Place (at Canonmills, near Powderhall Stadium) ☎ (031) 556 9805
11 (12.30 Sun)–midnight (11.45 Sat)
Draught Bass; Caledonian Deuchars IPA, 80/- Ⓗ; guest beer
Edwardian-style pub (estd. 1981), attracting a varied clientele. A relaxed atmosphere is enhanced by gas lighting and an unusual display of 19 hand-painted mirrors. Q ◖

Southsider
3–5 West Richmond Street (near Surgeon's Hall)
☎ (031) 667 2003
11–midnight (1am Fri); 12.30–11 Sun
Maclay 60/-, 70/-, 80/-, Kane's Amber Ale Ⓗ; guest beers
Busy Southside lounge bar, popular with students and discerning boozers alike. Can get hot and uncomfortably smoky. Four guest beers, Worthington White Shield and a few Belgian bottled beers always available. Family room lunchtime and afternoon. Eve meals Sun only, till 6pm.
♉ ◖ ⊞ ⇌ (Waverley) ♣

Stable Bar
Mortonhall Park, Frogston Road East (off B701, E of A702; down road by garden centre)
☎ (031) 664 0773
11–1am; 12.30–11 Sun
Caledonian 80/- Ⓗ
Friendly bar approached through an arch and a cobbled courtyard. Food is served all day (except Sun 3–6.30). Adjacent to a camping/caravan park in rural surroundings on the southern edge of the city. Children welcome. Skittle alley.
♨ Q ♉ ❀ ◖ ◗ ▲ P

Starbank Inn

64 Laverockbank Road, Newhaven (W of Leith)
☎ (031) 552 4141
11 (12.30 Sun)–11 (midnight Thu–Sat)
Belhaven 80/-; Taylor Landlord Ⓗ; guest beers
Recently refurbished by Belhaven to a very high standard and an example to other larger breweries. The bar serves an L-shaped, bare-floorboarded room which has a no-smoking conservatory extension. Fine views over the Forth to sunny Fife. Seven guest beers.
Q ◖ ◗ ⊟

Todd's Tap

42 Bernard Street
☎ (031) 556 4122
12 (12.30 Sun)–11 (midnight Thu–Sat)
Belhaven 60/-, 70/-, 80/-; Marston's Pedigree; Yates Bitter Ⓗ
Friendly, wee howff with a front bar and a back parlour, where there is a warming fire. The unique collection of specially commissioned photographs of extinct city breweries should not be missed. A veritable museum, with some outstanding breweriana. ♨ Q ◖ ⊟

Haddington

Pheasant

72 Market Street (off A1)
☎ (062 082) 6342
11 (12.30 Sun)–11 (midnight Thu–Sat)
Belhaven St Andrew's Ale; Caledonian 80/-; Ind Coope Burton Ale; Tetley Bitter Ⓗ; guest beer
Vibrant and often very noisy pub attracting young folk, especially at weekends. The long bar snakes through to the games area where Basil (surely a Norwegian Blue) holds court. ◖ ♣

Linlithgow

Four Marys

65 High Street
☎ (0506) 842171
12–2.30, 5–11 (midnight Fri); 12–midnight Sat; 12.30–2.30, 7–11 Sun
Belhaven 70/-, 80/- Ⓗ; guest beers
Attractive lounge bar with antique furniture and items reflecting the town's history. Good range of constantly changing guest beers and a large choice of malt whiskies. Twice-yearly beer festivals. CAMRA Forth Valley *Pub of the Year* 1993. No food Sun eve. ◖ ◗ ⇌

Lothianburn

Steading

118 Biggar Road (A702)
☎ (031) 445 1128
11–11.30 (midnight Fri & Sat); 12.30–11 Sun
Caledonian 70/-, Deuchars IPA, ERA, 80/-; Taylor Landlord; Tetley Bitter Ⓗ
Stone-built former cottages converted into an attractive bar and restaurant with a conservatory extension. A very popular eating establishment, but the drinking area has been preserved. Close to the Pentland Hills and an artificial ski slope. ♨ Q ❀ ◖ ◗ ♿ P

Musselburgh

Levenhall Arms

10 Ravenshaugh Road (off A199) ☎ (031) 665 3220
11 (12.30 Sun)–11 (1am Thu–Sat)
Caledonian Deuchars IPA, 80/-; Ind Coope Burton Ale Ⓗ
Busy public bar where colourful characters mix with the local clientele. Regular live music at weekends. Deservedly given the Burton Ale *Master Cellarman* award in 1993. ⊟ ♣ P

Volunteer Arms (Stagg's)

78–81 North High Street (behind Brunton Hall)
☎ (031) 665 6481
11–11; closed Sun
Draught Bass; Belhaven St Andrew's Ale; Caledonian Deuchars IPA, 80/- Ⓗ
Established in 1858, a traditional bar with wood panelling and a magnificent gantry with four polished casks and a rare brewery mirror. A busy, friendly local where the regular clientele mix with theatre-goers. ⊟ ♿ ♣ P

Newbridge

Newbridge Inn

31 Bridge Street (near M8/M9 roundabout)
☎ (031) 333 3220
11–2.30, 5–11 (midnight Thu & Fri); 11–midnight Sat; 12.30–4, 6.30–11 Sun
Caledonian 80/- Ⓗ
Former coaching inn, dating from 1683. The public bar is split into a games area (with pool table) and a drinking area; the lounge is tucked away at the rear. No food at weekends. ◖ ⊟ ♣

North Berwick

Dalrymple Arms

Quality Street ☎ (0620) 2969
11 (12.30 Sun)–11 (midnight Thu & Sat; 1am Fri)
Beer range varies Ⓗ
Popular locals' boozer in the centre of this seaside town. The cosy bar is made all the more welcoming by the blazing coal fire. TV/games room at the rear. Five guest beers and an impressive range of over 30 malt whiskies.
♨ ◖ ⊟ ⇌ ♣

The Symbols

♨	real fire	♿	easy wheelchair access
Q	quiet pub (at least one bar)	⛺	camping facilities at the pub or nearby
🐴	indoor room for children	⇌	near British Rail station
❀	garden or other outdoor drinking area	⊖	near underground station
🛏	accommodation	♣	pub games
◖	lunchtime meals	⌓	real cider
◗	evening meals	P	pub car park
⊟	public bar	⊬	no-smoking room or area

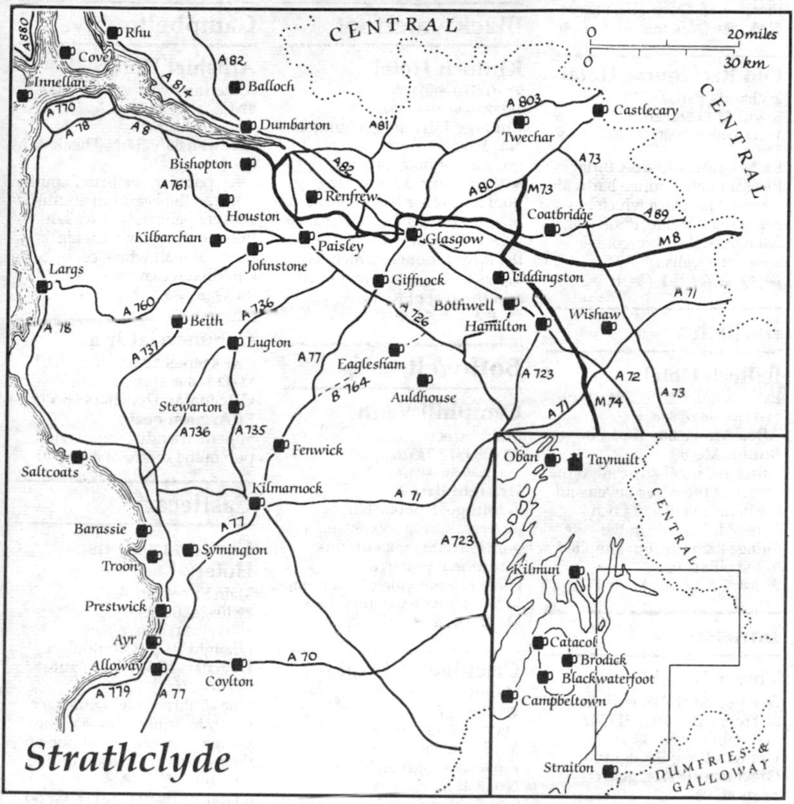

West Highland, Taynuilt

Note: licensing laws permit no entry after 11pm to pubs in the following locations: Bishopton, Houston, Johnstone, Kilbarchan, Paisley and Renfrew

Alloway

Balgarth

Dunure Road (A719, at Doonfoot, S of Ayr)
☎ (0292) 442441
11 (12.30 Sun)–11 (midnight Fri & Sat)
Whitbread Boddingtons Bitter, Flowers Original H
Former country hotel well refurbished into a Brewers Fayre pub/restaurant. The main bar features sporting activities. Children's certificate – families welcome. Opposite a popular garden centre. Food available all day.
Q P

Bellisle House Hotel (Tam O' Shanter Bar)

Bellisle Park, Doonfoot Road (A719, S of Ayr)
☎ (0292) 42331
11–11 (6 winter)
Alloa Arrol's 80/- E
Golfers' 19th hole, attached to an hotel in a splendid country park with two golf courses, gardens and a pets corner. Photos of famous golfers adorn the walls. Meals available in the cafeteria or hotel.
P

Auldhouse

Auldhouse Arms

Langlands Road (right from Strathaven Road, left at first roundabout) OS624502
☎ (035 52) 63242
12–2.30, 5–11; 12–midnight Fri & Sat; 12.30–11 Sun
Belhaven 80/- A
Rare example of a Scots country pub: several rooms and a superb wood-panelled bar. Open fires; excellent meals. Unchanged for many years.
Q P

Ayr

Chestnuts Hotel

52 Racecourse Road (A719, S of centre) ☎ (0292) 264393
11 (12 Sun)–midnight
Draught Bass; Broughton Special; guest beers H
Comfortable lounge bar with a vaulted ceiling and a collection of over 300 water jugs. Excellent bar meals. Children's certificate.
Q P

Geordie's Byre

103 Main Street (over river, N of centre) ☎ (0292) 264925
11 (12.30 Sun)–11 (midnight Thu–Sat)
Caledonian Deuchars IPA, 80/-; guest beers A
Friendly, traditional local. The back lounge (open weekends) has an interesting array of Victoriana and bric-a-brac. A monthly venue for 'Poets and

Pints' eyes. Three guest beers.
⊞ ♿ ≡ (Newton-on-Ayr) ♣

Old Racecourse Hotel
2 Victoria Park (A719, S of town) ☎ (0292) 262873
11 (12 Sun)–midnight (12.30am Fri & Sat)
S&N Theakston Best Bitter [H]
Pleasant hotel lounge bar with a central fireplace which has a copper hood/flue. Photos of winners at Ayr Racecourse adorn the walls.
♨ Q ❀ 🛏 ◐ ◑ ≡ P

Balloch

Balloch Hotel
Balloch Road ☎ (0389) 52579
11–11 (including Sun)
Alloa Arrol's 80/-; Ind Coope Burton Ale [H]
Attractive hotel adjacent to the source of the River Leven and the bonnie banks of Loch Lomond. Real ale in the lounge bar only, but supplied to the public bar.
❀ 🛏 ◐ ◑ ⊞ ▲ ≡ ♣ P

Barassie

Tower Hotel
Beach Road (B748, seafront, N of Troon) ☎ (0292) 311142
11–midnight; 12.30–11 Sun
Draught Bass; Broughton Greenmantle Ale; guest beers [H]
Attractive hotel on Troon's north beach, offering a fine view over the Firth of Clyde to Arran. Real ale is sold in both the lounge and public bars. Children welcome.
Q ❀ 🛏 ◐ ◑ ⊞ ♿ ≡ ♣ P

Beith

Anderson Hotel
17 Eglinton Street (B7049, S of centre) ☎ (050 55) 2034
11–1am (including Sun)
John Smith's Magnet [H]**; guest beer**
Small hotel on the edge of the centre of a small town between Glasgow and the main population centres of Ayrshire. Food always available. ♨ 🛏 ◐ ◑ ⊞ ♣ P

Bishopton

Golf Inn
28–30 Old Greenock Road
☎ (0505) 862303
11–2.30, 5–midnight (11.45 Sat)
Belhaven 80/-; guest beers [A]
The first-ever CAMRA meeting in Scotland was held here in 1974. A pub with a well-stocked off-licence.
Q ⊞ P

Blackwaterfoot

Kinloch Hotel
☎ (0770) 860444
11 (12.30 Sun)–12.30am
Courage Directors; Younger No. 3 [A]
Prominent hotel on the seafront with a swimming pool and other leisure facilities open to the public. The real ale is in the small public bar and the larger lounge, which has views to Campbeltown Loch and the rest of Kintyre.
☋ 🛏 ◐ ◑ ⊞ ♣ P

Bothwell

Camphill Vaults
Main Street
☎ (0698) 853526
11 (12.30 Sun)–11.45
Draught Bass [H]
A lounge, a public bar, alcoves, sitting rooms and a games room make up this traditional pub in a conservation village. Camping in Strathclyde Country Park.
Q ☋ ⊞ ▲ ♣ P

Cricklewood Hotel
Hamilton Road
☎ (0698) 853172
11 (12.30 Sun)–midnight
McEwan 80/-; Whitbread Flowers Original; Younger No. 3 [H]
Good family hotel, open at 7.30 for breakfast. High quality meals served until 11pm.
♨ ☋ ❀ 🛏 ◐ ◑ ♿ ▲ P

Brodick

Brodick Bar
Alma Road (behind Post Office) ☎ (0770) 302169
11 (12.30 Sun)–midnight
McEwan 80/-; S&N Theakston Best Bitter [H]
Modern public and lounge bars in a plain, single-storey building, just off the seafront. One of the few pubs on the island, where hotel bars are more common.
♨ ☋ ◐ ◑ ⊞

Duncan's Bar (Kingsley Hotel)
☎ (0770) 302531
11–midnight (including Sun) (11–2.30, 7.30–midnight winter; closed winter Sun)
McEwan 70/-, 80/-; S&N Theakston XB [H]
Large, comfortable bar to the side of a seashore hotel. The front garden enjoys an excellent view across the bay to Goat Fell. Regular folk and jazz nights in summer.
♨ ☋ ❀ 🛏 ◐ ◑ ♣ P

Campbeltown

Ardshiel Hotel
Kilkerran Road
☎ (0586) 552133
11–2.30, 5–midnight
McEwan 80/-; S&N Theakston XB [H]
Very popular, well-run, family hotel on the beautiful South Kintyre peninsula. Excellent home cooking and a wide range of malt whiskies. Children welcome.
♨ Q ❀ 🛏 ◐ ◑ P

Commercial Inn
Cross Street ☎ (0586) 553703
11 (12.30 Sun)–1am
Caledonian Deuchars IPA *or* **ERA; guest beer** [H]
Superb, friendly, family-run pub in the centre of town. ⊞

Castlecary

Castlecary House Hotel
Main Street (off A80)
☎ (0324) 840233
11–11 (11.30 Fri, Sat & Sun)
Draught Bass; Caledonian Deuchars IPA, 80/- [H]**; guest beers**
Fine country hotel with three separate drinking areas. The village is on the site of one of the major Roman forts on the Antonine Wall. Also nearby is a large railway viaduct. Good food in the hotel restaurant.
Q ❀ 🛏 ◐ ◑ ⊞ ♿ P

Catacol

Catacol Bay Hotel
☎ (0770) 830231
11–1am (including Sun)
Ruddles Best Bitter; John Smith's Magnet [H]**; guest beer**
Small, white-painted hotel on the shore in a hamlet, a mile south of Lochranza. Food is always available. Superb views to Kintyre. Next to the Twelve Apostles, an unusual listed terrace of houses.
♨ Q ☋ ❀ 🛏 ◐ ◑ ▲ ♣ P

Coatbridge

Carsons
Whifflet Street
☎ (0236) 422867
11–midnight; 12.30–11.45 Sun
Belhaven St Andrew's Ale; Broughton Greenmantle Ale [A]
Single-bar pub, refurbished with dark wood panels, cask ends and interesting murals. Children welcome in the lounge for meals, which are served all day until 6.30, except Sun. ◐ ◑ ⊞ P

Cove

Knockderry Hotel
Shore Road (B833)
☎ (043 684) 2283
11–midnight; 12.30–11 Sun
S&N Theakston Best Bitter; guest beer 🄷
Converted Victorian mansion, with a pleasant blend of architectural features, situated on the Rosneath peninsula. The magnificent wood-panelled lounge bar offers fine views over Loch Long. Good food. ♨ ❀ 🛏 ◖ ◗ P

Coylton

Finlayson Arms Hotel
Hillhead (A70, 4 miles E of Ayr) ☎ (0292) 570298
11–2.30, 5–midnight (1am Fri); 11–1am Sat; 12.30–midnight Sun
Broughton Special 🄷**; guest beer**
Village inn with a very comfortable lounge and excellent meals. Children welcome. Caravan Club approved site in the grounds.
♨ Q ☺ ❀ 🛏 ◖ ◗ ⊞ ▲ ♣ P

Dumbarton

Stag's Head
116 Glasgow Road
☎ (0389) 32642
11–midnight (1am Fri & Sat)
Alloa Arrol's 80/-; Ind Coope Burton Ale 🄰
Modern, open-plan bar with a lounge and traditional games areas. ❀ ◖ ◗ ≠ (East) ♣ P

Eaglesham

Cross Keys
Montgomery Street
☎ (035 53) 2002
11 (12.30 Sun)–11 (11.30 Thu, midnight Fri & Sat)
Belhaven St Andrew's Ale; Stones Best Bitter; Whitbread Flowers Original 🄷
A comfortable lounge contrasts with the traditional stone public bar in this friendly village pub. Good value food (not served Sun).
◖ ◗ ⊞

Eglinton Arms Hotel
Gilmour Street
☎ (035 53) 2631
11–2.30, 5–11 (midnight Thu–Sat)
McEwan 80/- 🄰
Popular, welcoming inn, where real ale is sold only in the cocktail bar. 🛏 ◖ ◗ P

Fenwick

King's Arms
89 Main Road (B7061, just off A77) ☎ (056 06) 276
11–2.30, 5–11.30 (midnight Thu); 11–midnight Fri & Sat; 12.30–11.30 Sun
S&N Theakston Best Bitter 🄷
Village inn on the edge of moorland; a listed building with an unusual exterior, although the lounge is standard mock 'olde-worlde'. The artwork of a well-known local cartoonist adorns the walls. Children are welcome in the snug. ☺ 🛏 ◖ ♣ P

Giffnock

MacDonald Hotel (Sportsman's Inn)
Mains Avenue, Eastwood Toll
☎ (041) 638 2225
11–11 (midnight Thu–Sat); 12.30–5, 6.30–11 Sun
S&N Theakston Best Bitter, XB, Old Peculier; Younger No. 3 🄷
Comfortable bar attached to a Thistle hotel. Two of the beers listed are available at any one time. 🛏 ≠ (Whitecraigs) P

Glasgow

Athena Taverna
780 Pollokshaws Road (1 mile from Shawlands Cross)
☎ (041) 424 0858
11–2.30, 5–11; closed Sun
Belhaven 80/-; Courage Directors 🄰**; guest beers**
Southside café-style bar with four guest ales and a selection of German and Belgian bottled beers. The adjoining Greek restaurant serves high quality food. ◖ ◗ ♿ ≠ (Queens Pk)

Babbity Bowster
16–18 Blackfriars Street
☎ (041) 552 5055
11 (12.30 Sun)–midnight
Maclay 70/-, 80/-, Kane's Amber Ale 🄰**; guest beer**
Fine Merchant City pub, popular with journalists, the legal profession and students. Excellent bar food. The only pub in the city with an outdoor drinking area. Folk band Sun night.
♨ Q ❀ 🛏 ◖ ◗ ≠ (High St) ♣ ⌓ P

Bon Accord
153 North Street (by M8, near Mitchell Library)
☎ (041) 248 2247
11–11.45; 6.30–11 Sun
Belhaven 80/-; Caledonian Deuchars IPA, 80/-, Golden Promise 🄷**; guest beers**
One-time Glasgow real ale flagship, striving to regain its former glory. Twelve beers normally available.
◖ ◗ ≠ (Charing Cross)

Boswell Hotel
27 Mansionhouse Road, Langside ☎ (041) 632 9812
11 (12.30 Sun)–11 (11.30 Tue, Fri & Sat)
Draught Bass; Belhaven 80/-; Caledonian 80/-; Courage Directors 🄷**; guest beers**
Known locally as the Country Club; a split-level bar and a separate public bar. Wide selection of guest ales, two guest ciders and many imported bottles. Most beers are in the lounge bar, which displays some amusing cartoons.
Q ☺ ❀ 🛏 ◖ ◗ ⊞ ♿ ≠ (Langside) ♣ ⌓ P

Brewery Tap
1055 Sauchiehall Street
☎ (041) 339 8866
12–11 (including Sun, midnight Fri & Sat)
Alloa Arrol's 80/- 🄴**; Belhaven 60/-** 🄰**; Harviestoun 70/-** 🄴**; Ind Coope Burton Ale** 🄷**; Tetley Bitter** 🄴**; guest beers**
Renovated pub overlooked by the art gallery and university. Its dark-painted interior is enlivened by a variety of posters and signs. Regular live music nights.
☺ ◖ ⊖ (Kelvinhall)

Mitre
12 Brunswick Street (near Tron Theatre) ☎ (041) 552 3764
11–11 (midnight Thu–Sat); 12.30–10 Sun
Caledonian 70/-; Ind Coope Burton Ale; Tetley Bitter; guest beer 🄷
Fine, small unspoilt pub with original (1866) Victorian decor, including a mini-horseshoe bar with dividing screens. Selection of bottled Belgian beers. A friendly welcome provides respite from the nearby busy street (Trongate). Meals till 6pm.
◖ ◗ ⊞ ≠ (Argyle St) ⊖ (St Enoch) ♣

Station Bar
75 Port Dundas Road
11–midnight (11.45 Sat); 12.30–11.45 Sun
Draught Bass; Caledonian Deuchars IPA; guest beer 🄷
Bar taking its name from the railway terminal formerly across the road. The decor reflects the wide range of trades in the locality. HQ of Partick Thistle's International Supporters Club and runs its own golf tournament.
≠ (Queen St)
⊖ (Cowcaddens)

Tennents
191 Byres Road
☎ (041) 339 0649
11 (12.30 Sun)–11 (midnight Fri & Sat)
Draught Bass; Broughton Greenmantle Ale, Old Jock; Caledonian Deuchars IPA, Double Amber Ale; Maclay Kane's Amber Ale 🄷**; guest beers**

Large, open and often busy pub with a rectangular bar. Usually 12 beers on offer and an annual beer festival.
◐ ⊖ (Hillhead)

Three Judges
141 Dumbarton Road (at Partick Cross)
☎ (041) 334 5569
11 (12.30 Sun)–11 (midnight Fri & Sat)
Maclay 80/-, Oat Malt Stout H**; guest beers**
Tenement corner pub. The only regular outlet for small cider producers in the West of Scotland. ⇌ (Partick)
⊖ (Kelvin Hall)

Ubiquitous Chip
Ashton Lane ☎ (041) 334 5007
11 (12.30 Sun)–11 (midnight Fri & Sat)
Caledonian Deuchars IPA, 80/- A
Part of a converted coaching inn, this former store room boasts some original features. Excellent food is served all day. Frequented by the arts and literary fraternity. Connected with one of Glasgow's finest restaurants, which does not serve chips (of course)!
Q ◐ ◑ ⊖ (Hillhead)

Victoria Bar
157–159 Bridgegate (just N of Victoria Bridge)
☎ (041) 552 6040
11–midnight (including Sun)
Broughton Greenmantle Ale, Oatmeal Stout; Jennings Cumberland Ale; Maclay 70/-, 80/- A
Well-known locally as the Vicky, a basic old-style bar with wood panelling. Friendly bar staff and regulars. Frequent folk music.
Q ⇌ (Argyle St) ⊖ (St Enoch)

Hamilton

George
18 Campbell Street
☎ (0698) 424225
11–11.45; 6.30–11 Sun
Maclay 80/-, Oat Malt Stout H**; guest beer**
Not always as reputable as it is today; even in recent years this town-centre lounge has had its ups and downs, but it is currently on an up. Children welcome in the afternoon.
◐ ⇌ (Central)

Houston

Fox & Hounds
Main Street ☎ (0505) 612248
11–1am (11.45 Sat); 12.30–11 Sun
Broughton Greenmantle Ale A**; Maclay 70/-** H

Large pub with three bars. Real ale is available in the Huntsman Lounge and the upstairs bar/restaurant. Beware of the mynah bird (mark IV). ◐ ◑ P

Innellan

Braemar Hotel
On A815 ☎ (0369) 83792
12 (12.30 Sun)–midnight
S&N Theakston Best Bitter H
Built in the 19th century as the superb seaside home of textile magnate JP Coates, with a splendid view over the Firth of Clyde from the large outdoor seating area. Children's play area. ◐ ◑ P

Johnstone

Coanes
High Street ☎ (0505) 22925
11 (6.30 Sun)–11 (midnight Thu–Fri, 11.45 Sat)
Draught Bass; Broughton Greenmantle Ale; Caledonian Deuchars IPA; Marston's Pedigree; Whitbread Boddingtons Bitter H**; guest beers**
Comfortable, town-centre pub. The bar is wood panelled, with a town house appearance, while the lounge is in modern, open-plan style. Both drinking areas are decorated with period pictures and memorabilia. No food Sun.
◐ ⇌

Kilbarchan

Trust Inn
Low Barholm ☎ (0505) 72401
5 (11 Thu–Sat)–midnight
Ind Coope Burton Ale; Tetley Bitter H
Olde-worlde pub with an atmosphere to match, set in a village steeped in local weaving history. The old weaver's cottage is situated nearby. No food Sun.
◐ ◑ ⇌ (Miliken Pk)

Kilmarnock

Hunting Lodge
14 Glencairn Square (opp. Safeway, S of centre)
☎ (0563) 22920
11–3, 5–midnight; 11–midnight Thu–Sat; 12.30–midnight Sun
Draught Bass; Broughton Greenmantle Ale; Caledonian 80/-; guest beers H
Pub with a Tudor-style interior, friendly atmosphere and good bar food at reasonable prices. Children welcome. The venue for Kilmarnock Folk Club (Thu). Occasional mini-festivals and ceilidhs held. The widest real ale choice in Ayrshire (five guests). ◐ ◑ ⇌

Kilmun

Coylet Inn
Loch Eck (A815, 9 miles N of Dunoon) ☎ (036 984) 426
11 (12.30 Sun)–2.30, 6.30–11 (5–midnight Fri & Sat)
Caledonian Deuchars IPA E**; McEwan 80/-; Younger No. 3** A
Attractive and inviting lochside bar where you can relax around the open fire after a day touring or walking in the hills. Good bar food.
◐ ◑ P

Largs

Clachan
Bath Street (B7025, just off A78) ☎ (0475) 672224
11 (12.30 Sun)–midnight (1am Thu–Sat)
Belhaven 70/-, 80/- A
Cheery, popular, single-bar pub in a side street just behind the seafront. Very busy at weekends with young people.
◐ ⇌

Lugton

Paraffin Lamp
Beith Road (A736/B777 jct)
☎ (0505) 85510
11 (12 Sun)–11
Whitbread Flowers Original; guest beer H
Brewers Fayre country pub where food is available all day. Pine furniture, flowery wallpaper and Art Deco lampshades feature. Can be very busy at times but is difficult to reach by public transport. The guest beer is from the Whitbread range. The garden has a playground.
◐ P

Oban

Oban Inn
Stafford Street ☎ (0631) 62484
11–1am (including Sun)
McEwan 80/-; S&N Theakston Best Bitter A
Fine harbourside pub which fully deserves its place as the town's best-known hostelry. The public bar has a nautical flavour, while the upstairs lounge boasts some stained-glass panels. ◐ ◑ ⇌

Paisley

Abbey Bar
Lawn Street ☎ (041) 889 8451
11–11 (1am Fri, 11.45 Sat)
McEwan 80/- H
Small town tavern situated across from the magnificent Paisley Abbey. Offers a variety of social events and runs buses

to the St Mirren games. Cosy, homely atmosphere, with friendly bar staff. ⇌ (Gilmour St)

Ale House

Shuttle Street ☎ (041) 848 7403
12–midnight (1am Fri, 11.45 Sat); 6.30–11 Sun
Beer range varies Ⓗ/Ⓐ
Pub where the pool room doubles as a function suite (live bands as advertised on blackboards). Good selection of malts; most Scottish ales available, plus occasional offerings from small English breweries (see the blackboard for a list). Requests for special beers invited. Occasional mini-festivals. Lunch served Sat. ⇌ (Canal St/Gilmour St)

Bar Point

42 Wellmeadow Street (near University) ☎ (041) 889 5188
11 (12.30 Sun)–11 (midnight Thu, 1am Fri, 11.45 Sat)
Belhaven 80/- Ⓗ
Not to be missed. The friendly, enterprising owners have made this one-bar local popular with young and old. Regular quiz nights, live bands, sporting events and outings create a club atmosphere. Children's licence till 8, if sampling the great food. ❀ ◐ ◑ ♣

Buddies

23 Broomlands Street (near University) ☎ (041) 889 5314
11–midnight (11.45 Sat); 12.30–11 Sun
Belhaven St Andrew's Ale Ⓗ
Recent decoration, including wood panelling, has enhanced this already fine corner pub which has a library, and angling and chess clubs. Good selection of bottled beers. Large, comfortable lounge.
⊟ ♿ ♣

Bull Inn

New Street ☎ (041) 887 8545
11–midnight (1am Fri, 11.45 Sat); 12–11 Sun
Belhaven 80/- Ⓐ**; Whitbread Boddingtons Bitter; Flowers Original** Ⓗ
Paisley's oldest hostelry (1901). On the Paisley Heritage Trail, with wood-panelled walls in the bar and multi-coloured snugs at the back (watch out for the pennyfarthing on the wall). Food served 12–2.30, when children are welcome.
♔ ◐ ⇌ (Gilmour St/ Canal St)

Cellar Bar

Lady Lane
11–midnight (12.30am Fri, 11.45 Sat); 6.30–11 Sun
McEwan 80/-; S&N Theakston XB Ⓗ
Bar with a comfortable lounge; busy with students during term-time. Also a haunt for DJs from the local radio station next door. ◐

Dusty Miller

31 Causeyside Street (opp. Paisley Centre shopping arcade) ☎ (041) 889 5529
11–11 (including Sun, midnight Thu & Fri, 11.45 Sat)
Caledonian 80/-; Ind Coope Burton Ale Ⓗ
Traditional bar in a busy town centre. Meals available in a separate restaurant; bar snacks served. The pub takes its name from a popular salmon fly, hence the fishing theme in the decor. ⇌ (Gilmour St)

Jays Bar

98 Causeyside Street
☎ (041) 889 5522
11–11 (midnight Thu, 1am Fri, 11.45 Sat)
Bass Worthington BB Ⓗ
Carpeted, split-level bar and lounge, with the bar on the lower level. Happy hour 4–6 Mon–Fri. Regular bar quizzes on Wed. Q ◐ ◑ ⇌ (Canal St)

RH Finlay's

33 Causeyside Street
☎ (041) 889 9036
11–midnight (1am Fri, 11.45 Sat); 6.30–11 Sun
Draught Bass Ⓗ
Attractive, refurbished, town-centre lounge and bar, recommended for its food, and ideal for the new shopping centre. Known to locals as Nancy's, after the legendary former barmaid!
◐ ⇌ (Gilmour St/Canal St)

Tannahills

100 Neilston Road (1 mile from centre) ☎ (041) 889 2491
11–11 (including Sun, midnight Thu & Fri, 11.45 Sat)
Caledonian Deuchars IPA Ⓐ
Olde-worlde-style pub with plenty of pictures of old Paisley and its poet, Robert Tannahill. ◐

Tap & Spile

Terminal Building, Glasgow Airport ☎ (041) 848 4869
10 (12.30 Sun)–11 (1am Fri, 11.45 Sat)
Alloa Arrol's 80/-; Maclay Scotch Ale; Mitchell's Best Bitter Ⓗ**; guest beers**
Formerly the Bonnie and Clyde Bar, within the main terminal, converted to a Tap & Spile in April 1992. Cask ales (including five guests) have proved very popular. ♿ P ⊁

Wee Howff

53 High Street
☎ (041) 889 2095
11–11 (11.30 Fri & Sat); closed Sun
Ind Coope Burton Ale; Tetley Bitter Ⓗ**; guest beers**
Small town-centre pub with friendly and efficient bar staff. The publican was the first *Burton Master Cellarman* in Scotland. ⇌ (Gilmour St)

Prestwick

Golf Inn

154 Main Street (A79)
☎ (0292) 77616
11–11.30 (midnight Wed, 12.30am Thu & Fri, 11.45 Sat)
Draught Bass Ⓗ
Town-centre lounge bar, convenient for public transport, with mock olde-worlde decor. Note the large photograph of an archetypal 'old worthy' over the fireplace.
☋ ❀ ◐ ♿ ⇌ ♠ P

Parkstone Hotel

Central Esplanade
☎ (0292) 77286
11 (12.30 Sun)–12.30am (1am Fri & Sat)
Belhaven 80/- Ⓗ
Comfortable lounge bar in a seafront hotel with views over to Arran. A long-established outlet for Belhaven. Children welcome at lunchtime.
♔ Q ❀ ⛿ ◐ ◑ ♿ ⇌ P

Renfrew

Ferry Inn

Clyde Street ☎ (041) 886 2104
11–11 (midnight Fri, 11.45 Sat)
Belhaven 80/- Ⓗ
Riverside local displaying photographs of the Clyde's shipbuilding past and present. Mini-beer festivals are held twice a year. Cyclists and dogs welcome. ♔ Q

Rhu

Rhu Inn

Gareloch Road (A814)
☎ (0436) 821048
11–11.45; 12.30–10.45 Sun
Broughton Greenmantle Ale, Oatmeal Stout Ⓐ**; S&N Theakston Best Bitter** Ⓗ
Small, multi-roomed village local with a drinking corridor and possibly the smallest public bar in the Strathclyde region. A very popular pub that can get packed at times.
♔ ☋ ⛿ ⊟ P

Saltcoats

Windy Ha'

31 Bradshaw Street
☎ (0294) 63688
11–midnight; 12.30–5, 7–11 Sun
Broughton Greenmantle Ale Ⓔ
Traditional, western Scotland down-to-earth local, close to the town centre and harbour; an island bar and a small snug.

Takes part in inter-pub competitions in pool, darts, dominoes and football. Probably the cheapest pint in Ayrshire. ⊞ ≢ ♣

Stewarton

Millhouse Hotel

8 Dean Street (B769 N of centre) ☎ (0560) 82255
11–midnight (including Sun)
Draught Bass [H]; Belhaven 80/- [A]
Distinctive, stone-built, riverside hotel with a small wood-panelled bar, a comfortable lounge and a function suite, where meals are served. A welcome return of real ale to Stewarton.
🛏 ◑ ◗ ⊞ ≢ ♣ P

Straiton

Black Bull Hotel

21 Main Street (B7045)
☎ (065 57) 240
11 (12 Sun)–midnight (1am Fri & Sat)
Draught Bass [H]
One of the oldest inns in the area, in a picturesque conservation village, amongst hills near the northern edge of Galloway Forest Park. Low ceilings; scenes of country life are portrayed on the walls.
🔥 Q 👶 ❀ 🛏 ◑ ◗ ⊞ P

Symington

Halfway House Hotel

Kilmarnock Road (A77, dual carriageway outside village)
☎ (0563) 830240
11–11 (including Sun)
Draught Bass; S&N Theakston Old Peculier; guest beers [H]
Recently modernised hotel on the main road from Glasgow to the Ayrshire coast, with a comfortable lounge bar and a separate function room. Wheelchair access at the rear.
Q ❀ 🛏 ◑ ◗ ♿ P

Wheatsheaf Inn

Main Street (off A77)
☎ (0563) 830307
11–2.30, 5–midnight; 11–midnight Fri–Sun
Belhaven 80/- [A]
Attractive country pub in a conservation village: a busy locals' public bar, a comfortable lounge and a dining room. Its pleasant garden is overlooked by lion sculptures. Renowned for food. 🔥 ❀ ◑ ◗ ⊞ ♿ ♣ P

Troon

Anchorage Hotel

149 Templehill (B749)
☎ (0292) 317448
11–12.30am (including Sun)
Broughton Greenmantle Ale; Caledonian 80/-; Tetley Bitter; guest beers [H]
The oldest licensed premises in Troon, renowned for the range of beers (three guests). Nautical theme; close to Troon harbour and marina, with open views to the Firth of Clyde. Petanque court. Children are welcome till 9.30. Occasional mini-festivals.
🔥 🛏 ◑ ◗ ♿ ≢ ♣ P

Harbour Bar

169 Templehill (B749)
☎ (0292) 312668
11–12.30am; 12.30–midnight Sun
Broughton Greenmantle Ale; guest beers [H]
Popular locals' bar close to the harbour and marina. One bar serves the recently refurbished lounge and public bar areas. The public bar has a pool table and three dartboards. A welcome return to the *Guide* of an old favourite. Q ♿ ≢ ♣

McKay's

69 Portland Street (A759)
☎ (0292) 311079
11 (12.30 Sun)–midnight (1am Fri & Sat)
Maclay 80/-; Mansfield Old Baily; guest beer [H]
Town-centre lounge bar with wine bar-style decor: Impressionist prints, etc. Normally quiet and relaxing, but noisier on Sat nights, when the clientele is more young and trendy. A welcome addition to Troon's real ale pubs. ❀ ◑ ◗ ≢

Twechar

Quarry Inn

Main Street ☎ (0236) 821496
11 (12.30 Sun)–11.30 (1am Fri)
Maclay 60/-, 70/-, 80/- [H]
Traditional, lively village pub in a former mining area. The bar is decorated with many brewery mirrors and warmed by old pot-bellied stoves. Famous for its Oktoberfest. Petanque played. Good prices.
🔥 ⊞ ♣ P

Uddingston

Rowan Tree

62 Old Mill Road
☎ (0698) 812678
11–11.45; 12.30–11 Sun
Maclay 80/-, Oat Malt Stout [A]
Edwardian pub comprising a public bar, lounge and a games/function room and boasting some splendid mirrors. No food Sun.
🔥 Q 👶 ◑ ⊞ ♿ ≢ P

Wishaw

Imperial (Tam Parks)

121 Main Street
☎ (0698) 372320
11–midnight; 12.30–11 Sun
S&N Theakston Old Peculier; Younger No. 3 [H]
Very much a man's pub with snug rooms (not even a ladies' loo!). ≢

Tayside

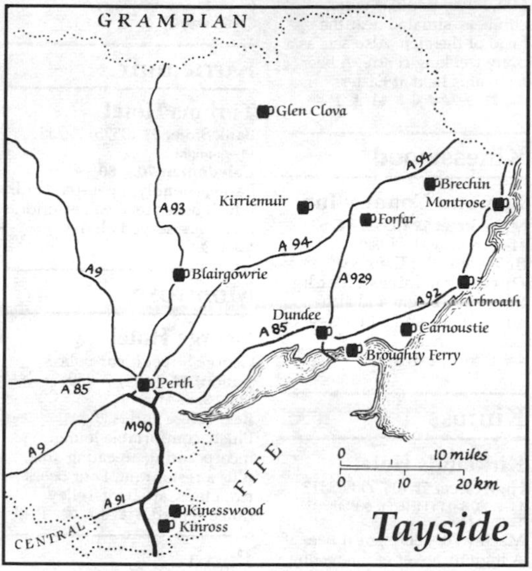

Arbroath

Victoria
15 Catherine Street
☎ (0241) 74589
11–2.30, 5–11; 11–midnight Fri & Sat; 12.30–2.30 Sun
McEwan 80/-; S&N Theakston Best Bitter; guest beers Ⓗ
Friendly, town-centre bar popular with the locals. Darts competitions Mon eve.
Q 🛏 ◐ ⊞ ▲ ≇ ♣

Blairgowrie

Kintrae House Hotel
Balmoral Road, Rattray
☎ (0250) 872106
11–2.30, 5.30–11 (11.45 Fri & Sat); 12–2, 6.30–11 Sun
Belhaven 80/-; guest beers Ⓗ
Excellent bar in a small hotel.
♛ Q 🛏 ◐ ◑ P

Brechin

Dalhousie Bar
Market Street ☎ (035 662) 2096
11 (12.30 Sun)–11
Beer range varies Ⓗ
Popular, friendly locals' bar: a wood-panelled interior with a high ceiling and a horseshoe bar. Two guest ales are served.
◐ ⊞ ♣

Broughty Ferry

Fisherman's Tavern
12 Fort Street ☎ (0382) 75941
11–midnight; 12.30–11 Sun
Belhaven 60/-, 80/-, St Andrew's Ale; Maclay 80/- Ⓗ**; guest beers**
Twenty years in the *Guide* and 1993 CAMRA National *Urban Pub of the Year* – need we say more? Q 🛏 ⊞ ≇ (limited service) ♣

Old Anchor Inn
Gray Street ☎ (0382) 737899
11.30–11.30 (midnight Fri & Sat); 6.30–11 Sun
Caledonian Deuchars IPA; McEwan 80/-; S&N Theakston Best Bitter, XB; Whitbread Boddingtons Bitter, Flowers Original Ⓐ
Long-standing bar, pleasantly refurbished with a nautical theme. Can be busy at weekends. No smoking area only at lunchtime.
◐ ♿ ≇ (limited service) ⚟

Carnoustie

Morven Hotel
28 West Path (200 yds off main road near high school)
☎ (0241) 52385
11–2.30, 4.30–midnight; 11–midnight Fri–Sun
Courage Directors; Ind Coope Burton Ale; guest beers Ⓗ
Small hotel with views over the River Tay. Beer festival held every summer, usually in June. Two guest beers.
Q ☋ ❀ 🛏 ◐ ◑ ▲ ≇ P

Dundee

Belushi's
66 North Lindsay Street (behind Overgate shopping centre) ☎ (0382) 200008
11–midnight; closed Sun & Mon
Broughton Greenmantle Ale; Caledonian 80/-; Jennings Cumberland Ale; Maclay Kane's Amber Ale; Taylor Landlord; guest beers Ⓗ
Large upstairs lounge with an up-market image. The extensive menu caters for a variety of tastes (eve meals end at 8). ◐ ◑ ≇

Frew's Bar
117 Strathmartine Road (top of Hilltown, opp. Coldside library) ☎ (0382) 810975
11–11.45; 12.30–11 Sun
Draught Bass Ⓗ
Friendly local retaining a traditional decor and atmosphere. Close to football grounds. A wide range of bottled beers includes Worthington White Shield.
⊞ ♿

Galleon Bar
2 Whitehall Crescent (near City Square) ☎ (0382) 24376
10–midnight; 12–11 Sun
Alloa Arrol's 80/-; Caledonian Deuchars IPA, 80/-; Ind Coope Burton Ale Ⓗ**; guest beers**
Large, one-room pub where any available space is crammed with memorabilia, providing much interest. Beer festivals are held during March and Oct. More ales are available at weekends, when demand increases. ◐ ◑ ≇

Mercantile Bar
100 Commercial Street (near Albert Square) ☎ (0382) 25500
11–11 (midnight Thu–Sat); 7–11 Sun
Belhaven St Andrew's Ale; Caledonian 80/-; Ind Coope Burton Ale; McEwan 80/-; Maclay 80/-; S&N Theakston Best Bitter Ⓗ
Impressive circular bar with numerous mirrors and finely crafted wooden gantries. The upstairs eating area has a no-smoking section. ◐ ◑ ≇

Phoenix
103–105 Nethergate (near university) ☎ (0382) 200014
11–midnight; 12.30–11 Sun
Beer range varies Ⓗ
Very popular, Victorian-style pub where five guest beers are taken from a wide range and are always changing. Bottled fruit beers also available.
◐ ◑ ≇

Planet Bar
161 South Road, Lochee (200 yds W of Lochee bypass south roundabout) ☎ (0382) 623258
11–11.30 (midnight Fri & Sat); 12.30–11 Sun
Harviestoun Old Manor; guest beer Ⓗ
Large lounge and a bar in fairly modern style in a popular local with a friendly atmosphere. Regulars organise wide-ranging sporting and social events. The guest beer is always from a Scottish independent brewer. ⊞ ♿ P

Speedwell Bar
165 Perth Road (1 mile W of centre) ☎ (0382) 67783
11 (12.30 Sun)–2.30, 5 (7 Sun)–11 (11.30 Wed & Thu); 11–midnight Fri & Sat
Courage Directors; Ind Coope Burton Ale Ⓗ; guest beer
Unspoilt Edwardian house, rich in mahogany; the L-shaped bar boasts snob screens and there is a separate no-smoking sitting room. Worthington White Shield available. Q ⊬

Tavern
168–172 Perth Road
☎ (0382) 27135
11–2.30, 5–11.30; 11–11.30 Wed & Thu; 11–midnight Fri & Sat; 7–11 Sun
Draught Bass; Caledonian 80/-; Stones Best Bitter Ⓗ
Popular pub with students and locals, very busy when sports events are televised. Friendly landlord and hospitable interior. ◖ ◗ ♿

Forfar

Osnaburg Bar
23 Osnaburg Street
☎ (0307) 63380
11–midnight; 12.30–11 Sun
Belhaven 80/- Ⓗ; guest beer
Friendly locals' bar situated near a home-brewing shop. Bar snacks are served all day.
◖ ⊟

Glen Clova

Clova Hotel
On B955, 15 miles N of Kirriemuir ☎ (057 55) 222
11–11; 12.30–midnight Sun
Maclay 80/-; Orkney Dark Island Ⓗ; guest beer
Hotel very popular with climbers, situated near the head of the glen. Also acts as a pony trekking centre. A beer festival is held at Easter.
♨ ⛑ ❀ ⛿ ◖ ◗ ⊟ ▲ P

Kinesswood

Lomond Country Inn
Main Street ☎ (0592) 84253
11–11 (midnight Fri & Sat)
Belhaven 80/-; Courage Directors; Jennings Bitter Ⓗ
Inn with a bright and airy atmosphere, and a fine view of Loch Leven. ♨ Q ⛑ ❀ ⛿ ◖ ◗ ♿ ▲ P ⊬

Kinross

Kirklands Hotel
High Street ☎ (0577) 863313
11–2.30, 5–11 (11.45 Fri & Sat); 12.30–11 Sun
Maclay 70/-, 80/-; guest beer Ⓗ
A high turnover of interesting guest beers (nearly 200 in the last two years) ensures local popularity here. Particularly busy at weekends. Children's certificate. ⛑ ⛿ ◖ ◗ ⊟

Muirs Inn
49 The Muirs (Milnathort road, N of centre) ☎ (0577) 862270
11–2.30, 5–11 (11.45 Fri); 11–11.45 Sat; 12.30–11 Sun
Belhaven 80/-, 90/-; Caledonian Deuchars IPA; Harviestoun Ptarmigan; Orkney Dark Island Ⓗ; guest beers
Former coaching inn displaying a number of items from a local defunct distillery in the lounge. Draws custom from a wide area. Bar snacks or restaurant meals.
Q ❀ ⛿ ⊟ ♿ ▲ P

Kirriemuir

Thrums Hotel
Bank Street ☎ (0575) 72758
11–midnight
Caledonian 70/-, 80/- Ⓗ
Large, friendly, open-plan pub which belies its bleak exterior. Meals are served all day.
⛿ ◖ ◗

Montrose

George Hotel
George Street (near police station) ☎ (0674) 75050
11 (12 Sun)–11
Beer range varies Ⓗ
Plush, comfortable lounge incorporating an eating area, plus a restaurant. Four beers from the Carlsberg-Tetley range served. ⛿ ◖ ◗ ⇌ P ⊬

Perth

Greyfriars
South Street ☎ (0738) 33036
11 (12.30 Sun)–11 (11.45 Fri & Sat)
Alloa Arrol's 80/-; Ind Coope Burton Ale; guest beers Ⓗ
Small, friendly, city-centre pub near the river. Eve meals served Fri and Sat only.
◖ ◗ ⇌ ♣

Old Ship Inn
Skinnergate ☎ (0738) 24929
11–2.30, 5–11; 11–11 Fri & Sat; closed Sun
Alloa Arrol's 80/-; Caledonian 70/-, Deuchars IPA Ⓗ
Quiet gem of a pub – Perth's oldest (established in 1665). Eve meals on Sat only.
Q ◖ ⊟ ♣

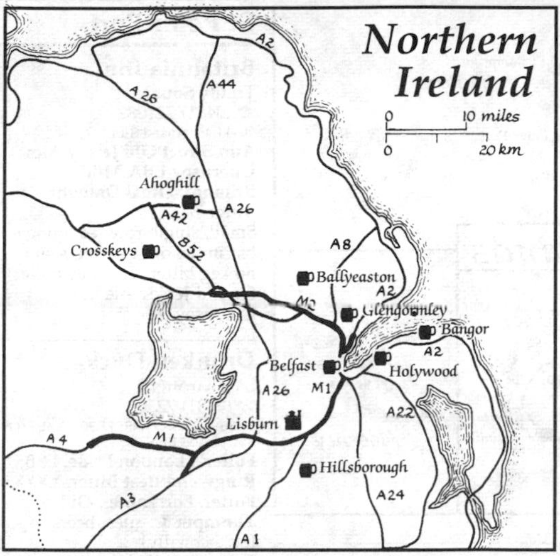

Hilden, Lisburn

Ahoghill

Rowan Arms
The Diamond ☎ (0266) 871459
11.30–11.30; closed Sun
S&N Theakston Best Bitter [H]; **Worthington White Shield**
Old, established, family-run village inn; comfortable and multi-roomed, with two fires, clocks, jugs and local memorabilia. ♔ Q ⊞ ♣ P

Ballyeaston

Carmichaels (Staffie's)
16 Ballyeaston Village
12–11; closed Sun
Worthington White Shield
Unspoilt, one-roomed country bar with agricultural appointments. No draught beer. A gem. ♔ Q P

Bangor

Jenny Watts
High Street ☎ (0247) 270401
11.30–11; 12.30–2.30, 7–10.30 Sun
S&N Theakston Best Bitter [H]
Agreeable, town-centre, Victorian-style bar and lounge with local memorabilia. Can get crowded eves.
♔ Q ❀ ◖ ⇌ (NIR)

Belfast

Bittles
100 Upper Church Lane (off Victoria Sq) ☎ (0232) 311088
11.30–11.30; 12–3 Sun, closed Sun eve
Worthington White Shield
Bijou, triangular, multi-level lounge with thespian and literary aspirations. Well conducted and cosy.
◖ ⇌ (Central NIR)

Kings Head
829 Lisburn Road (A1, opp. Kings Hall) ☎ (0232) 667805
12–11 (11.30 Fri & Sat); 7–10 Sun
Hilden Ale [H]
A series of comfortable bars and lounges around a central servery, in two adjoining Victorian villas with a modern extension. Q ❀ ◖ ⊞
⇌ (Balmoral NIR) P

Kitchen Bar & Parlour Bar
18 Victoria Square/6 Telfair Street ☎ (0232) 324901
11.30–11 (may close earlier eves); usually closed Sun
S&N Theakston Best Bitter; guest beers [H]
Two long, interconnecting bars of traditional character in a city-centre backwater. Haunt of beer buffs, railway preservationists and folk musicians. Family-run with super service and legendary lunches. Beer festivals. Don't miss.
♔ Q ◖ ⊞ ⇌ (Central NIR)

Morrisons
Bedford Street
☎ (0232) 248458
12–midnight (1 am Wed–Sat); 7–10 Sun
S&N Theakston Best Bitter; guest beers [H]
Vast recreation of a spirit grocer, with snugs, counters, whiskey mirrors and *Five Boys* memorabilia. Frequently busy with media personalities. Function room/lounge upstairs. ◖ ♿ ⇌ (Botanic NIR)

Crosskeys

Crosskeys Inn
Grange Road, Toome (off B52, 7 miles from Randalstown)
☎ (0648) 50694
11–11; 7–10.30 Sun
Worthington White Shield
Untarnished, stone wall and thatch country pub: an ex-spirit grocer and post office dating back 350 years. A listed bar, lounge and a quiet room with turf fires and local memorabilia. Irish trad. session music.
♔ Q ❀ ⊞ ♿ P

Glengormley

Crown & Shamrock
585 Antrim Road (A6, 1½ miles W of centre)
11.30–11; 7–10.30 Sun
Worthington White Shield
Unspoilt, family-run, country pub: a plain public bar with a low, panelled ceiling, traditional service and appointments, and an adjoining, intimate sitting room. Occasional draught beers. ♔ Q ❀ ⊞ P

Whittleys
Kings Moss (B56, 2½ miles NW of centre) ☎ (0232) 832438
11.30–11; closed Sun
Worthington White Shield
Old, low-ceilinged public bar with a stone tile and wood floor; lounge; railway-themed restaurant. Children catered for. ♔ Q ❀ ◖ ◗ ⊞ P

Hillsborough

Hillside
Main Street ☎ (0846) 682765
12–11; 12.30–2.30, 7–10 Sun
Hilden Ale, Great Northern Porter [H]
Comfortable village inn with stone flooring and nooks and crannies. Renowned restaurant above. ♔ Q ❀ ◖ ◗ ⊞

Plough Inn
The Square ☎ (0846) 682985
11.30–11; 12.30–2, 7–10 Sun
S&N Theakston Best Bitter [H]
Country village pub (estd. 1758) with wood-panelled seats, ceiling beams, china and memorabilia. Good restaurant (book). ♔ Q ❀ ◖ ◗ P

Holywood

Bear Tavern
High Street ☎ (0232) 426837
11.30–11 (1 am Wed–Sat); 12.30–2.30, 7–10.30 Sun
Worthington White Shield
Lively, long, narrow bar with mahogany fittings, mirrors and glass. Cosy inglenooks and a sloping stone floor beneath a Paris Docks-style, first-floor lounge. Occasional draught beer.
♔ ❀ ◖ ♿ ⇌ (NIR)

Channel Islands

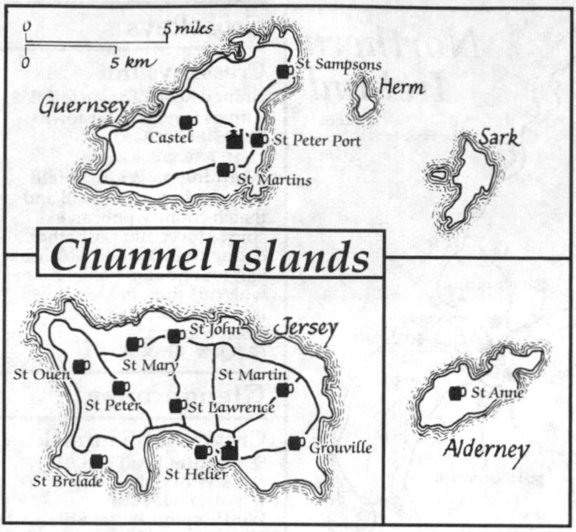

Ann Street, *St Helier;* ***Guernsey, Randalls***, *St Peter Port*

Alderney

St Anne

Coronation Inn
High Street ☎ (048 182) 2630
11 (12 Sun)–2, 5 (8 Sun)–midnight
Randalls Best Bitter [G]
Unspoilt town local with a welcoming atmosphere. Regular charity events.
♛ Q ⊞ ♣

Try also: Georgian House Hotel, Victoria St (Ringwood)

Guernsey

Castel

Fleur du Jardin
Kings Mills ☎ (0481) 57996
11–2.30, 5–11.45; closed Sun
Guernsey Real Draught Bitter [H]
Comfortable hotel in an attractive setting, named after a cow! Renovated in keeping with its farmhouse origins. The garden has a play area.
♛ Q ❀ ⊨ ◑ ◗ ⅄ P

Le Friquet Country Hotel
Le Friquet ☎ (0481) 56509
10.30–11.45; closed Sun
Randalls Best Bitter [H]
Comfortable lounge and several small rooms off, in a plush hotel with an excellent restaurant. The owner, from the North of England, is proud of the head on his ale.
ಶ ❀ ⊨ P

Try also: Venture Inn, La Villiaze, Forest (Randalls)

St Martins

Captains Hotel
La Fosse ☎ (0481) 38990
10.30–11.45; closed Sun
Guernsey Real Draught Bitter [H]
Attractive lounge bar boasting an impressive handpump. Moulin Huet Pottery and Bay are nearby. Eve meals Wed–Sat. ❀ ⊨ ◑ ◗ ♣ P

Greenacres Hotel
Les Hubits ☎ (0481) 35711
12–11.45 (12–3, 6–11.45 winter); closed Sun
Guernsey Real Draught Bitter [H]
Comfortable hotel in the countryside: a relaxed atmosphere in a cosy bar and a long lounge overlooking a pool. ♛ ❀ ⊨ ◑ P ⅄

L'Auberge Divette
Jerbourg ☎ (0481) 38485
10.30–11.45; closed Sun
Guernsey LBA Mild, Real Draught Bitter [H]
Well-run country pub with a good atmosphere, set on a cliff-bound peninsula with panoramic views from the lounge and the large, suntrap garden. Easy access to cliff paths. No eve meals Thu.
♛ ಶ ❀ ◑ ◗ ⊞ ♣ P

Try also: La Barbarie Hotel (Randalls)

St Peter Port

Britannia Inn
Trinity Square
☎ (0481) 721082
10–11.45; closed Sun
Ann Street Old Jersey Ale; Guernsey LBA Mild, Britannia, Real Draught Bitter [H]
Small, single-roomed lounge bar in the old quarter, selling no keg bitter. The only outlet for Old Jersey Ale in Guernsey. ♣

Drunken Duck
La Charotterie
☎ (0481) 725045
11.30–2.30, 4–11.45; 11.30–11.45 Fri & Sat; closed Sun
Fuller's London Pride, ESB; Ringwood Best Bitter, XXXX Porter, Fortyniner, Old Thumper [G]; guest beers (occasionally)
Cosy, friendly, two-roomed pub on the southern edge of town. Impromptu folk night Tue and regular quiz nights. Occasional ciders. ◑ ♣

Foresters Inn
St Georges Esplanade
☎ (0481) 723583
10.30–2, 5.30–11.45; 10.30–11.45 Fri & Sat; closed Sun
Guernsey LBA Mild [H]
Lively local overlooking Belle Greve Bay, with a functional bar and a comfortable lounge.
⊨ ◑ ⊞ ♣

Prince of Wales
Manor Place (top of Smith Street) ☎ (0481) 720166
10–11.45; closed Sun
Randalls Best Mild [G], **Best Bitter** [H]
Interesting old hostelry on the edge of the shopping area. Real ale is served in the upper bar only. ◑ ♣

Rohais Inn
Rohais ☎ (0481) 720060
10.30–2, 4–11.45; 10.30–11.45 Sat; closed Sun
Guernsey LBA Mild [G]
Unsophisticated local with one large bar and very limited parking; situated on the western outskirts of town. Specialises in pub games.
⊞ ♣ P

Ship & Crown
North Pier Steps
☎ (0481) 721368
10–11.45; closed Sun
Guernsey Real Draught Bitter [H]
Busy town pub opposite the main marina for visiting yachts. Decorated with pictures of ships and local shipwrecks, and popular with

bankers and yachtsmen at lunchtime. ◐

Thomas de la Rue

The Pollet ☎ (0481) 714990
10–11.45; closed Sun
Guernsey LBA Mild (summer), **Real Draught Bitter** Ⓗ
Small lower bar and a split-level lounge with views over the harbour. The famous banknote printer, de la Rue, set up business here in the 18th century. The atmosphere varies from professional workers at lunchtime to a vibrant disco-bar in the eve.
◐ ♿

Try also: Salerie Inn, Glategny Esplanade (Guernsey)

St Sampsons

Pony Inn

Petites Capelles
☎ (0481) 44374
10.30–11.45; closed Sun
Guernsey LBA Mild, Real Draught Bitter Ⓗ
Popular local with three varied bars. Handy for Guernsey Candles and Oatlands Craft Centre. Regular meat draws are held. Eve meals in winter, Fri and Sat only.
❀ ◐ ◗ ⊟ ♣ P

Jersey

Grouville

Seymour Inn

La Rocque (Gorey coast road)
☎ (0534) 54558
10–11; 11–1, 4.30–11 Sun
Ann Street Old Jersey Ale, Ann's Treat, Winter Ale; Guernsey LBA Mild, Real Draught Bitter Ⓗ
Popular coastal pub with a real ale bar, good food, good atmosphere and friendly staff. No meals Sun.
♨ Q ❀ ◐ ◗ ⊟ ♿ ♣ P

Try also: Grouville Tavern (Ann Street); **Pembroke** (Randalls)

St Brelade

La Pulente

La Pulente (southern end of St Ouen's Bay) ☎ (0534) 41760
9–11; 11–1, 4.30–11 Sun
Draught Bass; Whitbread Boddingtons Bitter Ⓗ**; guest beers**
Situated on the unspoilt western coast with panoramic views, a comfortable lounge and a lively locals' bar. Good value food includes some unusual special dishes (not served Sun).
♨ Q ♉ ❀ ◐ ◗ ⊟ ♣ P

Olde Smugglers Inn

Ouaisne Bay ☎ (0534) 41510
11–11; 11–1, 4.30–11 Sun
Draught Bass; Whitbread Boddingtons Bitter Ⓗ**; guest beers**
Historic pub where a folk club meets Sun nights. Good food (not served Sun); good for families and near the beach.
♨ Q ♉ ◐ ◗ P

Try also: Olde Portelet (Randalls)

St Helier

Cock & Bottle

Royal Square ☎ (0534) 22184
10–11; 11–1, 4.30–11 Sun
Guernsey Real Draught Bitter Ⓗ
Historic pub, recently refurbished and situated by the seat of Government. No food Sun. Q ◐

Lamplighter

Mulcaster Street
☎ (0534) 23119
10–11; 11–1, 4.30–11 Sun
Draught Bass; Whitbread Boddingtons Bitter Ⓗ**; guest beers**
Entertaining, gas-lit town pub with a good ambience and a varied clientele. Jersey's only outlet for real cider (Bulmers). No food Sun. Q ◐ ♣ ⌓

Peirson

Royal Square ☎ (0534) 22726
10–11; 11–1, 4.30–11 Sun
Bass Worthington BB, Draught Bass Ⓗ
Historic pub near the seat of Government, with a restaurant upstairs (no food Sun). Q ◐

Try also: Customs, Esplanade; **Don,** The Parade (both Randalls)

St John

Les Fontaines

Route du Nord
☎ (0534) 862707
10–11; 11–1, 4.30–11 Sun
Whitbread Boddingtons Bitter Ⓗ
14th-century granite pub with a traditional locals' bar, situated by the cliffs on the north coast. No food Sun.
♨ Q ♉ ❀ ◐ ◗ ⊟ ♿ P

St Lawrence

British Union

Main Road ☎ (0534) 861070
10.30–11; 11–1, 4.30–11 Sun
Guernsey LBA Mild, Real Draught Bitter Ⓗ
One of the best pubs on the island: good local flavour with friendly staff and good food. Brilliant for families, with games for children.
♨ Q ♉ ❀ ◐ ◗ ⊟ ♣

St Martin

Anne Port Bay Hotel

Anne Port ☎ (0534) 52058
11–2.30 (1 Sun), 5 (4.30 Sun)–11; 11–11 Sat
Draught Bass; Marston's Pedigree Ⓖ**; guest beers**
Cosy east coast hotel above a picturesque bay. No food Sun.
Q ♉ 🛏 ◐ ◗ P

Rozel Bay Inn

Rozel Bay ☎ (0534) 863438
10–11; 11–1, 4.30–11 Sun
Draught Bass; Whitbread Boddingtons Bitter Ⓗ
Small, traditional two-bar pub situated near a picturesque harbour. No food Sun.
♨ Q ◐ ⊟ P

St Mary

St Mary's Country Hotel

☎ (0534) 481561
10–11; 11–1, 4.30–11 Sun
Bass Worthington BB, Draught Bass Ⓗ
Smart country pub with a good, extensive menu. No food Sun; eve meals Fri and Sat only. Spacious children's area.
♨ Q ♉ ❀ ◐ ◗ ⊟ ♣ P

St Ouen

Moulin de Lecq

Greve de Lecq Bay
☎ (0534) 482818
11–11; 11–1, 4.30–11 Sun
Ann Street Old Jersey Ale, Ann's Treat, Winter Ale; Guernsey LBA Mild, Real Draught Bitter Ⓗ
Interesting pub with an old working water wheel. A good-sized outdoor area hosts summer barbecues.
♨ Q ♉ ❀ ◐ ◗ P

St Peter

Star (& Tipsy Toad Brewery)

La Route de Beaumont
☎ (0534) 485556
10–11; 11–1, 4.30–11 Sun
Tipsy Toad Cyril's Bitter, Agile Frog, JB, Horny Toad, Pale Ale, Star Drooper Ⓗ**; guest beers**
Beautifully restored and extended Victorian pub, incorporating Jersey's microbrewery. Good food (not served Sun); frequent live music. Note: The beers served here are kept under a blanket of nitrogen, a system currently under review by CAMRA.
♨ ♉ ❀ ◐ ◗ ♿ ♣ P

Isle of Man

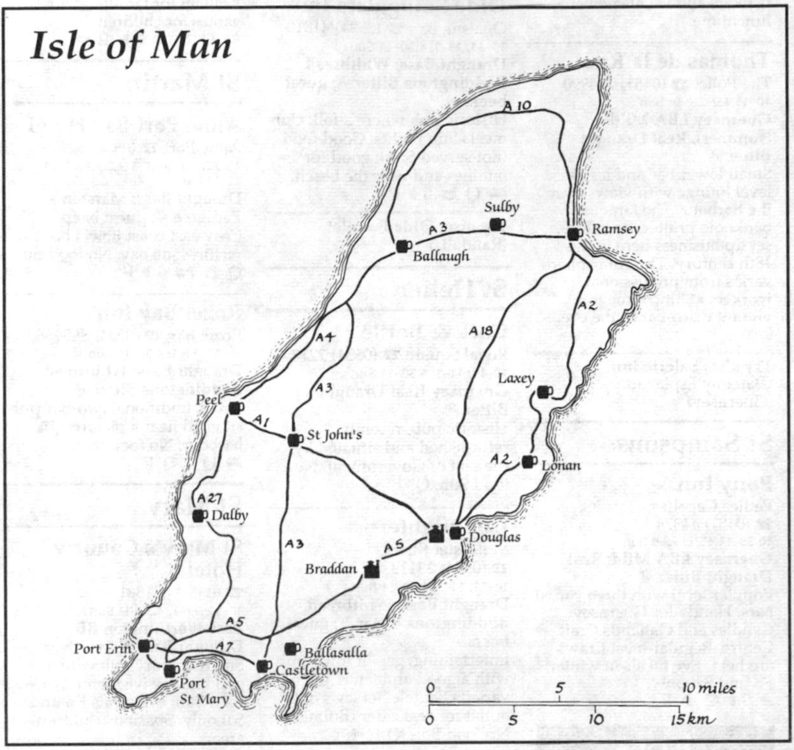

🏭 ***Bushy's**, Braddan; **Isle of Man**, Douglas*

Sunday hours on the Isle of Man are 12–1.30, 8–10

Ballasalla

Whitestone

At A5/A8 jct ☎ (0624) 822334
12–10.45
Okells Bitter Ⓗ
Excellent village pub serving good lunches, including daily specials. Popular with locals and visitors. Well decorated and spacious.
Q ❀ ◐ ♿ ⇌ (IMR) ♣ P

Ballaugh

Raven

Ballaugh Bridge
☎ (0624) 897272
12–10.45
Marston's Pedigree; Okells Bitter; Whitbread Boddingtons Mild Ⓗ
Recently refurbished village pub on the TT course. The outdoor balcony is good for watching riders negotiate the notorious Ballaugh bridge.
Q ❀ ◐ ▲ ♣ P

Try also: Mitre, Kirk Michael (Okells)

Castletown

Castle Arms (Glue Pot)

Quayside ☎ (0624) 824673
12–10.45
Cains Mild, Bitter; Tetley Bitter Ⓗ
Tastefully extended, rather than gutted, the 'Glue Pot' retains its loyal local support. What more comfortable source of refreshment could complement historic Castle Rushen? No food Sun. ◐

Duck's Nest

Station Road
☎ (0624) 823282
12–10.45
Bushy's Mild, Best Bitter, Old Bushy Tail Ⓗ**; guest beers**
An excellent excuse for leaving the steam train, the 'Duck' offers much improved facilities without great changes to the layout. Note the fine wooden flooring and bar counter. Bushy's 'flagship' in the south. No food Sun.
🔥 ❀ ◐ ⇌ (IMR) ♣

Union

☎ (0624) 823214
11.30–10.45
Okells Bitter Ⓗ
For a New Year's Day charity dip in the harbour, contact the Ale-Drinkers' Society based here. The less adventurous may stick to the friendly and comfortable surroundings, unsullied by the aromas of pub catering. ♣

Dalby

Ballacallin Hotel

On A27
☎ (0624) 842030
12–2.30, 5.30–10.45; 12–10.45 Sat & summer
Okells Bitter Ⓗ
Friendly country pub/hotel with good views to the sea and the Mountains of Mourne; superb summer sunsets. Large dining/function room as well as two bars. Minibus for parties of eight or more. Check before taking children. Superb food.
🔥 ❀ 🛏 ◐ ◑ ♣ P

Douglas

Albert
3 Chapel Row (next to bus station) ☎ (0624) 673632
11–10.45
Okells Mild, Bitter Ⓗ
Straightforward drinkers' pub popular with the locals. Toasties lunchtime.
⇌ (IMR) ♣

Bushy's Bar
Victoria Street (opp. sea terminal) ☎ (0624) 675139
12–10.45
Bushy's Mild, Best Bitter, Piston Brew, Old Bushy Tail Ⓗ
Bushy's caters for all tastes and ages, serving good lunches and breakfasts. Very lively at night – late licence in the music room with live bands. TT memorabilia.
♨ 👪 ❀ ◐ ⇌ (IMR) ♣

Foresters Arms
St Georges Street
☎ (0624) 676509
12–10.45
Okells Mild, Bitter Ⓗ
Traditional Manx pub serving the finance district. Very popular with locals and business people. Toasties and baps all day. ♨ ⇌ (IMR) ♣

Old Market Inn
Chapel Row (opp. bus station)
☎ (0624) 675202
12–10.45
Bushy's Best Bitter; Okells Bitter Ⓗ
Look for the mural over the bar in this very popular local with a community spirit and excellent atmosphere.
♨ ⊟ ⇌ (IMR) ♣

Terminus Tavern
Strathallan Crescent
☎ (0624) 624312
12–10.30
Okells Mild, Bitter Ⓗ
Pub at the end of the promenade, by the electric tram terminus. Very good selection of home-cooked food.
♨ Q ❀ ◐ ◑ ⊟ ♿
⇌ (MER) ♣ P

Tramshunters Arms
Harris Promenade
☎ (0624) 621521
12–10.45
Okells Mild, Bitter Ⓗ**; guest beers**
Stylish pub catering for all tastes, attached to the Sefton Hotel. Always 14 cask ales; a popular haunt for beer enthusiasts. Excellent value lunches: the beef baps have to be seen! Pictures and prints of trams. 🛏 ◐ ♿ ♣ P

Waterloo
Strand Street ☎ (0624) 676833
12 (11 summer)–10.45
Okells Mild, Bitter Ⓗ
Traditional and hospitable local in the heart of a shopping area. A wonderful haven from the hustle and bustle. ♣

Laxey

New Inn
New Road ☎ (0624) 861077
12–10.45
Bushy's Best Bitter; Okells Bitter; guest beers Ⓗ
Traditional, very friendly village pub with a great display of photographs for soap fans. Regular turnover of guest beers; very genial host. No meals Sun. ❀ 🛏 ◐ ◑
⊟ ▲ ⇌ (MER) ♣ P

Shore
Old Laxey ☎ (0624) 861509
12–2.30 (not Mon or Tue in winter), 4.30–10.45 (12–10.45 summer)
Bushy's Best Bitter; Okells Bitter Ⓗ
Riverside pub near the harbour, with a popular garden. The spacious bar has a strong nautical flavour, with a bar front rescued from an old church. Pleasant riverside walks nearby. Children's play area. Breakfasts during TT week. ♨ ❀ ◐ ◑ ▲ P

Lonan

Liverpool Arms
Onchan (main Onchan–Laxey coast road) ☎ (0624) 674787
12–10.30
Okells Mild, Bitter Ⓗ
Old halfway house with a convivial atmosphere. Good lunches; pool and darts played. The lounge tables are converted Singer sewing machines. ♨ Q ❀ ◐ ⊟
⇌ (MER) ♣ P

Peel

Royal
Athol Street (opp. bus station)
☎ (0624) 842217
11–10.45
Okells Mild, Bitter Ⓗ
Popular local with a small front room, a main bar and a side room leading to the garden, which includes a covered area. Handy for the shops. Q ❀ ▲

Whitehouse
Tynwald Road
☎ (0624) 842252
11–11
Draught Bass; Bushy's Best Bitter; Cains Bitter; Marston's Pedigree; Okells Mild, Bitter; Whitbread Flowers Original Ⓗ
Comfortable, friendly pub with a cosy snug (Captain's Cabin) and games and music rooms (Manx music Sat nights). Old local prints. CAMRA IOM *Pub of the Year* 1992. ♨ Q ❀ ▲ ♣ P

Port Erin

Falcon's Nest Hotel
Station Road ☎ (0624) 834077
11–10.45
Bushy's Best Bitter; Okells Bitter; Tetley Bitter; Whitbread Boddingtons Bitter Ⓗ
The wood-panelled lounge of this traditional hotel overlooks the beach. Popular with locals; friendly service.
♨ 🛏 ◐ ◑ ⇌ (IMR) P

Port St Mary

Albert
Athol Street ☎ (0624) 832118
12–10.45
Bushy's Best Bitter; Okells Bitter; Tetley Bitter Ⓗ
Excellent, traditional pub overlooking the harbour: a friendly public bar, cosy lounge and a pool room. Popular with locals and fishermen. Good value food.
♨ Q ◐ ⊟ ♣ P

Ramsey

Britannia
Waterloo Road
☎ (0624) 816547
11.30–10.45
Okells Mild, Bitter Ⓗ
Recently refurbished to provide a pleasant lounge whilst retaining the character of the traditional bar. Excellent location, opposite the electric railway station. ♨ Q ❀ ◐
⊟ ♿ ⇌ (MER) ♣

St John's

Central
Station Road ☎ (0624) 801372
6.30 (2 Wed, 4 Thu & Fri, 12 Sat)–10.45 (12–10.45 summer)
Bass Worthington BB; Cains Bitter; Okells Bitter Ⓗ**; guest beers**
Recently refurbished pub next to the cattle market, with roadside tables. A welcome stop for walkers on the Heritage Trail. The Tynwald Ceremony takes place up the road (5th July). Live music Sun and occasionally other nights.
♨ ❀ ◐ ♣ P

Sulby

Sulby Glen Hotel
Main Road (on TT course)
☎ (0624) 897240
12–10.45
Bushy's Best Bitter; Okells Bitter Ⓗ
Good example of a Manx country pub, displaying local history plus TT memorabilia. A good mix of local activities and visitor interest. Ideal for exploring the north. Excellent all round.
♨ ❀ 🛏 ◐ ◑ ⊟ ▲ ♣ P

THE BREWERIES

THE 1994 BREWERIES SECTION is the biggest ever, undisputable evidence that the real ale boom continues apace. Around thirty new names appear in the Independents section, some are brew pubs which have expanded their operations, others are brand new enterprises chancing their arm in a highly competitive guest beer market. When added to the twenty or so new breweries last year, this means that the Independents section has expanded by more than 30% in two years. And the trend looks set to continue, as more and more microbreweries are planned.

The major developments in the brewing industry this year thankfully do not concern mergers and take-overs, although the threat of acquisition has not disappeared. Will Greene King dare to bid again for Morland, for instance, or will Greenalls, new owners of Devenish, be looking for other pub groups or breweries to take under its wing?

The real changes have come on the technical side. In June 1993, a new system of assessing the duty on beer payable by breweries to Customs and Excise came into force. In the past, the original gravity (OG) of a beer was the marker employed to work out a brewery's tax bill; now it is the alcohol by volume figure (ABV). The difference is that the former is a reading of the potential strength of the beer taken before fermentation begins, and the latter is the actual alcohol content of the finished brew.

The change was introduced to benefit small brewers. Under the old system, a 6% allowance was given to producers to cover wastage between the time of the OG reading and the beer leaving the brewery. The larger brewers were able to minimise wastage through streamlining production and gained unfairly from the system. Now all brewers are treated equally. Sadly, the big brewers have not been satisfied and some have looked to offset the losses resulting from the new system by reducing the ABV of some beers. In other words, they have weakened the beer in order to pay less tax. The most notable cases involve Courage, whose Webster's Yorkshire Bitter amongst other ales, and Holsten Pils primarily amongst lagers, have suffered. It is noticeable that prices in the pub have not been reduced accordingly.

Another consequence of the change in duty assessment is that the OG figure is no longer declared by some brewers. Whilst all brewers, big and small, must now publish their ABV ratings, not all had done so before we went to press. The result is that some beers listed have OG figures but no

ABVs, and some newer beers have ABVs but no OGs. Hopefully, details will be uniform next year.

Brewing Fashions

IF THE TREND LAST YEAR was to porters and stouts, this year's movement has been towards seasonal and special brews. Many new breweries produce beers geared to the time of year, Coach House for example, but this has now been copied by larger independents like Shepherd Neame and even a national like Whitbread, which now brews Summer Ale as well as Winter Royal. McMullen and Marston's are just two breweries which have launched special, limited-period ales, through their Special Reserve and Head Brewer's Choice, respectively.

On the down side, the Carlsberg-Tetley merger was finally approved, bringing further rationalisation to the British brewing industry, and it was depressing to see Whitbread draw to a close over 100 years of production at Sheffield's Exchange Brewery, leaving the giant with only three cask beer plants to its name. Some microbreweries have also felt the pinch of competition and have not survived. Forbes in Suffolk, Keystone in Yorkshire and Pack Horse in Kent spring to mind. Pub groups continue to flourish and hopefully, as they grow in stature, they may broaden their beer ranges and give opportunities to smaller breweries and not just national brand producers who seem to have sewn up much of this particular market.

About the Breweries Section

THE BREWERIES SECTION is, as usual, divided into four parts. The Independents come first, followed by the Nationals. Brew Pubs, brewing mostly for their own consumption rather than a free trade, come next, with the country's major Pub Groups following. Many other smaller pub-owning companies exist, some off-shoots of the national brewers, but these are the biggest independent operators.

The real ales produced by all the breweries are listed in ascending original gravity order and most are furnished with tasting notes by CAMRA tasting panels. The panels operate throughout the year, tasting beers in pubs, not brewery sample rooms or laboratories, so that the descriptions relate to beer which the public actually finds on sale. Those beers which have not been officially tasted are marked with an asterisk. The tankard symbol alongside the names of some beers indicates that they are *Good Beer Guide Beers of the Year*. These have been chosen by CAMRA tasting panels, by votes from the general public at CAMRA beer festivals, and from a poll of CAMRA members. A full list of *Beers of the Year* can be found on page 225.

The Independents

ADNAMS — **Adnams and Company PLC, Sole Bay Brewery, Southwold, Suffolk IP18 6JW. Tel. (0502) 722424**

East Anglia's seaside brewery, established in 1890, whose local deliveries are still made by horse drays. Real ale is available in all its 115 pubs (50 leased from Whitbread in June 1992). It also supplies almost 500 other outlets direct, with over 80% of beer production now sold outside the Adnams estate. Adnams Extra has been relaunched to make it more widely available.

Mild (OG 1034, ABV 3.2%) Classic dark mild. The aroma is an inviting blend of fruit, malts and hops which leads through to a malty and fruity flavour. Long dry finish.

Bitter (OG 1036, ABV 3.6%) Good session beer with an abundance of hops and bitterness throughout. Dry, often citrus-like aftertaste.

Old (OG 1042, ABV 4.1%) Rich red/brown winter ale. The flavour and aroma are a well-balanced blend of roast grain, malt and fruit. A rich bittersweet finish lingers.

Extra (OG 1043, ABV 4.3%) This amber beer is somewhat of a rarity in Suffolk, but worth the search. The overwhelmingly hoppy aroma and flavour of citrus fruits are complemented by a tangy, dry aftertaste. *Champion Beer of Britain* 1993.

Broadside (OG 1049, ABV 4.4%) A full-bodied beer with a welcoming aroma of fruit and malt. This leads through to a well-balanced blend of malt, hops and fruit, with a bittersweet edge. Dry, faintly fruity finish.

Tally Ho (OG 1075, ABV 6.2%) Rich seasonal brew whose aroma of malt and fruit conjures up the spirit of Christmas. On the palate, bittersweet fruit flavours linger through to the finish.

ALLIED BREWERIES — See Nationals, Carlsberg-Tetley.

ALLOA — See Nationals, Carlsberg-Tetley.

ANN STREET — **Ann Street Brewery, Ann Street, St Helier, Jersey, CI JE1 1BZ. Tel. (0534) 31561**

Brewery owning 51 pubs which started brewing cask beer again in 1992 after a break of 30 years. Since then it has increased its range to include a winter ale and a summer ale. The number of its own pubs taking the beer has increased this year by ten to a total of 14. Guernsey Brewery beers are also available.

Old Jersey Ale* (OG 1036, ABV 3.6%)

Ann's Treat* (OG 1050, ABV 5%) Initially a summer beer.

Mary Ann Winter Ale (OG 1078, ABV 8.5%) New beer available October–April.

ANSELLS — See Nationals, Carlsberg-Tetley.

ARCHERS — **Archers Ales Ltd., Station Ind. Estate, London Street, Swindon, Wilts. SN1 5DY. Tel. (0793) 496789**

A small brewery, set up in 1979, which has grown very successfully and now supplies 180 free trade outlets from Oxford to Bath (via wholesalers), plus four tied houses. Brewing close to capacity, it is now ready for its second expansion.

Village Bitter (OG 1035, ABV 3.5%) Dry and well balanced, with a full body for its gravity. Malty and fruity in the nose, then a fresh, hoppy flavour with balancing malt, and a hoppy, fruity finish.

Best Bitter (OG 1040, ABV 4%) Slightly sweeter and rounder than Village Bitter, with a malty, fruity aroma and a pronounced bitter finish.

Black Jack Porter (OG 1046, ABV 4.6%) A winter brew: a black beer with intense roast malt dominant on the tongue. The aroma is fruity and there is some sweetness on the palate, but the finish is pure roast grain.

Golden Bitter (OG 1046, ABV 4.7%) A full-bodied, hoppy, straw-coloured brew with an underlying fruity sweetness. Very little aroma, but a strong bitter finish.

Old Cobleigh's* (OG 1065, ABV 6.5%) Formerly known as Headbanger. Almost a barley wine in style, enjoying a full flavour. Sweet and powerful, with a pleasant, dry finish.

ARKELL'S

Arkell's Brewery Ltd., Kingsdown, Swindon, Wilts. SN2 6RU. Tel. (0793) 823026

Established in 1843 and now one of the few remaining breweries whose shares are all held by a family; Managing Director, James Arkell, is a great-great-grandson of founder John Arkell. A gradual expansion is taking place in the tied estate with single pubs being acquired, mainly in the M4 corridor. Almost all 82 tied pubs serve real ale (four still use top pressure). Also supplies 160 free trade outlets.

2B (OG 1032, ABV 3.2%) Well-balanced, pale beer. Essentially bitter, but with a hint of fruit and honey. A most refreshing session or lunchtime beer with good body for its OG.

Mash Tun Mild (OG 1036, ABV 3.5%) A very dark, almost black mild ale with a predominantly malt/roast flavour and a similar faint aroma. There is bitterness and roast in the aftertaste. Hard to find on its home territory.

3B (OG 1040, ABV 4%) An unusual darkish bitter which is coloured by the use of crystal malt, giving a nutty flavour which persists throughout and combines with bitterness in the aftertaste.

Kingsdown Ale (OG 1052, ABV 5%) A darker, stronger version of 3B with which it is sometimes parti-gyled (derived from the same original brew). A distinct roast/fruit flavour persists with a lingering dry aftertaste.

Noel Ale (OG 1055, ABV 5.5%) Worth spending Christmas in Swindon for. A sweetish nose followed by powerful fruit/hop flavour with lingering bittersweet aftertaste.

3A (Anniversary Ale)* (OG 1075, ABV 6%) New on draught in autumn 1993 for the brewery's 150th anniversary.

ARUNDEL

Arundel Brewery, Ford Airfield Estate, Ford, Arundel, W. Sussex BN18 0BE. Tel. (0903) 733111

Set up in 1992, the first brewery in this historic town for over 50 years. All the beers are from authentic Sussex recipes, brewed without additives. Old Knucker was named after a local legend of a dragon, Knucker, who allegedly terrorised the townsfolk for many years before being slain by a local hero, whose grave can still be visited today.

Best Bitter (OG 1040, ABV 4%) Pale tawny brew with a good hop and fruit aroma with underlying malt. Its dry, hoppy flavour is balanced by malt and fruit and leads through to a fruity, dry aftertaste.

Stronghold (OG 1050, ABV 5%) Rich malt predominates in this brew, with a good balance of roast, fruit and hops on a bittersweet base.

> Beers marked with an asterisk have not been tasted by official CAMRA tasting panels. However, some of these beers do carry brief descriptions derived from limited samplings or other sources, and can be used for rough guidance.

Old Knucker (OG 1055, ABV 5.5%) Dark, full-bodied beer, with strong roast malt character throughout. The flavour is a complex blend of sweet fruit and caramel maltiness, which balances the dry roast bitterness. This is mirrored in the aftertaste; in the aroma the roast malt is complemented by fruit, caramel and malt with some hops.

ASH VINE **Ash Vine Brewery (South West) Ltd., The White Hart, Trudoxhill, Frome, Somerset BA11 5DP. Tel. (0373) 836344**

Set up in 1987 near Taunton, but moved to the White Hart in January 1989 and bought a second tied house at the same time. Also supplies over 50 free trade outlets locally, and others nationwide via wholesalers. Black Bess Porter is the latest addition to the beer range.

Trudoxhill (OG 1035, ABV 3.3%) An amber beer, with a light floral hop aroma. A refreshing taste with good bitter dryness and a long finish. A light beer retaining the distinctive Ash Vine taste.

Bitter (OG 1039, ABV 3.8%) A light gold brew with a strong floral hop aroma with malt and fruit undertones. A powerful, bitter hoppiness dominates the taste and leads to a dry, hoppy finish. An unusual and distinctive brew.

Challenger (OG 1044, ABV 4.1%) A mid brown beer with a solid malt flavour balanced by its good hoppy bitterness and subtle citrus fruits. Can be sulphurous and slightly metallic.

Black Bess Porter (OG 1045, ABV 4.2%) A dark copper brown, bitter porter with roast malt, hops and a sweet fruitiness. Malt and hop nose, and a dry, bitter finish. Occasionally sulphurous and metallic.

Tanker (OG 1049, ABV 4.7%) A tawny-coloured beer with a well developed balance of malt, bitter hops, fruit and subtle sweetness. A hoppy aroma and a bitter, dry finish.

Hop & Glory (OG 1059, ABV 5.5%) Copper-coloured with malt, fruit and hop aroma. The taste is bittersweet, with hops in abundance and some citrus fruits. A complex, rich and warming, satisfying winter ale.

ASTON MANOR **Aston Manor Brewery Company Ltd., 173 Thimblemill Lane, Aston, Birmingham, W. Midlands B7 5HS. Tel. (021) 328 4336**

Founded by ex-Ansells employees in 1983, Aston Manor moved very rapidly into the take-home trade, and discontinued brewing cask ale in 1986. Although still not its main income, the company resumed brewing real ale in 1990 under contract to Chandler's Brewery Company Ltd., and plans to expand this side of the business. Supplies two local free trade outlets on a regular basis.

Mild (Chandler's Dolly's Dark Mild) (OG 1032, ABV 3%) A roast and hop-flavoured mild with a hint of bitterness and sweetness. Dry, bitter finish.

Bitter (Chandler's JCB) (OG 1038, ABV 3.6%) Mid brown, hoppy and bitter beer with a sweet and bitter aftertaste.

Old Deadlies Winter Ale* (OG 1060, ABV 6.4%)

ATLAS See Preston.

AYLESBURY (ABC) See Nationals, Carlsberg-Tetley.

BALLARD'S **Ballard's Brewery Ltd., Unit C, The Old Sawmill, Nyewood, Rogate, Petersfield, Hants. GU31 5HA. Tel. (0730) 821301**

Founded in 1980 at Cumbers Farm, Trotton, the brewery moved in 1985 to the Ballards pub (now the Elsted Inn) and then to Nyewood (in West Sussex, despite the postal address). Supplies 55 free trade outlets and plans to increase production by up to 50% in the next three years. It has a tradition of brewing Christmas ales with different names and appropriate gravities each year, e.g. Old Episscopal (OG 1092) for 1992.

Midhurst Mild* (OG 1035, ABV 3.4%) A new dark mild.

Trotton Bitter (OG 1036, ABV 3.5%) A well-flavoured session bitter, amber/tawny in colour. The good balance of malt and hops runs through from the aroma to the finish, with a slight fruitiness also present.

Best Bitter (OG 1042, ABV 4.1%) Copper-red, with a malty aroma. Indeed, a notably malty beer altogether, but well-hopped and with a satisfying finish.

Wassail (OG 1060, ABV 5.8%) A strong, full-bodied, fruity beer with a predominance of malt throughout, but also an underlying hoppiness. Tawny/red in colour.

BANKS & TAYLOR

Banks & Taylor Brewery Ltd., The Brewery, Shefford, Beds. SG17 5DZ. Tel. (0462) 815080/816789

Founded in 1981 in a small industrial unit, this successful brewery is still growing steadily. It has ten tied houses, all of which sell real ale, and its free trade in the Home Counties and East Anglia has now increased to some 250 outlets. The extensive range of beers is well regarded and several seasonal brews are also offered. SOD is often sold under house names.

Shefford Mild (OG 1035, ABV 3.5%) A dark beer with a well-balanced taste. Sweetish, roast malt aftertaste.

Shefford Bitter (OG 1038, ABV 3.8%) A very drinkable, hoppy beer, with some malt and fruit flavours. Hoppy aroma and a bitter, hoppy aftertaste.

Shefford Pale Ale (SPA) (OG 1041, ABV 4%) A well-balanced beer, with hops and malt present throughout and hints of fruit in the aroma and taste. Dry, bitter aftertaste.

Edwin Taylor's Extra Stout (OG 1045, ABV 4.5%) A dark stout with predominant roast malt characteristics and a dry aftertaste.

Shefford Old Dark (SOD) (OG 1050, ABV 5%) Dark, reddish-brown ale with similar characteristics to SOS, but with added caramel flavouring.

Shefford Old Strong (SOS) (OG 1050, ABV 5%) A deceptively drinkable sweetish beer. A hoppy, malty aroma with hints of fruit leads to a well-balanced taste of hops and malt. Sweetish, malty finish with discernible fruit.

2XS (OG 1058, ABV 5.8%) A reddish beer with a strong, fruity, hoppy aroma. The taste is full-flavoured and the finish strong and sweetish.

Black Bat (OG 1064, ABV 6.4%) A powerful sweet, fruity, malty beer. Fruity, nutty aroma; strong roast malt aftertaste.

Old Bat (OG 1080, ABV 8%) Powerful-tasting sweet beer, with bitterness coming through in the aftertaste. Fruit is present in both aroma and taste.

BANKS'S

The Wolverhampton & Dudley Breweries PLC, Park Brewery, Lovatt Street, Wolverhampton, W. Midlands WV1 4NY. Tel. (0902) 711811

Unspoilt by Progress

Wolverhampton & Dudley Breweries was formed in 1890 by the amalgamation of three local companies. Hanson's was acquired in 1943, but its Dudley brewery was closed in 1991. Hanson's Mild is now brewed at Wolverhampton, but Hanson's Bitter has been discontinued in cask form. The 150 Hanson's pubs keep their own livery. In January 1992 W&D bought Camerons Brewery and 51 pubs from Brent Walker. These have now been added to and bring the tied estate for the whole group to almost 950 houses, most of them serving traditional ales, virtually all through electric, metered dispense. Extensive free trade in pubs and clubs. Through a reciprocal trading arrangement with Marston's, Pedigree is now sold in W&D pubs, with Banks's Mild available in Marston's houses. Camerons Strongarm is now being test marketed around Wolverhampton.

Hanson's Mild (OG 1036, ABV 3.5%) Mid to dark brown mild with a malty roast flavour and roast malt predominating the aftertaste.

Mild (OG 1036, ABV 3.5%) A mid brown, malty mild with a hint of bitterness. Touches of roast and caramel, but malt and bitter flavours make it drink like a dark bitter.

Bitter (OG 1038, ABV 3.8%) Malty, pale brown bitter with a dry, malty, sweet aftertaste fighting with a touch of bitterness.

BASS See Nationals.

BATEMAN

George Bateman & Son Ltd., Salem Bridge Brewery, Mill Lane, Wainfleet, Skegness, Lincs. PE24 4JE. Tel. (0754) 880317

A family-owned and -run brewery, established in 1874 by the present chairman's grandfather, then a bankrupt farmer, to serve local landworkers. In the mid-1980s, a family dispute threatened the brewery's future, but, after a three-year battle, Chairman George Bateman secured the brewery's independence and it is now steadily expanding its sales area to cover nearly the whole of the UK. All its 62 tied houses serve real ale, and around 220 free trade outlets are supplied directly by the brewery, which is planning to increase its brewing capacity to keep up with demand.

Dark Mild (OG 1033, ABV 3.1%) Some roast taste and a slight hint of fruit are balanced by a hoppy and bitter flavour and finish. Happily a beer which is enjoying a gentle revival.

XB (OG 1036, ABV 3.8%) A predominantly hoppy and bitter beer throughout, satisfying and slightly dry. Popular in the tied estate, but overshadowed by its heavier brothers in the free trade.

Valiant* (OG 1042, ABV 4.3%) A new addition to the range; a bitter launched in summer 1993.

XXXB (OG 1048, ABV 5%) Although some malt and fruitiness are evident in the aroma and flavour, the hoppy and bitter characteristics always come through. A worthy past winner of CAMRA awards.

Salem Porter (OG 1049, ABV 5%) Complex, dark beer with an aroma of roasted grain, a dry, nutty malt taste and a hoppy finish.

Victory Ale (OG 1056, ABV 6%) A warming and powerful, strong beer with malt and sweet flavours masked by a bitter and hoppy presence, which gives a lighter, crisper taste, leading the unwary to underestimate its strength.

BATHAM

Bathams (Delph) Ltd., Delph Brewery, Delph Road, Brierley Hill, W. Midlands DY5 2TN. Tel. (0384) 77229

Small brewery, hidden behind one of the Black Country's most famous pubs, the 'Bull & Bladder'. This family firm has not only managed to survive successfully since 1877, it is now brewing to full capacity and having difficulty maintaining its free trade supplies (around 30 outlets) due to the increased demand in its own nine tied houses. The long-term plans are to slowly build on its tied estate, to refurbish existing pubs and to extend the brewery.

Mild Ale (OG 1037, ABV 3.5%) Sweet and well-balanced dark brown ale with a hoppy, fruity finish.

Best Bitter ⊕ (OG 1044, ABV 4.5%) A straw-coloured bitter which initially seems sweet, but a complex dry, hoppy taste soon predominates. Probably the best example of the traditional Black Country style of bitter.

XXX (OG 1064, ABV 6.5%) A Christmas ale, mid brown in colour and strong, with a malty, fruity taste. Hop flavour is present but malt predominates through to the aftertaste.

BEER ENGINE **The Beer Engine, Newton St Cyres, Exeter, Devon EX5 5AX. Tel. (0392) 851282**

Successful brew pub now serving an expanding free trade. Stands next to the Barnstaple branch railway line, hence the names. Owns one other pub, the Sleeper in Seaton. Occasionally produces a bottle-conditioned beer.

Rail Ale (OG 1037, ABV 3.8%) Yellow-coloured beer with a malty aroma and hoppy flavour and aftertaste.

Piston Bitter (OG 1044, ABV 4.6%) Tawny-coloured with a strong malt and fruit aroma and flavour, and a hoppy, malty aftertaste.

Sleeper Heavy (OG 1055, ABV 5.6%) Tawny-coloured beer with a fruity taste and a malty aftertaste.

Whistlemas (OG 1072, ABV 7.5%) Produced for Christmas; mid brown in colour with a fruity aroma, malty taste and sweet aftertaste.

BELHAVEN **Belhaven Brewery Co. Ltd., Spott Road, Dunbar, Lothian EH42 1RS. Tel. (0368) 62734**

Although established as far back as 1719, making it the oldest brewery in Scotland, Belhaven has been owned since 1989 by the London-based property and leisure group, Control Securities PLC but it has managed to continue to produce award-winning beers, increasing its production by almost a quarter from 1991 to 1992. Three-quarters of its 62 tied houses take cask beer, which is also supplied direct to 200 or so free trade outlets.

60/- Ale* (OG 1031, ABV 2.6%) Dark and malty.

70/- Ale* (OG 1035, ABV 3.2%) Light and hoppy.

Sandy Hunter's Traditional Ale* (OG 1037, ABV 3.6%)

80/- Ale* (OG 1041, ABV 3.9%) Heavy, full-bodied ale.

St Andrew's Ale* (OG 1046, ABV 4.5%)

90/- Ale* (OG 1070, ABV 7.3%) An occasional, rich brew.

BENSKINS See Nationals, Carlsberg-Tetley.

BENTLEY See Nationals, Whitbread.

BERROW **Berrow Brewery, Coast Road, Berrow, Burnham-on-Sea, Somerset TA8 2QU. Tel. (0278) 751345**

Brewery founded in June 1982 and now supplying pubs and clubs locally, amounting to about ten free trade outlets.

Best Bitter (BBBB or 4Bs) (OG 1038, ABV 3.8%) A pleasant, pale brown session beer, with a fruity aroma, a malty, fruity flavour and bitterness in the palate and finish.

Topsy Turvy (TT) (OG 1055, ABV 6%) An excellent, straw-coloured beer. Its aroma is of malt and hops, which are also evident in the taste, together with sweetness. The aftertaste is malty. Very easy to drink. Beware!

BIG END See Daleside.

The tankard symbol indicates the *Good Beer Guide Beers of the Year*, finalists in the *Champion Beer of Britain* contest held at the *Great British Beer Festival* at Olympia in August 1993.

BIG LAMP **Big Lamp Brewers, 1 Summerhill Street, Newcastle upon Tyne, Tyne & Wear NE4 6EJ. Tel. (091) 261 4227**

Big Lamp was set up in 1982 and changed hands at the end of 1990. Currently supplies one tied house and a growing free trade (about 55 outlets). ESB has just been reintroduced to the beer list.

Bitter (OG 1038, ABV 3.9%) Hoppy and complex with a lasting fruit and bitter finish. An impressive range of flavours go towards making this basic bitter a truly satisfying drink.

Summerhill Stout (OG 1044, ABV 4.4%) Another beer with many features, including a rich roast aroma and a malty mouthfeel. Look for a light bitterness and some sweetness.

Prince Bishop Ale (OG 1044, ABV 4.8%) A light-coloured beer for its gravity with a clean hoppiness and well-balanced aroma, taste and mouthfeel.

ESB (OG 1046, ABV 5%) A complex beer with a red hue. Hops balance malt against a background fruitiness and a lingering bitterness. A distinctive and special bitter.

Winter Warmer (OG 1048, ABV 5.2%) Maltiness and roast dominate the aroma and taste. Bitterness is evident throughout. More of a strong bitter than a winter warmer.

Old Genie (OG 1070, ABV 7.4%) An occasional beer. A dark and strong, well-balanced ale. Sweetness dominates the taste and aftertaste, although there are some roast and fruit elements in the aroma.

Blackout (OG 1100, ABV 11%) Rich and powerful beer with a cauldron of flavour. Hops, malt and roast match a strong, sweet character with a slowly declining bitterness.

BLACKAWTON **Blackawton Brewery, Washbourne, Totnes, Devon TQ9 7UF. Tel. (0803) 732339**

Situated just outside the village of Washbourne, this small family brewery was only founded in 1977 but it is the oldest in Devon. It originated in the village of Blackawton, but moved to its present site in 1981 and, although changing ownership in 1988, retains a loyal local following. Serves around 50 free trade outlets, having no pubs of its own.

Bitter (OG 1037.5, ABV 3.8%) Tawny in colour, with no detectable aroma. A good bitter, fruity taste with a bitter aftertaste.

Devon Gold* (OG 1040.5, ABV 4.1%) A summer brew, available April–October. A very pleasant, straw-coloured beer.

44 Special (OG 1044.5, ABV 4.5%) Pale brown, malty, fruity, sweet-tasting beer with a distinct malty aroma. A slightly sweet beer.

Headstrong (OG 1051.5, ABV 5.2%) Pale brown, malty, aromatic beer. Sweet, malty taste and finish.

BLACKBEARD **Blackbeard Trading Company, Nelson Inn, Rocks Green, Ludlow, Shropshire SY8 2DN. Tel. (0584) 872908**

Beer wholesaler which brews no beer of its own, but has its own brands contract-brewed by Hanby and Freeminer.

BLACK SHEEP **The Black Sheep Brewery PLC, Wellgarth, Masham, Ripon, N. Yorks. HG4 4EN. Tel. (0765) 689227**

New brewery instigated in 1992 by Paul Theakston, a member of Masham's famous brewing family, in the former Wellgarth Maltings. Future plans include adding to the three slate Yorkshire square fermenters to allow for increased capacity. Currently supplies 65 outlets direct.

Best Bitter (OG 1038, ABV 3.8%) Subtle aroma of malt, with traces of fruit and hops. The flavour is malty with underlying faint fruit and hop bitterness. Dry finish but little depth of flavour.

Special Strong Bitter* (OG 1044, ABV 4.4%)

BODDINGTONS See Nationals, Whitbread, and Pub Groups.

BORDER

Border Brewery Company Ltd., The Old Kiln, Brewery Lane, Tweedmouth, Berwick-upon-Tweed, Northumberland TD15 2AH. Tel. (0289) 303303

Not to be confused with the Wrexham brewery taken over and closed by Marston's, this new operation opened in 1992 on the site of the town's original Border Brewery which was established in the 17th century, but which lay idle for 50 years. Supplies its own pub and ten other outlets.

Old Kiln Bitter* (OG 1036, ABV 3.8%)

Old Kiln Ale (OG 1038, ABV 4%) A light-tasting bitter with a hoppy and fruity character and lasting sweetness.

BRAINS

SA Brain & Co. Ltd., The Old Brewery, 49 St Mary Street, Cardiff, S. Glamorgan CF1 1SP. Tel. (0222) 399022

A traditional brewery which has been in the Brain family since Samuel Brain and his Uncle Joseph bought the Old Brewery in 1882. Now the largest independent brewery in Wales, it supplies cask-conditioned beer to all its 114 pubs and a substantial free trade. The company has diversified in recent years with interests in hotel, tourism and leisure projects in Wales and the West Country. MA (OG 1035, ABV 3.5%) – a mix of Dark and Bitter – is only available at the Crown Hotel, Skewen.

Dark (OG 1035, ABV 3.5%) A full-bodied, dark brown mild with traces of chocolate followed by a rounded bittersweet finish.

Bitter (OG 1035, ABV 3.7%) A distinctively bitter beer, pale and somewhat malty with an intense, dry finish. Commonly known as 'Light'.

SA Best Bitter (OG 1042, ABV 4.2%) A full-bodied, malty premium bitter; well-balanced, with a smooth and strong dry finish.

BRAKSPEAR

WH Brakspear & Sons PLC, The Brewery, New Street, Henley-on-Thames, Oxfordshire RG9 2BU. Tel. (0491) 573636

A brewery can be traced back to before 1700 on the present Henley site, but Brakspear came into being in 1799 when Robert Brakspear started up a partnership with Richard Hayward. Robert's son, William Henry, greatly expanded the brewery and its trade. Brakspear boasts many excellent, unspoilt pubs and all 114 tied houses serve traditional ales. It also supplies over 250 free trade outlets, and Bitter is widely available as a guest beer. The new beer, OBJ, launched in 1993, is an acronym for 'Oh Be Joyful', the local name given to the original Henley Strong Ale. The 27% stake in Brakspear owned by Whitbread was reduced to less than 15% in 1992.

Mild (OG 1030, ABV 2.8%) Thin beer with a red/brown colour and a sweet, malty, fruity aroma. The well-balanced taste of malt, hops and caramel has a faint bitterness, complemented by a sweet, fruity flavour, having hints of black cherries. The main characteristics extend through to the bittersweet finish.

Bitter (OG 1035, ABV 3.4%) Amber in colour, with a good fruit, hop and malt nose. The initial taste of malt and the dry, well-hopped bitterness quickly dissolves into a predominantly bitter, sweet and fruity aftertaste.

Old Ale (OG 1043, ABV 4%) Red/brown with good body. The strong, fruity aroma is well complemented by malt, hops and roast caramel. Its pronounced taste of malt, with discernible sweet, roast and caramel flavours, gives way to fruitiness. The aftertaste is of bittersweet chocolate, even though chocolate malt is not present.

Special (OG 1043, ABV 4%) Tawny/amber in colour, its good, well-balanced aroma has a hint of sweetness. The initial taste is moderately sweet and malty, but is quickly overpowered by the dry bitterness of the hops, before a slightly sweet fruitiness. A distinct, dry, malty finish.

OBJ* (OG 1051, ABV 5%)

BRANSCOMBE VALE **Branscombe Vale Brewery, Great Seaside Farm, Branscombe, Seaton, Devon EX12 3DP. Tel. (0297) 80511**

Brewery set up in July 1992 in two former cowsheds owned by the National Trust, by former dairy workers, Paul Dimond and Graham Luxton. Graham's wife runs one of the village pubs, the Fountain Head, where the beers are always available. Ten other regular outlets, and 40 more on an occasional basis.

Branoc (OG 1040, ABV 3.8%) Pale brown beer with a hoppy aroma. Distinctly bitter taste and aftertaste.

Olde Stoker (OG 1055, ABV 5.4%) Dark brown with a distinct roast aroma and a roast, bitter taste and aftertaste.

BREWERY ON SEA **The Brewery on Sea Ltd., 24 Winston Business Centre, Chartwell Road, Lancing, W. Sussex BN15 8TU. Tel. (0903) 851482**

New brewery established by former Pitfield/Premier brewer Rob Jones and Jon Sale, whose Spinnaker beers had been brewed under contract by Premier in previous years. The first brews were produced in early summer 1993.

Spinnaker Bitter* (OG 1035, ABV 3.5%)

Spinnaker Mild* (OG 1035, ABV 3.5%)

Spinnaker Classic* (OG 1040, ABV 4%)

Special Crew* (OG 1050, ABV 5.5%)

Black Rock* (OG 1051, ABV 5.5%)

Riptide* (OG 1060, ABV 6.5%)

BRIDGWATER **Bridgwater Brewing Company, Unit 1, Lovedere Farm, Goathurst, Bridgwater, Somerset TA5 2DD. Tel. (0278) 663996**

The good villagers of Goathurst (pronounced Go-thurst), need go thirsty no more. Since spring 1993, this new brewery has been established in a village which formerly had no hostelry at all. An initial output of ten barrels a week is supplied to around eight local outlets.

Carnival Special Brew* (OG 1035, ABV 3.5%) Seasonal, brewed for the carnival months of October and November.

Coppernob* (OG 1045, ABV 4.4%)

Sunbeam* (OG 1052, ABV 5.4%)

BRITISH OAK **British Oak Brewery, Salop Street, Eve Hill, Dudley, W. Midlands DY1 3AX. Tel. (0384) 236297**

Started as a family-run brew pub, in May 1988, and now supplies 15 free trade outlets, as well as a second pub of its own. Also produces traditional cider.

Eve'ill Bitter (OG 1042, ABV 4%) A fruity, malty beer with a bitter aftertaste.

Colonel Pickering's Porter (OG 1046, ABV 4.3%) Dark, fruity and bitter; a full-bodied, creamy, distinctive beer.

Dungeon Draught (OG 1050, ABV 4.8%) A mid to dark brown fruity ale with plenty of malt and hops.

Old Jones (OG 1062, ABV 6%) Available September–April; dark, sweet, rich and malty.

BROUGHTON — **Broughton Brewery Ltd., Broughton, Peeblesshire, Borders ML12 6HQ. Tel. (089 94) 345**

Go-ahead brewery, founded in 1980 by former S&N executive David Younger to brew and distribute real ale in central and southern Scotland (over 200 outlets and a single tied house in Dumfries). While this remains the priority, an increasing amount of bottled beer (not bottle-conditioned) is distributed nationally. The draught Scottish Oatmeal Stout took a CAMRA award soon after its 1992 launch, and Merlin's Ale is the latest addition to the range.

Greenmantle Ale (OG 1038, ABV 4%) Beer lacking aroma. Bittersweet in taste, with a hint of fruit, and a very dry finish.

Special Bitter* (OG 1038, ABV 4%) A dry-hopped version of Greenmantle.

Scottish Oatmeal Stout* (OG 1039, ABV 3.8%)

Merlin's Ale* (OG 1042, ABV 4.2%)

Old Jock (OG 1069, ABV 6.7%) Strong, sweetish and fruity in the finish.

MATTHEW BROWN See Nationals, Scottish & Newcastle.

BRUNSWICK — **Brunswick Brewing Co. Ltd., 1 Railway Terrace, Derby DE1 2RU. Tel. (0332) 290677**

Brewery based at the Brunswick Inn, an historic building partly restored by the Derbyshire Historic Building Trust, then bought by the present owners in 1987. The first brew was produced in June 1991 and it now supplies 12 other outlets from its extensive range of beers.

Recession Ale* (OG 1033, ABV 3.3%)

Celebration Mild* (OG 1034, ABV 3.4%)

First Brew* (OG 1036, ABV 3.6%)

Fat Boy Stout* (OG 1040, ABV 3.8%)

Second Brew* (OG 1042, ABV 4.2%)

Railway Porter* (OG 1045, ABV 4.3%)

Festival Ale* (OG 1046, ABV 4.6%) An occasional brew.

Old Accidental* (OG 1050, ABV 5%)

Owd Abusive* (OG 1066, ABV 6%)

BUCKLEY See Crown Buckley.

BULLMASTIFF — **Bullmastiff Brewery, 14 Bessemer Close, off Hadfield Road, Leckwith, Cardiff, S. Glamorgan CF1 8AQ. Tel. (0222) 665292**

Small brewery set up in Penarth in 1987 by a fanatical home-brewer. Supplies about 30 outlets locally, but not on a regular basis, so the beers are rather hard to find on the brewery's home patch. Much of the production is sold right across the country through wholesalers. Moved to new, larger premises in summer 1992.

Bitter (OG 1035, ABV 3.5%) A pale brown, bitter beer with a malty aroma and a dry finish. A popular session beer.

> OG stands for Original Gravity, the reading taken before fermentation of the amount of fermentable material in the brew. It is a rough indicator of strength. More reliable is the ABV (Alcohol by Volume) rating, which gives the percentage of alcohol in the finished beer.

Ebony Dark (OG 1042, ABV 4%) As its name suggests, a very dark brown beer with a roast malt flavour and aroma. Very drinkable, with a rich, malt aftertaste.

Best Bitter (OG 1043, ABV 4%) A well-balanced, malty, bitter beer with a smooth, fruity finish. Very drinkable.

Son of a Bitch (OG 1062, ABV 6.4%) A full-bodied, notably hoppy, malty beer. This premium bitter has both a distinctive aroma and aftertaste.

BUNCES

Bunces Brewery, The Old Mill, Netheravon, Wilts. SP4 9QB. Tel. (0980) 70631

Brewery housed in a listed building on the Wiltshire Avon, established in 1984 but sold by Tony and Robin Bunce to a Danish couple in summer 1993. It delivers cask-conditioned beers to around 40 free trade outlets within a radius of 50 miles, and supplies a number of wholesalers.

Vice Beer* (OG 1033, ABV 3.2%) A wheat beer; a summer brew.

Benchmark (OG 1035, ABV 3.5%) A pleasant, bitter ale of remarkable character, which maintains one's interest for a long time. The taste is malty, the aroma subtle and the very long finish is quite dry on the palate.

Pigswill* (OG 1040, ABV 4%) A beer first brewed for the Two Pigs at Corsham, now more widely available.

Best Bitter (OG 1042, ABV 4.1%) A first-rate beer. The piquant aroma introduces a complex malty and bitter taste with a hint of fruit. Long, fresh, bitter aftertaste.

Old Smokey (OG 1050, ABV 5%) A delightful, warming, dark bitter ale, with a roasted malt taste and a hint of liquorice surrounding a developing bitter flavour. Very appealing to the eye.

BURTON BRIDGE

Burton Bridge Brewery, 24 Bridge Street, Burton upon Trent, Staffs. DE14 1SY. Tel. (0283) 510573

Established in 1982, with one tied outlet at the front of the brewery. The adjoining premises are gradually being refurbished into a new brewhouse and this will allow for an extension of the pub into the old brewery buildings. Supplies guest beers to around 250 outlets virtually nationwide, and specialises in commemorative bottled beers to order. *Bottle-conditioned beer: Burton Porter (OG 1045, ABV 4.6%)*

Summer Ale* (OG 1038, ABV 3.8%) Only available during British Summer Time.

XL Bitter (OG 1040, ABV 4%) A golden/amber, malty drinking bitter, with a dry palate and finish. A faint hoppiness and fruitiness come through in the aroma and taste.

Bridge Bitter (OG 1042, ABV 4.2%) Again, golden/amber in colour, robust and malty, with a hoppy and bitter palate and aftertaste. Though malt and hops are both present throughout, the dry, hoppy character dominates the finish. Some balancing fruitiness and sweetness.

Burton Porter (OG 1045, ABV 4.5%) A dark, ruby-red, sweetish porter. The malty, slightly fruity aroma is followed by a roast malt and fruit flavour, and a malty and fairly bitter finish.

Top Dog Stout* (OG 1050, ABV 5%) A winter brew.

Hearty Ale* (OG 1050, ABV 5.1%) A new Christmas offering.

Burton Festival Ale (OG 1055, ABV 5.5%) Strong, sweetish and full-bodied. The nose is malty and slightly hoppy, and the palate has similar characteristics, with a pronounced fruitiness. Copper-coloured; a little cloying and heavy.

Old Expensive* (OG 1065, ABV 6.7%) Winter only; a dark, warming beer, also known as OX.

The Independents

BURTONWOOD **Burtonwood Brewery PLC, Burtonwood Village, Warrington, Cheshire WA5 4PJ. Tel. (0925) 225131**

A family-run public company, established in 1867 on farmland by James Forshaw who had learnt his trade at Bath Springs Brewery in Ormskirk. In the 1980s, Burtonwood embarked on a £6 million pound extension plan and its new brewhouse was completed in 1990. Supplies real ale to 300 of its 427 tied houses, 138 of which are on long lease from Carlsberg-Tetley. Has a 35% stake in the Paramount pub chain and is continuing to develop trading relationships with other pub groups. Also supplies 300 free trade outlets direct and in summer 1993 began brewing Chester's Best Bitter following the closure of Whitbread's Exchange Brewery.

Mild (OG 1032, ABV 3%) A smooth, dark brown, malty mild with a good roast flavour, some caramel and a hint of bitterness. Slightly dry finish.

Bitter (OG 1036, ABV 3.8%) A well-balanced, refreshing and malty bitter, with good hoppiness and a little sweetness. Malty and bitter aftertaste.

James Forshaw's Bitter (OG 1038, ABV 4%) Hoppy and bitter beer. Fairly sweet with a hint of fruit. More hoppy and characterful than the ordinary bitter.

Top Hat* (OG 1045, ABV 4.8%) Cask version of Burtonwood's strong bitter, only available in a handful of outlets.

For Whitbread:

Chester's Best Bitter* (OG 1033, ABV 3.6%)

BURTS See Island.

BUSHY'S **Mount Murray Brewing Co. Ltd., Mount Murray, Castletown Road, Braddan, Isle of Man. Tel. (0624) 661244**

Set up in 1986 as Bushy's Brewpub, but, when demand outgrew the capacity, it moved to its present site in 1990, and also increased its range of beers (which are brewed to the stipulations of the Manx Brewers' Act of 1874). The brewery has benefited from the closure of Castletown Brewery and the sale of pubs from the Isle of Man Breweries' tied estate, which has widened the free trade market on the island. Four tied houses are also supplied.

Dark Mild (OG 1035, ABV 3.7%) With a hoppy aroma, and notes of chocolate and coffee to the malty flavour, this rich, creamy, fruity, very dark brew is reminiscent of a porter.

Best Bitter (OG 1038, ABV 3.7%) An aroma full of pale malt and hops introduces you to a beautifully hoppy, bitter beer. Despite the predominant hop character, malt is also evident. Fresh and clean tasting.

Old Bushy Tail (OG 1045, ABV 4.7%) An appealing reddish-brown beer with a pronounced hop and malt aroma, the malt tending towards treacle. Slightly sweet and malty on the palate, with distinct orangey tones. The full finish is malty and hoppy, with hints of toffee.

Piston Brew* (OG 1045, ABV 4.5%) Available during the TT races (June) and Manx Grand Prix (September) only.

Lovely Jubbely Christmas Ale (OG 1060, ABV 6.2%) A rich, satisfying, mid brown beer with a pronounced aroma of malt and fruit. Sweet and malty on the palate; the finish is balanced with some hop bitterness.

BUTCOMBE **Butcombe Brewery Ltd., Butcombe, Bristol, Avon BS18 6XQ. Tel. (0275) 472240**

One of the most successful of the new wave of breweries, set up in 1978 by a former Courage Western MD, Simon Whitmore. During 1992/93, the brewery was virtually doubled in size (for the third time), allowing for an 80-barrel brew, and almost all the old plant was replaced. Real ale is supplied to its three houses (which are not tied) and over 300 other outlets, mostly within a 50-mile radius of the brewery.

Bitter (OG 1039, ABV 4.1%) An amber beer with a pleasant, malty, bitter taste, some hop and occasional fruit. It has a hoppy, malty aroma and a bitter finish, which can be very drying. A clean, crisp, refreshing beer. It is sometimes served too young, when it lacks complexity.

BUTTERKNOWLE **The Butterknowle Brewery Co., The Old School House, Lynesack, Butterknowle, Bishop Auckland, Co. Durham DL13 5QF. Tel. (0388) 710109**

Since its launch in August 1990, Butterknowle has continued to prosper and grow by producing award-winning ales, gaining second place both in the *Bitter* and *Best Bitter* (with Conciliation) categories at the Great British Beer Festival in 1992. It now supplies 40 outlets on a regular basis, and over 100 with guest beers from its impressive range. New plant recently purchased from the New Forest Brewery will increase its production by almost 50%. The brewery is situated in Victorian buildings once home to the Lynesack National School.

West Auckland Mild* (OG 1034, ABV 3.3%) An occasional brew. The name is used by permission of The Cameron Brewery Co.

Bitter (OG 1036, ABV 3.6%) A good, hoppy bitter. Very drinkable, with a light bitterness and malty aftertaste.

Festival Stout (OG 1038, ABV 3.6%) Originally brewed for the sixth Darlington Spring Festival; a beer with a roast, slightly smoky flavour, a hoppy aroma and a sweetish aftertaste.

Conciliation Ale (OG 1042, ABV 4.2%) Butterknowle's flagship brand: a rich ale, with a good balance of fruit and bitterness. Well-hopped in both aroma and palate with a dry aftertaste.

Black Diamond (OG 1050, ABV 4.8%) Actually red-brown in colour. A richly pungent ale with a good body and sweet taste. Hop and bitter flavours are mild, leaving a grainy finish.

High Force (OG 1060, ABV 6.2%) A smooth strong ale, well hopped, with some fruity sweetness. A good depth of flavour develops in the aftertaste: a multi-dimensional beer.

Old Ebenezer (OG 1080, ABV 8%) A splendid, rich and fruity, seasonal barley wine: liquid Christmas cake with a potent punch. Surprisingly moreish, if only in sips!

CAINS **Robert Cain & Co. Ltd., Stanhope Street, Liverpool, Merseyside L8 5XJ. Tel. (051) 709 8734**

Robert Cain's brewery was first established on this site in 1850 and the present brewery completed in 1902. It was bought out by Higsons in the 1920s, then by Boddingtons in 1985. When Whitbread took control of the latter's interests in 1990, it soon closed the brewery, switching the brewing of Higsons to Sheffield. The site was then bought by GB Breweries to brew canned beers, but with enthusiastic staff and CAMRA support, it soon started brewing cask beers to supply around 250 outlets via wholesalers. The Robert Cain name was then revived and the first tied house was opened in summer 1993. The company is now owned by the Brewery Group Denmark AS (formerly Faxe Jyske).

Dark Mild (OG 1033, ABV 3.2%) Dry, roasty dark mild with some bitterness and hints of sweetness and fruit. Can be thin and lacking in character when young.

Traditional Bitter (OG 1039, ABV 4.1%) Darkish, malty and full-bodied. More hoppy and less bitter than last year, with a good, hoppy nose. Well-balanced and distinctive.

Formidable Ale (FA) (OG 1048, ABV 5.1%) A hoppy and bitter beer with some fruit. Good, hoppy nose and a strong, bitter aftertaste. Sharp, clean and dry – can be quite aggressive.

CALEDONIAN

The Caledonian Brewing Company Ltd., Slateford Road, Edinburgh, Lothian EH11 1PH. Tel. (031) 337 1286

Described by Michael Jackson as a 'living, working museum of beer making', Caledonian (or Caley) operates from a Victorian brewhouse, using the last three direct-fired open coppers in Britain – one of which dates back to 1869 when the brewery was started by George Lorimer and Robert Clark. It was taken over by Vaux of Sunderland in 1919, who continued to brew there until 1987, when, under threat of closure, it was acquired by a management buy-out team. No tied estate, but around 300 free trade outlets are supplied.

60/- Ale* (OG 1032, ABV 3.3%) A flavoursome light ale.

70/- Ale* (OG 1036, ABV 3.5%) Soft and malty in flavour.

Deuchars IPA (OG 1038, ABV 3.8%) A well-hopped session beer, with a balance of malt and hops in the taste and a peppery aroma.

Edinburgh Real Ale or ERA* (OG 1041, ABV 4.2%)

80/- Ale* (OG 1043, ABV 4.2%) Malty and flavoursome, with hops well in evidence.

Porter* (OG 1043, ABV 4.2%) Dry and nutty.

Campbell, Hope & King's Double Amber Ale* (OG 1046, ABV 4.6%) A new beer introduced in early summer 1993.

Golden Promise* (OG 1048, ABV 4.8%) An organic beer.

Merman XXX* (OG 1050, ABV 5%) Dark, sweetish heavy beer, based on a Victorian recipe.

Edinburgh Strong Ale or ESA* (OG 1078, ABV 8%) Rich and deceptively strong.

CAMERONS

The Cameron Brewery Company, Lion Brewery, Hartlepool, Cleveland TS24 7QS. Tel. (0429) 266666

This major brewer of real ale went through a difficult period when it was bought by the ill-fated Brent Walker group in 1989. However, its fortunes have turned since being bought, in 1992, by Wolverhampton and Dudley Breweries (Banks's and Hanson's) who have invested heavily in the brewery and in a programme of pub refurbishments. It has acquired some 30 new pubs since the take-over and now sells cask-conditioned ales in most of its 83 tied houses, as well as supplying roughly 550 free trade outlets. The beers were relaunched in September 1992, and Strongarm is also being test marketed in W&D pubs in the West Midlands.

Bitter (OG 1036, ABV 3.6%) A light beer with a good balance of malt and hops and a true bitter finish. An excellent session beer when in good form but quality does vary.

Strongarm (OG 1042, ABV 4%) A pleasant, medium-bodied ale with a lot of character. Darkish in colour, with a full, well-balanced flavour of malt and hops and a dry, bitter finish. Again, quality can vary and there is a trend in some pubs to serve it too cold to be appreciated.

> Beers marked with an asterisk have not been tasted by official CAMRA tasting panels. However, some of these beers do carry brief descriptions derived from limited samplings or other sources, and can be used for rough guidance.

CANNON ROYAL **Cannon Royal Brewery, 3 Highfield Road, Kidderminster, Hereford & Worcester DY10 2TL. Tel. (0562) 743262**

A new brewery set up in 1993 at the Fruiterer's Arms pub in Uphampton, by the former brewer of the Fox & Hounds brew pub in Stottesdon.

Arrowhead Bitter* (OG 1039, ABV 3.9%)

Buckshot Bitter* (OG 1045, ABV 4.5%)

Millward's Musket Mild* (OG 1046, ABV 4.5%)

Christmas Merry* (OG 1062, ABV 6%)

CASTLE EDEN See Nationals, Whitbread.

CASTLETOWN See Isle of Man Breweries.

CHANDLER'S See Aston Manor.

CHARRINGTON See Nationals, Bass.

CHERITON **The Cheriton Brewhouse, Cheriton, Alresford, Hants. SO24 0QQ. Tel. (0962) 771166**

A new purpose-built brewery, opened at Easter 1993 by Paul Tickner, licensee of the Flower Pots Inn next door, and two partners. Its beer has quickly picked up a local following, and is available in 15 outlets. A new stronger ale is also in the pipeline.

Pots Ale* (ABV 3.8%) Golden in colour and quite well hopped.

CHESTER'S See Nationals, Whitbread.

CHILTERN **The Chiltern Brewery, Nash Lee Road, Terrick, Aylesbury, Bucks. HP17 0TQ. Tel. (0296) 613647**

Set up in 1980 on a small farm, Chiltern specializes in an unusual range of beer-related products, like beer mustards, Old Ale chutneys, cheeses and malt marmalade. These products are available from the brewery shop and also a dozen other retail outlets. Brewery tours are very popular. The beer itself is regularly supplied to around 20 free trade outlets (no tied houses). *Bottle-conditioned beer: Three Hundreds Old Ale (OG 1050, ABV 4.9%); Bodgers Barley Wine (OG 1080, ABV 8.5%)*

Chiltern Ale* (OG 1038, ABV 3.7%) A distinctive, tangy light bitter.

Beechwood Bitter* (OG 1043, ABV 4.3%) Full-bodied and nutty.

Three Hundreds Old Ale* (OG 1050, ABV 4.9%) A strong, rich, deep chestnut-coloured beer.

CLARK'S **HB Clark & Co. (Successors) Ltd., Westgate Brewery, Wakefield, W. Yorks. WF2 9SW. Tel. (0924) 373328**

The only brewery in Wakefield, founded in 1905. Ceased brewing during the keg revolution of the sixties and seventies, although it continued to operate as a drinks wholesaler. Resumed cask ale production in 1982 and, within two months, Clark's Traditional Bitter was voted *Best Bitter* at the Great British Beer Festival in Leeds. T'Owd Dreadnought, originally brewed for beer festivals, has now become part of the regular range. Supplies real ale to its three tied houses and around 25 free trade outlets. The beers are now available more widely, including in Scotland via beer agencies.

Traditional Bitter (OG 1038, ABV 3.8%) An amber-coloured standard bitter with a pleasing hoppy, fruity aroma. A fine hop flavour is dominant in the palate, with malt and fruit. A good, clean-tasting bitter with a long, hoppy finish.

Festival Ale (OG 1042, ABV 4.2%) A light-tasting, smooth hoppy bitter, with balancing sweetness and malt, plus fruit notes. The finish is of hoppy bitterness and fruit, which is also evident in the aroma.

Burglar Bill (OG 1044, ABV 4.6%) A good, hoppy aroma precedes the excellent, strong hop flavour, combined with rich malt and fruit. A long finish of hops and malt completes this full-bodied, strong bitter.

Rams Revenge (OG 1046, ABV 4.8%) A dark brown beer with a reddish hue and a taste dominated by roast malt and caramel. The aroma is fruity, with roast malt, and the finish is dry and malty but short.

Hammerhead (OG 1055, ABV 5.7%) Rich malt in the mouth, but with hop flavour and bitterness to balance. The malty, hoppy aroma is faint, but the finish is long, malty and dry. A robust, strong bitter.

Winter Warmer (OG 1060, ABV 6.4%) A dark brown, powerful strong ale. A strong mouth-filling blend of roast malt, hop flavour, sweetness and fruit notes concludes with a satisfying finish of bittersweet roast malt.

T'Owd Dreadnought* (OG 1080, ABV 9%)

COACH HOUSE

The Coach House Brewing Company Ltd., Wharf Street, Howley, Warrington, Cheshire WA1 2DQ. Tel. (0925) 232800

Built in 1991 and run mainly by ex-Greenall Whitley employees. Despite unfulfilled promises of trading agreements with Greenalls and Paramount PLC, the company has gone from strength to strength and has now extended its trading area into northern Scotland and southern England via the Tap & Spile chain. Negotiations have also begun with a national brewer to supply Coach House beers to their tenancies. Currently some 350 outlets are supplied direct, although the beers are still hard to find on their home patch. Seasonal beers and interesting recipes are company policy, with several new additions since the last edition.

Coachman's Bitter (OG 1037, ABV 3.7%) A well-hopped, malty bitter, moderately fruity with a hint of sweetness. Good hoppy nose. A refreshing beer which improves with longer conditioning.

Gunpowder Strong Mild (OG 1037, ABV 3.8%) Full-bodied and roasty dark mild. Hints of vanilla and treacle with chocolate overtones. Malty aroma and full finish.

Ostlers Summer Pale Ale (OG 1038, ABV 3.9%) Light, refreshing and very bitter, with a hint of pepper and a very dry finish. German hops are used in this summer ale.

Squires Gold Spring Ale (OG 1042, ABV 4.2%) A golden spring beer. New Zealand hops give intense bitterness which is followed by a strong chocolate flavour from amber malt. Bitterness mellows in older samples. Uncompromising and characterful.

Innkeeper's Special Reserve (OG 1045, ABV 4.5%) A darkish, full-flavoured bitter. Quite fruity with a strong, bitter aftertaste.

Bootleg Valentines Ale (OG 1050, ABV 5%) Fruity, bitter and fairly sweet with a very dry aftertaste. A well-balanced beer, brewed in February.

Taverners Autumn Ale (OG 1050, ABV 5%) Fruity and bitter; golden in colour. Slightly dry aftertaste. A warming and autumnal ale.

Posthorn (OG 1050, ABV 5%) Well-hopped and very fruity with bitterness and malt also prominent. Hoppy aroma and fruity aftertaste.

Blunderbus Old Porter (OG 1055, ABV 5.2%) A super winter beer. The intense roast flavour is backed up by coffee, chocolate and liquorice, and hints of spice and smoke. Very well-hopped; massive mouthfeel. An intense, chewy pint which is surprisingly refreshing and moreish.

Anniversary Ale (OG 1060, ABV 6%) Fruity and sweet bitter, produced each July to commemorate the brewery's founding.

Burns Auld Skeekit (OG 1060, ABV 6%) Malty and fruity beer whose sweetness can be slightly cloying. A January brew.

Three Kings Christmas Ale (OG 1060, ABV 6%) A strong, hoppy and fruity ale with intense bitterness. Much improved with age when malt and almond flavours come through.

COMMERCIAL

Commercial Brewing Co. Ltd., Worth Brewery, Worth Way, Keighley, W. Yorks. BD21 5LP. Tel. (0535) 611914

Set up in a former garage, this ambitious brewery's first beer was produced in February 1992 and was soon joined by a further six. Commercial acquired its first tied house in December 1992 and there are plans for more. Some 120 other outlets are supplied direct. *Bottle-conditioned beers: Alesman (ABV 3.7%); Porter (ABV 4.6%); Old Toss (ABV 6.5%); Master James Strong Ale (ABV 8.1%); Santa's Toss (ABV 8%)*

Becksider* (OG 1034, ABV 3.5%)

Keighlian Mild* (OG 1034, ABV 3.5%) A summer brew.

Keighlian Bitter (OG 1036, ABV 3.7%) Clean, fruity beer with pungent hop/citrus fruit character on the nose. Bitter fruit aftertaste.

Worth Best Bitter* (OG 1045, ABV 4.5%)

Worth Porter* (OG 1045, ABV 4.6%)

Old Toss* (OG 1065, ABV 6.5%)

Santa's Toss* (OG 1080, ABV 8%) A winter brew.

COOK'S

The Cook Brewery Co., 44 Burley Road, Bockhampton, Christchurch, Dorset BH23 7AJ. Tel. (0425) 73721

After 15 years as a brewing plant engineer, Nigel Cook started brewing in Twickenham in 1988 and selling his polypins to local off-licences. He moved to Dorset in 1989 with plant from the ex-Swannell's brewery in Hertfordshire and went into production there in May 1991. Currently supplies 20 outlets, with steady growth continuing into the guest beer market in the southern New Forest.

Yardarm Special Bitter* (OG 1051, ABV 5.2%) A hoppy premium bitter.

CORNISH

See Nationals, Whitbread, and Pub Groups, Devenish.

COTLEIGH

Cotleigh Brewery, Ford Road, Wiveliscombe, Somerset TA4 2RE. Tel. (0984) 24086

Continued growth has taken this brewery a long way from its first home – a stable block at Cotleigh Farmhouse in 1979. 1985 saw the completion of a purpose-built brewhouse and there was further expansion in 1991 and 1993 with the purchase of adjoining premises and the doubling of brewing capacity. Harrier SPA, Tawny and Old Buzzard are the regular brews, the others are made available to customers on a monthly guest beer rota. Serves over 100 outlets, mostly in Devon and Somerset, although the beers are also available across the country via wholesalers. No longer has a tied house. Brews occasionally for East-West Ales wholesalers.

Harrier SPA (OG 1036, ABV 3.6%) A straw-coloured beer with a very hoppy aroma and flavour, and a hoppy, bitter finish. Plenty of flavour for a light, low gravity beer.

Nutcracker Mild* (OG 1036, ABV 3.6%) A dark mild, an occasional brew.

Tawny Bitter (OG 1040, ABV 3.8%) A mid brown-coloured, very consistent beer. A hoppy aroma, a hoppy but quite well-balanced flavour, and a hoppy, bitter finish.

Barn Owl Bitter* (OG 1048, ABV 4.5%) Brewed only occasionally, in aid of the brewery's adopted charity, the Hawk and Owl Trust.

Old Buzzard (OG 1048, ABV 4.8%) Dark ruby-red beer, tasting strongly of roast malt, balanced with hops. Roast malt again in the finish, with bitterness. Very drinkable once the taste is acquired.

Rebellion* (OG 1050, ABV 5%) An occasional brew.

Red Nose Reinbeer* (OG 1060, ABV 5.6%) A dark and warming Christmas brew.

For East-West Ales:

Aldercote Ale* (OG 1042, ABV 4.2%) An occasional brew.

COURAGE See Nationals.

CROPTON **Cropton Brewery Co., The New Inn, Cropton, Pickering, N. Yorks. YO18 8HH. Tel. (075 15) 330**

Set up in 1984 just to supply the New Inn, the brewery was expanded in 1988 to supply its additive-free beers to a growing local free trade and now sells to around 30 outlets. King Billy is the latest addition to the range.

King Billy Bitter (OG 1037, ABV 3.6%) Specially brewed for the King William pub in Hull: a gold-coloured, beautifully clean, hoppy bitter, light on the palate but with strong hop flavour and bitterness. Long, hoppy and bitter finish but only a slight aroma.

Two Pints Best Bitter (OG 1040, ABV 4%) A hop aroma precedes a powerful, flowery hop character with some malt and bitterness. Long, smooth hoppy and sweet finish. A fine, distinctive bitter.

Scoresby Stout (OG 1042, ABV 4.2%) A rich assault of predominantly roast malt and bitterness, moving to a long, bitter finish of roast malt and chocolate. Jet black, and a stout in every sense.

Special Strong Bitter* (OG 1060, ABV 6.3%) A powerful winter ale.

CROUCH VALE **Crouch Vale Brewery Ltd., 12 Redhills Road, South Woodham Ferrers, Chelmsford, Essex CM3 5UP. Tel. (0245) 322744**

Started in 1981 by two CAMRA enthusiasts, Crouch Vale has expanded gradually and now has six full-time employees, and, with the opening up of guest beer markets, the future still looks rosy. Its single tied house, the Cap & Feathers at Tillingham was the CAMRA national *Pub of the Year* in 1989. 250 free trade outlets in Suffolk, Essex and Greater London.

Best Mild (OG 1035, ABV 3.5%) Dark reddish brown, with a roast aroma and hints of malt and caramel. Good roast flavour, with a sharper bitter aftertaste, tinged with a lingering dryness.

Woodham IPA (OG 1035, ABV 3.5%) Amber beer with a fresh, hoppy nose with a slight fruitiness. A refreshing lunchtime drink that gives a bitter aftertaste to the hoppy, fruity texture.

Best Bitter (OG 1040, ABV 4%) A rich, balanced red/brown-coloured beer with a hoppy, fruity aroma. The taste is of fruit and malt, with hops leading to a dry, bitter aftertaste.

Millennium Gold (OG 1042, ABV 4.2%) A wonderful golden beer featuring a strong, hoppy nose with maltiness. A powerful mixture of hops and fruit combines with pale malt to give a final sharp, bitter flavour with malty undertones.

Strong Anglian Special or SAS (OG 1048, ABV 5%) A tawny-coloured beer with a fruity nose. A balanced brew with a sharp bitterness and a dry aftertaste.

> The tankard symbol indicates the *Good Beer Guide Beers of the Year*, finalists in the *Champion Beer of Britain* contest held at the *Great British Beer Festival* at Olympia in August 1993.

Essex Porter (OG 1050, ABV 5%) Dark brew with a malt and roast malt aroma with some hops and fruit. The flavour is fruity and slightly nutty on a sweet base. Well-rounded sweet aftertaste.

FPA or Fine Pale Ale* (OG 1050, ABV 5%) Very occasional brew.

Santa's Revenge (OG 1055, ABV 5.8%) A Christmas ale, also sold throughout the year under house names. Despite its strength, it is dry and winey, not sweet.

Willie Warmer (OG 1060, ABV 6.5%) A dark red ale, brimming with roast aromas and hints of fruit. The roast and fruit merge pleasantly to give a flavour of balanced sweetness and malt, tinged with pleasant aftertastes.

CROWN BUCKLEY

Crown Brewery PLC, Cowbridge Road, Pontyclun, Mid Glamorgan CF7 9YG. Tel. (0443) 225453

Following several take-overs, Buckley, the oldest brewery in Wales (estd. 1767) became merged with Crown Brewery (the former United Clubs Brewery) in 1989, with Harp financial backing. This ultimately meant that the new company was owned by Guinness but it represented a genuine lifeline for the company. During this time, Crown Buckley underwent a great deal of rationalisation and restructuring, which left the company with a tied estate of 90 pubs. A management buy-out in June 1993 resulted in the brewery becoming genuinely independent again and looking forward to a long-overdue period of growth and stability. All beer production is carried out at the Llanelli (Buckley) site; kegging and bottling is done at Pontyclun (the old Crown brewery).

Buckley's Dark Mild (OG 1034, ABV 3.4%) A very dark, malty mild, fairly sweet with traces of chocolate, followed by a nutty, bitter finish. Difficult to find in good condition.

Buckley's Best Bitter (OG 1036, ABV 3.8%) A well-balanced, medium gravity bitter which has a rather sweet, malty flavour and a pleasant, bitter finish.

Special Best Bitter (SBB) (OG 1036, ABV 3.8%) Distinctively malty and clean tasting, with a pronounced bitter flavour and a rather dry aftertaste.

Reverend James Bitter (OG 1045, ABV 4.5%) A malty, full-bodied bitter with fruity overtones, followed by a bittersweet aftertaste.

DALESIDE

Daleside Brewery, Camwal Road, Harrogate, N. Yorks. HG1 4PT. Tel. (0423) 880041

Formerly Big End brewery, founded in 1988 by Bill Witty and now run by Bill with his son, Craig. The move to new premises and a change of company name in the spring of 1992 also brought an improvement in quality and character to the beers. Supplies outlets within a 100-mile radius.

Bitter (OG 1038, ABV 3.6%) Pale brown bitter with a strong, fruity aroma. The clean, fruity taste with balancing malt and bitterness, is finished with a long bitter, fruit aftertaste. Can be sold under house names.

Dalesman Old Ale (OG 1042, ABV 4%) Satisfying, dark brown strong bitter, with rich malt and roast in the mouth, complemented by fruit and hop flavour. Light hop and roast malt finish. Can also have house names.

Monkey Wrench (OG 1056, ABV 5.4%) A strong aroma of fruit leads to a rich assault of malt/roast and a strong fruit flavour with balancing bitterness, ending in a long fruity, malty/bitter finish. Some sweetness throughout. A powerful strong ale, dark ruby/brown in hue. Can be difficult to find.

The Independents

DARLEY See Wards.

DAVENPORTS See Nationals, Carlsberg-Tetley, and Pub Groups, Greenalls.

DENT **Dent Brewery, Hollins, Cowgill, Dent, Cumbria LA10 5TQ. Tel. (0539) 625326**

Set up in a converted barn in the Yorkshire Dales in March 1990, originally to supply just three local pubs. Now has two tied houses and supplies over 100 outlets all over northern England. All Dent's beers are brewed using the brewery's own spring water. T'Owd Tup is a new addition to the range.

Bitter* (OG 1036, ABV 3.7%)

Ramsbottom Strong Ale* (OG 1046, ABV 4.5%)

T'Owd Tup (OG 1058, ABV 6%)

DEVENISH See Pub Groups and Nationals, Whitbread.

DONNINGTON **Donnington Brewery, Stow-on-the-Wold, Glos. GL54 1EP. Tel. (0451) 830603**

Possibly the most attractive brewery in the country, set in a 13th-century watermill in idyllic surroundings. Bought by Thomas Arkell in 1827, it became a brewery in 1865, and it is still owned and run by the family. Supplies 15 tied houses, and 12 free trade outlets. XXX is only available in a few outlets.

BB (OG 1036, ABV 3.5%) Little aroma, but a pleasing, bitter beer, with a good malt/hop balance. Not as distinctive as it used to be.

XXX (OG 1036, ABV 3.5%) Again, thin in aroma, but flavoursome. More subtle than others in its class. Some fruit and traces of chocolate and liquorice in the taste, with a notably malty finish.

SBA (OG 1046, ABV 4%) Malt dominates over bitterness in the flavour of this premium bitter. Subtle, with just a hint of fruit and a dry, malty finish. Faintly malty aroma.

DUNN PLOWMAN **The Dunn Plowman Brewery, 80 South Street, Leominster, Hereford & Worcester HR6 8JF. Tel. (0568) 615059**

Brewery founded in April 1992 next to the Black Horse pub and now supplying six other pubs locally, plus some outlets in West Wales through wholesalers.

BHB* (OG 1040, ABV 4%)

Woody's Crown* (OG 1045, ABV 4.5%)

Shire Horse Ale* (OG 1050, ABV 5%)

Muletide* (OG 1056, ABV 5.5%) A winter beer.

DYFFRYN CLWYD **Bracdy Dyffryn Clwyd Brewery, The Old Butter Market, Factory Ward, Denbigh, Clwyd.**

Denbigh's old Butter Market, a listed building, converted into a brewery by local pub landlord, Ioan Evans. The first barrels of beer rolled out in summer 1993. A winter porter may be added to its list.

Cysur Bitter* (ABV 4%)

Cwrw Castell* (ABV 5%)

EARL SOHAM **Earl Soham Brewery, The Victoria, Earl Soham, Woodbridge, Suffolk IP13 7RL. Tel. (0728) 685758**

Established in April 1985 to supply its own pub, the Victoria, and a few years' later acquired a second pub, the Tram Depot in Cambridge. This has now been sold to Everards. Supplies a few other free trade outlets.

Gannet Mild (OG 1032, ABV 3%) Unusual ale, more like a light porter than a mild, given the bitter finish and roast flavours which compete with the underlying maltiness.

Victoria (OG 1036, ABV 3.5%) A characterful, well-hopped malty beer whose best feature is the superbly tangy, hoppy aftertaste.

Albert Ale (OG 1044, ABV 4.3%) Hops predominate in every aspect of this beer but especially in the finish which some will find glorious, others astringent. A truly extreme brew.

Jolabrugg (OG 1060, ABV 5.4%) The recipe for this winter brew tends to change from batch to batch, but expect something rich, smooth and fruity with a bittersweet aftertaste.

EASTWOOD'S

Eastwood's Brewery, Unit A2A, Commercial Mills, Savile Street, Milnsbridge, Huddersfield, W. Yorks. HD3 3PG. Tel. (0484) 656024

Brewery established by John Eastwood, former licensee of the Dusty Miller pub in Huddersfield, in April 1993. A premium bitter and a strong ale may be added.

Best Bitter* (OG 1037, ABV 3.7%)

ELDRIDGE POPE

Eldridge, Pope & Co. PLC, Weymouth Avenue, Dorchester, Dorset DT1 1QT. Tel. (0305) 251251

Charles and Sarah Eldridge started the Green Dragon Brewery in Dorchester in 1837. By 1880, Edwin and Alfred Pope had bought into the company and it had moved to its present site, next to the railway, with its first pubs situated along the line. The brewery is still run by the Pope family, producing award-winning ales. Thomas Hardy's Ale has long been notable as the strongest naturally-conditioned bottled beer. Unfortunately a cask breather device is used in most of the 180 tied houses; those houses not using the device have been designated 'Traditional Ale Houses'. Free trade extends as far as London, Bristol and Exeter, and the brewery also brews under contract for Ross. *Bottle-conditioned beers: Thomas Hardy Country Bitter (OG 1040, ABV 4.2%); Thomas Hardy's Ale (OG 1125, ABV 12%)*

Dorchester Bitter (OG 1032, ABV 3.3%) A light session beer which is hoppy and bitter throughout, with some balancing malt.

Best Bitter (OG 1036, ABV 3.8%) A mixture of malt and hop, with a hint of fruit. Difficult to find in cask-conditioned form.

Blackdown Porter (OG 1040, ABV 4%) A dark beer with an intense roast malt aroma. There are traces of coffee, chocolate and blackcurrant in the taste, leading into a dry, bitter finish. Deliberately served chilled in some outlets.

Thomas Hardy Country Bitter (OG 1040, ABV 4.2%) A dry, hoppy beer, with faint undertones of malt and fruit. The taste is smooth despite a bitter edge which continues into the aftertaste.

Royal Oak (OG 1048, ABV 5%) A full-bodied beer with a distinctive banana aroma and a mainly sweet, fruity taste. This is balanced by malt and some hop, and there is a fruity finish to this smooth, well-rounded brew.

For Ross:

Bottle-conditioned beer: Saxon Strong Ale (OG 1050, ABV 5%)

ELGOOD'S

Elgood & Sons Ltd., North Brink Brewery, Wisbech, Cambs. PE13 1LN. Tel. (0945) 583160

From its classical Georgian, riverside premises (converted in the 1790s from a mill and granary and acquired by Elgood's in 1878), this brewery supplies all but seven of its 49 tied houses with real ale. A mini-brewery has been set up to produce a variety of beers in small volumes to be sold as guests. A visitors' centre and brewery museum is planned to coincide with the brewery's bicentenary in 1995. Serves around 100 free trade outlets in East Anglia.

Black Dog Mild* (OG 1037, ABV 3.6%) A seasonal brew for the spring.

Cambridge Bitter (OG 1037, ABV 3.8%) A pleasant beer but can be bland. The good balance of malt and hops on the palate combines with sharp pungent bitterness that lingers in the aftertaste. Malt in the aroma is often accompanied by sulphury hoppiness.

Barleymead* (OG 1048, ABV 4.8%) A seasonal, autumn brew.

Greyhound Strong Bitter or GSB (OG 1049, ABV 5.2%) A rare beer, but one that has improved. An aroma of malt and raisin-like fruit leads into a well-balanced flavour of malt, fruit and hops on a bittersweet base. Bitter fruit finish.

Sir Henry's Porter* (OG 1055, ABV 5%) An autumn offering, named after the now-retired head brewer, Sir Henry Holder.

Winter Warmer (OG 1080, ABV 9%) A rich red/brown winter ale. Wine-like, with a full, fruity, bittersweet flavour that also has a yeasty/Marmite component. Fruity aroma and bittersweet finish.

ENVILLE

Enville Ales, Enville Brewery, Cox Green, Enville, Stourbridge, W. Midlands DY7 5LG. Tel. (0384) 873770

A newly commissioned brewery (1993) on a picturesque Victorian farm complex, in a village where brewing ceased in the 1920s. Using the same water source as the original brewery, it now serves around 20 free trade outlets. Enville is in Staffordshire, despite the West Midlands postal address.

Ale* (OG 1046, ABV 4.8%)

Gothic Ale* (OG 1052, ABV 5.2%)

EVERARDS

Everards Brewery Ltd., Castle Acres, Narborough, Leicester LE9 5BY. Tel. (0533) 630900

A small brewery, entirely family owned and run, which was founded in Leicester in 1849, by the great-great-grandfather of the current chairman, Richard Everard. Over the years its beers were brewed in both Leicester and Burton upon Trent, until all production was transferred to Castle Acres in 1990. Most of its 142 tied houses sell real ale, but some use cask breathers; many offer guest beers. Everards also services some 500 free trade accounts and began brewing Chester's Best Mild in summer 1993, following the closure of Whitbread's Exchange Brewery.

Mild* (OG 1036, ABV 3.3%) A new mild, introduced in 1993, with a higher gravity than its predecessor.

Beacon Bitter (OG 1036, ABV 3.8%) Light, well-balanced tawny bitter with a hoppy aroma and flavour leading to a bitter finish.

Tiger Best Bitter (OG 1041, ABV 4.2%) Mid brown, with an aroma of malt and hops and a soft, malty palate. Good balance, with a finish that is bitter and hoppy. A good, medium-bodied bitter.

Old Original (OG 1050, ABV 5.2%) A beer with a smooth, distinctive palate and a faintly hoppy and fruity aroma. A complex beer with hops predominant, leading to an equally complex bitter finish.

Old Bill Winter Warmer* (OG 1068, ABV 7.3%) Brewed Dec–Jan.

> OG stands for Original Gravity, the reading taken before fermentation of the amount of fermentable material in the brew. It is a rough indicator of strength. More reliable is the ABV (Alcohol by Volume) rating, which gives the percentage of alcohol in the finished beer.

For Whitbread:

Chester's Best Mild* (OG 1032, ABV 3.5%)

EXE VALLEY

Exe Valley Brewery, Land Farm, Silverton, Exeter, Devon EX5 4HF. Tel. (0392) 860406

Barron Brewery was set up in 1984 by Richard Barron, and the company name changed when he was joined by Guy Sheppard. At the farm brewery, operating from an old barn (using the farm's own spring water), new plant was installed in 1993 which has effectively trebled the old equipment's capacity of 60 barrels a week. Some 35 local free trade outlets within a 25-mile radius are supplied on a regular basis (no tied estate).

Bitter (OG 1038, ABV 3.7%) Malty, pale brown bitter, with a fruity, hoppy taste and a fruity, bitter aftertaste.

Dob's Best Bitter (OG 1040, ABV 4.1%) Pale brown bitter with strong hop aroma, a pleasantly hoppy, fruity taste and a well-balanced, fruity, sweet aftertaste.

Devon Glory (OG 1047, ABV 4.7%) A tawny-coloured beer with an extremely fruity aroma and taste.

Exeter Old Bitter (OG 1047, ABV 4.8%) Tawny-coloured. The fruity aroma is followed by a pleasant, hoppy and fruity taste and aftertaste.

EXMOOR

Exmoor Ales Ltd., Golden Hill Brewery, Wiveliscombe, Somerset TA4 2NY. Tel. (0984) 23798

When it began production in 1980, this brewery won immediate national acclaim, as its Exmoor Ale took the *Best Bitter* award at CAMRA's Great British Beer Festival. Operating from the former Hancock's Brewery at Wiveliscombe (closed 1959), it has no ambitions for a tied estate but concentrates on supplying real ale to some 150 pubs in the region and to a wholesale network covering virtually the whole country.

Ale (OG 1039, ABV 3.8%) Pale brown beer with a malty aroma and a malty, dry taste. Bitter and malty finish. Very drinkable.

Dark* (OG 1042, ABV 4.1%) An occasional brew.

Gold (OG 1045, ABV 4.5%) Yellow/golden in colour, with a malty aroma and flavour, and a slight sweetness and hoppiness. Sweet, malty finish.

Stag (OG 1050, ABV 5.2%) Pale brown beer, with a malty taste and aroma, and a bitter finish. Slightly sweet. Very similar to Exmoor Ale and drinks as easily.

Beast* (OG 1066, ABV 6.6%) A winter brew: October–March.

FEATHERSTONE

Featherstone Brewery, Unit 2, Charnwood Ind. Units, Vulcan Road, Leicester. Tel. (0533) 531901

Small brewery, specializing in supplying custom beers to pubs for sale under house names. Six local outlets take the beers regularly and the brewery also acts as a wholesaler for producers. Plans to acquire a tied house.

Robins Bitter* (OG 1030, ABV 2.6%)

Mild* (OG 1035, ABV 3.6%)

Stout* (OG 1038, ABV 3.8%)

Best Bitter* (OG 1039, ABV 4.1%)

Porter* (OG 1048, ABV 5.1%)

Vulcan Bitter* (OG 1048, ABV 5.1%)

FEDERATION | **Northern Clubs Federation Brewery Ltd., Lancaster Road, Dunston, Tyne & Wear NE11 9JR. Tel. (091) 460 9023**

A co-operative, founded in 1919 to discover ways of overcoming the post-war beer shortage, which expanded to supply pubs and clubs through its own depots and wholesalers. The brewery is still owned by clubs and their business accounts for the majority of the brewery's trade, but only a tiny amount of the brewery's output is cask-conditioned.

Best Bitter (OG 1035, ABV 3.6%) Very difficult to find, especially on top form, when it has a pleasant aroma, a bitter flavour and a well-balanced aftertaste, with a hint of fruit throughout. Really an ordinary bitter, not a best.

Special Ale (OG 1039, ABV 4%) A pale brown bitter with balanced malt and hop character and lasting bitterness.

Buchanan's Original (OG 1044, ABV 4.5%) Rich, with a strong palate. More generous with malt character than hops or bitterness but with a balanced fruitiness.

FELINFOEL | **The Felinfoel Brewery Co. Ltd., Farmers Row, Felinfoel, Llanelli, Dyfed SA14 8LB. Tel. (0554) 773357**

This famous Welsh brewery was built in 1878 when the village brew pub could no longer keep up with local demand. Despite recent predators, it is managing to hang on to its independence. For a while Crown Buckley held a considerable stake, but, after investment in the latter company by Guinness, the Lewis family trust which runs Felinfoel was able to buy back a large number of Felinfoel shares. Supplies draught ale to all but one of its 85 houses (though some use top pressure) and serves roughly 300 free trade outlets. Also acts as a wholesaler for other draught ales.

Traditional Bitter (OG 1031, ABV 3.2%) A hoppy and slightly malty session beer. Very refreshing, with a hoppy aftertaste. Sometimes difficult to find but worth the effort.

Traditional Dark (OG 1031, ABV 3.2%) A dark brown/red mild, rather thin with roast malt overtones, followed by a more bitter flavour and aftertaste.

Cambrian Best Bitter (OG 1036, ABV 3.8%) Notably hopped and fairly malty pale brown beer. Somewhat fruity, with a pleasantly bitter aftertaste.

Double Dragon 'Premium' (OG 1048, ABV 5%) A fine, well-balanced, rich bitter with a nutty malt flavour, a fruity nose and a rounded bittersweet finish.

FLOWERS See Nationals, Whitbread.

FORBES | **Forbes Ales, Unit 2, Harbour Road Ind. Estate, Oulton Broad, Lowestoft, Suffolk NR32 3LZ. Tel. (0502) 587905**

Brewery set up in 1988. Not brewing at present and currently up for sale.

FOXLEY | **Foxley Brewing Company Ltd., Unit 3, Home Farm Workshops, Mildenhall, Marlborough, Wilts. SN8 2LR. Tel. (0672) 515000**

Rob Owen and Neil Collings, both keen home brewers, started this, their first commercial venture, in July 1992 to supply 30 pubs locally. Now available within a 50-mile radius, the Best Bitter has been joined by a stronger brew.

Best Bitter* (OG 1038, ABV 4%)

Strong Ale* (OG 1048, ABV 4.8%)

FRANKLIN'S — **Franklin's Brewery, Bilton Lane, Bilton, Harrogate, N. Yorks. HG1 4DH. Tel. (0423) 322345**

A brewery set up in 1980 by Sean Franklin, who devised a beer to copy the bouquet of the wines in which he specialised! Now run by Leeds CAMRA founder-member Tommy Thomas. Supplies around ten free trade outlets, and beer festivals.

Bitter — (OG 1038, ABV 3.9%) A tremendous hop aroma precedes a flowery hop flavour, combined with malt. Long hop and bitter finish. A fine, unusual amber bitter.

Blotto* — (OG 1055, ABV 6%) A winter and occasional brew.

FREEMINER — **Freeminer Brewery, Sling, Coleford, Glos. GL16 8JJ. Tel. (0594) 810408**

New brewery, set up at the edge of the Forest of Dean in November 1992 by partners Don Burgess and Chris Lewis. Also brews a draught cider, plus beers under contract for Blackbeard. Supplies 30 outlets direct, including several in the Manchester area, and others across the country via wholesalers.

Bitter* — (OG 1038, ABV 4%)

Speculation Ale* — (OG 1047, ABV 4.8%)

Deep Shaft Stout* — (OG 1050, ABV 5%)

Slaughter Porter* — (OG 1055, ABV 5.2%)

For Blackbeard Trading:

Three Bells* — (OG 1048, ABV 4.8%)

Stairway to Heaven* — (OG 1055, ABV 5%)

FREETRADERS — **Freetraders Group Ltd., Twyford Abbey Road, Park Royal, London NW10 7SB. Tel. (081) 965 0222**

Beer and soft drinks wholesaler whose one original beer, Twelve Bore Bitter, is brewed by King & Barnes (see King & Barnes).

FREMLINS — See Nationals, Whitbread.

FRIARY MEUX — See Nationals, Carlsberg-Tetley.

FULLER'S — **Fuller, Smith and Turner PLC, Griffin Brewery, Chiswick Lane, Chiswick, London W4 2QB. Tel. (081) 994 3691**

Beer has been brewed on the Fuller's site for over 325 years, John Fuller being joined by Henry Smith and John Turner in 1845. Descendants of the original partners are still on the board today, making Fuller's one of only two surviving independent London brewers after the 1960s take-over spree. The brewery recently completed a £1.6 million brewhouse redevelopment to cope with growing demand; the installation of new mash tuns in 1993 has meant an increase in capacity of 50%. All but three of its 203 tied houses serve real ale, and Fuller's supplies an extensive free trade both directly and through its subsidiary real ale distributor, Classic Ales. Hock, a dark mild phased out in the 1970s, was revived in 1993.

Hock* — (OG 1033, ABV 3.2%) Brewed March–October.

Chiswick Bitter — (OG 1034, ABV 3.5%) A distinctively hoppy beer when fresh, with strong maltiness and a fruity character. Finishes with a lasting, dry bitterness and a pleasing aftertaste. *Champion Beer of Britain* 1989.

London Pride — (OG 1040, ABV 4.1%) An excellent beer with a strong, malty base and a rich balance of well-developed hop flavours and powerful bitterness.

Mr Harry* (OG 1048, ABV 4.8%) Available November–February.

ESB (OG 1054, ABV 5.5%) A copper-red, strong, robust beer with great character. A full-bodied maltiness and a rich hoppiness are immediately evident and develop into a rich fruitiness with an underlying sweet fullness.

FURGUSONS See Nationals, Carlsberg-Tetley.

GALE'S **George Gale & Co. Ltd., The Hampshire Brewery, Horndean, Hants. PO8 0DA. Tel. (0705) 571212**

Hampshire's major brewery, Gale's was founded in 1847. The building was largely destroyed by fire and a new, enlarged brewery was built on the original site in 1869. It grew slowly and steadily during the early 20th century, taking over other small local breweries along the way. It has now sold off 13 of its pubs to Maritime Taverns, but all the remaining 131 tied houses, which include some very attractive old inns, serve real ale. Gale's also supplies other outlets via the big breweries and brews for Whitbread. Its light mild has now been dropped. *Bottle-conditioned beer: Prize Old Ale (OG 1094, ABV 9%)*

XXXD* (OG 1031, ABV 2.9%)

BBB or Butser Brew Bitter (OG 1035, ABV 3.6%) Golden brown in colour, with little aroma; fairly sweet-tasting, with the sweetness not appearing to come entirely from malt. Some grain and maltiness are also present, with some bitterness and hop flavour to finish.

Best Bitter (OG 1040, ABV 3.8%) Probably the best-balanced beer of the Gale's range: sweet and malty, with some fruit leading to a malty finish with some hop character. A reddish-brown brew.

5X (OG 1044, ABV 4.2%) Available October–March. A very fruity beer, occasionally with liquorice and aniseed, too. There is a winey fruitiness to the nose and some bitterness in the finish.

HSB (OG 1050, ABV 5%) Too sugary-sweet for some palates. A deep brown beer with little aroma but some malt grain and mixed fruit (apples, bananas and damson), leading to a dry, hoppy finish.

Prize Old Ale (OG 1094, ABV 9%) Draught version of the bottle-conditioned beer, available in only a few outlets at Christmastime. Perhaps less full-tasting than from the bottle, with a flavour of woody port and roast malt, which builds up to a slightly bitter finish balanced by tangerines. A very dark brown, vinous brew.

For Whitbread:

Pompey Royal (OG 1043, ABV 4.5%) A brown beer with a hint of redness. Low in aroma, with the flavour dominated by sweetness and pear fruit. The finish can be a little cloying.

GIBBS MEW **Gibbs Mew PLC, Anchor House, Netherhampton Road, Salisbury, Wilts. SP2 8RA. Tel. (0722) 411911**

Established in 1898 by the amalgamation of Salisbury brewers Bridger Gibbs & Sons and Herbert Mew & Co. Charrington bought a stake in the company in the 1960s, which the Gibbs family bought back in 1972, and, in 1992, with CAMRA support, it saw off predators Brierly Investments. The tied estate has grown considerably in the last ten years, partly due to a bulk purchase of pubs from Grand Metropolitan, but some houses are likely to be sold on in the near future. Real ale is now supplied to all 120 pubs (ten of which are not tied), as well as a growing free trade in southern and south-western England.

> Beers marked with an asterisk have not been tasted by official CAMRA tasting panels. However, some of these beers do carry brief descriptions derived from limited samplings or other sources, and can be used for rough guidance.

Timothy Chudley Local Line Bitter (OG 1036, ABV 3.6%) A clean-tasting bitter to be savoured. Moderately-hopped and slightly fruity. An ideal lunchtime ale.

Wiltshire Traditional Bitter (OG 1036, ABV 3.6%) A pleasant enough flavour of malt and hops, but frankly bland and uninspiring. Dry finish.

Premium Bitter (OG 1042, ABV 4%) A truly bland and uninteresting beer. A small, corky taste and an overbearing sweetness are only tempered by bitterness in the aftertaste.

Salisbury Best Bitter (OG 1042, ABV 4%) A rather chewy, sweet ale, decidedly lacking in bitterness. All the same, a pleasant beer.

Deacon* (OG 1051, ABV 5%) The latest addition to the range.

The Bishop's Tipple (OG 1066, ABV 6.5%) Weaker than the average barley wine, but not lacking in flavour. The full-bodied taste is marvellously malty with a kick that leaves the brain rather less clear than the beer.

GLENNY See Wychwood.

GOACHER'S

P&DJ Goacher, Hayle Mill Cottages, Bockingford, Maidstone, Kent ME15 6DT. Tel. (0622) 682112

Kent's most successful small independent brewer, set up in 1983 by Phil and Debbie Goacher, producing all-malt ales with Kentish hops for about 30 free trade outlets in the Maidstone area. Acquired its first tied house in 1992, and a porter has been added to the range. Special, a 75%/25% mix of Light and Dark, is also available to pubs for sale under house names. Brewing takes place at a nearby trading estate in Tovil.

Real Mild Ale* (OG 1033, ABV 3.4%) A full-flavoured malty ale with a background bitterness.

Fine Light Ale* (OG 1036, ABV 3.7%) Pale, golden brown bitter ale with a strong hoppy aroma and aftertaste. A very hoppy and moderately malty session beer.

Best Dark Ale (OG 1040, ABV 4.1%) Intensely bitter beer, balanced by a moderate maltiness, with a complex aftertaste. Lighter in colour than it once was, but still darker than most bitters.

Gold Star* (OG 1050, ABV 5.1%) A new summer pale ale.

Porter* (OG 1050, ABV 5.1%) A new dark ruby winter beer with a roast malt flavour.

Old 1066 Ale* (OG 1066, ABV 6.7%) Black, potent old ale, produced in winter only.

GOLDFINCH

Goldfinch Brewery, 47 High East Street, Dorchester, Dorset DT1 1HU. Tel. (0305) 264020

Brewery established in 1987 at Tom Brown's Public House whose theme is broadly based on *Tom Brown's Schooldays*. It has expanded from a one-barrel to a four-barrel plant and has plans for future growth. Supplies Tom Brown's (which is run as a free house) and an increasing free trade.

Tom Brown's Best Bitter (OG 1039, ABV 4%) A pale-coloured bitter which is fruity in both aroma and taste, with hop and some malt. The bittersweet taste gives way to a predominantly bitter finish.

Flashman's Clout Strong Ale (OG 1043, ABV 4.5%) A beer with an attractive, honeyed aroma, and, again, a bittersweet taste with malt and some hop. Tawny/mid brown in colour, with hoppiness coming through to give a bitter edge to the aftertaste.

Midnight Blinder (OG 1050, ABV 5%) A ruby-red-coloured beer with an intense fruit aroma. Malt, hop and fruit combine to give the familiar bittersweet taste of Goldfinch beers, leading into a marvellous hoppy, bitter finish.

GOOSE EYE **Goose Eye Brewery, Ingrow Bridge, South Street, Keighley, W. Yorks. BD21 5AX. Tel. (0535) 605807**

After an absence of three years from the brewing scene, Goose Eye was reopened in 1991 in a converted carpet warehouse by Bryan Eastell, with a new partner, Jack Atkinson. The beers are supplied to 50 free trade outlets, and plans are in hand to acquire a free house.

Black Goose Mild* (OG 1037) A new mild.

Bitter* (OG 1038, ABV 3.9%)

Wharfedale Bitter* (OG 1045, ABV 4.5%)

Pommie's Revenge* (OG 1052, ABV 5.2%)

GRAND METROPOLITAN See Nationals, Courage, and Pub Groups, Chef & Brewer and Inntrepreneur.

GREENALLS See Pub Groups and Nationals, Carlsberg-Tetley.

GREENE KING **Greene King PLC, Westgate Brewery, Westgate Street, Bury St Edmunds, Suffolk IP33 1QT. Tel. (0284) 763222**

East Anglia's largest regional brewery (established 1799), producing cask-conditioned beers at Bury; it closed the Rayments brewery at Furneux Pelham in 1987 and its Biggleswade brewery is now entirely given over to lager production. In May 1992, Greene King bought up the Whitbread Investment Company's stake in Morland, but its bid to take full control (and close the Abingdon brewery) flopped disastrously. All Greene King's 835 tied houses serve cask ale, with only a minority still applying a blanket of CO_2 and a cask breather. Extensive free trade, but XX Mild is still threatened by declining sales.

XX Mild (OG 1032, ABV 3%) Considering its low gravity, this ale usually offers a surprisingly full-bodied maltiness, backed up with caramel and chocolate.

IPA (OG 1036, ABV 3.6%) Strong hop aromas lead into a formidably hoppy palate and a long bitter finish. Harsh, one-dimensional examples do often occur, however.

Rayments Special Bitter (OG 1040, ABV 4%) Significantly sweeter and richer than the other Greene King beers. Some find it pleasantly fruity, others consider it a bit bland.

Abbot Ale (OG 1049, ABV 5%) A complex strong ale whose multiplicity of flavours is not always easily kept in balance, but, when on form, it is a richly satisfying brew. Hop oils can be intrusive.

Winter Ale (OG 1060, ABV 6%) Available November–January and usually served from polypins on the bar. A dark red/brown old ale of substance, like a good wine in many ways. A predominantly fruity nose with some chocolate leads through to a rich blend of fruit, roast malt and some sweetness in the taste. A surprisingly dry aftertaste rounds off this warming brew.

GUERNSEY **The Guernsey Brewery Co. (1920) Ltd., South Esplanade, St Peter Port, Guernsey, CI GY1 1BJ. Tel. (0481) 720143**

One of two breweries on this Channel Isle, serving its stronger than average real ales in 13 of its 32 tied houses. Free trade takes in some 60 outlets on Alderney, Herm, Sark and Jersey. Originally opened as the London Brewery in 1865, it became a Guernsey registered company in 1920 upon the introduction of income tax on the mainland. It was taken over by Jersey's Ann Street Brewery in 1988 and Guernsey real ale is available in selected Ann Street houses. Britannia Bitter is often sold under house names.

LBA Mild (OG 1037, ABV 3.8%) Copper-red in colour, with a complex aroma of malt, hops, fruit and toffee. The rich, mellow flavour combines malt, fruit, hops and butterscotch. The finish has malt and hops. Full-flavoured and surprisingly dry.

Britannia Bitter (OG 1042, ABV 4%) A brewery mix of Mild and Bitter. Amber/tawny in colour, with an aroma of malt, fruit and toffee. Very malty on the palate and again in the finish. Full-bodied and satisfying.

Real Draught Bitter (OG 1045, ABV 4.2%) Golden in colour, with a fine malt aroma. Malt and fruit are strong on the palate and the beer is quite dry for its strength. Excellent, dry malt and hop finish.

GUINNESS See Nationals.

HP&D See Nationals, Carlsberg-Tetley.

HADRIAN **Hadrian Brewery Ltd., Unit 10, Hawick Crescent Ind. Estate, Newcastle upon Tyne, Tyne & Wear NE6 1AS. Tel. (091) 276 5302**

Brewery started with a five-barrel plant in 1987. It grew steadily, and was forced to move to new premises at the end of 1991 in order to expand to a 20-barrel plant. Financial problems followed, but the brewery was saved from receivership. Forty free trade outlets.

Gladiator Bitter (OG 1039, ABV 4%) Hoppiness dominates in this light and drinkable bitter.

Centurion Best Bitter (OG 1045, ABV 4.5%) Excellently-balanced beer with prolonged malt and bitter character and a lingering hoppy aftertaste.

Emperor Ale (OG 1050, ABV 5%) A beautiful old ale, well-crafted and with a good balance of hop, malt, fruit and bitter elements providing a strong aroma.

Yule Fuel (OG 1060, ABV 6.2%) Fruity and bitter Christmas ale. Well hopped.

For The Village Brewer (non-brewing company):

Zetland Best Bitter* (OG 1042, ABV 4.2%)

HALL & WOODHOUSE **Hall & Woodhouse Ltd., The Brewery, Blandford Forum, Dorset DT11 9LS. Tel. (0258) 452141**

Founded as the Ansty Brewery in 1777 by Charles Hall, whose son, Robert, took Mr GEI Woodhouse into partnership in 1847. More usually known as 'Badger's', the brewery serves cask beer in 140 of its 149 houses (although an increasing number now use cask breathers), as well as around 500 free trade outlets in southern England. Also owns the Gribble Inn brew pub.

Badger Best Bitter (OG 1041, ABV 4%) A fine best bitter whose taste is strong in hop and bitterness, with underlying malt and fruit. A hoppy finish with a bitter edge.

Hard Tackle (OG 1045, ABV 4.5%) A well-balanced, tawny-coloured beer. The nose is fruity and hoppy with some malt, and the palate has similar characteristics. A mainly bitter aftertaste.

Tanglefoot (OG 1048, ABV 5%) A pale-coloured beer with a full fruit character throughout. Some malt and hop are also present in the palate, whilst the finish is bittersweet. Dangerously drinkable.

HALLS See Nationals, Carlsberg-Tetley.

HAMBLETON **Hambleton Ales, Holme-on-Swale, Thirsk, N. Yorks. YO7 4JE. Tel. (0845) 567460**

Brewery set up in March 1991 in a Victorian barn on the banks of the River Swale. The production target of 20 barrels a week was quickly achieved and overtaken; capacity has now been increased to such an extent that relocation is a distinct possibility. Supplies over 100 free trade outlets.

Bitter* (ABV 3.6%)

Porter* (ABV 3.6%)

Stallion* (ABV 4.2%)

For The Village Brewer (non-brewing company):

White Boar Bitter* (OG 1037, ABV 3.8%)

Old Raby Ale* (OG 1048, ABV 4.8%)

HAMPSHIRE

Hampshire Brewery, 5 Anton Trading Estate, Andover, Hants. SP10 2NJ. Tel. (0264) 336699

Set up in 1992 by a former Bunces head brewer, Simon Paine, and his partner, Steve Winduss, with a 25-barrel plant built to their own specification. Their first brew was named after Alfred the Great, whose parliament resided in Andover. A further three beers have since been added to the range and a strong beer has been tested. It supplies around 100 carefully targeted pubs.

King Alfred's (OG 1038, ABV 3.8%) A good session beer; the well-hopped, fruity, slightly perfumed flavour has a lingering bitter finish.

Lionheart* (OG 1042, ABV 4.2%)

Porter* (OG 1044, ABV 4.4%)

Pendragon* (OG 1048, ABV 4.8%)

HANBY

Hanby Ales Ltd., New Brewery, Aston Park, Soulton Road, Wem, Shropshire SY4 5SD. Tel. (0939) 232432

Following the closure of Wem Brewery by Greenalls in 1988, the former head brewer, Jack Hanby, set up his own brewery with a partner, Peter Simmonds. Brewing commenced the following spring and by February 1990 they had moved into a new, larger brewhouse, which was altered and expanded again in 1991 to cope with the large volume and range of products. The business is supplemented by wholesaling other breweries' beers.

Black Magic Mild* (OG 1033, ABV 3.3%)

Drawwell Bitter (OG 1039, ABV 3.9%) Full-flavoured, with plenty of hop character, right through to the finish.

Shropshire Stout* (OG 1045, ABV 4.4%)

Treacleminer Bitter* (OG 1046, ABV 4.6%)

Nutcracker Bitter* (OG 1060, ABV 6%)

Cocklewarmer Bitter* (OG 1080, ABV 7.6%)

For Blackbeard Trading:

Happy Jack* (OG 1030, ABV 3%)

Black Betty* (OG 1045, ABV 4.4%)

Cherry Bomb* (OG 1060, ABV 5.9%)

Joy Bringer* (OG 1060, ABV 5.9%)

Queen Ann's Revenge* (OG 1080, ABV 7.6%)

HANCOCK'S See Nationals, Bass.

HANSON'S See Banks's.

HANSEATIC **Hanseatic Trading Company Ltd., Manor House, Hambleton, Oakham, Leics. LE15 8TH. Tel. (0572) 722215**

Non-brewing company founded by ex-Ruddles brewer Jim Pryor in 1993. Its bottle-conditioned beers (no draught) are contract-brewed by McMullen (see McMullen) and mostly sold by the Oddbins off-licence chain.

HARDINGTON **Hardington Brewery, Albany Buildings, Dean Lane, Bedminster, Bristol, Avon BS3 1BT. Tel. (0272) 636194**

Set up in April 1991, Hardington's has little connection with the old Somerset brewery of the same name. Demand for its beers has been steadily increasing and it now serves 50 outlets as well as its first tied house, acquired in 1992.

Traditional Bitter (OG 1037, ABV 3.7%) An amber, clean, refreshing beer. Floral hop and citrus fruit aroma and taste, with balancing malt and a little sweetness. Long, dry, bitter finish.

Best Bitter (OG 1042, ABV 4.2%) Crisp, refreshing amber beer with a malty, slightly sweet, bitter taste, and a dry finish. Floral hop and citrus fruit aroma. Moreish.

Moonshine (OG 1048, ABV 5%) Yellow/gold beer, with a wheaty malt and slightly citrus fruit aroma. A smooth, pale malt, sweetish taste, with hints of fruit and spice, and a dry, bitter finish. Enigmatic.

Jubilee (OG 1050, ABV 5%) A mid brown, smooth, complex, fruity and warming beer. Beautifully balanced throughout.

Old Lucifer (OG 1054, ABV 6%) A smooth, powerful and distinctive, pale brown beer: sweet, fruity and warming. A complex malt and hop balance with pleasant bitterness. A superb, full-bodied ale.

Old Ale (OG 1065, ABV 6.5%) A rich, copper-red, full-bodied, warming ale; well-balanced, with a fruity, hoppy, roast malt aroma. A similar bittersweet, vinous taste with fruit undertones. Complex finish. A powerful, superbly well-crafted old ale.

HARDYS & HANSONS **Hardys & Hansons PLC, Kimberley Brewery, Nottingham NG16 2NS. Tel. (0602) 383611**

Established in 1832 and 1847 respectively, Hardys and Hansons were two competitive breweries until a merger in 1930 produced the present company. Nottingham's last independent brewery is controlled by descendants of the original Hardy and Hanson families, who are committed to keeping it that way. Its good value real ales are supplied to 150 of its 256 tied houses but there is still a tendency to spoil them with top pressure (never used on the strong Kimberley Classic). The brewery supplies around 50 other free trade outlets and has now started supplying pubs further afield via wholesalers.

Best Mild (OG 1034, ABV 3.1%) A dark, sweetish mild, slightly malty. Can have fruity notes.

Best Bitter (OG 1039, ABV 3.9%) Golden/straw-coloured, distinctive, faintly fruity beer. Subtle in aroma; malt is more prominent than hop character and balancing bitterness.

Kimberley Classic* (OG 1048, ABV 4.8%) A light-coloured, deceptively strong beer.

HARTLEYS See Robinson's.

HARVEYS **Harvey & Son (Lewes) Ltd., The Bridge Wharf Brewery, 6 Cliffe High Street, Lewes, E. Sussex BN7 2AH. Tel. (0273) 480209**

Established in the late 18th century by John Harvey, on the banks of the River Ouse, this Georgian brewery was partly rebuilt in 1880 and the Victorian Gothic tower and brewhouse remain a very attractive feature in the town centre. Still a family-run company, offering real ale in all 33 tied pubs and about 350 free trade outlets in Sussex and Kent. Frequently produces commemorative beers – occasionally on draught. *Bottle-conditioned beer: 1859 Porter (OG 1053, ABV 4.8%)*

XX Mild Ale (OG 1030, ABV 3%) A dark, malty brew with some roast in the aroma. The flavour also sees some fruity sweetness. Roasty finish.

Sussex Pale Ale (OG 1033, ABV 3.5%) An amber ale with a hoppy, fruity aroma and some malt. This leads through to a refreshing hop and fruit flavour on a bitter base, with some malt, too. Good dry finish.

Sussex Best Bitter (OG 1040, ABV 4%) Fruit and hops are prominent all the way through this drinkable southern bitter. The bitter palate also has some caramel maltiness. Bitter hop/fruit finish.

XXXX or Old Ale (OG 1043, ABV 4.3%) Brewed October-May: a rich, dark beer with a good malty nose, with some undertones of roast, hops and fruit. The flavour is a complex blend of roast malt, grain, fruit and hops with some caramel. Malty caramel finish with roast flavour.

Armada Ale (OG 1046, ABV 4.5%) Full-bodied brew with a good bitter-fruit and hoppy finish. This balance of hops and fruit is present throughout, with some grain and malt. Bitterness in the flavour makes it very drinkable.

1859 Porter* (OG 1053, ABV 4.8%) Available only in March.

Tom Paine* (OG 1055, ABV 5.5%) A summer offering, brewed only in July.

Elizabethan* (OG 1090, ABV 8.3%) December or occasional brews only; a silky-smooth barley wine.

HARVIESTOUN **Harviestoun Brewery Ltd., Devon Road, Dollar, Clackmannanshire, Central FK14 7LX. Tel. (0259) 42141**

Hand-built in a 200-year-old stone byre by two home-brew enthusiasts in 1985, this small brewery operates from a former dairy at the foot of the Ochil Hills, near Stirling. To cope with demand, a new, custom-built brew plant was installed in 1991, and a visitor centre is planned. Currently serves some 50 outlets in central Scotland. No tied houses.

Waverley 70/-* (OG 1037, ABV 3.7%) A light session beer with hints of roast in the aftertaste.

Original 80/-* (OG 1042, ABV 4.2%) A malty brew with hop flavour.

Ptarmigan 85/-* (OG 1045, ABV 4.5%) The first known 85/- ale, brewed with Bavarian hops and Scottish malt.

Old Manor* (OG 1050, ABV 5.1%) A dark beer with a roast malt flavour.

Nouveau* (OG 1094, ABV 10.5%) A winter brew for Christmas and the New Year. The gravity increases with the years: i.e. 1094 for 1994, etc.

HERITAGE **Heritage Brewery Ltd. (Museum Trust), Anglesey Road, Burton upon Trent, Staffs. DE14 3PF. Tel. (0283) 510246**

The brewing company of the Heritage Brewery Museum, based in the former Everards Tiger Brewery which was built in 1881 for Liverpool brewer Thomas Sykes. Purchased in 1985 for preservation, the more modern equipment has recently been removed to restore the brewery to its original condition. Whilst rebuilding work is carried out in the brewhouse, the brewing has been sub-contracted. Thomas Sykes Ale is the speciality brew, sold mostly in corked bottles for celebrations and commemorations, but also available on draught. The beers are sold at the brewery itself, and in the free trade via Lloyds Country Beers. *Bottle-conditioned beer: Thomas Sykes Ale (OG 1103, ABV 10%) also sold as Christmas Ale*

Bitter* (OG 1045, ABV 4.2%)

Thomas Sykes Ale* (OG 1103, ABV 10%)

HESKET NEWMARKET **Hesket Newmarket Brewery, Old Crown Barn, Hesket Newmarket, Cumbria CA7 8JG. Tel. (069 74) 78288**

Brewery set up in a barn behind the owners' pub in an attractive North Lakes village. Most of the beers are named after local fells and are supplied to the Old Crown and eight other pubs in the north, plus a further 30 or so outlets from Edinburgh down to Kent on an occasional or guest beer basis. Brewery tours are available by prior arrangement. Refurbishment and expansion are planned.

Great Cockup Porter* (OG 1035, ABV 2.6%) A refreshing, chocolate-tasting beer.

Skiddaw Special Bitter* (OG 1035, ABV 3.1%) A golden session beer, despite its name.

Blencathra Bitter* (OG 1035, ABV 3.5%) A ruby-coloured bitter.

Doris's 90th Birthday Ale* (OG 1045, ABV 4.3%) A fruity premium ale.

Old Carrock Strong Ale* (OG 1060, ABV 5.9%) A dark red, powerful ale.

Ay Ala's Angel (OG 1080, ABV 7.1%) Brewed for Christmas.

HEXHAMSHIRE **Hexhamshire Brewery, Leafields, Ordley, Hexham, Northumberland NE46 1SX. Tel. (0434) 673031**

Set up in November 1992 by the owner of the Dipton Mill Inn, using equipment manufactured from former milk tanks, which, the owners report, were an excellent choice. No adjuncts are used in the beers (whose strengths and names may change) which are produced for the inn and around 15 other local outlets.

Low Quarter Ale (OG 1035, ABV 3.5%) Nice, full-bodied, bitter, hoppy ale.

Bitter (OG 1037, ABV 3.8%) Very light-coloured, very bitter (dry) and very quaffable. Little body.

Devil's Water (OG 1042, ABV 4.2%) A darker, mid brown beer; malty with some hop taste.

HIGHGATE See Nationals, Bass.

HIGSONS See Cains and Nationals, Whitbread.

HILDEN **Hilden Brewery, Hilden House, Lisburn, Co. Antrim BT27 4TY. Tel. (0846) 663863**

Mini-brewery beside a Georgian country house, set up in 1981 to counter the local all-keg Guinness/Bass duopoly. Presently the only real ale brewery in Northern Ireland, supplying two free trade outlets and some pubs in England.

Ale (OG 1038) An amber-coloured beer with an aroma of malt, hops and fruit. The balanced taste is slightly slanted towards hops, and hops are also prominent in the full, malty finish. Bitter and refreshing.

Great Northern Porter (OG 1039) A new brew with a rich, tawny colour and a pronounced malty aroma. Crystal malt is dominant in both the flavour and aftertaste.

Special Reserve (OG 1040) Dark red/brown in colour and superbly aromatic – full of dark malts, producing an aroma of liquorice and toffee. Malt, fruit and toffee on the palate, with a sweet, malty finish. Mellow and satisfying, but not regularly available.

HOBSONS

Hobsons Brewery & Co., The Brewery, Cleobury Ind. Estate, Cleobury Mortimer, Kidderminster, Hereford & Worcester DY14 8DP. Tel: (0299) 270837

Established at Easter 1993 in a former sawmill, Hobsons is run by Nick Davies and his parents, supplying 11 outlets within a 20-mile radius. The brewery is actually in Shropshire, despite the postal address. A Christmas Ale is likely.

Best Bitter* (OG 1038, ABV 3.8%) A hoppy, bitter, nutty beer.

HOGS BACK

Hogs Back Brewery, Manor Farm, The Street, Tongham, Surrey GU10 1DE. Tel. (0252) 783000

This purpose-built brewery was set up in a restored farm building (circa 1768) in August 1992. The business began by supplying guest beers and bottled foreign beers to local pubs, but now its own beers are regularly sold to over 100 outlets and the purchase of a pub is planned.

Dark Mild* (OG 1036, ABV 3.4%) A smooth mild, occasionally brewed.

Tongham Traditional English Ale (TEA) (OG 1044, ABV 4.2%) Pale brown bitter with a good balance of malt and hops. Slightly fruity.

Special* (OG 1048, ABV 4.6%) Another occasional brew; a light golden ale.

Rip Snorter* (OG 1052, ABV 5%) A strong special bitter.

Olde Tongham Tastie (OTT)* (OG 1066, ABV 6.5%) A winter ale.

Santa's Wobble (OG 1077, ABV 7.5%) Fruity Christmas beer with hints of banana and coconut in the flavour. Also sold occasionally in summer under the name of Still Wobbling.

HOLDEN'S

Holden's Brewery Ltd., Hopden Brewery, George Street, Woodsetton, Dudley, W. Midlands DY1 4LN. Tel. (0902) 880051

One of the long-established family breweries of the Black Country, which started as a brew pub at the Park (now the brewery tap) in 1916. It produces a good range of real ales for its 20 pubs and around 90 free trade customers and more tied houses are planned, as finances allow. Also bottles its own beers and others under contract at the only remaining bottling hall in the Black Country.

Stout (OG 1036, ABV 3.7%) A dark brown, near black beer, with a bitter, malty flavour. Hints of liquorice in the aftertaste. Not regularly available.

Mild (OG 1037, ABV 3.7%) A smooth blend of malt, hops, roast and fruitiness. Drinks with the body of a much stronger beer.

Bitter (OG 1039, ABV 3.9%) Again, smooth, with a blend of malt and hops and a dry, crisp, bitter finish.

XB* (OG 1042, ABV 4.1%) Sold mainly as a house beer, under house names. A sweeter, fruitier version of the bitter.

Special (OG 1051, ABV 5%) A strong, sweet and malty pale ale, full-bodied, with a bittersweet aftertaste.

XL (OG 1092, ABV 9%) Usually only available at Christmas: a very strong, sweet and dark ale.

HOLT

Joseph Holt PLC, Derby Brewery, Empire Street, Cheetham, Manchester M3 1JD. Tel. (061) 834 3285

Successful family brewery, founded in 1849 (not to be confused with Carlsberg-Tetley's Midlands company Holt, Plant & Deakin).

> OG stands for Original Gravity, the reading taken before fermentation of the amount of fermentable material in the brew. It is a rough indicator of strength. More reliable is the ABV (Alcohol by Volume) rating, which gives the percentage of alcohol in the finished beer.

All 106 tied houses serve real ale, most of them taking hogsheads (54-gallon casks) because their low prices make them so popular. The beers are increasingly in demand as guests and free trade is growing all the time, so much so that extensions to the brewery were set in motion in 1992.

Mild (OG 1032, ABV 3.2%) Very dark beer with a complex aroma and taste. Roast malt is prominent, but so are hops and fruit. Strong in bitterness for a mild and has a long-lasting, satisfying aftertaste.

Bitter (OG 1039, ABV 4%) Tawny beer with a strong hop aroma. Although balanced by malt and fruit, the uncompromising bitterness can be a shock to the unwary and extends into the aftertaste.

HOLTS See Nationals, Carlsberg-Tetley.

HOME See Nationals, Scottish & Newcastle.

HOOK NORTON

The Hook Norton Brewery Co. Ltd., Hook Norton, Banbury, Oxfordshire OX15 5NY. Tel. (0608) 737210

Built by John Harris on the family farm in 1850, Hook Norton remains one of the most delightful traditional Victorian tower breweries in Britain. It retains much of its original plant and machinery, the showpiece being the 25-horsepower stationary steam engine which still pumps the Cotswold well water used for brewing. The brewery boasts some fine old country pubs, with all 35 of its tied houses serving real ale, and some 450 free trade outlets also supplied.

Best Mild (OG 1032, ABV 2.9%) A dark, red/brown mild with a malty aroma and a malty, sweetish taste, tinged with a faint hoppy balance. Malty in the aftertaste. Splendid and highly drinkable.

Best Bitter (OG 1036, ABV 3.3%) An excellently-balanced, golden bitter. Malty and hoppy on the nose and in the mouth, with a hint of fruitiness. Dry, but with some balancing sweetness. A hoppy bitterness dominates the finish.

Old Hooky (OG 1049, ABV 4.3%) An unusual, tawny beer with a strong fruity and grainy aroma and palate, balanced by a hint of hops. Full-bodied, with a bitter, fruity and malty aftertaste.

Twelve Days (OG 1058, ABV 5.4%) A dark brown Christmas brew. The flavour is predominantly dry and chocolatey with a blend of hops and sweetish fruit as a base. Dry, roasty finish.

HOP BACK

Hop Back Brewery, 27 Estcourt Road, Salisbury, Wilts. SP1 3AS. Tel. (0722) 328594

Originally a brew pub, set up in May 1987 with a five-barrel plant and producing award-winning beers. Moved production to a new brewery at Downton in May 1992 to cope with increased demand but the brewery at the pub is still used for trial and speciality beers, including the mild and wheat beer which have now been added permanently to the range. Supplies two tied houses and a growing free trade (currently 25 outlets).

Mild* (OG 1032, ABV 3.2%)

GFB (OG 1035, ABV 3.5%) Golden, with the sort of light, clean, tasty quality which makes an ideal session ale. Hoppy aroma and taste, leading to a good dry finish. Refreshing.

Special (OG 1040, ABV 4%) A medium bitter. Slightly sweet, but with a good balance of malt and hops and a long finish.

Wilt Alternative* (OG 1042, ABV 4.2%)

Entire Stout (OG 1042, ABV 4.8%) A rich, dark stout with a strong roasted malt flavour and a long, sweet and malty aftertaste. A vegan beer.

Summer Lightning (OG 1050, ABV 5%) Light, well-balanced, but deceptively strong. Very hoppy and sweetish. Winner of many CAMRA awards.

Wheat Beer* (OG 1052, ABV 5.2%)

HOSKINS

Hoskins Brewery PLC, Beaumanor Brewery, 133 Beaumanor Road, Leicester LE4 5QE. Tel. (0533) 661122

Established in 1877 and the smallest remaining tower brewery in the country, Hoskins was family-owned until 1983 when it was taken over and expanded by the present owners. It sold eight pubs to Wolverhampton & Dudley in 1992, reducing its tied estate to seven, but it is intending to buy other pubs; all the tied houses serve real ale. A recent increase in brewing capacity now allows its beers to be sold via a growing list of wholesalers, as well as through the ten outlets it supplies direct. Unfortunately, the beer quality is felt by many to be occasionally inconsistent.

Beaumanor Bitter (OG 1039, ABV 3.9%) A drinkable and refreshing, amber-coloured beer. An aroma of malt and hops leads into a hoppy taste and an astringent, bitter, hoppy aftertaste.

Penn's Ale (OG 1045, ABV 4.3%) A full-bodied, easy-drinking beer, golden in colour and with a slightly fruity aroma. Rich, malty and well-balanced in flavour, followed by a clean, dry, crystal malt finish.

Premium* (OG 1050, ABV 4.6%) An occasional brew.

Churchill's Pride* (OG 1050, ABV 4.8%) An occasional brew for the free trade.

Old Nigel (OG 1060, ABV 5.7%) Malt and hints of liquorice are present in the robust flavour of this winter beer (December–February). Fruity in aroma and sweet-tasting, with a lasting, pleasantly fruity finish. Russet in colour.

HOSKINS & OLDFIELD

Hoskins & Oldfield Brewery Ltd., North Mills, Frog Island, Leicester LE3 5DH. Tel. (0533) 532191

Set up by two members of Leicester's famous brewing family, Philip and Stephen Hoskins, in 1984, after the sale of the old Hoskins Brewery. With three new brews since the last edition, a wide range of beers is produced for a scattered free trade and the number of outlets is gradually increasing.

HOB Mild (OG 1036, ABV 3.5%) A dark ruby mild with a chocolate and coffee aroma, and a dry, stout-like flavour. Heavy and creamy, with a lasting, dry, malty finish.

Brigadier Bitter* (OG 1036, ABV 3.6%)

HOB Bitter (OG 1041, ABV 4%) Golden in colour, with an aroma of peardrops. Its flavour is fruity and hoppy, with a harsh, hoppy, but sweet aftertaste.

Little Matty (OG 1041, ABV 4%) Very complex brown/red beer. Hops and fruit blend with malt for an almost 'nuts and raisins' aroma. The flavour is a good balance of hops and bittersweet citrus fruits. Long, dry aftertaste.

Tom Kelly's Stout (OG 1043, ABV 4.2%) A satisfying stout, dark in colour, with an attractive, golden, creamy head and an aroma of malt and fruit. The flavour is exceedingly bitter but malty, and the finish is dry and chocolatey.

Tom Hoskins Porter* (OG 1050, ABV 4.8%) Brewed using honey and oats.

EXS Bitter* (OG 1051, ABV 5%)

Tom Kelly's Christmas Pudding Porter* (OG 1052, ABV 5%) A festive beer, also brewed using honey and oats.

Old Navigation Ale (OG 1071, ABV 7%) Ruby/black beer, with an aroma reminiscent of sherry. Sweet and fruity, with a stout-like malt flavour.

Christmas Noggin (OG 1100, ABV 10%) Russet-coloured beer with a spicy, fruity aroma. The taste is of malt and fruit, and the finish balances malt and hops. Sweet but not cloying. Available throughout the year.

SARAH HUGHES

Sarah Hughes Brewery, Beacon Hotel, 129 Bilston Street, Sedgley, Dudley, W. Midlands DY3 1JE. Tel. (0902) 883380

Brewery reopened in 1988 after lying idle for 30 years, to serve the village pub and a few other outlets. Now produces for the free trade. A Victorian-style conservatory acts as a reception area for brewery visits (always welcome during opening hours). Plans for bottling have still not materialised.

Sedgley Surprise (OG 1048, ABV 5%) A sweet and malty pale ale that tastes lighter than its gravity. Bittersweet and malty with underlying fruitiness.

Original Dark Ruby Mild (OG 1058, ABV 6%) A rich ruby ale that unleashes a salvo of different flavours at the taste buds. Sweet, malty and fruity in the mouth with a lingering hoppy and malty finish.

HULL

Hull Brewery Co. Ltd., 144–148 English Street, Hull, Humbs. HU3 2BT. Tel. (0482) 586364

Hull Brewery was resurrected in 1989 after a 15-year gap, by two local businessmen, originally as a mild-only operation; the other beers were added over the next three years. It acquired its first tied house in May 1992 and plans to open a second. Free trade has grown from a base in the Hull club scene to around 60 outlets in West Yorkshire and South Humberside.

Mild* (OG 1033, ABV 3.2%)

Bitter* (OG 1037, ABV 3.6%)

Governor Strong Ale* (OG 1047, ABV 4.8%)

HYDES' ANVIL

Hydes' Anvil Brewery Ltd., 46 Moss Lane West, Manchester M15 5PH. Tel. (061) 226 1317

Family-controlled, traditional brewery, first established at the Crown Brewery, Audenshaw, Manchester in 1863 and on its present site, a former vinegar brewery, since the turn of the century. The smallest of the established Manchester breweries, it is continuing its gradual expansion by buying pubs from the Nationals and supplies cask ale to all its 61 tied houses. Brews Harp lager under contract.

Mild (OG 1032, ABV 3.5%) A light, refreshing, slightly fruity drink with little aftertaste. Fruity aroma, with a hint of malt.

Dark Mild* (OG 1034, ABV 3.5%) A mild with a caramel and fruit aroma. Quite sweet and fruity with a pleasant aftertaste. Sold mainly in the company's Welsh pubs – rare in the Manchester area.

Light (OG 1034, ABV 3.7%) A lightly-hopped session beer, complex in character, with malt dominating before a brief but dry finish. Available more in southern Manchester than Mild, and vice-versa in northern parts of the city.

Bitter (OG 1036, ABV 3.8%) A good-flavoured bitter, with a malty and hoppy nose, fruity background and malt and hops in the finish. A hint of bitterness and astringency throughout.

IND COOPE

See Nationals, Carlsberg-Tetley.

ISLAND **Island Brewery, 16 Manners View, Dodnor Ind. Site, Newport, Isle of Wight PO30 5FA. Tel. (0983) 528098**

An ambitious new brewery set up in 1991 by the Hampshire-based soft drinks firm Hartridge's. When the island's only other brewery, Burts, closed, its assistant brewer joined Island and trade increased sooner than expected, leading to the installation of a larger plant in 1992. In 1993, Island announced that it had purchased the Burts name and brands and would be dropping the Island name. Burts VPA may be re-introduced but Newport Best could be discontinued. Hartridge's owns five pubs on the mainland.

Nipper Bitter* (OG 1038, ABV 3.8%)

Newport Best Bitter* (OG 1045, ABV 4.6%)

ISLE OF MAN **Isle Of Man Breweries Ltd., Falcon Brewery, Murrays Road, Douglas, Isle of Man. Tel. (0624) 661140**

The main brewery on the island, having taken over and closed the rival Castletown brewery in 1986. Production of Castletown beers ceased completely in 1992 after a period at the Falcon Brewery. The remaining real ales are produced under the unique Manx Brewers' Act 1874 (permitted ingredients: water, malt, sugar and hops only) at the impressive Okells Victorian tower brewhouse near the centre of Douglas, but work on a new brewery at Kewaigue is to start soon. It has 53 pubs, 42 of which are tied, and all but one sell real ale. Limited free trade.

Okells Mild (OG 1034, ABV 3.4%) A genuine, well-brewed mild ale, with a fine aroma of hops and crystal malt. Reddish-brown in colour, this beer has a full malt flavour with surprising bitter hop notes and a hint of blackcurrants and oranges. Full malty finish.

Okells Bitter (OG 1035, ABV 3.7%) Golden, malty and superbly hoppy in aroma, with a hint of honey. Rich and malty on the tongue, with a wonderful, dry malt and hop finish. A complex but rewarding beer.

JENNINGS **Jennings Bros PLC, Castle Brewery, Cockermouth, Cumbria CA13 9NE. Tel. (0900) 823214**

Brewery founded in 1828 and on the present site for over 100 years, and still using the local well water. It gradually expanded over the years, particularly during the 1920s, by taking over other smaller local breweries and their pubs. It now supplies a growing network of free trade outlets, wholesalers and other brewers across the UK, and real ale is also available at 87 of the 93 tied houses.

Dark Mild* (OG 1031, ABV 3.1%) A dark, mellow mild.

Bitter (OG 1035, ABV 3.4%) An excellent, distinctive, red/brown brew with a hoppy, malty aroma. A good, strong balance of grain and hops in the taste, with a moderate bitterness, developing into a lingering, dry, malty finish.

Cumberland Ale* (OG 1040, ABV 3.8%) A hoppy, golden bitter.

Oatmeal Stout* (OG 1040, ABV 3.8%)

Sneck Lifter* (OG 1055, ABV 5.1%) A dark, strong warmer.

> Beers marked with an asterisk have not been tasted by official CAMRA tasting panels. However, some of these beers do carry brief descriptions derived from limited samplings or other sources, and can be used for rough guidance.

JOLLY ROGER **Jolly Roger Brewery Ltd., The Faithful City Brewery, 31–33 Friar Street, Worcester WR1 2NA. Tel. (0905) 22222**

Founded as a brew pub in Upton upon Severn in 1982, Jolly Roger made its new home in Worcester in 1985 and expanded quickly thereafter. However, a few setbacks in 1993 led to changes in control and a scaling down of operations. Now supplies four of its own outlets in Worcester and some local free trade. The Jolly Roger Brewery Tap no longer brews, but the Hereford brew pub is still active (see Brew Pubs). *Bottle-conditioned beer: Winter Wobbler (OG 1094, ABV 11%)*

Ale* (OG 1038, ABV 3.8%)

Quaff* (OG 1038, ABV 3.8%)

Shipwrecked* (OG 1040, ABV 4%)

Flagship* (OG 1052, ABV 5.2%)

Winter Wobbler* (OG 1094, ABV 11%) A winter ale.

JUDGES **Judges Brewery, Unit 5, Church Lawford Business Centre, Church Lawford, Warwickshire CV23 9HD. Tel. (0203) 545559**

Brewery set up by Graham and Ann Judge in early summer 1992 in a sleepy Warwickshire village. It fills the gap in Warwickshire brewing left by the demise of Thornley's in 1968.

Barristers Bitter* (OG 1037, ABV 3.4%) A light, delicately hopped beer, a good session beer.

Old Gavel Bender* (OG 1050, ABV 4.7%) A very deceptive, strong bitter, leaving a good aftertaste. Full-bodied and distinctive.

Santa's Surprise* (OG 1052) A very dark (black) winter porter.

KELHAM ISLAND **Kelham Island Brewery, 23 Alma Street, Sheffield, S. Yorks. S3 8SA. Tel. (0742) 781867**

Brewery opened in 1990 at the Fat Cat pub, using equipment purchased from the former Oxford Brewery and Bakehouse. Its range of real ales has increased and future plans include the production of bottled fruit and wheat beers. Free trade is growing, with around 100 outlets in Derbyshire, Nottinghamshire and South Yorkshire.

Hallamshire Bitter* (OG 1036, ABV 3.6%)

Bitter (OG 1038, ABV 3.8%) A light-coloured, hoppy bitter with a faint hop aroma and a short but dry finish. Lemon notes sometimes in the mouth; usually feels a bit thin. A clean session bitter.

Porter* (OG 1043, ABV 4.3%)

Celebration* (OG 1046, ABV 4.6%)

Bête Noire* (OG 1055, ABV 5.5%) A winter beer.

KEMPTOWN **The Kemptown Brewery Co. Ltd., 33 Upper St James's Street, Kemptown, Brighton, E. Sussex BN2 1JN. Tel. (0273) 602521**

Brewery established in 1989, built in the 'tower' tradition behind the Hand in Hand pub. It takes its name and logo from the former Kemptown Brewery, situated 500 yards away. Supplies 12 outlets direct.

Budget Bitter* (OG 1035, ABV 3.6%)

Mild* (OG 1038, ABV 3.8%)

Bitter* (OG 1040, ABV 4%)

Celebrated Staggering Ale* (OG 1050, ABV 5%)

Staggering in the Dark (SID)* (OG 1052, ABV 5.2%)

Old Grumpy* (OG 1065, ABV 6.5%) A Christmas ale.

KEYSTONE **Keystone Brewing Company, Sherburn in Elmet, N. Yorks.** Brewery closed.

KING & BARNES **King & Barnes Ltd., The Horsham Brewery, 18 Bishopric, Horsham, W. Sussex RH12 1QP. Tel. (0403) 270470**

Long-established brewery, dating back almost 200 years and in the present premises since 1850. It is run by the fifth generation of the King family, having united with the Barnes family brewery in 1906. Its 'Fine Sussex Ales' are served in all 58 country houses and in an extensive free trade, mostly within a radius of 40 miles. A new beer, Twelve Bore Bitter, is produced for the Freetraders Group wholesalers. *Bottle-conditioned beer: Festive (OG 1050, ABV 5.3%)*

Mild Ale (OG 1033, ABV 3.5%) A smooth, malty, dark brown mild, with a bittersweet finish and a fruity, malty aroma. Tends to be displaced by Old Ale in winter.

Sussex (OG 1034, ABV 3.5%) A hoppy, tawny-coloured bitter, with good malt balance and a dry finish.

Broadwood (OG 1040, ABV 4.2%) Pale brown with a faint malt aroma. A good marriage of malt and hops is present in the taste, with malt slightly dominating.

Old Ale ⊟ (OG 1046, ABV 4.5%) A classic, almost black old ale. A fruity, roast malt flavour, with some hops, leads to a bittersweet, malty finish. Lovely roast malt aroma. Available October–Easter.

Festive (OG 1050, ABV 4.5%) Tawny/red with a malty aroma. The flavour is fruity and malty, with a noticeable hop presence. Malt dominates the finish.

For Freetraders:

Twelve Bore Bitter* (OG 1035, ABV 3.7%)

LARKINS **Larkins Brewery Ltd., Chiddingstone, Edenbridge, Kent TN8 7BB. Tel. (0892) 870328**

Larkins brewery was started by the Dockerty family in 1986 with the purchase of the Royal Tunbridge Wells Brewery, but then moved to a converted barn at the owner's farm in 1990. An additional brewing copper and fermenter were acquired in June 1991 to keep up with the growing local free trade: the additive-free beers can now be found in around 60 pubs in the South-East. Only Kent hops are used, some from the farm itself.

Traditional Bitter* (OG 1035, ABV 3.5%) A tawny-coloured beer.

Sovereign (OG 1040, ABV 4%) A malty and slightly fruity, bitter ale, with a very malty finish. Copper-red in colour.

Best Bitter (OG 1045, ABV 4.7%) Full-bodied, slightly fruity and unusually bitter for its gravity. Dangerously drinkable!

Porter (OG 1052, ABV 5.5%) Each taste and smell of this potent black winter beer reveals another facet of its character. An explosion of roasted malt, bitter and fruity flavours leaves a bittersweet aftertaste.

LASTINGHAM — **The Lastingham Brewery Company Ltd., Unit 4, Showfield Lane Ind. Estate, Malton, N. Yorks. YO17 0BT. Tel. (0653) 696155**

New brewery founded in June 1993 and serving around 20 outlets.

Church Bitter* (OG 1038, ABV 3.7%)

Curate's Downfall* (OG 1044)

LEES — **JW Lees & Co. (Brewers) Ltd., Greengate Brewery, Middleton Junction, Manchester M24 2AX. Tel. (061) 643 2487**

Family-owned brewery, founded in 1828 by John Willie Lees, a retired cotton manufacturer. The existing brewhouse dates from 1876 but has been expanded in recent years. Serves real ale in all 173 of its tied houses and clubs (mostly in northern Manchester). Free trade in the North-West extends to about 120 outlets and the bitter is increasingly popular as a guest beer.

GB Mild (OG 1032, ABV 3.5%) Malty and fruity in aroma. The same flavours are found in the taste, but do not dominate in a beer with a rounded and smooth character. Dry, malty aftertaste. Low turnover in some outlets.

Bitter (OG 1038, ABV 4.2%) Pale beer with a malty, hoppy aroma and a distinctive, malty, dry and slightly metallic taste. Clean, dry Lees finish.

Moonraker (OG 1073, ABV 7%) Reddish-brown in colour, having a strong, malty, fruity aroma. The flavour is rich and sweet, with roast malt, and the finish is fruity yet dry. Only available in a handful of outlets.

LICHFIELD — **Lichfield Brewery, 3 Europa Way, Boley Park, Lichfield, Staffs. WS14 9TZ. Tel. (0543) 419919**

Two CAMRA members began brewing at Lichfield in 1992, bringing production back to the city after 60 years. Using a five-barrel plant, they now supply ten regular outlets, plus others with guest beers.

Inspired* (OG 1040, ABV 4%)

Xpired* (OG 1050, ABV 5%)

LINFIT — **Linfit Brewery, Sair Inn, Lane Top, Linthwaite, Huddersfield, W. Yorks. HD7 5SG. Tel. (0484) 842370**

A 19th-century brew pub which recommenced brewing in 1982, producing an impressive range of ales for sale at the Sair and for free trade as far away as Manchester (12 regular outlets). New plant installed in 1993 has doubled its capacity.

Mild (OG 1032, ABV 3%) Roast malt dominates in this straightforward dark mild. Some hop aroma; slightly dry flavour. The finish is malty.

Bitter (OG 1035, ABV 3.7%) Good session beer. A dry-hopped aroma leads to a clean-tasting, hoppy bitterness, balanced with some maltiness. The finish is well balanced, too, but sometimes has an intense bitterness.

Special (OG 1041, ABV 4.3%) Dry-hopping again provides the aroma for this rich and mellow bitter. Very soft profile and character; it fills the mouth with texture rather than taste. Clean, rounded finish.

English Guineas Stout (OG 1050, ABV 5.3%) A fruity, roasted aroma preludes a smooth, roasted, chocolatey flavour which is bitter but not too dry. Excellent appearance; good, bitter finish.

Old Eli (OG 1050, ABV 5.3%) Excellent, well-balanced premium bitter with a dry-hopped aroma and a fruity, bitter finish.

Leadboiler (OG 1063, ABV 6.6%) Flowery and hoppy in aroma, with a very moreish, strong bitter flavour which provides a soft mouthfeel, well-balanced by a prominent maltiness. Rounded, bitter finish.

Enoch's Hammer (OG 1080, ABV 8.6%) Straw-coloured, vinous bitter with no pretentions about its strength or pedigree. A full, fruity aroma leads on to a smooth, alcoholic, hoppy, bitter taste, with an unexpectedly bitter finish.

Xmas Ale (OG 1082, ABV 8.6%) A hearty and warming ale. The flavour is strong in roasted malt, with some bitterness. Extremely vinous, with a slightly yeasty, metallic taste. Bitter finish. An adaptation of Enoch's Hammer.

LION'S

Lion's Original Brews Ltd., Griffin Brewery, Unit 6, Belshaw Court, Billington Road, Burnley, Lancs. BB1 5UB. Tel. (0282) 830156

Brewery which started trading in October 1991. Originally a six-barrel plant, it was expanded during summer 1992, and the mild is the latest addition to the range. Supplies around 50 free trade outlets.

Dark Mild* (OG 1033, ABV 3.2%)

Original Bitter (OG 1038, ABV 4.1%) A good example of a classic Lancashire bitter. A pungent, hoppy aroma leads through into a well-hopped, dry flavour that also has good malt and fruit presence. Very dry, hoppy aftertaste.

Owd Edgar* (OG 1068, ABV 7%) A seasonal brew.

LITTLE AVENHAM

The Little Avenham Brewery, 30 Avenham Street, Preston, Lancs. PR1 3BN. Tel. (0772) 51380

After winning a local CAMRA *Pub of the Year* award for their pub, Gaston's Real Ale and Fine Wine Pub, the owners and licensee decided to brew their own beer. The first brew was produced in 1992 and proved so popular that they started supplying other outlets (currently around 20), as well as a second tied house.

Pickled Priest* (OG 1036, ABV 3.5%)

Clog Dancer* (OG 1038, ABV 4%)

Hedgerow Bitter* (OG 1038, ABV 4%) Autumn beer using locally picked hops.

Torchlight Bitter* (OG 1050, ABV 5%)

Pierrepoints Last Drop* (OG 1064, ABV 7%)

LLOYDS

Lloyds Country Beers Ltd., John Thompson Brewery, Ingleby, Derbyshire DE7 1HW. Tel. (0332) 863426

Lloyds is the separate business set up to supply the beers brewed at the John Thompson Inn (see Brew Pubs) to the free trade: over 60 outlets, mainly in the Midlands. It also distributes Heritage Bitter from the Heritage Brewery.

Derby Mild* (OG 1033, ABV 3.3%)

Classic* (OG 1038, ABV 3.7%) Available in summer only.

Derby Bitter or Country Bitter or JTS XXX* (OG 1042, ABV 4.2%) Full and fruity.

Porter* (OG 1045, ABV 4.5%) A winter beer.

VIP (Very Important Pint)* (OG 1048, ABV 4.7%) Heavier, darker version of the bitter.

Overdraft* (OG 1067.5, ABV 6.2%) An occasional brew.

Skullcrusher (OG 1067.5, ABV 6.2%) A full-bodied Christmas ale. The intense, sulphury aroma has some fruit, and the fruity, bittersweet flavour has a slightly smoky malt edge. Dry but short finish.

LONGSTONE

Longstone Brewery, Station Road, Belford, Northumberland NE70 7DT. Tel. (0668) 213031

Brewery operational since 1991, the first in Northumberland for many years. A second, stronger beer is due to be launched, both as a cask ale and in a bottle-conditioned form. Supplies 16 free trade outlets regularly in the north, and others further afield via beer agencies.

Bitter (OG 1039, ABV 4%) Pungent and sometimes undefinable flavours can lie in this imaginative beer. Hop character dominates but notice also the underlying fruit and lasting sweetness.

LORIMER & CLARK

See Vaux and Caledonian.

McEWAN

See Nationals, Scottish & Newcastle.

THOMAS MCGUINNESS

Thomas McGuinness Brewing Company, Cask & Feather, 1 Oldham Road, Rochdale, Lancs. OL16 1UA. Tel. (0706) 711476

Brewery established in 1991 behind the Cask & Feather pub, starting with one beer, but soon producing four. Supplies real ale to its own three pubs (which are not tied), and to a growing free trade. As a promotional gambit, it recently acquired the 'talking' shire horses that featured in the Webster's advertisements, to pull the dray wagon to shows and pub events.

Mild* (OG 1034, ABV 3.4%)

Best Bitter (OG 1038, ABV 4.1%) Gold in colour with a hoppy aroma: a clean, refreshing beer with a balance of hops and grainy malt, which extends to the aftertaste. Also a hint of grapefruit in the flavour.

Junction Bitter (OG 1038, ABV 4.1%) Fruit and malt aroma. Fruit, hops and malt feature in the taste, with a varying degree of sweetness.

Tommy Todd Porter (OG 1050, ABV 5.2%) A winter warmer, with a fruit and roast aroma, leading to a balance of malt and roast malt flavours, with a touch of chocolate. Not too sweet for its gravity.

MACLAY

Maclay & Co. Ltd., Thistle Brewery, Alloa, Clackmannanshire, Central FK10 1ED. Tel. (0259) 723387

Family-run business, founded in 1830 by James Maclay and moved to the present Victorian tower brewery in 1869. It still uses traditional brewing methods and direct-fired coppers and the beers are produced using only bore-hole water (the only Scottish brewery to do so) without any adjuncts. Two new beers have been added to the range since the last edition. Half of the 30 tied houses offer real ale, which is also supplied to 200 other outlets.

60/- Ale* (OG 1034, ABV 3.4%) A flavoursome, dark session beer.

70/- Ale* (OG 1036, ABV 3.6%) A well-hopped, quenching beer.

80/- Export* (OG 1040, ABV 4%) Well-balanced and rich.

Kane's Amber Ale* (OG 1040, ABV 4%)

Oat Malt Stout* (OG 1045, ABV 4.5%)

Scotch Ale* (OG 1050, ABV 5%)

Old Alloa Ale (OG 1070, ABV 6.5%) A winter beer.

> The tankard symbol indicates the *Good Beer Guide Beers of the Year*, finalists in the *Champion Beer of Britain* contest held at the *Great British Beer Festival* at Olympia in August 1993.

McMULLEN

McMullen & Sons Ltd., The Hertford Brewery, 26 Old Cross, Hertford, Herts. SG14 1RD. Tel. (0992) 584911

Hertfordshire's oldest independent brewery, founded in 1827 by Peter McMullen. The Victorian tower brewery, which houses the original oak and copper-lined fermenters still in use today, was built on the site of three wells. In April 1993, the company launched a new initiative, McMullen Special Reserve, a series of seasonal cask-conditioned ales for sale through selected McMullen and free trade pubs for a limited period. Real ale is served in all McMullen's 150 pubs in Hertfordshire, Essex and London, and also supplied to around 180 free trade outlets. The company also brews bottle-conditioned beers for Hanseatic Trading Company.

Original AK (OG 1033, ABV 3.8%) A light bitter with a hoppy aroma. The malty, hoppy flavour is followed by a distinctive, dry aftertaste which has bitterness, hoppiness and a touch of malt.

Country Best Bitter (OG 1041, ABV 4.6%) Well-rounded taste of malt, hops and fruit. The aroma has hops and malt, and there is a distinctive finish with bitterness, malt and hops.

Stronghart (OG 1070, ABV 7%) A sweet, rich, dark beer; a single brew for the winter months. It has a malty aroma, with hints of hops and roast malt which carry through to the taste.

For Whitbread:

Wethered Bitter* (OG 1035, ABV 3.6%)

For Hanseatic:

Bottle-conditioned beers: BCA (OG 1045, ABV 4.5%); IPA (OG 1045, ABV 4.5%); Black Russian (OG 1048, ABV 4.8%)

MALTON

Malton Brewery Company Ltd., Crown Hotel, Wheelgate, Malton, N. Yorks. YO17 0HP. Tel. (0653) 697580

Malton began brewing in 1985 in a stable block at the rear of the Crown Hotel, where the former Grand National winner Double Chance was once stabled, hence the name of the bitter. Steady growth in the sales of the additive-free beers, and occasional special brews, led to the installation of more fermenting vessels. Now supplies around 20 free trade outlets regularly, as well as guest beers to several pubs in North and West Yorkshire.

Pale Ale (OG 1034, ABV 3.6%) A light, but fresh, hoppy nose leads into a hoppy, bitter taste with a delicate dryness at the finish. A fine, clean session ale that is darker and less malty than last year.

Double Chance Bitter (OG 1038, ABV 4%) Strong hop aroma and taste with hints of malt and fruit on the palate. The bitter, dry aftertaste is light in the mouth but does not hide itself. Again, it seems less malty than last year.

Pickwick's Porter ⊟ (OG 1042, ABV 4.2%) A revelation this year, a porter of character. Lots of roast and malt in the nose and mouth, with a dry balance of tart fruit and dark chocolate. A dry, nutty finish rounds off this jet-black brew.

Owd Bob ⊟ (OG 1055, ABV 5.8%) A rich, warming, multi-layered beer with a hop and roast aroma, a complex hop, fruit and chocolate taste and a dry, slightly cloying but bitter finish. Dark brown with red hints, it belies its strength.

MANSFIELD

Mansfield Brewery PLC, Littleworth, Mansfield, Notts. NG18 1AB. Tel. (0623) 25691

Founded in 1855, and now one of the country's leading regional brewers, Mansfield stopped brewing cask beer in the early 1970s. It resumed real ale production in 1982 as an experiment and has not looked back since. Its excellent ales are all fermented in traditional Yorkshire squares and have enjoyed steadily rising sales, aided in

1991 by the acquisition of a substantial number of pubs from Courage, and another dozen from S&N in 1993. Now most of its 450-odd pubs serve cask beer. Supplies an extensive free trade (particularly East Midlands clubs), enjoys a reciprocal trading arrangement with Charles Wells, and has just begun brewing Home Mild for S&N.

Old Shilling* (OG 1030, ABV 3%) Primarily a brew for the Boddington Pub Company, not sold in the Mansfield estate.

Riding Dark Mild (OG 1035, ABV 3.4%) Dark ruby-coloured and quite rich for a mild, with a complex aroma of malt, roast and fruit. The dry, roasty flavour, with traces of bittersweet fruit, follows through into a dry aftertaste.

Riding Traditional Bitter (OG 1036, ABV 3.5%) Pale brown, with a malty, hoppy nose. A firm malt background is overlaid with a good bitter bite and hop flavours.

Old Baily (OG 1045, ABV 4.7%) Resembles a Scottish heavy, but with a fine balance of hop, malt and fruit flavours. Dark copper-red in colour, with an aroma of malt and fruit.

For Scottish & Newcastle:

Home Mild* (OG 1036, ABV 3.6%)

MARSTON MOOR **Marston Moor Brewery, The Crown Inn, Kirk Hammerton, York, N. Yorks. YO5 8DD. Tel. (0423) 330341**

Small, but expanding brewery, set up in 1983 and acquiring its first tied house, the Crown, in 1988, and now negotiating for a second. The growing free trade (around 50 outlets over a wide area in the North) has led to a 50% expansion in output.

Cromwell Bitter* (OG 1037, ABV 3.7%) A distinctive, bitter beer.

Brewers Pride* (OG 1042 ABV 4.2%) An amber-coloured, premium beer.

Porter* (OG 1042, ABV 4.2%) A seasonal brew (October–May), ruby-coloured and stout-like.

Black Tom Stout* (OG 1045, ABV 4.5%) An occasional brew, usually in winter.

Brewers Droop* (OG 1050, ABV 5.2%) A potent, straw-coloured ale.

ESB* (OG 1050, ABV 5.2%)

Troopers Ale* (OG 1050, ABV 5.2%) An occasional brew.

MARSTON'S **Marston, Thompson & Evershed PLC, Shobnall Road, Burton upon Trent, Staffs. DE14 2BW. Tel. (0283) 31131**

The only brewery still using the Burton Union system of fermentation for its stronger ales and Marston's commitment to this method was reinforced in 1992 with a £1 million investment in a new Union room. Real ale is available in most of its 856 pubs, stretching from Yorkshire to Hampshire, and the enormous free trade is helped by many Whitbread and other national brewers' houses stocking Pedigree Bitter. There has been a rationalisation of the beer range in the last year: the Border beers (relics of Marston's 1984 take-over of the Border Wrexham brewery) have been axed, as has Mercian Mild, while Burton Best Bitter has been relaunched as Marston's Bitter. During 1993 selected Marston's pubs offered special brews promoted under the title of Head Brewer's Choice and Banks's Mild is also now available in Marston's pubs.

Bitter (OG 1037, ABV 3.7%) Formerly Burton Best Bitter. An amber/tawny session beer which can often be markedly sulphury in the aroma and taste. At its best, a splendid, subtle balance of malt, hops and fruit follows a faintly hoppy aroma and develops into a balanced, dry aftertaste.

Merrie Monk (OG 1043, ABV 4.5%) A smooth, dark brew. Has a creamy, slightly sweet flavour, with traces of caramel, roast malt and fruit. Sweet, malty finish.

Pedigree Bitter (OG 1043, ABV 4.5%) A famous beer whose quality now varies enormously following its national availability. Can be less than ordinary and rarely reaches its former heights. Prone to a sulphury aroma when fresh.

Owd Rodger (OG 1080, ABV 7.6%) A dark, ruby-red barley wine, with an intense fruity nose before a deep, winey, heavy fruit flavour, with malt and faint hops. The finish is dry and fruity (strawberries). Misunderstood, moreish and strong.

MAULDONS **Mauldons Brewery, 7 Addison Road, Chilton Ind. Estate, Sudbury, Suffolk CO10 6YW. Tel. (0787) 311055**

Set up in 1982 by former Watney's brewer Peter Mauldon, whose family once had its own brewery. Its extensive beer list changes frequently and is supplied to 150 free trade outlets in East Anglia and Hertfordshire, as well as more widely via wholesalers. Provides house beers for local pubs and wholesales other guest beers and ciders.

Bitter (OG 1037, ABV 3.8%) Malt and fruit are predominant throughout, with little balancing hop or bitterness.

Old Porter (OG 1042, ABV 3.8%) A black beer with malt and roast flavours dominating. Some hop in the finish.

Old XXXX (OG 1042, ABV 4%) Winter ale with a reddish brown appearance. The taste is complex, with fruit, malt, caramel, hop and bitterness all present.

Squires (OG 1044, ABV 4.2%) A best bitter with a good, malty aroma. The taste is evenly balanced between malt and a hoppy bitterness.

Special (OG 1045, ABV 4.2%) By far the most hoppy of the Mauldons beers, with a good, bitter finish. Some balancing malt.

Suffolk Punch (OG 1050, ABV 4.8%) A full-bodied, strong bitter. The malt and fruit in the aroma are reflected in the taste and there is some hop character in the finish. Deep tawny/red in colour.

Black Adder (OG 1055, ABV 5.3%) A dark stout. Roast is very strong in the aroma and taste, but malt, hop and bitterness provide an excellent balance and a lingering finish. *Champion Beer of Britain* 1991.

White Adder (OG 1055, ABV 5.3%) A new amber beer full of citrus spiciness, with a hoppy/fruitiness dominating the aroma and the flavour. Clean, dry finish.

Suffolk Comfort* (OG 1065, ABV 6.6%)

Christmas Reserve (OG 1065, ABV 6.7%) A sweet Christmas ale with malt and fruit. Typically for this type of ale, it has little bitterness. Fairly pale in colour for a strong beer, with red tints.

MILL **Mill Brewery, Unit 18c, Bradley Lane, Newton Abbot, Devon TQ12 4JW. Tel. (0626) 63322**

Brewery founded in 1983 on the site of an old watermill. Special brews, based on Janner's Old Original, are often sold under local pub names, 'Janner' being the local term for a Devonian. Serves nine regular outlets and the free trade in southern Devon and Torbay.

Janner's Ale (OG 1038) Pale brown beer, with little aroma. A light lunchtime beer.

Janner's Old Dark Ale (OG 1040) Red-coloured beer with a malt and bitter taste and aftertaste.

> OG stands for Original Gravity, the reading taken before fermentation of the amount of fermentable material in the brew. It is a rough indicator of strength. More reliable is the ABV (Alcohol by Volume) rating, which gives the percentage of alcohol in the finished beer.

Janner's Old Original (OG 1045) Golden beer with plenty of fruit and hops present in both aroma and flavour.

Janner's Christmas Ale* (OG 1050) The festive beer.

MINERS ARMS See Mole's.

MITCHELL'S

Mitchell's of Lancaster (Brewers) Ltd., 11 Moor Lane, Lancaster LA1 1QB. Tel. (0524) 63773

The only surviving independent brewery in Lancaster (estd. 1880), wholly owned and run by direct descendants of founder William Mitchell. The company is very traditional: many of the casks are still wooden and its award-winning beers are brewed with natural spring well water. Real ale is sold in all but four of its 53 pubs and virtually countrywide in the free trade, and the company is building a strong reputation as a supplier of guest ales in the North-West.

Dark Mild (OG 1034, ABV 3.3%) Black with ruby-red tints. Malty in aroma and taste, with a faint fruitiness. A smooth and highly drinkable mild.

Olde Priory Porter (OG 1035, ABV 3.3%) Quite dry, dark beer with a spicy nose. Roasted barley features before a slightly woody, satisfying, long aftertaste.

Best Bitter (OG 1036, ABV 3.5%) A golden bitter with a malty aroma and a superb, dry, malty flavour, with a faint balance of hops. The delicate bitter aftertaste usually demands more of the same.

Fortress (OG 1042, ABV 4.2%) Pale yellow/brown beer with hop on the nose but little hop in the soft palate which is faintly malty. Good body; not sweet.

Old Clog (OG 1045, ABV 4.2%) Dark brown beer with red highlights. Light and thin in body, flavour and aroma. Treacly, with some liquorice. Fairly dry and somewhat disappointing.

ESB (OG 1050, ABV 5%) Creamy in texture; malty in aroma. The flavour is also malty and fruity, with a hoppy finish.

Single Malt (OG 1064, ABV 7.2%) A seasonal brew, mid brown in colour and suggestive of malt whisky in aroma and flavour. Strongly malty throughout, with a subtle bittersweet, hoppy balance in the taste.

MITCHELLS & BUTLERS (M&B) See Nationals, Bass.

MOLE'S

Mole's Brewery (Cascade Drinks Ltd.), 5 Merlin Way, Bowerhill, Melksham, Wilts. SN12 6TJ. Tel. (0225) 704734

Brewery built in 1982 by former Ushers brewer Roger Catté (the brewery name came from his nickname). Now runs 12 tied houses and serves a growing free trade in the West Country, supplying other parts of the country via beer agencies. Mole's also brews under contract occasionally for the inoperative Miner's Arms brewery and acts as a distributor for other members of the Small Independent Brewers Association (SIBA). Looking to expand the brewery and produce seasonal beers.

IPA (OG 1035, ABV 3.5%) A pale brown beer with a trace of maltiness in the aroma. The flavour is thin, malty and dry, with little finish. May be renamed Brewery Tap Bitter.

Cask Bitter (OG 1040, ABV 4%) A pale brown/golden-coloured beer with a light malt aroma. A clean, dry, malty taste, with some bitterness and delicate floral hop flavour. A well-balanced, light ale. May be renamed Best Bitter.

Landlord's Choice* (OG 1045, ABV 4.5%) A dark beer.

Brew 97 (OG 1050, ABV 5%) A mid brown, full-bodied beer with a gentle malt and hop aroma. The rich flavour is malty, with fruit, hop and traces of vanilla. A wonderfully warming, malty ale.

XB* (OG 1065, ABV 6.5%) A winter ale, available for about two months around Christmas.

For Miner's Arms:

Own Ale (OG 1038, ABV 3.8%) Pale brown beer with a mostly malty, bitter taste, a malty aroma and a dry finish. Since being contract brewed, it has become noticeably sweeter and more consistent.

Guvnor's Special Brew (OG 1048, ABV 4.8%) A golden, malty brew with a faint, hoppy aroma and a dry, slightly sour palate, with some citrus fruit. A dry, malty, lasting finish.

MOORHOUSE'S

Moorhouse's Brewery (Burnley) Ltd., 4 Moorhouse Street, Burnley, Lancs. BB11 5EN. Tel. (0282) 422864

Long-established (1870) producer of hop bitters, which in 1978 began brewing cask beer. Has since had several owners; the latest, Bill Parkinson, took over eight years ago and invested in a new brewhouse to meet increased demand for the award-winning beers. The brewery is also building up its tied estate; it now has six pubs, all offering real ale, and also supplies around 200 free trade outlets.

Black Cat Mild* (OG 1034, ABV 3.4%)

Premier Bitter (OG 1038, ABV 3.8%) Pale brown in colour, this brew has a superb hop flower aroma, with some fruit and malt. On the palate, citrus flavours are balanced by malt and hoppy bitterness. Dry, hoppy finish.

Pendle Witches Brew (OG 1050, ABV 5%) A good hoppy aroma leads through to a full-bodied, malty sweetness, with a trace of hop bitterness. Bitter-sweet aftertaste.

Owd Ale* (OG 1065, ABV 6.4%) A winter brew.

MORLAND

Morland & Co. PLC, PO Box 5, Ock Street, Abingdon, Oxfordshire OX14 5DD. Tel. (0235) 553377

Old regional brewery, established in 1711. In 1992, it survived a take-over bid by Greene King, who after buying Whitbread Investment Company's 43.4% stake, tried (but failed) to pick up a further 6.7% to take overall control and close the brewery. Now also brews under contract for Courage. Nearly all Morland's 370 pubs serve real ale, but in many cases the licensee uses a cask-breather. Morland cask ales are also available in the club and free trade (over 500 outlets).

Original Bitter (OG 1035, ABV 4%) A light amber beer with a malty, hoppy nose with a hint of fruitiness. The distinct, but lightish malt and hops carry over to the flavour and leave a sweet but dry, hoppy aftertaste.

Old Masters (OG 1040, ABV 4.6%) A well-balanced tawny/amber beer with not outstandingly strong flavours. The initial aroma of malt and hops leads to a moderately malty, but dry and hoppy flavour, with a hint of fruit which can be faintly sulphurous. Dry, bitter finish.

Old Speckled Hen (OG 1050, ABV 5.2%) Morland's most distinctive beer, deep tawny/amber in colour. A well-balanced aroma of roasted malt and hops is complemented by a good hint of caramel. An initial sweet, malty, fruity, roast caramel taste soon allows the dry hop flavour through, leaving a well-balanced aftertaste.

	For Courage:
Wilson's Original Mild*	(OG 1032, ABV 3%)

MORRELLS

1782
MORRELLS BREWERY
Oxford

Morrells Brewery Ltd., The Lion Brewery, St Thomas' Street, Oxford OX1 1LA. Tel. (0865) 792013

The only brewery in Oxford is run by the Morrell family, as it has been since 1782. Of its 136 pubs, over 50 are within the city limits and all but one of the outlets serve real ale, though some employ blanket pressure. Also brews Whitbread's Strong Country Bitter under contract and acts as a drinks wholesaler. Over 100 free trade outlets stock the beers.

Bitter (OG 1036, ABV 3.7%) Golden in colour and light in body, but not in flavour, with a good aroma of hops complemented by malt and fruitiness. An initial dry hop bitterness is well balanced by malt, which gives way to a refreshing, slightly sweet fruitiness, with a hint of roast caramel. A bittersweet, hoppy finish.

Mild* (OG 1037, ABV 3.7%)

Varsity (OG 1041, ABV 4.3%) A tawny/amber beer. Malt, hops and fruit are the main features in both aroma and taste, but are well balanced. The slightly sweet, malty, fruity start fades away to a distinctive, bittersweet finish.

Graduate (OG 1048, ABV 5.2%) An intense malt and roast aroma is complemented by a moderate hoppiness in the taste. Pleasant, bitter finish.

College* (OG 1072, ABV 7.3%) A winter brew.

For Whitbread:

Strong Country Bitter* (OG 1037, ABV 3.9%)

MUNDANE

Mundane Ales, The Old Cooperage, Dallow Bridge, Dallow Street, Burton upon Trent, Staffs. DE14 2PQ. Tel. (0283) 517779

A beer wholesaler which opened its own brewery in January 1993 to supply its pub in Halesowen and other regular customers. Like the brewery, the beers have tongue-in-cheek names. A dark stout is also in the pipeline.

Average Ale* (OG 1035)

Opening Medicine* (OG 1040, ABV 4%)

NENE VALLEY

Nene Valley Brewery, Unit 1, Midland Business Centre, Midland Road, Higham Ferrers, Northants. NN9 8PN. Tel. (0933) 412411

A brewery which opened with a single-barrel outfit in April 1992 before moving to its present site where it now turns over 15 barrels a week. Supplies over 40 outlets.

Trojan Bitter (OG 1038 ABV 3.8%) A well-presented beer, but with little depth of flavour. Clean and dry, with a dried grass hop character and a palate-cleansing dry finish.

Shopmates* (OG 1044, ABV 4.4%)

Rawhide* (OG 1050, ABV 5%)

Medusa Ale* (OG 1090, ABV 8%)

Santa's Tipple* (OG 1130, ABV 13%) Winter beer.

NETHERGATE — **Nethergate Brewery Co. Ltd., 11–13 High Street, Clare, Suffolk CO10 8NY. Tel. (0787) 277244**

Small brewer of award-winning beers, set up in 1986. Only traditional methods are used: no sugars, no colourings and no hop extracts. Brewing capacity increased to 180 barrels a week in 1993 and there are plans to expand the tied estate from the current two pubs to a total of 15 by the end of 1994. Nearly 140 free trade outlets are supplied, mostly in East Anglia.

IPA (OG 1036, ABV 3.6%) Splendid session beer, refreshing and quaffable. The hoppiness on the tongue is balanced by malt and a peachy fruitiness, but the lingering finish is all hops.

Bitter (OG 1039, ABV 4.1%) Delightful malt and hop aromas give way to a beautifully balanced palate packed with flavour: Golding hops, rich malts and hints of fruit. Deep and powerfully hoppy finish.

Old Growler (OG 1055, ABV 5.5%) A complex and deeply satisfying strong porter. Lots of roasty bitterness on the tongue, but fruit and chocolate also feature, followed by a typical Nethergate hoppy finish.

NEW FOREST — **New Forest Brewery, Old Lyndhurst Road, Cadnam, Hants. SO4 2NL. Tel. (0703) 812766**

No longer a brewery, but a wholesaler. Takes Charles Wells ales (Eagle, Bombardier and keg beers) and re-badges them under its own name.

NICHOLSON'S — See Nationals, Carlsberg-Tetley.

NIX WINCOTT — **Nix Wincott Brewery, Three Fyshes Inn, Bridge Street, Turvey, Beds. MK43 8ER. Tel. (0234) 881264**

Brew pub, founded in 1987, which has expanded production in response to demand from the local free trade and wholesalers. Plans are in hand to expand still further. The latest addition to the range, Turvey Bitter, was introduced in early 1993. Supplies eight outlets regularly, as well as the Three Fyshes.

Turvey Bitter (OG 1034, ABV 3.4%) An unusual toffee aroma leads through into a toffee malt flavour with a hint of hops. Clean, slightly astringent, dry aftertaste.

Two Henrys Bitter (OG 1039, ABV 3.9%) A dry, fruity beer with some malt in the flavour and a very bitter, slightly hoppy aftertaste. Hops, malt and some fruit in the nose.

THAT (OG 1048, ABV 4.8%) Fruit is present throughout in this mid brown brew. A flavour of malt, hops and fruit on a bitter base leads through into a bitter fruit finish. 'THAT' stands for Two Henrys Alternative Tipple.

Old Nix (OG 1057, ABV 5.9%) This pungent, almost wine-like beer has an overwhelming fruit and malt aroma, characteristics carried through to the flavour which also has a bitter, slightly hoppy base. Dry, fruity finish.

Winky's Winter Warmer* (OG 1060, ABV 6.1%) A dark, Christmas ale.

Winky Wobbler (OG 1070, ABV 7.3%) A potent winter brew that has an aroma of fruit and wine. The flavour is a powerful combination of bitter-sweet malt, fruit, roast and some hops. A dry, fruity aftertaste.

> Beers marked with an asterisk have not been tasted by official CAMRA tasting panels. However, some of these beers do carry brief descriptions derived from limited samplings or other sources, and can be used for rough guidance.

The Independents

NORTH YORKSHIRE

North Yorkshire Brewing Co., 80–84 North Ormesby Road, Middlesbrough, Cleveland TS4 2AG. Tel. (0642) 226224

Company started in March 1990 with a purpose-built brewery, but demand for its additive-free beers was such that the capacity had to be increased in 1992 and there are plans to expand again in 1994 to a 200-barrel plant. The IPA has been replaced by new brew, Yorkshire Brown. Supplies two tied houses and over 100 free trade outlets.

Best Bitter (OG 1036, ABV 3.6%) Light and very refreshing. Surprisingly full-flavoured for a pale, low gravity beer. A complex, bittersweet mixture of malt, hops and fruit carries through into the aftertaste.

Yorkshire Brown* (OG 1040, ABV 3.8%)

Yorkshire Porter* (OG 1040, ABV 3.8%)

Erimus Dark (OG 1046, ABV 4.5%) A dark, full-bodied, sweet brew with lots of roast malt and caramel, and an underlying hoppiness. At its best, it is very smooth indeed, with a tight, creamy head and a sweet, malty finish.

Flying Herbert (OG 1048, ABV 4.8%) A refreshing, red/brown beer with a hoppy aroma. The flavour is a pleasant balance of roast malt and sweetness which predominates over the hops. The malty, bitter finish develops slowly.

Dizzy Dick (OG 1080, ABV 7.7%) A smooth, strong, dark, aromatic ale with an obvious bite, although too sweet for some. The very full, roast malt and caramel flavour has hints of fruit and toffee. The malty sweetness persists in the aftertaste.

OAK

Oak Brewing Company Ltd., Phoenix Brewery, Green Lane, Heywood, Gtr. Manchester OL10 2EP. Tel. (0706) 627009

Brewery established in 1982 in Ellesmere Port which moved in 1991 to Heywood and now supplies over 60 free trade outlets from West Cheshire to West Yorkshire. Plans to open a brewery tap have been brought forward since an old station opposite the brewery was re-opened as a tourist attraction in the summer of 1993.

Hopwood Bitter* (OG 1034, ABV 3.5%)

Best Bitter (OG 1038, ABV 3.9%) A tawny, hoppy session beer with some balancing malt in the aroma and taste. A strong, dry and hoppy finish.

Tyke Bitter* (OG 1042, ABV 4.3%) Originally brewed for the West Riding Brewery (currently inoperative), but available throughout Oak's free trade.

Midsummer Madness* (OG 1044, ABV 4.5%) A new summer beer.

Old Oak Ale (OG 1044, ABV 4.5%) A well-balanced, brown beer with a multitude of mellow fruit flavours. Malt and hops balance the strong fruitiness in the aroma and taste, and the finish is malty, fruity and dry.

Double Dagger (OG 1050, ABV 5.1%) A pale brown, malty brew, more pleasantly dry and light than its gravity would suggest. Moderately fruity throughout and a hoppy bitterness in the mouth balances the strong graininess.

Porter* (OG 1050, ABV 5.1%) Now available all-year round.

Wobbly Bob (OG 1060, ABV 6.1%) A red/brown beer with a malty, fruity aroma. Strongly malty and fruity in flavour and quite hoppy, with the sweetness yielding to a dryness in the aftertaste.

Humbug* (OG 1069, ABV 7%) A new winter beer.

OAKHILL **The Old Brewery, High Street, Oakhill, Bath, Avon BA3 5AS. Tel. (0749) 840134**

Situated high in the Mendip Hills in Somerset (despite the Avon address), the brewery was set up by a farmer in 1984 in an old fermentation room of the original Oakhill Brewery (estd. 1767). However, the old Maltings building in Oakhill has now been bought as a new brewery site. Two tied houses have been acquired and Oakhill also supplies around 300 other outlets.

Best Bitter (OG 1038, ABV 3.8%) Amber-coloured, with a hoppy, malty aroma. Hoppy and bitter in the mouth, with balancing malt. There is a similar balance in the strong finish. Can be sulphury.

Black Magic (OG 1044, ABV 4%) A black/brown bitter stout with moderate roast malt and a touch of fruit in the nose. Smooth roast malt and bitterness in the taste, with mellow coffee and chocolate. Slightly fruity and sweet, with a long lasting, bitter, dry, roast finish.

Yeoman Strong Ale (OG 1049, ABV 4.8%) A mid brown beer with a hoppy, malty aroma and a malty, fruity, bittersweet taste. The strong finish is fruity, hoppy and dry.

OKELLS See Isle of Man Breweries.

OLDHAM See Nationals, Whitbread, and Pub Groups, Boddington.

OLD LUXTERS **Chiltern Valley Wines, Old Luxters Farmhouse, Hambleden, Henley-on-Thames, Oxfordshire RG9 6JW. Tel. (0491) 638330**

Brewery set up in May 1990 in a 17th-century barn by David Ealand, owner of Chiltern Valley Wines. Apart from the brewery and vineyard, the site also houses a fine art gallery. Extra fermentation tanks were added recently and sales have increased threefold, with the brewery now supplying 12 free houses in the area and some further afield. Plans are in hand to bottle the Barn Ale. Hambleden is in Buckinghamshire, despite the brewery's postal address.

Barn Ale (OG 1042.5, ABV 4.4%) Predominantly malty, fruity and hoppy in taste and nose, and tawny/amber in colour. Fairly rich and strong in flavours: the initial, sharp, malty and fruity taste leaves a dry, bittersweet, fruity aftertaste, with hints of black cherry. Can be slightly sulphurous.

OLD MILL **Old Mill Brewery Ltd., Mill Street, Snaith, Goole, Humbs. DN14 9HS. Tel. (0405) 861813**

Small brewery, started in 1983 in a 200-year-old former malt kiln and corn mill. New equipment was installed in 1991 to increase the brew length to 60 barrels. Slowly building up its tied estate and now has ten pubs, all serving real ale, as well as a free trade of around 150 accounts.

Traditional Mild (OG 1034, ABV 3.5%) A dark brown/red beer, with roast and chocolate aromas and taste, embellished sometimes with fruit and hop notes. Short finish. More body this year than last.

Traditional Bitter (OG 1037, ABV 4%) Malt and hop on the nose, and in the mouth. Fruit notes are present in the taste but hoppy bitterness dominates into a slow and deep finish. This brown and amber beer has improved over the last year.

Bullion (OG 1044, ABV 4.7%) A malty and hoppy aroma: malt and fruit mix in the mouth; the finish is dry and bitter. A dark brown beer with hints of other colours, this is a smoother, almost bittersweet premium, yet quaffable, ale.

The Independents

ORKNEY — **The Orkney Brewery, Quoyloo, Orkney KW16 3LT. Tel. (0856) 84802**

The Orkneys' first brewery in living memory, set up in 1988 by former licensee Roger White. Initially only brewing keg beer for local palates, his personal commitment to real ale has proved so successful that cask ales now represent 90% of sales (mostly to central Scotland). Orkney's beers are now bottled by Holden's of Dudley for export to Canada and other countries.

Raven Ale (OG 1038, ABV 3.8%) Still mainly keg on the island, but worth seeking out when in 'real' form. Smooth, mellow and malty, with a distinctive aroma and finish.

Dragonhead Stout* (OG 1040, ABV 4%)

Dark Island* (OG 1045, ABV 4.6%)

Skullsplitter* (OG 1080, ABV 8.5%)

OTTER — **Otter Brewery, Mathayes, Luppitt, Honiton, Devon EX14 0SA. Tel. (0404) 891285**

Otter started brewing in November 1990 and, quickly exceeding its owners' expectations, has since doubled in size. Some 30 pubs take the beers, which are brewed using local malt and the brewery's own spring water.

Bitter (OG 1036, ABV 3.6%) Pale brown-coloured beer: a pleasant, malty, aroma with a hoppy taste and a hoppy, bitter finish.

Ale (OG 1043, ABV 4.5%) Tawny-coloured, well-balanced beer with a hoppy, bitter taste and aftertaste.

Head (OG 1054, ABV 5.8%) Tawny-coloured beer with a strong, fruity aroma, and a taste and aftertaste of malt and fruit.

PACKHORSE — **The Packhorse Brewing Company, Ashford, Kent.**
Brewery closed.

PALMERS — **JC & RH Palmer Ltd., The Old Brewery, West Bay Road, Bridport, Dorset DT6 4JA. Tel. (0308) 422396**

Britain's only thatched brewery is situated by the sea in former mill buildings where brewing has taken place for 200 years. It was bought by JC Palmer in 1896 and is now managed by his great-grandsons. Plans to increase its tied estate of 65 houses over the next few years by very selective acquisitions. All its pubs serve real ale although top pressure and cask breathers are widely in use. Serves about 30 direct free trade outlets, but its beers are reaching a wider audience throughout the South via wholesalers.

Bridport Bitter or BB (OG 1032, ABV 3.2%) A light beer with a hoppy aroma, a bitter, hoppy taste with some malt, and a bitter aftertaste.

Best Bitter or IPA (OG 1040, ABV 4.2%) An uninspiring beer. Hoppy and bitter throughout, with some balancing fruit and malt. Difficult to find in good condition.

Tally Ho! (OG 1046, ABV 4.7%) A dark and complex brew with a mainly malty aroma. The nutty taste is dominated by roast malt, balanced with some bitterness. Malty and bitter aftertaste. Limited availability, especially in winter.

PARISH — **Parish Brewery, The Old Brewery Courtyard, Somerby, Leics. LE14 2PZ. Tel. (066 477) 781**

The first brewery to be established in Somerby since the 16th century, Parish started life at the Stag and Hounds, Burrough on the Hill, and moved in July 1990 for greater capacity, following increased sales. Baz's Bonce Blower is the strongest draught beer available all-year round in the UK. In addition to the neighbouring Old Brewery Inn, which is a free house, Parish directly supplies 20 outlets.

Mild (OG 1035, ABV 3.5%) A thin, dark brew with a faint malty aroma. The palate is caramel and fruit with a dry roast finish.

Special Bitter or PSB (OG 1038, ABV 3.8%) A tasty, well-balanced bitter with hops predominating throughout. A slight yeastiness does not spoil this pale brown, thin-bodied beer.

Somerby Premium Bitter (OG 1040, ABV 4%) A tawny, medium-bodied best bitter with notes of orange imposing upon the hoppy flavour and dry aftertaste.

Rainbow Porter* (OG 1048, ABV 4.5%) A winter beer.

Poachers Ale (OG 1060, ABV 6%) A complex, full-flavoured ale which encompasses malt, hops, fruit and acidity. It has a dark ruby colour with hints of yeast on the palate.

Baz's Bonce Blower or BBB (OG 1110, ABV 12%) A robust and vigorous Christmas pudding of a beer, black in colour with a splendid rich palate and aftertaste.

PILGRIM **Pilgrim Brewery, West Street, Reigate, Surrey RH2 9BL. Tel. (0737) 222651**

Surrey brewery which celebrated its tenth anniversary in 1992. Sales of all the beers are now being concentrated in the brewery's own locality, with pub promotions being something of a speciality.

Surrey Pale Ale or SPA (OG 1037, ABV 3.7%) A well-balanced pale brown bitter with an underlying fruitiness. Hop flavour comes through in the finish. A good session beer.

Porter (OG 1041, ABV 4%) A dark brown beer with a roast malt flavour. The finish is balanced by a faint developing hoppiness.

Progress Best Bitter (OG 1041, ABV 4%) Reddish-brown in colour, with a predominantly malty flavour and aroma, although hops are also evident in the taste.

Crusader Premium Bitter (OG 1047, ABV 4.7%) Light, golden beer with a malty bitterness. A very drinkable summer brew.

Saracen Stout* (OG 1047, ABV 4.7%) An occasional stout.

Talisman (OG 1048, ABV 4.8%) A strong ale with a dark red colour, a fruity, malt flavour and roast overtones. Available all year, but more common in winter.

PITFIELD **Chainmaker Beer Co. Ltd., Stourbridge Estate, Mill Race Lane, Stourbridge, W. Midlands DY8 1JN. Tel. (0384) 442040**

PITFIELD'S

The UB Group (United Breweries of India) now wholly owns the Chainmaker Beer Company, which produces the former Premier/Pitfield beers and the Wiltshire Brewery brands. The total tied estate is now 78 pubs, all but three of which sell real ale. A further 200 free trade outlets are also supplied.

Mild* (OG 1035, ABV 3.4%)

Bitter (OG 1036, ABV 3.6%) A faint hop aroma leads through into a dry, hoppy flavour with underlying fruit and malt sweetness. Dry, slightly astringent aftertaste; little depth of flavour.

Wiltshire Stonehenge Bitter* (OG 1036, ABV 3.6%)

> The tankard symbol indicates the *Good Beer Guide Beers of the Year*, finalists in the *Champion Beer of Britain* contest held at the *Great British Beer Festival* at Olympia in August 1993.

ESB (OG 1044, ABV 4.2%) A pale brown, malty-flavoured bitter. Quite hoppy and slightly sweet.

Hoxton Heavy (OG 1048, ABV 4.8%) A copper-red beer, quite hoppy in taste and aroma. Slightly sweet.

Wiltshire Old Grumble* (OG 1048, ABV 4.8%)

Dark Star (OG 1049, ABV 5%) A malt and roast-flavoured, black beer, slightly fruity, with a hop and bitter finish.

Black Knight Stout* (OG 1051, ABV 5%)

Wiltshire Stonehenge Ginger Beer* (OG 1060, ABV 6.5%)

Maiden's Ruin* (OG 1076, ABV 7.5%)

Santa's Downfall* (OG 1076, ABV 7.5%)

PLASSEY

Plassey Brewery, The Plassey, Eyton, Wrexham, Clwyd LL13 0SP. Tel. (0978) 780922

Brewery founded in 1985 by former Border brewer, Alan Beresford. Following his death in 1989, it was taken over by another ex-Border man, Ian Dale, in partnership with Tony Brookshaw, owner of the farm on which the brewery is sited. The farm also includes a touring caravan and leisure park, a craft centre and a licensed outlet for Plassey's ales. The brewery now supplies about ten free trade outlets, with Dragon's Breath the latest (seasonal) addition to the range.

Bitter ⊟ (OG 1039, ABV 4%) Excellent, straw-coloured beer, well-hopped and bitter, with blackcurrant fruitiness. Light and refreshing.

Cwrw Tudno (OG 1047, ABV 5%) More malty and sweet and less bitter than the bitter, but has a fairly dry aftertaste.

Dragon's Breath (OG 1060) A fruity, strong bitter, smooth and quite sweet, though not cloying, with an intense, fruity aroma. A dangerously drinkable winter warmer.

POOLE

The Brewhouse Brewery, 68 High Street, Poole, Dorset BH15 1DA. Tel. (0202) 682345

Brewery established in 1981, two years before the Brewhouse pub/brewery was opened. When an extension to the Brewhouse was completed in 1990, the entire brewing operation was transferred there and further expansion is now underway. The Brewhouse pub keeps the beer under blanket pressure, but 15 other outlets also take Poole products, and it brews Ansty Ale (OG 1080, ABV 8.5%) for the Fox at Ansty.

Poole Best Bitter or Dolphin* (OG 1038, ABV 3.8%) An amber-coloured, balanced bitter.

Bosun Bitter* (OG 1045, ABV 4.6%) Amber and rich.

SAM POWELL

See Wood.

PREMIER

See Pitfield.

PRESTON

The Preston Brewing Co. Ltd., Atlas Brewery, Brieryfield Road, Preston, Lancs. PR1 8SR. Tel. (0772) 883055

Set up in a disused foundry in 1992, the Atlas Brewery's beers have quickly found favour with the local people and are stocked semi-permanently by some 75 outlets. There are plans to increase capacity to 100 barrels a week and make the beers more widely available via wholesalers.

Pride Dark Mild*	(ABV 3.6%)
Pride Ale*	(OG 1036, ABV 3.8%)
Atlas Special Bitter*	(ABV 4.5%)
Walburge's Splendid Porter*	(OG 1042, ABV 4.5%)
Atlas Really Strong Export*	(OG 1060, ABV 6.5%)

RCH — **RCH Brewery, Royal Clarence Hotel, The Esplanade, Burnham-on-Sea, Somerset TA8 1BQ. Tel (0278) 783138**

RCH Brewery

Brew pub, set up ten years ago, now supplying many other outlets in the West Country on an occasional basis via its own wholesale agency.

Clarence Pride (OG 1036, ABV 3.6%) A pale brown beer with a hoppy/malty aroma, a hoppy, strongly bitter taste and a bitter, hoppy finish.

Pitchfork* (OG 1043, ABV 4.3%)

Old Slug Porter* (OG 1045, ABV 4.5%)

Clarence Regent* (OG 1050, ABV 5.2%) A dark brown/black winter brew.

RANDALLS — **RW Randall Ltd., Vauxlaurens Brewery, St Julian's Avenue, St Peter Port, Guernsey, CI GY1 3JG. Tel. (0481) 720134**

The smaller of Guernsey's two breweries, which was purchased by RH Randall from Joseph Gullick in 1868. Successive generations have continued to run the business, except during the period of the German occupation when brewing ceased until after the war. Owns 16 houses, but only four serve real ale; supplies eight other free trade outlets.

Best Mild (OG 1033, ABV 3.2%) Copper-red, with a malty and fruity aroma and a hint of hops. The fruity character remains throughout, with a sweetish, malty undertone.

Best Bitter (OG 1046, ABV 5%) Amber in colour, with a malt and fruit aroma. Sweet and malty both in the palate and finish.

RANDALLS (JERSEY) — See Pub Groups.

RAYMENTS — See Greene King.

REBELLION — **Rebellion Beer Company, The Marlow Brewery, Unit J, Rose Ind. Estate, Marlow Bottom Road, Marlow, Bucks. SL7 3ND. Tel. (0628) 476594**

REBELLION BEER CO.

A new brewery, opened in 1993, which hopes to fill the gap left by Wethered and is in fact discussing the possibility of taking over part of the old Wethered site in Marlow which was closed by Whitbread in 1988. The brewery water is being 'Marlowised', i.e. treated to recreate the mineral composition of the water used by the former Wethered brewery.

IPA* (OG 1039, ABV 3.9%)

REDRUTH — **Redruth Brewery Ltd., The Brewery, Redruth, Cornwall TR15 1AT. Tel. (0209) 212244**

The old Cornish Brewery, originally founded in 1792 and now back under its original name, following a management buy-out from Devenish in July 1991. The only real ale brewed is Cornish

Original, for Whitbread to supply to Devenish! With no tied estate and most local pubs being tied to other breweries, Redruth has no outlets for beers of its own and therefore concentrates on contract packaging and brewing.

For Whitbread:

Cornish Original Bitter* (OG 1036, ABV 3.4%)

REEPHAM **Reepham Brewery, Unit 1, Collers Way, Reepham, Norfolk NR10 4SW. Tel. (0603) 871091**

Family brewery, founded in 1983 by a former Watney's research engineer with a purpose-built plant in a small industrial unit. The company was launched on a single beer, Granary Bitter, but now produces quite a range, which varies from year to year and includes some award-winners. Thirty local outlets are supplied directly, plus more through wholesalers. *Bottle-conditioned beer: Rapier Pale Ale (OG 1042, ABV 4.2%)*

Granary Bitter (OG 1038, ABV 3.8%) An amber beer which is well-balanced and makes easy drinking. The malt and hops are complemented by a pleasing amount of bitterness and hints of fruitiness.

Dark* (OG 1039, ABV 3.9%) A strong mild.

Summer Velvet* (OG 1040, ABV 4%)

Rapier Pale Ale (OG 1042, ABV 4.2%) Beer with a distinctly flowery aroma which is unlike the complex palate which has a grainy maltiness, mixed with a fruity, hoppy background and a hint of woodiness. Very drinkable.

Velvet Stout (OG 1042, ABV 4.2%) The fruity, malt aroma of this darkish brown beer gives way to a sweet, mellow taste explosion of malt, roast, fruit and hops. This subsides to a pleasant aftertaste with hints of liquorice. Still excellent.

Smugglers Stout (OG 1045, ABV 4.5%) A dark red/brown beer with a well-balanced roast and bitter finish. It needs more body and bitterness to be a proper stout, but a good beer nonetheless. A fruity, malty aroma; an initial sweetness with roast malt in the mouth.

Old Bircham Ale (OG 1046, ABV 4.6%) An amber/tawny beer with good body for its gravity. The fruity aroma precedes a complex, malty, hoppy palate, which also has a sweetness that dies away in the malty, dry finish. A winter brew.

Brewhouse* (OG 1052, ABV 5%) A strong winter ale.

REINDEER **Reindeer Trading Company Ltd., 10 Dereham Road, Norwich, Norfolk NR2 4AY. Tel. (0603) 666821**

Brew pub which opened in 1987 and since the summer of 1992 has been brewing at least four times a week to keep up with the demand from the free trade (currently 15 outlets) and the guest beer market. Plans to expand the brewery further in future. At the pub the main beers are stored in cellar tanks, about half of them under blanket pressure. The Pale Ale and Porter are the latest additions to a growing range.

Moild (OG 1034, ABV 3.5%) Full bodied (for a mild) and definitely full flavoured; the palate has a malt and roast base with hop, sweetness and some bitterness. Usually a dry mild, but can be initially quite fruity. Not your average mild.

Pale Ale or RPA (OG 1034, ABV 3.5%) A pale brown beer without much aroma, but lots of hop and bitterness in the palate which lingers in the aftertaste. Quite astringent for a beer of this type.

Bevy (OG 1037, ABV 4%) A session beer which has a good quantity of hoppiness and bitterness, and more maltiness than the RPA. There is also a touch of roast and sweetness, with some astringency in the aftertaste.

Gnu Bru (OG 1042, ABV 4.5%) Basically, a hoppy/bitter beer, particularly in the dry aftertaste. There is also a quantity of malt in the aroma and complex aftertaste.

Porter (OG 1045, ABV 5%) A dark red/brown beer with a lot of roast in the palate, also some hop and a hint of fruit. Not much bitterness; dry, lasting aftertaste.

Bitter (OG 1047, ABV 5%) A full-bodied beer which is complex and flavoursome. Sweeter than the weaker beers, it is fruity and malty throughout, with some lingering hop bitterness.

Red Nose (OG 1057, ABV 6%) A dark red/brown, very full-bodied beer. Mainly fruity and malty, it is a rich, complex brew, good for cold evenings, although some may find it a touch cloying.

Sanity Claus (OG 1067, ABV 6.8%) Brewed for Christmas, this beer's inviting fruit and malt aroma leads to a very smooth, complex palate. Fruit and malt are the main features of this dangerously drinkable beer, with some roast and hop flavours but little bitterness. Very good.

RIDLEYS

TD Ridley & Sons Ltd., Hartford End Brewery, Chelmsford, Essex CM3 1JZ. Tel. (0371) 820316

In 1992, Ridleys celebrated 150 years of brewing, in the same buildings on the River Chelmer where miller Thomas Dixon Ridley began production in 1842. After closing three small pubs in 1992, it acquired three busier ones from national breweries and is currently undergoing a programme of improving existing tied houses, all 65 of which sell real ale. Around 300 other outlets are also supplied, at the lowest prices in the South-East.

Mild (OG 1034, ABV 3.5%) Dark brown with mixed aromas of roast and caramels. A bitter taste, studded with strong roast flavour; bitter aftertastes. More a bitter with caramel and roast accents than a mild. Found only in a handful of tied pubs.

IPA Bitter (OG 1034, ABV 3.5%) A hoppy and well-balanced bitter with hints of malt. The dry, bitter aftertaste lingers, with hops and a slight fruit flavour.

Winter Ale* (OG 1050, ABV 5%) The seasonal offering.

RINGWOOD

Ringwood Brewery Ltd., 138 Christchurch Road, Ringwood, Hants. BH24 3AP. Tel. (0425) 471177

Hampshire's first new brewery in the real ale revival, founded in 1978 and housed in attractive 18th-century buildings, formerly part of the old Tunks brewery, though plans are in hand for a new brewhouse. Famous for its award-winning Old Thumper, it has two tied houses and around 300 free trade accounts, from Weymouth to Chichester and the Channel Isles.

Best Bitter (OG 1038, ABV 4%) A golden brown, moreish beer, with flavours for all. The aroma has a hint of hops and leads to a malty sweetness, which becomes dry, with a hint of orange. Malt and bitterness in the finish.

XXXX Porter (OG 1048, ABV 4.7%) Sadly only available October–March: a rich, dark brew with a strong aroma of roasted malt, hops and fruit. Rich in flavour, with coffee, vanilla, damsons, apples and molasses present. The overall roast maltiness continues into the drying, hoppy, bitter finish.

Fortyniner (OG 1048, ABV 4.8%) A good premium beer, with malt and hops in good balance. The flavours slowly increase to a fruity finish.

Old Thumper (OG 1058, ABV 5.8%) A golden beer with a surprisingly bitter aftertaste, which follows a middle period tasting of various fruits. May be a little sweet for some.

RISING SUN

The Rising Sun Brewery, Knowle Bank Road, Shraley Brook, Audley, Stoke-on-Trent, Staffs. ST7 8DS. Tel. (0782) 720600

Brewing began in June 1989 at the Rising Sun pub and currently around 35 outlets are supplied on a semi-regular basis. A second tied house is being sought and there are plans to brew a bottle-conditioned fruit beer from the pub's own damsons. *Bottle-conditioned beers: Total Eclipse (OG 1072, ABV 6.9%); Solar Flare (OG 1100, ABV 11.5%)*

Mild* (OG 1034, ABV 3.5%)

Sunlight* (OG 1036, ABV 3.5%) Summer only.

Rising* (OG 1040, ABV 3.9%)

Setting* (OG 1045, ABV 4.4%)

Sun Stroke* (OG 1056, ABV 5.6%)

Total Eclipse* (OG 1072, ABV 6.9%)

Solar Flare* (OG 1100, ABV 11.5%) Winter only.

ROBINSON'S

Frederic Robinson Ltd., Unicorn Brewery, Hillgate, Stockport, Cheshire SK1 1JJ. Tel. (061) 480 6571

Major family brewery, founded in 1838. Took over Hartleys of Ulverston in 1982, but closed that brewery in October 1991 and is now planning to demolish some of the buildings (including a listed chimney). Only Hartleys XB is still brewed (at Stockport). Most of its 409 tied houses (70 from the Hartleys Cumbrian estate, but most in southern Manchester and Cheshire) sell real ale. Best Bitter is widely available, but Bitter can be found in only about 20 outlets.

Best Mild (OG 1032, ABV 3.3%) A pale brown, well-balanced beer, with a sweet aftertaste. A good, refreshing drink.

Dark Best Mild (OG 1032, ABV 3.3%) Toffee/malt-tasting, with a slight bitterness. Very quaffable, enjoying a fruity/malt aroma and a dry finish. Not commonly available.

Bitter (OG 1035, ABV 3.5%) Fresh-tasting, with an aniseed tinge. Characteristic aroma and a smooth but brief finish.

Hartleys XB (OG 1040, ABV 4%) Little aroma. Malty with some hop bitterness and a dry finish.

Best Bitter (OG 1041, ABV 4.2%) An amber beer with a malty, hoppy nose. A well-balanced taste precedes a slight, bitter finish.

Old Tom (OG 1080, ABV 8.5%) A full-bodied, dark, fruity beer, similar in texture to a barley wine. The aroma is fruity and mouthwatering; the aftertaste is bittersweet. A beer to be sipped respectfully by a roaring winter fire.

> OG stands for Original Gravity, the reading taken before fermentation of the amount of fermentable material in the brew. It is a rough indicator of strength. More reliable is the ABV (Alcohol by Volume) rating, which gives the percentage of alcohol in the finished beer.

ROBINWOOD **Robinwood Brewers & Vintners, Todmorden, W. Yorks.**

A company which commenced brewing in 1988 and at one time had three tied houses. However, in 1993, brewing ceased and the Todmorden premises were put up for sale. The brewery was poised to resume production at a different Yorkshire location. *Bottle-conditioned beer: Old Fart (OG 1059, ABV 6%)*

Best Bitter* (OG 1036, ABV 4.1%)

XB* (OG 1046, ABV 4.7%)

Old Fart* (OG 1060, ABV 6%)

ROOSTER'S **Rooster's Brewery, Unit 20, Claro Business Park, Claro Road, Harrogate, N. Yorks. HG1 4BA. Tel. (0423) 561861**

Another of the rash of new breweries set up in 1992, this one in September, by Sean Franklin, formerly of Franklin's Brewery. Currently supplies up to 30 outlets, but demand is growing and new equipment is being installed to increase the capacity. *Bottle-conditioned beers: Yankee (OG 1042, ABV 4.3%); Rooster's (OG 1046, ABV 4.7%)*

Yankee (OG 1042, ABV 4.3%) Straw-coloured beer with a delicate aroma. The flavour is an interesting mix of malt and hops with a gentle sweetness and a bite of orange peel, leading to a short, pleasant finish.

Rooster's (OG 1046, ABV 4.7%) Light amber beer with a subtle, sweet, slightly hoppy nose. Intense malt flavours, reminiscent of treacle toffee with chocolate and orange undertones, and an unexpected hoppy finish.

ROSS **Ross Brewing Company, The Bristol Brewhouse, 117–119 Stokes Croft, Bristol, Avon BS1 3RW. Tel. (0272) 420306**

Set up in Hartcliffe in 1989, Ross was the first brewery to brew with organic Soil Association barley, initially producing bottle-conditioned beers only. The brewery has now moved to the Bristol Brewhouse pub and the one remaining bottled beer, Saxon Strong Ale, is brewed under contract by Eldridge Pope (see Eldridge Pope). Ross instead now brews cask beers for consumption in the pub and in a very limited free trade.

Clifton Dark (OG 1045, ABV 4.5%) A subtle, but complex copper brown mild. A bitter, dry taste with malt, roast and caramel throughout and a hint of fruit. The bitter finish is slightly metallic.

Hartcliffe Bitter (OG 1045, ABV 4.5%) A pale brown, malty beer with a balancing bitter sweetness. Little aroma and a dry, malt finish. The quality is variable.

Kingsdowner* (OG 1045, ABV 4.5%) An occasional brew.

Medieval Porter (OG 1045, ABV 4.5%) A distinctive, copper brown porter. The roast malt and hop aroma has traces of ginger and herbs. The taste is similar, with bitterness and a sweet fruitiness. A dry, spicy finish.

Pale Ale* (OG 1050, ABV 5%)

ROYAL CLARENCE See RCH.

RUDDLES **Ruddles Brewery Ltd., Langham, Oakham, Leics. LE15 7JD. Tel. (0572) 756911**

Famous real ale brewery, founded in 1858, which lost its independence when it was taken over by Grand Metropolitan in 1986. Ruddles beers subsequently became national brands. Acquired by Dutch lager giant Grolsch in 1992, after a time under Courage.

Best Bitter (OG 1037, ABV 3.7%) Medium-bodied, tawny bitter with an aroma of sulphur and hops leading to a bitter, hoppy flavour and dry finish.

County (OG 1050, ABV 4.9%) Hoppy bitterness, softened by malt, characterizes this mid brown beer. A well-bodied bitter, it has improved of late, but is still nothing like the County of old.

RUDGATE

Rudgate Brewery Ltd., 2 Centre Park, Marston Business Park, Rudgate, Tockwith, York, N. Yorks. YO5 8QF. Tel. (0423) 358382

Brewery founded in April 1992 and bought by two former Bass executives in November that year. It operates from an old armoury building on the edge of Tockwith's disused airfield and now supplies 50 regular outlets, from Tyneside to Nottingham.

Viking* (OG 1039, ABV 3.9%)

Battleaxe* (OG 1044, ABV 4.4%)

RYBURN

Ryburn Brewery, Mill House, Mill House Lane, Sowerby Bridge, W. Yorks. HX6 3LN. Tel. (0422) 835413

Brewery founded with a tiny, two-barrel plant in a former dye works, in 1990, whose beers were only available sporadically until 1991 when it began supplying the Stanley Arms in Stockport on a regular basis. Now supplies 12, mostly local outlets and is planning to purchase a tied house. Produces occasional special brews.

Mild (OG 1033, ABV 3.3%) Stout-like in taste and colour, with a rich roast malt flavour and balancing bitterness, which is reflected in the finish and aroma.

Bitter* (OG 1038, ABV 3.8%)

Stout* (OG 1040, ABV 4%) A winter brew

Porter* (OG 1042, ABV 4.2%) A Christmas brew.

Rydale Bitter* (OG 1044, ABV 4.4%) Mid brown in colour with little aroma. A smooth, malty bitter with hop character and bitterness, plus some fruit notes. Long, malty and bitter finish.

Stabbers Bitter (OG 1050, ABV 5%) A malty aroma leads to a rich maltiness in the mouth with bittersweet, fruity elements, concluding in a malty and bitter finish. A mid brown, powerful strong ale.

Strong Mild (OG 1050, ABV 5%) Dark ruby, strong beer. Sweet caramel and malt on the palate, with good fruit presence, ending with a similar finish. Faint aroma.

ST AUSTELL

St Austell Brewery Co. Ltd., 63 Trevarthian Road, St Austell, Cornwall PL25 4BY. Tel. (0726) 74444

Brewing company set up in 1851 by maltster and wine merchant Walter Hicks. It moved to the present site in 1893 and remains a family business, with many of Hicks's descendants employed in the company. Its 140 tied houses are spread right across Cornwall, nearly all of them serving traditional ale, and some 300 free trade outlets are also supplied. The recently-opened visitors' centre is proving to be a great success.

Bosun's Bitter (OG 1036, ABV 3.4%) A refreshing session beer, sweetish in aroma and bittersweet in flavour. Lingering, hoppy finish.

XXXX Mild (OG 1039, ABV 3.6%) Little aroma, but a strong, malty, caramel-sweetish flavour is followed by a good, lingering aftertaste, which is sweet but with a fruity dryness. Very drinkable.

Tinners Ale (OG 1039, ABV 3.7%) A deservedly-popular, golden beer with an appetising malt aroma and a good balance of malt and hops in the flavour. Lasting finish.

Hicks Special Draught or HSD (OG 1051, ABV 5%) An aromatic, fruity, hoppy bitter which is initially sweet and has an aftertaste of pronounced bitterness, but whose flavour is fully-rounded.

Winter Warmer*	(OG 1060, ABV 6%) Available November–February.

SCOTTIES See Scott's.

SCOTT'S

Scott's Brewing Company, Crown Hotel, 151 High Street, Lowestoft, Suffolk NR31 1HR. Tel. (0502) 569592

Brewery founded in June 1989 and now supplying beer to its own four pubs (none of which are tied) and around 20 free trade outlets.

Golden Best Bitter (OG 1038, ABV 3.4%) A golden beer which is not at all strong tasting. What flavour it has is a reasonable balance of malt and (pungent) hop. The latter dominates in the aftertaste.

Blues and Bloater (OG 1039, ABV 3.7%) This pleasant malty, fruity beer is let down by the taste which is light, lacking in bitterness and a bit cloying. More of a light mild than a bitter.

Dark Oast (OG 1047, ABV 4.7%) A winter beer, red/brown in colour, with less body than its gravity would suggest. The taste has roast malt as its main characteristic, with hoppiness prominent in the aftertaste.

William French (OG 1047, ABV 4.7%) A full and beautifully-balanced beer. A faint, malty aroma leads into a palate with strong malt and hop flavours, and considerable fruitiness. A full and balanced aftertaste, too.

SCOTTISH & NEWCASTLE See Nationals.

SELBY

Selby (Middlesbrough) Brewery Ltd., 131 Millgate, Selby, N. Yorks. YO8 0LL. Tel. (0757) 702826

Old family brewery which resumed brewing in 1972 after a gap of 18 years and is now mostly involved in wholesaling. Real ale is available primarily through its Brewery Tap off-licence in Selby, and not at the company's single pub.

Strong Ale* (OG 1045, ABV 4.5%)

Old Tom (OG 1069, ABV 6.5%) Deceptively strong, tawny-hued ale. Mouth-filling malt, roast and tangy hop on the palate, with a distinctive 'smoky' character. Hoppy and malty finish, but the aroma is not marked. Excellent but rather rare beer.

SHEPHERD NEAME

Shepherd Neame Ltd., 17 Court Street, Faversham, Kent ME13 7AX. Tel. (0795) 532206

A fine old brewery retaining many original features, with a visitors' reception centre in a restored medieval hall. Believed to be the oldest continuous brewer in the land (since 1698), and only Kent hops are used in its beers. The tied estate has been increased by 50% since 1990 and now comprises 371 pubs, all selling real ale, but, sadly, it is still company policy to encourage tenants to keep beers under low blanket pressure. Offers regional guest beers to its tenants via a beer club and directly supplies 200 free trade outlets.
Bottle-conditioned beer: Spitfire (ABV 4.7%)

Master Brew Bitter (OG 1036, ABV 3.8%) A very distinctive bitter, mid brown in colour, with a very hoppy aroma. Well-balanced with a nicely aggressive bitter taste from its hops, leaving a hoppy/bitter finish, tinged with sweetness.

Best Bitter (OG 1039, ABV 4%) Mid brown, with less marked characteristics than the bitter. However, the nose is very well balanced and the taste enjoys a malty, bitter smokiness. A malty, well-rounded finish.

Masons Dark Ale* (ABV 4.2%) A new dark mild for summer.

Spitfire Ale* (OG 1044, ABV 4.7%) A commemorative brew (Battle of Britain) for the RAF Benevolent Fund's appeal, now a permanent feature.

Original Porter (ABV 5.2%) Rich, black, full-bodied, winter brew. The good malt and roast aroma also has a fine fruit edge. The complex blend of flavours is dominated by roast malt, which is also present in a very dry aftertaste.

Bishops Finger* (OG 1053, ABV 5.4%) A well-known bottled beer, introduced in cask-conditioned form in 1989.

SHIPSTONE'S See Nationals, Carlsberg-Tetley, and Pub Groups, Greenalls.

SMILES

Smiles Brewing Co. Ltd., Colston Yard, Colston Street, Bristol, Avon BS1 5BD. Tel. (0272) 297350

Established in 1977 to supply a local restaurant, and started full-scale brewing early in 1978. Changed hands in 1991. Noted for its quality ales and good pubs (a winner of CAMRA's *Pub Design* awards), Smiles celebrated its 15th anniversary by brewing Bristol Stout, which proved so successful it has been added to the permanent beer range. Supplies five managed pubs and 200 free trade outlets, and is looking to acquire more tied houses.

Bitter (OG 1037, ABV 3.7%) A golden/amber, light beer with plenty of malt and hops for its gravity. Its bitter, fruit palate is balanced by a pleasant, dry finish. Has a malty, hoppy aroma.

Best Bitter (OG 1041, ABV 4.1%) A mid brown, fruity beer with some malt and hops in both nose and taste. Slightly sweet, but a well-rounded beer with a bitter, dry finish.

Bristol Stout (OG 1046, ABV 4.7%) A dark, red/brown stout with a malt and roast aroma. The predominantly malty taste features some hops and fruit. A roast, bitter, dry finish. Available September–March.

Exhibition (OG 1051, ABV 5.2%) A deep copper-red beer, a complex collection of rich flavours. The pronounced roast malt, hop and fruit taste leads into a dry, bittersweet finish. Individual fruit flavours are sometimes discernible.

JOHN SMITH'S See Nationals, Courage.

SAMUEL SMITH

Samuel Smith Old Brewery (Tadcaster), Tadcaster, N. Yorks. LS24 9SB. Tel. (0937) 832225

Small company operating from the oldest brewery in Yorkshire, dating from 1758 and once owned by John Smith. Although John Smith's is now Courage-owned, 'Sam's' remains family-owned and firmly independent. Beers are brewed from well water without the use of any adjuncts and all cask beer is fermented in Yorkshire stone squares and racked into wooden casks provided by the brewery's own cooperage. Real ale is served in the majority of its 200-plus tied houses, which include 27 in London, representing good value for the capital; also supplies some free trade outlets.

Old Brewery Bitter (OBB) (OG 1040, ABV 3.8%) Malt dominates the nose, the taste and aftertaste, although this is underscored at all stages by a gentle hoppiness. A 'big' beer with loads of flavour, complemented by an attractive amber colour.

Museum Ale (OG 1050, ABV 5%) Deep amber in colour, which gives some idea of the fruitiness to be found in the nose, taste and finish. A sweet beer with winey flavours, despite no sugar being used in the brewing process.

SNOWDONIA

Snowdonia Brewery, Gellilydan, Blaenau Ffestiniog, Gwynedd LL41 4EH. Tel. (0766) 85379

Beginning as a brew pub, Barry's Brewery at the Bryn Arms took on a partner in March 1993, in order to expand its range of beers and outlets. Currently serves around three outlets.

Mêl y Moelwyn Bitter (OG 1037, ABV 3.7%) A well-balanced and hoppy beer with a dry, fruity aftertaste. Full-flavoured with honey notes.

Choir Porter* (OG 1045, ABV 4.5%) The first porter to be brewed in Wales: a dark, malty brew.

Snowdon Strong Bitter (OG 1050, ABV 5.2%) A smooth, mellow and well-rounded, strong bitter. Fairly sweet but not cloying, it is well-hopped and eminently drinkable.

SPRINGFIELD See Nationals, Bass.

SPRINGHEAD

Springhead Brewery, Main Street, Sutton on Trent, Newark, Notts. NG23 6PE. Tel. (0636) 821000

Possibly the smallest brewery in the country, occupying a mere 12 square yards of floor space. Began production in 1990 and has expanded from a single barrel to a seven and a half barrel plant. A second beer is planned and over 50 free trade outlets are supplied.

Bitter* (OG 1038, ABV 4%)

STEAM PACKET

The Steam Packet Brewery, Steam Packet Inn, Racca Green, Knottingley, W. Yorks. WF11 8AT. Tel. (0977) 674176

Brewery which began producing beers for the pub in November 1990, but which expanded to supply almost 50 outlets, mainly in the North-West. New brews are regularly added to its already substantial range of beers which are picking up a good following, partly helped by very reasonable prices.

Mellors Gamekeeper Bitter* (OG 1036, ABV 3.6%) A malty brew, with a dry, malty initial taste, but it can be very weak in aftertaste. Light brown in colour.

Chatterley* (OG 1037, ABV 3.7%) Wheat malt brew, with a light golden colour and a quite fruity, hoppy taste. A session beer with a lemon aftertaste.

Foxy* (OG 1039, ABV 3.9%) A new, russet-coloured beer with a small amount of wheat malt. The very well-balanced malt and hop flavour is also fruity, with a slight lemon flavour in the aftertaste.

Bitter Black* (OG 1040, ABV 4%) A dark, malty brew with a well-balanced taste of malt and a lightly vinous nose and aftertaste. Like a dark strong mild.

Bargee* (OG 1048, ABV 4.8%) A Belgian-style beer of a slightly darker colour than Foxy, with a very malty initial taste which bursts into a fruity aftertaste.

Poacher's Swag* (OG 1050, ABV 5%) A pale-coloured, strong, dry beer with a real taste of alcohol; dry in aftertaste.

Giddy Ass* (OG 1080, ABV 8%) A new beer with a winey taste and no hint of sweetness. Dangerously drinkable.

STOCKS

Stocks Brewery, The Hallcross, 33–34 Hallgate, Doncaster, S. Yorks. DN1 3NL. Tel. (0302) 328213

Brewery founded in December 1981 as a brew pub in a former baker's shop and now running two other tied houses. Supplies 12 local outlets direct and has an expanding free trade, including the Tap & Spile chain.

Best Bitter (OG 1037, ABV 3.6%) A clean but thin session beer, this mid brown/tawny ale has a faint aroma, a malt and hoppy bitter taste, and a moderately dry finish. An ordinary, rather than a best bitter.

Select (OG 1044, ABV 4.3%) Light aroma and mouthfeel, though more body this year than last. Malt in the mouth and a short bitter finish. A smooth yet delicate mid-brown beer with red hints.

Old Horizontal (OG 1056, ABV 5.3%) A dark brown beer with ruby hints, this bre has fruit, roast and chocolate, but malt predominates in t flavour, as it does in the nose. Short finish, but rich overall fee pint for sipping quietly.

The Independents

STONES — See Nationals, Bass.

STRONG — See Morrells and Nationals, Whitbread.

SUMMERSKILLS — **Summerskills Brewery, Unit 15, Pomphlett Farm Ind. Estate, Broxton Drive, Billacombe, Plymouth, Devon PL9 7BG. Tel. (0752) 481283**

SEMPER FIDELIS AD BACCUM

Summerskills was initially set up in 1983 in a vineyard, but was only operational for two years. It was relaunched by new owners in 1990, with plant from the old Penrhos brewery, and production has grown at a steady rate. Supplies around 30 free trade outlets directly and others nationally via wholesalers. Also acts as a wholesaler of other small independents' beers. The brewery logo comes from the ship's crest of HMS Bigbury Bay.

Best Bitter (OG 1042, ABV 4.3%) Mid brown with a malty, hoppy aroma and taste. Strong hoppy, bitter aftertaste.

Whistle Belly Vengeance* (OG 1046, ABV 4.7%) Mid brown, multi-flavoured beer – predominantly roast malt and hops, with a hoppy, bitter finish. Tastes stronger than it is.

Ninjabeer (OG 1049, ABV 5%) A new brew. An amber-coloured, sweet-tasting beer with a fruity aroma. Its colour belies its strength.

TAYLOR — **Timothy Taylor & Co. Ltd., Knowle Spring Brewery, Keighley, W. Yorks. BD21 1AW. Tel. (0535) 603139**

TIMOTHY TAYLOR TRADITIONAL REAL ALES CHAMPIONSHIP BEERS

The fame of Timothy Taylor's prize-winning ales stretches far beyond West Yorkshire and the brewery's 29 pubs. Founded in 1858, though a new brewhouse came on stream in spring 1991 and was immediately brewing to capacity. Supplies over 200 free trade outlets.

Golden Best (OG 1033, ABV 3.5%) A golden beer with a light hop and malt nose. A soft and smooth, slightly sweet, malty taste ends in a short malt and hop finish with just a hint of bitterness. Very quaffable.

Dark Mild (OG 1034, ABV 3.5%) Dark brown with red hints. The caramel conceals the Golden Best it is based on until the finish, when a short, light but dry aftertaste hits the back of the throat. Less sweet and more rounded of late.

Best Bitter (OG 1037, ABV 4%) A light and delicate nose of hop, fruit and malt leads into a much more bitter taste than previously, cascading into a deep, dry nutty finish. Less complex than of old, but very drinkable. A fine brew.

Landlord (OG 1042, ABV 4.3%) Long regarded as king, but is the crown slipping? Still hoppy, but the fruit notes are now engulfed in bitterness. Lemon can still be detected in the nose, but the flowers seem to have gone. Remains a fine beer.

Porter (OG 1043, ABV 3.5%) Roast malt and caramel dominate the whole drink until the aftertaste, when sweetness wins through. In an age of new, true porters, this brew looks lost. Perhaps that is why it is increasingly difficult to find.

Ram Tam (XXXX) (OG 1043, ABV 4.3%) The caramel is not as daunting as last year, allowing greater access to the dry hop bitterness in the taste and finish. More rounded, yet it still displays harsh hop character; a slight sweetness lingers.

TAYLOR WALKER — See Nationals, Carlsberg-Tetley.

ENNENT ALEDONIAN — See Nationals, Bass.

HUA TETLEY — See Nationals, Carlsberg-Tetley.

THEAKSTON See Nationals, Scottish & Newcastle.

THOMPSON'S

Thompson's Brewery, Unit 1, Brewery Meadow, Ashburton, Devon TQ13 7DG. Tel. (0364) 53737

FINE TRADITIONAL ALES

Started brewing in 1981 for its own pub, the London Inn, which remains its sole tied house. Free trade, however, has been increasing rapidly of late throughout the South-West. A major expansion programme is underway at the brewery, starting with a new brewhouse which opened in early 1992. The beer range tends to change from year to year.

Best Bitter (OG 1040, ABV 4.2%) Pale brown, fairly thin dry bitter.

Celebration Porter* (OG 1040, ABV 4.2%)

IPA (OG 1044, ABV 4.6%) Pale brown ale with malt and fruit in the aroma, a distinct hoppy, fruity flavour and a dry, bitter finish. A well-rounded beer.

Botwrights Man of War (OG 1050, ABV 5%) Golden beer with a fruity sweet taste and aftertaste.

Figurehead (OG 1050, ABV 5.2%) Reddish beer with a strong, fruity aroma. Full of fruity flavour, with a bitter aftertaste.

THWAITES

Daniel Thwaites PLC, PO Box 50, Star Brewery, Blackburn, Lancs, BB1 5BU. Tel. (0254) 54431

Lancashire brewery, founded by excise officer Daniel Thwaites in 1807 and now run by his great-great-grandson. Still uses shire horse drays and, unusually, produces two milds. Most of the 400 tied houses serve real ale, and a substantial free trade is also supplied.

Mild (OG 1031, ABV 3%) Dark brown/copper beer with a fine malty quality in both aroma and flavour. No perceptible finish.

Best Mild (OG 1034, ABV 3.2%) A rich, dark mild presenting a smooth, malty flavour and a pleasant, slightly bitter finish.

Bitter (OG 1036, ABV 3.4%) A gently-flavoured, clean-tasting bitter. Malt and hops lead into a full, lingering, bitter finish.

Craftsman* (OG 1042, ABV 4.2%)

TITANIC

Titanic Brewery, Unit G, Harvey Works, Lingard Street, Burslem, Stoke-on-Trent, Staffs. ST6 1ED. Tel. (0782) 823447

This brewery, named in honour of the Titanic's Captain Smith who hailed from Stoke, was founded in 1985 but soon fell into difficulties and ceased trading for a while. However, the tide turned and to such an extent that a move to larger premises in 1992 was needed to cope with increased demand for the beers. Some 150 free trade outlets are supplied, as well as a single tied house. A porter may be added. *Bottle-conditioned beer: Christmas Ale (OG 1080, ABV 7.8%, Wreckage matured for one year)*

Best Bitter* (OG 1036, ABV 3.6%) A summer beer, satisfyingly bitter.

Lifeboat Ale (OG 1040, ABV 4%) A fruity and malty, red/brown, bitter beer, with a slight caramel character. The finish is dry and fruity. Almost like a strong dark mild.

Premium Bitter (OG 1042, ABV 4.2%) A red/brown beer with a fruity aroma, a malty, fruity taste and aftertaste, and a lingering bitterness.

Anniversary* (OG 1050, ABV 5%) An occasional brew.

Captain Smith's Strong Ale (OG 1050, ABV 5%) Another red/brown beer, but this one is hoppy and bitter with a balancing, malty sweetness. A hoppy aroma; a dry, malty finish. Highly drinkable.

Wreckage* (OG 1080, ABV 7.8%) A winter brew.

The Independents

TOLLY COBBOLD — **Tollemache & Cobbold Brewery Ltd., Cliff Road, Ipswich, Suffolk IP3 0AZ. Tel. (0473) 231723**

One of the oldest breweries in the country, founded by Thomas Cobbold in 1723 at Harwich, which survived several changes in ownership until the Brent Walker take-over in 1989, when the Cliff Brewery was closed and production transferred to Camerons in Hartlepool. However, a management buy-out, led by former Tolly directors Brian Cowie and Bob Wales, saved the day and Tolly Cobbold Ipswich-brewed ales were back on sale in September 1990. The new company acquired no pubs from Brent Walker, but secured a five-year trading agreement, supplying a total of over 500 pubs. Opened a brewery tap, its only tied house, in June 1992.

Mild (OG 1032, ABV 3.2%) A malty, dark mild with roasty notes and a hoppy finish to balance the malt. The aroma is mostly of malt.

Bitter (OG 1035, ABV 3.5%) A light-bodied session bitter with the old Tolly maltiness. Some hoppiness, mainly in the finish, but not a particularly bitter beer.

Original Best Bitter (OG 1038, ABV 3.8%) A beer with a hoppy and bitter taste, with balancing maltiness. The finish is dry.

Old Strong Winter Ale (OG 1047, ABV 4.6%) Available November–February. A dark winter ale with a good malt and roast aroma. These characteristics are also evident in the initial flavour, along with caramel. The finish is bittersweet, with a lasting dryness.

Tollyshooter Premium Bitter* (OG 1052, ABV 5%) A new premium bitter, named after the Sir John Harvey-Jones TV series, *Troubleshooter*, in which Tolly featured.

TRAQUAIR HOUSE — **Traquair House Brewery, Innerleithen, Peeblesshire, Borders, EH44 6PW. Tel. (0896) 830323**

This 18th-century brewhouse is situated in one of the wings of Traquair House (over 1,000 years old) and was rediscovered by the 20th Laird, Peter Maxwell Stuart, in 1965. He began brewing again using all the original equipment (which remained intact, despite having lain idle for over 100 years). Today the bottled product, Traquair House Ale (not bottle-conditioned), is exported worldwide, although production is only set at around 5,000 gallons a year. This beer is available on draught only at the White Horse in Parsons Green, London, but four outlets are supplied with the cask-conditioned Bear Ale. The brewery passed to Catherine Maxwell Stuart in 1990.

Bear Ale* (OG 1050, ABV 5%) A strong bitter.

Ale* (OG 1070, ABV 7.2%) Dark and potent.

TRING — **Tring Brewery Company Ltd., 81–82 Akeman Street, Tring, Herts. HP23 6AF. Tel. (0442) 890740**

Established in December 1992, brewing the first beer in the town for almost 60 years, Tring has been so successful that expansion is already being considered. Death or Glory is brewed on October 25 to commemorate the Charge of the Light Brigade in 1854.

Ridgeway Bitter* (ABV 4%)

Old Icknield Ale* (ABV 4.8%)

Death or Glory* (ABV 6.8%)

TROUGH — **Trough Brewery Ltd., Louisa Street, Idle, Bradford, W. Yorks. BD10 8NE. Tel. (0274) 613450**

Brewery which started in 1981 and enjoyed rapid expansion in the guest beer and club market. Its market share has been reduced somewhat, but it is fighting back with an attractive pricing strategy. Nearly all Trough's 60 free trade outlets and three tied houses are within a 20-mile range of the brewery. New plant was commissioned in 1992, doubling production capacity.

Bitter (OG 1035, ABV 3.5%) Now gold in colour, like all Trough beers (except Blind Pugh). An inviting hop aroma and a fine, strong hop flavour with malt balance, lead to a long, hop and bitter finish with fruit notes. A good, refreshing standard bitter.

Wild Boar (OG 1039, ABV 4%) A good fruity, hoppy aroma leads to a rich malty, hop and fruit flavour in the mouth, finished by a long, hoppy and fruity aftertaste.

Festival Ale (OG 1048, ABV 5%) An excellent strong ale with a good hop and fruit aroma. A deceptively strong bitter with a lightness on the palate, yet packed with flavours of malt, hops and fruit. Long bittersweet and hoppy finish.

Blind Pugh (OG 1050, ABV 5.2%) Jet-black stout characterized by a strong roast malt taste and a sharp bitterness, both on the tongue and in the long aftertaste, which has chocolate notes. Moderate roast aroma.

ULEY

Uley Brewery Ltd., The Old Brewery, Uley, Dursley, Glos. GL11 5TB. Tel. (0453) 860120

Brewing at Uley began in 1833, but Price's Brewery, as it was then, remained inactive for most of this century. Work commenced on restoring the premises in 1984 and Uley Brewery was reborn in 1985. Current expansion work will allow for an extra brew per week. Has no pubs of its own but serves 30 free trade outlets in the Cotswolds area. Pig's Ear is only brewed to order.

Bitter or Hogshead or UB40 (OG 1040, ABV 4%) Copper-coloured beer with malt, hops and fruit in the aroma and a malty, fruity taste, underscored by a hoppy bitterness. The finish is dry, with a balance of hops and malt.

Old Spot Prize Ale (OG 1050, ABV 5%) A fairly full-bodied, red/brown ale with a fruity aroma, a malty, fruity taste (with a hoppy bitterness), and a strong, balanced aftertaste.

Pig's Ear Strong Beer (OG 1050, ABV 5%) A pale-coloured, light beer, deceptively strong. Notably bitter in flavour, with a hoppy, fruity aroma and a bitter finish.

Pigor Mortis (OG 1058, ABV 5.5%) A Christmas brew, another beer which belies its strength. No distinct aroma, but a sweet, smooth flavour, with hints of fruit and hops. Dry finish.

USHERS

Ushers of Trowbridge PLC, Directors House, 68 Fore Street, Trowbridge, Wilts. BA14 8JF. Tel. (0225) 763171

This famous West Country brewery was founded in 1824, but lost its identity after being swallowed up by Watney (later Grand Met) in 1960. A successful management buy-out from Courage in 1992 has given Ushers back its independence. Purchased 26 pubs in the same year, with further acquisitions planned, and over £2 million has been invested in new plant. Supplies real ale to 90% of its 459 tied houses and to Courage/Grand Met Inntrepreneur pubs.

Best Bitter (OG 1037, ABV 3.8%) Dry bitter, lacking malt character, but has a faint hop aroma and a hop oil palate. The dry finish can sometimes be metallic; very variable.

Founders Ale (OG 1045, ABV 4.5%) A pale brown beer with a bitter hop taste, balanced by sweet maltiness and a hint of citrus. A predominantly bitter finish. Variable, it can be thin for its gravity.

1824 Particular (OG 1060, ABV 6.2%) This winter beer has a light malt and carame[l] aroma and taste, balanced by some bittersweetness in the flavou[r] and finish.

The Independents

VAUX

Vaux Breweries Ltd., The Brewery, Sunderland, Tyne & Wear SR1 3AN. Tel. (091) 567 6277

First established in 1837 and now one of the country's largest regional brewers, Vaux remains firmly independent. Owns Wards of Sheffield, but sold off Lorimer & Clark in Edinburgh to Caledonian in 1987. Real ale is sold in over 300 of its 700 tied houses (which include those run by Wards and Vaux Inns Ltd.) and is also provided to 10% of its 700 free trade customers. Looking to increase its tied estate, buying pubs in Yorkshire, the North-West and elsewhere from national brewers. Vaux Extra Special (OG 1047, ABV 5%) is produced at Wards (see Wards), but Vaux Mild is Wards Mild rebadged.

Lorimers Best Scotch (OG 1036, ABV 3.6%) A difficult beer to catch in prime condition. Aroma is often lacking, but, when fresh, there can be a subtle hop character to balance a sweet and malty taste. A replica of the original Scottish Scotch.

Bitter* (OG 1036, ABV 3.9%) Recently relaunched and distributed mainly outside the North-East.

Samson (OG 1041, ABV 4.1%) A light-bodied beer with complex tastes. May give a sulphury aroma when fresh, but hop dominates. Sweetness is evident and may persist.

Double Maxim (OG 1044, ABV 4.2%) A smooth brown ale, now more commonly on draught. Malt and hop balance well with a lasting fruit taste and notable body.

VILLAGE BREWER

The Village Brewer, Aldborough St John, Richmond, N. Yorks. DL11 7TJ. Tel. (0325) 374887

Non-brewing company whose beers are produced by Hadrian and Hambleton.

WADWORTH

Wadworth & Co. Ltd., Northgate Brewery, Devizes, Wilts. SN10 1JW. Tel. (0380) 723361

Delightful market town tower brewery set up in 1885 by Henry Wadworth. Solidly traditional, it still runs horse-drawn drays. The brewery continues to expand and is producing up to 2,000 barrels a week to supply a wide-ranging free trade in the South of England and its own 185 tied houses (a figure which it is always looking to increase). All the pubs serve real ale and 6X remains one of the South's most famous beers.

Henry's Original IPA (OG 1034, ABV 3.8%) A golden brown-coloured beer with a gentle, malty and slightly hoppy aroma, a good balance of flavours, with maltiness gradually dominating, and then a long-lasting aftertaste to match, eventually becoming biscuity. A good session beer.

6X (OG 1040, ABV 4.3%) Mid brown in colour, with a malty and fruity nose and some balancing hop character. The flavour is similar, with some bitterness and a lingering malty, but bitter finish. Full-bodied and distinctive.

Malt & Hops* (OG 1045, ABV 4.4%) A seasonal brew, produced at hop harvest time.

Farmer's Glory (OG 1046, ABV 4.5%) Can be delightfully hoppy and fruity, but is variable in flavour and conditioning. The aroma is of malt and it should have a dryish, hoppy aftertaste.

Old Timer (OG 1055, ABV 5.8%) Available in winter/spring only. A rich, copper-brown beer with a strong, fruity, malty aroma. The flavour is full-bodied and complete, with hints of butterscotch and peaches, beautifully balanced by a lasting, malty, dry finish. A classic beer.

TER WALKER See Nationals, Carlsberg-Tetley.

The Independents

WARDS — **SH Ward & Co. Ltd., Sheaf Brewery, Ecclesall Road, Sheffield, S. Yorks. S11 8HZ. Tel. (0742) 755155**

Established in 1840 by Joshua Kirby, but a subsidiary of Vaux of Sunderland since 1972. Since the closure of the neighbouring Thorne brewery in 1986, Wards has also produced Darley's beers. Real ale is available in half of the 280 tied houses (this figure includes pubs run by Vaux Inns) and almost 600 free trade outlets are supplied.

Mild or Darley's Dark Mild (OG 1032, ABV 3.2%) Also sold as Vaux Mild. A rich malt aroma heads a roast malt taste but unfortunately little else except for an occasional hint of chocolate. The finish is longer than before and may be drier. The lovely red/brown colour remains.

Thorne Best Bitter (OG 1037, ABV 3.9%) A pale brown, session drinkers' brew, with a gentle malt aroma under siege from hops. The beer now has a thin, hoppy air on a light malt base and is not unpleasant. Nevertheless, it remains unexciting.

Sheffield Best Bitter (OG 1038, ABV 4%) Malt dominates the aroma but hops are present. The taste is also malty, but hops come through to the bitter finish. Sometimes it has a hint of sweetness and often feels thin, but there is usually a clean edge.

Kirby Strong Beer (OG 1045, ABV 5%) A malty nose and a malt and fruit taste lead to a mildly bitter aftertaste. Remains a difficult beer to find.

For Vaux:

Extra Special Bitter (OG 1046, ABV 5%) Can be a rich beer with a fruity aroma and pleasant mouthfeel – not always achieved in its limited distribution.

WATNEY — See Nationals, Courage.

WEBSTER'S — See Nationals, Courage.

WEETWOOD — **Weetwood Ales, Weetwood Grange, Weetwood, Tarporley, Cheshire CW6 0NQ. Tel. (0829) 52377**

New brewery set up at an equestrian centre in 1993, with its first brew on sale in March. Ten free trade customers.

Best Cask Bitter (ABV 3.8%) A bitter, fruity and clean-tasting beer, with a hoppy nose and a strong dry finish.

WELLS — **Charles Wells Ltd., The Eagle Brewery, Havelock Street, Bedford, Beds. MK40 4LU. Tel. (0234) 272766**

Successful, family-owned brewery, established in 1876 and on this site since 1976. Work to expand the brewhouse was completed in the summer of 1992 and has effectively doubled the brewing capacity. Wells widened the area of its tied estate in 1991 by buying 38 pubs from Bass, but it is now undergoing a rationalisation programme and up to 40 houses may be closed. All but ten of the current 350 tied pubs serve real ale, but about 50% apply cask breathers. The brewery supplies 125 other outlets direct.

Eagle IPA (OG 1035, ABV 3.6%) A well-balanced drinking beer; the hoppy aroma has a hint of citrus and often of sulphur. Malt and hops on the palate are complemented by an orangey bitterness that leads through to a very dry finish.

Bombardier Best Bitter (OG 1042, ABV 4.2%) A beer that seems to have improved of late. The flavour is complex but is a well-balanced blend of malt, fruit and hops on a bitter base. Bitter finish with some fruit. Fruit and hops in the aroma.

WELSH BREWERS — See Nationals, Bass.

WEST COAST

West Coast Brewing Co. Ltd., Justin Close, Chorlton-on-Medlock, Manchester M13 9UX. Tel. (061) 273 6366

Enterprising brewery set up in 1989 by consultant brewer Brendan Dobbin to serve his own pub, the Kings Arms. Outside demand grew (currently around 20 free trade outlets) and led to the expansion of the brewery. It moved a few hundred yards away in 1993 to premises adjacent to its second tied house.

Dobbin's North Country (DNC) Dark Mild (OG 1032, ABV 3%) Very full-flavoured for its gravity; dark and rather fruity.

DNC Best Bitter (OG 1038, ABV 4%) A pale beer with malt, hops and fruit in the aroma. Fresh, clean taste – hoppy and bitter, with some malt and a dry finish.

DNC Guiltless Stout (OG 1039, ABV 4%) Very dark in colour, with roast malt predominant in the aroma and taste. A long, dry aftertaste.

DNC Kangaroo XXXX Pale Ale* (OG 1040, ABV 4.2%) The latest addition: a hoppy, light-coloured premium bitter.

DNC Big Heavy Jimmie* (OG 1045, ABV 4.5%) A pale beer with a greater malt emphasis than is usual for the brewery. A recreation of an old-style Scottish heavy.

DNC Ginger Beer* (OG 1050, ABV 5%) Originally brewed as a strong summer 'refresher', its popularity has led to year-round production.

DNC Yakima Grande Porter* (OG 1050, ABV 5.5%) Rich, mellow and dark, brewed with the same American hops as the Pale Ale below.

DNC Yakima Grande Pale Ale (OG 1050, ABV 6%) A pale beer with a strong, hoppy nose. Hops are also very evident in the flavour. A well-attenuated beer, making it strong and very dry.

DNC Extra Special Bitter (OG 1060, ABV 7%) A powerful, mid brown beer with a strong, complex aroma, malt and hops on the tongue (with sweetish, fruity undertones), and a full, predominantly bitter, hoppy finish.

DNC Old Soporific* (OG 1084, ABV 10%) Dobbin's winter offering, but only one or two brews are produced each year.

WEST HIGHLAND

West Highland Brewers, Old Station Brewery, Taynuilt, Argyll, Strathclyde PA35 1JB. Tel. (086 62) 246

Brewery constructed in November 1989 in listed buildings, part of the last remaining station of the Callander and Oban Railway. Has one tied house, the station tap, and supplies 12 free trade outlets.

Highland Heavy* (OG 1038, ABV 3.8%)

Old Station Porter* (OG 1041, ABV 4.2%)

Highland Severe* (OG 1050, ABV 4.8%)

WETHERED

See McMullen and Nationals, Whitbread.

WHITBREAD

See Nationals.

WHITBY'S

Whitby's Own Brewery Ltd., St Hilda's, The Ropery, Whitby, N. Yorks. YO22 4ET. Tel. (0947) 605914

Brewery opened in a former workhouse in 1988 and moved 50 yards in 1992 into newer, larger premises. Free trade (mostly as guest beers) extends from Newcastle upon Tyne to Huddersfield and takes in roughly 50 outlets. Still looking for the first tied house.

Merryman's Mild* (OG 1036, ABV 3.6%)

Ammonite Bitter (OG 1038, ABV 3.8%) A light, refreshing beer, pleasant and fruity, with a hoppy aftertaste. Difficult to track down, but well worth the effort.

Woblle (OG 1045, ABV 4.5%) A copper-red, full-bodied, malty bitter, with a burnt roast flavour and a dry, hoppy finish.

Force Nine (OG 1055, ABV 5.5%) Strong and dark, with a well-balanced blend of contrasting flavours: sweet and fruity, dry and malty, with a strong, bitter finish. A beer of the winter ale type, excellent in its class.

WHITWORTH HALL

Whitworth Hall Brewery, Whitworth Lane, Spennymoor, Co. Durham DL16 7QX. Tel. (0388) 817419

A small brewery set up mainly to supply Whitworth Hall, which attracts summer visitors to the house and grounds. Also supplies the Manor House, Ferryhill on a regular basis, but outside sales have been limited by the brewery's lack of small casks. A plum beer, using the Hall's own plums, has also been produced (only available by special request).

Bonnie Bobby Shafto* (OG 1062, ABV 6%) Belgian-styled brown beer.

Plum Beer* (OG 1062, ABV 8%) Bobby Shafto further fermented with plum juice.

WICKWAR

Wickwar Brewing Co., The Old Cider Mill, Station Road, Wickwar, Avon GL12 8NB. Tel. (0454) 294168

Launched on the 'Glorious First of May 1990' (guest beer law day) by two Courage tenants, Brian Rides and Ray Penny, with the aim of providing guest ales for their three tenancies. The business has been so successful that they have now doubled the capacity to 60 barrels a week and dropped their tenancies to concentrate on supplying their 30 regular outlets. The brewery operates from an old cider mill, originally the site of Arnold, Perrett & Co. Ltd. brewery.

Coopers WPA (OG 1036, ABV 3.5%) A yellow/gold, well-balanced, light, refreshing brew with hops, citrus fruit and a delicate, sweet maltiness. Bitter, dry finish.

Brand Oak Bitter (OG 1039, ABV 4%) A distinct blend of hops, malt and citrus fruits. The slightly sweet taste turns into a fine, dry bitterness with a lasting finish. Moreish. Known locally as 'Bob'.

Olde Merryford Ale (OG 1049, ABV 5.1%) A pale brown, full-flavoured, well-balanced beer, with malt, hops and fruit elements throughout. Slightly sweet, with a long lasting, malty, dry finish.

Station Porter (OG 1060, ABV 6.1%) A smooth, warming, dark copper-brown Christmas ale with a roast malt, coffee and rich fruit aroma. It has a similarly complex, dry, bittersweet taste and a long, warming finish. A superb, strong porter – almost an old ale.

WILSONS See Morland, and Nationals, Courage.

WILTSHIRE See Pitfield.

WOLVERHAMPTON & DUDLEY See Banks's and Camerons.

WOOD

The Wood Brewery Ltd., Wistanstow, Craven Arms, Shropshire SY7 8DG. Tel. (0588) 672523

Village brewery, founded by the Wood family in 1980, which has enjoyed steady growth in recent years, culminating in a major extension of the brewery during the winter of 1991/92. Now also brews Sam Powell beers after rescuing them from receivership in 1991. Still just one tied house, the Plough next to the brewery, but it is considering further acquisitions. Also serves 75 other outlets. Specialises in producing commemorative bottled beers.

Sam Powell Best Bitter* (OG 1034, ABV 3%)

101* (OG 1035, ABV 3.5%) A new brew.

Sam Powell Original Bitter* (OG 1038, ABV 3.5%)

Parish Bitter* (OG 1040, ABV 3.75%) A light, refreshing bitter.

Special Bitter* (OG 1043, ABV 4%) A full-flavoured, sweetish beer.

Sam Powell Old Sam* (OG 1048, ABV 4.3%)

Wonderful* (OG 1050, ABV 4.75%) Strong and dark.

Christmas Cracker* (OG 1060, ABV 6%) A dark winter warmer (November–January).

WOODFORDE'S **Woodforde's Norfolk Ales (Woodforde's Ltd.), Broadland Brewery, Woodbastwick, Norwich, Norfolk NR13 6SW. Tel. (0603) 720353**

WOODFORDE'S
Norfolk Ales
BROADLAND BREWERY
WOODBASTWICK
NORWICH NR13 6SW
Tel: (0603) 720353

Founded in late 1980 in Norwich to bring much-needed choice to a long Watney-dominated region. Moved to a converted farm complex, with greatly increased production capacity, in the picturesque Broadland village of Woodbastwick in 1989. Brews an extensive range of beers which changes from year to year, including several seasonal and occasional brews. Has two tied houses, the brewery tap being the latest acquisition, opened in December 1992. Supplies 150 other outlets on a regular basis. *Bottle-conditioned beer: Norfolk Nip (OG 1080, ABV 8.6%) sometimes also on draught*

Broadsman Bitter (OG 1035, ABV 3.5%) A session beer which is a straightforward combination of malt and hops. The aroma has a light, flowery hop character, with bitterness coming through in the palate to dominate the aftertaste.

Mardler's Mild ⊟ (OG 1035, ABV 3.5%) A red/brown mild which is smooth and malty, and well balanced with some fruitiness. The aftertaste is malty, fruity and short. Enjoyable.

Wherry Best Bitter (OG 1039, ABV 3.8%) This award-winning, amber beer has a distinctly hoppy nose and a well-balanced palate with pronounced bitterness and, usually, a flowery hop character. A long-lasting, satisfying, bitter aftertaste.

Norfolk Porter (OG 1043, ABV 4.1%) Now only brewed occasionally and light-tasting for its strength and colour, this red/brown beer has a fruity aroma, fleshed out with roast malt and hops. The taste is well balanced, with roast malt and hops; the aftertaste is mainly bitter.

Old Bram* (OG 1043, ABV 4.1%)

John Brown* (OG 1043, ABV 4.2%) Malt is the most noticeable component of this beer, particularly in the aftertaste. Little bitterness, but the hop and fruitiness (neither very strong) help make this a complex beer for its strength.

Nelson's Revenge (OG 1045, ABV 4.4%) This premium bitter has quite a strong, pleasant, malty, fruity, hoppy aroma which the rounded and complex, malty palate doesn't quite live up to. The hoppiness and bitterness come through more distinctly at the end to give a good, lasting aftertaste.

Norfolk Nog ⊟ (OG 1049, ABV 4.5%) A full-bodied red/brown beer with plenty of flavour and aroma. Roast malt balances the sweeter components of the palate. A very good, dark winter brew. *Champion Beer of Britain* 1992.

Baldric (OG 1052, ABV 5.2%) Noticeably a strong bitter, with fruit, hops and malt on the nose and in the full-flavoured palate, where bitterness mingles with the other flavours. A pleasant fruit and hop aftertaste.

Headcracker ⊟ (OG 1069, ABV 7%) This fairly pale brown barley wine is full bodied and fruity throughout. The sweetness in the palate is balanced by the hoppiness and bitterness. The aftertaste is definitely warming.

WORLDHAM — **Worldham Brewery, Smith's Farm, East Worldham, Alton, Hants. GU34 3AT. Tel. (0420) 83383**

It took 18 months for Worldham to convert a hop kiln into a ten-barrel brewery, using plant acquired from a number of different breweries, and it eventually launched its only beer at the 1991 CAMRA Farnham Beerex. Now serves around 50 free trade outlets, but this number is steadily expanding.

Old Dray Bitter (OG 1043, ABV 4.4%) Mid to deep brown beer, low in aroma and with a dry flavour with some grain. Strong on hops in the slightly cloying finish.

WORTH See Commercial.

WORTHINGTON See Nationals, Bass.

WORTLEY — **Wortley Brewery, Halifax Road, Wortley, Sheffield, S. Yorks. S30 7DB. Tel. (0742) 882245**

Brewery opened in December 1991 in the cellar of the Wortley Arms Hotel, initially to produce beer for the pub and now supplying 15 other outlets regularly. Survived a brief closure in April 1992 during which all brewing equipment was removed. A third, stronger beer is planned.

Bitter (ABV 3.6%) A light, malty and hoppy-nosed, newish beer with a moderate to strong malt and fruit taste, ending in a gentle bitter finish.

Earls Ale (ABV 4.2%) Beer with a malty base to which hops and fruit add depth and character. Not as obviously hoppy in taste as last year, but the aftertaste remains clean and dry. A fine bitter, still feeling its way.

WYCHWOOD — **The Wychwood Brewery, Two Rivers, Station Lane, Witney, Oxfordshire OX8 6BH. Tel. (0993) 702574**

Formerly Glenny Brewery, set up in 1983 in the old maltings of the extinct Clinch's brewery, and moved to its own premises in 1987. The brewery was radically revamped during 1992 and now runs ten pubs in the South, from Brighton to Bristol. All have been refurbished in a studenty 'Firkin' style and bear names like Hobgoblin and Dr Thirsty's Surgery. All take real ale, which is also supplied to 74 other outlets.

Shires Bitter (OG 1034, ABV 3.4%) A pleasantly hoppy and malty, light brown session beer, with a roast malt and fruit aroma.

Fiddlers Elbow* (OG 1040, ABV 4%) Brewed May–October.

Best (OG 1042, ABV 4.2%) Mid brown, full-flavoured premium bitter. Moderately strong in hop and malt flavours, with pleasing, fruity overtones which last through to the aftertaste.

Dr Thirsty's Draught* (OG 1050, ABV 5.2%) Primarily aimed at the guest beer market.

Hobgoblin (OG 1058, ABV 6%) Powerful, full-bodied, copper-red, well-balanced brew. Strong in roasted malt, with a moderate, hoppy bitterness and a slight fruity character.

WYE VALLEY — **Wye Valley Brewery, 69 St Owen Street, Hereford HR1 2JQ. Tel. (0432) 274968**

Brewery which started production in March 1985 and moved to its present address in October 1986. New plant was installed in 1992 to increase capacity and cater for a rapidly growing free trade; the number of outlets has doubled since the last edition of this guide. Runs one tied house (Barrels in Hereford).

Hereford Bitter (OG 1036, ABV 3.6%) Very little nose, but a crisp, dry and truly bitter taste, with a balancing malt flavour. The initial bitter aftertaste mellows to a pleasant, lingering malt.

Hereford Pale Ale or HPA (OG 1040, ABV 4%) Beer with a distinctive colour of old pine and a malty nose. On the tongue, it is malty, with some balancing bitterness and a hint of sweetness. Good, dry finish.

Hereford Supreme (OG 1043, ABV 4.3%) This rich, copper-red beer has a good malty, fruity aroma. In the complex variety of flavours, the malt, fruit and bitterness are distinctive. The finish has bitterness but can be cloyingly malty.

Brew 69 (OG 1055, ABV 5.5%) A pale beer which disguises its strength. Has a well-balanced flavour and finish, without the sweetness which normally characterizes beer of this strength.

YATES

Yates Brewery, Ghyll Farm, Westnewton, Aspatria, Cumbria CA5 3NX. Tel. (069 73) 21081

Small, traditional brewery set up in 1986 by Peter and Carol Yates in an old farm building on their smallholding, where a herd of pedigree goats makes good use of the brewery's by-products. Brews award-winning beers to its capacity of 34 barrels a week during summer and other peak times, but at present has no plans to expand further. Directly serves 20 free trade outlets.

Bitter (OG 1035, ABV 3.8%) A fruity, bitter, straw-coloured ale with malt and hops in the aroma and a long, bitter aftertaste.

Premium (OG 1048, ABV 5.2%) Available at Christmas and a few other times of the year. Straw-coloured, with a strong aroma of malt and hops, and full-flavoured, with a slight toffee taste. The malty aftertaste becomes strongly bitter.

Best Cellar (OG 1052, ABV 5.3%) Brewed only in winter. An excellent, red/brown beer with a fruity aroma and a sweet, malty flavour, contrasted by a hoppy bitterness. The finish is a bittersweet balance, with grain and some hops.

YOUNGER

See Nationals, Scottish & Newcastle.

YOUNG'S

Young & Co.'s Brewery PLC, The Ram Brewery, High Street, Wandsworth, London SW18 4JD. Tel. (081) 870 0141

Founded in 1675 by the Draper family, and bought by Charles Young and Anthony Bainbridge in 1831. Their partnership was dissolved in 1884 and the business was continued by the Young family. Now a public company, it is still very much a family affair. The only London brewer not to hitch its drays to the keg revolution in the 1970s, Young's brews award-winning beers in the traditional manner, with some of its pub deliveries still made by horse-drawn drays. Around 600 free trade outlets are supplied, mostly within the M25 ring, though the brewery's presence is extending westward. The tied estate has now increased to 180 houses.

Bitter (OG 1036, ABV 3.7%) A light and distinctive bitter with well-balanced malt and hop characters. A strong bitterness is followed by a delightfully astringent and hoppy aftertaste.

Porter (OG 1040, ABV 4%) Beer with a roasted grain and chocolatey aroma, leading to a flavour of malt and hops and a dry coffee/chocolate finish.

Special (OG 1046, ABV 4.8%) A strong, full-flavoured, bitter beer with a powerful hoppiness and a malty aroma. Hops persist in the aftertaste, with a rich fruitiness and lasting fullness.

Winter Warmer (OG 1055, ABV 5%) A dark brown ale with a malty, fruity aroma, a sweet and fruity flavour, with roast malt and some balancing bitterness, and a bittersweet finish, including some lingering malt.

BASS

Bass

Bass Brewers Ltd., 137 High Street, Burton upon Trent, Staffs. DE14 1JZ Tel. (0283) 511000

Britain's biggest brewer, founded by William Bass in 1777. Today it commands some 23% of all beer production in the UK, with two of the company's ale brands (Stones Best Bitter and Worthington Best Bitter) featuring amongst the top five sellers, and Draught Bass the biggest-selling premium cask ale. Following the announced closure of the breweries in Edinburgh (Heriot), Sheffield (Hope) and Wolverhampton (Springfield), Bass will now be operating from just nine sites, with those at Alton, Glasgow, Belfast and Tadcaster producing only keg beer.

Bass continues to promote its leading brands. Both Stones and Worthington Best Bitter have been supported by extensive advertising campaigns, to the detriment of one brand in particular, Charrington IPA. This beer, originally from London, but now produced in Birmingham, has been in decline for some time and could well be phased out in the near future. However, the resurgence in darker beers has given a boost to Highgate Mild, promoted by Bass as Highgate Dark in the South-East. The famous bottle-conditioned beer, Worthington White Shield, has been relaunched in new, non-returnable bottles and at a much higher price, gaining a mixed reception in the trade.

Another move that has not gone down well with drinkers has been the surreptitious drop in some beer strengths during the last year or so. Although ABVs have been lowered by more than 0.1% in some cases, there has been no commensurate drop in price – in other words, there has been a back-door price rise.

Bass has also drawn criticism for the use of handpump imagery on its so-called 'draught' beers in a can. These are not the same as handpulled real ales, despite the company's attempts to persuade drinkers otherwise, and the belated withdrawal of the handpump pictures from the can packaging has only happened after much pressure.

On the pub side, Bass Taverns controls 3,000 pubs out of a company total of around 4,550 houses. The remaining 1,350 pubs, excluding 200 Toby Restaurants, are operated by the Bass Lease Company. Many pubs still bear the liveries of former Bass trading divisions like Charrington, Tennents, M&B and Welsh Brewers. Overall, Bass has sold about 2,730 pubs to comply with the DTI Orders, although many of these have been to new pub chain companies which have also agreed to take their beer from Bass. Free trade represents some 49% of sales; the tied estate accounts for 31%, and the balance comes from the take-home trade, which Bass sees as an area for growth.

BURTON — **Burton Brewery, Station Street, Burton upon Trent, Staffs. DE14 1JZ. Tel. (0283) 513578**

The original home of Bass, producing one of Britain's most famous ales, available throughout its estate and the free trade.

Draught Bass — (OG 1043, ABV 4.4%) Formerly one of Britain's classic beers, this tawny ale can vary widely in character, depending on its age. A fruity and malty aroma and taste are balanced by an underlying hoppy dryness when at its best, though the palate is usually sweetish. The finish is bittersweet, with some lingering malt. Often served too green, but, when it's good, it's still a classic pint.

The Nationals

BIRMINGHAM	**Cape Hill Brewery, PO Box 27, Smethwick, Birmingham, W. Midlands B16 0PQ. Tel. (021) 558 1481**
	One of the largest cask beer production centres in the country, subject of a £55 million investment programme in the past year.
M&B Mild	(OG 1033.5, ABV 3.3%) A dark brown quaffing mild with roast and malt flavours. Dry, slightly bitter finish.
Charrington IPA*	(OG 1036.5, ABV 3.4%)
M&B Brew XI	(OG 1038, ABV 3.9%) A sweet, malty beer with a hoppy, bitter aftertaste.

WALSALL	**Highgate Brewery, Sandymount Road, Walsall, W. Midlands WS1 3AP. Tel. (0922) 23168**
	Built in 1895 and now a listed building, the Highgate Brewery is the smallest in the Bass group and has remained unchanged for many years.
M&B Highgate Mild	(OG 1034.5, ABV 3.2%) A smooth, well-balanced ruby/dark brown mild with hints of fruit, roast and bittersweet maltiness. Sold as Highgate Dark in the South-East.
M&B Springfield Bitter	(OG 1035.5, ABV 3.5%) A pale, sweetish, malty bitter. Highgate's distinctive, slightly blood-like taste marks it out from the Springfield original. The keg version is brewed at Cape Hill.
M&B Highgate Old Ale	(OG 1055.5, ABV 5.3%) November-January only: a dark brown/ruby-coloured old ale. A full-flavoured, fruity, malty ale with a complex aftertaste, with hints of malt, roast, hops and fruit.

SHEFFIELD	**Cannon Brewery, Rutland Road, Sheffield, S. Yorks. S3 8BE. Tel. (0742) 349433**
	The original home of William Stones Ltd., taken over by Bass in 1968.
Light	(OG 1030, ABV 3.2%) An amber-coloured mild: a lightly-flavoured blend of malt, sweetness and bitterness. At its best, has a delicate, pleasing, flowery taste, but can too often be bland. A disappointing, short, sweetish finish and little aroma.
Mild XXXX	(OG 1031, ABV 3.2%) A pleasant, smooth, dark mild with a faint aroma of caramel, which leads to a caramel and roast, rich taste, with complementing sweetness and bitterness. A good, long, satisfying, roast malt and caramel-sweet finish.
Special Bitter	(OG 1035, ABV 3.4%) Certainly not special. Pale brown in hue, with little aroma. The generally bland taste has sweetness, malt and a slight bitterness. The poor, sweet and dryish finish can be cloying. Unexciting.
Stones Best Bitter	(OG 1037.5, ABV 4.1%) A fine mixture of malt, hop and fruit in the nose extends into a bitter, hoppy taste, ending in a clean yet mellow bitter finish. Has become softer as the straw colour has become more golden.
	Hope Brewery, Claywheels Lane, Wadsley Bridge, Sheffield, S. Yorks. S6 1NB. Tel. (0742) 349433
	Bass's specialist bottled beer brewery, founded in 1892 but now planned for closure. White Shield will be transferred to Cape Hill. *Bottle-conditioned beer: Worthington White Shield (OG 1050.5, ABV 5.6%)*

Beers marked with an asterisk have not been tasted by official CAMRA tasting panels. However, some of these beers do carry brief descriptions derived from limited samplings or other sources, and can be used for rough guidance.

CARDIFF — **The Brewery, Crawshay Street, Cardiff, S. Glamorgan CF1 1TR. Tel. (0222) 233071**

The Hancock's brewery (founded in 1884) which was taken over by Bass Charrington in 1968. Real ale has now become more prominent in the valleys pubs it serves and Worthington Best Bitter is now a national brand.

Worthington Dark (OG 1032.5, ABV 3.3%) A dark brown, creamy mild with some maltiness and a sweet finish. Well worth finding, but now mainly confined to the Swansea area.

Hancock's HB (OG 1036.5, ABV 3.8%) A slightly malty, bitter beer, with a bitter-sweet aftertaste. A popular but not particularly distinctive beer.

Worthington Best Bitter (OG 1037, ABV 3.6%) A fairly malty, light brown beer, with a somewhat bitter finish.

CARLSBERG-TETLEY

107 Station Street, Burton upon Trent, Staffs. DE14 1BZ. Tel. (0283) 31111

The new company formed by Allied Breweries and Danish giant Carlsberg. Allied was established in 1961 with the merger of Ansells, Tetley Walker and Ind Coope. Carlsberg has long been a world-famous brewer, with quality lagers in its own country but lacklustre copies in Britain. It has owned no pubs, but, with its modern Northampton brewery now added to Allied's already under-capacity sites, there are new worries about brewery closures. The Romford keg brewery has already ceased production and Allied's lager plant at Wrexham still looks vulnerable. The company's biggest ale brand is the heavily promoted Tetley Bitter, but Ind Coope Burton Ale has been much less successful of late.

On the pub front, the company is keen to keep its local brewery image. Though the newly-formed Tetley Pub Company now manages the former Joshua Tetley and Tetley Walker pubs, the traditional brewery liveries still decorate the pubs, as they do in the South-East, where Ind Coope Retail runs the former pubs of Friary Meux, Benskins, ABC and Halls. In London, Taylor Walker is complemented by the small Nicholson's chain of upmarket pubs, and the Ansells trademark is very prominent in the Midlands and South Wales. However, many former Allied pubs have been sold to regional breweries and pub chains, and over 700 have been leased by Pubmaster (with the Allied beer tie still in place).

ALLOA — **Alloa Brewery Company Ltd., Whins Road, Alloa, Clackmannanshire, Central FK10 3RB. Tel. (0259) 723539**

Allied's Scottish arm, established in 1810, which was taken over by Archibald Arrol in 1866. It fell to Ind Coope & Allsopp's in 1951, becoming part of Allied in the 1961 merger. Took over Drybroughs from Watney in 1987. Less than a third of Alloa pubs sell real ale, but some offer Maclay and Caledonian beers as guests.

Archibald Arrol's 80/-* (OG 1041, ABV 4.2%) A full-flavoured beer with dry hop character.

FURGUSONS — **Furgusons Plympton Brewery, Valley Road, Plympton, Plymouth, Devon PL7 3LQ. Tel. (0752) 330171**

Set up in the Halls Plympton depot in 1984, this brewery's business has expanded rapidly over the last four years and continues t grow. It now offers three ales of its own for sale to Ansells pubs the area and to free trade in the South-West (about 200 account

Dartmoor Best Bitter (OG 1038, ABV 3.7%) Mid brown to red beer with a malty aroma and a sweet, malty flavour and aftertaste.

Dartmoor Strong (OG 1044, ABV 4.3%) A pale brown, fruity and sweet-tasting beer with a fruity aroma.

Cockleroaster (OG 1060, ABV 5.8%) Around Christmas only. An amber-coloured, full-bodied beer. Smooth and well balanced, yet slightly sweet-tasting, with a strong, multi-flavoured finish.

HP&D **Holt, Plant & Deakin Ltd., Dudley Road, Wolverhampton, W. Midlands, WV2 3AF. Tel. (0902) 450504**

Trades under the name of Holts, but do not confuse it with Manchester's Joseph Holt brewery: a Black Country company set up in 1984 and now running 47 traditional pubs, all serving real ale. Holts Mild and Bitter are brewed by Tetley Walker in Warrington (see Tetley Walker), though Mild may move to Wolverhampton. Some Entire is still produced at the company's old brewery in Oldbury.

Entire (OG 1043, ABV 4.4%) An amber, hoppy beer with an aromatic bouquet and a splendid, complex, hoppy aftertaste.

Deakin's Downfall* (OG 1060, ABV 5.9%) A winter ale.

Plant's Progress* (OG 1060, ABV 5.9%) A second winter brew.

IND COOPE **Ind Coope Burton Brewery Ltd., 107 Station Street, Burton upon Trent, Staffs. DE14 1BZ. Tel. (0283) 31111**

The major brewery in the group which resulted from the merger of the adjoining Allsopp's and Ind Coope breweries in 1934. It currently has a capacity of two and a half million barrels a year and brews eight real ales for the South and the Midlands, providing beer for the Ansells, Ind Coope Retail, Taylor Walker and Nicholson's trading divisions. These 'local' beers are derived from two mashes: ABC, Friary and Taylor Walker from one, Benskins and Nicholson's from the other. Lumphammer (OG 1039) is brewed for the Worcestershire-based Little Pub Co. chain, but the Greenalls beers it produced have been transferred to Tetley Walker.

For Ind Coope Retail:

ABC Best Bitter* (OG 1035, ABV 3.5%) A light, refreshing bitter, owing much of its character to dry hopping.

Benskins Best Bitter (OG 1035, ABV 3.5%) A hoppy aroma, taste and finish. Can be a bit thin on occasions, when any malt and fruit flavours are lost. Otherwise, it's a pleasant, suppable pint.

Friary Meux Best Bitter (OG 1035, ABV 3.5%) Malt just dominates over hops in the aroma and flavour of this tawny beer. A strange, fruity flavour lurks in the background.

Ind Coope Burton Ale (OG 1047, ABV 4.8%) Full of hop and malt flavours with hints of fruit and sweetness. It has a hoppy, malty aroma with a faint smell of fruit and a bitter, hoppy finish. *Champion Beer of Britain* 1990.

For Ansells:

Ansells Bitter (OG 1035, ABV 3.5%) A pale brown, malty bitter, balanced by hoppiness. Bittersweet aftertaste.

Ansells Mild (OG 1035.5, ABV 3.2%) A dark brown, malty beer with hints of roast caramel and sweetness. Well-balanced aftertaste.

For Taylor Walker and Nicholson's:

Nicholson's Best Bitter* (OG 1035, ABV 3.5%)

Taylor Walker Best Bitter* (OG 1035, ABV 3.5%) Light, malty bitter.

The Nationals

JOSHUA TETLEY **Joshua Tetley & Son Ltd., PO Box 142, The Brewery, Leeds, W. Yorks. LS1 1QG. Tel. (0532) 435282**

Yorkshire's best-known brewery, founded in 1822 by maltster Joshua Tetley. The brewery site covers 20 acres and includes a brewhouse opened in May 1989 to handle the increased demand for Tetley Bitter, though versions of both Tetley Bitter and Mild are also brewed at the Tetley Walker plant in Warrington, with no point of origin declared on the pump clips. A new visitor centre is due to open at Easter 1994.

Mild (OG 1033, ABV 3.2%) Red/brown in colour, with a light hint of malt and caramel in the aroma. A rounded taste of malt and caramel follows, with balancing bitterness, then a generally dry finish. A smooth, satisfying mild.

Bitter (OG 1035.5, ABV 3.6%) An amber-coloured standard bitter with a faint hoppy aroma. A good, refreshing, smooth balance of hop, bitterness and grain in the mouth, finishing with a long, dry aftertaste. Quality can vary.

TETLEY WALKER **Tetley Walker Ltd., Dallam Lane, Warrington, Cheshire WA2 7NU. Tel. (0925) 31231**

Brewery founded by the Walker family in 1852 which merged with Joshua Tetley in 1960 and currently brews Tetley Walker, Peter Walker, HP&D and Greenalls brands. The Tetley Mild and Bitter brewed here are versions of the beers from Tetley's Leeds brewery but are sold with identical pump clips. In the *Good Beer Guide* pub section, we state Tetley Walker instead of Tetley when we are aware that the beer comes from Warrington and not Leeds.

Tetley Dark Mild (OG 1032, ABV 2.9%) A smooth, dark, malty mild with balanced roast and caramel flavours, and a hint of fruit and liquorice. Some dryness. Much improved over the last year.

Walker Mild (OG 1032, ABV 2.9%) Smooth, dark mild with fruit and hints of caramel, roast and bitterness. The malty aftertaste quickly gives way to a faint dryness.

Tetley Mild (OG 1032, ABV 3.2%) A smooth, malty mild with some fruitiness and bitter notes. The aftertaste is malty, with a little dryness. A refreshing, darkish mild.

Walker Bitter (OG 1033, ABV 3.3%) A light, refreshing, well-balanced bitter with some hop and a little fruit.

Walker Best Bitter (OG 1036, ABV 3.3%) A bitter beer with a dry finish. The bitterness is sometimes astringent and can mask other flavours. Reasonably hoppy.

Tetley Bitter (OG 1036, ABV 3.6%) A fruity session beer with a dry finish. Bitterness tends to dominate malt and hop flavours. Sharp, clean-tasting and popular.

Wild Rover (OG 1055, ABV 5.6%) A well-balanced, strong bitter which can be quite sweet but is not cloying. Brewed occasionally for Tetley's in-pub beer festivals and appears under various names.

Walker Winter Warmer (OG 1060, ABV 5.8%) Brewed November-February. A smooth, dark and sweet winter ale, with a strong, fruity flavour, balanced to some degree by a bitter taste and the dry character of the finish. Improves with age as sweetness declines and other flavours emerge. At its best, it is dangerously drinkable.

For HP&D:

HP&D Bitter (OG 1036, ABV 3.4%) Brewed not to give offence: pale, sweet, malty and brown.

OG stands for Original Gravity, the reading taken before fermentation of the amount of fermentable material in the brew. It is a rough indicator of strength. More reliable is the ABV (Alcohol by Volume) rating, which gives the percentage of alcohol in the finished beer.

HP&D Mild (OG 1036, ABV 3.4%) An innocuous mild that doesn't trouble the tastebuds. Dark brown, sweet and malty.

For Greenalls:

Greenalls Mild (OG 1032, ABV 3.1%) A dark, malty mild with a faint malt and fruit aroma. Quite fruity, with hints of roast, caramel and a little bitterness. Good when on form but often thin and bland.

Shipstone's Mild* (OG 1034, ABV 3.4%)

Greenalls Bitter (OG 1036, ABV 3.8%) A well-balanced beer which is quite fruity and well hopped, with a good, dry finish.

Davenports Traditional Bitter* (OG 1037, ABV 3.9%)

Shipstone's Bitter* (OG 1037, ABV 4%)

Thomas Greenall's Original Bitter (OG 1045, ABV 4.4%) Astringent bitterness tends to dominate malt and hop flavours; fairly fruity and a little sweet.

COURAGE

Courage Ltd., Ashby House, 1 Bridge Street, Staines, Surrey TW18 4TP. Tel. (0784) 466199

Since 1991, Courage, owned by Foster's of Australia, has been a brewer without pubs. Indulging in a pubs-for-breweries swap with Grand Metropolitan (the old Watney's, Manns and Truman breweries), as a means of avoiding the full implications of the 1989 Beer Orders, it divested itself of all its pub estate, gaining at the same time all Grand Met's breweries and giving itself 20% of all UK beer production. The ex-Courage pubs, together with most of Grand Met's pubs, were amalgamated into Inntrepreneur Estates (see Pub Groups) for leasing out on long contracts to existing tenants or other businessmen. These pubs are obliged to take Courage beers for seven years, though this agreement may well continue beyond this time.

The brewery closures feared when the deal was announced have yet to materialise, though the future of the old Webster's brewery in Halifax is still in some doubt. Webster's Choice has already been killed off by the heavy promotion of Directors, and all non-production staff have been transferred to John Smith's in Tadcaster. Courage sold off the Ruddles brewery to Dutch lager giant Grolsch (see Independents), and Ushers of Trowbridge is now independent, thanks to a management buy-out (again see Independents). Courage also operates keg beer plants in Mortlake and on the outskirts of Reading, and owns the Beamish & Crawford brewery in Cork, Ireland.

Like Bass, Courage has reduced the alcohol content of some beers.

BRISTOL **Bristol Brewery, Counterslip, Bristol, Avon BS1 6EX. Tel. (0272) 297222**

The former Georges brewery, now Courage's only real ale brewery in the South. Growing demand for cask beer has resulted in expansion at this plant in recent years, with Best and Directors very well promoted nationally but Bitter Ale sales confined mostly to the West Country and South-East Wales. However, the three beers are all diluted versions of the same original high gravity brew.

Bitter Ale (OG 1031, ABV 3.3%) A pale, light-bodied bitter, with a delicately hoppy, bitter, grainy malt taste. A dry bitter finish and a hoppy aroma.

Best Bitter (OG 1039, ABV 4%) A pale brown bitter with a balance of bitter hops, grainy malt (sometimes fruit), and a slight sweetness. The aroma is hoppy; the finish is bitter and dry, with some hops. Variable.

Directors (OG 1046, ABV 4.8%) A well-balanced, red/brown malty ale, with hops and fruit in the nose. The similar taste has a faint fruitiness, and develops into a bitter, dry finish. All too often served below par, when it can be harshly bitter and lacking in body.

JOHN SMITH'S

John Smith's Brewery, Tadcaster, N. Yorks. LS24 9SA. Tel. (0937) 832091

A business founded at the Old Brewery in 1758 and taken over by John Smith (brother of Samuel Smith, see Independents) in 1847. The present brewery was built in 1884 and became part of the Courage empire in 1970. John Smith's Bitter is Courage's best-known ale, thanks to extensive television advertising. *Bottle-conditioned beer: Imperial Russian Stout (OG 1098, ABV 10%), a famous export beer which may be transferred to the Courage Reading brewery*

Bitter (OG 1039, ABV 3.8%) Copper-coloured beer with a pleasant mix of hops and malt in the nose. Malt dominates the taste but hops take over in the finish. The brewery's quality control for this beer is excellent. Widely available nationally.

Magnet (OG 1040, ABV 4%) A well-crafted beer, almost ruby-coloured. Hops, malt and citrus fruit can be identified in the nose and there are complex flavours of nuts, hops and fruit, giving way to a long, malty finish.

FOUNTAIN HEAD

Fountain Head Brewery, Ovenden Wood, Halifax, W. Yorks. HX2 0TL. Tel. (0422) 357188

The original Samuel Webster brewery, merged by Watney in 1985 with Wilson's of Manchester, a move which saw the closure of Wilson's own brewery. Webster's Yorkshire Bitter appeared to be threatened by the Grand Met deal, as Courage was already committed to John Smith's Bitter, but the Halifax brew has proved surprisingly resilient and still benefits from a sizeable advertising budget. It may be the one beer to survive if Courage does close the Halifax brewery. Already Wilson's Mild has been contracted out to Morland (see Independents).

Webster's Green Label Best (OG 1034, ABV 3.2%) A faint, hoppy aroma, with a little fruitiness at times. Some sweetness in the malty taste, and a bitter finish. A boy's bitter.

Wilson's Original Bitter (OG 1036, ABV 3.5%) A fairly thin, golden beer with a malty and fruity aroma and a flowery hop flavour, which can be very bitter at times. Malty overtones in taste and finish.

Webster's Yorkshire Bitter (OG 1037, ABV 3.5%) A disappointing beer with a faintly malty and fruity aroma (sometimes metallic). Often very bland in taste to offend no-one. If you are lucky, it can have a good, fresh, hoppy-bitter flavour and finish (but very rare!).

GUINNESS

Guinness Brewing (GB), Park Royal Brewery, London NW10 7RR. Tel. (081) 965 7700

No real ale – sad words with which to begin a description of one of the world's great breweries. The last naturally-conditioned beer, the bottled Guinness Original, was discontinued in April 1993, despite loud protests from beer-lovers. This was a strange move, especially at a time when both stouts and bottle-conditioned beers were attracting so much interest. Guinness Original is still on sale, but only in a brewery-conditioned, pasteurised version, which lacks the complexity and freshness of the bottle-conditioned beer.

All Draught Guinness sold in the UK is keg. In Ireland, Draught Guinness (OG 1038, brewed at Arthur Guinness, St James's Gate, Dublin 8) is not pasteurised but is served with gas pressure. Canned 'Draught' Guinness is also pasteurised and produces its tight, creamy head by use of a small plastic sparkler at the bottom of the can.

S&N

SCOTTISH & NEWCASTLE

Scottish & Newcastle Breweries PLC, Abbey Brewery, 111 Holyrood Road, Edinburgh, Lothian EH8 8YS. Tel. (031) 556 2591

The 1960 merger between Scottish Brewers Ltd. (the former Younger and McEwan breweries) and Newcastle Breweries Ltd. has had a major influence on the British brewing industry. It may not be officially classed as a 'National', because it does not own more than 2,000 pubs, but S&N is a giant brewer in every other way. It has a massive presence in the free trade (particularly through McEwan and Theakston brands and the infamous Newcastle Brown Ale) and also dominates many free houses through the loan-tie system of offering loans in return for beer sales.

The closure of its Matthew Brown subsidiary in Blackburn in 1991, despite earlier assurances that the brewery was 'sacrosanct', enraged drinkers and fears grew for Theakston, too, when S&N began to produce Theakston beers at the Tyne Brewery in Newcastle. Today most of Theakston's production comes from Newcastle.

S&N currently operates a total of 1,850 pubs, 800 managed and 1,050 tenanted, with over 50% selling cask-conditioned beer. There are currently five breweries, including a keg beer plant in Manchester. However, rumours persist about the company leaving brewing and possibly merging with another producer, such as Whitbread.

FOUNTAIN

Fountain Brewery, 159 Fountainbridge, Edinburgh, Lothian EH3 9YY. Tel (031) 229 9377

The Scottish production centre, formerly the home of William McEwan & Co. Ltd, founded in 1856. Its beers are sold under two separate names – McEwan and Younger, depending on the trading area, but such is the promotion of Theakston products that the futures of 70/-/Younger Scotch Bitter and No. 3 remain in doubt.

McEwan 70/- or Younger Scotch Bitter*

(OG 1036, ABV 3.7%) A well-balanced, sweetish brew, becoming more and more rare.

McEwan 80/- or Younger IPA*

(OG 1042, ABV 4.5%) Malty and sweet-flavoured, with some graininess and a dry finish.

Younger No. 3*

(OG 1042, ABV 4.5%) Rich and dark.

TYNE	**Tyne Brewery, Gallowgate, Newcastle upon Tyne, Tyne & Wear NE99 1RA. Tel (091) 232 5091**
	The home of Newcastle Breweries Ltd., formed in 1890 as an amalgamation of five local breweries. In recent years it brewed no cask beer, until most of Theakston's production was transferred here (see Theakston). No indication is given at the point of sale or in advertising that Theakston beers are brewed in Newcastle.
Theakston Mild Ale	(OG 1035, ABV 3.5%)
Theakston Best Bitter	(OG 1038, ABV 3.8%)
Theakston XB	(OG 1044, ABV 4.5%)
Theakston Old Peculier	(OG 1056, ABV 5.6%)

HOME	**Home Brewery, Mansfield Road, Daybrook, Nottingham NG5 6BU. Tel. (0602) 675030**
	Founded in 1875 and acquired by S&N in 1986, Home's tied estate offers real ale in 180 of its 400 pubs. Extensive free trade in the Midlands and the North. Now brews the beers from the closed Matthew Brown brewery in Blackburn and these are still sold in 184 of the 403 Matthew Brown pubs in the North-West. Home Mild (OG 1036, ABV 3.6%), however, is now contract-brewed at Mansfield (see Independents), and there are real worries about its future.
Matthew Brown Dark Mild*	(OG 1030.5, ABV 3.1%)
Matthew Brown Bitter*	(OG 1034, ABV 3.5%)
Home Bitter	(OG 1038, ABV 3.8%) The flavour balances malt and hops well, with a smooth, initial taste and a lingering, dry, bitter finish. Golden/copper in colour; little aroma.

THEAKSTON	**T&R Theakston Ltd., Wellgarth, Masham, Ripon, N. Yorks. HG4 4PX. Tel (0765) 689544**
	Company formed in 1827 and based at this brewery since 1875. Became part of S&N when its parent company, Matthew Brown, was swallowed up. More than £1 million has been spent on this brewery in the last few years, reflecting the 'national' status its brews have been given by S&N. Although Theakston itself runs just ten tied houses, the free trade is enormous and, consequently, most of Theakston's production now takes place in Newcastle. The same pump clips are used for Masham and Newcastle beers, so the consumer is still not told whether the beer actually comes from Theakston's brewery.
Mild Ale	(OG 1035, ABV 3.5%) Very dark amber in colour, with a mix of malt and hops in the nose. A smooth, full mild with malt and chocolate flavours and a delicate, hoppy aftertaste which comes from dry hopping.
Best Bitter	(OG 1038, ABV 3.8%) A rather thin bitter with a hoppy and sulphurous aroma and a developing dryness in the aftertaste.
XB	(OG 1044, ABV 4.5%) A light drinking bitter with little body or aftertaste. Hop and fruit dominate, with low bitterness.
Old Peculier	(OG 1056, ABV 5.6%) A rich and complex beer with a fruity aroma and a well-balanced taste. The mouthfeel is smooth and assertive, with developing dryness. Still retaining the magic of its original acclaim.

WHITBREAD

The Whitbread Beer Company, Porter Tun House, Capability Green, Luton, Beds. LU1 3LS. Tel. (0582) 391166

Whitbread has once again gone down the road of brewery closures. Having destroyed the likes of Strong's of Romsey, Wethered of Marlow, Fremlins of Faversham, Chester's of Salford and Higsons of Liverpool, this time it was the Exchange Brewery at Sheffield which was given the chop, despite great investment in recent years. The result is that Trophy Bitter and beers which bear the Higsons and Chester's names have been on the move once more. Now only three cask ale plants remain and some beers have been farmed out to other breweries.

At the same time, Whitbread has been putting large sums of money into promoting its cask ale portfolio, and the retail side of the company has turned a number of pubs into 'alehouses' to support this initiative. Boddingtons Bitter, purchased along with the Strangeways Brewery in 1989, and Flowers Original have been the major beneficiaries, though the new Porter was also well publicised initially.

Whitbread brews for the Devenish pub chain, and also dominates the beer supply in many of its former pubs which have been sold off to new pub groups. In addition to the cask beer breweries, the company also operates keg beer factories in Magor in South Wales and Samlesbury in Lancashire.

Whitbread's 4,600 pubs are controlled by two divisions: Whitbread Inns (managed houses) and Whitbread Pub Partnerships (pubs leased out, usually on 20-year terms). Each group has about 2,300 pubs.

BODDINGTONS

Strangeways Brewery, PO Box 23, Strangeways, Manchester M60 3WB. Tel. (061) 828 2000

Brewery established in 1778 whose Bitter has long been one of Britain's best-known traditional beers. Whitbread acquired the brewery when the Boddingtons company, which had already taken-over and closed Oldham Brewery, retreated to pub owning and other leisure enterprises. Now Whitbread is pushing Boddingtons Bitter relentlessly nationwide and it takes up 90% of the brewery's already expanded production capacity.

OB Mild (OG 1032, ABV 3%) Copper-red in colour, with a malty aroma. A smooth roast malt and fruit flavour follows, then a malty aftertaste.

Boddingtons Mild (OG 1033, ABV 3%) A thin, dark mild with a malty flavour, somewhat drier in character of late. Short aftertaste. The number of outlets still appears to be in decline.

Boddingtons Bitter (OG 1035, ABV 3.8%) A pale beer in which agreeable hoppiness and bitterness can be spoiled by a rather cloying sweetness in flavour and aftertaste.

OB Bitter (OG 1037, ABV 3.8%) Pale beer with an aroma of malt and fruit. The flavour is malty and bitter, with a bittersweet tinge and a dry, malty finish.

The tankard symbol indicates the *Good Beer Guide Beers of the Year,* finalists in the *Champion Beer of Britain* contest held at the *Great British Beer Festival* at Olympia in August 1993.

The Nationals

CASTLE EDEN — **Castle Eden Brewery, PO Box 13, Castle Eden, Hartlepool, Cleveland TS27 4SX. Tel. (0429) 836007**

Originally attached to a 17th-century coaching inn, the old Nimmo's brewery (established in 1826) was purchased by Whitbread in 1963. It actually stands in County Durham, despite the Cleveland postal address, and now produces some of Whitbread's better quality beers, including the new Porter. Winter Royal, once brewed by Wethered of Marlow, has arrived here after a time at Gale's in Horndean, as have the Higsons beers from Sheffield – all helping to secure the future of this small brewery, which also produces keg Campbells beer for the Scottish market.

Higsons Mild* (OG 1032, ABV 3.1%)

Higsons Bitter* (OG 1037, ABV 3.8%)

Castle Eden Ale (OG 1041, ABV 4%) A rich, hoppy bitter with well-developed hop character and moderate body and mouthfeel. When fresh, has a good balance, with a slight sweetness. Now available nationwide.

Whitbread Porter (OG 1052, ABV 4.6%) Although the original trial brew may be rarely matched, this is a deservedly proud beer, rich in coffee and chocolate flavours, with fine hop character and an impressive aftertaste. However, sales have been affected by its high price and it is now likely to be available only February-May.

Winter Royal* (OG 1055, ABV 5.5%) The former Wethered winter ale.

FLOWERS — **The Flowers Brewery, Monson Avenue, Cheltenham, Glos. GL50 4EL. Tel. (0242) 261166**

Brewery established in 1760 by banker John Gardner, which became the Cheltenham Original Brewery when rebuilt in 1898. It merged in 1958 with Stroud Brewery to form West Country Breweries Ltd. and was acquired by Whitbread in 1963. The Flowers brewing operation and title were transferred from Stratford-upon-Avon in 1968. In recent years, it has become the centre for Whitbread cask ale in the South, absorbing the Wethered, Strong and Fremlins production as these breweries were closed. Wethered Bitter (see McMullen), Pompey Royal (see Gale's) and Strong Country Bitter (see Morrells) have since been contracted out to other breweries, while Fremlins Bitter has been joined at Cheltenham by Royal Wessex Bitter (for Devenish) and Trophy and Bentley's Yorkshire Bitter (following the closure of Sheffield's Exchange brewery in 1993).

West Country Pale Ale (WCPA) (OG 1030.5, ABV 3%) Hoppy in aroma, but not as distinctive as it used to be. Light, refreshing and hoppy, with a clean, dry finish.

Fremlins Bitter* (OG 1035.5, ABV 3.5%)

Flowers IPA (OG 1036, ABV 3.6%) Pale brown, with little aroma, perhaps a faint maltiness. Moderately dry taste and finish, but no discernible hoppiness. Thin and uninspiring.

Summer Ale* (OG 1036, ABV 3.6%)

Whitbread Best Bitter* (OG 1036, ABV 3.6%) Also available in keg form.

Bentley's Yorkshire Bitter* (OG 1036, ABV 3.8%)

Trophy* (OG 1036, ABV 3.8%)

Flowers Original (OG 1045, ABV 4.5%) Hoppy aroma and hops in the taste, with some malt and a hint of fruit. A notably bitter finish.

For Devenish:

Royal Wessex Bitter* (OG 1040.5, ABV 4%)

Brew Pubs

ABINGTON PARK BREWERY CO.
Wellingborough Road, Northampton NN1 4EY. Tel. (0604) 31240
Cobblers Ale (OG 1037, ABV 3.3%)
Becket (OG 1040, ABV 3.6%)
Dark (OG 1044, ABV 3.6%)
Extra (OG 1047, ABV 4.3%)
A Chef & Brewer Victorian-styled brew pub, opened in 1984 and incorporating a five-barrel plant. Stores beer in cellar tanks under CO_2 at atmospheric pressure.

ALE HOUSE
79 Raglan Road, Leeds, W. Yorks. LS2 9DZ. Tel. (0532) 455447
Monster Mash (OG 1042)
XB (OG 1045)
No. 9 (OG 1046)
White Rose Ale (OG 1064)
Housewarmer (OG 1079) Brewed at Christmas.
Real ale off-licence next to Leeds University. Started brewing in late 1987 and now offers eight handpumps, with weekly guest beers and four real ciders. Brewed special beers for the Leeds Centenary festival in 1993.

ALFORD ARMS
Frithsden, Hemel Hempstead, Herts. HP1 3DD. Tel. (0442) 864480
Cherry Pickers (OG 1036, ABV 3.6%)
Pickled Squirrel (OG 1045, ABV 4.5%)
Rudolf's Revenge (OG 1058, ABV 5.8%)
Now brewing full-time and supplying 13 other Whitbread pubs with its malt extract beers. Occasional one-off brews.

ALL NATIONS (Mrs Lewis's)
Coalport Road, Madeley, Telford, Shropshire TF7 5DP. Tel. (0952) 585747
Pale Ale (OG 1032)
One of four brew pubs left before the new wave arrived. The others were the Blue Anchor, Old Swan and Three Tuns. Still known as Mrs Lewis's, the inn has been in the same family since 1934 and has been brewing for 200 years.

ANCIENT DRUIDS
Napier Street, Cambridge CB1 1HR. Tel. (0223) 324514
Mild (OG 1035, ABV 3.2%)
Kite Bitter (OG 1035, ABV 3.5%)
Druids Special (OG 1047, ABV 4.3%)
Merlin (OG 1055, ABV 6%)
The Bee's Knees (OG 1060, ABV 6.2%) Occasional.
Frostbiter (OG 1070, ABV 7.5%) Winter only.
Set up in 1984. Uses malt extract.

BIRD IN HAND
Paradise Brewery Ltd., Paradise Park, Hayle, Cornwall TR27 4HY. Tel. (0736) 753974
Paradise Bitter (OG 1040)
Miller's Ale (OG 1044)
Artists Ale (OG 1055)
Victory Ale (OG 1070) Winter only.
Unusual brewery in a bird park, founded in 1980. Three other pubs are supplied, plus more in summer.

BLACK HORSE
Leominster, Hereford & Worcester.
See Independents, Dunn Plowman.

BLACK HORSE & RAINBOW
The Liverpool Brewing Company Ltd., 21–23 Berry Street, Liverpool, Merseyside L1 9DF. Tel. (051) 709 5055
LBC Bitter (OG 1038) Occasional.
Rainbow Bitter (OG 1038) Occasional.
Black Horse Bitter (OG 1044)
Winter Bitter (OG 1045)
Celebration (OG 1050)
Five-barrel brewery opened in July 1990. Special brews are produced for events like university graduation and freshers weeks. Uses cellar tanks with a blanket of CO_2. The plant can be viewed both from within the pub and from the street.

BLUE ANCHOR
50 Coinagehall Street, Helston, Cornwall TR13 8EL. Tel. (0326) 562821
Middle (OG 1050)
Best (OG 1053)
Special (OG 1066 summer, 1076 winter)
Historic thatched brew pub, originating as a monks' resting place in the 15th century. Produces powerful ales known locally as 'Spingo' beers. Put on the market in 1993.

BORVE BREW HOUSE
Ruthven, Huntly, Grampian AB54 4SR. Tel. (046 687) 343
Borve Ale (OG 1040, ABV 3.8%)
Tall Ships IPA (OG 1050, ABV 4.9%)
Bishop Elphinstone Ale (OG 1053, ABV 4.7%)
Cairm Porter (OG 1060)
Moved from its original site on the Isle of Lewis in 1988 to a former school on the mainland, now converted to a pub with the brewery adjacent. Supplies about half a dozen free trade outlets. *Bottle-conditioned beers: Borve Ale (OG 1040, ABV 3.8%); Extra Strong Ale (OG 1085, ABV 10%)*

BRISTOL BREWHOUSE
Bristol, Avon.
See Independents, Ross.

BRUNSWICK INN
Derby.
See Independents, Brunswick.

BRYN ARMS
Gellilydan, Gwynedd.
See Independents, Snowdonia.

CANNON PUBLIC HOUSE
Parker & Son Brewers Ltd., Cannon Street, Wellingborough, Northants. NN8 4DL. Tel. (0933) 279629
Cannon Pride (OG 1041, ABV 4.2%)
Cannon Fodder (OG 1055, ABV 5.5%)
Brewery founded in January 1993 with equipment supplied by Banks & Taylor. Now serves five other pubs. Cannon Special (ABV 4.8%) is a blend of the two beers above; Cannon Dark (ABV 4.8%) is Cannon Special with added caramel.

CONCERTINA BAND CLUB
9a Dolcliffe Road, Mexborough, S. Yorks. S64 9AZ. Tel. (0709) 580841
Bitter (OG 1038, ABV 4%)
Brew club which began production in 1992. Plans to expand the range and supply outside establishments.

THE CYDER HOUSE INN
SHACKLEFORD BREWERY CO.

CYDER HOUSE INN
Shackleford Brewery Co., Peperharow Lane, Shackleford, Godalming, Surrey GU8 6AN. Tel. (0483) 810360
Piston Broke (OG 1040, ABV 4%)
Old Shackle (OG 1048, ABV 4.7%)
Ted's Tipple (OG 1058, ABV 5.8%) A winter porter.
Full mash brewery set up in 1992. The landlord intends to open a second pub brewery in the near future.

DUKE OF NORFOLK BREWERY
202–204 Westbourne Grove, London W11. Tel. (071) 229 3551
No longer brews but sells beer from the Greyhound Brewery.

FARMERS ARMS
Mayhem's Brewery, Ledbury Road, Apperley, Glos. GL19 4DR. Tel. (0452) 780307
Oddas Light (OG 1038, ABV 3.8%)
Sundowner (OG 1044, ABV 4.5%)
Brewery opened in 1992, which also produces its own cider.

FELLOWS, MORTON & CLAYTON BREWHOUSE COMPANY
54 Canal Street, Nottingham NG1 7EH. Tel. (0602) 506795
Samuel Fellows Bitter (OG 1040, ABV 4%)
Matthew Clayton's Original Strong Ale (OG 1048, ABV 5%)
Easter Xtra Nectar (OG 1058, ABV 6%)
New Year Nectar (OG 1060, ABV 5.9%)
Pub leased from Whitbread, brewing since 1980 from malt extract. The brewery may be resited at the rear and full mash brewing introduced.

FIRST IN, LAST OUT
14–15 High Street, Old Town, Hastings, E. Sussex TN34 3EY. Tel. (0424) 425079
Crofters (OG 1040)
Cardinal (OG 1044) A stout.
Pub in the historic part of town, with a brewery installed in 1985. Production has more than doubled in the last five years.

FLAMINGO BREWERY COMPANY
88 London Road, Kingston upon Thames, Surrey KT2 6PX. Tel. (081) 541 3717
Fairfield Bitter (OG 1037)
Royal Charter (OG 1045)
Coronation (OG 1057)
Previously the Flamingo & Firkin, now owned by Saxon Inns. Cellar tanks are used for Fairfield Bitter.

FLOWER POTS INN
Cheriton, Hants.
See Independents, Cheriton.

FOX & HOUNDS
Barley Brewery, Barley, Royston, Herts. SG8 8HU. Tel. (0763) 848459
Old Dragon (OG 1036)
Flame Thrower (OG 1044)
Early member of the pub brewing revival, using a 19th-century brewhouse at what used to be the Waggon & Horses before changing its name.

FOX & HOUNDS
High Street, Stottesdon, Shropshire DY14 8TZ. Tel. (074 632) 222
Wust (OG 1039, ABV 3.7%)
Bostin Bitter (OG 1043, ABV 4.1%)
Gobstopper (OG 1065, ABV 6.5%) A winter ale.
Pub which started brewing in the 1970s and which has had a succession of brewers leading to today's landlord. A few other pubs are supplied. 'Wust' and 'Bostin' are Black Country expressions meaning worst and best. A mild may be added.

FOX & NEWT
9 Burley Street, Leeds, W. Yorks. LS9 1LD. Tel. (0532) 432612
No longer brews.

Brew Pubs

FROG & PARROT
64 Division Street, Sheffield, S. Yorks. S1 4SG. Tel. (0742) 721280
Old Croak (OG 1040, ABV 3.3%)
Reckless (OG 1050, ABV 4.5%)
Conqueror (OG 1066, ABV 6.7%)
Roger & Out (OG 1125, ABV 16.9%)
Whitbread malt extract brew pub whose Roger & Out is listed in the *Guinness Book of Records* as the world's strongest beer. Beers are kept under a nitrogen blanket in casks and are sometimes available in a handful of other pubs. *Bottle-conditioned beer: Roger & Out (OG 1125, ABV 16.9%)*

GASTONS BAR
Preston, Lancs.
See Independents, Little Avenham.

GREEN DRAGON
Broad Street, Bungay, Suffolk, NR35 1EE. Tel (0986) 892681
Chaucer Ale (OG 1037, ABV 3.6%)
Bridge Street Bitter (OG 1046, ABV 4.5%)
Dragon (OG 1055, ABV 5.5%)
Pub purchased from Brent Walker in 1991. Buildings at the rear were then adapted to house stainless steel milk equipment, converted for use in brewing.

GREEN DRAGON
Murphy Associates Ltd., The Evesham Brewery, Oat Street, Evesham, Hereford & Worcester. Tel. (0386) 443462
Asum Ale (OG 1038)
New brewery supplying this pub and one other local. 'Asum' is an old local pronunciation of 'Evesham'.

GREYHOUND BREWERY COMPANY LTD
151 Greyhound Lane, Streatham Common, London SW16 5NJ. Tel. (081) 677 9962
XXXP Pedigree Mild (OG 1036, ABV 3.6%)
Special Ale (OG 1038, ABV 3.8%)
Streatham Strong (OG 1048, ABV 4.9%)
Streatham Dynamite (OG 1055, ABV 5.5%)
Brew pub, set up in 1984. Special beers are brewed for bank holidays and other occasions. Cellar tanks with a blanket of CO_2 are used at the pub, but a few other outlets are supplied with cask beer.

GRIBBLE INN
Oving, Chichester, W. Sussex PO20 6BP. Tel. (0243) 786893
Harvest Gold (OG 1030, ABV 3%)
Gribble Ale (OG 1042, ABV 4.2%)
Reg's Tipple (OG 1055, ABV 5.5%)
Black Adder II (OG 1062.5, ABV 6.1%)
Wobbler (OG 1080, ABV 7.8%)
Brew pub owned by Hall & Woodhouse which recommenced brewing in autumn 1991 after a gap of 18 months. The beers may sometimes be found in other Hall & Woodhouse pubs. Black Adder II is not to be confused with the *Champion Beer of Britain* 1991 from Mauldons.

HAND IN HAND
Brighton, E. Sussex.
See Independents, Kemptown.

HEDGEHOG & HOGSHEAD
100 Goldstone Villas, Hove, E. Sussex BN3 3RX. Tel. (0273) 733660
Brighton Breezy Bitter (OG 1043, ABV 4.3%)
Hogbolter (OG 1058, ABV 5.8%)
Prickletickler (OG 1075, ABV 7.3%) An occasional brew.
Slay Bells (OG 1080, ABV 8%) Christmas only.
The first of David Bruce's new ventures, which opened in July 1990. Both casks and tanks are used for storage and a cask breather is used on slower sellers.

HEDGEHOG & HOGSHEAD
163 University Road, Highfield, Southampton, Hants SO2 1TS. Tel. (0703) 581124
Belcher's Best Bitter (OG 1043, ABV 4.3%)
Bob's Bootleg Bitter (OG 1052, ABV 5.2%)
Hogbolter (OG 1058, ABV 5.8%)
Prickletickler (OG 1075, ABV 7.3%) Winter only.
Slay Bells (OG 1080, ABV 8%) Christmas only.
The second in the new chain. The same storage and cask breather systems are used as in the Brighton pub.

HIGHLANDER
William Clark Brewing, 15–16 Esplanade, South Cliff, Scarborough, N. Yorks. YO11 2AF. Tel. (0723) 365627
XXXPS (OG 1036)
Mild (OG 1038)
EXB (OG 1040)
Thistle Bitter (OG 1040)

No. 68 (OG 1042)
Brewery set up behind a Victorian hotel, which used to sell its Scotch-style beers to the free trade, but now only brews for itself.

JOHN THOMPSON INN
John Thompson Brewery, Ingleby, Derbyshire DE7 1HW. Tel. (0332) 862469
JTS XXX (OG 1042, ABV 4.2%) Sold elsewhere as Lloyds Derby Bitter.
15th-century farmhouse, converted to a pub in 1969. Has brewed since 1977, with its other beers supplied to the free trade through Lloyds Country Beers (see Independents), a separate enterprise.

JOLLY ROGER
The Original Hereford Brewing Company Ltd., 88 St Owen Street, Hereford HR1 2QD. Tel. (0432) 274998
Quaff Ale (OG 1040, ABV 4%)
Goodness Stout (OG 1042, ABV 4.2%)
Blackbeard (OG 1045, ABV 4.5%)
Old Hereford Bull (OG 1050, ABV 5%)
An off-shoot of the Worcester Jolly Roger (see below), established in October 1990. The bar takes the shape of a galleon.

JOLLY ROGER BREWERY AND TAP
50 Lowesmoor, Worcester WR1 2SG. Tel. (0905) 21540
Not currently brewing.

LASS O'GOWRIE
36 Charles Street, Manchester M1 7DB. Tel. (061) 273 6932
LOG 35 (OG 1035)
Jepson Scully (OG 1038)
LOG 42 (OG 1042)
Centurion (OG 1052)
Graduation (OG 1056)
Victorian pub, revamped and re-opened as a Whitbread malt extract brew pub in 1983. Beer is stored in cellar tanks without a blanket of gas. Centurion and Graduation are only brewed three or four times a year.

MARISCO TAVERN
Lundy Island Brewery, Lundy Island, Bristol Channel EX39 2LY. Tel. (0237) 431831
John O's (OG 1036)
Old Light Bitter (OG 1040)
Brewery opened in 1984 but closed and relocated in 1992. Recommenced brewing in spring 1993, producing beers from malt extract for visitors to the island.

MARKET PORTER
9 Stoney Street, Borough Market, London SE1 9AA. Tel. (071) 407 2495
No longer brews, but the former brewer may supply this and other pubs from a new brewery close by.

MASONS ARMS
Lakeland Brewing Co., Strawberry Bank, Cartmel Fell, Cumbria LA11 6NW. Tel. (053 95) 68686
Amazon Bitter (OG 1038, ABV 4%)
Great Northern (OG 1047, ABV 5%)
Big Six (OG 1064, ABV 6%)
Damson Beer (OG 1070, ABV 9%)
Famous pub, known for its large selection of bottled beers, which began brewing in May 1990. Beer names are based on books by local author Arthur Ransome. *Bottle-conditioned beers: Great Northern, Big Six and Damson Beer (OGs and ABVs as above).* Damson Beer is made from the pub's own damsons to a kriek recipe, using 12lbs of fruit per gallon. Has also produced a real cider.

MINERVA
Nelson Street, Hull, Humbs. HU1 1XE. Tel. (0482) 26909
Pilots Pride (OG 1039)
Joshua Tetley full mash brew pub, set up in 1983 and storing its beer under blanket pressure in cellar tanks.

MIN PIN INN
North Cornwall Brewers, Tregatta Corner, Tintagel, Cornwall PL34 0DX.
Tel. (0840) 770241
Legend Bitter (OG 1035, ABV 3.6%)
Brown Willy Bitter (OG 1055, ABV 4.3%)
Converted farmhouse with possibly the only entirely female-operated brewery in the country (established in 1985). Malt extract used.

OLD SWAN (Ma Pardoe's)
Halesowen Road, Netherton, Dudley, W. Midlands DY2 1BT.
Famous old brew pub which is not currently brewing.

ORANGE BREWERY
37–39 Pimlico Road, London SW1W 8NE. Tel. (071) 730 5984

Pimlico Light (OG 1033.5, ABV 3%)
SW1 (OG 1040, ABV 3.5%)
Pimlico Porter (OG 1045.5, ABV 4.2%)
SW2 (OG 1049.5, ABV 4.5%)
Angels Downfall (OG 1082, ABV 7.5%) Christmas ale.

Brewery opened in 1983. The full mash brews are stored in cellar tanks and, with the exception of SW1, are kept under blanket pressure. Also brews a stout and a lager.

PLOUGH INN
Bodicote Brewery, Bodicote, Banbury, Oxfordshire OX15 4BZ. Tel. (0295) 262327
Bitter (OG 1035, ABV 3.5%)
No. 9 (OG 1045, ABV 4.2%)
Old English Porter (OG 1045, ABV 4.3%) October-April only.
Triple XXX (OG 1055, ABV 5.3%) November-May only.

Brewery founded in 1982 in a pub which has now been in the same hands for 35 years.

ROSE STREET BREWERY
55 Rose Street, Edinburgh, Lothian EH2 2NH. Tel. (031) 220 1227
Auld Reekie 80/- (OG 1043, ABV 4%)
Auld Reekie 90/- (OG 1057, ABV 5.5%)

Brew pub founded in 1983, run by Alloa Brewery and now supplying half a dozen other Alloa outlets. Malt extract used.

ROYAL CLARENCE,
Burnham-on-Sea, Somerset.
See Independents, RCH.

ROYAL INN & HORSEBRIDGE BREWERY
Horsebridge, Tavistock, Devon PL19 8TJ. Tel. (082 287) 214
Tamar (OG 1039, ABV 3.9%)
Horsebridge Best (OG 1045, ABV 4.5%)
Heller (OG 1060, ABV 6%)

15th-century country pub, once a nunnery, which began brewing in 1981. After a change of hands, and a period of inactivity, the single-barrel plant recommenced brewing in 1984.

SHIP & PLOUGH
The Promenade, Kingsbridge, Devon TQ7 1JD. Tel. (0548) 852485
Blewitt's Best Bitter (OG 1038)
King's Ale (OG 1040)
Blewitt's Head Off (OG 1050, may vary)

Brewery started in 1991 which may expand to serve other pubs.

STAR & TIPSY TOAD
St Peters Village, St Peter, Jersey, CI.
Tel. (0534) 485556
Agile Frog (OG 1036)
Cyril's Bitter (OG 1036)
Jimmy's Bitter (JB) (OG 1040)
Horny Toad (OG 1050)
Pale Ale (OG 1050)
Star Drooper (OG 1060) Winter only.

Half-million pound refurbishment of the old Star pub. The first brew appeared in spring 1992. Both casks and cellar tanks are used and beer is kept under a blanket of nitrogen. A second brew pub is planned for St Helier.

STEAM PACKET INN,
Knottingley, W. Yorks.
See Independents.

TALLY HO COUNTRY INN
14 Market Street, Hatherleigh, Devon EX20 3JN. Tel. (0837) 810306
Dark Mild (OG 1034, ABV 2.8%)
Potboiler's Brew (OG 1036, ABV 3.5%)
Tarka Tipple (OG 1042, ABV 4%)
Nutters (OG 1048, ABV 4.6%)
Janni Jollop (OG 1066, ABV 6.6%) Winter only.

Brew pub whose first beer went on sale at Easter 1990. Full mash, no additives. A second fermenter was added in 1992. *Bottle-conditioned beer: Thurgia (OG 1056, ABV 5.7%)*

THREE TUNS BREWERY
Salop Street, Bishop's Castle, Shropshire SY9 5BW. Tel. (0588) 638797
Light Mild (OG 1035)
XXX (OG 1042)
Old Scrooge (OG 1055) Christmas only.
Jim Wood's (OG 1058)

Historic brew pub which first obtained a brewing licence in 1642. The tower brewery was built in 1888 and is still in use, but the pub and brewery are now up for sale.

WHEATSHEAF INN
Fromes Hill Brewery, Fromes Hill, Ledbury, Hereford & Worcester HR8 1HT.
Tel. (0531) 640888
Buckswood Dingle (OG 1036)

Brewery founded in April 1993, using local hops for its one bitter. A stronger beer may be added. One other outlet is also supplied.

WILLY'S
17 High Cliff Road, Cleethorpes, Humbs. DN35 8RQ. Tel. (0472) 602145
Original Bitter (OG 1038, ABV 3.6%)
Burcom Bitter (OG 1044, ABV 4.2%)
Coxswains Special Bitter (OG 1049, ABV 4.9%)
Old Groyne (OG 1060, ABV 6.2%)
Brewery opened in May 1989 to supply the seafront pub and some free trade. Old Groyne is becoming popular as a guest beer through wholesalers. Another outlet, SWIGS (Second Willy's In Grimsby), was bought in December 1989.

YORKSHIRE GREY
2–6 Theobalds Road, London WC1X 8PN. Tel. (071) 405 2519
Headline Bitter (OG 1037, ABV 3.5%)
Holborn Best Bitter (OG 1047, ABV 4.5%)
Regiment Strong Ale (OG 1055.5, ABV 5.1%)
Malt extract brew pub on the corner of Gray's Inn Road. CO_2 blanket on cellar tanks.

THE FIRKIN PUBS
114 Lots Road, Chelsea, London SW10 0RJ. Tel. (071) 352 6645
Pub brewery chain founded by David Bruce in 1979, relaunching the brew pub concept in what used to be run-down national brewers' houses. The pubs were refurbished in a back-to-basics fashion and were given in-house breweries, tucked away behind viewing windows. The Bruce's Brewery chain rapidly grew in number until 1988, when he sold all the pubs to Midsummer Leisure (later European Leisure), who, in turn, sold them to Stakis Leisure in September 1990. Now the chain is owned by the Taylor Walker wing of Carlsberg-Tetley. Not all the Firkin pubs now brew; some are supplied by the others, so only the actual brew pubs are listed here. Three basic brews are available, sold under house names, a 1036 OG/3.6% ABV bitter, a stronger bitter at 1043/4.1%, and Dogbolter (OG 1058, ABV 5.6%). Some pubs offer extra brews like milds, summer or winter beers and real ginger ales. All the brews are full mash and most pubs now offer some cask-conditioned beer with no additional gas applied. However, cellar tanks with mixed gas breathers are still widely used for many beers. More pubs are likely to be added to the chain.

FALCON & FIRKIN
360 Victoria Park Road, Hackney, London E9 7BT. Tel. (081) 985 0693
The largest of the Firkin brew pubs which also supplies cask-conditioned beers for the Flower & Firkin (at Kew Gardens), the Fox & Firkin, the Frigate & Firkin, the Frog & Firkin, the Fusilier & Firkin and the Pheasant & Firkin.

FERRET & FIRKIN
114 Lots Road, Chelsea, London SW10 0RJ. Tel. (071) 352 6645
'The Ferret & Firkin in the Balloon up the Creek', as it is properly known. Opened in 1983.

FIDDLER & FIRKIN
14 South End, Croydon CR0 1DL.
Tel. (081) 680 9728
New brew pub, opened in 1993.

FLAMINGO & FIRKIN
Becket Street, Derby DE1 1HT.
Tel. (0332) 45948
Established in 1988, one of only two brewing Firkins outside London. Beers here are casked, with no extraneous gas applied.

FLEA & FIRKIN
137 Grosvenor Street, Manchester M1 7DZ. Tel. (061) 274 3682
Opened in 1990 and serves a few other outlets.

FLOUNDER & FIRKIN
54 Holloway Road, London N7 8JL.
Tel. (071) 609 9574
Opened in 1985.

FOX & FIRKIN
316 Lewisham High Street, London SE13 3HL. Tel. (081) 690 8925
The second Bruce's pub, opened in 1980. Special brews for the Firkin chain are produced here.

GOOSE & FIRKIN
47–48 Borough Road, Southwark, London SE1 1DR. Tel. (071) 403 3590
The first of the Firkin pubs, a former Truman house. It was converted in 1993 to a full mash brewery and, during the refurbishment, the beers were provided by the Flounder & Firkin and the Falcon & Firkin.

PHOENIX & FIRKIN
5 Windsor Walk, Camberwell, London SE5 8BB. Tel. (071) 701 8282
An award-winning reconstruction of the burnt-out Denmark Hill railway station, opened in 1984.

BEARDS OF SUSSEX LTD
Stella House, Diplock Way, Hailsham, E. Sussex BN27 3JF. Tel. (0323) 847888

Former brewing company which opted out of production in 1959. Currently runs 32 traditional pubs in Sussex, which can sell any beers from the company's wholesaling division. Over 30 breweries feature on the list.

BELHAVEN INNS
Bury House, 31 Bury Street, London EC3A 5AR. Tel. (071) 815 0805

A wholly-owned subsidiary of Control Securities PLC, the parent company of Belhaven brewery. Belhaven Inns, however, are not confined to Scotland but spread across the country. There are currently 591 pubs run by the group, roughly half-tenanted, half-leased, and they sell beers from Courage and Carlsberg-Tetley, with no guest beers allowed.

BODDINGTON PUB COMPANY
West Point, 501 Chester Road, Manchester M16 9HX. Tel. (061) 876 4292

Famous Manchester brewing name which sold its Strangeways and Higsons breweries to Whitbread in 1989. Had previously taken over and closed the neighbouring Oldham Brewery. Now runs 473 pubs in the North-West, 263 managed, three on short leases and the rest tenanted. The pubs sell the Boddingtons, Oldham and Higsons beers from Whitbread, as well as Tetley, John Smith's and Theakston brews, plus Cains beers in the Liverpool area. There is also a selection from the group's Guest Ale Club and some pubs have been designated 'Boddingtons Ale Houses'.

QUALITY • SERVICE
BODDINGTON
PUBS
VALUE • CHOICE

CM GROUP LTD
Magnet House, Station Road, Tadcaster, N. Yorks. LS24 9JF. Tel. (0937) 833311

Eighty-strong pub chain in North-East England, expanded from ten in 1992. Most of the pubs have been leased from Whitbread, with half tenanted, half managed. No guest beers are available to managers or tenants, with supplies coming from Whitbread, Courage and S&N.

CAFE INNS PLC
16 Grimshaw Street, Preston, Lancs. PR1 3DD. Tel. (0772) 882990

Company established in 1986 and now running 125, mostly tenanted pubs in the North-West. Fifty-two of the pubs are leased from Burtonwood and are operated under the Vantage Inns banner, a company jointly owned by Café Inns and Burtonwood.

CENTRIC PUB COMPANY LTD
Star Chambers, 412 Radford Road, Nottingham NG7 7NP. Tel. (0602) 790066

Pub group established with the leasing of 200 pubs from Bass in 1992. Now runs 203 pubs, mostly tenanted, in the Midlands and the North-West and tenants can only buy beers from the nominated suppliers – Bass (for draught) and S&N (for bottled). Former Bass tenants have lost their guest beer rights.

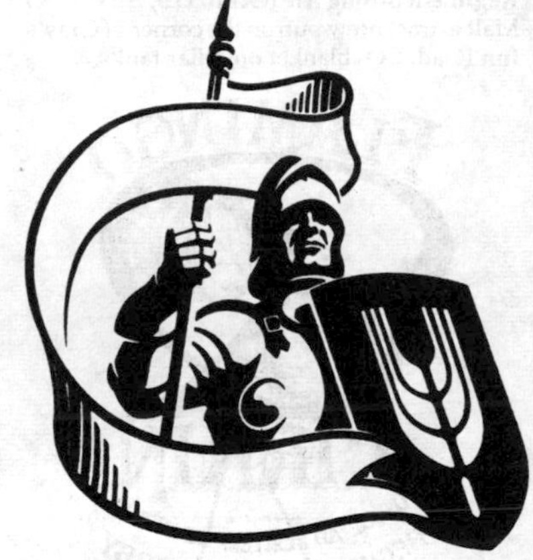

CENTURY INNS LTD
Belasis Business Centre, Coxwold Way, Billingham, Cleveland TS23 4EA. Tel. (0642) 343426

Company formed in 1991 by Camerons employees with the purchase of 185 pubs from Bass. The intention was to establish a pub estate for a buy-out of the Camerons brewery, but this was scuppered by Brent Walker. The number of pubs now stands at 301, all traditionally tenanted and located down the north-eastern side of the country, from Teesside to Lincolnshire. Beer sales are still mostly confined to Bass products, with some Courage and S&N beers.

CHEF & BREWER GROUP LTD
PO Box 112, Riverside House, Riverside Way, Northampton NN1 5ND. Tel. (0604) 239000

The managed house division of Grand Metropolitan PLC, operating 1,600 pubs and pub-restaurants, including 330 acquired from Courage in 1991. Pubs are tied to Courage beers until 1995. (See also Inntrepreneur Estates Ltd.)

DEAN ENTERTAINMENTS LTD
Dean House, Victoria Road, Kirkcaldy, Fife KY1 2SA. Tel. (0592) 200417

Scottish-based company owning 25 pubs, two hotels and three discos in the Fife and Tayside area. Fifteen of the pubs came from Tennent Caledonian.

JA DEVENISH PLC
Hope Square, Weymouth, Dorset DT4 8TP. Tel. (0305) 761111

Company founded in 1742 and now a member of the family of ex-breweries which only run pubs. Having closed the Weymouth brewery in 1985, it signed up a supply deal with Whitbread in 1991, leaving its Redruth brewery to a management buy-out team. Whitbread now supplies Devenish with Royal Wessex Bitter from Cheltenham, as well as Cornish Original, produced for Whitbread by the new regime at Redruth. The 540 pubs (spread across the country and about half managed) include 50 bought and 115 leased from Whitbread. Devenish has also bought the Roast Inns chain from Whitbread. Former Whitbread tenants have lost their guest beer rights. As we went to press, it was announced that a bid from Greenalls to take over the company and its pubs had been successful.

ENTERPRISE INNS LTD
Friars Gate, Stratford Road, Solihull, W. Midlands B90 4BN. Tel. (021) 733 7700

Midlands-based company founded in 1991 with the purchase of 372 pubs from Bass. Most of these are now run on a 21-year lease basis, with beers provided by Bass. Lessees are not allowed to buy beers outside the company, though the choice of suppliers may be extended.

DISCOVERY INNS
Discovery House, Westpoint Row, Great Park Road, Almondsbury Park, Bristol, Avon BS12 4QG. Tel. (0454) 619234

Company founded in 1992 and now running 223 pubs which it picked up from Whitbread, mostly on a freehold basis. The pubs are offered out on three-year tenancies but all guest beer rights have been taken away and only a limited choice from Whitbread's portfolio, with some Bass, Courage and regional brewers' beers, is offered to tenants. Most of the pubs are in the West Country and South Wales, with others in the North and London.

SIR JOHN FITZGERALD LTD
Café Royal Buildings, 8 Nelson Street, Newcastle upon Tyne, Tyne & Wear NE1 5AW. Tel. (091) 232 0664

Long-established, family-owned, property and pubs company, dating from the end of the last century. Its pubs convey a 'free house' image, all 27 (26 managed) being in the North-East.

GRAY & SONS (CHELMSFORD) LTD
Rignals Lane, Galleywood, Chelmsford, Essex. Tel. (0245) 75181

A brewery which ceased production at its Chelmsford brewery in 1974 and which now supplies its 49 Essex pubs with beers from Greene King (IPA, Rayments Special and Abbot Ale) and Ridleys (Mild) instead.

GREENALLS GROUP PLC
Wilderspool House, Greenalls Avenue, Warrington, Cheshire WA4 6RH. Tel. (0925) 51234

Former brewing giant which destroyed many fine independent breweries before turning its back on brewing in 1991. On a 1980s rampage, Greenalls stormed the Midlands, taking over and closing the Wem, Davenports, Simpkiss and Shipstone's breweries. Greenalls beers are now brewed by Carlsberg-Tetley. Guest beers in its 1,500 pubs (600 managed, 900 tenanted) include Tetley Bitter, Stones Best Bitter and, in a few outlets, ales from Cains, Adnams, Greene King, Young's and Coach House. However, this company demonstrated its contempt for brewing and pub traditions by bulldozing the famous Tommy Ducks pub in Manchester under the cover of night, ignoring local planning legislation. Last orders were called on a Saturday evening, with even bar staff unaware of the impending demolition. On Sunday morning only a heap of rubble remained. For yet another act of criminal vandalism, Greenalls deserves nothing but condemnation. In summer 1993, the Greenalls empire was extended even further with the take-over of Devenish.

GROSVENOR INNS PLC
The Old Schoolhouse, London Road, Shenley, Herts. WD7 9DX. Tel. (0923) 855837

Group running 27 pubs in London and the Midlands, 19 of which are Inntrepreneur houses tied to Courage beers. Guest beers are offered from Whitbread (Boddingtons), Fuller's and Wadworth. Once known as Cromwell Taverns and now a publicly-quoted company, launched on the USM in May 1992. Plans to develop its estate within the M25 ring.

HEAVITREE BREWERY PLC
Trood Lane, Matford, Exeter, Devon EX2 8YP. Tel. (0392) 58406

West Country brewery which gave up production in 1970 to concentrate on running pubs. The current estate stands at 115: 11 managed, 81 tenanted and 23 leased out (mostly on 21-year contracts). The pubs are tied to taking beers from Whitbread, Bass and Eldridge Pope.

INN BUSINESS LTD
Woodrow Farm, Wiggington, Tring, Herts. HP23 6HT. Tel. (0442) 891508

Company running 80 pubs, obtained from Whitbread, as well as a handful of Morland and Carlsberg-Tetley leases in the South. Strong Whitbread beer presence, but some Harveys and Banks & Taylor beers are also sold.

INNTREPRENEUR ESTATES LTD
Mill House, Aylesbury Road, Thame, Oxfordshire OX9 3AT. Tel. (0844) 261526

The pub-owning company formed by Courage and Grand Metropolitan as part of the pubs-for-breweries swap in 1991. In the deal, Courage bought up all Grand Met's (Watney's) breweries, with most of Courage's pubs taken over by Inntrepreneur (330 went directly to Grand Met). Not all Grand Met pubs were absorbed into this new company: some are still operated by the Chef & Brewer division. Inntrepreneur has led the way with the long lease (20 years) as a replacement for the traditional tenancy. As a result, many former Courage tenants have left the trade. The company currently operates 6,830 pubs, 4,250 of which it is allowed to keep tied, under the Government's Beer Orders. The others (some leased to other pub groups) became free houses on 1 November 1992. The tied pubs will take Courage beers until 1998, after which they will be free, unless another supply deal is negotiated.

LEISURETIME INNS PLC
Attlee House, St Aldates Courtyard, Oxford OX1 1BN. Tel. (0865) 251681

Company formed in 1988 and now owning just 33 pubs, having halved its estate in the last year. All pubs are within an 80-mile radius of Oxford and follow two styles: the Slug & Lettuce, bare boards, traditional pub idiom, and the County Taverns, olde-worlde eating house pattern, with beams and open fires. Beers are mainly supplied by Bass and Courage.

MARITIME TAVERNS LTD
Queens Gate, Queens Terrace, Southampton, Hants. SO1 1BP. Tel. (0703) 338177

A subsidiary of John Labatt (UK) Ltd., operating 140 pubs across southern Britain. Most pubs are tenanted, though 20 are on 21-year leases. Licensees have a choice of national brewers' beers (Bass, Whitbread, Carlsberg-Tetley and Courage), plus Eldridge Pope and Brains in some outlets. The choice of cask ales may be increased as this new company develops its beer policy.

MARR TAVERNS LTD
156 Tooley Street, London SE1 2NR.
Tel. (071) 403 1140

Pub group owning 195 pubs and aiming at over 700 by the end of the decade. Nearly all pubs are tenanted on traditional three-year contracts, but there are no guest beer rights at present. Beers are supplied by Courage and Bass, plus some local suppliers.

MOLYNEUX LEISURE GROUP PLC
Molyneux House, Kingsway, South Woodham Ferrers, Chelmsford, Essex CM3 5QH. Tel. (0245) 323014

Three-year-old company currently running 160 pubs in East Anglia and London but on the look-out for more high barrelage free houses. Some pubs are branded 'Henry Molyneux's Fine Ale and Dining Establishments' and they serve mainly Courage beers.

MORGAN PINDER
328a Central Market, West Smithfield, London EC1A 9DU.

Company running 80 managed pubs in England and Wales, supplied by Courage and Carlsberg-Tetley. The pubs were taken over by a new company, Greenland Leisure, as we went to press.

ORIGINAL PUB HOLDINGS
Springfield, 146 Springfield Road, Brighton, E. Sussex BN1 6DE. Tel. (0273) 881313

A four-year-old company operating 26 pubs in the South, derived from a variety of sources, including Bass and Courage. All are free houses.

PARAMOUNT PLC
St Werburgh Chambers, Chester, Cheshire CH1 2EP. Tel. (0244) 321171

Ambitious company part-owned by Greenalls (25%), Burtonwood (20%) and Bass (10%). Most of its 115 pubs were purchased from these three operators and S&N. Also a partner in Real Inns (50 pubs) with Labatts, and manages 50 pubs for Whitbread under the Wirral Taverns name. The pubs are centred within 100 miles of Chester and nearly all are leased out on long contracts. Licensees are encouraged to sell cask ale, but are restricted to the Burtonwood and Bass lists. Wirral Taverns offer the Whitbread portfolio.

PUB MANAGEMENT CO. LTD
4 Column Barn, Broughton Hall Business Park, Skipton, N. Yorks. BD23 3AE.
Tel. (0756) 792717

Company running 71 pubs in West Yorkshire, on a mixture of short leases and tenancies. Aiming for 100 pubs. Carlsberg-Tetley has a supply arrangement.

Pub Groups

PUBMASTER LTD
Greenbank, Hartlepool, Cleveland TS24 7QS. Tel. (0429) 266666

Company formed in 1991 to take over the pub estate of Brent Walker (ex-Camerons and Tolly Cobbold pubs). In 1992, 734 houses were leased from Allied, and 174 from Whitbread. Pubmaster currently runs 2,043 pubs across the country, most tenanted. Its most famous trading name is Tap & Spile, a chain of 25 traditional alehouses offering an excellent choice of beers. The other Pubmaster pubs stock beers from Bass, Carlsberg-Tetley, Whitbread and some regional independents. Shares control of 80 Maple Leaf Inns with Labatts.

RANDALLS VAUTIER LTD
PO Box 43, Clare Street, St Helier, Jersey, CI JE4 8NZ. Tel. (0534) 887788

Brewery which had produced no real ale for some time but which stopped brewing altogether in September 1992. Now runs 30 pubs on Jersey which sell Bass and Marston's Pedigree. Not to be confused with Randalls of Guernsey.

REGENT INNS PLC
Northway House, 1379 High Road, Whetstone, London N20 9LP. Tel. (081) 445 5016

Company founded in 1980 and now owning 35 pubs in London and the Home Counties. Once known as Lockton Inns. Floated on the Stock Market in 1993.

RYAN ELIZABETH HOLDINGS PLC
Ryan Precinct, 33 Fore Street, Ipswich, Suffolk IP4 1JL. Tel. (0473) 217458

This company's 52 pubs in East Anglia (bought from national brewers) are leased to individual operators on 35-year contracts. Most are free, but around 20% have a tie to Bass or S&N.

SAXON INNS LTD
142–146 Whitecross Street, London EC1Y 8QJ. Tel. (071) 490 4161

Company formed in 1987 which developed a small managed chain of ex-free houses and Inntrepreneur leases until taking over 14 pubs from Bass in 1992. These are now run as tenancies. The company currently controls 39 pubs, most within the M25 ring, including the Flamingo Brewery brew pub (see Brew Pubs). Guest beers are dictated by head office, with Fuller's London Pride widely available.

SCORPIO INNS LTD
Zealley House, Greenhill Way, Newton Abbot, Devon TQ12 3TB. Tel. (0626) 334888

Pub group formed in 1991. After initially managing pubs in Plymouth for Grand Met, it obtained over 100 pubs from Whitbread on short leases, bringing the number of pubs controlled to 136. Despite being 'free of tie', these pubs stock Whitbread lagers and keg beers, plus a Whitbread cask ale. A guest beer from a short list of well-known brands is also available to tenants. Pubs are located in South Wales, the Bristol area and along the M4 corridor to Berkshire. Some have been externally redecorated in company colours. Scorpio is also looking to purchase a further 100 pubs in conjunction with Courage.

Pub Groups

SMITHINNS PLC
Bridge House, Station Road, Scunthorpe, Humbs. DN15 6PY. Tel. (0724) 861703

Five-year-old company operating 41 managed pubs in Yorkshire, Humberside and northern Lincolnshire. Eleven pubs are leased from big brewers and tied to their products, with the other 30 selling beers from national and certain regional brewers. Plans to develop the Honest Lawyer mini-chain of pubs which offer at least seven ales.

SURREY FREE INNS PLC
Newtown House, 38 Newtown Road, Liphook, Hants. GU30 7DX.
Tel. (0428) 725248

Established in 1986 to run a series of pubs in the South and now controls 30 outlets which tend to have a commitment to food. Twenty-eight are managed houses and two are on 20-year leases. Seven pubs are leased from Inntrepreneur, two are leased from Carlsberg-Tetley; the others are private purchases, including two former Berni Inns. The company is supplied by Courage and S&N, but a guest beer programme is also operated and two house beers are sold. These are No Name Bitter (rebadged John Smith's Bitter) and Auld Soxx (rebadged Courage Directors).

SYCAMORE TAVERNS LTD
1 Guildford Street, Chertsey, Surrey KT16 9BG. Tel. (0932) 571545

Company operating around 300 pubs bought from Allied. Tenants are allowed a guest beer from the Bass and Courage lists, though most beers still come from Carlsberg-Tetley.

THORNABY LEISURE LTD
Enterprise House, Valley Street North, Darlington, Co. Durham, DL1 1GY.
Tel. (0325) 489619

Company set up in 1987 which currently has 34 pubs in North-East England, some bought from S&N. Looking to expand into the Midlands. Beers are supplied by S&N, Bass and Courage.

TOM COBLEIGH LTD
Phoenix House, Mansfield Road, Sutton-in-Ashfield, Notts. NG17 4HD.
Tel. (0623) 442144

Company established in 1991 with two pubs. Since then the estate has grown to 75, two-thirds tenanted, the remainder managed. The pubs, which conform to the company's motto of 'Unspoilt pubs for nice people', are located in Yorkshire, Humberside and the north-eastern Midlands. Seven pubs are leased from Devenish, and 51 from Whitbread, though these are held by a subsidiary called The Nice Pub Company. Licensees choose beers from a head office range of national and regional ales.

TRENT TAVERNS LTD
PO Box 1061, Gringley on the Hill, Doncaster, S. Yorks. DN10 4ED. Tel. (0777) 817408

Company set up by a former S&N employee. Its 67 pubs in the Midlands are leased from Whitbread and sell only Whitbread and S&N beers.

JD WETHERSPOON ORGANISATION PLC
735 High Road, North Finchley, London N12 0BP. Tel. (081) 446 9099

Ambitious London-based group which opened its first pub in 1979 and went public in 1992. Currently owns over 60 pubs in and around the capital, all managed, with the goal being 100 pubs in three years' time. Many of the pubs are conversions from shops, including ex-Woolworth stores. Common names are JJ Moon's and other 'Moon' titles. No music is played in any of the pubs and all pubs offer a no-smoking area. Three beers are always sold: S&N Theakston XB and Younger Scotch, and Courage Directors, with Greene King IPA and Abbot Ale, Wadworth 6X and Theakston Best Bitter also widely available. Licensees also have a choice of guest beers.

JAMES WILLIAMS (NARBERTH)
7 Spring Gardens, Narberth, Dyfed SA67 7BP. Tel. (0834) 860318

Privately-owned concern, founded in 1830 and operating 51 pubs in Dyfed (all tenanted), which has invested heavily in its estate since 1986. Tenants have a choice of selected beers from Brains, Crown Buckley, Felinfoel, Bass, Carlsberg-Tetley, Courage, Whitbread, Wadworth and Ruddles.

The Beers Index

Who brews Bishops Finger, Kimberley Classic or White Adder? What about Bear Ale, Clog Dancer or Rip Snorter? By using this Index, you will be able to match such beers to their breweries. The page numbers given refer to the breweries section of the *Guide*, where more information about the beer can be obtained.

A

B

C

The Beers Index

D

E

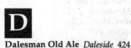

F

The Beers Index

The Beers Index

The Beers Index

The Beers Index

READERS' RECOMMENDATIONS

Suggestions for pubs to be included or excluded

All pubs are surveyed by the local branches of CAMRA. If you would like to draw their attention to a pub already featured, or any you think should be featured, please fill in the form below (or a copy of it) and send it to the address indicated. We also welcome letters, if readers feel strongly about pub entries.

Pub Name:

Address:

Reason for recommendation/criticism:

Pub Name:

Address:

Reason for recommendation/criticism:

Your name and address:

Please send to: GBG, CAMRA Ltd., 34 Alma Road, St Albans, Herts. AL1 3BW

CAMRA BOOKS AND GIFTS

CAMRA produces a wide range of books and other items to complement the *Good Beer Guide*. The major titles are listed below, but a full catalogue of CAMRA products (including local guides) is available on request. Tear out or copy this form for ease of ordering.
All prices include UK postage and packing.

	Quantity	Price each	Amount
GUIDES			
CAMRA Guide to Good Pub Food (3rd edition)		£9.95	
The Best Waterside Pubs (1st edition)		£7.99	
Good Beer Guide to Belgium and Holland		£8.99	
Beer, Bed & Breakfast (Robson Books: 4th edition)		£7.99	
OTHER TITLES			
CAMRA Guide to Home Brewing (2nd edition)		£6.99	
Brew Your Own Real Ale at Home		£6.99	
Bedside Book of Beer (an ale anthology)		£6.99	
Called to the Bar (CAMRA: the first 21 years)		£6.99	
OTHER PRODUCTS			
CAMRA Tie		£5.50	
CAMRA T-shirt (white: M, L, XL, XXL – state size)		£6.50	
CAMRA Bar Towel		£1.95	
		Total	£

Please send to CAMRA Ltd., 34 Alma Road, St Albans, Herts. AL1 3BW (cheques made payable to CAMRA Ltd. must accompany all orders). Allow 28 days for delivery. To place a credit card order, phone (0727) 867201 and ask for the Products Secretary.

Name
Address
Post Code

INSTRUCTIONS TO YOUR BANK TO PAY DIRECT DEBITS

Please complete parts 1 to 4 to instruct your bank to make payments directly from your account.

Return the form to Campaign for Real Ale Limited, 34 Alma Road, St Albans, Herts. AL1 3BW

To the Manager

Bank

____

____

____

1 Please write the full postal address of your bank branch in the box.

2 Name(s) of account holders(s) ______________________________

Address ______________________________

____

Post Code ______________________________

3 Account number

Banks may refuse to accept instructions to pay direct debits from some types of account.

Direct debit instructions should only be addressed to banks in the United Kingdom.

CAMRA Computer Membership No. (for office use only)

0	0					

Originator's Identification No.

9	2	6	1	2	9

4 Your instructions to the bank, and signature.

- I instruct you to pay direct debits from my account at the request of Campaign for Real Ale Limited.
- The amounts are variable and are to be debited annually.
- I understand that Campaign for Real Ale Limited may change the amount only after giving me prior notice.
- PLEASE CANCEL ALL PREVIOUS STANDING ORDER INSTRUCTIONS IN FAVOUR OF CAMPAIGN FOR REAL ALE LIMITED.
- I will inform the bank in writing if I wish to cancel this instruction.
- I understand that if any direct debit is paid which breaks the terms of this instruction, the bank will make a refund.

Signature(s) ______________________________

____

Date ______________________________

JOIN CAMRA–FREE

Finally, here's an offer we hope you cannot refuse!

The Campaign for Real Ale has been fighting for Britain's pubs and breweries for 23 years. Our current membership stands at nearly 40,000 and we are now offering *Good Beer Guide* readers the chance to discover what CAMRA is all about, with a no-obligation, three-months' free trial membership.

AS A CAMRA MEMBER YOU GET

- Generous discounts on all CAMRA products, including the *Good Beer Guide*
- *What's Brewing*, CAMRA's informative and entertaining newspaper, delivered free to your door each month, bringing you up-to-the-minute news of events in the brewing industry ● a free members' handbook, packed with information about real ale and good beer ● reduced or free entrance to CAMRA beer festivals nationwide

AS A CAMRA MEMBER YOU CAN

- Help save your local pubs and breweries
- Attend local branch meetings, join brewery trips and other social events
- Vote for and survey entries for the *Good Beer Guide* and nominate beers for the *Champion Beer of Britain* contest
- Help decide national policy at the annual conference
- Become involved in running beer festivals

By taking advantage of this free trial membership, you will receive all the above benefits. Just fill in the direct debit form overleaf and sign the application form below (or copies of them). If, after three months, you do not wish to continue your membership, all you need do is return your membership card and you will owe nothing.

If you do not want to take up this offer, but wish to join anyway, just fill in the application form below and send it to us with a cheque for your first year's subscription. Do not fill in the direct debit form. For payment by credit card, contact the Membership Secretary on (0727) 867201.

Help us protect your pleasure! Join CAMRA now!

Full membership £12; Joint husband and wife membership £14; Life membership £120/£140
Please delete as appropriate:

- ☐ **I/We wish to take advantage of the trial membership, and have completed the instructions overleaf.**
- ☐ **I/We wish to become members of CAMRA.**
- ☐ **I/We agree to abide by the memorandum and articles of association of the company.**
- ☐ **I/We enclose a cheque/p.o. for £ (payable to CAMRA Ltd.)**

Name(s)

Address

Signature(s)

CAMRA Ltd., 34 Alma Road, St Albans, Herts. AL1 3BW